SOCIAL SECURITY LEGISLATION 2017/18

VOLUME V: UNIVERSAL CREDIT

SOCIAL SECURITY LEGISLATION 2017/18

General Editor
Nick Wikeley, M.A. (Cantab)

VOLUME V: UNIVERSAL CREDIT

Commentary By

John Mesher, B.A., B.C.L. (Oxon), LL.M. (Yale)

Richard Poynter, B.C.L., M.A. (Oxon)
District Tribunal Judge
Judge of the Upper Tribunal

Nick Wikeley, M.A. (Cantab)
Judge of the Upper Tribunal
Emeritus Professor of Law, University of Southampton

Consultant Editor
Child Poverty Action Group

SWEET & MAXWELL THOMSON REUTERS

Published in 2017 by
Thomson Reuters trading as Sweet & Maxwell
Registered in England & Wales, Company No 1679046.
Registered Office and address for service:
5 Canada Square, Canary Wharf,
London E14 5AQ

Typeset by Servis Filmsetting Ltd, Stockport, Cheshire
Printed and bound by CPI Group (UK) Ltd,
Croydon, CR0 4YY

For further information on our products and services,
visit www.sweetandmaxwell.co.uk

No natural forests were destroyed to make this product.
Only farmed timber was used and re-planted.

A CIP catalogue record for this book is
available from the British Library

ISBN 978–0–414–06448–5

FOREWORD

It is immensely reassuring to have available to those who prepare and attend hearings a steadfast source of reliable information and guidance, in a familiar format, that will effectively assist us in our common endeavour to deliver access to justice for those seeking redress. In the face of ongoing complex reform as well as the continuing development of the jurisprudence applicable to the existing legislation it remains an essential reference and I am happy to once again endorse the publication of these volumes. We owe a tremendous debt of gratitude to all those who contribute to making the Social Security Legislation series such a success.

Judge John Aitken
Chamber President, Social Entitlement Chamber
Social Security and Child Support,
Criminal Injuries Compensation,
Asylum Support.

PREFACE

Universal Credit is Volume V of the series *Social Security Legislation 2017/18*. The companion volumes are Hooker, Poynter, White, Wikeley, Mesher and Mitchell, Volume I: *Non-Means Tested Benefits and Employment and Support Allowance*; Mesher, Poynter and Wikeley, Volume II: *Income Support, Jobseeker's Allowance, State Pension Credit and the Social Fund*; Rowland and White, Volume III: *Administration, Adjudication and the European Dimension*; and Wikeley, Mitchell and Hooker, Volume IV: *Tax credits and HMRC-administered Social Security Benefits*. Each of the volumes in the series provides a legislative text, clearly showing the form and date of amendments, and commentary up to date to April 10, 2017. The commentary sometimes includes references to some later case law.

Neither the outcome of the EU referendum of June 23, 2016 nor the Prime Minister's letter of March 29, 2017 triggering art.50 of the Treaty on European Union immediately alters the United Kingdom's membership of the Union. The United Kingdom will remain a Member State and European Union law will continue to apply until such time as the exit arrangements provided for in art.50 are completed.

The introduction of universal credit is the biggest change to the social security system since the abolition of supplementary benefit and its replacement with income support thirty years ago. Universal credit is intended to simplify the social security system and to ensure that claimants will always be better off in work. In the medium to long term, the Government intends to abolish six existing benefits and tax credits: income support, income-based jobseeker's allowance, income-related employment and support allowance, housing benefit, child tax credit and working tax credit and replace them all with universal credit. In the short term, however, universal credit is being introduced on a phased basis, so the old and new systems are co-existing side by side. During this transitional period, universal credit is not a replacement benefit but an additional benefit. Originally the new benefit was available only to a so-called "Pathfinder Group" of claimants, i.e. those who both met certain criteria or 'gateways' and also lived in certain districts (set out in a series of Commencement Orders), known as the universal credit 'Live Service'. Increasingly, however, the universal credit 'Full Service' or 'Digital Service' is being rolled out, in which the gateway conditions do not need to be met.

Volume V is divided into five Parts. Part I provides a clear and comprehensive narrative overview and analysis of the scope and structure of universal credit. Part II comprises the relevant primary legislation, principally provisions in the Welfare Reform Act 2012, but also including sections from the Social Security Administration Act 1992 and the Social Security Act 1998. Part III for the most part consists of the main regulations, the Universal Credit Regulations 2013. Part IV contains the Universal Credit (Transitional Provisions) Regulations 2014 as well as all relevant Commencement Orders to date, along with phasing provisions. Finally,

Part V includes regulations governing both claims and payments and also decisions and appeals as they relate to universal credit. The text includes both the key statutory material and detailed commentary. The following new aspects of the universal credit regime from April 2017 are covered: the restriction of the child element to two children per family for new claimants (subject to certain exceptions); the abolition of the limited capability for work element; the reduction in the universal credit taper; and the new rules on the housing costs element for 18 and 19 year-olds.

We should put on record that this is the first edition of this volume which has been produced without the input of Penny Wood, a key member of the original authors' team, who retired earlier this year. Penny's contribution both to this volume and Volume II has been immense; for a full acknowledgement of our debt to her please see the Preface to Volume II.

As always, revising and updating the legislative text and commentary has required considerable flexibility on the part of the publisher and a great deal of help from a number of sources, including CPAG as advisory editor to the series. We remain grateful for this assistance in our task of providing an authoritative reflection on the current state of the law. To maximise space for explanatory commentary in books which seem to grow in size year on year, we have provided lists of definitions only where the commentary to the provision is substantial, or where reference to definitions is essential for a proper understanding. Users of the book should always check whether particular words or phrases they are called on to apply have a particular meaning ascribed to them in legislation. Generally the first or second regulation in each set of regulations contains definitions of key terms (check the "Arrangements of Regulations" at the beginning of each set for an indication of the subject matter covered by each regulations). There are also definition or "interpretation" sections in primary legislation.

Users of the series, and its predecessor works, have over the years contributed to their effectiveness by providing valuable comments on our commentary, as well as pointing out where the text of some provision has been omitted in error, or become garbled, or not been brought fully up to date. In some cases, this has drawn attention to an error which might otherwise have gone unnoticed. In providing such feedback, users of the work have helped to shape the content and ensure the accuracy of our material, and for that we continue to be grateful. This is all the more important in the context of this new benefit. We therefore hope that users of the work will continue to provide such helpful input and feedback. Please write to the General Editor of the series, Professor Nick Wikeley, c/o School of Law, University of Southampton, Highfield, Southampton SO17 1BJ, email: njw@soton.ac.uk, and he will pass on any comments received to the appropriate commentator.

Our gratitude also goes to the President of the Social Entitlement Chamber of the First-tier Tribunal and his colleagues there for continuing the now long tradition of help and encouragement in our endeavours.

August 31, 2017.

John Mesher
Richard Poynter
Nick Wikeley

CONTENTS

PART I
INTRODUCTION

PART II
UNIVERSAL CREDIT: STATUTES

PART III
UNIVERSAL CREDIT: REGULATIONS

PART IV A
TRANSITIONAL PROVISIONS

Contents

PART IV B
COMMENCEMENT ORDERS

Contents

Contents

USING THIS BOOK: AN INTRODUCTION TO
LEGISLATION AND CASE LAW

Introduction

This book is not a general introduction to, or general textbook on, the law relating to social security but it is nonetheless concerned with both of the principal sources of social security law—*legislation* (both primary and secondary) and *case law*. It sets out the text of the most important legislation, as currently in force, and then there is added commentary that refers to the relevant case law. Lawyers will be familiar with this style of publication, which inevitably follows the structure of the legislation.

This note is designed primarily to assist readers who are not lawyers to find their way around the legislation and to understand the references to case law, but information it contains about how to find social security case law is intended to be of assistance to lawyers too.

Primary legislation

Primary legislation of the United Kingdom Parliament consists of *Acts of Parliament* (also known as *Statutes*). They will have been introduced to Parliament as *Bills*. There are opportunities for Members of Parliament and peers to debate individual clauses and to vote on amendments before a Bill is passed and becomes an Act (at which point the clauses become sections). No tribunal or court has the power to disapply, or hold to be invalid, an Act of Parliament unless it is inconsistent with European Union law.

An Act is known by its "short title", which incorporates the year in which it was passed (e.g. the Social Security Contributions and Benefits Act 1992), and is given a chapter number (abbreviated as, for instance, "c.4" indicating that the Act was the fourth passed in that year). It is seldom necessary to refer to the chapter number but it appears in the running heads in this book.

Each *section* (abbreviated as "s." or, in the plural, "ss.") of an Act is numbered and may be divided into *subsections* (abbreviated as "subs." and represented by a number in brackets), which in turn may be divided into *paragraphs* (abbreviated as "para." and represented by a lower case letter in brackets) and *subparagraphs* (abbreviated as "subpara." and represented by a small roman numeral in brackets). Subparagraph (ii) of para.(a) of subs. (1) of s.72 will usually be referred to simply as "s.72(1)(a)(ii)". Upper case letters may be used where additional sections or subsections are inserted by amendment and additional lower case letters may be used where new paragraphs and subparagraphs are inserted. This accounts for the rather ungainly s.171ZS of the Social Security Contributions and Benefits Act 1992 (in Vol.IV).

Sections of a large Act may be grouped into a numbered *Part*, which may even be divided into *Chapters*. It is not usual to refer to a Part or a Chapter unless referring to the whole Part or Chapter.

Where a section would otherwise become unwieldy because it is necessary to include a list or complicated technical provisions, the section may simply refer to a *Schedule* at the end of the Act. A Schedule (abbreviated as "Sch.") may be divided into paragraphs and subparagraphs and further divided into heads and subheads. Again, it is usual to refer simply to, say, "para.23(3)(b)(ii) of Schedule 3". Whereas it is conventional to speak of a section *of* an Act, it is usual to speak of a Schedule *to* an Act.

When Parliament wishes to change the law, it may do so by passing a new Act that amends a previous Act or it may do so by passing a freestanding Act, although even then consequential amendments to other legislation are usually required. Thus, for instance, when incapacity benefit was introduced by the Social Security (Incapacity for Work) Act 1994, the changes were largely made by inserting sections 30A to 30E and Part XIIA into the Social Security Contributions and Benefits Act 1992 and repealing the provisions in that Act dealing with sickness and invalidity benefit. In contrast, when jobseeker's allowance was introduced by the Jobseekers Act 1995, it was decided that the main provisions relating to the new benefit would be found in the 1995 Act itself and the 1992 Act was amended only so as to repeal, or amend, the provisions dealing with, or referring to, unemployment benefit.

When there has been a proliferation of Acts or Acts have been very substantially amended, the legislation may be consolidated in a new Act, for which there is a fast track procedure in Parliament. Only limited amendments may be made by a consolidation Act but such an Act reorganises and tidies up the legislation. Because social security law is so frequently amended, it tends to be consolidated every decade or two. The last consolidation Acts relevant to this book were the Social Security Contributions and Benefits Act 1992 (in Vols I, II and IV) and the Social Security Administration Act 1992 (in this volume).

Secondary legislation

Secondary legislation (also known as *subordinate legislation* or *delegated legislation*) is made by *statutory instrument* in the form of a set of *Regulations* or a set of *Rules* or an *Order*. The power to make such legislation is conferred on ministers and other persons or bodies by Acts of Parliament. To the extent that a statutory instrument is made beyond the powers (in Latin, ultra vires) conferred by primary legislation, it may be held by a tribunal or court to be invalid and ineffective. Secondary legislation must be laid before Parliament. However, most secondary legislation is not debated in Parliament and, even when it is, it cannot be amended although an entire statutory instrument may be rejected.

A set of Regulations or Rules or an Order has a name indicating its scope and the year it was made and also a number, as in the Social Security (Disability Living Allowance) Regulations 1991 (SI 1991/2890) (the 2890th statutory instrument issued in 1991). Because there are over 3,000 statutory instruments each year, the number of a particular statutory instrument is important as a means of identification and it should usually be cited the first time reference is made to that statutory instrument.

Sets of Regulations or Rules are made up of individual *regulations* (abbreviated as "reg.") or *rules* (abbreviated as "r." or, in the plural, "rr."). An Order is made up of *articles* (abbreviated as "art."). Regulations, rules and articles may be divided into paragraphs, subparagraphs and heads. As in Acts, a set of Regulations or Rules or an Order may have one or more Schedules attached to it. The style of numbering used in statutory instruments is the same as in sections of, and Schedules to, Acts of Parliament. As in Acts, a large statutory instrument may have regulations or rules grouped into Parts and, occasionally, Chapters. Statutory instruments may be amended in the same sort of way as Acts.

Northern Ireland legislation

Most of the legislation set out in this series applies only in Great Britain, social security not generally being an excepted or reserved matter in relation to Northern Ireland. However, Northern Irish legislation—both primary legislation, most relevantly in the form of *Orders in Council* (which, although statutory instruments, had the effect of primary legislation in Northern Ireland while there was direct rule from Westminster) and *Acts of the Northern Ireland Assembly*, and subordinate legislation, in the form of *statutory rules*—has, until recently, largely replicated legislation in Great Britain so that much of the commentary in this book will be applicable to equivalent provisions in Northern Ireland legislation. Latterly, there has been a greater reluctance to maintain parity with Great Britain and, initially at least, the provisions in the Welfare Reform Act 2012 were not replicated in Northern Ireland.

However, following a lengthy impasse, on November 18, 2015, the Northern Ireland Assembly consented to the stalled Northern Ireland (Welfare Reform) Bill 2015 being taken forward by the Westminster Parliament and approved the welfare clauses of the Welfare Reform and Work Bill as initially introduced at Westminster and the draft Welfare Reform (Northern Ireland) Order 2015. Subsequently, the Northern Ireland (Welfare Reform) Act 2015 received the Royal Assent on November 25, 2015. The purpose of the Act was to provide a power by Order in Council to legislate for welfare reform in Northern Ireland and confer power on the Secretary of State or on a Northern Ireland department to make further provision by regulations or order.

The Welfare Reform (Northern Ireland) Order 2015 (SI 2015/2006) was duly made and came into force on December 10, 2015. The Order makes provision equivalent to the Welfare Reform Act 2012 and will implement the reforms contained in that Act in Northern Ireland with some limited specific changes. The Order confers powers on the Northern Ireland Department for Social Development (now renamed the Department for Communities) to make regulations with respect to the reforms in Northern Ireland. The reforms are gradually being rolled out across the jurisdiction in 2016 and 2017 (see e.g. the Welfare Reform (Northern Ireland) Order 2015 (Commencement No. 1) Order 2016 (SR No 46/2016).

In addition, the Northern Ireland Act 1998 (Modification) Order 2016 (SI 2016/160) adds the Welfare Reform Act 2012 and the Welfare Reform (Northern Ireland) Order 2015, together with certain pensions legislation to the legislation listed in s.87(6) of the Northern Ireland Act 1998 (which requires the Secretary of State for Work and Pensions and the Minister with responsibility for social security in Northern Ireland to consult each other to ensure, to the extent they agree, that the relevant legislation achieves single systems of social security, child support and pensions for the UK).

To that extent parity in welfare provision has been restored. Alongside these statutory changes the Northern Ireland Executive has announced allocations from Executive funds to 'top-up' the UK welfare arrangements in Northern Ireland, so as to mitigate the effects of these changes, with a review planned for 2018/2019.

European Union legislation

The United Kingdom is a Member State of the European Union, and European Union legislation has effect within the United Kingdom. The outcome of the EU referendum of June 23, 2016 does not immediately alter the United Kingdom's membership of the Union; the United Kingdom will remain a Member State and European Union law will continue to apply until such time as the exit arrangements provided for in art.50 of the Treaty on European Union are completed. The primary legislation is in the form of the *Treaties* agreed by the Member States. Relevant subordinate legislation is in the form of *Regulations,* adopted to give effect to the provisions of the Treaties, and *Directives,* addressed to Member States and requiring them to incorporate certain provisions into their domestic laws. Directives are relevant because, where a person brings proceedings against an organ of the State, as is invariably the case where social security is concerned, that person may rely on the Directive as having direct effect if the Member State has failed to comply with it. European Union Treaties, Regulations and Directives are divided into *Articles* (abbreviated as "Art.") United Kingdom legislation that is inconsistent with European Union legislation may be disapplied. The most relevant provisions of European Union legislation are set out in Part III of this volume.

Finding legislation in this book

If you know the name of the piece of legislation for which you are looking, use the list of contents at the beginning of each volume of this series which lists the pieces of legislation contained in the volume. That will give you the paragraph reference to enable you to find the beginning of the piece of legislation. Then, it is easy to find the relevant section, regulation, rule, article or Schedule by using the running heads on the right hand pages. If you do not know the name of the piece of legislation, you will probably need to use the index at the end of the volume in order to find the relevant paragraph number but will then be taken straight to a particular provision.

The legislation is set out as amended, the amendments being indicated by numbered sets of square brackets. The numbers refer to the numbered entries under the heading "AMENDMENTS" at the end of the relevant section, regulation, rule, article or Schedule, which identify the amending statute or statutory instrument. Where an Act has been consolidated, there is a list of "DERIVATIONS" identifying the provisions of earlier legislation from which the section or Schedule has been derived.

Finding other legislation

Legislation in both its amended and its unamended form may now be found on *http://www.legislation.gov.uk* and so the "Blue Volumes" at *http://lawvolumes.dwp.gov.uk/the-law-relating-to-social-security/* are no longer being

updated (as from October 2015). Northern Ireland social security legislation may be found at *http://www.communities-ni.gov.uk/law_relating_to_
social_security*. European Union legislation may be found at *http://eur-lex.
europa.eu/collection/eu-law.html*.

Interpreting legislation

Legislation is written in English and generally means what it says. However,
more than one interpretation is often possible. Most legislation itself contains definitions. Sometimes these are in the particular provision in which a
word occurs but, where a word is used in more than one place, any definition will appear with others. In an Act, an interpretation section is usually
to be found towards the end of the Act or of the relevant Part of the Act. In
a statutory instrument, an interpretation provision usually appears near the
beginning of the statutory instrument or the relevant Part of it. In the more
important pieces of legislation in this series, there is included after every
section, regulation, rule, article or Schedule a list of "DEFINITIONS",
showing where definitions of words used in the provision are to be found.

However, not all words are statutorily defined and there is in any event
more to interpreting legislation than merely defining its terms. Decision-
makers and tribunals need to know how to apply the law in different types
of situations. That is where case law comes in.

Case law and the commentary in this book

In deciding individual cases, courts and tribunals interpret the relevant
law and incidentally establish legal principles. Decisions on questions of
legal principle of the superior courts and appellate tribunals are said to be
binding on decision-makers and the First-tier Tribunal, which means that
decision-makers and the First-tier Tribunal must apply those principles.
Thus the judicial decisions of the superior courts and appellate tribunals
form part of the law. The commentary to the legislation in this series, under
the heading "GENERAL NOTE" after a section, regulation, rule, article or
Schedule, refers to this *case law*.

Much case law regarding social security benefits is still in the form of decisions of Social Security Commissioners and Child Support Commissioners.
However, while there are still Commissioners in Northern Ireland, which
has a largely separate judiciary and tribunal system, the functions of
Commissioners in Great Britain were transferred to the Upper Tribunal
and allocated to the Administrative Appeals Chamber of that tribunal on
November 3, 2008. Consequently, social security case law is increasingly to
be found in decisions of the Upper Tribunal.

The commentary in this series is not itself binding on any decision-maker
or tribunal because it is merely the opinion of the author. It is what is actually said in the legislation or in the judicial decision that is important. The
legislation is set out in this series, but it will generally be necessary to look
elsewhere for the precise words used in judicial decisions. The way that
decisions are cited in the commentary enables that to be done.

The reporting of decisions of the Upper Tribunal and Commissioners

About 50 of the most important decisions of the Administrative Appeals
Chamber of the Upper Tribunal are selected to be "reported" each year

in the Administrative Appeals Chamber Reports (AACR), using the same criteria as were formerly used for reporting Commissioners' decisions in Great Britain. The selection is made by an editorial board of judges and decisions are selected for reporting only if they are of general importance and command the assent of at least a majority of the relevant judges. The term "reported" simply means that they are published in printed form as well as on the Internet (see *Finding case law*, below) with headnotes (i.e. summaries) and indexes, but there are two other important consequences of a decision being reported. Reported decisions are available in all tribunal venues and can be consulted in local social security offices and some main libraries. They also have a greater precedential status than ordinary decisions (see *Judicial precedent* below).

A handful of Northern Ireland Commissioners' decisions are also selected for reporting in the Administrative Appeals Chamber Reports each year, the selection being made by the Chief Social Security Commissioner in Northern Ireland.

Citing case law

As has been mentioned, much social security case law is still to be found in decisions of Social Security Commissioners and Child Support Commissioners, even though the Commissioners have now effectively been abolished in Great Britain.

Reported decisions of Commissioners were known merely by a number or, more accurately, a series of letters and numbers beginning with an "R". The type of benefit in issue was indicated by letters in brackets (e.g. "IS" was income support, "P" was retirement pension, and so on) and the year in which the decision was selected for reporting or, from 2000, the year in which it was published as a reported decision, was indicated by the last two digits, as in *R(IS) 2/08*. In Northern Ireland there was a similar system until 2009, save that the type of benefit was identified by letters in brackets after the number, as in *R 1/07 (DLA)*.

Unreported decisions of the Commissioners in Great Britain were known simply by their file numbers, which began with a "C", as in *CIS/2287/2008*. The letters following the "C" indicated the type of benefit in issue in the case. Scottish and, at one time, Welsh cases were indicated by a "S" or "W" immediately after the "C", as in *CSIS/467/2007*. The last four digits indicated the calendar year in which the case was registered, rather than the year it was decided. A similar system operated in Northern Ireland until 2009, save that the letters indicating the type of benefit appeared in brackets after the numbers and, from April 1999, the financial year rather than the calendar year was identified, as in *C 10/06-07 (IS)*.

Decisions of the Upper Tribunal, of courts and, since 2010, of the Northern Ireland Commissioners are generally known by the names of the parties (or just two of them in multi-party cases). Individuals are anonymised through the use of initials in the names of decisions of the Upper Tribunal and the Northern Ireland Commissioners and occasionally in the names of decisions of courts. In this series, the names of official bodies may also be abbreviated (e.g. "SSWP" for the Secretary of State for Work and Pensions, "HMRC" for Her Majesty's Revenue and Customs, "CMEC" for the Child Maintenance and Enforcement Commission and "DSD" for the Department for Social Development in Northern Ireland). Since 2010, decisions of the Upper

Tribunal and of Northern Ireland Commissioners have also been given a "flag" in brackets to indicate the subject matter of the decision, which in social security cases indicates the principal benefit in issue in the case. Thus, the name of one jobseeker's allowance case is *SSWP v JB (JSA)*.

Any decision of the Upper Tribunal, of a court since 2001 or of a Northern Ireland Commissioner since 2010 that has been intended for publication has also given a *neutral citation number* which enables the decision to be more precisely identified. This indicates, in square brackets, the year the decision was made (although in relation to decisions of the courts it sometimes merely indicates the year the number was issued) and also indicates the court or tribunal that made the decision (e.g. "UKUT" for the Upper Tribunal, "NICom" for a Northern Ireland Commissioner, "EWCA Civ" for the Civil Division of the Court of Appeal in England and Wales, "NICA" for the Court of Appeal in Northern Ireland, "CSIH" for the Inner House of the Court of Session (in Scotland), "UKSC" for the Supreme Court and so on). A number is added so that the reference is unique and finally, in the case of the Upper Tribunal or the High Court in England and Wales, the relevant chamber of the Upper Tribunal or the relevant division or other part of the High Court is identified (e.g. "(AAC)" for the Administrative Appeals Chamber, "(Admin)" for the Administrative Court and so on). Examples of decisions of the Upper Tribunal and a Northern Ireland Commissioner with their neutral citation numbers are *SSWP v JB (JSA)* [2010] UKUT 4 (AAC) and *AR v DSD (IB)* [2010] NICom 6.

If the case is reported in the Administrative Appeals Chamber Reports or another series of law reports, a reference to the report usually follows the neutral citation number. Conventionally, this includes either the year the case was decided (in round brackets) or the year in which it was reported (in square brackets), followed by the volume number (if any), the name of the series of reports (in abbreviated form, so see the Table of Abbreviations at the beginning of each volume of this series) and either the page number or the case number. However, before 2010, cases reported in the Administrative Appeals Chamber Reports or with Commissioners' decisions were numbered in the same way as reported Commissioners' decisions. *Abdirahman v Secretary of State for Work and Pensions* [2007] EWCA Civ 657; [2008] 1 W.L.R. 254 (also reported as *R(IS) 8/07*) is a Court of Appeal decision, decided in 2007 but reported in 2008 in volume 1 of the Weekly Law Reports at page 254 and also in the 2007 volume of reported Commissioners' decisions. *NT v SSWP* [2009] UKUT 37 (AAC), *R(DLA) 1/09* is an Upper Tribunal case decided in 2009 and reported in the Administrative Appeals Chamber Reports in the same year. *Martin v SSWP* [2009] EWCA Civ 1289; [2010] AACR 9 is a decision of the Court of Appeal that was decided in 2009 and was the ninth decision reported in the Administrative Appeals Chamber Reports in 2010.

It is usually necessary to include the neutral citation number or a reference to a series of reports only the first time a decision is cited in any document. After that, the name of the case is usually sufficient.

All decisions of the Upper Tribunal that are on their website have neutral citation numbers. If you wish to refer a tribunal or decision-maker to a decision of the Upper Tribunal that does not have a neutral citation number, contact the office of the Administrative Appeals Chamber (*adminappeals@ hmcts.gsi.gov.uk*) who will provide a number and add the decision to the website.

Decision-makers and claimants are entitled to assume that judges of both the First-tier Tribunal and the Upper Tribunal have immediate access to reported decisions of Commissioners or the Upper Tribunal and they need not provide copies, although it may sometimes be helpful to do so. However, where either a decision-maker or a claimant intends to rely on an unreported decision, it will be necessary to provide a copy of the decision to the judge and other members of the tribunal. A copy of the decision should also be provided to the other party before the hearing because otherwise it may be necessary for there to be an adjournment to enable that party to take advice on the significance of the decision.

Finding case law

The extensive references described above are used so as to enable people easily to find the full text of a decision. Most decisions of any significance since the late 1990s can be found on the Internet.

Decisions of the Upper Tribunal and of the Commissioners in Great Britain may be found at *https://www.gov.uk/administrative-appeals-tribunal-decisions*. This includes reported decisions since 1991 and other decisions considered likely to be of interest to tribunals and tribunal users since about 2000, together with a few older decisions. Decisions of Commissioners in Northern Ireland may be found on *https://www.communities-ni.gov.uk/services/northern-ireland-digest-case-law*.

The Administrative Appeals Chamber Reports, which include not only reported decisions of the Administrative Appeals Chamber of the Upper Tribunal but also reported decisions of the Northern Ireland Commissioners and decisions of the courts in related areas of law, are available on the HMCTS website at *http://www.osscsc.gov.uk/Decisions/admin AppealsChamberReports.htm*. They are also published by the Stationery Office in bound volumes which follow on from the bound volumes of Commissioners' decisions published from 1948.

Copies of decisions of the Administrative Appeals Chamber of the Upper Tribunal or of Commissioners that are otherwise unavailable may be obtained from the offices of the Upper Tribunal (Administrative Appeals Chamber) or, in Northern Ireland, from the Office of the Social Security and Child Support Commissioners.

Decisions of a wide variety of courts and tribunals in the United Kingdom may be found on the free website of the British and Irish Legal Information Institute, *http://www.bailii.org*. It includes all decisions of the Supreme Court and provides fairly comprehensive coverage of decisions given since about 1996 by the House of Lords and Privy Council and most of the higher courts in England and Wales, decisions given since 1998 by the Court of Session and decisions given since 2000 by the Court of Appeal and High Court in Northern Ireland. Some earlier decisions have been included, so it is always worth looking and, indeed, those decisions dating from 1873 or earlier and reported in the English Reports may be found through a link to *http://www.commonlii.org/uk/cases/EngR/*.

Decisions of the European Court of Justice (concerned with the law of the European Union) are all to be found on *http://curia.europa.eu*.

Decisions of the European Court of Human Rights are available at *http://www.echr.coe.int*.

Most decisions of the courts in social security cases, including decisions of the European Court of Justice on cases referred by United Kingdom courts and tribunals, are reported in the Administrative Appeals Chamber Reports or with the reported decisions of Commissioners and may therefore be found on the same websites and in the same printed series of reported decisions. So, for example, *R(I) 1/00* contains Commissioner's decision *CSI/12/1998*, the decision of the Court of Session upholding the Commissioner's decision and the decision of the House of Lords in *Chief Adjudication Officer v Faulds*, reversing the decision of the Court of Session. The most important decisions of the courts can also be found in the various series of law reports familiar to lawyers (in particular, in the *Law Reports*, the *Weekly Law Reports*, the *All England Law Reports*, the *Public and Third Sector Law Reports*, the *Industrial Cases Reports* and the *Family Law Reports*) but these are not widely available outside academic or other law libraries, although the *All England Law Reports* are occasionally to be found in the larger public libraries. See the Table of Cases at the beginning of each volume of this series for all the places where a decision mentioned in that volume is reported.

If you know the name or number of a decision and wish to know where in a volume of this series there is a reference to it, use the Table of Cases or the Table of Commissioners' Decisions 1948–2009 in the relevant volume to find the paragraph(s) where the decision is mentioned.

Judicial precedent

As already mentioned, decisions of the Upper Tribunal, the Commissioners and the higher courts in Great Britain become *case law* because they set binding precedents which must be followed by decision-makers and the First-tier Tribunal in Great Britain. This means that, where the Upper Tribunal, Commissioner or court has decided a point of legal principle, decision-makers and appeal tribunals must make their decisions in conformity with the decision of the Upper Tribunal, Commissioner or court, applying the same principle and accepting the interpretation of the law contained in the decision. So a decision of the Upper Tribunal, a Commissioner or a superior court explaining what a term in a particular regulation means, lays down the definition of that term in much the same way as if the term had been defined in the regulations themselves. The decision may also help in deciding what the same term means when it is used in a different set of regulations, provided that the term appears to have been used in a similar context.

Only decisions on points of law set precedents that are binding and, strictly speaking, only decisions on points of law that were necessary to the overall conclusion reached by the Upper Tribunal, Commissioner or court are binding. Other parts of a decision (which used to be known as obiter dicta) may be regarded as helpful guidance but need not be followed if a decision-maker or the First-tier Tribunal is persuaded that there is a better approach. It is particularly important to bear this in mind in relation to older decisions of Social Security Commissioners because, until 1987, the right of appeal to a Commissioner was not confined to points of law.

Where there is a conflict between precedents, a decision-maker or the First-tier Tribunal is generally free to choose between decisions of equal status. For these purposes, most decisions of the Upper Tribunal and decisions of Commissioners are of equal status. However, a decision-maker or First-tier Tribunal should generally prefer a reported decision to an unreported one unless the unreported decision was the later decision and the Commissioner or Upper Tribunal expressly decided not to follow the earlier reported decision. This is simply because the fact that a decision has been reported shows that at least half of the relevant judges of the Upper Tribunal or the Commissioners agreed with it at the time. A decision of a Tribunal of Commissioners (i.e. three Commissioners sitting together) or a decision of a three-judge panel of the Upper Tribunal must be preferred to a decision of a single Commissioner or a single judge of the Upper Tribunal.

A single judge of the Upper Tribunal will normally follow a decision of a single Commissioner or another judge of the Upper Tribunal, but is not bound to do so. A three-judge panel of the Upper Tribunal will generally follow a decision of another such panel or of a Tribunal of Commissioners, but similarly is not bound to do so, whereas a single judge of the Upper Tribunal will always follow such a decision.

Strictly speaking, the Northern Ireland Commissioners do not set binding precedent that must be followed in Great Britain but their decisions are relevant, due to the similarity of the legislation in Northern Ireland, and are usually regarded as highly persuasive with the result that, in practice, they are generally given as much weight as decisions of the Great Britain Commissioners. The same approach is taken in Northern Ireland to decisions of the Upper Tribunal on social security matters and to decisions of the Great Britain Commissioners.

Decisions of the superior courts in Great Britain and Northern Ireland on questions of legal principle are almost invariably followed by decision-makers, tribunals and the Upper Tribunal, even when they are not strictly binding because the relevant court was in a different part of the United Kingdom or exercised a parallel – but not superior – jurisdiction.

Decisions of the European Court of Justice come in two parts: the Opinion of the Advocate General and the decision of the Court. It is the decision of the Court which is binding. The Court is assisted by hearing the Opinion of the Advocate General before itself coming to a conclusion on the issue before it. The Court does not always follow its Advocate General. Where it does, the Opinion of the Advocate General often elaborates the arguments in greater detail than the single collegiate judgment of the Court. Decision-makers, tribunals and Commissioners must apply decisions of the European Court of Justice, where relevant to cases before them, in preference to other authorities binding on them.

The European Court of Human Rights in Strasbourg is quite separate from the European Court of Justice in Luxembourg and serves a different purpose: interpreting and applying the European Convention on Human Rights, which is incorporated into United Kingdom law by the Human Rights Act 1998. Since October 2, 2000, public authorities in the United Kingdom, including courts, Commissioners, tribunals and decision-makers have been required to act in accordance with the incorporated provisions of the Convention, unless statute prevents this. They must take into account the Strasbourg case law and are required to interpret domestic legislation, so far as it is possible to do so, to give effect to the incorporated Convention rights. Any court or tribunal may declare secondary legislation incompatible with those rights and, in certain circumstances, invalidate it. Only the higher courts can declare a provision of primary legislation to be incompatible with those rights, but no court, tribunal or Upper Tribunal can invalidate primary legislation. The work of the Strasbourg Court and the impact of the Human Rights Act 1998 on social security are discussed in the commentary in Part IV of this volume.

See the note to s.3(2) of the Tribunals, Courts and Enforcement Act 2007 in Part V of this volume for a more detailed and technical consideration of the rules of precedent.

Other sources of information and commentary on social security law

For a comprehensive overview of the social security system in Great Britain, CPAG's *Welfare Benefits and Tax Credits Handbook*, published annually each spring, is unrivalled as a practical introduction from the claimant's viewpoint.

From a different perspective, the Department for Work and Pensions publishes the 14-volume *Decision Makers' Guide* at *https://www.gov.uk/government/collections/decision-makers-guide-staff-guide* and the new *Advice for Decision Making*, which covers personal independence payment, universal credit and the "new" versions of Jobseeker's Allowance and Employment and Support Allowance, at *https://www.gov.uk/government/publications/advice-for-decision-making-staff-guide*. Similarly, Her Majesty's Revenue and Customs publish manuals relating to tax credits, child benefit and guardian's allowance, which they administer, see *http://www.hmrc.gov.uk/thelibrary/manuals-a-z.htm*. (Note that the *Child Benefit Technical Manual* also covers guardian's allowance.) These guides and manuals are extremely useful but their interpretation of the law is not binding on tribunals and the courts, being merely internal guidance for the use of decision-makers.

There are a number of other sources of valuable information or commentary on social security case law: see in particular publications such as the *Journal of Social Security Law*, CPAG's *Welfare Rights Bulletin*, *Legal Action* and the *Adviser*. As far as online resources go there is little to beat *Rightsnet* (*http://www.rightsnet.org.uk*). This site contains a wealth of resources for people working in the welfare benefits field but of special relevance in this context are Commissioners'/Upper Tribunal Decisions section of the "Toolkit" area and also the "Briefcase" area which contains summaries of the decisions (with links to the full decisions). Sweet and Maxwell's online subscription service *Westlaw* is another valuable source (*http://www.westlaw.co.uk*), as is the Merrill Corporation's *Casetrack* (*http://www.casetrack.com/ct/casetrack.nsf/index?openframeset*) and LexisNexis *Lexis* (*http://www.lexis.com*).

Conclusion

The internet provides a vast resource but a search needs to be focused. Social security schemes are essentially statutory and so in Great Britain the legislation which is set out in this series forms the basic structure of social security law. However, the case law shows how the legislation should be interpreted and applied. The commentary in this series should point the way to the case law relevant to each provision and the Internet can then be used to find it where that is necessary.

EFFECTIVE DATES OF CHANGES TO UNIVERSAL CREDIT LEGISLATION

Once universal credit has been awarded, the general rule is that a superseding decision based on a change of circumstances, takes effect from the first day of the assessment period in which that change occurred or is expected to occur (see the Decisions and Appeals Regulations 2013 reg.35 and Sch.1, Pt.III). This follows the rule for the "legacy" benefits (IS, HB, JSA(IB), and ESA(IR)) in which changes took effect from the first day of the benefit week in which they occurred or were expected to occur (see, e.g., the Social Security and Child Support (Decisions and Appeals) Regulations 1999 Schs 3A and 3C).

The administrative advantages of having a bright line rule about the effective dates for changes in circumstances are obvious: it avoids having to carry out more than one benefit calculation for each period by reference to which entitlement is administered.

However, the "legacy" benefits were paid on a weekly basis, so claimants could neither gain nor lose more than a week's benefit if a change in circumstances was taken into account early. By contrast, universal credit is administered by reference to monthly assessment periods. Having an adverse change that occurs towards the end of an assessment period taken into account up to a month early can have serious consequences for claimants (e.g., where a claimant ceases to be liable to pay rent and therefore to be eligible for the housing costs element).

It is therefore important to note that where the change in circumstances is a change in *legislation* the opposite rule often applies. In such cases, the amending Regulations may contain a provision in the following (or similar terms):

"(2) Where the amendments made by these Regulations apply in respect of an existing award of universal credit, they have effect for the purposes of that award—

  (a) on [date] if there is an assessment period for that award that begins on that day; or

  (b) if sub-paragraph (a) does not apply, on the first day of the next assessment period for the award beginning after that day.

(3) For the purposes of this regulation, "existing award of universal credit" means an award of universal credit that exists on [date]."

The effect is that the amended law apples to new claims for universal credit from the outset. However, where there is an existing award of universal credit, the amendment takes effect from the first day of the following assessment period.

In such cases, the Amendment sections of the commentary in this volume refer to "Assessment periods beginning on or after" the date on which the amending regulation comes into force (or similar), rather than just stating that date.

TABLE OF CASES

TABLE OF COMMISSIONERS' DECISIONS

TABLE OF ABBREVIATIONS USED IN THIS SERIES

1975 Act	Social Security Act 1975
1977 Act	Marriage (Scotland) Act 1977
1979 Act	Pneumoconiosis (Workers' Compensation) Act 1979
1986 Act	Social Security Act 1986
1996 Act	Employment Rights Act 1996
1998 Act	Social Security Act 1998
2002 Act	Tax Credits Act 2002
2004 Act	Gender Recognition Act 2004
2006 Act	Armed Forces Act 2006
2008 Act	Child Maintenance and Other Payments Act 2008
2013 Act	Marriage (Same Sex Couples) Act 2013
2014 Act	Marriage and Civil Partnership (Scotland) Act 2014
A1P1	Art.1 of Protocol 1 to the European Convention on Human Rights
AA	Attendance Allowance
AA 1992	Attendance Allowance Act 1992
AAC	Administrative Appeals Chamber
AACR	Administrative Appeals Chamber Reports
A.C.	Law Reports, Appeal Cases
A.C.D.	Administrative Court Digest
Admin	Administrative Court
Admin L.R.	Administrative Law Reports
Administration Act	Social Security Administration Act 1992
Administration Regulations	Statutory Paternity Pay and Statutory Adoption Pay (Administration) Regulations 2002
AIP	assessed income period
All E.R.	All England Reports
All E.R. (E.C.)	All England Reports (European Cases)
AMA	Adjudicating Medical Authorities
AO	Adjudication Officer
AOG	*Adjudication Officers Guide*
art.	article
Art.	Article
ASD	Autistic Spectrum Disorder
ASPP	Additional Statutory Paternity Pay

Table of Abbreviations used in this Series

A.T.C.	Annotated Tax Cases
Attendance Allowance Regulations	Social Security (Attendance Allowance) Regulations 1991
AWT	All Work Test
BA	Benefits Agency
Benefits Act	Social Security Contributions and Benefits Act 1992
B.H.R.C.	Butterworths Human Rights Cases
B.L.G.R.	Butterworths Local Government Reports
Blue Books	*The Law Relating to Social Security*, Vols 1–11
B.P.I.R.	Bankruptcy and Personal Insolvency Reports
B.T.C.	British Tax Cases
BTEC	Business and Technology Education Council
B.V.C.	British Value Added Tax Reporter
B.W.C.C.	Butterworths Workmen's Compensation Cases
c.	chapter
C	Commissioner's decision
C&BA 1992	Social Security Contributions and Benefits Act 1992
CAA 2001	Capital Allowances Act 2001
CAB	Citizens Advice Bureau
CAO	Chief Adjudication Officer
CB	Child Benefit
CBA 1975	Child Benefit Act 1975
CBJSA	Contribution-Based Jobseeker's Allowance
C.C.L. Rep.	Community Care Law Reports
CCM	HMRC *New Tax Credits Claimant Compliance Manual*
C.E.C.	European Community Cases
CERA	cortical evoked response audiogram
CESA	Contribution-based Employment and Support Allowance
CFS	chronic fatigue syndrome
Ch.	Chancery Division Law Reports; Chapter
Citizenship Directive	Directive 2004/38/EC of the European Parliament and of the Council of April 29, 2004
CJEC	Court of Justice of the European Communities
CJEU	Court of Justice of the European Union
Claims and Payments Regulations	Social Security (Claims and Payments) Regulations 1987
Claims and Payments Regulations 1979	Social Security (Claims and Payments) Regulations 1979
Claims and Payments Regulations 2013	Universal Credit, Personal Independence Payment, Jobseeker's Allowance and Employment and Support Allowance (Claims and Payments) Regulations 2013
CM	Case Manager

CMA	Chief Medical Adviser
CMEC	Child Maintenance and Enforcement Commission
C.M.L.R.	Common Market Law Reports
C.O.D.	Crown Office Digest
COLL	*Collective Investment Schemes Sourcebook*
Community, The	European Community
Computation of Earnings Regulations	Social Security Benefit (Computation of Earnings) Regulations 1978
Computation of Earnings Regulations 1996	Social Security Benefit (Computation of Earnings) Regulations 1996
Consequential Provisions Act	Social Security (Consequential Provisions) Act 1992
Contributions and Benefits Act	Social Security Contributions and Benefits Act 1992
Contributions Regulations	Social Security (Contributions) Regulations 2001
COPD	chronic obstructive pulmonary disease
CP	Carer Premium; Chamber President
CPAG	Child Poverty Action Group
CPR	Civil Procedure Rules
Cr. App. R.	Criminal Appeal Reports
CRCA 2005	Commissioners for Revenue and Customs Act 2005
Credits Regulations 1974	Social Security (Credits) Regulations 1974
Credits Regulations 1975	Social Security (Credits) Regulations 1975
Crim. L.R.	Criminal Law Review
CRU	Compensation Recovery Unit
CSA 1995	Children (Scotland) Act 1995
CSIH	Inner House of the Court of Session (Scotland)
CSM	Child Support Maintenance
CS(NI)O 1995	Child Support (Northern Ireland) Order 1995
CSOH	Outer House of the Court of Session (Scotland)
CSPSSA 2000	Child Support, Pensions and Social Security Act 2000
CTA	Common Travel Area
CTA 2009	Corporation Tax Act 2009
CTA 2010	Corporation Tax Act 2010
CTB	Council Tax Benefit
CTC	Child Tax Credit
CTC Regulations	Child Tax Credit Regulations 2002
CTF	child trust fund
CTS	Carpal Tunnel Syndrome
DAC	Directive 2011/16/ EU (Directive on administrative co-operation in the field of taxation)

Table of Abbreviations used in this Series

DAT	Disability Appeal Tribunal
dB	decibels
DCA	Department for Constitutional Affairs
DCP	Disabled Child Premium
Decisions and Appeals Regulations 1999	Social Security Contributions (Decisions and Appeals) Regulations 1999
Dependency Regulations	Social Security Benefit (Dependency) Regulations 1977
DfEE	Department for Education and Employment
DHSS	Department of Health and Social Security
Disability Living Allowance Regulations	Social Security (Disability Living Allowance) Regulations
DIY	do it yourself
DLA	Disability Living Allowance
DLA Regs 1991	Social Security (Disability Living Allowance) Regulations 1991
DLAAB	Disability Living Allowance Advisory Board
DLADWAA 1991	Disability Living Allowance and Disability Working Allowance Act 1991
DM	Decision Maker
DMA	Decision-making and Appeals
DMG	*Decision Makers' Guide*
DMP	Delegated Medical Practitioner
DP	Disability Premium
DPT	diffuse pleural thickening
DPTC	Disabled Person's Tax Credit
DRO	Debt Relief Order
DSD	Department for Social Development (Northern Ireland)
DSM IV; DSM-5	Diagnostic and Statistical Manual of Mental Disorders of the American Psychiatric Association
DSS	Department of Social Security
DTI	Department of Trade and Industry
DWA	Disability Working Allowance
DWP	Department for Work and Pensions
DWPMS	Department for Work and Pensions Medical Service
EAA	Extrinsic Allergic Alveolitis
EAT	Employment Appeal Tribunal
EC	European Community
ECHR	European Convention on Human Rights
ECJ	European Court of Justice
E.C.R.	European Court Reports
ECSC	European Coal and Steel Community

ECSMA	European Convention on Social and Medical Assistance
EEA	European Economic Area
EEC	European Economic Community
EESSI	Electronic Exchange of Social Security Information
E.G.	Estates Gazette
E.G.L.R.	Estates Gazette Law Reports
EHC plan	education, health and care plan
EHIC	European Health Insurance Card
EHRC	European Human Rights Commission
E.H.R.R.	European Human Rights Reports
EL	employers' liability
E.L.R	Education Law Reports
EMA	Education Maintenance Allowance
EMP	Examining Medical Practitioner
Employment and Support Allowance Regulations	Employment and Support Allowance Regulations 2008
EPS	extended period of sickness
Eq. L.R.	Equality Law Reports
ERA	evoked response audiometry
ERA scheme	Employment, Retention and Advancement scheme
ES	Employment Service
ESA	Employment and Support Allowance
ESA Regs 2013	Employment and Support Allowance Regulations 2013
ESA Regulations	Employment and Support Allowance Regulations 2008
ESA WCAt	Employment and Support Allowance Work Capability Assessment
ESC	employer supported childcare
ESE Scheme	Employment, Skills and Enterprise Scheme
ESE Regulations	Jobseeker's Allowance (Employment, Skills and Enterprise Scheme) Regulations 2011
ESES Regulations	Jobseeker's Allowance (Employment, Skills and Enterprise Scheme) Regulations 2011
ETA 1973	Employment and Training Act 1973
ETA(NI) 1950	Employment and Training Act (Northern Ireland) 1950
ETS	European Treaty Series
EU	European Union
Eu.L.R.	European Law Reports
EWCA Civ	Civil Division of the Court of Appeal (England and Wales)
EWHC Admin	Administrative Court Division of the High Court (England and Wales)

FA 1993	Finance Act 1993
FA 1996	Finance Act 1996
FA 2004	Finance Act 2004
Fam. Law	Family Law
FAS	Financial Assistance Scheme
F.C.R.	Family Court Reporter
FEV	forced expiratory volume
FIS	Family Income Supplement
FISMA 2000	Financial Services and Markets Act 2000
F.L.R.	Family Law Reports
FME	further medical evidence
F(No.2)A 2005	Finance (No.2) Act 2005
FOTRA	Free of Tax to Residents Abroad
FRAA	flat rate accrual amount
FRS Act 2004	Fire and Rescue Services Act 2004
FSCS	Financial Services Compensation Scheme
FTT	First-tier Tribunal
General Benefit Regulations 1982	Social Security (General Benefit) Regulations 1982
General Regulations	Statutory Shared Parental Pay (General) Regulations 2014
GMCA	Greater Manchester Combined Authority
GMFRA	Greater Manchester Fire and Rescue Authority
GMP	Guaranteed Minimum Pension
GMWDA	Greater Manchester Waste Disposal Authority
GNVQ	General National Vocational Qualification
GP	General Practitioner
GRA	Gender Recognition Act 2004
GRB	Graduated Retirement Benefit
GRP	Graduated Retirement Pension
HB	Housing Benefit
HB (WSP) R (NI) 2017	Housing Benefit (Welfare Social Payment) Regulations (Northern Ireland) 2017
HBRB	Housing Benefit Review Board
HCA	Homes and Communities Agency
HCD	House of Commons Debates
HCP	healthcare professional
HCV	Hepatitis C virus
Health Service Act	National Health Service Act 2006
Health Service (Wales) Act	National Health Service (Wales) Act 2006
HIV	Human Immunodeficiency Virus
HL	House of Lords
H.L.R.	Housing Law Reports
HMIT	Her Majesty's Inspector of Taxes

HMRC	Her Majesty's Revenue and Customs
HMSO	Her Majesty's Stationery Office
Hospital In-Patients Regulations 1975	Social Security (Hospital In-Patients) Regulations 1975
HP	Health Professional
HPP	Higher Pensioner Premium
HRA 1998	Human Rights Act 1998
H.R.L.R.	Human Rights Law Reports
HRP	Home Responsibilities Protection
HSE	Health and Safety Executive
IAC	Immigration and Asylum Chamber
IAP	Intensive Activity Period
IB	Incapacity Benefit
IB PCA	Incapacity Benefit Personal Capability Assessment
IB Regs	Social Security (Incapacity Benefit) Regulations 1994
IB Regulations	Social Security (Incapacity Benefit) Regulations 1994
IB/IS/SDA	Incapacity Benefits Regime
IBJSA	Income-Based Jobseeker's Allowance
IBS	Irritable Bowel Syndrome
ICA	Invalid Care Allowance
I.C.R.	Industrial Cases Reports
ICTA 1988	Income and Corporation Taxes Act 1988
IFW Regulations	Incapacity for Work (General) Regulations 1995
IH	Inner House of the Court of Session
I.I.	Industrial Injuries
IIAC	Industrial Injuries Advisory Council
IIDB	Industrial Injuries Disablement Benefit
ILO	International Labour Organization
Imm. A.R.	Immigration Appeal Reports
Incapacity for Work Regulations	Social Security (Incapacity for Work) (General) Regulations 1995
Income Support General Regulations	Income Support (General) Regulations 1987
IND	Immigration and Nationality Directorate of the Home Office
I.N.L.R.	Immigration and Nationality Law Reports
I.O.	Insurance Officer
IPPR	Institute of Public Policy Research
IRESA	Income-Related Employment and Support Allowance
I.R.L.R.	Industrial Relations Law Reports
IS	Income Support

Table of Abbreviations used in this Series

IS Regs	Income Support Regulations
IS Regulations	Income Support (General) Regulations 1987
ISA	Individual Savings Account
ISBN	International Standard Book Number
ITA 2007	Income Tax Act 2007
ITEPA 2003	Income Tax, Earnings and Pensions Act 2003
I.T.L. Rep.	International Tax Law Reports
I.T.R.	Industrial Tribunals Reports
ITS	Independent Tribunal Service
ITTOIA 2005	Income Tax (Trading and Other Income) Act 2005
IVB	Invalidity Benefit
IW (General) Regs	Social Security (Incapacity for Work) (General) Regulations 1995
IW (Transitional) Regs	Incapacity for Work (Transitional) Regulations
Jobseeker's Allowance Regulations	Jobseeker's Allowance Regulations 1996
Jobseeker's Regulations 1996	Jobseeker's Allowance Regulations 1996
JSA	Jobseeker's Allowance
JSA 1995	Jobseekers Act 1995
JSA (NI) Regulations	Jobseeker's Allowance (Northern Ireland) Regulations 1996
JSA (Transitional) Regulations	Jobseeker's Allowance (Transitional) Regulations 1996
JSA Regs 1996	Jobseeker's Allowance Regulations 1996
JSA Regs 2013	Jobseeker's Allowance Regulations 2013
JS(NI)O 1995	Jobseekers (Northern Ireland) Order 1995
J.S.S.L.	Journal of Social Security Law
J.S.W.L.	Journal of Social Welfare Law
K.B.	Law Reports, King's Bench
L.& T.R.	Landlord and Tenant Reports
LCW	limited capability for work
LCWA	Limited Capability for Work Assessment
LCWRA	limited capability for work-related activity
LDEDC Act 2009	Local Democracy, Economic Development and Construction Act 2009
LEA	local education authority
LEL	Lower Earnings Limit
LET	low earnings threshold
L.G. Rev.	Local Government Review
L.G.L.R.	Local Government Reports
L.J.R.	Law Journal Reports
LRP	liable relative payment
L.S.G.	Law Society Gazette
Luxembourg Court	Court of Justice of the European Union (also referred to as CJEC and ECJ)

MA	Maternity Allowance
MAF	Medical Assessment Framework
Maternity Allowance Regulations	Social Security (Maternity Allowance) Regulations 1987
MDC	Mayoral development corporation
ME	myalgic encephalomyelitis
Medical Evidence Regulations	Social Security (Medical Evidence) Regulations 1976
MEN	Mandatory Employment Notification
Mesher and Wood	*Income Support, the Social Fund and Family Credit: the Legislation* (1996)
M.H.L.R.	Mental Health Law Reports
MHP	mental health problems
MIF	minimum income floor
MIG	minimum income guarantee
Migration Regulations	Employment and Support Allowance (Transitional Provisions, Housing Benefit and Council Tax Benefit (Existing Awards) (No.2) Regulations 2010
MP	Member of Parliament
MRSA	methicillin-resistant Staphylococcus aureus
MS	Medical Services
MWA Regulations	Jobseeker's Allowance (Mandatory Work Activity Scheme) Regulations 2011
MWAS Regulations	Jobseeker's Allowance (Mandatory Work Activity Scheme) Regulations 2011
NCB	National Coal Board
NDPD	Notes on the Diagnosis of Prescribed Diseases
NHS	National Health Service
NI	National Insurance
N.I..	Northern Ireland Law Reports
NICA	Northern Ireland Court of Appeal
NICom	Northern Ireland Commissioner
NICs	National Insurance Contributions
NINO	National Insurance Number
NIRS 2	National Insurance Recording System
N.L.J.	New Law Journal
NMC	Nursing and Midwifery Council
Northern Ireland Contributions and Benefits Act	Social Security Contributions and Benefits (Northern Ireland) Act 1992
N.P.C.	New Property Cases
NRCGT	non-resident capital gains tax
NTC Manual	Clerical procedures manual on tax credits
NUM	National Union of Mineworkers
NUS	National Union of Students
OCD	obsessive compulsive disorder

Ogus, Barendt and Wikeley	A. Ogus, E. Barendt and N. Wikeley, *The Law of Social Security* (1995)
Old Cases Act	Industrial Injuries and Diseases (Old Cases) Act 1975
OPB	One Parent Benefit
O.P.L.R.	Occupational Pensions Law Reports
OPSSAT	Office of the President of Social Security Appeal Tribunals
Overlapping Benefits Regulations	Social Security (Overlapping Benefits) Regulations 1975
P	retirement pension case
P. & C.R.	Property and Compensation Reports
para.	paragraph
Pay Regulations	Statutory Paternity Pay and Statutory Adoption Pay (General) Regulations 2002; Statutory Shared Parental Pay (General) Regulations 2014
PAYE	Pay As You Earn
PC	Privy Council
PCA	Personal Capability Assessment
PCC	Police and Crime Commissioner
PD	Practice Direction; prescribed disease
Pens. L.R.	Pensions Law Reports
Pensions Act	Pension Schemes Act 1993
PEP	Personal Equity Plan
Persons Abroad Regulations	Social Security Benefit (Persons Abroad) Regulations 1975
Persons Residing Together Regulations	Social Security Benefit (Persons Residing Together) Regulations 1977
PIE	Period of Interruption of Employment
PILON	pay in lieu of notice
Pilot Scheme Regulations	Universal Credit (Work-Related Requirements) In Work Pilot Scheme and Amendment Regulations 2015
PIP	Personal Independence Payment
P.I.Q.R.	Personal Injuries and Quantum Reports
Polygamous Marriages Regulations	Social Security and Family Allowances (Polygamous Marriages) Regulations 1975
PPF	Pension Protection Fund
Prescribed Diseases Regulations	Social Security (Industrial Injuries) (Prescribed Diseases) Regulations 1985
PSCS	Pension Service Computer System
Pt	Part
PTA	pure tone audiometry
P.T.S.R.	Public and Third Sector Law Reports
PTWR 2000	Part-time Workers (Prevention of Less Favourable Treatment) Regulations 2000

PVS	private and voluntary sectors
Q.B.	Queen's Bench Law Reports
QBD	Queen's Bench Division
QCS Board	Quality Contract Scheme Board
QEF	qualifying earnings factor
QYP	qualifying young person
r.	rule
R	Reported Decision
R.C.	Rules of the Court of Session
REA	Reduced Earnings Allowance
reg.	regulation
RIPA	Regulation of Investigatory Powers Act 2000
RMO	Responsible Medical Officer
rr.	rules
RR	reference rate
RSI	repetitive strain injury
RTI	Real Time Information
R.V.R.	Rating & Valuation Reporter
s.	section
S	Scottish Decision
SAP	Statutory Adoption Pay
SAPOE Regulations	Jobseeker's Allowance (Schemes for Assisting Persons to Obtain Employment) Regulations 2013
SAWS	Seasonal Agricultural Work Scheme
SAYE	Save As You Earn
SB	Supplementary Benefit
SBAT	Supplementary Benefit Appeal Tribunal
SBC	Supplementary Benefits Commission
S.C.	Session Cases
S.C. (H.L.)	Session Cases (House of Lords)
S.C. (P.C.)	Session Cases (Privy Council)
S.C.C.R.	Scottish Criminal Case Reports
S.C.L.R.	Scottish Civil Law Reports
Sch.	Schedule
SDA	Severe Disablement Allowance
SDP	Severe Disability Premium
SEC	Social Entitlement Chamber
SEN	special educational needs
SERPS	State Earnings Related Pension Scheme
ShPP	statutory shared parental pay
ShPP Regulations	Statutory Shared Parental Pay (General) Regulations 2014
SI	Statutory Instrument

SIP	Share Incentive Plan
S.J.	Solicitors Journal
S.J.L.B.	Solicitors Journal Law Brief
SLAN	statement like an award notice
S.L.T.	Scots Law Times
SMP	Statutory Maternity Pay
SMP (General) Regulations 1986	Statutory Maternity Pay (General) Regulations 1986
SPC	State Pension Credit
SPC Regulations	State Pension Credit Regulations 2002
SPCA 2002	State Pension Credit Act 2002
SPL Regulations	Shared Parental Leave Regulations 2014
SPP	Statutory Paternity Pay
ss.	sections
SS (No.2) A 1980	Social Security (No.2) Act 1980
SSA 1975	Social Security Act 1975
SSA 1977	Social Security Act 1977
SSA 1978	Social Security Act 1978
SSA 1979	Social Security Act 1979
SSA 1981	Social Security Act 1981
SSA 1986	Social Security Act 1986
SSA 1988	Social Security Act 1988
SSA 1989	Social Security Act 1989
SSA 1990	Social Security Act 1990
SSA 1998	Social Security Act 1998
SSAA 1992	Social Security Administration Act 1992
SSAC	Social Security Advisory Committee
SSAT	Social Security Appeal Tribunal
SSCBA 1992	Social Security Contributions and Benefits Act 1992
SSCB(NI)A 1992	Social Security Contributions and Benefits (Northern Ireland) Act 1992
SSCPA 1992	Social Security (Consequential Provisions) Act 1992
SSD	Secretary of State for Defence
SSHBA 1982	Social Security and Housing Benefits Act 1982
SSHD	Secretary of State for the Home Department
SSI	Scottish Statutory Instrument
SS(MP)A 1977	Social Security (Miscellaneous Provisions) Act 1977
SSP	Statutory Sick Pay
SSP (General) Regulations	Statutory Sick Pay (General) Regulations 1982
SSPA 1975	Social Security Pensions Act 1975
SSPP	statutory shared parental pay
SSWP	Secretary of State for Work and Pensions

Table of Abbreviations used in this Series

State Pension Credit Regulations	State Pension Credit Regulations 2002
S.T.C.	Simon's Tax Cases
S.T.C. (S.C.D.)	Simon's Tax Cases: Special Commissioners' Decisions
S.T.I.	Simon's Tax Intelligence
STIB	Short-Term Incapacity Benefit
subpara.	subparagraph
subs.	subsection
T	Tribunal of Commissioners' Decision
T.C.	Tax Cases
TCA 1999	Tax Credits Act 1999
TCA 2002	Tax Credits Act 2002
TCC	Technology and Construction Court
TCEA 2007	Tribunals, Courts and Enforcement Act 2007
TCGA 1992	Taxation of Chargeable Gains Act 2002
TCTM	*Tax Credits Technical Manual*
TEC	Treaty Establishing the European Community
TENS	transcutaneous electrical nerve stimulation
TEU	Treaty on European Union
TFC	tax-free childcare
TFEU	Treaty on the Functioning of the European Union
TIOPA 2010	Taxation (International and Other Provisions) Act 2010
TMA 1970	Taxes Management Act 1970
T.R.	Taxation Reports
Transfer of Functions Act	Social Security Contributions (Transfer of Functions etc.) Act 1999
Tribunal Procedure Rules	Tribunal Procedure (First-tier Tribunal)(Social Entitlement Chamber) Rules 2008
UB	Unemployment Benefit
UC	Universal Credit
UC Regs 2013	Universal Credit Regulations 2013
UCITS	Undertakings for Collective Investments in Transferable Securities
UKAIT	UK Asylum and Immigration Tribunal
UKBA	UK Border Agency of the Home Office
UKCC	United Kingdom Central Council for Nursing, Midwifery and Health Visiting
UKFTT	United Kingdom First-tier Tribunal Tax Chamber
UKHL	United Kingdom House of Lords
U.K.H.R.R.	United Kingdom Human Rights Reports
UKSC	United Kingdom Supreme Court
UKUT	United Kingdom Upper Tribunal

Table of Abbreviations used in this Series

UN	United Nations
Universal Credit Regulations	Universal Credit Regulations 2013
URL	uniform resource locator
USI Regs	Social Security (Unemployment, Sickness and Invalidity Benefit) Regulations 1983
USI Regulations	Social Security (Unemployment, Sickness and Invalidity Benefit) Regulations 1983
UT	Upper Tribunal
VAT	Value Added Tax
VCM	vinyl chloride monomer
Vol.	Volume
VWF	Vibration White Finger
W	Welsh Decision
WCA	Work Capability Assessment
WCAt	limited capability for work assessment
WFHRAt	Work-Focused Health-Related Assessment
WFI	work-focused interview
WFTC	Working Families Tax Credit
Wikeley, Annotations	N. Wikeley, "Annotations to Jobseekers Act 1995 (c.18)" in *Current Law Statutes Annotated* (1995)
Wikeley, Ogus and Barendt	Wikeley, Ogus and Barendt, *The Law of Social Security* (2002)
W.L.R.	Weekly Law Reports
Workmen's Compensation Acts	Workmen's Compensation Acts 1925 to 1945
WP	Widow's Pension
WPS	War Pensions Scheme
WRA 2007	Welfare Reform Act 2007
WRA 2009	Welfare Reform Act 2009
WRA 2012	Welfare Reform Act 2012
W-RA Regulations	Employment and Support Allowance (Work-Related Activity) Regulations 2011
WRAAt	Work-Related Activity Assessment
WRPA 1999	Welfare Reform and Pensions Act 1999
WRP(NI)O 1999	Welfare Reform and Pensions (Northern Ireland) Order 1999
WSP (LCP) R (NI) 2016	Welfare Supplementary Payment (Loss of Carer Payments) Regulations (Northern Ireland) 2016
WSP (LDRP) R (NI) 2016	Welfare Supplementary Payment (Loss of Disability-Related Premiums) Regulations (Northern Ireland) 2016
WSPR (NI) 2016	Welfare Supplementary Payment Regulations (Northern Ireland) 2016
WTC	Working Tax Credit
WTC Regulations	Working Tax Credit (Entitlement and Maximum Rate) Regulations 2002

PART I

INTRODUCTION

Universal Credit—An Introduction

If the information technology on which it depends can be made to work, universal credit is destined to become the future of working-age social security in Great Britain. Its introduction is the biggest change to the social security system since the abolition of supplementary benefit and its replacement with income support ("IS") by the Social Security Act 1986.

However, there have been problems with the speed at which the new benefit has been introduced, and changes to the structure and rate of the "work allowance" that took effect in April 2016 have dramatically reduced some of the incentives to work previously offered by universal credit.

The problem: complexity and disincentives to work

Readers of Vols I to IV of this work will require no persuading that the social security system as a whole is complex. However, the changes since 1996—including the introduction of jobseeker's allowance ("JSA") in October 1996, the new tax credits in April 2003, and employment and support allowance ("ESA") in October 2008—have destroyed the previous position of IS as a single benefit for all those poor enough to satisfy the means-test. Instead, the changes have created a system for claimants of working age (i.e., who have yet to attain the qualifying age for state pension credit ("SPC")) that is more than usually Byzantine.

Before the introduction of universal credit, people of working age who needed to claim benefit because they were not working (or, though working, were not earning enough to meet their basic needs) had to choose from a complex array of benefits some of which complemented each other and others of which were mutually exclusive.

Those who were able to work, but could not find a job, generally had to claim JSA, entitlement to which was either "contribution-based", or "income-based" ("JSA(IB)") which was a euphemism for "means-tested". Those who could not work because they were prevented from doing so by illness or disability claimed ESA, which again could be contributory or "income-related" ("ESA(IR)"). Those who could not be expected to work for other reasons (e.g., because they were caring for a young child or for a disabled person) could claim IS, entitlement to which was based on a means-test and had no contributory component.

The three benefits listed above were administered by the Department for Work and Pensions ("DWP") and included elements to help meet a claimant's housing costs if (broadly speaking) the claimant was an owner-occupier. However, for claimants who rented their homes, help for housing costs was provided by a fourth benefit, housing benefit ("HB") which was administered by local authorities.

Moreover, ESA(IR) and—except in a limited class of transitional cases—JSA(IB) and IS were "adults only" benefits. For claimants whose families included children or "qualifying young persons" (people aged between 16 and 20 who are in education or training) state help for the cost of feeding, clothing and bringing up the child or qualifying young person was provided by HM Revenue & Customs ("HMRC") through two further benefits, child benefit and child tax credit ("CTC").

Finally, people working more than 16 hours a week were excluded from IS, JSA(IB) and ESA(IR). However, they could sometimes claim working tax credit ("WTC"), which was not open to anyone working fewer than 16 hours a week. HB had no hours rule (although, of course, the more hours a person worked, the more likely their claim might fail on income grounds).

The complexity of that system, in which a claimant with children living in rented property might have to claim four different benefits from three different agencies was further aggravated by the fact entitlement to tax credits was normally calculated with respect to, and paid over, an entire tax year whereas entitlement to IS, JSA(IB), ESA(IR) and HB was calculated weekly and usually paid fortnightly or, in the case of HB, four-weekly or monthly. It was often difficult to ensure that the two different calculation and payment systems meshed together properly, not least because the mechanisms for sharing information between the DWP, HMRC and local authorities were less than perfect. The whole system operated against the background that a mistake, whether by the claimant or the administering authority, could result in an overpayment, leaving the claimant in debt, often for thousands of pounds.

The old system had the further effect of providing financial disincentives to work at certain levels of income. Under the means-tests for IS, JSA(IB) and ESA(IR) only relatively small amounts of earnings were ignored. Claimants whose earnings exceeded those "disregards" had their benefits reduced penny for penny by the amount of the excess and therefore derived no further benefit from their earnings until they earned enough to lose entitlement to benefit altogether.

This is not the place for a detailed discussion of the poverty trap. An example should suffice to make the point.

During 2017/2018, a single claimant, call her Jane, aged over 25 on the basic rate of JSA(IB) receives £73.10 per week. Jane's weekly earnings disregard is £5.00. Suppose she does one hour's work a week at the national minimum wage of £7.50 per hour. The first £5 of those earnings is disregarded but her JSA(IB) is reduced by £2.50 (the amount by which £7.50 exceeds £5) to £70.60. Jane's total weekly income is thus £78.10 (£7.50 in earnings plus JSA(IB) of £70.60).

Now, suppose Jane increases her working hours to ten per week. Her weekly earnings are now £75.00 (£7.50 × 10) but her earnings disregard is still £5. Therefore her weekly entitlement to JSA(IB) is reduced by £70.00 (£75.00-£5.00) from £73.10 to £3.10, giving her a total weekly income of £78.10 (£75.00 in earnings plus £3.10 in JSA(IB)). In short, Jane's income remains exactly the same whether she works one hour per week or ten. It is only once she works 11 hours a week, taking her earnings to £82.50 and losing entitlement to JSA(IB) altogether, that Jane begins to be better off. And at that stage, if she is in rented accommodation, she is likely to lose 65 pence in HB for each additional pound that she earns. She will also lose entitlement to "passported" advantages such as free prescriptions, which will provide a further disincentive to work.

Universal credit and the new system

Universal credit is designed to get rid of both the problems outlined above by simplifying the social security system and ensuring that claimants will always be better off in work.

The planned simplification of the system was meant to be achieved by abolishing six of the seven benefits referred to above (IS, JSA(IB), ESA(IR) HB, CTC and WTC) and replacing them with universal credit. As universal credit is administered and paid by the DWP, the effect will be to end the role of local authorities in social security administration and to restrict the role of HMRC to the administration of child benefit and guardian's allowance.

In the new system, child benefit continues unaffected and two new benefits, confusingly called "jobseeker's allowance" and "employment and support allowance"—and referred to as "new style" JSA and ESA to distinguish them from the older, identically–named, "old style" benefits—will be paid without any means-test, but for limited periods, to those who meet the contribution conditions.

The proposed new structure is undoubtedly simpler than the system it will replace.

Unfortunately, the aim of simplification is currently being frustrated by the decision to phase universal credit in over a period of years. That decision is entirely understandable, given the new benefit's reliance on information technology. It would be a recipe for disaster for universal credit to be introduced on a general basis before it had been established in pilot areas that it could be properly administered.

However, the effect of a phased introduction is that the two systems continue to co-exist, so that what has been achieved is not a simplification of the benefits system but a significant complication. During the transition, universal credit is not a *replacement* benefit but an *additional* benefit.

Moreover, it is inherent in the design of universal credit that it overlaps with each of the older benefits it is eventually intended to replace. That overlap means that, in addition to the complication of the old and new systems existing side-by-side (including having two different and mutually exclusive benefits both called JSA and two called ESA), it is also necessary to have legislation defining which set of rules applies to any particular claimant at any given time. That legislation is now to be found first, in the Universal Credit (Transitional Provisions) Regulations 2014 ("the 2014 Regulations") and, second, in a series of Commencement Orders that, even by the high standards set by past social security legislation, are bewilderingly complex.

If that were not enough, the procedures by which universal credit has been introduced mean that, at least in relation to some issues, the benefit now exists in two forms with different substantive rules: see *Introduction of universal credit* below.

As a final complication, the need to devote departmental resources to the introduction of universal credit appears to have delayed the extension of the housing costs element of SPC to cover rent and other payments made by those who are not owner-occupiers. Further, even claimants who have become subject to the universal credit rules may still claim HB if they live in "exempt accommodation" (see the definition in Sch.1, para.1 to the Universal Credit Regulations, below). The effect is that local authorities will need to retain their benefits departments—and incur the associated costs and overheads that might otherwise have been saved—to deal with claims for HB from those who are above working age and in exempt accommodation.

All of that might not matter if the transition from the old system to the new were relatively swift. However, that has not happened. On June 8, 2017—the latest date for which statistics are available, and more than four years after the benefit was introduced—there were 540,000 people on universal credit. This compares with the original projection by the Office for Budget Responsibility in March 2013 that there would be 6.1 million people on universal credit in 2016-17. On the current timetable, the benefit will not be fully "rolled-out" to all new claimants until September 2018. The process of migrating claimants who are in receipt of IS, JSA(IB), ESA(IR) HB, CTC and WTC to the new benefit will then begin in July 2019 and is not now expected to end before March 2022 (see the written statement by the Secretary of State for Work and Pensions on July 20, 2016 (Hansard HCWS96)).

The slow pace of the transition also means that, for the vast majority of existing working age claimants, the benefits system continues to be as described in the opening paragraphs of this introduction: they will continue to deal with up to three different authorities and to be subject to disincentives to work from the poverty trap.

That having been said, the new scheme has some positive features.

First—and with the notable exception of the Commencement Orders—the legislation is better structured and easier to follow than social security lawyers have become accustomed to. The drafting still has some eccentricities. For example, the Regulations use the words "claimant" and "person" in an inconsistent and confusing way that assumes that they are precise synonyms for each other; and it is surprising to find what used to be the permitted work rule for those who have limited capability for work hidden away in a regulation (reg.41) that appears to be about when a work capability assessment may be carried out. However, overall, the Regulations and the 2014 Regulations are not unnecessarily opaque or complex, even though the rules for any benefit that replaces six other benefits are inevitably going to be detailed.

Second, although the universal credit scheme embodies political judgments about what claimants should be required to do in return for their benefit with which it is possible to disagree, progress has been made towards eliminating the poverty trap.

If we return to the example given above and suppose that, instead of claiming JSA, Jane had been eligible to claim universal credit, then her basic entitlement to universal credit (ignoring housing costs as we did implicitly in the JSA example) would be her "maximum amount" which would consist of the standard allowance for a single person aged at least 25, namely £317.82 per month. That equates to £73.34 per week (£317.82 × 12 ÷ 52) and is therefore a few pence higher than the equivalent personal allowance for JSA.

Jane then begins to work one hour a week at the minimum wage of £7.50 per hour. In an average month she would earn £32.50 (£7.50 × 52 ÷ 12). From April 2016, Jane would no longer be entitled to a work allowance (i.e., because she does not have responsibility for a child or qualifying young person and does not have limited capability for work). There would therefore be no equivalent of the £5 weekly disregard in the JSA calculation. However, under universal credit, from April 2017 only 63% of Jane's earnings will be deducted from the maximum amount, not the full amount of her (undisregarded) earnings as in JSA. In cash terms, the deduction is £20.47 (£32.50 × 63%) giving a monthly universal credit award of £297.35 (£317.82 − £20.47), equivalent to £68.62 per week (£297.35 × 12 ÷ 52). Jane's equivalent weekly income is therefore £76.12 (£68.62 in universal credit + £7.50 in earnings).

That figure compares unfavourably with Jane's weekly income of £78.10 on JSA (although she is still slightly better off than if she had not worked at all). However, not many people work for just one hour a week and the more work Jane does, the more the universal credit rules begin to operate in her favour. If Jane works for even two hours a week, her equivalent weekly income from universal credit and earnings is £78.89, which is (just) higher than the £78.10 JSA figure. And if she works ten hours a week (at which level, it will be remembered, her combined weekly earnings and benefit under JSA would still have been £78.10), the equivalent weekly income from universal credit and earnings is £101.09.

However, Jane is considerably worse off under the new universal credit rules than she would have been under the rules that existed before April 2016 (see *The amounts to be deducted,* below).

Note also that the rules about housing costs mean that many owner-occupiers will be substantially worse off as a result of working and some of them will be worse off than they would have been under IS/JSA/ESA (see below).

Introduction of universal credit

Universal credit raises two transitional issues. The first is whether a person making a fresh claim for benefit is free to claim IS/HB/JSA/ESA or whether he or she must now claim universal credit. The second is in what circumstances existing recipients of IS/HB/JSA/ESA will be moved from those benefits to universal credit.

Although the Act contains powers to migrate existing claimants, there are no plans to start the migration process before July 2019 (by which time it is intended that universal credit will be in place for all new claimants). If the way in which timescales have slipped in the past are any guide to the future, migration will probably not begin until well after that date. This introduction will therefore focus on the first issue.

The process of introducing universal credit was begun by the Universal Credit (Transitional Provisions) Regulations 2013 ("the 2013 Regulations"). The text of those Regulations (which have now been revoked) is set out on pp.305-354 of the 2013/14 edition of this volume. In summary, they provided that claimants may (and must) claim universal credit rather than IS/JSA/ESA if, at the time their claim was made or treated as made, they resided in one of the "relevant districts" and were either in the Pathfinder Group or had formerly been jointly entitled to universal credit as a member of a former couple. The relevant districts were postcode areas linked to particular Jobcentres and specified in the various Commencement Orders (see Pt IV below). The extension of universal credit proceeded by issuing further Commencement Orders that widened the geographical scope of the rules by adding further "relevant districts".

Membership of the Pathfinder Group was governed by regs 4-12 of the 2013 Regulations (pp.312-323 of the 2013/14 edition). The criteria for membership of the Pathfinder Group were so narrowly drawn that it, in summary, it only included single, adult, British citizens who would otherwise have had to claim JSA. The issues that were likely to give rise to disputes were narrower still because any claimant whose circumstances were likely to give rise to complications had been excluded from the Pathfinder Group and therefore had to continue to claim IS/JSA/ESA. Unsurprisingly in those circumstances, the initial experience of the Social Entitlement Chamber of the First-tier Tribunal is that universal credit appeals have overwhelmingly been about backdating and the imposition of sanctions.

The 2013 Regulations were revoked by the 2014 Regulations with effect from June 16, 2014. Nothing equivalent to the former Pathfinder conditions appeared in the 2014 Regulations. Instead, a policy decision was taken that new "Gateway conditions" would be specified in Commencement

Orders. This approach gave the government flexibility to vary those conditions for different areas, or to include no Gateway conditions at all.

That flexibility has been used to establish two different models for the implementation of universal credit. From November 11, 2014, the No.20 Commencement Order (see Pt IV below) allowed (and required) claimants who lived in a small area of the SM5 postcode in the London Borough of Sutton to claim universal credit without having to satisfy the Gateway conditions. On the same day, the Universal Credit (Digital Service) Amendment Regulations 2014 (SI 2014/2887) came into force and made substantive changes to the Universal Credit Regulations, that only apply in what are described as "digital service" areas. At that time, the SM5 2 postcode area was the only such area. However, subsequent Commencement Orders have expanded the areas covered by the digital service and further statutory instruments (SI 2014/3225 and SI 2015/1647) have introduced additional amendments to the Universal Credit Regulations that only apply in such areas.

In keeping with its long-standing institutional reluctance to call anything by its correct statutory name, the DWP now refers to digital service areas as "full service" areas and distinguishes them from the areas in which the Gateway conditions still apply by referring to the latter as "live service" areas.

The distinction reflects the fact that universal credit is now administered using two separate and incompatible IT systems, depending on whether the claimant lives in a full/digital service area or a live service area.

At the time of going to press, the rules for universal credit are in force on at least a live service basis (i.e., for claimants who satisfy the Gateway Conditions) throughout Great Britain and on a full/digital service basis in an increasing number of areas. The further roll-out of universal credit therefore consists of a process of "de-gatewayfication": instead of Commencement Orders extending universal credit to new geographical areas by prescribing additional relevant districts, they convert existing live service areas to full/digital service areas by revoking the Gateway conditions in those areas.

But even claims by people who live (or lived) in live service areas can raise issues that, if they had existed at the time of the original claim, would have meant that the Gateway conditions were not satisfied. This is because of what is known colloquially as the "lobster pot" principle. The editors of this volume profess no expertise in catching marine crustaceans, but it is understood that the analogy is to the fact that the route into a lobster pot is a narrow one, but that once inside there is more room and, most importantly, the lobster cannot get back out. The principle applies to universal credit because the Commencement Orders are structured so that the provisions of the Act that abolish JSA(IB) and ESA(IR) come into force in relation to a particular claimant when he or she makes a valid claim for, or is actually awarded universal credit. From that point on, the claimant cannot go back to the those benefits (i.e., because, in relation to him or her, they no longer exist) and must therefore continue to claim universal credit even if he or she no longer lives in a relevant district or has had a change of circumstances that is incompatible with the Gateway conditions. The other "legacy" benefits (IS, CTC, WTC and, in most cases, HB) cease to apply because regs 5-8 of the 2014 Regulations exclude those who are in receipt of universal credit from entitlement and prevent those who are not actually in receipt of universal credit but count as a universal credit claimant from making a new claim for them. In full/digital service areas, the relevant commencement orders prevent anyone living within the area from claiming a "legacy" benefit.

There are two morals for those who advise on universal credit or have to adjudicate on universal credit appeals. The first is that is important to ascertain whether universal credit was claimed, or awarded, under the full service rules or the live service rules because that may make a difference to the applicable law. The second is that the common perception that universal credit is at present a benefit that can only give rise to straightforward issues is no longer correct. All the detailed rules in this Volume are now in force in the full service areas and the continuing extension of those areas, together with the effect of the lobster pot, mean that the number of people who are affected by those rules continues to increase. Since the first edition of this Volume in 2013/14, universal credit has not merely spread geographically: it has become more complex.

The relevant law

The universal credit scheme is established by Part 1 of the Welfare Reform Act 2012 ("WRA 2012" or "the Act") and by the Schedules to the Act that are given effect by provisions in Part 1. The Act has subsequently been amended by the Welfare Reform and Work Act 2016 (WR & RA 2016). As is common in social security law, the Act sets out the structure of the scheme and confers extensive powers on the Secretary of State to make regulations prescribing matters of detail. The main regulations are the Universal Credit Regulations 2013 ("the Universal Credit Regulations" or "the Regulations"), but there are others including the 2014 Regulations and regulations dealing with claims and payments, and decisions and appeals, for universal credit, personal independence payment ("PIP"), new style JSA and new style ESA.

This volume contains all the statute law that directly affects entitlement to universal credit, including procedural issues. Provisions that relate indirectly to universal credit, i.e., by amending the rules for other benefits so that they refer to universal credit are taken into account in Vols I to IV.

The structure of universal credit

Any description of the structure of universal credit will involve at least an implicit decision about the level of detail that should be included. Almost any general proposition about social security law will be subject to qualifications and exceptions. Failing to note those qualifications and exceptions risks giving an unhelpfully approximate explanation of how the structure is meant to work. However, dealing with them in full risks obscuring the view of the wood by concentrating on the trees.

We have the advantage that the detailed rules about universal credit are dealt with in the annotations to the legislation in Parts II to V. The purpose of this introduction is to give the big picture. It therefore discusses details only where a particular rule is entirely new, or markedly different from the equivalent rules for existing benefits, or is likely to have important practical effects, or to give rise to disputes. There is never any substitute for looking at the actual words of the legislative text. Until they have checked both that text and the commentary to it, readers should assume that everything in this introduction is subject to unstated exceptions, particularly when such exceptions are implied by the use of words such as "normally" and "usually".

Universal credit is a non-contributory, means-tested, working age, social security benefit. That means that it is not "universal". With very limited exceptions, people who are not of working age are excluded from entitlement, as are (with no exceptions) those who do not satisfy the means-test.

Moreover, as is the case with all non-contributory benefits, the rules contain residence and presence conditions (including a right to reside test) which exclude those who are felt not have a legitimate connection with Great Britain or who have been absent from the UK for an extended period.

In addition, the fact that universal credit is a social security benefit means that it is not "credit" in the sense in which that word is used in ordinary speech. Universal credit is a *payment*, made as a matter of legal right to those who meet the conditions of entitlement, not a *loan* to tide claimants over a period of reduced income. With the sole exception of the hardship payments made to those who have been sanctioned, universal credit that has been correctly paid does not have to be repaid.

Couples

One of the basic principles of universal credit is that it cannot usually be claimed by one member of a couple: WRA 2012 s.2(1) provides that a claim for universal credit may only be made a single person or by members of a couple jointly. It is implicit that any award of universal credit made on a joint claim will be a joint award to both members of the couple.

The basic conditions

Entitlement to universal credit depends upon satisfying both the "basic conditions" and the "financial conditions" set out in the Act (WRA 2012, s.3(1)). Where a joint claim is made, those conditions must usually be satisfied by both members of the couple (WRA 2012, s.3(2)).

The basic conditions are set out in s.4(1) of the Act. They are that the claimant:

- must be at least 18 years old;
- must not have reached the qualifying age for SPC;
- is in Great Britain;
- is not receiving education; and
- has accepted a claimant commitment.

The last three of those conditions are further defined, or partially defined, in regulations. For example, a person who does not have a right to reside in the UK is treated as not being habitually resident here and hence as not being "in Great Britain": see reg.9 of the Universal Credit Regulations. All of those conditions are subject to exceptions which are specified in regulations. In addition, a person who meets the basic conditions cannot acquire entitlement to universal credit if he or she falls within the restrictions specified in s.6 of the Act and reg.19 of the Regulations.

It should be noted that it is not a condition of entitlement to universal credit that any claimant should be, or should not be, in remunerative work. The only way in which work affects universal credit is through the income that is earned from undertaking it.

The financial conditions

The financial conditions are set out in s.5 of the Act. They are that
- the claimant's capital (or, for couples, joint capital) is not greater than a prescribed amount (currently fixed at £16,000 by reg.18 of the Regulations); and that
- the claimant's income (or, for couples, joint income) is "such that, if the claimant were entitled to universal credit, the amount payable

would not be less than any prescribed minimum" (currently fixed at one penny by reg.17 of the Regulations).

As is discussed above and below, entitlement to universal credit reduces as a claimant's income increases. The effect of the convoluted wording quoted in the second bullet point above is that if, as a result of that reduction, the amount of universal credit payable would be less than one penny (i.e., nil), the financial conditions are not satisfied. In other words, one cannot be entitled to universal credit at a nil rate.

As would be expected, the calculation of a claimant's income and capital are the subject of detailed provisions in the Regulations.

Assessment periods

Universal credit is a monthly benefit. Entitlement is normally assessed by reference to the claimant's circumstances during an "assessment period", which is defined by WRA 2012 s.7(2) and reg.21(1) of the Regulations as "a period of one month beginning with the first date of entitlement and each subsequent period of one month during which entitlement subsists". That entitlement is then normally paid monthly in arrears after the end of the assessment period to which the payment relates (see reg.47 of the Universal Credit, Personal Independence Payment, Jobseeker's Allowance and Employment and Support Allowance (Claims and Payments) Regulations 2013).

Calculation of entitlement to universal credit

Under s.8(1) of the Act, the amount of an award of universal credit is the balance of the "maximum amount" less "the amounts to be deducted".

The amount so calculated will normally be reduced by the "benefit cap" (see below) if the claimant's total entitlement to specified social security benefits would otherwise exceed the amount of the cap.

The maximum amount

The maximum amount is a monthly amount. It is conceptually equivalent to the weekly "applicable amount" used in the calculation of entitlement to IS, JSA(IB) and ESA(IR). It is the total of the standard allowance (equivalent to the personal allowances for IS/JSA/ESA) established by WRA 2012, s.9 and reg.36 of the Regulations, and any of the following amounts to which the claimant is (or the joint claimants are) entitled:

- the child element

  Under WRA 2012, s.10 and regs.24 & 36 of the Regulations, an amount is allowed for each child or qualifying young person for whom a claimant is responsible, up to (subject to exceptions and transitional savings) a maximum of two children or qualifying young persons. An additional amount is allowed for each child or qualifying young person who is entitled to disability living allowance ("DLA") or PIP. The amount is higher if entitlement is to the highest rate of the care component of DLA or the enhanced rate of the daily living component of PIP or if the child or qualifying young person is registered blind.

- the housing costs element

  The housing costs element is payable under WRA 2012, s.11 and regs 25 & 26 of, and Schs 1-5 to the Regulations. The rules are summarised below, but note in particular that owner occupiers who have any earned income are not entitled to housing costs (see Sch. 5, Pt.2, para.4).

- the LCWRA element

  This is payable where the claimant has limited capability for work-related activity. It is equivalent to, but paid at a considerably higher rate than, the support component of ESA (see WRA 2012, s.12 and regs 27(1)(b) & 36 of the Regulations). The former LCW element (equivalent to the former work-related activity component of ESA) was abolished with effect from April 3, 2017 and is now only payable to claimants with transitional protection.

- the carer element

  This is equivalent to, and is paid at approximately the same rate as, the carer premium for IS/JSA/ESA (see WRA 2012, s.12 and regs 29 & 36 of the Regulations). To qualify, a claimant must satisfy the conditions of entitlement to carer's allowance other than having earnings below the prescribed limit and making a claim for that benefit (see regs 30(1) & (2) of the Regulations).

- the childcare costs element

  The childcare costs element is 85% of the charges incurred by a claimant for relevant childcare (defined in reg.35 of the Regulations) subject to a maximum of £646.35 pcm for one child or £1,108.04 pcm for two or more children (regs 34(1) and 36) and also to anti-abuse rules in reg.34(2). To qualify, a claimant must satisfy both the work condition (reg. 32) and the childcare costs condition (reg.33)

  The childcare costs element is not subject to the benefits cap (reg. 81(1)(b) and (2)).

The amounts of the standard allowance and the various elements are specified in a table that forms part of reg.36 of the Regulations.

The amounts to be deducted

Once the maximum amount has been ascertained, it is necessary to calculate the amounts to be deducted from it. By WRA 2012, s.8(3) & reg.22 of the Universal Credit Regulations, those amounts are:

- All the claimant's, or the claimants' combined, *unearned* income;
- Either (where the claimant does not have responsibility for a child or qualifying young person and does not have limited capability for work) 63% of his or her *earned* income; or
- (where the claimant has responsibility for a child or qualifying young person or has limited capability for work) 63% of the amount by which the claimant's, or the claimants' combined, *earned* income exceeds the work allowance.

The "work allowance" is what is described in IS/HB/JSA/ESA as an "earnings disregard". There are two rates, which are specified in a table that forms part of reg.22. The higher work allowance of £397 is applicable if the award of universal credit does not include the housing costs element: otherwise the lower work allowance of £192 applies.

Until April 2016, all claimants with earned income had work allowances, but, as indicated above, work allowances are now only available when the claimant (or at least one joint claimant) has responsibility for a child or qualifying young person or has limited capability for work. In addition, some of pre-April allowances were higher than is now the case. For some claimants who have responsibility for a child, the reduction in the work allowances were at least partially offset by the April 2016 increases in the maximum rates of the childcare costs elements (reg.36 of the Regulations) and the percentage of relevant childcare charges that is eligible to be met by universal credit (reg.34). However, the maximum increase in the child care costs element was £114.06 per month for one child and £192.54 for two or more children, By contrast, the higher work allowance for a single person with children was cut by £337 from £734 to £397.

In fairness, the cuts in the lower work allowance are considerably less than in the higher allowance (and it is likely that many claimants who have responsibility for a child or qualifying young person will have housing costs and so only be eligible for the lower allowance). So the combined effect of the cut in the work allowance and the increase in the childcare costs element will often be a modest increase in entitlement to universal credit.

However, that has been achieved at the cost of a swinging reduction in work incentives for able-bodied, childless, claimants. Revisiting the example above, readers will remember that by working for ten hours a week at the minimum wage, Jane (who is able-bodied and childless) was able to obtain an equivalent weekly income of £101.09 from universal credit and her earnings. That figure was calculated as follows:

1. Jane's (monthly) maximum amount is £317.82.

2. 10 hours @ the minimum wage of £7.50 per hour = £75.00

3. £75.00 per week is equivalent to £325.00 per month.

4. As the £325.00 is earned income, only 63% (i.e., £204.75) is deducted from Jane's maximum amount of £317.82, giving a monthly universal credit award of £113.07, which is equivalent to £26.54 per week.

5. Adding Jane's weekly equivalent universal credit of £26.09 to her weekly earnings of £75.00 gives £101.09.

However, before April 2016, Jane would have been eligible for a work allowance of £111.00 and so (at 2015/16 rates) her equivalent weekly income from universal credit and her earnings would have been £112.00 as follows:

1. Jane's (monthly) maximum amount would have been the same namely £317.82.

2. 10 hours @ the (October 2015) minimum wage of £6.70 per hour = £67.00

3. £67.00 per week is equivalent to £290.33 per month.

4. Jane's work allowance of £111.00 would have been deducted from her monthly earnings of £290.33 to give £179.33.

5. Until April 2017, the taper was 65%, rather than 63%, so 65% of the reduced figure of £179.33 (i.e., £116.56) would then have been deducted from Jane's maximum amount of £317.82, giving a monthly universal credit award of £201.26, which is equivalent to £46.44 per week.

6. Adding Jane's weekly equivalent universal credit of £46.44 to her weekly earnings of £67.00 gives £113.44.

Overall, despite the subsequent increase in the maximum amount and increases in the national minimum wage, Jane remains £11.54 per week (£113.44–£101.90) worse off as a result of the April 2016 changes. That is a cut of over 10% (and the equivalent figure for 2016/17 was a cut of over 13%: see p.14 of Vol.V of the 2016/17 edition). The cut took effect from the first assessment period beginning on or after April 11, 2016 and there was no transitional protection for existing claimants.

Calculation of income

Earned income

Employees

The treatment of the earned income of employees is another new feature of the universal credit scheme and one of the areas in which the benefit depends heavily upon the efficient operation of information technology. Most employers are now obliged to submit their PAYE returns to HMRC online and on a monthly basis under the "Real-Time Information" system. The idea is that that PAYE information should then be used to calculate the claimant's entitlement to universal credit for that month. If the system works, it has the advantage that claimants need not report fluctuations in their earnings (and therefore need not fear having to repay overpayments if they omit to do so). The possibility of treating earned income in this way was the main reason for establishing universal credit as a monthly, rather than weekly, benefit and for providing that payment should be in arrears after the end of the assessment period.

For those advantages to accrue the way in which earnings from employment are calculated are different from those for IS/HB/JSA/ESA. First, earnings are to be taken as the actual amount received by the claimant during the assessment period (see reg.54(1)). Then, reg.55 defines "earned income" by reference to the income tax definition. Finally reg.61 provides that where the claimant's employer is a "Real Time Information employer", the information on which the Secretary of State bases his calculation of earned income is to be the information reported by that employer through the PAYE system and the claimant is normally treated as having received those earnings in the same assessment period as the Secretary of State received the information.

The self-employed

The principle in reg.54(1) of the Universal Credit Regulations that earnings are to be taken as the actual amount received by the claimant during the assessment period also applies to self-employed earnings. Under reg.57(2), a person's self-employed earnings in respect of an assessment period are to be calculated by taking that person's "gross profits" (defined by reg.57(3) as "the actual receipts in [the assessment] period less any deductions for expenses allowed under regulation 58 or 59") and then deducting any payments of income tax and Class 2 and 4 national insurance contributions actually made to HMRC in that period and any "relievable pension contributions made" (as defined in s.188 of the Finance Act 2004, i.e., contributions to a registered pension scheme for which tax relief is available). Regs 58 & 59 establish an exhaustive list of the expenses that can be deducted. In particular, reg.59 provides for flat rate deductions for business mileage and the use of the claimant's home for business purposes.

Self-employed earnings are subject to a "minimum income floor" (see regs 62-64). The minimum income floor is usually an amount representing the person's "individual threshold" (see below) converted to a monthly figure and subjected to a notional deduction to reflect the tax and national insurance contributions payable on that level of self-employed earnings. Except during a start-up period (reg.63) self-employed claimants whose earnings in any assessment period are less than their minimum income floor are treated as having earnings equal to that floor. The policy behind that provision is explained below.

Unearned income

Unearned income is deducted from the maximum amount without any disregard or taper. However, in contrast to the rules for IS/JSA/ESA and working-age HB, not all types of unearned income fall within the definition. Those that do are set out in reg.66 of the Universal Credit Regulations and include:

- retirement pension income;

- certain social security benefits (including "new style" JSA and ESA);

- spousal maintenance payments;

- student income (e.g., student loans and grants: see reg.68);

- payments under permanent health insurance policies and certain mortgage protection policies;

- income from (non-retirement) annuities and from trusts unless disregarded as compensation for personal injury (regs 75 & 76);

- income treated as the yield from capital under reg.72 (see below);

- miscellaneous income that is taxable under Part 5 of Income Tax (Trading and Other Income) Act 2005;

Unearned income is calculated as a monthly amount but—in contrast to earned income—does not necessarily represent the amount actually received by the claimant in the assessment period for which the award is made. Regulation 73 contains detailed rules for converting unearned income (other than student income) received in respect of periods other than a month into a monthly equivalent. Student income has its own detailed rules, which are set out in regs 69-71.

Treatment of capital

Capital is relevant to universal credit entitlement in two ways. First, there is a maximum capital limit of £16,000 for both single and joint claimants (see reg.18 of the Universal Credit Regulations). Claimants who have capital in excess of that limit do not satisfy the first financial condition (see WRA 2012 s.5) and are therefore not entitled to benefit. Second, claimants with capital of more than £6,000 but less than £16,000 are treated as receiving an amount of unearned income equal to an "assumed yield" on that income. Reg.72 of the Universal Credit Regulations provides that that assumed yield is to be £4.35 per assessment period for each £250 (or part thereof). Readers who are familiar with IS/HB/JSA/ESA will recognise the "tariff income" rule under a different name.

The calculation of capital is governed by regs.45-50. By reg.46(1) and (2), the whole of a claimant's capital (other than his or her personal possessions) is to be taken into account unless it is treated as income under regs 46(3) and (4) or disregarded under reg. 48 and Sch.10. The valuation rules closely follow those for IS/HB/JSA/ESA and reg.50 contains a notional capital rule which is similar, though not identical, to that for the older working age benefits.

The benefit cap

Awards of universal credit are subject to the "benefit cap" established by ss.96-97 of the Act and regs 78-83 of the Universal Credit Regulations. This means that, subject to limited exceptions, if an award of universal credit would lead to the claimant's total entitlement to social security benefits exceeding the level of the cap then the amount of universal credit that the claimant would otherwise be awarded for the assessment period is reduced by the amount of the excess.

The cap is fixed at £2,167 per assessment period–equivalent to £500 per week or £26,500 per annum–for joint claimants or those responsible for a child or qualifying young person, or £1,517 per assessment period–equivalent to £350 per week or £18,200 per annum–for single claimants who are not responsible a child or a qualifying young person).

The cap is fixed at for different levels. If the claimant is (or joint claimants are) resident in Greater London, the cap is £23,000 per annum–equivalent to £442.30 per week–for joint claimants or those responsible for a child or qualifying young person and £15,410 per annum—£296.35 per week—for other claimants. If the claimant is (or joint claimants are) not resident in Greater London, the equivalent levels are £20,000 per annum and £13,400 per annum (£384.62 per week and £257.69 per week). The higher levels in Greater London are intended to reflect the higher cost of accommodation in the capital. However, the childcare costs element of universal credit is not subject to the cap and the cap does not apply at all if the universal credit award contains the LCWRA element; if a claimant is receiving certain other benefits including new style ESA with the support component, industrial injuries disablement benefit and attendance allowance; or if any member of the household is receiving DLA or PIP.

Housing costs

Section 8(2)(c) of the Act provides that the maximum amount is to include "any amount included under s.11 (housing costs)". Section 11(1) says that an award of universal credit must include "an amount in respect of any liability of a claimant to make payments in respect of the accommodation they occupy as their home". By s.11(2), the accommodation must be in Great Britain and must be residential accommodation but need not be self-contained. The remainder of s.11 confers powers for the Secretary of

State to make regulations, which have been used to make regs 25 and 26 of, and Schs 1-5 to, the Universal Credit Regulations.

Regulation 25 establishes three conditions for eligibility, the "payment condition", the "liability condition" and the "occupation condition"(see reg.25(5)(b)).

The payment condition (reg.25(1)(a) and (2) is that payments must be rent payments (as defined in Sch.1, paras.2 and 3), owner-occupier payments (Sch.1, paras.4-6) or service charges payments (Sch.1, para.7). The inclusion of rent payments is a major change. Previously help with rent was given through HB which was administered by local authorities rather than the DWP. Many—but not all—of the rules about rental payments are similar to those for HB. A further change from IS/JSA/ESA is that for interest payments to count as an owner-occupier payment, it is only necessary that the loan under which the interest is payable should be "secured on the accommodation in respect of which the claimant meets the occupation condition": there is no requirement that the loan should have been taken out to acquire an interest in the accommodation.

The liability condition (reg.25(1)(b) and (3)) is that the claimant (or either joint claimant) must either be liable to make the payments on a commercial basis, or treated as liable to make the payments (Pt 1 of Sch.2) and must not be treated as not liable to make the payments (Pt 2 of Sch.2).

The occupation condition (reg.25(1)(c) and (4)) is that the claimant must normally be treated as occupying the accommodation as his or her home (Pt 1 of Sch.3) and not be treated as not occupying it (Pt 2 of Sch.3)

The rules for the calculation of the housing costs element are set out in Schs 4 (for renters) and 5 (for owner occupiers).

One notable feature of the latter schedule is that if the claimant (or either joint claimant) is an owner-occupier and either of them has any earned income, no housing costs element is payable (Sch.5, para.4). This is a marked change from the old system (where mortgage interest payments could be paid as part of IS or JSA even if the claimant was working for up to 16 hours a week). The following example shows that this rule has the potential to frustrate the stated policy aim that universal credit will ensure that claimants will always be better off in work

> The (joint) claimants are a couple with a young daughter. Neither is in work. The mother is the responsible carer for the daughter. She receives child benefit of £20.70 per week (£89.70 per month). However child benefit is not taken into account as unearned income for universal credit so their unearned income is nil.
>
> They own their home and have eligible housing costs of £500 per month.
>
> Their universal credit entitlement is £1,230.56 as follows:

	£	£
Standard allowance for joint claimants where one is aged over 25	498.89	
Child element	231.67	
Housing costs element	500.00	
Maximum Amount	£1,230.56	1,230.56
Less Amounts to be deducted	0.00	
Entitlement		**£1,230.56**

Their monthly income is £1,320.26 (universal credit of £1,230.56 + child benefit of £89.70), which leaves them with £820.26 (or £182.29 per week) once their housing costs have been paid.

Suppose the father starts work for 10 hours a week for the minimum wage, so his earnings are £75.00 per week or £325.00 per month. The mother continues not to work so the couple incur no childcare charges.

As the father now has earned income, the couple are no longer entitled to the housing costs element. However, they do get the benefit of the higher work allowance. For joint claimants responsible for a child, that is £397 per month.

To calculate the father's earned income for the purposes of universal credit, deduct the work allowance of £397 from the earned income of £325.00. As this is less than nil, the couple's earned income for universal credit purposes remains nil.

The couple's entitlement to universal credit is now £730.56 as follows

	£	£
Standard allowance for joint claimants where one is aged over 25	498.89	
Child element	231.67	
Housing costs element	0.00	
Maximum Amount	£730.56	730.56
Less Amounts to be deducted	0.00	0.00
Entitlement		**£730.56**

Their monthly income is £1,145.26 (universal credit of £730.56 + child benefit of £89.70 + earnings of £325.00), which leaves them with £645.26 (or £148.90 per week) once their housing costs have been paid.

The family is £30.98 (£182.29—£151.31) per week worse off because the father has started work.

Claimant responsibilities and the claimant commitment

The claimant commitment

Under s.4(1)(e) of the Act, it is a basic condition of entitlement to universal credit that the claimant "has accepted a claimant commitment". By s.14, a claimant commitment is "a record of a claimant's responsibilities in relation to an award of universal credit" and is to include a record of the requirements with which the claimant must comply, any prescribed information, and any other information the Secretary of State considers it appropriate to include. However, the claimant commitment does not itself impose requirements on the claimant and the condition that the clamant should accept it appears to have been included so that there is no doubt about what requirements have, in fact, been imposed. Any failure to comply with a requirement is dealt with by a sanction rather than by ending entitlement to benefit.

Claimant responsibilities

Work-related requirements

Section 13(1) of the Act empowers the Secretary of State "to impose work-related requirements with which claimants must comply". There are four different types of work-related requirement:

- the work-focused interview requirement (WRA 2012 s.15)

  As its name suggests, this is a "requirement that a claimant participate in one or more work-focused interviews as specified by the Secretary of State".

- the work preparation requirement (WRA 2012 s.16)

  This is a "requirement that a claimant take particular action specified by the Secretary of State for the purpose of making it more likely in the opinion of the Secretary of State that the claimant will obtain paid work (or more paid work or better-paid work)". Section 16(3) gives the following examples of actions that the Secretary of State may specify:

  o attending a skills assessment
  o improving personal presentation
  o participating in training
  o participating in an employment programme
  o undertaking work experience or a work placement
  o developing a business plan
  o any prescribed action

  In addition any claimant with limited capability for work may also be required to participate in a work-focused health-related assessment.

- work search requirements (WRA 2012 s.17 and reg.95)

  There are two of these. The first is that a claimant must take all reasonable action for the purpose of obtaining paid work (or more paid work or better-paid work). The second is that he or she must also take any particular action specified by the Secretary of State for that purpose. Section 17(3) gives the following examples of actions that the Secretary of State may specify

  o carrying out work searches;
  o making applications;
  o creating and maintaining an online profile;
  o registering with an employment agency;
  o seeking references;
  o any prescribed action.

Under reg.95, claimants are treated as not having complied with the first work search requirement unless they have spent at least the "expected number of hours each week minus any relevant deductions" taking action to obtain paid work unless the Secretary of State is satisfied that the claimant has taken all reasonable action for that purpose despite having spent fewer hours taking action.

Reg.88 provides that the expected number of hours is 35 per week unless the claimant has caring responsibilities or is physically or mentally impaired and the Secretary of State agrees to a lesser number of hours. Reg.95(2) specifies that relevant deductions means the total of any time agreed by the Secretary of State for the claimant to carry out paid work, voluntary work, a work preparation requirement, or voluntary work preparation in that week or to deal with temporary childcare responsibilities, a domestic emergency, funeral arrangements or other temporary circumstances.

- work availability requirements (WRA 2012 s.18 and reg.96)

    This is a requirement that the claimant be available for work which is defined as "able and willing immediately to take up paid work (or more paid work or better-paid work)"

The work-related requirements which may be imposed on a claimant depend on which of the following groups the claimant falls into—

- Claimants subject to no work-related requirements (WRA 2012 s.19 and regs 89-90);

    These include claimants with limited capability for work and work-related activity, claimants with regular and substantial caring responsibilities for a severely disabled person, and claimants who are the responsible carer for a child under the age of 1, the claimant has reached the qualifying age for state pension credit; pregnant women within 11 weeks of the expected date of confinement and new mothers within 15 weeks of the birth, recent adopters, certain claimants in education and foster parents of children under 1.

    Claimants also fall within this group if they are in work and their earnings equal or exceed the threshold that applies to them. For most people that threshold will be the amount they would earn if they worked for their expected number of hours (usually 35 per week) at the minimum wage converted to a monthly figure. At current rates, that threshold is £1,137.50 (£7.50 x 35 x 52 ÷ 12) for those aged 25 or over. Lower thresholds apply to those aged less than 25, those who would otherwise be subject to the work-focused interview requirement only, or the work preparation requirement only, and apprentices. Couples have a joint threshold that applies to their combined weekly earnings.

- Claimants subject to the work-focused interview requirement only (WRA 2012 s.20 and reg.91);

    This group comprises the responsible carers of children who are aged 1 or more but are under 3 and certain foster parents and others caring for children

- Claimants subject to the work-focused interview and work preparation requirements only (WRA 2012 s.21 and reg.91A);

    This group comprises claimants who have limited capability for work, but do not also have limited capability for work-related activity, or are responsible carers of children aged 3 or 4.

- Claimants subject to all work-related requirements (WRA 2012 s.22 and reg.92).

    This group comprises every claimant who is not in any of the other groups. The Secretary of State *must* impose the work search requirement and the work availability requirement on everyone in this group and *may* also impose the work-focused interview requirement and a work preparation requirement.

Reg.98 establishes special rules for the victims of domestic violence.

Connected requirements

Under s.23 of the Act, the Secretary of State may also impose a "connected requirement". There are three of these. First, claimants may be required to participate in an interview in connection with a work-related requirement. Second, they may be required to provide evidence to verify that they have complied with work-related requirements that have been imposed on them. Finally, they may be required to report specified changes in their circumstances which are relevant to work-related requirements.

Sanctions

It is not a condition of entitlement to universal credit that claimants should comply with requirements imposed by the Secretary of State under the provisions summarised above. Instead, compliance is enforced by the imposition of sanctions under which the amount of universal credit payable is reduced. Under regs 110-111 of the Universal Credit Regulations, the maximum reduction is the amount of the standard allowance applicable to the award of universal credit for the assessment period that is being considered or, where the sanction has only been imposed on one of two joint claimants, half the amount of that standard allowance.

There are four levels of sanction.

Higher-level sanctions are imposed under s.26 of the Act, which specifies that various actions or omissions by the claimant are to be "sanctionable failures". The definition of each of those failures is technical but, in broad terms, higher-level sanctions apply where, for no good reason, a claimant fails to undertake a work placement or apply for a vacancy when required to do so; fails to take up an offer of paid work; ceases work or loses pay voluntarily or through misconduct (whether before or after claiming universal credit). The sanction period is fixed by reg.102 of the Universal Credit Regulations. Again the rules are technical but for adults who commit a sanctionable failure during the currency of a claim, length of the sanction period depends upon whether there has been a previous sanctionable failure within the previous 365 days (including the date of the failure that led to the imposition of the current sanction. If not, then the sanction period is 91 days; if there was one previous sanctionable failure within the period, it is 182 days; and, for a third or subsequent sanctionable failure within the 365 day period it is 1095 days (3 years). Shorter periods apply if the claimant was under 18 when the sanctionable failure occurred or in the case of a failure that occurred before the claim for universal credit. Reg.102 is subject to reg.113 which specifies a number of circumstances in which a sanctionable failure does not result in a reduction of universal credit.

Medium-level sanctions, low-level sanctions and *lowest-level sanctions* are imposed under s.27 of the Act. That section provides that it is to be a sanctionable failure for a claimant to fail, for no good reason, to comply with a work-related requirement or a connected requirement unless that failure would also be a sanctionable failure under s.26, in which case the higher-level sanction applies. The level of sanction that such a failure attracts is prescribed in regs.103-105. The regulations themselves do not say so but it is important to remember that, by virtue of s.27, each of the failures discussed below is only sanctionable if it occurred for no good reason. Moreover, regs.103-105 are subject to reg.113 which specifies a number of circumstances in which a sanctionable failure does not result in a reduction of universal credit.

A failure to take all reasonable action to obtain paid work in breach of a work search requirement under s.17(1)(a) or a failure to comply with a work availability requirement attracts a medium-level sanction under reg.103. The sanction period is 28 days for the first such failure in any 365 day period and 91 days for a second or subsequent failure in that period.

Reg.104 provides that low-level sanctions apply to claimants who are subject to the work preparation requirement or to all work-related requirements and who have failed to comply with a work-focused interview requirement, a work preparation requirement, or a connected requirement, or failed to take a particular action specified by the Secretary of State to obtain work in breach of a work search requirement. The sanction lasts until 7, 14 or 28 days (depending on the number of previous such failures in the preceding 65 days) after the claimant complies with the requirement, or has a change of circumstances so that he or she is not longer subject to any work-related requirements, or the requirement is withdrawn, or the award of universal credit ends. Again, the period for 16 and 17 year-olds is shorter.

Lowest-level sanctions are governed by reg.105. They apply to claimants who are subject to the work-focused interview requirement only (i.e., under WRA 2012, s.20) and who fail to comply with that requirement. The sanction continues until the claimant complies with the requirement, or has a change of circumstances so that he or she is no longer subject to any work-related requirements, or the award of universal credit ends.

When deciding whether there has been a previous sanctionable failure within the 365 day period, failures occurring in the 14 days immediately preceding the failure in question are disregarded (reg.101(4)).

The total of all outstanding sanction periods in relation to a particular claimant, cannot exceed 1095 days (reg.101(3)).

Under reg.109, a sanction terminates (irrespective of the length of the unexpired sanction period) if, since the most recent sanction was imposed, the claimant has been in paid work for six months (not necessarily consecutively) and during each of those months his or her earnings were equal to or exceeded the applicable threshold (see above).

Regulations provide for the date on which the sanction period is to begin. Where a claimant is subject to more than one sanction, they run consecutively (reg.101(2)).

Where a 100% sanction has been imposed (but not where there has been a 40% reduction), the Secretary of State must make a hardship payment under WRA 2012, s.28 in the (very limited) circumstances prescribed by regs 115-118. Under reg.119, hardship payments are usually recoverable in accordance with s.71ZH of the Social Security Administration Act 1992. However, any hardship payment ceases to be recoverable if, since the last date on which the award of universal credit was subject to a sanction, the claimant (or the joint claimants) has (or have) been in paid work for six months (not necessarily consecutively) and during each of those months his or her earnings (or their joint earnings) were equal to or exceeded the applicable threshold (see above).

PART II

UNIVERSAL CREDIT: STATUTES

Social Security Administration Act 1992

(1992 c.5)

An Act to consolidate certain enactments relating to the administration of social   1.2
security and related matters with amendments to give effect to recommendations of
the Law Commission and the Scottish Law Commission.

[13th February 1992]

GENERAL NOTE

For the main provisions of this Act ("the SSAA 1992") and extensive commen-   1.3
tary, see Vol.III of this series. This Volume only includes certain of the amendments
made to SSAA 1992 by the WRA 2012, namely the insertion of new ss.71ZB to
71ZH inclusive.

Recovery of benefit payments

[¹ Recovery of overpayments of certain benefits

71ZB.—(1) The Secretary of State may recover any amount of the   1.4
following paid in excess of entitlement—
  (a) universal credit;
  (b) jobseeker's allowance;
  (c) employment and support allowance, *and*
  (d) *except in prescribed circumstances, housing credit (within the meaning of*
       the State Pension Credit Act 2002).
(2) An amount recoverable under this section is recoverable from—
  (a) the person to whom it was paid, or
  (b) such other person (in addition to or instead of the person to whom it
       was paid) as may be prescribed.
(3) An amount paid in pursuance of a determination is not recoverable
under this section unless the determination has been—
  (a) reversed or varied on an appeal, or
  (b) revised or superseded under section 9 or section 10 of the Social
       Security Act 1998,

25

except where regulations otherwise provide.

(4) Regulations may provide that amounts recoverable under this section are to be calculated or estimated in a prescribed manner.

(5) Where an amount of universal credit is paid for the sole reason that a payment by way of prescribed income is made after the date which is the prescribed date for payment of that income, that amount is for the purposes of this section paid in excess of entitlement.

(6) In the case of a benefit referred to in subsection (1) which is awarded to persons jointly, an amount paid to one of those persons may for the purposes of this section be regarded as paid to the other.

(7) An amount recoverable under this section may (without prejudice to any other means of recovery) be recovered—

(a) by deduction from benefit (section 71ZC);
(b) by deduction from earnings (section 71ZD);
(c) through the courts etc (section 71ZE);
(d) by adjustment of benefit (section 71ZF).]

AMENDMENT

1.5   1. Welfare Reform Act 2012 s.105(1) (April 29, 2013 for certain purposes, but at a date appointed for remaining purposes).

GENERAL NOTE

1.6   This new section marks a fundamental shift in the law relating to the recovery of overpayments of benefit. It deals (at present only) with the recovery of overpaid universal credit, JSA, ESA and the new housing credit element of state pension credit. However, it is not yet fully in force—see further below. Furthermore, so far as ESA and JSA are concerned, the present effect of the commencement provisions is that the new test applies only to overpayments of the new-style contributory versions of ESA and JSA, introduced as part of the universal credit regime.

The Secretary of State is given the power to recover any amount of Universal Credit, JSA and ESA, which has been paid in excess of entitlement (subs.(1)(a)–(c)). The same principle applies also to housing credit which has been paid in excess of entitlement, except in circumstances that will be prescribed in regulations (subs.(1)(d)). There is no requirement on the Secretary of State to establish either a misrepresentation or failure to disclose as a precondition for recovery. It follows that any payment of one of the relevant benefits in excess of the claimant's appropriate entitlement will be a recoverable overpayment, including those overpayments which arise purely as a result of official error. The underlying philosophy is that even the need for the Department to take responsibility for its own mistakes "does not give people the right to keep taxpayers' money that they are not entitled to" (Explanatory Memorandum to the Social Security (Overpayments and Recovery) Regulations 2013, para.7.2).

The overpaid benefit can be recovered from the person to whom it was paid or such other person as is prescribed (subs.(2); see further Security (Overpayments and Recovery) Regulations 2013 (SI 2013/384) reg.4). There must have been a relevant revision, supersession or appellate decision (subs.(3)). This requirement is broadly equivalent to the existing s.71(5A) of the SSAA 1992. However, note that reg.5 of the Security (Overpayments and Recovery) Regulations 2013 provides that "Section 71ZB(3) of the Act (recoverability of an overpayment dependent on reversal, variation, revision or supersession) does not apply where the circumstances of the overpayment do not provide a basis for the decision pursuant to which the payment was made to be revised under section 9 of the Social Security Act 1998 or superseded under section 10 of that Act."

Subsection (5) has the effect that where another income or benefit that would affect the award of universal credit is paid late, any amount of universal credit, which would not have been paid had the other income or benefit been paid on time, is treated as an overpayment and is recoverable from the universal credit recipient.

Where an award of benefit is made to persons jointly, an amount paid to one member of the couple may be treated as paid to the other and so recovered (subs. (6)).

The various methods of recovery are set out in subs.(7), namely deduction from benefit (s.71ZC), by deduction from earnings (s.71ZD) (a new method akin to attachment of earnings), through the courts (s.71ZE) or by adjustment of subsequent benefit payments (s.71ZF).

Note that this section is not fully in force. Article 5(3)(a) of the Welfare Reform Act 2012 (Commencement No.8 and Savings and Transitional Provisions) Order 2013 (SI 2013/358) provided for the amending s.105(1) of the WRA 2012 to have effect in so far as it was not already in force "except in so far as it inserts section 71ZB(1)(d) of the 1992 Act and the word 'and' immediately preceding it" (the italicised text above). The Commencement No.8 Order was then modified by art.23(3) of the Welfare Reform Act 2012 (Commencement No.9 and Transitional and Transitory Provisions and Commencement No.8 and Savings and Transitional Provisions (Amendment)) Order 2013 (SI 2013/983), which provides that new s.71ZB(1)(b) and (c) "come into force on 29th April 2013 only in so far as they relate respectively to a new style JSA award and a new style ESA award".

1.7

Deduction from benefit

[¹ **71ZC.**—(1) An amount recoverable from a person under section 71ZB may be recovered by deducting the amount from payments of prescribed benefit.

(2) Where an amount recoverable from a person under section 71ZB was paid to the person on behalf of another, subsection (1) authorises its recovery from the person by deduction—

(a) from prescribed benefits to which the person is entitled;

(b) from prescribed benefits paid to the person to discharge (in whole or in part) an obligation owed to that person by the person on whose behalf the recoverable amount was paid, or

(c) from prescribed benefits paid to the person to discharge (in whole or in part) an obligation owed to that person by any other person.

(3) Where an amount is recovered as mentioned in paragraph (b) of subsection (2), the obligation specified in that paragraph shall in prescribed circumstances be taken to be discharged by the amount of the deduction.

(4) Where an amount is recovered as mentioned in paragraph (c) of subsection (2), the obligation specified in that paragraph shall in all cases be taken to be so discharged.]

1.8

AMENDMENT

1. Welfare Reform Act 2012 s.105(1) (July 1, 2012 for the purpose only of prescribing under s.71ZC(1) the benefits from which deductions may be made in order to recover penalties, October 1, 2012 to the extent that it inserts s.71ZC(1) for the purpose only of enabling recovery of the penalties to take place by these methods; and April 29, 2013 for remaining purposes).

GENERAL NOTE

This section provides for the recovery of overpayments under the new s.71ZB by deduction from benefit. Thus overpayments of universal credit, JSA, ESA and the housing credit can be recovered by making deductions from payments of

1.9

prescribed benefits (subs.(1)). Where universal credit, JSA, ESA or the housing credit is paid to a third party (e.g. a landlord) on the claimant's behalf, overpayments of those benefits may be recovered from prescribed benefits to which the third party is entitled; ongoing payments of prescribed benefits to the third party being made on the benefit claimant's behalf; or ongoing payments of prescribed benefits paid to the third party on other benefit claimants' behalf (e.g. if a landlord has other tenants who are in receipt of universal credit or housing credit) (subs.(2)). Furthermore, in circumstances to be prescribed by regulations, where deductions are made from payments of prescribed benefits to the third party on the claimant's behalf, then the claimant's obligations to the third party will be discharged, e.g. the landlord would not be able to put the claimant into arrears with their rent (subs.(3)). Similarly, in all cases where deductions are made from payments of prescribed benefits to the third party on behalf of other benefit claimants, the other claimants' obligations to the third party will likewise be discharged (and so the landlord would not be able to hold those other claimants as being in arrears with their rent) (subs.(4)). See further Social Security (Overpayments and Recovery) Regulations 2013 (SI 2013/384) P5 (regs 10–16) and especially reg.15.

Deduction from earnings

1.10   [¹ 71ZD.—(1) Regulations may provide for amounts recoverable under section 71ZB to be recovered by deductions from earnings.

(2) In this section "earnings" has such meaning as may be prescribed.

(3) Regulations under subsection (1) may include provision—

(a) requiring the person from whom an amount is recoverable ("the beneficiary") to disclose details of their employer, and any change of employer, to the Secretary of State;

(b) requiring the employer, on being served with a notice by the Secretary of State, to make deductions from the earnings of the beneficiary and to pay corresponding amounts to the Secretary of State;

(c) as to the matters to be contained in such a notice and the period for which a notice is to have effect;

(d) as to how payment is to be made to the Secretary of State;

(e) as to a level of earnings below which earnings must not be reduced;

(f) allowing the employer, where the employer makes deductions, to deduct a prescribed sum from the beneficiary's earnings in respect of the employer's administrative costs;

(g) requiring the employer to keep records of deductions;

(h) requiring the employer to notify the Secretary of State if the beneficiary is not, or ceases to be, employed by the employer;

(i) creating a criminal offence for non-compliance with the regulations, punishable on summary conviction by a fine not exceeding level 3 on the standard scale;

(j) with respect to the priority as between a requirement to deduct from earnings under this section and—

(i) any other such requirement;

(ii) an order under any other enactment relating to England and Wales which requires deduction from the beneficiary's earnings;

(iii) any diligence against earnings.]

AMENDMENT

1. Welfare Reform Act 2012 s.105(1) (July 1, 2012).

DEFINITION

"earnings"—see subs.(2).

GENERAL NOTE

Under the previous arrangements, the Secretary of State typically recovered overpayment debts through deductions from ongoing benefit entitlement. However, once a claimant subject to an overpayment liability stopped receiving benefit, further recovery relied heavily on the debtor's compliance with repayment. The DWP estimates that about 350,000 people who are no longer in receipt of benefit owe some £500 million (DWP Impact Assessment, *Direct Earnings Attachment to Recover Overpaid Social Security Benefits*, September 2011, p.7). If a former claimant chose not to pay the money owed, then the Department's only option was to take court action, which was not always cost effective. In principle, however, the Department has always been able to apply to the magistrates' court for an attachment of earnings order as a means of recovering outstanding overpayments. Indeed, in the six months from April 2010, the Department obtained 824 orders under the Attachment of Earnings Act 1971, suggesting an annual case load of about 1,650 such cases (DWP Impact Assessment, p.9).

This new section for the first time empowers both the Department and local authorities to recover debt by attachment of earnings without the need for an application to court. The new Direct Earnings Attachments (DEA) are thus designed to act as an incentive to those liable for overpayments to make arrangements to repay their debts and, if they still refuse to repay, to provide the Department (or local authority) with a simpler alternative means to secure recovery. See further Social Security (Overpayments and Recovery) Regulations 2013 (SI 2013/384), especially Pt 6 (regs 17–30). These Regulations set out the circumstances in which a DEA can be issued, the type of earnings from which a deduction can be taken, the responsibilities of employers and the relevant rates of deduction where a DEA is in place.

The new DEA system may just be an interim measure. The DWP has also considered the possibility of recovering overpayments from former claimants who are now in employment through the PAYE system (DWP Impact Assessment, pp.6–7). However, this method could not be implemented for some years, presumably for operational or technical reasons as much as anything else. But note in this regard the increased powers for information sharing between the DWP and HMRC (see WRA 2012, s.127).

Court action etc.

[¹ **71ZE.**—(1) Where an amount is recoverable under section 71ZB from a person residing in England and Wales, the amount is, if [² the county court] so orders, recoverable—

(a) under section 85 of the County Courts Act 1984; or

(b) otherwise as if it were payable under an order of the court.

(2) Where an amount is recoverable under section 71ZB from a person residing in Scotland, the amount recoverable may be enforced as if it were payable under an extract registered decree arbitral bearing a warrant for execution issued by the sheriff court of any sheriffdom in Scotland.

(3) Any costs of the Secretary of State in recovering an amount of benefit under this section may be recovered by him as if they were amounts recoverable under section 71ZB.

(4) In any period after the coming into force of this section and before the coming into force of section 62 of the Tribunals, Courts and Enforcement Act 2007, subsection (1)(a) has effect as if it read "by execution issued from the county court".]

1.11

1.12

AMENDMENTS

1. Welfare Reform Act 2012 s.105(1) (October 1, 2012, for the purpose only of enabling recovery of the penalties to take place by these methods and April 29, 2013 for other purposes).
2. Crime and Courts Act 2013 s.17(5) and Sch.9(3) para.52(1)(b) (April 22, 2014).

GENERAL NOTE

1.13   This section provides for the recovery of overpayments under new s.71ZB through the courts. Thus overpayments are recoverable through the county courts for claimants residing in England and Wales (subs.(1)) and through the sheriff courts for those residing in Scotland (subs.(2)). The Secretary of State's normal practice is to try and recover court costs when there is a court judgment in his favour. However, under the previous law there was no mechanism for the Secretary of State to recover such associated costs in the same way as if they formed part of the overpayment debt (e.g. by deduction from benefit or by adjustment of subsequent payments of benefit). Accordingly, subs.(3) allows the Secretary of State to recover costs by the same method as the overpayment itself is recovered.

Adjustment of benefit

1.14   [¹ **71ZF**. —Regulations may for the purpose of the recovery of amounts recoverable under section 71ZB make provision—
   (a) for treating any amount paid to a person under an award which it is subsequently determined was not payable—
      (i) as properly paid, or
      (ii) as paid on account of a payment which it is determined should be or should have been made,
and for reducing or withholding arrears payable by virtue of the subsequent determination;
   (b) for treating any amount paid to one person in respect of another as properly paid for any period for which it is not payable in cases where in consequence of a subsequent determination—
      (i) the other person is entitled to a payment for that period, or
      (ii) a third person is entitled in priority to the payee to a payment for that period in respect of the other person,
and by reducing or withholding any arrears payable for that period by virtue of the subsequent determination.]

AMENDMENTS

1. Welfare Reform Act 2012 s.105(1) (April 29, 2013).
2. Welfare Reform Act 2012 Sch.14(4) para.1 (April 29, 2013).

GENERAL NOTE

1.15   This section concerns the recovery of overpayments under new s.71ZB using the method of adjusting subsequent benefit payments. It provides that the Secretary of State may prescribe in regulations that in certain circumstances, amounts paid but subsequently determined as not payable, can be treated as properly paid and be set against future payments of benefit or against certain payments to third parties.

1.15.1   [¹ **71ZG Recovery of payments on account**
(1) The Secretary of State may recover any amount paid under section 5(1)(r) (payments on account).

(2) An amount recoverable under this section is recoverable from—

(a) the person to whom it was paid, or

(b) such other person (in addition to or instead of the person to whom it was paid) as may be prescribed.

(3) Regulations may provide that amounts recoverable under this section are to be calculated or estimated in a prescribed manner.

(4) In the case of a payment on account of a benefit which is awarded to persons jointly, an amount paid to one of those persons may for the purposes of this section be regarded as paid to the other.

(5) Sections 71ZC, 71ZD and 71ZE apply in relation to amounts recoverable under this section as to amounts recoverable under section 71ZB.]

AMENDMENT

1. Welfare Reform Act 2012, s.105(1) (April 29, 2013 for certain purposes, but at a date appointed for remaining purposes).

[¹ **71ZH Recovery of hardship payments etc**   1.15.2

(1) The Secretary of State may recover any amount paid by way of—

(a) a payment under section 28 of the Welfare Reform Act 2012 (universal credit hardship payments) which is recoverable under that section,

(b) [² ...]

(c) a payment of a jobseeker's allowance under paragraph 8 or 8A of Schedule 1 to that Act (exemptions), where the allowance is payable at a prescribed rate under paragraph 9 of that Schedule and is recoverable under that paragraph,

(d) a payment of a jobseeker's allowance under paragraph 10 of that Schedule (claims yet to be determined etc) which is recoverable under that paragraph, or

(e) a payment which is recoverable under section 6B(5A)(d) or (7)(d), 7(2A)(d) or (4)(d), 8(3)(aa), (4)(d) or 9(2A)(d) or (4)(d) of the Social Security Fraud Act 2001.

(2) An amount recoverable under this section is recoverable from—

(a) the person to whom it was paid, or

(b) such other person (in addition to or instead of the person to whom it was paid) as may be prescribed.

(3) Regulations may provide that amounts recoverable under this section are to be calculated or estimated in a prescribed manner.

(4) Where universal credit or a jobseeker's allowance is claimed by persons jointly, an amount paid to one claimant may for the purposes of this section be regarded as paid to the other.

(5) Sections 71ZC to 71ZF apply in relation to amounts recoverable under this section as to amounts recoverable under section 71ZB.]

AMENDMENT

1. Welfare Reform Act 2012, s.105(1) (April 29, 2013 for certain purposes, but at a date appointed for remaining purposes).

2. Welfare Reform Act 2012 Sch.14(4) para.1 (April 29, 2013).

GENERAL NOTE

See further reg.119 of the Universal Credit Regulations.   1.15.3

Social Security Act 1998

(1998 c.14)

An Act to make provision as to the making of decisions and the determination of appeals under enactments relating to social security, child support, vaccine damage payments and war pensions; to make further provision with respect to social security; and for connected purposes.

[21st May 1998]

GENERAL NOTE

1.17   For the main provisions of this Act ("the SSA 1998"), see Vol.III of this series. This Volume only includes the core provisions in the SSA 1998 which are essential to understanding the structure of decision-making and appeals for universal credit. For detailed commentary on these and other provisions, see Vol.III.

CHAPTER II

SOCIAL SECURITY DECISIONS AND APPEALS

Decisions

Decisions by Secretary of State

1.18   **8.**—(1) Subject to the provisions of this Chapter, it shall be for the Secretary of State—
    (a) to decide any claim for a relevant benefit;
    (b) [6 . . .] [1 and]
    (c) subject to subsection (5) below, to make any decision that falls to be made under or by virtue of a relevant enactment; [1 . . .]
    (d) [1 . . .]
    (2) Where at any time a claim for a relevant benefit is decided by the Secretary of State—
    (a) the claim shall not be regarded as subsisting after that time; and
    (b) accordingly, the claimant shall not (without making a further claim) be entitled to the benefit on the basis of circumstances not obtaining at that time.
    (3) In this Chapter "relevant benefit" [2 . . .] means any of the following, namely—

(a) benefit under Parts II to V of the Contributions and Benefits Act;
[⁸(aa) universal credit;]
[⁹ (ab)state pension or a lump sum under Part 1 of the Pensions Act 2014;]
[¹⁰ (ac) bereavement support payment under section 30 of the Pensions Act 2014;]
(b) a jobseeker's allowance;
[⁵(ba) an employment and support allowance;]
[⁷(baa) personal independence payment;]
[³(bb) state pension credit;]
(c) *income support*;
(d) [⁴ ...]
(e) [⁴ ...]
(f) a social fund payment mentioned in section 138(1)(a) or (2) of the Contributions and Benefits Act;
(g) child benefit;
(h) such other benefit as may be prescribed.

(4) In this section "relevant enactment" means any enactment contained in this Chapter, the Contributions and Benefits Act, the Administration Act, the Social Security (Consequential Provisions) Act 1992 [³, the Jobseekers Act] [⁵, the State Pension Credit Act 2002 [⁸, Part 1 of the Welfare Reform Act 2007, Part 1 of the Welfare Reform Act 2012] [⁷ [⁹, Part 4 of that Act or Part 1 of the Pensions Act 2014]], [¹⁰ or section 30 of that Act] other than one contained in—

(a) Part VII of the Contributions and Benefits Act so far as relating to housing benefit and council tax benefit; or
(b) Part VIII of the Administration Act (arrangements for housing benefit and council tax benefit and related subsidies).

[¹ (5) Subsection (1)(c) above does not include any decision which under section 8 of the Social Security Contributions (Transfer of Functions, etc) Act 1999 falls to be made by an officer of the Inland Revenue.]

AMENDMENTS

1. Social Security Contributions (Transfer of Functions, etc.) Act 1999 s.18 and Sch.7, para.22 (April 1, 1999).   **1.19**
2. Welfare Reform and Pensions Act 1999 s.88 and Sch.13 (April 6, 2000).
3. State Pension Credit Act 2002 s.11 and Sch.1, para.6 (July 2, 2002 for the purpose of exercising any power to make regulations or orders and April 7, 2003 for other purposes).
4. Tax Credits Act 2002 s.60 and Sch.6 (April 8, 2003, subject to a saving in respect of outstanding questions concerning working families' tax credit and disabled person's tax credit—see Tax Credits Act 2002 (Commencement No.4, Transitional Provisions and Savings) Order 2003 (SI 2003/962), art.3(1)–(3)).
5. Welfare Reform Act 2007 s.28(1) and Sch.3, para.17(1)(and (3) (March 18, 2008 for regulation-making purposes and July 27, 2008 for other purposes).
6. Welfare Reform Act 2012 s.147 and Sch.14, Pt 8 (April 1, 2013).
7. Welfare Reform Act 2012 s.91 and Sch.9, paras 37 and 39 (February 25, 2013 for regulation-making purposes and April 8, 2013 for other purposes).
8. Welfare Reform Act 2012 s.31 and Sch.2, paras 43 and 45 (February 25, 2013 for regulation-making purposes and April 29, 2013 for other purposes).
9. Pensions Act 2014 Sch.12(1) para.33 (April 6, 2016).
10. Pensions Act 2014 Sch.16 paras 39(2) and (3) (April 6, 2017).

1.20 DEFINITIONS

"the Administration Act"—see SSA 1998 s.84.

"claim"—by virtue of SSA 1998 s.39(2), see SSAA 1992, s.191.

"claimant"—see SSA 1998 s.39(1), and by virtue of SSA 1998 s.39(2), see SSAA 1992 s.191.

"the Contributions and Benefits Act"—see SSA 1998 s.84.

"Inland Revenue"—by virtue of SSA 1998 s.39(2), see SSAA 1992 s.191 but note that the Inland Revenue has been merged into HMRC (Her Majesty's Revenue and Customs) by the Commissioners for Revenue and Customs Act 2005.

"the Jobseekers Act"—see SSA 1998 s.84.

"prescribed"–*ibid*.

"relevant benefit"—see subs.(3).

"relevant enactment"—see subs.(4).

Revision of decisions

1.21   **9.**—(1) [¹ . . .] Any decision of the Secretary of State under section 8 above or section 10 below may be revised by the Secretary of State—

(a) either within the prescribed period or in prescribed cases or circumstances; and

(b) either on an application made for the purpose or on his own initiative;

and regulations may prescribe the procedure by which a decision of the Secretary of State may be so revised.

(2) In making a decision under subsection (1) above, the Secretary of State need not consider any issue that is not raised by the application or, as the case may be, did not cause him to act on his own initiative.

(3) Subject to subsections (4) and (5) and section 27 below, a revision under this section shall take effect as from the date on which the original decision took (or was to take) effect.

(4) Regulations may provide that, in prescribed cases or circumstances, a revision under this section shall take effect as from such other date as may be prescribed.

(5) Where a decision is revised under this section, for the purpose of any rule as to the time allowed for bringing an appeal, the decision shall be regarded as made on the date on which it is so revised.

(6) Except in prescribed circumstances, an appeal against a decision of the Secretary of State shall lapse if the decision is revised under this section before the appeal is determined.

AMENDMENT

1. Welfare Reform Act 2012 s.147 and Sch.14, Pt 8 (April 1, 2013).

DEFINITION

"prescribed"—see SSA 1998 s.84.

Decisions superseding earlier decisions

1.22   **10.**—(1) Subject to [¹ subsection (3)] [⁴ . . .] below, the following, namely—

(a) any decision of the Secretary of State under section 8 above or this section, whether as originally made or as revised under section 9 above; [³ . . .]

34

[³(aa) any decision under this Chapter of an appeal tribunal or a Commissioner; and]

(b) any decision under this Chapter [² of the First-tier Tribunal or any decision of the Upper Tribunal which relates to any such decision],

may be superseded by a decision made by the Secretary of State, either on an application made for the purpose or on his own initiative.

(2) In making a decision under subsection (1) above, the Secretary of State need not consider any issue that is not raised by the application or, as the case may be, did not cause him to act on his own initiative.

(3) Regulations may prescribe the cases and circumstances in which, and the procedure by which, a decision may be made under this section.

(4) [¹ . . .]

(5) Subject to subsection (6) and section 27 below, a decision under this section shall take effect as from the date on which it is made or, where applicable, the date on which the application was made.

(6) Regulations may provide that, in prescribed cases or circumstances, a decision under this section shall take effect as from such other date as may be prescribed.

[³ (7) In this section—

"appeal tribunal" means an appeal tribunal constituted under Chapter 1 of this Part (the functions of which have been transferred to the First-tier Tribunal);

"Commissioner" means a person appointed as a Social Security Commissioner under Schedule 4 (the functions of whom have been transferred to the Upper Tribunal), and includes a tribunal of such persons.]

AMENDMENTS

1. Social Security Contributions (Transfer of Functions, etc.) Act 1999, s.18 and Sch.7, para.23 (April 1, 1999).

2. Transfer of Functions Order 2008 (SI 2008/2833) art.6 and Sch.3, paras 14 and 148 (November 3, 2008).

3. Welfare Reform Act 2012 s.103 and Sch.12, para.4 (check date, 2013).

4. Welfare Reform Act 2012 s.147 and Sch.14, Pt 8 (April 1, 2013).

DEFINITIONS

"appeal tribunal"—see subs.(7).
"Commissioner"—*ibid.*
"prescribed"—SSA 1998 s.84.

Appeals

Appeal to [² First-tier Tribunal]

12.—(1) This section applies to any decision of the Secretary of State under section 8 or 10 above (whether as originally made or as revised under section 9 above) which—

(a) is made on a claim for, or on an award of, a relevant benefit, and does not fall within Schedule 2 to this Act; [¹ or]

(b) is made otherwise than on such a claim or award, and falls within Schedule 3 to this Act; [¹ . . .]

(c) [¹ . . .]

1.22.1

[¹ (2) In the case of a decision to which this section applies, the claimant and such other person as may be prescribed shall have a right to appeal to [² the First-tier Tribunal], but nothing in this subsection shall confer a right of appeal—

[³(a)] in relation to a prescribed decision, or a prescribed determination embodied in or necessary to a decision;

(b) where regulations under subsection (3A) so provide.]]

(3) Regulations under subsection (2) above shall not prescribe any decision or determination that relates to the conditions of entitlement to a relevant benefit for which a claim has been validly made or for which no claim is required.

[³(3A) Regulations may provide that, in such cases or circumstances as may be prescribed, there is a right of appeal under subsection (2) in relation to a decision only if the Secretary of State has considered whether to revise the decision under section 9.

(3B) The regulations may in particular provide that that condition is met only where—

(a) the consideration by the Secretary of State was on an application;

(b) the Secretary of State considered issues of a specified description, or

(c) the consideration by the Secretary of State satisfied any other condition specified in the regulations.

(3C) The references in subsections (3A) and (3B) to regulations and to the Secretary of State are subject to any enactment under or by virtue of which the functions under this Chapter are transferred to or otherwise made exercisable by a person other than the Secretary of State.]

[⁵(3D) In the case of a decision relating to child benefit or guardian's allowance, the making of any appeal under this section against the decision as originally made must follow the Commissioners for Her Majesty's Revenue and Customs first deciding, on an application made for revision of that decision under section 9, not to revise the decision.]

(4) Where the Secretary of State has determined that any amount is recoverable under or by virtue of section 71[⁴, 71ZB, 71ZG, 71ZH,] or 74 of the Administration Act, any person from whom he has determined that it is recoverable shall have the same right of appeal to [² the First-tier Tribunal] as a claimant.

(5) In any case where—

(a) the Secretary of State has made a decision in relation to a claim under Part V of the Contributions and Benefits Act; and

(b) the entitlement to benefit under that Part of that Act of any person other than the claimant is or may be, under Part VI of Schedule 7 to that Act, affected by that decision,

that other person shall have the same right of appeal to [² the First-tier Tribunal] as the claimant.

(6) A person with a right of appeal under this section shall be given such notice of a decision to which this section applies and of that right as may be prescribed.

(7) Regulations may—

[³(a)] make provision as to the manner in which, and the time within which, appeals are to be brought;

[(b) provide that, where in accordance with regulations under subsection (3A) there is no right of appeal against a decision, any purported appeal may be treated as an application for revision under section 9].

(8) In deciding an appeal under this section, [² the First-tier Tribunal]—

(a) need not consider any issue that is not raised by the appeal; and

(b) shall not take into account any circumstances not obtaining at the time when the decision appealed against was made.

(9) The reference in subsection (1) above to a decision under section 10 above is a reference to a decision superseding any such decision as is mentioned in paragraph (a) or (b) of subsection (1) of that section.

AMENDMENTS

1. Social Security Contributions (Transfer of Functions, etc.) Act 1999 s.18 and Sch.7, para.25 (April 1, 1999).

2. Transfer of Functions Order 2008 (SI 2008/2833) art.6 and Sch.3, paras 143 and 149 (November 3, 2008).

3. Welfare Reform Act 2012 s.102(1)–(4) (February 25, 2013).

4. Welfare Reform Act 2012 s.105(6) (April 29, 2013).

5. Tax Credits, Child Benefit and Guardian's Allowance Reviews and Appeals Order 2014/886 art.4(1) (April 6, 2014).

DEFINITIONS

"the Administration Act"—see SSA 1998 s.84.

"claim"—by virtue of SSA 1998 s.39(2), see SSAA 1992 s.191.

"claimant"—see SSA 1998 s.39(1), and by virtue of SSA 1998 s.39(2), see SSAA 1992 s.191.

"the Contributions and Benefits Act"—see SSA 1998 s.84.

"prescribed"—*ibid.*

"relevant benefit"—see s.8(3).

Finality of decisions

17.—(1) Subject to the provisions of this Chapter [¹ and to any provision made by or under Chapter 2 of Part 1 of the Tribunals, Courts and Enforcement Act 2007], any decision made in accordance with the foregoing provisions of this Chapter shall be final; and subject to the provisions of any regulations under section 11 above, any decision made in accordance with those regulations shall be final.

1.23

(2) If and to the extent that regulations so provide, any finding of fact or other determination embodied in or necessary to such a decision, or on which such a decision is based, shall be conclusive for the purposes of—

(a) further such decisions;

(b) decisions made under the Child Support Act; and

(c) decisions made under the Vaccine Damage Payments Act.

AMENDMENT

1. Transfer of Functions Order 2008 (SI 2008/2833) art.6 and Sch.3, paras 143 and 155 (November 3, 2008).

DEFINITIONS

"the Child Support Act"—see SSA 1998 s.84.

"the Vaccine Damage Act"—*ibid.*

SCHEDULE 2

DECISIONS AGAINST WHICH NO APPEAL LIES

Jobseeker's allowance for persons under 18

1.24   **1.** In relation to a person who has reached the age of 16 but not the age of 18, a decision—
    (a) whether section 16 of the Jobseekers Act is to apply to him; or
    (b) whether to issue a certificate under section 17(4) of that Act.

Christmas bonus

2. A decision whether a person is entitled to payment under section 148 of the Contributions and Benefits Act.

Priority between persons entitled to [³ carer's allowance]

3. A decision as to the exercise of the discretion under section 70(7) of the Contributions and Benefits Act.

Priority between persons entitled to child benefit

4. A decision as to the exercise of the discretion under paragraph 5 of Schedule 10 to the Contributions and Benefits Act.

Persons treated as if present in Great Britain

5. A decision whether to certify, in accordance with regulations made under section 64(1), 71(6), 113(1) or 119 of the Contributions and Benefits Act, that it is consistent with the proper administration of that Act to treat a person as though he were present in Great Britain.

[¹ Work-focused interviews

5A. A decision terminating or reducing the amount of a person's benefit made in consequence of any decision made under regulations under section 2A [⁴ or 2AA] of the Administration Act (work-focused interviews).]

Alteration of rates of benefit

6. A decision as to the amount of benefit to which a person is entitled, where it appears to the Secretary of State that the amount is determined by—
    (a) the rate of benefit provided for by law; or
    (b) an alteration of a kind referred to in—
        (i) section 159(1)(b) of the Administration Act (income support); [² ...]
        (ii) section 159A(1)(b) of that Act (jobseeker's allowance)[;²
        (iii) section 159B(1)(b) of that Act (state pension credit)]][⁵;
        (iv) section 159C(1)(b) of that Act (employment and support allowance)][⁷; or
        (v) section 159D(1)(b) of that Act (universal credit)].

Increases in income support due to attainment of particular ages

7. A decision as to the amount of benefit to which a person is entitled, where it appears to the Secretary of State that the amount is determined by the recipient's entitlement to an increased amount of income support or income-based jobseeker's allowance in the circumstances referred to in section 160(2) or 160A(2) of the Administration Act.

[⁸ Increases in universal credit due to attainment of particular ages

7A. *A decision as to the amount of benefit to which a person is entitled, where it appears to the Secretary of State that the amount is determined by the recipient's entitlement to an increased amount of universal credit in the circumstances referred to in section 160C(2) of the Administration Act.]*

Reduction in accordance with reduced benefit decision

8. A decision to reduce the amount of a person's benefit in accordance with a reduced benefit decision (within the meaning of section 46 of the Child Support Act).

[⁶ *Reduction on application of benefit cap*

8A. A decision to apply the benefit cap in accordance with regulations under section 96 of the Welfare Reform Act 2012.]

Power to prescribe other decisions

9. Such other decisions as may be prescribed.

AMENDMENTS

1. Welfare Reform and Pensions Act 1999 s.81 and Sch.11, para.87 (November 11, 1999).

2. State Pension Credit Act 2002 s.11 and Sch.1, para.11 (July 2, 2002 for the purpose of exercising any power to make regulations or orders and October 6, 2003 for all other purposes).

3. Regulatory Reform (Carer's Allowance) Order 2002 (SI 2002/1457) art.2(1) and Sch., para.3(b) September 2002 for the purposes of exercising powers to make subordinate legislation and October 28, 2002 for all other purposes).

4. Employment Act 2002 s.53 and Sch.7, para.51 (July 5, 2003).

5. Welfare Reform Act 2007 Sch.3, para.17(1) and (8) (October 27, 2008).

6. Welfare Reform Act 2012 s.97(6) (April 15, 2013).

7. Welfare Reform Act 2012 s.31, Sch.2, paras 43, 50(1), (2) (April 29, 2013).

8. *Welfare Reform Act 2012 s.31, Sch.2, paras 43, 50(1), (3) (not yet in force).*

DEFINITIONS

"the Administration Act"—see SSA 1998, s.84.
"benefit"—see SSA 1998, s.39(1), and by virtue of SSA 1998 s.39(2), see SSAA 1992, s.191.
"the Child Support Act"—see SSA 1998, s.84.
"the Contributions and Benefits Act"—*ibid.*
"the Jobseekers Act"—*ibid.*
"prescribed"—*ibid.*

Section 12(1)

SCHEDULE 3

DECISIONS AGAINST WHICH AN APPEAL LIES

PART I

BENEFIT DECISIONS

Entitlement to benefit without a claim

1. In such cases or circumstances as may be prescribed, a decision whether a person is entitled to a relevant benefit for which no claim is required.   **1.25**

2. If so, a decision as to the amount to which he is entitled.

Payability of benefit

3. A decision whether a relevant benefit (or a component of a relevant benefit) to which a person is entitled is not payable by reason of—

   (a) any provision of the Contributions and Benefits Act by which the person is disqualified for receiving benefit;

   (b) regulations made under section 72(8) of that Act (disability living allowance);

   (c) regulations made under section 113(2) of that Act (suspension of payment);

   (d) [⁸ . . .]

[⁵ (da) [⁸ . . .]]

  [¹ (e) [⁶ . . .] [² or

   (f) section [⁷ 6B,] 7, 8 or 9 of the Social Security Fraud Act 2001][⁴; [¹⁰ . . .]

   (g) section 18 of the Welfare Reform Act 2007];

[¹⁰ (h) regulations made under section 85(1) or 86(1) of the Welfare Reform Act 2012; or

    (i) section 87 of that Act].

[⁹ **3A.** A decision as to the amount of a relevant benefit that is payable to a person by virtue of regulations under section 6B, 7, 8 or 9 of the Social Security Fraud Act 2001.]

Payments to third parties

4. Except in such cases or circumstances as may be prescribed, a decision whether the whole or part of a benefit to which a person is entitled is, by virtue of regulations, to be paid to a person other than him.

Recovery of benefits

5. A decision whether payment is recoverable under section 71 or 71A of the Administration Act.

6. If so, a decision as to the amount of payment recoverable.

[¹¹**6A.** *A decision as to whether payment of housing credit (within the meaning of the State Pension Credit Act 2002) is recoverable under section 71ZB of the Administration Act.*]

¹⁰**6B.** A decision as to the amount of payment recoverable under section 71ZB, 71ZG or 71ZH of the Administration Act.]

State pension: prisoners and overseas residents

[¹²**6C.** A decision that a state pension under Part 1 of the Pensions Act 2014 is not payable by reason of regulations under section 19 of that Act (prisoners).

6D. A decision that a person is not entitled to increases in the rate of a state pension under Part 1 of the Pensions Act 2014 by reason of regulations under section 20 of that Act (overseas residents).]

Industrial injuries benefit

7. A decision whether an accident was an industrial accident for the purposes of industrial injuries benefit.

Jobseekers' agreements

8. A decision in relation to a jobseeker's agreement as proposed to be made under section 9 of the Jobseekers Act, or as proposed to be varied under section 10 of that Act.

[⁵*State Pension Credit*

8A. A decision whether to specify a period as an assessed income period under section 6 of the State Pension Credit Act 2002.

8B. If so, a decision as to the period to be so specified.

8C. A decision whether an assessed income period comes to an end by virtue of section 9(4) or (5) of that Act.

8D. If so, a decision as to when the assessed income period so ends.]

Power to prescribe other decisions

9. Such other decisions relating to a relevant benefit as may be prescribed.

Part II

Contributions Decisions

10.–15. *[Omitted]*.

Responsibilities at home

1.26

16. A decision whether a person was (within the meaning of regulations) precluded from regular employment by responsibilities at home.

Earnings and contributions credits

17. A decision whether a person is entitled to be credited with earnings or contributions in accordance with regulations made under section 22(5) of the Contributions and Benefits Act.

18.–29. *[Omitted]*.

AMENDMENTS

1. Child Support, Pensions and Social Security Act 2000, s.66 and Sch.9, Pt V (October 15, 2001).
2. Social Security Fraud Act 2001, s.12(2) (April 1 2002).
3. State Pension Credit Act 2002, Sch.1, para.12 (July 2, 2002 for the purpose of exercising any power to make regulations or orders and October 6, 2003 for other purposes).
4. Welfare Reform Act 2007, Sch.3, para.17(1) and (9) (October 27, 2008).
5. Welfare Reform Act 2009, s.1(4) and Sch.3, para.4 (November 12, 2009).
6. Welfare Reform Act 2009, Sch.7 (March 22, 2010).
7. Welfare Reform Act 2009, Sch.4, para.10 (April 1, 2010).
8. Welfare Reform Act 2012, s.46(4) (October 22, 2012).
9. Welfare Reform Act 2012, s.31 and Sch.2, paras 43 and 51 (April 1, 2013).
10. Welfare Reform Act 2012, s.91 and Sch.9, paras 37 and 43 (April 8, 2013).
11. Welfare Reform Act 2012, s.105(7) (April 29, 2013).
12. Pensions Act 2014 Sch.12(1) para.37 (April 6, 2016).

DEFINITIONS

"the Administration Act"—see SSA 1998 s.84.
"benefit"—see SSA 1998 s.39(1), and by virtue of SSA 1998, s.39(2) see SSAA 1992 s.191.
"claim"—*ibid*.
"the Child Support Act"—see SSA 1998 s.84.
"the Contributions and Benefits Act"—*ibid*.
"industrial injuries benefit"—see SSA 1998 s.39(1), and by virtue of SSA 1998 s.39(2), see SSAA 1992 s.191.
"the Jobseekers Act"—see SSA 1998 s.84.
"prescribed"—*ibid*.
"relevant benefit"—see SSA 1998 s.8(3).

Welfare Reform Act 2012

(2012 c.5)

ARRANGEMENT OF SECTIONS

PART 1

UNIVERSAL CREDIT

CHAPTER 1

ENTITLEMENT AND AWARDS

Introductory

1.27

Entitlement

CHAPTER 3

SUPPLEMENTARY AND GENERAL

Supplementary and consequential

Universal credit and other benefits

General

Regulations

PART 5

SOCIAL SECURITY: GENERAL

Benefit cap

PART 7

FINAL

SCHEDULES

An Act to make provision for universal credit and personal independence payment; to make other provision about social security and tax credits; to make provision about the functions of the registration service, child support maintenance and the use of jobcentres; to establish the Social Mobility and Child Poverty Commission and otherwise amend the Child Poverty Act 2010; and for connected purposes.

[8th March 2012]

PART 1

UNIVERSAL CREDIT

CHAPTER 1

ENTITLEMENT AND AWARDS

Introductory

1.31   **Universal credit**

1.—(1) A benefit known as universal credit is payable in accordance with this Part.

(2) Universal credit may, subject as follows, be awarded to—

(a) an individual who is not a member of a couple (a "single person"), or

(b) members of a couple jointly.

(3) An award of universal credit is, subject as follows, calculated by reference to—

(a) a standard allowance;

(b) an amount for responsibility for children or young persons;

(c) an amount for housing; and

(d) amounts for other particular needs or circumstances.

DEFINITIONS

"child"—see s.40.
"couple"—see ss.39 and 40.

GENERAL NOTE

1.32   Part 1 of the Welfare Reform Act 2012 ("WRA 2012") contains the provisions and confers regulation-making powers in relation to universal credit. Universal credit is to be the new means-tested, non-contributory benefit for people of working age. It replaces income support, income-based jobseeker's allowance (JSA), income-related employment and support allowance (ESA), housing benefit, working tax credit and child tax credit. Thus it will be paid to people both in and out of work. State pension credit will continue for people who are over the qualifying age for state pension credit (this is gradually rising in line with the staged increase in pensionable age for women until it reaches 65 in November 2018 and will increase to 66 by October 2020)—see s.4(4), which applies the definition of "the qualifying age" for state pension credit in s.1(6) of the State Pension Credit Act 2002 (see Vol.II in this series) for the purposes of universal credit. ESA and JSA will also continue but as contributory benefits only.

Note that "a person who is subject to immigration control" is not entitled to universal credit (Immigration and Asylum Act 1999, s.115, as amended by WRA 2012, Sch.2, para.54 with effect from April 29, 2013).

Initially universal credit was introduced only for people in the "pathfinder group" and only on an extremely limited geographical basis. See the Introduction and the General Note at the beginning of Part IV of this Volume for a summary of the process by which universal credit has been "rolled out" on a national basis up to August 8, 2016.

As usual, Part 1 creates the legislative framework and the detail is to be found in the Universal Credit Regulations 2013 (SI 2013/376)—on which see Pt III of this Volume.

Subs.(2)

This provides that in the case of a couple awards are to be made to the couple jointly. Note the definition of "claimant" in s.40, which states that "claimant" in Pt 1 of the Act means "a single claimant or each of joint claimants".   **1.33**

Subs.(3)

Depending on the claimant's (or claimants') circumstances, an award of universal credit will include a standard allowance (see s.9 and reg.36 of the Universal Credit Regulations), an amount for children and young persons for whom the claimant is responsible (see s.10 and regs 24 and 36 of the Universal Credit Regulations), housing costs (see s.11 and regs 25–26 of, and Schs 1–5 to, the Universal Credit Regulations) and an amount for "other particular needs or circumstances" (see s.12 and regs 23(2) and 27–35 of, and Schs 6-9 to, the Universal Credit Regulations). Note that although subs.(3)(b) refers to an amount for children and young persons, in the case of the latter, s.10 restricts this to "qualifying young persons". For who counts as a "qualifying young person" see s.40 and reg.5 of the Universal Credit Regulations.   **1.34**

Claims

2.—(1) A claim may be made for universal credit by—   **1.35**

(a) a single person; or

(b) members of a couple jointly.

(2) Regulations may specify circumstances in which a member of a couple may make a claim as a single person.

Definitions

"claim"—see s.40.
"couple"—see ss.39 and 40.
"single person"—see s.40.

General Note

In the case of a couple, claims for universal credit are to be made jointly. This does not apply in prescribed circumstances (subs.(2)). On subs.(2), see reg.3(3) of the Universal Credit Regulations and note reg.3(4)-(6).   **1.36**

For the rules for claims for universal credit see the Universal Credit, Personal Independence Payment, Jobseeker's Allowance and Employment and Support Allowance (Claims and Payments) Regulations 2013 (SI 2013/380) in Part V of this Volume. Generally a claim for universal credit has to be made online. Note reg.6 (claims not required for entitlement to universal credit in certain cases).

Entitlement

Entitlement

1.37   **3.**—(1) A single claimant is entitled to universal credit if the claimant meets—

(a) the basic conditions; and

(b) the financial conditions for a single claimant.

(2) Joint claimants are jointly entitled to universal credit if—

(a) each of them meets the basic conditions; and

(b) they meet the financial conditions for joint claimants.

DEFINITIONS

"claim"—see s.40.
"claimant"—*ibid.*
"joint claimants"—*ibid.*
"single claimant"—*ibid.*

GENERAL NOTE

1.38   This sets out the general conditions of entitlement to universal credit. A single claimant has to meet all of the basic conditions (see s.4) and the financial conditions (i.e., the means-test) (see s.5). In the case of joint claimants, both of them have to meet all of the basic and the financial conditions. Note, however, s.4(2) which allows for regulations to provide for exceptions from any of these conditions, either in the case of a single claimant, or one or both joint claimants.

Basic conditions

1.39   **4.**—(1) For the purposes of section 3, a person meets the basic conditions who—

(a) is at least 18 years old;

(b) has not reached the qualifying age for state pension credit;

(c) is in Great Britain;

(d) is not receiving education; and

(e) has accepted a claimant commitment.

(2) Regulations may provide for exceptions to the requirement to meet any of the basic conditions (and, for joint claimants, may provide for an exception for one or both).

(3) For the basic condition in subsection (1)(a) regulations may specify a different minimum age for prescribed cases.

(4) For the basic condition in subsection (1)(b), the qualifying age for state pension credit is that referred to in section 1(6) of the State Pension Credit Act 2002.

(5) For the basic condition in subsection (1)(c) regulations may—

(a) specify circumstances in which a person is to be treated as being or not being in Great Britain;

(b) specify circumstances in which temporary absence from Great Britain is disregarded.

(c) modify the application of this Part in relation to a person not in Great Britain who is by virtue of paragraph (b) entitled to universal credit.

(6) For the basic condition in subsection (1)(d) regulations may—

(a) specify what "receiving education" means;

(b) specify circumstances in which a person is to be treated as receiving or not receiving education.

(7) For the basic condition in subsection (1)(e) regulations may specify circumstances in which a person is to be treated as having accepted or not accepted a claimant commitment.

DEFINITIONS

"claim"—see s.40.
"claimant"—*ibid.*
"joint claimants"—*ibid.*

GENERAL NOTE

Subsection (1) lists the basic conditions that have to be satisfied for entitlement to universal credit. Subsection (2) allows for regulations to provide for exceptions from any of these conditions, either in the case of a single claimant, or one or both joint claimants.   **1.40**

Subs.(1)(a)

The minimum age for entitlement to universal credit is generally 18. However, under subs.(3) regulations can provide for a lower age in certain cases. See reg.8 of the Universal Credit Regulations for the cases where the minimum age is 16.   **1.41**

Subs.(1)(b)

This subsection excludes the possibility that a person could be entitled to both state pension credit and universal credit by providing that no person who has reached "the qualifying age for state pension credit" will meet the basic conditions for universal credit. But note subs.(2) and see reg.3(2) of the Universal Credit Regulations. The effect of reg.3(2) is that a couple may still be entitled to universal credit even if one member is over the qualifying age for state pension credit, provided that the other member of the couple is under that age.   **1.42**

Subsection (4) applies the definition of "the qualifying age" for state pension credit in s.1(6) of the State Pension Credit Act 2002 (see Vol.II in this series) for the purposes of universal credit. The effect of that definition is that the qualifying age for state pension credit for both men and women is the pensionable age for women (this was 60 but since April 2010 has been gradually rising and will reach 65 in November 2018).

Subs.(1)(c)

It is a basic condition of entitlement to universal credit that the person is in Great Britain. Note subs.(5) under which regulations may treat a person as being or not being in Great Britain (see reg.9 of the Universal Credit Regulations for when a person is treated as not being in Great Britain, and reg.10 on Crown servants and armed forces) and may provide for the circumstances in which temporary absence from Great Britain is ignored (see reg.11).   **1.43**

Subs.(1)(d)

A person must not be "receiving education" to be eligible for universal credit. For the regulations made under subs.(6) see regs 12–14 of the Universal Credit Regulations.   **1.44**

Subs. (1) (e)

1.45   The concept of a claimant commitment as a condition of receiving benefit is an important part of the underlying policy behind the Government's welfare benefit reforms. See s.14 below and the notes to that section. Note that the condition is met merely by having accepted the most up-to-date version of the claimant commitment. A failure to comply with the claimant commitment does not entail any breach of subs.(1)(e), nor is that in itself any ground for a sanction, although sanctions may be imposed for failures to comply with work-related and connected requirements that are recorded in the claimant commitment and other legal consequences may follow from failures to carry out other obligations. Under subs.(7) regulations may specify the circumstances in which a person can be treated as having accepted or not accepted a claimant commitment—see regs 15–16 of the Universal Credit Regulations.

Financial conditions

1.46   **5.**—(1) For the purposes of section 3, the financial conditions for a single claimant are that—

(a) the claimant's capital, or a prescribed part of it, is not greater than a prescribed amount, and

(b) the claimant's income is such that, if the claimant were entitled to universal credit, the amount payable would not be less than any prescribed minimum.

(2) For those purposes, the financial conditions for joint claimants are that—

(a) their combined capital, or a prescribed part of it, is not greater than a prescribed amount, and

(b) their combined income is such that, if they were entitled to universal credit, the amount payable would not be less than any prescribed minimum.

DEFINITIONS

   "claim"—see s.40.
   "claimant"—*ibid.*
   "joint claimants"—*ibid.*
   "prescribed"—*ibid.*
   "single claimant"—*ibid.*

GENERAL NOTE

1.47   This section contains the means-test for universal credit. Both the capital and the income condition have to be met. For joint claimants it is their combined capital and their combined income that counts (subs.(2)).

Capital

1.48   The capital limit for universal credit for both a single claimant and joint claimants is £16,000 (see reg.18(1) of the Universal Credit Regulations). Note that where a claimant who is a member of a couple makes a claim as a single person (see reg.3(3) of the Universal Credit Regulations for the circumstances in which this may occur) the capital of the other member of the couple counts as the claimant's (reg.18(2)).

   Thus the capital limit for universal credit is the same as for income support, income-based JSA, income-related ESA and housing benefit. There is no capital limit for working tax credit and child tax credit. See further the notes to s.134(1) SSCBA 1992 in Vol. II of this series.

   For the rules on calculating capital see regs 45–50 and 75–77 of, and Sch 10 to, the Universal Credit Regulations.

Income

The effect of subs.(1)(b) in the case of a single claimant and subs.(2)(b) in the case of joint claimants is that there will be no entitlement to universal credit if the amount payable is less than the minimum amount. The minimum amount is 1p (see reg.17 of the Universal Credit Regulations and note reg.6(1) on rounding). Thus it is possible for a person to be entitled to universal credit of 1p.

Note that where a claimant who is a member of a couple makes a claim as a single person (see reg.3(3) of the Universal Credit Regulations for the circumstances in which this may occur) the combined income of the couple is taken into account when calculating an award (reg.22(3)(a)).

Any income of a child is not taken into account.

See also the regulation-making powers as regards the calculation of capital and income in para.4 of Sch.1.

1.49

Restrictions on entitlement

6.—(1) Entitlement to universal credit does not arise—

1.50

(a) in prescribed circumstances (even though the requirements in section 3 are met);

(b) if the requirements in section 3 are met for a period shorter than a prescribed period.

(c) for a prescribed period at the beginning of a period during which those requirements are met.

(2) A period prescribed under subsection (1)(b) or (c) may not exceed seven days.

(3) Regulations may provide for exceptions to subsection (1)(b) or (c).

DEFINITION

"prescribed"—see s.40.

GENERAL NOTE

This enables regulations to be made which provide that a person will not be entitled to universal credit: (i) even though s/he meets the basic and financial conditions (subs.(1)(a)); (ii) if s/he meets those conditions for seven days or less (subs.(1)(b) and subs.(2)); or (iii) for a period of seven days or less at the beginning of a period during which those conditions are met (subs.(1)(c) and subs.(2)).

1.51

The power conferred by subs.(1)(a) has been exercised to make reg.19 of the Universal Credit Regulations and that conferred by subs.(1)(c) to make reg.19A. No regulations have yet been made under subs.(1)(b).

Awards

Basis of awards

7.—(1) Universal credit is payable in respect of each complete assessment period within a period of entitlement.

1.52

(2) In this Part an "assessment period" is a period of a prescribed duration.

(3) Regulations may make provision—

(a) about when an assessment period is to start;

(b) for universal credit to be payable in respect of a period shorter than an assessment period;

(c) about the amount payable in respect of a period shorter than an assessment period.

(4) In subsection (1) "period of entitlement" means a period during which entitlement to universal credit subsists.

GENERAL NOTE

1.53 See the commentary to reg.21 of the Universal Credit Regulations.

Calculation of awards

1.54 **8.**—(1) The amount of an award of universal credit is to be the balance of—

(a) the maximum amount (see subsection (2)), less
(b) the amounts to be deducted (see subsection (3)).

(2) The maximum amount is the total of—

(a) any amount included under section 9 (standard allowance);
(b) any amount included under section 10 (responsibility for children and young persons);
(c) any amount included under section 11 (housing costs), and
(d) any amount included under section 12 (other particular needs or circumstances).

(3) The amounts to be deducted are—

(a) an amount in respect of earned income calculated in the prescribed manner (which may include multiplying some or all earned income by a prescribed percentage), and
(b) an amount in respect of unearned income calculated in the pre-scribed manner (which may include multiplying some or all unearned income by a prescribed percentage).

(4) In subsection (3)(a) and (b) the references to income are—

(a) in the case of a single claimant, to income of the claimant, and
(b) in the case of joint claimants, to combined income of the claimants.

DEFINITIONS

"claim"—see s.40.
"claimant"—*ibid.*
"joint claimants"—*ibid.*
"prescribed"—*ibid.*
"single claimant"—*ibid.*

GENERAL NOTE

1.55 See the commentary to reg.22 of the Universal Credit Regulations.

Elements of an award

Standard allowance

1.56 **9.**—(1) The calculation of an award of universal credit is to include an amount by way of an allowance for—

(a) a single claimant, or
(b) joint claimants.

(2) Regulations are to specify the amount to be included under subsection (1).

(3) Regulations may provide for exceptions to subsection (1).

DEFINITIONS

"claim"—see s.40.
"claimant"—*ibid.*

GENERAL NOTE

See the commentary to regs 23 and 36 of the Universal Credit Regulations.　1.57

Responsibility for children and young persons

10.—(1) The calculation of an award of universal credit is to include an　1.58
amount for each child or qualifying young person for whom a claimant is
responsible.

[¹ (1A) But the amount mentioned in subsection (1) is to be available in
respect of a maximum of two persons who are either children or qualifying
young persons for whom a claimant is responsible.]

(2) Regulations may make provision for the inclusion of an additional
amount [¹ for each] child or qualifying young person [¹ for whom a claimant
is responsible who] is disabled.

(3) Regulations are to specify, or provide for the calculation of, amounts
to be included under subsection (1) or (2).

(4) Regulations may provide for exceptions to subsection (1) [¹ or (1A)].

(5) In this Part, "qualifying young person" means a person of a prescribed description.

AMENDMENT

1. Welfare Reform and Work Act 2016 s.14(1)-(4) (April 6, 2017).

DEFINITIONS

"child"—see s.40.
"disabled"—*ibid.*

GENERAL NOTE

See the commentary to regs 24 and 36 of the Universal Credit Regulations.　1.59

Housing costs

11.—(1) The calculation of an award of universal credit is to include an　1.60
amount in respect of any liability of a claimant to make payments in respect
of the accommodation they occupy as their home.

(2) For the purposes of subsection (1)—

(a)　the accommodation must be in Great Britain;

(b)　the accommodation must be residential accommodation;

(c)　it is immaterial whether the accommodation consists of the whole or
part of a building and whether or not it comprises separate and self-
contained premises.

(3) Regulations may make provision as to—

(a)　what is meant by payments in respect of accommodation for the purposes of this section (and, in particular, the extent to which universal
credit payments include mortgage payments);

(b) circumstances in which a claimant is to be treated as liable or not liable to make such payments;

(c) circumstances in which a claimant is to be treated as occupying or not occupying accommodation as their home (and, in particular, for temporary absences to be disregarded);

(d) circumstances in which land used for the purposes of any accommodation is to be treated as included in the accommodation.

(4) Regulations are to provide for the determination or calculation of any amount to be included under this section.

(5) Regulations may—

(a) provide for exceptions to subsection (1);

(b) provide for inclusion of an amount under this section in the calculation of an award of universal credit—

(i) to end at a prescribed time, or

(ii) not to start until a prescribed time.

DEFINITIONS

"claim"—see s.40.
"claimant"—*ibid.*
"prescribed"—*ibid.*

GENERAL NOTE

1.61   This provides for an award of universal credit to include an amount in respect of the claimant's (or claimants') liability to make payments in respect of the accommodation they occupy as their home. It will cover payments both by people who are renting their homes and by owner occupiers (as well as service charges).

Under subs.(2), the accommodation must be residential accommodation and must be in Great Britain. It can be the whole or part of a building and need not comprise separate and self-contained premises.

For the rules relating to housing costs see regs 25–26 of, and Schs 1–5 to, the Universal Credit Regulations.

Other particular needs or circumstances

1.62   **12.**—(1) The calculation of an award of universal credit is to include amounts in respect of such particular needs or circumstances of a claimant as may be prescribed.

(2) The needs or circumstances prescribed under subsection (1) may include—

(a) [¹ . . .]

(b) the fact that a claimant has limited capability for work and work-related activity;

(c) the fact that a claimant has regular and substantial caring responsibilities for a severely disabled person.

(3) Regulations are to specify, or provide for the determination or calculation of, any amount to be included under subsection (1).

(4) Regulations may—

(a) provide for inclusion of an amount under this section in the calculation of an award of universal credit—

(i) to end at a prescribed time, or

(ii) not to start until a prescribed time;

(b) provide for the manner in which a claimant's needs or circumstances are to be determined.

AMENDMENT

1. Welfare Reform and Work Act 2016 s.16 (April 3, 2017).

DEFINITIONS

"claim"—see s.40.
"claimant"—*ibid.*
"limited capability for work"—*ibid.*
"prescribed"—*ibid.*
"work"—*ibid.*

GENERAL NOTE

See the commentary to regs 27–36 of the Universal Credit Regulations.   **1.63**

CHAPTER 2

CLAIMANT RESPONSIBILITIES

Introductory

Work-related requirements: introductory

13.—(1) This Chapter provides for the Secretary of State to impose   **1.64**
work-related requirements with which claimants must comply for the purposes of this Part.
    (2) In this Part "work-related requirement" means—
    (a) a work-focused interview requirement (see section 15);
    (b) a work preparation requirement (see section 16);
    (c) a work search requirement (see section 17);
    (d) a work availability requirement (see section 18).
    (3) The work-related requirements which may be imposed on a claimant
depend on which of the following groups the claimant falls into—
    (a) no work-related requirements (see section 19);
    (b) work-focused interview requirement only (see section 20);
    (c) work-focused interview and work preparation requirements only (see
        section 21);
    (d) all work-related requirements (see section 22).

GENERAL NOTE

    The remaining sections of this Chapter of the WRA 2012 in the main set out what   **1.65**
sort of work-related requirements can be imposed on which universal credit claimants, as well as the system for imposing sanctions (reductions in benefit) on claimants for failure to comply with those requirements. Although s.13(1) refers only to
work-related requirements as defined in ss.15–18, s.23 allows the Secretary of State
to require a claimant to participate in an interview for various related purposes
and to provide information and evidence. A failure to comply with a requirement
under s.23 can lead to a sanction under s.27(2)(b) in the same way as can a failure
to comply with any work-related requirement. Section 14 contains rules about the
"claimant commitment", acceptance of which is a condition of entitlement under
s.4(1)(e).

There is a handy summary of the sanctions framework in Chapter 48.2 of CPAG's *Welfare Benefits and Tax Credits Handbook* (2017/2018 edn.).

Note that if a claimant is entitled to both universal credit and new style JSA, reg.5 of the JSA Regulations 2013 provides that no work-related requirements can be imposed under the new style JSA regime (ss.6B-6G of the new style Jobseekers Act 1995) and that the provisions for reduction of JSA on sanctions under ss.6J and 6K of that Act do not apply. See the annotations to reg.5 in Vol.II of this series for discussion of the consequences, and the notes to reg.111 of and Sch.11 to the Universal Credit Regulations. There is an equivalent provision in reg.42 of the ESA Regulations 2013 in relation to new style ESA.

Claimant commitment

1.66   **14.**—(1) A claimant commitment is a record of a claimant's responsibilities in relation to an award of universal credit.

(2) A claimant commitment is to be prepared by the Secretary of State and may be reviewed and updated as the Secretary of State thinks fit.

(3) A claimant commitment is to be in such form as the Secretary of State thinks fit.

(4) A claimant commitment is to include—

(a) a record of the requirements that the claimant must comply with under this Part (or such of them as the Secretary of State considers it appropriate to include),

(b) any prescribed information, and

(c) any other information the Secretary of State considers it appropriate to include.

(5) For the purposes of this Part a claimant accepts a claimant commitment if, and only if, the claimant accepts the most up-to-date version of it in such manner as may be prescribed.

DEFINITIONS

"claimant"—see s.40.
"prescribed"—*ibid.*

GENERAL NOTE

1.67   Under s.4(1)(e) the final basic condition of entitlement is that the claimant has accepted a claimant commitment. Section 14 defines the nature of a claimant commitment and there are further provisions in regs 15 and 16 of the Universal Credit Regulations. Where a claim has to be made jointly by both members of a couple, both are claimants and subject to this condition.

Note that the condition is met merely by having accepted the most up-to-date version of the claimant commitment, as discussed below. A failure to comply with the claimant commitment does not entail any breach of s.4(1)(e), nor is that in itself any ground for a sanction, although sanctions may be imposed for failures to comply with work-related and connected requirements that are recorded in the claimant commitment and other legal consequences may follow from failures to carry out other obligations.

It is an important element of the universal credit scheme, in contrast to the schemes that it has replaced, that the acceptance of the claimant commitment is a condition of entitlement for all categories of claimant, not merely those who would previously have been within the ambit of old style JSA. However, for those other categories the commitment can only be a much more generalised statement of responsibilities (see below), since the application of "conditionality" in the full sense to the claimant's personal circumstances will not be in issue.

Subsections (1) and (2) define a claimant commitment as a record prepared by the Secretary of State (in such form as he thinks fit: subs.(3)) of a claimant's responsibilities in relation to an award of universal credit. In particular, by subs.(4)(a), the record is to include the requirements that the particular claimant must comply with under the WRA 2012. These will in the main be work-related and connected requirements (see ss.15-25). However, in relation to those with limited capability for work or work-related activity the requirements will include those to provide information or evidence and to submit to a medical examination (s.37(5)-(7) and regs 43 and 44 of the Universal Credit Regulations). Work-related requirements can sometimes be to take specific action (e.g. to participate in a particular interview under s.15 or to take particular action to improve prospects of paid work under s.16 or to obtain paid work under s.17), so that the document will need to be detailed and closely related to the claimant's circumstances as they are from time to time. As such, it may be subject to frequent change, although there is a discretion in subs.(4)(a) to omit requirements if appropriate. The process of review and updating under subs.(2) appears to be completely informal, in stark contrast to the process for variation of a jobseeker's agreement under s.10 of the old style Jobseekers Act 1995, so can accommodate that. Each updating will trigger a new requirement to accept the most up-to-date version. Subsection (4)(b) requires the record to contain any prescribed information. Regulations have not as yet prescribed any such information. Subsection (4)(c) allows the record to contain any other information (note, information, not a further requirement) that the Secretary of State considers appropriate. For the claimant commitment to serve the basic purpose discussed below, that information must at least include information about the potential consequences under the Act of receiving a sanction for failure to carry out a requirement.

Since subs.(4) is, though, not an exhaustive statement of what a claimant commitment can contain, merely a statement of elements that it must contain, there is no reason why other responsibilities in relation to an award of universal credit cannot also be recorded, along with any appropriate accompanying information. For instance, the general obligations under regs 38 and 44 of the Claims and Payments Regulations 2013 to supply information and evidence in connection with an award and to notify changes of circumstances should probably be recorded, as it is in the example mentioned below.

Very limited exceptions from the application of the basic condition in s.4(1)(e) are set out in reg.16 of the Universal Credit Regulations. The WRA 2012 does not seek to define what is meant by acceptance of a claimant commitment beyond the provision in subs.(5) that it must be the most up-to-date version that has been accepted in such manner as prescribed in regulations. Regulation 15 of the Universal Credit Regulations provides for the time within which and the manner in which the claimant commitment must be accepted, but says nothing about what accepting the commitment entails in substance.

Since the commitment is the record of the particular claimant's responsibilities as imposed by or under the legislation itself it does not seem that acceptance can mean much more than an acknowledgement of its receipt or possibly also that the claimant understands the implications of the requirements set out. There can be no question of a claimant having to express any agreement with the justice or reasonableness of the requirements, let alone of the policy behind universal credit. Nor does acceptance seem to involve any personal commitment to carrying out the stated requirements, despite the language used in the example mentioned below. A failure to comply with any requirement imposed by the Secretary of State is a matter for a potential sanction under ss.26 or 27, not for a conclusion that the basic condition of entitlement in s.4(1)(e) is no longer met. There is no direct sanction for a failure to comply with a requirement just because it is included in the claimant commitment, nor does such a failure show that the claimant commitment has ceased to be accepted in the sense suggested above.

However, this distinction may be of little significance in practice, since inclusion in the claimant commitment appears to be a sufficient means of notifying a

1.68

claimant of the imposition of a requirement (see s.24(4) below) and a failure for no good reason to comply with any work-related requirement attracts a sanction under s.27(2) at the least. For instance, if the Secretary of State acting under s.17(2)(b) (work search requirement) specifies in the claimant commitment an impossibly large or internally inconsistent number of actions per week, then a failure to carry out the actions is at least prima facie a sanctionable failure and the question of whether what was specified was unreasonable would appear to be relevant only to "good reason" (though see the further discussion in the notes to ss.26 and 27). It is not like the actively seeking employment condition in old style JSA where, whatever was set out in a jobseeker's agreement, the fundamental test was whether claimants had in any week taken such steps as they could reasonably have been expected to have done to have the best prospects of securing employment.

Chapter J1 of *Advice for Decision Making* says that the claimant commitment is generated as the result of a conversation with the claimant (para.J1010) and that claimants who fall into the all work-related requirements group or the work preparation group will need to have a discussion with an adviser before a claimant commitment can be drawn up and accepted. Claimant commitments for claimants not in either of those groups may be accepted as part of the normal claims process (para.J1011). The meaning of that last phrase is not entirely clear, but may refer to those groups of claimants on whom it is clear from the outset that no personalised requirements will be imposed. There is a recognition that claimants may well not feel able to accept on the spot at a first interview with an adviser (now called a work coach) the full range of requirements set out in the claimant commitment, so that if the claimant declines to accept the document then, a "cooling-off period" of a maximum of seven days must be allowed for reconsideration (para.J1010). The legislative basis for this is under reg.15(1) of the Universal Credit Regulations, which provides that s.4(1)(e) is to be treated as satisfied from the outset when the claimant commitment is accepted within such period after the making of the claim as the Secretary of State specifies. It must in law be open to an adviser, depending on the particular circumstances, to specify a longer period or to alter the period initially specified. See the notes to reg.15 for further discussion of the dates on which claimant commitments are deemed to be accepted.

The notion of the claimant commitment is in many ways at the heart of what "conditionality" is meant to achieve under universal credit. It looks on its face to be an expression of what Charles Reich in his classic essay *The New Property* (1964) 73 Yale Law Journal 733 called "the New Feudalism". The universal credit claimant not only has, as the price of securing entitlement to the benefit, to accept a defined status that involves the giving up of some rights normally enjoyed by ordinary citizens, but appears to have to undertake some kind of oath of fealty by accepting a commitment to the feudal duties of that status. However, in reality the claimant commitment is a much more prosaic, and more sensible, thing. In its interesting paper *Universal Credit and Conditionality* (Social Security Advisory Committee Occasional Paper No. 9, 2012) the SSAC reported research findings that many claimants of current benefits subject to a sanctions regime did not understand what conduct could lead to a sanction, how the sanctions system worked (some not even realising that they had been sanctioned) and in particular what the consequences of a sanction would be on current and future entitlement. Paragraph 3.12 of the paper states:

"The lessons to be learned from the research ought to be relatively straightforward to implement, although providing the appropriate training for a large number of Personal Advisers may present a considerable challenge:

- claimants need to have the link between conditionality and the application of sanctions fully explained at the start of any claim
- clear and unambiguous communication about the sanctions regime between advisers and claimants is vital at the start of any claim and must form a key element in the Claimant Commitment

- claimants need to know when they are in danger of receiving a sanction and to be told when a sanction has been imposed, the amount and the duration
- claimants need to know what actions they have to take to reverse a sanction—the process and consequences of re-compliance."

If one of the main aims of conditionality, of encouraging claimants to avoid behaviour that would impede a possible return to or entry into work and thus reducing the incidence of the imposition of sanctions or of more severe sanctions, is to be furthered, it therefore makes sense to build into the system a requirement to set out each claimant's responsibilities and the consequences of not meeting them in understandable terms. However, as the SSAC suggests, the nature of the personal interaction between personal advisers, now known as work coaches, and claimants may be much more important than a formal written document in getting over the realities of the situation and in encouraging claimants to take steps to avoid or reduce dependence on benefit.

A similar line of thought seems to be behind what was set out in paras 65 and **1.69**
66 of the joint judgment of Lords Neuberger and Toulson in *R (on the application of Reilly and Wilson) v Secretary of State for Work and Pensions* [2013] UKSC 68; [2014] 1 A.C. 453, in relation to the JSA regime, after noting the serious consequence of imposing a requirement to engage in unpaid work on a claimant on pain of discontinuance of benefits:

"65. Fairness therefore requires that a claimant should have access to such information about the scheme as he or she may need in order to make informed and meaningful representations to the decision-maker before a decision is made. Such claimants are likely to vary considerably in their levels of education and ability to express themselves in an interview at a Jobcentre at a time when they may be under considerable stress. The principle does not depend on the categorisation of the Secretary of State's decision to introduce a particular scheme under statutory powers as a policy: it arises as a matter of fairness from the Secretary of State's proposal to invoke a statutory power in a way which will or may involve a requirement to perform work and which may have serious consequences on a claimant's ability to meet his or her living needs.
66. Properly informed claimants, with knowledge not merely of the schemes available, but also of the criteria for being placed on such schemes, should be able to explain what would, in their view, be the most reasonable and appropriate scheme for them, in a way which would be unlikely to be possible without such information. Some claimants may have access to information downloadable from a government website, if they knew what to look for, but many will not. For many of those dependent on benefits, voluntary agencies such as Citizens Advice Bureaus play an important role in informing and assisting them in relation to benefits to which they may be entitled, how they should apply, and what matters they should draw to the attention of their Jobcentre adviser."

These principles were discussed by the Court of Appeal in *SSWP v Reilly and Hewstone* and *SSWP v Jeffrey and Bevan* [2016] EWCA Civ 413; [2017] Q.B. 657, [2017] AACR 14 in relation to Mr Bevan's cross-appeal against the decision of the three-judge panel of the Upper Tribunal in *SSWP v TJ (JSA)* [2015] UKUT 56 (AAC). There was a detailed description and discussion of the decision in *TJ* in the 2015/16 edition of Vol.II, which need not be repeated here in the light of the Court of Appeal's decision. The Upper Tribunal had concluded, in the terms of its own summary in para.13(vi), that in the case of schemes which were mandatory both at the stages of referral onto them and once on them, no basis could be identified on which *meaningful* representations could be made prior to the decision to refer, in the sense of those representations being able to affect the decision to refer. In the 2015/16 edition of Vol.II there was some criticism of the Upper Tribunal's use of the word "mandatory" in this context.

The Court of Appeal first held that the Upper Tribunal had been right on the particular facts of Mr Bevan's case (where his complaint was that he could not afford the bus fare to attend the appointment given, so needed payment in advance rather than a refund) to find that it would have made no difference to what he would have said to the provider about the fares if he had known about what *The Work Programme Provider Guidance* issued by the DWP said about ability to use transportation.

So far as the Upper Tribunal's general guidance is concerned, the Court said this in para.172 about the submission that the Upper Tribunal had erred in saying that there was no scope for making representations in connection with a decision to refer a claimant to the Work Programme since referral was mandatory:

> "We do not believe that that is a fair reading of what the Tribunal said; and if it is properly understood there does not seem to be any dispute of principle between the parties. The Tribunal was not laying down any absolute rule. The Secretary of State's policy, embodied in the guidance, is that referral to the Programme should be automatic (ignoring the specified exceptions) if the criteria are met. All that the Tribunal was doing was to point out that, that being so, any representations would have to address the question why he should depart from the policy; and that it was not easy to see what such representations might be. That seems to us an obvious common sense observation, particularly since referral to the Work Programme does not as such involve any specific obligation: see para.151 above. But it does not mean that there could never be such cases, and indeed para.224 is expressly addressed to that possibility. The Tribunal did not depart from anything that the Supreme Court said in [*Reilly and Wilson*]. It was simply considering its application in the particular circumstances of referral to the Work Programme."

The Court considered that in the real world application of the prior information duty was unlikely to be important at the point of initial referral to the Work Programme under the old style JSA legislation, as claimants were unlikely to object at that stage, before any specific requirements were imposed. Problems were likely to emerge when particular requirements were imposed on claimants that they considered unreasonable or inappropriate. The Upper Tribunal had appeared to say in para.249 of its decision that there was little or no scope for the operation of the duty at that stage. The Court of Appeal says this in paras 177 and 178:

> "177. Mr de la Mare [counsel for Mr Bevan] submitted that that is wrong. If it is indeed what the Tribunal meant, we agree. So also does Ms Leventhal [counsel for the Secretary of State], who explicitly accepted in her written submissions that 'the requirements of fairness continue to apply after referral'. In principle, JSA claimants who are required, or who it is proposed should be required, under the Work Programme to participate in a particular activity should have sufficient information to enable them to make meaningful representations about the requirement – for example, that the activity in question is unsuitable for them or that there are practical obstacles to their participation. The fact that participation is mandatory if the requirement is made is beside the point: the whole purpose of the representations, and thus of the claimant having the relevant information to be able to make them, is so that the provider may be persuaded that the requirement should not be made, or should be withdrawn or modified.
>
> 178. However we should emphasise that the foregoing is concerned with the position in principle. It is quite another matter whether the Work Programme as operated in fact fails to give claimants such information. The Secretary of State's evidence before the Tribunal was that the relevant guidance in fact provides for them to be very fully informed. We have already referred to the Tribunal's findings about the information given at the referral interview. But it was also the evidence that at the initial interview with the provider post-referral, which is designed to find out how the claimant can be best supported, and in the subsequent inter-

actions between claimant and provider claimants are supposed to be given both information and the opportunity to make representations. Whether in any particular case there has nevertheless been a failure to give information necessary to enable the claimant to make meaningful representations will have to be judged on the facts of the particular case. Tribunals will no doubt bear in mind the point made in [*Reilly and Wilson*] that it is important not to be prescriptive about how any necessary information is provided: see para.74 of the judgment of Lord Neuberger and Lord Toulson."

It is now understood that Mr Bevan, who had been represented by CPAG, has abandoned the possibility of applying for permission to appeal to the Supreme Court against the Court of Appeal's decision, having been unable to obtain legal aid. The Supreme Court has refused Mr Hewstone's application for permission to appeal on the ground that it did not raise a point of law that deserved consideration at that point, as the outcome would not have affected the position of the parties to the case. That was because the claimants had succeeded on the point on art.6 of the ECHR and had only been seeking a declaration of incompatibility with the ECHR. The judges did indicate, though, that the issue whether the 2013 Act breached art.1 of Protocol 1 of the ECHR might deserve consideration in another case in which its resolution could affect the outcome. The government has not yet made any statement in response to the Court of Appeal's declaration of incompatibility. It thus remains possible that claimants affected may be offered some tangible further benefit.

In relation to the universal credit scheme, there might well be scope therefore for the application of the general principle of fairness at the stage of the application of a work-related or connected requirement and at the stage of specification of particular actions or activities. However, the process of discussion leading to the drawing up of a claimant commitment and its notification of the requirements imposed, as described above, certainly gives full opportunity for the provision of sufficient information to enable claimants to make meaningful representations about the content of the claimant commitment and to decide whether or not to accept initially and to make meaningful representations and decisions about taking particular specified actions further down the line. But the crucial questions in any appeals will most likely be, as suggested in para.178 of *Jeffrey and Bevan*, how the process was actually carried out in the particular case in question.

In *NM v SSWP (JSA)* [2016] UKUT 351 (AAC) Judge Wright held, as eventually conceded by the Secretary of State, that the inability to show that relevant DWP guidance had been considered before the claimant was given notice to participate in a Mandatory Work Activity scheme meant either that the claimant should not have been referred to the scheme (because the officer either would have followed the guidance or could have been persuaded to do so on representations from the claimant) or that he had good reason for not participating in the scheme. The appeal related to a sanction for failing to participate, through behaviour on the scheme. The guidance, in something called *Mandatory Work Activity Guidance* or *Operational Instructions–Procedural Guidance–Mandatory Work Activity –January 2012*, was relevant because at the time it instructed that claimants should not be considered for referral to Mandatory Work Activity if, among other circumstances, they were currently working (paid or voluntary). The claimant had been volunteering in a Sue Ryder shop, which he had to give up to attend the required scheme as a volunteer in a Salvation Army shop. The Secretary of State submitted that the guidance had since been changed to introduce an element of discretion about referral of claimants doing voluntary work. Judge Wright held that this would not excuse a failure by an officer of the Secretary of State to consider his own guidance or, on any appeal, a failure to provide the guidance to a First-tier Tribunal in accordance with the principles of natural justice.

A sample claimant commitment has been produced by the DWP in response to a freedom of information request (available at *https://www.gov.uk/government/publications/foi-query-universal-credit-claimant-commitment-example* (accessed January 27,

2014), or through a link in the universal credit part of the discussion forum on the Rightsnet website). The document puts things in terms of what the claimant says he or she will do. It is suggested above that that is not quite what the legislation requires, but there is obviously a tension with an attempt to use everyday and simple language. Nevertheless, the document is long and complicated. In the sample, there is no attempt to specify the precise length of the sanction that would be imposed for a failure for no good reason (the document says "without good reason") to comply with a requirement, but the maximum possible duration is included, plus the words "up to". It is arguable that this information is insufficiently precise.

There is some difficulty in working out what remedies a claimant would have who disagrees with the imposition of a requirement included in the claimant commitment. If the claimant declines to accept the Secretary of State's form of the record, at the outset of the claim or as later reviewed and up-dated, then any initial disallowance of the claim or subsequent supersession of an awarding decision would be appealable. However, it is not clear whether such an appeal could succeed on the basis that a requirement in fact included in the claimant commitment should not have been imposed under the conditions in ss.19–24. If the requirement was one whose imposition was prohibited by the legislation and the claimant was prepared to accept everything else in the document, it is submitted that it could properly be concluded that the condition in s.4(1)(e) had been satisfied (compare the approach of Judge Rowland in *CJSA/1080/2002* and *GM v SSWP (JSA)* [2014] UKUT 57 (AAC) in holding that a claimant was to be accepted as satisfying a condition of attendance at a Jobcentre when he had in fact not attended after being informed that he was not entitled to JSA so that attendance was pointless: see further the notes to reg.23 of the JSA Regulations 1996 in Vol.II). If it was a matter of the Secretary of State's discretion under s.22(3), the result might be different. A claimant who accepts a claimant commitment under protest about some requirement may no doubt request the Secretary of State not to impose the challenged requirement and in consequence to review the claimant commitment. However, it appears that the claimant cannot appeal directly either against the imposition of the requirement or the content of the claimant commitment or against a refusal by the Secretary of State to remove a requirement and to review the claimant commitment. See the discussion in the note to s.24 below, which would apply equally to any of the kinds of decision mentioned. None of them are "outcome" decisions.

Work-related requirements

Work-focused interview requirement

1.70   **15.**—(1) In this Part a "work-focused interview requirement" is a requirement that a claimant participate in one or more work-focused interviews as specified by the Secretary of State.

(2) A work-focused interview is an interview for prescribed purposes relating to work or work preparation.

(3) The purposes which may be prescribed under subsection (2) include in particular that of making it more likely in the opinion of the Secretary of State that the claimant will obtain paid work (or more paid work or better-paid work).

(4) The Secretary of State may specify how, when and where a work-focused interview is to take place.

DEFINITION

"claimant"—see s.40.

GENERAL NOTE

This section defines what a "work-focused interview" is and makes the related 1.71
requirement "participation" in the interview. This is for the purposes of ss.20–22,
and in particular s.20, which applies the requirement to participate in such an interview to the great majority of claimants within the JSA ambit, although on a discretionary basis. Also note the circumstances specified in and under s.19 in which no
work-related requirement may be imposed.

Under subss.(2) and (3) regulations must prescribe the purposes, relating to work
or work preparation, for which an interview may be required. The prescription, in
very wide terms, is in reg.93 of the Universal Credit Regulations. "Paid work" is not
defined in the Act, but when that phrase is used in reg.93 the definition in reg.2 will
apply (see the note to reg.93). The Secretary of State is allowed under subss.(1) and
(4) to specify how, when and where the interview is to take place, so that there is
no straightforward limit on the number or frequency of the interviews that may be
specified, or on the persons who may conduct the interview. The interviews must of
course properly be for one of the purposes prescribed in reg.93. The requirement
to participate in an interview cannot be used for punitive purposes or simply as a
means of control of a claimant. No doubt it is also to be implied that only rational
requirements may be imposed, so that a specification of two interviews in different
places at the same time or so that they could not practicably be coordinated could
be disregarded (see the approach of Judge Rowland in *GM v SSWP (JSA)* [2014]
UKUT 57 (AAC): notes to s.14 above). Rationality would also require that what
was specified should not be incompatible with other requirements, in particular the
work search and work availability requirements where there is no discretion under
s.22(2) about their imposition. Thus a claimant could not validly be required to
attend so many interviews that it made it impossible to take work search actions
for the hours specified under s.17, unless there was a corresponding reduction in
the s.17 requirements. These are rather extreme examples, which it is hoped would
not arise in practice. Because, as discussed in the notes to s.24, there is no right
of appeal against an imposition of a work-related or connected requirement as
such, the issues will normally arise in the course of challenges to or appeals against
removal of entitlement for failing to accept a claimant commitment containing the
requirement(s) in questions or against reductions in benefit following a sanction for
non-compliance. The main focus in the latter case may be on whether the claimant
had a good reason for not complying with the requirement, but sight should not be
lost of whether there had been non-compliance with the requirement as properly
interpreted (see below).

There is no requirement that the specification under subs.(4) of how, when and
where an interview is to take place should be in writing or in other permanent form.
However, good practice, plus the potential need for acceptable evidence of the existence and terms of the specification in the light of the principle that the claimant
should in sanctions cases be given the benefit of any doubt that might reasonably
arise (*DL v SSWP (JSA)* [2013] UKUT 295 (AAC)), must surely point to the need
for written or computer records to be kept and to be available to the claimant for
reference.

Note that the requirement, as now for both old style and new style JSA, is not
attendance at an interview at the specified time and date, but participation in it. This
would appear to mean that a claimant can be required to participate in an interview
over the telephone, providing that that manner of conducting it has been specified
under subs.(4). In an ambiguous (so far as JSA is concerned) Parliamentary answer
on 24 November 2015 (UIN 17005), the Minister of State Priti Patel said:

"Under JSA, claimants are not sanctioned for failing to answer their telephone.
In Universal Credit, claimants who have a prearranged telephone interview
with their Work Coach, and who fail to participate without good reason, can be
referred for a sanction decision."

There is no further provision about what participating in a work-focused interview entails. It must at least entail turning up at the place and time specified, although the decision of Judge Knowles in *SA v SSWP (JSA)* [2015] UKUT 454 (AAC) (see the notes to s.27 for full discussion) would indicate that tribunals should consider, in cases where the claimant arrives not very late, whether it is proportionate to the nature of all the circumstances to regard that as a failure to participate in an interview. There were all sorts of mitigating circumstances in *SA*, that may well not be present in other cases.

The requirement to participate must also extend to making some meaningful contribution to the interview, but the limits will probably not be established until there have been some more sanctions appeals in JSA or universal credit that reach the Upper Tribunal. Behaviour that leads to the premature termination of the interview may well amount to a failure to participate (see the facts of *DM v SSWP (JSA)* [2015] UKUT 67 (AAC) in the notes to s.27(2)(b)). There may, though, in cases of uncooperative claimants or heavy-handed officials or a combination, be difficult questions about when an interview has ceased to exist, so that subsequent behaviour cannot be relevant to whether there has been a failure to participate (see *PH v SSWP (ESA)* [2016] UKUT 119 (AAC) on failing to submit to a medical examination). A failure for no good reason to comply with any work-related requirement is sanctionable under s.27(2)(a). That is the context in which what amounts to a failure to comply will be identified, as well as what might amount to a good reason for non-compliance. For instance, there appear to be no provisions prescribing the length of notice of an interview to be given or how far a claimant can be required to travel, but there could plainly be a good reason for failing to comply with unreasonable requirements, especially if the claimant had attempted in advance to draw any problem with attendance to the Secretary of State's attention.

Note that under s.23(1) the Secretary of State is empowered to require a claimant to attend an interview relating to the imposition of a work-related requirement on the claimant or assisting the claimant to comply with a requirement.

Work preparation requirement

1.72   **16.**—(1) In this Part a "work preparation requirement" is a requirement that a claimant take particular action specified by the Secretary of State for the purpose of making it more likely in the opinion of the Secretary of State that the claimant will obtain paid work (or more paid work or better-paid work).

(2) The Secretary of State may under subsection (1) specify the time to be devoted to any particular action.

(3) Action which may be specified under subsection (1) includes in particular—

(a) attending a skills assessment;

(b) improving personal presentation;

(c) participating in training;

(d) participating in an employment programme;

(e) undertaking work experience or a work placement;

(f) developing a business plan;

(g) any action prescribed for the purpose in subsection (1).

(4) In the case of a person with limited capability for work, the action which may be specified under subsection (1) includes taking part in a work-focused health-related assessment.

(5) In subsection (4) "work-focused health-related assessment" means an assessment by a health care professional approved by the Secretary of State which is carried out for the purpose of assessing—

(a) the extent to which the person's capability for work may be improved by taking steps in relation to their physical or mental condition, and

(b) such other matters relating to their physical or mental condition and the likelihood of their obtaining or remaining in work or being able to do so as may be prescribed.

(6) In subsection (5) "health care professional" means—

(a) a registered medical practitioner,

(b) a registered nurse,

(c) an occupational therapist or physiotherapist registered with a regulatory body established by an Order in Council under section 60 of the Health Act 1999, or

(d) a member of such other profession regulated by a body mentioned in section 25(3) of the National Health Service Reform and Health Care Professions Act 2002 as may be prescribed.

DEFINITIONS

"claimant"—see s.40.
"limited capability for work"—*ibid.*

GENERAL NOTE

This section defines "work preparation requirement" for the particular purposes of ss.21 and 22. The requirement is to take particular action specified by the Secretary of State for the purpose of making it more likely that the claimant will obtain paid work or obtain more or better-paid such work. Subsection (3) gives a non-exhaustive list of actions that may be specified, including under para.(g) any action prescribed in regulations. No regulations have as yet been made under para.(g). The list is in fairly broad terms, not further defined in the legislation, even "employment programme". The sorts of activities required do not themselves have to be paid, so long as they can legitimately be related to the purpose of improving prospects of obtaining paid work or more or better paid work (see below and the notes to s.26(2)(a)). So unpaid work experience or placements (e.g. as an intern) or voluntary work can be made mandatory. See the notes to s.15 above for the need for the co-ordination with the practical application of other work-related or connected requirements for the specification of any particular work preparation requirement to be rational.

1.73

The Secretary of State has a discretion under ss.21 and 22(3) whether to impose a work preparation requirement in any particular case. Also note the circumstances specified in and under s.19 in which no work-related requirement may be imposed.

The Secretary of State may under subs.(2) specify the time to be devoted to any particular action, but in practice this is likely to be less controversial than the similar power in s.17(2) in relation to a work search requirement. Subsections (4)–(6) allow the application of a particular requirement to take part in a work-focused health-related assessment to claimants with limited capability for work (only claimants who also have limited capability for work-related activity being exempted from all work-related requirements under s.19(2)(a)). Paragraph 15 of *JS v SSWP (ESA)*; [2013] UKUT 635 (AAC) suggests that if a claimant is patently not going to be able to obtain work at any stage or is already in a suitable apprenticeship or placement no action could make it more likely that work or more work would be obtained, so that no action could be legitimately specified.

There is no requirement that the specification under subss.(1) and (2) of the particular action to be taken and the time to be devoted to it should be in writing or in other permanent form. However, good practice, plus the potential need for acceptable evidence of the existence and terms of the specification in the light of the principle that the claimant should in sanctions cases be given the benefit of any doubt that might reasonably arise (*DL v SSWP (JSA)* [2013] UKUT 295 (AAC)), must surely point to the need for written or computer records to be kept and to be available to the claimant for reference. See *NM v SSWP (JSA)* [2016] UKUT 351 (AAC), discussed in para.1.169 above, for circumstances in which failure to consider relevant DWP guidance about the circumstances in which there should or should not be referral to a scheme, with sufficient information to the claimant to allow the making of meaningful representations, undermines the applicability of any sanction for failure to comply with a requirement. The principles of natural justice require that the terms of the relevant guidance be provided to a tribunal on any appeal.

A failure for no good reason by a claimant subject to all work-related requirements to comply with a requirement under this heading to undertake a work placement of a prescribed description (i.e. the Mandatory Work Activity Scheme: reg.114 of the Universal Credit Regulations) is sanctionable under s.26(2)(a) (higher-level sanctions). Outside that limited category, failure for no good reason to comply with any work-related requirement is sanctionable under s.27(2)(a). That is the main context in which there will be exploration of what action can be said to make it more likely that the claimant will obtain paid work or more or better-paid work, since the addition of the Secretary of State's opinion in subs.(1) will not be allowed to take away the power of tribunals to reach their own conclusions on that matter. What amounts to a failure to comply will also be identified, as well as what might amount to a good reason for non-compliance. The issue may also arise in challenges to the removal of entitlement following a failure to accept a claimant commitment containing a disputed work preparation requirement (see the notes to s.14).

Note that under s.23(1) the Secretary of State is empowered to require a claimant to participate in an interview relating to the imposition of a work-related requirement on the claimant or assisting the claimant to comply with a requirement. Under s.23(3) he can require the provision of information and evidence for the purpose of verifying compliance and that the claimant confirm compliance in any manner.

Work search requirement

1.74   **17.**—(1) In this Part a "work search requirement" is a requirement that a claimant take—
   (a) all reasonable action, and
   (b) any particular action specified by the Secretary of State,
for the purpose of obtaining paid work (or more paid work or better-paid work).
   (2) The Secretary of State may under subsection (1)(b) specify the time to be devoted to any particular action.
   (3) Action which may be specified under subsection (1)(b) includes in particular—
   (a) carrying out work searches;
   (b) making applications;
   (c) creating and maintaining an online profile;
   (d) registering with an employment agency;
   (e) seeking references;
   (f) any action prescribed for the purpose in subsection (1).
   (4) Regulations may impose limitations on a work search requirement by reference to the work to which it relates; and the Secretary of State may in any particular case specify further such limitations on such a requirement.
   (5) A limitation under subsection (4) may in particular be by reference to—
   (a) work of a particular nature,
   (b) work with a particular level of remuneration,
   (c) work in particular locations, or
   (d) work available for a certain number of hours per week or at particular times,
and may be indefinite or for a particular period.

DEFINITION

"claimant"—see s.40.

GENERAL NOTE

This section defines "work search requirement" for the particular purpose of   1.75
s.22, under which the requirement must be imposed on all claimants except those
exempted by s.19, 20 or 21. It is a requirement that a claimant take both all reasonable action (subs.(1)(a)) and any particular action specified by the Secretary of State
(subs.(1)(b)) for the purpose of obtaining paid work or more or better-paid work.
"Paid work" is not defined in the Act, nor is it defined in regulations for the specific
purpose of ss.17 and 22. However, under the power in s.25, regs 94 and 95 of the
Universal Credit Regulations deem the work search requirement not to have been
complied with in certain circumstances and make references to "paid work". For
those purposes, the definition in reg.2 will apply, i.e. work done for payment or in
expectation of payment, excluding work for a charity or voluntary organisation, or
as a volunteer, in return for expenses only. Regulation 87 adds nothing to the terms
of s.17 itself. Thus it appears that both self-employment and employment can be
considered both under the reg.2 definition and under the ordinary meaning of the
phrase "paid work" and that voluntary work or unpaid internships or work placements are excluded. According to the then Minister of State Esther McVey (House
of Commons written answers April 2, 2014 and September 1, 2014) guidance to
Jobcentre Plus staff is that, in contrast to the position for JSA, universal credit claimants can be mandated to apply for vacancies for zero hours contracts. At the time
it appeared not to matter whether there was an exclusivity clause in the contract
or not, but such clauses were made unenforceable from May 26, 2015 by the new
s.27A of the Employment Rights Act 1996. There will be a question in challenges
to and appeals against sanctions decisions whether claimants have a good reason for
not complying with a requirement to search for zero hours contracts.

Subsections (4) and (5) allow regulations to impose limitations on the kind of
work search which can be required and also allow the Secretary of State to specify
further limitations. Regulation 97 contains the prescribed limitations, in terms
of hours of work for carers and those with a disability, of the maximum time for
travel to and from work and of the type of work recently undertaken. See the notes
to reg.97. There appears to be no limitation on the number of hours a week that
work could involve while still falling for consideration, apart from in the cases of
the particular categories of claimant identified in reg.97(2). Note also that reg.99
exempts claimants from the work search requirement in a variety of individual circumstances that would make the carrying out of any work search impracticable. See
the notes to reg.99 for the details. The circumstances include several to do with care
of children, the carrying out of various worthwhile activities, unfitness for work for
short and (subject to conditions) more extended periods and, particularly important
to the structure of universal credit, where earnings are at a defined level. Regulation
98 exempts recent victims of domestic violence for a fixed period.

What is "all reasonable action" under subs.(1)(a) for the purpose of obtaining paid
work within any applicable limitations is obviously in general a matter of judgment.
That includes a judgment about what counts as "action" and about the significance
of any potential action that has not been taken. The actions mentioned in subs.(3)
might be a starting point, but other things could plainly count, such as carrying out
research into the job market or potential for self-employment. No doubt just sitting
and thinking falls the other side of the line, but can often form an essential element
of the hours devoted to some more active action. Subsection (3) does not include in
its list accepting an offer of suitable work. However, it could certainly be argued that
a claimant who failed to accept such an offer had failed to take all reasonable action
for the purpose of obtaining paid work. A medium-level sanction could then follow
under s.27(2)(a) if the failure was for no good reason unless the case fell within
s.26(2)(c) (failing for no good reason to comply with a work availability requirement

by taking up an offer of paid work). There is a certain artificiality to the s.26(2)(c) sanction (see the notes to that section) but no doubt in practice decision-makers will prefer to use that provision first in a case where an offer of work has not been taken up. If for any reason that provision does not apply, it can be argued that s.27(2)(a) and s.17(1)(a) should be considered in addition. It seems very unlikely that in practice the Secretary of State would ever be in a position to specify under sub.(1) that a claimant should accept a particular offer of paid work.

Regulation 95 of the Universal Credit Regulations deems a claimant not to have complied with the requirement unless quite stringent conditions about the weekly hours devoted to work search are satisfied. See the notes to reg.95 and remember that the sanctions in s.26(4)(a), in relation to having, before claiming universal credit, failed to take up an offer of paid work, and s.27(2)(a) can only be imposed when there was no good reason for the failure to comply. Paragraph 15 of *JS v SSWP (ESA)* [2013] UKUT 635 (AAC) suggests that if a claimant is patently not going to be able to obtain work at any stage or is already in a suitable apprenticeship or placement no action could make it more likely that work or more work would be obtained, so that no action could be legitimately specified.

1.76   The particular action that can be specified by Secretary of State under subs.(1)(b) can, by subs.(3), include a number of actions, including those prescribed in regulations. No relevant regulation has yet been made. The list includes, at (c), creating and maintaining an online profile. That is relied on by the DWP to support requiring claimants to create a public profile and a public CV in Universal Jobmatch. There is helpful guidance on this in Memo ADM 15/16 of June 2016, which recognises that claimants cannot be mandated to do that or create an email account from day one of their claim, merely encouraged, and that mandation is not to follow until the claimant has had an initial work search interview with a work coach. The requirement is not to be imposed unless the benefits of Universal Jobmatch have been explained, its use is reasonable in the claimant's individual circumstances (including health, learning problems, whether English is a second language, lack of appropriate literacy and numeracy skills), the claimant has access to the internet (including at a Jobcentre) and the cookies fact sheet has been issued.

Particular vacancies can also be notified to a claimant within Universal Jobmatch and a requirement to apply notified through the claimant commitment. A failure for no good reason to comply with such a requirement leads to a higher-level sanction under s.26(2)(b). Memo ADM 15/16 suggests that if a claimant subject to such a sanction has also failed to take all reasonable action for the purposes of obtaining paid work by not applying for enough notified vacancies, there can also be a medium-level sanction under s.27(2)(a). However, it is arguable that an imposition of the medium-level sanction in those circumstances would contravene s.27(3) (no s.27 sanction if failure is also a s.26 sanctionable failure).

Where a claimant has been required to apply for a particular vacancy, reg.94 of the Universal Credit Regulations deems the work search requirement not to have been complied with where the claimant fails to participate in an interview offered in connection with the vacancy.

There is no requirement that the specification under subss.(1)(b), (2) and (3) of the particular actions to be taken and the time to be devoted to them should be in writing or in other permanent form. However, good practice, plus the potential need for acceptable evidence of the existence and terms of the specification in the light of the principle that the claimant should in sanctions cases be given the benefit of any doubt that might reasonably arise (*DL v SSWP (JSA)* [2013] UKUT 295 (AAC)), must surely point to the need for written or computer records to be kept and to be available to the claimant for reference.

Note that under s.23(1) the Secretary of State is empowered to require a claimant to participate in an interview relating to the imposition of a work-related requirement on the claimant or assisting the claimant to comply with a requirement. Under s.23(3) he can require the provision of information and evidence for the purpose of verifying compliance and that the claimant confirm compliance in any manner. A failure for no good reason to comply with any of those connected requirements is also sanctionable under s.27(2)(b).

Work availability requirement

18.—(1) In this Part a "work availability requirement" is a requirement   1.77
that a claimant be available for work.

(2) For the purposes of this section "available for work" means able and willing immediately to take up paid work (or more paid work or better-paid work).

(3) Regulations may impose limitations on a work availability requirement by reference to the work to which it relates; and the Secretary of State may in any particular case specify further such limitations on such a requirement.

(4) A limitation under subsection (3) may in particular be by reference to—

(a) work of a particular nature,

(b) work with a particular level of remuneration,

(c) work in particular locations, or

(d) work available for a certain number of hours per week or at particular times,

and may be indefinite or for a particular period.

(5) Regulations may for the purposes of subsection (2) define what is meant by a person being able and willing immediately to take up work.

DEFINITION

"claimant"—see s.40.

GENERAL NOTE

This section defines "work availability requirement" for the particular purpose of   1.78
s.22, under which the requirement must be imposed on all claimants except those exempted by s.19, 20 or 21. It requires in general that a claimant be able and willing immediately to take up paid work, or more or better-paid work. "Paid work" is not defined in the Act, nor is it defined in regulations for the specific purpose of ss.18 and 22. However, under the power in s.25, reg.96 of the Universal Credit Regulations deems the work availability requirement not to have been complied with in certain circumstances and to have been satisfied in other circumstances and makes references to "paid work". For those purposes, the definition in reg.2 will apply, i.e. work done for payment or in expectation of payment, excluding work for a charity or voluntary organisation, or as a volunteer, in return for expenses only. Regulation 87 adds nothing to the terms of s.18 itself. Thus it appears that willingness to take up both self-employment and employment can be considered. Under the ordinary meaning of the phrase "paid work" it would seem that voluntary work or unpaid internship or work placements are excluded (but see s.16 on work preparation).

For some suggestions as to a common sense approach to "immediately", in the specific context of reg.7 of the JSA Regulations 1996, see Simon Browne LJ in *Secretary of State for Social Security v David*, reported in *R(JSA) 3/01*, at paras 25 and 26:

"That 'immediately' means within a very short space of time indeed is clear not only from the word itself but also from regulation 5 which provides for exceptions to this requirement in the case of those with caring responsibilities or engaged in voluntary work (who need only be willing and able to take up employment on 48 hours' notice) and certain others engaged in providing a service (who get 24 hours' notice). No doubt the requirement for immediate availability allows the claimant time to wash, dress and have his breakfast, but strictly it would seem inconsistent with, say, a claimant's stay overnight with a friend or relative, or attendance at a weekend cricket match, or even an evening at the cinema (unless perhaps he had left a contact number and had not travelled far).

26. In these circumstances, claimants ought clearly to be wary of entering into an agreement which offers unrestricted availability throughout the entire week, day and night, weekdays and weekends."

Subsections (3) and (4) allow regulations to impose limitations on the kind of work for which a claimant can be required to be available and also allow the Secretary of State to specify further limitations. Regulation 97 contains the prescribed limitations, in terms of hours of work for carers and those with a disability, of the maximum time for travel to and from work and of the type of work recently undertaken. See the notes to reg.97. There appears to be no limitation on the number of hours a week that work could involve while still falling for consideration, apart from in the cases of the particular categories of claimant identified in reg.97(2).

Subsection (5) allows regulations to define what is meant in subs.(1) by being able and willing immediately to take up work. Regulation 99(1)(b) of the Universal Credit Regulations uses this power to provide that claimants in any of the circumstances set out in reg.99(3), (4), (4A) or (5) are regarded as being available for work if able and willing to take up paid work or attend an interview immediately after the relevant circumstance ceases to apply. See also the provisions of reg.99(2B) with (5A) and reg.99(2C) with (5B). Regulation 96(1) deems the work availability requirement not to be complied with if the claimant is not able and willing immediately to attend an interview in connection with finding paid work. Regulation 96(2) to (5) defines circumstances in which carers, those doing voluntary work and those in paid employment are to be treated as having complied with the requirement, where it is accepted that some longer notice than "immediately" is needed. Those provisions can only apply subject to any modifications to the availability requirement made by reg.99. Regulation 98 prevents the imposition of any work-related requirement on recent victims of domestic violence.

1.79 It is notable, by contrast with the position that will be familiar to many readers from old style JSA and, before it, unemployment benefit, that being available for work is not a condition of entitlement to universal credit, failure to satisfy which means that there can be no entitlement to benefit at all. Instead, a failure to comply with the work availability requirement, if imposed on a claimant, is merely a potential basis for a sanction under ss.26 or 27. Under s.26(2)(c) a higher-level sanction can be imposed if a claimant fails for no good reason to comply by not taking up an offer of paid work. Section 27(2)(a) allows the imposition of a medium-level sanction for a failure for no good reason to comply with any work-related requirement.

Note that under s.23(1) the Secretary of State is empowered to require a claimant to participate in an interview relating to the imposition of a work-related requirement on the claimant or assisting the claimant to comply with a requirement. Under s.23(3) he can require the provision of information and evidence for the purpose of verifying compliance and that the claimant confirm compliance in any manner. A failure for no good reason to comply with any of those connected requirements is also sanctionable under s.27(2)(b).

Application of work-related requirements

Claimants subject to no work-related requirements

1.80 **19.**—(1) The Secretary of State may not impose any work-related requirement on a claimant falling within this section.

(2) A claimant falls within this section if—

(a) the claimant has limited capability for work and work-related activity,

(b) the claimant has regular and substantial caring responsibilities for a severely disabled person,

(c) the claimant is the responsible carer for a child under the age of 1, or

(d) the claimant is of a prescribed description.

(3) Regulations under subsection (2)(d) may in particular make provision by reference to one or more of the following—

(a) hours worked;

(b) earnings or income;

(c) the amount of universal credit payable.

(4) Regulations under subsection (3) may—

(a) in the case of a claimant who is a member of the couple, make provision by reference to the claimant alone or by reference to the members of the couple together;

(b) make provision for estimating or calculating any matter for the purpose of the regulations.

(5) Where a claimant falls within this section, any work-related requirement previously applying to the claimant ceases to have effect.

(6) In this Part "responsible carer", in relation to a child means—

(a) a single person who is responsible for the child, or

(b) a person who is a member of a couple where—

    (i) the person or the other member of the couple is responsible for the child, and

    (ii) the person has been nominated by the couple jointly as responsible for the child.

DEFINITIONS

"claimant"—see s.40.
"limited capability for work"—*ibid.*
"limited capability for work-related activity"—*ibid.*
"regular and substantial caring responsibilities"—*ibid.*
"severely disabled"—*ibid.*
"work-related requirement"—see ss.40 and 13(2).

GENERAL NOTE

The default position in s.22 is that a claimant is, unless falling within ss.19—21, **1.81** to be subject to all work-related requirements, i.e. the work search and work availability requirements, with the optional additions of a work-focused interview and/ or a work preparation requirement. Section 19 defines the circumstances in which no work-related requirement at all may be imposed. Under reg.98 of the Universal Credit Regulations, made under s.24(5) below, recent victims of domestic violence must be free of any work-related requirement for a period of 13 weeks, subject to an extension for a further 13 weeks in relation to the work search and work availability requirements for responsible carers of children (reg.98(1A)). Where a claim has to be made jointly by both members of a couple, both are claimants and it must be asked separately whether work-related requirements can be imposed on each. Note that a claimant who cannot, by virtue of s.19, have any work-related requirement imposed may nevertheless be required by the Secretary of State under s.23(1) (a) to participate in an interview relating to the possible imposition of any such requirement.

Subsection (2)

Three categories are specifically identified in subs.(2)(a)—(c). Others can, and **1.82** have been, prescribed in regulations (subss.(2)(d) and (3)–(4)):

(a) Claimants who have limited capability for work and for work-related activity cannot have any work-related requirement imposed. Once claimants who currently qualify for employment and support allowance (ESA) fall within the ambit of universal credit, limited capability will be tested in essentially the same way as for ESA. Note that claimants who do not fall within s.19(2)(a) are exempted from the application of the work search and work availability requirements if they have limited capability for work, but not limited capability for work-related activity (s.21(1)(b)). Under reg.99 of the Universal Credit Regulations claimants who are unfit for work (not further defined) and provide prescribed evidence cannot have the work search requirement imposed and have the work availability requirement modified, for limited periods. See the notes to reg.99 for the details of the various permutations of circumstances covered.

(b) Claimants who have regular and substantial caring responsibilities for a severely disabled person cannot have any work-related requirement imposed. Although s.40 allows the meaning of "regular and substantial caring responsibilities" and "severely disabled person" to be prescribed separately in regulations, reg.30 of the Universal Credit Regulations defines the two phrases in combination in terms of meeting the conditions of entitlement to carer's allowance, disregarding the earnings conditions. There seems no reason why that should not be valid. The test is therefore, in brief, that the person cared for is entitled to attendance allowance, at least the middle rate of the care component of disability living allowance, the standard or enhanced rate of the daily living component of personal independence payment or armed forces independence payment and that the carer devotes at least 35 hours per week to caring for such a person. But note that by virtue of reg.30(3) anyone who derives any earnings from the caring is excluded from the definition. See the extension in reg.89(1)(b) of the Universal Credit Regulations, under para.(d) below.

(c) Claimants who are the responsible carer for a child under the age of one cannot have any work-related requirement imposed. By subs.(6) a responsible carer is a person who is responsible for a child or a member of a couple where the other member is responsible. Regulation 4 of the Universal Credit Regulations, made under para.5 of Sch.1 to the WRA 2012, sets out how responsibility is to be determined. See the notes to reg.4.

(d) Regulations 89 and 90 of the Universal Credit Regulations set out the additional categories of claimant who cannot have any work-related requirement imposed. Regulation 90 covers the special rules needed by virtue of the special characteristic of universal credit as both an in-work and an out-of-work benefit. It thus exempts claimants whose earnings are of an amount at least equal to a threshold figure, calculated by reference to the national minimum wage and differing weekly hours for different groups of claimants. That in most cases produces a relatively high figure. For claimants with earnings below that threshold, see the effect of reg.99 on the work search and work availability requirements.

Regulation 89 covers more general categories. Regulation 89(1)(b) allows in some claimants who do not quite meet the conditions of subs.(2)(b). Regulation 89(1)(d) and (f) allow in some claimants who do not quite meet the conditions of subs.(2)(c). Regulation 89(1)(a) applies to claimants who have reached the qualifying age for state pension credit, i.e. state pension age. Regulation 89(1)(c) brings in women for shortish periods before and after confinement. Regulation 89(1)(e) brings in some claimants in education.

Claimants subject to work-focused interview requirement only

1.83   **20.**—(1) A claimant falls within this section if—

(a) the claimant is the responsible carer for a child who is aged [[1]1], on

(b) the claimant is of a prescribed description.

(2) The Secretary of State may, subject to this Part, impose a work-focused interview requirement on a claimant falling within this section.

(3) The Secretary of State may not impose any other work-related requirement on a claimant falling within this section (and, where a claimant falls within this section, any other work-related requirement previously applying to the claimant ceases to have effect).

AMENDMENT

1. Welfare Reform and Work Act 2016 s.17(1)(a) (April 3, 2017).

DEFINITIONS

"claimant"—see s.40.
"responsible carer"—see ss.40 and 19(6).
"work-focused interview requirement"—see ss.40 and 15(1).
"work-related requirement"—see ss.40 and 13(2).

GENERAL NOTE

The default position in s.22 is that a claimant is, unless falling within ss.19–21,   1.84
to be subject to all work-related requirements, i.e. the work search and work availability requirements, with the optional additions of a work-focused interview and/or a work preparation requirement. Section 20 defines the circumstances in which a claimant who does not fall within s.19 (no work-related requirements) can have a work-focused interview requirement, but not any other requirement, imposed. If the conditions of s.20(1) are met, there is a discretion whether actually to impose the work-focused interview requirement (subs.(2): "may"). Where a claim has to be made jointly by both members of a couple, both are claimants and it must be asked separately whether work-related requirements can be imposed on each. Note that under s.23 the Secretary of State may require a claimant to participate in an interview for purposes relating to the imposition of any work-related requirement, verifying compliance with any work-related requirement or assisting the claimant's compliance with any work-related requirement. He may also require the reporting of relevant changes of circumstances.

See s.24 for the process of imposing a requirement.

Section 19(1)(c) exempts responsible carers (defined in s.19(6)) of children under the age of one from all work-related requirements (and there are slight extensions in reg.89 of the Universal Credit Regulations). So no further protection is needed where a child is under the age of one. The scope of the protection given by s.20 to limit the permissible work-related requirements that can be imposed on a claimant has been narrowed considerably since April 2013. Initially, in combination with reg.91(1), subs.(1)(a) applied where the child in question was aged less than five. In April 2014, the crucial age was reduced to three, but with some further protection under s.21(1)(b) in combination with a new reg.91A for responsible carers of children aged three or four, who could not have any work-related requirements other than the work-focused interview or work preparation requirement imposed. The April 2017 amendments limit subs.(1)(a) to responsible carers of a child aged one (not under or over that age) and take away the power to prescribe any different age in regulations. As a result, reg.91(1), which had carried out the prescription previously required by subs.(1)(a), has been revoked. The further protection under s.21(1) has been limited to responsible carers of children aged two (subs.(1)(aa)) and reg.91A has been revoked.

Under s.20(1)(b), reg.91(2) continues to extend the effect of the provision to responsible foster carers of any child aged from one to 15 and to certain categories of foster parents and "friend and family carers". It seems anomalous that "ordinary" responsible carers should be treated less favourably then those groups, but no challenge under the Human Rights Act 1998 on the ground of discrimination could lead to any finding that the amendments were invalid, since they were all carried out by primary legislation.

The nature of the requirement and the purposes of the interview are defined in s.15 and reg.93 of the Universal Credit Regulations.

Claimants subject to work preparation requirement

1.85   **21.**—(1) A claimant falls within this section if the claimant does not fall within section 19 or 20 and—

(a) the claimant has limited capability for work,

[¹ (aa) the claimant is the responsible carer for a child who is aged 2,] or

(b) the claimant is of a prescribed description.

(2) The Secretary of State may, subject to this Part, impose a work preparation requirement on a claimant falling within this section.

(3) The Secretary of State may also, subject to this Part, impose a work-focused interview requirement on a claimant falling within this section.

(4) The Secretary of State may not impose any other work-related requirement on a claimant falling within this section (and, where a claimant falls within this section, any other work-related requirement previously applying to the claimant ceases to have effect).

(5) [¹ . . .]

AMENDMENT

1. Welfare Reform and Work Act 2016 s.17(1) (April 3, 2017).

DEFINITIONS

"claimant"—see s.40.
"limited capability for work"—see ss.40 and 37(1).
"prescribed"—see s.40.
"responsible carer"—see ss.40 and 19(6).
"work preparation requirement"—see ss.40 and 16(1).
"work-focused interview requirement"—see ss.40 and 15(1).
"work-related requirement"—see ss.40 and 13(2).

GENERAL NOTE

1.86   The default position in s.22 is that a claimant is, unless falling within ss.19–21, to be subject to all work-related requirements, i.e. the work search and work availability requirements, with the optional additions of a work-focused interview and/or a work preparation requirement. Section 21 defines the circumstances in which a claimant who does not fall within ss.19 or 20 (no work-related requirements or work-focused interview requirement only) can have a work preparation requirement and, under subs.(3), a work-focused interview requirement, but not any other requirement, imposed. Under s.23(1) the Secretary of State is empowered to require a claimant to attend an interview relating to the imposition of a work-related requirement, verifying compliance with any work-related requirement or assisting the claimant's compliance with any work-related requirement. He may also require the reporting of relevant changes of circumstances. Where a claim has to be made jointly by both members of a couple, both are claimants and it must be asked separately whether work-related requirements can be imposed on each.

See s.24 for the process of imposing a requirement. Note that there is a discretion ("may") to impose the requirement if the conditions are met.

Initially, the only claimants covered by s.21 were those with limited capability for work (but not limited capability for work-related activity, which would take the claimant into s.19(2)(a)) under subs.(1)(a), because no regulations had been made under subs.(1)(b). The duty in subs.(5) to make regulations did not arise in practice because any claimant who was the responsible carer for a child aged three or four fell within s.20(1)(b) by virtue of reg.91(1) of the Universal Credit Regulations as they stood at the time. In the period from April 6, 2014, when the crucial age under s.20(1)(a) was reduced to three, a prescription became necessary, which produced a new reg.91A. With effect from April 3, 2017 and the restriction of the effect of s.20(1)(a) to children aged one (and not under or over that age), the protection of s.21 has been limited to responsible carers of a child aged two (and not under or over that age). The former duty in subs.(5) to make regulations in certain circumstances has been removed and reg.91A has been revoked.

The nature of the work preparation requirement is defined in s.16.

Claimants subject to all work-related requirements

22.—(1) A claimant not falling within any of sections 19 to 21 falls within this section.   1.87

(2) The Secretary of State must, except in prescribed circumstances, impose on a claimant falling within this section—

(a) a work search requirement, and

(b) a work availability requirement.

(3) The Secretary of State may, subject to this Part, impose either or both of the following on a claimant falling within this section—

(a) a work-focused interview requirement;

(b) a work preparation requirement.

DEFINITIONS

"claimant"—see s.40.
"prescribed"—*ibid.*
"work availability requirement"—see ss.40 and 18(1).
"work preparation requirement"—see ss.40 and 16(1).
"work search requirement"—see ss.40 and 17(1).
"work-focused interview requirement"—see ss.40 and 15(1).

GENERAL NOTE

This section sets out the default position that a claimant of universal credit is,   1.88
unless falling within ss.19–21, to be subject to all work-related requirements, i.e. the work search and work availability requirements, with the optional additions of a work-focused interview and/or a work preparation requirement. Under s.23(1) the Secretary of State is empowered to require a claimant to attend an interview relating to the imposition of a work-related requirement, to the verification of compliance or to assisting the claimant to comply with a requirement. By contrast with other provisions, where this section applies the work search and work availability requirements *must*, subject to the exceptions prescribed in reg.99 of the Universal Credit Regulations, be imposed (subs.(2)), but there is a discretion about the other requirements (subs.(3)). See the notes to ss.19–21 for the circumstances in which either no or only some work-related requirements may be imposed. The content of the requirements is set out in ss.15–18 and associated regulations. Where a claim has to be made jointly by both members of a couple, and both are claimants it must be asked separately whether work-related requirements can be imposed on each. See s.24 for the process of imposing a requirement.

Work-related requirements: supplementary

Connected requirements

1.89   **23.**—(1) The Secretary of State may require a claimant to participate in an interview for any purpose relating to—

(a) the imposition of a work-related requirement on the claimant;

(b) verifying the claimant's compliance with a work-related requirement;

(c) assisting the claimant to comply with a work-related requirement.

(2) The Secretary of State may specify how, when and where such an interview is to take place.

(3) The Secretary of State may, for the purpose of verifying the claimant's compliance with a work-related requirement, require a claimant to—

(a) provide to the Secretary of State information and evidence specified by the Secretary of State in a manner so specified;

(b) confirm compliance in a manner so specified.

(4) The Secretary of State may require a claimant to report to the Secretary of State any specified changes in their circumstances which are relevant to—

(a) the imposition of work-related requirements on the claimant;

(b) the claimant's compliance with a work-related requirement.

DEFINITIONS

"claimant"—see s.40.

"work-related requirement"—see ss.40 and 13(2).

GENERAL NOTE

1.90   This section gives the Secretary of State power to require a claimant to do various things related to the imposition of work-related requirements, verifying compliance and assisting claimants to comply: to participate in an interview (subss.(1) and (2)); for the purpose of verifying compliance, to provide specified information and evidence or to confirm compliance (subs.(3)); or to report specified changes in a claimant's circumstances relevant to the imposition of or compliance with requirements. Such requirements do not fall within the meaning of "work-related requirement", but there is a separate ground of sanction under s.27(2)(b) for failing for no good reason to comply with them, but only for claimants subject to all work-related requirements or to the work preparation requirement (see reg.104(1) of the Universal Credit Regulations in conjunction with regs 102, 103 and 105). The Secretary of State is allowed under subs.(2) to specify how, when and where any interview under subs.(1) is to take place, so that there is no straightforward limit on the number or frequency of the interviews that may be specified, or on the persons who may conduct the interview. The interviews must of course properly be for one of the purposes specified in subs.(1). The requirement to participate in an interview cannot be used for punitive purposes or simply as a means of control of a claimant. The requirement, as now for new style JSA, is not attendance at an interview at the specified time and date, but participation in it. This would appear to mean that a claimant can be required to participate in an interview over the telephone, providing that that manner of conducting it has been specified under subs.(2). In an ambiguous (so far as JSA is concerned) Parliamentary answer on 24 November 2015 (UIN 17005), the Minister of State Priti Patel said:

"Under JSA, claimants are not sanctioned for failing to answer their telephone. In Universal Credit, claimants who have a prearranged telephone interview with their Work Coach, and who fail to participate without good reason, can be referred for a sanction decision."

There is no further provision about what participating in a work-focused inter-view entails. It must at least entail turning up at the place and time specified, although the decision of Judge Knowles in *SA v SSWP (JSA)* [2015] UKUT 454 (AAC) (see the notes to s.27 for full discussion) would indicate that tribunals should consider, in cases where the claimant arrives not very late, whether it is proportion-ate to the nature of all the circumstances to regard that as a failure to participate in an interview. There were all sorts of mitigating circumstances in *SA*, that may well not be present in other cases.

The requirement to participate must also extend to making some meaning-ful contribution to the interview, but the limits will probably not be established until some more sanctions appeals in JSA or universal credit reach the Upper Tribunal. Behaviour that leads to the premature termination of the interview may well amount to a failure to participate (see the facts of *DM v SSWP (JSA)* [2015] UKUT 67 (AAC) in the notes to s.27(2)(b)). There may, though, in cases of uncooperative claimants or heavy-handed officials or a combination, be dif-ficult questions about when an interview has ceased to exist, so that subsequent behaviour cannot be relevant to whether there has been a failure to participate (see *PH v SSWP (ESA)* [2016] UKUT 119 (AAC) on failing to submit to a medical examination).

The compulsory imposition of a sanction for failure for no good reason to report specified changes in circumstances, to provide specified information and evidence or to confirm compliance with a work-related requirement is a new departure.

See s.24 for the process of imposing a requirement.

Imposition of requirements

24.—(1) Regulations may make provision—   1.91
  (a) where the Secretary of State may impose a requirement under this Part, as to when the requirement must or must not be imposed;
  (b) where the Secretary of State may specify any action to be taken in relation to a requirement under this Part, as to what action must or must not be specified;
  (c) where the Secretary of State may specify any other matter in relation to a requirement under this Part, as to what must or must not be specified in respect of that matter.

(2) Where the Secretary of State may impose a work-focused interview requirement, or specify a particular action under section 16(1) or 17(1)(b), the Secretary of State must have regard to such matters as may be prescribed.

(3) Where the Secretary of State may impose a requirement under this Part, or specify any action to be taken in relation to such a requirement, the Secretary of State may revoke or change what has been imposed or specified.

(4) Notification of a requirement imposed under this Part (or any change to or revocation of such a requirement) is, if not included in the claimant commitment, to be in such manner as the Secretary of State may determine.

(5) Regulations must make provision to secure that, in prescribed circum-stances, where a claimant has recently been a victim of domestic violence—
  (a) a requirement imposed on that claimant under this Part ceases to have effect for a period of 13 weeks, and
  (b) the Secretary of State may not impose any other requirement under this Part on that claimant during that period.

(6) For the purposes of subsection (5)—
  (a) "domestic violence" has such meaning as may be prescribed;
  (b) "victim of domestic violence" means a person on or against whom domestic violence is inflicted or threatened (and regulations under

subsection (5) may prescribe circumstances in which a person is to be treated as being or not being a victim of domestic violence);

(c) a person has recently been a victim of domestic violence if a prescribed period has not expired since the violence was inflicted or threatened.

DEFINITIONS

"claimant"—see s.40.
"work-focused interview requirement"—see ss.40 and 15(1).

GENERAL NOTE

1.92   This section contains a variety of powers and duties in relation to the imposition by the Secretary of State of either a work-related requirement or a connected requirement under s.23. It makes the imposition of a requirement and the notification to the claimant a moderately formal process, which raises the question of whether the decision of the Secretary of State to impose a requirement is a decision that is appealable to a First-tier Tribunal under s.12(1) of the SSA 1998, either as a decision on a claim or award or one which falls to be made under the WRA 2012 as a "relevant enactment" (s.8(1)(a) and (c) of the SSA 1998). However, if it is a decision not made on a claim or award, it is not covered in Sch.3 to the SSA 1998 (or in Sch.2 to the Decisions and Appeals Regulations 2013 (see below and in Vol.III)), so could not be appealable under that heading. The discussion in the note to s.12(1) of the SSA 1998 in Vol.III would indicate that, since the imposition of a requirement is not an "outcome" decision determining entitlement or payability of universal credit or the amount payable, it is not appealable under s.12(1)(a) as a decision on a claim or award or as a decision on another basis.

Thus, it appears that a direct challenge to the imposition of any particular requirement, including any element specified by the Secretary of State, and/or its inclusion in a claimant commitment under s.14 of this Act, can only be made by way of judicial review in the High Court, with the possibility of a discretionary transfer to the Upper Tribunal. Otherwise, a challenge by way of appeal appears not be possible unless and until a reduction of benefit for a sanctionable failure is imposed on the claimant for a failure to comply with a requirement. It must therefore be arguable that in any such appeal the claimant can challenge whether the conditions for the imposition of the requirement in question were met, with the result that, if that challenge is successful, the sanction must be removed. That appears to have been the assumption of the Supreme Court in *R. (on the application of Reilly and Wilson) v Secretary of State for Work and Pensions* [2013] UKSC 68; [2014] 1 A.C. 453. In para.29 of their judgment, Lords Neuberger and Toulson mentioned without any adverse comment Foskett J's holding at first instance that a consequence of a breach of a regulation requiring a claimant to be given notice of a requirement to participate in a scheme was that no sanctions could lawfully be imposed on the claimants for failure to participate in the scheme.

Subsection (1)

1.93   Regulation 99 of the Universal Credit Regulations is made in part under para.(a), reg.98 on domestic violence falling more specifically under subss.(5) and (6). No regulations appear to have been made under paras (b) and (c).

Subsection (2)

1.94   No regulations appear to have been made under this provision.

Subsection (3)

1.95   The inclusion of this express power to revoke or change any requirement, or any specification of action, is an indication of the formality entailed in the imposition of a requirement. However, there appears to be no restriction on the circumstances in which the Secretary of State may carry out such a revocation or change, subject of course to the legislative conditions being met for whatever the new position is. A mere change of mind without any change in circumstances or mistake or error as to the existing circumstances will do.

Subsection (4)

This provision allows the Secretary of State to notify the claimant of the imposi-   **1.96** tion of any requirement, if not included in a claimant commitment under s.14, in any manner. Thus, it may be done orally (or presumably even through the medium of mime), but it is a necessary implication that a requirement must be notified to the claimant. That in turn implies that, whatever the manner of notification, the content must be such as is reasonably capable of being understood by the particular claimant with the characteristics known to the officer of the Secretary of State (so perhaps the medium of mime will not do after all). Less flippantly, this principle may be important for claimants with sensory problems, e.g. hearing or vision dif- ficulties. The expectation of course is that the requirements imposed under the Act will be included in the claimant commitment, one of whose aims is to ensure that claimants know and understand what is being required of them and the potential consequences of failing to comply. However, it is clear in law that the validity of a requirement is not dependent on inclusion in the claimant commitment. There is no such express condition and under s.14(4)(a) the Secretary of State is only under a duty to record in the claimant commitment such of the requirements under the Act as he considers it appropriate to include. It may be that the fact that a requirement is not recorded in the claimant commitment could be put forward as part of an argu- ment for there having been a good reason for failing to comply with the requirement.

Subsections (5) and (6)

The duty to make regulations providing that no work-related requirement or   **1.97** connected requirement under s.23 may be imposed for a period of 13 weeks on a claimant who has recently been a victim of domestic violence is partially carried out in reg.98 of the Universal Credit Regulations. Most of the meat is in the regulation, including the definition of "domestic violence", which has been amended since April 2013. See the note to reg.98 for the details. However, subs.(6)(b) does define "victim" to include not just those on whom domestic violence is inflicted but also those against whom it is threatened.

Regulation 98 appears to be defective in that it applies only to work-related requirements, which in accordance with the definition in s.13(2) do not include connected requirements under s.23. Thus the duty in subs.(5) in relation to any requirement under Part 1 of the Act has not been fulfilled in relation to connected requirements. That defect cannot affect the application of reg.98 to work-related requirements.

Compliance with requirements

25. Regulations may make provision as to circumstances in which a   **1.98** claimant is to be treated as having—

   (a) complied with or not complied with any requirement imposed under this Part or any aspect of such a requirement, or

   (b) taken or not taken any particular action specified by the Secretary of State in relation to such a requirement.

Gᴇɴᴇʀᴀʟ Nᴏᴛᴇ

Under subs.(a) regulations may deem a claimant either to have or not to have   **1.99** complied with any work-related requirement or connected requirement under s.23 in particular circumstances. Regulations 94–97 of the Universal Credit Regulations make use of this power, mainly in treating claimants as not having complied. No regulations appear to have been made as yet under subs.(b).

Reduction of benefit

Higher-level sanctions

1.100   **26.**—(1) The amount of an award of universal credit is to be reduced in accordance with this section in the event of a failure by a claimant which is sanctionable under this section.

(2) It is a failure sanctionable under this section if a claimant falling within section 22—

    (a) fails for no good reason to comply with a requirement imposed by the Secretary of State under a work preparation requirement to undertake a work placement of a prescribed description;

    (b) fails for no good reason to comply with a requirement imposed by the Secretary of State under a work search requirement to apply for a particular vacancy for paid work;

    (c) fails for no good reason to comply with a work availability requirement by not taking up an offer of paid work;

    (d) by reason of misconduct, or voluntarily and for no good reason, ceases paid work or loses pay.

(3) It is a failure sanctionable under this section if by reason of misconduct, or voluntarily and for no good reason, a claimant falling within section 19 by virtue of subsection (3) of that section ceases paid work or loses pay so as to cease to fall within that section and to fall within section 22 instead.

(4) It is a failure sanctionable under this section if, at any time before making the claim by reference to which the award is made, the claimant—

    (a) for no good reason failed to take up an offer of paid work, or

    (b) by reason of misconduct, or voluntarily and for no good reason, ceased paid work or lost pay,

and at the time the award is made the claimant falls within section 22.

(5) For the purposes of subsections (2) to (4) regulations may provide—

    (a) for circumstances in which ceasing to work or losing pay is to be treated as occurring or not occurring by reason of misconduct or voluntarily;

    (b) for loss of pay below a prescribed level to be disregarded.

(6) Regulations are to provide for—

    (a) the amount of a reduction under this section;

    (b) the period for which such a reduction has effect, not exceeding three years in relation to any failure sanctionable under this section.

(7) Regulations under subsection (6)(b) may in particular provide for the period of a reduction to depend on either or both of the following—

    (a) the number of failures by the claimant sanctionable under this section;

    (b) the period between such failures.

(8) Regulations may provide—

    (a) for cases in which no reduction is to be made under this section;

    (b) for a reduction under this section made in relation to an award that is terminated to be applied to any new award made within a prescribed period of the termination;

    (c) for the termination or suspension of a reduction under this section.

DEFINITIONS

"claimant"—see s.40.
"prescribed"—*ibid.*

"work availability requirement"—see ss.40 and 18(1).
"work preparation requirement"—see ss.40 and 16(1).
"work search requirement"—see ss.40 and 17(1).

GENERAL NOTE

Sections 26–28 set up a very similar structure of sanctions leading to reductions **1.101** in the amount of universal credit to that already imposed in the new ss.19–20 of the old style Jobseekers Act 1995 substituted by the WRA 2012 and in operation from October 22, 2012 (see the 2013/14 edition of Vol.II of this series). The similarity is in the creation of higher-level sanctions, here under s.26, and of medium, low and lowest-level sanctions, here under s.27, and in the stringency of the periods and the amount of reductions to be imposed, in particular for higher-level sanctions. See the discussion in the notes to s.19 of the Jobseekers Act 1995 in Vol.II. There are even more similarities to the structure of sanctions in ss.6J and 6K of the new style Jobseekers Act 1995, also introduced by the WRA 2012 and only in operation in relation to claimants to whom the universal credit provisions have started to apply. There are, however, some differences in the wording of otherwise similar provisions made by different parts of the WRA 2012, which will be noted below. The sanctions framework is limited to the operation of work-related and connected requirements, so that universal credit claimants who fall outside that ambit cannot be sanctioned (although other consequences might follow failure to comply with some requirements). That result is secured through the general restriction of the application of s.26 to claimants who are subject to all work-related requirements under s.22 (except under subs.(3)) and through the scope of s.27 being limited to failures to comply with work-related or connected requirements.

Note the important provision in reg.5 of the JSA Regulations 2013 that, if a claimant is entitled to both universal credit and new style JSA, no work-related requirements can be imposed under the new style JSA regime (ss.6B-6G of the new style Jobseekers Act 1995) and that the provisions for reduction of JSA on sanctions under ss.6J and 6K of that Act do not apply. See the annotations to reg.5 in Vol.II for discussion of the consequences.

The central concept under these provisions is of a "sanctionable failure", which under s.26(1) (subject to reg.113 of the Universal Credit Regulations), and s.27(1), is to lead to a reduction in the amount of an award of universal credit. For higher-level sanctions under s.26, the reduction for most adult claimants is in brief of 100 per cent of the claimant's individual standard universal credit allowance for about 13 weeks for a first higher-level failure, 26 weeks for second such failure within a year and 156 weeks for a third or subsequent such failure within a year. As noted below, regulations set out the amount and period of the reduction. There is no discretion under either ss.26 or 27 as to whether or not to apply a reduction if the conditions are met and no discretion under the regulations as to the amount and period of the reduction as calculated under the complicated formulae there. Regulation 113 of the Universal Credit Regulations, made under ss.26(8)(a) and 27(9)(a), sets out circumstances in which no reduction is to be made for a sanctionable failure. There is also provision for hardship payments under s.28.

As a matter of principle, a claimant has to be able, in any appeal against a reduction in benefit on the imposition of a sanction, to challenge whether the conditions for the imposition of sanction were met. See the note to s.24.

Another important concept is that of a "good reason" for the conduct or failure to comply with a requirement under the WRA 2012. Most of the definitions of sanctionable failures in ss.26 and 27 incorporate the condition that the failure was "for no good reason". Paragraph 8 of Sch.1 to the Act allows regulations to prescribe circumstances in which a claimant is to be treated as having or as not having a good reason for an act or omission and to prescribe matters that are or are not to be taken into account in determining whether a claimant has a good reason. No regulations have been made under this power. There is no equivalent to reg.72 of the JSA

Regulations 1996 (but the problem dealt with there is covered for universal credit by the allowance of limitations on work search and work availability requirements).

1.102   Thus, the concept remains a fairly open-ended one, no doubt requiring consideration of all relevant circumstances but also containing a large element of judgment according to the individual facts of particular cases. The amount and quality of information provided to the claimant in the claimant commitment or otherwise about responsibilities under the WRA 2012 and the consequences of a failure to comply will no doubt be relevant, especially in the light of the approach of the Supreme Court in paras 65 and 66 of *R (on the application of Reilly and Wilson) v Secretary of State for Work and Pensions* [2013] UKSC 68; [2014] 1 A.C. 453 and of the Court of Appeal in *SSWP v Reilly and Hewstone* and *SSWP v Jeffrey and Bevan* [2016] EWCA Civ 413; [2017] Q.B. 657; [2017] AACR 14 (see the notes to s.14 above). Probably, in addition, as in the previously familiar concept of "just cause", a balancing is required between the interests of the claimant and those of the community of those whose contributions and taxes finance the benefit in question. See the discussion under the heading of "Without a good reason" in the note to s.19 of the old style Jobseekers Act 1995 in Vol.II of this series.

In *SA v SSWP (JSA)* [2015] UKUT 454 (AAC), a decision on s.19A(2)(c) of the old style Jobseekers Act 1995 and failing to carry out a jobseeker's direction, Judge Knowles accepted the Secretary of State's submission that in determining whether a good reason had been shown for the failure all the circumstances should be considered and that the question was whether those circumstances would have caused a reasonable person (with the characteristics of the claimant in question) to act as the claimant did. Expressing the approach in such terms tends to point away from the notion of a balance.

However, there is a potentially significant difference in wording. In ss.26 and 27 and in ss.6J and 6K of the new style Jobseekers Act 1995 the condition is that the claimant fails "for no good reason", not that the claimant acts or omits to act "without a good reason". It may eventually be established that these two phrases have the same meaning, but in the ordinary use of language the phrase "for no good reason" carries a suggestion that something has been done or not done capriciously or arbitrarily, without any real thought or application of reason. It could therefore be argued that it is easier for a claimant to show that s/he did not act for no good reason and on that basis that the balancing of interests mentioned above could not be applicable. It would be enough that the claimant acted or failed to act rationally in the light of his or her own interests. It can of course be objected that such an argument fails to give the proper weight to the identification of what is a good reason and that it would seem contrary to the overall policy of the legislation if it was much easier to escape a universal credit sanction than an old style JSA sanction. On the other hand, it can be asked why Parliament chose to use a different phrase for the purposes of universal credit sanctions than "without a good reason" when the latter phrase could have fitted happily into ss.26 and 27. It is to be hoped that the ambiguity will be resolved in early decisions of the Upper Tribunal.

Subsections (2)–(4) set out what can be a sanctionable failure for the purposes of s.26 and higher-level sanctions. All except subs.(3) are restricted to claimants who are at the time of the imposition of the sanction subject to all work-related requirements under s.22. Thus, claimants excused from all work-related requirements under s.19 (e.g. those with limited capability for work and work-related activity or with specified caring responsibilities) or from some element of such requirements under s.20 or 21 cannot be subject to higher level sanctions. They can be subject to s.27 sanctions. Subsections (5)–(8) give regulation-making powers.

Subsection (2)

1.103   (a) It is a higher-level sanctionable failure for a claimant subject to all work-related requirements to fail for no good reason (on which see the note above) to comply with a work preparation requirement under s.16 to undertake a work placement of a description prescribed in regulations. Regulation 114(1) of the

Universal Credit Regulations prescribes Mandatory Work Activity as a work placement for the purposes of this provision and reg.114(2) in its substituted form gives
sufficient details of the scheme to satisfy the requirement in subs.(2)(a) to give a
description and not just a label (the problem identified by the Court of Appeal in
relation to the then state of the JSA legislation in *R (on the application of Reilly and
Wilson) v Secretary of State for Work and Pensions* [2013] EWCA Civ 66; [2013] 1
W.L.R. 2239), as approved by the Supreme Court ([2013] UKSC 68; [2014] 1
A.C.453). That was decided in relation to s.17A(1) of the old style Jobseekers Act
1995 and reg.2 of the Jobseeker's Allowance (Mandatory Work Activity Scheme)
Regulations 2011 (where the description of the scheme is in substance the same as
in reg.114) by Hickinbottom J in *R (Smith) v Secretary of State for Work and Pensions*
[2014] EWHC 843 (Admin). That conclusion and the judge's reasoning was in
essence endorsed by the Court of Appeal on the claimant's appeal ([2015] EWCA
Civ 229).

Before undertaking a Mandatory Work Activity scheme can have become a work
preparation requirement under s.16 it must have been specified for the claimant in
question by the Secretary of State and meet the condition of improving the particular claimant's work prospects. See *DM v SSWP (JSA)* [2015] UKUT 67 (AAC) on
the sanction for failing to carry out a jobseeker's direction under s.19A(2)(c) and
(11) of the old style Jobseekers Act 1995. There Judge Rowley, having referred to
official guidance in the DMG, held that to be valid a direction had to be personalised and appropriate to the individual claimant. There was insufficient evidence
to show that the "Group Information Session" in which the claimant had been
directed to participate and which apparently turned out to be about the sanctions
regime would have assisted the particular claimant to find employment or improve
his prospects of doing so, so that a sanction should not have been applied. The
requirement is to take the action specified by the Secretary of State, so that the detail
of the specification will be important in determining what amounts to a failure to
comply with the requirement. There will be familiar issues, e.g. whether turning up
to a scheme and then declining to co-operate or doing so only grudgingly amounts
to a failure to comply.

In *PL v DSD (JSA)* [2015] NI Com 72, the Chief Commissioner for Northern
Ireland has approved and applied the *obiter* suggestion of Judge Ward in *PL v SSWP
(JSA)* [2013] UKUT 227 (AAC) (on the pre-October 2012 form of the Great
Britain legislation) that in deciding whether a claimant had good cause for failing to
avail himself of a reasonable opportunity of a place on a training scheme or employment programme a tribunal erred in law, where the circumstances raised the issue,
in failing to consider the appropriateness of the particular scheme or programme to
the claimant in the light of his skills and experience and previous attendance on any
placements. Judge Ward's suggestion had been that the test was whether the claimant had reasonably considered that what was provided would not help him. It seems
likely that a similar general approach will be taken to issues of "good reason" under
s.26(2)(a) and (b) and, in the particular context of para.(a), the appropriateness of
the work placement. It may though still need to be sorted out how far the issue turns
on the claimant's subjective view, within the bounds of reasonableness, in the light
of the information provided at the time, as against a tribunal's view of the appropriateness of what was to be provided. The Chief Commissioner made no comment on
the treatment of the claimant's refusal to complete and sign forms with information
about criminal convictions and health, that the First-tier Tribunal had found were
reasonably required by the training provider as part of its application process for the
scheme, as a failure by the claimant to avail himself of a reasonable opportunity of
a place on the training scheme.

In *NM v SSWP (JSA)* [2016] UKUT 351 (AAC) Judge Wright held, as eventually conceded by the Secretary of State, that the inability to show that relevant DWP
guidance had been considered before the claimant was given notice to participate
in a Mandatory Work Activity scheme meant either that the claimant should not
have been referred to the scheme (because the officer either would have followed

the guidance or could have been persuaded to do so on representations from the claimant) or that he had good reason for not participating in the scheme. The appeal related to a sanction for failing to participate, through behaviour on the scheme. The guidance, in something called *Mandatory Work Activity Guidance* or *Operational Instructions – Procedural Guidance – Mandatory Work Activity – January 2012*, was relevant because at the time it instructed that claimants should not be considered for referral to Mandatory Work Activity if, among other circumstances, they were currently working (paid or voluntary). The claimant had been volunteering in a Sue Ryder shop, which he had to give up to attend the required scheme as a volunteer in a Salvation Army shop. The Secretary of State submitted that the guidance had since been changed to introduce an element of discretion about referral of claimants doing voluntary work. Judge Wright held that this would not excuse a failure by an officer of the Secretary of State to consider his own guidance or, on any appeal, to provide the guidance to a First-tier Tribunal in accordance with the principles of natural justice. The claimant in *NM* might also have had a good argument that in the light of his existing voluntary work the condition of making it more likely that the claimant would obtain paid work was not met.

For a further example on its own facts (and no more than that) of a potential good reason for not undertaking a placement, see *GR v SSWP (JSA)* [2013] UKUT 645 (AAC), where it was held that a claimant with a genuine fear that prevented him going to the town where a course was to take place had good cause (under reg.7 of the Jobseeker's Allowance (Employment, Skills and Enterprise Scheme) Regulations 2011) for failing to participate in the scheme.

(b) It is a higher-level sanctionable failure for a claimant subject to all work-related requirements to fail for no good reason (on which see the note above) to comply with a work search requirement under s.17 to apply for a particular vacancy for paid work. It would seem that for there to have been a requirement to apply for a particular vacancy the taking of that action must have been specified by the Secretary of State under s.17(1)(b). See the note to s.17 for discussion of the meaning of "paid work", the notification of vacancies through Universal Jobmatch and requirements to apply for vacancies in the claimant commitment. It appears in the nature of the word "vacancy" that it is for employment as an employed earner, or possibly some form of self-employment that is closely analogous to such employment, e.g. through an agency.

In *MT v SSWP (JSA)* [2016] UKUT 72 (AAC) doubts were expressed whether registration with an employment agency could fall within the equivalent provision for old style JSA (s.19(2)(c) of the old style Jobseekers Act 1995), at least without evidence of some specific vacancy. It is not entirely clear whether a vacancy has actually to exist at the time that the Secretary of State specifies that the claimant is to apply for it or whether it is enough that a vacancy is about to arise at that point (compare the terms of s.19(2)(c)). A claimant can hardly "fail" to apply for a vacancy while it does not actually exist. Some doubt was expressed in *CJSA 4179/1997* whether the offer of a "trial" as a part-time car washer properly fell within s.19(2)(c). It was suggested that if it did not, the case should have been considered under s.19(2)(d) (neglect to avail oneself of a reasonable opportunity of employment), to which there is no direct equivalent in the universal credit legislation (see the notes to para.(c) below). But if applying for or accepting the offer of the trial had been specified by the Secretary of State as a work search action under s.17, failure to comply for no good reason would be a sanctionable failure under s.27(2)(a) of the WRA 2012.

There is no express provision that the vacancy is for work that it is suitable for the claimant in question. However, plainly the question of suitability would be relevant to the issue of whether a claimant had no good reason for failing to apply for the vacancy, even in the absence of the decisions in *PL v DSD (JSA)* and *PL v SSWP (JSA)* discussed in the note to para.(a) above. Regulation 113(1)(a) of the Universal Credit Regulations prevents any reduction in benefit being made when the vacancy was because of a strike arising from a trade dispute. According to the then Minister of State Esther McVey (House of Commons written answers April 2, 2014 and

September 1, 2014) the instruction to Jobcentre Plus staff not to mandate claimants to apply for zero hours contracts applies only to JSA, not universal credit. However, again, and even though exclusivity clauses have been made unenforceable from May 26, 2015 by the new s.27A of the Employment Rights Act 1996, the suitability of such a contract for the particular claimant will certainly be relevant to the issue of no good reason.

Failure to apply for a vacancy no doubt encompasses an outright refusal to apply   **1.104** and also behaviour that is "tantamount to inviting a refusal by the employer to engage [the claimant]" (*R(U) 28/55*, para.7). In that case the claimant had presented himself for an interview for a job as a parcel porter in what the employer had described as a dirty and unshaven state, as a result of which he was not engaged. The Commissioner accepted that on the employer's evidence the claimant had neglected to avail himself of a reasonable opportunity of suitable employment. There is no reason why that general approach should not also apply in the present context.

It has long been accepted that a refusal or failure to complete an unobjectionable application form can amount to a failure to apply (see *R(U) 32/52* and *CJSA 2692/1999*). As Commissioner Howell noted in para.5 of *CJSA 4665/2001* there will be cases:

> "where the way a claimant completes or spoils a job application will be unsatisfactory and unfit to put in front of any employer so as to prevent it counting as a genuine application at all, so that he or she will have 'failed to apply': it is all a question of fact."

In *CJSA 4665/2001* itself, though, the Employment Service had refused to pass on otherwise properly completed application forms because the claimant had included criticisms of the Service and of government training initiatives. The Commissioner held that in the absence of any evidence that employers had been or would have been put off from considering the claimant by his comments or of any evidence of an intention to spoil his chances it had not been shown that he had failed to apply for the vacancies. A similar approach has been taken by Commissioner Rowland in a case in which the claimant disputed the necessity of including a photograph with the application form (*CJSA 2082/2002* and *CJSA 5415/2002*). As the employment officer did not have clear information from the employer contrary to the claimant's contention and had not tested the matter by submitting a form without a photograph, the sanction should not have been applied.

See the notes to para.(a) above for further discussion of good reason. Apart from the suitability and location of the work, personal, domestic and financial circumstances might be relevant. No doubt, as in the past, conscientious or religious objections would need particularly careful consideration. For instance, in *R(U) 2/77* (on neglect to avail) the claimant's sincerely held objection on what he described as moral grounds to joining a trade union were held to make to make an opportunity of employment unsuitable and unreasonable (and see *R(U) 5/71* for a case where a more intellectual conviction against joining a teachers' registration scheme did not have that effect). For a further example on its own facts (and no more than that) of a potential good reason for not applying for a vacancy, see *GR v SSWP (JSA)* [2013] UKUT 645 (AAC), where it was held that a claimant with a genuine fear that prevented him going to the town where a course was to take place had good cause (under reg.7 of the Jobseeker's Allowance (Employment, Skills and Enterprise Scheme) Regulations 2011) for failing to participate in the scheme.

Regulation 94 of the Universal Credit Regulations deems a claimant not to have complied with a requirement to apply for a particular vacancy for paid work where the claimant fails to participate in an interview offered in connection with the vacancy. Participation must at least entail turning up at the place and time for the interview, although the decision of Judge Knowles in *SA v SSWP (JSA)* [2015] UKUT 454 (AAC) (see the notes to s.27 for full discussion) would indicate that tribunals should consider, in cases where the claimant arrives not very late, whether it is proportionate to the nature of all the circumstances to regard that as a failure to participate in an interview. There were all sorts of mitigating circumstances in *SA*, that may well not be present in other cases. Participation must also extend to making some meaningful contribution to the interview, but the limits will probably not be established until there have been some more sanctions appeals to the Upper Tribunal. Behaviour that leads to the premature termination of the interview may well amount to a failure to participate (see the facts of *DM v SSWP (JSA)* [2015] UKUT 67 (AAC) in the notes to s.27(2)(b)). There may, though, in cases of uncooperative claimants or heavy-handed officials or a combination, be difficult questions about when an interview has ceased to exist, so that subsequent behaviour cannot be relevant to whether there has been a failure to participate (see *PH v SSWP (ESA)* [2016] UKUT 119 (AAC) on failing to submit to a medical examination).

Where non-compliance with the requirement to apply for a vacancy is constituted by failure to participate in an interview, good reason must extend to good reason for that failure to participate. There appear to be no provisions prescribing the length of notice of an interview to be given or how far a claimant can be required to travel, but there could plainly be a good reason for failing to comply with unreasonable requirements, especially if the claimant had attempted in advance to draw any problem with attendance to the attention of the Secretary of State or the potential employer. See reg.113(1)(a) of the Universal Credit Regulations excluding reductions in benefit on consideration of vacancies due to strikes arising from trade disputes.

(c) It is a higher-level sanctionable failure for a claimant subject to all work-related requirements to fail for no good reason (on which see the note above) to comply with a work availability requirement under s.18 by not taking up an offer of paid work. See the note to s.17 for discussion of the meaning of "paid work". Since the requirement under s.18 is in the very general terms of being able and willing immediately to take up paid work, the relevance of not taking up an offer can only be in revealing an absence of such ability or willingness. Therefore, both any limitations under reg.97 of the Universal Credit Regulations on the kinds of paid work that a claimant must be able and willing to take up immediately and the provisions of reg.96(2)–(5) on when a claimant is deemed to have complied with the requirement despite not being able to satisfy the "immediately" condition must be taken into account in determining whether a claimant has failed to comply with the requirement. See the discussion in the note to s.19(2)(c) of the old style Jobseekers Act 1995 in Vol.II of this series for what might amount to refusing or failing without a good reason to accept a situation, if offered, in any employment, but note that there may be differences between failing to accept a situation in employment and failing to accept an offer of paid work. Presumably a claimant escapes a sanction under this head by showing either a good reason for not accepting the particular offer, if that offer is compatible with the availability requirements currently imposed by the Secretary of State, or a good reason why those requirements should have been different in some way. See the notes to para.(a) above for discussion of the relevance of the suitability of the work in question for the particular claimant. See also reg.113(1)(a) of the Universal Credit Regulations excluding reductions in benefit on consideration of vacancies due to strikes arising from trade disputes.

(d) It is a higher-level sanctionable failure for a claimant subject to all work-related requirements to cease paid work or lose pay by reason of misconduct or voluntarily and for no good reason (on which see the note above). Since by definition the claimant must, if already subject to s.22, have an award of universal credit, this sanction can only apply to those claimants who are entitled to the benefit while in work. See the note to s.17 for discussion of the meaning of "paid work". See the note to subs.(4) below for discussion of the meanings of "misconduct" and "voluntarily and for no good reason", as well as of the implications of fixed and severe sanctions for losing pay apparently no matter what the amount of loss, subject to the exception from reductions in benefit in reg.113(1)(g) of the Universal Credit Regulations (earnings have not fallen below the level set in reg.99(6)). See the further exceptions in reg.113(1)(b) (trial periods in work where the claimant attempts hours additional to a limitation under ss.17(4) or 18(3)); (c) (voluntarily ceasing paid work or losing pay because of a strike); (d) (voluntarily ceasing paid work or losing pay as a member of the regular or reserve forces); and (f) (volunteering for redundancy or lay-off or short-time).

Subsection (3)

This provision applies to claimants with an award of universal credit who are **1.105** subject to no work-related requirements under s.19(2)(d) because reg.90 of the Universal Credit Regulations, made under the specific powers in s.19(3), applies s.19 where the claimant's earnings equal or exceed the individual threshold. If the claimant ceases the paid work from which those earnings are derived or loses pay so that the earnings are then below the individual threshold, either by reason of misconduct or voluntarily and for no good reason (on which see the note above), and does not fall within either ss.20 or 21, a higher-level sanction is to be imposed. See the note to subs.(4) below for discussion of the meanings of "misconduct" and "voluntarily and for no good reason". The exception in reg.113(1)(g) of the Universal Credit Regulations (earnings have not fallen below the level set in reg.99(6)) cannot by definition apply if this provision applies. If reg.99(6) (weekly earnings exceed amount of old style JSA personal allowance by £5 or £10) applies to the new level of earnings, no work search requirement can be imposed and the claimant therefore does not fall within s.22 (subject to all work-related requirements). In that case, subs.(3) cannot apply under its own terms and no exception is needed. If, as part of the ongoing process of working out an acceptable approach to in-work conditionality by subjecting claimants to pilot schemes under the Universal Credit (Work-Related Requirements) In Work Pilot Scheme and Amendment Regulations 2015 (in Part III below and see the notes to reg.99(6) and (6A) of the Universal Credit Regulations for discussion), entitlement is to be determined on the basis that reg.99(6) does not exist, then the terms of the exception in reg.113(1)(g) cannot apply either. A very slight decrease in earnings could, in a marginal case, have the effect identified in subs.(3), yet (no regulations having been made under subs.(5)(b)) the full force of the higher-level sanction must be imposed. It may be that in such circumstances it will be correspondingly easier for a claimant to show that a voluntary loss of pay was not "for no good reason". These issues will have to be worked out during the operation of the in-work conditionality pilot schemes mentioned above, which apparently expose claimants subject to them to very severe sanctions rules, although the DWP has stated that sanctions will be applied for failures to comply with in-work requirements under a pilot scheme "in the last resort" (see the notes to reg.99(6) and (6A)). See also the further exceptions in reg.113(1) (c) (voluntarily ceasing paid work or losing pay because of a strike); (d) (voluntarily ceasing paid work or losing pay as a member of the regular or reserve forces); and (f) (volunteering for redundancy or applying for a redundancy payment after lay-off or short-time).

Subsection (4)

Where a claimant has an award of universal credit and is subject to all work-related **1.106** requirements under s.22 it is a higher-level sanctionable failure if before making the claim relevant to the award the claimant for no good reason failed to take up an offer of paid work (para.(a)) or by reason of misconduct or voluntarily and for no good reason ceased paid work or lost pay (para.(b)). A practical limit to how far back before the date of claim such action or inaction can be to lead to a reduction of benefit is set by regs 102(4) and 113(1)(e) of the Universal Credit Regulations. If the gap between the action or inaction and the date of claim is longer than or equal to the period of the reduction that would otherwise be imposed, there is to be no reduction. Thus a lot depends on whether it is a first, second or subsequent "offence" within a year. These two grounds of sanction are the most similar to the familiar JSA grounds now in s.19(2)(a), (b) and (c) of the old style Jobseekers Act 1995.

Under para.(a), see the discussion in the note to subs.(2)(c), but note that this sanction applies to any offer of paid work. Therefore, all questions of whether the work is suitable for the claimant and whether or not it was reasonable for the claimant not to take it up will have to be considered under the "no good reason" condition. See the introductory part of the note to this section for the meaning of that phrase as compared with "without a good reason".

Under para.(b), it would appear that misconduct and voluntarily ceasing work will have the same general meaning as misconduct and leaving employment voluntarily for the purposes of old style JSA and, before it, unemployment benefit. See the extensive discussion in the notes to s.19(2)(a) and (b) of the old style Jobseekers Act 1995 in Vol.II of this series, which will not even be summarised here. The scope of the sanction has to be wider to take account of the nature of universal credit. Ceasing paid work certainly has a significantly wider meaning than losing employment as an employed earner if it encompasses self-employment in addition, as suggested in the note to s.17. The notion of ceasing paid work seems in itself wider than that of losing employment and to avoid difficulties over whether suspension from work without dismissal and particular ways of bringing a contract of employment to an end are covered. But remember that under reg.113(1)(f) of the Universal Credit Regulations a reduction cannot be applied on the ground of voluntarily ceasing work where the claimant has volunteered for redundancy or has claimed a redundancy payment after being subject to lay-off or short-time working, although the action remains a sanctionable failure. See also the exceptions for voluntarily ceasing paid work or losing pay because of a strike arising from a trade dispute or as a member of the regular or reserve forces (reg.113(1)(c) and (d)).

1.107   The other particularly significant widening of the scope of the sanction as compared with those in old style JSA is in the application of this and the similar sanctions under previous subsections to losing pay as well as to ceasing paid work. This is necessary, both in relation to circumstances before the date of claim and later, because it is possible for a claimant to be entitled to universal credit while still in paid work. If the earnings from the work are below the amount of the claimant's work allowance (varied according to circumstances) they are disregarded in the calculation of any award. If they exceed that amount, 63 per cent of the excess is taken into account as income to be set against the maximum amount of universal credit. There are also the rules, under s.19(2)(d) and (3), in reg.90 of the Universal Credit Regulations making a claimant subject to no work-related conditions if earnings are at least equal to an individual threshold (in the standard case the National Minimum Wage for 35 hours per week, with lesser hours used in defined circumstances). The sanction regime under s.26 can only apply when at the time of the award in question the claimant is subject to all work-related requirements under s.22 and so cannot be receiving earnings at or above that individual threshold. Subsection (3) above deals with the situation where during the course of an award of universal credit a claimant moves from having earnings at least equal to the individual threshold to a situation where the earnings are lower than that threshold. For loss of pay, short of the ceasing of work, prior to the date of claim to trigger the application of the sanction under subs.(3) it must be within a fairly narrow limit. To bring the claimant within the scope of s.22 the loss of pay must leave earnings below the individual threshold.

Subsection (5)

1.108   Regulations may deem ceasing work or losing pay not to be by reason of misconduct or voluntarily in certain circumstances and may provide that loss of pay below a prescribed level is to be disregarded. No such regulations have been made. Regulation 113 of the Universal Credit Regulations is made under the powers in subs.(8)(a) and only affects whether a reduction in benefit is to be imposed, not whether there is or is not a sanctionable failure.

Subsections (6) and (7)
See regs 101 and 106—111 of the Universal Credit Regulations for the amount   **1.109**
and period of the reduction in benefit under a higher-level sanction. The three-year
limit is imposed in subs.(6)(b) and cannot be extended in regulations.

Subsection (8)
Under para.(a), see reg.113 of the Universal Credit Regulations. Under para.(b),   **1.110**
see reg.107. Under para.(c), see regs 108 and 109.

Other sanctions

27.—(1) The amount of an award of universal credit is to be reduced in   **1.111**
accordance with this section in the event of a failure by a claimant which is
sanctionable under this section.

(2) It is a failure sanctionable under this section if a claimant—

(a) fails for no good reason to comply with a work-related requirement;

(b) fails for no good reason to comply with a requirement under section
23.

(3) But a failure by a claimant is not sanctionable under this section if it
is also a failure sanctionable under section 26.

(4) Regulations are to provide for—

(a) the amount of a reduction under this section, and

(b) the period for which such a reduction has effect.

(5) Regulations under subsection (4)(b) may provide that a reduction
under this section in relation to any failure is to have effect for—

(a) a period continuing until the claimant meets a compliance condition
specified by the Secretary of State,

(b) a fixed period not exceeding 26 weeks which is—

(i) specified in the regulations, or

(ii) determined in any case by the Secretary of State, or

(c) a combination of both.

(6) In subsection (5)(a) "compliance condition" means—

(a) a condition that the failure ceases, or

(b) a condition relating to future compliance with a work-related
requirement or a requirement under section 23.

(7) A compliance condition specified under subsection (5)(a) may be—

(a) revoked or varied by the Secretary of State;

(b) notified to the claimant in such manner as the Secretary of State may
determine.

(8) A period fixed under subsection (5)(b) may in particular depend on
either or both the following—

(a) the number of failures by the claimant sanctionable under this section;

(b) the period between such failures.

(9) Regulations may provide—

(a) for cases in which no reduction is to be made under this section;

(b) for a reduction under this section made in relation to an award that is
terminated to be applied to any new award made within a prescribed
period of the termination;

(c) for the termination or suspension of a reduction under this section.

DEFINITIONS

"claimant"—see s.40.
"work-related requirement"—see ss.40 and 13(2).

GENERAL NOTE

1.112   See the introductory part of the note to s.26 for the general nature of the universal credit sanctions regime under ss.26 and 27 and for discussion of the meaning of "for no good reason". Section 27(1) and (2) requires there to be a reduction, of the amount and period set out in regulations, wherever the claimant has failed for no good reason to comply with any work-related requirement or a connected requirement under s.23. There is no general discretion whether or not to apply the prescribed deduction, but that is subject first to the rule in subs.(3) that if a failure is sanctionable under s.26 (and therefore subject to the higher-level regime) it is not to be sanctionable under s.27 and to the rules in reg.113 of the Universal Credit Regulations about when a reduction is not to be applied although there is a sanctionable failure (none of which currently apply to s.27). While the power and duty under subs.(4) for regulations to provide for the amount and period of the reduction to be imposed is in fact more open-ended than that in s.26(6), because it does not have the three-year limit, subss. (5)–(7) introduce the specific power (that does not of course have to be used) for regulations to provide for the period of the reduction for a particular sanctionable failure to continue until the claimant meets a "compliance condition" (subs.(6)) or for a fixed period not exceeding 26 weeks specified in regulations or determined by the Secretary of State or a combination of both. The 26-week limit in subs.(5)(b) appears not to have any decisive effect because a longer period could always be pre-scribed under subs.(4)(b), unless "may" is to be construed as meaning "may only".

In practice, the powers have been used in the Universal Credit Regulations to set up a structure of medium-level (reg.103), low-level (reg.104) and lowest-level (reg.105) sanctions. See the notes to those regulations for the details.

The medium-level sanction applies only to failures to comply with a work search requirement under s.17(1)(a) to take all reasonable action to obtain paid work etc. or to comply with a work availability requirement under s.18(1). A failure to comply with a work search requirement under s.17(1)(b) to apply for a particular vacancy attracts a higher-level sanction under s.26(2)(b) if the claimant is subject to all work-related requirements. The reduction period under reg.103 is 28 days for a first "offence" and 91 days for a second "offence" or subsequent offence within a year of the previous failure (7 and 14 days for under-18s).

1.113   The low-level sanction under reg.104 applies where the claimant is subject either to all work-related requirements under s.22 or to the work preparation requirement under s.21 and fails to comply with a work-focused interview requirement under s.15(1), a work preparation requirement under s.16(1), a work search requirement under s.17(1)(b) to take any action specified by the Secretary of State or a connected requirement in s.23(1), (3) or (4). Note that this is the sanction that applies to a failure for no good reason to report specified changes in circumstances (s.23(4)) or to provide specified information and evidence (s.23(3)) as well as to failure to participate in an interview. The reduction period under reg.104 lasts until the claim-ant complies with the requirement in question, comes within s.19 (no work-related requirements), a work preparation requirement to take particular action is no longer imposed or the award terminates, plus seven days for a first "offence", 14 days for a second "offence" within a year of the previous failure and 28 days for a third or subsequent "offence" within a year (plus seven days in all those circumstances for under-18s).

The lowest-level sanction under reg.105 applies where a claimant is subject to s.20 and fails to comply with a work-focused interview requirement. The reduction period under reg.105 lasts until the claimant complies with the requirement, comes within s.19 (no work-related requirements), a work preparation requirement to take particular action is no longer imposed or the award terminates.

For the purposes of regs 104 and 105, "compliance condition" is defined in subs. (6) to mean either a condition that the failure to comply ceases or a condition relat-ing to future compliance. A compliance condition may be revoked or varied by the Secretary of State, apparently at will, and may be (not must be) notified to the claimant in such manner as the Secretary of State might determine (subs.(7)). But under regs 104 and 105 a compliance condition has to be "specified" by the Secretary of State. On the one hand, it is difficult to envisage it being decided that the Secretary of State can specify such a condition to himself, rather than to the claimant. On the other hand, it is difficult to envisage it being decided that a claimant who has in fact complied with a requirement has not met a compliance condition merely because the Secretary of State failed to give proper notice of the condition.

Regulation 113 of the Universal Credit Regulations, made in part under subs.(9)   1.114
(a), prescribes circumstances in which no reduction is to be made for a sanctionable failure under s.27, but none of the circumstances covered seem relevant to s.27.

Under para.(b) of subs.(9), see reg.107. Under para.(c), see regs 108 and 109.

Many of the requirements that can give rise to sanctions under s.27 involve undertaking or participating in interviews, courses, assessments, programmes etc that that have a specified start time. In *SA v SSWP (JSA)* [2015] UKUT 454 (AAC) the claimant, who had hearing difficulties and wore a hearing aid in one ear, was directed by an employment officer to attend and complete a CV writing course with Learn Direct two days later from 11.15 a.m. to 12.15 p.m. He was given a letter to confirm the time and date. The claimant arrived at 11.25 a.m. and was told that he was too late and so had been deemed to have missed his appointment. He immediately went to the Jobcentre Plus office to rebook an appointment for the course and explained that he had misheard the time for the appointment as 11.50, the time that he normally signed on. A fixed four-week sanction for failing, without a good reason, to carry out a reasonable jobseeker's direction was imposed. On appeal the claimant said that at the meeting with the employment officer he had not been wearing his hearing aid and that he had not thought to check the time of the appointment on the letter as he genuinely thought that it was the same as his two previous appointments. The First-tier Tribunal regarded it as clear that the direction had been reasonable and that the claimant had failed to comply with it, so that the sole question was whether he had had a good reason for the failure. On that question, the tribunal concluded that, although the error was genuine, that did not in itself give him a good reason and that he had failed to take reasonable steps to confirm the time of the appointment and dismissed his appeal. In setting aside the tribunal's decision and substituting her own decision reversing the imposition of the sanction (as had been suggested by the Secretary of State), Judge Knowles held that the tribunal had erred in law by failing to consider the question of whether the claimant had failed to comply with the direction. In the substituted decision, she concluded that, the claimant not having refused to carry out the direction and taking into account that his error was genuine and that he took immediate steps to rebook, it was disproportionate to treat his late arrival in isolation as amounting to a failure to comply with the direction. That can only be regarded as a determination on the particular facts that does not constitute any sort of precedent to be applied as a matter of law in other cases. The outcome may have reflected an understandable desire in a deserving case to get around the absence of any scope for varying the fixed period of four weeks for a sanction under s.19A of the old style Jobseekers Act 1995 for a "first offence". However, there could have been nothing unreasonable about a conclusion that arriving 10 minutes after the beginning of a course that only lasted for an hour amounted to a failure to comply with a direction to attend and complete the course, no matter how genuine the error that led to the late arrival.

Hardship payments

28.—(1) Regulations may make provision for the making of additional   1.115
payments by way of universal credit to a claimant ("hardship payments") where—

   (a) the amount of the claimant's award is reduced under section 26 or 27, and

(b) the claimant is or will be in hardship.

(2) Regulations under this section may in particular make provision as to—

    (a) circumstances in which a claimant is to be treated as being or not being in hardship;

    (b) matters to be taken into account in determining whether a claimant is or will be in hardship;

    (c) requirements or conditions to be met by a claimant in order to receive hardship payments;

    (d) the amount or rate of hardship payments;

    (e) the period for which hardship payments may be made;

    (f) whether hardship payments are recoverable.

DEFINITION

"claimant"—see s.40.

GENERAL NOTE

1.116   The provision of hardship payments is an important part of the sanctions regime for universal credit. The payments are to be made by way of universal credit. However, it will be seen that s.28, first, does not require the making of provision for hardship payments in regulations and, second, gives almost complete freedom in how any regulations define the conditions for and amounts of payments. The provisions made are in regs 115–119 of the Universal Credit Regulations, which contain stringent conditions and a restricted definition of "hardship", which nevertheless retains a number of subjective elements. Payments are generally recoverable, subject to exceptions. See the notes to those regulations for the details and the relevant parts of Ch.51 of CPAG's *Welfare benefits and tax credits handbook 2017/2018* for helpful explanations and examples. There seems to be no reason why a decision of the Secretary of State to make or not to make hardship payments on an application under reg.116(1)(c) should not be appealable to a First-tier Tribunal.

Administration

Delegation and contracting out

1.117   **29.**—(1) The functions of the Secretary of State under sections 13 to 25 may be exercised by, or by the employees of, such persons as the Secretary of State may authorise for the purpose (an "authorised person").

(2) An authorisation given by virtue of this section may authorise the exercise of a function—

    (a) wholly or to a limited extent;

    (b) generally or in particular cases or areas;

    (c) unconditionally or subject to conditions.

(3) An authorisation under this section—

    (a) may specify its duration;

    (b) may be varied or revoked at any time by the Secretary of State;

    (c) does not prevent the Secretary of State or another person from exercising the function to which the authorisation related.

(4) Anything done or omitted to be done by or in relation to an authorised person (or an employee of that person) in, or in connection with, the

exercise or purported exercise of the function concerned is to be treated for all purposes as done or omitted to be done by or in relation to the Secretary of State or (as the case may be) an officer of the Secretary of State.

(5) Subsection (4) does not apply—

(a) for the purposes of so much of any contract made between the authorised person and the Secretary of State as relates to the exercise of the function, or

(b) for the purposes of any criminal proceedings brought in respect of anything done or omitted to be done by the authorised person (or an employee of that person).

(6) Where—

(a) the authorisation of an authorised person is revoked, and

(b) at the time of the revocation so much of any contract made between the authorised person and the Secretary of State as relates to the exercise of the function is subsisting,

the authorised person is entitled to treat the contract as repudiated by the Secretary of State (and not as frustrated by reason of that revocation).

DEFINITION

"person"—see Interpretation Act 1978, Sch.1.

GENERAL NOTE

This section allows the Secretary of State to authorise other persons (which word **1.118** in accordance with the Interpretation Act 1978 includes corporate and unincorporated associations, such as companies) and their employees to carry out any of his functions under ss.13–25. Any such authorisation will not in practice cover the making of regulations, but may well (depending on the extent of the authorisations given) extend to specifying various matters under those sections. The involvement of private sector organisations, operating for profit, in running various schemes within the scope of the benefit system is something that claimants sometimes object to. Such a generalised objection, even if on principled grounds, is unlikely to amount in itself to a good reason for failing to engage with a scheme in question (although see the discussion in the note to s.26 on whether "for no good reason" has a restricted meaning). An objection based on previous experience with the organisation concerned or the nature of the course may raise more difficult issues. See also the discussion in *R(JSA) 7/03* plus *CSJSA/495/2007* and *CSJSA/505/2007*.

In *DH v SSWP (JSA)* [2016] UKUT 355 (AAC), an old style JSA case under the Jobseeker's Allowance (Schemes for Assisting Persons to Obtain Employment) Regulations 2013, it was held that the First-tier Tribunal erred in law in apparently dismissing the claimant's objections to attending a Work Programme run by a particular provider (on the grounds that staff of the company concerned had lied in a police statement and in court about whether travel expenses had been refunded to him and had bullied him) as, even if true, irrelevant to whether he had a good reason for failing to comply with requirements to attend. The tribunal had said that the claimant's remedies were to contact the police and to use appropriate complaints procedures, not to refuse to attend interviews or courses. The judge asked the rhetorical question in para.20 what could amount to good reason if such matters did not. The circumstances are to be distinguished from those in *R(JSA) 7/03*, not mentioned in *DH*, where the claimant's objection was a generalised one to the involvement of private companies in the provision of such schemes.

CHAPTER 3

SUPPLEMENTARY AND GENERAL

Supplementary and consequential

Supplementary regulation-making powers

1.119   **30.** Schedule 1 contains supplementary regulation-making powers.

Supplementary and consequential amendments

1.120   **31.** Schedule 2 contains supplementary and consequential amendments.

Power to make supplementary and consequential provision etc.

1.121   **32.**—(1) The appropriate authority may by regulations make such consequential, supplementary, incidental or transitional provision in relation to any provision of this Part as the authority considers appropriate.

(2) The appropriate authority is the Secretary of State, subject to subsection (3).

(3) The appropriate authority is the Welsh Ministers for—

(a) provision which would be within the legislative competence of the National Assembly for Wales were it contained in an Act of the Assembly;

(b) provision which could be made by the Welsh Ministers under any other power conferred on them.

(4) Regulations under this section may amend, repeal or revoke any primary or secondary legislation (whenever passed or made).

Universal credit and other benefits

Abolition of benefits

1.122   **33.**—(1) The following benefits are abolished—

(a) income-based jobseeker's allowance under the Jobseekers Act 1995;

(b) income-related employment and support allowance under Part 1 of the Welfare Reform Act 2007;

(c) income support under section 124 of the Social Security Contributions and Benefits Act 1992;

(d) housing benefit under section 130 of that Act;

(e) council tax benefit under section 131 of that Act;

(f) child tax credit and working tax credit under the Tax Credits Act 2002.

(2) In subsection (1)—

(a) "income-based jobseeker's allowance" has the same meaning as in the Jobseekers Act 1995;

(b) "income-related employment and support allowance" means an employment and support allowance entitlement to which is based on section 1(2)(b) of the Welfare Reform Act 2007.

(3) Schedule 3 contains consequential amendments.

DEFINITIONS

"income-related employment and support allowance"—see subs(2)(b).
"income-based jobseeker's allowance"—see subs.(2)(a).

GENERAL NOTE

Subs. (1)

The purpose of this provision is simple enough. Sub-section (1) provides for the abolition of income-based JSA, income-related ESA, income support, housing benefit, council tax benefit, child tax credit and working tax credit. The implementation of this section is much less straightforward. Council tax benefit was abolished in favour of localised schemes from April 2013. As a general rule abolition of the other benefits will only happen when all claimants have been transferred to universal credit. The exception to this rule is that when a claimant in the Pathfinder Group claims JSA, ESA or universal credit, this action of itself triggers the abolition at that point (and for that individual) of income-based JSA and income-related ESA (see Commencement Order No.9, art.4).

This sub-section is modelled on the drafting of s.1(3) of the Tax Credits Act (TCA) 2002, which provided for the abolition of e.g. the personal allowances for children in the income support and income-based JSA schemes. Section 1(3) of the TCA 2002 has never been fully implemented. The fate of subs.(1) here remains to be seen.

Subs. (3)

This introduces Sch.3, which makes consequential amendments relating to the abolition of these benefits. Those changes remove references in other legislation to contributory ESA or JSA, as these will be unnecessary once ESA and JSA are contributory benefits only, and update references to other legislation which has been amended.

Universal credit and state pension credit

34. Schedule 4 provides for a housing element of state pension credit in consequence of the abolition of housing benefit by section 33.

GENERAL NOTE

This section provides for a new housing credit element of state pension credit to replace housing benefit for claimants above the qualifying age for state pension credit. In its original form under the SPCA 2002, state pension credit was made up of two elements: the guarantee credit (performing the same function as income support used to) and the savings credit (providing a small top-up for those claimants with modest savings). Schedule 4 amends the SPCA 2002 to create a new third credit to cover housing costs. This will provide support for people who have reached the qualifying age for state pension credit (or for couples where both members have reached the qualifying age) once housing benefit is no longer available following the introduction of universal credit.

Universal credit and working-age benefits

35. Schedule 5 makes further provision relating to universal credit, jobseeker's allowance and employment and support allowance.

GENERAL NOTE

This section (and Sch.5) deals with the inter-relationship between universal credit, JSA and ESA. After the introduction of universal credit, ESA and JSA will continue to be available but only as contributory benefits.

Migration to universal credit

36. Schedule 6 contains provision about the replacement of benefits by universal credit.

GENERAL NOTE

This section gives effect to Sch.6, which makes provision relating to the replacement of the benefits that will be abolished under s.33, as well as any other

1.123

1.124

1.125

1.126

1.127

1.128

1.129

1.130

prescribed benefits, and the consequential migration (or transfer) of claimants to universal credit.

General

Capability for work or work-related activity

1.131   37.—(1) For the purposes of this Part a claimant has limited capability for work if—

(a) the claimant's capability for work is limited by their physical or mental condition, and

(b) the limitation is such that it is not reasonable to require the claimant to work.

(2) For the purposes of this Part a claimant has limited capability for work-related activity if—

(a) the claimant's capability for work-related activity is limited by their physical or mental condition, and

(b) the limitation is such that it is not reasonable to require the claimant to undertake work-related activity.

(3) The question whether a claimant has limited capability for work or work-related activity for the purposes of this Part is to be determined in accordance with regulations.

(4) Regulations under this section must, subject as follows, provide for determination of that question on the basis of an assessment (or repeated assessments) of the claimant.

(5) Regulations under this section may for the purposes of an assessment—

(a) require a claimant to provide information or evidence (and may require it to be provided in a prescribed manner or form);

(b) require a claimant to attend and submit to a medical examination at a place, date and time determined under the regulations.

(6) Regulations under this section may make provision for a claimant to be treated as having or not having limited capability for work or work-related activity.

(7) Regulations under subsection (6) may provide for a claimant who fails to comply with a requirement imposed under subsection (5) without a good reason to be treated as not having limited capability for work or work-related activity.

(8) Regulations under subsection (6) may provide for a claimant to be treated as having limited capability for work until—

(a) it has been determined whether or not that is the case, or

(b) the claimant is under any other provision of regulations under subsection (6) treated as not having it.

(9) Regulations under this section may provide for determination of the question of whether a claimant has limited capability for work or work-related activity even where the claimant is for the time being treated under regulations under subsection (6) as having limited capability for work or work-related activity.

DEFINITIONS

"claim"—see s.40.
"claimant"—*ibid.*

"limited capability for work"—*ibid.*
"prescribed"—*ibid.*
"work search requirement"—*ibid.*

GENERAL NOTE

If a person has limited capability for work or limited capability for work and work-related activity, this is relevant to universal credit in three ways. Firstly, it affects the amount of the award of universal credit (see ss.1(3)(d) and 12(2)(a) and (b) and regs 27–28 and 36 of the Universal Credit Regulations). Secondly, it determines the work-related requirements that can be imposed. Under s.19(1) and (2)(a) no work-related requirements can be imposed on a claimant who has limited capability for work and work-related activity and under s.21(1)(a) a claimant who has limited capability for work (and who does not fall within s.19 or 20) is only subject to the work preparation requirement. Thirdly, it enables the application of the appropriate work allowance (see s. 8(3)(a) and reg. 22 of the Universal Credit Regulations).   **1.132**

This section contains provisions that are broadly equivalent to those in ss.1(4), 2(5), 8 and 9 of the Welfare Reform Act 2007. Thus the question of whether a person has limited capability for work or limited capability for work and work-related activity, will be determined in the same way as for ESA.

In relation to subs.(7), note also the regulation-making power in para.8 of Sch.1.

Information

38. Information supplied under Chapter 2 of this Part or section 37 is to be taken for all purposes to be information relating to social security.   **1.133**

Couples

39.—[¹ ² (1) In this Part "couple" means—   **1.134**
- (a) two people who are married to, or civil partners of, each other and are members of the same household; or
- (b) two people who are not married to, or civil partners of, each other but are living together as a married couple.]

(2) [¹ ² . . .]

(3) For the purposes of this section regulations may prescribe—
- (a) circumstances in which the fact that two persons are [¹ ² married] or are civil partners is to be disregarded;
- (b) circumstances in which [¹ ² two people are to be treated as living together as a married couple];
- (c) circumstances in which people are to be treated as being or not being members of the same household.

AMENDMENTS

1. Marriage (Same Sex Couples) Act 2013 (Consequential and Contrary Provisions and Scotland) Order 2014 (SI 2014/560) art.2 and Sch.1, para.36 (March 13, 2014). This amendment extended to England and Wales only.

2. Marriage and Civil Partnership (Scotland) Act 2014 and Civil Partnership Act 2004 (Consequential Provisions and Modifications) Order 2014 (SI 2014/3229) art.29 and Sch.5, para.20 (December 16, 2014). This amendment extended to Scotland only. However, as it was in the same terms as the amendment made in England and Wales by SI 2014/560 (see above), the effect is that the law is now the same throughout Great Britain.

GENERAL NOTE

1.135   See the commentary to reg.3 of the Universal Credit Regulations.

Interpretation of Part 1

1.136   **40.** In this Part—

"assessment period" has the meaning given by section 7(2);

"child" means a person under the age of 16;

"claim" means claim for universal credit;

"claimant" means a single claimant or each of joint claimants;

"couple" has the meaning given by section 39;

"disabled" has such meaning as may be prescribed;

"joint claimants" means members of a couple who jointly make a claim or in relation to whom an award of universal credit is made;

"limited capability for work" and "limited capability for work-related activity" are to be construed in accordance with section 37(1) and (2);

"prescribed" means specified or provided for in regulations;

"primary legislation" means an Act, Act of the Scottish Parliament or Act or Measure of the National Assembly for Wales;

"qualifying young person" has the meaning given in section 10(5);

"regular and substantial caring responsibilities" has such meaning as may be prescribed;

"responsible carer", in relation to a child, has the meaning given in section 19(6);

"secondary legislation" means an instrument made under primary legislation";

"severely disabled" has such meaning as may be prescribed;

"single claimant" means a single person who makes a claim for universal credit or in relation to whom an award of universal credit is made as a single person;

"single person" is to be construed in accordance with section 1(2)(a);

"work" has such meaning as may be prescribed;

"work availability requirement" has the meaning given by section 18(1);

"work preparation requirement" has the meaning given by section 16(1);

"work search requirement" has the meaning given by section 17(1);

" work-focused interview requirement" has the meaning given by section 15(1);

"work-related activity", in relation to a person, means activity which makes it more likely that the person will obtain or remain in work or be able to do so;

"work-related requirement" has the meaning given by section 13(2).

Regulations

Pilot schemes

1.137   **41.**—(1) Any power to make—

(a) regulations under this Part,

(b) regulations under the Social Security Administration Act 1992 relating to universal credit, or

(c) regulations under the Social Security Act 1998 relating to universal credit, may be exercised so as to make provision for piloting purposes.

(2) In subsection (1), "piloting purposes", in relation to any provision, means the purposes of testing—

(a) the extent to which the provision is likely to make universal credit simpler to understand or to administer,

(b) the extent to which the provision is likely to promote—
    (i) people remaining in work, or
    (ii) people obtaining or being able to obtain work (or more work or better-paid work), or

(c) the extent to which, and how, the provision is likely to affect the conduct of claimants or other people in any other way.

(3) Regulations made by virtue of this section are in the remainder of this section referred to as a "pilot scheme".

(4) A pilot scheme may be limited in its application to—

(a) one or more areas;

(b) one or more classes of person;

(c) persons selected—
    (i) by reference to prescribed criteria, or
    (ii) on a sampling basis.

(5) A pilot scheme may not have effect for a period exceeding three years, but—

(a) the Secretary of State may by order made by statutory instrument provide that the pilot scheme is to continue to have effect after the time when it would otherwise expire for a period not exceeding twelve months (and may make more than one such order);

(b) a pilot scheme may be replaced by a further pilot scheme making the same or similar provision.

(6) A pilot scheme may include consequential or transitional provision in relation to its expiry.

GENERAL NOTE

This section was brought into force for all purposes on September 15, 2014 by   **1.138** art.6 of the Welfare Reform Act 2012 (Commencement No. 19 and Transitional and Transitory Provisions and Commencement No. 9 and Transitional and Transitory Provisions (Amendment)) Order 2014 (SI 2014/2321).

This important provision is similar to that in s.29 of the Jobseekers Act 1995. It contains the power to pilot changes in regulations across particular geographical areas and/or specified categories of claimants for up to three years, although this period can be extended, or the pilot scheme can be replaced by a different pilot scheme making the same or similar provision (subs.(5)). The power can only be exercised in relation to the types of regulation listed in subs.(1) and with a view to assessing whether the proposed changes are likely to make universal credit simpler to understand or administer, to encourage people to find or remain in work (or more or better-paid work) or "to affect the conduct of claimants or other people in any other way" (subs.(2)). Regulations made under this section are subject to the affirmative resolution procedure (s.43(4)). On past experience in relation to JSA, it seems likely that this power will be exercised on a fairly regular basis.

Regulations: general

42.—(1) Regulations under this Part are to be made by the Secretary of   **1.139** State, unless otherwise provided.

(2) A power to make regulations under this Part may be exercised—

(a) so as to make different provision for different cases or purposes;

(b) in relation to all or only some of the cases or purposes for which it may be exercised.

(3) Such a power includes—

(a) power to make incidental, supplementary, consequential or transitional provision or savings;

(b) power to provide for a person to exercise a discretion in dealing with any matter.

(4) Each power conferred by this Part is without prejudice to the others.

(5) Where regulations under this Part provide for an amount, the amount may be zero.

(6) Where regulations under this Part provide for an amount for the purposes of an award (or a reduction from an award), the amount may be different in relation to different descriptions of person, and in particular may depend on—

(a) whether the person is a single person or a member of couple.

(b) the age of the person.

(7) Regulations under section 11(4) or 12(3) which provide for the determination or calculation of an amount may make different provision for different areas.

DEFINITIONS

"couple"—see ss.39 and 40.
"single person"—see s.40.
"work"—*ibid.*

Regulations: procedure

1.140   43.—(1) Regulations under this Part are to be made by statutory instrument.

(2) A statutory instrument containing regulations made by the Secretary of State under this Part is subject to the negative resolution procedure, subject as follows.

(3) A statutory instrument containing the first regulations made by the Secretary of State under any of the following, alone or with other regulations, is subject to the affirmative resolution procedure—

(a) section 4(7) (acceptance of claimant commitment);

(b) section 5(1)(a) and (2)(a) (capital limits);

(c) section 8(3) (income to be deducted in award calculation);

(d) section 9(2) and (3) (standard allowance);

(e) section 10(3) and (4) (children and young persons element);

(f) section 11 (housing costs element);

(g) section 12 (other needs and circumstances element);

(h) section 18(3) and (5) (work availability requirement);

(i) section 19(2)(d) (claimants subject to no work-related requirements);

(j) sections 26 and 27 (sanctions);

(k) section 28 (hardship payments);

(l) paragraph 4 of Schedule 1 (calculation of capital and income);

(m) paragraph 1(1) of Schedule 6 (migration), where making provision under paragraphs 4, 5 and 6 of that Schedule.

(4) A statutory instrument containing regulations made by the Secretary of State by virtue of section 41 (pilot schemes), alone or with other regulations, is subject to the affirmative resolution procedure.

(5) A statutory instrument containing regulations made by the Secretary of State under this Part is subject to the affirmative resolution procedure if—

(a) it also contains regulations under another enactment, and

(b) an instrument containing those regulations would apart from this section be subject to the affirmative resolution procedure.

(6) For the purposes of subsections (2) to (5)—

(a) a statutory instrument subject to the "negative resolution procedure" is subject to annulment in pursuance of a resolution of either House of Parliament;

(b) a statutory instrument subject to the "affirmative resolution procedure" may not be made unless a draft of the instrument has been laid before, and approved by resolution of, each House of Parliament.

(7) A statutory instrument containing regulations made by the Welsh Ministers under section 32 may not be made unless a draft of the instrument has been laid before, and approved by resolution of, the National Assembly for Wales.

DEFINITIONS

"child"—see s.40.
"claim"—*ibid.*
"claimant"—*ibid.*
"work"—*ibid.*
"work availability requirement"—*ibid.*

PART 5

SOCIAL SECURITY: GENERAL

Benefit cap

Benefit cap

96.—(1) Regulations may provide for a benefit cap to be applied to the welfare benefits to which a single person or couple is entitled.   1.141

(2) For the purposes of this section, applying a benefit cap to welfare benefits means securing that, where a single person's or couple's total entitlement to welfare benefits in respect of the reference period exceeds the relevant amount, their entitlement to welfare benefits in respect of any period of the same duration as the reference period is reduced by an amount up to or equalling the excess.

(3) In subsection (2) the "reference period" means a period of a prescribed duration.

(4) Regulations under this section may in particular—

(a) make provision as to the manner in which total entitlement to welfare benefits for any period, or the amount of any reduction, is to be determined;

(b) make provision as to the welfare benefit or benefits from which a reduction is to be made;

(c) provide for exceptions to the application of the benefit cap;

(d) make provision as to the intervals at which the benefit cap is to be applied;

(e) make provision as to the relationship between application of the benefit cap and any other reduction in respect of a welfare benefit;

(f) provide that where in consequence of a change in the relevant amount, entitlement to a welfare benefit increases or decreases, that increase or decrease has effect without any further decision of the Secretary of State;

(g) make supplementary and consequential provision.

[¹ (5) Regulations under this section may make provision for determining the "relevant amount" for the reference period applicable in the case of a single person or couple by reference to the annual limit applicable in the case of that single person or couple.

(5A) For the purposes of this section the "annual limit" is—

(a) £23,000 or £15,410, for persons resident in Greater London;

(b) £20,000 or £13,400, for other persons.

(5B) Regulations under subsection (5) may—

(a) specify which annual limit applies in the case of—

    (i) different prescribed descriptions of single person;

    (ii) different prescribed descriptions of couple;

(b) define "resident" for the purposes of this section;

(c) provide for the rounding up or down of an amount produced by dividing the amount of the annual limit by the number of periods of a duration equal to the reference period in a year.]

(6) [¹ . . .]

(7) [¹ . . .]

(8) [¹ . . .]

(9) Regulations under this section may not provide for any reduction to be made from a welfare benefit—

(a) provision for which is within the legislative competence of the Scottish Parliament;

(b) provision for which is within the legislative competence of the National Assembly for Wales;

(c) provision for which is made by the Welsh Ministers, the First Minister for Wales or the Counsel General to the Welsh Assembly Government.

(10) In this section—

"couple" means two persons of a prescribed description;

"prescribed" means prescribed in regulations;

"regulations" means regulations made by the Secretary of State;

"single person" means a person who is not a member of a couple;

"welfare benefit" [¹ means—

(a) bereavement allowance (see section 39B of the Social Security Contributions and Benefits Act 1992),

(b) child benefit (see section 141 of the Social Security Contributions and Benefits Act 1992),

(c) child tax credit (see section 1(1)(a) of the Tax Credits Act 2002),

(d) employment and support allowance (see section 1 of the Welfare

Reform Act 2007), including income-related employment and support allowance (as defined in section 1(7) of the Welfare Reform Act 2007),

(e) housing benefit (see section 130 of the Social Security Contributions and Benefits Act 1992),

(f) incapacity benefit (see section 30A of the Social Security Contributions and Benefits Act 1992),

(g) income support (see section 124 of the Social Security Contributions and Benefits Act 1992),

(h) jobseeker's allowance (see section 1 of the Jobseekers Act 1995), including income-based jobseeker's allowance (as defined in section 1(4) of the Jobseekers Act 1995),

(i) maternity allowance under section 35 or 35B of the Social Security Contributions and Benefits Act 1992,

(j) severe disablement allowance (see section 68 of the Social Security Contributions and Benefits Act 1992),

(k) universal credit,

(l) widow's pension (see section 38 of the Social Security Contributions and Benefits Act 1992),

(m) widowed mother's allowance (see section 37 of the Social Security Contributions and Benefits Act 1992), or

(n) widowed parent's allowance (see section 39A of the Social Security Contributions and Benefits Act 1992).

(11) [¹ . . .]

AMENDMENT

1. Welfare Reform and Work Act 2016 s.8(1)-(5) (assessment periods beginning on or after November 7, 2016: see SI 2016/910).

GENERAL NOTE

See the commentary to regs 78–83 of the Universal Credit Regulations.   1.142

[¹ Benefit cap: review

96A.—(1) The Secretary of State must at least once in each Parliament   1.143
review the sums specified in section 96(5A) to determine whether it is appropriate to increase or decrease any one or more of those sums.

(2) The Secretary of State may, at any other time the Secretary of State considers appropriate, review the sums specified in section 96(5A) to determine whether it is appropriate to increase or decrease any one or more of those sums.

(3) In carrying out a review, the Secretary of State must take into account—

(a) the national economic situation, and

(b) any other matters that the Secretary of State considers relevant.

(4) After carrying out a review, the Secretary of State may, if the Secretary of State considers it appropriate, by regulations amend section 96(5A) so as to increase or decrease any one or more of the sums specified in section 96(5A).

(5) Regulations under subsection (4) may provide for amendments of section 96(5A) to come into force—

(a) on different days for different areas;

(b) on different days for different cases or purposes.

(6) Regulations under subsection (4) may make such transitional or transitory provision or savings as the Secretary of State considers necessary or expedient in connection with the coming into force of any amendment made by regulations under subsection (4).

(7) Regulations under subsection (6) may in particular—

(a) provide for section 96(5A) to have effect as if the amendments made by regulations under subsection (4) had not been made, in relation to such persons or descriptions of persons as are specified in the regulations or generally, until a time or times specified in a notice issued by the Secretary of State;

(b) provide for the Secretary of State to issue notices under paragraph (a) specifying different times for different persons or descriptions of person;

(c) make provision about the issuing of notices under paragraph (a), including provision for the Secretary of State to issue notices to authorities administering housing benefit that have effect in relation to persons specified, or persons of a description specified, in the notices.

(8) Section 176 of the Social Security Administration Act 1992 (consultation with representative organisations) does not apply in relation to regulations under subsection (4).

(9) If an early parliamentary general election is to take place in accordance with section 2 of the Fixed-term Parliaments Act 2011, the duty in subsection (1) is to be disregarded.]

AMENDMENT

1. Welfare Reform and Work Act 2016 (c.7) s.9(1) (November 7, 2016).

Benefit cap: supplementary

1.144   **97.**—(1) Regulations under section 96 [³ or 96A] may make different provision for different purposes or cases.

(2) Regulations under section 96 [³ or 96A] must be made by statutory instrument.

(3) [² ...]

(4) A statutory instrument containing [² ...] regulations under section 96 is subject to annulment in pursuance of a resolution of either House of Parliament.

[³ (4A) A statutory instrument containing regulations under section 96A may not be made unless a draft of the instrument has been laid before, and approved by a resolution of, each House of Parliament.]

(5) [¹ ...]

(6) In Schedule 2 to the Social Security Act 1998 (decisions against which no appeal lies) after paragraph 8 there is inserted—

"Reduction on application of benefit cap

8A A decision to apply the benefit cap in accordance with regulations under section 96 of the Welfare Reform Act 2012."

AMENDMENTS

1. Welfare Reform and Work Act 2016 s.9(6) (March 16, 2016).
2. Welfare Reform and Work Act 2016 s.8(6) (assessment periods beginning on or after November 7, 2016: see SI 2016/910).
3. Welfare Reform and Work Act 2016 s.9(2)-(5) (November 7, 2016).

See the commentary to regs 78–83 of the Universal Credit Regulations.　　　**1.145**

PART 7

FINAL

Repeals

147. *[Omitted]*　　　**1.146**

Financial provision

148. There shall be paid out of money provided by Parliament—　　**1.147**
(a) sums paid by the Secretary of State by way of universal credit or personal independence payment;
(b) any other expenditure incurred in consequence of this Act by a Minister of the Crown or the Commissioners for Her Majesty's Revenue and Customs;
(c) any increase attributable to this Act in the sums payable under any other Act out of money so provided.

Extent

149.—(1) This Act extends to England and Wales and Scotland only,　**1.148**
subject as follows.
(2) The following provisions extend to England and Wales, Scotland and Northern Ireland—
(a) section 32 (power to make consequential and supplementary provision: universal credit);
(b) section 33 (abolition of benefits);
(c)–(f) *[Omitted]*
(g) this Part, excluding Schedule 14 (repeals).
(3) *[Omitted]*
(4) Any amendment or repeal made by this Act has the same extent as the enactment to which it relates.

Commencement

150.—(1) The following provisions of this Act come into force on the day　**1.149**
on which it is passed—
(a)–(e) *[Omitted]*
(f) this Part, excluding Schedule 14 (repeals).
(2) *[Omitted]*
(3) The remaining provisions of this Act come into force on such day as the Secretary of State may by order made by statutory instrument appoint.
(4) An order under subsection (3) may—
(a) appoint different days for different purposes;
(b) appoint different days for different areas in relation to—

(i) any provision of Part 1 (universal credit) or of Part 1 of Schedule 14;

(ii)–(iii) *[Omitted]*

(iv) section 102 (consideration of revision before appeal);

(c) make such transitory or transitional provision, or savings, as the Secretary of State considers necessary or expedient.

Short title

1.150

151. This Act may be cited as the Welfare Reform Act 2012.

SCHEDULES

Section 30

SCHEDULE 1

UNIVERSAL CREDIT: SUPPLEMENTARY REGULATION-MAKING POWERS

Entitlement of joint claimants

1.151
1. Regulations may provide for circumstances in which joint claimants may be entitled to universal credit without each of them meeting all the basic conditions referred to in section 4.

Linking periods

2. Regulations may provide for periods of entitlement to universal credit which are separated by no more than a prescribed number of days to be treated as a single period.

Couples

3.—(1) Regulations may provide—

(a) for a claim made by members of a couple jointly to be treated as a claim made by one member of the couple as a single person (or as claims made by both members as single persons);

(b) for claims made by members of a couple as single persons to be treated as a claim made jointly by the couple.

(2) Regulations may provide—

(a) where an award is made to joint claimants who cease to be entitled to universal credit as such by ceasing to be a couple, for the making of an award (without a claim) to either or each one of them—

(i) as a single person, or

(ii) jointly with another person;

(b) where an award is made to a single claimant who ceases to be entitled to universal credit as such by becoming a member of a couple, for the making of an award (without a claim) to the members of the couple jointly;

(c) for the procedure to be followed, and information or evidence to be supplied, in relation to the making of an award under this paragraph.

Calculation of capital and income

4.—(1) Regulations may for any purpose of this Part provide for the calculation or estimation of—

(a) a person's capital,

(b) a person's earned and unearned income, and

(c) a person's earned and unearned income in respect of an assessment period.

(2) Regulations under sub-paragraph (1)(c) may include provision for the calculation to be made by reference to an average over a period, which need not include the assessment period concerned.

(3) Regulations under sub-paragraph (1) may—

(a) specify circumstances in which a person is to be treated as having or not having capital or earned or unearned income;

(b) specify circumstances in which income is to be treated as capital or capital as earned income or unearned income;

(c) specify circumstances in which unearned income is to be treated as earned, or earned income as unearned;

(d) provide that a person's capital is to be treated as yielding income at a prescribed rate;

(e) provide that the capital or income of one member of a couple is to be treated as that of the other member.

(4) Regulations under sub-paragraph (3)(a) may in particular provide that persons of a prescribed description are to be treated as having a prescribed minimum level of earned income.

(5) In the case of joint claimants the income and capital of the joint claimants includes (subject to sub-paragraph (6)) the separate income and capital of each of them.

(6) Regulations may specify circumstances in which capital and income of either of joint claimants is to be disregarded in calculating their joint capital and income.

Responsibility for children etc

5.—(1) Regulations may for any purpose of this Part specify circumstances in which a person is or is not responsible for a child or qualifying young person.   **1.152**

(2) Regulations may for any purpose of this Part make provision about nominations of the responsible carer for a child (see section 19(6)(b)(ii)).

Vouchers

6.—(1) This paragraph applies in relation to an award of universal credit where the calculation of the amount of the award includes, by virtue of any provision of this Part, an amount in respect of particular costs which a claimant may incur.

(2) Regulations may provide for liability to pay all or part of the award to be discharged by means of provision of a voucher.

(3) But the amount paid by means of a voucher may not in any case exceed the total of the amounts referred to in sub-paragraph (1) which are included in the calculation of the amount of the award.

(4) For these purposes a voucher is a means other than cash by which a claimant may to any extent meet costs referred to in sub-paragraph (1) of a particular description.

(5) A voucher may for these purposes—

(a) be limited as regards the person or persons who will accept it;

(b) be valid only for a limited time.

Work-related requirements

7.—Regulations may provide that a claimant who—

(a) has a right to reside in the United Kingdom under the EU Treaties, and

(b) would otherwise fall within section 19, 20 or 21, is to be treated as not falling within that section.

Good reason

8.—Regulations may for any purpose of this Part provide for—   **1.153**

(a) circumstances in which a person is to be treated as having or not having a good reason for an act or omission;

(b) matters which are or are not to be taken into account in determining whether a person has a good reason for an act or omission.

DEFINITIONS

"assessment period"—see s.40 and s.7(2).
"child"—see s.40.
"claim"—*ibid.*
"claimant"—*ibid.*
"couple"—see ss.39 and 40.
"joint claimants"—see s.40.
"prescribed"—*ibid.*
"single claimant"—*ibid.*
"single person"—*ibid.*

SCHEDULE 2

UNIVERSAL CREDIT: AMENDMENTS

[Omitted]

SCHEDULE 3

ABOLITION OF BENEFITS: CONSEQUENTIAL AMENDMENTS

Social Security Contributions and Benefits Act 1992 (c.4)

1.154
1. The Social Security Contributions and Benefits Act 1992 is amended as follows.

2. In section 22 (earnings factors), in subsections (2)(a) and (5), for "a contributory" there is substituted "an".

3. In section 150 (interpretation of Part 10), in subsection (2), in the definition of "qualifying employment and support allowance", for "a contributory allowance" there is substituted "an employment and support allowance".

Social Security Administration Act 1992 (c.5)

1.155
4. The Social Security Administration Act 1992 is amended as follows.

5. In section 7 (relationship between benefits), in subsection (3), for "subsections (1) and (2)" there is substituted "subsection (1)".

6. In section 73 (overlapping benefits), in subsections (1) and (4)(c), for "a contributory" there is substituted "an".

7. In section 159B (effect of alterations affecting state pension credit), for "a contributory", wherever occurring, there is substituted "an".

8. In section 159D (as inserted by Schedule 2 to this Act) (effect of alterations affecting universal credit), for "a contributory", wherever occurring, there is substituted "an".

Immigration and Asylum Act 1999 (c.33)

1.156
9. In the Immigration and Asylum Act 1999, in section 115 (exclusion from benefits of persons subject to immigration control)—

(a) in subsection (1), after paragraph (ha) there is inserted "or";

(b) in subsection (2)(b) for "(a) to (j)" substitute "(a) to (i)".

Child Support, Pensions and Social Security Act 2000 (c.19)

1.157
10. The Child Support, Pensions and Social Security Act 2000 is amended as follows.

11. (1) Section 69 (discretionary financial assistance with housing) is amended as follows.

(2) In subsection (1)—

(a) for "relevant authorities" there is substituted "local authorities";

(b) in paragraph (a), the words from "housing benefit" to "both," are repealed.

(3) In subsection (2)—

(a) in paragraph (b), for "relevant authority" there is substituted "local authority";

(b) in paragraph (e), for "relevant authorities" there is substituted "local authorities";

(c) in paragraphs (f), (g) and (h), for "relevant authority" there is substituted "local authority".

(4) In subsection (5), for "relevant authorities" there is substituted "local authorities".

(5) In subsection (7), for the definition of "relevant authority" there is substituted—

""local authority" has the meaning given by section 191 of the Social Security Administration Act 1992."

12.(1) Section 70 (grants towards cost of discretionary housing payments) is amended as follows.

(2) In subsection (1), after "payments" there is inserted "("grants")".

(3) For subsection (2) there is substituted—

"(2)The amount of a grant under this section shall be determined in accordance with an order made by the Secretary of State with the consent of the Treasury."

(4) In subsection (8)—

(a) for the definition of "relevant authority" there is substituted—

""local authority" has the same meaning as in section 69;";

(b) the definition of "subsidy" is repealed.

13. After section 70 there is inserted—

"70A. Payment of grant

(1) A grant under section 70 shall be made by the Secretary of State in such instalments, at **1.158** such times, in such manner and subject to such conditions as to claims, records, certificates, audit or otherwise as may be provided by order of the Secretary of State with the consent of the Treasury.

(2) The order may provide that if a local authority has not complied with the conditions specified in it within such period as may be specified in it, the Secretary of State may estimate the amount of grant under section 70 payable to the authority and employ for that purpose such criteria as he considers relevant.

(3) Where a grant under section 70 has been paid to a local authority and it appears to the Secretary of State that—

(a) the grant has been overpaid, or

(b) there has been a breach of any condition specified in an order under this section, he may recover from the authority the whole or such part of the payment as he may determine.

(4) Without prejudice to the other methods of recovery, a sum recoverable under this section may be recovered by withholding or reducing subsidy.

(5) An order under this section may be made before, during or after the end of the period to which it relates.

(6) In this section "local authority" has the same meaning as in section 69.

(7) Section 70(5) to (7) applies to orders under this section."

Capital Allowances Act 2001 (c.2)

14. In Schedule A1 to the Capital Allowances Act 2001 (first-year tax credits), in paragraph **1.159** 17(1)(b) after "sick pay," there is inserted "or".

Social Security Fraud Act 2001 (c.11)

15. The Social Security Fraud Act 2001 is amended as follows. **1.160**

16. In section 6B (loss of benefit for conviction etc), in subsection (5), for "to (10)" there is substituted "and (8)".

17. In section 7 (loss of benefit for repeated conviction etc), in subsection (2), for "to (5)" there is substituted "and (4A)".

18. In section 11 (regulations), in subsection (3)(c), for the words from "section" to the end there is substituted "section 6B(5A) or (8), 7(2A) or (4A) or 9(2A) or (4A)".

Commissioners for Revenue and Customs Act 2005 (c.11)

19. The Commissioners for Revenue and Customs Act 2005 is amended as follows. **1.161**

20. In section 5 (initial functions), in subsection (1), after paragraph (a) there is inserted "and".

21. In section 44 (payment into Consolidated Fund), in subsection (3), after paragraph (b) there is inserted "and".

Welfare Reform Act 2007 (c. 5)

22. The Welfare Reform Act 2007 is amended as follows. **1.162**

23. In section 1 (employment and support allowance), in subsection (3)(d), at the end there is inserted "and".

24. In section 2 (amount of contributory allowance), in subsection (1), for "In the case of a contributory allowance, the amount payable" there is substituted "The amount payable by way of an employment and support allowance".

25.(1) Section 27 (financial provisions) is amended as follows.

(2) In subsection (1), for the words from "so much of" to the end there is substituted "any sums payable by way of employment and support allowance".

(3) In subsection (3), for "contributory" there is substituted "employment and support".

26. In each of the following provisions, for "a contributory allowance" there is substituted "an employment and support allowance"

   (a) section 1A(1), (3), (4), (5) and (6) (as inserted by section 51 of this Act);

   (b) section 1B(1) (as inserted by section 52 of this Act);

   (c) section 3(2)(d);

   (d) section 18(4);

   (e) section 20(2), (3)(a), (b) and (c), (4), (5)(a), (b) and (c), (6), (7)(a), (b) and (c);

   (f) in Schedule 1, paragraphs 1(5)(d) and 3(2)(a);

   (g) in Schedule 2, paragraphs 6 and 7(2)(d).

Corporation Tax Act 2009 (c. 4)

1.163   27. The Corporation Tax Act 2009 is amended as follows.

28. In section 1059 (relief relating to SME R&D: total amount of company's PAYE and NICs liabilities), in subsection (5) after "sick pay" there is inserted "or".

29. In section 1108 (relief relating to vaccine research etc: total amount of company's PAYE and NICs liabilities), in subsection (5) after "sick pay" there is inserted "or".

GENERAL NOTE

1.164   The amendments contained in this Schedule to other primary legislation fall into two main categories.

First, and for the most part, the amendments are consequential upon the abolition of income support, housing benefit, council tax benefit, child tax credit, working tax credit and the income-based forms of ESA and JSA. So, for example, references in other Acts to "a contributory employment and support allowance" are changed to "an employment and support allowance". This is because, after the full implementation of universal credit, the only form of ESA which will be available will be a contributory allowance.

The second category of amendments concerns those made to the Child Support, Pensions and Social Security Act 2000. These amend the provisions relating to discretionary housing payments and are consequential on the abolition of council tax benefit and housing benefit.

SCHEDULE 4

HOUSING CREDIT ELEMENT OF STATE PENSION CREDIT

PART 1

AMENDMENTS TO STATE PENSION CREDIT ACT 2002

State Pension Credit Act 2002 (c.16)

1.165   1. The State Pension Credit Act 2002 is amended as follows.

2. In section 1 (entitlement), in subsection (2)(c), at the end there is inserted "or (iii) the conditions in section 3A(1) and (2) (housing credit)."

3. In that section, in subsection (3)—

   (a) after paragraph (b)   there is inserted "or

   (c) to a housing credit, calculated in accordance with section 3A, if he satisfies the conditions in subsections (1) and (2) of that section,";

   (b) for the words from "(or to both)" to the end there is substituted "(or to more than one of them, if he satisfies the relevant conditions)".

4. After section 3 there is inserted—

"3A. Housing credit

(1) The first of the conditions mentioned in section 1(2)(c)(iii) is that the claimant is liable to make payments in respect of the accommodation he occupies as his home.

(2) The second of the conditions mentioned in section 1(2)(c)(iii) is that the claimant's capital and income are such that the amount of the housing credit payable (if he were entitled to it) would not be less than a prescribed amount.

(3) Where the claimant is entitled to a housing credit, the amount of the housing credit shall be an amount calculated in or determined under regulations (which may be zero).

(4) For the purposes of subsection (1)—

  (a) the accommodation must be in Great Britain;

  (b) the accommodation must be residential accommodation;

  (c) it is immaterial whether the accommodation consists of the whole or part of a building and whether or not it comprises separate and self-contained premises.

(5) Regulations may make provision as to—

  (a) the meaning of "payments in respect of accommodation" for the purposes of this section (and, in particular, as to the extent to which such payments include mortgage payments);

  (b) circumstances in which a claimant is to be treated as liable or not liable to make such payments;

  (c) circumstances in which a claimant is to be treated as occupying or not occupying accommodation as his home (and, in particular, for temporary absences to be disregarded);

  (d) circumstances in which land used for the purposes of any accommodation is to be treated as included in the accommodation.

(6) Regulations under this section may make different provision for different areas."

5. In section 7 (fixing of retirement provision for assessed income period), at the end there is inserted—

"(10) Regulations may prescribe circumstances in which subsection (3) does not apply for the purposes of determining the amount of a housing credit to which the claimant is entitled."

6. In section 12 (polygamous marriages), in subsection (2)(b), after "savings credit" there is inserted "or housing credit".

7. In section 17 (interpretation), in subsection (1), after the definition of "guarantee credit" there is inserted—""housing credit" shall be construed in accordance with sections 1 and 3A;".

8. In Schedule 2 (consequential amendments etc), paragraph 9(5)(a) is repealed.

1.166

PART 2

AMENDMENTS TO OTHER ACTS

Social Security Administration Act 1992 (c.5)

9. The Social Security Administration Act 1992 is amended as follows.

1.167

10. In section 5 (regulations about claims and payments) in subsection (6), before "subsection" there is inserted "or housing credit (within the meaning of the State Pension Credit Act 2002)".

11. In section 15A (mortgage interest)—

  (a) in subsection (1A)—

    (i) in paragraph (b), for "the appropriate minimum guarantee for the purposes of" there is substituted "entitlement to";

    (ii) in the closing words, for "appropriate minimum guarantee for the purposes of" there is substituted "entitlement to";

  (b) in subsection (4), the definition of "appropriate minimum guarantee" is repealed.

12.(1)Section 122F (supply by rent officers of information) is amended as follows.

(2) In subsection (3)(a) at the end of the words in brackets there is inserted "or housing credit".

(3) In subsection (4) at the end there is inserted "or housing credit".

(4) After that subsection there is inserted—

"(5) In this section "housing credit" has the same meaning as in the State Pension Credit Act 2002".

Housing Act 1996 (c.52)

1.168   13.(1) Section 122 of the Housing Act 1996 (rent officers) is amended as follows.

(2) In the heading, at the end there is inserted "and housing credit".

(3) In subsection (1), at the end there is inserted "or housing credit (within the meaning of the State Pension Credit Act 2002)".

Child Support, Pensions and Social Security Act 2000 (c.19)

1.169   14. In section 69 of the Child Support, Pensions and Social Security Act 2000 (discretionary financial assistance with housing), in subsection (1)(a), after "universal credit" there is inserted "or housing credit (within the meaning of the State Pension Credit Act 2002)".

GENERAL NOTE

1.170   Schedule 4 (which at the time of writing is not yet in force) amends the State Pension Credit Act 2002 to create a new type of credit within state pension credit to cover housing costs. This will provide support for people who qualify for state pension credit once housing benefit is no longer available. The key provision is para.4, which inserts a new s.3A into the SPCA 2002. This provision sets out the conditions of entitlement to the housing credit (subss.(1) and (2)); it also provides the power to set out the manner in which the housing credit is to be calculated or determined in regulations (subs.(3)). The policy intention is that claimants will be entitled to broadly the same amount of support under the housing credit as they would previously have been entitled to by way of housing benefit. Subsection (5) of new s.3A simply adds detail to the power in subs.(3) by listing a number of specific matters in respect of which regulations may be made. Subsection (6) provides that regulations may make different provision for different areas. The underlying aim is to ensure that persons in different but abutting areas may be treated in a different manner depending on the circumstances obtaining in that area (e.g. to reflect different local taxation applied by different local authorities).

The other provision of note is para.5, which inserts a new s.7(10) into the SPCA 2002. Section 7 provides for assessed income periods in state pension credit, during which a person's retirement provision as assessed at the start of the period is taken to be the same throughout the period. The power exists in s.6(2)(b) to prescribe circumstances in which an assessed income period may not be set. The new s.7(10) provides that regulations may prescribe circumstances in which a person's retirement provision is not taken to be the same throughout the assessed income period for the purposes of determining the amount of housing credit to which a person is entitled. This power is inserted in order to replicate the current position in respect of housing benefit, which does not operate a system based on assessed income periods.

SCHEDULE 5

UNIVERSAL CREDIT AND OTHER WORKING-AGE BENEFITS

General

1.171   1.(1) In this Schedule "relevant benefit" means—

(a) jobseeker's allowance, or

(b) employment and support allowance.

(2) In this Schedule "work-related requirement" means—

(a) a work-related requirement within the meaning of this Part,

(b) a work-related requirement within the meaning of the Jobseekers Act 1995, or

(c) a work-related requirement within the meaning of Part 1 of the Welfare Reform Act 2007.

(3) In this Schedule "sanction" means a reduction of benefit under—

(a) section 26 or 27,

(b) section 6J or 6K of the Jobseekers Act 1995, or

(c) section 11J of the Welfare Reform Act 2007.

Dual entitlement

2. (1) Regulations may make provision as to the amount payable by way of a relevant benefit where a person is entitled to that benefit and universal credit.

(2) Regulations under sub-paragraph (1) may in particular provide for no amount to be payable by way of a relevant benefit.

(3) Regulations may, where a person is entitled to a relevant benefit and universal credit—
    (a) make provision as to the application of work-related requirements;
    (b) make provision as to the application of sanctions.

(4) Provision under sub-paragraph (3)(a) includes in particular—
    (a) provision securing that compliance with a work-related requirement for a relevant benefit is to be treated as compliance with a work-related requirement for universal credit;
    (b) provision disapplying any requirement on the Secretary of State to impose, or a person to comply with, a work-related requirement for a relevant benefit or universal credit.

(5) Provision under sub-paragraph (3)(b) includes in particular—
    (a) provision for the order in which sanctions are to be applied to awards of relevant benefit and universal credit;
    (b) provision to secure that the application of a sanction to an award of a relevant benefit does not result in an increase of the amount of an award of universal credit.

Movement between working-age benefits

3. Regulations may provide—
    (a) in a case where a person ceases to be entitled to universal credit and becomes entitled to a relevant benefit, for a sanction relating to the award of universal credit to be applied to the award of the relevant benefit;
    (b) in a case where a person ceases to be entitled to a relevant benefit and becomes entitled to universal credit, for a sanction relating to the award of the relevant benefit to be applied to the award of universal credit;
    (c) in a case where a person ceases to be entitled to one relevant benefit and becomes entitled to the other, for a sanction relating to the award of the former to apply to the award of the latter.

Hardship payments

4. Regulations under section 28 (hardship payments) may be made in relation to a person whose award of universal credit is reduced by virtue of regulations under paragraph 2(3)(b) or 3(b) as in relation to a person whose award is reduced under section 26 or 27.

Earnings tapers

5. In section 4 of the Jobseekers Act 1995 (amount payable by way of a jobseeker's allowance), in subsection (1)(b)—
    (a) after "making" there is inserted—
"(i) deductions in respect of earnings calculated in the prescribed manner (which may include multiplying some or all earnings by a prescribed percentage), and
    (b) "earnings," (before "pension payments") is repealed.

6. (1) Section 2 of the Welfare Reform Act 2007 (amount of contributory allowance) is amended as follows.

(2) In subsection (1)(c), after "making" there is inserted—
"(i) deductions in respect of earnings calculated in the prescribed manner (which may include multiplying some or all earnings by a prescribed percentage), and

(3) At the end there is inserted—
"(6) In subsection (1)(c)(i) the reference to earnings is to be construed in accordance with sections 3, 4 and 112 of the Social Security Contributions and Benefits Act 1992."

DEFINITIONS

"relevant benefit"—para.1(1)
"sanction"—para.1(3)
"work-related requirement"—para.1(2)

GENERAL NOTE

1.176   Schedule 5 makes provision to allow the Secretary of State to prescribe details of the relationship between universal credit on the one hand and ESA and JSA on the other. At the time of writing only paras 1-3 inclusive are in force; paras 4-6 are yet to be brought into force.

Para. 2

1.177   In certain circumstances claimants may meet the conditions of entitlement to both universal credit and JSA or ESA (as contributory benefits only). Paragraph 2 enables the Secretary of State to make provision as to the amount of contributory benefit payable where a person is entitled to both a contributory benefit and universal credit. According to the Department, Memorandum from the Department for Work and Pensions, *Welfare Reform Bill, as brought from the House of Commons on 16 June 2011,* House of Lords Select Committee on Delegated Powers and Regulatory Reform (at para.166):

> "It is intended that the power will in particular be used to:
> a) specify whether, in cases where the claimant might be entitled to both universal credit and either ESA or JSA, the claimant will be paid to only universal credit, or only the contributory benefit, or to both.
> b) make provision in relation to cases where a claimant might be able to choose which benefit to claim, in the event of them being potentially entitled to both.
> c) provide for exceptions, if appropriate, from the general rule.
> d) prescribe how work-related requirements are to apply in such cases.
> e) set out, if sanctions are applicable, which benefit is to be reduced first (in a case where a claimant is receiving both), what limitations any reductions are subject to, and to provide, if appropriate, that the application of a sanction to one benefit does not increase payment of the other."

Para. 3

1.178   Paragraph 3(a) and (b) allows for regulations to provide that where a person is entitled to universal credit and has their award reduced by a sanction, and then becomes entitled to JSA or ESA, the sanction can be applied to the new JSA or ESA award. This is obviously designed to ensure that claimants cannot avoid a sanction simply because they move between universal credit and JSA or ESA. Paragraph 3(c) makes similar provision for regulations to provide that sanctions imposed on claimants entitled to JSA or ESA can be applied to a subsequent award of the other benefit.

Para. 4

1.179   This allows for regulations made under s.28 (hardship payments) to apply to a person whose universal credit award is reduced by virtue of either para.2(3)(b) or 3(b) above. Section 28 only allows for universal credit hardship payments to be made to claimants who have their universal credit award reduced under ss.26 or 27, and so para.4 allows for claimants whose awards are reduced under other provisions to also be eligible for universal credit hardship payments.

Para. 5

1.180   This amendment to s.4 of the Jobseekers Act 1995 creates a power which allows the Secretary of State to deduct earnings which have been calculated in a prescribed manner, which may include multiplying some or all of the earnings by a prescribed percentage. The intention is to make provision for the amount of benefit payable to be tapered as earnings increase and to allow for some earnings to be disregarded before the taper is applied.

Para. 6

This amends s.2 of the Welfare Reform Act 2007, and has similar effect on provision for the calculation of earnings in ESA as does para.(5) in relation to JSA.   1.181

SCHEDULE 6

MIGRATION TO UNIVERSAL CREDIT

General

1.(1) Regulations may make provision for the purposes of, or in connection with, replacing   1.182
existing benefits with universal credit.
(2) In this Schedule "existing benefit" means—
  (a) a benefit abolished under section 33(1);
  (b) any other prescribed benefit.
(3) In this Schedule "appointed day" means the day appointed for the coming into force of
section 1.

Claims before the appointed day

2. (1) The provision referred to in paragraph 1(1) includes—   1.183
  (a) provision for a claim for universal credit to be made before the appointed day for a
      period beginning on or after that day;
  (b) provision for a claim for universal credit made before the appointed day to be treated
      to any extent as a claim for an existing benefit;
  (c) provision for a claim for an existing benefit made before the appointed day to be
      treated to any extent as a claim for universal credit.
(2) The provision referred to in paragraph 1(1) includes provision, where a claim for universal credit is made (or is treated as made) before the appointed day, for an award on the claim to be made in respect of a period before the appointed day (including provision as to the conditions of entitlement for, and amount of, such an award).

Claims after the appointed day

3. (1) The provision referred to in paragraph 1(1) includes—   1.184
  (a) provision permanently or temporarily excluding the making of a claim for universal
      credit after the appointed day by—
       (i) a person to whom an existing benefit is awarded, or
       (ii) a person who would be entitled to an existing benefit on making a claim for it;
  (b) provision temporarily excluding the making of a claim for universal credit after the
      appointed day by any other person;
  (c) provision excluding entitlement to universal credit temporarily or for a particular
      period;
  (d) provision for a claim for universal credit made after the appointed day to be treated to
      any extent as a claim for an existing benefit;
  (e) provision for a claim for an existing benefit made after the appointed day to be treated
      to any extent as a claim for universal credit.
(2) The provision referred to in paragraph 1(1) includes provision, where a claim for universal credit is made (or is treated as made) after the appointed day, for an award on the claim to be made in respect of a period before the appointed day (including provision as to the conditions of entitlement for, and amount of, such an award).

Awards

4.(1) The provision referred to in paragraph 1(1) includes—   1.185
  (a) provision for terminating an award of an existing benefit;
  (b) provision for making an award of universal credit, with or without application, to a
      person whose award of existing benefit is terminated.
(2) The provision referred to in sub-paragraph (1)(b) includes—
  (a) provision imposing requirements as to the procedure to be followed, information to
      be supplied or assessments to be undergone in relation to an award by virtue of that
      sub-paragraph or an application for such an award;
  (b) provision as to the consequences of failure to comply with any such requirement;
  (c) provision as to the terms on which, and conditions subject to which, such an award is
      made, including—

      (i) provision temporarily or permanently disapplying, or otherwise modifying, conditions of entitlement to universal credit in relation to the award;

     (ii) provision temporarily or permanently disapplying, or otherwise modifying, any requirement under this Part for a person to be assessed in respect of capability for work or work-related activity;

  (d) provision as to the amount of such an award;

  (e) provision that fulfilment of any condition relevant to entitlement to an award of an existing benefit, or relevant to the amount of such an award, is to be treated as fulfilment of an equivalent condition in relation to universal credit.

(3) Provision under sub-paragraph (2)(d) may secure that where an award of universal credit is made by virtue of sub-paragraph (1)(b)—

  (a) the amount of the award is not less than the amount to which the person would have been entitled under the terminated award, or is not less than that amount by more than a prescribed amount;

  (b) if the person to whom it is made ceases to be entitled to universal credit for not more than a prescribed period, the gap in entitlement is disregarded in calculating the amount of any new award of universal credit.

Work-related requirements and sanctions

1.186

5.(1) The provision referred to in paragraph 1(1) includes—

  (a) provision relating to the application of work-related requirements for relevant benefits;

  (b) provision relating to the application of sanctions.

(2) The provision referred to in sub-paragraph (1)(a) includes—

  (a) provision that a claimant commitment for a relevant benefit is to be treated as a claimant commitment for universal credit;

  (b) provision that a work-related requirement for a relevant benefit is treated as a work-related requirement for universal credit;

  (c) provision for anything done which is relevant to compliance with a work-related requirement for a relevant benefit to be treated as done for the purposes of compliance with a work-related requirement for universal credit;

  (d) provision temporarily disapplying any provision of this Part in relation to work-related requirements for universal credit.

(3) The provision referred to in sub-paragraph (1)(b) includes—

  (a) provision for a sanction relevant to an award of a relevant benefit to be applied to an award of universal credit;

  (b) provision for anything done which is relevant to the application of a sanction for a relevant benefit to be treated as done for the purposes of the application of a sanction for universal credit;

  (c) provision temporarily disapplying any provision of this Part in relation to the application of sanctions.

(4) In this paragraph—

"relevant benefit" means—

  (a) jobseeker's allowance,

  (b) employment and support allowance, and

  (c) income support;

"work-related requirement" means—

  (a) for universal credit, a work-related requirement within the meaning of this Part;

  (b) for jobseeker's allowance, a requirement imposed—

      (i) by virtue of regulations under section 8 or 17A of the Jobseekers Act 1995,

     (ii) by a jobseeker's direction (within the meaning of section 19A of that Act),

    (iii) by virtue of regulations under section 2A, 2AA or 2D of the Social Security Administration Act 1992, or

    (iv) by a direction under section 2F of that Act;

  (c) for employment and support allowance, a requirement imposed—

      (i) by virtue of regulations under section 8, 9, 11, 12 or 13 of the Welfare Reform Act 2007,

     (ii) by a direction under section 15 of that Act,

    (iii) by virtue of regulations under section 2A, 2AA or 2D of the Social Security Administration Act 1992, or

    (iv) by a direction under section 2F of that Act;

  (d) for income support, a requirement imposed—

      (i) by virtue of regulations under section 2A, 2AA or 2D of the Social Security Administration Act 1992, or

(ii) by a direction under section 2F of that Act;
"sanction" means a reduction of benefit under—
  (a) section 26 or 27 above,
  (b) section 19, 19A or 19B of the Jobseekers Act 1995,
  (c) section 11, 12 or 13 of the Welfare Reform Act 2007, or
  (d) section 2A, 2AA or 2D of the Social Security Administration Act 1992.

Tax credits

6. In relation to the replacement of working tax credit and child tax credit with universal credit, the provision referred to in paragraph 1(1) includes—   **1.187**
  (a) provision modifying the application of the Tax Credits Act 2002 (or of any provision made under it);
  (b) provision for the purposes of recovery of overpayments of working tax credit or child tax credit (including in particular provision for treating overpayments of working tax credit or child tax credit as if they were overpayments of universal credit).

Supplementary

7. Regulations under paragraph 1(1) may secure the result that any gap in entitlement to an existing benefit (or what would, but for the provisions of this Part, be a gap in entitlement to an existing benefit) is to be disregarded for the purposes of provision under such regulations.   **1.188**

DEFINITIONS

"appointed day"—see para.1(3).
"existing benefit"—see para.1(2).
"relevant benefit"—see para.5(4).
"sanction"—*ibid.*
"work-related requirement"—*ibid.*

GENERAL NOTE

Schedule 6 (which at the time of writing is partly in force and partly not yet in force) contains regulation-making powers to make provision in connection with replacing the existing means-tested benefits system with universal credit, and more particularly with the "migration" of claimants from one benefit to the other. Regulations made under this Schedule were subject to the affirmative resolution procedure where the power in para.1(1) was used in a way described in paras.4, 5 or 6 for the first time.   **1.189**

Para.1
The principal such regulations are the Transitional Provisions Regulations 2014.   **1.190**

Para.2
Regulations may specify when a claim can be treated as a claim for an existing benefit and when a claim can be treated as a claim for universal credit. For example, regulations may provide that a claim for an existing benefit made before the day that universal credit comes into effect, but for a period beginning after universal credit is introduced, (i.e. people making advance claims), can be treated as a claim for universal credit.   **1.191**

Para.3
Regulations may provide that after the appointed day (i.e. the day universal credit is introduced), existing benefits cannot be claimed (see Transitional Provisions Regulations 2014 regs 5 and 6). Regulations can also provide for a claim to universal credit to be treated as a claim for existing benefit. This might be used where e.g. a claimant's benefit is backdated to a period before universal credit was introduced. Regulations may also provide that these cases may be awarded universal credit on terms, which match wholly or partly, the existing benefit.   **1.192**

Para. 4

1.193   Regulations will be able to make provision for the "migration" of existing claimants onto universal credit. Such migration may be voluntary or mandatory. Regulations can prescribe the timing, conditions, kind and amount of any such entitlement to universal credit which was previously an award for an existing benefit. As regards para.4(1), see further the Transitional Provisions Regulations 2014.

Para. 5

1.194   This makes provision for the continuity of both work-related requirements and sanctions; see further especially regs 30–34 of the Transitional Provisions Regulations 2014 as regards sanctions.

Para. 6

1.195   This provides that the Secretary of State may, through regulations, modify any provision of the Tax Credits Act 2002 (or regulations) as necessary for the purposes of transferring people from working tax credit and child tax credit to universal credit. This power may be used to align certain tax credit rules more closely with universal credit to facilitate the transition process (para.(a)). Paragraph 6 also makes it clear that for overpayments of tax credits could, through the transitional regulations, be treated as overpayments of universal credit (para.(b)). See further regs 11-12A of the Transitional Provisions Regulations 2014.

Welfare Reform and Work Act 2016

(2016 c.7)

Sections Reproduced

Welfare benefits

An Act to make provision about reports on progress towards full employment and the apprenticeships target; to make provision about reports on the effect of certain support for troubled families; to make provision about life chances; to make provision about the benefit cap; to make provision about social security and tax credits; to make provision for loans for mortgage interest and other liabilities; and to make provision about social housing rents.
[March 16, 2016]

Sections 8-21 of, and Schedule 1 to, this Act are of potential relevance to entitle-   **1.196.1**
ment to social security benefits and tax credits. They have been reproduced below
to the extent that they are in force, do not make amendments that have been reproduced in the text of other legislation in this work, and have not been reproduced in
other volumes.

Sections 1-7 concern social policy, section 22 governs an aspect of social security
administration that cannot give rise to an appeal and sections 23-33 make provision
about social housing rents. They are therefore beyond the scope of this work,

Welfare benefits

Benefit cap

8.—(1)-(7) *[Omitted]*   **1.197**
(8) Regulations made by the Secretary of State may make such transitional or transitory provision or savings as the Secretary of State considers
necessary or expedient in connection with the coming into force of subsections (1) to (6).

(9) Regulations under subsection (8) may in particular—

(a) provide for section 96 to have effect as if the amendments made by
   subsections (2) to (5) and (7) had not been made, in relation to such
   persons or descriptions of persons as are specified in the regulations
   or generally, until a time or times specified in a notice issued by the
   Secretary of State;

(b) provide for the Secretary of State to issue notices under paragraph
   (a) specifying different times for different persons or descriptions of
   person;

(c) make provision about the issuing of notices under paragraph (a),
   including provision for the Secretary of State to issue notices to
   authorities administering housing benefit that have effect in relation
   to persons specified, or persons of a description specified, in the
   notices.

(10) Section 176 of the Social Security Administration Act 1992 (consultation with representative organisations) does not apply in relation to
regulations under subsection (8).

(11) Regulations under subsection (8) must be made by statutory instrument.

(12) A statutory instrument containing regulations under subsection (8)
is subject to annulment in pursuance of a resolution of either House of
Parliament.

GENERAL NOTE

Section 8 was brought into force on March 16, 2016 for the purpose of making   **1.198**
regulations (s.36(3)(a)), and on November 7, 2016 for all purposes (SI 2016/910,
reg.2(1)). It extends to England, Wales and Scotland (s.35(3)). Subss.(1)-(6)
amend WRA 2012 ss.96 and 97 (above) and subs.(7) revokes Pensions Act 2014
Sch.12 para.52. The regulation-making powers conferred by subs.(8)-(12) have
been exercised to make the Benefit Cap (Housing Benefit and Universal Credit)
(Amendment) Regulations 2016 (SI 2016/909).

Changes to child element of universal credit

1.199   **14.**—(1)-(5) *[Omitted]*

(6) The Secretary of State may by regulations make such transitional or transitory provision or savings as the Secretary of State considers necessary or expedient in connection with the coming into force of this section.

(7) Regulations under subsection (6) must be made by statutory instrument.

(8) A statutory instrument containing regulations under subsection (6) is subject to annulment in pursuance of a resolution of either House of Parliament.

General Note

1.200   Subss.(1)-(5), which amend Welfare Reform Act 2012 s.10 and Universal Credit Regulations, reg.24 came into force on April 6, 2017 (see SI 2017/111 reg.4). The other sub-sections came into force on February 8, 2017 (see SI 2017/111 reg.2(a)). The section as a whole extends to England and Wales and Scotland (s.35(3)(c)).

The regulation-making powers in subss.(6)-(8) have been used to make the Social Security (Restrictions on Amounts for Children and Qualifying Young Persons) Amendment Regulations 2017 (SI 2017/376) which amend Universal Credit Regulations, regs 2 and 24 and introduce new regs 24A and 24B and a new Sch.12 into those Regulations: see the commentary to regs 24-24B below.

Loans for mortgage interest etc

Loans for mortgage interest etc

1.201   **18.**—(1) The Secretary of State may by regulations provide for loans to be made in respect of a person's liability to make owner-occupier payments in respect of accommodation occupied by the person as the person's home.

(2) The regulations may make provision about eligibility to receive a loan under the regulations.

(3) Regulations under subsection (2) may in particular require that a person—

(a) is entitled to receive income support, income-based jobseeker's allowance, income-related employment and support allowance, state pension credit or universal credit;

(b) has received such a benefit for a period prescribed by the regulations.

(4) The regulations may make provision about the liabilities in respect of which a loan under the regulations may be made.

(5) Regulations under subsection (4) may in particular provide that a loan under the regulations may only be made if, and to the extent that, a person's liability to make owner-occupier payments was incurred for purposes prescribed by the regulations.

(6) Regulations under subsection (4) may in particular make provision about—

(a) determining or calculating the amount of a person's liabilities;

(b) the maximum amount of a person's liabilities in respect of which a loan under the regulations may be made.

(7) The regulations may—

(a) make provision about determining or calculating the amount that may be paid by way of loan under the regulations;

(b) require that a loan under the regulations be secured by a mortgage of or charge over a legal or beneficial interest in land or, in Scotland, by a heritable security.

(8) The regulations may define "owner-occupier payment".

(9) Regulations under this section may make different provision for different purposes.

(10) Regulations under this section must be made by statutory instrument.

(11) A statutory instrument containing regulations under this section is subject to annulment in pursuance of a resolution of either House of Parliament.

GENERAL NOTE

This section (and ss.19 & 21 below) came into force on April 3, 2017 (SI 2017/111 reg.3(d)-(f)). Section 20, which makes consequential amendments to, and repeals of, primary legislation has yet to be brought into force and is not reproduced. All four sections extend to England and Wales and Scotland (s.35(3)(g)).   1.202

Taken together, ss.18, 19 and 21 confer powers on the Secretary of State to make regulations which replace the housing costs element for owner-occupiers under Universal Credit Regulations, reg.25(2) and Sch.5 (and the equivalent payments under IS Regulations, Sch.3; Jobseeker's Allowance Regulations 1996, Sch.2; SPC Regulations, Sch.2; and ESA Regulations, Sch.6) with repayable loans.

However, by the final date for the inclusion of legislation in this edition (and also at the time of going to press) no regulations had been made and so the legislation listed in the previous paragraph remains in force. It is understood that the Department intends to begin replacing owner-occupier payments with loans from April 2018. The existence of the powers to make transitional provision in s.21 suggest that the new rules may be piloted and then "rolled out" rather than introduced for all claimants and in all areas at the same time.

Section 18: further provision

19.—(1) This section makes further provision about regulations under section 18.   1.203

(2) The regulations may make provision about—

(a) circumstances in which a person is to be treated as liable or not liable to make owner-occupier payments;

(b) circumstances in which a person is to be treated as occupying or not occupying particular accommodation as a home.

(3) The regulations may include—

(a) provision about applying for a loan;

(b) provision requiring a person to satisfy requirements prescribed by the regulations before a loan may be made under the regulations, including requirements about receiving financial advice;

(c) provision about entering into an agreement (which may contain such terms and conditions as the Secretary of State thinks fit, subject to what may be provided in the regulations);

(d) provision about the time when, and manner in which, a loan must be repaid;

(e) provision about other terms upon which a loan is made;

(f) provision about the payment of interest, including provision prescribing or providing for   the determination of the rate of interest;

(g) provision enabling administrative costs to be charged;

(h) provision about adding administrative costs to the amount of a loan;

(i) provision about accepting substituted security.

(4) The regulations may make provision—

(a) requiring that, in circumstances prescribed by the regulations, money lent in respect of a person's liability to make owner-occupier payments—

(i) is paid directly to the qualifying lender;

(ii) is applied by the qualifying lender towards discharging the person's liability to make owner-occupier payments;

(b) for the costs of administering the making of payments to qualifying lenders to be defrayed, in whole or in part, at the expense of the qualifying lenders, whether by requiring them to pay fees prescribed by the regulations, by deducting and retaining such part as may be prescribed by the regulations of the amounts that would otherwise be paid to them or otherwise;

(c) for requiring a qualifying lender, in a case where by virtue of paragraph (b) the amount paid to the lender is less than it would otherwise have been, to credit against the liability in relation to which the amount is paid the amount of the difference (in addition to the payment actually made);

(d) for enabling a body which, or person who, would otherwise be a qualifying lender to elect not to be regarded as a qualifying lender for the purposes of this section (other than this paragraph);

(e) for the recovery from any body or person—

(i) of any sums paid to that body or person by way of payment under the regulations that ought not to have been so paid;

(ii) of any fees or other sums due from that body or person by virtue of paragraph (b);

(f) for cases where the same person is liable to make owner-occupier payments under more than one agreement to make such payments.

(5) The regulations may provide for the Secretary of State to make arrangements with another person for the exercise of functions under the regulations.

(6) The regulations may include—

(a) provision requiring information and documents to be provided;

(b) provision authorising the disclosure of information.

(7) The bodies and persons who are "qualifying lenders" for the purposes of this section are—

(a) a deposit taker;

(b) an insurer;

(c) a county council, a county borough council, a district council, a London Borough Council, the Common Council of the City of London or the Council of the Isles of Scilly;

(d) a council constituted under section 2 of the Local Government etc. (Scotland) Act 1994;

(e) a new town corporation;

(f) other bodies or persons prescribed by regulations under section 18.

(8) In this section—

"deposit taker" means—

(a) a person who has permission under Part 4A of the Financial Services and Markets Act 2000 to accept deposits, or

(b) an EEA firm of the kind mentioned in paragraph 5(b) of Schedule 3 to that Act which has permission under paragraph 15 of that

Schedule (as a result of qualifying for authorisation under paragraph 12 of that Schedule) to accept deposits;

"insurer" means—

(a) a person who has permission under Part 4A of the Financial Services and Markets Act 2000 to effect and carry out contracts of insurance, or

(b) an EEA firm of the kind mentioned in paragraph 5(d) of Schedule 3 to that Act which has permission under paragraph 15 of that Schedule (as a result of qualifying for authorisation under paragraph 12 of that Schedule) to effect and carry out contracts of insurance.

(9) The definitions of "deposit taker" and 'insurer" in this section must be read with—

(a) section 22 of the Financial Services and Markets Act 2000;

(b) any relevant order under that section;

(c) Schedule 2 to that Act.

GENERAL NOTE

See the General note to s.18 above.   **1.204**

Transitional provision

21.—(1) Regulations made by the Secretary of State may make such tran-   **1.205**
sitional or transitory provision or savings as the Secretary of State considers necessary or expedient in connection with the coming into force of sections 18 to 20.

(2) The regulations may include provision for temporarily excluding the making of a loan under regulations under section 18 after the coming into force of sections 18 to 20.

(3) Regulations under subsection (2) may in particular—

(a) provide for a temporary exclusion to continue until a time or times specified in a notice issued by the Secretary of State;

(b) enable the Secretary of State to issue notices under paragraph (a) specifying different times for different persons or descriptions of person.

(4) The regulations may include provision for enabling assistance with payments in respect of accommodation occupied as a home to be given by means of a qualifying benefit after the coming into force of sections 18 to 20 (including where the making of loans is temporarily excluded).

(5) Regulations under subsection (4) may in particular—

(a) provide for legislation that has been repealed or revoked to be treated as having effect;

(b) provide for assistance by means of a qualifying benefit to continue until a time or times specified in a notice issued by the Secretary of State;

(c) enable the Secretary of State to issue notices under paragraph (b) specifying different times for different persons or descriptions of person.

(6) In this section "qualifying benefit" means income support, income-based jobseeker's allowance, income-related employment and support allowance, state pension credit or universal credit.

(7) Regulations under this section may make different provision for different areas, cases or purposes.

(8) Regulations under this section must be made by statutory instrument.

(9) A statutory instrument containing regulations under this section is subject to annulment in pursuance of a resolution of either House of Parliament.

GENERAL NOTE

1.206   See the General note to s.18 above.

Final

Power to make consequential provision

1.207   34.—(1) The Secretary of State may by regulations make such amendments and revocations of subordinate legislation (whenever made) as appear to the Secretary of State to be necessary or expedient in consequence of any provision of this Act.

(2) In this section "subordinate legislation" has the same meaning as in the Interpretation Act 1978.

(3) Regulations under this section must be made by statutory instrument.

(4) A statutory instrument containing regulations under this section is subject to annulment in pursuance of a resolution of either House of Parliament.

PART III

UNIVERSAL CREDIT: REGULATIONS

The Universal Credit Regulations 2013

(SI 2013/376)

Made on February 25, 2013 by the Secretary of State for Work and Pensions in exercise of the powers conferred by sections 2(2), 4(2), (3), (5), (6) and (7), 5, 6(1)(a) and (3), 7(2) and (3), 8(3), 9(2) and (3), 10(2) to (5), 11(3) to (5), 12(1), (3) and (4), 14(5), 15(2), 17(3) and (4), 18(3) and (5), 19(2)(d), (3) and (4), 20(1), 22(2), 24(1), (5) and (6), 25, 26(2)(a), (6) and (8), 27(4), (5), (9), 28, 32(1), 37(3) to (7), 39(3)(a), 40, 96 and 97 of, and paragraphs 1, 4, 5 and 7 of Schedule 1 and paragraphs 2 and 3 of Schedule 5 to, the Welfare Reform Act 2012; a draft having been laid before Parliament in accordance with section 43(3) of the Welfare Reform Act 2012 and approved by a resolution of each House of Parliament; and without the instrument having been referred to the Social Security Advisory Committee because it contains only regulations made by virtue of or consequential on Part 1 and sections 96 and 97 of, and Schedules 1 and 5 to, the Welfare Reform Act 2012 and is made before the end of the period of 6 months beginning with the coming into force of those provisions.

2.1

[In force April 2013 but see Pt IV]

ARRANGEMENT OF REGULATIONS

PART 1

INTRODUCTION

2.2

PART 2

ENTITLEMENT

PART 3

AWARDS

PART 4

ELEMENTS OF AN AWARD

PART 5

CAPABILITY FOR WORK OR WORK-RELATED ACTIVITY

PART 6

CALCULATION OF CAPITAL AND INCOME

CHAPTER 1

CAPITAL

PART 7

THE BENEFIT CAP

PART 8

CLAIMANT RESPONSIBILITIES

CHAPTER 1

WORK-RELATED REQUIREMENTS

CHAPTER 2

SANCTIONS

CHAPTER 3

HARDSHIP

SCHEDULES

PART 1

INTRODUCTION

Citation and commencement

2.4   **1.**—These Regulations may be cited as the Universal Credit Regulations 2013 and come into force on 29th April 2013.

GENERAL NOTE

2.5   Although the Regulations come into force on April 29, 2013, they do not apply to all claimants, or in all parts of the country. See further the Universal Credit (Transitional Provisions) Regulations 2014 and the commencement orders in Pt IV of this Volume.

Interpretation

2.6   **2.**—In these Regulations—
"the Act" means the Welfare Reform Act 2012;
[8 ...]
[2 "adopter" has the meaning in regulation 89(3)(a);]
"attendance allowance" means—
(a) an attendance allowance under section 64 of the Contributions and Benefits Act;
(b) an increase of disablement pension under section 104 or 105 of that Act (increases where constant attendance needed and for exceptionally severe disablement);
(c) [3 ...]
(d) a payment by virtue of article 14, 15, 16, 43 or 44 of the Personal Injuries (Civilians) Scheme 1983 or any analogous payment;
(e) any payment based on the need for attendance which is paid as an addition to a war disablement pension;
[1(f) armed forces independence payment under the Armed Forces and Reserve Forces (Compensation Scheme) Order 2011;]
"bereavement allowance" means an allowance under section 39B of the Contributions and Benefits Act;
[6 "blind" means certified as severely sight impaired or blind by a consultant ophthalmologist;]
"care leaver" has the meaning in regulation 8;
"carer's allowance" means a carer's allowance under section 70 of the Contributions and Benefits Act;
"carer element" has the meaning in regulation 29;
"childcare costs element" has the meaning in regulation 31;
"child element" has the meaning in regulation 24;
"close relative", in relation to a person, means—
(a) a parent, parent-in-law, son, son-in-law, daughter, daughter-in-law, step-parent, step-son, step-daughter, brother or sister; and
(b) if any of the above is a member of a couple, the other member of the couple;
"confinement" has the meaning in regulation 8;

"Contributions and Benefits Act" means the Social Security Contributions and Benefits Act 1992;

"course of advanced education" has the meaning in regulation 12;

"disability living allowance" means an allowance under section 71 of the Contributions and Benefits Act;

"earned income" has the meaning in Chapter 2 of Part 6;

"EEA Regulations" means the Immigration (European Economic Area) Regulations 2006;

"employment and support allowance" means an allowance under Part 1 of the Welfare Reform Act 2007 as amended by Schedule 3 and Part 1 of Schedule 14 to the Welfare Reform Act 2012 (removing references to an income-related allowance);

[4 "enactment" includes an enactment comprised in, or an instrument made under, an Act of the Scottish Parliament or the National Assembly of Wales;]

"ESA Regulations" means the Employment and Support Allowance Regulations 2013;

"expected number of hours per week" has the meaning in regulation 88;

"foster parent" means—

(a) in relation to England, a person with whom a child is placed under the Fostering Services Regulations 2011;

(b) in relation to Wales, a person with whom a child is placed under the Fostering Services (Wales) Regulations 2003;

(c) in relation to Scotland, a foster carer or kinship carer with whom a child is placed under the Looked After Children (Scotland) Regulations 2009;

"grant" has the meaning in regulation 68;

"health care professional" means (except in regulation 98)—

(a) a registered medical practitioner;

(b) a registered nurse; or

(c) an occupational therapist or physiotherapist registered with a regulatory body established by Order in Council under section 60 of the Health Act 1999;

"housing costs element" has the meaning in regulation 25;

"individual threshold" has the meaning in regulation 90(2);

"industrial injuries benefit" means a benefit under Part 5 of the Contributions and Benefits Act;

"ITEPA" means the Income Tax (Earnings and Pensions) Act 2003;

"jobseeker's allowance" means an allowance under the Jobseekers Act 1995 as amended by Part 1 of Schedule 14 to the Act (removing references to an income-based allowance);

"local authority" means—

(a) in relation to England, a county council, a district council, a parish council, a London borough council, the Common Council of the City of London or the Council of the Isles of Scilly;

(b) in relation to Wales, a county council, a county borough council or a community council;

(c) in relation to Scotland, a council constituted under section 2 of the Local Government etc. (Scotland) Act 1994;

[12 "LCWRA element" has the meaning in regulation 27;]

"looked after by a local authority" in relation to a child or young person means a child or young person who is looked after by a local authority within the meaning of section 22 of the Children Act 1989 [[10]], section 17(6) of the Children (Scotland) Act 1995 or section 74 of the Social Services and Well-being (Wales) Act 2014];

"maternity allowance" means a maternity allowance under section 35 [[5] or 35B] of the Contributions and Benefits Act;

"Medical Evidence Regulations" means the Social Security (Medical Evidence) Regulations 1976;

[[9] "monthly earnings" has the meaning in regulation 90(6);]

"national insurance contribution" means a contribution under Part 1 of the Contributions and Benefits Act;

[[11] "National Minimum Wage Regulations" means the National Minimum Wage Regulations 2015;]

"[[8] . . .] statutory paternity pay" means [[8] . . .] statutory paternity pay under Part 12ZA of the Contributions and Benefits Act;

"paid work" means work done for payment or in expectation of payment and does not include being engaged by a charitable or voluntary organisation, or as a volunteer, in circumstances in which the payment received by or due to be paid to the person is in respect of expenses;

"partner" means (except in regulation 77) the other member of a couple;

"personal independence payment" means an allowance under Part 4 of the Welfare Reform Act 2012;

"prisoner" means—

(a) a person who is detained in custody pending trial or sentence upon conviction or under a sentence imposed by a court; or

(b) is on temporary release in accordance with the provisions of the Prison Act 1952 or the Prisons (Scotland) Act 1989,

other than a person who is detained in hospital under the provisions of the Mental Health Act 1983 or, in Scotland, under the provisions of the Mental Health (Care and Treatment) (Scotland) Act 2003 or the Criminal Procedure (Scotland) Act 1995;

"qualifying young person" has the meaning in regulation 5;

"redundancy" has the meaning in section 139(1) of the Employment Rights Act 1996;

[[6] . . .]

"regular and substantial caring responsibilities for a severely disabled person" has the meaning in regulation 30;

"relevant childcare" has the meaning in regulation 35;

"responsible for a child or qualifying young person" has the meaning in regulation 4;

"statutory adoption pay" means a payment under Part 12ZB of the Contributions Benefits Act;

"statutory maternity pay" means a payment under Part 12 of the Contributions and Benefits Act;

[[7] "statutory shared parental pay" means statutory shared parental pay payable in accordance with Part 12ZC of the Contributions and Benefits Act;]

"statutory sick pay" means a payment under Part 11 of the Contributions and Benefits Act;

[[13] "step-parent", in relation to a child or qualifying young person ("A"), means a person who is not A's parent but—

(a) is a member of a couple, the other member of which is a parent of A, where both are responsible for A; or

(b) was previously a member of a couple, the other member of which was a parent of A, where immediately prior to ceasing to be a member of that couple the person was, and has since continued to be, responsible for A.]

"student loan" has the meaning in regulation 68;

"terminally ill" means suffering from a progressive disease where death in consequence of that disease can reasonably be expected within 6 months;

"total outstanding reduction period" has the meaning in regulation 101(5);

"trade dispute" has the meaning in section 244 of the Trade Union and Labour Relations (Consolidation) Act 1992;

"unearned income" has the meaning in Chapter 3 of Part 6;

"war disablement pension" means any retired pay, pension or allowance payable in respect of disablement under an instrument specified in section 639(2) of ITEPA;

[¹ . . .]

"widowed mother's allowance" means an allowance under section 37 of the Contributions and Benefits Act;

"widowed parent's allowance" means an allowance under section 39A of the Contributions and Benefits Act;

"widow's pension" means a pension under section 39 of the Contributions and Benefits Act.

AMENDMENTS

1. Armed Forces and Reserve Forces Compensation Scheme (Consequential Provisions: Subordinate Legislation) Order 2013 (SI 2013/591) art.7 and Sch., para.54 (April 8, 2013).

2. Universal Credit (Miscellaneous Amendments) Regulations 2013 (SI 2013/803) reg.2(1) and (2) (April 29, 2013).

3. Social Security (Miscellaneous Amendments) (No.2) Regulations 2013 (SI 2013/1508) reg.3(1) and (2) (October 29, 2013).

4. Universal Credit and Miscellaneous Amendments Regulations 2014 (SI 2014/597) reg.2(1) and (2) (April 28, 2014).

5. Social Security (Maternity Allowance) (Miscellaneous Amendments) Regulations 2014 (SI 2014/884) reg.6(1) (May 18, 2014).

6. Universal Credit and Miscellaneous Amendments (No.2) Regulations 2014 (SI 2014/2888) reg.3(1)(a) (Assessment periods beginning on or after November 26, 2014).

7. Shared Parental Leave and Statutory Shared Parental Pay (Consequential Amendments to Subordinate Legislation) Order 2014 (SI 2014/3255) art.28(1) and (2)(c) (December 31, 2014).

8. Shared Parental Leave and Statutory Shared Parental Pay (Consequential Amendments to Subordinate Legislation) Order 2014 (SI 2014/3255) art.28(1) and (2)(a) and (b) (April 5, 2015). The amendments are subject to the transitional provision in art.35 (see below).

9. Universal Credit and Miscellaneous Amendments Regulations 2015 (SI 2015/1754) reg.2 (Assessment periods beginning on or after November 4, 2015).

10. Universal Credit (Care Leavers and Looked After Children) Amendment Regulations 2016 (SI 2016/543) reg.2(1) and (2) (May 26, 2016).

11. Social Security (Jobseeker's Allowance, Employment and Support Allowance and Universal Credit) (Amendment) Regulations 2016 (SI 2016/678) reg.5(1) and (2) (July 25, 2016).

12. Employment and Support Allowance and Universal Credit (Miscellaneous Amendments and Transitional and Savings Provisions) Regulations 2017 (SI 2017/204) reg. 4(1) and (2) (April 3, 2017).

13. Social Security (Restrictions on Amounts for Children and Qualifying Young Persons) Amendment Regulations 2017 (SI 2017/376) reg.2(1) and (2) (April 6, 2017).

DEFINITIONS

"child"—see WRA 2012 s.40.
"couple"—see WRA 2012 ss.39 and 40.
"disabled"—see WRA 2012 s.40.
"qualifying young person"—see WRA 2012 ss.40 and 10(5).
"work"—see WRA 2012 s.40.

GENERAL NOTE

2.7   Most of these definitions are either self-explanatory, or references to definitions in other regulations, or discussed in the commentary to the regulations where the defined terms are used. A number are similar to terms defined for the purposes of IS, JSA and ESA: see further the commentary to reg.2(1) of the ESA Regulations 2008 in Vol.I of this series and to reg.2(1) of the IS Regulations and reg.1(2) of the JSA Regulations 1996 in Vol.II.

The Benefit Unit

Couples

2.8   **3.**—(1) This regulation makes provision in relation to couples, including cases where both members of a couple may be entitled to universal credit jointly without each of them meeting all the basic conditions referred to in section 4 of the Act (see paragraph (2)) and cases where a person whose partner does not meet all the basic conditions [¹ or is otherwise excluded from entitlement to universal credit] may make a claim as a single person (see paragraph (3)).

(2) A couple may be entitled to universal credit as joint claimants where—
(a) one member does not meet the basic condition in section 4(1)
    (b) (under the qualifying age for state pension credit) if the other member does meet that condition; or
(b) one member does not meet the basic condition in section 4(1)(d) (not receiving education) and is not excepted from that condition if the other member does meet that condition or is excepted from it.

(3) A person who is a member of a couple may make a claim as a single person if the other member of the couple—
(a) does not meet the basic condition in section 4(1)(a) (at least 18 years old) and is not a person in respect of whom the minimum age specified in regulation 8 applies;
(b) does not meet the basic condition in section 4(1)(c) (in Great Britain);
(c) is a prisoner; [¹ . . .]
(d) is a person other than a prisoner in respect of whom entitlement does not arise by virtue of regulation 19 (restrictions on entitlement) [; or
(e) is a person to whom section 115 of the Immigration and Asylum Act 1999 (exclusion from benefits) applies,]
and regulations 18 (capital limit), 36 (amount of elements) and 22 (deduction of income and work allowance) provide for the calculation of the award in such cases.

(4) Where two people are parties to a polygamous marriage, the fact that they are husband and wife is to be disregarded if—

(a) one of them is a party to an earlier marriage that still subsists; and

(b) the other party to that earlier marriage is living in the same household,

and, accordingly, the person who is not a party to the earlier marriage may make a claim for universal credit as a single person.

(5) In paragraph (4) "polygamous marriage" means a marriage during which a party to it is married to more than one person and which took place under the laws of a country which permits polygamy.

(6) Where the claimant is a member of a couple, and the other member is temporarily absent from the claimant's household, they cease to be treated as a couple if that absence is expected to exceed, or does exceed, 6 months.

DEFINITIONS

"claim"—see WRA 2012 s.40.
"claimant"—*ibid.*
"prisoner"—see reg.2.
"single person"—see WRA 2012 ss.40 and 1(2)(a).
"couple"—see WRA 2012 ss.39 and 40.

AMENDMENT

1. Universal Credit (Consequential, Supplementary, Incidental and Miscellaneous Provisions) Regulations 2013 (SI 2013/630) reg.8(1) and (2) (April 29, 2013).

GENERAL NOTE

This regulation is the first of four under the sub-heading, "The Benefit Unit". 2.9 That phrase is used extensively in departmental guidance (e.g., Chapter E2 of ADM) but is not defined anywhere in WRA 2012 or these Regulations. The Department intends the phrase to mean all the people in a given household who may, or must, be included in a claim for universal credit. That is consistent with these Regulations because identifying those people is also the subject-matter of regs 3–5 inclusive, which appear under the sub-heading.

It is not generally possible for a person who is a member of a couple to claim, or be awarded, universal credit as a single person. By s.2(1) WRA 2012, members of a couple must claim jointly and by s.1(2) any award of benefit is made jointly to both members of the couple. Further, under s.3(2)(a), the basic conditions of entitlement must be met by both members of the couple and, by ss.3(2)(b) and 5(2), whether or not they satisfy the financial conditions is assessed by reference to their combined income and capital.

It is therefore important for claimants to know whether or not they are members of a couple. The word is defined by s.39(1) and (2) WRA 2012 in terms which follow the standard definition for income-related benefits (e.g., in s.137 SSCBA 1992). It covers:

- two people who are married to each other (whether they are of different sexes or the same sex), or are civil partners of each other, and are members of the same household; and

- two people who are not married to, or civil partners of, each other but are living together as a married couple

see further the commentary to reg.2(1) of the IS Regulations in Vol.II. Note also the commentary to para.(6) below as regards temporary absence.

Para. (2)

2.10   Under s.4(2) WRA 2012, the Secretary of State has a general power to make regulations which provide for exceptions to the requirement to meet any of the basic conditions for universal credit. In the case of joint claimants, that power can be used to make an exception for one or both of them. Similarly, WRA 2012 Sch.1, para.1 empowers the Secretary of State to make regulations providing for circumstances in which joint claimants may be entitled to universal credit without each of them meeting all the basic conditions referred to in s.4. Those powers have been exercised to make para.(2) (among other regulations).

Under s.4(1)(b) it is a basic condition for universal credit that a person should not have reached the qualifying age for SPC (as defined in s.4(4) and s.1(6) SPCA 2002). However, under para.2(a) a couple may be jointly entitled to universal credit if one member is over that age, as long as the other member is under it. In those circumstances, the couple may be better off if the older member claims SPC. That will depend on a number of circumstances, the most important of which are likely to be whether either member has housing costs or is responsible for a child or qualifying young person. The universal credit rules include a 63% taper for earned income and, in some cases, a "work allowance" (see reg.22) which may well be more generous than the equivalent rules for SPC. However, for universal credit, owner occupiers who have earned income get a higher work allowance but do not get any amount for housing costs as part of universal credit (see para.4 of Sch.5), whereas, under SPC housing costs are paid. A couple where one member is over SPC age, and the other is not, should therefore seek advice about which benefit to claim.

Under s.4(1)(d), it is a basic condition for universal credit that a person should not be "receiving education". For the definition of that phrase, see regs 12 and 13. Note also that by s.4(2) and reg.14 some people are exempt from the condition imposed by s.4(1)(b). The effect of para.(2)(b) is that a couple may be jointly entitled to universal credit even though one member is receiving education (and does not fall within reg.14) as long as the other member is not receiving education (or does fall within reg.14).

Note that couples who fall within para.(2) must still claim universal credit jointly. The exceptions are from the requirement that both should meet the basic conditions, not the requirement for a joint claim.

Para. (3)

2.11   By contrast, a member of a couple who falls within para.(3) may claim universal credit as a single person.

The paragraph is made under s.3(2) WRA 2012 which empowers the Secretary of State to make regulations that "specify circumstances in which a member of a couple may make a claim as a single person". There is no express power to make regulations which disapply the requirement in s.1(2) that universal credit must be awarded jointly where the claimants are members of a couple. However, it is implicit that a member of a couple who may lawfully *claim* universal credit as a single person may also lawfully be *awarded* benefit in that capacity.

Under para.(3) a member of a couple may claim universal credit as a single person if the other member:

- is aged less than 18 (and is not a person who is entitled to claim universal credit from the age of 16 under reg.8): para.(3)(a);

- is not in Great Britain for the purposes of s.4(1)(c) WRA 2012 (see reg.9): para.(3)(b);

- is a prisoner (as defined in reg.2): para.(3)(c).

  (Note that, under reg.19(2), certain prisoners retain entitlement to the housing costs element of universal credit during the first six months of their sentence. However, para.(3)(c) applies whenever the other member of the couple is a prisoner. There is no additional requirement, as there is under para.(3)(d)—which also covers people who fall within reg.19—that the other member of the couple should be excluded from entitlement by that regulation. The implication is that the member of the couple who is not in prison can immediately make a claim as a single person.)

- is a member of a religious order or serving a sentence of imprisonment detained in hospital and excluded from entitlement to universal credit by reg.19: para.(3)(d); or

- is a person subject to immigration control who is excluded from entitlement to benefit under s.115 Immigration and Asylum Act 1999 (see in particular s.115(3) and (9) and the commentary to the 1999 Act in Vol.II): para.(3)(e)

There are special rules for calculating entitlement under claims made by virtue of para.(3). Under reg.36(3) the claimant's maximum amount is calculated using the standard allowance for a single claimant. However, under reg.22(3) the couple's combined income is taken into account when calculating the income to be deducted from that amount. and, under reg.18(2), the claimant's capital is treated as including the capital of the other member of the couple.

Note that the restricted standard allowance under reg.36(3) only applies to a member of a couple who claims as a single person under para.(3). It does *not* affect claims by those who are able to make a joint claim by virtue of para.(2).

Under reg.9(1) of the Claims and Payments Regulations 2013, if a person who is a member of a couple but is entitled to claim as a single person under para.(3), instead makes a joint claim, that claim is treated as made by that person as a single person.

Paras (4) and (5)

Paragraphs (4) and (5) apply to those in a polygamous marriage. "Polygamous marriage" is defined by para.(5) as "a marriage during which a party to it is married to more than one person and which took place under the laws of a country which permits polygamy". That definition could clearer. A possible interpretation is that once a party to the marriage has been married to more than one person, the marriage is to be treated as polygamous for as long as it lasts (i.e., because it is a marriage "during which" there were, at least for a period, more than two members). However, it is suggested that in the context of the regulation of the whole, that interpretation is not correct. The use of the present tense ("is married") and the provisions made by para.(4)—which can only apply if the marriage has more than two members—indicate that the head (a) of the definition is to be read as meaning that a marriage is polygamous *during any period in which* a party to it is married to more than one person. In other words, the definition preserves the distinction, which applies elsewhere in social security law, between a marriage that is actually polygamous and one that is only potentially polygamous, so that where neither party is actually married to more than one person, the marriage is not polygamous for universal credit purposes.

For the definition to apply, the party who is married to more than one person must be legally married to them under the law of England and Wales or the law of Scotland (as the case may be). This can raise complex issues of the private international law: see further the commentary to the Social Security and Family Allowances Regulations 1975 (SI 1975/561) in Vol.I and s.4 of Ch.17 of Dicey, Morris & Collins *The Conflict of Laws* 15th edn (Sweet & Maxwell, London, 2012).

The effect of para.(4) is that where a marriage is actually polygamous, and at least three members of that marriage live in the same household, the parties to the earlier or earliest marriage are treated as a couple and all other members of the marriage may make a claim for universal credit as a single person. Where such member of the marriage actually makes a joint claim with another member, that claim is treated as a claim made by that member as a single person (reg.9(2) and (3) of the Claims and Payments Regulations 2013).

2.12

Para. (6)

2.13   At first sight, the drafting of para.6 is puzzling. It seems to draw a distinction between the member of the couple who is "the claimant" who, it is implied, is the head of "the claimant's household" and that person's partner who is "the other member", when, as noted above, the structure of universal credit is that if a claim is to be made by a member of a couple, *both* parties must normally be *joint* claimants. However, WRA 2012, s.40, defines "claimant" as including "each of joint claimants". Therefore, the effect of para.(6) is that when either member of the couple is temporarily absent from the household, they cease to be treated as a couple if the absence is expected to last, or actually lasts, for more than six months.

Relationship formation and breakdown

2.14   TCA 2002 s.3, which requires couples to make a joint claim for tax credits, contains an express provision (s.3(4)), that entitlement to tax credits ceases if the claim was made by a couple and the members of that couple split up ("could no longer make a joint claim") or if, in the case of a single claim, the claimant becomes a member of a couple ("could no longer make a single claim"). By contrast, WRA 2012 does not include any such provision relating to universal credit. Various provisions in these Regulations and of the Claims and Payments Regulations 2013 *assume* that a joint award comes to an end when a couple separate and that an award to a single claimant ends if the claimant becomes a member of a couple. However, it is not permissible to interpret primary legislation on the basis of assumptions made in the secondary legislation made under it. It is more persuasive that the same assumption is made by WRA 2012, Sch.1, para.3(2), but even that paragraph empowers the Secretary of State to make regulations about what happens *if* an award of universal credit comes to an end because of a relationship change, rather than saying that is automatically the case.

One can argue that it is inherent in the concept of a joint award to a couple, that it should come to an end if that couple no longer exists. But if that is the case, why was it felt necessary to make express provision for the situation in TCA 2002? And, when one thinks about it further, it becomes less and less clear why—in the absence of any provision equivalent to s.3(4) TCA 2002—ceasing to be a couple, or becoming one, should not be treated like any other change of circumstances, like a change of address, or a change in the amount of income or capital, rather than as a change which brings the award of benefit to an end irrespective of the circumstances of the claimants after that change. The rules in reg.9(6)-(8) and (10) of the Claims and Payments Regulations (which dispense with the need for a fresh claim where people who have been awarded universal credit become, or cease to be, members of a couple) and reg.21(3)-(3B) (under which new awards of universal credit in such cases adopt the assessment periods of the old awards) mean that, in practice, that will often be the effect of relationship formation and breakdown, even though, formally, the regulations assume that a previous entitlement to universal credit comes to an end in such circumstances.

When a person is responsible for a child or qualifying young person

2.15   **4.**—(1) Whether a person is responsible for a child or qualifying young person for the purposes of Pt 1 of the Act and these Regulations is determined as follows.

(2) A person is responsible for a child or qualifying young person who normally lives with them.

(3) But a person is not responsible for a qualifying young person if the two of them are living as a couple.

(4) Where a child or qualifying young person normally lives with two or more persons who are not a couple, only one of them is to be treated as responsible and that is the person who has the main responsibility.

(5) The persons mentioned in paragraph (4) may jointly nominate which

of them has the main responsibility but the Secretary of State may determine that question—

(a) in default of agreement; or

(b) if a nomination or change of nomination does not, in the opinion of the Secretary of State, reflect the arrangements between those persons.

(6) [¹ Subject to regulation 4A,] a child or qualifying young person is to be treated as not being the responsibility of any person during any period when the child or qualifying young person is—

(a) looked after by a local authority; or

(b) a prisoner,

[¹ . . .]

(7) Where a child or qualifying young person is temporarily absent from a person's household the person ceases to be responsible for the child or qualifying young person if—

(a) the absence is expected to exceed, or does exceed, 6 months; or

(b) the absence is from Great Britain and is expected to exceed, or does exceed, one month unless it is in circumstances where an absence of a person for longer than one month would be disregarded for the purposes of regulation 11(2) or (3) (medical treatment or convalescence or death of close relative etc.).

DEFINITIONS

"the Act"—see reg.2.
"child"—see WRA 2012 s.40.
"couple"—see WRA 2012 ss.39 and 40.
"looked after by a local authority"—see reg.2.
"qualifying young person"—see WRA 2012 s.40 and 10(5) and regs 2 and 5.

AMENDMENT

1. Social Security (Miscellaneous Amendments) (No.2) Regulations 2013 (SI 2013/1508) reg.3(1) and (3) (July 29, 2013).

GENERAL NOTE

Whether or not a claimant is responsible for a child or qualifying young person is relevant to their maximum amount under Pt 4, to the level of any work allowance under reg.22 and to the imposition of work-related requirements under Pt 8.

Paras (1)–(5)

The general rule is that a person is responsible for a child or qualifying young person who normally lives with them (para.(2)) unless (in the case of a qualifying young person) the two of them are living together as a couple (para.(3)).

Where a child or qualifying young person normally lives with two people who are a couple, both members of the couple are responsible for him or her (because that is the effect of para.(2) and no other rule applies).

However, where he or she lives with two or more persons who are not a couple, only one of them is to be treated as responsible and that is the person who has the main responsibility for him or her (para.(4)). In those circumstances. the people with whom the child or qualifying young person lives may agree which of them has the main responsibility. However, the Secretary of State may overrule that agreement, if in his opinion, it does not reflect the arrangements those people have made (i.e., for the care of the child or qualifying young person) (para.(5)(b)). The Secretary of State may also decide who has main responsibility if the people with

2.16

2.17

whom the child or qualifying young person lives do not agree who has the main responsibility (para.(5)(a)).

Para. (6)

2.18   Children or qualifying young persons who are being looked after by a local author-ity or are prisoners (as defined in reg.2) are treated as not being the responsibility of any person. The effect is that the child or qualifying young person is disregarded for the purposes of reg.22, Pt 4 and Pt 8 even if he or she normally lives with the claimant or claimants.

However, para.(6) is subject to reg.4A, so that the child or qualifying young person is not treated as not being the responsibility of any person during any period in which he or she is being looked after by a local authority and either:

- his or her absence is "in the nature of a planned short term break, or is one of a series of such breaks, for the purpose of providing respite for the person who normally cares for" him or her; or

- (though being formally looked after by a local authority) the child or qualify-ing young person is placed with, or continues to live with, their parent or a person who has parental responsibility for them. For the definition of paren-tal responsibility, see reg.4A(2).

Para. (7)

2.19   Paragraph 7 deals with the temporary absence of a child or qualifying young person from a claimant's (or the claimants') household. In those circumstances, the person who was previously responsible for the child or qualifying young person ceases to be so as soon as the absence is expected to exceed six months or if, unex-pectedly, it actually exceeds six months (para.7(a)). That period is reduced to one month if the child or qualifying young person is also absent from Great Britain unless that absence would be disregarded under reg.11(1) by virtue of reg.11(2) or (3).

[¹ Responsibility for children looked after by a local authority

2.20   **4A.**—(1) There is excluded from regulation 4(6)(a)—

(a) any period which is in the nature of a planned short term break, or is one of a series of such breaks, for the purpose of providing respite for the person who normally cares for the child or qualifying young person;

(b) any period during which the child or qualifying young person is placed with, or continues to live with, their parent or a person who has parental responsibility for them.

(2) For the purposes of this regulation, a person has parental responsibil-ity if they are not a foster parent and—

(a) in England and Wales, they have parental responsibility within the meaning of section 3 of the Children Act 1989; or

(b) in Scotland, they have any or all of the legal responsibilities or rights described in sections 1 or 2 of the Children (Scotland) Act 1995.]

AMENDMENT

1. Social Security (Miscellaneous Amendments) (No.2) Regulations 2013 (SI 2013/1508) reg.3(1) and (4) (July 29, 2013).

DEFINITIONS

"child"—see WRA 2012 s.40.
"qualifying young person"—see WRA 2012 ss.40 and 10(5) and regs 2 and 5.
"looked after by a local authority"—see reg.2.
"local authority"—*ibid.*

See the general note to reg.4(6) above.   2.20.1

Meaning of "qualifying young person"

5.—(1) A person who has reached the age of 16 but not the age of 20 is   2.21
a qualifying young person for the purposes of Part 1 of the Act and these
Regulations—
   (a) up to, but not including, the 1st September following their 16th
       birthday; and
   (b) up to, but not including, the 1st September following their 19th
       birthday, if they are enrolled on, or accepted for, approved training
       or a course of education—
       (i) which is not a course of advanced education,
       (ii) which is provided at a school or college or provided elsewhere
            but approved by the Secretary of State, and
       (iii) where the average time spent during term time in receiving
             tuition, engaging in practical work or supervised study or taking
             examinations exceeds 12 hours per week.
   (2) Where the young person is aged 19, they must have started the education or training or been enrolled on or accepted for it before reaching that
age.
   (3) The education or training referred to in paragraph (1) does not
include education or training provided by means of a contract of employment.
   (4) "Approved training" means training in pursuance of arrangements
made under section 2(1) of the Employment and Training Act 1973 or
section 2(3) of the Enterprise and New Towns (Scotland) Act 1990 which
is approved by the Secretary of State for the purposes of this regulation.
   (5) A person who is receiving universal credit, an employment and
support allowance or a jobseeker's allowance is not a qualifying young
person.

MODIFICATION

With effect from June 16, 2014, reg. 5 is modified by reg. 28 of the Universal
Credit (Transitional Provisions) Regulations 2014 (SI 2014/1230) (see Pt IV
of this book). The modification applies where a person who would otherwise
be a "qualifying young person" within the meaning of reg. 5 is entitled to an
"existing benefit" (namely income-based JSA, income-related ESA, income
support, housing benefit, child tax credit or working tax credit: see reg.2(1) of SI
2014/1230). The modifications are (i) that such a person is not a qualifying young
person for the purposes of the Universal Credit Regulations, and (ii) that reg.
5(5) applies as if, after "a person who is receiving" there were inserted "an existing benefit (within the meaning of the Universal Credit (Transitional Provisions)
Regulations 2014),".

DEFINITIONS

"employment and support allowance"—see reg.2.
"jobseeker's allowance"—*ibid.*

GENERAL NOTE

Under s.8(2)(b) and s.10(1) WRA 2012 the calculation of an award of universal   2.22
credit includes an amount for a qualifying young person for whom the claimant

is responsible. Regulation 5 defines who is a qualifying young person. The definition is similar to that which applies for the purposes of child benefit (see by way of comparison regs 3, 7 and 8 of the Child Benefit (General) Regulations 2006 in Vol.IV of this series) but not quite. In particular, the concept of "terminal date" has gone.

Under reg.5, a person who is aged 16 or over but under 20 counts as a qualifying young person:

(i) up to (but not including) the 1st September following his/her 16th birthday if s/he is aged 16; or

(ii) up to (but not including) the 1st September following his/her 19th birthday if s/he is aged 16–19 and has been accepted for (or has enrolled on) approved training (defined in para.(4)) or non-advanced education at a school or college (or elsewhere as approved by the Secretary of State; note that in the case of education provided other than at a school or college there is no requirement that the qualifying young person must have been receiving such education before s/he became 16, as there is for child benefit (see reg.3(3) of the 2006 Regulations in Vol.IV of this series and *JH v HMRC (CHB)* [2015] UKUT 479 (AAC)). In the case of a course of education at least 12 hours on average a week must be spent on tuition, practical work, supervised study or examinations. Meal breaks and unsupervised study are not included. *R(F) 1/93* held that "supervised study" (in reg.5 of the Child Benefit Regulations 1976) "would normally be understood to import the presence or close proximity of a teacher or tutor". If the person is aged 19, s/he must have started (or been accepted for or enrolled on) the education or training before reaching 19. The education or training must not be provided as part of a contract of employment.

But note that if a person is receiving universal credit, new style ESA or new style JSA in his/her own right, s/he cannot be a qualifying young person (para.(5)). Note also the modification to para.(5) in reg. 28 of SI 2014/1230 referred to above, which has the effect that if the person is receiving income-based JSA, income-related ESA, income support, housing benefit, child tax credit or working tax credit s/he is not a qualifying young person.

See also reg.12(1) which provides that if a person is a qualifying young person s/he is regarded as receiving education and so will not meet the basic condition in s.4(1)(d) WRA 2012 (unless s/he comes within one of the exceptions to this requirement in reg.14).

Rounding

2.23   **6.**—(1) Where the calculation of an amount for the purposes of these Regulations results in a fraction of a penny, that fraction is to be disregarded if it is less than half a penny and otherwise it is to be treated as a penny.

[¹ (1A) Where the calculation of an amount for the purposes of the following [³ provisions] results in a fraction of a pound, that fraction is to be disregarded—

[² (za) regulation 82(1)(a) (exceptions – earnings);]

(a) regulation 90 (claimants subject to no work-related requirements – the earnings thresholds); and

(b) regulation 99(6) (circumstances in which requirements must not be imposed) [³; and

(c) paragraph 4C of Schedule 4 (persons to whom paragraph 4A does not apply – periods of work).]

(2) This regulation does not apply to the calculation in regulation 111 (daily rate for a reduction under section 26 or 27 of the Act).

AMENDMENTS

1. Universal Credit and Miscellaneous Amendments Regulations 2015 (SI 2015/1754), reg.4 (November 4, 2015, or in the case of existing awards, the first assessment period beginning on or after November 4, 2015).

2. Universal Credit (Benefit Cap Earnings Exception) Amendment Regulations 2017 (SI 2017/138) reg.2(2) (April 1, 2017).

3. Universal Credit (Housing Costs Element for claimants aged 18 to 21) (Amendment) Regulations 2017 (SI 2017/252) reg.2(2) (April 1, 2017).

DEFINITION

"the Act"—see reg.2.

PART 2

ENTITLEMENT

Introduction

7. This Part contains provisions about— 2.24
- (a) the requirement to meet the basic conditions in section 4 of the Act, including exceptions from that requirement;
- (b) the maximum amount of capital and the minimum amount of universal credit for the financial conditions in section 5 of the Act; and
- (c) cases where no entitlement to universal credit arises even if the basic conditions and the financial conditions are met.

DEFINITION

"the Act"—see reg.2.

Minimum age

Cases where the minimum age is 16

8.—(1) For the basic condition in section 4(1)(a) of the Act (at least 18 2.25
years old), the minimum age is 16 years old where a person—
- (a) has limited capability for work;
- (b) is awaiting an assessment under Part 5 to determine whether the person has limited capability for work and has a statement given by a registered medical practitioner in accordance with the Medical Evidence Regulations which provides that the person is not fit for work;
- (c) has regular and substantial caring responsibilities for a severely disabled person;
- (d) is responsible for a child;
- (e) is a member of a couple the other member of which is responsible for a child or a qualifying young person (but only where the other member meets the basic conditions in section 4 of the Act);

(f) is pregnant, and it is 11 weeks or less before her expected week of confinement, or was pregnant and it is 15 weeks or less since the date of her confinement; or

(g) is without parental support (see paragraph (3)).

(2) Sub-paragraphs (c), (f) and (g) of paragraph (1) do not include any person who is a care leaver.

(3) For the purposes of paragraph (1)(g) a young person is without parental support where that person is not being looked after by a local authority and—

(a) has no parent;

(b) cannot live with their parents because—
   (i) the person is estranged from them, or
   (ii) there is a serious risk to the person's physical or mental health, or that the person would suffer significant harm if the person lived with them; or

(c) is living away from their parents, and neither parent is able to support the person financially because that parent—
   (i) has a physical or mental impairment,
   (ii) is detained in custody pending trial or sentence upon conviction or under a sentence imposed by a court, or
   (iii) is prohibited from entering or re-entering Great Britain.

(4) In this regulation—

"parent" includes any person acting in the place of a parent;

"care leaver" means—

(a) in relation to England [¹ ...], an eligible child for the purposes of paragraph 19B of Schedule 2 to the Children Act 1989 or a relevant child for the purposes of section 23A of that Act;

[¹ (b) in relation to Scotland, a person under the age of 18 who—
   (i) is looked after by a local authority; or
   (ii) has ceased to be looked after by a local authority but is a person to whom a local authority in Scotland is obliged to provide advice and assistance in terms of section 29(1) of the Children (Scotland) Act 1995 or a person who is being provided with continuing care under section 26A of that Act,
   and who, since reaching the age of 14 has been looked after by a local authority for a period of, or periods totalling, 3 months or more (excluding any period where the person has been placed with a member of their family);

(c) in relation to Wales, a category 1 young person or category 2 young person within the meaning of section 104(2) of the Social Services and Well-being (Wales) Act 2014.]

"confinement" means—

(a) labour resulting in the birth of a living child; or

(b) labour after 24 weeks of pregnancy resulting in the birth of a child whether alive or dead,
   and where a woman's labour begun on one day results in the birth of a child on another day she is to be taken to be confined on the date of the birth.

AMENDMENT

1. Universal Credit (Care Leavers and Looked After Children) Amendment Regulations 2016 (SI 2016/543) reg.2(3) (May 26, 2016).

DEFINITIONS

"the Act"—see reg.2.
"child"—see WRA 2012, s.40.
"limited capability for work"—see WRA 2012, ss.40 and 37(1).
"local authority"—see reg.2.
"looked after by a local authority"—*ibid.*
"Medical Evidence Regulations"— *ibid.*
"qualifying young person"—see regs 2 and 5.
"regular and substantial caring responsibilities"—see WRA 2012, s.40 and reg.30.
"responsible for a child or qualifying young person"—see reg.4.

GENERAL NOTE

One of the basic conditions for entitlement to universal credit is that the claimant must be at least 18 years old (s.4(1)(a) WRA 2012). Regulation 8 provides for the exceptions to that rule.   **2.26**

Under para.(1) a person aged 16 or 17 (who satisfies the other basic conditions) can qualify for universal credit if s/he:

(a) has limited capability for work; or
(b) is waiting for a work capability assessment and has submitted a medical certificate stating that s/he is not fit for work; or
(c) has "regular and substantial caring responsibilities for a severely disabled person" (see reg.30), but not if s/he is a "care leaver" (defined in para. (4)); or
(d) is responsible for a child (see reg.4 for when a person is responsible for a child); or
(e) is a member of a couple and the other member satisfies the basic conditions and is responsible for a child or a qualifying young person (see reg.5 for who counts as a qualifying young person); or
(f) is pregnant and it is 11 weeks or less before her expected week of confinement (defined in para.(4)), or was pregnant and it is 15 weeks or less since the date of confinement, but not if s/he is a care leaver; or
(g) is "without parental support" (defined in para.(3)), but not if s/he is a care leaver.

In relation to the definition of "care leaver", for who is an "eligible child" for the purposes of para.19B of Sch.2 to the Children Act 1989 or a "relevant child" for the purposes of s.23A of that Act, or a "category 1 young person" or "category 2 young person" within the meaning of s.104(2) of the Social Services and Well-being (Wales) Act 2014, see the Children (Leaving Care) Act 2000 and the notes to that Act in Vol.II of this series.

A care leaver who is aged 16 or 17 is not entitled to a housing costs element for rent payments (see Sch.4, para.4) But note that a person aged 18-21, who was a care leaver before s/he became 18, is exempt from the "shared accommodation rate" for renters (see para.29(2) of Sch.4). In addition, a care leaver, or a person who is aged under 22 and is claiming universal credit for the first time and who was a care leaver before reaching 18, is exempt from the seven waiting days rule (see reg. 19A(1) and(3)(b)(iii)).   **2.27**

On para.(1)(g), a young person is "without parental support" if s/he is not being looked after by a local authority and comes within one of the categories listed in para.(3). These categories are similar to those in reg.13(2)(c), (d) and (e) of the Income Support Regulations (see the notes to those provisions in Vol.II of this series). Note the definition of "parent" in para.(4). On para.(3)(b)(ii), para.E1055 of ADM gives examples of "serious risk" as: (i) having a brother or sister who is a drug addict, which poses a risk to the young person who is exposed to the drugs at the parental home; (ii) having a history of mental illness which is made worse by the parent's attitude; or (iii) suffering from chronic bronchitis, which is made worse by the damp conditions of the parent's home. A 16 or 17 year old who is without parental support is exempt from the seven waiting days rule (see reg.19A(1) and (3) (b)(iv)).

Note that under reg.3(3)(a) a person who is a member of a couple (and is either 18 or over or falls within para.(1)) but whose partner is under 18 and does not fall within para.(1) can claim universal credit as a single person.

A person is not normally eligible for universal credit if s/he is receiving education (see s.4(1)(d) WRA 2012). However, see reg.14 for the exceptions.

In Great Britain

Persons treated as not being in Great Britain

2.28   **9.**—(1) For the purposes of determining whether a person meets the basic condition to be in Great Britain, except where a person falls within paragraph (4), a person is to be treated as not being in Great Britain if the person is not habitually resident in the United Kingdom, the Channel Islands, the Isle of Man or the Republic of Ireland.

(2) A person must not be treated as habitually resident in the United Kingdom, the Channel Islands, the Isle of Man or the Republic of Ireland unless the person has a right to reside in one of those places.

(3) For the purposes of paragraph (2), a right to reside does not include a right which exists by virtue of, or in accordance with—

(a) regulation 13 of the EEA Regulations or Article 6 of Council DirectiveNo.2004/38/EC; [² . . .]

[² (aa) regulation 14 of the EEA Regulations(3), but only in cases where the right exists under that regulation because the person is–
    (i) a qualified person for the purposes of regulation 6(1) of those Regulations as a jobseeker; or
    (ii) a family member (within the meaning of regulation 7 of those Regulations) of such a jobseeker; or]

(b) regulation 15A(1) of the EEA Regulations, but only in cases where the right exists under that regulation because the claimant satisfies the criteria in regulation 15A(4A) of those Regulations or article 20 of the Treaty on the Functioning of the European Union (in a case where the right to reside arises because a British citizen would otherwise be deprived of the genuine enjoyment of their rights as a European citizen).

(4) A person falls within this paragraph if the person is—

(a) a qualified person for the purposes of regulation 6 of the EEA Regulations as a worker or a self-employed person;

(b) a family member of a person referred to in sub-paragraph (a) within the meaning of regulation 7(1)(a), (b) or (c) of the EEA Regulations;

(c) a person who has a right to reside permanently in the United Kingdom by virtue of regulation 15(1)(c), (d) or (e) of the EEA Regulations;

(d) a refugee within the definition in Article 1 of the Convention relating to the Status of Refugees done at Geneva on 28th July 1951, as extended by Article 1(2) of the Protocol relating to the Status of Refugees done at New York on 31st January 1967;

[¹(e) a person who has been granted, or who is deemed to have been granted, leave outside the rules made under section 3(2) of the Immigration Act 1971 where that leave is—

   (i) discretionary leave to enter or remain in the United Kingdom,

   (ii) leave to remain under the Destitution Domestic Violence concession, or

   (iii) leave deemed to have been granted by virtue of regulation 3 of the Displaced Persons (Temporary Protection) Regulations 2005;]

  (f) a person who has humanitarian protection granted under those rules; or

  (g) a person who is not a person subject to immigration control within the meaning of section 115(9) of the Immigration and Asylum Act 1999 and who is in the United Kingdom as a result of their deportation, expulsion or other removal by compulsion of law from another country to the United Kingdom.

AMENDMENT

1. Social Security (Miscellaneous Amendments) (No.2) Regulations 2013 (SI 2013/1508) reg.3(1) and (5) (October 29, 2013).

2. Universal Credit (EEA Jobseekers) Amendment Regulations 2015 (SI 2015/546) reg.2 (June 10, 2015).

DEFINITION

"EEA Regulations"—see reg.2.

GENERAL NOTE

Under s.4(1)(c) WRA 2012, it is a basic condition of entitlement to universal credit that the claimant is "in Great Britain" and s.4(5)(a) empowers the Secretary of State to make regulations specifying "circumstances in which a person is to be treated as being, or not being, in Great Britain". Regulation 9 is made under that power. The general rule (para.(1)) is that to be "in Great Britain" a person must be habitually resident in the United Kingdom, the Channel Islands, the Isle of Man or the Republic of Ireland. Apart from people who fall within para.(4), everyone who is not so habitually resident is treated as not being in Great Britain.　　**2.29**

The habitual residence test in para.(1) is supplemented by para.(2) which establishes an ancillary right to reside test: no-one may treated as habitually resident in the United Kingdom, the Channel Islands, the Isle of Man or the Republic of Ireland for universal credit purposes unless the person has a right to reside in one of those places, other than a right to reside specified in para.(3).

For a detailed analysis of the habitual residence and right to reside tests, see the commentary to reg.21AA of the IS Regulations in Vol.II and the provisions of EU law in Pt III of Vol.III and in the Supplement to those volumes.

Crown servants and members of Her Majesty's forces posted overseas

10.—(1) The following persons do not have to meet the basic condition to be in Great Britain—　　**2.30**

  (a) a Crown servant or member of Her Majesty's forces posted overseas;

  (b) in the case of joint claimants, the partner of a person mentioned in sub-paragraph (a) while they are accompanying the person on that posting.

(2) A person mentioned in paragraph (1)(a) is posted overseas if the person is performing overseas the duties of a Crown servant or member of Her Majesty's forces and was, immediately before their posting or the first of consecutive postings, habitually resident in the United Kingdom.

(3) In this regulation—

"Crown servant" means a person holding an office or employment under the Crown; and

"Her Majesty's forces" has the meaning in the Armed Forces Act 2006.

DEFINITIONS

"joint claimants"—see WRA 2012 s.40.

"partner"—see reg.2.

GENERAL NOTE

2.31   Under s.4(1)(c) WRA 2012, it is a basic condition of entitlement to universal credit that the claimant is "in Great Britain". However s.4(2) empowers the Secretary of State to make regulations that "provide for exceptions to the requirement to meet any of the basic conditions". Regulation 10 is made under that power.

Crown Servants and members of Her Majesty's forces who are posted overseas (as defined in para.(2)) do not have to meet the basic condition to be in Great Britain.

Neither does the partner of such a Crown Servant or member of Her Majesty's forces, if a joint claim for universal credit is made. However, as it seems probable that a Crown Servant or member of Her Majesty's forces who has been posted overseas will be in full-time work, many such joint claims seem likely to fail on the basis that the financial conditions are not met.

By para.(3), the phrase "Her Majesty's forces" has the meaning in the Armed Forces Act 2006. However, that phrase is not defined in that Act except to the extent that ""Her Majesty's forces" ... do not include any Commonwealth force" (see s.374). "Commonwealth force" is defined by the same section as meaning "a force of a Commonwealth country".

Temporary absence from Great Britain

2.32   **11.**—(1) A person's temporary absence from Great Britain is disregarded in determining whether they meet the basic condition to be in Great Britain if—

(a) the person is entitled to universal credit immediately before the beginning of the period of temporary absence; and

(b) either—

(i) the absence is not expected to exceed, and does not exceed, one month, or

(ii) paragraph (3) or (4) applies.

(2) The period of one month in paragraph (1)(b) may be extended by up to a further month if the temporary absence is in connection with the death of—

(a) the person's partner or a child or qualifying young person for whom the person was responsible; or

(b) a close relative of the person, or of their partner or of a child or qualifying young person for whom the person or their partner was responsible,

and the Secretary of State considers that it would be unreasonable to expect the person to return to Great Britain within the first month.

(3) This paragraph applies where the absence is not expected to exceed, and does not exceed, 6 months and is solely in connection with—

(a) the person undergoing—
- (i) treatment for an illness or physical or mental impairment by, or under the supervision of, a qualified practitioner, or
- (ii) medically approved convalescence or care as a result of treatment for an illness or physical or mental impairment, where the person had that illness or impairment before leaving Great Britain; or

(b) the person accompanying their partner or a child or qualifying young person for whom they are responsible for treatment or convalescence or care as mentioned in sub-paragraph (a).

(4) This paragraph applies where the absence is not expected to exceed, and does not exceed, 6 months and the person is—

(a) a mariner; or

(b) a continental shelf worker who is in a designated area or a prescribed area.

(5) In this regulation—

"continental shelf worker" means a person who is employed, whether under a contract of service or not, in a designated area or a prescribed area in connection with any activity mentioned in section 11(2) of the Petroleum Act 1998;

"designated area" means any area which may from time to time be designated by Order in Council under the Continental Shelf Act 1964 as an area within which the rights of the United Kingdom with respect to the seabed and subsoil and their natural resources may be exercised;

"mariner" means a person who is employed under a contract of service either as a master or member of the crew of any ship or vessel, or in any other capacity on board any ship or vessel where—

(a) the employment in that other capacity is for the purposes of that ship or vessel or its crew or any passengers or cargo or mails carried by the ship or vessel; and

(b) the contract is entered into in the United Kingdom with a view to its performance (in whole or in part) while the ship or vessel is on its voyage;

"medically approved" means certified by a registered medical practitioner;

"prescribed area" means any area over which Norway or any member State (other than the United Kingdom) exercises sovereign rights for the purpose of exploring the seabed and subsoil and exploiting their natural resources, being an area outside the territorial seas of Norway or such member State, or any other area which is from time to time specified under section 10(8) of the Petroleum Act 1998;

"qualified practitioner" means a person qualified to provide medical treatment, physiotherapy or a form of treatment which is similar to, or related to, either of those forms of treatment.

DEFINITIONS

"child"—see WRA 2012 s.40.
"close relative"—see reg.2.
"partner"—*ibid.*

"prescribed"—see WRA 2012 s.40.
"responsible for a child or qualifying young person"—see regs 2, 4 and 4A.
"qualifying young person"—see WRA 2012 s.40 and 10(5) and regs 2 and 5.

GENERAL NOTE

2.33   Under s.4(1)(c) WRA 2012, it is a basic condition of entitlement to universal credit that the claimant is "in Great Britain". However s.4(5)(b) and (c) empowers the Secretary of State to make regulations that specify circumstances in which temporary absence from Great Britain is disregarded (subs.(5)(b)) and modify the application of WRA 2012 in relation to a person who is not in Great Britain but who is entitled to universal credit by virtue of subs.(5)(b) (subs.(5)(c)). Regulation 11 is made under the former power.

Paras (1) and (2)
    The general rule is that a person who is entitled to universal credit retains that entitlement during a temporary absence—for whatever reason—that is not expected to exceed one month and does not in fact exceed that period (para.(1)(b)(i)). By para.(1)(a), there must be an existing entitlement to universal credit for the rule to apply. It is not possible to claim universal credit for the first time while temporarily absent abroad.
    The one-month period in para.(1)(b)(i) can be extended by up to a further month in the circumstances set out in para.(2)(a) and (b) if the Secretary of State considers it would be unreasonable to expect the person to return home during the first month.

Paras (3) and (4)
2.34   The one-month period in para.(1)(b)(i) is also extended to six months if either para.(3) or para.(4) applies. Those paragraphs are not subject to the condition that the Secretary of State should consider that it would be unreasonable to expect the person to return home sooner.
    Paragraph (3) permits an extended temporary absence for medical treatment, physiotherapy, or a treatment that is similar to either of those forms of treatment, or medically approved convalescence in the circumstances set out in para.(3)(a) and (b). Note the definitions of "medically approved" and "qualified practitioner" in para.(5). The phrase, "registered medical practitioner" is further defined by para.1 of Sch.1 Interpretation Act 1978 as meaning "a fully registered person within the meaning of the Medical Act 1983 who holds a licence to practise under that Act."
    Paragraph (4) permits an extended temporary absence for a "mariner" and a "continental shelf worker" who is in a "designated area" or a "prescribed area". All four of those terms are defined in para.(5). The definition of "mariner" is self-explanatory. The definition of "continental shelf worker" is more technical but, to summarise, it means a person working on an oil or gas rig in a specified area. Readers are referred to the Continental Shelf Act 1964, the Petroleum Act 1998 and the Orders in Council made under those Acts for further details of the areas concerned.
2.35   Note that paras (2) and (3) are also relevant to the question whether a person remains responsible for a child or qualifying young person during the temporary absence of that child or qualifying young person: see the commentary to reg.4(7) above.

Receiving education

Meaning of "receiving education"

2.36   **12.**—[¹ (1) This regulation applies for the basic condition in section 4(1)(d) of the Act (not receiving education).

(1A) A qualifying young person is to be treated as receiving education, unless the person is participating in a traineeship.

(1B) In paragraph (1A) "traineeship" means a course which—

(a) is funded (in whole or in part) by, or under arrangements made by, the—

    (i) Secretary of State under section 14 of the Education Act 2002, or

    (ii) Chief Executive of Skills Funding;

(b) lasts no more than 6 months;

(c) includes training to help prepare the participant for work and a work experience placement; and

(d) is open to persons who on the first day of the course have reached the age of 16 but not 25;]

(2) [¹ Except in circumstances where paragraph (1A) applies] "receiving education" means—

(a) undertaking a full-time course of advanced education; or

(b) undertaking any other full-time course of study or training at an educational establishment for which a student loan or grant is provided for the person's maintenance.

(3) In paragraph (2)(a) "course of advanced education" means—

(a) a course of study leading to—

    (i) a postgraduate degree or comparable qualification,

    (ii) a first degree or comparable qualification,

    (iii) a diploma of higher education,

    (iv) a higher national diploma; or

(b) any other course of study which is of a standard above advanced GNVQ or equivalent, including a course which is of a standard above a general certificate of education (advanced level), or above a Scottish national qualification (higher or advanced higher).

(4) A claimant who is not a qualifying young person and is not undertaking a course described in paragraph (2) is nevertheless to be treated as receiving education if the claimant is undertaking a course of study or training that is not compatible with any work-related requirement imposed on the claimant by the Secretary of State.

AMENDMENT

1. Social Security (Traineeships and Qualifying Young Persons) Amendment Regulations 2015 (SI 2015/336) reg.4 (March 27, 2015).

DEFINITIONS

"claimant"—see WRA 2012 s.40.
"qualifying young person"—see WRA 2012 ss.40 and 10(5) and regs 2 and 5.

GENERAL NOTE

It is a condition of entitlement to universal credit that the person is not receiving education (s.4(1)(d) WRA 2012) (but see reg.14 for the exceptions to this rule).

2.37

Note that a couple may be entitled to universal credit as joint claimants even where one member of the couple is receiving education (and does not come within reg.14), provided that the other member is not receiving education, or comes within reg.14 (see reg.3(2)(b)).

Regulation 12 defines who counts as receiving education. Firstly, a qualifying young person (see reg.5 for who is a qualifying young person) is deemed to be receiving education, unless s/he is participating in a traineeship (para.(1A)).

"Traineeship" is defined in para.(1B) (note that the office of the Chief Executive of Skills Funding has been abolished but para.(1B) has not been updated to reflect this). If s/he is participating in a traineeship, s/he will not count as receiving education for the purposes of s.4(1)(d).

If para.(1A) does not apply, receiving education means being on a full-time course of advanced education (defined in para.(3)) or on another full-time course of study or training at an educational establishment for which a student loan or grant is provided for the person's maintenance (para.(2)). But in addition a claimant will also be treated as receiving education if s/he is on a course of study or training that is not compatible with the work-related requirements imposed on him/her (para.(4)).

The definition of "course of advanced education" in reg.12(3) is the same as the definition in reg.61(1) of the Income Support Regulations (see Vol.II in this series). "Full-time" is not defined.

See reg.13 for when a person is regarded as being on a course.

Meaning of "undertaking a course"

2.38   **13.**—(1) For the purposes of these Regulations a person is to be regarded as undertaking a course of education [¹, study] or training—

  (a) throughout the period beginning on the date on which the person starts undertaking the course and ending on the last day of the course or on such earlier date (if any) as the person finally abandons it or is dismissed from it; or

  (b) where a person is undertaking a part of a modular course, for the period beginning on the day on which that part of the course starts and ending—

    (i) on the last day on which the person is registered as undertaking that part, or

    (ii) on such earlier date (if any) as the person finally abandons the course or is dismissed from it.

  (2) The period referred to in paragraph (1)(b) includes—

  (a) where a person has failed examinations or has failed to complete successfully a module relating to a period when the person was undertaking a part of the course, any period in respect of which the person undertakes the course for the purpose of retaking those examinations or completing that module; and

  (b) any period of vacation within the period specified in paragraph (1)(b) or immediately following that period except where the person has registered to attend or undertake the final module in the course and the vacation immediately follows the last day on which the person is to attend or undertake the course.

  (3) In this regulation "modular course" means a course which consists of two or more modules, the successful completion of a specified number of which is required before a person is considered by the educational establishment to have completed the course.

  (4) A person is not to be regarded as undertaking a course for any part of the period mentioned in paragraph (1) during which the following conditions are met—

  (a) the person has, with the consent of the relevant educational establishment, ceased to attend or undertake the course because they are ill or caring for another person;

  (b) the person has recovered from that illness or ceased caring for that person within the past year, but not yet resumed the course; and

  (c) the person is not eligible for a grant or student loan.

AMENDMENT

1. Universal Credit (Consequential, Supplementary, Incidental and Miscellaneous Provisions) Regulations 2013 (SI 2013/630) reg.38(3) (April 29, 2013).

DEFINITIONS

"grant"—see regs 2 and 68(7).
"student loan"—*ibid.*

GENERAL NOTE

Paragraphs (1) to (3) of reg.13 reproduce the rules in reg.61(2) to (4) of the   2.39
Income Support Regulations. See the notes to reg.61 in Vol.II of this series.

Paragraph (4) is similar to the provision in reg.1(3D) and (3E) of the JSA Regulations 1996 (see Vol.II in this series). The person must have recovered from the illness or his/her caring responsibilities must have ended within the past year for para.(4) to apply (see para.(4)(b)).

Exceptions to the requirement not to be receiving education

14. A person does not have to meet the basic condition in s.4(1)(d) of the   2.40
Act (not receiving education) if—
  (a) the person—
      (i) is undertaking a full-time course of study or training which is not a course of advanced education,
      (ii) is under the age of 21, or is 21 and reached that age whilst undertaking the course, and
      (iii) is without parental support (as defined in regulation 8(3));
  (b) the person is entitled to attendance allowance, disability living allowance or personal independence payment and has limited capability for work;
  (c) the person is responsible for a child or a qualifying young person;
  (d) the person is a single person and a foster parent with whom a child is placed;
  (e) the person is a member of a couple, both of whom are receiving education, and the other member is—
      (i) responsible for a child or qualifying young person, or
      (ii) a foster parent with whom a child is placed; or
  (f) the person—
      (i) has reached the qualifying age for state pension credit, and
      (ii) is a member of a couple the other member of which has not reached that age.

DEFINITIONS

"the Act"—see reg.2.
"attendance allowance"—*ibid.*
"child"—see WRA 2012 s.40.
"couple"—see WRA 2012 ss.39 and 40.
"course of advanced education"—see reg.12(3).
"disability living allowance"—see reg.2.
"foster parent"—*ibid.*
"personal independence payment"—*ibid.*
"qualifying young person"—see WRA 2012 ss.40 and 10(5) and regs 2 and 5.
"qualifying age for state pension credit"—see WRA 2012 s.4(4), SPCA 2002 s.1(6).

GENERAL NOTE

2.41   This regulation sets out the exceptions to the rule in s.4(1)(d) WRA 2012 that a person must not be receiving education. Note that most student funding will count as income—see regs 68–71. If a person who comes within reg.14 has student income in relation to the course that s/he is undertaking which is taken into account in the calculation of his/her universal credit award, s/he will not have any work requirements (see reg.89(1)(e)(ii)).

The following are exempt from the condition in s.4(1)(d):

-   a person who is on a course which is not a course of advanced education (see reg.12(3) for what counts as a course of advanced education) and who is under 21 (or is 21 and reached that age while on the course) and who is "without parental support" (see reg.8(3) for who counts as without parental support) (para.(a)). Such a person will have no work requirements (see reg.89(1)(e)(i));

-   a person who has limited capability for work (see reg.39(1)) and who is entitled to disability living allowance, personal independence payment, attendance allowance or armed forces independence payment (see the definition of "attendance allowance" in reg.2 which includes armed forces independence payment) (para.(b));

-   a person who is responsible for a child or qualifying young person (para.(c));

-   a single person who is a foster parent with whom a child is placed (para.(d));

-   a member of a couple, both of whom are receiving education, whose partner is responsible for a child or qualifying young person or is a foster parent with whom a child is placed (para.(e)); or

-   a member of a couple who has reached the qualifying age for state pension credit but whose partner is below that age (para.(f)).

Note that a person who falls within reg.13(4) is not regarded as undertaking a course and so is not treated as receiving education (see reg.12(2)).

Note also that a couple may be entitled to universal credit as joint claimants even where one member of the couple is receiving education (and does not come within this regulation), provided that the other member is not receiving education, or comes within this regulation (see reg.3(2)(b)).

Accepting a claimant commitment

Claimant commitment—date and method of acceptance

2.42   **15.**—(1) For the basic condition in section 4(1)(e) of the Act, a person who has accepted a claimant commitment within such period after making a claim as the Secretary of State specifies is to be treated as having accepted that claimant commitment on the first day of the period in respect of which the claim is made.

(2) In a case where an award may be made without a claim, a person who accepts a claimant commitment within such period as the Secretary of State specifies is to be treated as having accepted a claimant commitment on the day that would be the first day of the first assessment period in relation to the award in accordance with regulation 21(3) [¹or (3A)].

(3) The Secretary of State may extend the period within which a person is required to accept a claimant commitment or an updated claimant commitment where the person requests that the Secretary of State review—

(a) any action proposed as a work search requirement or a work availability requirement; or

(b) whether any limitation should apply to those requirements,
and the Secretary of State considers that the request is reasonable.

(4) A person must accept a claimant commitment by one of the following
methods, as specified by the Secretary of State—

(a) electronically;

(b) by telephone; or

(c) in writing.

AMENDMENT

1. Income Support (Digital Service) Amendment Regulations 2014 (SI
2014/2887) reg.3(1)(a) (November 26, 2014).

DEFINITIONS

"claimant commitment"—see WRA 2012 s.14(1)
"work availability requirement"—see WRA 2012 ss.40 and 18(1)
"work search requirement"—see WRA 2012 ss.40 and 17(1)

GENERAL NOTE

By virtue of s.4(1)(e) of the WRA 2012 it is one of the basic conditions for making   **2.43**
an award of universal credit that a claimant, including each of joint claimants, has
accepted a claimant commitment, the meaning of which is then set out in s.14. See
that provision and its annotations for the nature of a claimant commitment (i.e. a
record of the claimant's responsibilities under the WRA 2012) and what is entailed
in accepting such a record. There are exceptions from the basic condition in reg.16
below. Regulation 15 deals with the time within which and the method by which
a claimant commitment must be accepted. The relevant regulation-making powers
are in s.14(5) of the WRA 2012, which requires the most up-to-date version of a
claimant commitment to be accepted "in such manner as may be prescribed", and
in s.4(7), which allows regulations to specify circumstances in which a person is to
be treated as having or as not having accepted a claimant commitment.

Para. (1)

On a new claim, if the claimant commitment is accepted within the time speci-   **2.44**
fied by the Secretary of State (as extended under para.(3) if applicable), and by a
method prescribed in para.(4), the basic condition is deemed to be satisfied from
the first day of the period claimed for. Otherwise, the condition would only be
met from the date on which the acceptance by a prescribed method actually took
place. Paragraph (1) must therefore be made under s.4(7) of the WRA 2012. Under
s.14(2) of the WRA 2012, the Secretary of State may review and up-date a claimant commitment as he thinks fit and under s.14(5) a claimant has to accept the
most-up-date version. Such circumstances do not seem to fall within either paras
(1) or (2), although para.(3) refers to a period within which a claimant is required
to accept an up-dated claimant commitment and its possible extension. There is
doubt whether an acceptance under such circumstances strictly takes effect only
from its actual date or from the date of the preparation of the up-dated version, but
no-one is likely to complain if the Secretary of State gives retrospective effect to an
acceptance of an up-dated version within a specified time, as consistency would
suggest is fair.

Para. (2)

Where no claim is required to be made (see reg.6 of the Claims and Payments   **2.45**
Regulations 2013), effectively the same rule is applied as in para.(1) with effect from
the first day of the award.

Para. (3)

2.46   This paragraph allows the Secretary of State, in defined circumstances, to extend the period within which a person is required (which is only in the sense of required in order to take advantage of giving a retrospective effect to the acceptance) to accept a claimant commitment or an up-dated version. It is arguable that no such authorisation is needed to allow the Secretary of State to extend any period as first specified under paras (1) or (2), so that the form of the restrictions in sub-paras (a) and (b) may not matter too much. Those provisions purport to apply when a claimant has requested that the Secretary of State review any action proposed as a work search or work availability requirement (see ss.17(1)(b) and 18 of the WRA 2012) or whether any limitation should apply to those requirements (see reg.97 below). The main difficulty with them, apart from the fact that s.18 contains no power for the Secretary of State to specify particular action in relation to a work availability requirement, is that the legislation contains no formal process of review of the "proposals" mentioned. The reference must presumably be to the power under s.24(3) of the WRA 2012 for the Secretary of State to revoke or change any requirement imposed under the Act or any specification of action to be taken and to a request to exercise that power in relation to action specified under ss.17 or 18. Those difficulties perhaps reinforce the argument for the Secretary of State being able to extend the period for acceptance of the claimant whenever it appears reasonable to do so, although that would involve giving no effective force to para.(3).

Para. (4)

2.47   This paragraph, as allowed by s.14(5) of the WRA 2012, requires that any acceptance of a claimant commitment that can count for the purposes of s.4(1)(e) be done electronically, by telephone or in writing, with the Secretary of State able to specify which in any particular case. "Electronically" will no doubt cover a range of methods. It seems bizarre that acceptance orally or otherwise face-to-face is not allowed, although the telephone is covered. Both methods are capable of being recorded in some permanent form. In so far as no account is taken of the circumstances of claimants with disabilities and the problem cannot be taken care of under reg.16 this provision must be vulnerable to a challenge under the Human Rights Act 1998 for discrimination contrary to art.14 of the European Convention on Human Rights.

Claimant commitment—exceptions

2.48   **16.** A person does not have to meet the basic condition to have accepted a claimant commitment if the Secretary of State considers that—

       (a) the person cannot accept a claimant commitment because they lack the capacity to do so; or

       (b) there are exceptional circumstances in which it would be unreasonable to expect the person to accept a claimant commitment.

DEFINITION

"claimant commitment"—see WRA 2012 s.14(1)

GENERAL NOTE

2.49   The basic condition in s.4(1)(e) of the WRA 2012 does not have to be met where the claimant either lacks the capacity to accept a claimant commitment (para. (a)) or there are exceptional circumstances in which it would be unreasonable to expect the claimant to accept a claimant commitment (para.(b)). Both provisions, but especially para.(b), contain elements of judgment. If "accepting" a claimant commitment has the restricted meaning suggested in the notes to s.14 of the WRA

2012, that will affect when it might be unreasonable to expect a claimant to do so. If a claimant would be unable or experience undue difficulty in accepting a claimant commitment by one of the methods required by reg.15(4), that would suggest that it would be unreasonable to expect the claimant to take those steps to accept the claimant commitment. It is unclear whether, in a case in which a claimant is entitled to both universal credit and new style JSA (so that in accordance with reg.5 of the JSA Regulations 2013 no work-related or connected requirements can be imposed in relation to JSA), the claimant would still be required to accept a claimant commitment to retain entitlement to JSA. Even if the claimant is so required, the effect of reg.5 would be that it was the universal credit claimant commitment that was the controlling document.

Financial conditions

Minimum amount

17. For the purposes of section 5(1)(b) and (2)(b) of the Act (financial conditions: amount payable not less than any prescribed minimum) the minimum is one penny.

2.50

DEFINITION

"the Act"—see reg.2.

Capital limit

18.—(1) For the purposes of section 5(1)(a) and (2)(a) of the Act (financial conditions: capital limit)—

2.51

(a) the prescribed amount for a single claimant is £16,000; and

(b) the prescribed amount for joint claimants is £16,000.

(2) In a case where the claimant is a member of a couple, but makes a claim as a single person, the claimant's capital is to be treated as including the capital of the other member of the couple.

DEFINITIONS

"claimant"—see WRA 2012 s.40.
"couple"—see WRA 2012 ss.39 and 40.
"joint claimants"—see WRA 2012 s. 40.
"prescribed"—*ibid.*
"single claimant"—*ibid.*
"single person"—see WRA 2012 ss.40 and 1(2)(a).

GENERAL NOTE

This provides that the capital limit for universal credit for both a single claimant and joint claimants is £16,000. Thus the capital limit for universal credit is the same as for income support, income-based JSA, income-related ESA and housing benefit (there is no capital limit for working tax credit and child tax credit). See further the notes to s.134(1) SSCBA 1992 in Vol.II of this series.

2.52

Under para.(2), where a claimant who is a member of a couple makes a claim as a single person (see reg.3(3) for the circumstances in which this may occur) the capital of the other member of the couple counts as the claimant's.

For the rules on calculating capital see regs 45–50 and 75–77 and Sch.10.

Restrictions on entitlement

Restrictions on entitlement—prisoners etc.

2.53 **19.**—(1) Entitlement to universal credit does not arise where a person is—

(a) a member of a religious order who is fully maintained by their order;

(b) a prisoner; or

(c) serving a sentence of imprisonment detained in hospital.

(2) Paragraph (1)(b) does not apply during the first 6 months when the person is a prisoner where—

(a) the person was entitled to universal credit immediately before becoming a prisoner, and the calculation of their award included an amount for the housing costs element; and

(b) the person has not been sentenced to a term in custody that is expected to extend beyond that 6 months.

(3) In the case of a prisoner to whom paragraph (2) applies, an award of universal credit is not to include any element other than the housing costs element.

(4) In paragraph (1)(c) a person serving a sentence of imprisonment detained in hospital is a person who is—

(a) being detained—

(i) under section 45A or 47 of the Mental Health Act 1983 (power of higher courts to direct hospital admission; removal to hospital of persons serving sentence of imprisonment etc), and

(ii) before the day which the Secretary of State certifies to be that person's release date within the meaning of section 50(3) of that Act (in any case where there is such a release date); or

(b) being detained under—

(i) section 59A of the Criminal Procedure (Scotland) Act 1995 (hospital direction), or

(ii) section 136 of the Mental Health (Care and Treatment) (Scotland) Act 2003 (transfer of prisoners for treatment of mental disorder).

DEFINITIONS

"housing costs element"—see regs 2 and 25.

"prisoner"—see reg.2.

GENERAL NOTE

2.54 WRA 2012, s.6(1)(a) provides that "entitlement to universal credit does not arise ... in prescribed circumstances even though the requirements of section 3 [i.e., the requirements to satisfy the basic conditions and the financial conditions] are met". Regulation 19 is made under that power. Its effect is that, where a person's circumstances fall within para.(1), entitlement to universal credit "does not arise" even though that person otherwise meets all the conditions of entitlement. Those circumstances as that the claimant is a fully maintained member of a religious order, a prisoner (subject to para.(2)), or serving a sentence of imprisonment in a hospital (as defined in para.(4)).

The wording "entitlement ... does not arise" in both s.6 and reg.19 creates problems. It would have been more natural to say that a person whose circumstances fall within para.(1) "is not entitled to Universal Credit" even if he or she satisfies s.3.

One possibility is that the wording may have been chosen to forestall any suggestion that the rules in reg.19 amount to conditions of disentitlement or disqualification (in which case, subject to the principles enunciated by the House of Lords in *Kerr v Department of Social Development*, [2004] UKHL 23 (also reported as *R 1/04 (SF)*), the burden would be on the Secretary of State to show that affected claimants were not entitled to universal credit, rather than for the claimants to prove that they were). However, this seems unlikely. Whether or not a person is a fully maintained member of a religious order, a prisoner, or serving a sentence of imprisonment in a hospital are not questions that would normally raise difficult issues of proof. And if this was the intention, it is not entirely clear that s.6 and reg.19 achieve it.

Whatever the reason for the wording, the problem it creates is that (to use prisoners as an example) although departmental policy is that prisoners should generally have no entitlement to universal credit other than under reg.19(2) (see ADM E3030 and E3040), that is not what s.6 and reg.19 say. They only say that entitlement does not arise where a person is a prisoner. But that does not cover the position in which entitlement has already arisen but the claimant subsequently becomes a prisoner. If s.6 and reg.19 contained a clear statement that a person who is a prisoner "is not entitled" to universal credit (except where reg.19(2) applies), then imprisonment would be a relevant change of circumstances and a ground for superseding the decision awarding universal credit. As it is, the effect of reg.19 appears to be limited to cases in which a new claim is made by a person who is already a prisoner because it is only in such cases that there is any issue about whether entitlement has "arisen". This view is reinforced by s.6(1)(b) and (c) and (2) which provide that entitlement to universal credit does not arise if the basic conditions or the financial conditions are met for a period shorter than a prescribed period or for up to seven days at the beginning of a period during which those conditions are met. In those provisions the "entitlement . . . does not arise" wording is being applied to circumstances where there is no existing entitlement, as is apt. 2.55

Paras (2) and (3)

The above analysis, creates some difficulties in the interpretation of para.(2). This says that para.(1)(b) "does not apply" during the first six months when the person is a prisoner where that person was entitled to universal credit immediately before becoming a prisoner, and certain other circumstances exist. If what is said above is correct, then para.(1)(b) does not apply at all in such a case, irrespective of the other circumstances. (That is not an objection to the analysis. The "entitlement . . . does not arise" wording is in primary legislation and the way in which the Secretary of State has interpreted that wording when making secondary legislation is not a guide to what it actually means). 2.56

The policy which para.(2) seeks to implement is that where someone with an existing award of universal credit that includes the housing costs element is sentenced to a term in custody that is not expected to extend beyond that 6 months, entitlement to universal credit is retained but the award may not include any element other than the housing costs element.

See also the commentary under the headings *Members of religious orders* and *Person serving a sentence of imprisonment in hospital* in the General Note to reg.21 of the IS Regulations in Vol.II.

[¹ **Waiting Days**

19A.—(1) Entitlement to universal credit does not arise in the first 7 days of the period in respect of which the claim is made if— 2.57

    (a) on the first day of that period ("the relevant date") the claimant, or either of joint claimants, falls within section 22 of the Act (claimants subject to all work-related requirements); and

(b) none of the exceptions in paragraph (3) applies.

(2)   A claimant who may fall outside section 22 of the Act only because they have limited capability for work is to be taken to fall within that section for the purposes of this regulation.

(3)   The exceptions are—

(a) where a new award of universal credit is made—

    (i) to a single claimant as a consequence of a previous award having ended when the claimant ceased to be a member of a couple or to joint claimants as a consequence of two previous awards having ended when the claimants became a couple; or

    (ii) in any other circumstances in which the assessment periods for that award are to begin on the same day of each month as the assessment periods for a previous award (see regulation 21); or

(b) where, on the relevant date, the claimant (or either of joint claimants)—

    (i) is terminally ill;

    (ii) has recently been a victim of domestic violence (as determined in accordance with regulation 98(2));

    (iii) is a care leaver [³ or a person under the age of 22 who is claiming universal credit for the first time and was a care leaver before reaching the age of 18];

    (iv) is aged 16 or 17 and without parental support (as determined in accordance with regulation 8(3));

    (v) has been a prisoner within the month ending on the relevant date; or

    (vi) has been entitled to a jobseeker's allowance or an employment and support allowance within the 3 months ending on the relevant date.

(4)   In order to determine whether a single claimant, or either of joint claimants, falls within section 22 of the Act for the purposes of this regulation, the definition of [² monthly] earnings in regulation 90(6) is to be read as if the reference to the current assessment period were a reference to the month that would be the first assessment period of the award if paragraph (1) of this regulation did not apply.]

Amendments

1. Universal Credit (Waiting Days) (Amendment) Regulations 2015 (SI 2015/1362) reg.2(1)(a) (August 3, 2015).

2. Universal Credit and Miscellaneous Amendments Regulations 2015 (SI 2015/1754) reg.2(3) (Assessment periods beginning on or after November 4, 2015).

3. Universal Credit and Miscellaneous Amendments Regulations 2015 (SI 2015/1754) reg.5 (Assessment periods beginning on or after November 4, 2015).

Definitions

"assessment period"—see WRA 2012 ss.40 and 7(2) and reg.21.
"care leaver"—see reg.8.
"claimant"—see WRA 2012 s.40.
"couple"—see WRA 2012 s.39.
"employment and support allowance"—see reg.2.
"jobseeker's allowance"—*ibid.*
"joint claimants"—see WRA 2012 s.40.
"prisoner"—see reg.2.

"terminally ill"—*ibid.*
"weekly earnings"—*ibid.*
"work-related requirements"—see WRA 2012 s.13.

GENERAL NOTE

WRA 2012 s.6(1)(c) provides that "entitlement to universal credit does not arise **2.58** . . . for a prescribed period at the beginning of a period during which" the claimant satisfies the basic and financial conditions for universal credit (i.e., as required by WRA 2012 s.3). By s.6(2), the period for which there is no entitlement may not exceed seven days.

Regulation 19A is made under the power conferred by s.6(1)(c). From August 3, 2015, entitlement to universal credit is normally deferred for seven "waiting days". The rule is similar to that which applies to JSA (see Jobseekers Act 1995 Sch.1, para.4 and JSA Regulations 1996 reg.46, and JSA Regulations 2013, reg.36) and ESA (see WRA 2007 Sch.2, para.2, ESA Regulations 2008 reg.144, and ESA Regulations 2013 reg.85).

Paras (1) and (2).
Whether the waiting days rule applies is assessed by reference to the "relevant **2.59** date", namely the first day of the period covered by the claim. Entitlement to universal credit is deferred if, on the relevant date:

- the claimant (or either joint claimant) is subject to all work-related requirements by virtue of WRA 2012 s.22 (para.(1)(a)); or

- would be so subject if he, she or they did not have limited capability for work (para.(2)); unless (in either case)

- one of the exceptions in para.(3) applies (para.(1)(b)).

Para. (3).
The waiting days rule does not apply where an award of universal credit is made **2.60** in circumstances in which the assessment periods for that award are to begin on the same day of each month as the assessment periods for a previous award (see regulation 21(3)-(3C) below); or where, on the relevant date, any claimant satisfies any of the conditions in heads (i)-(vi) of sub-para.(b). Those conditions are mostly self-explanatory. Note, however, that the definitions of "jobseeker's allowance" and "employment and support allowance" in reg.2 restrict the operation of head (vi) to new style (contributory) JSA and ESA. For circumstances in which a claimant becomes entitled to UC for the first time within three months of being entitled to old style JSA or ESA (in either case, whether contributory or income-related) or to IS, see reg.16A of the Transitional Provisions Regulations 2014 (as inserted by reg.2(2) of SI 2015/1362).

Para. (4).
Under WRA 2012 s.19(1) and (2)(d) and Universal Credit Regulations reg.90, **2.61** claimants whose "monthly earnings" are equal to or exceed their "individual thresholds" are subject to no work-related requirements. That has the effect that they are not "subject to all work-related requirements" under s.22 and, therefore, the waiting days rule does not apply to them (para.(1)(a)). Monthly earnings are normally assessed by reference to the "current assessment period" (see reg.90(6)) but, where the waiting days rule applies, the start of the first assessment period is postponed by seven days (see reg.21(1A)). Para.(4) provides that when deciding whether a person is "subject to all work-related requirements" for the purposes of para.(1)(a), monthly earnings are assessed over the month that would have been the assessment period if the waiting days rule did not apply.

PART 3

AWARDS

Introduction

2.62   **20.** This Part contains provisions for the purposes of sections 7 and 8 of the Act about assessment periods and about the calculation of the amount of an award of universal credit.

DEFINITIONS

"the Act"—see reg.2.
"assessment period"—see WRA 2012 ss.40 and 7(2).

GENERAL NOTE

2.63   Part 3 is made under powers conferred by ss.7 to 12 WRA 2012 and is concerned with the calculation of an award of universal credit. There are two underlying principles. The first is that an award is made by reference to an "assessment period" (s.7 and reg.21). The second is that the amount of the award is calculated by ascertaining the claimant's (or claimants') "maximum amount" and then deducting "the amounts to be deducted", namely all unearned income and some earned income (s.8 and reg.22).

[¹ **Awards**

2.64   **20A.** For the purpose of determining, under any legislation, whether a person is entitled to any benefit or other advantage by virtue of having an award of universal credit, save where the contrary intention is expressed in that legislation, a person is not treated as being awarded universal credit in respect of any day on which they are not entitled to universal credit.]

AMENDMENT

1. Universal Credit (Waiting Days) (Amendment) Regulations 2015 (SI 2015/1362) reg.2(1)(b) (August 3, 2015).

GENERAL NOTE

2.65   Reg.20A clarifies that where entitlement to another benefit is conditional on a person "having as award of universal credit" a person does not have such an award on any day when they are not entitled to universal credit (*e.g.*, on waiting days). The intention appears to be to prevent the reasoning of the Upper Tribunal in *SSWP v SJ (IS)* [2015] UKUT 0127 (AAC) (see the commentary to reg.7(3) and (4) of the Social Fund Maternity and Funeral Expenses (General) Regulations 2005 in Vol.II) from being extended to universal credit.

Assessment periods

2.66   **21.**—(1) An assessment period is, subject to paragraph (5), a period of one month beginning with the first date of entitlement and each subsequent period of one month during which entitlement subsists.

[² (1A) Where regulation 19A (waiting days) applies, the first day of entitlement for the purposes of paragraph (1) is the first day after the expiry of the 7 days referred to in paragraph (1) of that regulation.]

(2) Each assessment period begins on the same day of each month except as follows—

(a) if the first date of entitlement falls on the 31st day of a month, each assessment period begins on the last day of the month; and

(b) if the first date of entitlement falls on the 29th or 30th day of a month, each assessment period begins on the 29th or 30th day of the month (as above) except in February when it begins on the 27th day or, in a leap year, the 28th day.

[¹ (3) Where a new award is made to a single person without a claim by virtue of regulation 9(6)(a) or (10) of the Claims and Payments Regulations (old award has ended when the claimant ceased to be a member of a couple) each assessment period for the new award begins on the same day of each month as the assessment period for the old award.

(3A) Where a new award is made to members of a couple jointly without claim by virtue of regulation 9(6)(b) or (7) of the Claims and Payments Regulations (two previous awards have ended when the claimants formed a couple) each assessment period for the new award begins on the same day of each month as the assessment period for whichever of the old awards ended earlier.

(3B) Where a claim is treated as made by virtue of regulation 9(8) of the Claims and Payments Regulations (old award ended when a claimant formed a couple with a person not entitled to universal credit), each assessment period in relation to the new award begins on the same day of each month as the assessment period for the old award.

(3C) Where a claim is made by a single person or members of a couple jointly and the claimant (or either joint claimant) meets the following conditions—

(a) the claimant was previously entitled to an award of universal credit the last day of which fell within the 6 months preceding the date on which the claim is made; and

(b) during that 6 months—

(i) the claimant has continued to meet the basic conditions in section 4 of the Act (disregarding the requirement to have accepted a claimant commitment and any temporary period of absence from Great Britain that would be disregarded during a period of entitlement to universal credit); and

(ii) the claimant was not excluded from entitlement by regulation 19 (restrictions on entitlement – prisoners etc.),

each assessment period for the new award begins on the same day of each month as the assessment period for the old award or, if there was an old award in respect of each joint claimant, the assessment period that ends earlier in relation to the date on which the claim is made.

(3D) For the purposes of this regulation it does not matter if, at the beginning of the first assessment period of the new award, the following persons do not meet the basic conditions in section 4(1)(a) and (c) of the Act (at least 18 years old and in Great Britain) or if they are excluded from entitlement under regulation 19 (restrictions on entitlement – prisoners etc.) provided they meet those conditions (and are not so excluded) at the end of that assessment period—

(a) in a case to which paragraph (3B) applies, the member of the couple who was not entitled to universal credit; or

(b) in a case to which paragraph (3C) applies, the member of the couple who does not meet the conditions mentioned in that paragraph.

(3E) In this regulation "the Claims and Payments Regulations" means the Universal Credit, Personal Independence Payment, Jobseeker's Allowance and Employment and Support Allowance (Claims and Payments) Regulations 2013.]

(5) [¹ . . .]

(6) [¹ . . .]

AMENDMENTS

1. Universal Credit (Digital Service) Amendment Regulations 2014 (SI 2014/2887) reg.3(1) (November 26, 2014).The amendment is subject to the saving provision in reg.5 of SI 2014/2887 (see Pt IV).

2. Universal Credit (Waiting Days) (Amendment) Regulations 2015 (SI 2015/1362) reg.2(1)(c) (August 3, 2015).

DEFINITIONS

"assessment period"—see WRA 2012 ss.40 and 7(2).
"claim"—see WRA 2012 s.40.
"couple"—see WRA 2012 ss.39 and 40.
"jobseeker's allowance"—see reg.2.
"personal independence payment"—*ibid.*

GENERAL NOTE

2.67   The effect of the saving provision in reg.5 of SI 2014/2887 is that the text of the regulation reproduced above only applies in "Full Service" (or "Digital Service") areas (see *Universal Credit—An Introduction*, above). For claims that are subject to the "Live Service" rules, see the text of, and commentary, to reg.21 on pp.134-136 of the 2013-2014 edition (and, for the provisions governing repeat claims now contained in reg.21(3C), reg.6 of the Claims and Payments Regulations 2013 on pp.432-433). Note, however that the insertion of the new para.(1A) with effect from August 3, 2015 applies in both Full Service and Live Service cases.

WRA 2012, s.7(1) provides that universal credit "is payable in respect of each complete assessment period within a period of entitlement". "Assessment period" is defined by s.7(2) as a "period of prescribed duration" and "period of entitlement" is defined by s.7(4) as a "period during which entitlement to universal credit subsists". Section 7(3) empowers the Secretary of State to make regulations about when an assessment period is to start, for universal credit to be payable in respect of a period shorter than an assessment period and for the amount payable in respect of a period shorter than an assessment period. Regulation 21 is made under the powers conferred by s.7(2) and (3).

2.68   *Para. (1)* provides that an assessment period is a period of one month beginning with the first date of entitlement and each subsequent period of one month during which entitlement subsists.

2.69   *Para. (1A)* clarifies that where the waiting days rule applies (see the General Note to reg.19A), the first day of entitlement (and therefore the first day of the assessment period) is the day after the expiry of the seven waiting days.

2.70   *Para (2)* makes provision to avoid the administrative problems that would otherwise occur in shorter months. The general rule is that each assessment period begins on the same day of each month. But that is not always possible when the first assessment period began on the 29th, 30th or 31st of a month because not all months have more than 28 days. Therefore:

- if the first date of entitlement falls on the 31st day of a month, each subsequent assessment period begins on the last day of the month (para.(2)(a)); or

- if the first date of entitlement falls on the 29th or 30th day of a month, each subsequent assessment period begins on the 29th or 30th day of the month except in February when it begins on the 27th day or, in a leap year, the 28th day.

Paras (3)-(3B): Reg.9(6)-(8) and (10) of the Claims and Payments Regulations   2.71
2013 (see the definition in para.(3E)) specify circumstances in which it is possible
to become entitled to universal credit without making a claim for it. All of those
circumstances involve there having been a previous award of universal credit. Paras
(3)-(3B) govern the day on which the first assessment period begins under the new
award:

- *Para. (3)* applies where an award is made to a single person who had previously been awarded universal credit as one of two joint claimants, but who has ceased to be a member of a couple, either through relationship breakdown (reg.9(6)(a) of the Claims and Payments Regulations 2013) or through death (reg.9(10)). In such circumstances, each assessment period for the new award begins on the same period of each month as the assessment period for the old award.

- *Para. (3A)* applies either (1) where a joint award of universal credit ends because one former joint claimant has formed a new couple with a third person who is already entitled to universal credit (reg.9(6)(b)) or (2) where two single claimants who are already entitled to universal credit form a couple. In those cases, the dates on which the assessment periods began under the previous awards will not necessarily be the same, so para.(3A) provides that the assessment periods for the new award will begin on the same day of each month as the assessment period for whichever of the two old awards ended earlier.

- *Para. (3B)* applies if a joint award of universal credit ends because one former joint claimant has formed a new couple with a third person who was not previously entitled to universal credit (reg.9(8)), and provides that each assessment period for the new award begins on the same period of each month as the assessment period for the old award. This rule applies even if—at the beginning of the first assessment period under the new award—one member of the new couple was under 18, or was not in Great Britain, or was excluded from entitlement under reg.19, as long as s/he was 18 or over, in Great Brittan, and not excluded from entitlement at the end of that assessment period (para.(3D)).

Para. (3C) is not—or, at any rate, not necessarily—concerned with relationship   2.72
formation or breakdown, but rather with repeat claims. It applies if a new claim for
universal credit is made and the claimant (or either or both joint claimants) was (or
were) entitled to universal credit within the previous six months and, during the
period between the old award and the new claim, the claimant (or both claimants):

- were at least 18 years old, below state pension credit age, in Great Britain (other than for periods of temporary absence that would have been disregarded under reg.11 if there had been an award of universal credit at the time) and were not receiving education; and

- were not excluded from entitlement to universal credit by reg.19 as a member of a religious order, as a prisoner, or as a person serving a sentence of imprisonment detained in hospital.

If the new claim is made by a couple, and—at the beginning of the first assessment period under the new award—one member was under 18, or was not in Great

Britain, or was excluded from entitlement under reg.19, the conditions in the two bullet points above are treated as having been met provided was 18 or over, in Great Britain and not excluded from entitlement at the end of that assessment period (para.(3D)).

Where para.(3C) applies, each assessment period for the new award begins on the same day of the month as each assessment period of the old award or, if there were two old assessment periods (*i.e.,* because two people who were previously single claimants have formed a couple between the end of the old award and the new claim), on the same day of the month as whichever assessment period of the old award ended earlier.

Under reg.26(5) of the Claims and Payments Regulations 2013, a claim must be made before the end of the assessment period in respect of which it is made in order to benefit from para.(3C).

This will normally be more favourable to claimants that the rules for initial claims. The claims process for repeat claimants is intended to be simpler. In addition, the fact that the first assessment period of the new award will normally begin before the date of the new claim (*i.e.,* unless that date happens to coincide with the start of an assessment period) means that the claimant(s) will be entitled to universal credit before that date (although any income earned during the assessment period from a previous employment will be brought into account). However, where any claimant is not in work at the date of the new claim and has ceased being in paid work since the old award ended, the amount of universal credit paid for the first assessment period is reduced (technically, "apportioned") unless the new claim is made within seven days of the date on which work ceased: see reg.22A, below.

Note, finally, that where any of paras (3)-(3C) apply, the waiting days rule does not: see reg.19A(3)(a).

Deduction of income and work allowance

2.73

22.—(1) The amounts to be deducted from the maximum amount in accordance with section 8(3) of the Act to determine the amount of an award of universal credit are—

   (a) all of the claimant's unearned income (or in the case of joint claimants all of their combined unearned income) in respect of the assessment period; and

   [¹ (b) the following amount of the claimant's earned income (or, in the case of joint claimants, their combined earned income) in respect of the assessment period—

      (i) in a case where no work allowance is specified in the table below (that is where a single claimant does not have, or neither of joint claimants has, responsibility for a child or qualifying young person or limited capability for work), [² 63%] of that earned income; or

      (ii) in any other case, [² 63%] of the amount by which that earned income exceeds the work allowance specified in the table.]

(2) The amount of the work allowance is—

   (a) if the award contains no amount for the housing costs element, the applicable amount of the higher work allowance specified in the table below; and

   (b) if the award does contain an amount for the housing costs element, the applicable amount of the lower work allowance specified in that table.

   [¹ (3) In the case of an award where the claimant is a member of a couple, but makes a claim as a single person, the amount to be deducted from the maximum amount in accordance with section 8(3) of the Act is the same as the amount that would be deducted in accordance with paragraph (1) if the couple were joint claimants.]

[¹ Higher work allowance	
Single claimant—	
responsible for one or more children or qualifying young persons and/or has limited capability for work	£397
Joint claimants	
responsible for one or more children or qualifying young persons and/or where one or both have limited capability for work	£397
Lower work allowance	
Single claimant—	
responsible for one or more children or qualifying young persons and/or has limited capability for work	£192
Joint claimants—	
responsible for one or more children or qualifying young persons and/or where one or both have limited capability for work]	£192

AMENDMENTS

1. Universal Credit (Work Allowance) Amendment Regulations 2015 (SI 2015/1649) reg.2 (Assessment periods beginning on or after April 11, 2016).
2. Universal Credit (Reduction of the Earnings Taper Rate) Amendment Regulations 2017 (SI 2017/348) reg.2(1) and (2) (Assessment periods beginning on or after April 10, 2017).

DEFINITIONS

"the Act"—see reg.2.
"assessment period"—see WRA 2012, ss.40 and 7(2).
"child"—see WRA 2012, s.40.
"claimant"—*ibid*.
"couple"—see WRA 2012, ss.39 and 40.
"earned income"—see reg.2.
"housing costs element"—see regs 2 and 25.
"joint claimants"—see WRA 2012, s.40.
"limited capability for work"—see WRA 2012, ss.40 and 37(1).
"qualifying young person"—see WRA 2012, ss.40 and 10(5) and regs 2 and 5.
"responsible for a child or qualifying young person"—see regs 2, 4 and 4A.
"single claimant"—see WRA 2012, s.40.
"unearned income"—see reg.2.
"work"—see WRA 2012, s.40.

GENERAL NOTE

Under s.8(1) WRA 2012, the amount of an award of universal credit is the balance of the maximum amount less the amounts to be deducted which, by s.8(3), are to be two prescribed amounts, one in respect of earned income and the other in respect of unearned income. Regulation 22 is made under s.8(3) and specifies how those prescribed amounts are to be determined. **2.74**

Para.(1) contains the three general principles. First, the claimant's (or the claimants' combined) *unearned* income (i.e., as calculated in accordance with regs 65-74) **2.75** is deducted in full (para.(1)(a)). Second, where no claimant has either responsibility for a child or qualifying young person or limited capabilty for work, 63% of *earned* income (i.e., as calculated in accordance with regs 51-64) is deducted. Third, where any claimant has responsibility for a child or qualifying young person or limited capabilty for work, the deduction is 63% of the amount by which the claimant's (or the claimant's combined) earned income exceeds the "work allowance" specified in the table to the regulation (para.(1)(b)(ii)).

2.76   *Para. (3)* modifies those principles where a member of a couple is claiming as a single claimant under reg.3(3): the couple's combined income is take into account when calculation earned and unearned income, even though the circumstances of the other member of the couple will be excluded when calculating his or her maximum amount (see reg.36(3)).

Para. (1) (b) is—or, at any rate, was until April 11, 2016 see below—the main mechanism by which the policy that, under universal credit, claimants will always be better off in work is achieved. The "work allowance" is what would previously have been described as an earnings disregard: an amount deducted from a claimant's earnings before any means-test is carried out. But, even at the lowest rate, it is a more generous disregard than applied for the purposes of IS, income-based JSA and income-related ESA. Even where there is no responsibility for a child or qualifying young person—and therefore no work allowance—the 63% "taper" means that the claimant keeps 35 pence in every additional pound he or she earns, whereas under IS, income-based JSA and income-related ESA, benefit was reduced pound for pound so that, once a claimant's earnings exceeded the earnings disregard (and ignoring any potential entitlement to WTC), there was no financial incentive to work unless he or she could earn enough to come off income-related benefits altogether.

Before April 11, 2016, the work allowances specified in most cases were higher than those that now appear above. In addition, work allowances were also specified for claimants who were not responsible for a child or qualifying young person, For a more detailed discussion of the effects of the reduction and removal of work allowances in those cases, see *Universal Credit—An Introduction* above.

Para. (2)

2.77   The amount of the work allowance to be deducted from earned income in cases where a claimant has responsibility for a child or qualifying young person is specified in para.(2) and the table at the end of the regulation. The higher work allowance is applicable when the award of universal credit does not contain the housing costs element and the lower work allowance when it does. Very few universal credit claimants will not have to pay anything towards housing costs. The most likely recipients of the higher work allowance are, those living as non-dependants in another person's household, owner-occupiers whose earnings exclude them from entitlement to housing costs under Sch.5, para.4 and those renters treated as not liable to make payments under Sch.2, paras 5 to 10.

[¹ **Apportionment where re-claim delayed after loss of employment**

2.78   **22A.**—(1) This regulation applies where—
  (a) a new award is made in a case to which regulation 21(3C) (new claim within 6 months of a previous award) applies; and
  (b) the claimant (or either joint claimant) is not in paid work and has ceased being in paid work since the previous award ended, other than in the 7 days ending with the date on which the claim is made.
  (2) In calculating the amount of the award for the first assessment period in accordance with section 8 of the Act—
  (a) the amount of each element that is to be included in the maximum amount; and

(b) the amount of earned and unearned income that is to be deducted from the maximum amount,

are each to be reduced to an amount produced by the following formula—

$$N \times \left(\frac{A \times 12}{365} \right)$$

Where—

N is the number of days in the period beginning with the date on which the claim is made and ending with the last day of the assessment period; and

A is the amount of the element that would otherwise be payable for that assessment period or, as the case may be, the amount of earned and unearned income that would otherwise be deducted for that assessment period.

(3) The period of 7 days in paragraph (1)(b) may be extended if the Secretary of State considers there is good reason for the delay in making the claim.

AMENDMENT

1. Universal Credit (Digital Service) Amendment Regulations 2014 (SI 2014/2887) reg.3(1)(d) (November 26, 2014). The amendment is subject to the saving provision in reg.5 of SI 2014/2887 (see Pt.IV).

DEFINITIONS

"assessment period"—see WRA 2012 ss.40 and 7(2) and reg.21.
"claim"—see WRA 2012 s.40.
"claimant"—*ibid*.
"earned income"—see reg.2 and regs 51-64.
"joint claimants"—see WRA 2012 s.40.
"maximum amount"—see WRA 2012 s.8(2).
"unearned income"—see reg.2 and regs 65-74.

GENERAL NOTE

The effect of the saving provision in reg.5 of SI 2014/2887 is that the new reg.22A only applies in "Full Service" (or "Digital Service") areas (see *Universal Credit—An Introduction*, above). It does not affect claims that are subject to the "Live Service" rules (as to which see the commentary to reg.6 of the Claims and Payments Regulations 2013 (below) and pp.432-3 of the 2013/14 edition).   **2.79**

Until November 25, 2014, it was unnecessary in some circumstances to re-claim universal credit if there had been a gap in entitlement of no more than six months. However, in Full Service cases only, and from November 26, 2014, a claim is now necessary but such repeat claims are subject to more favourable rules (see reg.21(3C) above). In particular, the assessment period from the old award of universal credit is adopted, with the effect that the claimant will normally become entitled to universal credit before the date of his or her claim.

However, in cases where the new claim is made more than seven days after any claimant ceased paid work, reg.22A removes the benefit of that more favourable rule. The monthly amounts of each element included in the maximum amount for the assessment period and of the earned and unearned income received in the assessment period are apportioned by multiplying by 12 and dividing by 365 to give a daily rate and then multiplying by the number of days between the date of claim and the end of the assessment period. Note that the apportioned result is likely to less favourable to the claimant than simply starting a new assessment period on the date of claim would have been. Under the apportionment, income earned during the assessment period in the claimant's former employment is taken into account, albeit at a reduced rate. If the assessment period had started at the date of claim, that income would have been received before it started and would not be taken into account.

According to the explanatory memorandum to SI 2014/2887 reg,22A was introduced ". . . to encourage claimants to re-claim universal credit as quickly as possible. Evidence has shown that where claimants enter a conditionality regime within two weeks of losing a job it significantly decreases their time between periods of employment".

Under para.(3), the seven day time limit for re-claiming may be extended if the Secretary of State (and, on appeal, the First-tier Tribunal or Upper Tribunal) considers there is good reason for the delay in making the claim.

Note finally that, where reg.21(3C) applies, the waiting days rule does not: see reg.19A(3)(a)(ii).

PART 4

ELEMENTS OF AN AWARD

Introduction

2.80   **23.**—(1) This Part contains provisions about the amounts ("the elements") under—

(a) section 9 (the standard allowance);

(b) section 10 (responsibility for children and young persons);

(c) section 11 (housing costs); and

(d) section 12 (particular needs and circumstances),

of the Act that make up the maximum amount of an award of universal credit, as provided in section 8(2) of the Act.

(2) The elements to be included in an award under section 12 of the Act in respect of particular needs or circumstances are—

(a) [¹ . . .] the LCWRA element

(b) the carer element (see regulations 29 and 30); and

(c) the childcare costs element (see regulations 31 to 35).

AMENDMENT

1. Employment and Support Allowance and Universal Credit (Miscellaneous Amendments and Transitional and Savings Provisions) Regulations 2017 (SI 2017/204) reg. 4(1) and (3) (April 3, 2017).

DEFINITION

"the Act"—see reg.2.

GENERAL NOTE

2.81   The maximum amount for the purposes of s.8 WRA is the total of:

- the standard allowance: WRA 2012, s.9 and reg.36;

- an amount for each child or young person for whom a claimant is responsible ("the child element") WRA 2012,s.10 and reg.24;

- any amount included in respect of any liability of the claimant to make payments in respect of the accommodation they occupy as their home ("the housing costs element"): WRA 2012, s.11 and regs 25 and 26; or

- any amount included in respect of "other particular needs and circumstances": WRA 2012, s.12 and regs.27 to 35.

The amounts to be included in respect of other particular needs and circumstances are the LCWRA element (regs 27 and 28), the carer element (see regs 29 and 30) and the childcare costs element (regs 31–35). The former LCW element was abolished with effect from April 3, 2017 by the Employment and Support Allowance and Universal Credit (Miscellaneous Amendments and Transitional and Savings Provisions) Regulations 2017 (SI 2017/204) subject to the transitional and savings provisions in Sch.2, Pt.2 to those Regulations (see below).

Responsibility for children or young persons

The child element

24.—(1) The amount to be included in an award of universal credit for each child or qualifying young person for whom a claimant is responsible [² and in respect of whom an amount may be included under section 10] ("the child element") is given in the table in regulation 36.

2.82

(2) An additional amount as shown in that table is to be included in respect of each child or qualifying young person who is disabled and that amount is—

(a) the lower rate, where the child or qualifying young person is entitled to disability living allowance or personal independence payment (unless sub-paragraph (b) applies); or

(b) the higher rate where the child or qualifying young person is—

    (i) entitled to the care component of disability living allowance at the highest rate or the daily living component of personal independence payment at the enhanced rate, or

    (ii) [¹ . . .] blind.

AMENDMENTS

1. Universal Credit and Miscellaneous Amendments (No.2) Regulations 2014 (SI 2014/2888) reg.3(1)(b) (Assessment periods beginning on or after November 26, 2014).

2. Welfare Reform and Work Act 2016 (c.7) s.14(5)(a) (April 6, 2017).

DEFINITIONS

"blind"—see reg.2.

"child"—see WRA 2012, s.40.

"child element"—see reg.2.

"disability living allowance"—*ibid.*

"disabled"—see WRA 2012, s.40.

"personal independence payment"—see reg.2.

"responsible for a child or qualifying young person"—see regs 2, 4 and 4A.

"qualifying young person"—see WRA 2012, s.40 and 10(5) and regs 2 and 5.

GENERAL NOTE

The child element includes two amounts, which are specified in reg.36. The first, which is included for each child or qualifying young person for whom a claimant is responsible, is £231.67 per assessment period subject to a maximum of two children: see regs 24A and 24B and Sch.12.

2.83

Before April 6, 2017 the rate of the child element was higher for the first child or qualifying young person for whom the claimant was responsible. Under reg.43 of the Transitional Provisions Regulations 2014, the higher rate continues to apply where the claimant is responsible for a child or qualifying young person born before April 6, 2017. In 2017/2018, the transitionally protected higher rate is £277.08.

An additional amount is included for each child or qualifying young person who is entitled to disability living allowance or personal independence payment or is registered as blind. The higher amount of £367.92 per assessment period is included where the child or qualifying young person is blind or entitled to the highest rate of the care component of disability living allowance or the enhanced rate of personal independence payment; the lower amount of £126.11 is included in any other case.

[¹ Availability of the child element where maximum exceeded

2.84   **24A.**—(1) Where a claimant is responsible for more than two children or qualifying young persons, the amount mentioned in section 10(1) of the Act is to be available in respect of—

(a) the first and second children or qualifying young persons in the claimant's household; and

(b) the third and any subsequent child or qualifying young person in the claimant's household if—

(i) the child or qualifying young person is transitionally protected; or

(ii) an exception applies in relation to that child or qualifying young person.

(2) A reference in paragraph (1) to a child or qualifying young person being the first, second, third or subsequent child or qualifying young person in the claimant's household is a reference to the position of that child or qualifying young person in the order determined in accordance with regulation 24B.

(3) A child or qualifying young person is transitionally protected in the circumstances set out in regulation 40 of the Universal Credit (Transitional Provisions) Regulations 2014.

(4) An exception applies in relation to a child or qualifying young person in the circumstances set out in Schedule 12.]

AMENDMENT

1. Social Security (Restrictions on Amounts for Children and Qualifying Young Persons) Amendment Regulations 2017 (SI 2017/376) reg.2(1) and (3) (April 6, 2017).

GENERAL NOTE

2.84.1   From April 6, 2017 until October 31, 2018, the rules described in this Note apply to existing universal credit claimants only (including those who claim after April 6, 2017 and subsequently become responsible for two or more children or qualifying young persons). During that interim period, a person who is responsible for two or more children or qualifying young persons cannot make a new claim for universal credit—and will therefore need to claim IS/JSA/ESA and CTC (and, where relevant, HB) instead—unless the claim is made within six months of a previous award terminating under reg.21(3C) or is made by a single person within one month of an award of universal credit terminating because that person ceased to be a member of a couple. See generally, reg.39 of the Transitional Provisions Regulations 2014.

From April 6, 2017 s.10(1A) of the WRA 2012 (as inserted by WR&WA 2016, s.14(1)-(4)) provides that the child element of universal credit established by s.10(1) "is to be available in respect of a maximum of two persons who are either children or qualifying young persons for whom a claimant is responsible." However, s.10(4) provides that "[r]egulations may provide for exceptions to subsection (1) or (1A). Regulations 24A and 24B are made under that power. Reg.24A and Sch.12 create exceptions to the "two-child limit".

In the interests of brevity, the rest of this note will refer to "child" and "children" as if those words included qualifying young persons.

Para. (1) provides that where a claimant is responsible for two or more children, the child element is to be available in respect of the first and second (as determined in accordance with reg.24B: see para.(2)) and for any additional child where either s/he is transitionally protected by reg.40 of the Transitional Provisions Regulations 2014 (see para.(3)) or an exception in Sch.12 applies to him/her: see para.(4). **2.84.2**

Transitional protection

Reg.40 of the Transitional Provisions Regulations 2014 provides that a child is transitionally protected in the following circumstances: **2.84.3**

- (For assessment periods during the interim period from April 6, 2017 until October 31, 2018, including the assessment period during which the interim period begins), s/he was born before April 6, 2017 and there are at least two other children for whom the claimant (or either of joint claimants) is responsible who were born before April 6, 2017 and who precede him or her in the order determined by reg.24B.

- (For assessment periods after the interim period, including the assessment period during which the interim period ends) s/he was born before April 6, 2017 and the claimant (or either joint claimant) was either:

  - entitled to an award of universal credit (or was in a period of non-entitlement between connected awards) and was responsible for the child; or

  - within the six months immediately before the claimant first became entitled to universal credit after the interim period ended, the claimant was in receipt of an individual element of child tax credit for the child or was entitled to an award of IS or old style JSA where an amount in respect of the child was included in the applicable amount;

  and in either case the claimant has neither ceased to be responsible for the child or ceased to be entitled to universal credit (apart from a period of non-entitlement between connected awards). In this case, it is also necessary that there are at least two other children born before April 6, 2017 in respect of whom the claimant (either joint claimant) meets the conditions above and precede the first child in the order determined by reg.24B.

Exceptions

These are set out in Sch.12. They apply in certain cases where there has been: **2.84.4**

- a multiple birth (para.2);

- an adoption (para.3);

- a "non-parental caring arrangement" (para.4);

- non-consensual conception (para.5); or

- a previous exception where the claimant is a step-parent of the child.

Multiple births

The childcare element is available for the third or subsequent child in a household where that child was one of two or more children born as the result of the same pregnancy, the claimant is the child's (non-adoptive) parent and is responsible for at least two of the children born as a result of that pregnancy and the child is not the first in order (*i.e.*, under reg.24B) of the children born as a result of that pregnancy (see Sch.12, para.2). **2.84.5**

In plain English what this means is that the childcare element is included for all children born as a result of a multiple birth as long as the household did not already include two or more older children.

Adoption

2.84.6   The childcare element is available for an adoptive child (irrespective of how many other children the household already includes) except where, the claimant (or his/ her partner) was the child's step parent immediately before the adoption or is the child's (non-adoptive) parent (see Sch.12, para.3). There are also exceptions in certain cases where the child has been adopted in or from another country.

Non-parental caring arrangements

2.84.7   The childcare element is available for the third or subsequent child in a household where the child's parent is herself (or himself) a child (not, in this case, a qualifying young person) and the claimant (or either joint claimant) is responsible for the child's parent: see para.4(1)(b).

There is a further exception where the claimant (or either joint claimant) is a "friend or family carer" as defined in para.4(2): see para.4(1)(a). That definition covers people who are responsible for a child but who are not (and whose partner, if any, is not) a parent or step parent of the child and have care of the child under a variety of different statutes, or who are entitled to guardian's allowance for the child or who have undertaken the care of the child in circumstances where it is likely that the child would otherwise be looked after by a local authority.

Non-consensual conception

2.84.8   This exception applies where the claimant is the child's parent and the Secretary of State (or, on appeal, a Tribunal) accepts that the child "is likely to have been conceived as a result of sexual intercourse to which the claimant did not agree by choice or did not have the freedom and capacity to agree by choice": see para.5(1) (a) and (b). It is also a condition that the claimant "is not living at the same address as the other party to the intercourse". The use of the present tense ("is not living") suggests that the exception can apply if the claimant lived with the other party at the time of the non-consensual conception but no longer does so. That is implicitly confirmed by para.5(5)(b) (see below).

There is a partial definition of the circumstances in which the claimant is to be treated as not having the freedom or capacity to agree by choice to sexual intercourse in para.5(2). They include (but are not limited to) circumstances in which (at the time of conception) the two parties were "personally connected", the other party was "repeatedly or continuously engaging in behaviour towards [the claimant] that was controlling or coercive" and that behaviour had a "serious effect" on the claimant.

Under para.5(5), the claimant and other party are "personally connected" if, at or around the time of the conception, the were in an intimate personal relationship with each other, or were living together as members of the same family having previously been in an intimate personal relationship with each other.

Under para.5(6), behaviour is to be regarded as having a "serious effect" on the claimant if it caused her to fear, on at least two occasions, that violence would be used against her or caused her serious alarm or distress which had a substantial adverse effect on her day-to-day activities.

The Secretary of State may accept the claimant's unsupported word that she is not living at the same address as the other party (para.5(4). However, under para.5(3), he may only determine that the child is likely to have been conceived as a result of sexual intercourse to which the claimant did not agree by choice or did not have the freedom and capacity to agree by choice in two sets of circumstances.

The first set of circumstances apply if:

- there has been a conviction for rape or controlling or coercive behaviour in an intimate family relationship, or an analogous offence under the law of a country outside Great Britain; or

- an award of compensation has been made has been made under the Criminal Injuries Compensation Scheme in respect of a "relevant criminal injury" (as defined in para.5(7)); and

where the offence was committed, or the criminal injury caused, by the other party and resulted in the conception or diminished the claimant's freedom or capacity to agree by choice to the sexual intercourse that resulted in the conception (see para5(3)(b)).

The second set of circumstances apply if the claimant provides evidence from an "approved person" which demonstrates that the claimant has had contact with that, or another, approved person and her circumstances "are consistent with those of a person to whom" paras 5(1)(a) and (1)(b)(i) apply. "Approved person" is defined by para.5(7) as "a person of a description specified on a list approved by the Secretary of State ... and acting in their capacity as such". That list can be found in Form NCC1, *Support for a child conceived without your consent (England, Scotland and Wales)*, which those claiming to have conceived a child non-consensually must complete. The list reads:

- a healthcare professional in a Sexual Assault Referral Centre, or

- other healthcare professionals, such as a doctor, midwife, nurse or health visitor

- a registered social worker

- a specialist support worker from an approved organisation as listed on http://www.gov.uk/government/publications/support-for-a-child-conceived-without-your-consent

At the time of going to press, that website lists:

- members of The Survivors Trust;

- members of Rape Crisis England and Wales;

- Refuge;

- certain member organisations of Women's Aid Federation Northern Ireland and Women's Aid Federation of England.

Note that there is no restriction on when the claimant must have had contact with the approved person.

Under reg. 42 of the Transitional Provisions Regulations 2013, the Secretary of State may treat the requirement for evidence from an approved person as satisfied where the claimant has previously provided such evidence to HMRC for the purposes of the corresponding exception in relation to CTC.

Continuation of an existing exception for step-parents

Para.5 of Sch.12 applies where the claimant is the step-parent of a child ("A");   **2.84.9** has previously had the benefit of an exception in a joint award of universal credit with one of A's parents; in that award the claimant was also responsible for one or more children born as a result of the same pregnancy as A; A is not the first in order (*i.e.*, under reg.24B) of the children born as a result of that pregnancy; and that award ended because the step-parent and parent ceased to be a couple, or in any other circumstances in which the assessment periods for a later award begin and end on the same day of each month as an earlier award under reg.21.

In those circumstances, if the step-parent continues to be responsible for A, under the new award, the childcare element continues to be available for A, even if s/he is the third or subsequent child in a household.

Finally, under reg.41 of the Transitional Provisions Regulations 2014, a similar exception applies where, within 6 months before the step-parent became entitled to universal credit, s/he had an award of CTC, IS or old style JSA in which an exception corresponding with one of those set out above applied in respect of A.

[¹ **Order of children and qualifying young persons**

2.85   **24B.**—(1) Subject to paragraph (2), the order of children or qualifying young persons in a claimant's household is to be determined by reference to the following date in relation to each child or qualifying young person for whom the claimant is responsible ("A"), taking the earliest date first—

   (a) where the claimant, or if the claimant is a member of a couple, the other member, is A's parent or step-parent (in either case, other than by adoption), A's date of birth; or

   (b) in any other case, the date on which the claimant became responsible for A (or in the case of joint claimants where each of them became responsible for A on a different date, the earlier date).

   (2) In a case where—

   (a) the date in relation to two or more children or qualifying young persons for whom the claimant is responsible (as determined under paragraph (1)) is the same date; or

   (b) a claimant gave birth to a child less than 10 months after becoming responsible for a child or qualifying young person to whom paragraph 4 of Schedule 12 (exception for non-parental caring arrangements) applies,

the order of those children or qualifying young persons (as between themselves only) in the claimant's household is the order determined by the Secretary of State that ensures that the amount mentioned in section 10(1) of the Act is available in respect of the greatest number of children or qualifying young persons.

   (3) In this regulation and Schedule 12, "claimant" means a single claimant or either of joint claimants.]

AMENDMENT

1. Social Security (Restrictions on Amounts for Children and Qualifying Young Persons) Amendment Regulations 2017 (SI 2017/376) reg.2(1) and (3) (April 6, 2017).

GENERAL NOTE

2.85.1   This regulation establishes the rules for determining the order of children and qualifying young persons ("children" as in the General Note to reg.24A) in a household for the purposes of the "two-child limit" in s.10(1A) WRA 2012 (see the General Note to reg.24A above) by allocating a date to each child for whom the claimant is responsible. The child with the earliest date is first in the order and so on.

The general rule in *para. (1)* is that where the claimant (or either joint claimant) is the child's parent or step-parent (other than by adoption) the date is the child's date of birth. Otherwise, the date is the date on which the claimant became responsible for the child or, if two joint claimants became responsible on different dates, the earlier of those dates.

2.85.2   *Para. (2)* establishes a qualification and an exception to that general rule. The qualification applies where the para.(1) rule determines the same date for two or more children. The exception applies where a claimant gives birth to a child less than 10 months after becoming responsible for another child as a result of a "non-parental caring arrangement" (see Sch.12, para.4). In either case, the Secretary of State must determine the order of those children so as to maximise the number of children for whom the child element is available.

The housing costs element

25.—(1) Paragraphs (2) to (4) specify for the purposes of section 11 of   2.86
the Act (award of universal credit to include an amount in respect of any
liability of a claimant to make payments in respect of the accommodation
they occupy as their home)—

    (a) what is meant by payments in respect of accommodation (see paragraph (2));

    (b) the circumstances in which a claimant is to be treated as liable or not liable to make such payments (see paragraph (3));

    (c) the circumstances in which a claimant is to be treated as occupying or not occupying accommodation and in which land used for the purposes of any accommodation is to be treated as included in the accommodation (see paragraph (4)).

(2) The payments in respect of accommodation must be—

    (a) payments within the meaning of paragraph 2 of Schedule 1 ("rent payments");

    (b) payments within the meaning of paragraph 4 of that Schedule ("owner-occupier payments");

    (c) payments within the meaning of paragraph 7 of that Schedule ("service charge payments").

(3) The circumstances of the liability to make the payments must be such
that—

    (a) the claimant (or either joint claimant)—

        (i) has a liability to make the payments which is on a commercial basis, or

        (ii) is treated under Part 1 of Schedule 2 as having a liability to make the payments; and

    (b) none of the provisions in Part 2 of that Schedule applies to treat the claimant (or either joint claimant) as not being liable to make the payments.

(4) The circumstances in which the accommodation is occupied must be
such that—

    (a) the claimant is treated under Part 1 of Schedule 3 as occupying the accommodation as their home (including any land used for the purposes of the accommodation which is treated under that Part as included in the accommodation); and

    (b) none of the provisions in Part 2 of that Schedule applies to treat the claimant as not occupying that accommodation.

(5) References in these Regulations—

    (a) to the housing costs element are to the amount to be included in a claimant's award under section 11 of the Act;

    (b) to a claimant who meets the payment condition, the liability condition or the occupation condition are, respectively, to any claimant in whose case the requirements of paragraph (2), (3) or (4) are met (and any reference to a claimant who meets all of the conditions specified in this regulation is to be read accordingly).

DEFINITIONS

"the Act"—see reg.2.
"claimant"—see WRA 2012, s.40.

GENERAL NOTE

2.87   Since universal credit replaces benefits which can include an amount for house purchase costs (income support, income-based JSA and income-related ESA) and housing benefit, the housing costs element of universal credit covers payments both by people who are renting their homes and by owner-occupiers (as well as service charges).

Section 11 WRA 2012 allows for universal credit to include "an amount in respect of any liability of a claimant to make payments in respect of the accommodation they occupy as their home". It also provides that the accommodation must be residential accommodation and must be in Great Britain, and that the accommodation can be the whole or part of a building and need not comprise separate and self-contained premises. All the other detailed rules relating to the housing costs element are in this regulation and reg.26 and in Schs 1–5 to these Regulations (made under the powers in s.11).

Paragraphs (2) to (4) contain the three basic conditions for the payment of a housing costs element: the payment condition (para.(2)), the liability condition (para.(3)) and the occupation condition (para.(4)).

Under para.(2) and Sch.1 the payments in respect of the accommodation must be "rent payments", "owner-occupier payments" or "service charges" (referred to hereafter as "eligible payments"). See the notes to Sch.1 for further discussion.

Under para.(3) and Sch.2 the claimant (or either joint claimant) must be liable to make the eligible payments on a commercial basis, or be treated as liable to make them, and must not be treated as not liable to make them. See the notes to Sch.2.

Under para.(4) and Sch.3 the claimant (or each claimant in the case of joint claimants: s.40 WRA 2012) must be treated as occupying the accommodation as his/her home, and not be treated as not occupying it. See the notes to Sch.3.

Note:

- Paragraph 4 of Sch.4 which excludes any 16 or 17 year old who is a care leaver (defined in reg.8(4)) from entitlement to a housing costs element.

- If the claimant (and/or other member of the couple, in the case of couples) who is an owner-occupier has *any* earned income during an assessment period (i.e. month), no housing costs element will be payable (Sch.5, para.4, although in the case of a shared ownership tenancy (see reg.26(6)), rent payments and service charges can still be met).

- The lower work allowance applies if an award includes a housing costs element (reg.22(2)(b)). This will only affect people in rented accommodation because owner-occupiers cannot get a housing costs element if they have any earned income (see above).

- People who live in "specified accommodation" (see Sch.1, paras 3(h) and 3A, together with the definition of "exempt accommodation" in para.1 of Sch.1) do not receive help with housing costs through universal credit but for the time being at least this will continue to be provided by way of housing benefit.

- There are no deductions for non-dependants (referred to as a housing cost contribution) in the case of owner-occupiers.

Amount of the housing costs element—renters and owner-occupiers

26.—(1) This regulation provides for the amount to be included in an award in respect of an assessment period in which the claimant meets all the conditions specified in regulation 25.

2.88

(2) Schedule 4 has effect in relation to any claimant where—

(a) the claimant meets all of those conditions; and

(b) the payments for which the claimant is liable are rent payments (whether or not service charge payments are also payable).

(3) Schedule 5 has effect in relation to any claimant where—

(a) the claimant meets all of those conditions; and

(b) the payments for which the claimant is liable are—

(i) owner-occupier payments (whether or not service charge payments are also payable), or

(ii) service charge payments only.

(4) Where both paragraphs (2) and (3) apply in relation to a claimant who occupies accommodation under a shared ownership tenancy—

(a) an amount is to be calculated under each of Schedules 4 and 5; and

(b) the amount of the claimant's housing cost element is the aggregate of those amounts.

(5) But where, in a case to which paragraph (4) applies, there is a liability for service charge payments, the amount in respect of those payments is to be calculated under Schedule 4.

(6) "Shared ownership tenancy" means—

(a) in England and Wales, a lease granted on payment of a premium calculated by reference to a percentage of the value of accommodation or the cost of providing it;

(b) in Scotland, an agreement by virtue of which the tenant of accommodation of which the tenant and landlord are joint owners is the tenant in respect of the landlord's interest in the accommodation or by virtue of which the tenant has the right to purchase the accommodation or the whole or part of the landlord's interest in it.

DEFINITION

"claimant"—see WRA 2012 s.40.

GENERAL NOTE

This provides that the amount of the housing costs element for renters (whether or not service charges are also payable) is to be calculated in accordance with Sch.4 (para.(2)). The amount for owner-occupiers (whether or not service charges are also payable) is calculated in accordance with Sch.5 (para.(3)(a) and (b)(i)). Schedule 5 also applies if only service charges are payable (para.(3)(b)(ii)). If the claimant occupies the accommodation under a shared ownership tenancy (defined in para.(6)), the amount of the claimant's (or claimants') housing costs element is the aggregate of the amount calculated under Schs 4 and 5 (para.(4)); in the case of shared ownership any amount for service charges is calculated under Sch.4 (para.(5)).

2.89

Note reg.39(4) of the Decisions and Appeals Regulations 2013 which provides that if the Secretary of State considers that he does not have all the relevant information or evidence to decide what housing costs element to award, the decision will be made on the basis of the housing costs element that can immediately be awarded.

Particular needs or circumstances—capability for work

Award to include [¹ LCWRA element]

2.90   **27.**—[¹ (1) An award of universal credit is to include an amount in respect of the fact that a claimant has limited capability for work and work-related activity ("the LCWRA element").]

(2) The [¹ amount of that element is] given in the table in regulation 36.

(3) Whether a claimant has limited capability for [¹ . . .] work and work-related activity is determined in accordance with Part 5.

[¹ (4) In the case of joint claimants, where each of them has limited capability for work and work-related activity, the award is only to include one LCWRA element.]

AMENDMENT

1. Employment and Support Allowance and Universal Credit (Miscellaneous Amendments and Transitional and Savings Provisions) Regulations 2017 (SI 2017/204) reg.4(1) and (4) (April 3, 2017).

DEFINITIONS

"claimant"—see WRA 2012 s.40.
"limited capability for work"—see WRA 2012 ss.40 and 37(1).
"limited capability for work-related activity"—see WRA 2012 ss.40 and 37(2).
"work-related activity"— see WRA 2012 s.40.

GENERAL NOTE

2.91   Section 12(2)(a) and (b) WRA 2012 allows for an award of universal credit to include an additional element if the claimant (or each claimant in the case of joint claimants: s.40 WRA 2012) has limited capability for work and work-related activity ("LCWRA"). See reg.29(4) where the claimant also qualifies for the carer element (note if it is the other member of the couple that qualifies for the carer element reg.29(4) will not apply).

If both joint claimants have LCWRA, only one additional element will be included (para.(4)).

See reg.36 for the amount of the LCWRA element and reg.28 for when it will be included.

The former LCW element was abolished with effect from April 3, 2017 by the Employment and Support Allowance and Universal Credit (Miscellaneous Amendments and Transitional and Savings Provisions) Regulations 2017 (SI 2017/204) subject to the transitional and savings provisions in Sch.2, Pt.2 to those Regulations (see below). See pp.166-167 of the 2016/17 edition of this volume for the rules that apply if Sch.2. Pt.2 applies and both joint claimants are entitled to the LCW or LCWRA elements or one is entitled to the LCW element and the other is entitled to the LCWRA element.

LCW and LCWRA are assessed in accordance with Part 5 of these Regulations. Under reg.39(1) a claimant will have LCW if it has been decided on the basis of an assessment under these Regulations or Part 4 of the ESA Regulations 2013 that s/he has LCW, or if s/he is treated as having LCW because any of the circumstances in Sch.8 apply (see reg.39(6)). Similarly, under reg.40(1), a claimant will have LCWRA if it has been decided on the basis of an assessment under these Regulations that s/he has LCW and LCWRA or under Part 5 of the ESA Regulations 2013 that s/he has LCWRA, or if s/he is treated as having LCW and LCWRA because any of the circumstances in Sch.9 apply (see reg.40(5)).

See reg.41 as to when an assessment may be carried out.

Note regs 19 to 27 of the Universal Credit (Transitional Provisions) Regulations 2014 (see Pt IV of this Volume) which concern the transition from old style ESA, income support on the ground of incapacity for work or disability and other incapacity benefits to universal credit.

In relation to the effect of a determination of LCW (or not), see reg.40(1) and (2) of the Decisions and Appeals Regulations 2013 which is the equivalent of reg.10 of the Social Security and Child Support (Decisions and Appeals) Regulations 1999. See the notes to reg.10 in Vol.III of this series.

Period for which the [² . . .] LCWRA element is not to be included

28.—(1) An award of universal credit is not to include the [² . . .] LCWRA element until the beginning of the assessment period that follows the assessment period in which the relevant period ends.

(2) The relevant period is the period of three months beginning with—

(a) if regulation 41(2) applies (claimant with [¹ monthly] earnings equal to or above the relevant threshold) the date on which the award of universal credit commences or, if later, the date on which the claimant applies for the [² . . .] LCWRA element to be included in the award; or

(b) in any other case, the first day on which the claimant provides evidence of their having limited capability for work in accordance with the Medical Evidence Regulations.

(3) But where, in the circumstances referred to in paragraph (4), there has been a previous award of universal credit—

(a) if the previous award included the [² . . .] LCWRA element, paragraph (1) does not apply; and

(b) if the relevant period in relation to that award has begun but not ended, the relevant period ends on the date it would have ended in relation to the previous award.

(4) The circumstances are where—

(a) immediately before the award commences, the previous award has ceased because the claimant ceased to be a member of a couple or became a member of a couple; or

(b) within the six months before the award commences, the previous award has ceased because the financial condition in section 5(1)(b) (or, if it was a joint claim, section 5(2)(b)) of the Act was not met.

(5) Paragraph (1) also does not apply if—

(a) the claimant is terminally ill; or

(b) the claimant—

  (i) is entitled to an employment and support allowance that includes the support component [² . . .], or

  (ii) was so entitled on the day before the award of universal credit commenced and has ceased to be so entitled by virtue of section 1A of the Welfare Reform Act 2007 (duration of contributory allowance).

(6) [² . . .]

(7) Where, by virtue of this regulation, the condition in section 5(1)

2.92

(b) or 5(2)(b) of the Act is not met, the amount of the claimant's income (or, in the case of joint claimants, their combined income) is to be treated during the relevant period as such that the amount payable is the prescribed minimum (see regulation 17).

AMENDMENTS

1. Universal Credit and Miscellaneous Amendments Regulations 2015 (SI 2015/1754), reg.2(3) (November 4, 2015, or in the case of existing awards, the first assessment period beginning on or after November 4, 2015).

2. Employment and Support Allowance and Universal Credit (Miscellaneous Amendments and Transitional and Savings Provisions) Regulations 2017 (SI 2017/204) reg.4(1) and (5) (April 3, 2017).

DEFINITIONS

"the Act"—see reg.2.
"assessment period"—see WRA 2012 ss.40 and 7(2) and reg.21.
"claim"—see WRA 2012 s.40.
"claimant"—*ibid.*
"couple"—see WRA 2012 ss.39 and 40.
"employment and support allowance"—see reg.2.
"joint claimants"—see WRA 2012 s.40.
"LCW element"—see regs.2 and 27.
"LCWRA element"—*ibid.*
"limited capability for work"—see WRA 2012 ss.40 and 37(1).
"limited capability for work-related activity"—see WRA 2012 ss.40 and 37(2).
"Medical Evidence Regulations"—see reg.2.
"monthly earnings"—see regs 2 and 90(6).
"work-related activity"—see WRA 2012 s.40.

GENERAL NOTE

2.93   The LCWRA element will not normally be included until the beginning of the assessment period following the assessment period in which the "relevant period" ends (para.(1)), but see the exceptions below.

The "relevant period" is a three months waiting period, starting on the first day on which the claimant submits a medical certificate, or if reg.41(2) applies because the claimant has monthly earnings equal to or above the "relevant threshold" (16 × the national minimum national wage, which is £7.50 per hour from April 1, 2017, converted to a monthly amount by multiplying by 52 and dividing by 12), the date on which the claimant's universal credit award starts, or the date the claimant applies for the LCWRA element to be included, if later (para.(2)).

A claimant does not have to serve the three months waiting period if s/he:

- was previously entitled to universal credit including the LCWRA element, or the three months waiting period for the LCWRA element in relation to the previous award had started but not ended, and the previous award ended immediately before the current award started because the claimant had stopped being or become a couple, or ended in the six months before the current award started because the income condition was not met (and note para.(7)). If the three month waiting period in the previous award had not been completed, the claimant will have to serve the remainder of it (paras.(3) and (4));

- is terminally ill (para.(5)(a)); or

- is entitled to ESA that includes the support component, or was so entitled on the day before the universal credit award started but the ESA ended because of the 52 week limit on entitlement to contributory ESA (para.(5)(b)).

182

Particular needs or circumstances–carers

Award to include the carer element

29.—(1) An award of universal credit is to include an amount ("the 2.94
carer element") specified in the table in regulation 36 where a claimant has
regular and substantial caring responsibilities for a severely disabled person,
but subject to paragraphs (2) to (4).

(2) In the case of joint claimants, an award is to include the carer element
for both joint claimants if they both qualify for it, but only if they are not
caring for the same severely disabled person.

(3) Where two or more persons have regular and substantial caring
responsibilities for the same severely disabled person, an award of universal
credit may only include the carer element in respect of one them and that
is the one they jointly elect or, in default of election, the one the Secretary
of State determines.

[¹ (4) Where an amount would, apart from this paragraph, be included in
an award in relation to a claimant by virtue of paragraphs (1) to (3), and the
claimant has limited capability for work and work-related activity (and, in
the case of joint claimants, the LCWRA element has not been included in
respect of the other claimant), only the LCWRA element may be included
in respect of the claimant.]

AMENDMENT

1. Employment and Support Allowance and Universal Credit (Miscellaneous
Amendments and Transitional and Savings Provisions) Regulations 2017 (SI
2017/204) reg.4(1) and (6) (April 3, 2017).

DEFINITIONS

"carer element"—see reg.2.
"claimant"—see WRA 2012 s.40.
"disabled"—*ibid.*
"joint claimants"—see WRA 2012 s.40.
"LCW element"—see regs 2 and 27.
"LCWRA element"—*ibid.*
"limited capability for work"—see WRA 2012 ss.40 and 37(1).
"limited capability for work-related activity"—see WRA 2012 ss.40 and 37(2).
"regular and substantial caring responsibilities for a severely disabled person"—
   see regs 2 and 30.
"severely disabled"—*ibid.*
"work"—*ibid.*
"work-related activity"—*ibid.*

GENERAL NOTE

The carer element (£151.89 per assessment period: see reg.36) is included in the 2.95
maximum amount if a claimant has "regular and substantial caring responsibilities for a severely disabled person" (as defined in reg.30): para.(1). Where there is
a joint claim, and both parties have regular and substantial caring responsibilities
for a severely disabled person, the amount is included twice, as long as they are
caring for different severely disabled people: para.(2). However, if awards would
also include the LCWRA element (see regs 27 and 28) as well as the carer element,
then only the LCWRA element is included, unless (in the case of a joint claim), the

LCWRA element has been included in respect of the other member of the couple (see reg.27(4)). This reflects the fact that, at £151.89 per assessment period, the carer element is not as high as the LCWRA element at £318.76.

Paragraph (3) governs the situation where two or more people have regular and substantial caring responsibilities for the same person. Only one of those carers can have the carer element included in an award of universal credit. They can agree between them which it is to be but, if they do not do so, the Secretary of State will decide. Under reg.50(2) and Sch.3, para.4 of the Decisions and Appeals Regulations 2013, there is no right of appeal against the Secretary of State's decision on that point.

Meaning of "regular and substantial caring responsibilities for a severely disabled person"

2.96   **30.**—(1) For the purposes of Part 1 of the Act and these Regulations, a person has regular and substantial caring responsibilities for a severely disabled person if they satisfy the conditions for entitlement to a carer's allowance or would do so but for the fact that their earnings have exceeded the limit prescribed for the purposes of that allowance.

(2) Paragraph (1) applies whether or not the person has made a claim for a carer's allowance.

(3) But a person does not have regular and substantial caring responsibilities for a severely disabled person if the person derives earned income from those caring responsibilities.

DEFINITIONS

"carer's allowance"—see reg.2.
"disabled"—see WRA 2012 s.40.
"prescribed"—see WRA 2012 s.40.
"severely disabled"—see WRA 2012 s.40.

GENERAL NOTE

2.97   A claimant has regular and substantial caring responsibilities for a severely disabled person if he or she satisfies the conditions of entitlement to carer's allowance (see Vol.I) as long as he or she does not have earned income from those responsibilities. It is not necessary for the claimant to have claimed carer's allowance (para.(2)): it is enough that they would meet the conditions of entitlement if they did.

Particular needs or circumstances—childcare costs

Award to include childcare costs element

2.98   **31.** An award of universal credit is to include an amount in respect of childcare costs ("the childcare costs element") in respect of an assessment period in which the claimant meets both—

(a) the work condition (see regulation 32); and

(b) the childcare costs condition (see regulation 33).

Definition

"childcare costs element"—see reg.2.

General Note

The childcare costs element is included in the maximum amount if a claim-   **2.99**
ant satisfies both the work condition (reg.32) and the childcare costs condition
(reg.33). By reg.34, the amount of the element is 85 per cent cases of the charges
incurred by the claimant for "relevant childcare" up to a maximum of £646.35 per
assessment period for a single child or £1,108.04 for two or more children (reg.36).
The childcare costs element is not reduced under the benefit cap: see reg.81(1)
and (2).

The work condition

32.—(1) The work condition is met in respect of an assessment period   **2.100**
if—
  (a) the claimant is in paid work or has an offer of paid work that is due
       to start before the end of the next assessment period; and
  (b) if the claimant is a member of a couple (whether claiming jointly
       or as a single person), the other member is either in paid work or is
       unable to provide childcare because that person—
       (i)   has limited capability for work,
       (ii) has regular and substantial caring responsibilities for a severely
             disabled person, or
       (iii) is temporarily absent from the claimant's household.
  (2) For the purposes of meeting the work condition in relation to an
assessment period a claimant is to be treated as being in paid work if—
  (a) the claimant has ceased paid work—
       (i)   in that assessment period,
       (ii) in the previous assessment period, or
       (iii) if the assessment period in question is the first or second assess-
             ment period in relation to an award, in that assessment period
             or in the month immediately preceding the commencement of
             the award; or
  (b) the claimant is receiving statutory sick pay, statutory maternity pay,
       [² ...] statutory paternity pay, [² ...] statutory adoption pay [¹ ,
       statutory shared parental pay] or a maternity allowance.

Amendments

1. Shared Parental Leave and Statutory Shared Parental Pay (Consequential
Amendments to Subordinate Legislation) Order 2014 (SI 2014/3255) art.28(1)
and (3)(c) (December 31, 2014).
2. Shared Parental Leave and Statutory Shared Parental Pay (Consequential
Amendments to Subordinate Legislation) Order 2014 (SI 2014/3255) art.28(1)
and (3)(a) and (b) (April 5, 2015). The amendments are subject to the transitional
provision in art.35 (see below).

Definitions

"assessment period"—see WRA 2012, ss.40 and 7(2).
"claimant"—see WRA 2012, s.40.
"maternity allowance"—see reg.2.
"paid work"—ibid.

"single person"—see WRA 2012, ss.40 and 1(2)(a).
"statutory adoption pay"—see reg.2.
"statutory maternity pay"—*ibid.*
"statutory paternity pay"—*ibid.*
"statutory shared parental pay"—*ibid.*
"statutory sick pay"—*ibid.*
"work"—see WRA 2012, s.40.

GENERAL NOTE

2.101   A claimant satisfies the work condition if she or he is in paid work or has an offer of paid work that is due to start before the end of the next assessment period: para. (1)(a). For joint claims (or in cases where by a member of a couple claims as a single person under reg.3(3)) there is an additional condition that the other member is either in paid work or is unable to provide childcare for one of the reasons set out in heads (i)–(iii). Claimants are treated as if they were still in paid work if they have stopped work within the periods set out in para.(2)(a) or if they are receiving statutory sick pay, statutory maternity pay, statutory paternity pay, statutory shared parental pay, statutory adoption pay (see Vol.IV) or a maternity allowance (see Vol.I).

The childcare costs condition

2.102   **33.**—(1) The childcare costs condition is met in respect of an assessment period if—
[¹ (za) the claimant has paid charges for relevant childcare that are attributable to that assessment period (see regulation 34A) and those charges have been reported to the Secretary of State before the end of that assessment period;]
(a) [¹ the charges are in respect of]—
        (i) a child, or
        (ii) a qualifying young person who has not reached the 1st September following their 16th birthday,
for whom the claimant is responsible; and
(b) the charges are for childcare arrangements—
        (i) that are to enable the claimant to take up paid work or to continue in paid work, or
        (ii) where the claimant is treated as being in paid work by virtue of regulation 32(2), that are to enable the claimant to maintain childcare arrangements that were in place when the claimant ceased paid work or began to receive those benefits.
[¹ (2) The late reporting of charges for relevant childcare may be accepted in the same circumstances as late notification of a change of circumstances may be accepted under regulation 36 of the Universal Credit, Personal Independence Payment, Jobseeker's Allowance and Employment and Support Allowance (Decisions and Appeals) Regulations 2013 and, in such cases, subject to regulation 34A below, all or part of any such charges may be taken into account in any assessment period to which they relate.]

AMENDMENT

1. Universal Credit (Digital Service) Amendment Regulations 2014 (SI 2014/2887) reg.2(1) and (2) (November 26, 2014). The amendment is subject to the saving provision in reg.5 of SI 2014/2887 (see Pt.IV).

Definitions

"assessment period"—see WRA 2012, ss.40 and 7(2).
"claimant"—see WRA 2012, s.40.
"paid work"—see reg.2.
"relevant childcare"—see reg.35.
"responsible for a child or qualifying young person"—see regs 2, 4 and 4A.

General Note

The effect of the saving provision in reg.5 of SI 2014/2887 is that the amendments   2.103
to reg.33 with effect from November 26, 2014 only apply in "Full Service" (or
"Digital Service") cases (see *Universal Credit—An Introduction* above). For the text
of the unamended regulation (which continues to apply in "Live Service" cases) see
p.149 of the 2013/14 edition.
    A claimant satisfies the childcare costs condition in the circumstances set out in
para.(1)(za), (a) and (b). Those paragraphs are cumulative. All three must apply
before the childcare costs condition is satisfied.

Para.(1)(za) applies if a claimant pays charges for relevant childcare (as defined
in reg.35) that are attributable to the assessment period under consideration and,
subject to para.(2), have been reported to the Secretary of State before the end of
that period. Reg.34A governs the assessment period to which charges are attributable.

Para.(1)(a) applies if the charges are in respect of a child or a qualifying young   2.104
person for whom she the claimant is responsible. A qualifying young person ceases
to count for these purposes on September 1st following his or her 16th birthday.

Para.(1)(b) applies if the charges are for childcare arrangements to enable the   2.105
claimant to work or to maintain childcare arrangements that were in place before
a period when she or he is not in paid work but is treated by reg.32(2) as if she or
he were.
    Under para.(2) the Secretary of State may accept childcare charges that are
reported after the end of the assessment period after the end of the assessment
period to which they are attributable, in the same circumstances as any late notification of a change of circumstances may be accepted under reg.36 of the Decisions
and Appeals Regulations 2013 (see Pt.IV below).

Amount of childcare costs element

34.—(1) The amount of the childcare costs element for an assessment   2.106
period is the lesser of—
[¹ (a) [² 85%] of the charges paid for relevant childcare that are attribut-
        able to that assessment period; or]
   (b) the maximum amount specified in the table in regulation 36.
(2) In determining the amount of charges paid for relevant childcare,
there is to be left out of account any amount—
   (a) that the Secretary of State considers excessive having regard to the
        extent to which the claimant (or, if the claimant is a member of a
        couple, the other member) is engaged in paid work; or
   (b) that is met or reimbursed by an employer or some other person or is
        covered by other relevant support.
(3) "Other relevant support" means payments out of funds provided by
the Secretary of State or by Scottish or Welsh Ministers in connection with
the claimant's participation in work-related activity or training.

AMENDMENT

1. Universal Credit (Digital Service) Amendment Regulations 2014 (SI 2014/2887) reg.2(1) and (3) (November 26, 2014). The amendment is subject to the saving provision in reg.5 of SI 2014/2887 (see Pt.IV).

2. Universal Credit and Miscellaneous Amendments Regulations 2015 (SI 2015/1754) reg.6 (Assessment periods beginning on or after April 11, 2016).

DEFINITIONS

"childcare costs element"—see reg.2.
"claimant"—see WRA 2012, s.40.
"couple"—see WRA 2012, ss.39 and 40.
"relevant childcare"—see reg.2 and reg.35.
"work"—see WRA 2012, s.40.

GENERAL NOTE

2.107   *Para. (1)*: See the note to reg.31.

The effect of the saving provision in reg.5 of SI 2014/2887 is that the amendment to para.(1) with effect from November 26, 2014 (but not the increase in the rate at which childcare costs are met from 70% to 85% with effect from April 11, 2016) only applies in "Full Service" (or "Digital Service") cases (see *Universal Credit—An Introduction* above). For the text of para.(1) as it continues to apply in "Live Service" cases (except for the change from 70% to 85%), see p.150 of the 2013/14 edition.

2.108   *Paras (2) and (3)*: Charges for relevant childcare are not taken into account to the extent that the Secretary of State considers them excessive; if they are reimbursed by the claimant's employer or some other person; or if they are covered by "other relevant support" (as defined in para.(3)) paid to claimants participating in work-related activity or training.

[¹ Charges attributable to an assessment period

2.109   **34A.**—(1) Charges paid for relevant childcare are attributable to an assessment period where—

(a) those charges are paid in that assessment period for relevant child-care in respect of that assessment period; or

(b) those charges are paid in that assessment period for relevant child-care in respect of a previous assessment period; or

(c) those charges were paid in either of the two previous assessment periods for relevant childcare in respect of that assessment period.

(2)   For the purposes of paragraph (1)(c), where a claimant pays charges for relevant childcare in advance, the amount which they have paid in respect of any assessment period is to be calculated as follows:

Step 1

Take the total amount of the advance payment (leaving out of account any amount referred to in regulation 34(2)).

Step 2

Apply the formula—

$$\left(\frac{PA}{D} \right) \times AP$$

Where—

PA is the amount resulting from step 1;

D is the total number of days covered by the payment referred to in step 1, and

AP is the number of days covered by the payment which also fall within the assessment period in question.

(3)   In this regulation, a reference to an assessment period in which charges are paid, or in respect of which charges are paid, includes any month preceding the commencement of the award that begins on the same day as each assessment period in relation to a claimant's current award.

AMENDMENT

1. Universal Credit (Digital Service) Amendment Regulations 2014 (SI 2014/2887) reg.2(1) and (4) (November 26, 2014). The amendment is subject to the saving provision in reg.5 of SI 2014/2887 (see Pt IV).

DEFINITIONS

"assessment period"—see WRA 2012 ss.40 and 7(2) and reg.21.
"claimant"—see WRA 2012 s.40.
"relevant childcare"—see reg.2 and reg.35.

GENERAL NOTE

The effect of the saving provision in reg.5 of SI 2014/2887 is that reg.34A only applies in "Full Service" (or "Digital Service") cases (see *Universal Credit—An Introduction* above).   **2.110**

Reg.34A governs when childcare charges are attributable to an assessment period for the purposes of reg.33(1)(za).

Para. (1) provides that charges are attributable either:

• to the assessment period in which they are paid if they are for relevant childcare in that period or (in arrears) for relevant childcare in a previous assessment period (sub-paras (a) and (b)) including, in the latter case, periods before the start of the award of universal credit (para.(3)); or

• to the assessment period in which the relevant childcare is provided if they were paid in advance in one of the two previous assessment periods (sub-para.(1)(c)). In practice, this means that childcare charges can be paid at least two months, and sometimes up to three months, in advance. Again, the previous periods can be before the start of the award of universal credit (para. (3)).

Para. (2) sets out the formula for deciding the amount of childcare charges paid in advance under para.(1)(c) that is to be attributed to an assessment period. The full amount of the advance payment (other than sums that are to be left out of account under reg.34(2) because they are excessive or are met or reimbursed by another person) is divided it by the number of days to which it relates, to produce a daily rate, and then multiplied by the number of days in the assessment period.

Meaning of "relevant childcare"

35.—(1) "Relevant childcare" means any of the care described in paragraphs (2) to (5) other than care excluded by paragraph (7) or (8).   **2.111**

(2) Care provided in England for a child—

(a) by a person registered under Part 3 of the Childcare Act 2006; or

[¹(b) by or under the direction of the proprietor of a school as part of the school's activities—

    (i) out of school hours, where a child has reached compulsory school age, or

    (ii) at any time, where a child has not yet reached compulsory school age; or]

[¹(c) by a domiciliary care provider registered with the Care Quality Commission in accordance with the requirements of the Health and Social Care Act 2008.]

  (3) Care provided in Scotland for a child—

  (a) by a person in circumstances in which the care service provided by the person consists of child minding or of day care of children within the meaning of [¹ schedule 12 to the Public Services Reform (Scotland) Act 2010 and is registered under Part 5 of that Act; or]

  (b) by a childcare agency where the care service consists of or includes supplying, or introducing to persons who use the service, childcarers within the meaning of [¹ paragraph 5 of schedule 12 to the Public Services Reform (Scotland) Act 2010; or]

  (c) by a local authority in circumstances in which the care service provided by the local authority consists of child minding or of day care of children within the meaning of [¹ schedule 12 to the Public Services Reform (Scotland) Act 2010 and is registered under Part 5 of that Act].

  (4) Care provided in Wales for a child—

  (a) by a person registered under Part 2 of the Children and Families (Wales) Measure 2010;

  (b) in circumstances in which, but for articles 11, 12 or 14 of the Child Minding and Day Care Exceptions (Wales) Order 2010, the care would be day care for the purposes of Part 2 of the Children and Families (Wales) Measure 2010;

  (c) by a childcare provider approved in accordance with a scheme made by the National Assembly for Wales under section 12(5) of the Tax Credits Act 2002;

[¹(d) out of school hours, by a school on school premises or by a local authority;]

  (e) by a domiciliary care worker under the Domiciliary Care Agencies (Wales) Regulations 2004; or

  (f) by a foster parent in relation to the child (other than one whom the foster parent is fostering) in circumstances in which the care would be child minding or day care for the purposes of Part 2 of the Children and Families (Wales) Measure 2010 but for the fact that the child is over the age of the children to whom that Measure applies.

  (5) Care provided anywhere outside Great Britain by a childcare provider approved by an organisation accredited by the Secretary of State.

[¹ (5A) In paragraph (2)(b), "school" means a school that Her Majesty's Chief Inspector of Education, Children's Services and Skills is, or may be, required to inspect.]

  (6) In paragraphs (2)(b) and (4)(d)—

  (a) "proprietor", in relation to a school, means—

    (i) the governing body incorporated under section 19 of the Education Act 2002, or

    (ii) if there is no such governing body, the person or body of persons responsible for the management of the school; and

(b) "school premises" means premises that may be inspected as part of an inspection of the school.

(7) The following are not relevant childcare—

(a) care provided for a child by a close relative of the child, wholly or mainly in the child's home; and

(b) care provided by a person who is a foster parent of the child.

(8) Care is not within paragraph (2)(a) if it is provided in breach of a requirement to register under Part 3 of the Childcare Act 2006.

(9) In this regulation "child" includes a qualifying young person mentioned in regulation 33(1)(a)(ii).

DEFINITIONS

"child"—see WRA 2012 s.40 and para.(9).
"foster parent"—see reg.2.
"local authority"—*ibid.*
"qualifying young person"—see WRA 2012 s.40 and 10(5) and regs 2 and 5.

AMENDMENT

1. Social Security (Miscellaneous Amendments) (No.2) Regulations 2013 (SI 2013/1508) reg.3(1) and (6) (July 29, 2013).

GENERAL NOTE

Under reg.33(1)(a), charges only count for the purposes of the childcare costs condition if they are paid for "relevant childcare". Regulation 35 defines that phrase. By para.(1) care is "relevant childcare" if it falls within paras (2) to (5) unless it is excluded by paras (7) or (8).　　2.112

Paras (2)–(5): The details differ as between England, Scotland and Wales but the rule may be summarised as being that to qualify as relevant childcare, the care must be provided by a person authorised or approved by an organ of the state to do so. In England and Wales, it can also be provided by the "proprietor" of a "school" on "school premises". The words and phrase in quotation marks are defined in paras (5A) and (6).　　2.113

Paras (7) and (8): Care is not relevant childcare if it is provided by an unregistered childminder (para.(8)), by a foster parent (para.(7)(b) or by a close relative of the child (or qualifying young person: see para.(9)) wholly or mainly in the child's own home (para.(7)(a)).　　2.114

General

Table showing amounts of elements

36.—(1) The amounts of the standard allowance, the child element, the [³ LCWRA element] and the carer element (which are all fixed amounts) and the maximum amounts of the childcare costs element are given in the following table.　　2.115

(2) The amount of the housing costs element is dealt with in regulation 26.

(3) In the case of an award where the claimant is a member of a couple, but claims as a single person, the amounts are those shown in the table for a single claimant.

Element	Amount for each assessment period
Standard allowance—	
single claimant aged under 25	[¹£251.77]
single claimant aged 25 or over	[¹£317.82]
joint claimants both aged under 25	[¹£395.20]
joint claimants where either is aged 25 or over	[¹£498.89]
Child element—	
[⁵ . . .]	[⁵ . . .]
[⁵ each] child or qualifying young person	[⁵ £231.67]
Additional amount for disabled child or qualifying young person—	
lower rate	[¹£126.11]
higher rate	[⁵ £372.30]
[³ LCWRA element]—	
[³ . . .]	[³ . . .]
limited capability for work and work-related activity	[⁵ £318.76]
Carer element	[⁵ £151.89]
Childcare costs element—	
maximum amount for one child	[²£646.35]
maximum amount for two or more children	[²£1,108.04]

AMENDMENTS

1. Welfare Benefits Up-rating Order 2015 (SI 2015/30) art.13 and Sch. 5 (Assessment periods beginning on or after April 6, 2015).

2. Universal Credit and Miscellaneous Amendments Regulations 2015 (SI 2015/1754) reg.6 (Assessment periods beginning on or after April 11, 2016).

3. Employment and Support Allowance and Universal Credit (Miscellaneous Amendments and Transitional and Savings Provisions) Regulations 2017 (SI 2017/204) reg.4(1) and (7) (April 3, 2017).

4. Welfare Reform and Work Act 2016 s.14(5)(b) (April 6, 2017).

5. Social Security Benefits Up-rating Order 2017 (SI 2017/260) art.28(2) and Sch.16 (Assessment periods beginning on or after April 10, 2017).

DEFINITIONS

"assessment period"—see WRA 2012, ss.40 and 7(2).
"carer element"—see reg.2.
"child element"—*ibid.*
"childcare costs element"—see reg.2.
"claimant"—see WRA 2012, s.40.
"disabled"—*ibid.*
"housing costs element"—see regs 2 and 25.
"joint claimants"—see WRA 2012, s.40.
"LCWRA element"—see regs 2 and 27.

"limited capability for work"—see WRA 2012, ss.40 and 37(1).
"limited capability for work-related activity"—see WRA 2012, ss.40 and 37(2).
"qualifying young person"—see WRA 2012, s.40 and 10(5) and regs 2 and 5.
"single claimant"—see WRA 2012, s.40.

GENERAL NOTE

The amount of each element in the universal credit calculation is prescribed by **2.116** the table (other than the housing costs element, the amount of which is prescribed by reg.26(2)). Para.(3) provides that where a member of a couple claims as a single person (i.e., under reg.3(3)), it is the amounts for a single person that apply.

For the rules about entitlement to each of the elements, see the notes to the earlier regulations in Pt.4.

The amounts in the table have been up-rated twice since the first edition of this volume. The current amounts are as set out above and, with two exceptions, apply from April 6, 2015 (but see the note on p.xxv about when legislative changes to the rules for universal credit take effect in an individual case). From April 7, 2014 to April 6, 2015 (and again see the note on p.xxv), the amounts were

Element	Amount for each assessment period
Standard allowance—	
single claimant aged under 25	£249.28
single claimant aged 25 or over	£314.67
joint claimants both aged under 25	£391.29
joint claimants where either is aged 25 or over	£493.95
Child element—	
first child or qualifying young person	£274.58
second and each subsequent child or qualifying young person	£229.17
Additional amount for disabled child or qualifying young person—	
lower rate	£124.86
higher rate	£362.92
LCW and LCWRA elements—	
limited capability for work	£124.86
limited capability for work and work-related activity	£311.86
Carer element	£148.61
Childcare costs element—	
maximum amount for one child	£532.29
maximum amount for two or more children	£912.50

(see the Welfare Benefits Up-rating Order 2014 (SI 2014/147) art.13 and Sch.5, and the Social Security Benefits Up-rating Order 2014 (SI 2014/516) art.24(2) and Sch.16).

The two exceptions referred to above are the two amounts for the childcare costs element. The original 2013/14 rates of £532.29 and £912.50 were continued through 2014/2015 and 2015/2016 but have been increased from the first assessment period beginning on or after April 11, 2016.

The other current amounts would normally also have been up-rated in April 2016. However, on March 16, 2016, s.11 and Sch.1 of the Welfare Reform and

Work Act 2016 came into force. As a result the following amounts are frozen at their 2015/16 levels for four tax years (i.e., until April 6, 2020):

- all the rates of the standard allowance (para.1(j) of Sch.1 to the 2016 Act);
- the lower rate of the additional amount for a disabled child or qualifying young person (para.1(k)); and
- the LCW element (para.1(l)).

The amounts for the child element, the higher rate of the additional amount for a disabled child or qualifying young person, the LCWRA element, the carer element, the childcare costs element, and the housing costs element are not subject to the four-year freeze. However, they were not up-rated for 2016/17 as the Secretary of State decided that those amounts has maintained their value in relation to prices as measured by the Consumer Prices Index over the 12 month period ending September 2015 (which had showed negative inflation of 0.1%): see para.4.2 of the Explanatory Memorandum to SI 2016/230.

Before April 6, 2017 the rate of the child element was higher for the first child or qualifying young person for whom the claimant was responsible. Under reg.43 of the Transitional Provisions Regulations 2014, the higher rate continues to apply where the claimant is responsible for a child or qualifying young person born before April 6, 2017. In 2017/2018, the transitionally protected higher rate is £277.08.

Run-on after a death

2.117   **37.** In calculating the maximum amount of an award where any of the following persons has died—

    (a) in the case of a joint award, one member of the couple;

    (b) a child or qualifying young person for whom a claimant was responsible; [¹ ...]

    (c) in the case of a claimant who had regular and substantial caring responsibilities for a severely disabled person, that person [¹ ; or

    (d) a person who was a non-dependant within the meaning of paragraph 9(2) of Schedule 4,]

the award is to continue to be calculated as if the person had not died for the assessment period in which the death occurs and the following two assessment periods.

AMENDMENT

1. Universal Credit and Miscellaneous Amendments Regulations 2014 (SI 2014/597) reg.2(1) and (3) (April 28, 2014).

DEFINITIONS

    "assessment period"—see WRA 2012, ss.40 and 7(2).
    "claimant"—see WRA 2012, s.40.
    "couple"—see WRA 2012, ss.39 and 40.
    "regular and substantial caring responsibilities for a severely disabled person"—
      see regs 2 and 30.
    "responsible for a child or qualifying young person"—see regs 2, 4 and 4A.
    "severely disabled"—see WRA 2012, s.40.

GENERAL NOTE

2.118   Where a joint claimant, a child or qualifying young person for whom a claimant is responsible, a severely disabled person for whom a claimant had regular and substantial caring responsibilities or, from April 28, 2014, a non-dependant dies, the award of universal credit runs-on (i.e., it continues as if that person had not died) for the assessment period in which the death occurred and the following two assessment periods.

Part 5

Capability for work or work-related activity

Introduction

38. The question whether a claimant has limited capability for work, or for work and work-related activity, is to be determined for the purposes of the Act and these Regulations in accordance with this Part.

2.119

DEFINITIONS

"the Act"—see reg.2.
"work-related activity"—see WRA 2012, s.40.

GENERAL NOTE

The question of whether a person has limited capability for work ("LCW") or limited capability for work and work-related activity ("LCWRA") is relevant for three reasons. Firstly, if a person has LCW or LCWRA, it affects the work requirements that can or cannot be imposed on him/her (see ss.19(2)(a) and 21(1)(a) WRA 2012). Secondly, it will entitle him/her to an additional element as part of his/her universal credit (see regs 27–28), although note reg.29(4) where the claimant is also eligible for the carer element. Thirdly, it determines which level of the lower or higher work allowance (if applicable) applies (see reg. 22).

2.120

Note also that the minimum age for claiming universal credit is 16 (not 18) if a person has LCW or is waiting for a work capability assessment and has submitted a medical certificate stating that s/he is not fit for work (see reg.8(1)(a) and (b)). In addition, if a claimant's universal credit award includes the LCWRA element, or the claimant (or either or both joint claimants) is receiving new style ESA that includes the support component, the benefit cap does not apply (see reg.83(1)(a)).

Limited capability for work

39.—(1) A claimant has limited capability for work if—

2.121

(a) it has been determined that the claimant has limited capability for work on the basis of an assessment under this Part or under Part 4 of the ESA Regulations; or

(b) the claimant is to be treated as having limited capability for work (see paragraph (6)).

(2) An assessment under this Part is an assessment as to the extent to which a claimant who has some specific disease or bodily or mental disablement is capable of performing the activities prescribed in Schedule 6 or is incapable by reason of such disease or bodily or mental disablement of performing those activities.

(3) A claimant has limited capability for work on the basis of an assessment under this Part if, by adding the points listed in column (3) of Schedule 6 against each descriptor listed in column (2) of that Schedule that applies in the claimant's case, the claimant obtains a total score of at least—

(a) 15 points whether singly or by a combination of descriptors specified in Part 1 of that Schedule;

(b) 15 points whether singly or by a combination of descriptors specified in Part 2 of that Schedule; or

(c) 15 points by a combination of descriptors specified in Parts 1 and 2 of that Schedule.

(4) In assessing the extent of a claimant's capability to perform any activity listed in Schedule 6, it is a condition that the claimant's incapability to perform the activity arises—

(a) in respect of any descriptor listed in Part 1 of Schedule 6, from a specific bodily disease or disablement;

(b) in respect of any descriptor listed in Part 2 of Schedule 6, from a specific mental illness or disablement; or

(c) in respect of any descriptor or descriptors listed in—

(i) Part 1 of Schedule 6, as a direct result of treatment provided by a registered medical practitioner for a specific physical disease or disablement, or

(ii) Part 2 of Schedule 6, as a direct result of treatment provided by a registered medical practitioner for a specific mental illness or disablement.

(5) Where more than one descriptor specified for an activity applies to a claimant, only the descriptor with the highest score in respect of each activity which applies is to be counted.

(6) [¹ Subject to paragraph (7),] A claimant is to be treated as having limited capability for work if any of the circumstances set out in Schedule 8 applies.

[¹ (7) Where the circumstances set out in paragraph 4 or 5 of Schedule 8 apply, a claimant may only be treated as having limited capability for work if the claimant does not have limited capability for work as determined in accordance with an assessment under this Part.]

AMENDMENT

1. Universal Credit and Miscellaneous Amendments Regulations 2014 (SI 2014/597) reg. 2(4) (April 28, 2014).

DEFINITIONS

"the Act"—see reg.2.
"claimant"—see WRA 2012 s.40.
"ESA Regulations"—see reg.2.
"limited capability for work"—see WRA 2012 ss.40 and 37(1).

GENERAL NOTE

2.122   A claimant will have LCW if it has been decided on the basis of an assessment under these Regulations or Part 4 of the ESA Regulations 2013 that s/he has LCW, or if s/he is treated as having LCW because any of the circumstances in Sch.8 apply (paras (1) and (6)). The effect of para.(7) is that a claimant can only be treated as having LCW under para.4 of Sch.8 (substantial risk to his/her health or that of someone else) or para.5 of Sch.8 (life threatening disease) once a work capability assessment has been carried out and s/he has been assessed as not having LCW.

Note that if a claimant has reached the qualifying age for state pension credit (the qualifying age for state pension credit for both men and women is the pensionable age for women (s.4(4) WRA 2012 and s.1(6) State Pension Credit Act 2012) – since April 2010 this has been increasing from 60 and will reach 65 in November 2018) and is entitled to disability living allowance or personal independence payment, s/he is treated as having LCW (para.6 of Sch.8).

See Sch.6 for the activities and descriptors for assessing LCW. They are the same as the activities and descriptors in Sch.2 to the ESA Regulations 2008 for assessing LCW. See the notes to Sch.2 in Vol.I of this series. They are also the same as the activities and descriptors in Sch.2 to the ESA Regulations 2013.

Limited capability for work and work-related activity

40.—(1) A claimant has limited capability for work and work-related activity if—

  (a) it has been determined that—

    (i) the claimant has limited capability for work and work-related activity on the basis of an assessment under this Part, or

    (ii) the claimant has limited capability for work related activity on the basis of an assessment under Part 5 of ESA Regulations; or

  (b) the claimant is to be treated as having limited capability for work and work-related activity (see paragraph (5)).

(2) A claimant has limited capability for work and work-related activity on the basis of an assessment under this Part if, by reason of the claimant's physical or mental condition—

  (a) at least one of the descriptors set out in Schedule 7 applies to the claimant;

  (b) the claimant's capability for work and work-related activity is limited; and

  (c) the limitation is such that it is not reasonable to require that claimant to undertake such activity.

(3) In assessing the extent of a claimant's capability to perform any activity listed in Schedule 7, it is a condition that the claimant's incapability to perform the activity arises—

  (a) in respect of descriptors 1 to 8, 15(a), 15(b), 16(a) and 16(b)—

    (i) from a specific bodily disease or disablement; or

    (ii) as a direct result of treatment provided by a registered medical practitioner for a specific physical disease or disablement; or

  (b) in respect of descriptors 9 to 14, 15(c), 15(d), 16(c) and 16(d)—

    (i) from a specific mental illness or disablement; or

    (ii) as a direct result of treatment provided by a registered medical practitioner for a specific mental illness or disablement.

(4) A descriptor applies to a claimant if that descriptor applies to the claimant for the majority of the time or, as the case may be, on the majority of the occasions on which the claimant undertakes or attempts to undertake the activity described by that descriptor.

(5) [¹ Subject to paragraph (6),] A claimant is to be treated as having limited capability for work and work-related activity if any of the circumstances set out in Schedule 9 applies.

[¹ (6) Where the circumstances set out in paragraph 4 of Schedule 9 apply, a claimant may only be treated as having limited capability for work and work-related activity if the claimant does not have limited capability for work and work-related activity as determined in accordance with an assessment under this Part.]

2.123

AMENDMENT

1. Universal Credit and Miscellaneous Amendments Regulations 2014 (SI 2014/597) reg.2(5) (April 28, 2014).

DEFINITIONS

"the Act"—see reg.2.
"claimant"—see WRA 2012 s.40.
"ESA Regulations"—see reg.2.
"limited capability for work"—see WRA 2012 ss.40 and 37(1).
"limited capability for work-related activity"—see WRA 2012 ss.40 and 37(2).

GENERAL NOTE

2.124   A claimant will have LCW and LCWRA if it has been decided on the basis of an assessment under these Regulations that s/he has LCW and LCWRA or under Part 5 of the ESA Regulations 2013 that s/he has LCWRA, or if s/he is treated as having LCW and LCWRA because any of the circumstances in Sch.9 apply (see paras (1) and (5)). The effect of para.(6) is that a claimant can only be treated as having LCW and LCWRA under para.4 of Sch.9 (substantial risk to his/her health or that of someone else) once a work capability assessment has been carried out and s/he has been assessed as not having LCW and LCWRA.

Note that if a claimant has reached the qualifying age for state pension credit (the qualifying age for state pension credit for both men and women is the pensionable age for women (s.4(4) WRA 2012 and s.1(6) State Pension Credit Act 2012) – since April 2010 this has been increasing from 60 and will reach 65 in November 2018) and is entitled to the highest rate of the care component of disability living allowance, the enhanced rate of the daily living component of personal independence payment, attendance allowance or armed forces independence payment (see the definition of "attendance allowance" in reg.2 which includes armed forces independence payment) s/he is treated as having LCW and LCWRA (para.5 of Sch.9).

See Sch.7 for the activities and descriptors for assessing LCW and LCWRA. They are the same as the activities and descriptors in Sch.3 to the ESA Regulations 2008 for assessing LCWRA. See the notes to Sch.3 in Vol.1 of this series. They are also the same as the activities and descriptors in Sch.3 to the ESA Regulations 2013.

Work Capability Assessment

When an assessment may be carried out

2.125   **41.**—(1) The Secretary of State may carry out an assessment under this Part where—

(a) it falls to be determined for the first time whether a claimant has limited capability for work or for work and work-related activity; or

(b) there has been a previous determination and the Secretary of State wishes to determine whether there has been a relevant change of circumstances in relation to the claimant's physical or mental condition or whether that determination was made in ignorance of, or was based on a mistake as to, some material fact,

but subject to paragraphs (2) to (4).

(2) If the claimant has [¹ monthly] earnings that are equal to or exceed the relevant threshold, the Secretary of State may not carry out an assessment under this Part unless—

(a) the claimant is entitled to attendance allowance, disability living allowance or personal independence payment; or

(b) the assessment is for the purposes of reviewing a previous determination that a claimant has limited capability for work or for work and work-related activity that was made on the basis of an assessment under this Part or under Part 4 or 5 of the ESA Regulations,

and, in a case where no assessment may be carried out by virtue of this paragraph, the claimant is to be treated as not having limited capability for work unless they are treated as having limited capability for work or for work and work-related activity by virtue of regulation 39(6) or 40(5).

(3) The relevant threshold for the purposes of paragraph (2) is the amount that a person would be paid at the hourly rate set out in [² regulation 4 of the National Minimum Wage Regulations] for 16 hours a week [¹, converted to a monthly amount by multiplying by 52 and dividing by 12].

(4) If it has previously been determined on the basis of an assessment under this Part or under Part 4 or 5 of the ESA Regulations that the claimant does not have limited capability for work, no further assessment is to be carried out unless there is evidence to suggest that—

(a) the determination was made in ignorance of, or was based on a mistake as to, some material fact; or

(b) there has been a relevant change of circumstances in relation to the claimant's physical or mental condition.

AMENDMENTS

1. Universal Credit and Miscellaneous Amendments Regulations 2015 (SI 2015/1754), reg.2(4) (November 4, 2015, or in the case of existing awards, the first assessment period beginning on or after November 4, 2015).

2. Social Security (Jobseeker's Allowance, Employment and Support Allowance and Universal Credit) (Amendment) Regulations 2016 (SI 2016/678), reg.5(3) (July 25, 2016).

DEFINITIONS

"attendance allowance"—see reg.2.
"claimant"—see WRA 2012 s.40.
"disability living allowance"—see reg.2.
"ESA Regulations"—*ibid.*
"limited capability for work"—see WRA 2012 ss.40 and 37(1).
"limited capability for work-related activity"—see WRA 2012 ss.40 and 37(2).
"monthly earnings"–see regs 2 and 90(6).
"National Minimum Wage Regulations" – see reg. 2.
"personal independence payment"—*ibid.*
"work-related activity"—see WRA 2012 s.40.

GENERAL NOTE

Para. (1) 2.126

This provides when a work capability assessment can be carried out but it is subject to paras (2)–(4).

Paras (2) and (3) 2.127

The effect of these two paragraphs is that a claimant who has monthly earnings that are equal to or above the "relevant threshold" (16 × the national minimum national wage, which is £7.20 per hour from April 1, 2016, converted to a monthly amount by multiplying by 52 and dividing by 12) is treated as not having LCW (unless s/he is deemed to have LCW under reg.39(6) and Sch.8 or LCW and LCWRA under reg.40(5) and Sch.9) and no assessment may be carried out. But this rule does not apply if the claimant:

- is entitled to disability living allowance, personal independence payment, attendance allowance or armed forces independence payment (see the definition of "attendance allowance" in reg.2 which includes armed forces independence payment); or

- has already been assessed as having LCW or LCW and LCWRA under these Regulations or Pt 4 or 5 of the ESA Regulations 2013 and the purpose of the assessment is to review that determination.

Paragraphs (2) and (3) thus contain what could be viewed as a rump of a "permitted work rule" (somewhat oddly placed in a regulation that is also concerned with when an assessment may be carried out). But the effect of para.(2)(b) is that a claimant will only be treated as not having LCW under para.(2) if his/her weekly earnings are equal to or above the relevant threshold (see para.(3)) *and* s/he has not yet been assessed under the work capability assessment. If the claimant has already been assessed as having LCW or LCW and LCWRA, para.(2) will not apply, although the work capability assessment may well be re-applied in these circumstances. Until it is determined that the claimant does not have LCW or LCW and LCWRA, the claimant's universal credit award will continue to include the LCW or LCWRA element (as appropriate) (confirmed in para.G1035 ADM).

Note reg.40(1) and (2) of the Decisions and Appeals Regulations 2013 which provides that a determination that a person has, or does not have, LCW, or is to be treated as having, or not having, LCW, that has been made for the purposes of new style ESA or universal credit is conclusive for the purpose of any further decision relating to that benefit.

2.128   *Para. (4)*

If it has been decided that the claimant does not have LCW either under these Regulations or the ESA Regulations 2013, no further assessment will be carried out for the purposes of universal credit unless the evidence suggests that the decision was made in ignorance of or mistake as to a material fact or that there has been a relevant change in the claimant's physical or mental condition (para.(4)). Note that this provision applies without time limit.

Assessment—supplementary

2.129   **42.**—(1) The following provisions apply to an assessment under this Part.

(2) The claimant is to be assessed as if the claimant were fitted with or wearing any prosthesis with which the claimant is normally fitted or normally wears or, as the case may be, wearing or using any aid or appliance which is normally, or could reasonably be expected to be, worn or used.

(3) If a descriptor applies in the case of the claimant as a direct result of treatment provided by a registered medical practitioner for a specific disease, illness or disablement, it is to be treated as applying by reason of the disease, illness or disablement.

DEFINITION

"claimant"—see WRA 2012 s.40.

Information requirement

2.130   **43.**—(1) The information required to determine whether a claimant has limited capability for work or for work and work-related activity is—

(a) any information relating to the descriptors specified in Schedule 6 or 7 requested by the Secretary of State in the form of a questionnaire; and

(b) any additional information that may be requested by the Secretary of State.

(2) But where the Secretary of State is satisfied that there is enough information to make the determination without the information mentioned in paragraph (1)(a), that information is not required.

(3) Where a claimant fails without a good reason to comply with a request under paragraph (1), the claimant is to be treated as not having limited capability for work or, as the case may be, for work and work-related activity.

(4) But paragraph (3) does not apply unless the claimant was sent a further request to provide the information at least 3 weeks after the date of the first request and at least 1 week has passed since the further request was sent.

DEFINITIONS

"claimant"—see WRA 2012 s.40.
"limited capability for work"—see WRA 2012 ss.40 and 37(1).
"limited capability for work-related activity"—see WRA 2012 ss.40 and 37(2).
"work-related activity"—see WRA 2012 s.40.

GENERAL NOTE

On paras (3) and (4), see regs 22 and 37 of the ESA Regulations 2008 and the notes to those regulations in Vol.I of this series.   2.131

Medical examinations

44.—(1) Where it falls to be determined whether a claimant has limited capability for work or for work and work-related activity, the claimant may be called by or on behalf of a health care professional approved by the Secretary of State to attend a medical examination.   2.132

(2) Where a claimant who is called by or on behalf of such a health care professional to attend a medical examination fails without a good reason to attend or submit to the examination, the claimant is to be treated as not having limited capability for work or, as the case may be, for work and work-related activity.

(3) But paragraph (2) does not apply unless—

(a) notice of the date, time and place of the examination was given to the claimant at least 7 days in advance; or

(b) notice was given less than 7 days in advance and the claimant agreed to accept it.

DEFINITIONS

"claimant"—see WRA 2012 s.40.
"health care professional"—see reg.2.
"limited capability for work"—see WRA 2012 ss.40 and 37(1).
"limited capability for work-related activity"—see WRA 2012 ss.40 and 37(2).
"work-related activity"—see WRA 2012 s.40.

2.133   See regs 23 and 38 of the ESA Regulations 2008 and the notes to those regulations in Vol.I of this series. But note that unlike regs 23 and 38, the notice under reg.44 does not have to be in writing (see para.(3)).

PART 6

CALCULATION OF CAPITAL AND INCOME

CHAPTER 1

CAPITAL

Introduction

2.134   **45.** This Chapter provides for the calculation of a person's capital for the purpose of section 5 of the Act (financial conditions) and section 8 of the Act (calculation of awards).

DEFINITION

"the Act"—see reg.2.

GENERAL NOTE

2.135   A claimant's resources are either capital or income. There is nothing in between. On the distinction between capital and income, see the notes to reg.23 of the Income Support Regulations in Vol.II of this series.

Compared with income support, income-based JSA, income-related ESA and housing benefit, the rules for the treatment of capital under universal credit are refreshingly concise. For example, there are only 19 paragraphs in Sch.10 (capital to be disregarded), whereas Sch.10 to the Income Support Regulations has over 70 (although a few have been omitted over the years).

The capital limit for universal credit for both a single claimant and joint claimants is £16,000 (see reg.18(1)). Note that where a claimant who is a member of a couple makes a claim as a single person (see reg.3(3) for the circumstances in which this may occur) the capital of the other member of the couple counts as the claimant's (reg.18(2)).

What is included in capital?

2.136   **46.**—(1) The whole of a person's capital is to be taken into account unless—

(a) it is to be treated as income (see paragraphs (3) and (4)); or

(b) it is to be disregarded (see regulation 48).

(2) A person's personal possessions are not to be treated as capital.

(3) Subject to paragraph (4), any sums that are paid regularly and by reference to a period, for example payments under an annuity, are to be treated as income even if they would, apart from this provision, be regarded as capital or as having a capital element.

(4) Where capital is payable by instalments, each payment of an instalment is to be treated as income if the amount outstanding, combined with any other capital of the person (and, if the person is a member of a couple, the other member), exceeds £16,000, but otherwise such payments are to be treated as capital.

GENERAL NOTE

The whole of a claimant's capital, both actual and notional (see reg.50), counts towards the £16,000 limit, except if it is treated as income under paras (3) and (4), or is ignored under Sch.10 or regs 75 and 76 (para.(1)). In the case of joint claimants, it is their combined capital that counts towards the £16,000 limit (s.5(2) (a) WRA 2012). A child's capital is not taken into account.

2.137

Note reg.49 which maintains the rule that applies for income support, old style JSA, old style ESA and housing benefit that it is only if a debt is secured on a capital asset that it can be deducted.

The capital must of course be the claimant's, that is, s/he must be the beneficial owner of it. See the notes to reg.46 of the Income Support Regulations in Vol.II of this series on beneficial ownership and what can constitute capital.

Note that personal possessions are not treated as capital (para.(2)). There is no equivalent to the rule for income support, old style JSA, old style ESA and housing benefit that personal possessions are taken into account if they have been acquired for the purpose of reducing capital in order to secure, or increase, entitlement to benefit (see, e.g., para.10 of Sch.10 to the Income Support Regulations in Vol.II of this series). However, in such circumstances claimants may be found to have notional capital under reg.50(1) and (2), by reason of having deprived themselves of capital through the mechanism of acquisition of personal possessions. For reg.50(1) to operate, the deprivation must have been for the purpose of securing entitlement to or increasing the amount of universal credit (rather than any other benefit), which may significantly limit its effect in relation to acquisitions some way in the past. In addition, reg.50(2), in a provision not replicated in relation to any other benefits, prevents claimants being treated as having deprived themselves of capital if they have purchased goods or services and the expenditure was reasonable in the circumstances (see further in the notes to that provision).

R(H) 7/08 was a case about whether a moveable but static caravan, attached to mains services on a non-residential site, was a "personal possession" for the purposes of the disregard in the housing benefit legislation. A tribunal had decided that it was not, so that its value counted as capital. The Commissioner held that it erred in law in doing so. After a discursive discussion of the legislative background and the scant authority, he said this in para.53:

> "My conclusion is that 'personal possessions' mean any physical assets other than land and assets used for business purposes. . . . [This] avoids uncertainty of scope and difficulties of application. It is consistent with the legislative history of the disregard and the more humane approach to resource-related benefits that has increasingly been shown over the period of the welfare state. It recognises the increased emphasis that has been given over recent decades to ways of assisting claimants off welfare by not requiring particular categories of possessions to be disposed of for what may be a relatively short period on benefit."

That approach would seem to require that the actual value of items acquired mainly, or even solely, as investments be disregarded, but there will sometimes be very difficult lines to be drawn in particular circumstances even if that basis were accepted. At what point might coins, say, or gold bars cease to be regarded as personal possessions and be regarded as a way of holding capital in the same way as everyday cash?

Might it still be argued that, as Commissioner Jacobs was not directly concerned in *R(H) 7/08* with any line between personal possessions and investments, the decision does not exclude a conclusion that the adjective "personal" is an indication that something has to be used at least partly for personal or domestic or household purposes, not solely for investment? Prior to its amendment in October 2014 by s.3(1) of the Inheritance and Trustees' Powers Act 2014, the definition of "personal chattels" in s.55(1)(x) in the Administration of Estates Act 1925 (for the purposes of identifying how an estate is to be distributed on intestacy), as well as setting out a long list of specific items, included "articles of household or personal use or ornament". The courts, bearing in mind the test in terms of the use made of the article at the time of death, took quite a generous approach to when that use had a personal element. In one case, *Re Reynolds'Will Trusts* [1966] 1 W.L.R. 19, the aptly named Stamp J, having held the intestate's valuable stamp collection, built up since childhood as his main hobby, to be part of his personal chattels, suggested that if he had gone into a shop and bought a similar collection that he then installed in his flat it could hardly be said that that was an article of personal use. The definition in place from October 1, 2014, covers all tangible movable property, subject to exceptions including property held solely as an investment. That is regarded as an expression of the position that had been established by the case law on the previous definition. Regulation 49(2) makes no express reference to the use made of any possession, but it may be arguable that the word "personal" entails the exclusion of items with no element of personal enjoyment or cherishing (such as collections of jewellery, art work, stamps etc locked away in a safe or bank vault and never inspected). However, such an approach would again involve the drawing of difficult lines after careful investigation that it may be thought that the legislation was intended to avoid. It would have been helpful if matters had been made plainer on the face of the legislation.

No doubt, whatever the general answer, the more evidence there is that an item was acquired by a person for investment, the stronger the argument would be for its cost having been a deprivation of capital under reg.50(1), subject to the working out of the scope of the exception in reg.50(2)(b) for purchasing goods and services where the expenditure was reasonable.

Under paras (3) and (4), certain payments that might otherwise be capital are treated as income (and therefore do not count as capital).

Paragraph (4) deals with capital payable by instalments. If the amount outstanding plus the claimant's (including, in the case of couples, the other member of the couple's) other capital is more than £16,000, each instalment when paid is treated as income. Otherwise the payment counts as capital. See the notes to reg.41(1) of the Income Support Regulations in Vol.II of this series.

Paragraph (3) applies to sums (other than capital payable by instalments) that are paid regularly and by reference to a period, such as payments under an annuity, that may otherwise be capital or have a capital element. They are treated as income. This is wider than the existing rule in, e.g., reg.41(2) of the Income Support Regulations (which only applies to payments under an annuity) and would seem to be an attempt to draw more of a line between capital and income. See the notes to reg.23 of the Income Support Regulations in Vol.II of this series on the distinction between capital and income.

Capital that is treated as income under paras (3) or (4) is included in a person's unearned income (see reg.66(1)(l)).

Note the "assumed yield from capital" rule in reg.72 (the equivalent to the "tariff income rule" for income support, old style JSA, old style ESA and housing benefit). Actual income from capital (unless the capital is disregarded or the income is taken into account under reg.66(1)(i) or (j)) is treated as capital from the day it is due to be paid.

Jointly held capital

2.138   **47.** Where a person and one or more other persons have a beneficial interest in a capital asset, those persons are to be treated, in the absence of evidence to the contrary, as if they were each entitled to an equal share of the whole of that beneficial interest.

GENERAL NOTE

2.139   This provision is much the same in structure as the income support and income-based JSA equivalents (reg.52 of the Income Support Regulations and reg.115 of the JSA Regulations 1996), with the addition of the apparently significant words "in the absence of evidence to the contrary". However, close analysis suggests that those words are meaningless and ineffective and that reg.47, like its equivalents, achieves only limited results of substance.

That conclusion follows from the decision of the Court of Appeal in *Hourigan v Secretary of State for Work and Pensions* [2002] EWCA Civ 1890, reported as *R(IS) 4/03*. There the claimant bought her council house with a contribution of five-sixths of the purchase price from her son. The legal estate was transferred to her, but it was accepted that in those circumstances she held the legal estate on trust for herself and her son as tenants in common in the proportions of their contributions to the purchase price. The Secretary of State argued that reg.52 of the Income Support Regulations applied because the claimant and her son were beneficially entitled to the capital asset of the equitable interest in the house and that as a result she had to be treated as having a half share in the equitable interest, although her actual share was one-sixth. It was argued that it was that deemed half share that had to be valued as capital, in which case the claimant was not entitled to income support because the capital limit was breached. Brooke LJ held that it would be a misuse of language to say that the claimant and her son were both beneficially entitled to a capital asset in the form of the house because the beneficial interest of each as a tenant in common was a separately disposable asset. To interpret reg.52 in the way contended for by the Secretary of State would require very much clearer words. Not only was it unfair to the claimant to treat her as possessing more capital than she could actually realise, but the Secretary of State's argument could also work unfairly in favour of claimants (e.g. if it had been a claimant who had a five-sixths share who was deemed to have only a half-share). Thus it was only the claimant's actual one-sixth share as tenant in common that fell to be valued as capital.

Brooke LJ accepted that the language of reg.52 could apply to circumstances in which the claimant and one or more persons were jointly entitled to the equitable interest in the same capital asset. In that situation the effect of reg.52 was to treat the joint tenancy as severed and to deem the claimant to have an equal share (with the other joint tenants), with there being a tenancy in common as between the claimant and the other joint tenant(s).

That appears correct, but the limit of the effect of reg.52 would appear to be in deeming that there has been a severance of the joint tenancy of the beneficial interest (as can be carried out by a joint tenant at any time or by selling or otherwise alienating or attempting to alienate the interest as a joint tenant). The limit is because there is no need for any regulation to deem that the claimant's share on severance is proportionate to the number of former joint tenants (i.e. a half share if there were previously two, a third share if there were previously three etc). That consequence follows from the nature of a joint tenancy, where there is only one interest (the so-called unity of interest), so that the interest of each tenant must be the same in extent, nature and duration. There is no room at that stage for going back to, say, the amount of contribution to the purchase price, to justify anything other than an equal share. Thus, if the claimant in *Hourigan* had expressly had the council house conveyed to her to hold in trust for herself and her son as joint tenants, there could have been no escape, regardless of any regulations, from the consequence on a severance (actual or deemed) of the joint tenancy in the beneficial interest that her share as tenant in common was one-half. It could make no difference that the son had contributed five-sixths of the purchase price. It is a common elementary student error to think otherwise, one into which it appears that Auld LJ fell in *Hourigan*.

The upshot is that, once it is determined that reg.47 is restricted to joint tenancies, the reference to the absence of evidence to the contrary becomes redundant. The purported relevance of the phrase "in the absence of evidence to the contrary" to the deeming in reg.47 can only be to the shares in which the beneficial interest is to be held under the tenancy in common (the phrase "in equal shares" having long been accepted as indicating a tenancy in common). Evidence to the contrary cannot prevent the deeming of a tenancy in common because in all circumstances where there was still actually a joint tenancy there would be evidence to the contrary, i.e. whatever the evidence was that produced that actual result, and the regulation could then never apply at all. However, no evidence to the contrary can influence the shares under the deemed tenancy in common, because the equal shares follow from the nature of a joint tenancy as noted above.

In cases, like the above, involving real property, there will usually be no difficulty in identifying the property subject to a joint tenancy. It may not be so easy when the joint interest is in some other asset or in a bank or building society account. That is shown by *CIS 7097/1995*. There, the claimant's husband went to live permanently in a nursing home. To help finance the cost of that accommodation, £7,000 of the husband's National Savings certificates were cashed in and the proceeds paid into the couple's joint bank account, so that the nursing home could be paid regularly by direct debit. There was evidence that the intention had not been that the sum should form part of the joint money in the account. The £7,000 had been declared as the husband's own money in an application to the local authority for financial assistance with the fees and a separate tally was kept of the use of that money. The AO treated the claimant's capital as including half of the balance in the joint account, including the proceeds of the husband's National Savings certificates, which took her over the limit, so that she was not entitled to income support. The Commissioner reversed that decision. There was clear evidence that the normal presumption of joint beneficial ownership between a husband and wife operating a joint bank account did not apply in relation to the £7,000. It was obviously intended that the proceeds of the husband's National Savings certificates were to remain his sole property and had been paid into the joint account merely for convenience. They did not form part of the claimant's capital. The Commissioner also analysed the nature of joint beneficial ownership and ownership in equal shares in a way consistent with what is said above.

A similar approach was taken in the Scottish case of *JK v SSWP (JSA)* [2010] UKUT 437 (AAC), reported as [2011] AACR 26. The claimant contended that some of the money in his and his wife's joint bank account belonged to his mother-in-law. It was held that the First-tier Tribunal, instead of asking whether there was a trust in favour of the mother-in-law, should have considered, by reference to such oral or written evidence available to it that it accepted, whether under Scots law (see *Cairns v Davidson* 1913 S.C. 1053) the presumption in favour of all the money in the joint account belonging to the claimant and his wife had been rebutted, so as to establish whether or not some of it belonged to the mother-in-law.

See the notes to reg.52 of the Income Support Regulations in Vol.II of this series for discussion of problems in the valuation of a deemed share under a tenancy in common and for the complexities caused by the wording of the rule for jointly held capital in the past.

Capital disregarded

2.140 **48.**—(1) Any capital specified in Schedule 10 is to be disregarded from the calculation of a person's capital (see also regulations 75 to 77).

(2) Where a period of 6 months is specified in that Schedule, that period may be extended by the Secretary of State where it is reasonable to do so in the circumstances of the case.

GENERAL NOTE

2.141 The number of disregards in Sch.10 is considerably reduced from those that apply for income support, old style JSA, old style ESA and housing benefit but they cover many of the same items, such as premises, business assets, rights in pension schemes, earmarked assets, etc. But note that some of the disregards that are in Schedules for the purposes of income support, old style JSA, old style ESA and housing benefit are to be found elsewhere in these Regulations, e.g., in regs 46(2),

49(3), 75 and 76. See also reg.77 in relation to companies in which the person is like a sole trader or partner.

Note the general extension on the grounds of reasonableness that can be applied to the six months' period in any of the provisions in Sch.10 (para.(2)).

Valuation of capital

49.—(1) Capital is to be calculated at its current market value or surrender value less—

    (a) where there would be expenses attributable to sale, 10 per cent; and

    (b) the amount of any encumbrances secured on it.

(2) The market value of a capital asset possessed by a person in a country outside the United Kingdom is—

    (a) if there is no prohibition in that country against the transfer of an amount equal to the value of that asset to the United Kingdom, the market value in that country; or

    (b) if there is such a prohibition, the amount it would raise if sold in the United Kingdom to a willing buyer.

(3) Where capital is held in currency other than sterling, it is to be calculated after the deduction of any banking charge or commission payable in converting that capital into sterling.

2.142

GENERAL NOTE

The rules for the valuation of capital are the same as those for income support, old style JSA, old style ESA and housing benefit. See the notes to regs 49 and 50 of the Income Support Regulations in Vol. II of this series.

The provision in para.(3) previously took the form of a disregard—see, e.g., para.21 of Sch.10 to the Income Support Regulations.

2.143

Notional capital

50.—(1) A person is to be treated as possessing capital of which the person has deprived themselves for the purpose of securing entitlement to universal credit or to an increased amount of universal credit.

(2) A person is not to be treated as depriving themselves of capital if the person disposes of it for the purposes of—

    (a) reducing or paying a debt owed by the person; or

    (b) purchasing goods or services if the expenditure was reasonable in the circumstances of the person's case.

(3) Where a person is treated as possessing capital in accordance with this regulation, then for each subsequent assessment period (or, in a case where the award has terminated, each subsequent month) the amount of capital the person is treated as possessing ("the notional capital") reduces—

    (a) in a case where the notional capital exceeds £16,000, by the amount which the Secretary of State considers would be the amount of an award of universal credit that would be made to the person (assuming they met the conditions in section 4 and 5 of the Act) if it were not for the notional capital; or

    (b) in a case where the notional capital exceeds £6,000 but not £16,000 (including where the notional capital has reduced to an amount equal to or less than £16,000 in accordance with sub-paragraph (a)) by the amount of unearned income that the notional capital is treated as yielding under regulation 72.

2.144

DEFINITION

"unearned income"—see reg.2.

GENERAL NOTE

Paras (1) and (2)

2.145
Under universal credit the only circumstance in which a person will be treated as having notional capital is where s/he has deprived him/herself of it for the purpose of securing, or increasing, entitlement to universal credit (although note also reg.77(2) in relation to companies in which the person is like a sole trader or partner).

There is a considerable amount of case law on the "deprivation rule"—see the notes to reg.51(1) of the Income Support Regulations in Vol.II of this series. But note that some of the case law will need to be read in the light of para.(2). In particular, the principle laid down in *R(SB) 38/85* will no doubt be relevant, that once it is shown that a person did possess, or received, a capital asset, the burden shifts to that person to show that it has ceased to be part of his actual capital. If the person fails to show that, the proper conclusion is then that the asset remains part of his actual capital, rather than to invoke any notional capital rule (see *R(SB) 40/85*). Tribunals should therefore in such circumstances avoid vague formulations such as 'the claimant is treated as having capital of £x' and make it clear whether the conclusion is that the person has actual or notional capital of that amount. One consequence of the difference is that, if a person is found to have actual capital as a consequence of not having shown that some asset or assets have been disposed of, there is no statutory diminishing capital rule to be applied. Normally where a claimant is not entitled to benefit because the amount of capital exceeds the £16,000 limit (or the amount of assumed tariff income from capital over £6,000 precludes entitlement) the 'remedy' is to dip into the capital to meet living and/or other reasonable expenses and to claim again when the amount of capital has reduced to the level that allows entitlement. However, a claimant may be in difficulty in making such an argument while maintaining that the assets in question had been disposed of.

It should also be remembered that another result of *R(SB) 38/85* and *R(SB) 40/85* is that there is a deprivation of capital whenever a person ceases to possess some asset, even though some other asset is received in return. Otherwise it would be possible to convert capital that counts towards the limits into a form in which it is disregarded without falling foul of the notional capital rule. However, para.(2) of the present regulation sets out important limitations on the effect of that principle, which are not present in the income support or old style ESA or JSA legislation (see below).

There is a great deal of case law on when there has been a deprivation for the purpose of securing entitlement to or increasing the amount of benefit, including the issue of how much knowledge of the capital limits is necessary for it to be concluded that the deprivation had that purpose. See the notes to reg.51(1) of the Income Support Regulations in Vol.II of this series for extensive discussion. No doubt, the principle that it is enough that that purpose is a significant operative purpose and need not be the sole or main purpose will be maintained here. There is no equivalent in reg.50 to the rule in reg.60(2) (notional earned income) treating the prohibited purpose as having existed where entitlement or higher entitlement to universal credit did result and was a foreseeable and intended consequence of the deprivation.

The operation of para.(1) is restricted to circumstances where the person's purpose is related to entitlement to universal credit. That is in contrast to the terms of reg.113(1) of the JSA Regulations 1996 (which covers purposes related to both old style JSA and income support) and of reg.115(1) of the ESA Regulations 2008 (which covers purposes related to all of old style ESA and JSA and income support), but not to the terms of reg.51(1) of the Income Support Regulations (which is restricted to income support). *R(IS) 14/93* was concerned with a similar problem on the transfer to income support from the corresponding supplementary benefit provisions in 1988. That was whether claimants who deprived themselves of capital under the supplementary benefit regime, before income support existed, could be said to have done so for the purpose of securing entitlement to income support so as to be caught by reg.51(1) once the income support legislation had come into force. The decisions on the point do not now need to be examined in detail. *R(IS) 14/93* holds that the words "income support" in reg.51(1) cannot be taken to refer to means-tested benefits that previously went under the name of supplementary benefit. Thus, if a deprivation of capital occurs while a person is receiving, or contemplating a claim for, income support or old style JSA or ESA, it may be arguable, depending on the exact circumstances, that if there is later a claim for universal credit the purpose of the deprivation was not to secure entitlement to universal credit. It may also be slightly more onerous to establish the person's knowledge of the capital rules in universal credit, as a new and not yet familiar benefit.

Para. (2)

Paragraph (2)(a) provides that a person will not be treated as having deprived him/herself of capital if s/he has used it to repay or reduce a debt. This provision avoids a lot of difficult issues under the notional capital rules for other benefits about the exact circumstances in which paying off debts in whole or part might indicate that securing entitlement to or increasing the amount of benefit was not a significant operative purpose of the deprivation. It appears to have a very wide application. There is no requirement that the debt is legally enforceable, or even that it is due to be repaid, or any restriction as to the type of debt involved. It should therefore apply to the repayment of loans from family or friends (subject to possible issues about when there is sufficient evidence to establish the existence of the debt on the balance of probabilities) and to the repayment of overdrafts or credit card balances as well as mortgages, personal loans etc. Although para.(2)(a) expressly refers to debts owed by the person who carries out the deprivation, it is submitted that where the person is a member of a couple (whose capital would be aggregated under reg.18(2) or s.5(2) of the WRA 2012) payment of a debt owed by the other member of the couple would be covered.

2.145.1

Under para.(2)(b) the deprivation rule is not to apply if the deprivation takes the form of purchase of goods or services and the expenditure was reasonable in the circumstances of the person concerned. It is not at all clear what might be covered by the word "goods". Regulation 46(2) provides that personal possessions are not to be treated as capital. In the notes to that provision the approach in *R(H) 7/08* is mentioned, that personal possessions mean any physical assets other than land and assets used for business purposes, with no distinctions to be drawn, say to exclude assets acquired for investment. However, a question is raised there whether the use of the adjective "personal" could be taken to exclude items used solely as investments. It could be argued here that "goods" should not have any narrower meaning than whatever is the correct meaning of personal possessions in reg.46(2). Indeed, it would seem that in the absence of the adjective "personal" the meaning should include things used for business purposes. On the other hand, it could be argued that the word "goods" suggests items used in the course of daily living, even though they might be regarded as capital purchases, so that it would not cover items acquired for investment. The practical importance of such uncertainties may be lessened by the condition of reasonableness. That test must depend on reasonableness as at the date of the potential deprivation, rather than as assessed later with the benefit of hindsight. Although the relevant circumstances will include the person's financial situation and prospects at the time, including the likelihood of having to claim a means-tested benefit and how much the person actually knew about the capital limits for such benefits, it is submitted that the assessment of benefit must balance the principle that in general people are free to spend their own money on whatever they like against what is reasonable in relation to the community of taxpayers who fund universal credit.

Note that if neither of the two situations in para.(2) apply, it remains necessary to consider whether the person did deprive him/herself of the capital for the purpose of securing, or increasing, entitlement to universal credit.

There is no longer any specific exclusion from the notional capital rule for trusts that have been set up as a result of personal injury or funds administered by a court that relate to personal injury but it would seem that the intention of the extensive disregard in reg.75 is that the notional capital rule does not apply.

Para. (3)

2.146
This paragraph contains the diminishing notional capital rule for universal credit. If the notional capital is more than £16,000, it is reduced in each subsequent assessment period, or each subsequent month if the universal credit award has ceased, by the amount of universal credit that the person would have received but for the notional capital. In the case of a person who has notional capital of between £6,000 and £16,000, the notional capital reduces by the amount of income deemed to be generated by that amount of capital under the "assumed yield from capital" rule in reg.72.

This diminishing notional capital rule is different from that in income support (reg.51A of the Income Support Regulations), old style ESA (reg.116 of the ESA Regulations 2008) or old style JSA (reg.114 of the JSA Regulations 2006). Those provisions apply whenever taking the notional capital into account has either taken the claimant out of entitlement or resulted in a reduction in the amount of benefit received. Then the amount of notional capital is reduced week by week by the amount of benefit in question that would otherwise have been paid for that week. Thus the rule can apply regardless of the initial amount of the notional capital. What matters is whether the combination of actual capital (if any) and notional capital takes the claimant over a relevant limit. By contrast, para.(3) applies only where the amount of notional capital alone exceeds either £16,000 or £6,000. If a claimant has actual capital of £15,000 and is then fixed with £2,000 of notional capital, so that there can no longer be entitlement to universal credit, the terms of para.(3) are not met and there apparently can be no reduction in the £2,000 of notional capital. If the claimant had no actual capital and was fixed with £17,000 of notional capital para.(3) could apply. That difference in treatment within universal credit and between different means-tested benefits seems inequitable. However, it may be that there is unjustified double counting in the other benefits in favour of claimants who have actual capital. In the example quoted of £15,000 actual capital and £2,000 notional capital, the claimant would need to dip into actual capital to meet essential living expenses in the absence of the previous benefit payments, and that expenditure on goods and services would no doubt be accepted as reasonable under para.(2)(b). So once the actual capital had reduced below £14,000, there could be entitlement again. The difference is that a universal credit claimant cannot take advantage of a reduction in the amount of notional capital in addition to that reduction in actual capital, whereas it appears that income support, old style ESA and old style JSA claimants can.

Presumably a person's notional capital will be calculated in the same way as if it were actual capital, that is, by applying any relevant disregard, although reg.50 does not specifically state this. This is assumed in para.H1885 ADM.

CHAPTER 2

EARNED INCOME

Introduction

2.147
51. This Chapter provides for the calculation or estimation of a person's earned income for the purposes of section 8 of the Act (calculation of awards).

Definitions

"the Act"—see reg.2.
"earned income"—see reg.52.

General Note

In the case of joint claimants their income is aggregated (see s.8(4)(b) of the WRA 2012). If a member of a couple is claiming as a single person (see reg.3(3) for the circumstances in which this can happen) the income of the other member of the couple is taken into account when calculating the universal credit award (see reg.22(3)).

2.148

Any income of a child is ignored.

In calculating universal credit, 65 per cent of the amount by which the claimant's, or the claimants' combined, earned income exceeds the applicable work allowance is taken into account (see s.8(3) WRA 2012 and reg.22).

Regulations 51–64 deal with the calculation of earned income and regs 65–74 with unearned income. Regulations 75–77 contain a number of additional rules in relation to treatment of a person's capital and income.

Meaning of "earned income"

52. "Earned income" means—

2.149

(a) the remuneration or profits derived from—
(i) employment under a contract of service or in an office, including elective office,
(ii) a trade, profession or vocation, or
(iii) any other paid work; or
(b) any income treated as earned income in accordance with this Chapter.

Definition

"paid work"—see reg.2.

General Note

Paragraph (a) spells out what counts as earned income. It comprises earnings as an employee, as an office-holder, including a holder of elective office, such as a local councillor, self-employed earnings, and remuneration or profits from any other paid work (for the definition of "paid work" see reg.2).

2.150

What might fall within sub-para.(iii) as paid work that does not already fall within sub-para.(i) (contract of employment or office) or (ii) (self-employment) remains obscure. There are no other regulations saying how remuneration or profit derived from other paid work should be calculated or taken into account. Regulations 55 on employed earnings and 58 and 59 on self-employed earnings contain rules about the calculation of such earnings that involve disregards of certain kinds of receipts and deductions from gross receipts. It plainly cannot be the case that such elements come back into consideration under sub-para.(iii). The exclusion of their amount in the calculation process does not alter their status as remuneration or profit derived from employment or self-employment and so cannot count as derived from "other" paid work. Possibly the category is meant to cover casual and informal work that lacks the organisation to qualify as a trade, vocation or profession (see *Hakki v Secretary of State for Work and Pensions* [2014] EWCA Civ 530 on a "professional" poker player held not to be a self-employed earner on that ground).

It appears that para.(a) establishes an overarching condition that payments that would fall to be calculated as employed earnings or self-employed earnings be remuneration or profit derived from the sources specified.

On para.(b), see reg.55(4) and (4A). Note also reg.60 on notional earned income.

Meaning of other terms relating to earned income

2.151

53.—(1) In this Chapter—

"car" has the meaning in section 268A of the Capital Allowances Act 2001;

"employed earnings" has the meaning in regulation 55;

"gainful self-employment" has the meaning in regulation 64;

"HMRC" means Her Majesty's Revenue and Customs;

"motor cycle" has the meaning in section 268A of the Capital Allowances Act 2001;

"PAYE Regulations" means the Income Tax (Pay As You Earn) Regulations 2003;

"relievable pension contributions" has the meaning in section 188 of the Finance Act 2004;

"self-employed earnings" has the meaning in regulation 57; and

"start-up period" has the meaning in regulation 63.

(2) References in this Chapter to a person participating as a service user are to—

(a) a person who is being consulted by or on behalf of—

    (i) a body which has a statutory duty to provide services in the field of health, social care or social housing; or

    (ii) a body which conducts research or undertakes monitoring for the purpose of planning or improving such services,

in their capacity as a user, potential user, carer of a user or person otherwise affected by the provision of those services; or

[¹ (ab) a person who is being consulted by or on behalf of—

    (i) the Secretary of State in relation to any of the Secretary of State's functions in the field of social security or child support or under section 2 of the Employment and Training Act 1973; or

    (ii) a body which conducts research or undertakes monitoring for the purpose of planning or improving such functions,

in their capacity as a person affected or potentially affected by the exercise of those functions or the carer of such a person;]

(b) the carer of a person consulted under [¹ sub-paragraphs (a) or (ab)].

AMENDMENT

1. Social Security (Miscellaneous Amendments) Regulations 2015 (SI 2015/67) reg.2(1)(g) and (2) (February 23, 2015).

Calculation of earned income—general principles

2.152

54.—(1) The calculation of a person's earned income in respect of an assessment period is, unless otherwise provided in this Chapter, to be based on the actual amounts received in that period.

(2) Where the Secretary of State—

(a) makes a determination as to whether the financial conditions in section 5 of the Act are met before the expiry of the first assessment period in relation to a claim for universal credit; or

(b) makes a determination as to the amount of a person's earned income in relation to an assessment period where a person has failed to report information in relation to that earned income, that determination may be based on an estimate of the amounts received or expected to be received in that assessment period.

DEFINITIONS

"the Act"—see reg.2.
"assessment period"—see WRA 2012 ss.40 and 7(2) and reg.21.
"claim"—see WRA 2012 s.40.
"earned income"—see reg.52.

GENERAL NOTE

Under para.(1), the normal rule is that a person's earned income (as defined in   **2.153**
reg.52 and so covering both employed earnings and self-employed earnings as well
as remuneration or profit derived from other paid work, whatever that is) is to be
based on the actual amount received during an assessment period.

In *PT v SSWP (UC)* [2015] UKUT 696 (AAC) the claimant claimed universal
credit on January 6, 2015 and received his final wages from his previous job on
January 16, 2015. These were taken into account in calculating his entitlement to
universal credit in the first assessment period. The claimant contended that they
should not have been taken into account as his job had ended. Judge Jacobs raises
the question of how there can be an assessment period before a decision has been
made that the claimant is entitled to universal credit. He accepts the Secretary of
State's explanation that the answer lies in s.5(1)(b) of the WRA 2012. The assessment period is fixed by reference to the first date of entitlement (reg.21(1)). Until
the decision is made on entitlement, s.5(1)(b) provides for income to be calculated
on the assumption that an award will be made. The earnings were received during
the first assessment period and so fell to be taken into account under para.(1). It
did not matter that the employment had ceased to exist by the time the wages were
paid. Nor can it matter that the wages were earned in respect of weeks prior to the
first assessment period. It is the time of receipt that is crucial.

However, para.(2) allows an estimate to be made (i) where the calculation is made
before the expiry of the first assessment period or (ii) where there has been a failure
to report information about earned income in an assessment period.

An assessment period is normally a period of one month beginning with the first
day of entitlement to universal credit and each subsequent month while entitlement
continues (see reg.21(1)).

Employed earnings

55.—(1) This regulation applies for the purposes of calculating earned   **2.154**
income from employment under a contract of service or in an office, including elective office ("employed earnings").

(2) Employed earnings comprise any amounts that are general earnings,
as defined in section 7(3) of ITEPA, but excluding—

(a) amounts that are treated as earnings under Chapters 2 to 11 of Part
3 of ITEPA (the benefits code); and

(b) amounts that are exempt from income tax under Part 4 of ITEPA.

(3) In the calculation of employed earnings the following are to be disregarded—

(a) expenses that are allowed to be deducted under Chapter 2 of Part 5
of ITEPA; and

(b) expenses arising from participation as a service user (see regulation
53(2)).

(4) The following benefits are to be treated as employed earnings—

(a) statutory sick pay;

(b) statutory maternity pay;

(c) [³ ...] statutory paternity pay;

(d) [³ ...]

(e) statutory adoption pay [² ; and]

[² (f) statutory shared parental pay.]

[¹ (4A) A repayment of income tax or national insurance contributions received by a person from HMRC in respect of a tax year in which the person was in paid work is to be treated as employed earnings unless it is taken into account as self-employed earnings under regulation 57(4).]

(5) In calculating the amount of a person's employed earnings in respect of an assessment period, there are to be deducted from the amount of general earnings or benefits specified in paragraphs (2) to (4)—

(a) any relievable pension contributions made by the person in that period;

(b) any amounts paid by the person in that period in respect of the employment by way of income tax or primary Class 1 contributions under section 6(1) of the Contributions and Benefits Act; and

(c) any sums withheld as donations to an approved scheme under Part 12 of ITEPA (payroll giving) by a person required to make deductions or repayments of income tax under the PAYE Regulations.

AMENDMENTS

1. Universal Credit and Miscellaneous Amendments (No.2) Regulations 2014 (SI 2014/2888) reg.4(2) (November 26, 2014, or in the case of existing awards, the first assessment period beginning on or after November 26, 2014).

2. Shared Parental Leave and Statutory Shared Parental Pay (Consequential Amendments to Subordinate Legislation) Order 2014 (SI 2014/3255) art.28(4)(c) and (d) (December 31, 2014).

3. Shared Parental Leave and Statutory Shared Parental Pay (Consequential Amendments to Subordinate Legislation) Order 2014 (SI 2014/3255) art.28(4)(a) and (b) (April 5, 2015). The amendments are subject to the transitional provision in art.35 (see Pt IV of this book).

DEFINITIONS

"Contributions and Benefits Act"—see reg.2.
"earned income"—see reg.52.
"ITEPA"—see reg.2.
"relievable pension contributions" —see reg.53(1).
"PAYE Regulations" —*ibid.*
"statutory adoption pay"—see reg.2.
"statutory maternity pay"—*ibid.*
"statutory shared parental pay"—*ibid.*
"statutory sick pay"—*ibid.*

GENERAL NOTE

2.155 This regulation applies to employed earnings (i.e., under a contract of service or as an office holder) (para.(1)). By reason of the overarching definition of "earned income" in reg.52, payments must be derived from such employment. See reg.57 for the calculation of self-employed earnings.

Unlike income support, old style JSA, old style ESA and housing benefit, what counts as employed earnings for the purposes of universal credit is defined in terms of the income tax rules (paras (2) and (3)(a)). However, not all amounts that HMRC treats as earnings count for universal credit purposes (see para.(2)(a)).

Under para.(2))(a) benefits in kind, for example living accommodation provided by reason of the employment, are excluded.

The meaning of "general earnings" in s.7(3) of ITEPA, which the beginning of para.(2) makes the starting point for calculating earned income, is earnings within Chap.1 of Part 3 of ITEPA or any amount treated as earnings, excluding exempt earnings. Section 62 of ITEPA, which constitutes Chap.1 of Part 3, provides in subs. (2) that earnings means:

"(a)   any salary, wages or fee;

(b)   any gratuity or other profit or incidental benefit of any kind obtained by the employee if it is money or money's worth; and

(c)   anything else that constitutes an emolument of the employment."

That meaning is thus very broad, but is immediately narrowed by para.(2)(a) of reg.55 in the exclusion of amounts treated as earnings in Chaps 2–11 of Part 3 of ITEPA. Those items covers matters like expenses, vouchers, provision of living accommodation, cars, vans and related benefits and loans. The exclusion by para. (2)(b) of amounts exempt from income tax under Part 4 of ITEPA would have followed in any event under the terms of s.7(3) of ITEPA. Those exemptions include mileage or transport allowances, travel and subsistence allowances, benefits for training and learning, recreational benefits etc and some payments on the termination of employment (see the separate section below).

Under para.(3)(a) expenses that are deductible under ITEPA, Pt 5, Ch.2, are disregarded in calculating employed earnings—this includes, for example, expenses that are "wholly, exclusively and necessarily" incurred in the course of the claimant's employment (see s.336(1) of ITEPA). In addition, expenses from participation as a service user (defined in reg.53(2)) are ignored (para.(3)(b)), although payments for attendance at meetings, etc., will count as earnings.

Note that employed earnings also include statutory sick pay, statutory maternity pay, statutory paternity pay, statutory adoption pay and statutory shared parental pay (para.(4)).

Paragraph (4A), inserted with effect from November 26, 2014, treats a repayment of income tax or NI contributions in respect of a tax year in which the person was in paid work as employed earnings, unless it is taken into account as self-employed earnings. According to DWP (see Memo ADM 24/14), this will include repayments of income tax that relate to other sources, such as unearned income, as long as the claimant was in paid work in the tax year to which the repayment relates. Memo ADM 24/14 gives as an example a case in which a claimant receives a cheque for £200 from HMRC, which relates to an overpayment of £600 income tax in the tax year 2011/12 in which the claimant was in paid work and an underpayment of £400 in the following year. The amount that counts as employed earnings is £200, which is the repayment that the claimant received.

In calculating a person's employed earnings in an assessment period the following are deducted: any income tax and Class 1 contributions paid in that assessment period, together with any contributions to a registered pension scheme and any charity payments under a payroll giving scheme made in that period (para.(5)). Since the definition of "relievable pension contributions" in reg.53(1) is by reference only to s.188 of the Finance Act 2004 it is arguable that the annual and lifetime limits imposed in other sections of that Act are not incorporated for universal credit purposes.

Information on a person's employed earnings and deductions made will normally be taken from what is recorded on PAYE records. See further the note to reg.61.

Earnings on cessation of employment

There are no special provisions for the treatment of final earnings under universal credit. A claimant's final earnings will be taken into account in the assessment period in which they are paid under the general rule in reg.54(1). See in   **2.156** particular *PT v SSWP (UC)* [2015] UKUT 696 (AAC), discussed in the notes to reg.54. Termination payments (e.g., payments in lieu of notice and holiday pay) are "general earnings" under ss.7(3)(a) and 62 of ITEPA (see HMRC, *Employment Income Manual*, para.12850) and so will be taken into account for the purposes of universal credit. However, employment tribunal awards for unfair dismissal, damages for breach of contract and redundancy payments (statutory and contractual) will not count as they are only taxable under s.401 of ITEPA and so do not come within s.7(3) (see *Employment Income Manual*, paras 12960, 12970, 12978, 13005 and 13750). For other employment tribunal awards which do count as earnings see para.02550 of the *Employment Income Manual*.

Dividends

The overriding principle set out in reg.52(a) that earned income from employment under a contract of service or in an office must be remuneration or profit derived from that employment or office suggests that payments of dividends on shares cannot be earned income. They are derived from the ownership of the shares. However, sometimes payments that are described as dividends are not properly to be treated as such. The formal company law and accounting processes for declaring a dividend may not have been gone through or the whole transaction may be a sham. There may be other situations in which, although the payments are properly to be regarded as dividends they are derived from employment or an office. See the discussion in *H v SSWP and C (CSM)* [2015] UKUT 621 (AAC), citing extensively from the decision in *CCS 2533/2014* (not currently on the AAC website), which itself relied on the decision (described as instructive) of the Court of Appeal in the tax case of *HMRC v PA Holdings Ltd* [2011] EWCA Civ 1414. The overall approach adopted by the Court of Appeal is to look at the substance, not the form.

Dividends are chargeable to income tax under Part 4 of the Income Tax (Trading and Other Income) Act 2005 (ITTOIA), so cannot as such fall within the definition of general earnings in s.7(3) of ITEPA. However, if in substance the payments constitute remuneration derived from employment or an office they would fall within that definition. As a matter of principle, a decision-maker or tribunal would not be bound by HMRC having accepted payments as in substance of dividends taxable only under ITTOIA, but would have to come to an independent judgment on all the evidence available about whether payments were general earnings. However, how HMRC treated the payments would of course be a relevant factor to be considered., with the weight to be given to that treatment depending on how far it was based on a mere acceptance of statements on a tax return or on any further consideration of the particular circumstances.

Employee involved in trade dispute

2.157
56. A person who has had employed earnings and has withdrawn their labour in furtherance of a trade dispute is, unless their contract of service has been terminated, to be assumed to have employed earnings at the same level as they would have had were it not for the trade dispute.

DEFINITIONS

"employed earnings"—see regs 53(1) and 55.
"trade dispute"—see reg.2.

GENERAL NOTE

2.158
A person who is involved in a trade dispute but still employed is treated as having the same level of earnings as s/he would have had but for the trade dispute. "Trade dispute" has the same meaning as in s.244 of the Trade Union and Labour Relations (Consolidation) Act 1992 (reg.2).

Self-employed earnings

57.—(1) This regulation applies for the purpose of calculating earned   2.159
income that is not employed earnings and is derived from carrying on a
trade, profession or vocation ("self-employed earnings").

(2) A person's self-employed earnings in respect of an assessment period
are to be calculated by taking the amount of the gross profits (or, in the case
of a partnership, the person's share of those profits) of the trade, profession
or vocation and deducting from that amount—

(a) any payment made to HMRC in the assessment period in respect of
the trade, profession or vocation by way of—

(i) Class 2 contributions [² under section 11(2), (6) or (8)] of the
Contributions and Benefits Act or any Class 4 contributions
payable under section 15 of that Act, or

(ii) income tax; and

(b) any relievable pension contributions made by the person in the
assessment period (unless a deduction has been made in respect of
those contributions in calculating a person's employed earnings).

(3) The gross profits of the trade, profession or vocation in respect of an
assessment period are the actual receipts in that period less any deductions
for expenses allowed under regulation 58 or 59.

(4) The receipts referred to in paragraph (3) include receipts in kind
and any refund or repayment of income tax, value added tax or national
insurance contributions relating to the trade, profession or vocation.

[¹ (5) Where the purchase of an asset has been deducted as an expense
in any assessment period and, in a subsequent assessment period, the asset
is sold or ceases to be used for the purposes of a trade, profession or vocation carried on by the person, the proceeds of sale (or, as the case may be,
the amount that would be received for the asset if it were sold at its current
market value) are to be treated as a receipt in that subsequent assessment
period].

AMENDMENTS

1. Universal Credit and Miscellaneous Amendments (No.2) Regulations 2014 (SI
2014/2888) reg.4(3) (November 26, 2014, or in the case of existing awards, the first
assessment period beginning on or after November 26, 2014).

2. Social Security (Miscellaneous Amendments No.2) Regulations 2015 (SI
2015/478) reg.36 (April 6, 2015).

DEFINITIONS

"assessment period"—see WRA 2012, ss.40 and 7(2) and reg.21.
"Contributions and Benefits Act"—see reg.2.
"earned income"–see reg.52.
"employed earnings"—see regs 53(1) and 55.
"relievable pension contributions"—see reg.53(1).

GENERAL NOTE

This regulation applies for the purpose of calculating self-employed earnings.   2.160
As with employed earnings, it is the actual amount received during the assessment
period that is taken into account. Thus a person who is self-employed will need to
report his or her earnings every month.

Self-employed earnings are earnings that are not employed earnings and are
derived from carrying on a trade, profession or vocation (para.(1)). On the tests for

deciding whether a person is an employed earner or in self-employment, see, for example, *CJSA/4721/2001*. Whether particular earnings are self-employed earnings for the purposes of universal credit is not determined by how they have been treated for other purposes, e.g. contribution purposes (see *CIS/14409/1996* and para.H4017 ADM).

Thus the first question is whether the person is engaged in self-employment. The issue will have to be determined according to the facts. Paragraph H4013 ADM quotes as examples a person who sells his two classic cars after losing his job because he can no longer afford their upkeep (who is not engaged in a trade) and a person who buys 10,000 toilet rolls from a wholesaler with the intention of selling them for a profit (who is so engaged). If it is decided that the person is engaged in self-employment, the question of whether s/he is in "gainful self-employment" will also need to be considered for the purpose of applying the minimum income floor rule (see the note to reg.62). If the person is not in gainful self-employment, no minimum income floor will apply and the person's actual self-employed earnings will be taken into account for the purposes of calculating his/her universal credit award.

While the most common concern is to distinguish between employment and self-employment, there may be circumstances that fall outside both categories, in which case the category of "other paid work" in reg.52(a)(iii) would have to be considered. See the decision of the Court of Appeal in the child support case *Hakki v Secretary of State for Work and Pensions* [2014] EWCA Civ 530 in which a "professional" poker player was held not to be a self-employed earner on the ground that his activities lacked the necessary degree of organisation to amount to a trade, profession or vocation.

There are no specific rules excluding certain payments from being self-employed earnings (contrast, for example, reg.37(2) of the Income Support Regulations in Vol.II of this series).

The starting point for assessing the earnings of the self-employed is the amount of gross profits in an assessment period (i.e. month), from which the following are deducted: any income tax, Class 2 and Class 4 contributions paid in that assessment period, together with any contributions to a registered pension scheme made in that period (unless such pension contributions have already been deducted from the person's employed earnings) (para.(2)). Many self-employed people do not pay tax and NI contributions regularly but they can arrange with HMRC to make such payments monthly and for most people it will be to their advantage to do so for the purposes of universal credit.

The gross profits are the actual receipts from the self-employment in the assessment period (regardless of when they were earned), less amounts for any allowable expenses (see regs 58 and 59) paid in the assessment period (para.(3)). Under para.(4) receipts include receipts in kind and any refund or repayment of income tax, value added tax or national insurance contributions for the self-employment. This method of calculating self-employed earnings on the basis of receipts actually received and expenses actually paid is based on HMRC's "cash basis and simplified expenses accounting system" (the cash basis model, or "cash in/cash out"). According to para.H4141 ADM, self-employed claimants will be asked to report monthly between seven days before and 14 days after the end date of each assessment period details of actual income receipts and actual expenditure on allowable expenses during the assessment period that has just come to an end.

Under para.(5), where the purchase of an asset has been deducted as an expense in any assessment period, and in a subsequent assessment period the asset is sold, or ceases to be used for the purpose of the claimant's self-employment, the proceeds of sale, or the amount that would have been received if the asset had been sold at its current market value, will be treated as a receipt in that subsequent period. DWP guidance (Memo ADM 24/14) advises decision makers that the full amount of the proceeds of sale (or deemed proceeds of sale) is to be taken into account, even if only a proportion of the purchase price was deducted as a expense in the assessment period in which the asset was purchased because the claimant's self-employed earnings in that assessment period were less than the price of the asset. This provision would seem to embody a somewhat rigid approach which does not take into account the realities of self-employment which usually needs to be viewed over a much longer period than an assessment period (i.e., a month). To quote the example given by Memo ADM 24/14, if a claimant pays £400 for display material in an assessment period in which his/her earnings are only £100, so that only £100 of the expense is taken into account as this reduces his/her earnings to nil, it does not seem fair that the whole of the sale price (or deemed sale price) should count as a receipt in a subsequent assessment period, rather than the equivalent of the expenses reduction s/he was allowed.

Capital receipts, such as funds introduced by the self-employed person or loans from third parties for financing purposes, do not count (see *R(FC) 1/97* and the other cases discussed in the note to reg.37(1) of the Income Support Regulations in Vol.II of this series and para.H4190 ADM).

This method of calculation, even on the assumption that claimants will be able to supply accurate information month by month, might be expected in many cases to produce considerable fluctuations between assessment periods depending on the chance of when receipts come in and when expenses are incurred. In the case of fluctuations downwards, reg.62 on the minimum income floor may come into play. If a self-employed person is in gainful employment as defined in reg.64, would apart from the operation of reg.62 be subject to all work-related requirements and their actual earned income in an assessment period is below the minimum income floor (usually the hourly national minimum wage times 35), their earned income is deemed to be equal to that threshold. However, the test for gainful employment is quite strict. The person must be carrying on a trade, profession or vocation as their main employment and derive self-employed earnings from that. In addition, the trade, profession or vocation must be "organised, developed, regular and carried on in the expectation of profit". Those last conditions, and also the exclusion of the 12-month start-up period under reg.63, will exclude many claimants with fluctuating or more casual operations. See the notes to reg.64 for further discussion. If reg.62 does not apply, the actual level of self-employed earnings as calculated under the present regulation must be taken. Even if reg.62 does apply to some assessment periods, there is no mechanism for evening out fluctuations to a higher level for other assessment periods. If earned income exceeds the minimum income floor in any assessment period, the actual level must be taken.

See also reg.77 for the special rules that apply if a person's control of a company is such that s/he is like a sole trader or a partner. In those circumstances, amongst other things, the company's income or the person's share of it is to be treated as the person's income and calculated under reg.57 as if it were self-employed earnings. It is, though, far from clear how that notional conversion is to take place. Under reg.57, in the case of actual self-employed earnings, the calculation is based on gross profits in the sense of actual receipts in any assessment period less permitted deductions for expenses under regs 58 and 59. Presumably therefore, "the income of the company" does not mean the net income of the company as might be calculated for corporation tax purposes or under ordinary accounting principles. Presumably it means the actual receipts of the company in the assessment period in question less the deductions for expenses under regs 58 and 59, looking at expenditure on behalf of the company rather than by the person in question. It is difficult to say whether in practice information will be available as to such receipts and expenditure in a current assessment period of a month. A further problem is how to calculate the deductions from gross profits under para. (2)(a) and (b) for Class 2 and 4 national insurance contributions and income tax paid to HMRC in the assessment period and relievable pension contributions made in that period, when the person's actual tax and national insurance status will not have been as a self-employed earner. But some difficulties may be avoided by the provision in reg.77(3)(c) that if the person's activities in the course of the company's trade are their main employment reg.62 (minimum income floor) is to be applied.

Permitted expenses

2.161   **58.**—(1) The deductions allowed in the calculation of self-employed earnings are amounts paid in the assessment period in respect of—

(a) expenses that have been wholly and exclusively incurred for purposes of the trade, profession or vocation; or

(b) in the case of expenses that have been incurred for more than one purpose, an identifiable part or proportion that has been wholly and exclusively incurred for the purposes of the trade, profession or vocation,

excluding any expenses that were incurred unreasonably.

(2) Payments deducted under paragraph (1) may include value added tax.

(3) No deduction may be made for payments in respect of—

(a) expenditure on non-depreciating assets (including property, shares or other assets held for investment purposes);

(b) any loss incurred in respect of a previous assessment period;

(c) repayment of capital [¹ ...] in relation to a loan taken out for the purposes of the trade, profession or vocation;

(d) expenses for business entertainment.

[¹(3A) A deduction for a payment of interest in relation to a loan taken out for the purposes of the trade, profession or vocation may not exceed £41.]

(4) This regulation is subject to regulation 59.

AMENDMENT

1. Social Security (Miscellaneous Amendments) (No.2) Regulations 2013 (SI 2013/1508) reg.3(7) (July 29, 2013).

DEFINITIONS

"assessment period"—see WRA 2012, ss.40 and 7(2) and reg.21.
"self-employed earnings"—see reg 53(1) and 57.

GENERAL NOTE

2.162   This regulation, and reg.59, provide for the deductions that can be made from self-employed earnings. Only these deductions can be made in addition to those under reg.57(2)(a) and (b) for Class 2 and 4 national insurance contributions and income tax paid to HMRC and relievable pension contributions.

The amount of the deduction will normally be the actual amount of the permitted expenses paid in the assessment period, but note para.(4). The effect of para.(4) is that the alternative deductions under reg.59 in respect of the expenses referred to in paras (2)–(4) of that regulation may be made instead. However, note that in the case of a car, the actual costs involved in acquiring or using it are not allowable and the only deduction that can be made is a flat rate deduction for mileage under reg.59(2).

To be deductable, the expenses must have been paid in the assessment period, be reasonable and have been "wholly and exclusively" incurred for the purposes of the self-employment (para.(1)), but note para.(1)(b). See para.H4214 ADM for examples of allowable expenses. Permitted expenses include value added tax (para.(2)).

Paragraph (1)(b) specifically provides for the apportionment of expenses that have been incurred for more than one purpose (e.g., for business and private purposes). In such a case, a deduction will be made for the proportion of the expenses that can be identified as wholly and exclusively incurred for the purposes of the self-employment. See *R(FC) 1/91* and *R(IS) 13/91* which hold that any apportionment already agreed by HMRC should normally be accepted. But note the alternative flat-rate deductions for expenses if a person uses his/her home for business purposes in reg.59(3). See also reg.59(4) which provides for flat-rate deductions from expenses if business premises are also used for personal use.

No deduction can be made for the payments listed in para.(3). Note the rule in para.(3)(b) which provides that payments in respect of a loss in a previous assessment period cannot be deducted. In addition, a loss in one employment cannot be set off against a profit or earnings in another separate employment (see *R(FC) 1/93* and the other cases discussed in the note to reg.38(11) of the Income Support Regulations in Vol.II of this series). That rule does not appear on the face of reg.58, but follows from the condition in para.(1)(a) that the expenses have been incurred for the purposes of the particular trade, profession or vocation. There may sometimes be difficult questions as to whether a person is carrying on separate businesses or some combined business.

Repayments of capital on a loan taken out for the purposes of the self-employment are not deductable (para.(3)(c)) but deductions can be made for interest paid on such a loan up to a limit of £41 per assessment period (para.(3A)). Paragraph (3A) was introduced to bring universal credit into line with the tax rules which now allow a deduction of up to £500 annually for interest payments made on loans taken out for the purposes of a business. This will include interest on credit cards and overdraft charges if the original expense related to the business. According to para.H4217 ADM only £41 can be deducted in any assessment period, regardless of the number of relevant loans a person has and for what purposes. It might just be arguable that the terms of para.(3A) are sufficient to rebut the normal presumption under s.6(c) of the Interpretation Act 1978 that the singular includes the plural.

Flat rate deductions for mileage and use of home and adjustment for personal use of business premises

59.—(1) This regulation provides for alternatives to the deductions that would otherwise be allowed under regulation 58.

(2) Instead of a deduction in respect of the actual expenses incurred in relation to the acquisition or use of a motor vehicle, the following deductions are allowed according to the mileage covered on journeys undertaken in the assessment period for the purposes of the trade, profession or vocation—

    (a) in a car, van or other motor vehicle (apart from a motorcycle), 45 pence per mile for the first 833 miles and 25 pence per mile thereafter; and

    (b) on a motorcycle, 24 pence per mile,

and, if the motor vehicle is a car [1 . . .], the only deduction allowed for the acquisition or use of that vehicle is a deduction under this paragraph.

(3) Where a person carrying on a trade, profession or vocation incurs expenses in relation to the use of accommodation occupied as their home, instead of a deduction in respect of the actual expenses, a deduction is allowed according to the number of hours spent in the assessment period on income generating activities related to the trade, profession or vocation as follows—

    (a) at least 25 hours but no more than 50 hours, £10;

    (b) more than 50 hours but no more than 100 hours, £18;

2.163

(c) more than 100 hours, £26.

(4) Where premises which are used by a person mainly for the purposes of a trade, profession or vocation are also occupied by that person for their personal use, whether alone or with other persons, the deduction allowed for expenses in relation to those premises is the amount that would be allowed under regulation 58(1) if the premises were used wholly and exclusively for purposes of the trade, profession or vocation, but reduced by the following amount according to the number of persons occupying the premises for their personal use—

(a) £350 for one person;

(b) £500 for two persons;

(c) £650 for three or more persons.

AMENDMENT

1. Social Security (Miscellaneous Amendments) (No.2) Regulations 2013 (SI 2013/1508) reg.3(8) (July 29, 2013).

DEFINITIONS

"the Act"—see reg.2.
"assessment period"—see WRA 2012 ss.40 and 7(2) and reg.21.
"car"—see reg.53(1).
"motor cycle"—*ibid.*

GENERAL NOTE

2.164   This regulation provides for alternative deductions to those that would otherwise be permitted under reg.58 to be chosen (para.(1)). However, note that in the case of a car, there is no choice: only a flat rate deduction for mileage is allowed and no deduction can be made for the actual cost of buying or using the car (para.(2)). This does not apply to other motor vehicles.

Under para.(2), a deduction for mileage on journeys undertaken for the purposes of the business in the assessment period:

●   on a motorcycle, of 24 pence per mile; or

●   in a car, van or other motor vehicle (other than a motorcycle), of 45 pence per mile for the first 833 miles and 25 pence per mile after that,

can be made instead of the actual cost of buying or using the motor vehicle (in the case of a car this is the only permitted deduction).

If a person uses his/her own home for the purposes of his/her self-employment, a flat-rate deduction of:

●   £10 for at least 25 hours but no more than 50 hours;

●   £18 for more than 50 hours but no more than 100 hours; or

●   £26 for more than 100 hours,

of "income generating activities" related to the self-employment in an assessment period can be made instead of the actual expenses incurred in the use of the home (para.(3)). The guidance in paras H4241–H4242 ADM suggests that "income generating activities" include providing services to customers, general administration of the business (e.g. filing and record-keeping) and action to secure business (e.g. sales and marketing) but do not include being on call (e.g. a taxi driver waiting for customers to ring), the use of the home for storage or time spent on completing tax returns (presumably on this basis DWP would also discount any time spent collating evidence of actual receipts and expenses for the purposes of the person's universal credit claim).

For the alternative provision for apportionment of expenses, see reg.58(1)(b).

Paragraph (4) provides that if the person lives in premises that are mainly used for business purposes, the expenses that would be allowed if the premises were used wholly and exclusively for the purposes of the person's self-employment are to be reduced by a set amount depending on the number of people living in the premises. The reduction is £350 for one person, £500 for two and £650 for three or more people in each assessment period. It is not entirely clear but the reduction under this paragraph appears to be a set rule, rather than an alternative to an apportionment under reg.58(1)(b).

Notional earned income

60.—(1) A person who has deprived themselves of earned income, or whose employer has arranged for them to be so deprived, for the purpose of securing entitlement to universal credit or to an increased amount of universal credit is to be treated as possessing that earned income.

2.165

(2) Such a purpose is to be treated as existing if, in fact, entitlement or higher entitlement to universal credit did result and, in the opinion of the Secretary of State, this was a foreseeable and intended consequence of the deprivation.

(3) If a person provides services for another person and—

(a) the other person makes no payment for those services or pays less than would be paid for comparable services in the same location; and

(b) the means of the other person were sufficient to pay for, or pay more for, those services,

the person who provides the services is to be treated as having received the remuneration that would be reasonable for the provision of those services.

(4) Paragraph (3) does not apply where—

(a) the person is engaged to provide the services by a charitable or voluntary organisation and the Secretary of State is satisfied that it is reasonable to provide the services free of charge or at less than the rate that would be paid for comparable services in the same location;

(b) the services are provided by a person who is participating as a service user (see regulation 53(2)); or

(c) the services are provided under or in connection with a person's participation in an employment or training programme approved by the Secretary of State.

DEFINITIONS

"earned income"—see reg.52.
"a person who is participating as a service user"—see reg.53(2).

GENERAL NOTE

This regulation treats a person as having employed or self-employed earnings in two situations. For the rules relating to notional unearned income, see reg.74.

2.166

Paras (1)–(2)

This contains the deprivation of earnings rule for universal credit. It applies if a person has deprived himself/herself of earned income, for the purpose of securing entitlement to, or increasing the amount of, universal credit. It also applies if the person's employer has "arranged for" the deprivation. Presumably this will only apply if the person's purpose was to secure, or increase, entitlement to universal credit by way of the arrangement and the employer's purpose is not relevant.

2.167

See the notes to regs 42(1) and 51(1) of the Income Support Regulations in Vol. II of this series on the deprivation rule.

The operation of para.(1) is restricted to circumstances where the person's purpose is related to entitlement to universal credit. That is in contrast to the terms of reg.105(1) of the JSA Regulations 1996 (which covers purposes relating to both old style JSA and income support) and of reg.106(1) of the ESA Regulations 2008 and reg.42(1) of the Income Support Regulations (which both cover purposes relating to all of old style ESA and JSA and income support). *R(IS) 14/93* was concerned with a similar problem on the transfer to income support from the corresponding supplementary benefit provisions in 1988 in relation to the notional capital. That was whether claimants who deprived themselves of capital under the supplementary benefit regime, before income support existed, could be said to have done so for the purpose of securing entitlement to income support so as to be caught by reg.51(1) of the Income Support Regulations once the income support legislation had come into force. The Commissioner holds that the words "income support" in reg.51(1) cannot be taken to refer to means-tested benefits that previously went under the name of supplementary benefit. Thus, if a deprivation of earned income occurs while a person is receiving, or contemplating a claim for, income support or old style JSA or ESA, it may be arguable, depending on the exact circumstances, that if there is later a claim for universal credit the purpose of the deprivation was not to secure entitlement to universal credit. But there might in such circumstances be a continuing deprivation for that purpose if there was not an earlier permanent deprivation.

Note, however, para.(2). The effect of para.(2) is that the person will be deemed to have the necessary purpose if s/he did obtain universal credit, or more universal credit, and in the opinion of the Secretary of State, this was "a foreseeable and intended consequence" of the deprivation. To some extent para.(2) represents a codification of the case law on the "purpose" part of the deprivation rule. However, it seems likely that much will continue to depend on the view taken by the Secretary of State (and on appeal a tribunal) of the person's intention. It is far from clear what difference there is meant to be between "intended consequence" in para.(2) and "purpose" (interpreted as meaning significant operative purpose) in para.(1). If there is no difference there would be no point in including the deeming in para.(2). It may have been thought that the conditions in para.(2) are easier to determine one way or the other, but it is submitted that a consequence is not intended just because a person realises that it will result from the deprivation.

Paras (3)–(4)

2.168   This is similar but not identical to the notional earnings rule for income support, old style JSA, old style ESA and housing benefit. For example, the exception in para. (4)(a) only applies if the person is engaged to provide the services by a charitable or voluntary organisation and does not also include the situation where the person is simply a volunteer (on the meaning of "volunteer" see *R(IS) 12/92*).

See the notes to reg.42(6) and (6A) of the Income Support Regulations in Vol.II of this series.

[¹Information for calculating earned income – real time information etc

2.169   **61.**—(1) Unless paragraph (2) applies, a person must provide such information for the purposes of calculating their earned income at such times as the Secretary of State may require.

(2) Where a person is, or has been, engaged in an employment in respect of which their employer is a Real Time Information employer—

    (a) the amount of the person's employed earnings from that employment for each assessment period is to be based on the information which is reported to HMRC under the PAYE Regulations and is received by the Secretary of State from HMRC in that assessment period; and

(b) for an assessment period in which no information is received from HMRC, the amount of employed earnings in relation to that employment is to be taken to be nil.

(3) The Secretary of State may determine that paragraph (2) does not apply—

(a) in respect of a particular employment, where the Secretary of State considers that the information from the employer is unlikely to be sufficiently accurate or timely; or

(b) in respect of a particular assessment period where—

(i) no information is received from HMRC and the Secretary of State considers that this is likely to be because of a failure to report information (which includes the failure of a computer system operated by HMRC, the employer or any other person); or

(ii) the Secretary of State considers that the information received from HMRC is incorrect, or fails to reflect the definition of employed earnings in regulation 55, in some material respect.

(4) Where the Secretary of State determines that paragraph (2) does not apply, the Secretary of State must make a decision as to the amount of the person's employed earnings for the assessment period in accordance with regulation 55 (employed earnings) using such information or evidence as the Secretary of State thinks fit.

(5) When the Secretary of State makes a decision in accordance with paragraph (4) the Secretary of State may—

(a) treat a payment of employed earnings received by the person in one assessment period as received in a later assessment period (for example where the Secretary of State has received the information in that later period or would, if paragraph (2) applied, have expected to receive information about that payment from HMRC in that later period); or

(b) where a payment of employed earnings has been taken into account in that decision, disregard information about the same payment which is received from HMRC.

(6) Paragraph (5) also applies where the Secretary of State makes a decision under regulation 41(3) of the Universal Credit, Personal Independence Payment, Jobseeker's Allowance and Employment and Support Allowance (Decisions and Appeals) Regulations 2013 in a case where the person disputes the information provided by HMRC.

(7) In this regulation "Real Time Information Employer" has the meaning in regulation 2A(1) of the PAYE Regulations.]

AMENDMENT

1. Universal Credit and Miscellaneous Amendments (No.2) Regulations 2014 (SI 2014/2888) reg.4(4) (November 26, 2014, or in the case of existing awards, the first assessment period beginning on or after November 26, 2014).

DEFINITIONS

"assessment period"—see WRA 2012, ss.40 and 7(2) and reg.21.
"earned income"–see reg.52.
"employed earnings"—see regs 53(1) and 55.

"HMRC"—see reg.53(1).
"PAYE Regulations"—*ibid.*

GENERAL NOTE

2.170   This regulation is concerned with the collection of information in relation to employed earnings. One of the new features of universal credit is that normally PAYE information is to be used to calculate a person's employed earnings (and thus his/her entitlement to universal credit) and that direct reporting of employed earnings by a claimant (or "self-reporting") is only to be the fall-back position. It is mainly for this reason that universal credit is assessed on a monthly basis and paid in arrears after the end of the assessment period.

This regulation was re-cast on November 26, 2014 as DWP's "on-going process of monitoring and evaluation identified some circumstances where it is not appropriate for Universal Credit purposes simply to take the RTI [Real Time Information] at face value or where the Secretary of State should clarify contingency arrangements" (see the Explanatory Memorandum which accompanies SI 2014/2888). The re-casting involves a distinct change in emphasis, as well as clarifying a number of points.

Paragraph (1) contains a general rule that a claimant must provide the information that the Secretary of State requires for the purposes of calculating his/her earned income (note that earned income includes not only employed earnings, but also earnings as an office-holder, self-employed earnings, remuneration from any other paid work and income treated as earned income: see reg.52).

However, this is subject to para.(2) and it is para.(2) that will apply in most cases of employed earnings. Under para.(2), if the claimant's employer is a "Real Time Information employer" (defined in para. (7)), the calculation of the claimant's employed earnings is to be based on the information that is reported to HMRC through the PAYE system and received by the Secretary of State from HMRC in that assessment period (sub-para.(a)). If no information is received from HMRC for an assessment period, the claimant's earnings from that employment are to be taken as nil (sub-para.(b)).

Since October 6, 2013 most employers have been Real Time Information employers (see reg.2A(1)(d) of the Income Tax (Pay As You Earn) Regulations 2003 (SI 2003/2682) ("the PAYE Regulations"). Under reg.67B of the PAYE Regulations a Real Time Information employer is required to deliver specified information to HMRC before or at the time of making payments to an employee. During the period October 6, 2013 to April 5, 2014 this requirement was relaxed for Real Time Information employers with less than 49 employees in that they only had to provide the information by the last day of the tax month, i.e. by the 5th of the following calendar month. In December 2013 HMRC announced a further relaxation of this rule that applied only until April 2016 but only to existing employers with nine or fewer employees. They were required to provide the information on or before the last pay day of the month.)

Paragraph (3) allows the Secretary of State to decide that para.(2) does not apply

- in relation to a particular employment, where the information from the employer is "unlikely to be sufficiently accurate or timely"; or

- in respect of a particular assessment period where
    (i) no information is received from HMRC and this is likely to be due to a failure to report (including the failure of a computer system); or
    (ii) the information received from HMRC is incorrect, or the payment does not fall within the meaning of employed earnings in reg.55, in some material respect.

If the Secretary of State decides that para.(2) does not apply, he has to decide the amount of the claimant's employed earnings for the assessment period, using such information or evidence as he thinks fit (para.(4)). Presumably the claimant will be asked to provide the necessary information (see para.(1)). Note also the Secretary of State's power under reg. 54(2)(b) to estimate a claimant's employed earnings.

There would seem to be a relatively thin line between the circumstances in which para.(2)(b) (no information received from HMRC) will apply and those in which para.(3)(b)(i) (no information received from HMRC which is likely to be due to a failure to report) applies. Unless the claimant does not have employed earnings in a particular assessment period, it seems likely that in most instances the lack of information will be due to some failure to report (bearing in mind that failure to report includes the failure of a computer system: see para.(3)(b)(i)).

Under para.(5), if the Secretary of State makes a decision under para.(4), s/he can treat a payment of employed earnings received in one assessment period as received in a later assessment period, or, where the decision under para.(4) took account of a payment of employed earnings, disregard information about the same payment received from HMRC.

Paragraph (6) provides that the flexibility in para.(5) also applies where the Secretary of State makes a decision under reg.41(3) of the Decisions and Appeals Regulations 2013 and the claimant disputes the information provided by HMRC.

Under s.159D (effect of alterations affecting universal credit) of SSAA 1992, inserted by s.31 of, and para.23 of Sch.2 to, WRA 2012, and reg.41 of the Decisions and Appeals Regulations 2013, an alteration (i.e., an increase or decrease) in the amount of a claimant's employed earnings as a result of information provided to the Secretary of State by HMRC takes effect without any further decision by the Secretary of State. However, if the claimant disputes the figure used in accordance with reg.55 to calculate his/her employed earnings in any assessment period, s/he can ask the Secretary of State to give a decision in relation to that assessment period (which must be given within 14 days of the request, or as soon as practicable thereafter). The claimant will then be able to appeal against that decision.

See also para.22 of Sch.1 to the Decisions and Appeals Regulations 2013 which provides that a supersession decision made where a claimant's employed earnings have reduced and s/he has provided the information for the purpose of calculating those earnings at the times required by the Secretary of State takes effect from the first day of the assessment period in which that change occurred.

Gainful self-employment

[¹Minimum income floor

62.—(1) This regulation applies to a claimant who—   2.171
  (a) is in gainful self-employment (see regulation 64); and
  (b) would, apart from this regulation, fall within section 22 of the Act (claimants subject to all work-related requirements).

(2) Where this regulation applies to a single claimant, for any assessment period in respect of which the claimant's earned income is less than their individual threshold, the claimant is to be treated as having earned income equal to that threshold.

(3) Where this regulation applies to a claimant who is a member of a couple, for any assessment period in respect of which—
  (a) the claimant's earned income is less than their individual threshold; and
  (b) the couple's combined earned income is less than the couple threshold,
the claimant is to be treated as having earned income equal to their individual threshold minus any amount by which that amount of earned income

combined with their partner's earned income would exceed the couple threshold.

(4) In this regulation, references to the claimant's individual threshold and to the couple threshold are to the amounts set out in regulation 90(2) and 90(3) respectively, converted to net [² . . .] amounts by—

(a) [² . . .]

(b) deducting such amount for income tax and national insurance contributions as the Secretary of State considers appropriate.

(5) An assessment period referred to in this regulation does not include an assessment period which falls wholly within a start-up period or begins or ends in a start-up period.]

AMENDMENTS

1. Universal Credit and Miscellaneous Amendments (No.2) Regulations 2014 (SI 2014/2888) reg.4(5) (November 26, 2014, or in the case of existing awards, the first assessment period beginning on or after November 26, 2014).

2. Universal Credit and Miscellaneous Amendments Regulations 2015 (SI 2015/1754) reg.2(5) (November 4, 2015, or in the case of existing awards, the first assessment period beginning on or after November 4, 2015).

DEFINITIONS

"assessment period"—see WRA 2012, ss.40 and 7(2) and reg.21.
"claimant"—see WRA 2012, s.40.
"couple"—see WRA 2012, ss.39 and 40.
"earned income"–see reg.52.
"gainful self-employment"—see regs 53(1) and 64.
"individual threshold"–see regs 2 and 90(2).
"national insurance contribution"—see reg.2.
"start-up period"—see regs 53(1) and 63.
"work-related requirement"—see WRA 2012, ss.40 and 13(2).

GENERAL NOTE

2.172   This regulation provides for the "minimum income floor" which applies to certain self-employed claimants. It is an anti-abuse provision which has presumably been introduced because of the difficulties of checking the hours of work of self-employed people.

A new form of reg.62 was introduced on November 26, 2014 in order to make "clearer provision about the calculation of the MIF [minimum income floor] when a self-employed person is a member of a couple (or when both members of a couple are self-employed)" (see the Explanatory Memorandum which accompanies SI 2014/2888). It is a distinct improvement on the previous form of reg.62. However, some confusion still remains, partly because the phrase "individual threshold" as used in reg.62 does not have quite the same meaning as that phrase in reg.90, even though reg.62(4) cross-refers to reg.90. This is because under para.(4)(b) of this regulation "appropriate" deductions for income tax and NI contributions may be made when calculating a claimant's individual threshold, which is not the case under reg.90 (see below).

Regulation 62 will only apply if in any assessment period a claimant

- is in "gainful self-employment" (as defined in reg.64) (para.(1)(a)); *and*

- is not in a "start-up period" (see reg.63) (para. (5)); *and*

- would, apart from this regulation, fall within s. 22 WRA 2012 (claimant subject to all work-related requirements) (para.(1)(b)); *and*

    (i) in the case of a single claimant, his/her self-employed earnings, together with any other earned income (as defined in reg.52), are below his/her individual threshold (para.(2)); *or*

    (ii) in the case of a couple, his/her self-employed earnings, together with any other earned income, are below his/her individual threshold, and the couple's combined earned income is below the couple threshold (para. (3)).

See reg.55 which applies for the purpose of calculating earned income that is "employed earnings" and reg.57 which applies for the purpose of calculating earned income that is "self-employed earnings". Thus references to earned income in reg.62 would seem to be to employed earnings and self-employed earnings after the deductions that are allowed under regs 55 and 57 respectively have been made.

For a claimant's individual threshold for the purposes of reg.62, the starting point is reg.90(2). This provides that a claimant's individual threshold is the hourly rate of the national minimum wage for a claimant of that age multiplied by, in the case of a claimant who would otherwise be subject to all work-related requirements under s.22 of the WRA 2012, the expected number of hours per week (usually 35, see reg.88). In the case of a claimant who would otherwise fall within ss.20 or 21, the multiplier is 16. This amount is then multiplied by 52 and divided by 12 (to make it monthly), from which is deducted "such amount for income tax and national insurance contributions as the Secretary of State considers appropriate" (para.(4)). Presumably this will normally be the amount for income tax and NI contributions that would be payable if the claimant's actual earned income was at this level but para.(4)(b) does not actually say that.

If the claimant's earned income is less than this figure (the minimum income floor) s/he will be treated as having earned income equal to this figure (para.(2)). If it equals or exceeds this figure reg.62 does not apply and the claimant's actual earnings will be taken into account in the normal way.

Example 1

Michael is single, aged 25 and a self-employed plumber. He declares earnings of £580 (£700 less permitted expenses of £120) for the current assessment period. He also has employed earnings of £200 a month as he works in a hardware store on Saturday mornings. His minimum income floor is £1048.16 a month (35 hours a week x £7.50 x 52 divided by 12, less £89.32 for notional tax and NI contributions). As his self-employed earnings and employed earnings added together amount to £780, this is less than his minimum income floor and so he is treated as having earnings of £1048.16 and his universal credit is assessed on that basis.

    2.173

In the case of a couple, the position is more complicated. Under para.(3), in addition to the condition that the claimant's earned income is less than his/her individual threshold (as calculated under para.(4)), the couple's combined earned income must also be less than the couple threshold (as calculated under para.(4)) for reg.62 to apply. The starting point for calculating the couple threshold under para.(4) is reg.90(3). This provides that in the case of joint claimants their individual thresholds are added together (see reg.90(3)(b) for how the threshold is calculated in the case of a person who is a member of a couple but claims as a single person by virtue of reg.3(3)). This amount is then multiplied by 52 and divided by 12 (to make it monthly), from which is deducted "such amount for income tax and national insurance contributions as the Secretary of State considers appropriate" (para.(4)(b)).

If these two conditions are met, the claimant will be treated as having earned income equal to his/her individual threshold, less any amount by which that deemed earned income combined with his/her partner's earned income exceeds the couple threshold (para.(3)).

Example 2

2.174   Rafiq and Maggie are a couple and they have one child, Charlie, who is aged 2. Rafiq has a photography business and Maggie works in a pub in the evenings. Maggie's earnings are £600 and Rafiq's are £500 in the current assessment period.

Maggie has been accepted as the "responsible carer" for Charlie and so falls within s.20 of the WRA 2012. Her individual threshold is therefore £520 a month (16 hours a week x £7.50 x 52 divided by 12 = £520), with no tax or NI contribution deductions at this level of earnings.

Rafiq's individual threshold is £1,048.16 a month (35 hours a week x £7.50 x 52 divided by 12, less £89.32 for tax and NI contributions)

Rafiq and Maggie's actual combined earnings are £1,100 (£500 plus £600).

This is below the sum of their joint earnings thresholds of £1,568.16 (£1,048.16 for Rafiq plus £520 for Maggie).

However, adding Rafiq's minimum income floor to Maggie's actual earnings gives £1,648.16 (£1,048.16 plus £600). That is £80 above their joint earnings thresholds of £1,568.16, so Rafiq is treated as having earnings of £968.16 (£1,048.16 less £80). Their universal credit is assessed on the basis of earned income of £1,568.16 (Rafiq's deemed earnings of £968.16 plus Maggie's actual earnings of £600).

Note that if reg.62 does apply in an assessment period, a claimant will not be subject to work-related requirements in that assessment period (see reg.90(1) and (5)).

Note also that income a claimant is deemed to have by virtue of reg.62 does not count as earned income for the purpose of the benefit cap (see reg.82(4)).

Start-up period

2.175   **63.**—(1) A "start-up period" is a period of 12 months and applies from the beginning of the assessment period in which the Secretary of State determines that a claimant is in gainful self-employment where—

(a) the claimant has begun to carry on the trade, profession or vocation which is their main employment in the 12 months preceding the beginning of that assessment period; and

(b) the claimant is taking active steps to increase their earnings from that employment to the level of the claimant's individual threshold (see regulation 90).

(2) But no start-up period may apply in relation to a claimant where a start-up period has previously applied in relation to that claimant, whether in relation to the current award or any previous award of universal credit, unless that previous start-up period—

(a) began more than 5 years before the beginning of assessment period referred to in paragraph (1); and

(b) applied in relation to a different trade, profession or vocation which the claimant has ceased to carry on.

(3) The Secretary of State may terminate a start-up period at any time if the person is no longer in gainful self-employment or is no longer taking the steps referred to in paragraph (1)(b).

DEFINITIONS

"assessment period"—see WRA 2012 ss.40 and 7(2) and reg.21.
"claimant"—see WRA 2012 s.40.
"gainful self-employment"—see regs 53(1) and 64.
"individual threshold"—see regs 2 and 90(2).

If the claimant is in a "start-up period", the minimum income floor does not apply even if s/he is in gainful self-employment (as defined in reg.64) (see reg.62(5)).   **2.176**

A start-up period is a period of up to 12 months starting from the beginning of the assessment period in which the Secretary of State decides that the claimant is in gainful self-employment, provided that the claimant (i) started his/her trade, profession or vocation which is his/her main employment in the 12 months before the beginning of that assessment period and (ii) is taking active steps to increase his/her earnings from that self-employment to the level of his/her individual threshold under reg.90, i.e., the level at which s/he will no longer have to meet work-related requirements (para.(1)).

If the claimant is no longer in gainful self-employment, or is not taking active steps to increase his/her earnings as required by para.(1)(b), the Secretary of State can end the start-up period (para.(3)).

A claimant can only have one start-up period in relation to the same trade, profession or vocation. In addition, a claimant who has had a previous start-up period can only have a further start-up period in relation to a different trade, profession or vocation if the previous start-up period began more than five years before the start of the assessment period in which the new one begins (para.(2)).

Meaning of "gainful self-employment"

64. A claimant is in gainful self-employment for the purposes of regulations 62 and 63 where the Secretary of State has determined that—   **2.177**

    (a) the claimant is carrying on a trade, profession or vocation as their main employment;

    (b) their earnings from that trade, profession or vocation are self-employed earnings; and

    (c) the trade, profession or vocation is organised, developed, regular and carried on in expectation of profit.

"claimant"—see WRA 2012, s.40.
"self-employed earnings"—see regs 53(1) and 57.

This defines when a claimant is in "gainful self-employment". This is important because it determines whether the "minimum income floor" (see reg.62) applies to the claimant's earned income.   **2.178**

A claimant is in gainful self-employment if s/he is undertaking a trade, profession or vocation as his/her main employment, the earnings from which are self-employed earnings, and the trade, profession or vocation is "organised, developed, regular and carried on in expectation of profit". The mere hope of profit is not enough. There must be a realistic expectation not just of bringing money in, but of profit. If any of these conditions are not met, the claimant will not be in gainful self-employment.

In order to decide whether a claimant is in gainful self-employment, s/he will be asked to attend a Gateway interview soon after making a claim for universal credit or after declaring that s/he is in self-employment.

There is lengthy guidance on the gainful self-employment test at paras H4020–4058 ADM. This suggests that the question of whether the self-employment is the claimant's main employment will depend on a number of factors, such as the hours spent undertaking it each week, whether this is a significant proportion of the claimant's expected hours per week, how many hours (if any) the claimant spends on employed activity, the amount of income received, whether the claimant receives a greater proportion of his/her income from self-employed or employed activity, and whether self-employment is the claimant's main aim.

In order to decide whether the self-employment is "organised, developed, regular and carried on in expectation of profit", the guidance suggests that factors such as whether the work is undertaken for financial gain, the number of hours worked each week, whether there is a business plan, the steps being taken to increase the income from the work, whether the business is being actively marketed or advertised, how much work is in the pipeline and whether HMRC regard the activity as self-employment may be relevant. None of those factors seem related specifically to regularity, which will have to be determined in accordance with the overall pattern of activity. Difficult questions may arise where the nature of the trade etc carried on creates seasonal fluctuations or even seasonal periods of non-activity.

Clearly if the claimant's business is an established one that has been operating for some time and is still receiving income, it may be relatively straightforward to decide that the claimant is in gainful self-employment. If, however, the business is receiving little or no income, it may be that the self-employment is no longer "organised", "regular" or "carried on in expectation of profit". All the circumstances will need to be considered, including future prospects and whether this is part of the normal pattern of the claimant's work. A claimant may still be in gainful employment while unable to work through illness but in that situation should consider submitting medical certificates with a view to no longer being subject to all work-related requirements and thus the minimum income floor not applying. And at some point it would be said that the claimant had ceased to carry on the business.

If the claimant is not in gainful self-employment, the minimum income floor will not apply and the claimant's actual self-employed earnings will be taken into account.

CHAPTER 3

UNEARNED INCOME

Introduction

2.179   **65.** This Chapter provides for the calculation of a person's unearned income for the purposes of section 8 of the Act (calculation of awards).

DEFINITION

    "the Act"—see reg.2.

What is included in unearned income?

2.180   **66.**—(1) A person's unearned income is any of their income, including income the person is treated as having by virtue of regulation 74 (notional unearned income), falling within the following descriptions—
  (a) retirement pension income (see regulation 67);
  (b) any of the following benefits to which the person is entitled, subject to any adjustment to the amount payable in accordance with regulations under section 73 of the Social Security Administration Act 1992 (overlapping benefits)—
    (i) jobseeker's allowance,
    (ii) employment and support allowance,
    (iii) carer's allowance,
    (iv) [1 . . .],
    (v) widowed mother's allowance,
    (vi) widowed parent's allowance,

    (vii) widow's pension,

    (viii) maternity allowance, or

    (ix) industrial injuries benefit, excluding any increase in that benefit under section 104 or 105 of the Contributions and Benefits Act (increases where constant attendance needed and for exceptionally severe disablement);

(c) any benefit, allowance, or other payment which is paid under the law of a country outside the United Kingdom and is analogous to a benefit mentioned in sub-paragraph (b);

(d) payments made towards the maintenance of the person by their spouse, civil partner, former spouse or former civil partner under a court order or an agreement for maintenance;

(e) student income (see regulation 68);

(f) a payment made under section 2 of the Employment and Training Act 1973 or section 2 of the Enterprise and New Towns (Scotland) Act 1990 which is a substitute for universal credit or is for a person's living expenses;

(g) a payment made by one of the Sports Councils named in section 23(2) of the National Lottery etc. Act 1993 out of sums allocated to it for distribution where the payment is for the person's living expenses;

(h) a payment received under an insurance policy to insure against—

    (i) the risk of losing income due to illness, accident or redundancy, or

    (ii) the risk of being unable to maintain payments on a loan, but only to the extent that the payment is in respect of owner-occupier payments within the meaning of paragraph 4 of Schedule 1 in respect of which an amount is included in an award for the housing costs element;

(i) income from an annuity (other than retirement pension income), unless disregarded under regulation 75 (compensation for personal injury);

(j) income from a trust, unless disregarded under regulation 75 (compensation for personal injury) or 76 (special schemes for compensation);

(k) income that is treated as the yield from a person's capital by virtue of regulation 72;

(l) capital that is treated as income by virtue of regulation 46(3) or (4);

(m) income that does not fall within sub-paragraphs (a) to (l) and is taxable under Part 5 of the Income Tax (Trading and Other Income) Act 2005(miscellaneous income).

(2) In paragraph (1)(f) and (g) a person's living expenses are the cost of—

(a) food;

(b) ordinary clothing or footwear;

(c) household fuel, rent or other housing costs (including council tax), for the person, their partner and any child or qualifying young person for whom the person is responsible.

AMENDMENT

1. Pensions Act 2014 (Consequential, Supplementary and Incidental Amendments) Order 2017 (SI 2017/422) art.43(3) (April 6, 2017, subject to arts 2 and 3).

DEFINITIONS

"bereavement allowance"—see reg.2.
"carer's allowance" —*ibid.*
"child" —see WRA 2012 s.40
"employment and support allowance" —see reg.2.
"industrial injuries benefit" —*ibid.*
"jobseeker's allowance" —*ibid.*
"maternity allowance" —*ibid.*
"partner"—*ibid.*
"qualifying young person" —see WRA 2012 ss.40 and 10(5) and regs 2 and 5.
"widowed mother's allowance" —*ibid.*
"widowed parent's allowance" —*ibid.*
"widow's pension"—*ibid.*

MODIFICATION

With effect from June 16, 2014, reg.66 is modified by reg.25 of the Universal Credit (Transitional Provisions) Regulations 2014 (SI 2014/1230) (see Pt IV of this Volume). The modification applies where an award of universal credit is made to a claimant who is entitled to incapacity benefit or severe disablement allowance, in which case reg.66 applies as if incapacity benefit or, as the case may be, severe disablement allowance were added to the list of benefits in reg.66(1)(b).

2.181   GENERAL NOTE

Para. (1)
Universal credit adopts the approach taken in state pension credit of specifying what is to be included as unearned income. If a type of income is not listed as included, it is ignored and does not affect the claimant's (or claimants') award. Accordingly, there is no need for any general provisions disregarding specified kinds of unearned income (but see regs 75 and 76, expressly mentioned in para.(1)(i) and (j)).

In calculating universal credit, all of the claimant's, or the claimants' combined, unearned income that counts is taken into account in full (see s.8(3) of the WRA 2012 and reg.22).

Unearned income also includes notional unearned income (see reg.74).

On para.(1)(a) (retirement pension income), see the note to reg.67 and on para. (1)(e) (student income), see the note to reg.68.

Not all benefit income is taken into account—see para.(1)(b) for the benefits that do count (note that this will also includes incapacity benefit or severe disablement allowance if the claimant is entitled to either of these benefits: see the modification made to para.(1)(b) by reg.25 of SI 2014/1230 referred to above). Thus, for example, child benefit is ignored, as is disability living allowance, attendance allowance and personal independence payment. War disablement pension and war widows', widowers' or surviving civil partners' pensions are also ignored (for income support, old style JSA, old style ESA and housing benefit there is only a £10 disregard). Bereavement allowance, which has been abolished prospectively for deaths on or after April 6, 2017 has been taken out of the list of benefits in para.(1) (b), but remains in the list in relation to awards of the allowance made before April 6, 2017 or to awards made in relation to deaths before that date (see arts 2 and 3 of the amending Order, SI 2017/422). The monthly payments of the new bereavement support payment have not been put into the list, so will not count as income for universal credit purposes, whether paid on time or in arrears. In so far as any payment of arrears is to be treated as capital it is disregarded as such under para.18(1)(c) of Sch.10. The initial one-off lump sum payment appears to have the character of capital and is disregarded as such under the new para.20 of Sch.10.

Under para.(1)(d) payments "towards the maintenance of a person" from his/ her spouse, or former spouse, or civil partner, or former civil partner, under a court order or maintenance agreement count. Thus maintenance payments that are not made pursuant to an agreement (e.g., ad hoc voluntary payments) will be ignored. There is also no provision for treating such payments as unearned income if they are made directly to a third party. Maintenance for a child is ignored.

The list in reg.66 does not include charitable or voluntary payments and so these will be ignored. On the meaning of charitable and voluntary payments, see the notes to para.15 of Sch.9 to the Income Support Regulations in Vol.II of this series.

Payments from employment and training programmes under s.2 of the Employment and Training Act 1973 or s.2 of the Enterprise and New Towns (Scotland) Act 1990 are only taken into account in so far as they are a substitute for universal credit (e.g., a training allowance) or for a person's living expenses (para. (1)(f)). See para.(2) for what counts as "living expenses".

Under para.(1)(h) payments under an insurance policy count but only if the policy was to insure against the contingencies in heads (i) and (ii). Under head (ii) payments under a mortgage (or other loan) protection policy will only be taken into account if the payment is to pay interest on a mortgage or loan secured on the person's home or to meet "alternative finance payments" (see the notes to paras 4–6 of Sch.1) *and* if the person's universal credit award includes a housing costs element under para.4 of Sch.1. Thus insurance policy payments to meet, e.g., capital repayments or policy premiums, will be ignored.

Income from an annuity (other than retirement pension income) counts unless it was purchased with personal injury compensation—see reg.75, as does income from a trust (unless it is disregarded under regs 75 or 76) (para.(1)(i) and (j)).

On para.(1)(k), "assumed yield from capital" (the equivalent to the "tariff income rule" for income support, old style JSA, old style ESA and housing benefit), see the note to reg.72.

Paragraph (1)(l) includes as income capital that is treated as income under reg.46(3) or (4)—see the note to reg.46.

Paragraph (1)(m) covers income that does not fall within paras (1)(a)–(l) but which is taxable under Pt 5 of the Income Tax (Trading and Other Income) Act 2005. The types of income that are taxable under Pt 5 include royalty payments, income from films and sound recordings, and income from estates in administration.

Unearned income is calculated monthly in accordance with reg.73, except in the case of student income which is calculated in accordance with reg.71.

Meaning of "retirement pension income"

67.—(1) Subject to paragraph (2), in regulation 66(1)(a) "retirement pension income" has the same meaning as in section 16 of the State Pension Credit Act 2002 as extended by regulation 16 of the State Pension Credit Regulations 2002.

2.182

(2) Retirement pension income includes any increase in a Category A or Category B retirement pension mentioned in section 16(1)(a) of the State Pension Credit Act 2002 which is payable under Part 4 of the Contributions and Benefits Act in respect of a person's partner.

Definitions

"Contributions and Benefits Act"—see reg.2.
"partner"—*ibid.*

2.183 "Retirement pension income" has the same meaning for the purposes of universal credit as it does for state pension credit. See the notes to s.16 of the State Pension Credit Act 2002 and reg.16 of the State Pension Credit Regulations 2002 in Vol.II of this series. Presumably para.(2) is felt to be necessary because s.16(1)(a) of the 2002 Act does not refer to such increases (although in the case of a couple it is their combined income that counts (s.8(4)(b) of the WRA 2012)).

Person treated as having student income

2.184 **68.**—(1) A person who is undertaking a course [¹of education, study or training] (see regulation 13) and has a student loan[², a postgraduate master's degree loan] or a grant in respect of that course, is to be treated as having student income in respect of—

(a) an assessment period in which the course begins;

(b) in the case of a course which lasts for two or more years, an assessment period in which the second or subsequent year begins;

(c) any other assessment period in which, or in any part of which, the person is undertaking the course, excluding—

(i) an assessment period in which the long vacation begins or which falls within the long vacation, or

(ii) an assessment period in which the course ends.

(2) Where a person has a student loan [² or a postgraduate master's degree loan], their student income for any assessment period referred to in paragraph (1) is to be based on the amount of that loan.

(3) Where paragraph (2) applies, any grant in relation to the period to which the loan applies is to be disregarded except for—

(a) any specific amount included in the grant to cover payments which are rent payments in respect of which an amount is included in an award of universal credit for the housing costs element;

(b) any amount intended for the maintenance of another person in respect of whom an amount is included in the award.

(4) Where paragraph (2) does not apply, the person's student income for any assessment period in which they are treated as having that income is to be based on the amount of their grant.

(5) A person is to be treated as having a student loan [² or a postgraduate master's degree loan] where the person could acquire [² a student loan or a postgraduate master's degree loan] by taking reasonable steps to do so.

(6) Student income does not include any payment referred to in regulation 66(1)(f) (training allowances).

(7) In this regulation and regulations 69 to 71—

"grant" means any kind of educational grant or award, excluding a student loan or a payment made under a scheme to enable persons under the age of 21 to complete courses of education or training that are not advanced education;

"the long vacation" is a period of no less than one month which, in the opinion of the Secretary of State, is the longest vacation during a course which is intended to last for two or more years;

[² "postgraduate master's degree loan" means a loan which a student is eligible to receive under the Education (Postgraduate Master's Degree Loans) Regulations 2016;]

"student loan" means a loan towards a student's maintenance pursuant to any regulations made under section 22 of the Teaching and Higher Education Act 1998, section 73 of the Education (Scotland) Act 1980 or Article 3 of the Education (Student Support) (Northern Ireland) Order 1998 and includes, in Scotland, a young student's bursary paid under regulation 4(1)(c) of the Students' Allowances (Scotland) Regulation 2007.

AMENDMENTS

1. Universal Credit (Consequential, Supplementary, Incidental and Miscellaneous Provisions) Regulations 2013 (SI 2013/630) reg. 38(5) (April 29, 2013).
2. Social Security (Treatment of Postgraduate Master's Degree Loans and Special Support Loans) (Amendment) Regulations 2016 (SI 2016/743) reg. 6(2) (August 4, 2016).

DEFINITIONS

"assessment period"—see WRA 2012, ss.40 and 7(2) and reg.21.
"housing costs element"—see regs 2 and 25.

GENERAL NOTE

See the notes to reg.13 for when a person is regarded as undertaking a course of education, study or training. If a person who is exempt from the requirement not to be receiving education under reg.14 has student income that is taken into account in calculating his/her universal credit award, s/he will not have any work requirements (see reg.89(1)(e)(ii)). If the person leaves his/her course, student income is taken into account up to the end of the assessment period before the one in which s/he leaves the course. This is because the person is no longer undertaking the course and so para.(1) of this regulation does not apply (the change of circumstance will take effect from the first day of the assessment period in which it occurs—para.20 of Sch.1 to the Decisions and Appeals Regulations 2013). As any student income that is left over at the end of a course or when a person finally abandons or is dismissed from it does not fall within any other paragraph in reg.66(1), it will be ignored.

2.185

Para. (1)

This provides for the assessment periods (i.e. months) in which student income will be taken into account. These are any assessment periods during which, or during part of which, the person is undertaking the course of education, study or training, including the assessment period in which the course begins, or any subsequent year of the course begins. But student income will be ignored in the assessment period in which the course ends, in the assessment period in which the long vacation (defined in para.(7)) starts and in any assessment periods that fall wholly within the long vacation.

2.186

Paras (2)–(7)

These paragraphs define what counts as student income. It does not include training allowances and payment for living expenses taken into account under reg.66(1)(f) (para.(6)).

If a person has a student loan or a postgraduate master's degree loan (both defined in para.(7)), or is treated as having a student loan or a postgraduate master's degree loan under para.(5), the amount of that loan counts as income and any grant (defined in para.(7)) paid for the same period as the loan is ignored. But any specific amount included in the grant for rent payments which are being met by universal credit, or any amount intended for the maintenance of another person included in the person's universal credit award, will count as income (paras (2) and (3)).

2.187

If the person does not have, and is not treated under para.(5) as having, a student loan or a postgraduate master's degree loan, grant income is taken into account (para.4)).

Note the exclusion from the definition of "grant" of payments made to enable people under 21 to complete courses of non-advanced education or training. This means that payments from the "16–19 Bursary Fund" and educational maintenance allowances (in so far as they still exist) do not count as student income (they are fully disregarded for the purposes of income support, old style JSA, old style ESA and housing benefit). Paragraph H6008 ADM also states that grant income does not include any payment derived from Access Funds (although the basis for this is not clear).

"Student loan" for the purposes of regs 68–71 only includes a loan towards the student's maintenance (see para.(7)). In Scotland it also includes a young student's bursary. Any loan for tuition fees will be ignored.

See regs 69–71 for the calculation of student income. There is a disregard for student income of £110 per assessment period (reg.71).

Calculation of student income—student loans [¹ and postgraduate master's degree loans]

2.188   **69.**—(1) Where, in accordance with regulation 68(2), a person's student income is to be based on the amount of a student loan for a year, the amount to be taken into account is the maximum student loan (including any increases for additional weeks) that the person would be able to acquire in respect of that year by taking reasonable steps to do so.

[¹ (1A) Where, in accordance with regulation 68(2), a person's student income is to be based on the amount of a postgraduate master's degree loan for a year, the amount to be taken into account is 30 per cent. of the maximum postgraduate master's degree loan that the person would be able to acquire by taking reasonable steps to do so.]

(2) For the purposes of calculating the maximum student loan in paragraph (1) [¹ or the maximum postgraduate master's degree loan in paragraph (1A)] it is to be assumed no reduction has been made on account of—

(a) the person's means or the means of their partner, parent or any other person; or

(b) any grant made to the person.

AMENDMENT

1. Social Security (Treatment of Postgraduate Master's Degree Loans and Special Support Loans) (Amendment) Regulations 2016 (SI 2016/743) reg. 6(3) (August 4, 2016).

DEFINITIONS

"partner"—see reg.2.
"postgraduate master's degree loan--see reg.68(7).
"student loan"—see regs 2 and 68(7).

GENERAL NOTE

2.189   The amount of a student loan that is taken into account is the maximum amount (including any increases for additional weeks) that the person could obtain for that year if s/he took reasonable steps to do so (para.(1)). In the case of a postgraduate master's degree loan, it is 30 per cent. of the maximum postgraduate master's degree loan that the person could obtain for that year if s/he took reasonable steps to do so (para.(1A)). No reduction is made for any assessed contribution from a parent or partner (or any other person) or for any grant which may have reduced the loan.

See reg.71 for how the amount of student income to be taken into account in an assessment period is calculated (note the disregard of £110).

Calculation of student income—grants

70. Where, in accordance with regulation 68(4), a person's student income is to be based on the amount of a grant, the amount to be taken into account is the whole of the grant excluding any payment—

    (a) intended to meet tuition fees or examination fees;

    (b) in respect of the person's disability;

    (c) intended to meet additional expenditure connected with term time residential study away from the person's educational establishment;

    (d) intended to meet the cost of the person maintaining a home at a place other than that at which they reside during their course, except where an award of universal credit includes an amount for the housing costs element in respect of those costs;

    (e) intended for the maintenance of another person, but only if an award of universal credit does not include any amount in respect of that person;

    (f) intended to meet the cost of books and equipment;

    (g) intended to meet travel expenses incurred as a result of the person's attendance on the course; or

    (h) intended to meet childcare costs.

2.190

DEFINITION

"grant"—see regs 2 and 68(7).

GENERAL NOTE

If a grant counts as student income (on which see reg.68 and the note to that regulation), the whole of the grant is taken into account, subject to the disregards in paras (a)–(h). The disregards in paras (d) and (e) do not apply if the person's universal credit award includes an amount in respect of housing costs (para.(d)) or for the maintenance of another person (para.(e)) (see also reg.68(3)).

See reg.71 for how the amount of student income to be taken into account in an assessment period is calculated (note the disregard of £110).

2.191

Calculation of student income—amount for an assessment period

71. The amount of a person's student income in relation to each assessment period in which the person is to be treated as having student income in accordance with regulation 68(1) is calculated as follows.

2.192

Step 1

Determine whichever of the following amounts is applicable—

    (a) [¹ in so far as regulation 68(2) applies to a person with a student loan,] the amount of the loan (and, if applicable, the amount of any grant) in relation to the year of the course in which the assessment period falls; [¹ . . .]

    [¹ (aa) in so far as regulation 68(2) applies to a person with a postgraduate master's degree loan, 30 per cent. of the amount of the loan in relation to the year of the course in which the assessment period falls; or]

(b) if regulation 68(4) applies (person with a grant but no student loan [¹ or postgraduate master's degree loan]) the amount of the grant in relation to the year of the course in which the assessment period falls. But if the period of the course is less than a year determine the amount of the grant or loan in relation to the course.

Step 2

Determine in relation to—

(a) the year of the course in which the assessment period falls; or

(b) if the period of the course is less than a year, the period of the course, the number of assessment periods for which the person is to be treated as having student income under regulation 68(1).

Step 3

Divide the amount produced by step 1 by the number of assessment periods produced by step 2.

Step 4

Deduct £110.

AMENDMENT

1. Social Security (Treatment of Postgraduate Master's Degree Loans and Special Support Loans) (Amendment) Regulations 2016 (SI 2016/743) reg. 6(4) (August 4, 2016).

DEFINITIONS

"grant"—see regs 2 and 68(7).
"postgraduate master's degree loan" – see reg.68(7).
"student loan" – see regs 2 and 68(7).

GENERAL NOTE

2.193   The amount of a person's student income that is to be taken into account in each assessment period (i.e. month) is worked out as follows:

Step 1:

(a) if the person has, or is treated as having, a student loan, calculate the annual amount of the loan, plus, if applicable, the annual amount of any grant that is to be taken into account (see regs 68 and 70), for that year of the course; or

(b) if the person has, or is treated as having, a postgraduate master's degree loan, calculate 30 per cent. of the loan for that year of the course; or

(c) if the person has a grant but does not have, and is not treated as having, a student loan, or a postgraduate master's degree loan, calculate the amount of the grant for that year of the course; or

(d) if the course lasts for less than a year, calculate the amount of the loan and/ or grant for the course.

Step 2: calculate the number of assessment periods for which the person is to be treated as having student income in that year of the course, or if the course lasts for less than a year, during the course, in accordance with reg.68(1). Note that this will include assessment periods during which the person was undertaking the course and which count under reg.68(1), even if the person had not made a claim for universal credit at that time. See H6140-6144 ADM (example 2).

Step 3: divide the amount in Step 1 by the number of assessments periods in Step 2.

Step 4: deduct £110, as £110 of student income is ignored in each assessment period.

General

Assumed yield from capital

72.—(1) A person's capital is to be treated as yielding a monthly income   **2.194**
of £4.35 for each £250 in excess of £6,000 and £4.35 for any excess which is not a complete £250.

(2) Paragraph (1) does not apply where the capital is disregarded or the actual income from that capital is taken into account under regulation 66(1)(i) (income from an annuity) or (j) (income from a trust).

(3) Where a person's capital is treated as yielding income, any actual income derived from that capital, for example rental, interest or dividends, is to be treated as part of the person's capital from the day it is due to be paid to the person.

GENERAL NOTE

This contains the universal credit equivalent of the tariff income rule that applies   **2.195**
for income support, old style JSA, old style ESA and housing benefit. Under universal credit it is referred to as "assumed yield from capital".

If a person has capital above £6,000 but below £16,000, it is treated as producing £4.35 per month for each complete £250 above £6,000 and £4.35 per month for any odd amount left over (para.(1)). But this does not apply if the capital is disregarded (see Sch.10 and regs 75 and 76), or if the actual income is taken into account under reg.66(1)(i) (income from an annuity) or (j) (income from a trust) (para.(2)). And remember the deductions that must be made under reg.49 in reaching the value of capital.

If the assumed yield from capital rule does apply, actual income from the capital counts as part of the person's capital from the day it is due to be paid (para. (3)).

Unearned income calculated monthly

73.—(1) A person's unearned income is to be calculated as a monthly   **2.196**
amount.

(2) Where the period in respect of which a payment of income is made is not a month, an amount is to be calculated as the monthly equivalent, so for example—

(a) weekly payments are multiplied by 52 and divided by 12;
(b) four weekly payments are multiplied by 13 and divided 12;
(c) three monthly payments are multiplied by 4 and divided by 12; and
(d) annual payments are divided by 12.

[1(2A) Where the period in respect of which unearned income is paid begins or ends during an assessment period the amount of unearned income for that assessment period is to be calculated as follows—

$$N \times \left(\frac{M \times 12}{365} \right)$$

where N is the number of days in respect of which unearned income is paid that fall within the assessment period and M is the monthly amount referred to in paragraph (1) or, as the case may be, the monthly equivalent referred to in paragraph (2).]

(3) Where the amount of a person's unearned income fluctuates, the monthly equivalent is to be calculated—

(a) where there is an identifiable cycle, over the duration of one such cycle; or

(b) where there is no identifiable cycle, over three months or such other period as may, in the particular case, enable the monthly equivalent of the person's income to be determined more accurately.

(4) This regulation does not apply to student income.

AMENDMENT

1. Universal Credit (Digital Service) Amendment Regulations 2014 (SI 2014/2887) reg.4 (November 26, 2014). The amendment is subject to the saving provision in reg.5 of SI 2014/2887 (see Pt IV of this Volume).

DEFINITIONS

"assessment period"–see WRA 2012 ss.40 and 7(2) and reg.21.
"student income"—see reg.68.

GENERAL NOTE

Para. (1)

2.197   Unearned income is calculated as a monthly amount (paras (1) and (2)). But unlike earned income the amount taken into account in an assessment period (i.e. month) is not necessarily the amount actually received in that month. If the amount of the unearned income varies, the monthly equivalent is calculated in accordance with para.(3)).

Para. (2A)

2.198   This paragraph provides an exception to the general rule that unearned income is calculated as a monthly amount. For assessment periods (i.e. months) during which unearned income starts and/or finishes, only an amount based on the actual days for which the income is paid will be taken into account. This is likely to mainly affect benefit payments and pensions.

Note that the amendment which inserted para.(2A) is subject to a saving provision–see reg. 5 of the Universal Credit (Digital Service) Amendment Regulations 2014 in Part IV. The effect is that para.(2A) only applies to awards in relation to claims from people living in areas where the "digital service" (also referred to by DWP as the "full service") is in operation or from such persons who subsequently form a new couple or who separate after being part of a couple.

Para. (3)

2.199   This provides that if there is an identifiable cycle, the amount of unearned income received during that cycle is converted into a monthly amount (para.(3)(a)). If there is no cycle, the amount taken into account is averaged over three months, or over another period if this produces a more accurate monthly equivalent (para.(3)(b)). See the notes to reg.5(2)–(3A) of the Income Support Regulations in Vol.II of this series for discussion of when there is a recognisable cycle, making the necessary allowances for the present regulation applying only to unearned income. There is no equivalent to here to paras (3)–(3A) of reg.5. "Identifiable" cannot mean anything different from "recognisable".

Para. (4)

This regulation does not apply to the calculation of student income. See reg.71 for the amount of a person's student income that is to be taken into account in each assessment period.

2.200

Notional unearned income

74.—(1) If unearned income would be available to a person upon the making of an application for it, the person is to be treated as having that unearned income.

2.201

(2) Paragraph (1) does not apply to the benefits listed in regulation 66(1) (b).

(3) A person who has reached the qualifying age for state pension credit is to be treated as possessing the amount of any retirement pension income for which no application has been made and to which the person might expect to be entitled if a claim were made.

(4) The circumstances in which a person is to be treated as possessing retirement pension income for the purposes of universal credit are the same as the circumstances set out in regulation 18 of the State Pension Credit Regulations 2002 in which a person is treated as receiving retirement pension income for the purposes of state pension credit.

DEFINITION

"retirement pension income"—see reg.67.

GENERAL NOTE

Paras (1) and (2)

A person is treated as having unearned income if "it would be available [to him or her] upon the making of an application for it". But this does not apply to the benefits listed in reg.66(1)(b).

2.202

A person should only be treated as having unearned income under para.(1) if it is clear that it would be paid if an application for it was made. Thus, for example, para.(1) would not apply to payments from a trust that are within the discretion of the trustees.

Paras (3) and (4)

If a person has reached the qualifying age for state pension credit, he or she will be treated as having retirement pension income (defined in reg.67) in the same circumstances as he or she would be so treated for the purposes of state pension credit under reg.18 of the State Pension Credit Regulations 2002. See the notes to reg.18 in Vol.II of this series. The qualifying age for state pension credit was 60 but since April 2010 it has been gradually rising in line with the staged increase in pensionable age for women and will reach 65 in November 2018; thereafter state pension age for both men and women is set to rise from 65 in December 2018 until it reaches 66 by October 2020. Although it is a condition of entitlement to universal credit that a person is below the qualifying age for state pension credit (see s.4(1) (b) of the WRA 2012), a couple may still be entitled if one member of the couple is under that age (see reg.3(2)).

2.203

If a person below the qualifying age for state pension credit chooses not to apply for retirement pension income, he or she will not be caught by this rule.

For the rules relating to notional earned income, see reg.60.

Chapter 4

Miscellaneous

Compensation for personal injury

2.204   **75.**—(1) This regulation applies where a sum has been awarded to a person, or has been agreed by or behalf of a person, in consequence of a personal injury to that person.

(2) If, in accordance with an order of the court or an agreement, the person receives all or part of that sum by way of regular payments, those payments are to be disregarded in the calculation of the person's unearned income.

(3) If the sum has been used to purchase an annuity, payments under the annuity are to be disregarded in the calculation of the person's unearned income.

(4) If the sum is held in trust, any capital of the trust derived from that sum is to be disregarded in the calculation of the person's capital and any income from the trust is to be disregarded in the calculation of the person's unearned income.

(5) If the sum is administered by the court on behalf of the person or can only be disposed of by direction of the court, it is to be disregarded in the calculation of the person's capital and any regular payments from that amount are to be disregarded in the calculation of the person's unearned income.

(6) If the sum is not held in trust or has not been used to purchase an annuity or otherwise disposed of, but has been paid to the person within the past 12 months, that sum is to be disregarded in the calculation of the person's capital.

General Note

2.205   This regulation provides for an extensive disregard of compensation for personal injury, both as capital and income.

Firstly, the compensation is ignored for 12 months from the date it is paid to the person (para.(6)). Thus if it is spent during that 12 months or reduces to £6,000 or less, it will not have any effect on universal credit. Secondly, if the compensation is put in trust, it will be disregarded as capital indefinitely and any income from the trust will be disregarded in the calculation of the person's unearned income (para. (4) and reg.66(1)(j)). Similarly, if the compensation payment is administered by a court, or can only be disposed of by direction of a court, its capital value is ignored and any regular payments from it are ignored in the calculation of the person's unearned income (para.(5)). Thirdly, if the compensation is used to purchase an annuity, payments under the annuity are disregarded as unearned income (para.(3) and reg.66(1)(i)). Fourthly, if, in accordance with a court order or agreement, the person receives all or part of the compensation by way of regular payments, these are ignored as unearned income (see para.(2)).

Although paras (3)–(5) refer to "the sum" awarded or agreed, in contrast to para. (2), which refers to all or part of that sum, it is submitted that in the overall context, "the sum" in paras (3)–(5) must be interpreted to include part of that sum and amounts derived from the original award or agreement.

There appears to be no problem with the relationship with reg.50(1) on notional capital (deprivation for the purpose of securing entitlement to or increasing the amount of universal credit) if the court order or agreement directly requires the making of regular payments (para.(2)) or the holding of the compensation payment on trust (para.(4)) or control by a court (para.(5)). However, an apparent problem could arise in cases in which the payment has initially been paid to the person concerned and later some or all of the amount is placed into a trust or is used to purchase an annuity. If that action had not been taken, the disregard under para. (6) could not have lasted for longer than 12 months. Therefore, depending on the amounts involved and other circumstances, it could appear on the face of it that the transfer of the capital was for the purpose of securing entitlement to universal credit or increasing its amount after the running out of that 12 months, so that the person would be treated as still possessing the amount disposed of. There is no equivalent in reg.50 to reg.51(1)(a) of the Income Support Regulations (reg.113(1)(a) of the JSA Regulations 1996 and reg.115(1)(a) of the ESA Regulations 2008) excluding its operation where the capital disposed of is derived from a payment made in consequence of a personal injury and is placed on trust. However, as suggested in the notes to reg.50(1) above, the intention of reg.75 is so clearly that the holding of funds in the ways set out in paras (3)–(5) should not affect entitlement to universal credit that it is submitted that the notional capital rule cannot be applied in those circumstances.

See the notes to para.12 of Sch.10 to the Income Support Regulations in Vol.II of this series, as to what constitutes personal injury.

Special schemes for compensation etc.

76.—(1) This regulation applies where a person receives a payment from a scheme established or approved by the Secretary of State or from a trust established with funds provided by the Secretary of State for the purpose of—

   (a) providing compensation in respect of—

      (i) a person having been diagnosed with variant Creutzfeldt-Jacob disease or infected from contaminated blood products,

      (ii) the bombings in London on 7th July 2005,

      (iii) persons who have been interned or suffered forced labour, injury, property loss or loss of a child during the Second World War; or

   (b) supporting persons with a disability to live independently in their accommodation.

(2) Any such payment, if it is capital, is to be disregarded in the calculation of the person's capital and, if it is income, is to be disregarded in the calculation of the person's income.

(3) In relation to a claim for universal credit made by the partner, parent, son or daughter of a diagnosed or infected person referred to in paragraph (1)(a)(i) a payment received from the scheme or trust, or from the diagnosed or infected person or from their estate is to be disregarded if it would be disregarded in relation to an award of state pension credit by virtue of paragraph 13 or 15 of Schedule 5 to the State Pension Credit Regulations 2002.

2.206

DEFINITIONS

   "claim"—see WRA 2012 s.40.
   "partner"—see reg.2.

GENERAL NOTE

   This regulation disregards payments from various compensation schemes and schemes to support people with a disability to live independently set up or approved by the Government. Any payment from these schemes or trusts is ignored as capital if it is capital, and as income if it is income (para.(2) and reg.66(1)(j)). Payments of

2.207

capital under para.(3) that are made to a parent of a person diagnosed with variant Creutzfeldt-Jacob disease are disregarded for two years; in the case of a payment to a parent of a person infected from contaminated blood products they are ignored until two years after the date of the person's death.

Company analogous to a partnership or one person business

2.208

77.—(1) Where a person stands in a position analogous to that of a sole owner or partner in relation to a company which is carrying on a trade or a property business, the person is to be treated, for the purposes of this Part, as the sole owner or partner.

(2) Where paragraph (1) applies, the person is to be treated, subject to paragraph (3)(a), as possessing an amount of capital equal to the value, or the person's share of the value, of the capital of the company and the value of the person's holding in the company is to be disregarded.

(3) Where paragraph (1) applies in relation to a company which is carrying on a trade—

(a) any assets of the company that are used wholly and exclusively for the purposes of the trade are to be disregarded from the person's capital while they are engaged in activities in the course of that trade;

(b) the income of the company or the person's share of that income is to be treated as the person's income and calculated in the manner set out in regulation 57 as if it were self-employed earnings; and

(c) where the person's activities in the course of the trade are their main employment, the person is to be treated as if they were in gainful self-employment and, accordingly, regulation 62 (minimum income floor) applies [¹ . . .].

(4) Any self-employed earnings which the person is treated as having by virtue of paragraph (3)(b) are in addition to any employed earnings the person receives as a director or employee of the company.

(5) This regulation does not apply where the person derives income from the company that is employed earnings by virtue of Chapter 8 (workers under arrangements made by intermediaries) or Chapter 9 (managed service companies) of Part 2 of ITEPA.

(6) In paragraph (1) "property business" has the meaning in section 204 of the Corporation Tax Act 2009.

AMENDMENT

1. Universal Credit and Miscellaneous Amendments (No.2) Regulations 2014 (SI 2014/2888) reg.4(6) (November 26, 2014, or in the case of existing awards, the first assessment period beginning on or after November 26, 2014).

DEFINITIONS

"employed earnings"—see regs 53(1) and 55.
"ITEPA"—see reg.2.
"self-employed earnings"—see regs 53(1) and 57.

GENERAL NOTE

2.209

If a person's control of a company, which is carrying on a trade or a property business (defined in para.(6)), is such that s/he is like a sole trader or a partner, the value of the person's shareholding is disregarded and s/he is treated as having a proportionate share of the capital of the company (para.(2)) and a proportionate share of the company's income as if that was self-employed earnings (para.(3)(b)). However, the

246

general rule in para.(3)(a) is that so long as the person is engaged in activities in the course of the company's trade the company's assets are disregarded as capital. Those rules are similar to those in reg.51(4) and (5) of the Income Support Regulations (see the notes in Vol.II of this series), reg.115(6) and (7) of the ESA Regulations 2008 and reg.113(4) and (5) of the JSA Regulations 1996, but by no means identical. Some unpacking and identification of potential problems is necessary.

First, note that the regulation as a whole does not apply where the person concerned receives employed earnings from the company that are chargeable to income tax under Chapter 8 (workers under arrangements made by intermediaries) or 9 (managed service companies) of Part 2 of the Income Tax (Earnings and Pensions) Act 2003 (ITEPA). There is no such exclusion in the income support and old style JSA rules. Chapter 8 of Part 2 of ITEPA is concerned with what are known as IR35 arrangements, under which a person provides services to a client who would be an employer except that the arrangements are made by a third party to whom the client makes the payments in return for the services. Then, subject to conditions, the payments to the third party are treated as employed earnings of the person concerned and chargeable to income tax. Chapter 9 applies to similar effect where the intermediary is a managed service company, i.e. one under the control of the service provider(s).

Para. (1)

The addition of the reference to a property business in para.(1) is unique. The definition in s.204 of the Corporation Tax Act 2009, as referred to in para.(6), is unhelpful in itself, merely saying that the term includes both UK and overseas property businesses. One has to go on to ss.205-207 to find provisions: (a) that a property business consists of every business which the company carries on for generating income from land in the UK or outside, as the case may be, and every transaction entered into for that purpose otherwise than in the course of the business; and (b) that generating income from land means exploiting it as a source of rents or other income. It is not clear why it was felt necessary to add the reference to a property business. Presumably, it would have been regarded as a trade under the Income Support Regulations, the ESA Regulations 2008 and the JSA Regulations 1996 in the general meaning of the word, it being irrelevant that the profits of a company from trade are chargeable to tax under a different Part of the Corporation Tax Act 2009 from the profits of a property business. But the reference causes problems of interpretation mentioned below.

2.210

Para. (2)

The approach adopted in *R(IS) 13/93* to the income support rule must also apply to para.(2) in that the value of the company's capital (by reference to which the amount of the person's notional capital is assumed) means the net total value after liabilities have been taken into account. The fact that the company owns some particularly valuable asset or assets does not on its own mean that the claimant's notional capital must be over the limit. The net worth must be identified, no doubt by looking at accounts and using standard accounting practices. Where the person's position is not analogous to that of a sole owner, but to a partner, the identification of the proportionate share may raise difficult issues of judgment. In *R(IS) 13/93* the Commissioner seemed prepared to adopt the proportionate shareholding as the criterion. There should then be no difficulty in the disregarding under para.(2) of the actual value of the person's shareholding in the company.

2.211

Para. (3)

There are further departures from the income support and old style JSA position in para.(3), in deeming the person's proportionate share of the company's income to be self-employed earnings (sub-para.(b)) and in applying the minimum income floor where the person's activities in the trade are their main employment (sub-para. (c)). There is a preliminary problem in that para.(3) only applies where para.(1)

2.212

applies in relation to a company that is carrying on a trade. There is no mention of a company carrying on a property business. Can it really have been intended that the consequences in sub-paras.(b) and (c) and, more importantly, the disregard of the capital value of the company's assets under sub-para.(a) are not to be applied where a company is carrying on a property business? There seems no element of policy or logic behind such a difference of treatment. Accordingly, especially if it is accepted, as suggested above, that outside the particular context of the tax regime under the Corporation Tax Act 2009, a property business would be regarded as a trade, it may be that in context the reference in para.(3) to carrying on a trade is to all trades including property businesses. The discussion below proceeds on that basis. However, some authoritative elucidation of the relationship between paras (1) and (3) in relation to property businesses would be welcome.

Under para.(3)(b) the income of the company or a proportionate share is to be treated as income of the person concerned and calculated under reg.57 as if it were self-employed earnings. That appears to be so even if the person concerned undertakes no activities in the course of the business. It is far from clear how the notional conversion is to take place. Under reg.57, in the case of actual self-employed earnings, the calculation is based on gross profits in the sense of actual receipts in any assessment period less permitted deductions for expenses under regs 58 and 59. Presumably, therefore "the income of the company" does not mean the net income of the company as might be calculated for corporation tax purposes or under ordinary accounting principles. Presumably it means the actual receipts of the company in the assessment period in question less the deductions for expenses under regs 58 and 59, looking at expenditure on behalf of the company rather than by the person in question. It is difficult to say whether in practice information will be available as to such receipts and expenditure in a current assessment period of a month. Even if that is so, there might well be large fluctuations month by month. A further problem is how to calculate the deductions from gross profits under reg.57(2)(a) and (b) for Class 2 and 4 national insurance contributions and income tax paid to HMRC in the assessment period and relievable pension contributions made in that period, when the person's actual tax and national insurance status will not have been as a self-employed earner. See para.(4) for the effect of the person having employed earnings.

In the light of the difficulties with para.(3)(b), the effect of para.(3)(c) may be particularly important. Where the person's activities in the course of the company's trade are their main employment they are deemed to be in gainful self-employment, so that reg.62 on the minimum income floor applies. For any assessment period in which reg.62 applies (see the notes to that provision) and the claimant's earned income is less than his or her individual threshold, the earned income is deemed to be equal to that amount. The weekly amount is effectively the hourly national minimum wage multiplied by the expected number of hours under reg.88. That level of income exempts the claimant from all work-related requirements (reg.90(1) and (5) and s.19 of the WRA 2012), but the deemed amount would be taken into account in calculating the amount of benefit payable.

The other element of para.(3) is the disregard of assets of the company that would otherwise be deemed to be part of the claimant's capital by reason of the person's deemed status as sole owner or partner in the business (sub-para.(a)). There are two conditions. The person must be engaged in activities in the course of the company's trade. In reg.51(4) and (5) of the Income Support Regulations, reg.115(6) and (7) of the ESA Regulations 2008 and reg.113(4) and (5) of the JSA Regulations 1996 the condition is that the person undertakes activities in the course of the business of the company. On that form of words the Commissioner in *R(IS) 13/93* was satisfied that the claimant's wife, who took telephone messages and received mail for the company, as well as being a director, was taking part in the company's business. He also said that although the activities were low key, he was far from certain that they were de minimis. It is not entirely clear that he was intending to lay down a rule that any activity beyond something that was de minimis (i.e. so trivial as to be equivalent to nothing) would do, rather than merely describing the circumstances of the particular case, but a principle that anything of substance would do appears right. Does a test in the terms of being engaged in activities in the course of the company's trade require a different approach? In *Chief Adjudication Officer v Knight*, reported as part of *R(IS) 14/98*, the Court of Appeal was concerned with the disregard of the assets of a business in which a person was engaged as a self-employed earner. The claimant was described as a sleeping partner in a farming business with her son and his wife. The court held that that, including the risk of her assets in the business and her right to a share of profits, did not constitute a sufficient positive involvement to conclude that she was engaged in the business. But it was recognised that each case would have to be decided individually. That does not suggest any plain difference in approach, and it is submitted that the word "engaged" does not in its ordinary meaning require anything more extensive than "undertaking activities".

It should be noted that para.(3)(a) applies only while the person is actually engaged in activities. No doubt short breaks, such as for weekends or longer holidays, are to be ignored. But there is no provision in it, as there is in para.6 of Sch.10 to the Income Support Regulations and in para.8 of Sch.10 to the present Regulations (business assets) for an extension where the person has ceased to carry on a trade, business or vocation within the previous six months (extendable) in certain circumstances such as incapacity thought not to be permanent. It may be arguable that the disregard in para.8 of Sch.10 can apply to the notional capital to be possessed under para.(2) if its conditions would have applied if the person had actually previously been carrying on the business as a self-employed person.

The second condition for the disregard under para.(3)(a) is that the assets are used wholly and exclusively for the purposes of the company's trade. That is not a condition in reg.51(5) of the Income Support Regulations, reg.115(7) of the ESA Regulations 2008 or reg.113(5) of the JSA Regulations 1996, under which the whole of the person's deemed capital under the equivalent of para.(2) is disregarded. Does the phrase "wholly and exclusively" exclude the disregarding of the value of assets that have a dual use? An obvious example would be a vehicle used for both business and personal purposes. In relation to the deduction of expenses in the calculation of the net profits of self-employed earners under reg.38(3)(a) of the Income Support Regulations (reg.98(3)(a) of the ESA Regulations 2008 and reg.101(4)(a) of the JSA Regulations 1996), where it is a condition that the expenses were wholly and exclusively defrayed for the purposes of the employment, it has been held that apportionment can extend not only to items where specific different uses can be identified (e.g. telephone calls or petrol costs) but also to items where there can be an apportionment on a time basis (e.g. vehicle insurance): *R(FC) 1/91*, *CFC 26/1989* and *R(IS) 13/91*. However, there are still some expenses that are not capable of apportionment, such as the cost of clothing or lunches. Where the use of an asset is in issue, there will be less room for apportionment. To take the example of a vehicle to be used equally for business and for personal purposes, for example, although the expenditure on licence fees, insurance and maintenance costs could be apportioned just as much as fuel costs, when looked at as a single asset to be valued it is hard to see how it could be said to be wholly and exclusively used for the purposes of the company's trade if it was used for any non-trivial non-trade purpose. Nonetheless, there might possibly be some things, like money in a bank account or a stock of stationery that could be regarded as made up of some assets used wholly and exclusively for the purposes of the company's trade and some not so used. Nor is it necessarily fatal to a conclusion that the asset is used wholly and exclusively for the purposes of the company's trade that a person derives some private advantage from it (e.g. a particularly comfortable office chair or one adapted to a person's disability or physiology).

That second condition seems unfairly restrictive compared to the position in income support and old style ESA and JSA and also compared to the treatment under universal credit of those actually in self-employment. There, para.7 of Sch.10 requires the disregard of assets used "wholly or mainly" for the purposes of the trade, business or vocation being carried on. In view of the express condition in para.(3)(a), it appears that a person could not rely on the wider disregard in para.7 of Sch.10 in relation to their deemed notional capital, on the same basis as suggested above in relation to para.8 of Sch.10. Indeed, that may cast doubt on the validity of the argument about para.8.

Para. (4)

2.213   If someone treated as having self-employed earnings under para.(3)(b) also has employed earnings from the company, either as an employee or in the office of director, the two sources of income are both to be taken into account. Dividends are not normally employed earnings, being derived from the ownership of the shares on which they are paid. But sometimes the label of dividend cannot properly be applied to the payments made or dividends properly so called can constitute remuneration derived from a contract of employment or in an office. See the notes to reg.55 (employed earnings). Dividends cannot constitute unearned income because they do not appear in the exhaustive list in reg.66(1). They are not remuneration or profit derived from employment under a contract of employment or in an office (reg.52(a)(i)). Even if they were to be regarded as such, they are not general earnings as defined in s.7(3) of ITEPA, being chargeable to income tax under Chapters 3–5 of Part 4 of the Income Tax (Trading and Other Income) 2005 (ITTOIA). It might be different if the labelling of the payments as dividends was a sham, the payments in substance being earnings merely dressed up as dividends.

PART 7

THE BENEFIT CAP

GENERAL NOTE

Introduction

2.214   Regulations 78–83 are made under ss.96–97 of the WRA 2012. They establish a "benefit cap" under which affected claimants can receive no more in social security benefits than £23,000 pa or £15,410 pa in Greater London and £20,000 pa or £13,400 pa elsewhere. In both cases, the higher of those limits applies to joint claimants or those responsible for a child or qualifying young person and the lower to single claimants who are not responsible a child or a qualifying young person. The £23,000 limit is equivalent to £1,916.67 per assessment period or approximately £442.35 per week. The equivalents for £20,000 are £1,666.67 and £384.62; for £15,410 they are £1,284.17 and £296.35; and for £13,400 they are £1,116.67 and £257.69. The higher rates apply irrespective of how many people are in the benefit unit: families consisting of a couple with six children are capped at the same rate as a single parent with one.

How the benefit cap works

2.215   Under reg.79, the benefit cap applies where the total amount of the "welfare benefits" (as defined in WRA 2012 s.96(10)) exceed whichever "relevant amount" applies: see reg.80A. The amount of universal credit that the claimant would otherwise be awarded for the assessment period is reduced by the amount of the excess: reg.81.

Calculation of entitlement to welfare benefits

2.216   Regulation 80 deals with how the amount of the claimant's (or claimants') entitlement to "welfare benefits" is calculated. The rule is that the total entitlement to all specified benefits during the assessment period is taken into account except where that entitlement is not payable because of the overlapping benefit rules: reg.80(1). Under reg.66, many of the benefits listed in WRA 2012 s.96(10) are taken into account as unearned income when calculating entitlement to universal credit.

Regulation 80(4) provides that they are to be taken into account for benefit cap purposes at the same rate as they are taken into account under reg.66. Universal credit itself is (obviously) taken into account at the rate to which the claimant(s) would be entitled if the benefit cap did not apply: reg.80(2). Regulation 80(3) provides (presumably for the avoidance of doubt) that where a claimant is disqualified from receiving (new-style) ESA by virtue of reg.93 ESA Regulations 2013, that benefit is not taken into account. Finally, reg.80(5) provides that where a "welfare benefit" is awarded in respect of a period other than a month (which will always be the case, except for universal credit itself) the monthly equivalent is to be calculated in the same way as for other unearned income under reg.73.

Exceptions

There are a number of exceptions, where the benefit cap does not apply, or the reduction is less than the full amount of the excess. The benefit cap does not apply in any assessment period: 2.217

- where the award of universal credit includes the LCWRA element, or the carer element;, or a claimant (including one or more joint claimants) is receiving "new-style" ESA at a rate that includes the support component: reg.83(1)(a) and (j);

- during which a claimant or a qualifying young person for whom s/he is responsible is receiving carer's allowance or a claimant is receiving industrial injuries benefit, attendance allowance, disability living allowance or personal independence payment, or guardian's allowance: reg.83(1)(b), (c), (f), (g), (i) and (k) and note that—for obvious reasons—those benefits are not "welfare benefits" as defined in WRA 2012 s.96(10);

- a child or qualifying young person for whom a claimant is responsible is receiving disability living allowance or personal independence payment: reg.83(1)(f) and (g); and

- a claimant is receiving a war pension (as defined in reg.83(2))or certain payments under the Armed Forces and Reserve Forces Compensation Scheme: reg.83(1)(d) and (c).

Where a claimant (or a child or qualifying young person) is entitled to attendance allowance, disability living allowance, personal independence payment—or a war pension or a relevant payment under the Armed Forces Compensation Scheme—but is not receiving it because he or she is in a hospital or a care home, the benefit cap does not apply by virtue of reg.83(1)(h).

Under reg.82(1), the benefit cap does not apply if the claimant's earned income (or the claimants' combined earned income) in the assessment exceeds "the amount of earnings that a person would be paid at the hourly rate set out in regulation 4 of the National Minimum Wage Regulations for 16 hours per week, converted to a monthly amount by multiplying by 52 and dividing by 12" or during the nine month "grace period" as defined in reg.82(2). The rules on the "minimum income floor" in reg.62 (which, in this instance, would be advantageous for the claimant(s)) do not apply to the calculation of earned income in this context.

Finally, where the award of universal credit includes the childcare costs element, the amount of that element is deducted from the amount of the reduction under reg.81. If that amount exceeds the excess of the total entitlement to welfare benefits over the relevant amount, then no reduction is made: reg.81(1) and (2).

Legal challenges

On March 18, 2015, in *R (SG and others (previously JS and others) v Secretary of State for Work and Pensions* [2015] UKSC 16, the Supreme Court (Lords Reed, Carnwath and Hughes, Lady Hale and Lord Kerr dissenting) rejected a legal challenge to the benefit cap on the grounds that it unlawfully discriminated against   2.218

women in breach of art.14 of, read with art.1 of the First Protocol to, ECHR; and infringed art.3(1) of the United Nations Convention on the Rights of the Child.

On November 26, 2015, in *Hurley v Secretary of State for Work And Pensions* [2015] EWHC 3382 (Admin), Collins J held that the failure to exempt individual family carers caring for adult family members from the benefit cap constituted unlawful discrimination contrary to contrary to Art.14 of—taken together with Art.1 of the First Protocol to, or Art.8 of—the ECHR. The government responded to the judgment by removing carer's allowance from the list of "welfare benefits" in WRA 2012 s.96(10) (see WR&WA 2016 s.8(4)) and by adding exceptions to reg.83 where the claimant (or a qualifying young person for whom s/he is responsible) is entitled to carer's allowance; or where the carer element is included in the ward of universal credit; or where the claimant is entitled to guardian's allowance.

On June 22, 2017 in *R (DA and Others) v Secretary of State for Work and Pensions* [2107] EWHC 1446 (Admin), Collins J ruled that the application of the benefit cap (under the equivalent provisions of the Housing Benefit Regulations 2006) to lone parents of children under two infringed their Convention Rights under arts 8 and 14 ECHR taken together. In particular, the applicants were unable to work for 16 hours a week (i.e., so as to take advantage of the earnings exception: see reg.82) because of their caring responsibilities and the cost of childcare.

Introduction

2.219   **78.**—(1) This Part makes provision for a benefit cap under section 96 of the Act which, if applicable, reduces the amount of an award of universal credit.

(2) In this Part "couple" means—

(a) joint claimants; or

(b) a single claimant who is a member of a couple within the meaning of section 39 of the Act and the other member of that couple,

and references to a couple include each member of that couple individually.

DEFINITION

"the Act"—see reg.2.

Circumstances where the benefit cap applies

2.220   **79.**—(1) Unless regulation 82 or 83 applies, the benefit cap applies where the welfare benefits to which a single person or couple is entitled during the reference period exceed the relevant amount [¹ determined under regulation 80A (relevant amount)].

(2) The reference period for the purposes of the benefit cap is the assessment period for an award of universal credit.

(3) [¹. . .]

(4) [¹. . .]

AMENDMENT

1. Benefit Cap (Housing Benefit and Universal Credit) (Amendment) Regulations 2016 (SI 2016/909) reg.3(1) and (2) (assessment periods beginning on or after November 7, 2016).

DEFINITIONS

"assessment period"—see WRA 2012 ss.40 and 7(2).

"bereavement allowance"—see reg.2.

"carer's allowance"—*ibid.*
"child"—see WRA 2012 s.40.
"claimant"—*ibid.*
"Contributions and Benefits Act"—see reg.2.
"couple"—see reg.78(2).
"employment and support allowance"—see reg.2.
"jobseeker's allowance"—*ibid.*
"joint claimants"—see WRA 2012 s.40.
"maternity allowance"—see reg.2.
"qualifying young person"—see WRA 2012 s.40 and 10(5) and regs 2 and 5.
"responsible for a child or qualifying young person"—see regs 2, 4 and 4A.
"single claimant"—see WRA 2012 s.40.
"single person"—see WRA 2012 ss.40 and 1(2)(a).
"welfare benefit"—see WRA 2012 s.96(10).
"widowed mother's allowance"—see reg.2.
"widowed parent's allowance"—*ibid.*
"widow's pension"—*ibid.*

GENERAL NOTE

Although "couple" is defined by reg.78(2) as including a member of a couple   2.221
who is permitted to claim as a single person under reg.3(3), the higher "relevant
amount" in reg.79(3)(a) is only available to "joint claimants" and those responsible
for a child or a qualifying young person. A member of a couple claiming as a single
person who is not responsible for a child or a qualifying young person, will therefore
be capped at the lower rate.

The welfare benefits to which reg.79 applies are defined by WRA 2012 s.96(10)
as bereavement allowance, child benefit, child tax credit, ESA, housing benefit,
incapacity benefit, IS, JSA, maternity allowance, severe disablement allowance, universal credit, widow's pension, widowed mother's allowance and widowed parent's
allowance.

Manner of determining total entitlement to welfare benefits

80.—(1) Subject to the following provisions of this regulation, the   2.222
amount of a welfare benefit to be used when determining total entitlement
to welfare benefits is the amount to which the single person or couple
is entitled during the reference period subject to any adjustment to the
amount payable in accordance with regulations under section 73 of the
Social Security Administration Act 1992 (overlapping benefits).

(2) Where the welfare benefit is universal credit, the amount to be used
is the amount to which the claimant is entitled before any reduction under
regulation 81 or under section 26 or 27 of the Act.

[¹ (2A) Where the welfare benefit is housing benefit under section 130 of
the Contributions and Benefits Act, the amount to be used is nil.]

(3) Where a person is disqualified for receiving an employment and
support allowance by virtue of section 18 of the Welfare Reform Act 2007,
it is disregarded as a welfare benefit.

(4) Where an amount of a welfare benefit is taken into account in assessing a single person's or a couple's unearned income for the purposes of an
award of universal credit the amount to be used is the amount taken into
account as unearned income in accordance with regulation 66.

(5) Where a welfare benefit is awarded in respect of a period that is not a
month, the amount is to be calculated as the monthly equivalent as set out
in regulation 73 (unearned income calculated monthly).

AMENDMENT

1. Benefit Cap (Housing Benefit and Universal Credit) (Amendment) Regulations 2016 (SI 2016/909) reg.3(1) and (3) (assessment periods beginning on or after November 7, 2016).

DEFINITIONS

"couple"—see reg.78(2).
"earned income"—see reg.2.
"single person"—see WRA 2012 ss.40 and 1(2)(a).
"unearned income"—see reg.2.

[¹ **Relevant amount**

2.223   **80A.**—(1) The relevant amount is determined by dividing the applicable annual limit by 12.

(2) The applicable annual limit is—

(a) £15,410 for a single claimant resident in Greater London who is not responsible for a child or qualifying young person;

(b) £23,000 for—
    (i) joint claimants where either joint claimant is resident in Greater London;
    (ii) a single claimant resident in Greater London who is responsible for a child or qualifying young person;

(c) £13,400 for a single claimant not resident in Greater London who is not responsible for a child or qualifying young person;

(d) £20,000 for—
    (i) joint claimants not resident in Greater London;
    (ii) a single claimant not resident in Greater London who is responsible for a child or qualifying young person.

(3) For the purposes of section 96 of the Act (benefit cap) and this regulation a claimant is resident in Greater London if—

(a) where the housing costs element is included in the claimant's award of universal credit—
    (i) accommodation in respect of which the claimant meets the occupation condition is in Greater London; or
    (ii) the claimant is in receipt of housing benefit in respect of a dwelling (which has the meaning given in section 137 of the Contributions and Benefits Act) in Greater London;

(b) where the housing costs element is not included in the claimant's award of universal credit—
    (i) accommodation that the claimant normally occupies as their home is in Greater London; or
    (ii) where there is no accommodation that the claimant normally occupies as their home, the Jobcentre Plus office to which the Secretary of State has allocated their claim is in Greater London.]

AMENDMENT

1. Benefit Cap (Housing Benefit and Universal Credit) (Amendment) Regulations 2016 (SI 2016/909) reg.3(1) and (4) (assessment periods beginning on or after November 7, 2016).

Reduction of universal credit

81.—(1) Where the benefit cap applies in relation to an assessment period for an award of universal credit, the amount of the award for that period is to be reduced by—　　　　　　　　　　　　　　　　　**2.224**

(a) the excess; minus

(b) any amount included in the award for the childcare costs element in relation to that assessment period.

(2) But no reduction is to be applied where the amount of the childcare costs element is greater than the excess.

(3) The excess is the total amount of welfare benefits that the single person or the couple are entitled to in the reference period, minus the relevant amount [¹ determined under regulation 80A].

AMENDMENT

1. Benefit Cap (Housing Benefit and Universal Credit) (Amendment) Regulations 2016 (SI 2016/909) reg.3(1) and (5) (assessment periods beginning on or after November 7, 2016).

DEFINITIONS

"childcare costs element"—see reg.2.
"assessment period"—see WRA 2012 ss.40 and 7(2).

Exceptions—earnings

82.—(1) The benefit cap does not apply to an award of universal credit in relation to an assessment period where—　　　　　　　　　　　　　　　**2.225**

(a) the claimant's earned income or, if the claimant is a member of a couple, the couple's combined earned income, is equal to or exceeds [¹ the amount of earnings that a person would be paid at the hourly rate set out in regulation 4 of the National Minimum Wage Regulations for 16 hours per week, converted to a monthly amount by multiplying by 52 and dividing by 12]; or

(b) the assessment period falls within a grace period or is an assessment period in which a grace period begins or ends.

(2) A grace period is a period of 9 consecutive months that begins on the most recent of the following days in respect of which the condition in paragraph (3) is met—

(a) a day falling within the current period of entitlement to universal credit which is the first day of an assessment period in which the claimant's earned income (or, if the claimant is a member of a couple, the couple's combined earned income is [¹ less than—

　(i) where the assessment period began before 1st April 2017, £430; or

　(ii) in any other case, the amount calculated in accordance with paragraph (1)(a)];

(b) a day falling before the current period of entitlement to universal credit which is the day after a day on which the claimant has ceased paid work.

(3) The condition is that, in each of the 12 months immediately preceding that day, the claimant's earned income or, if the claimant was a member of a couple, the couple's combined earned income was equal to or [¹ exceeded—

    (a) in any month beginning before 1st April 2017, £430; and

    (b) in any other case, the amount calculated in accordance with paragraph (1)(a)].

(4) "Earned income" for the purposes of this regulation does not include income a person is treated as having by virtue of regulation 62 (minimum income floor).

AMENDMENT

1. Universal Credit (Benefit Cap Earnings Exception) Amendment Regulations 2017 (SI 2017/138) reg.2(1) and (3) (Assessment periods beginning on or after April 1, 2017).

DEFINITIONS

"assessment period"—see WRA 2012 ss.40 and 7(2).
"claimant"—see WRA 2012 s.40.
"couple"—see reg.78(2).
"earned income"—see reg.2 and para.(4).

Exceptions—entitlement or receipt of certain benefits

2.226   **83.**—(1) The benefit cap does not apply in relation to any assessment period where—

    (a) the LCWRA element is included in the award of universal credit or the claimant is receiving an employment and support allowance that includes the support component;

    (b) a claimant is receiving industrial injuries benefit;

    (c) a claimant is receiving attendance allowance;

    (d) a claimant is receiving a war pension;

    (e) a claimant is receiving a payment under article 15(1)(c) or article 29(1)(a) of the Armed Forces and Reserve Forces (Compensation Scheme) Order 2011;

    (f) a claimant, or a child or qualifying young person for whom a claimant is responsible, is receiving disability living allowance;

    (g) a claimant, or a qualifying young person for whom a claimant is responsible, is receiving personal independence payment;

    (h) a claimant, or a child or qualifying young person for whom a claimant is responsible, is entitled to a payment listed in [¹ sub-paragraphs (b) to (g)] but—

        (i) is not receiving it by virtue of regulation 6 (hospitalisation) or regulation 7 (persons in care homes) of the Social Security (Attendance Allowance) Regulations 1991,

       (ii) it is being withheld by virtue of article 53 of the Naval, Military and Air Forces etc (Disablement and Death) Service Pensions Order 2006 (maintenance in hospital or an institution),

     (iii) is not receiving it by virtue of regulation 8 (hospitalisation) or regulation 9 (persons in care homes) of the Social Security (Disability Living Allowance) Regulations 1991, or

     (iv) in the case of personal independence payment, is not receiving it by virtue of regulations under section 85 (care home residents) or 86 (hospital in-patients) of the Act.

    [¹ (i) a claimant, or a qualifying young person for whom a claimant is responsible, is entitled to carer's allowance;

(j) the carer element is included in the award of universal credit;

(k) a claimant is entitled to guardian's allowance under section 77 of the Contributions and Benefits Act.]

(2) For the purposes of this regulation, "war pension" means—

(a) any pension or allowance payable under any of the instruments listed in section 639(2) of ITEPA—

    (i) to a widow, widower or a surviving civil partner, or

    (ii) in respect of disablement;

(b) a pension payable to a person as a widow, widower or surviving civil partner under any power of Her Majesty otherwise than under an enactment to make provision about pensions for or in respect of persons who have been disabled or have died in consequence of service as members of the armed forces of the Crown;

(c) a payment which is made under any of—

    (i) the Order in Council of 19th December 1881,

    (ii) the Royal Warrant of 27th October 1884, or

    (iii) the Order by His Majesty of 14th January 1922,

    to a widow, widower or surviving civil partner of a person whose death was attributable to service in a capacity analogous to service as a member of the armed forces of the Crown and whose service in such capacity terminated before 31st March 1973;

(d) a pension paid by the government of a country outside the United Kingdom which is analogous to any of the pensions, allowances or payments mentioned in paragraphs (a) to (c).

AMENDMENT

1. Benefit Cap (Housing Benefit and Universal Credit) (Amendment) Regulations 2016 (SI 2016/909) reg.3(1) and (6) (assessment periods beginning on or after November 7, 2016).

DEFINITIONS

"the Act"—see reg.2.
"attendance allowance"—see reg.2.
"child"—see WRA 2012, s.40.
"claimant"—*ibid.*
"disability living allowance"—see reg.2.
"employment and support allowance"—*ibid.*
"industrial injuries benefit"—*ibid.*
"ITEPA"—*ibid.*
"partner"—see reg.2.
"personal independence payment"—see reg.2.
"responsible for a child or qualifying young person"—see regs 2, 4 and 4A.
"qualifying young person"—see WRA 2012, s.40 and 10(5) and regs 2 and 5.

AMENDMENT

1. Universal Credit (Consequential, Supplementary, Incidental and Miscellaneous Provisions) Regulations 2013 (SI 2013/630) reg.38(1) and (6) (April 29, 2013).

PART 8

CLAIMANT RESPONSIBILITIES

CHAPTER 1

WORK-RELATED REQUIREMENTS

Introductory

Introduction

2.227   **84.** This Chapter contains provisions about the work-related requirements under sections 15 to 25 of the Act, including the persons to whom they are to be applied, the limitations on those requirements and other related matters.

DEFINITION

"work-related requirement"—see WRA 2012 ss.40 and 13(2)

Meaning of terms relating to carers

2.228   **85.** In this Chapter—
"relevant carer" means—
(a) a parent of a child who is not the responsible carer, but has caring responsibilities for the child; or
(b) a person who has caring responsibilities for a person who has a physical or mental impairment; and
"responsible foster parent" in relation to a child means a person who is the only foster parent in relation to that child or, in the case of a couple both members of which are foster parents in relation to that child, the member who is nominated by them in accordance with regulation 86.

DEFINITIONS

"child"—see WRA 2012 s.40
"couple"—see WRA 2012 ss.40 and 39
"foster parent"—see reg.2
"responsible carer"—see WRA 2012 ss.40 and 19(6)

GENERAL NOTE

2.229   The definitions of "relevant carer" and "responsible foster parent" are relevant for the purposes of regs 86, 88, 89(1)(f), 91(2), 96(3) and 97(2). A child is a person under the age of 16. Responsibility for a child is to be determined in accordance with the rules in regs 4 and 4A, under which the basic test is whether the child normally lives with the person in question. The definition of "relevant carer" allows the inclusion into that category of people who do not count as responsible under the reg.4 rules but nevertheless have caring responsibilities (not further defined) for the child in question or have caring responsibilities for a person of any age who has a physical or mental impairment (not further defined). If a child has only one foster parent, that person is the "responsible foster parent". If both members of a couple are foster parents of the child, there must be a nomination of one of them under reg.86.

Nomination of responsible carer and responsible foster parent

86.—(1) This regulation makes provision for the nomination of the responsible carer or the responsible foster parent in relation to a child.

(2) Only one of joint claimants may be nominated as a responsible carer or a responsible foster parent.

(3) The nomination applies to all the children, where there is more than one, for whom either of the joint claimants is responsible.

(4) Joint claimants may change which member is nominated—

(a) once in a 12 month period, starting from the date of the previous nomination; or

(b) on any occasion where the Secretary of State considers that there has been a change of circumstances which is relevant to the nomination.

2.230

DEFINITIONS

"child"—see WRA 2012 s.40
"joint claimant"—*ibid.*
"responsible carer"—see WRA 2012 ss.40 and 19(6)
"responsible foster parent"—see reg.85

GENERAL NOTE

This regulation provides, for the purposes of s.19(6) of the WRA 2012 and reg.85, for the nomination by a couple of which one of them is to be the "responsible carer" or "responsible foster parent". Under s.19(6) the nomination has to be made jointly. Presumably that is implied where the nomination is of the responsible foster parent under reg.85. Where more than one child is involved, the same nomination must cover all of them. The nomination can be changed once within 12 months from the date of the previous nomination or when there has been a relevant change of circumstances

2.231

References to paid work

87. References in this Chapter to obtaining paid work include obtaining more paid work or better paid work.

2.232

DEFINITION

"paid work"—see reg.2

GENERAL NOTE

References to obtaining paid work, which appears to include self-employment as well as employment, includes obtaining more or better paid work. This provision does not appear to add anything to the conditions of most of the provisions to which obtaining paid work is relevant.

2.233

Expected hours

88.—(1) The "expected number of hours per week" in relation to a claimant for the purposes of determining their individual threshold in regulation 90 or for the purposes of regulation 95 or 97 is 35 unless some lesser number of hours applies under paragraph (2).

(2) The lesser number of hours is—

2.234

(a) where—
(i) the claimant is a relevant carer, a responsible carer or a responsible foster parent, and
(ii) the Secretary of State is satisfied that the claimant has reasonable prospects of obtaining paid work,
the number of hours that the Secretary of State considers is compatible with those caring responsibilities;
(b) where the claimant is a responsible carer for a child under the age of 13, the number of hours that the Secretary of State considers is compatible with the child's normal school hours (including the normal time it takes the child to travel to and from school); or
(c) where the claimant has a physical or mental impairment, the number of hours that the Secretary of State considers is reasonable in light of the impairment.

DEFINITIONS

"child"—see WRA 2012 s.40.
"claimant"—*ibid.*
"relevant carer"—see reg.85.
"responsible carer"—see WRA 2012 ss.40 and 19(6).
"responsible foster parent"—see reg.85.

GENERAL NOTE

2.235   Regulation 90 calculates the amount of earnings that will take a claimant out of being subject to all work-related requirements under s.22 of the WRA 2012 by reference to the "expected number of hours per week" and the national minimum wage. Regulation 95 uses the same number as one of the tests for the time that a claimant has to spend in action aimed at obtaining paid work to avoid being deemed not to have complied with the work search requirement under s.17 of the WRA 2012. Regulation 97(2) allows certain claimants to limit the work for which they must be available and for which they must search to work for the expected number of hours per week. Regulation 88 defines the expected number of hours for all these purposes.

The number under para.(1) is 35, unless some lesser number is applicable under para.(2). Can the number be reduced to zero? Why not? Zero is a number and it is less than 35. There are three alternative categories in para.(2). Sub-paragraph (a) applies where the claimant is a relevant carer, a responsible carer or a responsible foster parent (see s.19(6) of the WRA 2012 and reg.85 above), and so has some substantial caring responsibility. Then, if the claimant nonetheless has reasonable prospects of obtaining paid work (including obtaining more or better paid work), the expected hours are what is compatible with those caring responsibilities. Sub-paragraph (b) applies where the claimant is a responsible carer (as defined in s.19(6) of the WRA 2012) for a child under the age of 13, when the expected hours are those compatible with the child's normal school and travel hours. Sub-paragraph (c) applies where the claimant has physical or mental disablement (not further defined), when the expected hours are those reasonable in the light of the impairment. This is an important rule in the structure of the application of work-related requirements in a benefit not restricted to jobseekers, and one where the argument that the expected hours under reg.88 can be zero is particularly relevant.

Note that the application of the deeming of non-compliance with the work search requirement under reg.95(1) if the expected hours of action are not taken is subject to deductions of hours under reg.95(2), including for temporary circumstances. Also note regs 96–99 on circumstances in which the work availability and work search requirements cannot be imposed or are moderated, particularly reg.96(4) (voluntary work), reg.96(5) (existing employment), reg.97(2) (physical or mental impairment) and reg.99(4) and (5)(c) (unfitness for work for short periods).

Work-related groups

Claimants subject to no work-related requirements

89.—(1) A claimant falls within section 19 of the Act (claimants subject   2.236
to no work-related requirements) if—
 (a) the claimant has reached the qualifying age for state pension credit;
 (b) the claimant has caring responsibilities for one or more severely
   disabled persons for at least 35 hours a week but does not meet the
   conditions for entitlement to a carer's allowance and the Secretary of
   State is satisfied that it would be unreasonable to require the claimant to comply with a work search requirement and a work availability
   requirement, including if such a requirement were limited in accordance with section 17(4) or 18(3) of the Act;
 (c) the claimant is pregnant and it is 11 weeks or less before her expected
   week of confinement, or was pregnant and it is 15 weeks or less since
   the date of her confinement;
 (d) the claimant is an adopter and it is 12 months or less since—
    (i) the date that the child was placed with the claimant, or
    (ii) if the claimant requested that the 12 months should run from a
      date within 14 days before the child was expected to be placed,
      that date;
 (e) the claimant does not have to meet the condition in section 4(1)(d)
   of the Act (not receiving education) by virtue of regulation 14 and—
    (i) is a person referred to in paragraph (a) of that regulation (under
      21, in non-advanced education and without parental support), or
    (ii) has student income in relation to the course they are undertak-
      ing which is taken into account in the calculation of the award;
      or
 (f) the claimant is the responsible foster parent of a child under the age
   of 1.
 (2) In paragraph (1)(b) "severely disabled" has the meaning in section 70
of the Contributions and Benefits Act.
 (3) In paragraph (1)(d)—
 (a) "adopter" means a person who has been matched with a child for
   adoption and who is, or is intended to be, the responsible carer for
   the child, but excluding a person who is a foster parent or close relative of the child; and
 (b) a person is matched with a child for adoption when it is decided by
   an adoption agency that the person would be a suitable adoptive
   parent for the child.
 [[1](4) For the purposes of paragraph (1)(e)(ii), a claimant is not to be
treated as having student income where—
 (a) that income is a postgraduate master's degree loan; and
 (b) the course in respect of which the loan is paid is not a full-time course.
 (5) In paragraph (4), "postgraduate master's degree loan" has the
meaning given in regulation 68(7).]

AMENDMENT

1. Social Security (Treatment of Postgraduate Master's Degree Loans and Special
Support Loans) (Amendment) Regulations 2016 (SI 2016/743) reg.6(5) (August
4, 2016).

Definitions

"child"—see WRA 2012 s.40.
"claimant"—*ibid.*
"close relative"—see reg.2.
"Contributions and Benefits Act"—*ibid.*
"postgraduate master's degree loan"—see para.(5) and reg.68(7).
"responsible carer"—see WRA 2012 ss.40 and 19(6).
"responsible foster parent"—see reg.85.

General Note

2.237   Section 19(2) of the WRA 2012 sets out in paras (a), (b) and (c) three categories of claimants who can be subject to no work-related requirements: (a) those who have limited capability for work and work-related activity; (b) those who meet the definition of having regular and substantial caring responsibilities for a severely disabled person (i.e. satisfy the conditions, apart from level of earnings and claiming, for carer's allowance, but gain no earned income from the caring: reg.30); and (c) those who are the responsible carer for a child under the age of one. Paragraph (d) of s.19(2) includes claimants of a description prescribed in regulations. Regulation 89(1) sets out categories prescribed for this purpose, as noted below. Regulation 90 prescribes another category, dependent on earnings. See also reg.98 on recent victims of domestic violence.

(a) Claimants who have reached the qualifying age for state pension credit. The qualifying age for men is the same as for a woman born on the same day and for women depends on the date of birth in accordance with a complicated formula. See p.772 of and Appendix 12 to CPAG's *Welfare benefits and tax credits handbook* (2017/2018 edition) for the details. For anyone born before April 6, 1950 the age is 60. For those born on or after that date there is a sliding scale rising to 65 in November 2018, and scheduled to reach 66 by October 2020 and 67 by some date from 2026.

(b) Claimants who do not meet the conditions of entitlement for carer's allowance, but have caring responsibilities for at least 35 hours per week for a severely disabled person (defined in the same way as for carer's allowance: para.(2)), where it would be unreasonable to expect the claimant to comply with a work search and a work availability requirement, even with limitations. Some claimants who fall within this category will already be covered by s.19(2)(b) and it is not easy to work out who could benefit from the extension. Perhaps the main category would be those who are paid for the caring, who are expressly excluded from the scope of s.19(2)(b) by the definition in reg.30 above.

(c) Claimants who are pregnant in the period from 11 weeks before the expected date of confinement and 15 weeks after the date of confinement.

(d) Claimants who are "adopters" (i.e. who have been matched with a particular child for adoption under the complicated conditions in para.(3)) within 12 months or so of placement. It does not matter how old the child is, so long as below the age of 16. Any person who is actually the responsible carer of a child under the age of one is already covered by s.19(2)(c). It appears that para.(d) can continue to apply after the child has actually been adopted, for the 12 months following placement. See para.(f) for foster parents.

(e) Claimants who, by virtue of reg.14(1)(a), do not have to meet the basic condition in s.4(1)(d) of the WRA 2012 of not receiving education or who have student income (see regs 68–71) that is taken into account in the award of universal credit.

(f) Claimants who are the responsible foster parent (there can only be one under reg.85) of a child under the age of one. It appears that such a person cannot get within s.19(2)(c) because reg.4(6)(a) prevents their being treated as responsible for the child while the child is "looked after" by a local authority under s.22 of the Children Act 1989 or s.17(6) of the Children (Scotland) Act 1995.

Claimants subject to no work-related requirements—the earnings thresholds

90.—(1) A claimant falls within section 19 of the Act (claimants subject   2.238
to no work-related requirements) if the claimant's [¹monthly] earnings are
equal to or exceed the claimant's individual threshold.

(2) A claimant's individual threshold is the amount that a person of the
same age as the claimant would be paid at the hourly rate applicable under
[²regulation 4 or regulation 4A(1)(a) to (c)] of the National Minimum
Wage Regulations for—

(a) 16 hours per week, in the case of a claimant who would otherwise
    fall within section 20 (claimants subject to work-focused inter-
    view requirement only) or section 21 (claimants subject to work-
    preparation requirement) of the Act; or

(b) the expected number of hours per week in the case of a claimant who
    would otherwise fall within section 22 of the Act (claimants subject
    to all work-related requirements)[¹,

converted to a monthly amount by multiplying by 52 and dividing by 12].

(3) A claimant who is a member of a couple falls within section 19 of the
Act if the couple's combined [¹monthly] earnings are equal to or exceed
whichever of the following amounts is applicable—

(a) in the case of joint claimants, the sum of their individual thresholds; or

(b) in the case of a claimant who claims universal credit as a single
    person by virtue of regulation 3(3), the sum of—
    (i) the claimant's individual threshold, and
    (ii) the amount a person would be paid for 35 hours per week
        at the hourly rate specified in [²regulation 4] of the National
        Minimum Wage Regulations[,¹
    converted to a monthly amount by multiplying by 52 and dividing
    by 12].

(4) A claimant falls within section 19 of the Act if the claimant is
employed under a contract of apprenticeship and has [¹monthly] earnings
that are equal to or exceed the amount they would be paid for—

(a) 30 hours a week; or

(b) if less, the expected number of hours per week for that claimant,

at the rate specified in [² regulation 4A(1)(d)] of the National Minimum
Wage Regulations[¹, converted to a monthly amount by multiplying by 52
and dividing by 12].

(5) A claimant who is treated as having earned income in accordance with
regulation 62 (minimum income floor) in respect of an assessment period
is to be taken to have weekly earnings equal to their individual threshold in
respect of any week falling within that assessment period.

(6) [¹ A person's monthly earnings are]—

(a) [1the person's] earned income calculated or estimated in relation to
    the current assessment period before any deduction for income tax,
    national insurance contributions or relievable pension contributions;
    or

(b) in a case where the person's earned income fluctuates (or is likely to
    fluctuate) the amount of that income[¹, calculated or estimated before
    any deduction for income tax, national insurance contributions or
    relievable pension contributions, taken as a monthly average]—
    (i) where there is an identifiable cycle, over the duration of one
        such cycle, or

(ii) where there is no identifiable cycle, over three months or such other period as may, in the particular case, enable the [¹monthly] average to be determined more accurately,

[¹and the Secretary of State may, in order to enable monthly earnings to be determined more accurately, disregard earned income received in respect of an employment which has ceased.]

(7) [²...]

AMENDMENTS

1. Universal Credit and Miscellaneous Amendments Regulations 2015 (SI 2015/1754) reg.2(6) (November 4, 2015).

2. Social Security (Jobseeker's Allowance, Employment and Support Allowance and Universal Credit) (Amendment) Regulations 2016 (SI 2016/678) reg.5(4) (July 25, 2016).

DEFINITIONS

"the Act"—see reg.2.
"assessment period"—see WRA 2012 ss.40 and 7(2), and reg.21.
"claimant"—see WRA 2012 s.40(1).
"couple"—see WRA 2012 ss.40 and 39.
"earned income"—see regs 2 and 52.
"joint claimants"—see WRA 2012 s.40.
"National Minimum Wage Regulations"—see reg.2.
"single person"—see WRA 2012 ss.40 and 1(2)(a).

GENERAL NOTE

2.239   Regulation 90 prescribes additional circumstances, beyond those prescribed by reg.89, in which a claimant falls within s.19(2)(d) of the WRA 2012 and therefore can be subject to no work-related requirements. The basic test under para.(1) is that the claimant's monthly earnings are at least equal to his or her "individual threshold". This provision is necessary because universal credit, in contrast to the terms of pre-existing benefits, can be payable while a claimant is in work. The policy is that if a claimant is already earning above a minimum level there is no need to require them to do anything to seek further paid work. Entitlement then depends on the income calculation under s.8 of the WRA 2012. See further the notes to reg.99.

Paragraph (3) applies the para.(1) test to couples. For joint claimants their individual thresholds are added together, as are their monthly earnings. The threshold is calculated under para.(2) by multiplying the hourly rate of national minimum wage by, in the case of a claimant who would otherwise be subject to all work-related requirements under s.22 of the WRA 2012, the expected number of hours per week (see reg.88, usually 35). In the case of a claimant who would otherwise fall within s.20 or 21, the multiplier is 16.

Under para.(6) monthly earnings are earned income as calculated under Chapter 2 of Part 6 of the Universal Credit Regulations (i.e. regs 51–64) in each monthly assessment period but without deductions for income tax, national insurance contributions or pension contributions, subject to an averaging provision in sub-para.(b) where earned income fluctuates or is likely to fluctuate. The ordinary calculation in regs 51–64 involves the use of "real time" information. In the case of both employment and self-employment the calculation of earned income in respect of any assessment period (i.e. month) is to be based on amounts received in that assessment period (regs 54, 55 and 57). There will be obvious difficulties in carrying out that process, on which see the notes to those regulations. If the process does work, it may be proper for the amount of universal credit to fluctuate month by month or for the claimant to fall in and out of entitlement on the means test. However, if entitlement continues there are plainly arguments against a claimant drifting in and out of exemption from all work-related requirements on the basis of the amount of earned income. That is presumably the thinking behind para.(6)(b). The reference to fluctuation of earned income must be to fluctuation over more than one assessment period, because fluctuation within each assessment period does not affect the total for that month. Under sub-para.(i) it is not clear whether the identifiable cycle refers merely to the pattern of receipts or to the pattern of the employment or self-employment or other paid work that produces the income. It would appear that there cannot be an identifiable cycle until it has started and come to an end, which is by definition the start of the next cycle, at least once. Given the difficulties that the notion of a recognisable cycle has given in other contexts it may be that most cases will be dealt with by sub-para.(ii), which requires the taking of an average over the previous three months or such other period as in the particular case enables the weekly average to be determined more accurately. That gives a very wide discretion.

Note also the important power at the end of para.(6) to disregard earned income from an employment that has ceased.

In relation to the self-employment some of those problems will be avoided by the application of the reg.62 minimum income floor (para.(5)). Providing that a person meets the quite stringent conditions in reg.64 for being in gainful self-employment and is not in a 12-month start-up period (reg.63), earned income below the individual threshold is deemed to be at that level.

Claimants subject to work-focused interview requirement only

91.—(1) [¹ . . .].

2.240

(2) A claimant falls within section 20 of the Act if—

(a) the claimant is the responsible foster parent in relation to a child aged at least 1;

(b) the claimant is the responsible foster parent in relation to a qualifying young person, and the Secretary of State is satisfied that the qualifying young person has care needs which would make it unreasonable to require the claimant to comply with a work search requirement or a work availability requirement, including if such a requirement were limited in accordance with section 17(4) or 18(3) of the Act;

(c) the claimant is a foster parent, but not the responsible foster parent, in relation to a child or qualifying young person, and the Secretary of State is satisfied that the child or qualifying young person has care needs which would make it unreasonable to require the claimant to comply with a work search requirement or a work availability requirement, including if such a requirement were limited in accordance with section 17(4) or 18(3) of the Act;

(d) the claimant has fallen within paragraph (a), (b) or (c) within the past 8 weeks and has no child or qualifying young person currently placed with them, but expects to resume being a foster parent; or

(e) the claimant has become a friend or family carer in relation to a child within the past 12 months and is also the responsible carer in relation to that child.

(3) In paragraph (2)(e) "friend or family carer" means a person who is responsible for a child, but is not the child's parent or step-parent, and has undertaken the care of the child in the following circumstances—

(a) the child has no parent or has parents who are unable to care for the child; or

(b) it is likely that the child would otherwise be looked after by a local authority because of concerns in relation to the child's welfare.

AMENDMENT

1. Welfare Reform and Work Act 2016 s.17(2)(a) (April 3, 2017).

DEFINITIONS

"the Act"—see reg.2.
"child"—see WRA 2012 s.40.
"claimant"—*ibid.*
"foster parent"—see reg.2.
"qualifying young person"—see regs 2 and 5.
"responsible carer"—see WRA 2012 ss.40 and 19(6).
"responsible foster parent"—see reg.85.
"work availability requirement"—see WRA 2012 ss.40 and 18(1).
"work search requirement"—see WRA 2012 ss.40 and 17(1).

GENERAL NOTE

Para. (1)

2.241   Paragraph (1) had formerly prescribed the relevant maximum age of a child for the purposes of s.20(1)(a) of the WRA 2012 to enable a responsible carer to be exempted from all work-related requirements except the work-focused interview requirement (initially five and then, from April 2014, three). From April 3, 2017 the operation of s.20(1)(a) has by its terms been restricted to responsible carers of a child aged one (responsible carers of a child under one being exempted from all work-related requirements under s.19(1)(c)). There is no longer any power to prescribe an age in regulations.

Para. (2)

2.242   This provision prescribes the categories of claimant who are subject only to the work-focused interview requirement under s.20(1)(b) and any connected requirements under s.23. They cover mainly foster parents.

Under sub-para.(a) responsible foster parents of children of any age from one to 15 are covered. Responsible foster parents of children under one are exempted from all work-related requirements under reg.89(1)(f).

That is extended to young persons in education up to the age of 19 if it would be unreasonable to subject the claimant to other work-related requirements (sub-para. (b)).

Sub-paragraph (c) extends the scope of sub-paras (a) and (b) to foster parents who do not meet the condition of being "responsible" if the child or qualifying young person has care needs that make it unreasonable to subject the claimant to other work-related requirements.

Sub-paragraph (d) allows the effect of sub-paras (a)–(c) to continue for eight weeks after the claimant ceases to have any child or qualifying young person placed with them, if a new placement is expected.

Sub-paragraph (e) applies to claimants who are responsible carers of a child of any age up to 15 if they fall within the meaning of "friend or family carer" in para.(3).

[¹Claimants subject to work preparation requirement

2.243   **91A.** [² . . .].]

AMENDMENTS

1. Income Support (Work-Related Activity) Miscellaneous Amendments Regulations 2014 (SI 2014/1097) reg.16(3) (April 28, 2014).
2. Welfare Reform and Work Act 2016 s.17(2)(b) (April 3, 2017).

See the notes to s.21 of the WRA 2012. The operation of that section in so far as it exempts responsible carers of a child from all work-related requirements except the work-focused interview and work preparation requirement has from April 3, 2017 been directly controlled by the terms of s.21 (the child must be aged two and no less or more). There is thus no need for a prescription of conditions including an age in regulations and the former duty in s.21(5) so to do has also been removed.

2.244

Claimants subject to all work-related requirements—EEA jobseekers

92.[¹ . . .]

2.245

AMENDMENT

1. Universal Credit (EEA Jobseekers) Amendment Regulations 2015 (SI 2015/546) reg.3 (June 10, 2015).

GENERAL NOTE

For the discriminatory effect of this provision on the entitlement of certain EEA claimants with a right to reside before its revocation in June 2015 see the notes to the 2013/14 edition. Now see reg.9 above, as also amended in June 2015.

2.246

The work-related requirements

Purposes of a work-focused interview

93. The purposes of a work-focused interview are any or all of the following—

2.247

    (a) assessing the claimant's prospects for remaining in or obtaining paid work;

    (b) assisting or encouraging the claimant to remain in or obtain paid work;

    (c) identifying activities that the claimant may undertake that will make remaining in or obtaining paid work more likely;

    (d) identifying training, educational or rehabilitation opportunities for the claimant which may make it more likely that the claimant will remain in or obtain paid work or be able to do so;

    (e) identifying current or future work opportunities for the claimant that are relevant to the claimant's needs and abilities;

    (f) ascertaining whether a claimant is in gainful self-employment or meets the conditions in regulation 63 (start-up period).

DEFINITIONS

    "claimant"—see WRA 2012 s.40.
    "obtaining paid work"—see reg.87.
    "paid work"—see reg.2.

GENERAL NOTE

This provision prescribes the purposes of a work-focused interview under the definition in s.15(2) of the WRA 2012. The purposes could probably not be set out more widely, especially given that obtaining paid work includes obtaining more

2.248

or better paid work. Arguably, even if there is no realistic prospect of a claimant obtaining any kind of paid work, the purpose of assessing those prospects or lack of prospects in an interview could still be fulfilled.

Work search requirement—interviews

2.249   **94.** A claimant is to be treated as not having complied with a work search requirement to apply for a particular vacancy for paid work where the claimant fails to participate in an interview offered to the claimant in connection with the vacancy.

DEFINITIONS

"claimant"—see WRA 2012, s.40.
"paid work"—see reg.2.
"work search requirement"—see WRA 2012 ss.40 and 17(1).

GENERAL NOTE

2.250   This provision, made under s.25(a) of the WRA 2012, applies when the Secretary of State has required under s.17(1)(b) that the claimant take the particular action of applying for a specified vacancy for paid work. If the claimant fails to participate in an interview offered in connection with the vacancy the work search requirement is deemed not to have been complied with. See the notes to s.17, and the notes to ss.15 and 27 for "participation" in an interview.

Work search requirement—all reasonable action

2.251   **95.**—(1) A claimant is to be treated as not having complied with a work search requirement to take all reasonable action for the purpose of obtaining paid work in any week unless—
    (a) either—
        (i) the time which the claimant spends taking action for the purpose of obtaining paid work is at least the claimant's expected number of hours per week minus any relevant deductions, or
        (ii) the Secretary of State is satisfied that the claimant has taken all reasonable action for the purpose of obtaining paid work despite the number of hours that the claimant spends taking such action being lower than the expected number of hours per week; and
    (b) that action gives the claimant the best prospects of obtaining work.
(2) In this regulation "relevant deductions" means the total of any time agreed by the Secretary of State—
    (a) for the claimant to carry out paid work, voluntary work, a work preparation requirement, or voluntary work preparation in that week; or
    (b) for the claimant to deal with temporary childcare responsibilities, a domestic emergency, funeral arrangements or other temporary circumstances.
(3) For the purpose of paragraph (2)(a) the time agreed by the Secretary of State for the claimant to carry out voluntary work must not exceed 50% of the claimant's expected number of hours per week.
(4) "Voluntary work preparation" means particular action taken by a claimant and agreed by the Secretary of State for the purpose of making it more likely that the claimant will obtain paid work, but which is not specified by the Secretary of State as a work preparation requirement under section 16 of the Act.

DEFINITIONS

"claimant"—see WRA 2012 s.40.
"expected number of hours"—see regs 2 and 88.
"obtaining paid work"—see reg.87.
"paid work"—see reg.2.
"work preparation requirement"—see WRA 2012 ss.40 and 16(1).
"work search requirement"—see WRA 2012 ss.40 and 17(1).

GENERAL NOTE

This regulation, made under s.25(a) of the WRA 2012, deems certain claimants   2.252
not to have complied with a work search requirement under s.17(1)(a) of the WRA
2012 to take all reasonable action for the purpose of obtaining paid work (including
more or better paid work). Although in form reg.95 merely lifts the deeming of non-
compliance if its conditions are met, there would seem to be little point in making
such detailed provision if claimants were not to be positively treated as having complied if the conditions are met. See the notes to s.17 and see reg.97 for limitations
on the kind of work that needs to be searched for. A failure for no good reason to
comply with the requirement under s.17(1)(a) can lead to a medium-level sanction
under s.27(2)(a) of the WRA 2012 and reg.103(1)(a).

To avoid the deeming a claimant must get within *both* sub-paras.(a) *and* (b) of
para.(1).

Under (a), the primary rule is that the claimant must spend at least the
"expected number of hours per week" (reg.88), less deductions for work, voluntary
work or work-related activities or various emergency, urgent or other temporary
difficulties (para.(2), subject to the further rules in paras (3) and (4)), in taking
action for the purpose of obtaining paid work. Note that the starting point of
expected hours under reg.88 may be reduced from 35 (arguably to nil, if appropriate) to take account of regular caring responsibilities and physical or mental
impairments. The time to count as a deduction under para.(2) must be agreed by
the Secretary of State. The words might suggest that the agreement must come in
advance of the activity that might qualify. However, it would seem unrealistic for
claimants to predict, say, the future occurrence of domestic emergencies so as to
seek the Secretary of State's agreement in advance. Thus, it would seem, and would
be in line with the normal pattern of claimants signing a declaration that they have
been seeking work in the previous fortnight, that a subsequent agreement will do
(although no doubt it would be sensible for claimants to raise potential issues in
advance where possible). It must be the case that, while the Secretary of State
appears to have an open-ended discretion whether or not to agree to any particular
hours being deducted under para.(2), on appeal against any sanction for failure
to comply with the work search requirement under s.17(1)(a) of the WRA 2012
a tribunal is allowed to substitute its own judgment about what should have been
agreed. Even if it were to be held that whatever had or had not been agreed by the
Secretary of State has to control whether there had been a sanctionable failure, the
reasonableness or otherwise of the Secretary of State's view would be relevant to
whether a failure to comply was "for no good reason". The deductions for hours
spent in paid work and voluntary work are important, as is that for work preparation
requirements in securing a rational co-ordination among the various work-related
requirements. Would para.(2)(b) allow the Secretary of State to allow short "holidays" from work search responsibilities, under the heading of temporary circumstances or temporary child care responsibilities (cf. reg.19(1)(p) and (2) of the JSA
Regulations 1996)? Or would such an allowance fall more naturally under reg.99(5)
(b) (work search requirement not to be imposed where it would be unreasonable to
do so because of temporary child care responsibilities or temporary circumstances)?

If the claimant cannot meet the expected hours condition, which for the majority of claimants will be 35 hours per week, sub-para.(a) can nevertheless be satisfied through head (ii) if the claimant has taken all reasonable action in the week

in question for the purpose of obtaining paid work. This is an important provision which, if properly applied, would go a good way to meeting the commonly expressed criticism that in the real world it is impossible for many claimants to fill 35 hours week after week with meaningful work search action.

Under (b), the action under (a) must give the claimant the best prospects of obtaining work. Taken at face value that condition imposes an almost impossibly high standard, because there will nearly always be something extra that the claimant could do to improve prospects of obtaining work. The condition must therefore be interpreted in a way that leaves some work for condition (a) to do and with some degree of common sense, taking account of all the circumstances, especially any factors that have led to a reduction in the expected hours below 35 or a deduction under para.(1)(a)(i) and (2), as well as matters such as the state of the local labour market, what the claimant has done in previous weeks and how successful or otherwise those actions were (see reg.18(3) of the JSA Regulations 1996). The work search requirement in s.17(1)(a) of the WRA 2012 is only to take all reasonable action. The reference here in secondary legislation to the best prospects of obtaining work cannot be allowed to make the test as set out in the primary legislation stricter than that. There will of course be considerable difficulty in checking on the precise number of hours spent in taking relevant action, depending on what might count as action (see the notes to s.17), and in what might be required from claimants in the way of record keeping. It may be that it will be much easier to define non-compliance with the requirement in s.17(1)(b) to take particular action specified by the Secretary of State, although such a failure will only attract a low-level sanction under s.27(2)(a) and reg.104(1)(b)(iii).

Work availability requirement—able and willing immediately to take up paid work

2.253   **96.**—(1) Subject to paragraph (2) a claimant is to be treated as not having complied with a work availability requirement if the claimant is not able and willing immediately to attend an interview offered to the claimant in connection with obtaining paid work.

(2) But a claimant is to be treated as having complied with a work availability requirement despite not being able immediately to take up paid work, if paragraph (3), (4) or (5) applies.

(3) This paragraph applies where—

(a) a claimant is a responsible carer or a relevant carer;

(b) the Secretary of State is satisfied that, as a consequence the claimant needs a longer period of up to 1 month to take up paid work, or up to 48 hours to attend an interview in connection with obtaining work, taking into account alternative care arrangements; and

(c) the claimant is able and willing to take up paid work, or attend an interview, on being given notice for that period.

(4) This paragraph applies where—

(a) a claimant is carrying out voluntary work;

(b) the Secretary of State is satisfied that, as a consequence, the claimant needs a longer period of up to 1 week to take up paid work, or up to 48 hours to attend an interview in connection with obtaining work; and

(c) the claimant is able and willing to take up paid work, or attend an interview, on being given notice for that period.

(5) This paragraph applies where a claimant—

(a) is employed under a contract of service;

(b) is required by section 86 of the Employment Rights Act 1996, or by the contract of service, to give notice to terminate the contract;

   (c) is able and willing to take up paid work once the notice period has expired; and

   (d) is able and willing to attend an interview on being given 48 hours notice.

DEFINITIONS

"claimant"—see WRA 2012 s.40.
"obtaining paid work"—see reg.87.
"paid work"—see reg.2.
"relevant carer"—see reg.85.
"responsible carer"—see WRA 2012 ss.40 and 19(6).
"work availability requirement"—see WRA 2012 ss.40 and 18(1).

GENERAL NOTE

This regulation is made under s.25 of the WRA 2012 and relates to the work avail-   **2.254**
ability requirement under s.18(1) and (2) of being able and willing immediately to
take up paid work or more or better paid work. See reg.97 for limitations on the kind
of work for which a claimant must be available and reg.99, and in particular para.
(5), for other situations in which the ordinary test of being able and willing immediately to take up work or attend an interview is modified.

Para. (1)
Paragraph (1) simply confirms that the requirement of being able and willing   **2.255**
immediately to take up paid work extends to being able and willing immediately to
attend an interview in connection with obtaining paid work, subject to the exemptions in paras (3)-(5), through the operation of para.(2).

Paras (2) to (5)
A claimant who falls within paras (3), (4) or (5) is to be treated as complying with   **2.256**
the work availability requirement, including as extended by para.(1). Paragraph (3)
applies to those with child-care or other caring responsibilities who would need to
take up to one month to take up paid work or up to 48 hours to attend an interview
and are able and willing to do so if given that length of notice. Can para.(3)(b)
allow claimants with caring responsibilities (noting that such claimants do not need
to have sole or main responsibility) to have a holiday without needing to arrange
some means of taking up work offers or interviews immediately? Or would such an
allowance fall more naturally under reg.99(5A) or (5B) with (5)(b) (no need to be
available immediately where work search requirement not to be imposed because
it would be unreasonable to do so because of temporary child care responsibilities
or temporary circumstances)? Paragraph (4) applies to claimants doing voluntary
work (not further defined), subject to the same conditions. Paragraph (5) applies to
claimants in employment who are required to give notice to terminate their contract
of employment and who are able and willing to take up paid work once that notice
has expired and to attend an interview on 48 hours' notice.

Work search requirement and work availability requirement— limitations

97.—(1) Paragraphs (2) to (5) set out the limitations on a work search   **2.257**
requirement and a work availability requirement.

(2) In the case of a claimant who is a relevant carer or a responsible
carer or who has a physical or mental impairment, a work search and work
availability requirement must be limited to the number of hours that is
determined to be the claimant's expected number of hours per week in
accordance with regulation 88.

(3) A work search and work availability requirement must be limited to work that is in a location which would normally take the claimant—
  (a) a maximum of 90 minutes to travel from home to the location; and
  (b) a maximum of 90 minutes to travel from the location to home.

(4) Where a claimant has previously carried out work of a particular nature, or at a particular level of remuneration, a work search requirement and a work availability requirement must be limited to work of a similar nature, or level of remuneration, for such period as the Secretary of State considers appropriate, but only if the Secretary of State is satisfied that the claimant will have reasonable prospects of obtaining paid work in spite of such limitation.

(5) The limitation in paragraph (4) is to apply for no more than 3 months beginning with—
  (a) the date of claim; or
  (b) if later, the date on which the claimant ceases paid work after falling within section 19 of the Act by virtue of regulation 90 (claimants subject to no work-related requirements- the earnings thresholds).

(6) Where a claimant has a physical or mental impairment that has a substantial adverse effect on the claimant's ability to carry out work of a particular nature, or in particular locations, a work search or work availability requirement must not relate to work of such a nature or in such locations.

DEFINITIONS

  "claimant"—see WRA 2012 s.40.
  "expected number of hours per week"—see regs 2 and 88.
  "relevant carer"—see reg.85.
  "responsible carer"—see WRA 2012 ss.40 and 19(6).
  "work availability requirement"—see WRA 2012 ss.40 and 18(1).
  "work search requirement"—see WRA 2012 ss.40 and 17(1).

GENERAL NOTE

2.258   This regulation is made under ss.17(4) and (5) (work search requirement) and 18(3) and (4) (work availability requirement) of the WRA 2012. It sets out limitations on the kind of work that a claimant can be required to search for or be able and willing immediately to take up. See reg.99 for other situations in which the ordinary tests for those requirements are modified.

Para. (2)
2.259   This paragraph establishes an important limitation on the kind of work that can be considered, but only for the particular categories of claimant identified: those with child care responsibilities and the disabled. Those categories of claimant can only be required to search for or be able and willing to take up work for no more than the number of hours per week compatible with those circumstances, as worked out under reg.88. So, as far as the work search requirement is concerned, this limitation appears to apply as much to the sort of work in relation to which the Secretary of State may specify particular action under s.17(1)(b) of the WRA 2012 as to the requirement under s.17(1)(a) to take all reasonable action for the purpose of obtaining paid work or more or better paid work. Although the drafting of para.(2) appears to limit the hours for which either requirement is applicable, it can only, in view of the terms of the regulation-making powers in ss.17(4) and 18(3), relate to the hours of work to which the relevant requirement can be attached. See para.(6) for permissible limitations relating to the location and nature of employment.

    Note that under s.19(1)(a) no work-related requirements can be imposed on a claimant who has limited capability for work and work-related activity, nor can any be imposed on a claimant with regular and substantial caring responsibilities for a severely disabled person (s.19(1)(b)) or who is the responsible carer for a child under the age of one (s.19(1)(c)).

Para. (3)

    A work search or availability requirement cannot relate to work in a location   **2.260** where the claimant's normal travel time either from home to work or from work to home would exceed 90 minutes, subject to the further limitation in para.(6) for some disabled claimants. Travel times below that limit could be relevant in relation to a sanction for non-compliance with a requirement, on the question of whether the claimant had no good reason for the failure to comply. On that question all circumstances could be considered, including the effect of any physical or mental impairment not serious enough to count under para.(6), whereas under this provision time is the conclusive factor unless the location is completely excluded under para.(6).

Paras (4) and (5)

    A claimant who has previously carried out work of a particular nature or at a par-   **2.261** ticular level of remuneration is to have the kind of work to be considered limited to similar conditions for so long as considered appropriate up to three months from the date of claim or ceasing to fall within s.19 of the WRA 2012 by virtue of the level of earnings (para.(5)). But the rule only applies if and so long as the claimant will have reasonable prospects of work subject to that limitation.

Para. (6)

    A claimant who has a physical or mental impairment which has a substantial   **2.262** adverse effect on their ability to carry out work of a particular nature or in particular locations (a significant additional condition over and above that of impairment on its own) is to have the kind of work to be considered under the work search and work availability requirements limited to avoid such work.

Victims of domestic violence

    98.—(1) Where a claimant has recently been a victim of domestic vio-   **2.263** lence, and the circumstances set out in paragraph (3) apply—

    (a) a work-related requirement imposed on that claimant ceases to have effect for a period of 13 consecutive weeks starting on the date of the notification referred to in paragraph (3)(a); and

    (b) the Secretary of State must not impose any other work-related requirement on that claimant during that period.

    [³(1A) Where a claimant referred to in paragraph (1) is a person who falls within section 22 of the Act (claimants subject to all work-related requirements) and is the responsible carer of a child, the Secretary of State must not impose a work search requirement or a work availability requirement on that claimant for a further period of 13 consecutive weeks beginning on the day after the period in paragraph (1)(a) expires.]

    (2) A person has recently been a victim of domestic violence if a period of 6 months has not expired since the violence was inflicted or threatened.

    (3) The circumstances are that—

    (a) the claimant notifies the Secretary of State, in such manner as the Secretary of State specifies, that domestic violence has been inflicted on or threatened against the claimant by the claimant's partner or former partner or by a family member during the period of 6 months ending on the date of the notification;

    (b) this regulation has not applied to the claimant for a period of 12 months before the date of the notification;

    (c) on the date of the notification the claimant is not living at the same address as the person who inflicted or threatened the domestic violence; and

(d) as soon as possible, and no later than 1 month, after the date of the notification the claimant provides evidence from a person acting in an official capacity which demonstrates that—

(i) the claimant's circumstances are consistent with those of a person who has had domestic violence inflicted or threatened against them during the period of 6 months ending on the date of the notification, and

(ii) the claimant has made contact with the person acting in an official capacity in relation to such an incident, which occurred during that period.

(4) In this regulation—

[¹"coercive behaviour" means an act of assault, humiliation or intimidation or other abuse that is used to harm, punish or frighten the victim;

"controlling behaviour" means an act designed to make a person subordinate or dependent by isolating them from sources of support, exploiting their resources and capacities for personal gain, depriving them of the means needed for independence, resistance or escape or regulating their everyday behaviour;

"domestic violence" means any incident, or pattern of incidents, of controlling behaviour, coercive behaviour, violence or abuse, including but not limited to—

(a) psychological abuse;
(b) physical abuse;
(c) sexual abuse;
(d) emotional abuse;
(e) financial abuse,

regardless of the gender or sexuality of the victim;]

"family member", in relation to a claimant, means the claimant's grandparent, grandchild, parent, step-parent, parent-in-law, son, step-son, son-in-law, daughter, step-daughter, daughter-in-law, brother, step-brother, brother-in-law, sister, step-sister, sister-in law and, if any of those persons is member of a couple, the other member of the couple;

"health care professional" means a person who is a member of a profession regulated by a body mentioned in section 25(3) of the National Health Service Reform and Health Care Professions Act 2002;

"person acting in an official capacity" means a health care professional, a police officer, a registered social worker, the claimant's employer, a representative of the claimant's trade union, or any public, voluntary or charitable body which has had direct contact with the claimant in connection with domestic violence;

"registered social worker" means a person registered as a social worker in a register maintained by—

[² (a) The Health and Care Professions Council;]
[⁴(b) Social Care Wales;]
(c) The Scottish Social Services Council; or
(d) The Northern Ireland Social Care Council.

1. Social Security (Miscellaneous Amendments) (No.2) Regulations 2013 (SI 2013/1508) reg.3(1) (October 29, 2013).
2. Universal Credit and Miscellaneous Amendments Regulations 2014 (SI 2014/597) reg.2(6) (April 28, 2014).
3. Universal Credit and Miscellaneous Amendments (No.2) Regulations 2014 (SI 2014/2888) reg.8(2) (November 26, 2014).
4. Social Security (Social Care Wales) (Amendment) Regulations 2017 (SI 2017/291) reg.2 (April 1, 2017).

DEFINITIONS

"claimant"—see WRA 2012 s.40.
"partner"—see reg.2.
"victim of domestic violence"—see WRA 2012 s.24(6)(b).
"work-related requirement"—see WRA 2012 ss.40 and 13(2).

GENERAL NOTE

This regulation, made as required by s.24(5) and (6) of the WRA 2012, exempts recent victims of domestic violence from the imposition of any work-related requirements for a period of 13 weeks from the date of notification to the Secretary of State under para.(3)(a) and lifts the effect of any existing imposition for the same period. The regulation appears to be defective to the extent that it makes no provision for exemption from the imposition of a connected requirement under s.23 of the WRA 2012, which is not a "work-related requirement" as defined in s.13(2). Thus the duty in s.24(5) to exempt recent victims of domestic violence from any requirement under Part 1 of the Act has not been fully carried out, but that would not seem to affect the validity of what has been provided in reg.98.

2.264

Paragraph (1A), in effect from November 26, 2014, requires the extension of the normal 13-week suspension under para.(1) for a further 13 weeks where the claimant is the responsible carer (see ss.19(6) and 40 of the WRA 2012 and reg.4) of a child.

For these purposes, para.(4) now provides a comprehensive definition of "domestic violence", instead of the former reference to a particular page of a difficult to find Department of Health document. It uses the terms of the government's official approach to the meaning of domestic violence across departments, which had not previously been used as a statutory definition. Note that the new criminal offence of controlling or coercive behaviour in intimate or familial relationships under s.76 of the Serious Crime Act 2015, while using the terms of controlling and coercive behaviour (the meaning of which is discussed in Home Office Statutory Guidance of December 2015) contains conditions that are different from those in reg.98. While the definition here expressly includes coercive behaviour and controlling behaviour (both given their own definition in para.(4)), any other incident of abuse of any kind can come within the ambit of domestic violence. Thus, although the specific definition of "coercive behaviour" requires the act or abuse to be used to harm, punish or frighten the victim and the specific definition of "controlling behaviour" is restricted to acts designed to make the victim subordinate or dependant by particular means (as taken to extremes by the vile Rob Titchener in *The Archers*), abuse of similar kinds where that specific form of intention or purpose is not present or is difficult to prove can nonetheless be domestic violence. The width of that makes the specific conditions in para.(3) for the application of reg.98 particularly important.

Section 24(6)(b) of the WRA 2012 defines a victim of domestic violence as a person on or against whom domestic violence (as defined above) is inflicted or threatened. Under s.24(6)(c) and para.(2) a person is to be treated as having recently been a victim of domestic violence if no more than six months has expired since the infliction or threat.

Para. (3)

2.265   This paragraph lays down four quite restrictive conditions that must all be satisfied for reg.98 to apply. Under sub-para.(a) the claimant must have notified the Secretary of State of the infliction or threatening of domestic violence by a partner, former partner or family member (as defined in para.(4)) within the previous six months. Under sub-para.(b), reg.98 must not have applied within the 12 months before the notification. Under sub-para.(c), the claimant must not on the date of the notification have been living at the same address as the person named as the assailant. Under sub-para.(d), the claimant must also provide, as soon as possible and no more than one month after the notification, evidence from person acting in an official capacity (defined quite widely in para.(4)) both that the claimant's circumstances are consistent with having had domestic violence inflicted or threatened in the six months before notification and that the claimant had made contact (apparently not necessarily within the six months) with the person in relation to an incident of infliction or threat of domestic violence that occurred during the six months before notification.

Circumstances in which requirements must not be imposed

2.266   **99.**—(1) Where paragraph (3), (4)[², (4A)] [¹ . . .] or (6) applies—
   (a) the Secretary of State must not impose a work search requirement on a claimant; and
   (b) "able and willing immediately to take up work" under a work availability requirement means able and willing to take up paid work, or attend an interview, immediately once the circumstances set out in paragraph (3), (4)[², (4A)] [¹ . . .] or (6) no longer apply.
   (2) A work search requirement previously applying to the claimant ceases to have effect from the date on which the circumstances set out in paragraph (3), (4)[², (4A)] [¹ . . .] or (6) begin to apply.
   [¹(2A) Where paragraph (5) applies—
   (a) the Secretary of State must not impose a work search requirement on a claimant; and
   (b) a work search requirement previously applying to the claimant ceases to have effect from the date on which the circumstances set out in paragraph (5) begin to apply.
   (2B) Where paragraph (5A) applies "able and willing to take up work" under a work availability requirement means able and willing to take up paid work, or to attend an interview, immediately once the circumstances set out in paragraph (5A) no longer apply.
   (2C) Where paragraph (5B) applies, "able and willing to take up work" under a work availability requirement means—
   (a) able and willing to take up paid work immediately once the circumstances set out in paragraph (5B) no longer apply; and
   (b) able and willing to attend an interview before those circumstances no longer apply.]
   (3) This paragraph applies where—
   (a) the claimant is attending a court or tribunal as a party to any proceedings or as a witness;
   (b) the claimant is a prisoner;
   (c) regulation 11(3) (temporary absence from Great Britain for treatment or convalescence) applies to the claimant;
   (d) any of the following persons has died within the past 6 months—
      (i) where the claimant was a member of a couple, the other member,

(ii) a child or qualifying young person for whom the claimant or, where the claimant is a member of a couple, the other member, was responsible, or

(iii) a child, where the claimant was the child's parent;

(e) the claimant is, and has been for no more than 6 months, receiving and participating in a structured recovery-orientated course of alcohol or drug dependency treatment;

(f) the claimant is, and has been for no more than 3 months, a person for whom arrangements have been made by a protection provider under section 82 of the Serious Organised Crime and Police Act 2005; or

(g) the claimant is engaged in an activity of a kind approved by the Secretary of State as being in the nature of a public duty.

(4) This paragraph applies where the claimant—

(a) is unfit for work—

(i) for a period of no more than 14 consecutive days after the date that the evidence referred to in sub-paragraph (b) is provided, and

(ii) for no more than 2 such periods in any period of 12 months; and

(b) provides to the Secretary of State the following evidence—

(i) for the first 7 days when they are unfit for work, a declaration made by the claimant in such manner and form as the Secretary of State approves that the claimant is unfit for work, and

(ii) for any further days when they are unfit for work, if requested by the Secretary of State, a statement given by a doctor in accordance with the rules set out in Part 1 of Schedule 1 to the Medical Evidence Regulations which provides that the person is not fit for work.

[²(4A) This paragraph applies for one or more periods of one month, as provided for in paragraphs (4B) and (4C), where the claimant is the responsible carer of a child and an event referred to in sub-paragraph (a) or (b) has taken place in the last 24 months and has resulted in significant disruption to the claimant's normal childcare responsibilities—

(a) any of the following persons has died—

(i) a person who was previously the responsible carer of that child;

(ii) a parent of that child;

(iii) a brother or sister of that child; or

(iv) any other person who, at the time of their death, normally lived in the same accommodation as that child and was not a person who was liable to make payments on a commercial basis in respect that accommodation; or

(b) the child has been the victim of, or witness to, an incident of violence or abuse and the claimant is not the perpetrator of that violence or abuse.

(4B) Paragraph (4A) is not to apply for more than one period of one month in each of the 4 consecutive periods of 6 months following the event (and, if regulation 98 or paragraph (3)(d) of this regulation applies in respect of the same event, that month is to run concurrently with any period for which that regulation or paragraph applies).

(4C) Each period of one month begins on the date specified by the Secretary of State after the claimant has notified the Secretary of State of the circumstances in paragraph (4A) provided that the Secretary of State is satisfied that the circumstances apply.]

(5) This paragraph applies where the Secretary of State is satisfied that it would be unreasonable to require the claimant to comply with a work search requirement [¹ ...], including if such a requirement were limited in accordance with section 17(4) [¹ ...] of the Act, because the claimant—

    (a) is carrying out a work preparation requirement or voluntary work preparation (as defined in regulation 95(4));

    (b) has temporary child care responsibilities or is dealing with a domestic emergency, funeral arrangements or other temporary circumstances; or

    (c) is unfit for work for longer than the period of 14 days specified in paragraph (4)(a) or for more than 2 such periods in any period of 12 months and, where requested by the Secretary of State, provides the evidence mentioned in paragraph (4)(b)(ii).

[¹(5A) This paragraph applies where the Secretary of State is satisfied that it would be unreasonable to require the claimant to comply with a work availability requirement to be able and willing to—

    (a) take up paid work; and

    (b) attend an interview,

(including if such a requirement were limited in accordance with section 18(3) of the Act) because the claimant falls within sub-paragraph (a), (b) or (c) of paragraph (5).

(5B) This paragraph applies where the Secretary of State is satisfied that it would be—

    (a) unreasonable to require the claimant to comply with a work availability requirement to be able and willing to take up paid work because the claimant falls within sub-paragraph (a), (b) or (c) of paragraph (5); and

    (b) reasonable to require the claimant to comply with a work availability requirement to attend an interview,

including if such a requirement were limited in accordance with section 18(3) of the Act.]

[³[⁴(6) This paragraph applies where the claimant has monthly earnings or, if the claimant is a member of a couple, the couple has combined monthly earnings (excluding in either case any that are not employed earnings) that are equal to, or more than, the following amount multiplied by 52 and divided by 12—

    (a) in the case of a single claimant, £5 plus the applicable amount of the personal allowance in a jobseeker's allowance for a single person aged 25 or over (as set out in Part 1 of Schedule 1 to the Jobseeker's Allowance Regulations 1996); or

    (b) in the case of a claimant who is a member of a couple, £10 plus the applicable amount of the personal allowance in a jobseeker's allowance for a couple where both members are aged 18 or over (as set out in that Part).]

(6A) In paragraph (6) "employed earnings" has the meaning in regulation 55.]

(7) In this regulation "tribunal" means any tribunal listed in Schedule 1 to the Tribunals and Inquiries Act 1992.

AMENDMENTS

1. Universal Credit and Miscellaneous Amendments Regulations 2014 (SI 2014/597) reg.2(7) (April 28, 2014).

2. Universal Credit and Miscellaneous Amendments) (No. 2) Regulations 2014 (SI 2014/2888) reg.8(3) (November 26, 2014).

3. Universal Credit (Work-Related Requirements) In Work Pilot Scheme and Amendment Regulations 2015 (SI 2015/89) reg.3 (February 19, 2015).

4. Universal Credit and Miscellaneous Amendments Regulations 2015 (SI 2015/1754) reg.2(7) (November 4, 2015).

DEFINITIONS

"child"—see WRA 2012 s.40.
"claimant"—*ibid.*
"couple"—see WRA 2012, ss.40 and 39.
"Medical Evidence Regulations"—see reg.2.
"paid work"—*ibid.*
"prisoner"—*ibid.*
"qualifying young person"—see WRA 2012 ss.40 and 10(5).
"responsible carer"—see WRA 2012 ss.40 and 19(6).
"voluntary work preparation"—see reg.95(4).
"work availability requirement"—see WRA 2012 ss.40 and 18(1).
"work preparation requirement"—see WRA 2012 ss.40 and 16(1).
"work search requirement"—see WRA 2012 ss.40 and 17(1).

GENERAL NOTE

This regulation is made under ss.22(2) and 24(1)(a) of the WRA 2012 in respect   2.267
of the work search and availability requirements and under s.18(5) in respect of the
work availability requirement. Its structure was revised in 2014 to make its operation somewhat clearer, although at the cost of a more complicated interaction of
various paragraphs. Some requirements have been tightened and some relaxed, also.

The central rule is under paras (1) and (2) and operates where any of paras
(3), (4), (4A) (incorporating (4B) and (4C)) or (6) applies. Under para.(1)(a) no
work search requirement can be imposed in those circumstances (and any already
imposed requirement lapses: para.(2)) and under para.(1)(b) the work availability
requirement is adjusted to require only that the claimant be willing and able to take
up paid work or attend an interview immediately once the circumstances in question cease to apply. Paragraphs (3), (4), (4A) and (6) cover fairly specifically defined
circumstances, dealt with separately below.

Paragraph (2A) operates where para.(5) applies, to the same effect as under paras
(1)(a) and (2) on the work search requirement in relation to the circumstances in
para.(5). Paragraph (5) also covers fairly specifically defined circumstances, but
with the additional condition that it be unreasonable to require compliance with the
work search requirement, and is dealt with separately below.

Paragraph (2B) operates where para.(5A) applies, to the same effect as under
para.(1)(b) in relation to the circumstances in para.(5A). Paragraph (5A) involves
a judgment that it would be unreasonable to require the claimant to be able and
willing to take up paid work <u>and</u> attend an interview (see further below).

Paragraph (2C) operates where para.(5B) applies, but only so as to lift the
requirement to be willing and able to take up an offer of paid work, not to lift the
requirement to be willing and able to attend an interview. The judgment required
under para.(5B) is thus that it would be unreasonable to require the claimant to
be able and willing to take up paid work, but reasonable to require willingness and
ability to attend an interview (see further below).

Para. (3)

2.268   Paragraph (3) lists a number of categories of claimant where the circumstances mean that the claimant could not be expected to look for or take up work or attend an interview, generally of a temporary nature:

(a)   Attending a court or tribunal (defined in para.(7)) as a party to proceedings or as a witness, apparently so long as the hearing continues for a party and so long as attendance is required for a witness.

(b)   A prisoner, under the reg.2 definition covering those detained in custody pending trial or sentence on conviction or under sentence or on temporary release, but excluding anyone detained in hospital under mental health legislation.

(c)   Temporary absence from Great Britain in connection with medical treatment for illness etc or convalescence, or accompanying a partner or child or qualifying young person undergoing such treatment or convalescence, under the conditions in reg.11(3). See the notes to that provision.

(d)   The claimant's then partner, a child or qualifying young person for whom the claimant or partner was responsible or a child of the claimant has died within the previous six months. See para.(4A)(a) for circumstances in which the operation of paras (1) and (2) can be triggered by the death within the previous 24 months of various people connected with a child.

(e)   Attending a structured recovery-oriented course of alcohol or drug dependency treatment, for no more than six months.

(f)   Having protection arrangements made under s.82 of the Serious Organised Crime and Police Act 2005 (protection of persons involved in investigations or proceedings whose safety is considered to be at risk), for no more than three months. Arrangements for protection are made by protection providers (e.g. Chief Constables and any of the Commissioners for HMRC).

(g)   Any other activity of a kind approved by the Secretary of State as being in the nature of a public duty, apparently for as long as the activity and approval lasts. It is therefore unclear whether on any appeal against a sanction where the application of this paragraph is in issue a First-tier Tribunal is required to accept non-approval of an activity by the Secretary of State or can substitute its own judgment.

Para. (4)

2.269   A claimant who is unfit for work (not further defined) and provides a self-certificate for the first seven days and, if requested, a statement from a doctor under the Medical Evidence Regulations (see Vol.I of this series) for any further days falls within the basic rules in this regulation. But the benefit of para.(4) is limited to a period of no more than 14 days after the evidence is provided and to no more than two such periods in any 12 months. There is a possible extension of those restrictions under para.(5)(c) in relation to the work search requirement or under para. (5A) or (5B) in relation to the work availability requirement.

Paras (4A) to (4C)

2.270   Paragraph (4A) supplies a number of further circumstances, all related to children, in which paras (1) and (2) operate to lift the work search requirement and modify the work availability requirement. The claimant must be the responsible carer of a child (as defined in s.19(6) of the WRA 2012 and see regs 4 and 4A for how responsibility is determined). Then one of events specified in sub-paras (a) and (b) must have occurred in the 24 months prior to the week in question and have resulted in significant disruption to the claimant's normal childcare responsibilities. Although it is not entirely clear, it seems to be necessary that the event is continuing to result in significant disruption in the week in question, not just at or shortly after the time of the event. "Normal childcare responsibilities" should be given its ordinary everyday meaning.

Sub-paragraph (a) applies when one of the persons listed (i.e. a parent or responsible carer or brother or sister of the child or someone else who lived in the same accommodation other than a commercial lodger) has died. Sub-paragraph (b) applies where the child has been the victim of or has witnessed an incident of violence or abuse not perpetrated by the claimant.

Paragraphs (4B) and (4C) limit each application of para.(4A) to a period of one month and to no more than one such application in each of the four periods of six months following the incident in question. Note the possibility of the application of para.(5)(b) without those limits in some circumstances that could have fallen within para.(4A).

Note also that under s.19(2)(c) of the WRA 2012 no work-related requirements may be imposed on the responsible carer of a child under the age of one, that under s.20(1)(a) only the work-focused interview requirement may be imposed on a claimant who is the responsible carer of a child aged one and that under s.21(1)(b) only the work-focused interview and work preparation requirements may be imposed on a claimant who is the responsible carer of a child aged two.

Para. (5)

The direct operation of para.(5) is now (since April 28, 2014) limited to the work   2.271
search requirement. See paras (5A) and (5B) for the effect on the work availability requirement where one of the conditions in para.(5)(a)–(c) is satisfied.

In three sorts of circumstances the imposition of a work search requirement, even as limited under reg.97, is prohibited where it would be unreasonable for the claimant to comply. Sub-paragraph (a) applies if the claimant is carrying out a work preparation requirement (s.16(1) of the WRA 2012) or voluntary work preparation (reg.95(4)). It appears that voluntary work preparation could include the doing of voluntary work if agreed by the Secretary of State (see the definition in reg.95(4)). Sub-paragraph (b) applies if the claimant has temporary child care responsibilities (for any child) or is dealing with a domestic emergency, funeral arrangements (for a claimant who is already covered by para.(3)(d)) or with other temporary circumstances. Sub-paragraph (c) applies where the claimant is unfit for work and the restrictions in para.(4) have been exceeded.

Would para.(5)(b) allow the Secretary of State to allow short "holidays" from work search responsibilities (and a modification of work availability requirements under para.(5A) or (5B)), under the heading of temporary circumstances or temporary child care responsibilities if satisfied that it would be reasonable to do so (cf. reg.19(1)(p) and (2) of the JSA Regulations 1996)? It is a feature of the universal credit scheme that it will apply to claimants in substantial work, who will have statutory holiday entitlements, as will family members of claimants not themselves in work. If so allowed, there would then be no need to consider the possible application of reg.95(2)(b) or 96(3)(b).

Paras (5A) and (5B)

Where it would be unreasonable, because of the satisfaction of any of the con-   2.272
ditions in para.(5)(a)–(c), for the claimant to be required to be able and willing immediately either to take up paid work or attend an interview, the work availability requirement is adjusted to require the claimant to be willing and able to do so immediately the condition ceases to be satisfied (paras (5A) and (1)(b)). Paragraph (5B) produces the equivalent effect where it would be unreasonable to require the claimant to be willing and able immediately to take up paid work, but reasonable to require willingness and ability to attend an interview.

Paras (6) and (6A)

Where a claimant or joint claimants are not already free of all work-related   2.273
requirements by reason of having earnings of at least the individual earnings threshold or the combined thresholds (reg.90), the work search requirement is not to be imposed if the monthly earnings, converted to a weekly equivalent, exceed the

applicable amount of the personal allowance for a single person aged 25 or over in the JSA Regulations 1996 by £5 or more (£10 over the couple's personal allowance for a couple). In addition, the work availability requirement is adjusted to require only willingness and ability to take up paid work or attend an interview immediately after the earnings fall below the specified level.

Prior to February 19, 2015, the test was in terms of the earnings being at a level where the Secretary of State was satisfied that the work search and availability requirements should not be imposed at the time in question. According to para.7.4 of the Explanatory Memorandum to the Universal Credit (Work-Related Requirements) In Work Pilot Scheme and Amendment Regulations 2015, para.(6) was initially put in that form because it had not been worked out what form of intervention in support of the principle of conditionality was likely to be most effective in cases where claimants were in work. The test was therefore made discretionary, with the intention of usually applying the level of earnings that would take a claimant or claimants out of entitlement to old style income-based JSA and with the prospect that para.(6) would later be revoked completely (apparently because it would then be known how the work search and availability requirements could be operated in an appropriate way).

The Pilot Scheme Regulations (see later in this Volume) represent an interim position. The February 2015 form of para.(6) now applies a hard-edged limit, adjusted from November 2015 to take account of the general change to the calculation of earnings for UC purposes on a monthly basis. The Pilot Scheme Regulations allow the Secretary of State to select on a random basis certain "qualifying claimants" who would otherwise benefit from para.(6) to be treated on the basis that para.(6) does not exist. The other conditions under reg.7 of those Regulations for being a "qualifying claimant" are falling within s.22 of the WRA 2012 (subject to all work-related requirements), not falling within reg.98 (victims of domestic violence) and not falling within reg.99(3) (except sub-para.(a) or (g)) or (5)(c). That effect of the Regulations will expire after three years from February 19, 2015, but can be extended by order of the Secretary of State. This is a very important provision, allowing experiments to take place on how to apply the principle of conditionality to those in more than merely subsidiary work, a question apparently not worked out when the scheme to which in-work conditionality was central was legislated for or in the several years since. The claimants selected for the experiments will bear the brunt of any unfairness or rough justice or impracticability revealed in the experiments.

See the House of Commons Work and Pensions Committee's report on *In-work progression in Universal Credit* (Tenth Report of Session 2010-16, May 2016, HC 549) for a critical but supportive description of the pilot scheme. The government's response to the report was published as HC 585 on July 21, 2016, in which it was anticipated that the necessary 15,000 participants would have been identified by early autumn 2016 and that claimants would be supported until autumn 2017. The DWP's evidence to the Committee was that sanctions would be applied for failures to meet in-work requirements without good reason "as a last resort" (para.47 of HC 549), a phrase repeated in para.27 of HC 585. It is not clear how this can operate in practice, as a decision-maker has no discretion not to impose a sanction or to modify its effects if the statutory conditions for imposition are met. Presumably, the intention is that work coaches or other officers will only refer cases to a decision-maker for a sanction as a last resort. On March 23, 2017 the DWP published *In-Work Progression Trial Progress Update: April 2015 to October 2016*. This revealed that 15,455 people had been on the trial and that during the update period 319 sanctions had been imposed, mainly at the low level for failing to participate in meetings or telephone calls.

CHAPTER 2

SANCTIONS

Introduction

100.—(1) This Chapter contains provisions about the reduction in the amount of an award of universal credit in the event of a failure by a claimant which is sanctionable under section 26 or 27 of the Act ("a sanctionable failure").

[[1](1A) In this Chapter references to a "current sanctionable failure" are to a sanctionable failure in relation to which the Secretary of State has not yet determined whether the amount of an award of universal credit is to be reduced under section 26 or 27 of the Act.]

(2) How the period of the reduction for each sanctionable failure is to be determined is dealt with in regulations 101 to 105.

(3) When the reduction begins or ceases to have effect is dealt with in regulations 106 to 109.

(4) How the amount of a reduction is calculated for an assessment period in which the reduction has effect is set out in regulations 110 and 111.

(5) Regulations 112 to 114 provide for some miscellaneous matters (movement of sanctions from a jobseeker's allowance or an employment and support allowance, cases in which no reduction is made for a sanctionable failure and prescription of work placement scheme for the purposes of section 26(2)(a) of the Act).

2.274

AMENDMENT

1. Social Security (Jobseeker's Allowance, Employment and Support Allowance and Universal Credit) (Amendment) Regulations 2016 (SI 2016/678) reg.5(5) (July 25, 2016).

DEFINITIONS

"the Act"—see reg.2.
"assessment period"—see WRA 2012 ss.40 and 7(2) and reg.21.
"claimant"—see WRA 2012 s.40.
"employment and support allowance"—see reg.2.
"jobseeker's allowance"—*ibid.*

Reduction periods

General principles for calculating reduction periods

101.—(1) The number of days for which a reduction in the amount of an award is to have effect ("the reduction period") is to be determined in relation to each sanctionable failure in accordance with regulations 102 to 105, but subject to paragraphs (3) and (4).

(2) Reduction periods are to run consecutively.

(3) If the reduction period calculated in relation to a sanctionable failure in accordance with regulations 102 to 105 would result in the total outstanding reduction period exceeding 1095 days, the reduction period in relation to that failure is to be adjusted so that the total outstanding reduction period does not exceed 1095 days.

2.275

(4) [¹...]

(5) In paragraph (3) "the total outstanding reduction period" is the total number of days for which no reduction in an award under section 26 or 27 of the Act has yet been applied.

AMENDMENT

1. Social Security (Jobseeker's Allowance, Employment and Support Allowance and Universal Credit) (Amendment) Regulations 2016 (SI 2016/678) reg.5(6) (July 25, 2016).

DEFINITIONS

"the Act"—see reg.2.
"sanctionable failure"—see reg.100(1).

GENERAL NOTE

2.276   Under reg.100 and this provision the way in which a sanction bites is through a reduction in the amount of an award of universal credit for a period determined under regs 101–105 (the "reduction period": para.(1)) for each sanctionable failure. A sanctionable failure is a failure which is sanctionable under s.26 or 27 of the WRA 2012. This regulation contains some general rules on sanctions.

Under para.(2) reduction periods for separate reduction periods run consecutively. That is subject to the general overall three-year limit in paras (3) and (5). The drafting is fairly impenetrable, but the upshot seems to be that if adding a new reduction period to the end of an existing period or, more likely, chain of reduction periods would take the total days in the periods over 1095 days the new reduction period is to be adjusted to make the total 1095 days exactly. Now that the rule previously in para.(4), about previous sanctionable failures in the 13 days before another sanctionable failure not counting, has been incorporated into the specific provisions in regs 102 – 104 and tidied up, there can be no question of that rule qualifying the effect of para.(3) to allow a total outstanding reduction period to exceed 1095 days, as had been suggested in the 2013/14 edition of this Volume.

Note also the circumstances prescribed in reg.109 (earnings over the individual threshold for 26 weeks) in which a reduction is to be terminated and the circumstances prescribed in reg.113 where there is to be no reduction despite the existence of a sanctionable failure. Under reg.111(3) the amount of the reduction is nil in an assessment period at the end of which the claimant is subject to no work-related requirements because of having limited capability for work and work-related activity under s.19 of the WRA 2012.

Higher-level sanction

2.277   **102.**—(1) This regulation specifies the reduction period for a sanctionable failure under section 26 of the Act ("higher level sanction").

[¹(2) Where the sanctionable failure is not a pre-claim failure, the reduction in the circumstances described in the first column of the following table is the period set out in—

(a) the second column, where the claimant is aged 18 or over on the date of the sanctionable failure;

(b) the third column, where the claimant is aged 16 or 17 on the date of the sanctionable failure.

Circumstances in which reduction period applies	Reduction period where claimant aged 18 or over	Reduction period where claimant aged 16 or 17
Where there has been no previous sanctionable failure by the claimant giving rise to a higher-level sanction	91 days	14 days
Where there have been one or more previous sanctionable failures by the claimant giving rise to a higher-level sanction and the date of the most recent previous sanctionable failure is not within 365 days beginning with the date of the current sanctionable failure	91 days	14 days
Where there have been one or more previous sanctionable failures by the claimant giving rise to a higher-level sanction and the date of the most recent previous sanctionable failure is within 365 days, but not within 14 days, beginning with the date of the current sanctionable failure and the reduction period applicable to the most recent previous sanctionable failure is— (a) 14 days (b) 28 days (c) 91 days (d) 182 days (e) 1095 days	 – – 182 days 1095 days 1095 days	 28 days 28 days – – –
Where there have been one or more previous sanctionable failures by the claimant giving rise to a higher-level sanction and the date of the most recent previous sanctionable failure is within 14 days beginning with the date of the current sanctionable failure and the reduction period applicable to the most recent previous sanctionable failure is— (a) 14 days (b) 28 days (c) 91 days (d) 182 days (e) 1095 days	 – – 91 days 182 days 1095 days	 14 days 28 days – – –

(3) But where the other sanctionable failure referred to in paragraph (2) was a pre-claim failure it is disregarded in determining the reduction period in accordance with that paragraph.

(4) Where the sanctionable failure for which a reduction period is to be determined is a pre-claim failure, the period is the lesser of—

    (a) the period that would be applicable to the claimant under paragraph (2) if it were not a pre-claim failure; or

(b) where the sanctionable failure relates to paid work that was due to last for a limited period, the period beginning with the day after the date of the sanctionable failure and ending with the date on which the limited period would have ended,

minus the number of days beginning with the day after the date of the sanctionable failure and ending on the day before the date of claim.

[¹(5) In this regulation—

"higher-level sanction" means a sanction under section 26 of the Act;

"pre-claim failure" means a failure sanctionable under section 26(4) of the Act.]

AMENDMENT

1. Social Security (Jobseeker's Allowance, Employment and Support Allowance and Universal Credit) (Amendment) Regulations 2016 (SI 2016/678) reg.5(7) (July 25, 2016).

DEFINITIONS

"the Act"—see reg.2.
"claimant"—see WRA 2012 s.40.
"current sanctionable failure"—see reg.100(1A).
"reduction period"—see reg.101(1).
"sanctionable failure"—see reg.100(1).

GENERAL NOTE

2.278   Higher-level sanctions are applicable to failures under s.26 of the WRA 2012. Such failures fall outside the scope of regs 103–105 and no failures under s.27 can come within the present regulation. Note the effect of reg.113 in specifying circumstances in which no reduction is to be applied although there has been a sanctionable failure. There is a distinction between "pre-claim failures", i.e. a failure under s.26(4) (before the relevant claim failing for no good reason to take up an offer of paid work or ceasing paid work or losing pay by reason of misconduct or voluntarily and for no good reason), and other failures.

The form of para.(2), specifying the length of sanctions reduction periods for non-pre-claim failures, has been re-cast with effect from July 25, 2016 to spell out more precisely much the same effect as previously. It is unhelpful that the individual entries in the table are not numbered. Boxes have been added by the publishers to aid clarity. The rules for 16 and 17-year-olds are no longer separated out from those for claimants aged at least 18, but now appear in column 3 of the table. None of the rules set out below may take the overall length of a total outstanding reduction period (reduction periods run consecutively) over 1095 days (reg.101(2) and (3)).

The general rule for adults in the first entry in column 2 is that the reduction period is 91 days if there have been no other higher-level UC sanctionable failures (or equivalent new style ESA or JSA failures if the claimant moved to universal credit with some days of an ESA or JSA reduction period outstanding: reg.112 and Sch.11 para.3) within the previous 365 days (counting the day of the current sanctionable failure). Contrary to what was said in the note to reg.113 in the 2013/14 edition of this Volume, it appears that if no reduction of benefit was imposed in relation to a previous sanctionable failure, by reason of reg.113, that failure has not "given rise to" a higher-level sanction so as to count for the purposes of the table. However, if a reduction has been terminated under reg.109, the failure would appear to count because it has given rise to a sanction, even though the period of the reduction has not lasted as long as originally set. It might be argued, for the purposes of the later parts of the table, that the relevant period of reduction was no longer applicable, but the definition of "reduction period" in reg.101(1) is in terms of the initial fixing of the period, with no reference to the effect of reg.109. However, para.(3) secures that pre-claim sanctionable failures (only failures under s.26(4) of the WRA 2012: para. (5)) do not count in this process.

Matters become more complicated when there has been a previous relevant failure within the 365 days. To start at the end of the table, if the sole or most recent previous relevant failure was within the past period of 14 days including the date of the current sanctionable failure, the length of the reduction period depends on the length of the reduction period imposed for the most recent relevant failure and is of equal length to that. Note, especially in relation to a further 1095-day reduction period, the overall limit to total outstanding reduction periods of 1095 days (reg.101(2) and (3)). That result might appear to be much more onerous on claimants than the previous form of para.(1) and reg.101(4). Under those provisions, any previous relevant failure occurring in the past period of 14 days including the date of the current sanctionable failure was disregarded entirely, whatever the length of the reduction period attached. That might appear to have left a claimant who benefited from that rule rather better off than under the July 2016 provisions. That is not so, although the explanation is complicated. If, under the old rules, the reduction period for the disregarded previous relevant failure was 182 days (or 1095 days), rather than merely 91 days, by definition there must have been one (or two or more) previous sanctionable failure in the past 365 days beginning with the date of the disregarded previous relevant failure. That failure or failures, if occurring in the past 365 days beginning with the date of the current sanctionable failure, would not have been disregarded under reg.101(4). Thus, if the disregarded previous relevant failure attracted a reduction period of 182 days, the previous non-disregarded failure would have attracted a 91-day reduction period and the reduction period for the current sanctionable failure would have been 182 days. If the disregarded previous relevant failure had attracted a 1095-day reduction period, the previous non-disregarded failure would have attracted a 182-day reduction period and the reduction period for the current sanctionable failure would have been 1095 days. That is the same outcome as produced under the form of para.(1) in force from July 2016.

If the most recent previous relevant failure falls outside the 14-day rule but within the 365 days, then the reduction for the current sanctionable failure goes up one step, except where the reduction period for the most recent relevant failure was 1095 days, when 1095 must be imposed again, to run consecutively (reg.101(2)), subject to the overall limit to a total outstanding reduction period of 1095 days (reg.101(3)).

There is a similar structure for 16 and 17-year-olds, with only two levels of reduction period, at 14 and 28 days.

For pre-claim sanctionable failures, under para.(4) the number of days between the date of the failure and the date of the relevant claim is deducted from the number of days in the reduction period calculated as under para.(2). That is subject to the further rule that if the sanctionable failure relates to paid work that was due to last only for a limited period, the period down to the date when the work was due to end is substituted for the para.(2) period in the calculation. Presumably that is to give an incentive to people to take such work. See also reg.113(1)(e).

Medium-level sanction

103.—(1) This regulation specifies the reduction period for a sanctionable failure under section 27 of the Act (other sanctions) where it is a failure by the claimant to comply with—

    (a) a work search requirement under section 17(1)(a) (to take all reasonable action to obtain paid work etc.); or

    (b) a work availability requirement under section 18(1).

    [¹(2) The reduction in the circumstances described in the first column of the following table is the period set out in—

2.279

(a) the second column, where the claimant is aged 18 or over on the date of the sanctionable failure;

(b) the third column, where the claimant is aged 16 or 17 on the date of the sanctionable failure.

Circumstances in which reduction period applies	Reduction period where claimant aged 18 or over	Reduction period where claimant aged 16 or 17
Where there has been no previous sanctionable failure by the claimant that falls within paragraph (1)	28 days	7 days
Where there have been one or more previous sanctionable failures by the claimant that fall within paragraph (1) and the date of the most recent previous sanctionable failure is not within 365 days beginning with the date of the current sanctionable failure	28 days	7 days
Where there have been one or more previous sanctionable failures by the claimant that fall within paragraph (1) and the date of the most recent previous sanctionable failure is within 365 days, but not within 14 days, beginning with the date of the current sanctionable failure and the reduction period applicable to the most recent previous sanctionable failure is—		
(a) 7 days	–	14 days
(b) 14 days	–	14 days
(c) 28 days	91 days	–
(d) 91 days	91 days	–
Where there have been one or more previous sanctionable failures by the claimant that fall within paragraph (1) and the date of the most recent previous sanctionable failure is within 14 days beginning with the date of the current sanctionable failure and the reduction period applicable to the most recent previous sanctionable failure is—		
(a) 7 days	–	7 days
(b) 14 days	–	14 days
(c) 28 days	28 days	–
(d) 91 days	91 days	–."

AMENDMENT

1. Social Security (Jobseeker's Allowance, Employment and Support Allowance and Universal Credit) (Amendment) Regulations 2016 (SI 2016/678) reg.5(8) (July 25, 2016).

"the Act"—see reg.2.
"claimant"—see WRA 2012 s.40.
"current sanctionable failure"—see reg.100(1A).
"reduction period"—see reg.101(1).
"sanctionable failure"—see reg.100(1).

GENERAL NOTE

This regulation applies to failures for no good reason to comply with two par-   **2.280**
ticular work-related requirements to which the claimant in question is subject: the
requirement under s.17(1)(a) of the WRA 2012 to take all reasonable action to
obtain paid work (but note, not the requirement under s.17(1)(b) to take particular action specified by the Secretary of State, where only some failures to comply
fall under s.26 and the higher-level sanctions regime) and the work availability
requirement in s.18(1). Note that none of the circumstances specified in reg.113
(no reduction to be applied though sanctionable failure) are relevant to medium-
level sanctions under s.27.

The form of para.(2), specifying the length of the sanction reduction period, has
been re-cast with effect from July 25, 2016 to spell out more precisely much the
same effect as previously. It is unhelpful that the individual entries in the table are
not numbered. Boxes have been added by the publishers to aid clarity. The rules
for 16 and 17-year-olds are no longer separated out from those for claimants aged
at least 18, but now appear in column 3 of the table. None of the rules set out
below may take the overall length of a total outstanding reduction period (reduction
periods run consecutively) over 1095 days (reg.101(2) and (3)).

The general rule for adults in the first entry in column 2 is that the reduction
period is 28 days if there have been no other medium-level UC sanctionable failures (or equivalent new style ESA or JSA failures if the claimant moved to universal
credit with some days of an ESA or JSA reduction period outstanding: reg.112 and
Sch.11 para.3) within the previous 365 days (counting the day of the current sanctionable failure). Arguably, the effect of there having been no reduction of benefit
in relation to a previous sanctionable failure, by reason of reg.113, is not quite the
same as under reg.102, because here there is no reference to the previous failure
having "given rise to" a medium-level sanction. If reg.113 applies there is still a
sanctionable failure, although no reduction of benefit is to be applied. However,
for the purposes of the later parts of the table, a reduction period applicable to
the previous sanctionable failure must be identified. If reg.113 has been applied to
that failure there can be no reduction period applicable. Consequently it must be
arguable that for the purposes of the table as a whole previous sanctionable failures
to which reg.113 has been applied do not count. See the notes to reg.102 for the
opposite effect where a reduction period has been terminated under reg.109.

The reduction period under para.(1) as from July 25, 2016 is 28 days if there have
been no other medium-level sanctionable failures (or equivalent new style ESA or
JSA sanctionable failures) at all or only outside the past period of 365 days including
the date of the current sanctionable failure. If the most recent relevant sanctionable
failure was in the past period of 14 days including the date of the current sanctionable failure, the length of the reduction period is equal to that for the most recent
failure. Where the most recent relevant failure was further in the past but still within
the 365 days, the length of the reduction period is 91 days. That is in substance the
same result as under the previous form of reg.20 and reg.101(4).

There is a similar structure for 16 and 17-year-olds, with only two levels of reduction period, at seven and 14 days.

Low-level sanction

2.281   **104.**—(1) This regulation specifies the reduction period for a sanctionable failure under section 27 of the Act (other sanctions) where—

   (a) the claimant falls within section 21 (claimants subject to work preparation requirement) or 22 (claimants subject to all work-related requirements) of the Act on the date of that failure; and

   (b) it is a failure to comply with—

      (i) a work-focused interview requirement under section 15(1),

      (ii) a work preparation requirement under section 16(1),

      (iii) a work search requirement under section 17(1)(b) (to take any particular action specified by the Secretary of State to obtain work etc.), or

      (iv) a requirement under section 23(1), (3) or (4) (connected requirements: interviews and verification of compliance).

(2) Where the claimant is aged 18 or over on the date of the sanctionable failure, the reduction period is the total of—

   (a) the number of days beginning with the date of the sanctionable failure and ending with—

      (i) the day before the date on which the claimant meets a compliance condition specified by the Secretary of State,

      (ii) the day before the date on which the claimant falls within section 19 of the Act (claimant subject to no work-related requirements),

      (iii) the day before the date on which the claimant is no longer required to take a particular action specified as a work preparation requirement by the Secretary of State under section 16, or

      (iv) the date on which the award terminates (other than by reason of the claimant ceasing to be, or becoming, a member of a couple),

      whichever is soonest; and

   [¹(b) in the circumstances described in the first column of the following table, the number of days in the second column.

Circumstances applicable to claimant's case	*Number of days*
Where there has been no previous sanctionable failure by the claimant that falls within paragraph (1)	7 days
Where there have been one or more previous sanctionable failures by the claimant that fall within paragraph (1) and the date of the most recent previous sanctionable failure is not within 365 days beginning with the date of the current sanctionable failure	7 days
Where there have been one or more previous sanctionable failures by the claimant that fall within paragraph (1) and the date of the most recent previous sanctionable failure is within 365 days, but not within 14 days, beginning with the date of the current sanctionable failure and the reduction period applicable to the most recent previous sanctionable failure is— (a) 7 days (b) 14 days (c) 28 days	 14 days 28 days 28 days

Circumstances applicable to claimant's case	Number of days
Where there have been one or more previous sanctionable failures by the claimant that fall within paragraph (1) and the date of the most recent previous sanctionable failure is within 14 days beginning with the date of the current sanctionable failure and the reduction period applicable to the most recent previous sanctionable failure is—	
(a) 7 days	7 days
(b) 14 days	14 days
(c) 28 days	28 days.";

(3) Where the claimant is aged 16 or 17 years on the date of the sanctionable failure, the reduction period is—

  (a) the number of days beginning with the date of the sanctionable failure and ending with—

    (i) the day before the date on which the claimant meets a compliance condition specified by the Secretary of State,

    (ii) the day before the date on which the claimant falls within section 19 of the Act (claimant subject to no work-related requirements),

    (iii) the day before the date on which the claimant is no longer required to take a particular action specified as a work preparation requirement by the Secretary of State under section 16, or

    (iv) date on which the award terminates (other than by reason of the claimant ceasing to be, or becoming, a member of a couple),

  whichever is soonest; and

[¹(b) if there was another sanctionable failure of a kind mentioned in paragraph (1) within 365 days, but not within 14 days, beginning with the date of the current sanctionable failure, 7 days.]

AMENDMENT

1. Social Security (Jobseeker's Allowance, Employment and Support Allowance and Universal Credit) (Amendment) Regulations 2016 (SI 2016/678) reg.5(9) (July 25, 2016).

DEFINITIONS

"the Act"—see reg.2.
"claimant"—see WRA 2012 s.40.
"compliance condition"—see WRA 2012 s.27(6).
"current sanctionable failure"—see reg.100(1A).
"reduction period"—see reg.101(1).
"sanctionable failure"—see reg.100(1).

GENERAL NOTE

This regulation applies only to claimants who are subject to all work-related requirements under s.22 of the WRA 2012 or to the work preparation requirement under s.21 at the time of the sanctionable failure. Then a low-level sanction is attracted by a failure for no good reason to comply with a work-focused interview requirement under s.15(1), a work preparation requirement under s.16(1), a work search requirement under s.17(1)(b) to take particular action specified by the Secretary of State (see reg.103—medium-level sanction—for failures to comply

2.282

291

with the requirement to take all reasonable action to obtain paid work under s.17(1)(a)) or one of the extensive connected requirements under s.23.

The calculation of the reduction period under para.(2) is more complicated than that for higher and medium-level sanctions. It is made up of a period of flexible length depending on the ongoing circumstances under sub-para.(a) plus a fixed period of days under sub-para.(b) to be added to the sub-para.(a) period. Note that none of the circumstances specified in reg.113 (no reduction to be applied though sanctionable failure) are relevant to low-level sanctions under s.27.

The basic rule in sub-para.(a) is that the period runs until any compliance condition specified by the Secretary of State is met. See the notes to s.27(5) of the WRA 2012 for the authorisation for this provision. A compliance condition is either that the failure to comply ceases to exist (e.g. the claimant attends a work-focused interview) or a condition as to future compliance. The condition must in accordance with s.27(5)(a) and sub-para.(a)(i) be specified by the Secretary of State. Although s.27(7) allows the Secretary of State to notify a claimant of a compliance condition in such manner as he determines, the approach of the Supreme Court in *R (on the application of Reilly and Wilson) v Secretary of State for Work and Pensions* [2013] UKSC 68; [2014] 1 A.C. 453 and of the Court of Appeal in *SSWP v Reilly and Hewstone* and *SSWP v Jeffrey and Bevan* [2016] EWCA Civ 413; [2017] 3 Q.B. 657, [2017] AACR 14 to the "prior information duty" and the requirements of fairness might possibly be relevant to the substance of what must be specified (and see the further discussion in the notes to s.27(5)). The sub-para.(a) period will also end if the claimant becomes subject to no work-related requirements for any reason under s.19 of the WRA 2012, is no longer required to take a specific action as a work preparation requirement or the award of universal credit terminates.

Under sub-para.(b) the additional number of days is seven if there have been no other low-level sanctionable failures (or equivalent new style ESA or JSA failures if the claimant moved to universal credit with some days of an ESA or JSA reduction period outstanding: reg.112 and Sch.11 para.3) in the previous 365 days (counting the day of the current sanctionable failure). Arguably, the effect of there having been no reduction of benefit in relation to a previous sanctionable failure, by reason of reg.113, is not quite the same as under reg.102, because here there is no reference to the previous failure having "given rise to" a low-level sanction. If reg.113 applies there is still a sanctionable failure, although no reduction of benefit is to be applied. However, for the purposes of the later parts of the table, a reduction period applicable to the previous sanctionable failure must be identified. If reg.113 has been applied to that failure there can be no reduction period applicable. Consequently it must be arguable that for the purposes of the table as a whole previous sanctionable failures to which reg.113 has been applied do not count. See the notes to reg.102 for the opposite effect where a reduction period has been terminated under reg.109.

The second general rule, where there has been at least one previous low-level sanctionable failure in the 365 day period, is that the para.(b) reduction period is 14 days, where the reduction period for the most recent sanctionable failure was seven days and 28 days in all other cases (subject to the possible application of reg.101(3)). The exception to that general rule is where the most recent sanctionable failure occurred within 14 days before the current sanctionable failure, including the day of that failure. In that case, the reduction period is to be of the same length as that applicable to the previous sanctionable failure.

Under para.(3) for claimants aged under 18, the same rules as in para.(2)(a) apply, plus an additional seven days if there has been one or more low-level sanctionable failures in the previous 365 days (excluding the most recent 14 days).

Lowest-level sanction

2.283   **105.**—(1) This regulation specifies the reduction period for a sanctionable failure under section 27 of the Act (other sanctions) where it is a failure by a claimant who falls within section 20 of the Act (claimants subject to work-focused interview requirement only) to comply with a requirement under that section.

(2) The reduction period is the number of days beginning with the date of the sanctionable failure and ending with—

(a) the day before the date on which the claimant meets a compliance condition specified by the Secretary of State;

(b) the day before the date on which the claimant falls within section 19 of the Act (claimant subject to no work-related requirements); or

(c) the day on which the award terminates (other than by reason of the claimant ceasing to be, or becoming, a member of a couple),

whichever is soonest.

DEFINITIONS

"the Act"—see reg.2.
"claimant"—see WRA 2012 s.40.
"compliance condition"—see WRA 2012 s.27(6).
"reduction period"—see reg.101(1).
"sanctionable failure"—see reg.100(1).

GENERAL NOTE

This regulation applies only to claimants who are subject only to the work-focused   2.284
interview requirement under s.20 of the WRA 2012. The reduction period for a
sanctionable failure to comply with that requirement runs until the claimant meets
a compliance condition specified by the Secretary of State (see notes to reg.104),
becomes subject to no work-related requirements for any reason under s.19 or the
award of universal credit terminates.

When reduction to have effect

Start of the reduction

106. A reduction period determined in relation to a sanctionable failure   2.285
takes effect from—

(a) the first day of the assessment period in which the Secretary of State determines that the amount of the award is to be reduced under section 26 or 27 of the Act (but see also regulation 107(2));

(b) if the amount of the award of universal credit for the assessment period referred to in paragraph (a) is not reduced in that period, the first day of the next assessment period; or

(c) if the amount of the award for the assessment period referred to in paragraph (a) or (b) is already subject to a reduction because of a previous sanctionable failure, the first day in respect of which the amount of the award is no longer subject to that reduction.

DEFINITIONS

"the Act"—see reg.2.
"assessment period"—see WRA 2012 ss.40 and 7(2) and reg.21.
"claimant"—see WRA 2012 s.40.
"reduction period"—see reg.101(1).
"sanctionable failure"—see reg.100(1).

2.286   These rules for the start of the reduction period follow fairly logically from the structure of the sanctions regime. Where no other reduction period is running the reduction period starts either in the assessment period (month) in which the decision to make the reduction is made or in the following assessment period (paras. (a) and (b)). If there is already a reduction applied in that assessment period, then, unless affected by the overall limit in reg.101(3) and (5), the new period starts on the expiry of the existing one.

Reduction period to continue where award terminates

2.287   **107.**—(1) If an award of universal credit terminates while there is an outstanding reduction period, the period continues to run as if a daily reduction were being applied and if the claimant becomes entitled to a new award (whether as single or joint claimant) before that period expires, that award is subject to a reduction for the remainder of the total outstanding reduction period.

(2) If an award of universal credit terminates before the Secretary of State determines that the amount of the award is to be reduced under section 26 or 27 of the Act in relation to a sanctionable failure and that determination is made after the claimant becomes entitled to a new award the reduction period in relation to that failure is to have effect for the purposes of paragraph (1) as if that determination had been made on the day before the previous award terminated.

DEFINITIONS

"the Act"—see reg.2.
"claimant"—see WRA 2012 s.40.
"joint claimants"—*ibid.*
"reduction period"—see reg.101(1).
"sanctionable failure"—see reg.100(1).
"single claimant"—see WRA 2012 s.40.

GENERAL NOTE

2.288   If an award of universal credit terminates while there is an outstanding reduction period, subsequent days count as if an actual reduction of benefit were being applied, so that on any further claim for universal credit the claimant is subject to the reduction only for the remainder of the period (para.(1)). If an award of universal credit terminates before the Secretary of State has made a decision about a reduction for a sanctionable failure, but a new award is in place by the time the decision is made (so that under reg.106 the reduction period would otherwise take effect in the current assessment period), the reduction period starts as if the decision had been made on the day before the previous award terminated.

Note that if on or after the termination of entitlement to universal credit the claimant is entitled to new style JSA, the reduction of benefit under the universal credit sanction for its unexpired period transfers to the award of JSA (JSA Regulations 2013 reg.30)

Suspension of a reduction where fraud penalty applies

2.289   **108.**—(1) A reduction in the amount of an award under section 26 or 27 of the Act is to be suspended for any period during which the provisions of section 6B, 7 or 9 of the Social Security Fraud Act 2001 apply to the award.

(2) The reduction ceases to have effect on the day on which that period begins and begins again on the day after that period ends.

DEFINITION

"the Act"—see reg.2.

When a reduction is to be terminated

109.—(1) A reduction in the amount of an award under section 26 or 27   **2.290**
of the Act is to be terminated where—
  (a) since the date of the most recent sanctionable failure which gave rise
      to a reduction, the claimant has been in paid work for a period of, or
      for periods amounting in total to, at least [¹six months]; and
  (b) the claimant's [¹monthly] earnings during that period or those
      periods were equal to or exceeded—
        (i) the claimant's individual threshold, [²...]
     [²(ia) where the claimant has no individual threshold, the amount that
            a person would be paid at the hourly rate specified in regulation
            4 or regulation 4A(1)(a) to (c) of the National Minimum Wage
            Regulations for 16 hours per week, converted to a monthly
            amount by multiplying by 52 and dividing by 12, or]
       (ii) if paragraph (4) of regulation 90 applies (threshold for an
            apprentice) the amount applicable under that paragraph.
(2) The termination of the reduction has effect—
  (a) where the date on which paragraph (1) is satisfied falls within a
      period of entitlement to universal credit, from the beginning of the
      assessment period in which that date falls; or
  (b) where that date falls outside a period of entitlement to universal
      credit, from the beginning of the first assessment period in relation
      to any subsequent award.
(3) A claimant who is treated as having earned income in accordance
with regulation 62 (minimum income floor) in respect of an assessment
period is to be taken to have [¹ monthly] earnings equal to their individual
threshold in respect of [¹ . . .] that assessment period.

AMENDMENTS

1. Universal Credit and Miscellaneous Amendments Regulations 2015 (SI
2015/1754) reg.2(8) (November 4, 2015).
2. Social Security (Jobseeker's Allowance, Employment and Support Allowance
and Universal Credit) (Amendment) Regulations 2016 (SI 2016/678) reg.5(10)
(July 25, 2016).

DEFINITIONS

"the Act"—see reg.2.
"assessment period"—see WRA 2012, ss.40 and 7(2) and reg.21.
"claimant"—see WRA 2012, s.40.
"individual threshold"—see regs 2 and 90(2).
"sanctionable failure"—see reg.100(1).
"National Minimum Wage Regulations"—see reg.2.

GENERAL NOTE

Any reduction for any level of sanction or sanctions terminates where since the   **2.291**
date of the most recent sanctionable failure the claimant has been in paid work with
earnings at least equal to the appropriate individual threshold for at least six months,
not necessarily consecutive. It does not matter what the total outstanding reduction

period is. The claimant could have had a reduction period of 1095 days imposed, yet after six months' work (which will have reduced the outstanding period accordingly) the basis for the entire reduction disappears, just as much as if the outstanding period was much shorter. Paragraph (2) confirms that the termination takes effect immediately if the condition in para.(1) is met while the claimant is entitled to universal credit. If the claimant is not then entitled to universal credit the termination takes effect from the beginning of the first assessment period under any new award. Note that this regulation does not take away the status of any sanctionable failure(s) on which the terminated reduction period was based. Thus for the purpose of asking in the future whether there have been other sanctionable failures within 364 days of a new sanctionable failure all such sanctionable failures must be counted.

See also reg.119(3) below, under which any hardship payments made under the conditions in reg.116 cease to be recoverable where the claimant has had earnings of the same level as specified in reg.109 for six months after the last day on which a reduction was applied.

There was a technical difficulty in the operation of reg.109(1)(b) in that under the definition of "individual threshold" in reg.90(2) only claimants who would otherwise (if it were not for the effect of reg.90(1) and s.19 of the WRA 2012) be subject to some work-related requirement could have an individual threshold and so take advantage of the provision in para.(1). That gap has been filled by the new para.(1)(b)(ia), specifying an amount of earnings in terms of the national minimum wage hourly rate and 16 hours per week for claimants without an individual threshold as such.

Amount of reduction

Amount of reduction for each assessment period

2.292
110. Where it has been determined that an award of universal credit is to be reduced under section 26 or 27 of the Act, the amount of the reduction for each assessment period in respect of which a reduction has effect is to be calculated as follows.

Step 1

Take the number of days—
(a) in the assessment period; or
(b) if lower, the total outstanding reduction period,
and deduct any days in that assessment period for which the reduction is suspended in accordance with regulation 108.

Step 2

Multiply the number of days produced by step 1 by the daily reduction rate (see regulation 111).

Step 3

If necessary, adjust the amount produced by step 2 so that it does not exceed—
(a) the amount of the standard allowance applicable to the award; or
(b) in the case of a joint claim where a determination under section 26 or 27 of the Act applies only in relation to one claimant, half the amount of that standard allowance.

Step 4

Deduct the amount produced by steps 2 and 3 from the amount of the award for the assessment period after any deduction has been made in accordance with Part 7 (the benefit cap).

DEFINITIONS

"the Act"—see reg.2.
"assessment period"—see WRA 2012 ss.40 and 7(2) and reg.21.
"claimant"—see WRA 2012, s.40.
"standard allowance"—see WRA 2012, s.9.

GENERAL NOTE

This apparently complex calculation will work out easily enough in practice. Its main point is to translate the daily rate of reduction under reg.111 into the appropriate amount for an assessment period, depending on the number of days in the period affected by a reduction. There is a rule of substance concealed in step 3, in that the reduction can never exceed the amount of the claimant's standard allowance, or half of a couple's standard allowance.

2.293

However, see the notes to reg.111 below for discussion of the capricious results that can follow from the way in which the daily reduction rate is calculated under reg.111 and from the principle that in accordance with ss.26 and 27 of the WRA 2012 the reduction is to be applied to the overall award of universal credit, however that is made up.

See those notes and the notes to reg.5 of the JSA Regulations 2013 in Vol.II of this series and to paras 1 and 2 of Sch.11 to the present Regulations for further discussion of the anomalous results where a universal credit recipient is also entitled another social security benefit (in particular new style ESA or JSA) and for the non-use of regulation-making powers that could have avoided them.

Daily reduction rate

111.—(1) The daily reduction rate for the purposes of regulation 110 is, unless paragraph (2), or (3) applies, an amount equal to the amount of the standard allowance that is applicable to the award multiplied by 12 and divided by 365.

2.294

(2) The daily reduction rate is 40 per cent of the rate set out in paragraph (1) if, at the end of the assessment period—

(a) the claimant is aged 16 or 17;
(b) the claimant falls within section 19 of the Act (claimant subject to no work-related requirements) by virtue of—
    (i) subsection (2)(c) of that section (responsible carer for a child under the age of 1), or
    (ii) regulation 89(1)(c),(d) or (f) (adopter, claimant within 11 weeks before or 15 weeks after confinement or responsible foster parent of a child under the age of 1); or
(c) the claimant falls within section 20 (claimant subject to work-focused interview only).

(3) The daily reduction rate is nil if, at the end of the assessment period, the claimant falls within section 19 of the Act by virtue of having limited capability for work and work-related activity.

(4) The amount of the rate in [¹paragraphs (1) and (2)] is to be rounded down to the nearest 10 pence.

(5) In the case of joint claimants—

(a) each joint claimant is considered individually for the purpose of determining the rate applicable under paragraphs (1) to (3); and

(b) half of any applicable rate is applied to each joint claimant accordingly.

AMENDMENT

1. Universal Credit (Consequential, Supplementary, Incidental and Miscellaneous Provisions) Regulations 2013 (SI 2013/630) reg.38(7) (April 29, 2013).

DEFINITIONS

"the Act"—see reg.2.
"assessment period"—see WRA 2012 ss.40 and 7(2) and reg.21.
"claimant"—see WRA 2012, s.40.
"joint claimants"—*ibid.*
"limited capability for work and work-related activity"—see WRA 2012, ss.40 and 37(1) and (2).
"single claimant"—see WRA 2012, s.40.
"standard allowance"—see WRA 2012, s.9.

GENERAL NOTE

2.295   The basic rule under para.(1) is that the reduction for the purposes of the calculation in reg.110 is by the whole amount of the claimant's standard allowance under s.9 of the WRA 2012. There is on the face of it no reduction to the elements that can make up the maximum amount of universal credit for responsibility for children and young persons (s.10), housing costs (s.11) or particular needs and circumstances (s.12). In the case of joint claimants, under para.(5) each claimant is considered separately for the purposes of calculating the reduction and treated as having half of the standard allowance applicable to them as joint claimants.

Under para.(2) the reduction is by 40 per cent of the standard allowance, rather than 100 per cent, for claimants under 18, claimants subject to no work-related requirements under s.19 of the WRA 2012 by virtue of s.19(2)(c) (responsible carer of a child under one) or reg.89(1)(c), (d) or (f) and claimants subject to the work-focused interview requirement only under s.20.

Despite the apparent simplicity of these rules, there are a number of complicating elements that create a degree of uncertainty. First, the effect of the rounding down under para.(4) to the nearest 10p in producing the daily rate of reduction from the amount of the standard allowance, which is expressed in reg.36 as a monthly amount, i.e. for each assessment period, is fairly clear. When the daily rate is multiplied by the number of days affected by the sanction in each assessment period in step 2 of reg.110 the result will often be less than the exactly proportionate share of the actual standard allowance. If a claimant's universal credit award was made up only of the standard allowance, then even a 100% reduction could leave some small amount still payable.

Second, the specification of the reduction rate in terms of the amount of the standard allowance, rather than the amount of the claimant's award of universal credit, creates problems in certain circumstances. In particular, this is so where the claimant has income to be deducted from the "maximum amount" (the appropriate standard allowance plus any additional elements for children, childcare costs, housing costs etc). Take a simple example of a single universal credit claimant of 25 doing no work who is also entitled to new style JSA of £73.10 per week through satisfaction of the contribution-based conditions. The standard allowance is £317.82 per month, which is also the maximum amount. That would appear to produce a universal credit award of £1.06 per month. If the claimant were then made subject to a 100% sanction for a 30-day assessment period, multiplying the daily reduction rate of £10.40 by 30 would produce a figure of £312. But the concept of a reduction cannot allow the amount of universal credit otherwise payable to go below zero, so that the reduction could be by no more than £1.06 per month. It must not then be forgotten that reg.5 of the JSA Regulations 2013 prevents any reduction being applied to the claimant's JSA entitlement when there is also entitlement to universal credit, even though there may have been a sanctionable failure under the new style JSA legislation. Regulation 42 of the ESA Regulations 2013 does the same in relation to new style ESA.

However, things would become much more complicated if the claimant had a housing costs and/or a children element included in the universal credit maximum amount, so that the amount payable was higher. The basic calculation of the amount of the reduction under reg.110 by reference to the standard allowance would stay the same. But, since ss.26 and 27 of the WRA 2012 and reg.110 provide simply for the reduction of the amount of an award of universal credit by the amount calculated under reg.110, there appears to be nothing to prevent the reduction in this second case biting into potentially the whole of universal credit award, subject only to the limit under step 3 of reg.110 of the amount of the standard allowance. These results appear arbitrary and unrelated to the merits of cases, but equally appear to follow inexorably from the structure of the universal credit legislation. In the example used, the claimant will still have the £73.10 per week of JSA intact (or some other source of income in other cases), which can be used to meet essential expenses.

Those simple examples do no more than scratch the surface of other complexities that may arise. They make the existence of the provision for hardship payments, now restricted to 100% reduction cases, in regs 115-119 even more important, although the conditions for payment are extremely restrictive.

Under para.(3) a nil reduction is to be applied, apparently for a whole assessment period, if at the end of that period the claimant is subject to no work-related requirements under s.19 by virtue of having limited capability for work and work-related activity (see s.19(2)(a)). The effect of applying a daily reduction, but making the rate nil, appears to be that any assessment periods falling within para.(3) count as part of the period of reduction under the sanction in question.

See reg.113 for circumstances in which no reduction is to be applied despite the existence of a sanctionable failure that would otherwise trigger a reduction and reg.109 for the termination of all outstanding reductions if a claimant has earnings equal to the individual threshold (see reg.90(2)) for 26 weeks.

Miscellaneous

Application of ESA or JSA sanctions to universal credit

112. Schedule 11 has effect in relation to persons who are, or have been, entitled to an employment and support allowance or a jobseeker's allowance and who are, or become, entitled to universal credit.

2.296

DEFINITIONS

"employment and support allowance"—see reg.2.
"jobseeker's allowance"—*ibid.*

GENERAL NOTE

The general effect of Sch.11 is that if a claimant moves from new style ESA or JSA to universal credit with some days of an ESA or JSA reduction period outstanding, the reduction for those days translates to the universal credit awards. The failures giving rise to those reductions count as previous sanctionable failures at the equivalent level for the purpose of calculating the length of the reduction period for higher, medium and low-level sanctions under regs 102–104.

2.297

Failures for which no reduction is applied

2.298   **113.**—(1) No reduction is to be made under section 26 or 27 of the Act for a sanctionable failure where—

(a) the sanctionable failure is listed in section 26(2)(b) or (c) (failure to apply for a particular vacancy for paid work, or failure to take up an offer of paid work) and the vacancy is because of a strike arising from a trade dispute;

(b) the sanctionable failure is listed in section 26(2)(d) (claimant ceases paid work or loses pay), and the following circumstances apply—

　(i) the claimant's work search and work availability requirements are subject to limitations imposed under section 17(4) and 18(3) in respect of work available for a certain number of hours,

　(ii) the claimant takes up paid work, or is in paid work and takes up more paid work that is for a greater number of hours, and

　(iii) the claimant voluntarily ceases that paid work, or more paid work, or loses pay,

within a trial period;

(c) the sanctionable failure is that the claimant voluntarily ceases paid work, or loses pay, because of a strike arising from a trade dispute;

(d) the sanctionable failure is that the claimant voluntarily ceases paid work as a member of the regular or reserve forces, or loses pay in that capacity;

(e) the sanctionable failure is listed in section 26(4) (failure to take up an offer of paid work, or to cease paid work or lose pay before making a claim), and the period of the reduction that would otherwise apply under regulation 102(4) is the same as, or shorter than, the number of days beginning with the day after the date of the sanctionable failure and ending with the date of claim;

(f) the sanctionable failure is that the claimant voluntarily ceases paid work in one of the following circumstances—

　(i) the claimant has been dismissed because of redundancy after volunteering or agreeing to be dismissed,

　(ii) the claimant has ceased work on an agreed date without being dismissed in pursuance of an agreement relating to voluntary redundancy, or

　(iii) the claimant has been laid-off or kept on short-time to the extent specified in section 148 of the Employment Rights Act 1996, and has complied with the requirements of that section; or

(g) the sanctionable failure is that the claimant by reason of misconduct, or voluntarily and for no good reason, ceases paid work or loses pay, but the claimant's [¹ monthly] earnings (or, if the claimant is a member of a couple, their joint [¹ monthly] earnings) have not fallen below [¹the amount specified in] regulation 99(6) (circumstances in which requirements must not be imposed).

(2) In this regulation "regular or reserve forces" has the same meaning as in section 374 of the Armed Forces Act 2006.

AMENDMENT

1. Universal Credit and Miscellaneous Amendments Regulations 2015 (SI 2015/1754) reg.2(9) (November 4, 2015).

DEFINITIONS

"the Act"—see reg.2.
"claimant"—see WRA 2012 s.40.
"couple"—see WRA 2012 ss.40 and 39.
"paid work"—see reg.2.
"redundancy"—*ibid.*
"sanctionable failure"—see reg.100(1).
"trade dispute"—see reg.2.
"work availability requirement"—see WRA 2012 ss.40 and 18(1).
"work search requirement"—see WRA 2012 ss.40 and 17(1).

GENERAL NOTE

This is an important provision in prescribing, under ss.26(8)(a) and 27(9)(a) of the WRA 2012, cases of sanctionable failure for which no reduction of benefit can be imposed. However, none of the circumstances specified are relevant to medium, low or lowest-level sanctions arising under s.27. Note that if a case comes within this regulation that does not affect the status of the sanctionable failure in question. It can still count if in relation to a future sanctionable failure it has to be asked whether there have been any sanctionable failures at the equivalent level in the previous 365 days. See the notes to regs 103 and 104 for further discussion. It will be different if, as under reg.102, the question to be asked is whether there has been a previous sanctionable failure giving rise to a sanction. If reg.113 has applied, the failure would appear not have given rise to a sanction. There remains scope for argument that in some of the circumstances listed there is a good reason for the particular claimant's failure to comply with the requirement in question, so that there is not in fact a sanctionable failure.

2.299

The cases are as follows:

(a) Where the sanctionable failure is failing for no good reason to apply for a particular vacancy for paid work or to take up an offer of paid work (WRA 2012, s.26(2)(b) or (c)), no reduction is to be imposed if the vacancy arose because of a strike arising from a trade dispute. "Trade dispute" is defined in reg.2 by adopting the rather long definition in s.244 of the Trade Union and Labour Relations (Consolidation) Act 1992:

"(1) In this Part a "trade dispute" means a dispute between workers and their employer which relates wholly or mainly to one or more of the following—

(a) terms and conditions of employment, or the physical conditions in which any workers are required to work;

(b) engagement or non-engagement, or termination or suspension of employment or the duties of employment, of one or more workers;

(c) allocation of work or the duties of employment between workers or groups of workers;

(d) matters of discipline;

(e) a worker's membership or non-membership of a trade union;

(f) facilities for officials of trade unions; and

(g) machinery for negotiation or consultation, and other procedures, relating to any of the above matters, including the recognition by employers or employers' associations of the right of a trade union to represent workers in such negotiation or consultation or in the carrying out of such procedures.

(2) A dispute between a Minister of the Crown and any workers shall, notwithstanding that he is not the employer of those workers, be treated as a dispute between those workers and their employer if the dispute relates to matters which—

(a) have been referred for consideration by a joint body on which, by virtue of provision made by or under any enactment, he is represented, or

    (b) cannot be settled without him exercising a power conferred on him by or under an enactment.

(3) There is a trade dispute even though it relates to matters occurring outside the United Kingdom, so long as the person or persons whose actions in the United Kingdom are said to be in contemplation or further-ance of a trade dispute relating to matters occurring outside the United Kingdom are likely to be affected in respect of one or more of the matters specified in subsection (1) by the outcome of the dispute.

(4) An act, threat or demand done or made by one person or organisation against another which, if resisted, would have led to a trade dispute with that other, shall be treated as being done or made in contemplation of a trade dispute with that other, notwithstanding that because that other submits to the act or threat or accedes to the demand no dispute arises.

(5) In this section—

"employment" includes any relationship whereby one person personally does work or performs services for another; and

"worker", in relation to a dispute with an employer, means—

    (a) a worker employed by that employer; or

    (b) a person who has ceased to be so employed if his employment was terminated in connection with the dispute or if the termination of his employment was one of the circumstances giving rise to the dispute."

That is a fairly comprehensive definition, although as compared with s.35(1) of the Jobseekers Act 1995 it does not cover disputes between employees and employees. "Strike" is not defined. It is possible that vacancies could arise because of industrial action short of a strike. There seems no good reason why claimants who on principle are not prepared to apply for such vacancies or accept offers should not also be protected. Perhaps it is arguable that in any event they have a good reason for failing to comply with the requirement in question, so that there is no sanctionable failure.

(b)   This provision protects claimants who take up work for a trial period, but only current universal credit claimants who are required only to search for and be available for work subject to limitations as to hours of work under reg.97, made under ss.17(4) and 18(3) of the WRA 2012. Then if such a claimant takes up work, or more work, for more than the hours of limitation for a trial period, but then voluntarily gives up that work or extra work or loses pay within the trial period, there is to be no reduction. As above, it would be arguable there was good reason for such action, so no sanctionable failure.

(c)   This provision provides the same protection as under sub-para.(a) for volun-tarily ceasing paid work or losing pay because of a strike arising from a trade dispute.

(d)   Members of the armed forces, both regular and reserve forces, who voluntarily cease paid work as such or lose pay, cannot suffer a reduction on that ground, whatever the circumstances.

(e)   Where there is a pre-claim sanctionable failure and the reduction period nor-mally applicable would expire on or before the date of the relevant universal credit claim, there is to be no reduction. It may be that the same result is achieved by reg.102(4).

(f)   This provides protection in the same circumstances as prescribed in reg.71 of the Jobseeker's Allowance Regulations 1996 for JSA purposes (see the notes to reg.71 in Vol II), except that there the claimant is deemed not to have left employment voluntarily and so not subject to any sanction. Here the claimant is merely protected from having a reduction of benefit imposed, subject to any argument that there was a good reason under general principles for voluntarily ceasing work, so no sanctionable failure.

(g)   Under reg.99(6) it may be determined that a claimant's or joint claimants' earnings are at a level where a work search or work availability requirement is not to be imposed, although the earnings are below the individual threshold or combined individual thresholds that has to be reached to make the claimant(s) subject to no work-related requirements under s.19 of the WRA 2012 and reg.90. If that decision is made after a claimant by reason of misconduct or voluntarily and for no good reasons ceases paid work or loses pay, no reduction of benefit is to be imposed.

Sanctionable failures under section 26—work placements

[¹**114.**—(1) A placement on the Mandatory Work Activity Scheme is a prescribed placement for the purpose of section 26(2)(a) of the Act (sanctionable failure not to comply with a work placement).

2.300

(2) In paragraph (1) "the Mandatory Work Activity Scheme" means a scheme provided pursuant to arrangements made by the Secretary of State and known by that name that is designed to provide work or work-related activity for up to 30 hours per week over a period of 4 consecutive weeks with a view to assisting claimants to improve their prospects of obtaining employment.]

AMENDMENT

1. Universal Credit (Consequential, Supplementary, Incidental and Miscellaneous Provisions) Regulations 2013 (SI 2013/630) reg.38(8) (April 29, 2013).

DEFINITIONS

"the Act"—see reg.2.
"claimant"—see WRA 2012 s.40.
"paid work"—see reg.2.
"work-related activity"—see WRA 2012 s.40.

GENERAL NOTE

See the notes to s.26(2)(a) of the WRA 2012 for the validity of this provision in giving sufficient detail of the nature of the Mandatory Work Activity Scheme to constitute a description of the scheme, as required by s.26(2)(a), not just a label, and for the circumstances in which failure to comply with a requirement to undertake a placement could give rise to a sanction. Note that the scheme need not be designed to provide work that is paid and that prospects of employment (not further defined) can in their ordinary meaning include prospects of self-employment.

2.301

CHAPTER 3

HARDSHIP

Introduction

115. This Chapter contains provisions under section 28 of the Act for the making of hardship payments where the amount of an award is reduced under section 26 or 27 of the Act.

2.302

DEFINITION

"the Act"—see reg.2.

Conditions for hardship payments

2.303   **116.**—(1) The Secretary of State must make a hardship payment to a single claimant or to joint claimants only where—

(a) the claimant in respect of whose sanctionable failure the award has been reduced under section 26 or 27 of the Act is aged 18 or over;

(b) the single claimant or each joint claimant has met any compliance condition specified by the Secretary of State under regulation 104(2)(a)(i);

(c) the single claimant or either joint claimant completes and submits an application—

   (i) approved for the purpose by the Secretary of State, or in such other form as the Secretary of State accepts as sufficient, and

   (ii) in such manner as the Secretary of State determines;

(d) the single claimant or either joint claimant furnishes such information or evidence as the Secretary of State may require, in such manner as the Secretary of State determines:

(e) the single claimant or each joint claimant accepts that any hardship payments that are paid are recoverable;

(f) the Secretary of State is satisfied that the single claimant or each joint claimant has complied with all the work-related requirements that they were required to comply with in the 7 days proceeding the day on which the claimant or joint claimants submitted an application in accordance with sub-paragraph (c); [¹...]

(g) the Secretary of State is satisfied that the single claimant or each joint claimant is in hardship; [¹and

(h) the daily reduction rate in regulation 111(1) applies for the purposes of the reduction in respect of the claimant under section 26 or 27 of the Act.]

(2) For the purposes of paragraph (1)(g) a single claimant or joint claimants must be considered as being in hardship only where—

(a) they cannot meet their immediate and most basic and essential needs, specified in paragraph (3), or the immediate and most basic and essential needs of a child or qualifying young person for whom the single claimant or either of joint claimants is responsible, only because the amount of their award has been reduced—

   (i) under section 26 or 27 of the Act, by the daily reduction rate set out in [¹regulation 111(1)], or

   (ii) by the daily reduction rate prescribed in regulations made under section 6B(5A), 7(2A) or 9(2A) of the Social Security Fraud Act 2001 which is equivalent to the rate referred to in paragraph (i);

(b) they have made every effort to access alternative sources of support to meet, or partially meet, such needs; and

(c) they have made every effort to cease to incur any expenditure which does not relate to such needs.

(3) The needs referred to in paragraph (2) are—

(a) accommodation;

(b) heating;

(c) food;

(d) hygiene.

AMENDMENT

1. Universal Credit and Miscellaneous Amendments Regulations 2014 (SI 2014/597) reg.2(12) (April 28, 2014).

DEFINITIONS

"the Act"—see reg.2.
"claimant"—see WRA 2012 s.40.
"joint claimants"—*ibid.*
"sanctionable failure"—see reg.100(1).
"single claimant"—see WRA 2012 s.40.
"work-related requirement"—see WRA 2012 ss.40 and 13(2).

GENERAL NOTE

This regulation is made under s.28 of the WRA 2012 and sets out the very stringent conditions for the making of hardship payments to claimants to whom a sanction has been applied under s.26 or 27, that limitation being imposed by reg.115 and s.28(1)(a). The amount and period of any payment is dealt with in regs 117 and 118. Paragraph (1) of reg.116 lays down seven conditions, all of which must be satisfied. Paragraphs (2) and (3) provide a further exhaustive definition of when claimants can be considered to be in hardship for the purpose of condition (g). No payment can be made under reg.117 for any period prior to the date on which all the conditions in para.(1) are met.

The opening words of para.(1), by providing that the Secretary of State *must* make a hardship payment only where all its conditions are met, appear to open the door to the Secretary of State making payments on a discretionary basis where the conditions are not met. However, that is not the case, because s.28 only allows additional payments of universal credit to be made in hardship cases when regulations so provide. It must remain open to the Secretary of State to make payments, not of universal credit, on an extra-statutory basis, but no doubt the circumstances would have to be truly exceptional to persuade him to do so.

Para.(1)

The seven conditions are as follows:

(a) The claimant to whom the sanction has been applied must be aged at least 18. Under-18s can be sanctioned, but will not have the amount of benefit reduced to nil, as for most over-18s (see reg.111(1) and (2)).

(b) Under reg.104(2)(a) reduction periods for low-level sanctions last unless and until the claimant satisfies a compliance condition specified by the Secretary of State, i.e. the failure to comply with the work-related requirement in question has come to an end or a condition about future compliance is met (WRA 2012, s.27(6)), plus a fixed period on top. If such a compliance condition has been specified, a hardship payment can only be made after it has been met. The result is that in these cases a hardship payment can only be made during the final fixed period.

(c) The claimant or one of joint claimants must make an application for a hardship payment. The Secretary of State may accept an application in any sufficient form, but it is not clear what could also be required by the additional condition of the submission of the application being in such manner as determined by the Secretary of State. Condition (f) below can make the timing of an application important, but there seems nothing to stop multiple applications being made day by day.

(d) The claimant must have supplied any information or evidence required by the Secretary of State.

(e) The claimant or both joint claimants must accept that any hardship payments are recoverable. Since the recoverability is imposed by reg.119 and s.71ZH of the Administration Act, independent of any advance agreement by the

2.304

2.305

305

claimant, it is not clear quite what level or manner of acceptance will satisfy this condition. The claimant in a sense has no option but to submit to what the law requires, no matter how vehemently dislike of the result is expressed.

(f) The claimant or both joint claimants must have complied with all work-related requirements imposed in the seven days preceding, presumably immediately preceding, the day of submission of the application under condition (c).

(g) The most fundamental condition is that the claimant or both joint claimants are in hardship, presumably as at the date of making the payment or possibly as at the date of the application in question. Because of the use of the present tense, it is arguable that it is not a necessary condition that the claimant or claimants are expected to be in hardship for the duration of the period covered by the payment. Paragraphs (2) and (3) define when a claimant can be accepted as in hardship.

(h) The effect of this provision, operative from April 2014, is to prevent any entitlement to a hardship payment arising for a claimant whose reduction in benefit under the sanction is only by 40% under reg.111(2), rather than by 100% under reg.111(1).

Paras (2) and (3)

2.306   The use of the word "only" means that claimants can only be accepted as in hardship if they meet all three of the following conditions:

(a) The claimant or both joint claimants must be unable to meet their most immediate and basic and essential needs, or those of children or young person for whom they are responsible, only by reason of the reduction in benefit due to a sanction or of a reduction for a benefit offence under the Social Security Fraud Act 2001. The only needs to be considered are accommodation, heating, food and hygiene (para.(3)) and then this condition limits consideration to immediate, basic and essential needs of those kinds. That plainly involves a large element of judgment, but the highly restrictive intention is made clear. There is no specific category of need relating to children no matter how young, e.g. for bedding, clothing or education.

(b) The claimant or both joint claimants must have made every effort to access alternative sources of support to at least go towards meeting needs within condition (a). Some limitations must necessarily be implied either in terms of what efforts can be required or in terms of what alternative sources of support can be considered. The alternative source must at least be lawful. But presumably claimants are not to be required to beg on the streets. Are they to be required to go to back street or payday lenders? How far are they required to explore sources from which there is no practical possibility of support?

(c) The claimant or both joint claimants must have made every effort to cease to incur expenditure not related to condition (a) needs. Given the restrictive scope of those needs, the range of expenditure to be considered is wide. But again some notions of reasonableness and practicability must necessarily be implied, especially if avoiding immediate expenditure in the short term might lead to disproportionate financial penalties or burdens in the longer term.

The period of hardship payments

2.307   [¹**117.**—(1) A hardship payment is to be made in respect of a period which—

(a) begins with the date on which all the conditions in regulation 116(1) are met; and

(b) unless paragraph (2) applies, ends with the day before the normal payment date for the assessment period in which those conditions are met.

(2) If the period calculated in accordance with paragraph (1) would be

7 days or less, it does not end on the date referred to in paragraph (1)(b) but instead ends on the normal payment date for the following assessment period or, if earlier, the last day on which the award is to be reduced under section 26 or 27 of the Act or under section 6B(5A), 7(2A) or 9(3A) of the Social Security Fraud Act 2001.

(3) In this regulation "the normal payment date" for an assessment period is the date on which the Secretary of State would normally expect to make a regular payment of universal credit in respect of an assessment period in a case where payments of universal credit are made monthly in arrears.]

AMENDMENT

1. Universal Credit (Consequential, Supplementary, Incidental and Miscellaneous Provisions) Regulations 2013 (SI 2013/630) reg.38(9) (April 29, 2013).

DEFINITIONS

"assessment period"—see WRA 2012 ss.40 and 7(2) and reg.21.
"joint claimants"—see WRA 2012 s.40.
"single claimant"—*ibid.*

GENERAL NOTE

The substituted form of reg.117 (in operation from the outset of the universal credit scheme) represents a simplification and clarification of the original form. Each hardship payment is made for a limited period. Once each period expires a new application must be made. Under para.(1)(a) the period of a payment starts when all the conditions in reg.116(1) are met. For that to be so the claimant must, amongst other things, have completed and submitted an application either on the approved form or in some other manner accepted by the Secretary of State (reg.116(1)(c)). The period ends under the general rule in para.(1)(b) on the day before the normal payment day for the assessment period in which the application was made, following which a new application has to be made for the next period. Under para.(2), if the application of para.(1)(b) would result in a period of hardship payment of less than eight days the period extends to the day before the normal payment day for the next assessment period.

2.308

The amount of hardship payments

118. The amount of a hardship payment for each day in respect of which such a payment is to be made is to be determined in accordance with the formula—

2.309

$$60\% \ of \left(\frac{(A \times 12)}{365} \right)$$

where A is equal to the amount of the reduction in the single claimant's or joint claimants' award calculated under regulation 110 for the assessment period preceding the assessment period in which an application is submitted under regulation 116(1)(c).

DEFINITIONS

"assessment period"—see WRA 2012, ss.40 and 7(2), and reg.21.
"joint claimants"—see WRA 2012, s.40.
"single claimant"—*ibid.*

GENERAL NOTE

2.310   The amount of any hardship payment payable per day is effectively 60 per cent of the reduction in the amount of benefit in the assessment period before that in which the application is made. See reg.111 for the daily reduction rate for different categories of claimant.

Recoverability of hardship payments

2.311   **119.**—(1) Subject to paragraphs (2) and (3), hardship payments are recoverable in accordance with section 71ZH of the Social Security Administration Act 1992.

[¹(2) Paragraph (1) does not apply in relation to any assessment period in which—

  (a) the single claimant, or each joint claimant, falls within section 19 of the Act by virtue of regulation 90 (claimants subject to no work-related requirements – the earnings threshold);

  (b) where regulation 90 applies to one of the joint claimants only, the joint claimants' combined monthly earnings are equal to or exceed the amount of the individual threshold; or

  (c) where regulation 90 does not apply to the single claimant or to either of the joint claimants, that claimant or the joint claimants' combined monthly earnings are equal to or exceed the amount that a person of the same age as the claimant, or the youngest of the joint claimants, would be paid at the hourly rate specified in regulation 4 or regulation 4A(1)(a) to (c) of the National Minimum Wage Regulations for 16 hours per week, converted to a monthly amount by multiplying by 52 and dividing by 12,

(3) Paragraph (1) ceases to apply where, since the last day on which the claimant's or the joint claimants' award was subject to a reduction under section 26 or 27 of the Act—

  (a) the single claimant, or each joint claimant, has fallen within section 19 of the Act by virtue of regulation 90 (claimants subject to no work-related requirements – the earnings threshold);

  (b) where regulation 90 applied to one of the joint claimants only, the joint claimants' have had combined monthly earnings that are equal to or exceed the amount of the individual threshold; or

  (c) where regulation 90 did not apply to the single claimant or to either of the joint claimants, that claimant or the joint claimants' have had combined monthly earnings that are equal to or exceed the amount that a person of the same age as the claimant, or the youngest of the joint claimants, would be paid at the hourly rate specified in regulation 4 or regulation 4A(1)(a) to (c) of the National Minimum Wage Regulations for 16 hours per week, converted to a monthly amount by multiplying by 52 and dividing by 12,

for a period of, or more than one period where the total of those periods amounts to, at least 6 months.]

AMENDMENT

1. Social Security (Jobseeker's Allowance, Employment and Support Allowance and Universal Credit) (Amendment) Regulations 2016 (SI 2016/678) reg.5(11) (July 25, 2016).

Definitions

"the Act"—see reg.2.
"claimant"—see WRA 2012 s.40.
"individual threshold"—see regs 2 and 90(2).
"joint claimants"—see WRA 2012 s.40.
"National Minimum Wage Regulations"—see reg.2
"single claimant"—see WRA 2012 s.40.

General Note

The basic rule is that any hardship payment is recoverable from the person to   2.312
whom it was paid (Administration Act, s.71ZH(2)(a)), by the means provided in
ss.71ZC to 71ZF. A payment made to one of joint claimants is treated as also paid to
the other (s.71ZH(4)). The amount is not recoverable during any assessment period
in which the claimant or both joint claimants are subject to no work-related requirements by reason of having earnings of at least the individual threshold(s) under
reg.90 (para.(2)(a) and (b)). The same applies under the new provision in para.(2)
(c) to claimants who do not have an individual threshold as defined in reg.90(2)
because they would not otherwise have been subject to any work-related requirement who meet the test of earnings at the rate of 16 times the national minimum
wage hourly rate. It appears from the contrast with the terms of para.(3) that once
the reason for freedom from any work-related requirements ceases, the payment
becomes recoverable again. Under para.(3) recoverability ceases if since the end of
the sanction period the claimant or both joint claimants have had earnings of at least
the para.(2) level for a period or periods amounting to six months.

Regulation 25(2)

Schedule 1

Meaning of Payments in Respect of Accommodation

General

Interpretation
1. In this Schedule—   2.313
"approved premises" means premises approved by the Secretary of State under section 13
    of the Offender Management Act 2007 (which contains provision for the approval etc. of
    premises providing accommodation for persons granted bail in criminal proceedings or for
    or in connection with the supervision or rehabilitation of persons convicted of offences);
"care home"—
    (a) in England and Wales, means a care home within the meaning of section 3 of the Care
        Standards Act 2000;
    (b) in Scotland, means a care home service within the meaning of paragraph 2 of
        Schedule 12 to the Public Services Reform (Scotland) Act 2010; and
    (c) in either case, includes an independent hospital;
[¹ "exempt accommodation" has the meaning given in paragraph 4(10) of Schedule 3 to
    the Housing Benefit and Council Tax Benefit (Consequential Provisions) Regulations
    2006;]
"housing association" has the meaning given by section 1(1) of the Housing Associations
    Act 1985;
"independent hospital"—
    (a) in England, means a hospital as defined by section 275 of the National Health Service
        Act 2006 that is not a health service hospital as defined by that section;
    (b) in Wales, has the meaning assigned to it by section 2 of the Care Standards Act 2000;
    (c) in Scotland, means an independent health care service as defined in section 10F(1)(a)
        and (b) of the National Health Service (Scotland) Act 1978;
"registered charity" means a charity entered in the register of charities maintained under
    Part 4 of the Charities Act 2011 or a body entered on the register of charities maintained
    under the Charities and Trustee Investment (Scotland) Act 2005;

"shared ownership tenancy" has the meaning given in regulation 26(6);

"tent" means a moveable structure that is designed or adapted (solely or mainly) for the purpose of sleeping in a place for any period and that is not a caravan, a mobile home or a houseboat;

[¹ . . .]

"voluntary organisation" means a body (other than a public or local authority) whose activities are carried on otherwise than for profit.

Rent payments

Rent payments

2.314   2. "Rent payments" are such of the following as are not excluded by paragraph 3—
(a) payments of rent;
(b) payments for a licence or other permission to occupy accommodation;
(c) mooring charges payable for a houseboat;
(d) in relation to accommodation which is a caravan or mobile home, payments in respect of the site on which the accommodation stands;
(e) contributions by residents towards maintaining almshouses (and essential services in them) provided by a housing association which is—
    (i) a registered charity, or
    (ii) an exempt charity within Schedule 3 to the Charities Act 2011.

Payments excluded from being rent payments

2.315   3. The following are excluded from being "rent payments"—
(a) payments of ground rent;
(b) payments in respect of a tent or the site on which a tent stands;
(c) payments in respect of approved premises;
(d) payments in respect of a care home;
(e) [¹ . . .]
(f) payments which are owner-occupier payments within the meaning of paragraph 4;
(g) payments which are service charge payments within the meaning of paragraph 7.
[¹ (h) payments in respect of accommodation specified in paragraph 3A.]

[1 Specified accommodation

2.316   3A.—(1) The accommodation referred to in paragraph 3(h) is accommodation to which one or more of the following sub-paragraphs applies.
(2) This sub-paragraph applies to accommodation which is exempt accommodation.
(3) This sub-paragraph applies to accommodation—
(a) which is provided by a relevant body;
(b) into which the claimant has been admitted in order to meet a need for care, support or supervision; and
(c) where the claimant receives care, support or supervision.
(4) This sub-paragraph applies to accommodation which—
(a) is provided by a local authority or a relevant body to the claimant because the claimant has left the home as a result of domestic violence; and
(b) consists of a building, or part of a building, which is used wholly or mainly for the non-permanent accommodation of persons who have left their homes as a result of domestic violence.
(5) This sub-paragraph applies to accommodation—
(a) which would be a hostel within the meaning of paragraph 29(10) (renters excepted form shared accommodation) of Schedule 4 (housing costs element for renters) but for it being owned or managed by a local authority; and
(b) where the claimant receives care, support or supervision.
(6) In this paragraph—
"domestic violence" has the meaning given in regulation 98 (victims of domestic violence);
"relevant body" means a—
(a) council for a county in England for each part of which there is a district council;
(b) housing association;
(c) registered charity; or
(d) voluntary organisation].

Owner-occupier payments

Owner-occupier payments

2.317   4.—(1) "Owner-occupier payments" are—
(a) loan interest payments within the meaning of paragraph 5;

(b) alternative finance payments within the meaning of paragraph 6.

(2) Payments are excluded from sub-paragraph (1) if they are service charge payments within the meaning of paragraph 7.

Meaning of "loan interest payments"

5. "Loan interest payments" means payments of interest on a loan which is secured on the accommodation in respect of which the claimant meets the occupation condition.

2.318

Meaning of "alternative finance payments"

6.—(1) "Alternative finance payments" means payments that are made under alternative finance arrangements which were entered into to enable a person to acquire an interest in the accommodation in respect of which the claimant meets the occupation condition.

2.319

(2) "Alternative finance arrangements" has the same meaning as in Part 10A of the Income Tax Act 2007.

Service charge payments

Service charge payments

7.—(1) "Service charge payments" are payments which—

2.320

(a) fall within sub-paragraph (2);

(b) are not excluded by sub-paragraph (3); and

(c) in any case to which paragraph 8 applies, meet all of the conditions set out in that paragraph.

(2) The payments falling within this sub-paragraph are payments of amounts which are, in whole or in part—

(a) payments of, or towards, the costs of or charges for providing services or facilities for the use or benefit of persons occupying accommodation; or

(b) fairly attributable to the costs of or charges for providing such services or facilities connected with accommodation as are available for the use or benefit of persons occupying accommodation.

(3) Payments are excluded by this sub-paragraph where—

(a) a loan that falls within paragraph 5 was taken out for the purposes of making the payments; or

(b) the services or facilities to which the payments relate are provided for the use or benefit of any person occupying—

(i) a tent,

(ii) approved premises,

(iii) a care home, or

(iv) exempt accommodation.

(4) It is irrelevant for the purposes of sub-paragraph (2)—

(a) whether or not the payments are separately identified as relating to the costs or charges referred to in sub-paragraph (2);

(b) whether they are made in addition to or as part of any other payment (including a payment that would otherwise be regarded as a rent payment within the meaning of paragraph 2);

(c) whether they are made under the same or a different agreement as that under which the accommodation is occupied.

Additional conditions: social rented sector renters and owner-occupiers

8.—(1) This paragraph applies for the purposes of calculating the amount of housing costs element to be included in a claimant's award of universal credit but only as regards calculations made under—

2.321

(a) Part 5 of Schedule 4 (social rented sector other than temporary accommodation); or

(b) Schedule 5 (housing costs element for owner-occupiers).

(2) The following are the conditions referred to in paragraph 7(1)(c).

(3) The first condition is that making the payments is a condition on which the right to occupy the accommodation depends.

(4) The second condition is that the payments fall within one or more of the following categories:

Category A—Payments to maintain the general standard of the accommodation

Payments within this category are for—

(a) the external cleaning of windows, but only in relation to upper floors of a multi-storey building;

(b) other internal or external maintenance or repair of the accommodation, but only where the payments are separately identifiable as relating to such maintenance or repair and payable by—

    (i) a claimant who occupies accommodation under a shared ownership tenancy, or

    (ii) a claimant in whose case any amount of housing costs element to be included in their award in respect of those payments would fall to be calculated under Schedule 5.

Category B—Payments for the general upkeep of areas of communal use

Payments within this category are for ongoing maintenance or cleaning of, and the supply of water, fuel or any other commodity relating to the common use of, internal or external areas, including areas for reasonable facilities (such as laundry rooms or children's play areas).

Category C—Payments in respect of basic communal services

Payments within this category are for provision, ongoing maintenance, cleaning or repair in connection with basic services generally available to all persons living in the accommodation (such as refuse collection, communal lifts, secure building access or wireless or television aerials to receive a service free of charge).

Category D—Accommodation-specific charges

Payments within this category are specific to the particular accommodation occupied by a claimant but are limited to payments for the use of essential items contained in it (such as furniture or domestic appliances).

(5) The third condition is that the costs and charges to which the payments relate are of a reasonable amount and relate to services or facilities of such description as it is reasonable to provide.

(6) The fourth condition is that the payments are none of the following—

(a) payments to the extent that they relate to the costs of or charges for providing services or facilities in respect of which payments out of public funds might otherwise be made (irrespective of whether the claimant has any entitlement to payments so made);

(b) payments in connection with the use of an asset which result in the transfer of the asset or any interest in it;

(c) payments to the extent that they relate to the costs of or charges for providing food, medical services or personal services (including personal care) of any description.

(7) Payments that are not service charge payments within the meaning of paragraph 7 by reason only that they fail to meet any of the conditions set out in sub-paragraphs (3) to (6) are nevertheless to be treated as if they were such service charge payments for the purposes of paragraphs 3(g) and 4(2).

AMENDMENT

1. Housing Benefit and Universal Credit (Supported Accommodation) (Amendment) Regulations 2014 (SI 2014/771) reg.2(2) (November 3, 2014).

DEFINITION

"claimant"—see WRA 2012 s.40.

GENERAL NOTE

2.322   In order to be eligible for a housing costs element, the claimant (or claimants) must meet the three basic conditions in reg.25(2) to (4): the payment condition, the liability condition, and the occupation condition. This Schedule is concerned with the payment condition.

Under reg.25(2) there are three types of payments that can be met: rent payments, owner-occupier payments and service charge payments.

Paras 2, 3 and 3A

2.323   Paragraph 2 lists the payments that are eligible as rent payments and para.3 the payments that are not eligible. Note that the amount of the housing costs element may be restricted under Sch.4 if the rent is higher than allowed (private tenants and temporary accommodation) or the accommodation is larger than allowed (social rented sector).

The payments listed in para.2 include most of the payments that can be met by housing benefit but not all, e.g. payments by way of mesne profits (or, in Scotland, violent profits) are not included.

Under para.3 payments in respect of ground rent and in respect of a tent and the site on which it stands are excluded (para.3(a) and (b)). These qualify as "other housing costs" for income support, old style JSA and old style ESA but there seems to be no provision for such payments under universal credit.

Payments by Crown tenants no longer seem to be excluded (as they are for housing benefit).

Paragraph 3(h), together with para.3A, inserted with effect from November 3, 2014, excludes payments in respect of "specified accommodation". There are four categories of "specified accommodation", the first of which, exempt accommodation, was previously excluded under para. 3(e) (now omitted).

The four categories are: (i) "exempt accommodation" (as defined in para.1–this is accommodation which is a "resettlement place" or accommodation provided by a non-metropolitan county council, a housing association, a registered charity or a voluntary organisation, where care, support or supervision is provided to the claimant by that body or a person acting on its behalf); (ii) accommodation provided by a "relevant body" (as defined in para. 3A(6)) into which the claimant has been admitted because of a need for care, support or supervision, which s/he receives; (iii) temporary accommodation provided by a local authority or a relevant body for people who have left home because of domestic violence, e.g., a women's refuge (note the definition of "domestic violence" in reg. 98(4), which is quite wide); and (iv) hostels owned or managed by a local authority where the claimant receives care, support or supervision. Note that in the case of categories (ii) and (iv) the care, support or supervision does not have to be provided by the relevant body or on its behalf, or by the local authority or on its behalf, as it does in the case of exempt accommodation.

Claimants living in specified accommodation are eligible for housing benefit. Corresponding amendments have been made to the Housing Benefit Regulations 2006 (SI 2006/213), the effect of which is to exclude housing benefit paid to claimants living in specified accommodation from the HB benefit cap for housing benefit purposes (see regs 75C(2)(a) and 75H of those Regulations–the exemption previously only applied to claimants living in exempt accommodation). Housing benefit is not included in the list of welfare benefits in reg. 79(4) to which the universal credit benefit cap applies.

Paras 4–6

2.324

The owner-occupier payments that can be met are "loan interest payments" and "alternative finance payments". They do not include service charge payments that come within para.7.

Note the £200,000 limit on loans in step 3 of para.10(2) of Sch.5 (except for loans for adaptations for disablement needs: see para.10(3) of Sch.5) and on the purchase price of the accommodation in the case of alternative finance payments in step 2 of para.11(2) of Sch.5. Note also that any increase, or decrease, in the amount of a loan, or in the amount owing under the alternative financial arrangements, during the currency of an award is only taken into account from the anniversary date (see paras 10(4) and 11(4) respectively of Sch.5).

"Loan interest payments" are defined in para.5 as "payments of interest on a loan which is secured on the accommodation in respect of which the claimant meets the occupation condition".

Thus payments of interest will be eligible (as calculated under Sch.5), provided only that the loan is secured on the accommodation that the claimant (or claimants: s.40 WRA 2012) is occupying, or is treated as occupying, as his/her home. Note that there is no requirement as to the purpose for which the loan (or loans) was taken out. Compare the income support, old style JSA and old style ESA provisions under which the loan has to be taken out to acquire an interest in the home or for the purpose of repairs or improvements (but does not have to be secured on the home, although it normally will be). Thus this could include a loan taken out, for example, to pay service charges (payments on loans secured on a claimant's home which were taken out to meet service charges are not eligible as service charge payments (see para.7(1)(b) and (3)(a)), or for repairs. But it could also include a loan taken out for any other purpose, for example, to buy a car, as long as the loan is secured on the claimant's home. This does seem surprising but is acknowledged in the examples given in para.F4082 ADM. Furthermore, a remortgage to roll up arrears of interest would also be covered. Thus a claimant may receive a housing costs element in respect of interest payments on loans that include arrears of interest (provided that they are secured on the home), which is a significant change from the position under the income support, old style JSA and old style ESA housing costs rules.

"**Alternative finance payments**" are defined in para.6. This will cover home financing schemes designed to be compliant with Shari'a principles. Such schemes are not eligible for income support (or old style JSA or old style ESA) housing costs (see the notes to para.15 of Sch.3 to the Income Support Regulations in Vol.II of this series).

Note that there is normally a qualifying period (i.e. waiting period) for owner-occupier payments (and for service charge payments if these are also payable). In the case of a new award of universal credit on or after April 1, 2016 the waiting period is nine consecutive assessments periods (i.e. months) (see Pt 3 of Sch.5). Before April 1, 2016 the waiting period was only three consecutive months. The amendment which increased the waiting period to nine months is subject to a saving provision (see reg. 8 of the Social Security (Housing Costs Amendments) Regulations 2015 in Pt.IV of this Volume and see the note to paras 5-7 of Sch.5).

Note also that if the claimant (or other member of the couple, in the case of couples) has *any* earned income during an assessment period (i.e. month) no housing costs element will be payable (Sch.5, para.4), although in the case of a shared ownership tenancy (defined in reg.26(6)) rent payments and service charges can still be met (Sch.5, para.4(3)). In addition, any break in entitlement to a housing costs element under Sch.5 (e.g. because of earnings), or if the owner-occupier ceases to qualify for a housing costs element under Sch. 5 during a waiting period, means that a whole new waiting period has to be served (see Sch.5, para.5).

Unlike income support, old style JSA and old style ESA, there is no rule that a housing costs element cannot be paid if the loan was taken out while the claimant (or either joint claimant) was in receipt of universal credit.

Paras 7 and 8

2.325   Service charge payments are eligible payments if they fall within para.7(2) and are not excluded under para.7(3). They do not have to be separately identified, nor does it matter if they are paid in addition to, or as part of, any other payment (including a rent payment within the meaning of para.2), or if they are paid under the same or a different agreement than that under which the accommodation is occupied (para.7(4)).

Note the additional conditions in para.8 that have to be met in the case of service charge payments by social sector renters (other those in temporary accommodation) and owner-occupiers. This does not apply to private renters.

According to para.F2074 ADM, where service charges are for the provision of an eligible service, the relevant proportion of staffing costs of a person (e.g. a concierge, groundskeeper or caretaker) employed to provide the eligible service can be included, as can the relevant proportion of the costs of managing and administering eligible services, if the claimant is liable for these costs.

SCHEDULE 2

CLAIMANT TREATED AS LIABLE OR NOT LIABLE TO MAKE PAYMENTS

PART I

TREATED AS LIABLE TO MAKE PAYMENTS

Certain other persons liable to make payments

1.—(1) A claimant is to be treated as liable to make payments where the person who is liable   **2.326** to make the payments is—

   (a) any child or qualifying young person for whom the claimant (or if the claimant is a member of a couple, either member) is responsible; or

   (b) in the case of a claimant who is a member of a couple claiming as a single person, the other member of the couple.

(2) Sub-paragraph (1)(b) does not apply to a person who is claiming as a single person by virtue of regulation 3(4).

Failure to pay by the person who is liable

2.—(1) A claimant is to be treated as liable to make payments where all of the conditions   **2.327** specified in sub-paragraph (2) are met.

(2) These are the conditions—

   (a) the person who is liable to make the payments is not doing so;

   (b) the claimant has to make the payments in order to continue occupation of the accommodation;

   (c) the claimant's circumstances are such that it would be unreasonable to expect them to make other arrangements;

   (d) it is otherwise reasonable in all the circumstances to treat the claimant as liable to make the payments.

(3) In determining what is reasonable for the purposes of sub-paragraph (2)(d) in the case of owner-occupier payments, regard may be had to the fact that continuing to make the payments may benefit the person with the liability to make the payments.

Payments waived in return for repair work

3. A claimant is to be treated as liable to make payments where—   **2.328**

   (a) the liability to make payments is waived by the person ("P") to whom the liability is owed; and

   (b) the waiver of that liability is by way of reasonable compensation for reasonable repair or re-decoration works carried out by the claimant to the accommodation which P would otherwise have carried out or been required to carry out.

Rent free periods

4.—(1) Where the arrangements under which the claimant occupies the accommodation   **2.329** provide for rent free periods, the claimant is to be treated as liable to make rent payments and service charge payments in respect of accommodation for the whole of any rent free period.

(2) In paragraph (1), "rent free period" has the meaning given in paragraph 7(4) of Schedule 4.

PART 2

TREATED AS NOT LIABLE TO MAKE PAYMENTS

Liability to make rent and other payments to close relative

5.—(1) A claimant is to be treated as not liable to make rent payments where the liability to   **2.330** make them is owed to a person who lives in the accommodation and who is—

   (a) if the claimant is a member of a couple, the other member; or

   (b) a child or qualifying young person for whom—

     (i) the claimant is responsible, or

     (ii) if the claimant is a member of a couple, the other member is responsible; or

   (c) a close relative of—

     (i) the claimant, or

     (ii) if the claimant is a member of a couple, the other member, or

(iii) any child or qualifying young person who falls within paragraph (b).

(2) A claimant who is treated under sub-paragraph (1) as not liable to make rent payments to any person is also to be treated as not liable to make service charge payments where the liability to make the service charge payments is to the same person.

Liability to make rent and other payments to company

2.331
6.—(1) A claimant is to be treated as not liable to make rent payments where the liability to make them is owed to a company and the owners or directors of the company include—

(a) the claimant;

(b) if the claimant is a member of a couple, the other member;

(c) a qualifying young person for whom a person who falls within paragraph (a) or (b) is responsible; or

(d) a close relative of any of the above who lives in the accommodation with the claimant.

(2) A claimant who is treated under sub-paragraph (1) as not liable to make rent payments to the company is also to be treated as not liable to make service charge payments where the liability to make the service charge payments is to—

(a) the same company; or

(b) another company of which the owners or directors include any of the persons listed in sub-paragraph (1)(a) to (d).

(3) In this paragraph, "owner", in relation to a company ("C"), means a person ("A") who has a material interest in C.

(4) For the purposes of sub-paragraph (3), A has a material interest in C if A—

(a) holds at least 10% of the shares in C; or

(b) is able to exercise a significant influence over the management of C by virtue of A's shareholding in C; or

(c) holds at least 10% of the shares in a parent undertaking ("P") of C; or

(d) is able to exercise a significant influence over the management of P by virtue of A's shareholding in P; or

(e) is entitled to exercise, or control the exercise of, voting power in C which, if it consists of voting rights, constitutes at least 10% of the voting rights in C; or

(f) is able to exercise a significant influence over the management of C by virtue of A's entitlement to exercise, or control the exercise of, voting rights in C; or

(g) is entitled to exercise, or control the exercise of, voting power in P which, if it consists of voting rights, constitutes at least 10% of the voting rights in P; or

(h) is able to exercise a significant influence over the management of P by virtue of A's entitlement to exercise, or control the exercise of, voting rights in P.

(5) For the purposes of sub-paragraph (4), references to "A" are to—

(a) the person; or

(b) any of the person's associates; or

(c) the person and any of the person's associates taken together.

(6) For the purposes of sub-paragraph (5), "associate", in relation to a person ("A") holding shares in an undertaking ("X") or entitled to exercise or control the exercise of voting power in relation to another undertaking ("Y"), means—

(a) the spouse or civil partner of A;

(b) a child or step-child of A (if under 18);

(c) the trustee of any settlement under which A has a life interest in possession (in Scotland a life interest);

(d) an undertaking of which A is a director;

(e) a person who is an employee or partner of A;

(f) if A has with any other person an agreement or arrangement with respect to the acquisition, holding or disposal of shares or other interests in X or Y, that other person;

(g) if A has with any other person an agreement or arrangement under which they undertake to act together in exercising their voting power in relation to X or Y, that other person.

(7) In sub-paragraph (6)(c), "settlement" means any disposition or arrangement under which property is held on trust (or subject to comparable obligations).

(8) For the purposes of this paragraph—

"parent undertaking" has the same meaning as in the Financial Services and Markets Act 2000 (see section 420 of that Act);

"shares" means—

(a) in relation to an undertaking with shares, allotted shares (within the meaning of Part 17 of the Companies Act 2006);

(b) in relation to an undertaking with capital but no share capital, rights to share in the capital of the body;

(c) in relation to an undertaking without capital, interests—

    (i)   conferring any right to share in the profits, or liability to contribute to the losses, of the body, or

    (ii) giving rise to an obligation to contribute to the debts or expenses of the undertaking in the event of a winding up;

"voting power", in relation to an undertaking which does not have general meetings at which matters are decided by the exercise of voting rights, means the rights under the constitution of the undertaking to direct the overall policy of the undertaking or alter the terms of its constitution.

Liability to make rent and other payments to a trust

7.—(1) A claimant is to be treated as not liable to make rent payments where the liability to make them is owed to a trustee of a trust and the trustees or beneficiaries of the trust include—   **2.332**

    (a) the claimant;

    (b) if the claimant is a member of a couple, the other member;

    (c) a child or qualifying young person for whom a person who falls within paragraph (a) or (b) is responsible; or

    (d) a close relative of any of the above who lives in the accommodation with the claimant.

(2) A claimant who is treated under sub-paragraph (1) as not liable to make rent payments to the trustee of a trust is also to be treated as not liable to make service charge payments where the liability to make the service charge payments is to—

    (a) a trustee of the same trust; or

    (b) a trustee of another trust of which the trustees or beneficiaries include any of the persons listed in sub-paragraph (1)(a) to (d).

Liability to make owner-occupier and other payments to member of same household

8.—(1) A claimant is to be treated as not liable to make owner-occupier payments where the liability to make the payments is owed to a person who lives in the claimant's household.   **2.333**

(2) A claimant who is treated under sub-paragraph (1) as not liable to make owner-occupier payments to any person is also to be treated as not liable to make service charge payments where the liability to make the service charge payments is to the same person.

(3) A claimant is to be treated as not liable to make service charge payments where—

    (a) there is no liability to make rent payments or owner-occupier payments; but

    (b) the liability to make service charge payments is to a person who lives in the claimant's household.

Arrears of payments

9.—(1) A claimant is to be treated as not liable to make payments in respect of any amount which—   **2.334**

    (a) represents an increase in the sum that would be otherwise payable; and

    (b) is the result of—

        (i)   outstanding arrears of any payment or charge in respect of the accommodation,

        (ii) outstanding arrears of any payment or charge in respect of other accommodation, previously occupied by the claimant, or

        (iii) any other unpaid liability to make a payment or charge.

(2) Sub-paragraph (1) does not apply if the claimant is treated as not liable to make the payments under any of the preceding provisions of this Part of this Schedule.

Contrived liability

10.—(1) A claimant is to be treated as not liable to make payments where the Secretary of State is satisfied that the liability to make the payments was contrived in order to secure the inclusion of the housing costs element in an award of universal credit or to increase the amount of that element.   **2.335**

(2) Sub-paragraph (1) does not apply if the claimant is treated as not liable to make the payments under any of the preceding provisions of this Part of this Schedule.

DEFINITIONS

"child"—see WRA 2012 s.40.

"claimant"—*ibid*.

"close relative"—see reg.2.

"couple"—see WRA 2012 ss.39 and 40.

"partner"—see reg.2.

"qualifying young person"—see WRA 2012 ss.40 and 10(5) and regs 2 and 5.

"rent free period"—see Sch.4, para.7(4).
"single person"—see WRA 2012 ss.40 and 1(2)(a).

GENERAL NOTE

2.336   In order to be eligible for a housing costs element, the claimant (or claimants) must meet the three basic conditions in reg.25(2) to (4): the payment condition, the liability condition, and the occupation condition. This Schedule is concerned with the liability condition.

Under reg.25(3) the claimant (or either joint claimant) must be liable to make rent payments, owner-occupier payments or service charge payments on a commercial basis, or be treated as liable to make them, and must not be treated as not liable to make them. "Liable" is not defined but presumably requires a legal (as opposed to a moral) liability (see *R v Rugby BC HBRB ex parte Harrison* [1994] 28 HLR 36 and the discussion on the meaning of "liability" in the notes to reg. 8 of the Housing Benefit Regulations in *CPAG's Housing Benefit and Council Tax Reduction Legislation*; it is also the view taken in para.F2081 ADM).

For the meaning of "on a commercial basis", see the notes to "*Board and lodging accommodation*" in reg.2 of the Income Support Regulations in Vol.II of this series and the notes to reg.9(1)(a) of the Housing Benefit Regulations in *CPAG's Housing Benefit and Council Tax Reduction Legislation*.

Paras 1–4

2.337   Under para.1 a claimant is treated as liable to make payments if the person who is liable is (i) a child or qualifying young person for whom the claimant (or the other member of the couple in the case of a couple) is responsible (sub-para.(1)(a)); or (ii) the other member of the couple, if the claimant is a member of a couple but claiming as a single person (see reg.3(3) for the circumstances in which this can apply) (sub-para.(1)(b)); note that sub-para.(1)(b) does not apply in the case of polygamous marriages (sub-para.(2)).

A claimant is also treated as liable to make payments if the payments have been waived by the person to whom they were due (e.g. a landlord) as reasonable compensation for the claimant carrying out reasonable repair or redecoration works which the person would otherwise have had to carry out (para.3), or, in the case of rent and service charge payments, during rent free periods (para.4).

Paragraph 2 applies where the person who is liable to make the payments is not doing so. The claimant will be treated as liable if the claimant has to make the payments in order to continue to occupy the accommodation, it would be unreasonable to expect the claimant to make other arrangements and it is reasonable to treat the claimant as liable. These conditions are similar to those in, e.g., reg.8(1)(c) of the Housing Benefit Regulations and para.2(1)(b) of Sch.3 to the Income Support Regulations (see the notes to para.2 of Sch.3 in Vol.II of this series), except for the added condition that it would be unreasonable to expect the claimant to make other arrangements.

Note para.2(3) which provides that in the case of owner-occupier payments, in deciding whether it would be reasonable to treat the claimant as liable, account may be taken of the fact that the payments continuing to be made may benefit the person who is liable to make the payments. Paragraph F2090 ADM gives the following example of where this might apply. A couple split up and C, the member in whose name the mortgage is, moves out and refuses to pay the mortgage. The other member, P, remains in the property. A decision-maker decides not to include a housing costs element in P's universal credit award as C could still pay the mortgage.

Paras 5–10

2.338   These paragraphs deal with when the claimant will be treated as not liable to make payments in respect of his/her home. Note that some of the exclusions only apply to some types of eligible payments. The situations in which this rule applies to rent payments are reduced compared with housing benefit (see reg.9 of the Housing

Benefit Regulations). Note that the "on a commercial basis" requirement applies to any liability to make payments in respect of accommodation under universal credit (see reg.25(3)(a)(i)).

Paras 5–7

A claimant is treated as not liable to make rent payments and service charges pay-   2.339
ments if the liability is to the following:

- Someone who also lives in the accommodation, and who is (i) the other member of the couple if the claimant is a member of a couple; (ii) a child or qualifying young person for whom the claimant or other member of the couple is responsible (see reg.4); or (iii) a close relative (defined in reg.2) of the claimant, the other member of the couple or the child or qualifying person (para.5).

  "Lives in the accommodation" probably means the same as "resides in the dwelling" in reg.9(1)(b) of the Housing Benefit Regulations (see the notes to reg.9(1)(b) in *CPAG's Housing Benefit and Council Tax Reduction Legislation*).

- A company, and the owners or directors of the company include (i) the claimant; (ii) the other member of the couple if the claimant is a member of a couple; (iii) a qualifying young person for whom the claimant or other member of the couple is responsible; or (iv) a close relative of the claimant, other member of the couple or qualifying young person (in the case of a close relative, s/he must live in the accommodation with the claimant) (para.6(1) and (2)).

  Note that the claimant will also be treated as not liable to pay the service charges if the liability for them is to another company whose owners or directors include any of the people listed in para.6(1) (para.6(2)(b)).

  An owner of a company for the purposes of para.6 is a person who has a "material interest" in it (para.6(3)). See para.6(4)–(8) for the detail.

- A trustee of a trust, and the trustees or beneficiaries of the trust include (i) the claimant; (ii) the other member of the couple if the claimant is a member of a couple; (iii) a child or qualifying young person for whom the claimant or other member of the couple is responsible; or (iv) a close relative of the claimant, other member of the couple or child or qualifying young person (in the case of a close relative, s/he must live in the accommodation with the claimant) (para.7(1) and (2)).

  Note that the claimant will also be treated as not liable to pay the service charges if the liability for them is to a trustee of another trust whose trustees or beneficiaries include any of the people listed in para.7(1) (para.7(2) (b)).

  See the notes to reg.9(1)(e) and (f) of the Housing Benefit Regulations in *CPAG's Housing Benefit and Council Tax Reduction Legislation*.

Para. 8

Paragraph 8(1) and (2) are concerned with owner-occupier payments and service   2.340
charges payments. They treat a claimant as not liable to make owner-occupier payments and service charges payments if the liability is to a person who is lives in the claimant's household. Clearly this is different from "lives in the accommodation" under paras 5 to 8. On the meaning of "household", see the notes to "*couple*" (under the heading "*Spouses and civil partners*") in reg.2 of the Income Support Regulations in Vol.II of this series.

Under para.8(3) a claimant is treated as not liable to make service charges payments if s/he is not liable for rent payments or owner-occupier payments and the liability for the service charges is to someone who is a member of the claimant's household.

Para. 9

2.341   This paragraph only applies if paras 5–8 do not apply (sub-para.(2)). It applies to all types of eligible payments.

It treats a claimant as not liable to pay any increase in the amount that s/he would otherwise be liable to pay, if that increase is the result of outstanding arrears of any payment or charge in respect of his/her current or previous accommodation. This also applies in respect of "any other unpaid liability to make a payment or charge" (see sub-para.(1)(b)(iii)) but only if that results in an increase in the amount the claimant is liable to pay.

What does "an increase in the sum that would otherwise be payable" mean? According to para.F2136 ADM, in relation to owner-occupier payments, because any loan secured on the claimant's home is eligible for inclusion in the calculation of the housing costs element (see para.5 of Sch.1) (subject to the £200,000 limit on loans in step 3 of para.10(2) of Sch.5), any increase in the loan (or loans) does not "represent an increase in the sum that would otherwise be payable" and so is not caught by para.9. This will include the situation when the loan is a remortgage to roll up arrears of interest. Thus a claimant may receive a housing costs element in respect of interest payments on loans that include arrears of interest (provided that they are secured on the home), which is a significant change from the position under the income support, old style JSA and old style ESA housing costs rules. Presumably this is because the arrears of interest are not "outstanding" if the remortgage has rolled up the arrears of interest.

An example of a payment that would come within para.9 is where a tenant has agreed to pay off arrears of rent by paying an increased amount of rent each month. S/he will be treated under para.9 as not liable to pay the extra amount above the rent that was originally agreed.

Para. 10

2.342   This paragraph only applies if paras 5–8 do not apply (sub-para.(2)). It applies to all types of eligible payments.

It contains a similar rule to the contrived tenancy provision in housing benefit (see reg.9(1)(l) of the Housing Benefit Regulations). See the notes to reg.9(1)(l) in *CPAG's Housing Benefit and Council Tax Reduction Legislation*. But note that reg.9(1) (l) refers to the liability being "created to take advantage of the housing benefit scheme", whereas the test under para.10 is that the liability "was contrived in order to secure the inclusion of the housing costs element". There may be a distinction between "created" and "contrived".

Regulation 25(4)

Schedule 3

Claimant Treated as Occupying or not Occupying Accommodation

Part I

Treated as Occupying Accommodation

The occupation condition: the general rule

2.343   1.—(1) The general rule is that a claimant is to be treated as occupying as their home the accommodation which the claimant normally occupies as their home.

(2) Subject to the following provisions of this Part, no claimant is to be treated as occupying accommodation which comprises more than one dwelling.

(3) Where none of those provisions applies and the claimant occupies more than one dwelling, regard is to be had to all the circumstances in determining which dwelling the claimant normally occupies as their home, including (among other things) any persons with whom the claimant occupies each dwelling.

(4) "Dwelling"—

    (a) in England and Wales, means a dwelling within the meaning of Part 1 of the Local Government Finance Act 1992;

    (b) in Scotland, means a dwelling within the meaning of Part 2 of that Act.

Croft land included in accommodation

   2.—(1) Where accommodation which a claimant normally occupies as their home is situated on or pertains to a croft, croft land used for the purposes of the accommodation is to be treated as included in the accommodation.

   (2) "Croft" means a croft within the meaning of section 3(1) of the Crofters (Scotland) Act 1993.

2.344

Claimant living in other accommodation during essential repairs

   3.—(1) Where a claimant—
- (a) is required to move into accommodation ("the other accommodation") on account of essential repairs being carried out to the accommodation the claimant normally occupies as their home;
- (b) intends to return to the accommodation which is under repair; and
- (c) meets the payment condition and the liability condition in respect of either the other accommodation or the accommodation which they normally occupy as their home (but not both),

the claimant is to be treated as normally occupying as their home the accommodation in respect of which those conditions are met.

   (2) A claimant is subject to the general rule in paragraph 1 where—
- (a) sub-paragraph (1)(a) and (b) apply to the claimant; but
- (b) the claimant meets the payment condition and the liability condition in respect of both the other accommodation and the accommodation which they normally occupy as their home.

2.345

Claimant housed in two dwellings by provider of social housing

   4.—(1) In sub-paragraph (2), "relevant claimant" means a claimant who meets all of the following conditions—
- (a) the first condition is that the claimant has been housed in two dwellings ("accommodation A" and "accommodation B") by a provider of social housing on account of the number of children and qualifying young persons living with the claimant;
- (b) the second condition is that the claimant normally occupies both accommodation A and accommodation B with children or qualifying young persons for whom the claimant is responsible;
- (c) the third condition is that the claimant meets the payment condition and the liability condition in respect of both accommodation A and accommodation B (and for these purposes it is irrelevant whether the claimant's liability is to the same or a different person).

   (2) In the case of a relevant claimant, both accommodation A and accommodation B are to be treated as the single accommodation which the relevant claimant normally occupies as their home.

   (3) In sub-paragraph (1), "provider of social housing" has the meaning given in paragraph 2 of Schedule 4.

2.346

Moving home: adaptations to new home for disabled person

   5.—(1) Sub-paragraph (2) applies where—
- (a) the claimant has moved into accommodation ("the new accommodation") and, immediately before the move, met the payment condition and liability condition in respect of the new accommodation; and
- (b) there was a delay in moving in that was necessary to enable the new accommodation to be adapted to meet the disablement needs of a person specified in sub-paragraph (3).

   (2) The claimant is to be treated as occupying both the new accommodation and the accommodation from which the move was made ("the old accommodation") if—
- (a) immediately before the move, the claimant was entitled to the inclusion of the housing costs element in an award of universal credit in respect of the old accommodation; and
- (b) the delay in moving into the new accommodation was reasonable.

   (3) A person is specified in this sub-paragraph if the person is—
- (a) a claimant or any child or qualifying young person for whom a claimant is responsible; and
- (b) in receipt of—
  - (i) the care component of disability living allowance at the middle or highest rate,
  - (ii) attendance allowance, or
  - (iii) the daily living component of personal independence payment.

   (4) No claimant may be treated as occupying both the old accommodation and the new accommodation under this paragraph for more than one month.

2.347

Claimant living in other accommodation because of reasonable fear of violence

2.348   **6.**—(1) This paragraph applies where—

(a) a claimant is occupying accommodation ("the other accommodation") other than the accommodation which they normally occupy as their home ("the home accommodation"); and

(b) it is unreasonable to expect the claimant to return to the home accommodation on account of the claimant's reasonable fear of violence in the home, or by a former partner, against the claimant or any child or qualifying young person for whom the claimant is responsible; but

(c) the claimant intends to return to the home accommodation.

(2) The claimant is to be treated as normally occupying both the home accommodation and the other accommodation as their home if—

(a) the claimant meets the payment condition and the liability condition in respect of both the home accommodation and other accommodation; and

(b) it is reasonable to include an amount in the housing costs element for the payments in respect of both the home accommodation and the other accommodation.

(3) Where the claimant meets the payment condition and the liability condition in respect of one accommodation only, the claimant is to be treated as normally occupying that accommodation as their home but only if it is reasonable to include an amount in the housing costs element for the payments in respect of that accommodation.

(4) No claimant may be treated as occupying both the home accommodation and the other accommodation under sub-paragraph (2) for more than 12 months.

Moving in delayed by adaptations to accommodation to meet disablement needs

2.349   **7.**—(1) The claimant is to be treated as having occupied accommodation before they moved into it where—

(a) the claimant has since moved in and, immediately before the move, met the payment condition and the liability condition in respect of the accommodation;

(b) there was a delay in moving in that was necessary to enable the accommodation to be adapted to meet the disablement needs of a relevant person; and

(c) it was reasonable to delay moving in.

(2) "Relevant person" means a person specified in paragraph 5(3).

(3) No claimant may be treated as occupying accommodation under this paragraph for more than one month.

Moving into accommodation following stay in hospital or care home

2.350   **8.**—(1) The claimant is to be treated as having occupied accommodation before they moved into it where—

(a) the claimant has since moved in and, immediately before the move, met the payment condition and the liability condition in respect of that accommodation; and

(b) the liability to make the payments arose while the claimant was a patient or accommodated in a care home (or, in the case of a joint claim, while both joint claimants were patients or were accommodated in a care home).

(2) No claimant may be treated as occupying the accommodation under this paragraph for more than one month.

(3) In this paragraph—

"care home" has the meaning given in paragraph 1 of Schedule 1;

"patient" means a person who is undergoing medical or other treatment as an in-patient in any hospital or similar institution.

PART 2

TREATED AS NOT OCCUPYING ACCOMMODATION

Periods of temporary absence exceeding 6 months

2.351   **9.**—(1) Subject to sub-paragraphs (2) and (3), a claimant is to be treated as no longer occupying accommodation from which they are temporarily absent where the absence exceeds, or is expected to exceed, 6 months.

(2) Sub-paragraph (1) does not apply to a claimant who falls within paragraph 3.

(3) Where a claimant who falls within paragraph 6 is temporarily absent from the accommodation which they normally occupy as their home, the claimant is to be treated as no longer occupying that accommodation where the absence exceeds, or is expected to exceed, 12 months.

DEFINITIONS

"attendance allowance"—see reg.2.
"care home"—see Sch.1, para.1.
"child"—see WRA 2012 s.40.
"claimant"—*ibid.*
"disability living allowance"—see reg.2.
"partner"—*ibid.*
"personal independence payment"—*ibid.*
"provider of social housing"—see Sch.4, para.2.
"qualifying young person"—see WRA 2012 ss.40 and 10(5) and regs 2 and 5.

GENERAL NOTE

In order to be eligible for a housing costs element, the claimant (or claimants) must meet the three basic conditions in reg.25(2) to (4): the payment condition, the liability condition, and the occupation condition. This Schedule is concerned with the occupation condition.

Under reg.25(4) the claimant (or each claimant in the case of joint claimants: s.40 WRA 2012) must be treated as occupying the accommodation as his/her home and not be treated as not occupying it. Croft land is included (see para.2).

Para.1

This contains the general rule that the claimant must be normally occupying the accommodation as his/her home (sub-para(1)). On the meaning of "normally occupying", see the notes to "dwelling occupied as the home" in reg.2 of the Income Support Regulations in Vol.II of this series.

In addition, the claimant cannot usually be treated as occupying accommodation which comprises more than one dwelling (sub-para.(2)). However, there are exceptions to these rules (see below). Where these exceptions do not apply, and the claimant (or claimants: s.40 WRA 2012) occupies more than one dwelling, to decide which is the dwelling normally occupied as the home, all the circumstances, including the people who live with the claimant (or claimants) in each dwelling, are to be taken into account (sub-para.(3)).

On the question of whether in certain circumstances two physically separate buildings can constitute one "dwelling", see the notes to reg.2 of the Income Support Regulations in Vol.II of this series. Where a claimant is housed in two dwellings by a "provider of social housing" (defined in Sch.4, para.2), see para.4 below.

Para.3

If the claimant has to move into temporary accommodation because essential repairs (see *R(SB) 10/81*) are being carried out to his/her normal home, intends to return to that home, and satisfies the payment and liability conditions for either the temporary accommodation or his/her normal home (but not both), s/he is treated as occupying as his/her home the accommodation in respect of which the payment and liability conditions are met (sub-para.(1)). If the claimant satisfies the payment and liability conditions for both the temporary accommodation and his/her normal home, s/he is treated as occupying the accommodation that s/he normally occupies as his/her home (sub-para.(2)). This may not necessarily be the accommodation that was his/her normal home.

There is no time limit in para.3 itself as to how long it can apply.

Para.4

This allows a housing costs element to be paid for two dwellings in the following circumstances. If the claimant (or claimants: s.40 WRA 2012) has been housed in two dwellings by a "provider of social housing" (defined in para.2 of Sch.4) due to the number of children and qualifying young persons living with him/her, the claimant normally occupies both dwellings with children or qualifying young persons (see reg.5) for whom s/he is responsible (see reg.4) and the claimant meets the payment

2.352

2.353

2.354

2.355

and liability conditions in respect of both dwellings, the claimant will be treated as normally occupying both dwellings as his/her home.

This paragraph can apply without time limit.

See para.17 of Sch.4 as to how the housing costs element is calculated under para.4. A single calculation is made for both dwellings together. This will be carried out under Pt 5 of Sch.4 if the rent is paid to a social sector landlord for both dwellings and neither is temporary accommodation (see para.21 of Sch.4 for the meaning of "temporary accommodation"). Otherwise, the calculation is made under Pt 4 of Sch.4, including applying the four bedroom limit. Note that under para.25(3)–(4) of Sch.4, if the cap rent for the two dwellings is different (e.g. because they are in different areas), the cap rent that is lower at the time the housing costs element is first calculated is the cap rent that applies. The calculation of the renter's housing costs element will continue to be based on that cap rent for as long as the renter is housed in those two homes.

Paras 5 and 7

2.356 Under para.5 a claimant (or claimants) can be treated as occupying two homes for up to one month if the claimant:

    (i)   has moved into his/her new home;

    (ii) met the payment and liability conditions for that home immediately before s/he moved in,

    (iii) was entitled to a housing costs element in respect of his/her old home immediately before the move; and

    (iv) the delay in moving in was reasonable and was necessary to enable the new home to be adapted to the disablement needs (not defined) of the claimant (or claimants: s.40 WRA 2012) or any child or qualifying young person for whom the claimant (or claimants) is responsible. The person with the disablement needs must be in receipt of the middle or highest rate of the care component of disability living allowance, the daily living component of personal independence payment (either rate), attendance allowance or armed forces independence payment (note that the definition of "attendance allowance" in reg.2 includes armed forces independence payment).

If the above circumstances apply but the claimant was not receiving a housing costs element in respect of his/her old home immediately before s/he moved in, para.7 will apply to treat the claimant as occupying his/her home for up to one month before s/he moves in.

On the meaning of "moving in" see *R(H) 9/05* and on "adapting the accommodation to meet disablement needs" see the notes to para.3(7)(c)(i) of Sch.3 to the Income Support Regulations in Vol.II of this series.

See para.18 of Sch.4 as to how the housing costs element is calculated under para.5. Note that any housing cost contributions for non-dependants are only deducted from the housing costs element for the old home.

Para.6

2.357 If the claimant is living in accommodation other than the accommodation s/he normally occupies as his/her home because of a reasonable fear of violence in the home, or from a former partner against him/her or any child or qualifying young person (see reg.5) for whom s/he is responsible (see reg.4), and s/he intends to return to the accommodation s/he normally occupies as his/her home, she can be treated as occupying both for up to 12 months. This applies if s/he meets the payment and liability conditions in respect of both the accommodation s/he normally occupies as his/her home and the other accommodation, provided that it is reasonable to pay a housing costs element for both. If the claimant only satisfies the payment and liability conditions in respect of one accommodation, s/he will be treated as occupying that accommodation as his/her home but only if it is reasonable to pay a housing costs element for that accommodation.

If a claimant in these circumstances is living in a refuge, it is unlikely that s/he will meet the payment condition for that accommodation (see para.3(h), together with para.3A, of Sch.1, under which payments in respect of "specified accommodation" do not count as rent payments. "Specified accommodation" includes temporary accommodation provided by a local authority or a "relevant body" (defined in para.3A(6)) for people who have left home because of domestic violence (defined in reg.98(4)) (para.3A(4)). However, if s/he is living in "specified accommodation", s/he can claim housing benefit for that accommodation.

Note para.9(3) which provides that such a claimant can no longer be treated as temporarily absent from the accommodation which s/he normally occupies as his/her home if the absence lasts, or is expected to last, more than 12 months.

See para.19 of Sch.4 as to how the housing costs element is calculated under para.6 where the claimant is entitled to a housing costs element for both homes. This will be calculated for each home under Pt 4 of Sch.4 or under Pt 5 of Sch.4, as the case may be. Note that any housing cost contributions for non-dependants are only deducted from the housing costs element for the home that the claimant is normally occupying.

Para. 8

Under this paragraph a claimant can be treated as occupying his/her home for up to one month before s/he moves in if s/he met the payment and liability conditions immediately before moving in and s/he became liable to make the payments while s/he was a patient (defined in sub-para.(3)) or in a care home (defined in para.1 of Sch.1), or in the case of joint claimants, while both of them were patients or in a care home.

2.358

Para. 9

Unless the absence is due to essential repairs (see para.3) or a fear of violence (see para.6), if a claimant is temporarily absent from the accommodation, s/he will be treated as no longer occupying it if the absence has lasted, or is expected to last, more than six months.

2.359

This is a considerably simplified provision compared with the rules for temporary absence that apply for the purposes of housing benefit and income support, old style JSA and old style ESA housing costs.

If at any time during the six months it becomes clear that the absence is likely to exceed six months, the claimant will be treated as no longer occupying the accommodation from that point (this could apply from the start if the absence was expected to last more than six months from the beginning). However, if the claimant returns to the accommodation for a period, even a very short period (24 hours?), the six months should restart (see *R v Penrith DC Housing Benefit Review Board ex p. Burt* (1990) 22 H.L.R. 292). See further the notes to para.3(8) to (12) of Sch.3 to the Income Support Regulations in Vol. II of this series.

Note that if a person was entitled to universal credit which included a housing costs element immediately before becoming a prisoner (defined in reg.2), and s/he has not been sentenced to a term in custody which is expected to last more than six months, s/he will be entitled to universal credit consisting of a housing costs element only during his/her first six months' absence as a prisoner (see reg.19(2) and (3)).

Regulation 26(2)

SCHEDULE 4

HOUSING COSTS ELEMENT FOR RENTERS

PART I

GENERAL

Introduction

1.—(1) This Schedule contains provisions about claimants to whom regulation 26(2) applies.

2.360

(2) Claimants who fall within sub-paragraph (1) are referred to in this Schedule as "renters" (and references to "joint renters" are to joint claimants to whom regulation 26(2) applies).

(3) Part 2 of this Schedule sets out [¹² exceptions] to section 11(1) of the Act for certain renters in whose case an award of universal credit is not to include an amount of housing costs element calculated under this Schedule.

(4) The following Parts of this Schedule provide for the calculation of the amount of housing costs element to be included under regulation 26(2) in a renter's award of universal credit—

    (a) Part 3 contains general provisions that apply to all calculations, whether under Part 4 or Part 5;

    (b) Part 4 applies in relation to renters who occupy accommodation in the private rented sector or who occupy temporary accommodation; and

    (c) Part 5 applies in relation to renters who occupy accommodation in the social rented sector other than temporary accommodation.

Interpretation

2.361   **2.** In this Schedule—

    [⁸ "exempt accommodation" has the meaning given in paragraph 4(10) of Schedule 3 to the Housing Benefit and Council Tax Benefit (Consequential Provisions) Regulations 2006;]

    "extended benefit unit" has the meaning given in paragraph 9;

    "Housing Act functions" means functions under section 122 of the Housing Act 1996 (functions of rent officers in connection with universal credit, housing benefit and rent allowance subsidy and housing credit);

    "housing cost contribution" has the meaning given in paragraph 13;

    "joint renter" has the meaning given in paragraph 1(2);

    "listed persons", in relation to a renter, means—

        (a) the renter;

        (b) where the renter is a member of a couple, the other member of the couple; and

        (c) any child or qualifying young person for whom the renter (or either joint renter) is responsible;

    [¹ "member of the armed forces" means a member of the regular forces or the reserve forces within the meaning of section 374 of the Armed Forces Act 2006;]

    "non-dependant" has the meaning given in paragraph 9(2);

    "provider of social housing" means—

        (a) a local authority;

        (b) a non-profit registered provider of social housing;

        (c) in relation to accommodation which is social housing, a profit-making registered provider of social housing;

        (d) a registered social landlord;

    "registered social landlord" means—

        (a) a body which is registered in the register maintained by the Welsh Ministers under Chapter 1 of Part 1 of the Housing Act 1996;

        (b) a body which is registered in the register maintained by the Scottish Housing Regulator under section 20(1) of the Housing (Scotland) Act 2010;

    "relevant payments" has the meaning given in paragraph 3;

    "the Rent Officers Order 2013" means the Rent Officers (Universal Credit Functions) Order 2013;

    "renter" means a single renter within the meaning of paragraph 1(2) or each of joint renters;

    "renter who requires overnight care" is to be understood in accordance with paragraph 12(3) to (5);

    "shared accommodation" has the meaning given in paragraph 27;

    "social housing" has the meaning given in sections 68 to 77 of the Housing and Regeneration Act 2008.

"Relevant payments" for purposes of this Schedule

2.362   **3.**—(1) "Relevant payments" means one or more payments of any of the following descriptions—

        (a) rent payments;

        (b) service charge payments.

    (2) "Rent payments", in relation to any calculation under Part 4 or 5 of this Schedule, has the meaning given in paragraph 2 of Schedule 1.

    (3) "Service charge payments"—

        (a) for the purposes of calculations under Part 4 of this Schedule, has the meaning given in paragraph 7 of Schedule 1;

(b) for the purposes of calculations under Part 5 of this Schedule, is to be understood in accordance with paragraphs 7 and 8 of Schedule 1.

PART 2

[[12] EXCEPTIONS] TO INCLUSION OF HOUSING COSTS ELEMENT

No housing costs element for 16 or 17 year old care leavers

4. Section 11(1) of the Act (housing costs) does not apply to any renter who is 16 or 17 years old and is a care leaver.

2.363

[[12] No housing costs element for certain renters aged at least 18 but under 22

4A. Section 11(1) of the Act does not apply to a renter who—

(a) is at least 18 but under 22 years old;

(b) falls within section 22 of the Act (claimants subject to all work-related requirements); and

(c) is a single person (or a member of a couple claiming as a single person).

2.364

Persons to whom paragraph 4A does not apply – general

4B.—(1) Paragraph 4A does not apply where—

(a) the renter is responsible for a child or a qualifying young person;

(b) the renter satisfies paragraph 29(2), (5)(a) or (c), (6), (7), (8) or (9) (renters excepted from shared accommodation), whether or not the renter is a person to whom Part 4 (private rented sector and temporary accommodation) applies;

(c) the renter meets the occupation condition in respect of temporary accommodation (within the meaning of paragraph 21);

(d) the renter is unable to live with their parents because—

    (i) the renter has no parent; or

    (ii) neither parent occupies accommodation as their home in Great Britain;

(e) in the opinion of the Secretary of State it is inappropriate for the renter to live with each of their parents, including (but not limited to) in circumstances where there would be a serious risk to the renter's physical or mental health, or the renter would suffer significant harm, if the renter lived with them;

(f) the renter's expected number of hours per week determined under regulation 88 (expected hours) is fewer than 35;

(g) regulation 99(3) or (4) (circumstances in which requirements must not be imposed) applies to the renter; or

(h) domestic violence has been inflicted on or threatened against the renter by the renter's partner or former partner or by a family member.

(2) In this paragraph, "domestic violence" and "family member" have the meanings given in regulation 98 (domestic violence).

2.365

Persons to whom paragraph 4A does not apply – periods of work

4C.—(1) Paragraph 4A does not apply to a renter in an assessment period where the renter's earned income is equal to or exceeds the amount that a person would be paid at the hourly rate set out in—

(a) unless paragraph (b) applies, regulation 4A(1)(b) of the National Minimum Wage Regulations; or

(b) where the renter was employed under a contract of apprenticeship on the last day of the assessment period, regulation 4A(1)(d) of the National Minimum Wage Regulations,

for 16 hours per week, converted to a net monthly amount by multiplying by 52 and dividing by 12.

(2) Paragraph 4A does not apply to a renter for a period of 6 consecutive months that begins on the most recent of the following days in respect of which the relevant condition in sub-paragraph (3) is met—

(a) the first day of the renter's first assessment period;

(b) the first day of an assessment period (which is not the renter's first assessment period) in which the renter's earned income is less than the threshold.

(3) The relevant condition is—

(a) in the case of sub-paragraph (2)(a), the renter's earned income was equal to or exceeded the threshold in each of the 6 calendar months ending before the calendar month in which the claim for universal credit was made;

(b) in the case of sub-paragraph (2)(b)—

    (i) the renter's earned income was equal to or exceeded the threshold in each of

2.366

the 6 assessment periods immediately preceding the day mentioned in sub-paragraph (2)(b); or

    (ii) where there are fewer than 6 assessment periods immediately preceding that day, the renter's earned income was equal to or exceeded the threshold in each of the 6 months comprised of:

  (aa) the assessment periods immediately preceding the day mentioned in sub-paragraph (2)(b); and

  (ab) the number of calendar months (ending before the calendar month in which the claim for universal credit was made) that are required to complete the 6 month period.

(4) In this paragraph—

"earned income" does not include income a person is treated as having by virtue of regulation 62 (minimum income floor);

"threshold" is the amount that a person would be paid at the hourly rate set out in—

    (a) unless paragraph (b) applies, regulation 4A(1)(b) of the National Minimum Wage Regulations;

    (b) where the renter was employed under a contract of apprenticeship for the duration of the 6 month period applicable under sub-paragraph (3), regulation 4A(1)(d) of the National Minimum Wage Regulations,

for 16 hours per week, converted to a net monthly amount by multiplying by 52 and dividing by 12.]

PART 3

GENERAL PROVISIONS ABOUT CALCULATION OF AMOUNT OF
HOUSING COSTS ELEMENT FOR RENTERS

Application of Part 3

2.367   **5.** This Part contains provisions of general application in calculating the amount of a renter's housing costs element under Part 4 or 5 of this Schedule.

Payments taken into account

Relevant payments to be taken into account

2.368   **6.**—(1) Where a renter meets the payment condition, liability condition and occupation condition in respect of one or more descriptions of relevant payment, each such description is to be taken into account for the purposes of the calculation under Part 4 or 5 of this Schedule.

(2) No account is to be taken of any amount of a relevant payment to the extent that all of the conditions referred to in sub-paragraph (1) are not met in respect of that amount.

(3) Any particular payment for which a renter is liable is not to be brought into account more than once, whether in relation to the same or a different renter (but this does not prevent different payments of the same description being brought into account in respect of an assessment period).

Relevant payments calculated monthly

2.369   **7.**—(1) Where any relevant payment is to be taken into account under paragraph 6, the amount of that payment is to be calculated as a monthly amount.

(2) Where the period in respect of which a renter is liable to make a relevant payment is not a month, an amount is to be calculated as the monthly equivalent, so for example—

    (a) weekly payments are multiplied by 52 and divided by 12;

  [⁷ (aa) two-weekly payments are multiplied by 26 and divided by 12;]

    (b) four-weekly payments are multiplied by 13 and divided by 12;

    (c) three-monthly payments are multiplied by 4 and divided by 12; and

    (d) annual payments are divided by 12.

(3) Where a renter is liable for relevant payments under arrangements that provide for one or more rent free periods, [⁷ subject to sub-paragraph (3A),] the monthly equivalent is to be calculated over 12 months by reference to the total number of relevant payments which the renter is liable to make in that 12 month period.

  [⁷ (3A) Where sub-paragraph (3) applies and the relevant payments in question are—

    (a) weekly payments, the total number of weekly payments which the renter is liable to make in any 12 month period shall be calculated by reference to the formula—

$$52 - RFP;$$

    (b) two-weekly payments, the total number of two-weekly payments which the renter is liable to make in any 12 month period shall be calculated by reference to the formula—

$$26 - RFP;$$

(c) four-weekly payments, the total number of four-weekly payments which the renter is liable to make in any 12 month period shall be calculated by reference to the formula—

$$13 - RFP;$$

where "RFP" is the number of rent free periods in the 12 month period in question.].

(4) "Rent free period" means any period in respect of which the renter has no liability to make one or more of the relevant payments which are to be taken into account under paragraph 6.

Room allocation

Size criteria applicable to the extended benefit unit of all renters

8.—(1) In calculating the amount of the renter's housing costs element under Part 4 or 5 of this Schedule, a determination is to be made in accordance with the provisions referred to in sub-paragraph (2) as to the category of accommodation which it is reasonable for the renter to occupy, having regard to the number of persons who are members of the renter's extended benefit unit (see paragraph 9).

2.370

(2) The provisions referred to in this sub-paragraph are the following provisions of this Schedule—
  (a) in respect of a calculation under Part 4, paragraphs 9 to 12 and 26 to 29;
  (b) in respect of a calculation under Part 5, paragraphs 9 to 12.

Extended benefit unit of a renter for purposes of this Schedule

9.—(1) For the purposes of this Schedule, the members of a renter's extended benefit unit are—

2.371

  (a) the renter (or joint renters);
  (b) any child or qualifying young person for whom the renter or either joint renter is responsible; and
  (c) any person who is a non-dependant.

(2) A person is a non-dependant if the person [⁶ normally] lives in the accommodation with the renter (or joint renters) and is none of the following—
  (a) a person within sub-paragraph (1)(a) or (b);
  (b) where the renter is a member of a couple claiming as a single person, the other member of the couple;
  (c) a foster child;
  (d) a person who is liable to make payments on a commercial basis in respect of the person's occupation of the accommodation (whether to the renter, joint renters or another person);
  (e) a person to whom the liability to make relevant payments is owed or a member of their household;
  (f) a person who has already been treated as a non-dependant in relation to a claim for universal credit by another person liable to make relevant payments in respect of the accommodation occupied by the renter.
[⁶ (g) a child or qualifying young person for whom no-one in the renter's extended benefit unit is responsible.]

(3) "Foster child" means a child in relation to whom the renter (or either joint renter) is a foster parent.

Number of bedrooms to which a renter is entitled

10.—(1) A renter is entitled to one bedroom for each of the following categories of persons in their extended benefit unit—

2.372

  (a) the renter (or joint renters);
  (b) a qualifying young person for whom the renter or either joint renter is responsible;
  (c) a non-dependant who is not a child;
  (d) two children who are under 10 years old;
  (e) two children of the same sex;
  (f) any other child.

(2) A member of the extended benefit unit to whom two or more of the descriptions in sub-paragraph (1) apply is to be allotted to whichever description results in the renter being entitled to the fewest bedrooms.

(3) In determining the number of bedrooms to which a renter is entitled, the following must also be taken into account—
  (a) the provisions of paragraph 11 as to treatment of periods of temporary absence of members of the renter's extended benefit unit;
  (b) any entitlement to an additional bedroom in accordance with paragraph 12;

(c) for the purpose of any calculation under Part 4 of this Schedule, the additional requirements in paragraphs 26 to 29.

Temporary absence of member of renter's extended benefit unit

2.373   **11.**—(1) A member of the renter's extended benefit unit who is temporarily absent from the accommodation occupied by the renter is to be included in a determination of the number of bedrooms to which the renter is entitled ("relevant determination") in the circumstances specified in sub-paragraphs (2) to (4).

(2) In the case of a child or qualifying young person, the circumstances specified in this sub-paragraph are that the relevant determination relates to any time—

(a) during the first 6 months of the absence of a child or qualifying young person for whom the renter is treated as not being responsible in accordance with regulation 4(6)(a) (child or qualifying young person looked after by local authority) where, immediately before the local authority started looking after them, the child or qualifying young person was included in the renter's extended benefit unit and the renter's award included the housing costs element;

(b) during the first 6 months of the absence of a child or qualifying young person for whom the renter is treated as not being responsible in accordance with regulation 4(6)(b) (child or qualifying young person is a prisoner) where—

(i) immediately before becoming a prisoner, the child or qualifying young person was included in the renter's extended benefit unit and the renter's award included the housing costs element, and

(ii) the child or qualifying young person has not been sentenced to a term in custody that is expected to extend beyond that 6 months; or

(c) before the renter or joint renter ceases to be responsible for a temporarily absent child or qualifying young person in accordance with regulation 4(7) (absence exceeding specified duration).

(3) In the case of a renter, the circumstances specified in this sub-paragraph are that the relevant determination relates to any time when—

(a) the temporary absence from Great Britain of the renter is disregarded in accordance with regulation 11(1) or (2); or

(b) the renter is a prisoner to whom regulation 19(2) (existing award includes housing costs when person becomes a prisoner) applies.

(4) In the case of a non-dependant, the circumstances specified in this sub-paragraph are that—

(a) the relevant determination relates to any time during a period specified in sub-paragraph (5); and

(b) immediately before the start of that period, the non-dependant was included in the renter's extended benefit unit and [² , in the circumstances specified in sub-paragraph (5)(a) to (c),] the renter's award included the housing costs element.

(5) The specified periods are—

(a) the first month of the non-dependant's temporary absence from Great Britain and, if the circumstances of the non-dependant are such as would be disregarded for the purposes of regulation 11(2) (death of a close relative), a further one month;

(b) the first 6 months of the non-dependant's temporary absence from Great Britain in the circumstances described in regulation 11(3)(a) (absence solely in connection with treatment for illness or physical or mental impairment);

(c) the first 6 months that the non-dependant is a prisoner where the non-dependant has not been sentenced to a term in custody that is expected to extend beyond that 6 months.

[³ (d) any period during which a non-dependant who is the son, daughter, step-son or step-daughter of a renter or joint renters is a member of the armed forces away on operations.]

(6) Any non-dependant who is temporarily absent from the accommodation occupied by the renter in circumstances other than those specified in sub-paragraphs (4) and (5) is not to be treated as being a member of the renter's extended benefit unit if that absence exceeds, or is expected to exceed, 6 months.

[⁶ **Additional room**

2.374   **12.**—[¹¹ (A1) A renter is entitled to an additional bedroom if one or more of the following persons satisfies the overnight care condition (see sub-paragraph (3))—

(a) the renter;

(b) a person in the renter's extended benefit unit;

(c) a child in respect of whom the renter satisfies the foster parent condition (see sub-paragraphs (4) and (5)).]

(1) A renter is entitled to an additional bedroom if they satisfy any of the following conditions—

(a) [¹¹ . . .]
(b) the foster parent condition [¹¹ . . .]; or
(c) the disabled child condition (see sub-paragraph (6)) [¹¹;
(d) the disabled person condition (see sub-paragraph (6A))].

[¹¹ (2) Sub-paragraphs (A1) and (1) apply subject to sub-paragraphs (8) and (9).]

(3) [¹¹ A person satisfies] the overnight care condition if—

(a) they are in receipt of—
  (i) the care component of disability living allowance at the middle or highest rate;
  (ii) attendance allowance; or
  (iii) the daily living component of personal independence payment;
(b) one or more persons who do not live in the renter's accommodation are engaged to provide overnight [¹¹ care for the person] and stay overnight in the accommodation on a regular basis; and
(c) overnight care is provided under arrangements entered into for that purpose.

(4) A renter satisfies the foster parent condition if the renter is—

(a) a foster parent; or
(b) an adopter with whom a child has been placed for adoption.

(5) For the purposes of sub-paragraph (4) "foster parent" includes a person who would be a foster parent, but for the fact that they do not currently have any child placed with them, provided that any period since the date when their last placement ended (or, if they have not yet had a child placed with them, since the date when they were approved to be a foster parent) does not exceed 12 months.

(6) A renter satisfies the disabled child condition if they or another member of their extended benefit unit are responsible for a child who would (but for the provisions of this paragraph) be expected to share a bedroom and that child is—

(a) in receipt of the care component of disability living allowance at the middle or highest rate; and
(b) by virtue of their disability, not reasonably able to share a room with another child.

[¹¹ (6A) A renter satisfies the disabled person condition if they would (but for the provisions of this paragraph) be expected to share a bedroom with a joint renter and—

(a) the renter is in receipt of—
  (i) the care component of disability living allowance at the middle or highest rate;
  (ii) attendance allowance at the higher rate;
  (iii) the daily living component of personal independence payment; and
(b) the renter is, by virtue of their disability, not reasonably able to share a bedroom with the joint renter.]

(7) [¹¹ . . .]

(8) Where a renter, or one or both of joint renters, satisfy the disabled child condition in relation to one or more children, they are entitled to as many additional bedrooms as are necessary to ensure that each such child has their own bedroom.

[¹¹ (9) The renter is, or joint renters are, entitled to one additional bedroom for each of the following that apply—

(a) one or more persons satisfy the overnight care condition;
(b) the renter, or one or both of joint renters, satisfies the foster parent condition;
(c) the renter, or one or both of joint renters, satisfies the disabled child condition; or
(d) the renter, or one or both of joint renters, satisfies the disabled person condition.]]

Housing cost contributions

Housing cost contributions

13.—(1) In calculating the amount of the housing costs element under Part 4 or 5 of this Schedule, a deduction is to be made in respect of each non-dependant who is a member of the renter's extended benefit unit.

(2) Paragraph (1) is subject to paragraphs 15 and 16.

(3) Any amount to be deducted under sub-paragraph (1) is referred to in this Schedule as a "housing cost contribution".

2.375

Amount of housing cost contributions

14.—(1) The amount of each housing cost contribution to be deducted under paragraph 13 is [¹⁴ £70.06].

2.376

(2) Deductions are not to be made until the amount has been determined which results from all other steps in the calculation required in relation to the renter under Parts 4 and 5 of this Schedule.

(3) Where the sum of all the housing cost contributions to be deducted in the renter's case exceeds the amount referred to in sub-paragraph (2)—

(a) the amount determined under this Schedule is to be reduced to nil; but

(b) no further reduction in respect of housing cost contributions is to be made from the renter's award.

Exempt renters

2.377
15.—(1) No deduction is to be made under paragraph 13 in the case of—

(a) any renter who is a single person to whom sub-paragraph (2) applies; or

(b) any joint renter where at least one joint renter is a person to whom sub-paragraph (2) applies.

(2) This sub-paragraph applies to—

(a) a person who is [⁹ . . .] blind;

(b) a person in receipt of the care component of disability living allowance at the middle or highest rate;

(c) a person in receipt of attendance allowance;

(d) a person in receipt of the daily living component of personal independence payment;

(e) a person who is entitled to a payment within paragraph (b), (c) or (d) but is not receiving it under, as the case may be—

(i) regulation 8 of the Social Security (Disability Living Allowance) Regulations 1991,

(ii) regulation 6 of the Social Security (Attendance Allowance) Regulations 1991,

(iii) regulation 21 of the Social Security (General Benefit) Regulations 1982, or

(iv) regulations under section 86 of the Act (payment of personal independence payment while a person is a hospital in-patient).

No deduction for housing cost contributions in respect of certain non-dependants

2.378
16.—(1) No deduction is to be made under paragraph 13 in respect of any non-dependant who is a member of the renter's extended benefit unit to whom sub-paragraph (2) applies.

(2) This sub-paragraph applies to—

(a) a person who is under 21 years old;

(b) a person in receipt of state pension credit;

(c) a person in receipt of the care component of disability living allowance at the middle or highest rate;

(d) a person in receipt of attendance allowance;

(e) a person in receipt of the daily living component of personal independence payment;

(f) a person who is entitled to a payment within paragraph (c), (d) or (e) but is not receiving it under, as the case may be—

(i) regulation 8 of the Social Security (Disability Living Allowance) Regulations 1991,

(ii) regulation 6 of the Social Security (Attendance Allowance) Regulations 1991,

(iii) regulation 21 of the Social Security (General Benefit) Regulations 1982, or

(iv) regulations under section 86 of the Act (payment of personal independence payment while a person is a hospital in-patient);

(g) a person in receipt of carer's allowance;

(h) a person who is a prisoner;

(i) a person who is responsible for a child under 5 years old.

[⁴ (j) a person who is a member of the armed forces away on operations who—

(i) is the son, daughter, step-son or step-daughter of a renter or joint renters, and

(ii) resided with the renter or joint renters immediately before leaving to go on operations and intends to return to reside with the renter or joint renters at the end of the operations.]

Calculations involving more than one accommodation

Single calculation for renter treated as occupying single accommodation

2.379
17.—(1) This paragraph applies to any renter where, under paragraph 4 of Schedule 3 (claimant housed in two dwellings by provider of social housing), two dwellings ("accommodation A" and "accommodation B") occupied by a renter are treated as the single accommodation in respect of which the renter meets the occupation condition.

(2) The amount of the renter's housing costs element is to be determined by a single calculation in respect of accommodation A and accommodation B as if they were one, taking account of—

(a) all relevant payments in respect of accommodation A and all relevant payments in respect of accommodation B; and

(b) the total number of bedrooms in accommodation A and accommodation B taken together.

(3) The single calculation is to be made under Part 5 of this Schedule in any case where—

(a) the renter's liability to make rent payments in respect of accommodation A and accommodation B is to a provider of social housing; and

(b) neither accommodation A nor accommodation B is temporary accommodation within the meaning of paragraph 21.

(4) In any other case, the single calculation is to be made under Part 4 of this Schedule.

Calculation where move to new accommodation delayed for adaptations for disabled person

18.—(1) Sub-paragraph (2) applies to any renter where, under paragraph 5 of Schedule 3 (moving home: adaptations to new home for disabled person), the renter meets the occupation condition in respect of both the new accommodation and the old accommodation.

2.380

(2) The amount of the renter's housing costs element under this Schedule is to be calculated as follows.

Step 1

Calculate an amount in accordance with Part 4 or Part 5 of this Schedule (as the case may be) in respect of both—

(a) the new accommodation; and

(b) the old accommodation.

Step 2

Add together the amounts determined in step 1.

Step 3

If a deduction was made for housing cost contributions in respect of both the new accommodation and the old accommodation, take the amount of the housing costs contributions deducted in respect of the new accommodation and add that to the amount resulting from step 2.

(3) In this paragraph, references to "the new accommodation" and "the old accommodation" are to be understood in accordance with paragraph 5 of Schedule 3.

Calculation where renter moves out because of reasonable fear of violence

19.—(1) Sub-paragraph (2) applies to any renter where, under paragraph 6(2) of Schedule 3 (claimant living in other accommodation because of reasonable fear of violence), the renter meets the occupation condition in respect of both the home accommodation and the other accommodation.

2.381

(2) The amount of the renter's housing costs element under this Schedule is to be calculated as follows:

Step 1

Calculate an amount in accordance with Part 4 or Part 5 of this Schedule (as the case may be) in respect of—

(a) the home accommodation; and

(b) the other accommodation.

Step 2

Add together the amounts determined in step 1.

Step 3

If a deduction was made for housing cost contributions in respect of both the home accommodation and the other accommodation—

(c) determine which accommodation the renter normally occupies as their home; and

(d) take the amount of the housing costs contributions deducted in respect of the accommodation not so occupied and add that to the amount resulting from step 2.

(3) In this paragraph, references to "the home accommodation" and "the other accommodation" are to be understood in accordance with paragraph 6 of Schedule 3.

Part 4

Private Rented Sector and Temporary Accommodation

Application of Part 4

2.382   20.—(1) This Part applies to—

(a) renters who are liable to make rent payments to a person other than a provider of social housing; and

(b) renters who meet the occupation condition in respect of temporary accommodation (see paragraph 21).

(2) Sub-paragraph (1) applies irrespective of whether renters are also liable to make service charge payments.

Meaning of "temporary accommodation"

2.383   21.—(1) Accommodation is temporary accommodation for the purposes of paragraph 20(1) (b) if it falls within Case 1 or Case 2.

(2) Case 1 is where—

(a) rent payments are payable to a local authority;

(b) the local authority makes the accommodation available to the renter—

(i) to discharge any of the local authority's functions under Part 3 of the Housing Act 1985, Part 7 of the Housing Act 1996 or Part 2 of the Housing (Scotland) Act 1987, or

(ii) to prevent the person being or becoming homeless within the meaning of Part 7 of the Housing Act 1996 or Part 2 of the Housing (Scotland) Act 1987; and

(c) the accommodation is not exempt accommodation.

(3) Case 2 is where—

(a) rent payments are payable to a provider of social housing other than a local authority;

(b) that provider makes the accommodation available to the renter in pursuance of arrangements made with it by a local authority—

(i) to discharge any of the local authority's functions under Part 3 of the Housing Act 1985, Part 7 of the Housing Act 1996 or Part 2 of the Housing (Scotland) Act 1987, or

(ii) to prevent the renter being or becoming homeless within the meaning of Part 7 of the Housing Act 1996 or Part 2 of the Housing (Scotland) Act 1987; and

(c) the accommodation is not exempt accommodation.

(4) Sub-paragraph (1) applies irrespective of whether the renter is also liable to make service charge payments.

The calculation of the housing costs element under this Part

The amount of housing costs element under this Part

2.384   22. The amount of the renter's housing costs element under this Part is to be calculated as follows:

Step 1

Determine—

(a) the amount of the renter's core rent; and

(b) the amount of the renter's cap rent,

and identify which is the lower amount (if both amounts are the same, that is the identified amount).

Step 2

Deduct the sum of the housing cost contributions (if any) under paragraph 13 from the amount identified in step 1.

The result is the amount of the renter's housing costs element calculated under this Part.

Core rent

2.385   23. Except where paragraph 24 applies, the renter's core rent is to be determined as follows:

Step 1

Determine the amount of each relevant payment to be taken into account under paragraph 6.

Step 2

Determine the period in respect of which each relevant payment is payable and, in accordance with paragraph 7, determine the amount of the payment in respect of a month.

Step 3

If there is more than one relevant payment, add together the amounts determined in step 2 in relation to all relevant payments.

The result is the renter's core rent.

Core rent for joint tenants

24.—(1) This paragraph applies where, in respect of the accommodation occupied by the renter, one or more persons other than the renter are liable to make relevant payments which are of the same description as those for which the renter is liable and which are to be taken into account under paragraph 6.

(2) The following steps are to be taken in order to determine the renter's core rent.

2.386

Step 1

Determine the total of all relevant payments referred to in sub-paragraph (1) for which the renter and others are liable in respect of the accommodation taken as a whole.

Step 2

Determine the period in respect of which each relevant payment is payable and, in accordance with paragraph 7, determine the amount of the payment in respect of a month.

Step 3

Add together all of the amounts determined in step 2 in relation to all relevant payments.

Step 4

Find the allocated amount in accordance with whichever of sub-paragraphs (3) to (5) applies in the renter's case.

The result is the renter's core rent.

(3) Where the only persons liable to make relevant payments are listed persons, the allocated amount is the amount resulting from step 3 in sub-paragraph (2).

(4) Where the persons liable for the relevant payments are one or more listed persons and one or more other persons, the allocated amount is to be found by the applying the formula—

$$\left(\frac{A}{B}\right) \times C$$

where—

"A" is the amount resulting from step 3 in sub-paragraph (2),

"B" is the total number of all persons (including listed persons) liable to make the relevant payments, and

"C" is the number of listed persons [5 liable to make relevant payments].

(5) If the Secretary of State is satisfied that it would be unreasonable to allocate the amount resulting from step 3 in sub-paragraph (2) in accordance with sub-paragraph (4), that amount is to be allocated in such manner as the Secretary of State considers appropriate in all the circumstances, having regard (among other things) to the number of persons liable and the proportion of the relevant payments for which each of them is liable.

Cap rent

25.—(1) The renter's cap rent is to be determined as follows.

2.387

Step 1

Determine the category of accommodation to which the renter is entitled under paragraphs 8 to 12 and 26 to 29.

Step 2

Having regard to the determination at step 1, determine the maximum allowable amount for the renter under sub-paragraph (2) or (4) (as the case may be).

The result is the renter's cap rent.

(2) The maximum allowable amount to be used in relation to the renter is the local housing allowance which applies at the relevant time to—

    (a) the broad rental market area in which the renter's accommodation is situated; and

    (b) the category of accommodation determined at step 1 as that to which the renter is entitled.

(3) But the maximum allowable amount in relation to the renter is to be determined under sub-paragraph (4) in any case where—

    (a) paragraph 4 of Schedule 3 (claimant housed in two dwellings by provider of social housing) applies to the renter; and

    (b) the maximum allowable amount determined under sub-paragraph (2) for the renter in relation to accommodation A and the amount so determined in relation to accommodation B are different (references to accommodation A and accommodation B are to be understood in accordance with paragraph 4 of Schedule 3); and

    (c) a single calculation is to be made in relation to the renter under paragraph 17 (renter treated as occupying single accommodation).

(4) In any such case, the maximum allowable amount to be used in making the single calculation required by paragraph 17—

    (a) is to be determined by reference to the accommodation for which the amount referred to in sub-paragraph (3)(b) is lower when the calculation is first made; and

    (b) is to continue to be determined by reference to that accommodation for so long as paragraph 4 of Schedule 3 applies to the renter in respect of the same accommodation A and the same accommodation B; and

    (c) is to be re-determined in accordance with paragraphs (a) and (b) on each occasion when the renter is re-housed in any other accommodation, provided that paragraph 4 of Schedule 3 continues to apply to the renter.

(5) In this paragraph—

"broad rental market area" means the broad rental market area determined under article 3 of the Rent Officers Order 2013;

"local housing allowance", in relation to a broad rental market area, means the amount determined by a rent officer for that area under article 4 of the Rent Officers Order 2013;

"relevant time" means the time at which the amount of the renter's housing costs element is calculated under paragraph 22.

Further provisions about size criteria for cases to which this Part applies

Four bedroom limit

2.388   **26.** In calculating the amount of a renter's housing costs element under paragraph 22, no renter is entitled to more than 4 bedrooms.

Specified renters entitled to shared accommodation only

2.389   **27.**—(1) In calculating the amount of a renter's housing costs element under paragraph 22, any specified renter (within the meaning of paragraph 28) is entitled to shared accommodation only.

(2) "Shared accommodation" means the category of accommodation specified in paragraph 1(a) of Schedule 1 to the Rent Officers Order 2013.

Meaning of "specified renters"

2.390   **28.**—(1) For the purposes of paragraph 27, "specified renter" means a renter in respect of whom all of the following conditions are met.

(2) The first condition is that the renter is a single person (or a member of a couple claiming as a single person) who—

    (a) is under 35 years old; and

    (b) is not an excepted person under paragraph 29.

(3) The second condition is that the renter is not responsible for any children or qualifying young persons.

(4) The third condition is that no person is a non-dependant in relation to the renter.

Renters excepted from shared accommodation

2.391   **29.**—(1) "Excepted person" means any renter ("E") who falls within any of sub-paragraphs (2) to (9).

[[10] (2) E is at least 18 but under 22 years old and was a care leaver (within the meaning of regulation 8) before reaching the age of 18.]

(3) [[10] . . .]

(4) E is at least 25 but under 35 years old and—

(a) has, for a total of at least 3 months (whether or not continuously), lived in one or more hostels for homeless people; and

(b) whilst E was living in such a hostel, was offered and has accepted services which the Secretary of State considers are intended to assist E to be rehabilitated or resettled within the community.

(5) E is under 35 years old and is in receipt of—

(a) the care component of disability living allowance at the middle or highest rate;

(b) attendance allowance; or

(c) the daily living component of personal independence payment.

(6) In relation to England and Wales, E is under 35 years old and is the subject of active multi-agency management pursuant to arrangements established by a responsible authority under section 325(2) of the Criminal Justice Act 2003 (arrangements for assessing etc. risks posed by certain offenders).

(7) In relation to Scotland, E is under 35 years old and is the subject of active multi-agency risk management pursuant to arrangements established by the responsible authorities under section 10(1) of the 2005 Act (arrangements for assessing and managing risks posed by certain offenders).

(8) In relation to Scotland, E is under 35 years old and—

(a) section 10(1) of the 2005 Act does not apply to E by reason only of the fact that section 10(1)(b) or (d) has not been brought fully into force; and

(b) E is considered by the Secretary of State to be a person who may cause serious harm to the public at large.

(9) In relation to Scotland, E is under 35 years old and—

(a) section 10(1) of the 2005 Act does not apply to E by reason only of the fact that section 10(1)(e) has not been brought fully into force; and

(b) by reason of an offence of which E has been convicted, E is considered by the Secretary of State to be a person who may cause serious harm to the public at large.

(10) In this paragraph—

"the 2005 Act" means the Management of Offenders etc. (Scotland) Act 2005;

"care home", "registered charity" and "voluntary organisation" have the meaning given in Schedule 1;

"hostel" means a building—

(a) in which there is provided, for persons generally or for a class of persons, domestic accommodation, otherwise than in separate and self-contained premises, and either board or facilities for the preparation of food adequate to the needs of those persons, or both; and

(b) which—

(i) is managed or owned by a provider of social housing other than a local authority, or

(ii) is operated other than on a commercial basis and in respect of which funds are provided wholly or in part by a government department or agency or a local authority, or

(iii) is managed by a voluntary organisation or a registered charity and provides care, support or supervision with a view to assisting those persons to be rehabilitated or resettled within the community; and

(c) which is not a care home;

"hostel for homeless people" means a hostel the main purpose of which is to provide accommodation together with care, support or supervision for homeless people with a view to assisting such persons to be rehabilitated or resettled within the community.

PART 5

SOCIAL RENTED SECTOR OTHER THAN TEMPORARY ACCOMMODATION

Application of Part 5

30.—(1) This Part—   2.392

(a) applies to renters who are liable to make rent payments to a provider of social housing; but

(b) does not apply to any renter who falls within paragraph 20(1)(b) (temporary accommodation).

(2) Sub-paragraph (1) applies irrespective of whether renters are also liable to make service charge payments.

Reduction in certain cases of amounts to be taken into account

Deduction from relevant payments of amounts relating to use of particular accommodation

2.393   **31.** In determining the amount of any relevant payment to be taken into account under paragraph 6, a deduction is to be made for any amount which the Secretary of State is satisfied—

    (a) is included in the relevant payment; but

    (b) relates to the supply to the accommodation of a commodity (such as water or fuel) for use by any member of the renter's extended benefit unit.

Power to apply to rent officer if relevant payments excessive

2.394   **32.**—(1) Sub-paragraph (2) applies where it appears to the Secretary of State that the amount of any relevant payment for which the renter is liable in respect of accommodation occupied by the renter is greater than it is reasonable to meet by way of the housing costs element under this Part.

(2) The Secretary of State may apply to a rent officer for a determination to be made as to the amount of the relevant payment by the officer in exercise of the officer's Housing Act functions.

(3) Sub-paragraph (4) applies in any case where a rent officer determines that a landlord might, at the time of the application under sub-paragraph (2), reasonably have expected to obtain a lower amount of the description of relevant payment referred to the rent officer.

(4) The lower amount determined by the rent officer is to be used in making the calculation under this Part, instead of the amount of the relevant payment for which the renter is liable, unless the Secretary of State is satisfied that it is not appropriate to use that lower amount.

The calculation of the housing costs element under this Part

The amount of housing costs element

2.395   **33.** The amount of the renter's housing costs element under this Part is to be calculated by reference to the formula—

$$S - HCC$$

where—

"S" is the amount resulting from whichever of paragraph 34 or 35 applies in the renter's case, and

"HCC" is the sum of the housing cost contributions (if any) under paragraph 13.

Determining the amount from which HCC deductions are to be made

2.396   **34.** Except where paragraph 35 applies, amount S referred to in paragraph 33 is to be found as follows:

Step 1

Determine which relevant payments are to be taken into account under paragraph 6 and determine the amount of each of them (applying paragraphs 31 and 32(3) and (4) as necessary).

Step 2

Determine the period in respect of which each relevant payment is payable and, in accordance with paragraph 7, determine the amount of the payment in respect of a month.

Step 3

If there is more than one relevant payment, add together the amounts determined in step 2 in relation to all relevant payments.

Step 4

Determine under paragraph 36(1) whether an under-occupation deduction is to be made and, if one is to be made, determine the amount of the deduction under paragraph 36(2) and deduct it from the amount resulting from step 2 or 3 (as the case may be).

The result is amount S from which the sum of the housing costs contributions are to be deducted under paragraph 33.

Determining the amount from which HCC deductions are to be made: joint tenants

35.—(1) This paragraph applies where, in respect of the accommodation occupied by the renter, one or more persons other than the renter is liable to make relevant payments which are of the same description as those for which the renter is liable and which are to be taken into account under paragraph 6.

(2) Amount S referred to in paragraph 33 is to be found as follows:

Step 1

Determine the total of all relevant payments referred to in sub-paragraph (1) for which the renter and others are liable in respect of the accommodation taken as a whole (applying paragraphs 31 and 32(3) and (4) as necessary).

Step 2

Determine the period in respect of which each relevant payment is payable and, in accordance with paragraph 7, determine the amount of the payment in respect of a month.

Step 3

Add together all of the amounts determined in step 2 in relation to all relevant payments.

Step 4

Find amount S in accordance with whichever of sub-paragraphs (3) to (5) applies in the renter's case.

The result is amount S from which the sum of the housing costs contributions are to be deducted under paragraph 33.

(3) Where the only persons liable to make relevant payments are listed persons, amount S is the amount resulting from step 3 in sub-paragraph (2) less the amount of the under-occupation deduction (if any) required by paragraph 36.

(4) Where the persons liable for the relevant payments are one or more listed persons and one or more other persons, amount S is to be found by the applying the formula—

$$\left(\frac{A}{B}\right) \times C$$

where—

"A" is the amount resulting from step 3 in sub-paragraph (2),

"B" is the total number of all persons (including listed persons) liable to make the relevant payments, and

"C" is the number of listed persons [5 liable to make relevant payments].

(5) If the Secretary of State is satisfied that it would be unreasonable to determine amount S in accordance with sub-paragraph (4), amount S is to be determined in such manner as the Secretary of State considers appropriate in all the circumstances, having regard (among other things) to the number of persons liable and the proportion of the relevant payments for which each of them is liable.

Under-occupancy deduction

36.—(1) A deduction for under-occupancy is to be made under this paragraph where the number of bedrooms in the accommodation exceeds the number of bedrooms to which the renter is entitled under paragraphs 8 to 12.

(2) Where a deduction is to be made, the amount of the deduction is to be determined by the formula—

$$A \times B$$

where—

"A"—

    (a) in relation to any deduction under paragraph 34, is the amount resulting from step 2 or 3 in that paragraph (as the case may be), or

    (b) in relation to any deduction under paragraph 35(3), is the amount resulting from step 3 in paragraph 35(2);

"B" is the relevant percentage.

(3) The relevant percentage is 14% in the case of one excess bedroom.

2.397

2.398

(4) The relevant percentage is 25% in the case of two or more excess bedrooms.

(5) No deduction for under-occupation is to be made in calculating the amount of the renter's housing costs element under this Part in any case to which regulation 26(4) to (6) (shared ownership) applies.

AMENDMENTS

1. Universal Credit (Miscellaneous Amendments) Regulations 2013 (SI 2013/803), reg.2(3)(a) (April 29, 2013).
2. Universal Credit (Miscellaneous Amendments) Regulations 2013 (SI 2013/803), reg.2(3)(b)(i) (April 29, 2013).
3. Universal Credit (Miscellaneous Amendments) Regulations 2013 (SI 2013/803), reg.2(3)(b)(ii) (April 29, 2013).
4. Universal Credit (Miscellaneous Amendments) Regulations 2013 (SI 2013/803), reg.2(3)(e) (April 29, 2013).
5. Social Security (Miscellaneous Amendments) (No.2) Regulations 2013 (SI 2013/1508), reg.3(10) (July 29, 2013).
6. Housing Benefit and Universal Credit (Size Criteria) (Miscellaneous Amendments) Regulations 2013 (SI 2013/2828), reg.4 (December 4, 2013).
7. Universal Credit and Miscellaneous Amendments Regulations 2014 (SI 2014/597) reg.2(13) (April 28, 2014).
8. Housing Benefit and Universal Credit (Supported Accommodation) (Amendment) Regulations 2014 (SI 2014/771) reg.2(3) (November 3, 2014).
9. Universal Credit and Miscellaneous Amendments (No.2) Regulations 2014 (SI 2014/2888) reg.3(1)(c) (November 26, 2014, or in the case of existing awards, the first assessment period beginning on or after November 26, 2014).
10. Universal Credit (Care Leavers and Looked After Children) Amendment Regulations 2016 (SI 2016/543) reg.3 (May 26, 2016).
11. Housing Benefit and Universal Credit (Size Criteria) (Miscellaneous Amendments) Regulations 2017 (SI 2017/213) reg.6 (Assessment periods beginning on or after April 1, 2017).
12. Universal Credit (Housing Costs Element for claimants aged 18 to 21) (Amendment) Regulations 2017 (SI 2017/652) reg.2(1) and (3) (April 1, 2017).
13. Social Security Benefits Up-rating Order 2017 (SI 2017/260) art.28(3) (Assessment periods beginning on or after April 10, 2017).

DEFINITIONS

"the Act"—see reg.2.
"assessment period"—see WRA 2012 ss.40 and 7(2) and reg.21.
"attendance allowance"—see reg.2.
"blind"—*ibid.*
"care leaver"—see regs 2 and 8.
"carer's allowance"—see reg.2.
"child"—see WRA 2012 s.40.
"claim"—*ibid.*
"claimant"—see WRA 2012 s.40.
"couple"—see WRA 2012 ss.39 and 40.
"disability living allowance"—see reg.2.
"disabled"—see WRA 2012 s.40.
"foster parent"—see reg.2.
"joint claimants"—see WRA 2012 s.40.
"local authority"—see reg.2.
"personal independence payment"—*ibid.*
"prisoner"—*ibid.*
"qualifying young person"—see WRA 2012 ss.40 and 10(5) and regs 2 and 5.
"registered as blind"—see reg.2.
"single person"—see WRA 2012 ss.40 and 1(2)(a).

GENERAL NOTE

Paras 1–7   **2.399**

This Schedule concerns the calculation of the housing costs element for "renters" (see para.1(2)). For the definition of "renter" see para.2. References to "joint renters" are to joint claimants who are renters (para.1(2)).

For a renter (or joint renters) to be entitled to a housing costs element under this Schedule, s/he must meet the payment, liability and occupation conditions in respect of one or more "relevant payments" (para.6(1) and (2)).

"Relevant payments" for the purpose of Sch.4 mean rent payments (for the meaning of rent payments see para.2 of Sch.1 and note the exclusions in para.3) and service charges (on which see para. 7 of Sch.1 in relation to service charge payments calculated under Pt.4 of this Schedule and paras 7 and 8 of Sch.1 in relation to service charge payments calculated under Pt.5 of this Schedule (para.3)). Relevant payments are calculated as a monthly amount (see para.7). Where a renter has the benefit of rent and/or service charge free periods (see the definition of "rent free period" in para.7(4)), the conversion to a monthly figure is based on a standard 52 week year (see para. 7(3) and the formula in para.7(3A)).

Paras 4–4C set out two exceptions in which there no housing costs element is to be included in the universal credit award.

The first (in para.4) applies to any 16 or 17 year old renter who is a care leaver (as defined in reg.8(4)).

The second, in para.4A, excludes single renters (including a member of a couple claiming as a single person) aged between 18 and 21 and are subject to all work-related requirements. It applies from April 1, 2017 but is subject to paras 4B and 4C and to the transitional provisions in regs 3 and 4 of the Universal Credit (Housing Costs Element for claimants aged 18 to 21) (Amendment) Regulations 2017 (SI 2017/252); see Part IVC below.

Para.4B provides that the housing costs element is to be included in a universal credit award a renter aged between 18 and 21 if the renter is responsible for a child or qualifying young person; if the renter is excepted from the shared accommodation by virtue or para.29 (other than para.29(4) which applies to former residents of hostels for homeless people and para.29(5)(b), which can only apply to people over 65); if s/he is occupying temporary accommodation as defined in para.21; if s/he is unable to live with her/his parents, either because s/he has no parent, or neither parent lives in Great Britain or because the Secretary of State (or, on appeal, a Tribunal) accepts that it is inappropriate for the renter to live with her/his parents; if the renter's expected number of hours is less than 35 per week (see reg.88) or falls within reg.99(3) or (4) (which provide that no work-related requirements are to be imposed on people who, for various reasons, including being temporarily unfit for work, or being in prison or in rehab, cannot be expected to engage with the labour market); or if, in certain circumstances s/he has been the victim of actual or threatened domestic violence.

The policy behind some of these exceptions is unclear. For example, it is unclear why a 21 year-old renter who is excluded from the housing costs element by para.4A should suddenly become eligible for it by attending a court or tribunal as a party to any proceedings or a witness and so fall within reg.99(3)(a). On the face of it, the provision would seem to mean that an 18-21 year old can become eligible for the housing costs element, at least for a period merely by appealing against the decision to exclude him/her, requesting an oral hearing of that appeal and attending it. That, presumably, cannot be correct and it may be the case that the rules about when changes of circumstance take effect mean that the exception will only apply in practice where the renter attends the court or tribunal for a period that falls within more than one assessment period. Similar points can be made about short periods of unfitness for work within reg.93(4) which are expressly limited to a maximum period of 14 days and therefore cannot last for a whole assessment period.

Para. 4C provides a further exception for renters aged between 18 and 21 whose earnings are equivalent to 16 hours a week at the applicable National Minimum Wage and a protected period of six months where renters have earned that amount for at least six months in the immediate past.

The transitional protection established by SI 2017/252 provides that the new rules introduced by the SI only apply if, to summarise, the universal credit award is administered under the digital service (aka full service) rules and computer system: see reg.3 of SI 2017/252.

There is also transitional protection for claimants who already had an award of universal credit that included the housing costs element before the restrictions on housing costs for 18-21 year-olds came into force and to people who were receiving housing benefit immediately before becoming entitled to universal credit: see reg.4(1) of SI 2017/252. The transitional protection lasts until the claimant's award of universal credit ceases to include the housing costs element for some other reason: see reg.4(2).

Part 3 of this Schedule contains general provisions, which apply to all calculations under the Schedule. The rules in Pt 4 apply to renters in the private sector or who occupy temporary accommodation. Part 5 applies to renters in the social rented sector.

A housing costs element for renters is normally paid to the claimant as part of his/her universal credit award. However, it can be paid to another person (e.g. the claimant's landlord) if this appears to the Secretary of State to be necessary to protect the interest of the claimant, his/her partner, a child or qualifying young person for whom the claimant or his/her partner is responsible or a severely disabled person in respect of whom the claimant receives a carer element (see reg.58(1) of the Claims and Payments Regulations 2013).

Note also reg.39(4) of the Decisions and Appeals Regulations 2013 which provides that if the Secretary of State considers that he does not have all the relevant information or evidence to decide what housing costs element to award, the decision will be made on the basis of the housing costs element that can immediately be awarded.

Paras 8–12 and 26–29

2.400

In order to calculate the amount of a renter's housing costs element, it is first necessary to decide the number of bedrooms that s/he is allowed under "the size criteria" (para.8). This depends on who counts as a member of the renter's "extended benefit unit".

The extended benefit unit comprises the renter, or joint renters, any child or qualifying young person (see reg.5) for whom the renter or either joint renter is responsible (see reg.4), and any non-dependant (para.9(1)).

A non-dependant is a person who normally lives in the renter's (or joint renters') accommodation and who is not excluded under para.9(2). There is no definition of "normally lives in the accommodation" but see the notes to reg.3(1) of the Income Support Regulations in Vol.II of this series on the general meaning of "residing with".

See paras 10–12 for the number of bedrooms allowed. Para.12 has been amended with effect from April 1, 2017 by SI 2017/213 to reflect the judgment of the Supreme Court in *R (Carmichael and Rourke) (formerly known as MA and Others) v Secretary of State for Work and Pensions* [2016] UKSC 58 that the previous law discriminated unlawfully against adult couples who cannot share a bedroom because of the disabilities of at least one member of the couple and renters who need an extra room to accommodate an overnight carer for a disabled child. Bedroom is not defined.

Note that in the case of renters in the private sector or who occupy temporary accommodation (see para.21 for the meaning of "temporary accommodation") the maximum number of bedrooms allowed is four (see para.26). There is no limit for renters in the social rented sector. In addition, in the case of private sector renters and those in temporary accommodation, the housing costs element for single claimants (including a member of a couple who is claiming as a single person: see reg.3(3)) aged under 35, with no children or qualifying young persons for whom they are responsible and no non-dependants, is restricted to the local housing allowance rate for one bedroom shared accommodation, unless they are exempt from this restriction (see paras 27–29).

Under para.10, a renter is allowed one bedroom for each of the categories of people in his/her extended benefit unit listed in sub-para.(1). If a person falls into more than one category, s/he is treated as in the category that results in the renter being allowed the lowest number of bedrooms (see sub-para.(2)). Paragraph F3112 ADM gives the following example of when sub-para.(2) might apply. A couple have four children, two boys aged 15 and 6 and two girls aged 12 and 8. The two boys could be allocated one room and the two girls one room under sub-para.(1)(e). Alternatively, having allocated the two girls one room under sub-para.(1)(e), the boys could be allocated one room each under sub-para.(1)(f). But as the first alternative results in a fewer number of bedrooms, that will be the number of bedrooms (two) that is allocated.

Note that joint renters (i.e. joint claimants: see para.1(2)) are allowed one bedroom but a non-dependant couple will be allocated one bedroom each (although a housing cost contribution (see paras 13–16) may be made in respect of each of them).

Under para.12, a renter is allowed additional bedrooms for each of the following conditions that s/he meets: (i) the overnight care condition (for the test for this see sub-para.(3)); (ii) the foster parent condition (see sub-paras (4) and (5) for the test); or (iii) the disabled child condition (see sub-para.(6) for the test). If the renter satisfies two or more of the conditions, the number of additional bedrooms allowed will be the total for both or all conditions (sub-para.(9)).

If both joint renters (i.e. joint claimants: see para.1(2)) satisfy the overnight care condition, they will only be allowed one additional bedroom (sub-para.(7)). (Note that the overnight care condition does not apply in the case of a disabled child who needs overnight care, but see the Court of Appeal's judgment in *Rutherford* below.) Similarly, only one additional bedroom will be allowed if both joint renters meet the foster parent condition (sub-para.(7)). However, if one or both of them satisfies both these conditions, one additional bedroom will be allowed in respect of each condition.

Example

Amy and Nick are foster parents to two children. Nick also meets the overnight care condition. They are allowed two additional bedrooms. One for satisfying the overnight care condition and one for satisfying the foster parent condition.

2.401

If the disabled child condition is met, one additional bedroom will be allowed for each disabled child (see sub-para.(8)).

Note that the disabled child condition applies if it is the renter (or joint renters) *or* a member of the renter's extended benefit unit (i.e. including a non-dependant) who is responsible for the disabled child. The requirement under sub-para.(6)(b) that the child is "not reasonably able to share a room with another child" will be a matter of judgment, depending on the circumstances.

See para.11 for the circumstances in which a renter, a child or qualifying young person or a non-dependant will continue to count for the purpose of deciding the number of bedrooms allowed, despite being temporarily absent. Note also the temporary absence rule for a claimant (or claimants) in para.9 of Sch.3.

See also reg.37 (run-on after a death). Under this provision if a joint claimant, a child or qualifying young person (see reg.5) for whom a claimant was responsible (see reg.4), a severely disabled person for whom a claimant had regular and substantial caring responsibilities (see reg.30) or a non-dependant who was a member of the claimant's extended benefit unit (para.9(1)(c) and (2)) dies the claimant's universal credit award continues to be calculated as if the person had not died for the assessment period in which the death occurred and the following two assessment periods. Thus if such a death affects the number of bedrooms a renter is allowed, it will not do so for that run-on period.

The application of the size criteria has caused considerable controversy, particularly since its extension to tenants in the social rented sector for the purposes of housing benefit on April 1, 2013 and the introduction of the "under-occupation deduction" (see below). A number of challenges have been made to the legality of the size criteria, including *Burnip, Trengove and Gorry v Secretary of State for Work and Pensions* [2012] EWCA Civ 629. This has led to some extension of the criteria—see para.12. However, this extension still does not provide, for example, for couples who are unable to share a bedroom due to disability, claimants who have mental health problems or separated parents who have shared caring responsibilities.

A further challenge by a number of claimants with differing circumstances was mounted in *R (on the application of MA & Ors) v Secretary of State for Work and Pensions and Ors* [2013] EWHC 2213. The claimants lost but the matter was pursued to the Court of Appeal. On February 21, 2014, the Court of Appeal dismissed the appeal, ruling that while the under-occupation deduction discriminated against people with disabilities the discriminatory effect of the policy was justified.

The claimants' further appeal was heard by the Supreme Court on February 29 to March 2, 2016, together with the Secretary of State's appeal against the Court of Appeal's judgment in *R (on the application of Rutherford) v Secretary of State for Work and Pensions; R (on the application of A) v Secretary of State for Work and Pensions* [2016] EWCA Civ 29. *Rutherford* concerned the application of the under occupation penalty where an extra bedroom was required because a severely disabled child needed respite night time care from carers in his own home. *A* was a victim of serious domestic violence who was living in a house under a Sanctuary Scheme, which had a "safe room" into which she could escape if necessary (it is not entirely clear why this was classed as a "bedroom" in the first place). It was accepted that reg.B13 of the Housing Benefit Regulations 2006 (SI 2006/213) constituted *prima facie* discrimination on the grounds of disability (*Rutherford*) and sex (*A*). In *Rutherford* the Court of Appeal held that the provision in reg.B13 for carers of disabled adults but not for carers of disabled children was not justified. In *A* the Court of Appeal referred to the distinction that had been drawn in *MA* between a broad class for whom discretionary housing payments were appropriate and a narrow class for whom they were not. *A* was within the narrow class covered by the decision in *Burnip*. The Secretary of State was therefore not entitled to decide that the better way of providing for *A* and those in a similar position was by way of discretionary housing payments, even though that would be a more flexible approach. At the time of writing the Supreme Court's judgment is not yet available.

Paras 13–16

2.402   After the calculation of the renter's (or joint renters') housing costs element has been carried out under Pt 4 or 5 of this Schedule, a deduction (referred to as a "housing cost contribution") is made for non-dependants, unless they, or the renter, or joint renters, are exempt. The deduction has been £69.37 since April 6, 2015 for each non-dependant who is a member of the renter's extended benefit unit. It was originally £68 and was then increased to £68.68 with effect from April 7, 2014 by art.24(3)(a) of the Social Security Benefits Up-rating Order 2014 (SI 2014/516).

Paras 17–19

2.403   See the notes to paras 4, 5 and 6 of Sch.3.

Paras 20–25

2.404   The housing costs element for private sector renters and those in temporary accommodation (as defined in para.21) is calculated by taking the lower of the renter's core rent and his/her cap rent and deducting from that amount any housing cost contributions (para.22).

Core rent

2.405   If the renter is solely liable to make the relevant payments, his/her core rent is the total of the monthly equivalents of the rent payments (as defined in para.2 of Sch.1) and service charges (see para.7 of Sch.1) that s/he is liable (or treated as liable) to pay (para.23).

If the renter is jointly liable with another person or persons to make the relevant payments, his/her core rent is worked out by taking the total of the monthly equivalents of the rent payments and service charges for which s/he and the other person(s) are liable for the whole accommodation and applying the following rules.

If the only people who are jointly liable are "listed persons" (as defined in para.2) (i.e. the renter, his/her partner and any child or qualifying young person for whom either of them is responsible), the renter's core rent is that total amount (para.24(3)). If the liability is with one or more people who are not listed persons, the total amount is divided by the number of people who are liable and multiplied by the number of listed persons who are liable to make the relevant payments (para.24(4)). This is the renter's core rent. If, however, the Secretary of State (and on appeal a tribunal) is satisfied that it would be unreasonable to apportion the liability in this way, it is to be apportioned in a way that is appropriate in the circumstances (para.24(5)). Paragraph F3197 ADM gives the following example of where such an adjustment might be appropriate. Two brothers are joint tenants of a three bedroom property. One brother has his daughter living with him and pays two thirds of the rent. The decision maker considers that this is reasonable and that the appropriate core rent for that brother is two thirds (not half) of the rent payable.

Cap rent

A renter's cap rent depends on the category of dwelling, i.e. how many bedrooms, s/he is allowed under the size criteria, subject to the four bedroom limit (see paras 8–12 and 26–29). His/her cap rent is the local housing allowance that applies at the time his/her housing costs element is calculated for that category of dwelling in the area in which s/he lives (para.25(1) and (2)). For how the cap rent is calculated if para.4 of Sch.3 (claimant housed in two dwellings by provider of social housing) applies, see the note to para.4 of Sch.3.

2.406

Paras 30–36

The housing costs element for social sector renters (other than those in temporary accommodation, as defined in para.21) is calculated as follows. First, a deduction is made from any relevant payments (as defined in para.6) of any amount that is for the supply of a commodity (e.g. water or fuel) to the accommodation for use by the renter or any member of his/her extended benefit unit (para.31). Secondly, if, on the application of the Secretary of State, a rent officer has determined that a landlord might reasonably expect to get a lower amount than the amount of the relevant payment the renter pays, that lower figure will be used in the calculation of the renter's housing costs element, unless the Secretary of State (or on appeal a tribunal) considers that it is not appropriate to use that lower amount (para.32). An example might be where the rent is higher because it includes payment for modifications made to enable a disabled person to live in the property (see para.F3253 ADM) but the wording of para.32(4) is quite wide and is not restricted to this type of situation. Note, however, that (like housing benefit) there is no right of appeal against "so much of a decision as adopts a decision of a rent officer . . ." (para.6 of Sch.3 to the Decisions and Appeals Regulations 2013).

2.407

Thirdly, if the number of bedrooms in the accommodation is more than the number the renter is allowed under paras 8–12, an "under-occupation deduction" will be made. The reduction is 14 per cent in the case of one excess bedroom and 25 per cent in the case of two or more excess bedrooms (see para.36).

If a renter is solely liable to make the relevant payments, this deduction will be made from the monthly equivalent of the total of the rent payments and service charges that s/he is liable (or treated as liable) to pay, as reduced in accordance with paras 31 and 32(3) and (4), if applicable (para.34, step 4).

If the renter is jointly liable with another person or persons to make the relevant payments, an under-occupancy deduction will only be made if the only people who are jointly liable are "listed persons" (as defined in para.2) (i.e. the renter, his/her partner and any child or qualifying young person for whom either of them is responsible) (para.35(3)). If the joint liability is with one or more people who are not listed persons, no under-occupancy deduction will be made (there is no reference to such a deduction in para.35(4)).

Note also that no under-occupancy deduction is made in the case of a shared ownership tenancy (see para.36(5)).

Under para.35(3)-(5) the rules for working out the amount of the renter's housing costs element if s/he is jointly liable with another person or persons to make the relevant payments are the same that apply for the purpose of working out a renter's core rent under Part 4 of this Schedule (see above).

Finally, a deduction will be made for any housing cost contribution (para.33).

Regulation 26(3)

SCHEDULE 5

HOUSING COSTS ELEMENT FOR OWNER-OCCUPIERS

PART I

GENERAL

Introduction

2.408   1.—(1) This Schedule contains provisions about claimants to whom regulation 26(3) applies.

(2) Claimants who fall within sub-paragraph (1) are referred to in this Schedule as "owner-occupiers" (and references to "joint owner-occupiers" are to joint claimants to whom regulation 26(3) applies).

(3) Part 2 of this Schedule sets out an exception to section 11(1) of the Act for certain owner-occupiers in whose case an award of universal credit is not to include an amount of housing costs element calculated under this Schedule.

(4) Part 3 of this Schedule provides for a qualifying period that is to elapse before an amount of housing costs element calculated under this Schedule may be included in an owner-occupier's award of universal credit.

(5) Part 4 provides for the calculation of the amount of housing costs element to be included under this Schedule in an owner-occupier's award of universal credit.

Interpretation

2.409   2. In this Schedule—

[¹ "alternative finance arrangements" has the meaning given in paragraph 6(2) of Schedule 1;]

"alternative finance payments" has the meaning given in paragraph 6 of Schedule 1;

"joint owner-occupier" has the meaning given in paragraph 1;

"loan interest payments" has the meaning given in paragraph 5 of Schedule 1;

"owner-occupier" means a single owner-occupier within the meaning of paragraph 1(2) or each of joint owner-occupiers;

"qualifying period" has the meaning given in paragraph 5;

[¹ "relevant date" means, in relation to an owner-occupier, the date on which an amount of housing costs element calculated under this Schedule is first included in the owner-occupier's award;]

"relevant payments" has the meaning given in paragraph 3;

"standard rate" has the meaning given in paragraph 12.

"Relevant payments" for purposes of this Schedule

2.410   3.—(1) "Relevant payments" means one or more payments of any of the following descriptions—

(a) owner-occupier payments;

(b) service charge payments.

(2) "Owner-occupier payments" has the meaning given in paragraph 4 of Schedule 1.

(3) "Service charge payments" is to be understood in accordance with paragraphs 7 and 8 of that Schedule.

346

PART 2

EXCEPTION TO INCLUSION OF HOUSING COSTS ELEMENT

No housing costs element where owner-occupier has any earned income

4.—(1) Section 11(1) of the Act (housing costs) does not apply to any owner-occupier in relation to an assessment period where—

    (a) the owner-occupier has any earned income; or

    (b) if the owner-occupier is a member of a couple, either member of the couple has any earned income.

  (2) Sub-paragraph (1) applies irrespective of the nature of the work engaged in, its duration or the amount of the earned income.

  (3) Nothing in this paragraph prevents an amount calculated under Schedule 4 from being included in the award of any claimant who falls within regulation 26(4) to (6) (shared ownership).

2.411

PART 3

NO HOUSING COSTS ELEMENT FOR QUALIFYING PERIOD

No housing costs element under this Schedule for qualifying period

5.—(1) An owner-occupier's award of universal credit is not to include any amount of housing costs element calculated under this Schedule until the beginning of the assessment period that follows the assessment period in which the qualifying period ends.

  (2) "Qualifying period" means a period of—

    (a) in the case of a new award, [⁶ 9] consecutive assessment periods in relation to which—

        (i) the owner-occupier has been receiving universal credit, and

        (ii) would otherwise qualify for the inclusion of an amount calculated under this Schedule in their award;

    (b) in any case where an amount calculated under this Schedule has for any reason ceased to be included in the award, [⁶ 9] consecutive assessment periods in relation to which the owner-occupier would otherwise qualify for the inclusion of an amount calculated under this Schedule in their award.

  (3) Where, before the end of a qualifying period, an owner-occupier for any reason ceases to qualify for the inclusion of an amount calculated under this Schedule—

    (a) that qualifying period stops running; and

    (b) a new qualifying period starts only when the owner-occupier again meets the requirements of sub-paragraph (2)(a) or (b).

2.412

Application of paragraph 5: receipt of JSA and ESA

6.—(1) This paragraph applies to any owner-occupier who immediately before the commencement of an award of universal credit is entitled to—

    (a) a jobseeker's allowance; or

    (b) an employment and support allowance.

  (2) In determining when the qualifying period in paragraph 5 ends in relation to the owner-occupier, any period that comprises only days on which the owner-occupier was receiving a benefit referred to in sub-paragraph (1) may be treated as if it were the whole or part of one or more assessment periods, as determined by the number of days on which any such benefit was received.

2.413

Application of paragraph 5: joint owner-occupiers ceasing to be a couple

7.—(1) This paragraph applies where—

    (a) an award of universal credit to joint owner-occupiers is terminated because they cease to be a couple;

    (b) a further award is made to one of them (or to each of them); and

    (c) in relation to the further award (or in relation to each further award), the occupation condition is met in respect of the same accommodation as that occupied by the joint owner-occupiers as their home.

  (2) In determining when the qualifying period in paragraph 5 ends in relation to the further award (or each further award), the whole or part of any assessment period which would have counted in relation to the award that is terminated is to be carried forward and taken into account in relation to the further award (or each further award).

2.414

(3) But where, immediately before the joint owner-occupiers' award was terminated, an amount of housing costs element calculated under this Schedule was already included in the award, no qualifying period under paragraph 5 applies to the owner-occupier in relation to the commencement of the further award (or each further award).

(4) For the purposes of sub-paragraph (1)(b), it is irrelevant whether the further award—

    (a) is made on a claim; or

    (b) by virtue of regulation 9(6) of the Universal Credit, Personal Independence Payment, Jobseeker's Allowance and Employment and Support Allowance (Claims and Payments) Regulations 2013 is made without a claim.

PART 4

CALCULATION OF AMOUNT OF HOUSING COSTS ELEMENT FOR OWNER-OCCUPIERS

Payments to be taken into account

2.415   **8.**—(1) Where an owner-occupier meets the payment condition, liability condition and occupation condition in respect of one or more relevant payments and the qualifying period has ended, each of the relevant payments is to be taken into account for the purposes of the calculation under this Part.

(2) No account is to be taken of any amount of a relevant payment to the extent that the conditions referred to in sub-paragraph (1) are not met in respect of that amount.

(3) Any particular payment for which an owner-occupier is liable is not to be brought into account more than once, whether in relation to the same or a different owner-occupier (but this does not prevent different payments of the same description being brought into account in respect of an assessment period).

The amount of housing costs element

2.416   **9.** The amount of the owner-occupier's housing costs element under this Schedule is the aggregate of the amounts resulting from paragraphs 10, 11 and 13 in respect of all relevant payments which are to be taken into account under paragraph 8.

Amount in respect of interest on loans

2.417   **10.**—(1) This paragraph provides for the calculation of the amount to be included in the owner-occupier's housing costs element under this Schedule in respect of relevant payments which are loan interest payments.

(2) Subject to sub-paragraphs (3) to (5), the amount in respect of the loan or loans to which the payments relate is to be calculated as follows.

Step 1

Determine the amount of the capital for the time being owing in connection with each loan.

Step 2

If there is more than one loan, add together the amounts determined in step 1.

Step 3

Identify which is the lower of these two amounts—

    (a) the amount resulting from step 1 or 2 (as the case may be); and

    (b) £200,000,

and, if both amounts are the same, that is the identified amount.

Step 4

Apply the formula—

$$\frac{(A \times SR)}{12}$$

where—

"A" is the amount identified in step 3, and

"SR" is the standard rate that applies at the date of the calculation (see paragraph 12).

The result is the amount to be included under this Schedule in respect of loan interest payments.

(3) In the application of sub-paragraph (2) to a loan (or any part of a loan) which was taken out for the purpose of making necessary adaptations to the accommodation to meet the disablement needs of a person specified in paragraph 5 of Schedule 3—

    (a) the loan (or the part of the loan) is to be disregarded for the purposes of steps 2 and 3; and

    (b) "A" in step 4 is to be read as the amount resulting from step 1 in respect of the loan (or the sum of those amounts if there is more than one loan taken out for the purpose of making such adaptations) plus the amount (if any) resulting from step 3 in relation to any other loan or loans.

(4) Any variation in the amount of capital for the time being owing in connection with a loan is not to be taken into account after the relevant date until such time as the Secretary of State recalculates the amount under this Schedule by reference to the amount of capital owing in connection with the loan—

    (a) on the first anniversary of the relevant date; or

    (b) in respect of any variation after the first anniversary, on the next anniversary which follows the date of the variation.

(5) [^{2} . . .]

Amount in respect of alternative finance arrangements

    11.—(1) This paragraph provides for the calculation of the amount to be included in the owner-occupier's housing costs element under this Schedule in respect of relevant payments which are alternative finance payments.   **2.418**

(2) The amount in respect of the alternative finance arrangements to which the payments relate is to be calculated as follows.

Step 1

Determine the purchase price of the accommodation to which the alternative finance payments relate.

Step 2

Identify which is the lower of these two amounts—

    (a) the amount resulting from Step 1; and

    (b) £200,000,

and, if both amounts are the same, that is the identified amount.

Step 3

Apply the formula—

$$\frac{(A \times SR)}{12}$$

where—

"A" is the amount identified in step 2, and

"SR" is the standard rate that applies at the date of the calculation (see paragraph 12).

The result is the amount to be included under this Schedule in respect of alternative finance payments.

[^{3} (3) "Purchase price" means the price paid by a party to the alternative finance arrangements other than the owner-occupier in order to acquire the interest in the accommodation to which those arrangements relate less—

    (a) the amount of any initial payment made by the owner-occupier in connection with the acquisition of that interest; and

    (b) the amount of any subsequent payments made by the owner-occupier before the relevant date to another party to the alternative finance arrangements which reduce the amount owed by the owner-occupier under the alternative finance arrangements.

(4) Any variation in the amount for the time being owing in connection with alternative finance arrangements is not to be taken into account after the relevant date until such time as the Secretary of State recalculates the amount under this Schedule by reference to the amount that is owing in connection with the alternative finance arrangements—

    (a) on the first anniversary of the relevant date; or

    (b) in respect of any variation after the first anniversary, on the next anniversary which follows the date of the variation.]

Standard rate to be applied under paragraphs 10 and 11

    12.—(1) The standard rate is the average mortgage rate published by the Bank of England which, immediately before this Schedule comes into force, has effect for the purposes of paragraph 12 of Schedule 3 to the Income Support (General) Regulations 1987 (which makes provision as to the standard rate to be used in determining amounts applicable to a claimant in respect of income support).   **2.419**

(2) The standard rate is to be varied each time that sub-paragraph (3) applies.

(3) This sub-paragraph applies when, on any reference day, the Bank of England publishes an average mortgage rate which differs by [⁴ 0.5 percentage points] or more from the standard rate that applies on that reference day (whether it applies by virtue of sub-paragraph (1) or by virtue of a previous application of this sub-paragraph).

(4) The average mortgage rate published on that reference day then becomes the new standard rate in accordance with sub-paragraph (5).

(5) Any variation in the standard rate by virtue of sub-paragraphs (2) to (4) comes into effect—

    (a) for the purposes of sub-paragraph (3), on the day after the reference day referred to in sub-paragraph (4);

    (b) for the purpose of calculating the amount of housing costs element to be included under this Schedule in an owner-occupier's award, on the day specified by the Secretary of State for that purpose.

(6) At least 7 days before a variation of the standard rate comes into effect under sub-paragraph (5)(b), the Secretary of State must arrange for notice to be published on a publicly accessible website of—

    (a) the new standard rate; and

    (b) the day specified in relation to that rate under sub-paragraph (5)(b).

(7) In this paragraph—

"average mortgage rate" means the effective interest rate (non-seasonally adjusted) of United Kingdom resident banks and building societies for loans to households secured on dwellings published by the Bank of England in respect of the most recent period specified for that rate at the time of publication;

"reference day" means any day falling on or after the date on which this Schedule comes into force.

Amount in respect of service charge payments

2.420   **13.**—(1) This paragraph provides for the calculation of the amount to be included in the owner-occupier's housing costs element under this Schedule in respect of relevant payments which are service charge payments.

(2) The amount in respect of the service charge payments is to be calculated as follows.

Step 1

Determine the amount of each service charge payment.

Step 2

Determine the period in respect of which each service charge payment is payable and determine the amount of the payment in respect of a month (see sub-paragraphs (3) and (4)).

Step 3

If there is more than one service charge payment, add together the amounts determined in step 2.

The result is the amount to be included under this Schedule in respect of service charge payments.

(3) Where the period in respect of which an owner-occupier is liable to make a service charge payment is not a month, an amount is to be calculated as the monthly equivalent, so for example—

    (a) weekly payments are multiplied by 52 and divided by 12;

  [⁵ (aa) two-weekly payments are multiplied by 26 and divided by 12;]

    (b) four-weekly payments are multiplied by 13 and divided by 12;

    (c) three-monthly payments are multiplied by 4 and divided by 12; and

    (d) annual payments are divided by 12.

(4) Where an owner-occupier is liable for service charge payments under arrangements that provide for one or more service charge free periods, [⁵ subject to sub-paragraph (4A),] the monthly equivalent is to be calculated over 12 months by reference to the total number of service charge payments which the owner-occupier is liable to make in that 12 month period.

  [⁵ (4A) Where sub-paragraph (4) applies and the service charge payments in question are—

    (a) weekly payments, the total number of weekly service charge payments which the owner-occupier is liable to make in any 12 month period shall be calculated by reference to the formula—

$$52 - SCFP;$$

(b) two-weekly payments, the total number of two-weekly service charge payments which the owner-occupier is liable to make in any 12 month period shall be calculated by reference to the formula—

$$26 - SCFP;$$

(c) four weekly payments, the total number of four-weekly service charge payments which the owner-occupier is liable to make in any 12 month period shall be calculated by reference to the formula—

$$13 - SCFP;$$

where "SCFP" is the number of service charge free periods in the 12 month period in question.]

(5) "Service charge free period" means any period in respect of which the owner-occupier has no liability to make one or more of the service charge payments which are to be taken into account under paragraph 8.

AMENDMENTS

1. Universal Credit and Miscellaneous Amendments Regulations 2014 (SI 2014/597) reg.2(14)(a) (April 28, 2014).

2. Universal Credit and Miscellaneous Amendments Regulations 2014 (SI 2014/597) reg.2(14)(b) (April 28, 2014).

3. Universal Credit and Miscellaneous Amendments Regulations 2014 (SI 2014/597) reg.2(14)(c) (April 28, 2014).

4. Universal Credit and Miscellaneous Amendments Regulations 2014 (SI 2014/597) reg.2(14)(d) (April 28, 2014).

5. Universal Credit and Miscellaneous Amendments Regulations 2014 (SI 2014/597) reg.2(14)(e) (April 28, 2014).

6. Social Security (Housing Costs Amendments) Regulations 2015 (SI 2015/1647) reg.5(2) (April 1, 2016). The amendment is subject to the saving provision in reg.8 of SI 2015/1647 (see Pt IV).

DEFINITIONS

"the Act"—see reg.2.
"alternative finance arrangements"–see Sch.1, para.6(1).
"alternative finance payments"–see Sch.1, para.6(2).
"assessment period"—see WRA 2012, ss.40 and 7(2) and reg.21.
"claim"—see WRA 2012, s.40.
"claimant"—*ibid.*
"couple"—see WRA 2012, ss.39 and 40.
"earned income"—see reg.2.
"employment and support allowance"—*ibid.*
"jobseeker's allowance"—*ibid.*
"personal independence payment"—*ibid.*

GENERAL NOTE

Paras 1–4   2.421

This Schedule concerns the calculation of the housing costs element for "owner-occupiers" (see para.1(2)). For the definition of "owner-occupier" see para.2. References to "joint owner-occupiers" are to joint claimants who are owner-occupiers (para.1(2)).

For an owner-occupier (or joint owner-occupier) to be entitled to a housing costs element under this Schedule, s/he must meet the payment, liability and occupation conditions in respect of one or more "relevant payments" (as defined in para.3) and the qualifying period (see paras 5–7) must have ended.

"Relevant payments" for the purposes of Sch.5 are owner-occupier payments (for the meaning of owner-occupier payments see para.4 of Sch.1) and service charges (on which see paras 7 and 8 of Sch.1). If the claimant (or claimants) is only liable for service charges payments, these will be calculated under this Schedule (see reg.26(3)). But if the claimant has a shared ownership tenancy, any service charges are calculated in accordance with Sch.4 (reg.26(5)).

Note the significant exclusion in para.4 from entitlement to a housing costs element under Sch.5. If an owner-occupier, or if s/he is a member of a couple, either member of the couple, has *any* earned income in an assessment period (i.e. month), s/he will not be entitled to a housing costs element in that assessment period. However, in the case of a shared ownership tenancy, rent payments and service charges can still be met (para.4(3)).

Paras 5–7

2.422 There is a waiting period (referred to as "a qualifying period") for owner-occupier and service charges payments. In the case of a new award of universal credit, a housing costs element cannot be included until there have been nine consecutive assessment periods (i.e. months) during which the owner-occupier has been receiving universal credit *and* would otherwise have qualified for a housing costs element under Sch.5 (para.5(2)(a)). A housing costs element is included from the start of the next assessment period. If, once awarded, there is a break in entitlement to a housing costs element under Sch.5 (e.g. because of earnings), the owner-occupier has to serve a further nine consecutive months during which s/he would otherwise qualify for a housing costs element before s/he can be awarded a housing costs element under Sch.5 again (para.5(2)(b)). This applies even if the owner-occupier continues to be entitled to universal credit during the break in entitlement to a housing costs element under Sch.5. If during a waiting period an owner-occupier ceases to qualify for a housing costs element under Sch.5, that waiting period ends and a new waiting period will have to be served (para.5(3)).

Note that before April 1, 2016 the waiting period under para.5(2)(a) and (b) was only three consecutive assessment periods. The amendment which increased the waiting period to nine months is subject to a saving provision (see reg.8 of the Social Security (Housing Costs Amendments) Regulations 2015 in Pt IV of this Volume). The effect of the saving provision in relation to universal credit is that for those claimants who are entitled, or treated as entitled, to one or more relevant benefits (i.e., income support, old style JSA, old style ESA or universal credit) for a continuous period which includes March 31, 2016, the form of reg.5(2)(a) and (b) and of reg. 29 of the Universal Credit (Transitional) Regulations 2014 that were in force before the April 1, 2016 amendments continues to have effect. So for claimants who are in a waiting period on March 31, 2016 the waiting period for a housing costs element remains three consecutive assessment periods.

Paragraphs 6 and 7 contain exceptions to the rule in para.5.

If immediately before the owner-occupier's award of universal credit began, s/he was entitled to new style JSA or new style ESA, the days that s/he was only receiving one of these benefits can count towards the waiting period (para.6).

Under para.7, if a universal credit award made to joint owner-occupiers comes to an end because they have ceased to be a couple, and a further award is made to one of them who continues to occupy the same accommodation as they did when they were a couple, the further award will include a housing costs element under Sch.5 without a waiting period if a housing costs element was included in the joint award. If a housing costs element was not yet included in the joint award, any assessment period, or part of an assessment period, which counted towards the waiting period under the joint award counts towards the waiting period for the new award. If both members of the former couple remain in the same accommodation and both claim and are awarded universal credit again, this provision will apply to both of them.

The waiting period may also be extinguished or reduced under reg.29 of the Transitional Provisions Regulations 2014, which applies where in the one month before the claim for universal credit was made, or treated as made, the owner occupier, or his/her partner or former partner, was entitled to income support, old style JSA or old style ESA that included help with housing costs or did not yet do so only because a waiting period was being served.

Paras 8–13

There is an upper limit of £200,000 for eligible loans (see para.10(2), step 3) and **2.423** for the purchase price (defined in para.11(3)) of the accommodation and para.6(2) of Sch.1 in the case of alternative finance arrangements (see para.11(2), step 2). See para.2 and para.6(2) of Sch.1 for the definition of "alternative finance arrangements".

However, if a loan (or part of a loan) was taken out to make necessary adaptations to the accommodation to meet the disablement needs of the claimant (or claimants: s.40 WRA 2012) or any child or qualifying young person for whom the claimant (or either joint claimant) is responsible, that loan (or part of the loan) is disregarded in applying the £200,000 limit (para.10(3)). The person with disablement needs must be in receipt of the middle or highest rate of the care component of disability living allowance, the daily living component of personal independence payment (either rate), attendance allowance or armed forces independence payment (see the definition of "attendance allowance" in reg.2 which includes armed forces independence payment).

To calculate the housing costs element for loan interest payments, the amount of the capital outstanding on the eligible loan or loans (subject to the £200,000 limit) is multiplied by the standard rate (currently (in July 2016) 3.12 per cent) (para.10(2), steps 3 and 4). If the £200,000 limit applies, the housing costs element will also include loan interest payments on any loan (or part of a loan) for adaptations for disablement needs on top of loan interest payments on the £200,000 (para.10(3)).

In the case of alternative finance arrangements, the housing costs element is the "purchase price" of the accommodation (subject to the £200,000 limit) multiplied by the standard rate (para.11(2)). The "purchase price" of the accommodation is the price paid by a party to the alternative finance arrangements, other than the owner-occupier, to acquire an interest in the accommodation, minus (i) the amount of any initial payment made by the owner-occupier in acquiring that interest; and (ii) any subsequent payment by the owner-occupier made before the relevant date which reduces the amount owed by the owner-occupier under the alternative finance arrangements (para.11(3)). The relevant date is the date on which an amount for the housing costs element is first included in the owner-occupier's award (see para.2). Under para.11(4) variations in the amount owing under such alternative finance arrangements are taken into account on an annual basis, in the same way as for standard mortgages (on which see para.10(4)).

The amount for service charges that can be included in an owner-occupier's housing costs element is the monthly equivalent of the actual service charge payment or payments (see para.13). Where the owner-occupier has the benefit of service charge free periods (defined in para.13(5)), the conversion to a monthly figure is based on a standard 52 week year (see para. 13(4) and the formula in para.13(4A)).

Note:

- No "housing cost contribution" for a non-dependant is made in the case of amounts awarded under Sch.5 (this is to be contrasted with the position under income support, old style JSA and old style ESA).

- Any increase, or decrease, in the amount of a loan, or in the amount owing under alternative finance arrangements, during the currency of an award is only taken into account from the anniversary date (see paras 10(4) and 11(4) respectively). But if a *new* (i.e. additional) loan is taken out that is secured on the home (or *additional* alternative finance arrangements are made), arguably that is a change of circumstances (rather than a variation in the amount owing) and so should take effect in accordance with Part III of Sch.1 to the Decisions and Appeals Regulations 2013).

- A housing costs element that is awarded in respect of payments of interest on a loan will be paid direct to the lender (see reg.59 of, and Sch.5 to, the Claims and Payments Regulations 2013).

- Under reg.39(4) of the Decisions and Appeals Regulations 2013, if the Secretary of State considers that he does not have all the relevant information or evidence to decide what housing costs element to award, the decision will be made on the basis of the housing costs element that can immediately be awarded.

Regulation 39(2) and(3)

SCHEDULE 6

ASSESSMENT OF WHETHER A CLAIMANT HAS LIMITED CAPABILITY FOR WORK

PART I

2.424

PHYSICAL DISABILITIES

(1)	(2)		(3)
Activity	Descriptors		Points
1. Mobilising unaided by another person with or without a walking stick, manual wheelchair or other aid if such aid is normally or could reasonably be worn or used.	1 (a)	Cannot, unaided by another person, either: (i) mobilise more than 50 metres on level ground without stopping in order to avoid significant discomfort or exhaustion; or (ii) repeatedly mobilise 50 metres within a reasonable timescale because of significant discomfort or exhaustion.	15
	(b)	Cannot, unaided by another person, mount or descend two steps even with the support of a handrail.	9
	(c)	Cannot, unaided by another person, either: (i) mobilise more than 100 metres on level ground without stopping in order to avoid significant discomfort or exhaustion; or (ii) repeatedly mobilise 100 metres within a reasonable timescale because of significant discomfort or exhaustion.	9
	(d)	Cannot, unaided by another person, either: (i) mobilise more than 200 metres on level ground without stopping in order to avoid significant discomfort or exhaustion; or (ii) repeatedly mobilise 200 metres within a reasonable timescale because of significant discomfort or exhaustion.	6
	(e)	None of the above applies.	0
2. Standing and sitting.	2 (a)	Cannot move between one seated position and another seated position which are located next to one another without receiving physical assistance from another person.	15
	(b)	Cannot, for the majority of the time, remain at a work station: (i) standing unassisted by another person (even if free to move around);	9

(1)	(2)	(3)
Activity	Descriptors	Points
	(ii) sitting (even in an adjustable chair); or (iii) a combination of paragraphs (i) and (ii), for more than 30 minutes, before needing to move away in order to avoid significant discomfort or exhaustion.	
	(c) Cannot, for the majority of the time, remain at a work station: (i) standing unassisted by another person (even if free to move around); (ii) sitting (even in an adjustable chair); or (iii) a combination of paragraphs (i) and (ii), for more than an hour before needing to move away in order to avoid significant discomfort or exhaustion.	6
	(d) None of the above applies.	0
3. Reaching.	3 (a) Cannot raise either arm as if to put something in the top pocket of a coat or jacket.	15
	(b) Cannot raise either arm to top of head as if to put on a hat.	9
	(c) Cannot raise either arm above head height as if to reach for something.	6
	(d) None of the above applies.	0
4. Picking up and moving or transferring by the use of the upper body and arms.	4 (a) Cannot pick up and move a 0.5 litre carton full of liquid.	15
	(b) Cannot pick up and move a one litre carton full of liquid.	9
	(c) Cannot transfer a light but bulky object such as an empty cardboard box.	6
	(d) None of the above applies.	0
5. Manual dexterity.	5 (a) Cannot press a button (such as a telephone keypad) with either hand or cannot turn the pages of a book with either hand.	15
	(b) Cannot pick up a £1 coin or equivalent with either hand.	15
	(c) Cannot use a pen or pencil to make a meaningful mark with either hand.	9
	(d) Cannot single-handedly use a suitable keyboard or mouse.	9
	(e) None of the above applies.	0
6. Making self understood through speaking, writing, typing, or other means which are normally or could reasonably be used, unaided by another person.	6 (a) Cannot convey a simple message, such as the presence of a hazard.	15
	(b) Has significant difficulty conveying a simple message to strangers.	15
	(c) Has some difficulty conveying a simple message to strangers.	6
	(d) None of the above applies.	0
7. Understanding communication by:	7 (a) Cannot understand a simple message, such as the location	15

(1)	(2)	(3)
Activity	Descriptors	Points
(i) verbal means (such as hearing or lip reading) alone; (ii) non-verbal means (such as reading 16 point print or Braille) alone; or	of a fire escape, due to sensory impairment.	
	(b) Has significant difficulty understanding a simple message from a stranger due to sensory impairment.	15
	(c) Has some difficulty understanding a simple message from a stranger due to sensory impairment.	6
(iii) a combination of sub-paragraphs (i) and (ii), using any aid that is normally or could reasonably be used, unaided by another person.	(d) None of the above applies.	0
8. Navigation and maintaining safety using a guide dog or other aid if either or both are normally used or could reasonably be used.	8 (a) Unable to navigate around familiar surroundings, without being accompanied by another person, due to sensory impairment.	15
	(b) Cannot safely complete a potentially hazardous task such as crossing the road, without being accompanied by another person, due to sensory impairment.	15
	(c) Unable to navigate around unfamiliar surroundings, without being accompanied by another person, due to sensory impairment.	9
	(d) None of the above applies.	0
9. Absence or loss of control whilst conscious leading to extensive evacuation of the bowel and/or bladder, other than enuresis (bed-wetting), despite the wearing or use of any aids or adaptations which are normally or could reasonably be worn or used.	9 (a) At least once a month experiences: (i) loss of control leading to extensive evacuation of the bowel and/or voiding of the bladder; or (ii) substantial leakage of the contents of a collecting device, sufficient to require cleaning and a change in clothing.	15
	(b) The majority of the time is at risk of loss of control leading to extensive evacuation of the bowel and/or voiding of the bladder, sufficient to require cleaning and a change in clothing, if not able to reach a toilet quickly.	6
	(c) Neither of the above applies.	0
10. Consciousness during waking moments.	10 (a) At least once a week, has an involuntary episode of lost or altered consciousness resulting in significantly disrupted awareness or concentration.	15
	(b) At least once a month, has an involuntary episode of lost or altered consciousness resulting in significantly disrupted awareness or concentration.	6
	(c) Neither of the above applies.	0

PART II

MENTAL, COGNITIVE AND INTELLECTUAL FUNCTION ASSESSMENT

(1)	(2)	(3)
Activity	Descriptors	Points
11. Learning tasks.	11 (a) Cannot learn how to complete a simple task, such as setting an alarm clock.	15
	(b) Cannot learn anything beyond a simple task, such as setting an alarm clock.	9
	(c) Cannot learn anything beyond a moderately complex task, such as the steps involved in operating a washing machine to clean clothes.	6
	(d) None of the above applies.	0
12. Awareness of everyday hazards (such as boiling water or sharp objects).	12 (a) Reduced awareness of everyday hazards leads to a significant risk of: (i) injury to self or others; or (ii) damage to property or possessions, such that the claimant requires supervision for the majority of the time to maintain safety.	15
	(b) Reduced awareness of everyday hazards leads to a significant risk of: (i) injury to self or others; or (ii) damage to property or possessions, such that the claimant frequently requires supervision to maintain safety.	9
	(c) Reduced awareness of everyday hazards leads to a significant risk of: (i) injury to self or others; or (ii) damage to property or possessions, such that the claimant occasionally requires supervision to maintain safety.	6
	(d) None of the above applies.	0
13. Initiating and completing personal action (which means planning, organisation, problem solving, prioritising or switching tasks).	13 (a) Cannot, due to impaired mental function, reliably initiate or complete at least two sequential personal actions.	15
	(b) Cannot, due to impaired mental function, reliably initiate or complete at least two sequential personal actions for the majority of the time.	9
	(c) Frequently cannot, due to impaired mental function, reliably initiate or complete at least two sequential personal actions.	6
	(d) None of the above applies.	0
14. Coping with change.	14 (a) Cannot cope with any change to the extent that day to day life cannot be managed.	15
	(b) Cannot cope with minor planned change (such as a pre-arranged change to the routine time scheduled for a lunch break), to the extent that, overall, day to day life is made significantly more difficult.	9
	(c) Cannot cope with minor unplanned change (such as the timing of an	6

(1)	(2)	(3)
Activity	Descriptors	Points
	appointment on the day it is due to occur), to the extent that, overall, day to day life is made significantly more difficult.	
	(d) None of the above applies.	0
15. Getting about.	15 (a) Cannot get to any place outside the claimant's home with which the claimant is familiar.	15
	(b) Is unable to get to a specified place with which the claimant is familiar, without being accompanied by another person.	9
	(c) Is unable to get to a specified place with which the claimant is unfamiliar without being accompanied by another person.	6
	(d) None of the above applies.	0
16. Coping with social engagement due to cognitive impairment or mental disorder.	16 (a) Engagement in social contact is always precluded due to difficulty relating to others or significant distress experienced by the claimant.	15
	(b) Engagement in social contact with someone unfamiliar to the claimant is always precluded due to difficulty relating to others or significant distress experienced by the claimant.	9
	(c) Engagement in social contact with someone unfamiliar to the claimant is not possible for the majority of the time due to difficulty relating to others or significant distress experienced by the claimant.	6
	(d) None of the above applies.	0
17. Appropriateness of behaviour with other people, due to cognitive impairment or mental disorder.	17 (a) Has, on a daily basis, uncontrollable episodes of aggressive or disinhibited behaviour that would be unreasonable in any workplace.	15
	(b) Frequently has uncontrollable episodes of aggressive or disinhibited behaviour that would be unreasonable in any workplace.	15
	(c) Occasionally has uncontrollable episodes of aggressive or disinhibited behaviour that would be unreasonable in any workplace.	9
	(d) None of the above applies.	0

DEFINITIONS

"claimant"—see WRA 2012 s.40.
"limited capability for work"—see WRA 2012 ss.40 and 37(1).

GENERAL NOTE

2.426   The activities and descriptors for assessing whether a claimant has LCW are the same as the activities and descriptors in Sch.2 to the ESA Regulations 2008. See the notes to Sch.2 to the 2008 Regulations in Vol.I of this series. They are also the same as the activities and descriptors in Sch.2 to the ESA Regulations 2013.

Regulation 40(2) and (3)

SCHEDULE 7

2.427

ASSESSMENT OF WHETHER A CLAIMANT HAS LIMITED CAPABILITY FOR
WORK AND WORK-RELATED ACTIVITY

Activity	Descriptors
1. Mobilising unaided by another person with or without a walking stick, manual wheelchair or other aid if such aid is normally or could reasonably be worn or used.	1 Cannot either: (a) mobilise more than 50 metres on level ground without stopping in order to avoid significant discomfort or exhaustion; or (b) repeatedly mobilise 50 metres within a reasonable timescale because of significant discomfort or exhaustion.
2. Transferring from one seated position to another.	2. Cannot move between one seated position and another seated position located next to one another without receiving physical assistance from another person.
3. Reaching.	3 Cannot raise either arm as if to put something in the top pocket of a coat or jacket.
4. Picking up and moving or transferring by the use of the upper body and arms (excluding standing, sitting, bending or kneeling and all other activities specified in this Schedule).	4 Cannot pick up and move a 0.5 litre carton full of liquid.
5. Manual dexterity.	5 Cannot press a button (such as a telephone keypad) with either hand or cannot turn the pages of a book with either hand.
6. Making self understood through speaking, writing, typing, or other means which are normally, or could reasonably be, used unaided by another person.	6 Cannot convey a simple message, such as the presence of a hazard.
7. Understanding communication by: (i) verbal means (such as hearing or lip reading) alone; (ii) non-verbal means (such as reading 16 point print or Braille) alone; or (iii) a combination of sub-paragraphs (i) and (ii), using any aid that is normally, or could reasonably, be used unaided by another person.	7 Cannot understand a simple message, such as the location of a fire escape, due to sensory impairment.
8. Absence or loss of control whilst conscious leading to extensive evacuation of the	8 At least once a week experiences: (a) loss of control leading to extensive evacuation of the bowel and/or voiding of the bladder; or

359

Activity	Descriptors
bowel and/or voiding of the bladder, other than enuresis (bed-wetting), despite the wearing or use of any aids or adaptations which are normally or could reasonably be worn or used.	(b) substantial leakage of the contents of a collecting device sufficient to require the individual to clean themselves and change clothing.
9. Learning tasks.	9 Cannot learn how to complete a simple task, such as setting an alarm clock, due to cognitive impairment or mental disorder.
10. Awareness of hazard.	10 Reduced awareness of everyday hazards, due to cognitive impairment or mental disorder, leads to a significant risk of: (a) injury to self or others; or (b) damage to property or possessions, such that the claimant requires supervision for the majority of the time to maintain safety.
11. Initiating and completing personal action (which means planning, organisation, problem solving, prioritising or switching tasks).	11 Cannot, due to impaired mental function, reliably initiate or complete at least two sequential personal actions.
12. Coping with change.	12 Cannot cope with any change, due to cognitive impairment or mental disorder, to the extent that day to day life cannot be managed.
13. Coping with social engagement, due to cognitive impairment or mental disorder.	13 Engagement in social contact is always precluded due to difficulty relating to others or significant distress experienced by the claimant.
14. Appropriateness of behaviour with other people, due to cognitive impairment or mental disorder.	14 Has, on a daily basis, uncontrollable episodes of aggressive or disinhibited behaviour that would be unreasonable in any workplace.
15. Conveying food or drink to the mouth.	15 (a) Cannot convey food or drink to the claimant's own mouth without receiving physical assistance from someone else; (b) Cannot convey food or drink to the claimant's own mouth without repeatedly stopping or experiencing breathlessness or severe discomfort; (c) Cannot convey food or drink to the claimant's own mouth without receiving regular prompting given by someone else in the claimant's presence; or (d) Owing to a severe disorder of mood or behaviour, fails to convey food or drink to the claimant's own mouth without receiving: (i) physical assistance from someone else; or (ii) regular prompting given by someone else in the claimant's presence.
16. Chewing or swallowing food or drink.	16 (a) Cannot chew or swallow food or drink; (b) Cannot chew or swallow food or drink without repeatedly stopping or experiencing breathlessness or severe discomfort; (c) Cannot chew or swallow food or drink without repeatedly receiving regular prompting given by someone else in the claimant's presence; or

Activity	Descriptors
	(d) Owing to a severe disorder of mood or behaviour, fails to: (i) chew or swallow food or drink; or (ii) chew or swallow food or drink without regular prompting given by someone else in the claimant's presence.

DEFINITIONS

"claimant"—see WRA 2012 s.40.
"limited capability for work"—see WRA 2012 ss.40 and 37(1).
"limited capability for work-related activity"—see WRA 2012 ss.40 and 37(2).

GENERAL NOTE

The activities and descriptors for assessing whether a claimant has LCW and **2.428** LCWRA are the same as the activities and descriptors in Sch.3 to the ESA Regulations 2008 for assessing whether a claimant has LCWRA. See the notes to Sch.3 to the 2008 Regulations in Vol.I of this series. They are also the same as the activities and descriptors in Sch.3 to the ESA Regulations 2013.

Regulation 39(6)

SCHEDULE 8

CIRCUMSTANCES IN WHICH A CLAIMANT IS TO BE TREATED AS HAVING
LIMITED CAPABILITY FOR WORK

Receiving certain treatments
  1. The claimant is receiving—   **2.429**
    (a) regular weekly treatment by way of haemodialysis for chronic renal failure;
    (b) treatment by way of plasmapheresis; or
    (c) regular weekly treatment by way of total parenteral nutrition for gross impairment of enteric function,
or is recovering from any of those forms of treatment in circumstances in which the Secretary of State is satisfied that the claimant should be treated as having limited capability for work.

In hospital
  2.—(1) The claimant is—   **2.430**
    (a) undergoing medical or other treatment as [¹ a patient] in a hospital or similar institution; or
    (b) recovering from such treatment in circumstances in which the Secretary of State is satisfied that the claimant should be treated as having limited capability for work.
  (2) The circumstances in which a claimant is to be regarded as undergoing treatment falling within sub-paragraph (1)(a) include where the claimant is attending a residential programme of rehabilitation for the treatment of drug or alcohol dependency.
  (3) For the purposes of this paragraph, a claimant is to be regarded as undergoing treatment as a patient in a hospital or similar institution only if that claimant has been advised by a health care professional to stay [² for a period of 24 hours or longer] following medical or other treatment.

Prevented from working by law
  3.—(1) The claimant—   **2.431**
    (a) is excluded or abstains from work pursuant to a request or notice in writing lawfully made or given under an enactment; or
    (b) is otherwise prevented from working pursuant to an enactment,
by reason of it being known or reasonably suspected that the claimant is infected or contaminated by, or has been in contact with a case of, a relevant infection or contamination.
  (2) In sub-paragraph (1) "relevant infection or contamination" means—
    (a) in England and Wales—
      (i) any incidence or spread of infection or contamination, within the meaning of section 45A(3) of the Public Health (Control of Disease) Act 1984 in respect of

which regulations are made under Part 2A of that Act (public health protection) for the purpose of preventing, protecting against, controlling or providing a public health response to, such incidence or spread, or

    (ii) tuberculosis or any infectious disease to which regulation 9 of the Public Health (Aircraft) Regulations 1979 (powers in respect of persons leaving aircraft) applies or to which regulation 10 of the Public Health (Ships) Regulations 1979 (powers in respect of certain persons on ships) applies; and

  (b) in Scotland any—

    (i) infectious disease within the meaning of section 1(5) of the Public Health etc (Scotland) Act 2008, or exposure to an organism causing that disease; or

    (ii) contamination within the meaning of section 1(5) of that Act, or exposure to a contaminant,

to which sections 56 to 58 of that Act (compensation) apply.

Risk to self or others

2.432   **4.**—(1) The claimant is suffering from a specific illness, disease or disablement by reason of which there would be a substantial risk to the physical or mental health of any person were the claimant found not to have limited capability for work.

(2) This paragraph does not apply where the risk could be reduced by a significant amount by—

  (a) reasonable adjustments being made in the claimant's workplace; or

  (b) the claimant taking medication to manage their condition where such medication has been prescribed for the claimant by a registered medical practitioner treating the claimant.

Life threatening disease

2.433   **5.** The claimant is suffering from a life threatening disease in relation to which—

  (a) there is medical evidence that the disease is uncontrollable, or uncontrolled, by a recognised therapeutic procedure; and

  (b) in the case of a disease that is uncontrolled, there is a reasonable cause for it not to be controlled by a recognised therapeutic procedure.

Disabled and over the age for state pension credit

2.434   **6.** The claimant has reached the qualifying age for state pension credit and is entitled to disability living allowance or personal independence payment.

AMENDMENTS

1. Universal Credit (Consequential, Supplementary, Incidental and Miscellaneous Provisions) Regulations 2013 (SI 2013/630), reg.38(10) (April 29, 2013).

2. Social Security (Miscellaneous Amendments) (No.2) Regulations 2013 (SI 2013/1508), reg.3(11) (July 29, 2013).

DEFINITIONS

"claimant"—see WRA 2012 s.40.
"disability living allowance"—see reg.2.
"health care professional"–*ibid.*
"limited capability for work"—see WRA 2012 ss.40 and 37(1).

GENERAL NOTE

2.435   Paragraph 1 is similar, though not identical, to reg.26 of the ESA Regulations 2008; para. 2 is similar, though not identical, to reg.25 of those Regulations; and para. 3 is the same as reg.20(1)(c) and (2) of the 2008 Regulations. See the notes to regs 20, 25 and 26 of the 2008 Regulations in Vol.I of this series.

Note that Sch.8 does not contain provisions for treating a claimant who is (i) terminally ill; (ii) a pregnant woman whose health, or whose unborn child's health, is at serious risk of damage: or (iii) receiving treatment for cancer as having limited capability for work. Such a claimant will be treated as having LCW and LCWRA under paras 1 to 3 respectively of Sch.9 (see below).

There is no equivalent of para.6 in the ESA Regulations 2008.

Paragraphs 4 and 5 together contain very similar provisions to those in reg. 29 of the 2008 Regulations (see the notes to reg.29 in Vol.1 of this series). Note the amendment to reg. 39 made on April 28, 2014, the effect of which is that a claimant can only be treated as having LCW under paras 4 or 5 if s/he has been assessed as not having LCW. Regulation 29 of the 2008 Regulations already contains such a provision.

Regulation 40(5)

SCHEDULE 9

CIRCUMSTANCES IN WHICH A CLAIMANT IS TO BE TREATED AS HAVING LIMITED CAPABILITY FOR WORK AND WORK-RELATED ACTIVITY

Terminal illness
1. The claimant is terminally ill.

2.436

Pregnancy
2. The claimant is a pregnant woman and there is a serious risk of damage to her health or to the health of her unborn child if she does not refrain from work and work-related activity.

2.437

Receiving treatment for cancer
3. The claimant is—

2.438

    (a) receiving treatment for cancer by way of chemotherapy or radiotherapy;
    (b) likely to receive such treatment within 6 months after the date of the determination of capability for work and work-related activity; or
    (c) recovering from such treatment,
and the Secretary of State is satisfied that the claimant should be treated as having limited capability for work and work-related activity.

Risk to self or others
4. The claimant is suffering from a specific illness, disease or disablement by reason of which there would be a substantial risk to the physical or mental health of any person were the claimant found not to have limited capability for work and work-related activity.

2.439

Disabled and over the age for state pension credit
5. The claimant has reached the qualifying age for state pension credit and is entitled to attendance allowance, the care component of disability living allowance at the highest rate or the daily living component of personal independence payment at the enhanced rate.

2.440

DEFINITIONS

"attendance allowance"—see reg.2.
"child"—see WRA 2012, s.40.
"claimant"—*ibid*.
"limited capability for work"—see WRA 2012, ss.40 and 37(1).
"limited capability for work-related activity"—see WRA 2012, ss.40 and 37(2).
"personal independence payment"—see reg.2.

GENERAL NOTE

For the equivalent of (i) para.1, see regs 20(1)(a) and 35(1)(a) of the ESA Regulations 2008; (ii) para.2, see regs 20(1)(d) and 35(1)(c) of those Regulations; and (iii) para.3, see regs 20(1)(b) and 35(1)(b) of the 2008 Regulations. See the notes to regs 20 and 35 of the 2008 Regulations in Vol.I of this series.

2.441

There is no equivalent of para.5 in the ESA Regulations 2008.

Paragraph 4 contains very similar provisions to those in regs 29(2)(b) and 35(2) of the 2008 Regulations (see the notes to regs 29 and 35 in Vol.1 of this series). Note the amendment to reg. 40 made on April 28, 2014, the effect of which is that a claimant can only be treated as having LCW and LCWRA under para.4 if s/he has been assessed as not having LCW and LCWRA. Regulations 29 and 35 of the 2008 Regulations already contain such a provision.

SCHEDULE 10

CAPITAL TO BE DISREGARDED

Premises

2.442   **1.**—(1) Premises occupied by a person as their home.

(2) For the purposes of this paragraph and paragraphs 2 to 5, only one set of premises may be treated as a person's home.

2. Premises occupied by a close relative of a person as their home where that close relative has limited capability for work or has reached the qualifying age for state pension credit.

3. Premises occupied by a person's former partner as their home where the person and their former partner are not estranged, but living apart by force of circumstances, for example where the person is in residential care.

4.—(1) Premises that a person intends to occupy as their home where—

(a) the person has acquired the premises within the past 6 months but not yet taken up occupation;

(b) the person is taking steps to obtain possession and has commenced those steps within the past 6 months; or

(c) the person is carrying out essential repairs or alterations required to render the premises fit for occupation and these have been commenced within the past 6 months.

(2) A person is to be taken to have commenced steps to obtain possession of premises on the date that legal advice is first sought or proceedings are commenced, whichever is earlier.

5. Premises that a person has ceased to occupy as their home following an estrangement from their former partner where—

(a) the person has ceased to occupy the premises within the past 6 months; or

(b) the person's former partner is a lone parent and occupies the premises as their home.

6. Premises that a person is taking reasonable steps to dispose of where those steps have been commenced within the past 6 months.

Business assets

2.443   **7.** Assets which are used wholly or mainly for the purposes of a trade, profession or vocation which the person is carrying on.

8. Assets which were used wholly or mainly for a trade, profession or vocation that the person has ceased to carry on within the past 6 months if—

(a) the person is taking reasonable steps to dispose of those assets; or

(b) the person ceased to be engaged in carrying on the trade, profession or vocation because of incapacity and can reasonably expect to be reengaged on recovery.

Rights in pensions schemes etc.

9. The value of any policy of life insurance.

2.444   **10.**—(1) The value of any right to receive a pension under an occupational or personal pension scheme or any other pension scheme registered under section 153 of the Finance Act 2004.

(2) "Occupational pension scheme" and "personal pension scheme" have the meaning in section 1 of the Pension Schemes Act 1993.

11.—(1) The value of a funeral plan contract.

(2) "Funeral plan contract" means a contract under which the person makes payments to a person to secure the provision of a funeral and where the sole purpose of the plan is the provision of a funeral.

Amounts earmarked for special purposes

2.445   **12.** An amount deposited with a housing association as a condition of the person occupying premises as their home.

13. An amount received within the past 6 months which is to be used for the purchase of premises that the person intends to occupy as their home where that amount—

(a) is attributable to the proceeds of the sale of premises formerly occupied by the person as their home;

(b) has been deposited with a housing association as mentioned in paragraph 12; or

(c) is a grant made to the person for the sole purpose of the purchase of a home.

14. An amount received under an insurance policy within the past 6 months in connection with the loss or damage to the premises occupied by the person as their home or to their personal possessions.

15. An amount received within the past 6 months that is to be used for making essential repairs or alterations to premises occupied or intended to be occupied as the person's home where that amount has been acquired by the person (whether by grant or loan or otherwise) on condition that it is used for that purpose.

Other payments

16. A payment made within the past 12 months under Part 8 of the Contributions and Benefits Act (the social fund).

2.446

17.—(1) A payment made within the past 12 months by or on behalf of a local authority—

(a) under section 17, 23B, 23C or 24A of the Children Act 1989, section 12 of the Social Work (Scotland) Act 1968 or section 29 or 30 of Children (Scotland) Act 1995; or

(b) under any other enactment in order to meet a person's welfare needs related to old age or disability, other than living expenses.

(2) In sub-paragraph (1) "living expenses" has the meaning in regulation 66(2).

18.—(1) A payment received within the past 12 months by way of arrears of, or compensation for late payment of—

(a) universal credit;

(b) a benefit abolished by section 33 of the Act; or

(c) a social security benefit which is not included as unearned income under regulation 66(1)(a) or (b).

(2) "Social security benefit" means a benefit under any enactment relating to social security in any part of the United Kingdom.

19. A payment to a person by virtue of being a holder of the Victoria Cross or George Cross.

[¹**20.** A payment made within the past 12 months of bereavement support payment in respect of the rate set out in regulation 3(2) or (5) of the Bereavement Support Payment Regulations 2017 (rate of bereavement support payment).]

AMENDMENT

1. Pensions Act 2014 (Consequential, Supplementary and Incidental Amendments) Order 2017 (SI 2017/422) art.43(4) (April 6, 2017).

DEFINITIONS

"close relative"—see reg.2.
"grant"—see regs 2 and 68(7).
"partner"—see reg.2.

GENERAL NOTE

The list of capital that is ignored for the purposes of universal credit is greatly reduced compared with that which applies for the purposes of income support, old style JSA, old style ESA and housing benefit. Many of the provisions in Sch.10 are similar to those that apply for those benefits but not all. Paragraph 11—the disregard of the value of a funeral plan—is new.

2.447

The opportunity has been taken to group the disregards in a more coherent and easy to follow structure. The notes below follow that structure and note the equivalences with and differences from the provisions in Sch.10 to the Income Support Regulations (see Vol.II of this series for detailed discussion). The disregards can apply to notional capital.

Premises

Paragraph 1 (premises occupied as the home) is equivalent to para.1 of the income support Sch.10 except that it is in terms of premises rather than a dwelling. Only one set of premises (whatever the precise meaning of that might be: see the notes to reg.2(1) of the Income Support Regulations for cases on when separate properties could constitute one dwelling) can be treated as the home. That rule is expressly extended to paras 2–5, as is not done in the income support Sch.10. Presumably the premises need not be residential accommodation providing that they are lived in as a home.

2.448

Paragraph 2 (premises occupied by a close relative as their home) is the equivalent of para.4(a) of the income support Sch.10, except that it is restricted to close relatives of the claimant instead of any relative or a partner. The alternative test (to that of having attained state pension credit qualifying age) of the relative having limited capability for work may possibly be more restrictive than that of being incapacitated. Regulations 38–44 only apply to determining whether a *claimant* has limited capability for work, or for work and work-related activity. Thus it is arguable either that the words "limited capability for work" merely have their ordinary meaning or that it is not necessary that the relative be in receipt of any benefit or credit based on a determination as to limited capability for work.

Paragraph 3 (premises occupied by a former partner as their home) is the equivalent of para.4(b) of the income support Sch.10, but with slightly different conditions. The application of para.4(b) is excluded where there has been a divorce from the former partner or a dissolution of a civil partnership as well as where the claimant and the former partner are estranged. The application of para.3 is not automatically excluded by divorce or the dissolution of a civil partnership, but is where there is estrangement, which may or may not follow such procedures, especially after some lapse of time. More important is the positive condition, not present in para.4(b) of the income support Sch.10, that the two are living apart by force of circumstances. That will prevent the application of the disregard for many non-estranged former partners.

Paragraph 4(1)(a) (premises acquired within past 6 months and intends to occupy as the home) is the equivalent of para.2 of the income support Sch.10, with a very slightly wider application. Paragraph 2 requires any extension to the period of 26 weeks from acquisition to be reasonable in the circumstances to enable the claimant to obtain possession and commence occupation. Under para.4(1)(a), provided as always that there is an intention to occupy the premises as the home, the extension under reg.48(2) can be made whenever it is reasonable in the circumstances.

Paragraph 4(1)(b) (commenced steps to obtain possession of premises within the past 6 months) is the equivalent of para.27 of the income support Sch.10. The provisions in sub-para.(2) about when a person is to be deemed to have commenced steps to obtain possession make the conditions the same as under para.27, except that any extension to the period of 6 months under reg.48(2) can be made whenever it is reasonable in all the circumstances instead of being linked to enabling obtaining possession and commencing occupation.

Paragraph 4(1)(c) (essential repairs or improvements to render premises fit for occupation commenced within the past 6 months) is the equivalent of para.28 of the income support Sch.10, except for the similar effect of reg.48(2) as above.

Paragraph 5 (claimant ceased to occupy premises as home following estrangement from former partner) is the equivalent of para.25 of the income support Sch.10, except that it does not automatically apply on divorce or the dissolution of a civil partnership, only on estrangement. The 6 months under sub-para.(b) can be extended where reasonable in the circumstances under reg.48(2).

Paragraph 6 (commenced taking reasonable steps to dispose of premises within past 6 months) is the equivalent of para.26 of the income support Sch.10. The 6 months can be extended where reasonable in the circumstances under reg.48(2). In both provisions the disregard applies to any premises, not just premises occupied as the home.

Business assets

2.449   Paragraph 7 (assets of business being carried on) is the equivalent of the first part of para.6(1) of the income support Sch.10. Paragraph 6 uses the terms of assets of a business owned in whole or in part by the claimant for the purposes of which he is engaged as a self-employed earner. In view of the meaning of self-employed earner, the use of the terms "used wholly or mainly for the purposes of a trade, profession or vocation" comes to the same thing. Paragraph 7 applies while the claimant is carrying on that trade, profession or vocation.

Paragraph 8 (assets of business that ceased to carry on within the past 6 months) is the equivalent of the second part of para.6(1) and para.6(2) of the income support Sch.10. Under sub-para.(b) the person must have ceased to be engaged in the trade, profession or vocation because of incapacity. That is arguably narrower than para.6(2), which only requires the person currently not to be engaged in the business by reason of some disease or bodily or mental disablement. First, the person must have been carrying on the trade, profession or vocation previously, rather than hoping to take it up for the first time. Second, the incapacity must have been the reason for ceasing, rather than intervening after a ceasing for some other reason. But para.6(2) requires an intention to become engaged or re-engaged, while para.8(b) merely requires a reasonable expectation that the person will be reengaged on recovery. The period of 6 months since ceasing to be engaged can be extended where reasonable in the circumstances under reg.48(2).

Rights in pensions schemes etc.

Note first that many provisions in the income support Sch.10 disregarding the capital value of the right to receive various forms of income are not replicated in the present Schedule (e.g. paras 11 (annuities, but see reg.46(3)), 12 (trust funds derived from personal injury compensation, but see reg.75(4)), 13 (life interests and liferents), 16 (capital payable by instalments, but see reg.46(4)), 24 (rent)). **2.450**

Paragraph 9 (life insurance policies) is the equivalent of para.15 of the income support Sch.10. The latter refers to the surrender value. Paragraph 9 does not, but in the light of reg.49(1), the disregard must apply to whichever of the market value or surrender value has been applied to the policy.

Paragraph 10 (occupational or personal pension schemes) is the equivalent of para.23 of the income support Sch.10. As noted in Vol.II of this series, the right to receive a pension from the schemes mentioned is not capable of being bought or sold and so would have no capital value anyway. There is no equivalent in the present Schedule to para.23A of the income support Sch.10 disregarding the value of any funds held under a personal pension scheme. It is no doubt considered that such funds do not form part of the capital of the member of the scheme, whose interests are only in the rights under the scheme rather than in the fund itself.

Paragraph 11 (funeral plan contracts) has no equivalent in the income support Sch.10.

Amounts earmarked for special purposes

Paragraph 12 (housing association deposits as a condition of occupying the home) is the equivalent of para.9(a) of the income support Sch.10. The latter defines housing association. **2.451**

Paragraph 13(a) (amounts received within the past 6 months attributable to proceeds of sale of previous home to be used for the purchase of premises to be occupied as the home) is the equivalent of para.3 of the income support Sch.10. Under the latter, the sum must be directly attributable to the proceeds of sale, rather than merely attributable. The emphasis of the 6-month condition is different. Under para.3 the intention must be to occupy new premises within 26 weeks of the sale of the previous home. Under para.13(a) there is simply a limit (extendable under reg.48(2)) of 6 months from the receipt of the proceeds of sale and no condition that the intention be to occupy the new home within any particular period. See *R(IS) 7/01* on the effect of the test of "is to be used".

Paragraph 13(b) (amounts received within the past 6 months to be used for the purchase of premises to be occupied as the home that have been deposited with a housing association) is the equivalent of para.9(b) of the income support Sch.10.

Paragraph 13(c) (grant received in the past 6 months for sole purpose of purchase of a home) appears to be the equivalent of para.37(a) of the income support Sch.10, but without any limitation as to the source of the grant. The definition of "grant" in reg.68(7) (see reg.2) does not seem applicable in the context of para.13(c).

Paragraph 14 (amount received within the past 6 months under an insurance policy in connection with loss of or damage to the home or personal possessions) is the equivalent of para.8(a) of the income support Sch.10, but without the condition that the sum be intended for repair and replacement. The 6 months can be extended where reasonable in the circumstances under reg.48(2).

Paragraph 15 (amount received within the past 6 months to be used for essential repairs or alterations to premises occupied or to be occupied as the home, where condition that it be used for that purpose) is the equivalent of para.8(b) of the income support Sch.10. See *R(IS) 7/01* on the effect of the test of "is to be used". The 6 months can be extended where reasonable in the circumstances under reg.48(2).

Other payments

2.452
Paragraph 16 (social fund payments made within the past 12 months) is the equivalent of para.18 of the income support Sch.10. The 12 months is not extendable.

Paragraph 17 (local authority welfare payments made within the past 12 months) appears to be the equivalent of paras 17(1) and (2), 18A and 67 of the income support Sch.10. Under sub-para.(b) there is no restriction to any particular legislative provision as the source of the power to make the payment, but an exception for payments for living expenses. However, it must be asked whether payments constitute capital rather than income in the first place. If income, amounts will metamorphose into capital only after the end of the period to which they are attributable as income. The 12 months is not extendable.

Paragraph 18 (arrears or compensation for late payment received within the past 12 months of universal credit and certain social security benefits) is the equivalent of para.7 of the income support Sch.10, although the specification of the other benefits covered is through a different method. The benefits abolished by s.33 of the WRA 2012 are income-based JSA, income-related ESA, income support, housing benefit, council tax benefit (already abolished), child tax credit and working tax credit. Benefits falling outside reg.66(1)(a) and (b) will include attendance allowance, any care or mobility component of disability living allowance, any daily living component or mobility component of personal independence payment and the monthly payments of the new bereavement support payment. However, in principle payments of benefits that have the character of income should retain that character when paid as arrears (see *R(SB) 4/89*). So that it is only amounts left over after the period to which they would be attributable as income that would become capital and therefore potentially subject to a disregard under Sch.10. It is not clear how far that principle applies to payments that would not be treated as income for the purposes of universal credit.

Paragraph 19 (Victoria Cross and George Cross) is the equivalent of para.46 of the income support Sch.10.

Paragraph 20 (lump sum bereavement support payment received within the previous 12 months) is the equivalent of the new para.72 of the income support Sch.10. The 12 months is not extendable. Payments of arrears of the monthly payments are disregarded as capital for 12 months from the date of receipt under para.18. In so far as they retain their character as income they fall outside the specification of what is unearned income in reg.66 (see reg.66(1)(b) as amended).

Omissions

2.453
A number of categories disregarded for the purposes of income support and old style ESA and JSA are thus not included in the universal credit Sch.10. Some cover very specific circumstances, but all are apparently deserving. They include payments of expenses of attending various schemes relating to jobseeking, the value of the right to receive the outstanding amount of capital payable by instalments, the value of capital treated as income (arguably unnecessary), payments from various funds (e.g., for those suffering from haemophilia), payments under a council tax reduction scheme and educational maintenance allowances.

Note that where a period of six months is specified in the provisions in this Schedule, that period can be extended by the Secretary of State (and on appeal a tribunal) if this is reasonable in the circumstances of the case (see reg.48(2)).

Regulation 112

SCHEDULE 11

APPLICATION OF ESA OR JSA SANCTIONS TO UNIVERSAL CREDIT

Moving an ESA sanction to UC

1. (1) This paragraph applies where—

    (a) a person is, or has ceased to be, entitled to an employment and support allowance;

    (b) there is a reduction relating to the award of the employment and support allowance under section 11J of the Welfare Reform Act 2007; and

    (c) the person becomes entitled to universal credit.

(2) Any reduction relating to the award of the employment and support allowance is to be applied to the award of universal credit.

(3) The period for which the reduction is to have effect is the number of days which apply to the person under regulations 52 and 53 of the ESA Regulations minus—

    (a) any days which have already resulted in a reduction to the amount of the employment and support allowance; and

    (b) if the award of the employment and support allowance has terminated, any days falling after the date of that termination and before the date on which the award of universal credits starts, and that period is to be added to the total outstanding reduction period.

(4) The amount of the reduction in the award of universal credit for any assessment period in which the reduction is applied is the amount calculated in accordance with regulation 110.

2.454

Moving a JSA sanction to UC

2. (1) This paragraph applies where—

    (a) a person is, or has ceased to be, entitled to a jobseeker's allowance;

    (b) there is a reduction relating to the person's award of a jobseeker's allowance under section 6J or 6K of the Jobseekers Act 1995; and

    (c) the person becomes entitled to universal credit.

(2) Any reduction relating to the award of the jobseeker's allowance is to be applied to the award of universal credit.

(3) The period for which the reduction is to have effect is the number of days which apply to the person under regulations 19 to 21 of the Jobseeker's Allowance Regulations 2013 minus—

    (a) any days which have already resulted in a reduction to the amount of the jobseeker's allowance; and

    (b) if the award of the jobseeker's allowance has terminated, any days falling after the date of that termination and before the date on which the award of universal credits starts, and that period is to be added to the total outstanding reduction period.

(4) The amount of the reduction in the award of universal credit for any assessment period in which the reduction is applied is the amount calculated in accordance with regulation 110.

2.455

Effect of ESA or JSA sanction on escalation of UC sanction

3. Where—

    (a) a reduction in relation to an award of an employment and support allowance or an award of a jobseeker's allowance is applied to an award of universal credit by virtue of paragraph 1 or 2;

    (b) there is a subsequent sanctionable failure under section 26 or 27 of the Act; and

    (c) the failure giving rise to the reduction in relation to the award of an employment and support allowance or the award of a jobseeker's allowance ("the previous failure") and the reduction period determined for that failure correspond with a failure specified under section 26 or 27 of the Act to which the same reduction period would apply under Chapter 2 of Part 8 of these Regulations,

for the purposes of determining the reduction period for that subsequent failure, the previous failure is to be treated as if it were the corresponding failure under section 26 or 27 of the Act.

2.456

GENERAL NOTE

Paras. 1 and 2

2.457 Paragraphs 1 and 2 constitute an important element of the relationship between new style ESA and JSA and universal credit. They provide that where a claimant is entitled to new style ESA or JSA and is subject to a sanction under s.11J of the WRA 2007 or s.6J or 6K of the WRA 2012 and then becomes entitled to universal credit, and also where the claimant ceases to be entitled to new style ESA or JSA, the ESA or JSA reduction is to be applied to the universal credit award. That works in practice if entitlement to ESA or JSA has ceased, but if that entitlement continues, it is the case that the unreduced amount of ESA or JSA counts as income in the calculation of the amount of any universal credit award and so cuts into the amount available for reduction under the universal credit sanction. That sanction cannot as such reduce the amount of new style ESA or JSA payable. It is in the nature of a reduction in the amount of an award of benefit that the reduction cannot exceed the amount of that particular award. That has the anomalous results discussed in the notes to reg.5 of the JSA Regulations 2013 in Vol.II of this series.

The WRA 2012 contains a regulation-making power that could have been used to avoid these anomalous results. This is in para.2 of Sch.5, which applies when a claimant is entitled to both universal credit and a "relevant benefit", i.e. new style ESA or JSA. Paragraph 2(2) allows regulations in particular to provide in such circumstances for no amount to be payable by way of the relevant benefit. A Departmental memorandum to the House of Lords Select Committee on Delegated Powers and Regulatory Reform (see para.1.177 of Vol.V) indicated that among the intended uses of the powers in para.2 was to specify in cases of dual entitlement whether the claimant would be paid only universal credit or only the relevant benefit or both. It was also intended to set out, if sanctions were applicable, which benefit was to be reduced first and to provide, if appropriate, that the application of a sanction to one benefit did not increase the amount of another. However, no regulations have been made to carry out those intentions. The only use of para.2 appears to have been in making reg.42 of the ESA Regulations 2013 and reg.5 of the JSA Regulations 2013, under the power in para.2(3), para.2(2) not being mentioned in the list of statutory powers invoked in the preamble to the Regulations. If regulations had provided that when there was dual entitlement no amount of new style ESA or JSA was to be payable, then there would have been no income from the benefit concerned to be taken into account in the calculation of the amount of universal credit payable and any reduction of benefit under a sanction would bite on the whole amount of the universal credit in the ordinary way. The non-application of the work-related and connected requirements for new style JSA and the sanctions regime under new style ESA and JSA would then have been part of a coherent structure. But that is not the actual state of the legislation.

It might be asked whether the provisions for reduction periods under the universal credit provisions to be applied to a new style ESA or JSA award and vice versa supply a way out of the anomalies. The answer is no. Regulation 61 of the ESA Regulations 2013 and reg.30 of the JSA Regulations 2013 only apply where a claimant ceases to be entitled to universal credit and is or becomes entitled to new style ESA or JSA. In those circumstances any universal credit sanction reduction period is applied to the ESA or JSA award. Regulations 61 and 30 do not apply during any period of dual entitlement. By contrast, when the opposite direction is considered, reg.43 of the ESA Regulations 2013 and reg.6 of the JSA Regulations 2013 apply only where the claimant is entitled to new style ESA or JSA subject to a sanction reduction period, becomes entitled to universal credit and *remains* entitled to new style ESA or JSA. But the result is that the reduction ceases to be applicable to the ESA or JSA award. That appears merely to reinforce the position under reg.42 of the ESA Regulations 2013 and reg.5 of the JSA Regulations 2013. The unreduced amount of ESA or JSA counts as income in the calculation of the amount of the universal credit award and only the "topping up" element of universal credit can be subject to reduction.

Para. 3

Under para.3, where a new style ESA or JSA sanction has been applied to universal credit under para.1 or 2, it can count as a "previous sanctionable failure" for the purposes of calculating the length of the reduction period for a subsequent universal credit sanction under s.26 or 27 of the WRA 2012 (see regs 102–104). Where there have been previous universal credit (and these equivalent) sanctionable failures within the previous 365 days including the date of the current sanctionable failure (but not within the previous 14 days), that affects the length of the reduction period. Note that it is not every previous new style ESA or JSA sanction that has that effect under para.3. It is only such a sanction that has been applied to universal credit. The position is thus not the same as under regs 19–21 of the JSA Regulations 2013 where there is express reference to previous universal credit sanctions as well as new style JSA sanctions (and new style ESA sanctions in the case of reg.21) as capable of being previous sanctionable failures. Regulation 19 of the ESA Regulations 2013 refers to previous new style JSA sanctionable failures and universal credit sanctionable failures at the appropriate level as well as to previous new style ESA low-level sanctionable failures. It also appears that an old style ESA or JSA sanctionable failure occurring within the 365 days cannot count as a previous sanctionable failure.

[¹ Regulation 24A(4)

SCHEDULE 12

Availability of the Child Element where Maximum Exceeded – Exceptions

Introduction

1. This Schedule provides for cases where, for the purposes of regulation 24A, an exception applies in relation to a child or qualifying young person for whom a claimant is responsible ("A").

Multiple births

2. An exception applies where—
   (a) the claimant is a parent (other than an adoptive parent) of A;
   (b) A was one of two or more children born as a result of the same pregnancy;
   (c) the claimant is responsible for at least two of the children or qualifying young persons born as a result of that pregnancy; and
   (d) A is not the first in the order of those children or qualifying young persons as determined under regulation 24B.

Adoptions

3. An exception applies where A has been placed for adoption with, or adopted by, the claimant in accordance with the Adoption and Children Act 2002 or the Adoption and Children (Scotland) Act 2007, but not where—
   (a) the claimant (or, if the claimant is a member of a couple, the other member)—
       (i) was a step-parent of A immediately prior to the adoption; or
       (ii) has been a parent of A (other than by adoption) at any time;
   (b) the adoption order made in respect of A was made as a Convention adoption order (as   defined, in England and Wales, in section 144 of the Adoption and Children Act 2002 and in Scotland, in section 119(1) of the Adoption and Children Scotland Act 2007); or
   (c) prior to that adoption, A had been adopted by the claimant (or, if the claimant is a member of a couple, the other member) under the law of any country or territory outside the British Islands.

Non-parental caring arrangements

4.—(1) An exception applies where the claimant—
   (a) is a friend or family carer in relation to A; or
   (b) is responsible for a child who is a parent of A.
   (2) In this paragraph, "friend or family carer" means a person who is responsible for A, but is not (or, if that person is a member of a couple, neither member is) A's parent or step-parent and—

2.458

2.459

2.460

2.461

2.462

(a) is named in a child arrangements order under section 8 of the Children Act 1989, that is in force with respect to A, as a person with whom A is to live;

(b) is a special guardian of A appointed under section 14A of that Act;

(c) is entitled to a guardian's allowance under section 77 of the Contributions and Benefits Act in respect of A;

(d) in whose favour a kinship care order, as defined in section 72(1) of the Children and Young People (Scotland) Act 2014, subsists in relation to A;

(e) is a guardian of A appointed under section 5 of the Children Act 1989 or section 7 of the Children (Scotland) Act 1995;

(f) in whom one or more of the parental responsibilities or parental rights respectively described in section 1 and 2 of the Children (Scotland) Act 1995 are vested by a permanence order made in respect of A under section 80 of the Adoption and Children (Scotland) Act 2007;

(g) fell within any of paragraphs (a) to (f) immediately prior to A's 16th birthday and has since continued to be responsible for A; or

(h) has undertaken the care of A in circumstances in which it is likely that A would otherwise be looked after by a local authority.

Non-consensual conception

2.463

5.—(1) An exception applies where—

(a) the claimant ("C") is A's parent; and

(b) the Secretary of State determines that—

    (i) A is likely to have been conceived as a result of sexual intercourse to which C did not agree by choice, or did not have the freedom and capacity to agree by choice; and

    (ii) C is not living at the same address as the other party to that intercourse ("B").

(2) The circumstances in which C is to be treated as not having the freedom or capacity to agree by choice to the sexual intercourse are to include (but are not limited to) circumstances in which, at or around the time A was conceived—

(a) B was personally connected to C;

(b) B was repeatedly or continuously engaging in behaviour towards C that was controlling or coercive; and

(c) that behaviour had a serious effect on C.

(3) The Secretary of State may make the determination in sub-paragraph (1)(b)(i) only if—

(a) C provides evidence from an approved person which demonstrates that—

    (i) C had contact with that approved person or another approved person; and

    (ii) C's circumstances are consistent with those of a person to whom sub-paragraphs (1)(a) and (1)(b)(i) apply; or

(b) there has been—

    (i) a conviction for—

        (aa) an offence of rape under section 1 of the Sexual Offences Act 2003 or section 1 of the Sexual Offences (Scotland) Act 2009;

        (bb) an offence of controlling or coercive behaviour in an intimate or family relationship under section 76 of the Serious Crime Act 2015; or

        (cc) an offence under the law of a country outside Great Britain that the Secretary of State considers to be analogous to the offence mentioned in sub-paragraph (aa) or (bb) above; or

    (ii) an award under the Criminal Injuries Compensation Scheme in respect of a relevant criminal injury sustained by C,

where it appears likely to the Secretary of State that the offence was committed, or the criminal injury was caused, by B and resulted in the conception of A or diminished C's freedom or capacity to agree by choice to the sexual intercourse which resulted in that conception.

(4) The Secretary of State may make the determination in sub-paragraph (1)(b)(ii) where the only available evidence is confirmation by C that that sub-paragraph applies.

(5) For the purposes of sub-paragraph (2)(a), B was personally connected to C if, at or around the time A was conceived—

(a) they were in an intimate personal relationship with each other; or

(b) they were living together and—

    (i) were members of the same family; or

    (ii) had previously been in an intimate personal relationship with each other.

(6) For the purposes of sub-paragraph (2)(c), B's behaviour had a serious effect on C if—

(a) it caused C to fear, on at least two occasions, that violence would be used against C; or

(b) it caused C serious alarm or distress which had a substantial adverse effect on C's day-to-day activities.

(7) In sub-paragraph (3)—

"approved person" means a person of a description specified on a list approved by the Secretary of State for the purposes of sub-paragraph (3)(a) and acting in their capacity as such;

"Criminal Injuries Compensation Scheme" means the Criminal Injuries Compensation Scheme under the Criminal Injuries Compensation Act 1995; and

"relevant criminal injury" means—

(a) a sexual offence (including a pregnancy sustained as a direct result of being the victim of a sexual offence);

(b) physical abuse of an adult, including domestic abuse; or

(c) mental injury,

as described in the tariff of injuries in the Criminal Injuries Compensation Scheme.

(8) For the purposes of sub-paragraph (5)(b)(i), B and C were members of the same family if, at or around the time A was conceived—

(a) they were, or had been, married to each other;

(b) they were, or had been, civil partners of each other;

(c) they were relatives (within the meaning given by section 63(1) of the Family Law Act 1996);

(d) they had agreed to marry each other, whether or not the agreement had been terminated;

(e) they had entered into a civil partnership agreement (within the meaning given by section 73 of the Civil Partnership Act 2004), whether or not the agreement had been terminated;

(f) they were both parents of the same child; or

(g) they had, or had had, parental responsibility (within the meaning given in regulation 4A(2)) for the same child.

Continuation of existing exception in a subsequent award

6. An exception applies where—   **2.464**

(a) the claimant ("C") is A's step-parent;

(b) none of the exceptions under paragraphs 2 to 5 above apply;

(c) C has previously been entitled to an award of universal credit as a member of a couple jointly with a parent of A, in which an exception under paragraph 2, 3 or 5 above applied in relation to A;

(d) since that award terminated, each award of universal credit to which C has been entitled has been made—

(i) as a consequence of a previous award having ended when C ceased to be a member of a couple or became a member of a couple; or

(ii) in any other circumstances in which the assessment periods for that award begin on the same day of each month as the assessment periods for a previous award under regulation 21 (assessment periods); and

(e) where, in the award mentioned in sub-paragraph (c), an exception under paragraph 2 above applied in relation to A—

(i) C is responsible for one or more other children or qualifying young persons born as a result of the same pregnancy as A; and

(ii) A is not the first in the order of those children or qualifying young persons as determined under regulation 24B (order of children and qualifying young persons).

AMENDMENT

1. Social Security (Restrictions on Amounts for Children and Qualifying Young Persons) Amendment Regulations 2017 (SI 2017/376) reg.2(1) and (4) (April 6, 2017).

GENERAL NOTE

See the commentary to regs 24-24B.   **2.465**

The Rent Officers (Universal Credit Functions) Order 2013

(SI 2013/382) (AS AMENDED)

The Secretary of State for Work and Pensions makes the following Order in exercise of the powers conferred by section 122 of the Housing Act 1996.

[*In force April 29, 2013*]

Citation and commencement

2.466   **1.**—This Order may be cited as the Rent Officers (Universal Credit Functions) Order 2013 and comes into force on 29th April 2013.

Interpretation

2.467   **2.**—In this Order—

"Welfare Reform Act" means the Welfare Reform Act 2012;

"the Universal Credit Regulations" means the Universal Credit Regulations 2013;

"accommodation" means any residential accommodation whether or not consisting of the whole or part of a building and whether or not comprising separate and self-contained premises;

[² "assessment period" has the same meaning as in section 40 of the Welfare Reform Act.]

[¹ ...]

"assured tenancy"—

(a) in England and Wales, has the same meaning as in Part 1 of the Housing Act 1988, except that it includes—

   (i) a tenancy which would be an assured tenancy but for paragraph 2, 8 or 10 of Schedule 1 (tenancies which cannot be assured tenancies) to that Act; and

   (ii) a licence which would be an assured tenancy (within the extended meaning given in this definition) were it a tenancy; and

(b) in Scotland, has the same meaning as in Part 2 of the Housing (Scotland) Act 1988, except that it includes—

    (i) a tenancy which would be an assured tenancy but for paragraph 7 or 9 of Schedule 4 (tenancies which cannot be assured tenancies) to that Act; and

   (ii) any other form of occupancy which would be an assured tenancy (within the extended meaning given in this definition) were it a tenancy;

"broad rental market area" has the meaning given in article 3;

"housing payment" means a relevant payment within the meaning of paragraph 3 of Schedule 4 (housing costs element for renters) to the Universal Credit Regulations;

"local authority" means—

(a) in relation to England, the council of a district or London borough, the Common Council of the City of London or the Council of the Isles of Scilly;

(b) in relation to Wales, the council of a county or county borough; and

(c) in relation to Scotland, a council constituted under section 2 (constitution of councils) of the Local Government etc. (Scotland) Act 1994;

"provider of social housing" has the meaning given in paragraph 2 of Schedule 4 to the Universal Credit Regulations;

"relevant time" means the time the request for the determination is made or, if earlier, the date the tenancy ends;

"service charge payments" has the meaning given in paragraph 7 of Schedule 1 (meaning of payments in respect of accommodation) to the Universal Credit Regulations;

"tenancy" includes—

(a) in England and Wales, a licence to occupy premises; and

(b) in Scotland, any other right of occupancy,

    and references to rent, a tenant, a landlord or any other expression appropriate to a tenancy are to be construed accordingly;

"tenant" includes, where the tenant is a member of a couple within the meaning of section 39 of the Welfare Reform Act, the other member of the couple;

"working day" means any day other than—

(a) a Saturday or a Sunday;

(b) Christmas Day or Good Friday; or

(c) a day which is a bank holiday under the Banking and Financial Dealings Act 1971 in any part of Great Britain.

AMENDMENTS

1. Rent Officers (Housing Benefit and Universal Credit Functions) (Amendment) Order 2013 (SI 2013/1544), art.4(2) (September 1, 2013).

2. Rent Officers (Housing Benefit and Universal Credit Functions) (Local Housing Allowance Amendments) Order 2014 (SI 2014/3126) art.4(2) (January 8, 2015).

Broad rental market area determinations

3.—(1) Broad rental market area determinations taking effect on 29th   **2.468** April 2013 are determined in accordance with paragraph (7) and all other broad rental market area determinations are determined in accordance with paragraphs (2) to (6).

(2) A rent officer must, at such times as the rent officer considers appropriate and if the Secretary of State agrees—

(a) determine one or more broad rental market areas; and

(b) in respect of that broad rental market area, or those broad rental market areas, give to the Secretary of State a notice which identifies the local authority areas and the postcodes contained within the broad rental market area (or each of them).

[² (2A) The power in paragraph (2) is not limited by paragraph 2(2A) or (2B) of Schedule 1.]

(3) A broad rental market area is an area within which a person could reasonably be expected to live having regard to facilities and services for the purposes of health, education, recreation, personal banking and shopping, taking account of the distance of travel, by public and private transport, to and from those facilities and services.

(4) A broad rental market area must contain—

(a) residential premises of a variety of types, including such premises held on a variety of tenures; and

(b) sufficient privately rented residential premises to ensure that, in the rent officer's opinion, the local housing allowance for the categories of accommodation in the area for which the rent officer is required to determine a local housing allowance is representative of the rents that a landlord might reasonably be expected to obtain in that area.

(5) Every part of Great Britain must fall within a broad rental market area and a broad rental market area must not overlap with another broad rental market area.

(6) Any broad rental market area determination made in accordance with paragraph (2) is to take effect—

(a) on the day the determination is made for the purpose of enabling a rent officer to determine a local housing allowance for that area; and

(b) for all other purposes on the next [¹ 7th April] following the day on which the determination is made.

(7) For broad rental market area determinations that take effect on 29th April 2013, a rent officer must use the broad rental market area determinations determined in accordance with article 4B of, and Schedule 3B to, the Rent Officers (Housing Benefit Functions) Order 1997 or the Rent Officers (Housing Benefit Functions) (Scotland) Order 1997 that apply on 29th April 2013.

AMENDMENTS

1. Rent Officers (Housing Benefit and Universal Credit Functions) (Local Housing Allowance Amendments) Order 2013 (SI 2013/2978), art.4(2) (January 13, 2014).

2. Rent Officers (Housing Benefit and Universal Credit Functions) (Local Housing Allowance Amendments) Order 2016 (SI 2016/1179) art.4(1) and (2) (January 23, 2017).

Local housing allowance determinations

2.469 **4.**—(1)[⁵...]

[⁵ (1)] [¹ In 2014 and in each subsequent year, on the date specified in paragraph [⁵ (2)],] a rent officer must—

(a) for each broad rental market area determine, in accordance with Schedule 1, a local housing allowance for each of the categories of accommodation set out in paragraph 1 of Schedule 1; and

(b) notify the Secretary of State of the local housing allowance determination made in accordance with sub-paragraph (a) for each broad rental market area.

[¹[³ [⁵ (2)] The date specified for the purposes of paragraph [⁵ (1)] is the last working day of January.]]

[⁴ [⁵ (3) Any local housing allowance determination made in accordance with paragraph (1) is to take effect—

(a) in the case of a person with an existing UC entitlement—
  (i) on the relevant Monday where that is the first day of an assessment period for the person in question; or
  (ii) where the relevant Monday is not the first day of an assessment period for that person, on the first day of the next assessment period following that; or
(b) in any other case, on the relevant Monday.]]

[⁵ (4) For the purposes of this article—

"a person with an existing UC entitlement" means a person who is entitled to universal credit on the relevant Monday;

"relevant Monday" means the first Monday in the first tax year that commences following the day on which the determination is made;

"tax year" means a period beginning with 6th April in one year and ending with 5th April in the next.]

AMENDMENTS

1. Rent Officers (Housing Benefit and Universal Credit Functions) (Amendment) Order 2013 (SI 2013/1544), art.4(3) (September 1, 2013).

2. Rent Officers (Housing Benefit and Universal Credit Functions) (Local Housing Allowance Amendments) Order 2013 (SI 2013/2978), art.4(2) (January 13, 2014).

3. Rent Officers (Housing Benefit and Universal Credit Functions) (Local Housing Allowance Amendments) Order 2014 (SI 2014/3126) art.4(3) (January 8, 2015).

4. Rent Officers (Housing Benefit and Universal Credit Functions) (Local Housing Allowance Amendments) Order 2014 (SI 2014/3126) art.4(4) (January 8, 2015).

5. Rent Officers (Housing Benefit and Universal Credit Functions) (Local Housing Allowance Amendments) Order 2015 (SI 2015/1753) art.4(2) (November 2, 2015).

DEFINITIONS

"accommodation"—see art.2.
"assessment period"—*ibid.*
"broad rental market area"—see arts 2 and 3.

Housing payment determination

5.—Where a rent officer receives a request from the Secretary of State for a determination in respect of housing payments for accommodation let by a provider of social housing, the rent officer must—

2.470

(a) determine in accordance with Schedule 2 whether each of the housing payments specified by the Secretary of State in that request is reasonable for that accommodation; and
(b) where the rent officer determines that a housing payment is not reasonable, determine in accordance with Schedule 2 the amount that is reasonable for the accommodation and notify the Secretary of State of that amount.

"accommodation"—see art.2.
"assessment period"—*ibid.*
"housing payment"—see art.2 and Universal Credit Regs, Sch.4, para.3.

Redeterminations

2.471   **6.**—(1) Where a rent officer has made a determination under article 3, 4 or 5 ("the determination") and paragraph (2) applies, a rent officer must make a further determination ("a redetermination") and notify the Secretary of State of the redetermination.

(2) This paragraph applies where—

(a) the determination was made under article 3 or 4 and the rent officer considers that there is an error in relation to that determination; or

(b) the determination was made under article 5 and—

    (i) the Secretary of State requests that the rent officer makes a redetermination;

    (ii) the Secretary of State informs the rent officer that the information supplied when requesting the determination was incorrect or incomplete; or

    (iii) the rent officer considers that there is an error in relation to the determination.

(3) Where a rent officer makes a redetermination the rent officer must do so in accordance with the provisions of this Order that applied to the determination and use the same information that was used for the determination except that, where the information used was incorrect or incomplete, the rent officer must use the correct or complete information.

(4) Where a rent officer makes a redetermination by virtue of paragraph (2)(b)(i), the rent officer must have regard to the advice of at least one other rent officer in relation to that redetermination.

Information

2.472   **7.**—Where a rent officer considers that the information supplied by the Secretary of State or a landlord under regulation 40 (information to be provided to rent officers) of the Universal Credit, Personal Independence Payment, Jobseeker's Allowance and Employment and Support Allowance (Claims and Payments) Regulations 2013 is incomplete or incorrect, the rent officer must—

(a) notify the Secretary of State or the landlord of that fact; and

(b) request that the Secretary of State or the landlord supplies the further information or to confirm whether, in their opinion, the information already supplied is correct and, if they agree that it is not, to supply the correct information.

Means of giving notice

2.473   **8.**—Any notice given by a rent officer under this Order may be given in writing or by electronic means unless the Secretary of State requests that notice is given in writing only.

Article 4

SCHEDULE 1

LOCAL HOUSING ALLOWANCE DETERMINATIONS

Categories of accommodation

1. The categories of accommodation for which a rent officer is required to determine a local housing allowance in accordance with article 4 are—
  (a) accommodation where the tenant has the exclusive use of only one bedroom and where the tenancy provides for the tenant to share the use of one or more of—
    (i) a kitchen;
    (ii) a bathroom;
    (iii) a toilet; or
    (iv) a room suitable for living in;
  (b) accommodation where the tenant has the exclusive use of only one bedroom and exclusive use of a kitchen, a bathroom, a toilet and a room suitable for living in;
  (c) accommodation where the tenant has the use of only two bedrooms;
  (d) accommodation where the tenant has the use of only three bedrooms;
  (e) accommodation where the tenant has the use of only four bedrooms.

2.474

[¹ Local housing allowance for category of accommodation in paragraph 1

2.—(1) Subject to paragraph 5 (anomalous local housing allowances) the rent officer must determine a local housing allowance for each category of accommodation in paragraph 1 as follows.

(2) [⁴ . . .]

[⁵ (2A) For a broad rental market area not listed in column 1 of the table in paragraph 5A, the local housing allowance for any category of accommodation is the lower of the amounts set out in sub-paragraph (3)(a) and (b).

(2B) For a broad rental market area listed in column 1 of the table in paragraph 5A, the local housing allowance—
  (a) for a category of accommodation listed in the corresponding entry in column 2 of that table, is the lower of the amounts set out in sub-paragraph (3A)(a) and (b);
  (b) for a category of accommodation not so listed, is the lower of the amounts set out in sub-paragraph (3)(a) and (b).]

[⁴ (3) [⁵ The amounts referred to in sub-paragraphs (2A) and (2B)(b) are—]
  (a) the local housing allowance determined for that category of accommodation on 30th January 2015 (or, where the allowance is redetermined under article 6 (redeterminations), the allowance as so redetermined); [⁵ and]
  (b) the rent at the 30th percentile determined in accordance with paragraph 3 [⁵ . . .].]

[⁵ (3A) The amounts referred to in sub-paragraph (2B)(a) are—
  (a) the local housing allowance determined for that category of accommodation on 30th January 2015 (or, where the determination is amended under article 6 (redeterminations), the allowance as so redetermined), plus 3%; and
  (b) the maximum local housing allowance listed in column 2 of the following table for the category of accommodation—

2.475

1. Category of accommodation as defined in the following paragraphs of this Schedule	2. Maximum local housing allowance for that category of accommodation
paragraph 1(1)(a) (one bedroom, shared accommodation)	£1129.42
paragraph 1(1)(b) (one bedroom, exclusive use)	£1129.42
paragraph 1(1)(c) (two bedrooms)	£1310.13
paragraph 1(1)(d) (three bedrooms)	£1536.01
paragraph 1(1)(e) (four bedrooms)	£1807.07]

(4) Where the local housing allowance would otherwise not be a whole number of pence, it must be rounded to the nearest whole penny by disregarding any amount less than half a penny and treating any amount of half a penny or more as a whole penny.]

Rent at the 30th percentile

2.476   **3.**—(1) The rent officer must determine the rent at the 30th percentile in accordance with the following sub-paragraphs.

(2) The rent officer must compile a list of rents.

[¹ (3) The rent officer must compile a list of rents in ascending order of the monthly rents which, in the rent officer's opinion, are payable—

    (a) for accommodation let under an assured tenancy for each category of accommodation specified in paragraph 1; and

    (b) in the 12 month period ending on the 30th day of the September preceding the date of the determination.]

(4) The list must include any rents which are of the same amount.

(5) The criteria for including an assured tenancy on the list of rents in relation to each category of accommodation specified in paragraph 1 are that—

    (a) the accommodation let under the assured tenancy is in the broad rental market area for which the local housing allowance for that category of accommodation is being determined;

    (b) the accommodation is in a reasonable state of repair; and

    (c) the assured tenancy permits the tenant to use exclusively or share the use of, as the case may be, the same number and type of rooms as the category of accommodation in relation to which the list of rents is being compiled.

[¹ (6) Sub-paragraph (7) applies where the rent officer is not satisfied that the list of rents in respect of any category of accommodation would contain sufficient rents, payable in the 12 month period ending on the 30th day of the September preceding the date of the determination for accommodation in the broad rental market area, to enable a local housing allowance to be determined which is representative of the rents that a landlord might reasonably be expected to obtain in that area.]

(7) In a case where this sub-paragraph applies, the rent officer may add to the list rents for accommodation in the same category in other areas in which a comparable market exists.

(8) Where rent is payable other than monthly the rent officer must use the figure which would be payable if the rent were to be payable monthly by calculating the rent for a year and dividing the total by 12.

(9) When compiling the list of rents for each category of accommodation, the rent officer must—

    (a) assume that no-one had sought or is seeking the tenancy who would have been entitled to housing benefit under Part 7 of the Social Security Contributions and Benefits Act 1992(12) or universal credit under Part 1 of the Welfare Reform Act; and

    (b) exclude the amount of any rent which, in the rent officer's opinion, is fairly attributable to the provision of services performed or facilities (including the use of furniture) provided for, or rights made available to, the tenant and which would not be classed as service charge payments.

(10) The rent at the 30th percentile in the list of rents ("R") is determined as follows—

    (a) where the number of rents on the list is a multiple of 10, the formula is—

$$R = \frac{\text{the amount of the rent at P} + \text{the amount of the rent at P1}}{2}$$

    where—

      (i) P is the position on the list found by multiplying the number of rents on the list by 3 and dividing by 10; and

      (ii) P1 is the following position on the list;

    (b) where the number of rents on the list is not a multiple of 10, the formula is—

$$R = \text{the amount of the rent at P2}$$

    where P2 is the position on the list found by multiplying the number of rents on the list by 3 and dividing by 10 and rounding the result upwards to the nearest whole number.

[¹ Maximum local housing allowance

2.477   **4.** [² [⁴ . . .]]]

Anomalous local housing allowances

2.478   **5.** Where—

    (a) the rent officer has determined the local housing allowance for each of the categories of accommodation in paragraph 1 in accordance with the preceding paragraphs of this Schedule; and

(b) the local housing allowance for a category of accommodation in paragraph 1(b) to (e) is lower than the local housing allowance for any of the categories of accommodation which precede it,

that local housing allowance is to be the same as the highest local housing allowance which precedes it.

[⁵ 5A. The table referred to in paragraph 2(2A) and (2B) is as follows—

1. Broad rental market area	2. Category of accommodation as defined in the following paragraphs of this Schedule
Aylesbury	paragraph 1(1)(b) (one bedroom, exclusive use)
Aylesbury	paragraph 1(1)(c) (two bedrooms)
Barrow-in-Furness	paragraph 1(1)(a) (one bedroom, shared accommodation)
Bedford	paragraph 1(1)(d) (three bedrooms)
Bolton and Bury	paragraph 1(1)(a) (one bedroom, shared accommodation)
Bristol	paragraph 1(1)(b) (one bedroom, exclusive use)
Bristol	paragraph 1(1)(d) (three bedrooms)
Bury St. Edmunds	paragraph 1(1)(a) (one bedroom, shared accommodation)
Cambridge	paragraph 1(1)(c) (two bedrooms)
Cambridge	paragraph 1(1)(e) (four bedrooms)
Central London	paragraph 1(1)(a) (one bedroom, shared accommodation)
Central Norfolk and Norwich	paragraph 1(1)(a) (one bedroom, shared accommodation)
Chilterns	paragraph 1(1)(c) (two bedrooms)
Flintshire	paragraph 1(1)(a) (one bedroom, shared accommodation)
Harlow and Stortford	paragraph 1(1)(a) (one bedroom, shared accommodation)
Inner North London	paragraph 1(1)(a) (one bedroom, shared accommodation)
Kings Lynn	paragraph 1(1)(a) (one bedroom, shared accommodation)
Lothian	paragraph 1(1)(b) (one bedroom, exclusive use)
Luton	paragraph 1(1)(b) (one bedroom, exclusive use)
Luton	paragraph 1(1)(c) (two bedrooms)
Luton	paragraph 1(1)(d) (three bedrooms)
Luton	paragraph 1(1)(e) (four bedrooms)
Milton Keynes	paragraph 1(1)(d) (three bedrooms)
Milton Keynes	paragraph 1(1)(e) (four bedrooms)
Neath Port Talbot	paragraph 1(1)(a) (one bedroom, shared accommodation)
North West Kent	paragraph 1(1)(e) (four bedrooms)
North West London	paragraph 1(1)(b) (one bedroom, exclusive use)
Outer East London	paragraph 1(1)(a) (one bedroom, shared accommodation)
Outer East London	paragraph 1(1)(e) (four bedrooms)
Outer South London	paragraph 1(1)(b) (one bedroom, exclusive use)
Outer South London	paragraph 1(1)(c) (two bedrooms)
Outer South West London	paragraph 1(1)(a) (one bedroom, shared accommodation)
Outer West London	paragraph 1(1)(c) (two bedrooms)

Pembrokeshire	paragraph 1(1)(a) (one bedroom, shared accommodation)
Solihull	paragraph 1(1)(a) (one bedroom, shared accommodation)
South West Essex	paragraph 1(1)(a) (one bedroom, shared accommodation)
South West Herts	paragraph 1(1)(d) (three bedrooms)
Southend	paragraph 1(1)(a) (one bedroom, shared accommodation)
Southern Greater Manchester	paragraph 1(1)(a) (one bedroom, shared accommodation)
Stevenage & North Herts	paragraph 1(1)(b) (one bedroom, exclusive use)
Stevenage & North Herts	paragraph 1(1)(d) (three bedrooms)
Stevenage & North Herts	paragraph 1(1)(e) (four bedrooms)
Sunderland	paragraph 1(1)(a) (one bedroom, shared accommodation)
Swindon	paragraph 1(1)(a) (one bedroom, shared accommodation)
Swindon	paragraph 1(1)(b) (one bedroom, exclusive use)
Vale of Glamorgan	paragraph 1(1)(a) (one bedroom, shared accommodation)
Walton	paragraph 1(1)(a) (one bedroom, shared accommodation)
Warwickshire South	paragraph 1(1)(a) (one bedroom, shared accommodation)]

6. [^{1} [^{3} [^{4} . . .]]]

AMENDMENTS

1. Rent Officers (Housing Benefit and Universal Credit Functions) (Local Housing Allowance Amendments) Order 2013 (SI 2013/2978), art.4(3) (January 13, 2014).
2. Rent Officers (Housing Benefit and Universal Credit Functions) (Local Housing Allowance Amendments) Order 2014 (SI 2014/3126) art.4(5) (January 8, 2015).
3. Rent Officers (Housing Benefit and Universal Credit Functions) (Local Housing Allowance Amendments) Order 2014 (SI 2014/3126) art.4(6) and Sch.3 (January 8, 2015).
4. Rent Officers (Housing Benefit and Universal Credit Functions) (Local Housing Allowance Amendments) Order 2015 (SI 2015/1753) art.4(3) (November 2, 2015).
5. Rent Officers (Housing Benefit and Universal Credit Functions) (Local Housing Allowance Amendments) Order 2016 (SI 2016/1179) art.4(1) and (3) (January 23, 2017).

Article 5

SCHEDULE 2

HOUSING PAYMENT DETERMINATION

2.479   1. The rent officer must determine whether, in the rent officer's opinion, each of the housing payments payable for the tenancy of the accommodation at the relevant time is reasonable.
2. If the rent officer determines under paragraph 1 that a housing payment is not reasonable, the rent officer must also determine the amount of the housing payment which is reasonable.
3. When making a determination under this Schedule, the rent officer must—
   (a) have regard to the level of similar payments under tenancies for accommodation which—

    (i) is let by the same type of landlord;

    (ii) is in the same local authority area [¹ (but see paragraph 4)];

    (iii) has the same number of bedrooms; and

    (iv) is in the same reasonable state of repair,

as the accommodation in respect of which the determination is being made;

(b) exclude—

    (i) the cost of any care, support or supervision provided to the tenant by the landlord or by someone on the landlord's behalf;

    (ii) any payments for services performed or facilities (including the use of furniture) provided for, or rights made available to, the tenant which are not service charge payments; and

(c) where the accommodation is let at an Affordable Rent, assume that the rent is reasonable.

4. Where the rent officer is not satisfied that the local authority area contains sufficient accommodation to allow a determination of the housing payments which a landlord might reasonably have been expected to charge, the rent officer may have regard to the level of housing payments in one adjoining local authority area [¹ or one local authority area adjoining an adjoining local authority area or, if the rent officer considers it necessary, more than one such area].

5. For the purposes of this Schedule—

(a) a housing payment is reasonable where it is not higher than the payment which the landlord might reasonably have been expected to obtain for the tenancy at the relevant time;

(b) accommodation is let by the same type of landlord where—

    (i) in a case where the landlord of the accommodation in respect of which the determination is being made is a local authority, the landlord of the other accommodation is also a local authority; and

    (ii) in a case where the landlord of the accommodation in respect of which the determination is being made is a provider of social housing other than a local authority, the landlord of the other accommodation is also a provider of social housing other than a local authority;

(c) accommodation is let at an Affordable Rent where—

    (i) the rent is regulated under a standard by the Regulator of Social Housing under section 194 of the Housing and Regeneration Act 2008(13) ("the 2008 Act") which requires the initial rent to be set at no more than 80% of the local market rent (including service charges); or

    (ii) the accommodation is let by a local authority and, under arrangements between the local authority and the Homes and Communities Agency (as established by section 1 of the 2008 Act), the Greater London Authority or the Secretary of State, the rent payable is set on the same basis as would be the case if the rent were regulated under a standard set by the Regulator of Social Housing under section 194 of the 2008 Act which requires the initial rent to be set at no more than 80% of the local market rent (including service charges).

AMENDMENT

1. Rent Officers (Housing Benefit and Universal Credit Functions) (Local Housing Allowance Amendments) Order 2016 (SI 2016/1179) art.4(1) and (4) (January 23, 2017).

DEFINITIONS

"accommodation"—see art.2.

"housing payment"—see art.2 and Universal Credit Regs, Sch.4, para.3.

"local authority"—see art.2.

"provider of social housing"—see art.2 and Universal Credit Regs, Sch.4, para.4.

"relevant time"—see art.2.

"service charge payments"—see art.2 and Universal Credit Regs, Sch.1 para.7.

"tenancy"—see art.2.

"tenant"—*ibid.*

The Universal Credit (Work-Related Requirements) In Work Pilot Scheme and Amendment Regulations 2015

(SI 2015/89)

Made on January 29, 2015 by the Secretary of State under sections 18(5), 22(2), 41(1)(a), (2)(b) and (4) and 42(2) and (3) of the Welfare Reform Act 2012, Part 3 being made with a view to ascertaining the extent to which the provision made by that Part is likely to promote people already in paid work remaining in work, or obtaining or being able to obtain, more work or better paid work, a draft having been laid before, and approved by resolution of, each House of Parliament in accordance with section 43(4) and (6)(b) of the Act, and the Social Security Advisory Committee having agreed in accordance with section 173(1) of the Social Security Administration Act 1992 that proposals in respect of these Regulations should not be referred to it.

[In force February 19, 2015]

REGULATIONS REPRODUCED

PART 1

INTRODUCTORY

PART 2

AMENDMENT OF THE UNIVERSAL CREDIT REGULATIONS

PART 3

THE IN WORK PILOT SCHEME

GENERAL NOTE

2.480   See the annotation to reg.99(6) and (6A), the provisions affected by the amendment in reg.3 of the present Regulations, for the context in which the pilot schemes will operate.

PART 1

INTRODUCTORY

Citation and commencement

1. These Regulations may be cited as the Universal Credit (Work-Related   2.480.1
Requirements) In Work Pilot Scheme and Amendment Regulations 2015,
and come into force at the end of the period of 21 days beginning with the
day on which they are made.

Interpretation

2. In these Regulations—   2.481
"the Act" means the Welfare Reform Act 2012;
[¹"monthly earnings" has the meaning in regulation 90(6) of the
   Universal Credit Regulations;]
"qualifying claimant" has the meaning in regulation 7;
"the Universal Credit Regulations" means the Universal Credit
   Regulations 2013; and
[¹. . .].

AMENDMENT

1. Universal Credit and Miscellaneous Amendments Regulations 2015 (SI
2015/1754) reg.3(2) (November 4, 2015).

PART 2

AMENDMENT OF THE UNIVERSAL CREDIT REGULATIONS

New provision for suspension of mandatory work search and work availability requirements on account of earnings

3. – *The amendments effected by this regulation have been taken into account*   2.482
in the text of the Universal Credit Regulations 2013 elsewhere in this volume.

PART 3

THE IN WORK PILOT SCHEME

Provision made for piloting purposes

4.—(1) The following provision is made in accordance with section 41 of   2.483
the Act to test the extent to which the imposition of work-related requirements on persons already in paid work is likely to promote their remaining
in work, or obtaining or being able to obtain, more work or better-paid
work.

(2) Regulation 99 of the Universal Credit Regulations (which provides
for the suspension of work search requirements and work availability
requirements where the claimant's [¹ monthly] earnings from employment
or, if the claimant is a member of a couple, their combined [¹ monthly]
earnings from employment, reach a specified amount) is to apply as if paragraph (6) were omitted.

(3) The provision made by paragraph (2) is to apply only in relation to qualifying claimants who have been selected by the Secretary of State in accordance with regulation 5 and notified of that selection in accordance with regulation 6.

(4) The provision made by paragraph (2) ceases to apply to a person who has been selected in accordance with regulation 5 where—

(a) that person ceases to be a qualifying claimant (but see paragraph (5)); or

(b) the Secretary of State has determined that that provision should cease to apply because—

(i) the person has moved to live in a different geographical area; or

(ii) the Secretary of State has determined that the testing of particular work-related requirements that have been imposed on that person has concluded.

(5) Where a person has been selected in accordance with regulation 5 and, by reason only of an increase or decrease in their [¹ monthly] earnings (or, if they are a member of a couple, the [¹ monthly] earnings of the other member) the person is no longer a qualifying claimant, paragraph (2) applies again if the person becomes a qualifying claimant again unless, in the intervening period—

(a) paragraph (2) has ceased to apply for another reason; or

(b) the person has ceased to be entitled to universal credit for a continuous period of 6 months or more.

AMENDMENT

1. Universal Credit and Miscellaneous Amendments Regulations 2015 (SI 2015/1754) reg.3(3) (November 4, 2015).

DEFINITIONS

"the Act"—see reg.2.

"claimant"—see WRA 2012 s.40.

"monthly earnings"—see reg.2 and the Universal Credit Regulations 2013 reg.90(6).

"qualifying claimant"—see regs 2 and 7.

"the Universal Credit Regulations"—see reg.2

"work"—see WRA 2012 s.40.

"work availability requirement"—see WRA 2012 ss.40 and 18(2).

"work search requirement"—see WRA 2012 ss.40 and 17(1).

"work-related requirement"—see WRA 2012 ss.40 and 13(2).

Selection of participants

2.484   5.—(1) A selection for the purpose of regulation 4 is to be made by the Secretary of State on a random sampling basis from persons who, at the time of the selection, are qualifying claimants.

(2) The Secretary of State may make a selection in accordance with paragraph (1) on more than one occasion and, on each occasion, the Secretary of State may limit that selection to qualifying claimants living in a particular geographical area determined by the Secretary of State or to persons who have become qualifying claimants within a period determined by the Secretary of State.

DEFINITION

"qualifying claimant"—see regs 2 and 7.

Notification of participants

6.—(1) The Secretary of State must notify a claimant in writing when— 2.485
   (a) the claimant is selected in accordance with regulation 5; and
   (b) the provision made by regulation 4(3) ceases to apply to the claimant by virtue of regulation 4(4), unless it is because the claimant is no longer a qualifying claimant by reason only of a change in earnings.

(2) Where, for the purposes of this regulation, the Secretary of State sends a notice by post to the claimant's last known address, it is to be treated as having been given or sent on the day on which it was posted.

(3) Schedule 2 to the Universal Credit, Personal Independence Payments, Jobseeker's Allowance and Employment and Support Allowance (Claims and Payments) Regulations 2013 applies to the delivery of an electronic communication sent by the Secretary of State for the purposes of this regulation in the same manner as it applies to the delivery of electronic communications for the purposes of those Regulations.

DEFINITIONS

"claimant"—see WRA 2012 s.40.
"qualifying claimant"—see regs 2 and 7.

Meaning of "qualifying claimant"

7.—(1) A qualifying claimant is a person who— 2.486
   (a) falls within section 22 of the Act (claimants subject to all work-related requirements);
   (b) has [¹ monthly] earnings of such an amount (or, if the person is a member of a couple, the couple has combined [¹ monthly] earnings of such an amount) that, apart from regulation 4(2), regulation 99(6) of the Universal Credit Regulations would apply;
   (c) is not a person on whom the Secretary of State must not impose work-related requirements by virtue of regulation 98 of the Universal Credit Regulations (victims of domestic violence); and
   (d) is not a person to whom any of the following paragraphs of regulation 99 of the Universal Credit Regulations (circumstances in which requirements must not be imposed) applies—
      (i) paragraph (3) (which provides for suspension of work search and work availability requirements for various reasons, including imprisonment and treatment for alcohol or drug dependency), except sub-paragraph (a) (claimant attending court as a witness etc.) and sub-paragraph (g) (claimant engaged in a public duty); or
      (ii) paragraph (5)(c) (claimant unfit for work for longer than 14 days).

AMENDMENT

1. Universal Credit and Miscellaneous Amendments Regulations 2015 (SI 2015/1754) reg.3(3) (November 4, 2015).

DEFINITIONS

"the Act"—see reg.2.
"couple"—see WRA ss.40 and 39.
"monthly earnings"—see reg.2 and the Universal Credit Regulations 2013 reg.90(6).

"the Universal Credit Regulations"—see reg.2
"work availability requirement"—see WRA 2012 ss.40 and 18(2).
"work search requirement"—see WRA 2012 ss.40 and 17(1).

Expiry of the pilot scheme

2.487 **8.** This Part ceases to have effect at the end of the period of three years starting with the day on which these Regulations come into force, unless it continues in effect by order of the Secretary of State under section 41(5)(a) of the Act.

PART IVA

TRANSITIONAL PROVISIONS

The Universal Credit (Transitional Provisions) Regulations 2014

2014/1230 (AS AMENDED)

The Secretary of State for Work and Pensions makes the following Regulations in exercise of the powers conferred by section 42(2) and (3) of and paragraphs 1(1) and (2)(b), 3(1)(a) to (c), 4(1)(a), 5(1), (2)(c) and (d) and (3)(a) and 6 of Schedule 6 to the Welfare Reform Act 2012.

In accordance with section 172(1) of the Social Security Administration Act 1992 ("the 1992 Act"), the Secretary of State has referred proposals in respect of these Regulations to the Social Security Advisory Committee.

In accordance with section 176(1) of the 1992 Act and, in so far as these Regulations relate to housing benefit, the Secretary of State has consulted with organisations appearing to him to be representative of the authorities concerned in respect of proposals for these Regulations.

[In force: June 16, 2014]

ARRANGEMENT OF REGULATIONS

PART 1

PART 2

CHAPTER 1

CHAPTER 2

CHAPTER 3

GENERAL NOTE

3.1   The original Universal Credit (Transitional Provisions) Regulations 2013 (SI 2013/386) ("the 2013 Regulations") came into force on April 29, 2013 and provided for the introduction of universal credit to limited categories of claimant. A series of Commencement Orders has subsequently brought into force provisions relating to universal credit for claimants in specified postcodes, accompanied (in those areas) by repeals of the legislation relating to jobseeker's allowance and employment and support allowance for those claimants. The present Regulations ("the 2014 Transitional Regulations") made provision for the second phase of the introduction of universal credit, and represented a change from the structured plans for the roll out of universal credit set out in the 2013 Regulations. These Regulations accordingly provide for some of the more complex transitional situations that will arise when dealing with families and those on a wider range of existing benefits. The House of Lords' Secondary Legislation Scrutiny Committee expressed the following opinion on the draft 2014 Transitional Regulations (First Report, Session 2014/15, footnote omitted):

"20. In line with an announcement made on 5 December 2013, the Department for Work and Pensions now expects the "majority" of existing benefit claimants to be transferred to Universal Credit by the end of 2017, that is, around 6.5 million people. DWP officials state that "decisions on the later stages of Universal Credit (UC) roll out will be informed by the development of the enhanced IT but some Employment Support Allowance claimants may be moved on to UC more slowly because they have already experienced the move from the old Incapacity Benefit and they would not immediately benefit from the improved work incentives of Universal Credit". The Committee was surprised to see this instrument accompanied by the original cost/benefit analysis from 2012, despite the well-publicised changes to the programme. DWP officials state that "the Impact Assessment published in December 2012 provides information based on the situation once Universal Credit (UC) is fully rolled out. Therefore, as there has not been any significant change since the Impact Assessment was published, we have not published an updated impact assessment for this instrument". However, the House may wish to note that the end date for completion of the transition to Universal Credit has been made more flexible and can be "managed" if problems arise in a particular area. Such changes will be made by Commencement Orders, which are not subject to parliamentary scrutiny. These Regulations also now include provision to allow the Secretary of State discretion temporarily to stop taking Universal Credit claims in certain geographic areas or for certain groups of claimants, so that any issues can be resolved. Where this provision is exercised, anyone prevented from claiming Universal Credit will be able to claim existing benefits or credits."

PART 1

Citation and commencement

1. (1) These Regulations may be cited as the Universal Credit (Transitional Provisions) Regulations 2014.

(2) These Regulations come into force on 16th June 2014.

3.2

Interpretation

2. (1) In these Regulations—

"the 2002 Act" means the Tax Credits Act 2002;

"the 2007 Act" means the Welfare Reform Act 2007;

"the Act" means the Welfare Reform Act 2012;

"assessment period" has the same meaning as in the Universal Credit Regulations;

"the Claims and Payments Regulations" means the Universal Credit, Personal Independence Payment, Jobseeker's Allowance and Employment and Support Allowance (Claims and Payments) Regulations 2013;

"contributory employment and support allowance" means a contributory

3.3

allowance under Part 1 of the 2007 Act as that Part has effect apart from the amendments made by Schedule 3, and Part 1 of Schedule 14, to the Act that remove references to an income-related allowance; [¹ . . .]

"existing benefit" means income-based jobseeker's allowance, income-related employment and support allowance, income support, housing benefit and child tax credit and working tax credit under the 2002 Act, but see also regulation 25(2);

"First-tier Tribunal" has the same meaning as in the Social Security Act 1998;

"housing benefit" means housing benefit under section 130 of the Social Security Contributions and Benefits Act 1992;

"income-based jobseeker's allowance" has the same meaning as in the Jobseekers Act 1995;

"income-related employment and support allowance" means an income-related allowance under Part 1 of the 2007 Act;

"income support" means income support under section 124 of the Social Security Contributions and Benefits Act 1992;

"joint-claim jobseeker's allowance" means old style JSA, entitlement to which arises by virtue of section 1(2B) of the Jobseekers Act 1995;

"new claimant partner" has the meaning given in regulation 7;

"new style ESA" means an allowance under Part 1 of the 2007 Act as amended by the amendments made by Schedule 3, and Part 1 of Schedule 14, to the Act that remove references to an income-related allowance;

"new style JSA" means an allowance under the Jobseekers Act 1995 as amended by the amendments made by Part 1 of Schedule 14 to the Act that remove references to an income-based allowance;

"old style ESA" means an employment and support allowance under Part 1 of the 2007 Act as that Part has effect apart from the amendments made by Schedule 3, and Part 1 of Schedule 14, to the Act that remove references to an income-related allowance;

"old style JSA" means a jobseeker's allowance under the Jobseekers Act 1995 as that Act has effect apart from the amendments made by Part 1 of Schedule 14 to the Act that remove references to an income-based allowance;

"partner" in relation to a person ("A") means a person who forms part of a couple with A;

[² "qualifying young person" has the same meaning as in the Universal Credit Regulations, but see also regulation 28;]

[¹ "specified accommodation" means accommodation to which one or more of sub-paragraphs (2) to (5) of paragraph 3A of Schedule 1 to the Universal Credit Regulations applies;]

"tax credit" (including "child tax credit" and "working tax credit"), "tax credits" and "tax year" have the same meanings as in the 2002 Act;

"the Universal Credit Regulations" means the Universal Credit Regulations 2013;

"Upper Tribunal" has the same meaning as in the Social Security Act 1998.

(2) For the purposes of these Regulations—

(a) the date on which a claim for universal credit is made is to be determined in accordance with the Claims and Payments Regulations;

(b) where a couple is treated, in accordance with regulation 9(8) of the Claims and Payments Regulations, as having made a claim for universal credit, references to the date on which the claim is treated as made are to the date of formation of the couple;

(c) where a regulation refers to entitlement to an existing benefit on the date on which a claim for universal credit is made or treated as made, such entitlement is to be taken into account notwithstanding the effect of regulations 5, 7 and 8 or termination of an award of the benefit before that date by virtue of an order made under section 150(3) of the Act.

AMENDMENTS

1. Universal Credit (Transitional Provisions) (Amendment) Regulations 2014 (SI 2014/1626) reg.3 (November 3, 2014).

2. Social Security (Restrictions on Amounts for Children and Qualifying Young Persons) Amendment Regulations 2017 (2017/376) reg.3(2) (April 6, 2017).

DEFINITIONS

"the Act"–see reg.2(1).

GENERAL NOTE

Para. (1)

"new claimant partner": where a single universal credit claimant becomes a member   3.4
of a couple, and their award terminates, and the other member of the couple was not previously entitled to universal credit as a single person, but an award of universal credit is then made to the couple as joint claimants, then the other member of the couple is known as a "new claimant partner" (see also reg.7).

"new style ESA": in effect, this means (new variant) contribution-based ESA, shorn of its previous income-based element, and as defined in what were originally the Pathfinder areas as from April 29, 2013.

"new style JSA": similarly, this means (new variant) contribution-based JSA, again shorn of its income-related element, and as defined in those Pathfinder areas as from April 29, 2013.

Para. (2) (a)
The normal rule is that the date of a universal credit claim is the date the claim   3.5
is received, whether electronically or by telephone or, if later, the first day for which the claim is made: see Claims and Payments Regulations 2013, reg.10.

Revocation and saving of the Universal Credit (Transitional Provisions) Regulations 2013

3. (1) The Universal Credit (Transitional Provisions) Regulations 2013   3.6
("the 2013 Regulations") are revoked, subject to the savings in paragraphs (2) to (4).

(2) Chapters 2 and 3 of Part 2 (Pathfinder Group and treatment of invalid claims) of the 2013 Regulations continue to have effect in relation to a claim for universal credit—

(a) which was made before the date on which these Regulations come into force ("the commencement date"); and

(b) in respect of which no payment has been made to the claimant before the commencement date.

(3) Regulation 19 of the 2013 Regulations (advance payments of universal credit) continues to have effect in relation to an advance payment which was made in accordance with that regulation before the commencement date and regulation 17 of these Regulations does not apply to such a payment.

(4) Any other provision of the 2013 Regulations continues to have effect in so far as is necessary to give full effect to paragraphs (2) and (3).

DEFINITIONS

"the 2013 Regulations"–para.(1).
"the commencement date"–para.(2)(a).

GENERAL NOTE

3.7   This regulation provides for revocation of the Universal Credit (Transitional Provisions) Regulations 2013 (para.(1)), subject to certain savings (paras.(2)-(4)). These savings concern claimants who claimed universal credit before the date on which the 2014 Transitional Regulations came into force (June 16, 2014) and relate in particular to the treatment of invalid claims and recovery of advance payments of universal credit made under the 2013 Transitional Regulations. The intention is to ensure that the validity of a claim is judged in accordance with the provisions which were in force at the time the claim was made, and that advance payments made under the 2013 Transitional Regulations remain recoverable.

PART 2

CHAPTER 1

Secretary of State discretion to determine that claims for universal credit may not be made

3.8   **4.** (1) Where the Secretary of State considers it necessary, in order to—
   (a) safeguard the efficient administration of universal credit; or
   (b) ensure the effective testing of systems for the administration of universal credit,

to cease to accept claims in any area, or in any category of case (either in all areas or in a specified area), the Secretary of State may determine that claims for universal credit may not be made in that area, or in that category of case.

(2) A determination under paragraph (1) has effect until it ceases to have effect in accordance with a further determination made by the Secretary of State.

(3) More than one determination under paragraph (1) may have effect at the same time.

GENERAL NOTE

3.9   This regulation had no direct equivalent under the 2013 Transitional Regulations. It vests the Secretary of State with a discretion temporarily to exclude claims for universal credit in any area, or in any category of case, if he considers that this is necessary in order to safeguard the efficient administration of universal credit, or to ensure the effective testing of administrative systems. In the event that this provision is exercised, anyone prevented from claiming universal credit would be able to claim existing benefits or tax credits.

CHAPTER 1

Exclusion of entitlement to certain benefits

5. (1) Except as provided in paragraph (2), a claimant is not entitled to—   **3.10**

(a) income support;

(b) housing benefit;

(c) a tax credit; or

(d) state pension credit under the State Pension Credit Act 2002,

in respect of any period when the claimant is entitled to universal credit.

(2) Entitlement to universal credit does not preclude the claimant from entitlement—

(a) to housing benefit in respect of [¹ specified accommodation]; or

(b) during the first assessment period for universal credit, where the claimant is a new claimant partner, to—

   (i) income support, where an award to which the new claimant partner is entitled terminates, in accordance with regulation 7(4), after the first date of entitlement to universal credit;

  (ii) housing benefit, where regulation 7(5)(b) applies and an award of housing benefit to which the new claimant partner is entitled terminates after the first date of entitlement to universal credit; or

 (iii) a tax credit, where an award to which the new claimant partner is entitled terminates, in accordance with the 2002 Act, after the first date of entitlement to universal credit.

AMENDMENTS

1. Universal Credit (Transitional Provisions) (Amendment) Regulations 2014 (SI 2014/1626) reg.3 (November 3, 2014).

DEFINITIONS

"the 2002 Act"–see reg.2(1).
"assessment period"–*ibid.*
"housing benefit"–*ibid.*
"income support"–*ibid.*
"new claimant partner"–*ibid.*
"specified accommodation"–*ibid.*
"tax credit"–*ibid.*

GENERAL NOTE

This regulation broadly performs the same function as reg.15(1)-(2A) of the 2013   **3.11** Transitional Regulations. The basic rule is that entitlement to universal credit and entitlement to any of the benefits or tax credits in para.(1) are mutually exclusive. Provision is made to similar effect in relation to "old style JSA" and "old style ESA" by virtue of the various Commencement Orders made under s.150(3) of the Act, which bring into force repeals of the legislation relating to those benefits. References to "old style JSA" and "old style ESA" are to the versions of jobseeker's allowance and employment and support allowance which include an income-based, or income-related, allowance (see reg.2 above).

Exclusion of claims for certain existing benefits

3.12   **6.** (1) Except as provided in paragraphs (5) to (9) a universal credit claimant may not make a claim for income support, housing benefit or a tax credit.

(2) For the purposes of this regulation, a person is a universal credit claimant if—

  (a) the person is entitled to universal credit;

  (b) the person has made a claim for universal credit, a decision has not yet been made on that claim and the person has not been informed (in accordance with an order made under section 150(3) of the Act) that he or she is not entitled to claim universal credit;

[² (ba)(i)   the conditions in regulation 6(1)(a), (b) and (c) or 6(2)(a), (b) and (c) of the Claims and Payments Regulations (claims not required for entitlement to universal credit in certain cases) are met in relation to the person;

    (ii) he or she may be entitled to an award of universal credit without making a claim if the conditions in regulation 6(1)(d) and (e) or, as the case may be, 6(2)(d) and (e) of those Regulations are also met; and

    (iii) either the Secretary of State has no information in relation to the person which may indicate a change of circumstances as referred to in regulation 6(1)(e) or, as the case may be, 6(2)(e) of those Regulations, or the Secretary of State has such information but no decision has been made that the person is entitled to universal credit;]

  (c) the person was previously entitled to a joint award of universal credit which terminated because the person ceased to be a member of a couple, he or she is not exempt (by virtue of regulation 9(6) of the Claims and Payments Regulations) from the condition of entitlement to universal credit that he or she makes a claim for it and the period of one month, starting with the date on which the person notified the Secretary of State that he or she had ceased to be a member of a couple, has not expired;

[² (ca) the person may be entitled to an award of universal credit in circumstances where, by virtue of regulation 9(6), (7) or (10) of the Claims and Payments Regulations (claims for universal credit by members of a couple), it is not a condition of entitlement that he or she makes a claim for it, but no decision has yet been made as to the person's entitlement;]

  (d) the person is treated, under the Claims and Payments Regulations, as having made a claim for universal credit, [² . . .] but no decision has yet been made as to the person's entitlement;

  (e) a decision has been made that the person is not entitled to universal credit and—

    (i) the Secretary of State is considering whether to revise that deci-

sion under section 9 of the Social Security Act 1998, whether
on an application made for that purpose, or on the Secretary of
State's own initiative; or

(ii) the person has appealed against that decision to the First-tier
Tribunal and that appeal or any subsequent appeal to the Upper
Tribunal or to a court has not been finally determined.

(3) For the purposes of paragraph (1)—

(a) a universal credit claimant makes a claim for benefit mentioned in
that paragraph if the claimant takes any action which results in a
decision on a claim being required under the relevant Regulations;
and

(b) except as provided in [² paragraphs (5) to (7B)], it is irrelevant that
the effect of any provision of the relevant Regulations is that, for
the purposes of those Regulations, the claim is made or treated as
made at a time when the claimant was not a universal credit claimant.

(4) The relevant Regulations are—

(a) in relation to a claim for income support, the Social Security (Claims
and Payments) Regulations 1987 ("the 1987 Regulations");

(b) in relation to a claim for housing benefit, the Housing Benefit
Regulations 2006 ("the 2006 Regulations") or, as the case may
be, the Housing Benefit (Persons who have attained the qualifying
age for state pension credit) Regulations 2006 ("the 2006 (SPC)
Regulations");

(c) in relation to a claim for a tax credit, the Tax Credits (Claims and
Notifications) Regulations 2002.

(5) A universal credit claimant is not precluded from making a claim for
income support if—

(a) first notification of the claimant's intention to make that claim was
made, or deemed to be made, for the purposes of regulation 6(1A)
(c) [² or 6(A)] of the 1987 Regulations, before the date on which the
claim for universal credit was made or treated as made; and

(b) in accordance with the 1987 Regulations, the claimant's entitlement
to income support in connection with the claim will (if the claimant
is entitled to income support) pre-date—

(i) the date, or anticipated date, of the claimant's entitlement to
universal credit in connection with the current award or claim;
or

(ii) where the claimant is a new claimant partner and regulation
7(4) would apply to the award, the date on which it would terminate in accordance with that provision.

(6) A universal credit claimant is not precluded from making a claim for
housing benefit if—

(a) first notification of the claimant's intention to make that claim
was given (within the meaning of regulation 83(5)(d) of the 2006
Regulations or, as the case may be, regulation 64(6)(d) of the 2006
(SPC) Regulations before the date on which the claim for universal
credit was made or treated as made; and

(b) in accordance with the 2006 Regulations or, as the case may be,
the 2006 (SPC) Regulations, the claimant's entitlement to housing
benefit in connection with the claim will (if the claimant is entitled
to housing benefit) pre-date—

    (i) the date, or anticipated date, of the claimant's entitlement to universal credit in connection with the current award or claim; or

    (ii) where the claimant is a new claimant partner and regulation 7(5)(b) would apply to the award, the date on which it would terminate in accordance with the 2006 Regulations or, as the case may be, the 2006 (SPC) Regulations.

(7) A universal credit claimant is not precluded from correcting or completing a claim for housing benefit which was defective within the meaning of the 2006 Regulations or the 2006 (SPC) Regulations if—

  (a) the defective claim was made before the date on which the claim for universal credit was made or treated as made; and

  (b) in accordance with the 2006 Regulations or, as the case may be, the 2006 (SPC) Regulations, the claimant's entitlement to housing benefit in connection with the claim will (if the claimant is entitled to housing benefit) pre-date—

    (i) the date, or anticipated date, of the claimant's entitlement to universal credit in connection with the current award or claim; or

    (ii) where the claimant is a new claimant partner and regulation 7(5)(b) would apply to the award, the date on which it would terminate in accordance with the 2006 Regulations or, as the case may be, the 2006 (SPC) Regulations.

[² (7A) A claimant who is a universal credit claimant by virtue of sub-paragraph (ba) of paragraph (2) (and no other sub-paragraph) is not precluded from—

  (a) making a claim for income support for a period starting on or after the relevant date if first notification of the claimant's intention to make that claim was made, or deemed to be made, for the purposes of regulation 6(1A)(c) or 6A of the 1987 Regulations, during the period starting with the relevant date and ending with 15th November 2015;

  (b) making a claim for housing benefit for a period starting on or after the relevant date if first notification of the claimant's intention to make that claim was given (within the meaning of regulation 83(5) (d) of the 2006 Regulations or, as the case may be, regulation 64(6) (d) of the 2006 (SPC) Regulations, during the period starting with the relevant date and ending with 15th November 2015;

  (c) correcting or completing a claim for housing benefit for a period starting on or after the relevant date, where that claim was defective within the meaning of the 2006 Regulations or the 2006 (SPC) Regulations and was made during the period starting with the relevant date and ending with 15th November 2015.

(7B) For the purposes of paragraph (7A), the "relevant date" is—

(a) where the conditions in regulation 6(1)(a), (b) and (c) of the Claims and Payments Regulations are met in relation to the claimant, the day after the claimant's last day of entitlement to universal credit;

(b) where the conditions in regulation 6(2)(a), (b) and (c) of the Claims and Payments Regulations are met in relation to the claimant, the first date on which the claimant would have been entitled to universal credit if the claimant had been so entitled.]

(8) A universal credit claimant is not precluded from making a claim for housing benefit in respect of [¹ specified accommodation].

(9) A universal credit claimant is not precluded from making a claim for a tax credit which the claimant is treated as having made by virtue of regulation 7(7) or 8(4)(a).

AMENDMENTS

1. Universal Credit (Transitional Provisions) (Amendment) Regulations 2014 (SI 2014/1626) reg.3 (November 3, 2014).
2. Universal Credit (Transitional Provisions) (Amendment) Regulations 2015 (SI 2015/1780) reg.2 (November 16, 2015).

DEFINITIONS

"the 1987 Regulations"–para.(4)(a).
"the 2006 Regulations"–para.(4)(b).
"the 2006 (SPC) Regulations"–*ibid*.
"the Act"–see reg.2(1).
"the Claims and Payments Regulations"–*ibid*.
"First-tier Tribunal"–*ibid*.
"housing benefit"–*ibid*.
"income support"–*ibid*.
"new claimant partner"–*ibid*.
"relevant date"–para.(7B).
"specified accommodation"–see reg.2(1).
"tax credit" –*ibid*.
"Upper Tribunal"–*ibid*.

GENERAL NOTE

This regulation broadly performs the same function as reg.15(3)-(5) of the 2013 **3.13** Transitional Regulations, with various modifications. In summary, universal credit claimants are excluded from claiming income support, housing benefit or tax credits, except in certain cases where notice of intention to claim has previously been given, or a defective claim has previously been made, and entitlement will run from a date before the claimant became entitled to universal credit. Thus the new regulation allows for further exceptions to the general rule that a universal credit claimant may not also claim, or have entitlement to existing benefits. In particular, where the claimant has previously notified their intention to make a claim for certain existing benefits (paras (5) and (6)), or has made a defective claim (para. (7)), and entitlement to the existing benefit would pre-date the date of entitlement to universal credit, the claim may now be completed, so that the claimant is not disadvantaged by the move to universal credit. There is also provision for overlap of awards of universal credit and certain existing benefits during the first assessment period for universal credit, where this is necessary to protect the interests of a former partner of the universal claimant. As with reg.5, similar provision is made in relation to both "old style JSA" and "old style ESA" by Commencement Orders made under s.150(3) of the Act.

The effect of the subsequent amendments made by the Universal Credit (Transitional Provisions) (Amendment) Regulations 2015 (SI 2015/1780) is to add certain claimants to the definition of a "Universal Credit claimant" contained in para.(2) such that they too may not make a claim for income support, housing benefit or tax credits. The further category of excluded claimants comprises those who:

- have been awarded universal credit and their earnings have reduced their universal credit award to nil; or

- have made a claim for universal credit, but are not entitled to an award because of the level of their earned income; and

- have entered a six month 're-award' period, during which universal credit may be awarded without a further claim if their earnings drop or there is another change of circumstances that would make universal credit payable.

Where claimants have been awarded or make a claim to universal credit and their earnings have either reduced their award to nil (or they are not entitled to universal credit after making that claim after the work allowance and taper have been applied), they enter a six month re-award period during which universal credit may be awarded without a further claim (if either their earnings drop or there is another change of circumstances that would make universal credit payable). Before the 2015 amendments, where claimants entered the six month re-award period and so have no universal credit entitlement, they may claim existing benefits if so entitled. However, if their earnings then drop (or their circumstances change so that universal credit becomes payable again), universal credit would also be re-awarded. The parallel access both to existing benefits and universal credit created administrative complexity and the risk of overpayments because of the difficulty in ensuring that payments of existing benefits and universal credit are not made for the same or an overlapping period.

These 2015 amendments do not apply to areas where universal credit is administered under relevant regulations as amended by the Universal Credit (Digital Service) Amendment Regulations 2014 (SI 2014/2887). In these areas the provision to re-award universal credit without a claim in these cases is revoked; and provisions in the relevant Commencement Orders bar claims for incomes support, housing benefit or tax credits by claimants who live in the relevant postcode districts.

Termination of awards of certain existing benefits: new claimant partners

3.14   **7.** (1) This regulation applies where—
  (a) a person ("A") who was previously entitled to universal credit [2 . . .] ceases to be so entitled on becoming a member of a couple;
  (b) the other member of the couple ("the new claimant partner") was not entitled to universal credit [2 . . .] immediately before formation of the couple;
  (c) the couple is treated, in accordance with regulation 9(8) of the Claims and Payments Regulations, as having made a claim for universal credit; and
  (d) the Secretary of State is satisfied that the claimants meet the basic conditions specified in section 4(1)(a) to (d) of the Act (other than any of those conditions which they are not required to meet by virtue of regulations under section 4(2) of the Act).

(2) Subject to paragraphs (4) and (5), where this regulation applies, all awards of income support or housing benefit to which the new claimant partner would (were it not for the effect of these Regulations) have been entitled during the relevant period are to terminate, by virtue of this regulation—
  (a) on the day before the first date on which the joint claimants are entitled to universal credit in connection with the claim; or
  (b) if the joint claimants are not entitled to universal credit, on the day before the first date on which they would have been so entitled, if all of the basic and financial conditions applicable to them had been met; or

(c) if the new claimant partner became entitled to an award after the date on which it would otherwise terminate under sub-paragraph (a) or (b), at the beginning of the first day of entitlement to that award.

(3) For the purposes of this regulation, "the relevant period" is the period starting with the first day of the assessment period (in relation to A's award of universal credit) during which A and the new claimant partner formed a couple and ending with the date of formation of the couple.

(4) Where the new claimant partner was entitled during the relevant period to income support, he or she was at that time a member of a couple and the award included an amount in respect of the new claimant partner and their partner at that time ("P"), the award of income support terminates, by virtue of this regulation, on the date on which the new claimant partner and P ceased to be a couple for the purposes of the Income Support (General) Regulations 1987, unless it terminates on that date in accordance with other legislative provision, or terminated on an earlier date.

(5) An award of housing benefit to which the new claimant partner is entitled does not terminate by virtue of this regulation where—

(a) the award is in respect of [¹ specified accommodation]; or

(b) the new claimant partner leaves the accommodation in respect of which housing benefit was paid, in order to live with A.

(6) Where an award terminates by virtue of this regulation, any legislative provision under which the award terminates on a later date does not apply.

(7) Where the new claimant partner was, immediately before forming a couple with A, treated by regulation 11 as being entitled to a tax credit, the new claimant partner is to be treated, for the purposes of the 2002 Act, as having made a claim for the tax credit in question for the current tax year.

AMENDMENTS

1. Universal Credit (Transitional Provisions) (Amendment) Regulations 2014 (SI 2014/1626) reg.3 (November 3, 2014).

2. Universal Credit (Digital Service) Amendment Regulations 2014 (SI 2014/2887) reg.3(3) (November 26, 2014).

DEFINITIONS

"the 2002 Act"–see reg.2(1).
"A"–para.7(1)(a).
"the Act"–see reg.2(1).
"assessment period"–*ibid.*
"the Claims and Payments Regulations"–*ibid.*
"housing benefit"–*ibid.*
"income support"–*ibid.*
"new claimant partner"–*ibid.*
"partner"–*ibid.*
"the relevant period"–para.(3).
"specified accommodation"–see reg.2(1).
"tax year"–*ibid.*

GENERAL NOTE

In broad terms this provision performs the same function as reg.16 of the 2013 Transitional Regulations, with various modifications. As a general rule, all existing benefit or tax credit awards will terminate when an award of universal credit is made to a newly formed couple, one of whom was previously entitled to universal credit

3.15

and the other to an existing benefit (or tax credit). The mechanics of this process are different for existing benefit and tax credits awards respectively.

Thus where the conditions in para.(1) are met, the new claimant partner's award of income support or housing benefit will terminate as provided for in para.(2). Para.(4) deals with the timing of the termination of an earlier award of income support where the new claimant partner was receiving that benefit together with their own previous partner ("P"). Para.(5) provides for special cases where an award of housing benefit does not end, despite the general rule.

The process is rather more complicated with tax credits – where the new partner is treated as having an ongoing tax credit award by virtue of reg.11, then they are treated as having made a new claim for the current year, whether or not they actually have made such a claim (para.(7)), and any award made under such a deemed claim likewise terminates on the day before the start of the joint award of universal credit.

Para. (1)

3.16   The amendments to para.(1)(a) and (b) (the omission of the words "as a single parent") are each subject to the saving provision as set out in reg.5 of the Universal Credit (Digital Service) Amendment Regulations 2014 (SI 2014/2887).

Para. (7)

3.17   See further reg.11.

Termination of awards of certain existing benefits: other claimants

3.18   **8.** (1) This regulation applies where—
   (a) a claim for universal credit (other than a claim which is treated, in accordance with regulation 9(8) of the Claims and Payments Regulations, as having been made) is made; and
   (b) the Secretary of State is satisfied that the claimant meets the basic conditions specified in section 4(1)(a) to (d) of the Act (other than any of those conditions which the claimant is not required to meet by virtue of regulations under section 4(2) of the Act).

(2) Subject to paragraph (3), where this regulation applies, all awards of income support, housing benefit or a tax credit to which the claimant (or, in the case of joint claimants, either of them) is entitled on the date on which the claim is made are to terminate, by virtue of this regulation—
   (a) on the day before the first date on which the claimant is entitled to universal credit in connection with the claim; or
   (b) if the claimant is not entitled to universal credit, on the day before the first date on which he or she would have been so entitled, if all of the basic and financial conditions applicable to the claimant had been met.

(3) An award of housing benefit to which a claimant is entitled in respect of [¹ specified accommodation] does not terminate by virtue of this regulation.

(4) Where this regulation applies and the claimant (or, in the case of joint claimants, either of them) is treated by regulation 11 as being entitled to a tax credit—
   (a) the claimant (or, as the case may be, the relevant claimant) is to be treated, for the purposes of the 2002 Act and this regulation, as having made a claim for the tax credit in question for the current tax year; and

(b) if the claimant (or the relevant claimant) is entitled on the date on which the claim for universal credit was made to an award of a tax credit which is made in respect of a claim which is treated as having been made by virtue of sub-paragraph (a), that award is to terminate, by virtue of this regulation—
  (i) on the day before the first date on which the claimant is entitled to universal credit; or
  (ii) if the claimant is not entitled to universal credit, on the day before the first date on which he or she would have been so entitled, if all of the basic and financial conditions applicable to the claimant had been met.

(5) Where an award terminates by virtue of this regulation, any legislative provision under which the award terminates on a later date does not apply.

AMENDMENT

1. Universal Credit (Transitional Provisions) (Amendment) Regulations 2014 (SI 2014/1626) reg.3 (November 3, 2014).

DEFINITIONS

"the 2002 Act"–see reg.2(1).
"the Act"–*ibid.*
"the Claims and Payments Regulations"–*ibid.*
"housing benefit"–*ibid.*
"income support"–*ibid.*
"specified accommodation"–*ibid.*
"tax credit" –*ibid.*
"tax year"–*ibid.*

GENERAL NOTE

As a general rule, all existing benefit or tax credit awards will terminate when an award of universal credit is made to a claimant. This regulation essentially performs the same function as reg.7 but for claimants who do not have a new claimant partner.   **3.19**

Treatment of ongoing entitlement to certain benefits: benefit cap

9. (1) This regulation applies where a claimant who is a new claimant partner, or who has (in accordance with regulation 26 of the Universal Credit Regulations) been awarded universal credit in respect of a period preceding the date on which the claim for universal credit was made or treated as made—   **3.20**
  (a) is entitled, in respect of the whole or part of the first assessment period for universal credit, to a welfare benefit (other than universal credit) mentioned in regulation 79(4) of the Universal Credit Regulations (circumstances where the benefit cap applies); and
  (b) is entitled to housing benefit at any time during the first assessment period for universal credit, or would be so entitled were it not for the effect of these Regulations.

(2) Where this regulation applies, regulation 79 of the Universal Credit Regulations applies, in relation to the claimant, as if the benefit in question was not included in the list of welfare benefits in paragraph (4) of that regulation.

"assessment period"–see reg.2(1).
"housing benefit"–*ibid.*
"new claimant partner"–*ibid.*
"the Universal Credit Regulations"–*ibid.*

GENERAL NOTE

3.21   This regulation provides for entitlement to some benefits (i.e. those listed in reg.79(4) of the Universal Credit Regulations 2013) to be disregarded for the purposes of the benefit cap during the claimant's first assessment period for universal credit. This applies where a claimant is entitled to universal credit from a date before the date on which they made a claim, or were treated as making a claim, and they were also previously entitled to housing benefit (which may already have been subject to the benefit cap).

Treatment of overpayments

3.22   **10.** (1) This regulation applies where—

(a) an award of universal credit is made to a claimant who was previously entitled to an existing benefit other than a tax credit or a joint-claim jobseeker's allowance; and

(b) a payment of the existing benefit is made which includes payment ("the overpayment") in respect of a period—

　　(i) during which the claimant is not entitled to that benefit (including non-entitlement which arises from termination of an award by virtue of an order made under section 150(3) of the Act or regulation 7, 8, or 14); and

　　(ii) which falls within an assessment period for universal credit.

(2) Where this regulation applies, for the purposes of calculating the amount of an award of universal credit in respect of an assessment period—

(a) regulation 66 of the Universal Credit Regulations (what is included in unearned income?) applies as if the overpayment which was made in respect of that assessment period were added to the descriptions of unearned income in paragraph (1)(b) of that regulation; and

(b) regulation 73 of the Universal Credit Regulations (unearned income calculated monthly) does not apply to the overpayment.

(3) In so far as any overpayment is taken into account in calculating the amount of an award of universal credit in accordance with this regulation, that payment may not be recovered as an overpayment under—

(a) the Social Security (Payments on account, Overpayments and Recovery) Regulations 1988;

(b) the Housing Benefit Regulations 2006; or

(c) the Housing Benefit (Persons who have attained the qualifying age for state pension credit) Regulations 2006.

DEFINITIONS

"the Act"–see reg.2(1).
"assessment period"–*ibid.*
"existing benefit"–*ibid.*
"joint-claim jobseeker's allowance"–*ibid.*
"overpayment"–para.(1)(b).
"tax credit"–see reg.2(1).
"the Universal Credit Regulations"–*ibid.*

This regulation provides that overpayments of existing benefits (other than joint-claim jobseeker's allowance or tax credits) that may arise on transition to universal credit are to be off-set against entitlement to universal credit (para.(1)). Thus, over-payments of existing benefits which may arise on transition to universal credit can be offset as unearned income against the claimant's entitlement to universal credit (para.(2)) and may not then be recovered under other legislation (para.(3)). This is because it will be recovered as unearned income from the universal credit award rather than as an excess payment under existing overpayments legislation.

3.23

Ongoing awards of tax credits

11. (1) For the purposes of regulations 7(7) and 8(4)—

    (a) a person is to be treated as being entitled to working tax credit with effect from the start of the current tax year even though a decision has not been made under section 14 of the 2002 Act in respect of a claim for that tax credit for that tax year, if the person was entitled to working tax credit for the previous tax year and any of the cases specified in paragraph (2) applies; and

    (b) a person is to be treated as being entitled to child tax credit with effect from the start of the current tax year even though a decision has not been made under section 14 of the 2002 Act in respect of a claim for that tax credit for that tax year, if the person was entitled to child tax credit for the previous tax year and any of the cases specified in paragraph (2) applies.

(2) The cases are—

    (a) a final notice has not been given to the person under section 17 of the 2002 Act in respect of the previous tax year;

    (b) a final notice has been given, which includes provision by virtue of subsection (2) or (4) of section 17, or a combination of those subsections and subsection (6) and—

        (i) the date specified in the notice for the purposes of section 17(2) and (4) or, where different dates are specified, the later of them, has not yet passed and no claim for a tax credit for the current tax year has been made, or treated as made; or

        (ii) a claim for a tax credit has been made, or treated as made, on or before the date mentioned in paragraph (i), but no decision has been made in relation to that claim under section 14(1) of the 2002 Act;

    (c) a final notice has been given, no claim for a tax credit for the current year has been made, or treated as made, and no decision has been made under section 18(1) of the 2002 Act in respect of entitlement to a tax credit for the previous tax year; or

    (d) a final notice has been given and—

        (i) the person did not make a declaration in response to provision included in that notice by virtue of section 17(2)(a), (4)(a) or (6)(a), or any combination of those provisions, by the date specified in the notice;

        (ii) the person was given due notice that payments of tax credit under section 24(4) of the 2002 Act had ceased due to his or her failure to make the declaration; and

        (iii) the person's claim for universal credit is made during the period

3.24

of 30 days starting with the date on the notice referred to in paragraph (ii) or, where the person is a new claimant partner, notification of formation of a couple with a person entitled to universal credit is given to the Secretary of State during that period.

DEFINITIONS

"the 2002 Act"–see reg.2(1).
"new claimant partner"–*ibid.*
"tax credit" –*ibid.*
"tax year"–*ibid.*

GENERAL NOTE

3.25   This regulation provides for a claimant to be treated as entitled to an award of a tax credit in certain cases, for the purposes of regs.7 and 8.

Modification of tax credits legislation: overpayments and penalties

3.26   **12.** (1) This regulation applies where—
(a) a claim for universal credit is made, or is treated as having been made;
(b) the claimant is, or was at any time during the tax year in which the claim is made or treated as made, entitled to a tax credit; and
(c) the Secretary of State is satisfied that the claimant meets the basic conditions specified in section 4(1)(a) to (d) of the Act (other than any of those conditions which the claimant is not required to meet by virtue of regulations under section 4(2) of the Act).

(2) Where this regulation applies, the 2002 Act applies in relation to the claimant with the following modifications.

(3) In section 28—
(a) in subsection (1)—
(i) after "tax year" in both places where it occurs, insert "or part tax year";
(ii) at the end insert "or treated as an overpayment of universal credit";
(b) in subsections (3) and (4), after "repaid" insert "to the Board or, as the case may be, to the Secretary of State";
(c) omit subsection (5);
(d) in subsection (6) omit "(apart from subsection (5))".

[¹ (4) For section 29(4) substitute —

"(4) Where a notice states that this subsection applies in relation to an amount (or part of an amount), it may be recovered—

(a) subject to provision made by regulations, by deduction from payments of any tax credit under an award made for any period to the person, or either or both of the persons, to whom the notice was given; or
(b) subject to regulations made by the Secretary of State under the Social Security Administration Act 1992(2)—

(i) by deductions under section 71ZC of that Act (Deduction from benefit—including universal credit);
(ii) by deductions under section 71ZD of that Act (Deduction from earnings); or
(iii) as set out in section 71ZE of that Act (Court action etc).")]

(5) In section 48 after the definition of "overpayment" insert—

""part tax year" means a period of less than a year beginning with 6th April and ending with the date on which the award of a tax credit terminated,".

(6) In Schedule 2, in paragraph 6(1)(a) and (c) and (2)(a), after "for the tax year" insert "or part tax year".

AMENDMENT

1. Universal Credit (Transitional Provisions) (Amendment) Regulations 2016 (SI 2016/232) reg.2 (April 1, 2016).

DEFINITIONS

"the 2002 Act"–see reg.2(1).
"the Act"–*ibid.*
"tax credit"–*ibid.*
"tax year"–*ibid.*

GENERAL NOTE

This regulation provides that, where a claim for universal credit is made by a claimant who was previously entitled to a tax credit, the Tax Credits Act 2002 is to apply to that claimant with certain modifications. The effect is that that any overpayments of tax credits may be treated as overpayments of universal credit and appropriate time limits apply in relation to the imposition of penalties.   3.27

[¹ Modification of tax credits legislation: finalisation of tax credits

12A. (1) This regulation applies where—   3.28

(a) a claim for universal credit is made, or is treated as having been made;

(b) the claimant is, or was at any time during the tax year in which the claim is made or treated as made, entitled to a tax credit; and

(c) the Secretary of State is satisfied that the claimant meets the basic conditions specified in section 4(1)(a) to (d) of the Act (other than any of those conditions which the claimant is not required to meet by virtue of regulations under section 4(2) of the Act).

(2) Subject to paragraph (3), where this regulation applies, the amount of the tax credit to which the person is entitled is to be calculated in accordance with the 2002 Act and regulations made under that Act, as modified by the Schedule to these Regulations ("the modified legislation").

(3) Where, in the opinion of the Commissioners for Her Majesty's Revenue and Customs, it is not reasonably practicable to apply the modified legislation in relation to any case or category of cases, the 2002 Act and regulations made under that Act are to apply without modification in that case or category of cases.]

AMENDMENT

1. Universal Credit (Transitional Provisions) (Amendment) Regulations 2014 (SI 2014/1626) reg.4 (October 13, 2014).

DEFINITIONS

"the 2002 Act"–see reg.2(1).
"the 2002 Act"–*ibid.*

"the modified legislation"–para.(2).
"tax credit"–see reg.2(1).
"tax year"–*ibid.*

GENERAL NOTE

3.29   This amendment is designed to smooth the transition from receipt of tax credits to an award of universal credit. It re-instates provision for in-year finalisation of tax credits for universal credit claimants (there was no equivalent to reg.17 of, and the Schedule to, the 2013 Transitional Regulations in the original version of the 2014 Transitional Regulations). By doing so, this provision allows tax credits awards to be finalised during the relevant tax year when a tax credit claimant makes the transition to universal credit (see paras.(1) and (2) and the Schedule), rather than after the end of the tax year. This is intended to reduce administrative complexity and confusion for the claimant by providing a clean break from tax credits, thus avoiding the claimant having to revert to providing HMRC with information about their circumstances and income after they have been receiving universal credit for some time. It also should thereby, in theory at least, ensure the claimant has a single interaction with HMRC so that HMRC only have to deal with their case once, as both the stopping of a tax credits award and the finalising of the award are dealt with upon transition to universal credit. Although the intention is that in-year finalisation of tax credits awards is the default approach in the majority of cases, provision has been made (see para.(3)) to allow HMRC to continue to finalise tax credits awards after the end of the tax year, if they think that it is not practicable to apply the modified legislation to a particular case or class of case, e.g. where it proved difficult to verify income that is particularly complex, such as those cases including particular combinations of self-employed and other income. Para.(3) might also be invoked as a contingency to guard against unforeseen operational or IT difficulties.

Appeals etc relating to certain existing benefits

3.30   **13.** (1) This regulation applies where, after an award of universal credit has been made to a claimant—

(a) an appeal against a decision relating to the entitlement of the claimant to income support, housing benefit or a tax credit (a "relevant benefit") is finally determined;

(b) a decision relating to the claimant's entitlement to income support is revised under section 9 of the Social Security Act 1998 ("the 1998 Act") or superseded under section 10 of that Act;

(c) a decision relating to the claimant's entitlement to housing benefit is revised or superseded under Schedule 7 to the Child Support, Pensions and Social Security Act 2000; or

(d) a decision relating to the claimant's entitlement to a tax credit is revised under section 19 or 20 of the 2002 Act, or regulations made under section 21 of that Act, or is varied or cancelled under section 21A of that Act.

(2) Where the claimant is a new claimant partner and, as a result of determination of the appeal or, as the case may be, revision or supersession of the decision the claimant would (were it not for the effect of these Regulations) be entitled to income support or housing benefit during the relevant period mentioned in regulation 7(3), awards of those benefits are to terminate in accordance with regulation 7.

(3) Where the claimant is not a new claimant partner and, as a result of determination of the appeal or, as the case may be, revision, supersession, variation or cancellation of the decision, the claimant would (were it not

for the effect of these Regulations) be entitled to a relevant benefit on the date on which the claim for universal credit was made, awards of relevant benefits are to terminate in accordance with regulation 8.

(4) The Secretary of State is to consider whether it is appropriate to revise under section 9 of the 1998 Act the decision in relation to entitlement to universal credit or, if that decision has been superseded under section 10 of that Act, the decision as so superseded (in either case, "the UC decision").

(5) Where it appears to the Secretary of State to be appropriate to revise the UC decision, it is to be revised in such manner as appears to the Secretary of State to be necessary to take account of—

(a) the decision of the First-tier Tribunal, Upper Tribunal or court, or, as the case may be, the decision relating to entitlement to a relevant benefit, as revised, superseded, varied or cancelled; and

(b) any finding of fact by the First-tier Tribunal, Upper Tribunal or court.

DEFINITIONS

"the 1998 Act"–para.(1)(b).
"the 2002 Act"–see reg.2(1).
"First-tier Tribunal"–*ibid.*
"housing benefit"–*ibid.*
"income support"–*ibid.*
"new claimant partner"–*ibid.*
"relevant benefit"–para.(1)(a).
"tax credit"–see reg.2(1).
"the UC decision"–para.(4).
"Upper Tribunal"–see reg.2(1).

GENERAL NOTE

3.31

This regulation deals with appeals which are determined, and decisions about existing benefits which are revised or superseded, after the appellant has become entitled to universal credit (see para.(1)). Entitlement to income support, housing benefit or a tax credit arising from an appeal, revision or supersession will terminate in accordance with regulation 7 or 8 (paras.(2) and (3)) and a decision made about entitlement to universal credit may be revised to take account of any findings of fact by the relevant appeal body (paras.(4) and (5)). The equivalent provision in the 2013 Transitional Regulations (reg.18) applied only to new claimants partners; this provision applies to all claimants and not just new claimant partners.

Appeals etc relating to universal credit

3.32

14. (1) This regulation applies where—

(a) a decision is made that a claimant is not entitled to universal credit ("the UC decision");

(b) the claimant becomes entitled to income support, housing benefit or a tax credit (a "relevant benefit");

(c) an appeal against the UC decision is finally determined, or the decision is revised under section 9 of the Social Security Act 1998;

(d) an award of universal credit is made to the claimant in consequence of entitlement arising from the appeal, or from the decision as revised; and

(e) the claimant would (were it not for the effect of regulation 5 and this regulation) be entitled to both universal credit and a relevant benefit in respect of the same period.

(2) Subject to paragraph (3), where this regulation applies—

(a) all awards of a relevant benefit to which the claimant would (were it not for the effect of these Regulations) be entitled are to terminate, by virtue of this regulation, at the beginning of the first day of entitlement to that award; and

(b) any legislative provision under which an award would otherwise terminate on a later date does not apply.

(3) An award of housing benefit to which a claimant is entitled in respect of [¹ specified accommodation] does not terminate by virtue of this regulation.

AMENDMENT

1. Universal Credit (Transitional Provisions) (Amendment) Regulations 2014 (SI 2014/1626) reg.3 (November 3, 2014).

DEFINITIONS

"housing benefit"–see reg.2(1).
"income support"–*ibid.*
"relevant benefit"–para.(1)(b).
"specified accommodation"–see reg.2(1).
"tax credit" –*ibid.*
"the UC decision"–para.(1)(a).

GENERAL NOTE

3.33   This regulation concerns the situation where a claimant successfully appeals a decision that they are not entitled to universal credit, or such a decision is revised, but only after the claimant has become entitled to income support, housing benefit or a tax credit. In such a case, the award of the existing benefit terminates at the beginning of the first day of entitlement if there would otherwise be an overlap with the award of universal credit.

CHAPTER 3

Modification of Claims and Payments Regulations in relation to universal credit claimants

3.34   **15.** (1) Where a claim for universal credit is made by a person who was previously entitled to an existing benefit, regulation 26 of the Claims and Payments Regulations (time within which a claim for universal credit is to be made) applies in relation to that claim with the modification specified in paragraph (2).

(2) In paragraph (3) of regulation 26, after sub-paragraph (a) insert—

"(aa) the claimant was previously in receipt of an existing benefit (as defined in the Universal Credit (Transitional Provisions) Regulations 2014) and notification of expiry of entitlement to that benefit was not sent to the claimant before the date that the claimant's entitlement expired;".

DEFINITIONS

"the Claims and Payments Regulations"–see reg.2(1).
"existing benefit"–*ibid.*

Where a claim for universal credit is made by a claimant who was previously enti-   3.35
tled to an existing benefit, this regulation modifies the application of reg.26(3) of
the Claims and Payments Regulations 2013 in relation to the claimant. In practice
it means that the time for claiming universal credit may be extended by up to one
month, if the claimant was not given advance notice of termination of the award of
existing benefit. The aim is to ensure that the same rule applies to claimants making
the transition to universal credit from existing benefits as will apply in relation to
universal credit and other benefits after the transitional period.

Persons unable to act

16. (1) Paragraph (2) applies where—   3.36
(a) a person ("P2") has been appointed, or treated as appointed, under
regulation 33(1) of the Social Security (Claims and Payments)
Regulations 1987 ("the 1987 Regulations") (persons unable to act)
to exercise rights and to receive and deal with sums payable on behalf
of a person who is unable to act ("P1"); or
(b) a person ("P2") has been appointed under regulation 18(3) of the
Tax Credits (Claims and Notifications) Regulations 2002 ("the 2002
Regulations") (circumstances where one person may act for another
in making a claim – other appointed persons) to act for a person who
is unable to act ("P1") in making a claim for a tax credit.
(2) Where this paragraph applies and P1 is, or may be, entitled to universal credit, the Secretary of State may, if P2 agrees, treat the appointment of
P2 as if it were made under regulation 57(1) of the Claims and Payments
Regulations (persons unable to act) and P2 may carry out the functions set
out in regulation 57(4) of those Regulations in relation to P1.
(3) Paragraph (4) applies where a person ("P2") was appointed, or
treated as appointed, under regulation 57(1) of the Claims and Payments
Regulations to carry out functions in relation to a person who is unable to
act ("P1") and who was, or might have been, entitled to universal credit,
but who has ceased to be so entitled, or was not in fact so entitled.
(4) Where this paragraph applies—
(a) the Secretary of State may, if P2 agrees, treat the appointment of P2
as if it were made under regulation 33(1) of the 1987 Regulations
and P2 may exercise rights and receive and deal with sums payable
in respect of existing benefits on behalf of P1; and
(b) the Board (within the meaning of the 2002 Regulations) may, if P2
agrees, treat the appointment of P2 as if it were made under regulation 18(3) of the 2002 Regulations and P2 may act for P1 in making
a claim for a tax credit.

DEFINITIONS

"the 1987 Regulations"–para.(1)(a).
"the 2002 Regulations"–para.(1)(b).
"the Claims and Payments Regulations"–see reg.2(1).
"existing benefit"–*ibid.*
"tax credit"–*ibid.*

The effect of this regulation (which had no equivalent provision in the 2013   3.37
Transitional Regulations) is that a person who has been appointed to act on behalf

of a claimant in relation to existing benefits and/or tax credits may be treated as having been appointed to act on their behalf in relation to universal credit and *vice versa*. This may be particularly relevant where claimants have mental health problems or where they suffer from other conditions that make communication with the Department very difficult or impossible. The aim of the provision is to make the process of transition between existing benefits and universal credit easier for claimants who are in this position.

[¹ Waiting days

3.37.1   **16A.** (1) This regulation applies where a claimant (or, in the case of joint claimants, either of them)—

(a) was entitled to old style JSA, old style ESA or income support at any time during the period of three months ending with the first day of the period in respect of which the claimant makes a claim for universal credit and ceased to be so entitled on starting paid work; or

(b) does not fall within sub-paragraph (a) and was entitled to an existing benefit at any time during the period of one month ending on that day.

(2) Where this regulation applies, regulation 19A(3)(b) (waiting days) of the Universal Credit Regulations 2013 applies with the following modifications—

(a) at the end of paragraph (v) omit "or"; and

(b) after paragraph (vi) insert—

"(vii) was entitled to a benefit mentioned in paragraph (1)(a) of regulation 16A (waiting days) of the Universal Credit (Transitional Provisions) Regulations 2014 at any time during the period of three months ending on the relevant date and ceased to be so entitled on starting paid work; or

(viii) does not fall within sub-paragraph (vii) and was entitled to a benefit mentioned in paragraph (1)(b) of regulation 16A (waiting days) of the Universal Credit (Transitional Provisions) Regulations 2014 at any time during the period of one month ending on the relevant date.]

AMENDMENT

1. Universal Credit (Waiting Days) (Amendment) Regulations 2015 (SI 2015/1362) reg.2(2) (August 3, 2015).

Advance payments of universal credit

3.38   **17.** (1) This regulation applies where—

(a) the Secretary of State is deciding a claim for universal credit, other than a claim which is treated as having been made, in accordance with regulation 9(8) of the Claims and Payments Regulations;

(b) the claimant is, or was previously, entitled to an existing benefit ("the earlier award"); and

(c) if the earlier award terminated before the date on which the claim for universal credit was made, the claim for universal credit was made during the period of one month starting with the date of termination.

(2) Where this regulation applies—

(a) a single claimant may request an advance payment of universal credit;

(b) joint claimants may jointly request such a payment,

at any time during the first assessment period for universal credit.

(3) Where a request has been made in accordance with this regulation, the Secretary of State may make an advance payment to the claimant, or joint claimants, of such amount in respect of universal credit as the Secretary of State considers appropriate.

(4) After an advance payment has been made under this regulation, payments of any award of universal credit to the claimant or, in the case of joint claimants, to either or both of them, may be reduced until the amount of the advance payment is repaid.

DEFINITIONS

"assessment period"–see reg.2(1).
"the Claims and Payments Regulations"–*ibid.*
"the earlier award"–para.(1)(b).
"existing benefit"–see reg.2(1).

GENERAL NOTE

As a general rule universal credit is payable monthly in arrears (Claims and Payments Regulations 2013, reg.47(1)). Where a claim for universal credit is made by a claimant who was entitled to an existing benefit before they became entitled to universal credit, this regulation allows the claimant to apply for an advance payment of universal credit during their first assessment period (paras.(1) and (2)). The amount of any advance payment is at the discretion of the Secretary of State (para. (3)). Repayment is by reduction of subsequent payments (para.(4)).   **3.39**

This regulation differs from its predecessor in the 2013 Transitional Regulations (reg.19), in that new claimant partners are now no longer able to request such an advance. Instead, if the new couple require support they will have to apply for a universal credit (change of circumstances) advance. The justification for this change is that it is supposed to reduce complexity in the advance payment process.

Deductions from benefits

18. (1) This regulation applies where—   **3.40**
  (a) an award of universal credit is made to a claimant who—
      (i) was entitled to income-based jobseeker's allowance, income-related employment and support allowance or income support (a "relevant award") on the date on which the claim for universal credit was made or treated as made;
      (ii) is a new claimant partner who was, immediately before forming a couple with a person entitled to universal credit, the partner of a person ("P") who was at that time entitled to a relevant award; or
      (iii) is not a new claimant partner and was, immediately before making a claim for universal credit, the partner of a person ("P") who was at that time entitled to a relevant award, where the award of universal credit is not a joint award to the claimant and P; and
  (b) on the relevant date, deductions in respect of fuel costs or water charges were being made under regulation 35 of the Social Security (Claims and Payments) Regulations 1987, in accordance with Schedule 9 to those Regulations.
(2) In this regulation, the "relevant date" means—
  (a) where paragraph (1)(a)(i) applies and the claimant is not a new claimant partner, the date on which the claim for universal credit was made;

    (b) where paragraph (1)(a)(i) applies and the claimant is a new claimant partner, the date on which the claim for universal credit was treated as made;

    (c) where paragraph (1)(a)(ii) or (iii) applies, the date on which the claimant ceased to be the partner of P.

(3) Where this regulation applies, deductions in respect of fuel costs or, as the case may be, water charges, may be made from the award of universal credit in accordance with Schedule 6 to the Claims and Payments Regulations, without the need for any consent which would otherwise be required under paragraph 3(3) of that Schedule.

(4) For the purposes of this regulation, a deduction is to be taken into account even if the relevant award subsequently terminated by virtue of an order made under section 150(3) of the Act, regulation 7 or, as the case may be, regulation 8, before the date on which the deduction was first applied.

DEFINITIONS

    "the Act"–see reg.2(1).
    "the Claims and Payments Regulations"–*ibid.*
    "income-based jobseeker's allowance"–*ibid.*
    "income-related employment and support allowance"–*ibid.*
    "income support"–*ibid.*
    "new claimant partner"–*ibid.*
    "partner"–*ibid.*
    "relevant award"–para.(1)(a)(i).
    "relevant date"–para.(2).

GENERAL NOTE

3.41   Where certain deductions were made from an award of an existing benefit (e.g. for fuel costs or water charges), this regulation allows deductions in respect of the same items to be made from an award of universal credit without the need for the consents which might otherwise be required.

Transition from old style ESA

3.42   **19.** (1) This regulation applies where—

    (a) an award of universal credit is made to a claimant who was entitled to old style ESA on the date on which the claim for universal credit was made or treated as made ("the relevant date"); and

[¹ (b) on or before the relevant date it had been determined that the claimant had limited capability for work or limited capability for work-related activity (within the meaning of Part 1 of the 2007 Act).]

(2) Where, on or before the relevant date, it had been determined that the claimant [¹ had limited capability for work (within the meaning of Part 1 of the 2007 Act)]—

    (a) [¹ ...]

    (b) the claimant is to be treated as having limited capability for work for the purposes of [¹ ...] section 21(1)(a) of the Act.

(3) [¹ ...]

(4) Where, on or before the relevant date, it had been determined that the claimant [¹ had limited capability for work-related activity (within the meaning of Part 1 of the 2007 Act) or was treated as having limited capability for work-related activity]—

(a) regulation 27(3) of the Universal Credit Regulations does not apply; and

(b) the claimant is to be treated as having limited capability for work and work-related activity for the purposes of regulation 27(1)(b) of those Regulations and section 19(2)(a) of the Act.

(5) Unless the assessment phase applied and had not ended at the relevant date, in relation to a claimant who is treated as having limited capability for work and work-related activity under paragraph (4)(4)(b)—

(a) regulation 28 of the Universal Credit Regulations does not apply; and

(b) the LCWRA element is (subject to the provisions of Part 4 of the Universal Credit Regulations) to be included in the award of universal credit with effect from the beginning of the first assessment period.

(6) For the purposes of this regulation, a determination that the claimant [¹ had limited capability for work or, as the case may be, limited capability for work-related activity (within the meaning of Part 1 of the 2007 Act)], is to be taken into account even if the award of old style ESA subsequently terminated (in so far as it was an award of income-related employment and support allowance) before the date on which that determination was made, by virtue of an order made under section 150(3) of the Act.

(7) Where a claimant is treated, by virtue of this regulation, as having limited capability for work or, as the case may be, limited capability for work and work-related activity, the Secretary of State may at any time make a fresh determination as to these matters, in accordance with the Universal Credit Regulations.

(8) In this regulation and in regulations 20 to 27—

[¹ "assessment phase" has the same meaning as in the 2007 Act;]

"incapacity benefit" and "severe disablement allowance" have the same meanings as in Schedule 4 to that Act;

[¹ "LCWRA element" has the same meaning as in the Universal Credit Regulations.]

(9) For the purposes of this regulation and regulation 20, references to cases in which the assessment phase applied are references to cases in which sections 2(2)(a)[¹ and 4(4)(a)] of the 2007 Act applied and references to cases in which the assessment phase did not apply are references to cases in which those sections did not apply.

[¹ (10) For the purposes of this regulation, references to a determination that the claimant had limited capability for work do not include a determination made under regulation 30 of the Employment and Support Allowance Regulations 2008 (conditions for treating a claimant as having limited capability for work until a determination about limited capability for work has been made).]

AMENDMENT

1. Employment and Support Allowance and Universal Credit (Miscellaneous Amendments and Transitional and Savings Provisions) Regulations 2017 (SI 2017/204) reg.5(2) (April 3, 2017).

DEFINITIONS

"the Act"–see reg.2(1).
"assessment period"–*ibid.*

"assessment phase"–para.(8).
"incapacity benefit"–*ibid.*
"income-based jobseeker's allowance"–see reg.2(1).
"LCW element"–para.(8).
"LCWRA element"–*ibid.*
"old style ESA"–see reg.2(1).
"the relevant date"–para.(1)(a).
"severe disablement allowance"–para.(8).
"support component"–*ibid.*
"the Universal Credit Regulations"–see reg.2(1).
"work-related activity component"–para.(8).

GENERAL NOTE

3.43   The purpose of this apparently complex provision is relatively simple. It provides that a claimant may be treated as having limited capability for work, or limited capability for work and work-related activity, for the purposes of an award of universal credit, if they were previously so assessed for the purpose of old style ESA. If the claimant in question was in the process of assessment of their capability for work in connection with an award of employment and support allowance at the time the award terminated, the assessment period for universal credit will be adjusted accordingly, under reg.20.

Transition from old style ESA before the end of the assessment phase

3.44   **20.** (1) This regulation applies where—
   (a) an award of universal credit is made to a claimant who was entitled to old style ESA on the date on which the claim for universal credit was made or treated as made ("the relevant date"); and
   (b) on the relevant date, the assessment phase in relation to the claimant applied and had lasted for less than 13 weeks.
   (2) Where this regulation applies—
   (a) regulation 28(2) of the Universal Credit Regulations (period for which the [¹ . . .] LCWRA element is not to be included) does not apply; and
   (b) for the purposes of regulation 28 of those Regulations, the relevant period is—
      (i) the period of 13 weeks starting with the first day of the assessment phase; or
      (ii) where regulation 5 of the Employment and Support Allowance Regulations 2008 (the assessment phase – previous claimants) applied to the claimant, the period which ends when the sum of the periods for which the claimant was previously entitled to old style ESA and the period for which the claimant is entitled to universal credit is 13 weeks.
   (3) Where, on the relevant date, the assessment phase in relation to the claimant applied and had not ended and had lasted for more than 13 weeks—
   (a) regulation 28 of the Universal Credit Regulations does not apply;
   (b) [¹ . . .]
   (c) if it is subsequently determined in accordance with Part 5 of the Universal Credit Regulations that the claimant has limited capability for work and work-related activity the LCWRA element is (subject to the provisions of Part 4 of those Regulations) to be included in the

award of universal credit with effect from the beginning of the first assessment period.

(4) For the purposes of this regulation, the fact that an assessment phase applied in relation to a claimant on the relevant date is to be taken into account even if the award of old style ESA subsequently terminated (in so far as it was an award of income-related employment and support allowance) before that date by virtue of an order made under section 150(3) of the Act.

AMENDMENT

1. Employment and Support Allowance and Universal Credit (Miscellaneous Amendments and Transitional and Savings Provisions) Regulations 2017 (SI 2017/204) reg.5(3) (April 3, 2017).

DEFINITIONS

"the Act"–see reg.2(1).
"assessment period"–*ibid.*
"assessment phase"–see reg.19(8).
"income-based jobseeker's allowance"–*ibid.*
"LCW element"–see reg.19(8).
"LCWRA element"–*ibid.*
"old style ESA"–*ibid.*
"the relevant date"–para.(1)(a).
"the Universal Credit Regulations"–see reg.2(1).

GENERAL NOTE

This regulation provides that where a claimant was in the process of assessment of their capability for work in connection with an award of old style ESA at the time that award terminated, the assessment period for universal credit will be adjusted accordingly.

3.45

[¹ Transition from jobseeker's allowance following an extended period of sickness

20A.—(1) This regulation applies where—

(a) the claimant's first day of entitlement to universal credit ("the relevant date"), immediately follows the claimant's last day of entitlement to a jobseeker's allowance; and

(b) immediately before the relevant date, the claimant was treated as capable of work or as not having limited capability for work under regulation 55ZA of the Jobseeker's Allowance Regulations 1996 or regulation 46A of the Jobseeker's Allowance Regulations 2013 (extended period of sickness).

(2) Where this regulation applies—

(a) regulation 28(2) of the Universal Credit Regulations (period for which [¹ . . .] LCWRA element is not to be included) does not apply; and

(b) for the purposes of regulation 28 of those Regulations, the relevant period is the period starting with the first day of the period for which the claimant was treated as capable of work or as not having limited capability for work as specified in paragraph (1)(b).]

3.46

AMENDMENTS

1. Jobseeker's Allowance (Extended Period of Sickness) Amendment Regulations 2015 (SI 2015/339) reg.6 (March 30, 2015).
2. Employment and Support Allowance and Universal Credit (Miscellaneous Amendments and Transitional and Savings Provisions) Regulations 2017 (SI 2017/204) reg.5(4) (April 3, 2017).

DEFINITIONS

"the relevant date"–para.(1)(a).
"LCW element"–see reg.19(8).
"LCWRA element"–*ibid.*
"the Universal Credit Regulations"–see reg.2(1).

GENERAL NOTE

3.47   The Jobseeker's Allowance (Extended Period of Sickness) Amendment Regulations 2015 (SI 2015/339) enabled jobseeker's allowance claimants suffering from a short (or third) period of sickness to choose to remain on that benefit while on what is termed as an "extended period of sickness" (EPS) for a continuous period of up to 13 weeks in a 12 month period. The same regulations also made provision to enable the employment and support allowance assessment phase (before any additional ESA components become payable) and the universal credit relevant period (before any additional universal credit elements become payable) to be reduced by the time a claimant spends on an EPS. This regulation is accordingly designed to ensure that the calculation of the universal credit relevant period includes the EPS where jobseeker's allowance claimants make a claim for universal credit and move immediately into the universal credit relevant period.

Other claimants with limited capability for work: credits only cases

3.48   **21.** (1) This regulation applies where—
  (a) an award of universal credit is made to a claimant who was entitled to be credited with earnings equal to the lower earnings limit then in force under regulation 8B(2)(iv), (iva) or (v) of the Social Security (Credits) Regulations 1975 ("the 1975 Regulations") on the date on which the claim for universal credit was made or treated as made (the "relevant date"); and
  (b) neither regulation 19 nor regulation 20 applies to that claimant (whether or not, in the case of joint claimants, either of those regulations apply to the other claimant).

(2) Where, on or before the relevant date, it had been determined that the claimant would have limited capability for work (within the meaning of Part 1 of the 2007 Act) if he or she was entitled to old style ESA—
  (a) [¹ ...]
  (b) the claimant is to be treated as having limited capability for work for the purposes of [¹ ...] section 21(1)(a) of the Act.

(3) [¹ ...]

(4) Where, on or before the relevant date, it had been determined that the claimant would have limited capability for work-related activity (within the meaning of Part 1 of the 2007 Act) if he or she was entitled to old style ESA—
  (a) regulation 27(3) of the Universal Credit Regulations does not apply; and
  (b) the claimant is to be treated as having limited capability for work and

work-related activity for the purposes of regulation 27(1)(b) of those Regulations and section 19(2)(a) of the Act.

(5) Unless the notional assessment phase applied and had lasted for less than 13 weeks at the relevant date, in relation to a claimant who is treated as having limited capability for work and work-related activity under paragraph (4)—

   (a) regulation 28 of the Universal Credit Regulations does not apply; and

   (b) the LCWRA element is (subject to the provisions of Part 4 of the Universal Credit Regulations) to be included in the award of universal credit with effect from the beginning of the first assessment period.

(6) Where, on the relevant date, the notional assessment phase in relation to the claimant to whom the award was made applied and had lasted for less than 13 weeks—

   (a) regulation 28(2) of the Universal Credit Regulations does not apply; and

   (b) for the purposes of regulation 28 of those Regulations, the relevant period is the period of 13 weeks starting with the first day of the notional assessment phase.

(7) Where, on the relevant date, the notional assessment phase in relation to the claimant applied and had not ended and had lasted for more than 13 weeks—

   (a) regulation 28 of the Universal Credit Regulations does not apply;

   (b) [¹ ...]

   (c) if it is subsequently determined in accordance with Part 5 of those Regulations that the claimant has limited capability for work and work-related activity, the LCWRA element is (subject to the provisions of Part 4 of those Regulations) to be included in the award of universal credit with effect from the beginning of the first assessment period.

(8) Where a claimant is treated, by virtue of this regulation, as having limited capability for work or, as the case may be, limited capability for work and work-related activity, the Secretary of State may at any time make a fresh determination as to these matters, in accordance with the Universal Credit Regulations.

(9) For the purposes of this regulation—

   (a) a determination that the claimant would have limited capability for work or, as the case may be, limited capability for work-related activity, if the claimant was entitled to old style ESA is to be taken into account even if the claimant subsequently ceased to be entitled as mentioned in paragraph (1)(a) before the date on which that determination was made because he or she became entitled to universal credit;

   (b) the fact that a notional assessment phase applied in relation to a claimant on the relevant date is to be taken into account even if the claimant subsequently ceased to be entitled as mentioned in paragraph (1)(a) before that date because the claimant became entitled to universal credit.

   (c) references to a determination that the claimant would have limited capability for work if the claimant was entitled to old style ESA do not include a determination made under regulation 30 of the

Employment and Support Allowance Regulations 2008 (conditions for treating a claimant as having limited capability for work until a determination about limited capability for work has been made);

(d) references to cases in which the notional assessment phase applied are references to cases in which sections 2(2)(a) [¹ and 4(4)(a)] of the 2007 Act would have applied to the claimant if he or she had been entitled to old style ESA in addition to the entitlement mentioned in paragraph (1)(a), but do not include cases in which the claimant is entitled as mentioned in paragraph (1)(a) under regulation 8B(2)(iva) of the 1975 Regulations;

(e) subject to sub-paragraph (f), the "notional assessment phase" is the period of 13 weeks starting on the day on which the assessment phase would have started in relation to the claimant, if he or she had been entitled to old style ESA and sections 2(2)(a) [¹ and 4(4)(a)] of the 2007 Act had applied;

(f) the notional assessment phase has not ended if, at the end of the 13 week period referred to in sub-paragraph (e), no determination has been made as to whether a claimant would have limited capability for work (within the meaning of Part 1 of the 2007 Act) if the claimant was entitled to old style ESA.

AMENDMENT

1. Employment and Support Allowance and Universal Credit (Miscellaneous Amendments and Transitional and Savings Provisions) Regulations 2017 (SI 2017/204) reg.5(4) (April 3, 2017).

DEFINITIONS

"the 1975 Regulations"–para.(1)(a).
"the 2007 Act" –see reg.2(1).
"the Act"–*ibid.*
"assessment period"–*ibid.*
"assessment phase"–see reg.19(8).
"LCW element"–*ibid.*
"LCWRA element"–*ibid.*
"old style ESA"–*ibid.*
"the relevant date"–para.(1)(a).
"the Universal Credit Regulations"–see reg.2(1).

GENERAL NOTE

3.49   This regulation makes similar provision to reg.20 but for claimants who were not entitled to old style ESA, but who were entitled to credits of contributions and earnings on the grounds of limited capability for work.

Transition from income support payable on the grounds of incapacity for work or disability [¹ and other incapacity benefits]

3.50   **22.** (1) This regulation applies where an award of universal credit is made to a claimant [¹ (other than a claimant to whom regulation 23 or 24 applies)] who was entitled to income support on the grounds of incapacity for work or disability on the date on which the claim for universal credit was made or treated as made [¹ or is entitled to incapacity benefit or severe disablement allowance].

(2) Where this regulation applies—

(a) if it is determined in accordance with Part 5 of the Universal Credit Regulations that the claimant has limited capability for work—

   (i) the claimant is to be treated as having had limited capability for work for the purposes of regulation 27(1)(a) of the Universal Credit Regulations (award to include LCW and LCWRA elements) from the beginning of the first assessment period;

   (ii) regulation 28 of those Regulations (period for which the LCW or LCWRA element is not to be included) does not apply; and

   (iii) the LCW element is (subject to the provisions of Part 4 of the Universal Credit Regulations) to be included in the award with effect from the beginning of the first assessment period;

(b) if it is determined in accordance with Part 5 of the Universal Credit Regulations that the claimant has limited capability for work and work-related activity—

   (i) the claimant is to be treated as having had limited capability for work and work-related activity for the purposes of regulation 27(1)(b) of the Universal Credit Regulations from the beginning of the first assessment period;

   (ii) regulation 28 of those Regulations does not apply; and

   (iii) the LCWRA element is (subject to the provisions of Part 4 of the Universal Credit Regulations) to be included in the award of universal credit with effect from the beginning of the first assessment period.

(3) In this regulation—

"income support on the grounds of incapacity for work or disability" means an award of income support which is an "existing award" within the meaning of Schedule 4 to the 2007 Act.

AMENDMENT

1. Universal Credit (Transitional Provisions) (Amendment) Regulations 2014 (SI 2014/1626) reg.5(1) (October 13, 2014).

DEFINITIONS

"the 2007 Act" –see reg.2(1).
"assessment period"–*ibid.*
"incapacity benefit"–see reg.19(8).
"income support"–*ibid.*
"income support on the grounds of incapacity for work or disability"–para.(3).
"LCW element"–see reg.19(8).
"LCWRA element"–*ibid.*
"severe disablement allowance"–*ibid.*
"the Universal Credit Regulations"–see reg.2(1).

GENERAL NOTE

The process of transition from existing incapacity benefits to universal credit is dealt with in regs.22 to 25. Transition from income support awarded on the grounds of incapacity for work or disability is dealt with in reg. 22 and transition from incapacity benefit or severe disablement allowance is dealt with in regs.23 to 25. In both cases, the limited capability for work (LCW) or limited capability for work and work-related activity (LCWRA) elements may be included in an award of universal credit with effect from the start of the first assessment period, if the claimant is

3.51

subsequently assessed as having limited capability for work or, in the case of a claimant approaching pensionable age, is entitled to certain other benefits. Regulations 26 and 27 make similar provision to regs.22-25 but in respect of claimants who although they were not entitled to an incapacity benefit were entitled to credits of earnings on the grounds of incapacity for work.

The various amendments to regs 22-26 which came into effect on October 13, 2014 were designed to ensure that incapacity benefit or severe disablement allowance claimants can have the LCW or LCWRA elements applied to their universal credit award, from the start of the first assessment period where they joined or made a universal credit claim, as quickly as possible. This is sought to be achieved by ensuring they either:

- remain in the employment and support allowance conversion process and undergo a work capability assessment to determine whether their existing incapacity award qualifies for conversion to new style ESA, inclusive of either the WRA or support component and where it does, allow this decision to be used to apply the LCW or LCWRA element to their universal credit award; or

- enter the universal credit assessment process and undergo a universal credit work capability assessment to ascertain whether the LCW or LCWRA element should be applied to their award.

Before the October 2014 amendments, claimants who have not commenced ESA conversion had the choice of either entering the universal credit assessment process or waiting until they undergo conversion to ascertain whether the LCW or LCWRA element should be applied to their universal credit award. The amendments are intended to ensure that where the claimant has not entered the ESA conversion process they now have to enter the universal credit process, if they want to be assessed and have the LCW or LCWRA element backdated. The significance of this change is that if they do not enter the universal credit assessment process they would have to wait until they are scheduled for ESA conversion to see if their existing incapacity award qualified for conversion to new style ESA, before the LCW or LCWRA element could be applied to their universal credit award. This is supposed to avoid any delay in these claimants accessing the additional financial support they will be entitled to if it is decided that they have LCW or LCWRA.

The amending regulations also ensure that where incapacity benefit claimants are in receipt of National Insurance credits only, and are not entitled to the appropriate level or component of a prescribed benefit to allow them to qualify for the LCW or LCWRA element in universal credit, that they will be treated in the same way as those incapacity benefit or severe disablement allowance claimants and will not have to serve the universal credit relevant period but can have the LCW or LCWRA element applied to their universal credit award, with retrospective effect, back to the start of the first assessment period, if it is subsequently determined by a universal credit work capability assessment that they have either LCW or LCWRA.

Transition from other incapacity benefits [1: assessment under the 2010 Regulations]

3.52

23. (1) This regulation applies where—

(a) an award of universal credit is made to a claimant who is entitled to incapacity benefit or severe disablement allowance [1 ("the relevant award")]; and

[1(b) on or before the date on which the claim for universal credit is made or treated as made, a notice has been issued to the claimant under regulation 4 of the Employment and Support Allowance (Transitional Provisions, Housing Benefit and Council Tax Benefit) (Existing

Awards) (No.2) Regulations 2010 ("the 2010 Regulations") (notice commencing the conversion phase).]

[¹ (1A) Where this regulation applies, regulations 27(3) (award to include LCW and LCWRA elements) and 38 (determination of limited capability for work and work-related activity) of the Universal Credit Regulations do not apply and the question whether a claimant has limited capability for work, or for work and work-related activity, is to be determined, for the purposes of the Act and the Universal Credit Regulations, in accordance with this regulation.]

(2) [¹ Where it is determined in accordance with the 2010 Regulations that the relevant award qualifies for conversion into an award in accordance with regulation 7 of those Regulations (qualifying for conversion) and that award includes the work-related activity component]—

(a) [¹ ...];
(b) the claimant is to be treated as having had limited capability for work for the purposes of regulation 27(1)(a) of the Universal Credit Regulations from the beginning of the first assessment period;
(c) regulation 28(1) of those Regulations (period for which LCW or LCWRA element is not to be included) does not apply;
(d) the LCW element is (subject to the provisions of Part 4 of the Universal Credit Regulations) to be included in the award of universal credit with effect from the beginning of the first assessment period; and
(e) the claimant is to be treated as having limited capability for work for the purposes of section 21(1)(a) of the Act.

(3) [¹ Where it is determined in accordance with the 2010 Regulations that the relevant award qualifies for conversion into an award in accordance with regulation 7 of those Regulations and that award includes the support component]—

(a) [¹ ...];
(b) the claimant is to be treated as having had limited capability for work and work-related activity for the purposes of regulation 27(1)(b) of the Universal Credit Regulations from the beginning of the first assessment period;
(c) regulation 28(1) of those Regulations does not apply;
(d) the LCWRA element is (subject to the provisions of Part 4 of the Universal Credit Regulations) to be included in the award of universal credit with effect from the beginning of the first assessment period; and
(e) the claimant is to be treated as having limited capability for work and work-related activity for the purposes of section 19(2)(a) of the Act.

AMENDMENT

1. Universal Credit (Transitional Provisions) (Amendment) Regulations 2014 (SI 2014/1626) reg.5(2) (October 13, 2014).

DEFINITIONS

"the 2010 Regulations"–para.(1)(b).
"the Act"–see reg.2(1).
"assessment period"–*ibid.*
"incapacity benefit"–see reg.19(8).
"LCW element"–*ibid.*

"LCWRA element"–*ibid.*
"the relevant award"–para.(1)(a).
"severe disablement allowance"–see reg.19(8).
"support component"–*ibid.*
"the Universal Credit Regulations"–see reg.2(1).
"work-related activity component"–see reg.19(8).

GENERAL NOTE

3.53   See General Note to reg.22.

Transition from other incapacity benefits: claimants approaching pensionable age

3.54   **24.** (1) This paragraph applies where—

(a)   an award of universal credit is made to a claimant who is entitled to incapacity benefit or severe disablement allowance;

(b)   no notice has been issued to the claimant under regulation 4 (notice commencing the conversion phase) of the Employment and Support Allowance (Transitional Provisions, Housing Benefit and Council Tax Benefit) (Existing Awards) (No.2) Regulations 2010 ("the 2010 Regulations");

(c)   the claimant will reach pensionable age (within the meaning of the 2010 Regulations) within the period of one year; and

(d)   the claimant is also entitled to—

(i)   personal independence payment, where neither the daily living component nor the mobility component is payable at the enhanced rate;

(ii)   disability living allowance under section 71 of the Social Security Contributions and Benefits Act 1992 ("the 1992 Act"), where the care component is payable at the middle rate within the meaning of section 72(4) of that Act or the mobility component is payable at the lower rate within the meaning of section 73(11) of that Act (or both components are payable at those rates);

(iii)   attendance allowance under section 64 of the 1992 Act, where the allowance is payable at the lower rate in accordance with section 65 of that Act;

(iv)   an increase in the weekly rate of disablement pension under section 104 of the 1992 Act (increase where constant attendance needed), where the increase is of an amount which is equal to or less than the amount specified in paragraph 2(a) of Part V of Schedule 4 to that Act; or

(v)   any payment based on the need for attendance which is paid as an addition to a war disablement pension (which means any retired pay or pension or allowance payable in respect of disablement under an instrument specified in section 639(2) of the Income Tax (Earnings and Pensions) Act 2003), where the amount of that payment is equal to or less than the amount specified in paragraph 2(a) of Part V of Schedule 4 to the 1992 Act.

(2) Where paragraph (1) applies and paragraph (3) does not apply—

(a)   regulation 27(3) of the Universal Credit Regulations (award to include LCW and LCWRA elements) does not apply;

(b) the claimant is to be treated as having limited capability for work for the purposes of regulation 27(1)(a) of those Regulations from the beginning of the first assessment period;

(c) regulation 28(1) of the Universal Credit Regulations (period for which LCW or LCWRA element is not to be included) does not apply;

(d) the LCW element is (subject to the provisions of Part 4 of the Universal Credit Regulations) to be included in the award of universal credit with effect from the beginning of the first assessment period; and

(e) the claimant is to be treated as having limited capability for work for the purposes of section 21(1)(a) of the Act.

(3) This paragraph applies where—

(a) an award of universal credit is made to a claimant who is entitled to incapacity benefit or severe disablement allowance;

(b) no notice has been issued to the claimant under regulation 4 of the 2010 Regulations;

(c) the claimant will reach pensionable age (within the meaning of the 2010 Regulations) within the period of one year; and

(d) the claimant is also entitled to—

    (i) personal independence payment, where either the daily living component or the mobility component is (or both components are) payable at the enhanced rate;

    (ii) disability living allowance under section 71 of the 1992 Act, where the care component is payable at the highest rate within the meaning of section 72(4) of that Act or the mobility component is payable at the higher rate within the meaning of section 73(11) of that Act (or both components are payable at those rates);

    (iii) attendance allowance under section 64 of the 1992 Act, where the allowance is payable at the higher rate in accordance with section 65 of that Act;

    (iv) armed forces independence payment under the Armed Forces and Reserve Forces (Compensation Scheme) Order 2011;

    (v) an increase in the weekly rate of disablement pension under section 104 of the 1992 Act, where the increase is of an amount which is greater than the amount specified in paragraph 2(a) of Part V of Schedule 4 to that Act; or

    (vi) any payment based on the need for attendance which is paid as an addition to a war disablement pension (which means any retired pay or pension or allowance payable in respect of disablement under an instrument specified in section 639(2) of the Income Tax (Earnings and Pensions) Act 2003), where the amount of that payment is greater than the amount specified in paragraph 2(a) of Part V of Schedule 4 to the 1992 Act.

(4) Where paragraph (3) applies (whether or not paragraph (1) also applies)—

(a) regulation 27(3) of the Universal Credit Regulations does not apply;

(b) the claimant is to be treated as having limited capability for work and work-related activity for the purposes of regulation 27(1)(b) of those Regulations from the beginning of the first assessment period;

(c) regulation 28(1) of the Universal Credit Regulations does not apply;

(d) the LCWRA element is (subject to the provisions of Part 4 of the Universal Credit Regulations) to be included in the award of universal credit with effect from the beginning of the first assessment period; and

(e) the claimant is to be treated as having limited capability for work and work-related activity for the purposes of section 19(2)(a) of the Act.

DEFINITIONS

"the 1992 Act"–para.(1)(d)(ii).
"the 2010 Regulations"–para.(1)(b).
"the Act"–see reg.2(1).
"assessment period"–*ibid.*
"incapacity benefit"–see reg.19(8).
"LCW element"–*ibid.*
"LCWRA element"–*ibid.*
"severe disablement allowance"–*ibid.*
"the Universal Credit Regulations"–see reg.2(1).
"work-related activity component"–see reg.19(8).

GENERAL NOTE

3.55   See General Note to reg.22.

Transition from other incapacity benefits: supplementary

3.56   **25.** (1) Where an award of universal credit is made to a claimant who is entitled to incapacity benefit or severe disablement allowance, regulation 66 of the Universal Credit Regulations (what is included in unearned income?) applies to the claimant as if incapacity benefit or, as the case may be, severe disablement allowance were added to the descriptions of unearned income in paragraph (1)(b) of that regulation.

(2) For the purposes of regulations [[1] 22,] 23 and 24 and this regulation only, incapacity benefit and severe disablement allowance are prescribed benefits under paragraph 1(2)(b) of Schedule 6 to the Act.

AMENDMENT

1. Universal Credit (Transitional Provisions) (Amendment) Regulations 2014 (SI 2014/1626) reg.5(3) (October 13, 2014).

DEFINITIONS

"the Act"–see reg.2(1).
"incapacity benefit"–see reg.19(8).
"severe disablement allowance"–*ibid.*
"the Universal Credit Regulations"–see reg.2(1).

GENERAL NOTE

3.57   See General Note to reg.22.

Other claimants with incapacity for work: credits only cases where claimant is approaching pensionable age

3.58   **26.** (1) This regulation applies where—

(a) an award of universal credit is made to a claimant who was entitled to be credited with earnings equal to the lower earnings limit then in

428

force under regulation 8B(2)(a)(i), (ii) or (iii) of the Social Security (Credits) Regulations 1975 on the date on which the claim for universal credit was made or treated as made;

(b) the claimant will reach pensionable age within the meaning of the Employment and Support Allowance (Transitional Provisions, Housing Benefit and Council Tax Benefit) (Existing Awards) (No.2) Regulations 2010 within the period of one year; and

(c) [¹ none of regulations 22, 23 or 24 apply] to that claimant (whether or not, in the case of joint claimants, [¹ any] of those regulations apply to the other claimant).

(2) Where the claimant is entitled to a payment, allowance or increased rate of pension specified in regulation 24(1)(d) and is not entitled to a payment, allowance or increased rate of pension specified in regulation 24(3)(d)—

(a) regulation 27(3) of the Universal Credit Regulations (award to include LCW and LCWRA elements) does not apply;

(b) the claimant is to be treated as having limited capability for work for the purposes of regulation 27(1)(a) of those Regulations from the beginning of the first assessment period;

(c) regulation 28(1) of the Universal Credit Regulations (period for which the LCW or LCWRA element is not to be included) does not apply;

(d) the LCW element is (subject to the provisions of Part 4 of the Universal Credit Regulations) to be included in the award of universal credit with effect from the beginning of the first assessment period; and

(e) the claimant is to be treated as having limited capability for work for the purposes of section 21(1)(a) of the Act.

(3) Where the claimant is entitled to a payment, allowance or increased rate of pension specified in regulation 24(3)(d) (whether or not the claimant is also entitled to a payment, allowance or increased rate of pension specified in regulation 24(1)(d))—

(a) regulation 27(3) of the Universal Credit Regulations does not apply;

(b) the claimant is to be treated as having limited capability for work and work-related activity for the purposes of regulation 27(1)(b) of those Regulations from the beginning of the first assessment period;

(c) regulation 28(1) of the Universal Credit Regulations does not apply;

(d) the LCWRA element is (subject to the provisions of Part 4 of the Universal Credit Regulations) to be included in the award of universal credit with effect from the beginning of the first assessment period; and

(e) the claimant is to be treated as having limited capability for work and work-related activity for the purposes of section 19(2)(a) of the Act.

[¹ (4) Where the claimant is not entitled to a payment, allowance or increased rate of pension specified in either regulation 24(1)(d) or regulation 24(3)(d)—

(a) if it is determined in accordance with Part 5 of the Universal Credit Regulations that the claimant has limited capability for work—

   (i) the claimant is to be treated as having had limited capability for work for the purposes of regulation 27(1)(a) of the Universal Credit Regulations from the beginning of the first assessment period;

      (ii) regulation 28 of the Universal Credit Regulations does not apply; and

      (iii) the LCW element is (subject to the provisions of Part 4 of the Universal Credit Regulations) to be included in the award with effect from the beginning of the first assessment period; and

  (b) if it is determined in accordance with Part 5 of the Universal Credit Regulations that the claimant has limited capability for work and work-related activity—

      (i) the claimant is to be treated as having had limited capability for work and work-related activity for the purposes of regulation 27(1)(b) of the Universal Credit Regulations from the beginning of the first assessment period;

      (ii) regulation 28 of the Universal Credit Regulations does not apply; and

      (iii) the LCWRA element is (subject to the provisions of Part 4 of the Universal Credit Regulations) to be included in the award of universal credit with effect from the beginning of the first assessment period.]

AMENDMENT

1. Universal Credit (Transitional Provisions) (Amendment) Regulations 2014 (SI 2014/1626) reg.5(4) (October 13, 2014).

DEFINITIONS

"the Act"–see reg.2(1).
"assessment period"–*ibid.*
"LCW element"–see reg.19(8).
"LCWRA element"–*ibid.*
"the Universal Credit Regulations"–see reg.2(1).
"the work-related activity component"–see reg.19(8).

GENERAL NOTE

3.59   Regulations 26 and 27 make similar provision to regs 22-25 but in respect of claimants who although they were not entitled to an incapacity benefit were entitled to credits of earnings under the Social Security (Credits) Regulations 1975 (SI 1975/556) on the grounds of incapacity for work.

Other claimants with incapacity for work: credits only cases

3.60   **27.** (1) This regulation applies where—

  (a) an award of universal credit is made to a claimant who was entitled to be credited with earnings equal to the lower earnings limit then in force under regulation 8B(2)(a)(i), (ii) or (iii) of the Social Security (Credits) Regulations 1975 on the date on which the claim for universal credit was made or treated as made; and

  (b) none of regulations 22, 23, 24 or 26 apply to that claimant (whether or not, in the case of joint claimants, any of those regulations apply to the other claimant).

  (2) Where this regulation applies—

  (a) if it is determined in accordance with Part 5 of the Universal Credit Regulations that the claimant has limited capability for work—

      (i) the claimant is to be treated as having had limited capability for work for the purposes of regulation 27(1)(a) of the Universal Credit Regulations (award to include LCW and LCWRA elements) from the beginning of the first assessment period;

(ii) regulation 28 of the Universal Credit Regulations (period for which the LCW or LCWRA element is not to be included) does not apply; and

(iii) the LCW element is (subject to the provisions of Part 4 of the Universal Credit Regulations) to be included in the award with effect from the beginning of the first assessment period;

(b) if it is determined in accordance with Part 5 of the Universal Credit Regulations that the claimant has limited capability for work and work-related activity—

(i) the claimant is to be treated as having had limited capability for work and work-related activity for the purposes of regulation 27(1)(b) of the Universal Credit Regulations from the beginning of the first assessment period;

(ii) regulation 28 of the Universal Credit Regulations does not apply; and

(iii) the LCWRA element is (subject to the provisions of Part 4 of the Universal Credit Regulations) to be included in the award of universal credit with effect from the beginning of the first assessment period.

DEFINITIONS

"assessment period"–see reg.2(1).
"LCW element"–see reg.19(8).
"LCWRA element"–*ibid.*
"the Universal Credit Regulations"–see reg.2(1).

GENERAL NOTE

See General Notes to regs 22 and 26. **3.61**

Meaning of "qualifying young person"

28. Where a person who would (apart from the provision made by **3.62** this regulation) be a "qualifying young person" within the meaning of regulation 5 of the Universal Credit Regulations is entitled to an existing benefit—

(a) that person is not a qualifying young person for the purposes of the Universal Credit Regulations; and

(b) regulation 5(5) of those Regulations applies as if, after "a person who is receiving" there were inserted "an existing benefit (within the meaning of the Universal Credit (Transitional Provisions) Regulations 2014),".

DEFINITIONS

"existing benefit"–see reg.2(1).
"the Universal Credit Regulations"–*ibid.*

GENERAL NOTE

This regulation ensures that payments may not be made as part of an award of **3.63** universal credit in respect of a young person who is entitled to existing benefits in their own right. Such persons cannot be claimed for by a parent or carer for the purposes of the Universal Credit Regulations 2013.

Support for housing costs

3.64   **29.** (1) Paragraph (3) applies where—

    (a) an award of universal credit is made to a claimant who—

        (i) was entitled to income-based jobseeker's allowance, income-related employment and support allowance or income support (a "relevant award") at any time during the period of one month ending with the day on which the claim for universal credit was made or treated as made (or would have been so entitled were it not for termination of that award by virtue of an order made under section 150(3) of the Act or the effect of these Regulations); or

        (ii) was at any time during the period of one month ending with the day on which the claim for universal credit was made or treated as made, the partner of a person ("P") who was at that time entitled to a relevant award, where the award of universal credit is not a joint award to the claimant and P; and

    (b) on the relevant date, the relevant award included an amount in respect of housing costs under—

        (i) paragraphs 14 to 16 of Schedule 2 to the Jobseeker's Allowance Regulations 1996 ("the 1996 Regulations");

        (ii) paragraphs 16 to 18 of Schedule 6 to the Employment and Support Allowance Regulations 2008 ("the 2008 Regulations"); or, as the case may be,

        (iii) paragraphs 15 to 17 of Schedule 3 to the Income Support (General) Regulations 1987 ("the 1987 Regulations").

    (2) In this regulation, the "relevant date" means—

    (a) where paragraph (1)(a)(i) applies and the claimant was not entitled to the relevant award on the date on which the claim for universal credit was made or treated as made, the date on which the relevant award terminated;

    (b) where paragraph (1)(a)(i) applies, the claimant is not a new claimant partner and he or she was entitled to the relevant award on the date on which the claim for universal credit was made, that date;

    (c) where paragraph (1)(a)(i) applies, the claimant is a new claimant partner and he or she was entitled to the relevant award on the date on which the claim for universal credit was treated as made, that date;

    (d) where paragraph (1)(a)(ii) applies, the date on which the claimant ceased to be the partner of P or, if earlier, the date on which the relevant award terminated.

    (3) Where this paragraph applies, paragraph 5 of Schedule 5 to the Universal Credit Regulations (no housing costs element under this Schedule for qualifying period) does not apply.

    (4) Paragraph (5) applies where paragraph (1)(a) applies, but the relevant award did not include an amount in respect of housing costs because the claimant's entitlement (or, as the case may be, P's entitlement) was nil by virtue of—

    (a) paragraph 6(1)(c) or 7(1)(b) of Schedule 2 to the 1996 Regulations;

    (b) paragraph 8(1)(c) or 9(1)(b) of Schedule 6 to the 2008 Regulations; or, as the case may be,

(c) paragraph 6(1)(c) or 8(1)(b) of Schedule 3(4) to the 1987 Regulations.

(5) Where this paragraph applies—

(a) paragraph 5(2) of Schedule 5 to the Universal Credit Regulations does not apply; and

(b) the "qualifying period" referred to in paragraph 5 of that Schedule is the period of [¹ 273] days starting with the first day on which the claimant (or, as the case may be, P) was entitled to the relevant award, taking into account any period which was treated as a period of continuing entitlement under—

    (i) paragraph 13 of Schedule 2 to the 1996 Regulations;

    (ii) paragraph 15 of Schedule 6 to the 2008 Regulations; or, as the case may be,

    (iii) paragraph 14 of Schedule 3 to the 1987 Regulations,

provided that, throughout that part of the qualifying period after the award of universal credit is made, receipt of universal credit is continuous and the claimant otherwise qualifies for the inclusion of an amount calculated under Schedule 5 to the Universal Credit Regulations in their award.

(6) For the purposes of—

(a) paragraph (1)(b) of this regulation, inclusion of an amount in respect of housing costs in a relevant award is to be taken into account even if the relevant award subsequently terminated by virtue of an order made under section 150(3) of the Act, regulation 7 or, as the case may be, regulation 8, before the date on which that amount was included in the award;

(b) paragraph (5)(b) of this regulation, entitlement to a relevant award is to be treated as having continued until the relevant date even if the award subsequently terminated by virtue of an order made under section 150(3) of the Act, regulation 7 or, as the case may be, regulation 8, before that date.

AMENDMENT

1. Social Security (Housing Costs Amendments) Regulations 2015 (SI 2015/1647) reg.6 (April 1, 2016).

DEFINITIONS

"the 1987 Regulations"–para.(1)(b)(iii).
"the 1996 Regulations"–para.(1)(b)(i).
"the 2008 Regulations"–para.(1)(b)(ii).
"the Act" –see reg.2(1).
"income-based jobseeker's allowance"–*ibid.*
"income-related employment and support allowance"–*ibid.*
"income support"–*ibid.*
"new claimant partner"–*ibid.*
"partner"–*ibid.*
"qualifying period"–para.(5)(b).
"relevant award"–para.(1)(a)(i).
"relevant date"–para.(2).
"the Universal Credit Regulations"–see reg.2(1).

GENERAL NOTE

This is a hideously opaque regulation. Where a universal credit claimant or their partner was previously entitled to old style JSA, old style ESA or income support,

    3.65

this regulation allows for any support for housing costs which was included in that award (paras.(1) and (2)), or time spent waiting to qualify for such support (paras. (4)-(6)), to be carried over to the award of universal credit (para.(3)), providing the claimant is entitled to the universal credit housing element. The amendment to para.(5)(b) is subject to the saving provision in reg.8 of the Social Security (Housing Costs Amendments) Regulations 2015 (SI 2015/1647).

Sanctions: transition from old style ESA

3.66   **30.** (1) This regulation applies where—
  (a) an award of universal credit is made to a claimant who was previously entitled to old style ESA ("the ESA award"); and
  (b) on the relevant date, payments in respect of the ESA award were reduced under regulation 63 of the Employment and Support Allowance Regulations 2008 ("the 2008 Regulations").

(2) In this regulation, the "relevant date" means—
  (a) where the claimant was not entitled to old style ESA on the date on which the claim for universal credit was made or treated as made, the date on which the ESA award terminated;
  (b) where the claimant is not a new claimant partner and was entitled to old style ESA on the date on which the claim for universal credit was made, that date;
  (c) where the claimant is a new claimant partner and was entitled to old style ESA on the date on which the claim for universal credit was treated as made, that date.

(3) Where this regulation applies—
  (a) the failure which led to reduction of the ESA award ("the ESA failure") is to be treated, for the purposes of the Universal Credit Regulations, as a failure which is sanctionable under section 27 of the Act;
  (b) the award of universal credit is to be reduced in relation to the ESA failure, in accordance with the provisions of this regulation and Chapter 2 of Part 8 of the Universal Credit Regulations (sanctions), as modified by this regulation; and
  (c) the reduction is to be treated, for the purposes of the Universal Credit Regulations, as a reduction under section 27 of the Act.

(4) The reduction period for the purposes of the Universal Credit Regulations is a period of the number of days which is equivalent to the length of the fixed period applicable to the person under regulation 63(7) of the 2008 Regulations in relation to the ESA failure, minus—
  (a) the number of days (if any) in that period in respect of which the amount of old style ESA was reduced; and
  (b) if the ESA award terminated before the first date of entitlement to universal credit in connection with the current award, the number of days (if any) in the period after termination of that award, before the start of the universal credit award.

(5) Accordingly, regulation 101 of the Universal Credit Regulations (general principles for calculating reduction periods) applies in relation to the ESA failure as if, in paragraphs (1) and (3), for "in accordance with regulations 102 to 105", there were substituted "in accordance with regulation 30 of the Universal Credit (Transitional Provisions) Regulations 2014".

(6) For the purposes of this regulation, a determination that payments in respect of the ESA award are to be reduced under regulation 63 of

the 2008 Regulations is to be taken into account even if the ESA award subsequently terminated (in so far as it was an award of income-related employment and support allowance) on a date before the date on which that determination was made, by virtue of an order made under section 150(3) of the Act.

DEFINITIONS

"the 2008 Regulations"–para.(1)(b).
"the Act"–see reg.2(1).
"the ESA award"–para.(1)(a).
"the ESA failure"–para.(3)(a).
"income-related employment and support allowance"–*ibid.*
"new claimant partner"–*ibid.*
"old style ESA"–*ibid.*
"relevant date"–para.(2).
"the Universal Credit Regulations"–see reg.2(1).

GENERAL NOTE

Regulations 30 to 34 deal with the treatment of any sanctions which have been imposed on awards of old style JSA and old style ESA, prior to a claimant's transition to universal credit. The underlying principle is one of equivalence of treatment. Such pre-existing sanctions will continue to have effect by way of deductions from the award of universal credit and past sanctions will also be taken into account for the purposes of determining the level of sanction applicable to any future sanctionable failure. However, where there is a period of entitlement to an existing benefit between two periods of entitlement to universal credit, any sanctions arising prior to that intervening period will not be taken into account.   3.67

So, for example, where a new universal credit claimant was previously entitled to ESA, and subject to an ESA sanction for failure to take part in a work-focussed interview or to undertake a work-related activity, the ESA failure is treated as a sanctionable failure for the purposes of universal credit (paras.(1) and (3)). The reduction period is adjusted accordingly (para.(4)).

Escalation of sanctions: transition from old style ESA

31. (1) This regulation applies where an award of universal credit is made to a claimant who was at any time previously entitled to old style ESA.   3.68

(2) Where this regulation applies, for the purposes of determining the reduction period under regulation 104 of the Universal Credit Regulations (low-level sanction) in relation to a sanctionable failure by the claimant, other than a failure which is treated as sanctionable by virtue of regulation 30—

  (a) a reduction of universal credit in accordance with regulation 30; and

  (b) any reduction of old style ESA under the Employment and Support Allowance Regulations 2008 ("the 2008 Regulations") which did not result in a reduction under regulation 30,

is, subject to paragraph (3), to be treated as arising from a sanctionable failure for which the reduction period which applies is the number of days which is equivalent to the length of the fixed period which applied under regulation 63 of the 2008 Regulations.

(3) In determining a reduction period under regulation 104 of the Universal Credit Regulations in accordance with paragraph (2), no account is to be taken of—

  (a) a reduction of universal credit in accordance with regulation 30 if, at any time after that reduction, the claimant was entitled to an existing benefit;

(b) a reduction of old style ESA under the 2008 Regulations if, at any time after that reduction, the claimant was entitled to universal credit, new style ESA or new style JSA, and was subsequently entitled to an existing benefit.

DEFINITIONS

"the 2008 Regulations"–para.(2)(b).
"existing benefit" "–see reg.2(1).
"new style ESA"–*ibid.*
"new style JSA"–*ibid.*
"old style ESA"–*ibid.*
"the Universal Credit Regulations"–*ibid.*

GENERAL NOTE

3.69   This provision ensures that any previous ESA fixed period reductions are taken into account when deciding the appropriate reduction period for the purposes of a universal credit sanction.

Sanctions: transition from old style JSA

3.70   **32.** (1) This regulation applies where—

(a) an award of universal credit is made to a claimant who was previously entitled to old style JSA ("the JSA award");

(b) on the relevant date, payments in respect of the JSA award were reduced under section 19 (as it applied either before or after substitution by the Act) or section 19A of the Jobseekers Act 1995 ("the 1995 Act"), or under regulation 69B of the Jobseeker's Allowance Regulations 1996 ("the 1996 Regulations"); and

(c) if the JSA award was made to a joint-claim couple within the meaning of the 1995 Act and the reduction related to—

(i) in the case of a reduction under section 19 as it applied before substitution by the Act, circumstances relating to only one member of the couple; or,

(ii) in the case of a reduction under section 19 as it applied after substitution by the Act, a sanctionable failure by only one member of the couple,

the award of universal credit was made to that person.

(2) In this regulation, the "relevant date" means—

(a) where the claimant was not entitled to old style JSA on the date on which the claim for universal credit was made or treated as made, the date on which the JSA award terminated;

(b) where the claimant is not a new claimant partner and was entitled to old style JSA on the date on which the claim for universal credit was made, that date;

(c) where the claimant is a new claimant partner and was entitled to old style JSA on the date on which the claim for universal credit was treated as made, that date.

(3) Where this regulation applies—

(a) the circumstances or failure which led to reduction of the JSA award (in either case, "the JSA failure") is to be treated, for the purposes of the Universal Credit Regulations, as—

(i) a failure which is sanctionable under section 26 of the Act, where the reduction was under section 19 of the 1995 Act; or

(ii) a failure which is sanctionable under section 27 of the Act, where the reduction was under section 19A of the 1995 Act or regulation 69B of the 1996 Regulations;

(b) the award of universal credit is to be reduced in relation to the JSA failure, in accordance with the provisions of this regulation and Chapter 2 of Part 8 of the Universal Credit Regulations (sanctions), as modified by this regulation; and

(c) the reduction is to be treated, for the purposes of the Universal Credit Regulations, as a reduction under section 26 or, as the case may be, section 27 of the Act.

(4) The reduction period for the purposes of the Universal Credit Regulations is a period of the number of days which is equivalent to the length of the period of reduction which is applicable to the person under regulation 69, 69A or 69B of the 1996 Regulations, minus—

(a) the number of days (if any) in that period in respect of which the amount of old style JSA was reduced; and

(b) if the award of old style JSA terminated before the first date of entitlement to universal credit in connection with the current award, the number of days (if any) in the period after termination of that award, before the start of the universal credit award.

(5) Accordingly, regulation 101 of the Universal Credit Regulations applies in relation to the JSA failure as if, in paragraphs (1) and (3), for "in accordance with regulations 102 to 105", there were substituted "in accordance with regulation 32 of the Universal Credit (Transitional Provisions) Regulations 2014".

(6) Where the JSA award was made to a joint-claim couple within the meaning of the 1995 Act and the JSA failure related to only one member of the couple, the daily reduction rate for the purposes of the Universal Credit Regulations is the amount calculated in accordance with regulation 70(3) of the 1996 Regulations in respect of the JSA award, divided by seven and rounded down to the nearest 10 pence, unless regulation 111(2) or (3) of the Universal Credit Regulations (daily reduction rate) applies.

(7) Where the daily reduction rate is to be determined in accordance with paragraph (6), regulation 111(1) of the Universal Credit Regulations applies in relation to the JSA failure as if, for the words from "an amount equal to" to the end there were substituted the words "an amount determined in accordance with regulation 32 of the Universal Credit (Transitional Provisions) Regulations 2014".

(8) For the purposes of this regulation, a determination that payments in respect of the JSA award are to be reduced under regulation 69, 69A or 69B of the 1996 Regulations is to be taken into account even if the JSA award subsequently terminated (in so far as it was an award of income-based jobseeker's allowance) on a date before the date on which that determination was made, by virtue of an order made under section 150(3) of the Act.

DEFINITIONS

"the 1995 Act"–para.(1)(b).
"the 1996 Regulations"–para.(1)(b).
"the 2002 Act" –see reg.2(1).
"income-based jobseeker's allowance"–*ibid.*

"the JSA award"–para.(1)(a).
"the JSA failure"–para.(3)(a).
"new claimant partner" –see reg.2(1).
"new style ESA"–*ibid*.
"new style JSA"–*ibid*.
"old style JSA"–*ibid*.
"relevant date"–para.(2).
"the Universal Credit Regulations"–see reg.2(1).

GENERAL NOTE

3.71   This has similar effect for JSA as reg.30 does for ESA. It is designed to ensure that current JSA sanctions carry forward into the universal credit scheme.

Escalation of sanctions: transition from old style JSA

3.72   **33.** (1) This regulation applies where an award of universal credit is made to a claimant who was at any time previously entitled to old style JSA.

(2) Where this regulation applies, for the purposes of determining the applicable reduction period under regulation 102 (higher-level sanction), 103 (medium-level sanction) or 104 (low-level sanction) of the Universal Credit Regulations in relation to a sanctionable failure by the person, other than a failure which is treated as sanctionable by virtue of regulation 32—

(a) a reduction of universal credit in accordance with regulation 32; and

(b) any reduction of old style JSA under section 19 or 19A of the Jobseekers Act 1995 ("the 1995 Act"), or under regulation 69B of the 1996 Regulations which did not result in a reduction under regulation 32,

is, subject to paragraph (3), to be treated as arising from a sanctionable failure for which the reduction period is the number of days which is equivalent to the length of the period which applied under regulation 69, 69A or 69B of the 1996 Regulations.

(3) In determining a reduction period under regulation 102, 103 or 104 of the Universal Credit Regulations in accordance with paragraph (2), no account is to be taken of—

(a) a reduction of universal credit in accordance with regulation 32 if, at any time after that reduction, the claimant was entitled to an existing benefit;

(b) a reduction of old style JSA under section 19 or 19A of the 1995 Act, or under regulation 69B of the 1996 Regulations if, at any time after that reduction, the claimant was entitled to universal credit, new style ESA or new style JSA, and was subsequently entitled to an existing benefit.

DEFINITIONS

"the 1995 Act"–para.(2)(b).
"the 1996 Regulations"–see reg.32(1)(b).
"existing benefit"–see reg.2(1).
"new style ESA"–*ibid*.
"new style JSA"–*ibid*.
"old style JSA"–*ibid*.
"the Universal Credit Regulations"–*ibid*.

GENERAL NOTE

3.73   This is the JSA equivalent of reg.31, which applies to ESA.

Sanctions: temporary return to certain existing benefits

34. If an award of universal credit terminates while there is an outstand-   3.74
ing reduction period (within the meaning of regulation 107 of the Universal
Credit Regulations) and the claimant becomes entitled to old style JSA, old
style ESA or income support ("the relevant benefit") during that period—
  (a) regulation 107 of the Universal Credit Regulations (reduction period
      to continue where award terminates) ceases to apply; and
  (b) the reduction period is to terminate on the first date of entitlement
      to the relevant benefit.

DEFINITIONS

"income support"–see reg.2(1).
"old style ESA"–*ibid.*
"old style JSA"–*ibid.*
"relevant benefit"–see reg.34.
"the Universal Credit Regulations"–see reg.2(1).

GENERAL NOTE

This provision has the effect that where a claimant comes off universal credit and   3.75
claims one of the former benefits (e.g. JSA, because he is no longer in a relevant
area), then if he subsequently becomes entitled again to universal credit (e.g. by
forming a couple with a universal credit claimant) then the universal credit sanction does not bite, even if it had on the face of it not expired. This is because the
reduction period is deemed as having terminated on the first day of the award of the
existing benefit such as JSA.

Loss of benefit penalties: transition from existing benefits other than tax credits

35. (1) Subject to paragraph (6), this regulation applies in the cases set   3.76
out in paragraphs (2) to (4).
(2) The first case is where—
  (a) an award of universal credit is made to a claimant who is an offender;
  (b) the claimant was entitled to old style JSA, old style ESA, income
      support or housing benefit ("the earlier award") at any time during
      the period of one month ending with the date on which the claim for
      universal credit was made or treated as made (or would have been
      so entitled were it not for termination of that award by virtue of an
      order made under section 150(3) of the Act or, as the case may be,
      the effect of these Regulations); and
  (c) payments in respect of the earlier award were, on the relevant date,
      subject to a restriction under section 6B (loss of benefit in case
      of conviction, penalty or caution for benefit offence), 7 (repeated
      benefit fraud) or 8 (effect of offence on joint-claim jobseeker's allow-
      ance) of the 2001 Act.
(3) The second case is where—
  (a) an award of universal credit is made to a claimant who is an offender;
  (b) another person who was the offender's family member (but is no
      longer their family member) was entitled to old style JSA, old style
      ESA, income support or housing benefit ("the earlier award") at any
      time during the period of one month ending with the date on which
      the claim for universal credit was made or treated as made; and
  (c) payments in respect of the earlier award were, on the relevant date,

subject to a restriction under section 9 (effect of offence on benefits for members of offender's family) of the 2001 Act.

(4) The third case is where—

(a) an award of universal credit is made to a claimant who is an offender's family member;

(b) the offender, or the claimant, was entitled to old style JSA, old style ESA, income support or housing benefit ("the earlier award") at any time during the period of one month ending with the date on which the claim for universal credit was made or treated as made; and

(c) payments in respect of the earlier award were, on the relevant date, subject to a restriction under section 6B, 7, 8 or, as the case may be, 9 of the 2001 Act.

(5) Where this regulation applies—

(a) any subsequent payment of universal credit to the claimant in respect of an assessment period which falls wholly or partly within the remainder of the disqualification period applicable to the offender is to be reduced in accordance with regulation 36; and

(b) regulation 3ZB of the 2001 Regulations does not apply.

(6) This regulation does not apply if the earlier award was a joint-claim jobseeker's allowance and—

(a) payments in respect of the award were, on the relevant date, subject to a restriction under section 8(2) of the 2001 Act; or

(b) the award of universal credit is not made to joint claimants who were, on the relevant date, both entitled to the joint-claim jobseeker's allowance.

(7) In this regulation and in regulation 36—

"the 2001 Act" means the Social Security Fraud Act 2001;

"the 2001 Regulations" means the Social Security (Loss of Benefit) Regulations 2001;

"disqualification period" has the meaning given in the 2001 Act, interpreted in accordance with the 2001 Regulations;

"earlier award" is to be interpreted in accordance with paragraph (2)(b), (3)(b) or, as the case may be, (4)(b) and, for the purposes of regulation 36, where there is more than one earlier award, the term refers to the award to which the claimant became entitled most recently;

"offender" means an offender within the meaning of the 2001 Act;

"offender's family member" has the same meaning as in the 2001 Act;

"the relevant date" means—

(a) in relation to the first case—

  (i) where the claimant was not entitled to the earlier award on the date on which the claim for universal credit was made or treated as made, the date on which the earlier award terminated;

  (ii) where the claimant is not a new claimant partner and was entitled to the earlier award on the date on which the claim for universal credit was made, that date;

  (iii) where the claimant is a new claimant partner and was entitled to the earlier award on the date on which the claim for universal credit was treated as made, that date;

(b) in relation to the second case, the date on which the person entitled to the earlier award ceased to be the offender's family member or, if the award terminated before that date, the date on which the earlier award terminated;

   (c) in relation to the third case—

     (i) where the claimant was entitled to the earlier award but that entitlement terminated before the date on which the claim for universal credit was made or treated as made, the date on which the earlier award terminated;

    (ii) where the claimant is not a new claimant partner and was entitled to the earlier award on the date on which the claim for universal credit was made, that date;

   (iii) where the claimant is a new claimant partner and was entitled to the earlier award on the date on which the claim for universal credit was treated as made, that date;

   (iv) where the offender's family member was entitled to the earlier award, the date on which that person ceased to be the offender's family member or, if earlier, the date on which the earlier award terminated.

(8) For the purposes of this regulation, the fact that payments in respect of an earlier award were subject to a restriction is to be taken into account, even if the earlier award subsequently terminated before the date on which payments became subject to a restriction by virtue of an order made under section 150(3) of the Act (in so far as it was an award of income-based job-seeker's allowance or income-related employment and support allowance), regulation 7 or, as the case may be, regulation 8.

DEFINITIONS

   "the 2001 Act"–para.(7).
   "the 2001 Regulations"–*ibid.*
   "the 2002 Act"–see reg.2(1).
   "assessment period"–*ibid.*
   "the disqualification period"–para.(7).
   "earlier award"–*ibid.*
   "housing benefit"–see reg.2(1).
   "income support"–*ibid.*
   "income-based jobseeker's allowance"–*ibid.*
   "income-related employment and support allowance"–*ibid.*
   "joint-claim jobseeker's allowance"–*ibid.*
   "new claimant partner"–*ibid.*
   "offender"—para.(7)
   "offender's family member"—*ibid.*
   "old style ESA"–see reg.2(1).
   "old style JSA"–*ibid.*
   "the relevant date"–para.(7).

GENERAL NOTE

   This provision (taken with reg.36) has the effect that where a claimant moves to   **3.77** universal credit within one month of the end of an award of an existing benefit and is subject to a loss of benefit penalty, the penalty will in most cases continue on the basis of the rate applicable to the existing benefit for the remainder of the disqualification period. The usual rules relating to calculation of penalties within universal credit will not apply.

Loss of benefit penalties: reduction of universal credit

   36. (1) Subject to paragraph (6) [¹ and to regulation 38], where regula-   **3.78** tion 35 applies, the amount of a reduction of universal credit in respect of an assessment period is to be calculated by multiplying the daily reduction rate by the number of days in the assessment period, unless paragraph (2) applies.

(2) Where the disqualification period ends during an assessment period, the amount of the reduction for that assessment period is (subject to paragraph (6)) to be calculated by multiplying the daily reduction rate by the number of days in the assessment period which are within the disqualification period.

(3) Subject to paragraphs (4) and (5), the daily reduction rate where regulation 35 applies is an amount which is equal to—

(a) the monetary amount by which payments in respect of the earlier award were reduced in accordance with section 6B or 7 of the 2001 Act or, as the case may be, regulation 3, 3ZA or 17 of the 2001 Regulations in respect of the last complete week before the relevant date (within the meaning of regulation 35);

(b) multiplied by 52;

(c) divided by 365; and

(d) rounded down to the nearest 10 pence.

(4) Where the monetary amount by which payments in respect of the earlier award would have been reduced would, if the claimant had remained entitled to the earlier award, have changed during the disqualification period because of an order made under section 150 of the Social Security Administration Act 1992 (annual up-rating of benefits)—

(a) the daily reduction rate is to be calculated in accordance with paragraph (3), but on the basis of the new amount by which payments would have been reduced; and

(b) any adjustment to the reduction of universal credit is to take effect from the first day of the first assessment period to start after the date of the change.

(5) Where the earlier award was a joint-claim jobseeker's allowance, the daily reduction rate is an amount which is equal to—

(a) the amount of the standard allowance applicable to the joint claimants under regulation 36 of the Universal Credit Regulations (table showing amounts of elements);

(b) multiplied by 12;

(c) divided by 365;

(d) reduced by 60%; and

(e) rounded down to the nearest 10 pence.

(6) The amount of the reduction under this regulation in respect of any assessment period is not to exceed the amount of the standard allowance which is applicable to the claimant in respect of that period.

AMENDMENTS

1. Universal Credit (Transitional Provisions) (Amendment) Regulations 2014 (SI 2014/1626) reg.6(1) (October 13, 2014).

DEFINITIONS

"the 2001 Act"–see reg.35(7).
"the 2001 Regulations"–*ibid.*
"assessment period"–see reg.2(1).
"the disqualification period"–see reg.35(7).
"earlier award"–*ibid.*

"joint-claim jobseeker's allowance"–see reg.2(1).
"the relevant date"–see reg.35(7).
"the Universal Credit Regulations"–see reg.2(1).

GENERAL NOTE

See General Note to reg.35. Note also that as compared with reg.35 of the 2013   **3.79**
Transitional Regulations provision for the transfer of loss of benefit penalties for
fraudulent offences to a universal credit award has been amended in relation to the
transfer of penalties from joint-claim JSA awards to an award of universal credit
(para.(5)). In these cases the amount of the penalty applied to the universal credit
award is reduced by 60%, if only one of the joint JSA claimants is subject to a
penalty. This reflects the position in JSA where the member of the joint-claim couple
who is not the benefit fraud offender can be paid JSA at the single person's rate.

[1 Loss of benefit penalties: transition from working tax credit

37. (1) This regulation applies where an award of universal credit is made   **3.80**
to a claimant who—
  (a) was previously entitled to working tax credit; and
  (b) is an offender, within the meaning of the 2002 Act.
  (2) Where this regulation applies, the Social Security (Loss of Benefit)
Regulations 2001 apply as if in regulation 3ZB of those Regulations—
  (a) in paragraph (1) at the beginning there were inserted "Subject to
       regulation 38 of the Universal Credit (Transitional Provisions)
       Regulations 2014,";
  (b) "disqualification period" includes a disqualification period within
       the meaning of the 2002 Act;
  (c) "offender" includes an offender within the meaning of the 2002 Act;
       and
  (d) "offender's family member" includes a person who is a member
       of the family (within the meaning of section 137(1) of the Social
       Security Contributions and Benefits Act 1992 of a person who is an
       offender within the meaning of the 2002 Act.]

AMENDMENTS

1.   Universal Credit (Transitional Provisions) (Amendment) Regulations
2014 (SI 2014/1626) reg.6(2) (October 13, 2014).

DEFINITIONS

"the 2002 Act"–see reg.2(1).
"working tax credit"–*ibid.*

GENERAL NOTE

This regulation provides that where a working tax credit (WTC) claimant has a   **3.81**
fraud penalty applied to their WTC award, the fraud penalty will be applied to the
universal credit standard allowance, for the remaining period of that penalty. As a
consequence, reg.38 below ensures that where a claimant has been in receipt of
WTC and another existing benefit (e.g. housing benefit) and both awards have had
a fraud penalty applied to them, the combination of these penalties will not exceed
the universal credit standard allowance in any assessment period. This follows the
approach taken with existing Department for Work and Pensions benefits where
there is more than one fraud penalty applied to an existing benefit award upon the
transition to universal credit.

[¹ Loss of benefit penalties: maximum total reduction

3.82   **38.** Where regulations 35 and 37 both apply to a claimant, the total amount of a reduction of universal credit in respect of any assessment period under—

(a) regulation 36; and

(b) regulation 3ZB of the Social Security (Loss of Benefit) Regulations 2001,

must not exceed the amount of the standard allowance which is applicable to the claimant in respect of that period.]

AMENDMENT

1. Universal Credit (Transitional Provisions) (Amendment) Regulations 2014 (SI 2014/1626) reg.6(2) (October 13, 2014).

DEFINITIONS

"assessment period"–see reg.2(1).

GENERAL NOTE

3.83   See General Note to reg.37.

[¹ PART 3

ARRANGEMENTS REGARDING CHANGES TO THE CHILD ELEMENT FROM APRIL 2017

Restriction on claims for universal credit during the interim period

3.84   **39.**—(1) During the interim period, no claim may be made for universal credit by a person who is responsible for more than two children or qualifying young persons, unless it is—

(a) a claim to which regulation 21(3C) of the Universal Credit Regulations (new claim within 6 months of a previous award terminating) applies; or

(b) a claim made by a single person within one month of an award of universal credit terminating because that person ceased to be a member of a couple.

(2) For the purposes of this regulation and regulation 40, the interim period is the period beginning with 6th April 2017 and ending with 31st October 2018, but may be extended by the Secretary of State if the Secretary of State considers it necessary to do so in order to protect the efficient administration of universal credit.]

AMENDMENT

1. Social Security (Restrictions on Amounts for Children and Qualifying Young Persons) Amendment Regulations 2017 (2017/376) reg.3(3) (April 6, 2017).

GENERAL NOTE

See General Note to regs 24A and 24B of the Universal Credit Regulations.

[¹ Availability of the child element where maximum exceeded – transitionally protected children and qualifying young persons

3.85   **40.**—(1) A child or qualifying young person for whom the claimant is responsible ("A") is transitionally protected for the purposes of regulation 24A(4) of the Universal Credit Regulations (availability of the child element where maximum exceeded) in the following circumstances.

(2) For the purposes of calculating an award of universal credit in respect of an assessment period in which the interim period begins or that falls wholly within the interim period, the circumstances are that—

(a) A was born before 6th April 2017; and

(b) there are at least two other children or qualifying young persons for whom the claimant (or either of joint claimants) is responsible who were born before 6th April 2017 and who precede A in the order determined by regulation 24B(5) of the Universal Credit Regulations (order of children and qualifying young persons).

(3) For the purposes of calculating an award of universal credit in respect of an assessment period in which the interim period ends or that begins after the end of the interim period, the circumstances are that—

(a) A was born before 6th April 2017;

(b) the claimant (or either of joint claimants) meets the following condition in respect of A—

(i) on the last day of the interim period, the claimant was entitled to an award of universal credit (or was in a period of non-entitlement between connected awards) and was responsible for A; or

(ii) if paragraph (i) does not apply, within the 6 months immediately preceding the first day on which the claimant first became entitled to an award of universal credit after the interim period ended, the claimant was in receipt of an individual element of child tax credit for A or was entitled to an award of income support or old style JSA where an amount in respect of A was included in the applicable amount,

and since the day mentioned in paragraph (i) or (ii) (whichever is applicable), the claimant has not ceased to be responsible for A or ceased to be entitled to universal credit (apart from a period of non-entitlement between connected awards); and

(c) there are at least two other children or qualifying young persons born before 6th April 2017—

(i) in respect of whom the claimant (or either of joint claimants) meets the condition in sub-paragraph (b); and

(ii) who precede A in the order determined by regulation 24B of the Universal Credit Regulations.

(4) In paragraph (3)(b) two awards are connected awards if the later award was made—

(a) as a consequence of the earlier award having terminated when the claimant ceased to be a member of a couple or became a member of a couple; or

(b) in any other circumstances in which the assessment periods for the later award begin on the same day of each month as the assessment periods for the earlier award under regulation 21(6) of the Universal Credit Regulations (assessment periods).]

AMENDMENT

1. Social Security (Restrictions on Amounts for Children and Qualifying Young Persons) Amendment Regulations 2017 (2017/376) reg.3(3) (April 6, 2017).

See General Note to regs 24A and 24B of the Universal Credit Regulations.

[¹ Availability of the child element where maximum exceeded – continuation of exception from a previous award of child tax credit, income support or old style JSA

3.86

41.—(1) Where—

(a) the claimant ("C") is the step-parent of a child or qualifying young person ("A"); and

(b) within the 6 months immediately preceding the first day on which C became entitled to an award of universal credit, C had an award of child tax credit, income support or old style JSA in which an exception corresponding with an exception under paragraph 2, 3, 5 or 6 of Schedule 12 to the Universal Credit Regulations applied in respect of A,

paragraph 6 of that Schedule is to apply as if sub-paragraph (c) of that paragraph were satisfied, despite the fact that the previous award was not an award of universal credit.

(2) In this regulation, "step-parent" has the same meaning as in the Universal Credit Regulations.]

AMENDMENT

1. Social Security (Restrictions on Amounts for Children and Qualifying Young Persons) Amendment Regulations 2017 (2017/376) reg.3(3) (April 6, 2017).

[¹ Evidence for non-consensual conception where claimant previously had an award of child tax credit

3.87

42.—(1) This regulation applies for the purposes of paragraph 5 of Schedule 12(7) to the Universal Credit Regulations (exception for non-consensual conception).

(2) The Secretary of State may treat the condition in sub-paragraph (3)(a) of that paragraph 5 as met if the Secretary of State is satisfied that the claimant has previously provided the evidence referred to in that sub-paragraph to the Commissioners for her Majesty's Revenue and Customs for the purposes of the corresponding exception in relation to child tax credit.]

AMENDMENT

1. Social Security (Restrictions on Amounts for Children and Qualifying Young Persons) Amendment Regulations 2017 (2017/376) reg.3(3) (April 6, 2017).

[¹ Abolition of higher amount of the child element for first child or qualifying young person – saving where claimant responsible for a child or qualifying young person born before 6th April 2017

3.88

43. Section 14(5)(b) of the Welfare Reform and Work Act 2016(8) (which amends the Universal Credit Regulations by omitting the amount of the child element payable for the first child or qualifying young person) does not apply where the claimant is responsible for a child or qualifying young person born before 6th April 2017.]

AMENDMENT

1. Social Security (Restrictions on Amounts for Children and Qualifying Young Persons) Amendment Regulations 2017 (2017/376) reg.3(3) (April 6, 2017).

SCHEDULE

MODIFICATION OF TAX CREDITS LEGISLATION (FINALISATION OF TAX CREDITS)

Modifications to the Tax Credits Act 2002

1. Paragraphs 2 to 10 prescribe modifications to the application of the 2002 Act where regu-   **3.89**
lation 12A of these Regulations applies.
2. In section 7 (income test)—
   (a) in subsection (3), before "current year income" in each place where it occurs, insert
        "notional";
   (b) in subsection (4)—
        (i) for "current year" substitute "current part year";
        (ii) in paragraphs (a) and (b), before "tax year" insert "part";
   (c) after subsection (4), insert—

"(4A) In this section "the notional current year income" means—

   (a) in relation to persons by whom a joint claim for a tax credit is made, the aggregate
        income of the persons for the part tax year to which the claim relates, divided by
        the number of days in that part tax year, multiplied by the number of days in the
        tax year in which the part tax year is included and rounded down to the next whole
        number of pence; and
   (b) in relation to a person by whom a single claim for a tax credit is made, the income
        of the person for that part tax year, divided by the number of days in that part tax
        year, multiplied by the number of days in the tax year in which the part tax year is
        included and rounded down to the next whole number of pence.".

3. In section 17 (final notice)—
   (a) in subsection (1)—
        (i) omit "the whole or"; and
        (ii) in sub-paragraph (a), before "tax year" insert "part";
   (b) in subsection (3), before "tax year" insert "part";
   (c) in subsections (4)(a) and (4)(b), for "current year" in both places where it occurs,
        substitute "current part year";
   (d) in subsection (5)(a) for "current year" in both places where it occurs, substitute
        "current part year";
   (e) omit subsection (8).
4. In section 18 (decisions after final notice)—
   (a) in subsection (1), before "tax year" insert "part";
   (b) omit subsections (6) to (9);
   (c) in subsection (10), for "subsection (1), (5), (6) or (9)" substitute "subsection (1) or
        (5)";
   (d) in subsection (11)—
        (i)   after "subsection (5)" omit "or (9)";
        (ii) omit paragraph (a);
        (iii) in paragraph (b) omit "in any other case,";
        (iv) before "tax year" in each place where it occurs, insert "part".
5. In section 19 (power to enquire)—
   (a) in subsection (1)(a) and (b), before "tax year" insert "part";
   (b) in subsection (3), before "tax year" insert "part";
   (c) for subsection (5) substitute—

        "(5) "The relevant section 18 decision" means the decision under subsection (1) of
        section 18 in relation to the person or persons and the part tax year.";

   (d) for subsection (6) substitute—

        "(6) "The relevant section 17 date" means the date specified for the purposes of
        subsection (4) of section 17 in the notice given to a person or persons under that
        section in relation to the part tax year.";

   (e) in subsection (11), before "tax year" insert "part";
   (f) in subsection (12), before "tax year" in each place where it occurs, insert "part".

6. In section 20 (decisions on discovery)—
    (a) in subsection (1), before "tax year" insert "part";
    (b) in subsection (4)(a), before "tax year" insert "part";
    (c) in subsection (5)(b), before "tax year" insert "part";
    (d) in subsection (6)—
        (i) before "tax year" insert "part";
        (ii) in paragraph (a), for "section 18(1), (5), (6) or (9)" substitute "section 18(1) or (5)";
    (e) in subsection (7), before "tax year" in each place where it occurs, insert "part".
7. In section 21 (decisions subject to official error), for "18(1), (5), (6) or (9)" substitute "18(1) or (5)".
8. In section 23 (notice of decisions)—
    (a) in subsection (1), for "18(1), (5), (6) or (9)" substitute "18(1) or (5)";
    (b) in subsection (3)—
        (i) after "18(1)" omit "or (6)";
        (ii) for paragraph (b) substitute—

        "(b) the notice of the decision under subsection (1) of section 18,".

9. In section 30(1) (underpayments), before "tax year" in each place where it occurs, insert "part".
10. In section 38 (appeals)—
    (a) in subsection (1)(b), before "tax year" insert "part";
    (b) for subsection (2), substitute—

        "(2) "The relevant section 18 decision" means the decision under subsection (1) of section 18 in relation to the person or persons and the tax credit for the part tax year.".

Modifications to the Tax Credits (Definition and Calculation of Income) Regulations 2002

3.90
11. Paragraphs 12 to 23 prescribe modifications to the application of the Tax Credits (Definition and Calculation of Income) Regulations 2002 where regulation 12A of these Regulations applies.
12. In regulation 2(2) (interpretation), after the definition of "the Macfarlane Trusts" insert—
    ""part tax year" means a period of less than a year beginning with 6th April and ending with the date on which the award of a tax credit terminated;".
13. In regulation 3 (calculation of income of claimant)—
    (a) in paragraph (1)—
        (i) before "tax year" insert "part";
        (ii) in Steps 1 and 2, after "of the claimant, or, in the case of a joint claim, of the claimants" insert "received in or relating to the part tax year";
        (iii) in the second and third sentences of Step 4, before "year" insert "part";
    (b) in paragraph (6A), for the words from "ending on 31st March" to the end, substitute "ending on the last day of the month in which the claimant's award of a tax credit terminated";
    (c) in paragraph (8)(b), before "year" insert "part".
14. In regulation 4 (employment income)—
    (a) in paragraph (1)(a), before "tax year" insert "part";
    (b) in paragraph (1)(b), (c), (d), (e), (g) and (k), before "year" insert "part";
    (c) in paragraph (1)(f), after "ITEPA" insert "which is treated as received in the part tax year and in respect of which the charge arises in the part tax year";
    (d) in paragraph (1)(h), after "week" insert "in the part tax year";
    (e) in paragraph (1)(i), for "that year" substitute "the tax year" and after "ITEPA" insert "which is treated as received in the part tax year";
    (f) in paragraph (1)(j), after "applies" insert "which is received in the part tax year";
    (g) in paragraph (1)(l), for "that year" substitute "the tax year" and after "ITEPA" insert "in respect of which the charge arises in the part tax year";
    (h) in paragraph (1)(m), after "paid" insert "in the part tax year";
    (i) in paragraph (4), in the first sentence and in the title of Table 1, after "employment income" insert "received in the part tax year";
    (j) in paragraph (5), after "calculating earnings" insert "received in the part tax year".
15. In regulation 5 (pension income)—

(a) in paragraph (1), after ""pension income" means" insert "any of the following received in or relating to the part tax year";

(b) in paragraph (2), in the first sentence and in the title of Table 2, after "pension income" insert "received in or relating to the part tax year";

(c) in paragraph (3), after "income tax purposes", insert "in relation to the part tax year".

16. In regulation 6 (trading income)—

(a) re-number the existing regulation as paragraph (1);

(b) in paragraph (1) (as so re-numbered)—

    (i) in sub-paragraph (a), for "taxable profits for the tax year" substitute "actual or estimated taxable profits attributable to the part tax year";

    (ii) in sub-paragraph (b), for "taxable profit for the" substitute "actual or estimated taxable profit attributable to the part tax";

(c) after paragraph (1) insert—

"(2) Actual or estimated taxable profits attributable to the part tax year ("the relevant trading income") is to be calculated by reference to the basis period (determined by reference to the rules in Chapter 15 of Part 2 of ITTOIA) ending during the tax year in which the claimant made, or was treated as making, a claim for universal credit.

(3) The relevant trading income is to be calculated by—

(a) taking the figure for the actual or estimated taxable income earned in the basis period;

(b) dividing that figure by the number of days in the basis period to give the daily figure; and

(c) multiplying the daily figure by the number of days in the part tax year on which the trade, profession or vocation was carried on.".

17. In regulation 7 (social security income)—

(a) in paragraph (1), after "social security income" insert "received in the part tax year";

(b) in paragraph (3), in the opening words and in the title of Table 3, after "social security income" insert "received in the part tax year".

18. In regulation 8 (student income), after "in relation to a student" insert ", any of the following which is received in the part tax year".

19. In regulation 10 (investment income)—

(a) in paragraph (1), after "gross amount" insert "received in the part tax year";

(b) in paragraph (1)(e), before "year" insert "part tax";

(c) in paragraph (2), in the opening words and in the title of Table 4, after "investment income" insert "received in the part tax year".

20. In regulation 11(1) (property income)—

(a) omit "annual";

(b) after "taxable profits" insert "for the part tax year".

21. In regulation 12(1) (foreign income), before "year" insert "part tax".

22. In regulation 13 (notional income), after "means income" insert "received in the part tax year".

23. In regulation 18 (miscellaneous income), after "means income" insert "received in the part tax year".

Modifications to the Tax Credits (Income Thresholds and Determination of Rates) Regulations 2002

24. Paragraphs 25 to 27 prescribe modifications to the application of the Tax Credits (Income Thresholds and Determination of Rates) Regulations 2002 where regulation 12A of these Regulations applies.   **3.91**

25. In regulation 2 (interpretation)—

(a) after the definition of "the income threshold" insert—

""part tax year" means a period of less than a year beginning with 6th April and ending with the date on which the award of a tax credit terminated;";

(b) in the definition of "the relevant income" insert "as modified by the Universal Credit (Transitional Provisions) Regulations 2014" at the end.

26. In regulation 7(3) (determination of rate of working tax credit)—

(a) in Step 1, in the definition of "MR", after "maximum rate" insert "(determined in the manner prescribed at the date on which the award of the tax credit terminated)";

(b) in Step 3—

    (i) in the definition of "I", before "tax year" insert "part";

(ii) in the definition of "N1", before "tax year" insert "part".

27. In regulation 8(3) (determination of rate of child tax credit)—

(a) in Step 1, in the definition of "MR", after "maximum rate" insert "(determined in the manner prescribed at the date on which the award of the tax credit terminated)";

(b) in Step 3—

(i) in the definition of "I", before "tax year" insert "part";

(ii) in the definition of "N1", before "tax year" insert "part".

Modifications to the Tax Credits (Claims and Notifications) Regulations 2002

3.92   28. Paragraphs 29 to 34 prescribe modifications to the application of the Tax Credits (Claims and Notifications) Regulations 2002 where regulation 12A of these Regulations applies.

29. In regulation 4 (interpretation), omit paragraph (b).

30. Omit regulation 11 (circumstances in which claims to be treated as made).

31. Omit regulation 12 (further circumstances in which claims to be treated as made).

32. In regulation 13 (circumstances in which claims made by one member of a couple to be treated as also made by the other)—

(a) in paragraph (1), after "prescribed by paragraph" omit "(2) or";

(b) omit paragraph (2).

33. In regulation 15(1)(c) (persons who die after making a claim)—

(a) omit "the whole or" and "after the end of that tax year but"; and

(b) for "section 18(1), (5), (6) or (9)" substitute "section 18(1) or (5)".

34. In regulation 33 (dates to be specified in notices)—

(a) in paragraph (a), for the words from "not later than 31st July" to "if later", substitute "not less than 30 days after the date on which the notice is given";

(b) omit paragraph (b) and the "and" which precedes it.

Modification to the Tax Credits (Payment by the Commissioners) Regulations 2002

3.93   35. Paragraph 36 prescribes a modification to the application of the Tax Credits (Payment by the Commissioners) Regulations 2002 where regulation 12A of these Regulations applies.

36. Omit regulation 7 (prescribed circumstances for certain purposes).

Modification to the Tax Credits (Residence) Regulations 2003

3.94   37. Paragraph 38 prescribes a modification to the application of the Tax Credits (Residence) Regulations 2003 where regulation 12A of these Regulations applies.

38. In regulation 3(5)(a) (circumstances in which a person is treated as not being in the United Kingdom)(26), omit "under regulation 11 or 12 of the Tax Credits (Claims and Notifications) Regulations 2002 or otherwise".

AMENDMENTS

1. Universal Credit (Transitional Provisions) (Amendment) Regulations 2014 (SI 2014/1626) reg.4 (October 13, 2014).

GENERAL NOTE

3.95   See General Note to reg.12A.

PART IVB

COMMENCEMENT ORDERS

The Welfare Reform Act 2012 (Commencement No.9 and Transitional and Transitory Provisions and Commencement No.8 and Savings and Transitional Provisions (Amendment)) Order 2013

(SI 2013/983) (C. 41) (AS AMENDED)

The Secretary of State, in exercise of the powers conferred by section 150(3) and (4)(a), (b)(i) and (c) of the Welfare Reform Act 2012, makes the following Order:

ARRANGEMENT OF ARTICLES

23.   Amendment of the Welfare Reform Act 2012 (Commencement No 8 and
            Savings and Transitional Provisions) Order 2013
24.   Appeals relating to ESA and JSA

Schedule 1 Postcode districts
Schedule 2 Universal credit provisions coming into force in relation to certain
            claims and awards
Schedule 3 Commencement of repeals in Part 1 of Schedule 14 to the Act
Schedule 4 Modifications of the Transitional Provisions Regulations 2010
Schedule 5 The Gateway Conditions

GENERAL NOTE

3.96   This Commencement Order ("the Commencement No.9 Order") was the first
to "roll out" the new universal credit scheme. Originally it had to be read together
with the Transitional Provisions Regulations 2013. This Order accordingly brought
into force, albeit for limited purposes only, provisions of the WRA 2012 that related
to both the introduction of universal credit and the abolition of income-related ESA
and income-based JSA. This was achieved by reference to the specific categories of
cases set out in arts. 3 and 4. However, these provisions applied only to four postcode districts in Manchester, Oldham and Stockport (or "the relevant districts"; see
Sch.1) as from April 29, 2013 (also the date on which the Transitional Provisions
Regulations 2013 came into force). The justification for the limited "roll out" was
that it would "facilitate an evaluation of the Universal Credit business processes
and information technology functionality in a live environment before it is rolled
out nationally from October 2013" (*Explanatory Memorandum to the Transitional
Provisions Regulations 2013*, Para.7.64).

In this Order and its following companions (see further below), an award of ESA
under Part 1 of the Welfare Reform Act 2007, in a case where income-related ESA
has been abolished (i.e. in a Pathfinder area), is referred to as a "new style ESA
award". Likewise an award of JSA under the Jobseekers Act 1995, in a case where
income-based JSA has been abolished, is referred to as a "new style JSA award".
Conversely an award of ESA under Part 1 of the Welfare Reform Act 2007, in a case
where income-related ESA has not been abolished, is referred to as an "old style
ESA award". Similarly an award of JSA under the Jobseekers Act 1995, in a case
where income-based JSA has not been abolished, is referred to as an "old style JSA
award".

This Order was initially followed by the Commencement No.11 Order (certain
postcodes in Wigan ("the No.2 relevant districts") and Oldham and Warrington
("the No.3 relevant districts") as from July 1, 2013), the Commencement No.13
Order (certain postcodes in Hammersmith, Manchester and Wigan ("the No.4 relevant districts") as from October 28, 2013) and the Commencement No.14 Order
(certain postcodes in Rugby, Inverness and Perth ("the No.5 relevant districts")
as from November 25, 2013). See now, in addition, the Commencement Orders
No.15, No.16, No.17, No.19, No.20 and No.21 covering the No.6 to No.28 relevant districts and subsequent Commencement Orders below. See also the further
amendments made by the Welfare Reform Act 2012 (Commencement No.9, 11,
13, 14, 16 and 17 and Transitional and Transitory Provisions (Amendment)) Order
2014 (SI 2014/1661) Welfare Reform Act 2012 (Commencement No.9, 11, 13, 14,
16 and 17 and Transitional and Transitory Provisions (Amendment) (No.2)) Order
2014 (SI 2014/1923).

In addition, of course, a claimant who lived in one of the four originally specified
postcode districts had also to be a member of the Pathfinder Group, i.e. be a person
who met the requirements of regulations 5 to 12 of the Transitional Provisions
Regulations 2013. However, as noted above the No.9 Commencement Order (along
with the No.11, 13, 14 and 16 Commencement Orders) was amended by the Welfare
Reform Act 2012 (Commencement No.9, 11, 13, 14, 16 and 17 and Transitional

454

and Transitory Provisions (Amendment)) Order 2014 (SI 2014/1661). In conjunction with these changes, the Transitional Provisions Regulations 2013 were revoked and replaced by the Universal Credit (Transitional Provisions) Regulations 2014 (SI 2014/1230). At the same time, the "Pathfinder Group" conditions, previously contained in regs.5 to 12 of the Transitional Provisions Regulations 2013 were omitted from the Transitional Regulations 2014. Instead, similar conditions (known as the "gateway conditions") appeared in Sch.5 to the Commencement No.9 Order as inserted by art.16 of (SI 2014/1661).

Citation

1. This Order may be cited as the Welfare Reform Act 2012 (Commencement No.9 and Transitional and Transitory Provisions and Commencement No.8 and Savings and Transitional Provisions (Amendment)) Order 2013.   **3.97**

Interpretation

2.-(1) In this Order—   **3.98**
"the Act" means the Welfare Reform Act 2012 (apart from in Schedule 4);
"the 1995 Act" means the Jobseekers Act 1995;
"the 2007 Act" means the Welfare Reform Act 2007;
"the amending provisions" means the provisions referred to in article 4(1)(a) to (c);
[¹] [⁴ "claimant"—
(a) in relation to an employment and support allowance, has the same meaning as in Part 1 of the Welfare Reform Act 2007, save as mentioned in article 5(1A);
(b) in relation to a jobseeker's allowance, has the same meaning as in the Jobseekers Act 1995 (as it applies apart from the amendments made by Part 1 of Schedule 14 to the Act that remove references to an income-based jobseeker's allowance), save as mentioned in article 5(1A);
(c) in relation to universal credit, has the same meaning as in Part 1 of the Act
"appointed day" means the day appointed for the coming into force of the amending provisions in accordance with article 4(3);]
"the Claims and Payments Regulations 1987" means the Social Security (Claims and Payments) Regulations 1987;
"the Claims and Payments Regulations 2013" means the Universal Credit, Personal Independence Payment, Jobseeker's Allowance and Employment and Support Allowance (Claims and Payments) Regulations 2013;
"contribution-based jobseeker's allowance" means a contribution-based allowance under the 1995 Act as it has effect apart from the amendments made by Part 1 of Schedule 14 to the Act that remove references to an income-based allowance;
"contributory employment and support allowance" means a contributory allowance under Part 1 of the 2007 Act as it has effect apart from the amendments made by Schedule 3, and Part 1 of Schedule 14, to the Act that remove references to an income-related allowance;
[¹ "conversion decision" has the meaning given by the 2010 Transitional Regulations;]

"the Decisions and Appeals Regulations 2013" means the Universal Credit, Personal Independence Payment, Jobseeker's Allowance and Employment and Support Allowance (Decisions and Appeals) Regulations 2013;

[5 "the Digital Service Regulations 2014" means the Universal Credit (Digital Service) Amendment Regulations 2014;]

[6 "disability living allowance" means an allowance under section 71 of the Social Security Contributions and Benefits Act 1992;]

"employment and support allowance" means an employment and support allowance under Part 1 of the 2007 Act;

"the ESA Regulations 2008" means the Employment and Support Allowance Regulations 2008;

"the ESA Regulations 2013" means the Employment and Support Allowance Regulations 2013;

[1 [3 . . .]

"First-tier Tribunal" has the same meaning as in the Social Security Act 1998;

"gateway conditions" means the conditions specified in Schedule 5;

"housing benefit" means housing benefit under section 130 of the Social Security Contributions and Benefits Act 1992;]

"income-based jobseeker's allowance" means an income-based jobseeker's allowance under the 1995 Act;

"income-related employment and support allowance" means an income-related allowance under Part 1 of the 2007 Act;

[1 "income support" means income support under section 124 of the Social Security Contributions and Benefits Act 1992;]

"jobseeker's allowance" means an allowance under the 1995 Act;

[1 [2 "joint claimants"], in relation to universal credit, has the same meaning as in Part 1 of the Act;]

"the JSA Regulations 1996" means the Jobseeker's Allowance Regulations 1996;

"the JSA Regulations 2013" means the Jobseeker's Allowance Regulations 2013;

[1 "new style ESA" means an employment and support allowance under Part 1 of the 2007 Act as amended by the provisions of Schedule 3, and Part 1 of Schedule 14, to the Act that remove references to an income-related allowance and "new style ESA award" shall be construed accordingly;

"new style JSA" means a jobseeker's allowance under the 1995 Act as amended by the provisions of Part 1 of Schedule 14 to the Act that remove references to an income-based allowance and "new style JSA award" shall be construed accordingly;

"old style ESA" means an employment and support allowance under Part 1 of the 2007 Act as it has effect apart from the amendments made by Schedule 3, and Part 1 of Schedule 14, to the Act that remove references to an income-related allowance and "old style ESA award" shall be construed accordingly;

"old style JSA" means a jobseeker's allowance under the 1995 Act as it has effect apart from the amendments made by Part 1 of Schedule 14 to the Act that remove references to an income-based jobseeker's allowance and "old style JSA award" shall be construed accordingly;]

[⁶ "personal independence payment" means an allowance under Part 4 of the Act;]

"relevant districts" means the postcode districts specified in Schedule 1;

[¹ "single claimant", in relation to universal credit, has the same meaning as in Part 1 of the Act;

"state pension credit" means state pension credit under the State Pension Credit Act 2002;

"tax credit" (including "child tax credit" and "working tax credit") has the same meaning as in the Tax Credits Act 2002;]

[¹ ...];

"the 2010 Transitional Regulations" means the Employment and Support Allowance (Transitional Provisions, Housing Benefit and Council Tax Benefit)(Existing Awards)(No.2) Regulations 2010.

[¹ "the 2014 Transitional Regulations" means the Universal Credit (Transitional Provisions) Regulations 2014;

"the Universal Credit Regulations" means the Universal Credit Regulations 2013;

"Upper Tribunal" has the same meaning as in the Social Security Act 1998.]

[¹ (2) For the purposes of this Order—

(a) the Claims and Payments Regulations 2013 apply for the purpose of deciding—

    (i) whether a claim for universal credit is made or is to be treated as made; and

    (ii) the date on which such a claim is made; and

(b) where a couple is treated, in accordance with regulation 9(8) of the Claims and Payments Regulations 2013, as making a claim for universal credit, references to the date on which the claim is treated as made are to the date of formation of the couple.]

AMENDMENTS

1. Welfare Reform Act 2012 (Commencement No.9, 11, 13, 14 and 16 and Transitional and Transitory Provisions (Amendment)) Order 2014 (SI 2014/1452) art.4 (June 16, 2014).

2. Welfare Reform Act 2012 (Commencement No.9, 11, 13 14, 16 and 17 and Transitional and Transitory Provisions (Amendment)) Order 2014 (SI 2014/1661) art. 4(1) (June 30, 2014).

3. Welfare Reform Act 2012 (Commencement No.9, 11, 13, 14, 16 and 17 and Transitional and Transitory Provisions (Amendment) (No.2)) Order 2014 (SI 2014/1923) art. 4(2) (July 28, 2014).

4. Welfare Reform Act 2012 (Commencement No.9, 11, 13 14, 16, 17 and 19 and Transitional and Transitory Provisions (Amendment)) Order 2014 (SI 2014/3067) art.6(2)(a) (November 24, 2014).

5. Welfare Reform Act 2012 (Commencement No.20 and Transitional and Transitory Provisions and Commencement No.9 and Transitional and Transitory Provisions (Amendment)) Order 2014 (SI 2014/3094) art.7(2)(a) (November 26, 2014).

6. Welfare Reform Act 2012 (Commencement No.9, 11, 13, 14, 16, 17 and 19 and Transitional and Transitory Provisions (Amendment)) Order 2015 (SI 2015/32) art.4(2) (January 26, 2015).

Day appointed for commencement of the universal credit provisions in Part 1 of the Act

3.99 **3.**-(1) 29th April 2013 is the day appointed for the coming into force of-

(a) sections 29 (delegation and contracting out), 37(1), (2), (8) and (9) (capability for work or work-related activity), 38 (information) and 39(1), (2), (3)(b) and (c) (couples) of the Act;

(b) the following paragraphs of Schedule 2 to the Act (universal credit: amendments) and section 31 of the Act (supplementary and consequential amendments) in so far as it relates to those paragraphs, in so far as they are not already in force—

(i) paragraphs 1, 2, 32 to 35, 37 to 42, 52 to 55 and 65;

(ii) paragraphs 4, 8, 10 to 23, 25 and 27 to 31 and paragraph 3 in so far as it relates to those paragraphs; and

(iii) paragraphs 44, 45, 47, 49, 50(2) and 50(1) in so far as it relates to 50(2), and paragraph 43 in so far as it relates to those paragraphs and sub-paragraphs; and

(c) paragraph 1 of Schedule 5 to the Act (universal credit and other working-age benefits) and section 35 of the Act in so far as it relates to that paragraph.

(2) The day appointed for the coming into force of the provisions of the Act listed in Schedule 2, in so far as they are not already in force, in relation to the case of a claim referred to in paragraph (3)(a) to (d) and any award that is made in respect of such a claim, and in relation to the case of an award referred to in paragraph (3)(e) or (f), is the day appointed in accordance with paragraph (4).

[¹ (3) The claims and awards referred to are—

(a) a claim for universal credit where, on the date on which the claim is made, the claimant resides in one of the relevant districts and meets the gateway conditions;

[²(b) a claim for universal credit where—

(i) in the case of a single claimant, the claimant gives incorrect information regarding the claimant residing in a relevant district or meeting the gateway conditions and the claimant does not reside in such a district or does not meet the gateway conditions on the date on which the claim is made;

(ii) in the case of joint claimants, either or both of the joint claimants gives or give incorrect information regarding his or her (or their) residing in such a district or meeting the gateway conditions and one or both of them does not or do not reside in such a district or does not or do not meet those conditions on the date on which the claim is made; and

(iii) after a decision is made that the single claimant is, or the joint claimants are, entitled to universal credit and one or more payments have been made in respect of the single claimant or the joint claimants, the Secretary of State discovers that incorrect information has been given regarding residence or meeting the gateway conditions.]

(c) a claim for universal credit that is treated as made by a couple in the circumstances referred to in regulation 9(8) of the Claims and Payments Regulations 2013 (claims for universal credit by members of a couple) where the claim complies with paragraph (7);

[²(d) a claim for universal credit by a former member of a couple who were joint claimants of universal credit, whether or not the claim is made jointly with another person, where the former member is not exempt from the requirement to make a claim by virtue of regulation 9(6) of the Claims and Payments Regulations 2013 (claims for universal credit by members of a couple), where the claim is made during the period of one month starting with the date on which notification is given to the Secretary of State that the former joint claimants have ceased to be a couple, and where the claim complies with paragraph (8);]

   (e) an award of universal credit that is made without a claim in the circumstances referred to in regulation 6(1) or (2) of the Claims and Payments Regulations 2013 (claims not required for entitlement to universal credit in some cases) where the circumstances referred to in paragraph (9) apply; and

   (f) an award of universal credit that is made without a claim in the circumstances referred to in regulation 9(6), (7) or (10) of the Claims and Payments Regulations 2013 (claims for universal credit by members of a couple) where the circumstances referred to in paragraph (9) apply.]

(4) The day appointed in relation to the cases of the claims and awards referred to in paragraph (2) is—

   (a) in the case of a claim referred to in paragraph (3)(a) to (d), the first day of the period in respect of which the claim is made or treated as made;

   (b) in the case of an award referred to in paragraph (3)(e) or (f), the first day on which a person is entitled to universal credit under that award.

(5) [¹ ...];

(6) For the purposes of paragraph (4)(a), where the time for making a claim for universal credit is extended under regulation 26(2) of the Claims and Payments Regulations 2013, the reference to the first day of the period in respect of which the claim is made or treated as made is a reference to the first day of the period in respect of which the claim is, by reason of the operation of that provision, timeously made or treated as made.

[¹ (7) A claim that is treated as made by a couple in the circumstances referred to in regulation 9(8) of the Claims and Payments Regulations 2013 complies with this paragraph where, on the date on which the claim is treated as made, the member of the couple who did not previously have an award of universal credit [³ ...] is not entitled to state pension credit.

(8) A claim by a former member of a couple that is made in the circumstances referred to in paragraph (3)(d) complies with this paragraph where, on the date on which the claim is made, [³ neither the former member nor his or her partner (if any) is entitled to state pension credit].

(9) The circumstances referred to are where the relevant person is not entitled to state pension credit and, save where an award of universal credit is made in the circumstances referred to in regulation 9(7) of the Claims and Payments Regulations 2013, his or her partner (if any) is not entitled to [³ state pension credit].

   (10) For the purposes of paragraph (9), "relevant person" means—

   (a) where an award of universal credit is made in the circumstances referred to in regulation 6(1) or (2) of the Claims and Payments

Regulations 2013, the former claimant referred to in that regulation 6(1);

(b) where an award of universal credit is made in the circumstances referred to in paragraph (6) of regulation 9 of the Claims and Payments Regulations 2013, [³ as that paragraph has effect apart from the amendments made by the Digital Service Regulations 2014,] the member of the former couple referred to in that paragraph;

[³(ba) where an award of universal credit is made in the circumstances referred to in paragraph (6) of regulation 9 of the Claims and Payments Regulations 2013, as that paragraph has effect as amended by the Digital Service Regulations 2014, the former joint claimant of universal credit to whom a new award of universal credit is made as referred to in sub-paragraph (a) or (b) of that paragraph;]

(c) where an award of universal credit is made in the circumstances referred to in paragraph (7) of regulation 9 of the Claims and Payments Regulations 2013, each of the joint claimants referred to in that paragraph;

(d) where an award of universal credit is made in the circumstances referred to in paragraph (10) of regulation 9 of the Claims and Payments Regulations 2013, the surviving partner referred to in that paragraph.

[³ (10A) In paragraph (3)—

(a) in sub-paragraph (c), the reference to regulation 9(8) of the Claims and Payments Regulations 2013 is a reference to that provision both as it has effect as amended by the Digital Service Regulations 2014 and as it has effect apart from that amendment;

(b) in sub-paragraph (d), the reference to regulation 9(6) of the Claims and Payments Regulations 2013 is a reference to that provision as it has effect apart from the amendment made by the Digital Service Regulations 2014;

(c) in sub-paragraph (f), the reference to regulation 9(6) of the Claims and Payments Regulations 2013 is a reference to that provision both as it has effect as amended by the Digital Service Regulations 2014 and as it has effect apart from that amendment.]

(11) For the purposes of paragraphs (8) and (9), "partner" means a person who forms part of a couple with the person in question, where "couple" has the same meaning as it has in section 39 of the Act.]

AMENDMENTS

1. Welfare Reform Act 2012 (Commencement No.9, 11, 13, 14 and 16 and Transitional and Transitory Provisions (Amendment)) Order 2014 (SI 2014/1452) art.5 (June 16, 2014).

2. Welfare Reform Act 2012 (Commencement No.9, 11, 13, 14, 16 and 17 and Transitional and Transitory Provisions (Amendment) (No.2)) Order 2014 (SI 2014/1923) art. 4(3) (July 28, 2014).

3. Welfare Reform Act 2012 (Commencement No.20 and Transitional and Transitory Provisions and Commencement No.9 and Transitional and Transitory Provisions (Amendment)) Order 2014 (SI 2014/3094) art.7(2)(b) (November 26, 2014).

"the Act"–art. 2(1).
"the Claims and Payments Regulations 2013"–*ibid.*
"relevant districts"–*ibid.*
"the Transitional Regulations"–*ibid.*

GENERAL NOTE

Para. (1)
  This brings into force various provisions relating to universal credit (including   **3.100**
some supplementary and consequential provisions set out in Sch.2 to the 2012 Act)
on April 29, 2013.

Para. (2)
  This tortuously worded provision has the effect of bringing into force those pro-   **3.101**
visions relating to universal credit in Part 1 of the WRA 2012, as set out in Sch.2,
where one of the different categories of case referred to in art.3(3) applies. These
relate to claims for UC and any resulting award as well as to awards of universal
credit without a claim.

Para. (3)
  This specifies the various situations in which para.(2) has the effect of applying   **3.102**
the new universal credit rules.

Sub-Para. (3) (a)
  This covers the situation where a person makes a claim for universal credit in   **3.103**
respect of a period that begins on or after April 29, 2013 where that individual
both resides in a "relevant district" at the time that the claim is made and meets the
gateway conditions.

Sub-Para. (3) (b)
  Where a person claims universal credit and incorrectly states that they live in a   **3.104**
relevant district, that person remains subject to the new regime.

Sub-Para. (3) (c)
  This covers the case of a single person who becomes a member of a couple where   **3.105**
the other member was already entitled to universal credit.

Sub-Para. (3) (d)
  Where a couple separate, and the member of the couple who is not exempt from   **3.106**
making a claim for universal credit makes a claim within a period of one month, the
new rules apply.

Sub-Para. (3) (e)
  A person may be awarded universal credit without making a claim as a result of   **3.107**
changes in their income within six months of their income being such that they were
not previously entitled to universal credit.

Sub-Para. (3) (f)
  Again, a person may be awarded universal credit without making a claim where   **3.108**
a couple cease to be a couple and an award is made to the member of the couple
who is exempt from making a claim. Similarly, an award of universal credit may be
made without a claim to a couple where the members of the couple were previously
entitled to the new benefit as single claimants. In addition, the new regime applies
where an award of universal credit is made without a claim to a member of a couple
where the other member of the couple has died.

461

Paras. (4) – (11)

3.109   These make supplementary provision dealing with the effective date of universal credit claims and awards under the preceding rules.

[¹ [² [³ Incorrect information regarding residence in a relevant district or meeting the gateway conditions

3.110   **3A.** (1) This article applies where a claim for universal credit is made and it is subsequently discovered that the single claimant or either or both of two joint claimants gave incorrect information regarding his or her (or their) residing in one of the relevant districts or meeting the gateway conditions and the conditions referred to in paragraph (2) are met.

(2) The conditions referred to are that, on the date on which the claim was made, the claimant—

(a) did not reside in one of the relevant districts (unless paragraph (3) applies); or

(b) did reside in one of the relevant districts but did not meet the gateway conditions.

(3) This paragraph applies where the claimant resided in an area apart from the relevant districts with respect to which the provisions of the Act referred to in Schedule 2 were in force in relation to a claim for universal credit and the conditions (if any) that applied to such a claim, for those provisions to come into force, were met.

(4) Where the discovery is made before the claim for universal credit has been decided—

(a) the claimant is to be informed that the claimant is not entitled to claim universal credit;

(b) if the claimant (or, in the case of joint claimants, either of them) makes a claim for old style ESA, old style JSA or income support ("the specified benefit") and the date on which that claim is made (as determined in accordance with the Claims and Payments Regulations 1987) is after the date on which the claim for universal credit was made, but no later than one month after the date on which the information required by sub-paragraph (a) was given—

(i) the claim for the specified benefit is to be treated as made on the date on which the claim for universal credit was made or the first date on which the claimant would have been entitled to the specified benefit if a claim had been made for it on that date, if later; and

(ii) any provision of the Claims and Payments Regulations 1987 under which the claim for the specified benefit is treated as made on a later date does not apply;

(c) if the claimant (or, in the case of joint claimants, either of them) makes a claim for housing benefit and the date of that claim (as determined in accordance with the Housing Benefit Regulations 2006 or, as the case may be, the Housing Benefit (Persons who have attained the qualifying age for state pension credit) Regulations 2006 (together referred to as "the Housing Benefit Regulations")) is after the date on which the claim for universal credit was made, but no later than one month after the date on which the information required by sub-paragraph (a) was given—

(i) the claim for housing benefit is to be treated as made on the date on which the claim for universal credit was made or the first date on which the claimant would have been entitled to housing benefit if a claim had been made for it on that date, if later; and

(ii) any provision of the Housing Benefit Regulations under which the claim for housing benefit is treated as made on a later date does not apply;

(d) if the claimant (or, in the case of joint claimants, either of them) makes a claim for a tax credit and that claim is received by a relevant authority at an appropriate office (within the meaning of the Tax Credits (Claims and Notifications) Regulations 2002 ("the 2002 Regulations")) during the period of one month beginning with the date on which the information required by sub-paragraph (a) was given—

(i) the claim for a tax credit is to be treated as having been received by a relevant authority at an appropriate office on the date on which the claim for universal credit was made or the first date on which the claimant would have been entitled to a tax credit if a claim had been so received on that date, if later; and

(ii) any provision of the 2002 Regulations under which the claim is treated as having been made on a later date does not apply.

(5) Where the discovery is made after a decision has been made that the claimant is entitled to universal credit, but before any payment has been made—

(a) that decision is to cease to have effect immediately, by virtue of this article;

(b) the claimant is to be informed that they are not entitled to claim universal credit; and

(c) sub-paragraphs (b) to (d) of paragraph (4) apply.

(6) Where the discovery is made after a decision has been made that the claimant is entitled to universal credit and one or more payments have been made in respect of the claimant, the decision is to be treated as a decision under section 8 of the Social Security Act 1998.

(7) For the purposes of paragraph (4), a person makes a claim for old style ESA or old style JSA where he or she makes a claim for an employment and support allowance or a jobseeker's allowance and the claim is subject to Part 1 of the 2007 Act or the 1995 Act respectively as those provisions have effect apart from the amendments made by the amending provisions.]]]

AMENDMENTS

1. Welfare Reform Act 2012 (Commencement No.9, 11, 13, 14 and 16 and Transitional and Transitory Provisions (Amendment)) Order 2014 (SI 2014/1452) art.5 (June 16, 2014).

2. Welfare Reform Act 2012 (Commencement No.9, 11, 13 14, 16 and 17 and Transitional and Transitory Provisions (Amendment)) Order 2014 (SI 2014/1661) art. 4(3) (June 30, 2014).

3. Welfare Reform Act 2012 (Commencement No.9, 11, 13, 14, 16 and 17 and Transitional and Transitory Provisions (Amendment) (No.2)) Order 2014 (SI 2014/1923) art. 4(4) (July 28, 2014).

Definitions

"the 1995 Act"–see art. 2(1).
"the 2007 Act"–*ibid.*
"the 2002 Regulations"–para.(4)(d).
"the Act"–see art.2(1).
"the amending provisions"–*ibid.*
"the Claims and Payments Regulations 1987"–*ibid.*
"claimant"–*ibid.*
"employment and support allowance"–*ibid.*
"gateway conditions"–*ibid.*
"housing benefit"–*ibid.*
"the Housing Benefit Regulations"–para.(4)(c).
"income support"–see art.2(1).
"jobseeker's allowance"–*ibid.*
"joint claimants"–*ibid.*
"old style ESA"–*ibid.*
"old style JSA"–*ibid.*
"relevant districts"–*ibid.*
"single claimant"–*ibid.*
"the specified benefit"–para.(4)(b).
"tax credit"–see art.2(1).

General Note

3.111   This makes provision for the position where a person claims universal credit and provides incorrect information as to their place of residence or their compliance with the gateway conditions. This article is similar to reg.13 of the revoked 2013 Transitional Regulations.

Day appointed for the abolition of income-related employment and support allowance and income-based jobseeker's allowance

3.112   [¹**4.** (1) The day appointed for the coming into force of—
(a) section 33(1)(a) and (b) and (2) of the Act (abolition of benefits);
(b) paragraphs 22 to 26 of Schedule 3 to the Act (abolition of benefits: consequential provisions) and section 33(3) of the Act in so far as it relates to those paragraphs; and
(c) the repeals in Part 1 of Schedule 14 to the Act (abolition of benefits superseded by universal credit) that are referred to in Schedule 3,
in relation to the case of a claim referred to in paragraph (2)(a) to (d) and (g) and any award that is made in respect of such a claim, and in relation to the case of an award referred to in paragraph (2)(e) and (f), is the day appointed in accordance with paragraph (3).
(2) The claims and awards referred to are—
(a) a claim for universal credit, an employment and support allowance or a jobseeker's allowance where, on the date on which the claim is made [² or treated as made], the claimant—
(i)   resides in one of the relevant districts; and
(ii) meets the gateway conditions;
[² (b) a claim for universal credit where—
(i)   in the case of a single claimant, the claimant gives incorrect information regarding the claimant residing in a relevant district or meeting the gateway conditions and does not reside in such a district or does not meet the gateway conditions on the date on which the claim is made;

    (ii) in the case of joint claimants, either or both of the joint claim-
ants gives or give incorrect information regarding his or her (or
their) residing in such a district or meeting those conditions and
one or both of them does not or do not reside in such a district
or does not or do not meet those conditions on the date on
which the claim is made; and

    (iii) after a decision is made that the single claimant is, or the joint
claimants are, entitled to universal credit and one or more payments have been made in respect of the single claimant or the
joint claimants, the Secretary of State discovers that incorrect
information has been given regarding residence or meeting the
gateway conditions;]

(c) a claim for universal credit that is treated as made by a couple in
the circumstances referred to in regulation 9(8) of the Claims and
Payments Regulations 2013 (claims for universal credit by members
of a couple) where the claim complies with article 3(7) and [³ ...] ;

[²(d) a claim for universal credit by a former member of a couple who were
joint claimants of universal credit, whether or not the claim is made
jointly with another person, where the former member is not exempt
from the requirement to make a claim by virtue of regulation 9(6)
of the Claims and Payments Regulations 2013 (claims for universal
credit by members of a couple), where the claim is made during the
period of one month starting with the date on which notification is
given to the Secretary of State that the former joint claimants have
ceased to be a couple, and where the claim complies with article
3(8);]

(e) an award of universal credit that is made without a claim in the circumstances referred to in regulation 6(1) or (2) of the Claims and
Payments Regulations 2013 (claims not required for entitlement to
universal credit in some cases) where the circumstances referred to
in article 3(9) apply;

(f) an award of universal credit that is made without a claim in the circumstances referred to in regulation 9(6), (7) or (10) the Claims and
Payments Regulations 2013 (claims for universal credit by members
of a couple) where the circumstances referred to in article 3(9) apply;
and

(g) a claim for an employment and support allowance or a jobseeker's
allowance [² other than one referred to in sub-paragraph (a) that is
made or treated as made] —

    (i) during the relevant period by a single claimant of universal credit
or, in the case of joint claimants of universal credit, by either of
the joint claimants, where the single claimant has made or the
joint claimants have made, or been treated as having made, a
claim for universal credit within sub-paragraphs (a) to (d);

    (ii) during the relevant period by a single claimant of universal
credit or, in the case of joint claimants of universal credit, by
either of the joint claimants, where the single claimant has been
awarded, or the joint claimants have been awarded, universal
credit without a claim within sub-paragraph (e) or (f);

    (iii) by a person who is entitled to make a claim for universal credit
in the circumstances referred to in sub-paragraph (d) but has
not yet done so; or

> (iv) by a person who may be entitled to an award of universal credit in the circumstances referred to in sub-paragraph (e) or (f) but where no decision has yet been made as to the person's entitlement.

(3) Subject to paragraph (4), the day appointed in relation to the cases referred to in paragraph (2) is—

> (a) in the case of a claim referred to in paragraph (2)(a) to (d) and (g), the first day of the period in respect of which the claim is made or (in the case of a claim for universal credit) treated as made;
>
> (b) in the case of an award referred to in paragraph (2)(e) or (f), the first day on which a claimant is entitled to universal credit under that award.

(4) In relation to the case of a claim referred to in paragraph (2)(c) (claim for universal credit treated as made by a couple), where the member of the couple referred to in regulation 9(8)(b) of the Claims and Payments Regulations 2013 ("new claimant partner") was entitled during the prior period to an old style ESA award or an old style JSA award, the new claimant partner was at that time a member of a couple and the award included an amount in respect of the new claimant partner and his or her partner ("P"), the day appointed in relation to that case is the day after the day on which the new claimant partner and P ceased to be a couple for the purposes of the ESA Regulations 2008 or the JSA Regulations 1996 as the case may be.

(5) For the purposes of paragraph (4), the "prior period" means the period beginning with the first day of the period for which the claim for universal credit is treated as made and ending with the day before the day on which the claim for universal credit is treated as made.

(6) In paragraph (1), the reference to the case of a claim for universal credit referred to in paragraph (2)(a) to (d) (and any award made in respect of the claim), or of an award of universal credit referred to in paragraph (2) (e) and (f), includes a reference to—

> (a) a case where a notice under regulation 4 of the 2010 Transitional Regulations (the notice commencing the conversion phase in relation to an award of incapacity benefit or severe disablement allowance) is issued to a single claimant or in the case of joint claimants, either of those claimants, during the designated period;
>
> (b) where sub-paragraph (a) does not apply, a case where a conversion decision is made during that period in relation to an award of incapacity benefit or severe disablement allowance to which a single claimant or in the case of joint claimants, either of those claimants, is entitled; and
>
> (c) where sub-paragraphs (a) and (b) do not apply, a case where the effective date of a conversion decision in relation to such an award occurs during that period (where "effective date" has the same meaning as in the 2010 Transitional Regulations),

and any award of an employment and support allowance that is made consequent on a conversion decision that relates to the notice referred to in sub-paragraph (a), the conversion decision referred to in sub-paragraph (b) or the conversion decision referred to in sub-paragraph (c), as the case may be.

(7) For the purposes of paragraph (6), the designated period means—

> (a) in relation to a claim for universal credit referred to in paragraph (2)

    (a), (b)(i) [², (ii)] or (d), any period when a decision has not yet been made on the claim;

(b) in relation to a claim for universal credit that is treated as made as referred to in paragraph (2)(c), any period when no decision has yet been made as to the joint claimants' entitlement;

(c) any period, subsequent to the period referred to in sub-paragraph (a) or (b), when the single claimant or joint claimants is or are entitled to an award of universal credit in respect of the claim; and

(d) in relation to an award of universal credit referred to in paragraph (2) (e) or (f), any period when the single claimant or joint claimants to whom the award was made is or are entitled to that award.]

[³ (8) In paragraph (2)—

(a) in sub-paragraph (c), the reference to regulation 9(8) of the Claims and Payments Regulations 2013 is a reference to that provision both as it has effect as amended by the Digital Service Regulations 2014 and as it has effect apart from that amendment;

(b) in sub-paragraph (d), the reference to regulation 9(6) of the Claims and Payments Regulations 2013 is a reference to that provision as it has effect apart from the amendments made by the Digital Service Regulations 2014;

(c) in sub-paragraph (f), the reference to regulation 9(6) of the Claims and Payments Regulations 2013 is a reference to that provision both as it has effect as amended by the Digital Service Regulations 2014 and as it has effect apart from that amendment.]

[⁴ [⁵(9)] For the purposes of paragraph (1), the reference to the case of a claim for universal credit referred to in paragraph (2)(a) to (d) (and any award made in respect of the claim), or of an award of universal credit without a claim referred to in paragraph (2)(e) and (f), includes a reference to an old style ESA award or an old style JSA award that exists (or, as a result of an act as referred to in [⁵ paragraph (10)], is later found to have existed at that time) immediately before the day appointed (as referred to in paragraph (3) or (4)) in relation to that claim or award without a claim.

[⁵ (10)] For the purposes of [⁵ paragraph (9)], the acts referred to are–

(a) the revision of a decision that the claimant was not entitled to old style ESA or old style JSA; or

(b) an appeal to the First-tier Tribunal, the Upper Tribunal or a court against such a decision.]

AMENDMENTS

1. Welfare Reform Act 2012 (Commencement No.9, 11, 13, 14 and 16 and Transitional and Transitory Provisions (Amendment)) Order 2014 (SI 2014/1452) art.6 (June 16, 2014).

2. Welfare Reform Act 2012 (Commencement No.9, 11, 13, 14, 16 and 17 and Transitional and Transitory Provisions (Amendment) (No.2)) Order 2014 (SI 2014/1923) art. 4(5) (July 28, 2014).

3. Welfare Reform Act 2012 (Commencement No.20 and Transitional and Transitory Provisions and Commencement No.9 and Transitional and Transitory Provisions (Amendment)) Order 2014 (SI 2014/3094) art.7(2)(c) (November 26, 2014).

4. Welfare Reform Act 2012 (Commencement No.9, 11, 13, 14, 16, 17 and 19 and Transitional and Transitory Provisions (Amendment)) Order 2015 (SI 2015/32) art.4(3) (January 26, 2015).

5. Welfare Reform Act 2012 (Commencement No.22 and Transitional and Transitory Provisions) Order 2015 (SI 2015/101) art.7(2)(a) (February 11, 2015).

DEFINITIONS

"the Act"–art. 2(1).
"the Claims and Payments Regulations 2013"–*ibid.*
"employment and support allowance"–*ibid.*
"income-based jobseeker's allowance"–*ibid.*
"income-related employment and support allowance"–*ibid.*
"jobseeker's allowance"–*ibid.*
"relevant districts"–*ibid.*
"the Transitional Regulations"–*ibid.*
"the 2010 Transitional Regulations"–*ibid.*

GENERAL NOTE

Para. (1)

3.113   This brings into force provisions relating to the abolition of both income-related ESA and income-based JSA. This includes the repeal of various provisions relating to the abolished allowances as set out in Sch.3. However, these provisions are only brought into force where one of the various different categories of case set out in para.(2) applies.

Para. (2)

3.114   This sets out the various categories of case affected by the amendments made by para.(1).

Para. (2) (a)

3.115   Where a person (i) resides in a relevant district (see Sch.1); (ii) meets the gateway conditions; and (iii) makes a claim for universal credit, ESA or JSA, then the amendments made by para.(1) above govern both the claim and any award made in respect of that claim.

Para. (2) (b)

3.116   This covers the situation here a person claims universal credit and incorrectly states that they live in a relevant district, or provides incorrect information as to their meeting the Pathfinder Group conditions. Such a claim remains within the universal credit regime despite the error.

Para. (2) (c)

3.117   This is analogous to art.3(3)(c).

Para. (2) (d)

3.118   This is analogous to art.3(3)(d).

Para. (2) (e)

3.119   This is analogous to art.3(3)(e).

Para. (2) (f)

3.120   This is analogous to art.3(3)(f).

Provisions that apply in connection with the abolition of income-related employment and support allowance and income-based jobseeker's allowance under article 4

3.121   [¹ 5. (1) [². ..] [³ In determining, for the purposes of article 4(2)(a), whether a claim for an employment and support allowance or a jobseeker's allowance meets the gateway conditions, Schedule 5 is to be read as though—

(a) any reference in that Schedule to making a claim for universal credit included a reference to making a claim for an employment and support allowance or a jobseeker's allowance as the case may be; and

(b) the reference in paragraph 4 to a single claimant, or to joint claimants, of universal credit was a reference to a person who would be a single claimant of universal credit or to persons who would be joint claimants of universal credit, if the claimant of an employment and support allowance or a jobseeker's allowance had made a claim for universal credit.

(1A) For the purposes of article 4(2)(a), where a claim for an employment and support allowance or a jobseeker's allowance is made by a couple or a member of a couple, any reference in article 4(2)(a) or Schedule 5 (save in paragraph 4 of that Schedule) to "the claimant" is a reference to each member of the couple.

(1B) For the purposes of paragraph (1A), "couple" has the same meaning as it has in section 39 of the Act.]

(2) [⁴. ..]

(3) For the purposes of article 4(2)(g), "relevant period" means—

(a) in relation to a claim for universal credit within article 4(2)(a) to (d), any UC claim period, and any period subsequent to any UC claim period in respect of which the single claimant or the joint claimants is or are entitled to an award of universal credit in respect of the claim;

(b) in relation to an award of universal credit within article 4(2)(e) or (f), any period when the single claimant or the joint claimants to whom the award was made is or are entitled to the award.

(4) For the purposes of paragraph (3)(a), a "UC claim period" is a period when—

(a) a claim for universal credit within article 4(2)(a), (b)(i) [², (ii)] or (d) has been made but a decision has not yet been made on the claim;

(b) a claim for universal credit within article 4(2)(c) has been treated as made and no decision has yet been made as to the joint claimants' entitlement; or

(c) a decision has been made that a single claimant or joint claimants is or are not entitled to universal credit and—

(i) the Secretary of State is considering whether to revise that decision under section 9 of the Social Security Act 1998, whether on an application made for that purpose, or on the Secretary of State's own initiative; or

(ii) the single claimant or the joint claimants has or have appealed against that decision to the First-tier Tribunal and that appeal or any subsequent appeal to the Upper Tribunal or to a court has not been finally determined.

[⁵ (5) For the purposes of article 4(2)(a) and (g), the Claims and Payments Regulations 1987 apply, subject to paragraphs (6) and (7), for the purposes of deciding–

(a) whether a claim for an employment and support allowance or a jobseeker's allowance is made; and

(b) the date on which the claim is made or treated as made.

(6) Subject to paragraph (7),–

(a) a person makes a claim for an employment and support allowance or

a jobseeker's allowance if he or she takes any action which results in a decision on a claim being required under the Claims and Payments Regulations 1987; and

(b) it is irrelevant that the effect of any provision of the Claims and Payments Regulations 1987 is that, for the purposes of those Regulations, the claim is made or treated as made at a date that is earlier than the date on which that action is taken.

(7) Where, by virtue of–

(a) regulation 6(1F)(b) or (c) of the Claims and Payments Regulations 1987, in the case of a claim for an employment and support allowance; or

(b) regulation 6(4ZA) to (4ZD) and (4A)(a)(i) and (b) of those Regulations, in the case of a claim for a jobseeker's allowance,

a claim for an employment and support allowance or a jobseeker's allowance is treated as made at a date that is earlier than the date on which the action referred to in paragraph (6)(a) is taken, the claim is treated as made on that earlier date.]

(8) For the purposes of article 4(3)(a)—

(a) in the case of a claim for universal credit, where the time for making a claim is extended under regulation 26(2) of the Claims and Payments Regulations 2013 (time within which a claim for universal credit is to be made), the reference to the first day of the period in respect of which the claim is made is a reference to the first day of the period in respect of which the claim is, by reason of the operation of that provision, timeously made;

(b) in the case of a claim for an employment and support allowance or a jobseeker's allowance, where the time for making a claim is extended under regulation 19 of, and Schedule 4 to, the Claims and Payments Regulations 1987, the reference to the first day of the period in respect of which the claim is made is a reference to the first day of the period in respect of which the claim is, by reason of the operation of those provisions, timeously made.]

AMENDMENTS

1. Welfare Reform Act 2012 (Commencement No.9, 11, 13, 14 and 16 and Transitional and Transitory Provisions (Amendment)) Order 2014 (SI 2014/1452) art.7 (June 16, 2014).

2. Welfare Reform Act 2012 (Commencement No.9, 11, 13, 14, 16 and 17 and Transitional and Transitory Provisions (Amendment) (No.2)) Order 2014 (SI 2014/1923) art. 4(6) (July 28, 2014).

3. Welfare Reform Act 2012 (Commencement No.9, 11, 13 14, 16, 17 and 19 and Transitional and Transitory Provisions (Amendment)) Order 2014 (SI 2014/3067) art.6(2)(b) (November 24, 2014).

4. Welfare Reform Act 2012 (Commencement No.20 and Transitional and Transitory Provisions and Commencement No.9 and Transitional and Transitory Provisions (Amendment)) Order 2014 (SI 2014/3094) art.7(2)(d) (November 26, 2014).

5. Welfare Reform Act 2012 (Commencement No.9, 11, 13, 14, 16, 17 and 19 and Transitional and Transitory Provisions (Amendment)) Order 2015 (SI 2015/32) art.4(4) (January 26, 2015).

DEFINITIONS

"the Claims and Payments Regulations 1987"–art. 2(1).
"the Claims and Payments Regulations 2013"–*ibid.*
"income-based jobseeker's allowance"–*ibid.*
"income-related employment and support allowance"–*ibid.*
"jobseeker's allowance"–*ibid.*
"the Transitional Regulations"–*ibid.*

GENERAL NOTE

These provisions supplement and further define the provisions of art.4.   3.122

[¹ Transitional provision where Secretary of State determines that claims for universal credit may not be made: effect on claims for employment and support allowance and jobseeker's allowance

5A. (1) Where a person makes a claim for an employment and support   3.123
allowance or a jobseeker's allowance at a time when they would not be able
to make a claim for universal credit by virtue of a determination under
regulation 4(1) of the 2014 Transitional Regulations (claims for universal
credit may not be made in an area or category of case) [⁴, or by virtue of
regulation 39 of those Regulations (restriction on claims for universal credit
during the interim period)] [² and where the amending provisions would
otherwise have come into force in relation to the claim by virtue of article
4(2)(a) or any corresponding provision in any order made under section
150(3) of the Act other than this Order], then—

(a) in relation to a claim for an employment and support allowance, Part
1 of the 2007 Act and the Welfare Reform Act 2009 are to apply as
though the amending provisions and the provisions referred to in
article 7(1)(c), (d) and (f) had not come into force in relation to the
claim;

(b) in relation to a claim for a jobseeker's allowance, the 1995 Act, the
Social Security Administration Act 1992(2) and the Social Security
Act 1998(3) are to apply as though the amending provisions and the
provisions referred to in article 7(1)(a), (b) and (e) had not come
into force in relation to the claim.]

[² (2) Paragraph (1) does not apply in relation to a claim for an employment and support allowance ("ESA") or a jobseeker's allowance ("JSA")
where the claim is made or treated as made—

(a) where the claimant of ESA or JSA has made or been treated as
having made a claim for universal credit ("UC") within article 4(2)
(a) to (d) (whether or not the claim for UC is made jointly with
another person), or has been awarded UC without a claim within
article 4(2)(e) or (f) (whether or not the award is made to the claimant of ESA or JSA and another person as joint claimants), during the
"relevant period" in relation to that claim or award as referred to in
article 5(3)(a) or (b);

(b) where the claimant of ESA or JSA has made a claim for UC within
any provision of an order made under section 150(3) of the Act,
apart from this Order, that corresponds to article 4(2)(a) or (b)
(whether or not the claim for UC is made by the claimant of ESA
or JSA and another person as joint claimants), during the "relevant
period" in relation to that claim as referred to in the provision of that
order that corresponds to article 5(3)(a); or

(c) at a time when the claimant of ESA or JSA may be entitled to an award of UC without a claim in the circumstances referred to in article 4(2)(e) or (f) (whether or not the award may be made to the claimant of ESA or JSA and another person as joint claimants) but where no decision has yet been made as to the claimant's entitlement.]

[³ (3) For the purposes of this article, paragraphs (5) to (7) of article 5 apply for the purpose of deciding—

(a) whether a claim for ESA or JSA is made; and

(b) the date on which the claim is made or treated as made.]

AMENDMENTS

1. Welfare Reform Act 2012 (Commencement No.9, 11, 13, 14 and 16 and Transitional and Transitory Provisions (Amendment)) Order 2014 (SI 2014/1452) art.8 (June 16, 2014).

2. Welfare Reform Act 2012 (Commencement No.19 and Transitional and Transitory Provisions and Commencement No.9 and Transitional and Transitory Provisions (Amendment)) Order 2014 (SI 2014/2321) art.7 (September 15, 2014).

3. Welfare Reform Act 2012 (Commencement No.23 and Transitional and Transitory Provisions) Order (2015/634) art.8(5) (March 18, 2015).

4. Welfare Reform Act 2012 (Commencement No.9 and 21 and Transitional and Transitory Provisions (Amendment)) Order 2017 (SI 2017/483) art.2(2) (April 6, 2017).

GENERAL NOTE

3.124   This provision has the effect that where a person claims ESA or JSA, and they would *not* be able to claim universal credit by virtue of a determination made by the Secretary of State that a claim for universal credit may not be made in a specified class of case or area (see reg.4(1) of the 2014 Transitional Regulations), then Part 1 of the Welfare Reform Act 2007, the Jobseekers Act 1995 and other relevant provisions apply in relation to the ESA or JSA claim as if the amending provisions had not come into force (see para.(1), subject to the exceptions in paras.(2)).

Transitional provision: where the abolition of income-related employment and support allowance and income-based jobseeker's allowance is treated as not applying

3.125   6.-(1) Paragraph (2) applies where—

(a) a person has or had a new style ESA award or a new style JSA award ("the award") [¹ by virtue of the coming into force of the amending provisions under any secondary legislation];

(b) in respect of all or part of the period to which the award relates, the person—

(i) makes a claim, or is treated as making a claim, for universal credit; or

(ii) makes an application to the Secretary of State for supersession of the decision to make the award, on the basis of a relevant change of circumstances that would relate to the grounds for entitlement to an income-related employment and support allowance or an income-based jobseeker's allowance if the amending provisions had not come into force [¹ ...];

(c) if the amending provisions had not come into force under [¹ ...]

and, in the case of a claim for universal credit, an application for supersession of the decision to make the award had been made, the person would be entitled to an income-related employment and support allowance or an income-based jobseeker's allowance, as the case may be, with respect to the period for which the claim for universal credit or application for supersession is made;

(d) where the person makes an application for supersession of the decision to make the award, the period in respect of which the application is made does not include any period in respect of which the person has been awarded universal credit; [¹ and]

[¹(e)(i) on the date on which the claim for universal credit is made, or the application for supersession is received, as the case may be, the claim does not, or, in the case of an application for supersession, a claim for universal credit by the person would not, fall within any case (including a case with respect to which an award of universal credit may be made without a claim) in relation to which the provisions of the Act referred to in Schedule 2 are in force ("the UC commencement case"); or

(ii) on that date, the claim for universal credit does, or, in the case of an application for supersession, a claim for universal credit by the person would, fall within the UC commencement case, but the claim does or would fall within a case (including a case that relates in whole or in part to residence in an area) that is the subject of a determination made by the Secretary of State under regulation 4(1) of the 2014 Transitional Regulations (determination that claims for universal credit may not be made) [², or the claim is or would be one to which regulation 39 of those Regulations (restriction on claims for universal credit during the interim period) applies].]

(2) Where this paragraph applies, then, in relation to the award and with effect from the first day of the period in respect of which the claim is made or treated as made, or the application for supersession is made, the 1995 Act or Part 1 of the 2007 Act, as the case may be, is to apply as though the amending provisions had not come into force [¹ ...].

(3) For the purposes of paragraph (1) [¹ ...]—

(a) the Claims and Payments Regulations 2013 apply for the purpose of deciding—

(i) whether a claim for universal credit is made or is to be treated as made; and

(ii) the day on which the claim is made or is to be treated as made; [¹ ...]

(b) [¹ ...].

(4) For the purposes of paragraph (2), the reference to the period in respect of which the application for supersession is made is a reference to the period beginning with the day from which the superseding decision takes effect in accordance with section 10(5) of the Social Security Act 1998 and regulation 35 of, and Schedule 1 to, the Decisions and Appeals Regulations 2013 (effectives dates: Secretary of State decisions).

(5) For the purposes of paragraph (2), the reference to the first day of the period in respect of which the claim for universal credit is made or treated as made, in a case where the time for making a claim for universal credit is extended under regulation 26(2) of the Claims and Payments Regulations

2013, is a reference to the first day of the period in respect of which the claim is, by reason of the operation of that provision, timeously made or treated as made.

[¹ (6) For the purposes of this article, "secondary legislation" means an instrument made under an Act.]

AMENDMENTS

1. Welfare Reform Act 2012 (Commencement No.9, 11, 13, 14 and 16 and Transitional and Transitory Provisions (Amendment)) Order 2014 (SI 2014/1452) art.9 (June 16, 2014).
2. Welfare Reform Act 2012 (Commencement No.9 and 21 and Transitional and Transitory Provisions (Amendment)) Order 2017 (SI 2017/483) art.2(3) (April 6, 2017).

DEFINITIONS

"the 1995 Act"–art. 2(1).
"the 2007 Act"–*ibid.*
"the amending provisions"–*ibid.*
"the award"–para.1(a)
"the Claims and Payments Regulations 2013"–art.2(1).
"employment and support allowance"–*ibid.*
"the Decisions and Appeals Regulations 2013"–*ibid.*
"income-based jobseeker's allowance"–*ibid.*
"income-related employment and support allowance"–*ibid.*
"jobseeker's allowance"–*ibid.*
"new style ESA award"–*ibid.*
"new style JSA award"–*ibid.*
"relevant districts"–*ibid.*
"the Transitional Regulations"–*ibid.*

GENERAL NOTE

3.126   This makes transitional provision for cases where the conditions in para.(1) are met. These all concern cases where the claimant either moves out of a relevant district or is not in the Pathfinder Group. In these cases, the award is treated as though the provisions in art.4(1)(a)-(c) above had not come into force (para.(2); see further art.9(2)). In consequence the person concerned will be able to claim an existing benefit, i.e. income-related ESA or income-based JSA, once again. The six conditions set out in Para.(1) are (in summary) that (a) the claimant has a new style ESA award or new style JSA award; (b) s/he makes a claim for universal credit or applies for supersession of the decision to make the award; (c) s/he would otherwise be entitled to income-related ESA or income-based JSA; (d) any award of universal credit has come to an end; (e), any claim for universal credit does not fall within the category of a "UC commencement case" or, if so, is the subject of a determination made by the Secretary of State under reg.4(1) of the 2014 Transitional Regulations. Paras.(3)-(5) make supplementary provision for paras.(1) and (2).

Day appointed for commencement of provisions relating to claimant responsibilities with respect to employment and support allowance and jobseeker's allowance, and transitional provisions

3.127   7.-(1) The day appointed for the coming into force of—
(a) section 44(2) of the Act and section 44(1) of the Act in so far as it relates to section 44(2) (claimant commitment for jobseeker's allowance);

(b) section 49(2) and (3) to (5) of the Act (and section 49(1) of the Act in so far as it relates to those provisions) (claimant responsibilities for jobseeker's allowance);

(c) section 54(2) of the Act (and section 54(1) of the Act in so far as it relates to that provision) (claimant commitment for employment and support allowance);

(d) section 57(2), (4), (5) and (9) of the Act (and section 57(1) of the Act in so far as it relates to those provisions) (claimant responsibilities for employment and support allowance);

(e) the repeals in Part 4 of Schedule 14 to the Act (jobseeker's allowance: responsibilities after introduction of universal credit); and

(f) the repeals in Part 5 of Schedule 14 to the Act (employment and support allowance: responsibilities after introduction of universal credit),

in so far as they are not already in force, is, in relation to a particular case, the day on which the amending provisions come into force, under any secondary legislation, in relation to that case.

[1 (2) Where, under any secondary legislation, in relation to a new style JSA award, the 1995 Act applies as though the amending provisions had not come into force, then, with effect from the day on which the 1995 Act so applies, the 1995 Act, the Social Security Administration Act 1992 and the Social Security Act 1998 are to apply in relation to the award as though the provisions referred to in paragraph (1)(a), (b) and (e) had not come into force.

(3) Where, under any secondary legislation, in relation to a new style ESA award, Part 1 of the 2007 Act applies as though the amending provisions had not come into force, then, with effect from the day on which Part 1 of the 2007 Act so applies, Part 1 of the 2007 Act and the Welfare Reform Act 2009 are to apply in relation to the award as though the provisions referred to in paragraph (1)(c), (d) and (f) had not come into force.]

(4) For the purposes of paragraphs (1) to (3), "secondary legislation" means an instrument made under an Act.

AMENDMENTS

1. Welfare Reform Act 2012 (Commencement No.11 and Transitional and Transitory Provisions and Commencement No.9 and Transitional and Transitory Provisions (Amendment)) Order 2013 (SI 2013/1511) art.6 (July 1, 2013).

DEFINITIONS

"the Act"–art. 2(1).
"the 1995 Act"–*ibid.*
"the 2007 Act"–*ibid.*
"the amending provisions"–*ibid.*
"employment and support allowance"–*ibid.*
"jobseeker's allowance"–*ibid.*
"new style ESA award"–*ibid.*
"new style JSA award"–*ibid.*
"secondary legislation"–para.(4).

GENERAL NOTE

This provides for the appointed day and transitional provisions for the measures in the WRA 2012 that relate to claimant responsibilities in relation to a new style ESA award or a new style JSA award.   **3.128**

Day appointed for commencement of provisions concerning consideration of revision before appeal

3.129   **8.** 29th April 2013 is the day appointed for the coming into force of paragraphs 1 to 11 and 15 to 18 of Schedule 11 to the Act (power to require consideration of revision before appeal) and section 102(6) of the Act in so far as it relates to those paragraphs, to the extent that those provisions are not already in force.

DEFINITIONS

"the Act"–art.2(1).

GENERAL NOTE

3.130   This simply brings into force those provisions of Sch.11 to the Act concerning consideration of revision before appeal.

Transitional provision: conversion of incapacity benefits

3.131   **9.**-(1) Subject to paragraph (2), where the amending provisions come into force under article 4(1) in relation to the case of a claim referred to in article 4(2)(a) to (d) [¹ or (g)] and any award made in respect of the claim, or the case of an award referred to in article 4(2)(e) or (f), the 2010 Transitional Regulations are to apply in relation to that case as if the modifications set out in Schedule 4 were made.

(2) Where article 6(2) applies in relation to a new style ESA award (such that the award continues as an old style ESA award), the 2010 Transitional Regulations are to apply in relation to the award, in its continuation as an old style ESA award, as if those modifications had not been made.

AMENDMENTS

1. Welfare Reform Act 2012 (Commencement No.9, 11, 13, 14 and 16 and Transitional and Transitory Provisions (Amendment)) Order 2014 (SI 2014/1452) art.10 (June 16, 2014).

DEFINITIONS

"the amending provisions"–art.2(1).
"new style ESA award"–*ibid.*
"old style ESA award"–*ibid.*
"the 2010 Transitional Regulations"–*ibid.*

GENERAL NOTE

3.132   The introduction of universal credit was always going to be complicated. That complexity has been made worse by the fact that many existing awards of ESA have not been assessed for conversion, sometimes described as "reassessment", to ESA, even though that process began on October 11, 2010. This regulation allows for transitional provisions whereby, in relation to cases with respect to which art.4 has come into force, the Transitional Provisions Regulations 2010 are to be read as if the amendments set out in Sch.4 were made. Those amendments substitute references to provisions that apply to new style ESA awards, including the ESA Regulations 2013.

[¹ Transition from old style ESA]

10. [¹ (1) This article applies where a person—   3.133

(a) makes, or is treated as making, a claim for an employment and support allowance and, under article 4, Part 1 of the 2007 Act, as amended by the provisions of Schedule 3, and Part 1 of Schedule 14, to the Act that remove references to an income-related allowance, applies in relation to the claim; or

(b)(i) has an old style ESA award immediately before the appointed day in relation to a case of a claim for universal credit referred to in article 4(2)(a) to (d) (and any award made in respect of the claim), or an award of universal credit referred to in article 4(2) (e) or (f); and

(ii) the old style ESA award consists of or includes a contributory employment and support allowance (which allowance therefore continues as a new style ESA award),

and, in the case of sub-paragraph (a), the condition referred to in paragraph (1A) is satisfied.

(1A) The condition is that—

(a) the person previously made, or was treated as having made, a claim for an employment and support allowance and Part 1 of the 2007 Act, as it has effect apart from the provisions of Schedule 3, and Part 1 of Schedule 14, to the Act that remove references to an income-related allowance, applied in relation to the claim;

(b) a notice was issued to the person under regulation 4 of the 2010 Transitional Regulations and Part 1 of the 2007 Act, as that Part has effect apart from the provisions of Schedule 3, and Part 1 of Schedule 14, to the Act that remove references to an income-related allowance, applied in relation to the notice; or

(c) the person previously had a new style ESA award and article 6(2) applied in relation to the award (which award therefore continued as an old style ESA award).]

(2) Where this article applies, the ESA Regulations 2013 are to be read as if—

(a)(i) in the definitions of "period of limited capability for work" in regulations 2 (interpretation) and 3 (further interpretation), the reference to a period throughout which a person has, or is treated as having, limited capability for work included a reference to a period throughout which the person in question had, or was treated as having, limited capability for work under the ESA Regulations 2008; and

(ii) the reference, in the definition in regulation 2, to regulation 28 of the Claims and Payments Regulations 2013 (time within which a claim for employment and support allowance is to be made) included a reference to regulation 19 of, and Schedule 4 to, the Claims and Payments Regulations 1987 (prescribed times for claiming benefit);

(b) in regulation 6 (the assessment phase–previous claimants)—

(i) any reference to an employment and support allowance included a reference to an old style ESA award; and

(ii) in paragraph (2)(b)(v) and (c)(iii), the reference to regulation 26 (conditions for treating a claimant as having limited capability for work until a determination about limited capability for work has been made) included a reference to regulation 30 of the ESA Regulations 2008 (conditions for treating a claimant as having limited capability for work until a determination about limited capability for work has been made);

(c) in regulation 7 (circumstances where the condition that the assessment phase has ended before entitlement to the support component [³ . . .] arises does not apply)—

    (i) any reference to an employment and support allowance included a reference to an old style ESA award; and

    (ii) in paragraph (3)(b)(iv), (c)(iii), (c)(iv) and (d)(iii), the reference to regulation 26 included a reference to regulation 30 of the ESA Regulations 2008;

(d) in regulation 11 (condition relating to youth–previous claimants), any reference to an employment and support allowance included a reference to an old style ESA award;

(e) in regulation 15 (determination of limited capability for work)—

    (i) the reference in paragraph (7)(a) to a claimant having been determined to have limited capability for work included a reference to such a determination made under Part 5 of the ESA Regulations 2008; and

    (ii) the reference in paragraph (7)(b) to a person being treated as having limited capability for work included a reference to a person being so treated under regulation 20 (certain claimants to be treated as having limited capability for work), 25 (hospital patients), 26 (claimants receiving certain regular treatment) or 29 (exceptional circumstances) of the ESA Regulations 2008;

(f) in regulation 26 (conditions for treating a claimant as having limited capability for work until a determination about limited capability for work has been made)—

    (i) in paragraph (2)(b), the reference to regulation 18 (failure to provide information in relation to limited capability for work) and 19 (claimant may be called for a medical examination to determine whether the claimant has limited capability for work) included a reference to regulation 22 (failure to provide information in relation to limited capability for work) and 23 (claimant may be called for a medical examination to determine whether the claimant has limited capability for work) of the ESA Regulations 2008; and

    (ii) in paragraph (4)(c), the reference to regulation 18 included a reference to regulation 22 of the ESA Regulations 2008;

(g) in regulation 30(4) (determination of limited capability for work-related activity), the reference to a determination about whether a claimant has, or is to be treated as having or not having, limited capability for work-related activity included such a determination that was made under Part 6 of the ESA Regulations 2008; [¹ . . .]

[¹(ga) in regulation 39(6) (exempt work), the reference to an employment and support allowance included a reference to an old style ESA award;

(gb) in regulation 85(2)(a) (waiting days), where a claimant was entitled to an old style ESA award with effect from the first day of a period of limited capability for work by virtue of regulation 144(2)(a) of the

ESA Regulations 2008 and, with effect from [² a day between the second and the seventh day of that period (including the second and the seventh day)], that award continued as a new style ESA award in the circumstances referred to in paragraph (1)(b) of this article, the reference to an employment and support allowance included a reference to the old style ESA award;]

(h) in regulation 87(1) (claimants appealing a decision), the reference to a determination that the claimant does not have limited capability for work under the ESA Regulations 2013 included a reference to such a determination under the ESA Regulations 2008.

(i) in regulation 89 (short absence), where—

    (i) a claimant had an old style ESA award in the circumstances referred to in paragraph (1)(b) of this article;

    (ii) a temporary absence from Great Britain commenced when regulation 152 of the ESA Regulations 2008 applied to the claimant; and

    (iii) the first 4 weeks of the temporary absence had not ended immediately before the first day of entitlement to the new style ESA award,

the initial words of regulation 89 included a reference to the claimant being entitled to the new style ESA award during the remainder of the first 4 weeks of the temporary absence that commenced when regulation 152 of the ESA Regulations 2008 applied to the claimant;

(j) in regulation 90 (absence to receive medical treatment), where—

    (i) a claimant had an old style ESA award in the circumstances referred to in paragraph (1)(b) of this article;

    (ii) a temporary absence from Great Britain commenced when regulation 153 of the ESA Regulations 2008 applied to the claimant; and

    (iii) the first 26 weeks of the temporary absence had not ended immediately before the first day of entitlement to the new style ESA award,

the initial words of paragraph (1) of regulation 90 included a reference to the claimant being entitled to the new style ESA award during the remainder of the first 26 weeks of the temporary absence that commenced when regulation 153 of the ESA Regulations 2008 applied to the claimant;

(k) in regulation 93 (disqualification for misconduct etc)—

    (i) in paragraph (3), for "Paragraph (2) does" there were substituted "Paragraphs (2) and (5) do"; and

    (ii) after paragraph (4) there were inserted—

"(5) Subject to paragraph (3), a claimant is to be disqualified for receiving an employment and support allowance for any period determined by the Secretary of State under regulation 157(2) of the Employment and Support Allowance Regulations 2008(3) less any days during that period on which those Regulations applied to the claimant.

(6) Where paragraph (5) applies to a claimant, paragraph (2) is not to apply to that claimant with respect to any matter referred to in paragraph (1) that formed the basis for the claimant's disqualification under regulation 157(2) of the Employment and Support Allowance Regulations 2008.";

(l) in regulation 95 (treating a claimant as not having limited capability for work), the existing words became paragraph (1) and—

    (i) at the beginning of paragraph (1), there were inserted "Subject to paragraph (2),"; and

    (ii) after paragraph (1), there were inserted—

"(2) A claimant is to be treated as not having limited capability for work if—

(a) under Part 1 of the Act as it has effect apart from the amendments made by Schedule 3, and Part 1 of Schedule 14, to the Welfare Reform Act 2012 that remove references to an income-related allowance ("the former law"), the claimant was disqualified for receiving a contributory employment and support allowance during a period of imprisonment or detention in legal custody;

(b) Part 1 of the Act as amended by the provisions of Schedule 3, and Part 1 of Schedule 14, to the Welfare Reform Act 2012 that remove references to an income-related allowance ("the current law") applied to the claimant with effect from a day that occurred during the period of imprisonment or detention in legal custody referred to in sub-paragraph (a) and during the period of six weeks with effect from the day on which the claimant was first disqualified as referred to in sub-paragraph (a); and

(c) the total of—

    (i) the period for which the claimant was disqualified for receiving a contributory employment and support allowance during the period of imprisonment or detention in legal custody when the former law applied to the claimant; and

    (ii) the period for which the claimant was disqualified for receiving an employment and support allowance during the period of imprisonment or detention in legal custody when the current law applied to the claimant,

amounts to more than six weeks."]

[¹ (3) Subject to paragraph (4), where this article applies, the 2007 Act is to be read as though—

(a) the reference to an employment and support allowance in section 1A(1) and (4) to (6);

(b) the first reference to an employment and support allowance in section 1A(3); and

(c) the first reference to an employment and support allowance in section 1B(4),

included a reference to a contributory employment and support allowance.

(4) Where this article applies and the 2010 Transitional Regulations apply to a person, paragraph (3)(c) becomes paragraph (3)(b) and, for paragraph (3)(a) and (b), there is substituted—

"(a) in section 1A as substituted by the 2010 Transitional Regulations—

    (i) the reference to an employment and support allowance in section 1A(1), (4) and (5); and

    (ii) the first reference to an employment and support allowance in section 1A(3); and".

(5) Where this article applies and a claimant—

(a) had an old style ESA award in the circumstances referred to in paragraph (1)(b); and

(b) the old style ESA award had not been preceded by a new style ESA award in the circumstances referred to in paragraph (1A)(c),

the 2007 Act is to be read as if, in section 24(2), the beginning of the assessment phase (subject to section 24(3)) was the first day of the period for which the claimant was entitled to the old style ESA award.]

AMENDMENTS

1. Welfare Reform Act 2012 (Commencement No.11 and Transitional and Transitory Provisions and Commencement No.9 and Transitional and Transitory Provisions (Amendment)) Order 2013 (SI 2013/1511) art.8 (July 1, 2013).

2. Welfare Reform Act 2012 (Commencement No.9, 11, 13 14, 16, 17 and 19 and Transitional and Transitory Provisions (Amendment)) Order 2014 (SI 2014/3067) art.7(a) (November 24, 2014).

3. Employment and Support Allowance and Universal Credit (Miscellaneous Amendments and Transitional and Savings Provisions) Regulations 2017 (SI 2017/204) reg.7 and Sch.1 para.9(2) (April 3, 2017).

DEFINITIONS

"the amending provisions"–art. 2(1)
"appointed day"–*ibid.*
"the Claims and Payments Regulations 1987"–*ibid.*
"the Claims and Payments Regulations 2013"–*ibid.*
"contributory employment and support allowance"–*ibid.*
"employment and support allowance"–*ibid.*
"the ESA Regulations 2008"–*ibid.*
"the ESA Regulations 2013"–*ibid.*
"new style ESA award"–*ibid.*
"old style ESA award"–*ibid.*

GENERAL NOTE

This makes transitional provisions for assessments of limited capability for work **3.134** or for work and work-related activity where a person has a new style ESA award and previously had an old style ESA award. Article 11 deals with the converse position.

So, for example, under the new style ESA award the definition of a period of limited capability for work includes a period throughout which the claimant had, or was treated as having, limited capability for work for the purposes of old style ESA (para.(2)(a)). Similarly, where the old style and new style awards link, then days of entitlement to old styled ESA in the linked award are included in calculating the end of the assessment phase (para.(2)(b)). To the same end, any earlier period of limited capability for work under the old style ESA award is counted in working out whether the work related activity component or support component is payable from the first day of entitlement (para.(2)(c)). Likewise, the six months rule for the purposes of treating a claimant as having limited capability for work until a further determination is made includes having limited capability for work (or being treated as such) under an old style ESA award (subs.(2)(f)).

[¹ Transition from new style ESA]

11.- [¹ (1) This article applies where a person— **3.135**
(a) makes, or is treated as making, a claim for an employment and support allowance and Part 1 of the 2007 Act, as it has effect apart from the provisions of Schedule 3, and Part 1 of Schedule 14, to the Act that remove references to an income-related allowance, applies in relation to the claim; or

(b) has a new style ESA award and article 6(2) applies in relation to the award (which award therefore continues as an old style ESA award),

and, in the case of sub-paragraph (a), the condition referred to in paragraph (1A) is satisfied.

(1A) The condition is that—

(a) the person previously made, or was treated as having made, a claim for an employment and support allowance and, under article 4, Part 1 of the 2007 Act, as amended by the provisions of Schedule 3, and Part 1 of Schedule 14, to the Act that remove references to an income-related allowance, applied in relation to the claim;

(b) a notice was issued to the person under regulation 4 of the 2010 Transitional Regulations and, under article 4, Part 1 of the 2007 Act, as amended by the provisions of Schedule 3, and Part 1 of Schedule 14, to the Act that remove references to an income-related allowance, applied in relation to the notice; or

(c) the person previously—

(i) had an old style ESA award immediately before the appointed day in relation to a case of a claim for universal credit referred to in article 4(2)(a) to (d) (and any award made in respect of the claim), or an award of universal credit referred to in article 4(2)(e) or (f); and

(ii) the old style ESA award consisted of or included a contributory employment and support allowance (which allowance therefore continued as a new style ESA award).]

(2) Where this article applies, the ESA Regulations 2008 are to be read as if—

(a)(i) in the definitions of "period of limited capability for work" in regulation 2(1) and (5) (interpretation), the reference to a period throughout which a person has, or is treated as having, limited capability for work included a reference to a period throughout which the person in question had, or was treated as having, limited capability for work under the ESA Regulations 2013; and

(ii) the reference, in the definition in regulation 2(1), to regulation 19 of the Claims and Payments Regulations 1987 (time for claiming benefit) included a reference to regulation 28 of the Claims and Payments Regulations 2013 (time within which a claim for an employment and support allowance is to be made);

(b) in regulation 5 (the assessment phase–previous claimants)—

(i) any reference to an employment and support allowance included a reference to a new style ESA award; and

(ii) in paragraph (2)(b)(v) and (c)(iii), the reference to regulation 30 (conditions for treating a claimant as having limited capability for work until a determination about limited capability for work has been made) included a reference to regulation 26 of the ESA Regulations 2013 (conditions for treating a claimant as having limited capability for work until a determination about limited capability for work has been made);

(c) in regulation 7 (circumstances where the condition that the assessment phase has ended before entitlement to the support component [5 . . .] arises does not apply)—

    (i) any reference to an employment and support allowance included a reference to a new style ESA award; and

    (ii) in paragraph (1B)(b)(iv), (c)(iii), (c)(iv) and (d)(iii), the reference to regulation 30 included a reference to regulation 26 of the ESA Regulations 2013;

(d) in regulation 10 (condition relating to youth – previous claimants), any reference to an employment and support allowance included a reference to a new style ESA award;

(e) in regulation 19 (determination of limited capability for work)—

    (i) the reference in paragraph (7)(a) to a claimant having been determined to have limited capability for work included a reference to such a determination made under Part 4 of the ESA Regulations 2013; and

    (ii) the reference in paragraph (7)(b) to a person being treated as having limited capability for work included a reference to a person being so treated under regulation 16 (certain claimants to be treated as having limited capability for work), 21 (hospital patients), 22 (claimants receiving certain treatment) or 25 (exceptional circumstances) of the ESA Regulations 2013;

(f) in regulation 30 (conditions for treating a claimant as having limited capability for work until a determination about limited capability for work has been made)—

    (i) in the initial words of paragraph (2)(b), the reference to regulation 22 (failure to provide information in relation to limited capability for work) and 23 (claimant may be called for a medical examination to determine whether the claimant has limited capability for work) included a reference to regulation 18 (failure to provide information in relation to limited capability for work) and 19 (claimant may be called for a medical examination to determine whether the claimant has limited capability for work) of the ESA Regulations 2013; and

    (ii) in [² paragraph (4)(c)], the reference to regulation 22 included a reference to regulation 18 of the ESA Regulations 2013;

(g) in regulation 34(4) (determination of limited capability for work-related activity), the reference to a determination about whether a claimant has, or is to be treated as having or not having, limited capability for work-related activity included such a determination that was made under Part 5 of the ESA Regulations 2013; [¹ ...]

[¹(ga) in regulation 45(10) (exempt work), the reference to an employment and support allowance included a reference to a new style ESA award;

(gb) in regulation 144(2)(a) (waiting days), where the claimant was entitled to a new style ESA award with effect from the first day of a period of limited capability for work by virtue of regulation 85(2)(a) of the ESA Regulations 2013 and, with effect from [⁴ a day between the second and the seventh day of that period (including the second and the seventh day)], that award continued as an old style ESA award in the circumstances referred to in paragraph (1)(c) of this article, the reference to an employment and support allowance included a reference to the new style ESA award;]

(h) in regulation 147A(1) (claimants appealing a decision), the reference to a determination that the claimant does not have limited capability for work included a reference to such a determination under the ESA Regulations 2013.

(i) in regulation 152 (short absence), where—

    (i) a claimant had a new style ESA award in the circumstances referred to in paragraph (1)(b) of this article;

    (ii) a temporary absence from Great Britain commenced when regulation 89 of the ESA Regulations 2013 applied to the claimant; and

    (iii) the first 4 weeks of the temporary absence had not ended immediately before the first day of entitlement to the old style ESA award,

the initial words of regulation 152 included a reference to the claimant being entitled to the old style ESA award during the remainder of the first 4 weeks of the temporary absence that commenced when regulation 89 of the ESA Regulations 2013 applied to the claimant;

(j) in regulation 153 (absence to receive medical treatment)—

    (i) a claimant had a new style ESA award in the circumstances referred to in paragraph (1)(b) of this article;

    (ii) a temporary absence from Great Britain commenced when regulation 90 of the ESA Regulations 2013 applied to the claimant; and

    (iii) the first 26 weeks of the temporary absence had not ended immediately before the first day of entitlement to the old style ESA award,

the initial words of paragraph (1) of regulation 153 included a reference to the claimant being entitled to the old style ESA award during the remainder of the first 26 weeks of the temporary absence that commenced when regulation 90 of the ESA Regulations 2013 applied to the claimant;

(k) in regulation 157 (disqualification for misconduct etc)—

    (i) in paragraph (3), for "Paragraph (2) does" there were substituted "Paragraphs (2) and (4) do"; and

    (ii) after paragraph (3) there were inserted—

"(4) Subject to paragraph (3), a claimant is to be disqualified for receiving an employment and support allowance for any period determined by the Secretary of State under regulation 93(2) of the Employment and Support Allowance Regulations 2013 less any days during that period on which those Regulations applied to the claimant.

(5) Where paragraph (4) applies to a claimant, paragraph (2) is not to apply to that claimant with respect to any matter referred to in paragraph (1) that formed the basis for the claimant's disqualification under regulation 93(2) of the Employment and Support Allowance Regulations 2013.";
[² ...]

(l) in regulation 159 (treating a claimant as not having limited capability for work), the existing words became paragraph (1) and—

    (i) at the beginning of paragraph (1), there were inserted "Subject to paragraph (2),"; and

    (ii) after paragraph (1), there were inserted—

"(2) A claimant is to be treated as not having limited capability for work if—

(a) under Part 1 of the Act as amended by the provisions of Schedule 3, and Part 1 of Schedule 14, to the Welfare Reform Act 2012 that remove references to an income-related allowance ("the former law"), the claimant was disqualified for receiving an employment and support allowance during a period of imprisonment or detention in legal custody;

(b) Part 1 of the Act as it has effect apart from the amendments made by Schedule 3, and Part 1 of Schedule 14, to the Welfare Reform Act 2012 that remove references to an income-related allowance ("the current law") applied to the claimant with effect from a day that occurred during the period of imprisonment or detention in legal custody referred to in sub-paragraph (a) and during the period of six weeks with effect from the day on which the claimant was first disqualified as referred to in sub-paragraph (a); and

(c) the total of—

   (i) the period for which the claimant was disqualified for receiving an employment and support allowance during the period of imprisonment or detention in legal custody when the former law applied to the claimant; and

   (ii) the period for which the claimant was disqualified for receiving a contributory employment and support allowance during the period of imprisonment or detention in legal custody when the current law applied to the claimant,

amounts to more than six weeks."] [³ and

(m) in Schedule 6 (housing costs), in paragraphs 8(1) and 9(1), each reference to an employment and support allowance included a reference to new style ESA.]

[¹ (3) Subject to paragraph (4), where this article applies, the 2007 Act is to be read as though—

(a) the reference to a contributory allowance in section (1A)(1) and (4) to (6);

(b) the first reference to a contributory allowance in section (1A)(3); and

(c) the first reference to a contributory allowance in section 1B,

included a reference to a new style ESA award.

(4) Where this article applies and the 2010 Transitional Regulations apply to a person, paragraph (3)(c) becomes paragraph (3)(b) and, for paragraph (3)(a) and (b), there is substituted—

"(a) in section 1A as substituted by the 2010 Transitional Regulations—

   (i) the reference to a contributory allowance in section 1A(1), (4) and (5); and

   (ii) the first reference to a contributory allowance in section 1A(3); and".

(5) Where this article applies and a claimant—

(a) had a new style ESA award in the circumstances referred to in paragraph (1)(b); and

(b) the new style ESA award had not been preceded by an old style ESA award in the circumstances referred to in paragraph (1A)(c),

section 24(2) of the 2007 Act is to be read as if the beginning of the assessment phase (subject to section 24(3)) was the first day of the period for which the claimant was entitled to the new style ESA award.]

AMENDMENTS

1. Welfare Reform Act 2012 (Commencement No.11 and Transitional and Transitory Provisions and Commencement No.9 and Transitional and Transitory Provisions (Amendment)) Order 2013 (SI 2013.1511) art.9 (July 1, 2013).

2. Welfare Reform Act 2012 (Commencement No.13 and Transitional and Transitory Provisions) Order 2013 (SI 2013/2657) art. 5(a) (October 29, 2013).

3. Welfare Reform Act 2012 (Commencement No.9, 11, 13, 14 and 16 and Transitional and Transitory Provisions (Amendment)) Order 2014 (SI 2014/1452) art.11 (June 16, 2014).

4. Welfare Reform Act 2012 (Commencement No.9, 11, 13 14, 16, 17 and 19 and Transitional and Transitory Provisions (Amendment)) Order 2014 (SI 2014/3067) art.7(a) (November 24, 2014).

5. Employment and Support Allowance and Universal Credit (Miscellaneous Amendments and Transitional and Savings Provisions) Regulations 2017 (SI 2017/204) reg.7 and Sch.1 para.9(3) (April 3, 2017).

DEFINITIONS

"the Claims and Payments Regulations 1987"–art. 2(1)
"the Claims and Payments Regulations 2013"–*ibid.*
"employment and support allowance"–*ibid.*
"the ESA Regulations 2008"–*ibid.*
"the ESA Regulations 2013"–*ibid.*
"new style ESA award"–*ibid.*
"old style ESA award"–*ibid.*

GENERAL NOTE

3.136   This makes transitional provisions for assessments of limited capability for work or for work and work-related activity where a person has an old style ESA award and previously had a new style ESA award. Article 10 deals with the converse position. The modifications are to similar effect as in Art.10.

[¹ Transition from old style JSA

3.137   **12.** – (1) This article applies where a person—
   (a) makes, or is treated as making, a claim for a jobseeker's allowance and, under article 4, the 1995 Act, as amended by the provisions of Part 1 of Schedule 14 to the Act that remove references to an income-based jobseeker's allowance, applies in relation to the claim; or
   (b) (i) has an old style JSA award (whether or not the award was made to the person as a member of a joint-claim couple) immediately before the appointed day in relation to a case of a claim for universal credit referred to in article 4(2)(a) to (d) (and any award made in respect of the claim), or an award of universal credit referred to in article 4(2)(e) or (f); and
        (ii) the old style JSA award consists of or includes a contribution-based jobseeker's allowance (which allowance therefore continues as a new style JSA award),

and, in the case of sub-paragraph (a), the condition referred to in paragraph (2) is satisfied.
   (2) The condition is that the person previously—
   (a) made, or was treated as having made, a claim for a jobseeker's allowance (whether or not as a member of a joint-claim couple) and the 1995 Act, as it has effect apart from the provisions of Part 1 of Schedule 14 to the Act that remove references to an income-based jobseeker's allowance, applied in relation to the claim; or
   (b) had a new style JSA award and article 6(2) applied in relation to the award (which award therefore continued as an old style JSA award).

(3) Where this article applies, the JSA Regulations 2013 are to be read as if—

(a) in regulation 15(3)(b) (victims of domestic violence), the reference to regulation 15 applying to the claimant included a reference to the claimant having been treated as being available for employment under regulation 14A(2) or (6) of the JSA Regulations 1996;

(b) in regulation 36(1) (waiting days), where a person was entitled to an old style JSA award with effect from the first day of a jobseeking period by virtue of regulation 46(1)(a) of the JSA Regulations 1996 and, with effect from [² a day between the second and the seventh day of that period (including the second and the seventh day)], that award continued as a new style JSA award in the circumstances referred to in paragraph (1)(b) of this article, the reference to a jobseeker's allowance included a reference to the old style JSA award;

(c) in regulation 37 (jobseeking period)—

    (i) the jobseeking period in relation to a claimant included any period that, under regulation 47 of the JSA Regulations 1996 (jobseeking period), forms part of the jobseeking period for the purposes of the 1995 Act; and

    (ii) in paragraph (3), the reference to a day that is to be treated as a day in respect of which the claimant was entitled to a jobseeker's allowance included a reference to any day that, under regulation 47(4) of the JSA Regulations 1996, is to be treated as a day in respect of which the claimant was entitled to a contribution-based jobseeker's allowance;

(d) in regulation 41 (persons temporarily absent from Great Britain), where a person had an old style JSA award in the circumstances referred to in paragraph (1)(b) of this article, the reference in paragraph (2)(b), (3)(a) and (c), (5)(a) and (6)(b) to entitlement to a jobseeker's allowance included a reference to the old style JSA award; and

(e) in regulation 46 (short periods of sickness), after paragraph (5) there were inserted—

"(6) Where—

(a) a person has been treated under regulation 55(1) of the Jobseeker's Allowance Regulations 1996 as capable of work or as not having limited capability for work for a certain period; and

(b) these Regulations apply to that person with effect from a day ("the relevant day") within that period,

the person is to be treated for the part of that period that begins with the relevant day as capable of work or as not having limited capability for work.

(7) Where paragraph (6) applies to a person and the conditions in paragraph (1)(a) to (c) are fulfilled in relation to that person on any day within the part of a period referred to in paragraph (6), the requirement of paragraph (1) to treat the person as capable of work or as not having limited capability for work is to be regarded as satisfied with respect to the fulfilment of those conditions on that day.

(8) For the purposes of paragraph (3), where paragraph (6) applies to a person, paragraph (3) is to apply to the person as though the preceding provisions of this regulation had applied to the person with respect to the person having been treated for a period, under regulation 55(1) of the

Jobseeker's Allowance Regulations 1996 and paragraph (6), as capable of work or as not having limited capability for work.".

(4) Where this article applies, the 1995 Act is to be read as though, in section 5 of the 1995 Act, the reference to a jobseeker's allowance in subsection (1) and the first reference to a jobseeker's allowance in subsection (2) included a reference to a contribution-based jobseeker's allowance.

(5) For the purposes of this article, "joint-claim couple" has the meaning given in section 1(4) of the 1995 Act.]

AMENDMENTS

1. Welfare Reform Act 2012 (Commencement No.11 and Transitional and Transitory Provisions and Commencement No.9 and Transitional and Transitory Provisions (Amendment)) Order 2013 (SI 2013/1511) art.10 (July 1, 2013).

2. Welfare Reform Act 2012 (Commencement No.9, 11, 13 14, 16, 17 and 19 and Transitional and Transitory Provisions (Amendment)) Order 2014 (SI 2014/3067) art.7(a) (November 24, 2014).

DEFINITIONS

"the amending provisions"–art. 2(1).
"the appointed day"–*ibid.*
"contribution-based jobseeker's allowance"–*ibid.*
"jobseeker's allowance"–*ibid.*
"joint-claim couple"—see para.(5).
"the JSA Regulations 1996"–art. 2(1).
"the JSA Regulations 2013"–*ibid.*
"new style JSA award"–*ibid.*
"old style JSA award"–*ibid.*

GENERAL NOTE

3.138 This makes transitional provisions for the continuity of jobseeking periods where a person has a new style JSA award and previously had an old style JSA award. Article 13 deals with the converse position.

[¹ Transition from new style JSA

3.139 **13.** (1) This article applies where a person—
   (a) makes, or is treated as making, a claim for a jobseeker's allowance (whether or not as a member of a joint-claim couple) and the 1995 Act, as it has effect apart from the provisions of Part 1 of Schedule 14 to the Act that remove references to an income-based jobseeker's allowance, applies in relation to the claim; or
   (b) has a new style JSA award and article 6(2) applies in relation to the award such that it continues as an old style JSA award,
and, in the case of sub-paragraph (a), the condition referred to in paragraph (2) is satisfied.
   (2) The condition is that the person previously—
   (a) made, or was treated as having made, a claim for a jobseeker's allowance and, under article 4, the 1995 Act, as amended by the provisions of Part 1 of Schedule 14 to the Act that remove references to an income-based jobseeker's allowance, applied in relation to the claim; or
   (b)(i) had an old style JSA award immediately before the appointed day in relation to a case of a claim for universal credit referred

to in article 4(2)(a) to (d) (and any award made in respect of the claim), or an award of universal credit referred to in article 4(2)(e) or (f); and

    (ii) the old style JSA award consisted of or included a contributory employment and support allowance (which allowance therefore continued as a new style JSA award).

(3) Where this article applies, the JSA Regulations 1996 are to be read as if—

[²(za) in regulation 11, the references in paragraph (2)(a) and (b) to a jobseeker's allowance included a reference to new style JSA;]

  (a) in regulation 14A (victims of domestic violence), for the purposes of paragraph (3)(b) of that regulation, a person had been treated as available for employment on a day (under paragraph (2) of that regulation) where regulation 15 of the JSA Regulations 2013 applied to that person on that day;

[²(aa) in regulation 17A(7), in paragraph (a) of the definition of "benefit", the reference to a jobseeker's allowance included a reference to new style JSA;

  (ab) in regulation 19(1)(r), the reference to a jobseeker's allowance included a reference to new style JSA;]

  (b) in regulation 46 (waiting days)—

    (i) where a person was entitled to a new style JSA award with effect from the first day of a jobseeking period by virtue of regulation 36(1) of the JSA Regulations 2013 and, with effect from [³ a day between the second and the seventh day of that period (including the second and the seventh day)], that award continued as an old style JSA award in the circumstances referred to in paragraph (1)(b) of this article, the reference to a jobseeker's allowance in paragraph (1)(a) included a reference to the new style JSA award; and

    (ii) the second reference to a jobseeker's allowance in paragraph (1)(d) included a reference to a new style JSA award;

  (c) in regulation 47 (jobseeking period)—

    (i) the jobseeking period in relation to a claimant included any period that, under regulation 37 of the JSA Regulations 2013 (jobseeking period) forms part of the jobseeking period for the purposes of the 1995 Act; and

    (ii) in paragraph (4), the reference to any day that is to be treated as a day in respect of which the claimant was entitled to a contribution-based jobseeker's allowance included a reference to a day that, under regulation 37(3) of the JSA Regulations 2013 (jobseeking period), is to be treated as a day in respect of which the claimant was entitled to a jobseeker's allowance;

  (d) in regulation 50 (persons temporarily absent from Great Britain), where a person had a new style JSA award in the circumstances referred to in paragraph (1)(b) of this article, the reference in paragraph (2)(b), (3)(a) and (c), (5)(a) and (c), (6AA)(a) and (6D)(b) to entitlement to a jobseeker's allowance included a reference to the new style JSA award; [² . . .]

  (e) in regulation 55 (short periods of sickness), after paragraph (5) there were inserted—

"(6) Where—

(a) a person has been treated under regulation 46(1) of the Jobseeker's Allowance Regulations 2013 as capable of work or as not having limited capability for work for a certain period; and

(b) these Regulations apply to that person with effect from a day ("the relevant day") within that period,

the person is to be treated for the part of that period that begins with the relevant day as capable of work or as not having limited capability for work.

(7) Where paragraph (6) applies to a person and the conditions in paragraph (1)(a) to (c) are fulfilled in relation to that person on any day within the part of a period referred to in paragraph (6), the requirement of paragraph (1) to treat the person as capable of work or as not having limited capability for work is to be regarded as satisfied with respect to the fulfilment of those conditions on that day.

(8) For the purposes of paragraph (3), where paragraph (6) applies to a person, paragraph (3) is to apply to the person as though the preceding provisions of this regulation had applied to the person with respect to the person having been treated for a period, under regulation 46(1) of the Jobseeker's Allowance Regulations 2013 and paragraph (6), as capable of work or as not having limited capability for work.".

[²(f) in paragraphs 6(1) and 7(1) of Schedule 2 (housing costs), each reference to a jobseeker's allowance included a reference to new style JSA; and

(g) in paragraph 13 of Schedule 2 (housing costs)—

    (i) in paragraph (a) of sub-paragraph (1) (apart from sub-paragraph (ii)(bb) of that paragraph), each of the references to a jobseeker's allowance included a reference to new style JSA;

    (ii) in sub-paragraph (1)(b), the reference to a jobseeker's allowance included a reference to new style JSA; and

    (iii) in sub-paragraph (1)(c)(iv) and (f)(iii), the reference to the making of a claim for a jobseeker's allowance included a reference to the making of a claim for a jobseeker's allowance where the 1995 Act, as it has effect as amended by the amending provisions, applied to the claim and the new style JSA award that resulted from the claim continued as an old style JSA award by virtue of article 6 of this Order.]

(4) Where this article applies, the 1995 Act is to be read as though, in section 5 of the 1995 Act, the reference to a contribution-based jobseeker's allowance in subsection (1) and the first reference to a contribution-based jobseeker's allowance in subsection (2) included a reference to a new style JSA award.

(5) For the purposes of this article, "joint-claim couple" has the meaning given in section 1(4) of the 1995 Act.]

AMENDMENTS

1. Welfare Reform Act 2012 (Commencement No.11 and Transitional and Transitory Provisions and Commencement No.9 and Transitional and Transitory Provisions (Amendment)) Order 2013 (SI 2013.1511) art.11 (July 1, 2013).

2. Welfare Reform Act 2012 (Commencement No.9, 11, 13, 14 and 16 and Transitional and Transitory Provisions (Amendment)) Order 2014 (SI 2014/1452) art.12 (June 16, 2014).

3. Welfare Reform Act 2012 (Commencement No.9, 11, 13 14, 16, 17 and 19 and Transitional and Transitory Provisions (Amendment)) Order 2014 (SI 2014/3067) art.7(a) (November 24, 2014).

DEFINITIONS

"contribution-based jobseeker's allowance"–art. 2(1).
"jobseeker's allowance"–*ibid.*
"joint-claim couple"—see para.(5).
"the JSA Regulations 1996"–art. 2(1).
"the JSA Regulations 2013"–*ibid.*
"new style JSA award"–*ibid.*
"old style JSA award"–*ibid.*

GENERAL NOTE

This makes transitional provisions for the continuity of jobseeking periods where **3.140** a person has an old style JSA award and previously had a new style JSA award. Article 12 deals with the converse position.

Sanctions: transition from old style ESA in case of a new award

14.-(1) This article applies where— **3.141**
  (a) a person is entitled to a new style ESA award and they were previously entitled to an old style ESA award that was not in existence immediately before the first day on which the person in question is entitled to the new style ESA award; and
  (b) immediately before the old style ESA award terminated, payments were reduced under regulation 63 of the ESA Regulations 2008 (reduction of employment and support allowance).
(2) Where this article applies—
  (a) the failure which led to reduction of the old style ESA award ("the relevant failure") is to be treated for the purposes of Part 8 of the ESA Regulations 2013, as a failure which is sanctionable under section 11J of the 2007 Act (sanctions);
  (b) the new style ESA award is to be reduced in relation to the relevant failure, in accordance with the provisions of this article and Part 8 of the ESA Regulations 2013 as modified by this article; and
  (c) the reduction referred to in sub-paragraph (b) is to be treated, for the purposes of the ESA Regulations 2013, as a reduction under section 11J of the 2007 Act.
(3) The reduction period for the purposes of the ESA Regulations 2013 is to be the number of days which is equivalent to the length of the fixed period applicable to the person under regulation 63 of the ESA Regulations 2008 in relation to the relevant failure, minus—
  (a) the number of days (if any) in that fixed period in respect of which the amount of the old style ESA award was reduced; and
  (b) the number of days (if any) in the period starting with the day after the day on which the old style ESA award terminated and ending with the day before the first day on which the person is entitled to the new style ESA award.
(4) Accordingly, regulation 51 of the ESA Regulations 2013 (general principles for calculating reduction periods) applies in relation to the relevant failure as if—
  (a) in paragraph (1), for the words "in accordance with regulations 52 and 53" there were substituted the words "in accordance with article 14 of the Welfare Reform Act 2012 (Commencement No.9 and Transitional and Transitory Provisions and Commencement

No.8 and Savings and Transitional Provisions (Amendment)) Order 2013"; and

(b) in paragraph (3), for the words "in accordance with regulation 52 or 53" there were substituted the words "in accordance with article 14 of the Welfare Reform Act 2012 (Commencement No.9 and Transitional and Transitory Provisions and Commencement No.8 and Savings and Transitional Provisions (Amendment)) Order 2013".

DEFINITIONS

"the 2007 Act"–art. 2(1).
"employment and support allowance"–*ibid.*
"the ESA Regulations 2008"–*ibid.*
"the ESA Regulations 2013"–*ibid.*
"new style ESA award"–*ibid.*
"old style ESA award"–*ibid.*

GENERAL NOTE

3.142   This makes transitional provision in relation to sanctions where a person has a new style ESA award and previously had an old style ESA award and was subject to sanctions.

Sanctions: transition from old style ESA in case of a continuing award

3.143   15.-(1) This article applies where—

(a) the amending provisions have come into force under article 4(1) in relation to the case of a claim for universal credit referred to in [¹ article 4(2)(a)] to (d) (and any award that is made in respect of the claim) or an award of universal credit referred to in article 4(2)(e) or (f);

(b) the person in question had an old style ESA award immediately before the appointed day which consisted of or included a contributory allowance (which allowance therefore continues as a new style ESA award); and

(c) immediately before the appointed day, payments under that award were reduced in accordance with regulation 63 of the ESA Regulations 2008 (reduction of employment and support allowance).

(2) Where this article applies—

(a) the failure which led to reduction of the old style ESA award ("the relevant failure") is to be treated for the purposes of Part 8 of the ESA Regulations 2013, as a failure which is sanctionable under section 11J of the 2007 Act (sanctions);

(b) on and after the appointed day, the award (in its continuation as a new style ESA award) is to be reduced in relation to the relevant failure, in accordance with the provisions of this article and Part 8 of the ESA Regulations 2013 as modified by this article; and

(c) the reduction referred to in sub-paragraph (b) is to be treated, for the purposes of the ESA Regulations 2013, as a reduction under section 11J of the 2007 Act.

(3) The reduction period for the purposes of the ESA Regulations 2013

is to be the number of days which is equivalent to the length of the fixed period applicable to the person under regulation 63 of the ESA Regulations 2008 in relation to the relevant failure, minus the number of days (if any) in that period in respect of which the amount of the old style ESA award was reduced.

(4) Accordingly, regulation 51 of the ESA Regulations 2013 (general principles for calculating reduction periods) applies in relation to the relevant failure as if—

(a) in paragraph (1), for the words "in accordance with regulations 52 and 53" there were substituted the words "in accordance with article 15 of the Welfare Reform Act 2012 (Commencement No.9 and Transitional and Transitory Provisions and Commencement No.8 and Savings and Transitional Provisions (Amendment)) Order 2013"; and

(b) in paragraph (3), for the words "in accordance with regulation 52 or 53" there were substituted the words "in accordance with article 15 of the Welfare Reform Act 2012 (Commencement No.9 and Transitional and Transitory Provisions and Commencement No.8 and Savings and Transitional Provisions (Amendment)) Order 2013".

AMENDMENT

1. Welfare Reform Act 2012 (Commencement No.9, 11, 13, 14 and 16 and Transitional and Transitory Provisions (Amendment)) Order 2014 (SI 2014/1452) art.13 (June 16, 2014).

DEFINITIONS

"the 2007 Act"–art. 2(1)
"the amending provisions"–*ibid.*
"the appointed day"–*ibid.*
"employment and support allowance"–*ibid.*
"the ESA Regulations 2008"–*ibid.*
"the ESA Regulations 2013"–*ibid.*
"new style ESA award"–*ibid.*

GENERAL NOTE

This makes transitional provision in relation to sanctions where a person has an award of universal credit and previously had an old style ESA award which was subject to sanctions.

3.144

Escalation of sanctions: transition from old style ESA

16.-(1) This article applies where a person is entitled to a new style ESA award and, at any time previously, the person was entitled to an old style ESA award.

3.145

(2) Where this article applies, for the purposes of determining the reduction period under regulation 52 of the ESA Regulations 2013 (low-level sanction) in relation to a sanctionable failure by the person to whom the new style award referred to in paragraph (1) was made, other than a failure which is treated as sanctionable under article 14 or 15—

(a) a reduction of a new style ESA award in accordance with article 14 or 15 as the case may be; and

(b) a reduction of an old style ESA award under the ESA Regulations 2008 which did not result in a reduction under article 14 or 15,

is, subject to paragraph (3), to be treated as arising from a sanctionable failure for which the reduction period which applies is the number of days which is equivalent to the length of the fixed period which applied under regulation 63 of the ESA Regulations 2008 (reduction of employment and support allowance).

(3) In determining a reduction period under regulation 52 of the ESA Regulations 2013 in accordance with paragraph (2), no account is to be taken of—

(a) a reduction of a new style ESA award in accordance with article 14 or 15, as the case may be, if, at any time after that reduction, the person was entitled to an old style ESA award, an old style JSA award or income support;

(b) a reduction of an old style ESA award under the ESA Regulations 2008 if, at any time after that reduction, the person was entitled to universal credit, a new style ESA award or a new style JSA award, and was subsequently entitled to an old style ESA award, an old style JSA award or income support.

DEFINITIONS

"employment and support allowance"–art. 2(1).
"the ESA Regulations 2008"–*ibid.*
"the ESA Regulations 2013"–*ibid.*
"new style JSA award"–*ibid.*
"old style ESA award"–*ibid.*
"old style JSA award"–*ibid.*

GENERAL NOTE

3.146   This ensures that any previous old style ESA fixed period reductions are taken into account when deciding the appropriate reduction period for the purposes of new style ESA award.

Sanctions: transition from old style JSA in case of a new award

3.147   17.-(1) This article applies where—

(a) a person is entitled to a new style JSA award and they were previously entitled to an old style JSA award that was not in existence immediately before the first day on which the person in question is entitled to the new style JSA award;

(b) immediately before that old style award terminated, payments were reduced under section 19 (as it applied both before and after substitution by the Act) (before substitution: circumstances in which a jobseeker's allowance is not payable; after substitution: higher-level sanctions) or 19A (other sanctions) of the 1995 Act, or under regulation 69B of the JSA Regulations 1996 (the period of a reduction under section 19B : Claimants ceasing to be available for employment etc.); and

(c) if the old style JSA award was made to a joint-claim couple within the meaning of the 1995 Act and the reduction related to—

(i) in the case of a reduction under section 19 as it applied before substitution by the Act, circumstances relating to only one member of the couple; or

(ii) in the case of a reduction under section 19 as it applied after substitution by the Act, a sanctionable failure by only one member of the couple,

the new style JSA award was made to that member of the couple.

(2) Where this article applies—

(a) the circumstances or failure which led to reduction of the old style JSA award (in either case "the relevant failure") is to be treated, for the purposes of the JSA Regulations 2013, as—

(i) a failure which is sanctionable under section 6J of the 1995 Act (higher-level sanctions), where the reduction was under section 19 of the 1995 Act; or

(ii) a failure which is sanctionable under section 6K of the 1995 Act (other sanctions), where the reduction was under section 19A of the 1995 Act or regulation 69B of the JSA Regulations 1996;

(b) the award of new style JSA is to be reduced in relation to the relevant failure, in accordance with the provisions of this article and Part 3 of the JSA Regulations 2013 (sanctions), as modified by this article; and

(c) the reduction is to be treated, for the purposes of the JSA Regulations 2013, as a reduction under section 6J or, as the case may be, section 6K of the 1995 Act.

(3) The reduction period for the purposes of the JSA Regulations 2013 is to be the number of days which is equivalent to the length of the period of reduction of a jobseeker's allowance which is applicable to the person under regulation 69, 69A or 69B of the JSA Regulations 1996, minus—

(a) the number of days (if any) in that period in respect of which the amount of a jobseeker's allowance was reduced; and

(b) the number of days (if any) in the period starting with the day after the day on which the old style JSA award terminated and ending with the day before the first day on which the person is entitled to a new style JSA award.

(4) Accordingly, regulation 18 of the JSA Regulations 2013 (general principles for calculating reduction periods) applies in relation to the relevant failure as if—

(a) in paragraph (1), for the words "in accordance with regulations 19, 20 and 21", there were substituted the words "in accordance with article 17 of the Welfare Reform Act 2012 (Commencement No.9 and Transitional and Transitory Provisions and Commencement No.8 and Savings and Transitional Provisions (Amendment)) Order 2013"; and

(b) in paragraph (3), for the words "in accordance with regulation 19, 20 or 21", there were substituted the words "in accordance with article 17 of the Welfare Reform Act 2012 (Commencement No.9 and Transitional and Transitory Provisions and Commencement No.8 and Savings and Transitional Provisions (Amendment)) Order 2013".

Definitions

"the Act"–art.2(1).
"the 1995 Act"–*ibid*.
"jobseeker's allowance"–*ibid*.
"the JSA Regulations 1996"–*ibid*.

"the JSA Regulations 2013"–*ibid.*
"new style JSA award"–*ibid.*
"old style JSA award"–*ibid.*

GENERAL NOTE

3.148   This makes transitional provision in relation to sanctions where a person has a new style JSA award and previously had an old style JSA award and was subject to sanctions.

Sanctions: transition from old style JSA in case of a continuing award

3.149   **18.**-(1) This article applies where—

(a) the amending provisions have come into force under article 4(1) in relation to the case of a claim for universal credit referred to in [¹ article 4(2)(a)] to (d) (and any award that is made in respect of the claim) or an award of universal credit referred to in article 4(2)(e) or (f);

(b) the person in question had an old style JSA award immediately before the appointed day which consisted of or included a contribution-based allowance (which allowance therefore continues as a new style JSA award);

(c) immediately before the appointed day, payments under that award were reduced under section 19 (as it applied both before and after substitution by the Act) (before substitution: circumstances in which a jobseeker's allowance is not payable; after substitution: higher-level sanctions) or 19A (other sanctions) of the 1995 Act, or under regulation 69B of the JSA Regulations 1996) (the period of a reduction under section 19B : Claimants ceasing to be available for employment etc.); and

(d) if the old style JSA award was made to a joint-claim couple within the meaning of the 1995 Act and the reduction related to—

   (i) in the case of a reduction under section 19 as it applied before substitution by the Act, circumstances relating to only one member of the couple; or

   (ii) in the case of a reduction under section 19 as it applied after substitution by the Act, a sanctionable failure by only one member of the couple,

the new style JSA award was made to that member of the couple.

(2) Where this article applies—

(a) the circumstances or failure which led to reduction of the old style JSA award (in either case "the relevant failure") is to be treated, for the purposes of the JSA Regulations 2013, as—

   (i) a failure which is sanctionable under section 6J of the 1995 Act (higher-level sanctions), where the reduction was under section 19 of the 1995 Act; or

   (ii) a failure which is sanctionable under section 6K of the 1995 Act (other sanctions), where the reduction was under section 19A of the 1995 Act or regulation 69B of the JSA Regulations 1996;

(b) the award (in its continuation as a new style JSA award) is to be reduced in relation to the relevant failure, in accordance with the provisions of this article and Part 3 of the JSA Regulations (sanctions), as modified by this article; and

(c) the reduction is to be treated, for the purposes of the JSA Regulations 2013, as a reduction under section 6J or, as the case may be, section 6K of the 1995 Act.

(3) The reduction period for the purposes of the JSA Regulations 2013 is to be the number of days which is equivalent to the length of the period of reduction of a jobseeker's allowance which is applicable to the person under regulation 69, 69A or 69B of the JSA Regulations 1996, minus the number of days (if any) in that period in respect of which the amount of a jobseeker's allowance was reduced.

(4) Accordingly, regulation 18 of the JSA Regulations 2013 (general principles for calculating reduction periods) applies in relation to the relevant failure as if—

(a) in paragraph (1), for the words "in accordance with regulations 19, 20 and 21", there were substituted the words "in accordance with article 18 of the Welfare Reform Act 2012 (Commencement No.9 and Transitional and Transitory Provisions and Commencement No.8 and Savings and Transitional Provisions (Amendment)) Order 2013"; and

(b) in paragraph (3), for the words "in accordance with regulation 19, 20 or 21", there were substituted the words "in accordance with article 18 of the Welfare Reform Act 2012 (Commencement No.9 and Transitional and Transitory Provisions and Commencement No.8 and Savings and Transitional Provisions (Amendment)) Order 2013".

AMENDMENT

1. Welfare Reform Act 2012 (Commencement No.9, 11, 13, 14 and 16 and Transitional and Transitory Provisions (Amendment)) Order 2014 (SI 2014/1452) art.13 (June 16, 2014).

DEFINITIONS

"the Act"–art. 2(1).
"the 1995 Act"–*ibid.*
"the amending provisions"–*ibid.*
"the appointed day"–*ibid.*
"jobseeker's allowance"–*ibid.*
"the JSA Regulations 1996"–*ibid.*
"the JSA Regulations 2013"–*ibid.*
"new style JSA award"–*ibid.*
"old style JSA award"–*ibid.*

GENERAL NOTE

This is the JSA equivalent to reg.15.   3.150

Escalation of sanctions: transition from old style JSA

19.-(1) This article applies where a person is entitled to a new style JSA   3.151
award and, at any time previously, the person was entitled to an old style
JSA award.

(2) Where this article applies, for the purposes of determining the applicable reduction period under regulation 19 (higher-level sanction), 20 (medium-level sanction) or 21 (low-level sanction) of the JSA Regulations

2013 in relation to a sanctionable failure by the person other than a failure which is treated as sanctionable by virtue of article 17 or 18—

(a) a reduction of a new style JSA award in accordance with article 17 or 18; and

(b) a reduction of an old style JSA award under section 19 (as it applied both before and after substitution by the Act) or 19A of the 1995 Act, or under regulation 69B of the JSA Regulations 1996, which did not result in a reduction under article 17 or 18,

is, subject to paragraph (3), to be treated as arising from a sanctionable failure for which the reduction period is the number of days which is equivalent to the length of the period which applied under regulation 69, 69A or 69B of the JSA Regulations 1996.

(3) In determining a reduction period under regulation 19 (higher-level sanction), 20 (medium-level sanction) or 21 (low-level sanction) of the JSA Regulations 2013 in accordance with paragraph (2), no account is to be taken of—

(a) a reduction of a new style JSA award in accordance with article 17 or 18 if, at any time after that reduction, the person was entitled to an old style JSA award, an old style ESA award or income support;

(b) a reduction of an old style JSA award under section 19 (as it applied both before and after substitution by the Act) or 19A of the 1995 Act, or under regulation 69B of the JSA Regulations 1996, if, at any time after that reduction, the person was entitled to universal credit, a new style JSA award or a new style ESA award, and was subsequently entitled to an old style JSA award, an old style ESA award or income support.

DEFINITIONS

"the Act"–art. 2(1).
"the 1995 Act"–*ibid.*
"the JSA Regulations 1996"–*ibid.*
"the JSA Regulations 2013"–*ibid.*
"new style JSA award"–*ibid.*
"old style ESA award"–*ibid.*
"old style JSA award"–*ibid.*

GENERAL NOTE

3.152   This is the JSA equivalent to reg.16.

Termination of sanctions under a new style ESA or JSA award

3.153   **20.**-(1) Paragraph (2) applies where—

(a) a new style ESA award or new style JSA award terminates while there is an outstanding reduction period (within the meaning of regulation 55 of the ESA Regulations 2013 (reduction period to continue where award of employment and support allowance terminates) or regulation 23 of the JSA Regulations 2013 (reduction period to continue where award of jobseeker's allowance terminates)) and the claimant becomes entitled to an old style ESA award, an old style JSA award or income support during that period; or

(b) article 6(2) applies to a new style ESA award or new style JSA award (such that it continues as an old style ESA award or an old style JSA award) and there is such an outstanding reduction period on the last day of the period of the new style ESA award or new style JSA award.

(2) Where this paragraph applies—

(a) regulation 55 of the ESA Regulations 2013 or regulation 23 of the JSA Regulations 2013, as the case may be, are to cease to apply; and

(b) the reduction period is to terminate on the first day of entitlement to an old style ESA award, old style JSA award or income support as the case may be.

DEFINITIONS

"employment and support allowance"–art.2(1).
"the ESA Regulations 2013"–*ibid.*
"jobseeker's allowance"–*ibid.*
"the JSA Regulations 2013"–*ibid.*
"new style ESA award"–*ibid.*
"new style JSA award"–*ibid.*
"old style JSA award"–*ibid.*

GENERAL NOTE

This provides that where a claimant has a new style ESA (or new style JSA) **3.154** award, is subject to sanctions and subsequently becomes entitled to an old style ESA (or old style JSA) award or income support, then the sanctions cease to have effect.

Transitory provisions: appeals

21.-(1) Paragraph (2) applies where— **3.155**

(a) the amending provisions have come into force under article 4(1) in relation to the case of a claim referred to in article 4(2)(a) to (d) (and any award that is made in respect of the claim) or the case of an award referred to in article 4(2)(e) or (f);

(b) the person is sent notice of a decision relating to a new style ESA award or a new style JSA award; and

(c) the date of notification with respect to that decision is before 28th October 2013.

(2) Where this paragraph applies, the provisions mentioned in paragraph (3) apply for the purposes of any appeal in relation to that decision as if regulation 55 of the Decisions and Appeals Regulations 2013 (consequential amendments) did not apply in that person's case.

(3) The provisions referred to are the following provisions of the Social Security and Child Support (Decisions and Appeals) Regulations 1999—

(a) regulation 32 (late appeals);

(b) regulation 33 (notice of appeal); and

(c) regulation 34 (death of a party to an appeal).

(4) For the purposes of paragraph (1), "the date of notification" means the date on which the decision notice was posted to the person's last known address by the Secretary of State.

DEFINITIONS

"the amending provisions"–art.2(1).
"the Decisions and Appeals Regulations 2013"–*ibid.*
"new style JSA award"–*ibid.*

GENERAL NOTE

3.156   This makes limited transitory provision with respect to appeals where a person is sent a notice relating to a new style ESA award or a new style JSA award before October 29, 2013.

Transitional provision: references to contributory employment and support allowance and contribution-based jobseeker's allowance

3.157   22. Where the amending provisions have come into force under article 4(1) in relation to the case of a claim referred to in article 4(2)(a) to (d) [¹ or (g)] (and any award that is made in respect of the claim) or the case of an award referred to in article 4(2)(e) or (f), then, in relation to such a case, any reference in the Social Security Administration Act 1992 or the Social Security Contributions and Benefits Act 1992 to—

(a) a contributory employment and support allowance is to be read as if it included a reference to a new style ESA award; and

(b) a contribution-based jobseeker's allowance is to be read as if it included a reference to a new style JSA award.

AMENDMENT

1. Welfare Reform Act 2012 (Commencement No.9, 11, 13, 14 and 16 and Transitional and Transitory Provisions (Amendment)) Order 2014 (SI 2014/1452) art.14 (June 16, 2014).

DEFINITIONS

"the amending provisions"–*ibid.*
"contribution-based jobseeker's allowance"–*ibid.*
"contributory employment and support allowance"–*ibid.*
"new style JSA award"–*ibid.*

GENERAL NOTE

3.158   This provision seeks to ensure that new style ESA and JSA awards are to be treated to all intents and purposes as awards of a contributory employment or support allowance or to a contribution-based jobseeker's allowance respectively. It does so by providing that, in relation to a case with respect to which art.4 has come into force, references in the SSAA 1992 and the SSCBA 1992 are to be construed as if they included a reference to a new style ESA award or to a new style JSA award respectively.

Amendment of the Welfare Reform Act 2012 (Commencement No 8 and Savings and Transitional Provisions) Order 2013

3.159   23.-(1) Article 5 of the Welfare Reform Act 2012 (Commencement No 8 and Savings and Transitional Provisions) Order 2013 (appointed day and saving for provisions relating to overpayments) is amended as follows.

(2) In paragraph (3)(a), at the beginning insert "subject to paragraph (3A),".

(3) After paragraph (3) insert—

"(3A) In so far as section 105(1) of the 2012 Act inserts section 71ZB(1)(b) and (c) of the 1992 Act, those paragraphs come into force on 29th April 2013 only in so far as they relate respectively to a new style JSA award and a new style ESA award.".

(4) In paragraph (6), for "those benefits have been claimed before 29th April 2013" substitute "they relate respectively to an old style JSA award and an old style ESA award".

(5) After paragraph (6) add—

"(7) In this article, "old style JSA award", "new style JSA award", "old style ESA award" and "new style ESA award" have the same meaning as in article 2(1) of the Welfare Reform Act 2012 (Commencement No.9 and Transitional and Transitory Provisions and Commencement No.8 and Savings and Transitional Provisions (Amendment)) Order 2013.".

DEFINITIONS

"the appointed day"–art. 2(1).
"new style JSA award"–*ibid.*
"old style ESA award"–*ibid.*
"old style JSA award"–*ibid.*

GENERAL NOTE

This amends art.5 of the Commencement No.8 Order as regards overpayments. **3.160** It is intended to make it clear that the new rules applying to overpayments of employment and support allowance and of jobseeker's allowance under the WRA 2012 apply only to overpayments of a new style ESA award and a new style JSA award respectively (para.(3)). The amendments also clarify that the old rules relating to overpayments of those benefits will continue to apply to overpayments of an old style ESA award and an old style JSA award respectively (para.(4)).

[¹ Appeals relating to ESA and JSA

24. (1) This article applies where, after an award of universal credit has **3.161** been made to a claimant (where that award is made by virtue of the coming into force of the provisions of the Act referred to in Schedule 2, under any secondary legislation) —

  (a) an appeal against a decision relating to the entitlement of the claimant to an old style ESA award or an old style JSA award is finally determined; or

  (b) a decision relating to the claimant's entitlement to such an award is revised under section 9 of the Social Security Act 1998 ("the 1998 Act") or superseded under section 10 of that Act.

(2) Where this article applies, the Secretary of State is to consider whether it is appropriate to revise under section 9 of the 1998 Act the decision in relation to entitlement to universal credit or, if that decision has been superseded under section 10 of that Act, the decision as so superseded (in either case, "the UC decision").

(3) Where it appears to the Secretary of State to be appropriate to revise the UC decision, it is to be revised in such manner as appears to the Secretary of State to be necessary to take account of—

  (a) the decision of the First-tier Tribunal, Upper Tribunal or court, or, as the case may be, the decision relating to entitlement to an old style ESA award or an old style JSA award, as revised or superseded; and

  (b) any finding of fact by the First-tier Tribunal, Upper Tribunal or court.

(4) For the purposes of this article, "secondary legislation" means an instrument made under an Act.]

AMENDMENT

1. Welfare Reform Act 2012 (Commencement No.9, 11, 13, 14 and 16 and Transitional and Transitory Provisions (Amendment)) Order 2014 (SI 2014/1452) art.15 (June 16, 2014).

GENERAL NOTE

3.162   This makes provision relating to the possible revision of a decision to make a universal credit award in the situation where an appeal against a decision not to award old style ESA or old style JSA is made after a universal credit award has been made.

SCHEDULE 1

POSTCODE DISTRICTS

3.163
1. M43
2. OL6
3. OL7
4. SK16

Article 3(2)

SCHEDULE 2

UNIVERSAL CREDIT PROVISIONS COMING INTO FORCE IN RELATION TO CERTAIN CLAIMS AND AWARDS

3.164
1. Section 1 (universal credit).
2. Section 2(1) (claims).
3. Section 3 (entitlement).
4. Section 4(1) and (4) (basic conditions).
5. Section 5 (financial conditions).
6. Section 6 (restrictions on entitlement).
7. Section 7(1) and (4) (basis of awards).
8. Section 8 (calculation of awards).
9. Section 9(1) (standard allowance).
10. Section 10(1) (responsibility for children and young persons).
11. Section 11(1) and (2) (housing costs).
12. Section 12(1) and (2) (other particular needs or circumstances).
13. Section 13 (work-related requirements: introductory).
14. Section 14 (claimant commitment).
15. Section 15(1) and (4) (work-focused interview requirement).
16. Section 16 (work preparation requirement).
17. Section 17(1), (2), (3)(a) to (e), (4) and (5) (work search requirement).
18. Section 18 (work availability requirement).
19. Section 19(1), (2)(a) to (c), (5) and (6) (claimants subject to no work-related requirements).
20. Section 20 (claimants subject to work-focused interview requirement only).
21. Section 21 (claimants subject to work preparation requirement).
22. Section 22 (claimants subject to all work-related requirements).
23. Section 23 (connected requirements).
24. Section 24(2), (3) and (4) (imposition of requirements).
25. Section 26(1) to (5) (higher-level sanctions).
26. Section 27(1) to (3) and (6) to (8) (other sanctions).

SCHEDULE 3

COMMENCEMENT OF REPEALS IN PART 1 OF SCHEDULE 14 TO THE ACT

Article 9   **3.165**

Short title and chapter	Extent of repeal
Jobseekers Act 1995 (c.18)	Section 1(2A) to (2D) and (4). In section 2, in subsection (3C)(d), "contribution-based". Sections 3 to 3B. In section 4— (a) in subsection (1), "contribution-based"; (b) subsections (3), (3A) and (6) to (11A). Section 4A. In section 5— (a) in the heading and in subsection (1) "contribution-based"; (b) in subsection (2), "contribution-based" in the first two places; (c) in subsection (3), "contribution-based". Section 13. Sections 15 to 17. In section 17A(10), the definition of "claimant". Section 23. Sections 26. In section 35(1)— (a) in the definition of "claimant", the words from "except" to the end; (b) the definitions of "contribution-based jobseeker's allowance", "income-based jobseeker's allowance", "income-related employment and support allowance", "joint-claim couple", "joint-claim jobseeker's allowance" and "the nominated member". In section 38— (a) in subsections (3) and (4), "contribution-based"; (b) subsection (6). In Schedule 1— (a) in paragraph 6(1), "contribution-based"; (b) paragraphs 8 and 8A; (c) paragraphs 9 to 10; (d) in paragraph 11(1), "contribution-based"; (e) in paragraph 16(1) and (2)(d), "contribution-based"; (f) paragraph 18(b) and (c).
Welfare Reform and Pensions Act 1999 (c.30)	In Schedule 7, paragraphs 2(3) and (4), 4, 5(3) and (4), 6, 9 to 11, 15 and 16. In Schedule 8, paragraph 29(2).

Short title and chapter	Extent of repeal
State Pension Credit Act 2002 (c.16)	In Schedule 2, paragraphs 36 to 38.
Income Tax (Earnings and Payments) Act 2003 (c.1)	In Schedule 6, paragraphs 228 to 230.
Civil Partnership Act 2004 (c.33)	In Schedule 24, paragraphs 118 to 122.
Welfare Reform Act 2007 (c.5)	In section 1— (a) in subsection (2), in the opening words, "either"; (b) in subsection (2)(a), "Part 1 of" and "that Part of"; (c) subsection (2)(b) and the preceding "or"; (d) in subsection (3)(f), the words from "(and" to "allowance)"; (e) in subsection (3A), "Part 1 of"; (f) in subsection (6), the definition of "joint-claim jobseeker's allowance"; (g) subsections (6A) and (7). In subsection 1A— (a) in the heading "contributory"; (b) in subsections (1) (in both places), (3) and (4), "Part 1 of". Section 1B(2). In section 2, in the heading, "contributory". In section 3, in the heading, "contributory". Sections 4 to 6. Section 23. In section 24(1), the definitions of "contributory allowance" and "income-related allowance". In section 26(1)(a), "or 4(4)(c) or (5)(c)". Section 27(2)(a) and (4). In Schedule 1— (a) the heading to Part 1; (b) Part 2. In Schedule 2— (a) in the headings to paragraphs 6 and 7, "Contributory allowance:"; (b) paragraph 8; (c) paragraph 11(b) and (c); (d) paragraph 12, so far as not otherwise repealed.
Welfare Reform Act 2009 (c.24)	In Part 3 of Schedule 7, the entry relating to the Civil Partnership Act 2004.

Schedule 4

Modifications Of The 2010 Transitional Regulations

3.166 1. The 2010 Transitional Regulations are to be read as if the amendments set out in this Schedule were made.

2. (1) Regulation 2 (interpretation) is amended as follows.

(2) In paragraph (1)—

(a) insert at the appropriate places in the alphabetical order of the definitions—

""the Claims and Payments Regulations" means the Universal Credit, Personal

Independence Payment, Jobseeker's Allowance and Employment and Support Allowance (Claims and Payments) Regulations 2013;";

""the Decisions and Appeals Regulations" means the Universal Credit, Personal Independence Payment, Jobseeker's Allowance and Employment and Support Allowance (Decisions and Appeals) Regulations 2013;";

""the ESA Regulations" means the Employment and Support Allowance Regulations 2013;";

(b) omit—

    (i) the definition of "income-related allowance";

    (ii) paragraphs (a) to (d) of the definition of "relevant deduction";

(c) in the definition of "benefit week", for "the 2008 Regulations" substitute "the ESA Regulations".

(3) In paragraph (3), omit "or awards".

3. In regulation 4 (the notice commencing the conversion phase), omit paragraph (6).

4. In regulation 5 (deciding whether an existing award qualifies for conversion)—

(a) in paragraph (1), omit "or awards";

(b) in paragraph (2)(a), for "or awards qualify" substitute "qualifies";

(c) in paragraph (2)(b), for "or awards do" substitute "does";

(d) in paragraph (6)(b), omit "or awards".

5. In regulation 6(2) (application of certain enactments for purpose of making conversion decisions)—

(a) for sub-paragraphs (b) and (c), substitute—

    "(b) the ESA Regulations;

    (c) regulation 38(2) and (3) of the Claims and Payments Regulations (evidence and information in connection with an award);";

(b) for sub-paragraph (e), substitute—

    "(e) the Decisions and Appeals Regulations."

6. In regulation 7 (qualifying for conversion)—

(a) in paragraph (1)—

    (i) omit "or awards";

    (ii) for "qualify" substitute "qualifies";

(b) in paragraphs (2)(b) and (3)(b), for "regulation 30 of the 2008 Regulations" substitute "regulation 26 of the ESA Regulations".

7. In regulation 8(1) (amount of an employment and support allowance on conversion), for "the 2008 Regulations" substitute "the ESA Regulations".

8. In regulation 9(1) (determining entitlement to a transitional addition)—

(a) for "or awards qualify" substitute "qualifies";

(b) omit "or 11(2) (transitional addition: income support)".

9. In regulation 10 (transitional addition: incapacity benefit or severe disablement allowance)—

(a) in paragraph (1), omit "(and for these purposes it is irrelevant whether the person is also entitled to any existing award of income support)";

(b) in paragraph (4)(a), for "paragraph (2) of regulation 67 of the 2008 Regulations (prescribed amounts for purpose of calculating a contributory allowance)" substitute "paragraph (1) of regulation 62 of the ESA Regulations (prescribed amounts)".

10. Omit regulation 11 (transitional addition: income support).

11. In regulation 12 (regulations 10 and 11: supplementary)—

(a) in the title, for "Regulations 10 and 11" substitute "Regulation 10";

(b) in paragraph (1), for "regulations 10 and 11" substitute "regulation 10";

(c) in paragraph (2), for "Amounts A and C are" substitute "Amount A is" and for "Amounts B and D are" substitute "Amount B is";

(d) for paragraph (3)(a), substitute—

    "(a) by virtue of an order made under section 150 of the Administration Act (annual up-rating of benefits), there is an increase in the weekly rate which, in accordance with regulation 10(3) (transitional addition: incapacity benefit or severe disablement allowance), is to be used to calculate Amount A; and";

(e) in paragraph (4)(a), for "paragraph (3)(a)(i) or (ii)" substitute "paragraph (3)(a)";

(f) in paragraphs (3) and (4), omit "or C" and "or applicable amount (as the case may be)".

12. In regulation 13(3) (the effective date of a conversion decision), omit "or awards".

13. In regulation 14 (conversion decision that existing award qualifies for conversion)—

(a) in paragraph (1)—

    (i) for "Subject to paragraph (2A), paragraphs (2) to (6)" substitute "Paragraphs (2) to (5)";

  (ii) for "or awards qualify" substitute "qualifies";
 (b) for paragraph (2), substitute—
  "(2) On the effective date of the conversion decision P's existing award is by virtue of this paragraph converted into, and shall have effect on and after that date as, a single award of an employment and support allowance of such amount as is specified in the conversion decision.";
 (c) omit paragraphs (2A), (2B) and (6);
 (d) in paragraph (4), omit "or awards";
 (e) for paragraph (7), substitute—
  "(7) In this regulation paragraphs (2) to (5) are subject to regulation 17 (changes of circumstances before the effective date).".

14. In regulation 15 (conversion decision that existing award does not qualify for conversion)—
 (a) in paragraph (1)—
  (i) for "Subject to paragraphs (2A) and (4), paragraphs (2), (3) and (6)" substitute "Subject to paragraph (4), paragraphs (2) and (3)";
  (ii) for "or awards do" substitute "does";
 (b) for paragraph (2), substitute—
  "(2) P's entitlement to an existing award of incapacity benefit or severe disablement allowance shall terminate by virtue of this paragraph immediately before the effective date of P's conversion decision.";
 (c) omit paragraphs (2A), (2B) and (6);
 (d) in paragraph (4)(a)—
  (i) for "the 2008 Regulations" substitute "the ESA Regulations";
  (ii) in paragraph (i), for "regulation 22(1) (failure to provide information or evidence requested in relation to limited capability for work)" substitute "regulation 18(1) (failure to provide information in relation to limited capability for work)";
  (iii) in paragraph (ii), for "regulation 23(2) (failure to attend for a medical examination to determine whether the claimant has limited capability for work)" substitute "regulation 19(2) (claimant may be called for a medical examination to determine whether the claimant has limited capability for work)";
 (e) in paragraph (5)—
  (i) in sub-paragraph (c), omit "or awards";
  (ii) in sub-paragraph (d), omit "or those existing awards";
 (f) for paragraph (7), substitute—
  "(7) In this regulation paragraphs (2) and (3) are subject to regulation 17 (changes of circumstances before the effective date).".

15. In regulation 16 (application of other enactments applying to employment and support allowance)—
 (a) in paragraph (1A)(b), for "regulation 145(1) of the 2008 Regulations" substitute "regulation 86 of the ESA Regulations";
 (b) in paragraph (2)(e)(ii), for "the 2008 Regulations" substitute "the ESA Regulations";
 (c) in paragraph (2)(e)(iii), omit "(being regulations consequentially amended by regulations made under Part 1 of the 2007 Act)".

16. In regulation 17 (changes of circumstances before the effective date)—
 (a) omit "or awards" in both places where it occurs;
 (b) in paragraph (a)(ii)—
  (i) omit "regulation 14(2B)(a) (termination of an existing award of incapacity benefit or severe disablement allowance where entitlement to award of income support continues),";
  (ii) for "(termination of existing awards which do not qualify for conversion)" substitute "(termination of an existing award which does not qualify for conversion)";
 (c) omit paragraph (c).

17. In regulation 18 (reducing the transitional addition: general rule), for paragraph (2) substitute—
  "(2) For the purposes of paragraph (1), a relevant increase is an increase in any amount applicable to the person under regulation 62(1) or (2) of the ESA Regulations, which is not excluded by paragraph (3).".

18. In regulation 21 (termination of transitional addition)—
 (a) in paragraph (1)(b)—
  (i) for ", (3), (3A) and (4)" substitute ", (3) and (3A)"and (4)";

(ii) omit "an employment and support allowance (entitlement to which arises from sections 1(2)(a) or 1(2)(b) of the 2007 Act), or to" and "or to an income-related allowance";

(b) omit paragraph (4);

(c) in paragraph (5)(a), for "regulation 145(1) of the 2008 Regulations (linking rules)" substitute "regulation 86 of the ESA Regulations (linking period)";

(d) in paragraph (5)(c)(ii), for "regulation 30 of the 2008 Regulations" substitute "regulation 26 of the ESA Regulations";

(e) in paragraph (5A)(c), for "regulation 145(1) of the 2008 Regulations (linking rules)" substitute "regulation 86 of the ESA Regulations (linking period)";

(f) omit paragraph (6);

(g) in paragraph (7)—

(i) for ", 1A and 2" substitute "and 1A";

(ii) omit "or additions, as the case may be," in both places where it occurs;

(iii) for "an allowance which is referred to in paragraph (1)(b)" substitute "a contributory allowance".

19. In regulation 22 (disapplication of certain enactments following conversion decision), omit paragraphs (c) and (d).

20. In Schedule 1 (modification of enactments: making conversion decisions)—

(a) in paragraph 2(a), for the modified section 1(2) substitute—

"(2) Subject to the provisions of this Part, a notified person is entitled to an employment and support allowance if the person satisfies the basic conditions and is entitled to an existing award of incapacity benefit or severe disablement allowance.";

(b) for paragraph 6, substitute—

"6. Schedule 1 to the 2007 Act is to be read as if paragraphs 1 to 6 were omitted.";

(c) in the heading to Part 2, for "the 2008 Regulations" substitute "the ESA Regulations";

(d) in paragraph 10, for "Regulation 30" substitute "Regulation 26";

(e) omit paragraph 10A;

(f) in paragraph 11, for "Regulation 75" substitute "Regulation 68";

(g) in paragraph 12, for "Regulation 144" substitute "Regulation 85";

(h) in the sub-heading to Part 3, for "Social Security (Claims and Payments) Regulations 1987" substitute "The Claims and Payments Regulations";

(i) in paragraph 13—

(i) for "Regulation 32 of the Social Security (Claims and Payments) Regulations 1987" substitute "Regulation 38 of the Claims and Payments Regulations";

(ii) in sub-paragraph (a), for "paragraph (1)" substitute "paragraph (2)";

(iii) in sub-paragraph (b), for "paragraph (1A)" substitute "paragraph (3)".

21. (1) Schedule 2 (modification of enactments: after the conversion phase) is amended as follows.

(2) In paragraph 2—

(a) in sub-paragraph (a), in the modified section 1(2)–

(i) in paragraph (a), for "or awards into a single award of an employment and support allowance;" substitute "into an award of an employment and support allowance; and";

(ii) omit paragraph (c) and for "; and" at the end of paragraph (b) substitute ",";

(b) in sub-paragraph (b) in the modified section 1(7)—

[¹ (i) for the definition of "contributory allowance" substitute—

"employment and support allowance" means an employment and support allowance to which a person is entitled by virtue of the Employment and Support Allowance (Transitional Provisions, Housing Benefit and Council Tax Benefit) (Existing Awards)(No.2) Regulations 2010 which was based on an award of incapacity benefit or severe disablement allowance to which the person was entitled.] and for "; and" following that definition substitute "."];

(ii) omit the definition of "income-related allowance".

[¹ (2A) In paragraph 2A—

(a) in paragraph (1), omit "contributory"; and

(b) in paragraph (2), in the substituted section 1A

(i) in paragraphs (1) and (3) to (5), for " a contributory allowance" substitute "an employment and support allowance"; and

(ii) in paragraph (3), omit "Part 1 of".]

(3) In paragraph 3(b), for "regulation 147A of the 2008 Regulations" substitute "regulation 87 of the ESA Regulations".

(4) Omit paragraphs 4 and 4A.

(5) In paragraph 6A—
  (a) in sub-paragraph (a), after paragraph (iv) insert "and";
  (b) in sub-paragraph (b), for "; and" substitute ".";
  (c) omit sub-paragraph (c).
(6) In the heading to Part 3, for "the 2008 Regulations" substitute "the ESA Regulations".
(7) In paragraph 8, for "regulation 147A of the 2008 Regulations" substitute "regulation 87 of the ESA Regulations".
(8) In paragraph 10, for "regulation 30" substitute "regulation 26".
"(9) For paragraph 11, substitute—
> 11. Regulation 39 (exempt work) is to be read as if, in the definition of "work period" in paragraph (6), after "referred to in paragraph (1)(c)", in both places where it occurs, there were inserted ", or any work done in accordance with regula-tion 17(4)(a) of the Social Security (Incapacity for Work)(General) Regulations 1995.
(10) For paragraph 12, substitute—"
> "12. Regulation 62 (prescribed amounts) is to be read as if, in paragraph (1), for sub-paragraphs (a) and (b) there were substituted—
>   (a)(i) where the claimant satisfies the conditions set out in section 2(2) or (3) of the Act, £71.70; or
>   (ii) where the claimant does not satisfy the conditions set out in section 2(2) or (3) of the Act—
>   (aa) where the claimant is aged not less than 25, £71.70; or
>   (bb) where the claimant is aged less than 25, £56.80; and
>   (b) the amount of any transitional addition to which the person is entitled under regulation 10 of the Employment and Support Allowance (Transitional Provisions, Housing Benefit and Council Tax Benefit) (Existing Awards) (No.2) Regulations 2010."
(9) Omit paragraph 13.
(10) In paragraph 14—
  (a) for "Regulation 75" substitute "Regulation 68";
  (b) for "paragraph 38" substitute "paragraph 11".
(11) In paragraph 15—
  (a) in the introductory words, for "Regulation 147A" substitute "regulation 87";
  (b) in the inserted regulation—
      (i) in the description of the number of the regulation, for "147A.—" substitute "87.—";
      (ii) in paragraph (2), for "regulation 19" substitute "regulation 15";
      (iii) in paragraph (4)(a), for "regulation 22 or 23" substitute "regulation 18 or 19";
      (iv) for "regulation 30", in all places where it occurs, substitute "regulation 26";
      (v) in paragraph (5)(c), for the words from ", struck out" to "(notice of appeal)", substitute "or struck out";
      (vi) in paragraph (5A), for "either—" and sub-paragraphs (a) and (b), substitute "receives the First-tier Tribunal's notification that the appeal is dismissed, with-drawn or struck out.".
(12) Omit paragraph 16.
(13) In the sub-heading before paragraph 17, for "Social Security (Claims and Payments) Regulations 1987" substitute "The Claims and Payments Regulations".
(14) In paragraph 17, for "The Social Security (Claims and Payments) Regulations 1987" substitute "The Claims and Payments Regulations".
(15) For paragraph 18 substitute—
> "18. Regulation 7 (claims not required for entitlement to an employment and support allowance in certain cases) is to read as if—
>   (a) the existing provisions were renumbered as paragraph (1);
>   (b) after paragraph (1) there were inserted—
>   (2) It is also not to be a condition of entitlement to an employment and support allowance that a claim be made for it where any of the following conditions are met—
>   (a) the claimant—
>   (i) has made and is pursuing an appeal against a conversion decision made by virtue of the Employment and Support Allowance (Transitional Provisions, Housing Benefit and Council Tax Benefit) (Existing Awards) (No.2) Regulations 2010 which embodies a determination that the beneficiary does not have limited capability for work; or
>   (ii) was entitled to an employment and support allowance by virtue of the

Employment and Support Allowance (Transitional Provisions, Housing Benefit and Council Tax Benefit) (Existing Awards) (No.2) Regulations 2010 and has made and is pursuing an appeal against a later decision which embodies a determination that the claimant does not have limited capability for work; or

(b) the claimant is entitled to an existing award which is subject to conversion under the Employment and Support Allowance (Transitional Provisions, Housing Benefit and Council Tax Benefit) (Existing Awards) (No.2) Regulations 2010." "

(16) In paragraph 19, for "regulation 26C" substitute "regulation 51".

(17) In paragraph 20—

(a) for "regulation 32(1B)" substitute "regulation 38(4)";

(b) in sub-paragraph (a), for the words "sub-paragraph (a)" substitute "sub-paragraph (b)";

(c) in sub-paragraph (b), for "(ab)" substitute "(bb)".

(18) Omit paragraph 21.

(19) In paragraph 22, for "Schedule 9B" substitute "Schedule 7".

(20) In paragraph 22A, in the inserted text omit paragraph (2B).

(21) In paragraph 23, in the inserted text omit paragraph (2B).

(22) In paragraph 24, in the inserted text omit paragraph (2B).

(23) In paragraph 25, in the inserted text omit paragraph (2B).

(24) In the sub-heading before paragraph 25A, for "Social Security and Child Support (Decisions and Appeals) Regulations 1999" substitute "Universal Credit, Personal Independence Payment, Jobseeker's Allowance and Employment and Support Allowance (Decisions and Appeals) Regulations 2013".

(25) In paragraph 25A—

(a) in sub-paragraph (1), for "Regulation 3 of the Social Security and Child Support (Decisions and Appeals) Regulations 1999 (revision of decisions)" substitute "Regulation 5 of the Universal Credit, Personal Independence Payment, Jobseeker's Allowance and Employment and Support Allowance (Decisions and Appeals) Regulations 2013 (revision on any grounds)";

(b) in sub-paragraph (1)(b), for "paragraph (9)(a)" substitute "paragraphs (2)(a) and (b)";

(c) for sub-paragraph (1)(c), substitute—

"(c) in paragraph (2)(a), for "in the case of an advance award under regulation 32, 33 or 34 of the Claims and Payment Regulations 2013" there were substituted, "in the case of an advance award under regulation 32, 33 or 34 of the Claims and Payment Regulations 2013 or a conversion decision within the meaning of regulation 5(2)(a) of the Employment and Support Allowance (Transitional Provisions, Housing Benefit and Council Tax Benefit) (Existing Awards) (No.2) Regulations 2010".";

(d) for sub-paragraph (2), substitute—

"(2) Regulation 23(1)(a) of those Regulations (change of circumstances) is to be read as if for "in the case of an advance award under regulation 32, 33 or 34 of the Claims and Payments Regulations 2013" there were substituted "in the case of an advance award under regulation 32, 33 or 34 of the Claims and Payments Regulations 2013 or a conversion decision within the meaning of regulation 5(2) (a) of the Employment and Support Allowance (Transitional Provisions, Housing Benefit and Council Tax Benefit) (Existing Awards) (No.2) Regulations 2010." "

(26) Omit paragraph 27.

22. In Schedule 3—

(a) for "The Social Security (Claims and Payments) Regulations 1987" substitute "the Claims and Payments Regulations";

(b) for " The Social Security and Child Support (Decisions and Appeals) Regulations 1999" substitute "the Decisions and Appeals Regulations".

AMENDMENT

1. Welfare Reform Act 2012 (Commencement No.11 and Transitional and Transitory Provisions and Commencement No.9 and Transitional and Transitory Provisions (Amendment)) Order 2013 (SI 2013/1511) art.7 (July 1, 2013).

Article 2(1)

[¹ SCHEDULE 5

THE GATEWAY CONDITIONS

Personal characteristics

3.167   1. The claimant must be—
(a) aged at least 18 years, but under 60 years and six months;
(b) [³ . . .];
(c) a British citizen who—
(i)   has resided in the United Kingdom throughout the period of two years ending with the date on which the claim for universal credit is made; and
(ii) has not, during that period, left the United Kingdom for a continuous period of four weeks or more.

Fitness to work

3.168   2. (1) The claimant must not—
(a) be pregnant; or
(b) have been pregnant, if the date of her confinement occurred during the period of 15 weeks ending with the date on which the claim for universal credit is made.
(2) In this paragraph, "confinement" has the same meaning as in regulation 8(4) of the Universal Credit Regulations.
(3) The claimant—
(a) must not have obtained from a doctor a statement given in accordance with the rules set out in Part 1 of Schedule 1 to the Social Security (Medical Evidence) Regulations 1976(1) ("a statement of fitness for work") in respect of the date on which the claim for universal credit is made, unless it has been determined, since the statement was given, that the claimant does not have limited capability for work within the meaning of the 2007 Act;
(b) must not have applied for a statement of fitness for work;
(c) must declare that the claimant does not consider himself or herself to be unfit for work; and
(d) must not have been the subject of a determination that the claimant has limited capability for work within the meaning of the 2007 Act, unless it has subsequently been determined that the claimant does not have limited capability for work within the meaning of that Act.

Existing benefits

3.169   3. (1) The claimant must not be entitled to—
[² (a) old style ESA;
(b) old style JSA;
(c) income support;]
(d) incapacity benefit or severe disablement allowance, as defined in Schedule 4 to the 2007 Act;
(e) disability living allowance [⁴ . . .]; or
(f) personal independence payment [⁴ . . .].
(2) [² . . .]
(3) The claimant must not be awaiting—
[² (a) a decision on a claim for—
(i)   any benefit mentioned in sub-paragraph (1)(a) to (c);
(ii) a tax credit; or
(iii) housing benefit;]; or
(b) the outcome of an application—
(i)   to the Secretary of State to consider whether to revise, under section 9 of the Social Security Act 1998, a decision that the claimant is not entitled to old style JSA, old style ESA or income support; or
(ii) to the relevant authority (within the meaning of the Child Support, Pensions and Social Security Act 2000) to consider whether to revise, under Schedule 7 to that Act, a decision that the claimant is not entitled to housing benefit.
(4) If the claimant has appealed against a decision that he or she is not entitled to a benefit mentioned in sub-paragraph (1)(a) to (c), the Secretary of State must be satisfied—

(a) that the appeal to the First-tier Tribunal, and any subsequent appeal to the Upper Tribunal or to a court, is not ongoing; and

(b) where an appeal has been finally determined, that there is no possibility of a further appeal by any party.

(5) [² . . .]

(6) [² . . .]

Income and capital

[³ **4.** (1) If the claimant is a single claimant, the claimant must declare that, during the period of one month starting with the date on which the claim for universal credit is made, the claimant's earned income is expected not to exceed [⁴ £338].

3.170

(2) If the claim for universal credit is made by a couple as joint claimants, they must declare that, during the period of one month starting with the date on which the claim is made—

(a) in relation to each member of the couple, the earned income of that member is expected not to exceed [⁴ £338]; and

(b) the couple's total earned income is expected not to exceed [⁴ £541].

(3) If the claimant is a single claimant and is not a member of a couple, the claimant's capital must not exceed £6,000.

(4) If the claimant is a single claimant and is a member of a couple, the couple's total capital must not exceed £6,000.

(5) If the claim for universal credit is made by a couple as joint claimants, the couple's total capital must not exceed £6,000.

(6) For the purposes of this paragraph, "couple" has the same meaning as it has in section 39 of the Act and "earned income" and "capital" have the same meanings as they have in Part 6 of the Universal Credit Regulations.]

Housing

5. The claimant must not—

3.171

(a) be homeless (within the meaning of section 175 of the Housing Act 1996) and must currently reside at his or her usual address;

(b) reside in accommodation in which care, supervision, counselling, advice or other support services (other than services connected solely with the provision of adequate accommodation) are made available to the claimant by or on behalf of the person by whom the accommodation is provided, with a view to enabling the claimant to live there;

(c) reside in the same household as a person who is a member of the regular forces or the reserve forces (within the meaning of section 374 of the Armed Forces Act 2006) and who is absent from the household in connection with that role; or

(d) own, or partly own, the property in which he or she resides.

Caring responsibilities

6. [⁴ (1) There must not be a child or young person living with the claimant some or all of the time if the child or young person–

3.172

(a) has been certified as severely sight impaired or blind by a consultant ophthalmologist;

(b) is looked after by a local authority, within the meaning of section 22 of the Children Act 1989 or section 17(6) of the Children (Scotland) Act 1995, save where the child or young person is so looked after during any period referred to in regulation 4A(1)(a) of the Universal Credit Regulations; or

(c) is entitled to a disability living allowance or personal independence payment.]

(2) The claimant must not—

[⁴ (a) be an adopter (within the meaning of the Universal Credit Regulations) with whom a child has been placed during the period of 12 months ending immediately before the date on which the claim for universal credit is made or with whom a child is expected to be placed during the period of two months beginning with that date; or]

(b) be a foster parent;

(c) be liable to pay child support maintenance under the Child Support Act 1991; or

(d) have any responsibility for providing care to a person who has a physical or mental impairment, other than in the course of paid or voluntary employment.

(3) For the purposes of this paragraph—

(a) "child" has the same meaning as in Part 1 of the Act;

(b) "foster parent" means—

(i) in relation to England, a person who is approved as a foster parent under the Fostering Services (England) Regulations 2011;

(ii) in relation to Wales, a person who is approved as a foster parent under the Fostering Services (Wales) Regulations 2003;

(iii) in relation to Scotland, a person who is approved as a kinship carer or a foster carer under the Looked After Children (Scotland) Regulations 2009 [⁴;

(c) "young person" means a person–

(i) who is not a child but who is under the age of 20; and

(ii) for whom the claimant would be responsible for the purposes of regulation 4 of the Universal Credit Regulations, if the person were a qualifying young person within the meaning of regulation 5 of those Regulations.]

Other requirements

3.173   7. The claimant—

[² (a) must not be carrying on a trade, profession or vocation in respect of which he or she receives self-employed earnings (within the meaning of regulation 57 of the Universal Credit Regulations) and must declare that he or she does not expect to carry on such a trade, profession or vocation during the period of one month starting with the date on which the claim for universal credit is made;]

(b) must not be receiving education or undertaking a course of training of any kind and must declare that he or she does not intend to engage in education or training of any kind (other than where required to do so by the Secretary of State, or by agreement with the Secretary of State, in connection with an award of universal credit) during the period of one month starting with the date on which the claim for universal credit is made;

(c) must not have—

(i) a deputy appointed by the Court of Protection under Part 1 of the Mental Capacity Act 2005 ("the 2005 Act");

(ii) a receiver appointed under Part 7 of the Mental Health Act 1983 and treated as a deputy by virtue of the 2005 Act; or

(iii) any other person acting on the claimant's behalf in relation to the claim for universal credit;

(d) must have a national insurance number;

[⁴ (e) must have an account with a bank, a building society, the Post Office, or a Credit Union (within the meaning of the Credit Unions Act 1979] [⁵ or, in the case of joint claimants(2), either member of the couple must have such an account] [²;

(f) must not be—

(i) a company director, within the meaning of the Companies Act 2006; or

(ii) a member of a limited liability partnership, within the meaning of the Limited Liability Partnerships Act 2000.]

Declarations

3.174   8. [³ (1)] [²A] declaration which is required by paragraph 2(3)(c), 4(1) , [³ 4(2)] or 7(a) or (b) is to be made by such method as may be required by the Secretary of State in relation to the person by whom it is to be made.]

[³ (2) A declaration which is required by paragraph 4(2) in relation to a couple may be made on behalf of the couple by both members of the couple or by either of them.]

AMENDMENTS

1. Welfare Reform Act 2012 (Commencement No.9, 11, 13, 14 and 16 and Transitional and Transitory Provisions (Amendment)) Order 2014 (SI 2014/1452) art.16 (June 16, 2014).

2. Welfare Reform Act 2012 (Commencement No.9, 11, 13 14, 16 and 17 and Transitional and Transitory Provisions (Amendment)) Order 2014 (SI 2014/1661) art. 4(4) (June 30, 2014).

3. Welfare Reform Act 2012 (Commencement No.9, 11, 13, 14, 16 and 17 and Transitional and Transitory Provisions (Amendment) (No.2)) Order 2014 (SI 2014/1923) art. 4(7) (July 28, 2014).

4. Welfare Reform Act 2012 (Commencement No.9, 11, 13, 14, 16, 17 and 19 and Transitional and Transitory Provisions (Amendment)) Order 2015 (SI 2015/32) arts.4(5) and 5 (January 26, 2015).

5. Welfare Reform Act 2012 (Commencement No.24 and Transitional and Transitory Provisions and Commencement No.9 and Transitional and Transitory Provisions (Amendment)) Order 2015 (SI 2015/1537) art.5(2)(a) (July 21, 2015).

GENERAL NOTE

Paragraph 4

One of the gateway conditions is that a single claimant must declare that their earned income for the next month "is not expected to exceed" a set figure (originally £330, now £338). The question on the original on-line claim form is subtly different, namely "Are you expecting take-home pay of £330 or more in the next month?" See AM v SSWP (UC) [2017] UKUT 131 for a discussion of the difficulties this may create. As Judge Rowland observed:

3.174.1

> '25. The Secretary of State argues that, because those who are uncertain are not confident that they will receive take-home pay of £330 or more in the next month, the correct answer for them to give on the claim form is no. I accept that, as a matter of very strict logic, that is so and that therefore the advice given to the claimant on 20 July 2015 was, strictly speaking, correct insofar as it explained which answer on the claim form was appropriate. However, it seems to me to be unlikely that this claimant is the only one to have read the option no as requiring him to declare that he expected not to receive take-home pay of £330 or more in the next month even though he had no such clear expectation. People do not always distinguish between I am not expecting take-home pay of £330 or more in the next month and I am expecting not to receive take-home pay of £330 or more in the next month. Without some guidance, the claim form is apt to confuse and a cautious person may prefer to answer "yes" rather than "no" so as to avoid an apparent under-declaration that might be construed as deliberately misleading.'

Judge Rowland further held as a matter of law as follows (at para.23):

> '23. Whether or not "highly likely" is the right phrase, I accept that in both paragraph 4(1) of Schedule 5 to the Commencement No.9 Order and in the question posed on the claim form, "expect" or "expecting" is used in the sense of the person concerned being reasonably confident about what will happen.'

The Welfare Reform Act 2012 (Commencement No.11 and Transitional and Transitory Provisions and Commencement No.9 and Transitional and Transitory Provisions (Amendment)) Order 2013

(SI 2013/1511) (C. 60) (AS AMENDED)

The Secretary of State, in exercise of the powers conferred by section 150(3) and (4)(a), (b)(i) and (c) of the Welfare Reform Act 2012, makes the following Order:

ARRANGEMENT OF ARTICLES

GENERAL NOTE

3.175   This Commencement Order ("the Commencement No.11 Order") extended the universal credit scheme to certain postcode districts in Wigan ("the No.2 relevant districts") and Manchester, Oldham and Warrington ("the No.3 relevant districts") as from July 1, 2013. The Order accordingly brought into force in those areas the provisions of the WRA 2012 that relate to both the introduction of universal credit and the abolition of income-related ESA and income-based JSA. This was achieved by reference to the specific categories of cases set out in arts.3 and 4. In addition, of course, the claimant had to fall within the Pathfinder Group, i.e. be a person who meets the requirements of regs.5 to 12 of the Transitional Provisions Regulations 2013 (or now meet the "gateway conditions" as set out in Sch.5 to the Commencement No.9 Order (as amended)).

An award of ESA under Part 1 of the Welfare Reform Act 2007, in a case where income-related ESA has been abolished, is referred to as a "new style ESA award". Likewise an award of a JSA under the Jobseekers Act 1995, in a case where income-based JSA has been abolished, is referred to as a "new style JSA award". Conversely an award of ESA under Part 1 of the Welfare Reform Act 2007, in a case where income-related ESA has not been abolished, is referred to as an "old style ESA award". Similarly an award of JSA under the Jobseekers Act 1995, in a case where income-based JSA has not been abolished, is referred to as an "old style JSA award".

This Order also amends certain transitional provisions in the Commencement No.9 Order.

Citation

3.176   **1.** This Order may be cited as the Welfare Reform Act 2012 (Commencement No.11 and Transitional and Transitory Provisions and Commencement No.9 and Transitional and Transitory Provisions (Amendment)) Order 2013.

Interpretation

3.177   **2.**-(1) In this Order—
"the Act" means the Welfare Reform Act 2012;
"the 1995 Act" means the Jobseekers Act 1995;
"the 2007 Act" means the Welfare Reform Act 2007;
"the amending provisions" means the provisions referred to in article 4(1)(a) to (c) of the No.9 Order (day appointed for the abolition of income-related employment and support allowance and income-based jobseeker's allowance);
"appointed day" means the day appointed for the coming into force of the amending provisions in accordance with article 4(3) of the No.9 Order;
[1 . . .] [4 "claimant"—

(a) in relation to an employment and support allowance, has the same meaning as in Part 1 of the Welfare Reform Act 2007, save as mentioned in article 5(1A) of the No.9 Order as applied by article 4(7);

(b) in relation to a jobseeker's allowance, has the same meaning as in the Jobseekers Act 1995 (as it applies apart from the amendments made by Part 1 of Schedule 14 to the Act that remove references to an income-based jobseeker's allowance), save as mentioned in article 5(1A) of the No.9 Order as applied by article 4(7);

(c) in relation to universal credit, has the same meaning as in Part 1 of the Act;]

"contribution-based jobseeker's allowance" means a contribution-based allowance under the 1995 Act as it has effect apart from the amendments made by Part 1 of Schedule 14 to the Act that remove references to an income-based allowance;

"contributory employment and support allowance" means a contributory allowance under Part 1 of the 2007 Act as it has effect apart from the amendments made by Schedule 3, and Part 1 of Schedule 14, to the Act that remove references to an income-related allowance;

"employment and support allowance" means an employment and support allowance under Part 1 of the 2007 Act;

[¹ "First-tier Tribunal" has the same meaning as in the Social Security Act 1998;

[¹ ²] [⁴ ...] [⁵ gateway conditions" means the conditions specified in Schedule 5 to the No.9 Order;";]

"jobseeker's allowance" means an allowance under the 1995 Act;

[³ "joint claimants", in relation to universal credit, has the same meaning as in Part 1 of the Act;]

"joint-claim couple" has the meaning given in section 1(4) of the 1995 Act;

"new style ESA award" means an award of an employment and support allowance under Part 1 of the 2007 Act as amended by the provisions of Schedule 3, and Part 1 of Schedule 14, to the Act that remove references to an income-related allowance;

"new style JSA award" means an award of a jobseeker's allowance under the 1995 Act as amended by the provisions of Part 1 of Schedule 14 to the Act that remove references to an income-based jobseeker's allowance;

"No.2 relevant districts" means the postcode districts and part-districts specified in Part 1 of the Schedule;

"No.3 relevant districts" means the postcode districts and part-districts specified in Part 2 of the Schedule;

"the No.9 Order" means the Welfare Reform Act 2012 (Commencement No.9 and Transitional and Transitory Provisions and Commencement No.8 and Savings and Transitional Provisions (Amendment)) Order 2013;

"old style ESA award" means an award of an employment and support allowance under Part 1 of the 2007 Act as it has effect apart from the amendments made by Schedule 3, and Part 1 of Schedule 14, to the Act that remove references to an income-related allowance;

"old style JSA award" means an award of a jobseeker's allowance under the 1995 Act as it has effect apart from the amendments made by Part

1 of Schedule 14 to the Act that remove references to an income-based jobseeker's allowance;

[³ "single claimant", in relation to universal credit, has the same meaning as in Part 1 of the Act;]

[⁵ ...]

[¹ ...]

[¹ "Upper Tribunal" has the same meaning as in the Social Security Act 1998.]

[¹ (2) For the purposes of this Order, the Universal Credit, Personal Independence Payment, Jobseeker's Allowance and Employment and Support Allowance (Claims and Payments) Regulations 2013 apply for the purpose of deciding—

(a) whether a claim for universal credit is made; and

(b) the date on which such a claim is made.]

[⁴ [⁵ ...]]

AMENDMENTS

1. Welfare Reform Act 2012 (Commencement No.9, 11, 13, 14 and 16 and Transitional and Transitory Provisions (Amendment)) Order 2014 (SI 2014/1452) art.18(2) (June 16, 2014).

2. Welfare Reform Act 2012 (Commencement No.9, 11, 13 14, 16 and 17 and Transitional and Transitory Provisions (Amendment)) Order 2014 (SI 2014/1661) art.5(a) (June 30, 2014).

3. Welfare Reform Act 2012 (Commencement No.9, 11, 13, 14, 16 and 17 and Transitional and Transitory Provisions (Amendment) (No.2)) Order 2014 (SI 2014/1923) art.6(2) (July 28, 2014).

4. Welfare Reform Act 2012 (Commencement No.9, 11, 13 14, 16, 17 and 19 and Transitional and Transitory Provisions (Amendment)) Order 2014 (SI 2014/3067) art.4(a), (b) and art.6(3) (November 24, 2014).

5. Welfare Reform Act 2012 (Commencement No.9, 11, 13, 14, 16, 17 and 19 and Transitional and Transitory Provisions (Amendment)) Order 2015 (SI 2015/32) art.7 (January 26, 2015).

Day appointed for commencement of the universal credit provisions in Part 1 of the Act

3.178   **3.**-(1) The day appointed for the coming into force of the provisions of the Act listed in Schedule 2 to the No.9 Order, in so far as they are not already in force, in relation to the case of a claim referred to in paragraph (2), and any award that is made in respect of the claim, is the day appointed in accordance with paragraph (3).

[¹ (2) The claims referred to are—

(a) a claim for universal credit where, on the date on which the claim is made, the claimant resides in one of the No.2 or No.3 relevant districts and meets the gateway conditions; and

[³(b) a claim for universal credit where—

    (i) in the case of a single claimant, the claimant gives incorrect information regarding the claimant residing in a No.2 or a No.3 relevant district or meeting the gateway conditions and the claimant does not reside in such a district or does not meet the gateway conditions on the date on which the claim is made;

    (ii) in the case of joint claimants, either or both of the joint claimants gives or give incorrect information regarding his or her (or

their) residing in such a district or meeting the gateway conditions and one or both of them does not or do not reside in such
a district or does not or do not meet those conditions on the
date on which the claim is made; and

(iii) after a decision is made that the single claimant is, or the joint
claimants are, entitled to universal credit and one or more payments have been made in respect of the single claimant or the
joint claimants, the Secretary of State discovers that incorrect
information has been given regarding residence or meeting the
gateway conditions.]

(3) The day appointed in relation to the case of a claim referred to in
paragraph (2), and any award that is made in respect of the claim, is the first
day of the period in respect of which the claim is made [² . . .].

(4) [¹ . . .]

(5) Article 3(6) of the No.9 Order applies for the purposes of paragraph
(3) as it applies for the purposes of article 3(4)(a) of the No.9 Order.

[¹ [³ (6) Article 3A of the No.9 Order applies in connection with a claim
for universal credit where a single claimant, or, as the case may be, either or
both of joint claimants, gives incorrect information regarding his or her (or
their) residing in a No.2 or a No.3 relevant district or meeting the gateway
conditions, as it applies in connection with the giving of incorrect information regarding a claimant residing in a relevant district (as defined in the
No.9 Order) or meeting the gateway conditions.]]

AMENDMENTS

1. Welfare Reform Act 2012 (Commencement No.9, 11, 13, 14 and 16 and
Transitional and Transitory Provisions (Amendment)) Order 2014 (SI 2014/1452)
art.18(3) (June 16, 2014).

2. Welfare Reform Act 2012 (Commencement No.9, 11, 13 14, 16 and 17 and
Transitional and Transitory Provisions (Amendment)) Order 2014 (SI 2014/1661)
art. 5(b) (June 30, 2014).

3. Welfare Reform Act 2012 (Commencement No.9, 11, 13, 14, 16 and 17 and
Transitional and Transitory Provisions (Amendment) (No.2)) Order 2014 (SI
2014/1923) art. 6(3) (July 28, 2014).

DEFINITIONS

"the Act"–art. 2(1).
"No.2 relevant districts"–*ibid.*
"No.3 relevant districts"–*ibid.*
"the No.9 Order"–*ibid.*

GENERAL NOTE

Para. (1)

This brings into force provisions relating to universal credit in Part 1 of the WRA   **3.179**
2012, as set out in Sch.2 to the Commencement No.9 Order in relation to the different categories of case set out in para.(2).

Para. (2) (a)

This covers the making of a claim for universal credit on or after July 1, 2013 in   **3.180**
respect of a period that begins on or after that date where a person lives in a "No.2
or No.3 relevant districts" at the time that the claim is made. The "No.2 relevant
districts" are those Wigan postcodes described in Part 1 of the Schedule. The "No.3

relevant districts", described in Part 2 of the Schedule, cover certain postcodes in Manchester, Oldham and Warrington. The other conditions for making a claim for universal credit, originally known as the "Pathfinder Group conditions", were set out in the Transitional Provisions Regulations 2013. These have now been superseded by the "gateway conditions" in Sch.5 to the Commencement No.9 Order (as amended) – except now in those areas where the so-called "full service" operates, under which a claimant simply has to live in the relevant area to come within the universal credit scheme.

Para. (2) (b)

3.181   This relates to the making of a claim for universal credit on or after July 1, 2013 in respect of a period that begins on or after that date but the claimant provides incorrect information as to either their residence in a relevant district or their meeting the gateway conditions, and this is only discovered once payments of universal credit have been made. Such a claim remains within the universal credit regime despite the error.

Para. (3)

3.182   The day appointed for the commencement of the universal credit provisions in the above cases is the first day of the period in respect of which the claim is made.

Para. (5)

3.183   Article 3(6) of the Commencement No.9 Order deals with the situation where there is an extension of time for making a claim.

Para. (6)

3.184   Article 3A of the Commencement No.9 Order makes consequential provision for cases where a claimant gives incorrect information about either their area of residence or meeting the gateway conditions. In particular, it provides for certain consequences to follow (i) where the discovery of the error is made before the claim for universal credit has been decided, (ii) where the discovery is made after an entitlement decision has been made, but before any payment of universal credit has been made, and (iii) where it is made after an entitlement decision and after one or more such payments have been made.

Day appointed for the abolition of income-related employment and support allowance and income-based jobseeker's allowance

3.185   [¹ 4. (1) The day appointed for the coming into force of the amending provisions, in relation to the case of a claim referred to in paragraph (2) and any award that is made in respect of the claim, is the day appointed in accordance with paragraph (3).

(2) The claims referred to are—

(a) a claim for universal credit, an employment and support allowance or a jobseeker's allowance where, on the date on which the claim is made [³ or treated as made], the claimant—

(i) resides in one of the No.2 or No.3 relevant districts; and

(ii) meets the gateway conditions;

[³(b) a claim for universal credit where—

(i) in the case of a single claimant, the claimant gives incorrect information regarding the claimant residing in a No.2 or a No.3 relevant district or meeting the gateway conditions and the claimant does not reside in such a district or does not meet the gateway conditions on the date on which the claim is made;

(ii) in the case of joint claimants, either or both of the joint claimants gives or give incorrect information regarding his or her (or their) residing in such a district or meeting the gateway conditions and one or both of them does not or do not reside in such a district or does not or do not meet those conditions on the date on which the claim is made; and

(iii) after a decision is made that the single claimant is, or the joint claimants are, entitled to universal credit and one or more payments have been made in respect of the single claimant or the joint claimants, the Secretary of State discovers that incorrect information has been given regarding residence or meeting the gateway conditions;

(c) a claim for an employment and support allowance or a jobseeker's allowance other than one referred to in sub-paragraph (a) that is made or treated as made during the relevant period by a single claimant of universal credit or by either of two joint claimants of universal credit who has or have made a claim for universal credit within sub-paragraph (a) or (b).]

(3) The day appointed in relation to the case of a claim referred to in paragraph (2), and any award that is made in respect of the claim, is the first day of the period in respect of which the claim is made.

(4) For the purposes of paragraph (2)(c), "relevant period" means, in relation to a claim for universal credit referred to in paragraph (2)(a) or (b), any UC claim period, and any period subsequent to any UC claim period in respect of which the claimant is entitled to an award of universal credit in respect of the claim.

(5) For the purposes of paragraph (4), a "UC claim period" is a period when—

(a) a claim for universal credit as referred to in paragraph (2)(a) or [² [³ (b)(i) (or (ii)]]] has been made but a decision has not yet been made on the claim; or

(b) a decision has been made that the claimant is not entitled to universal credit and—

    (i) the Secretary of State is considering whether to revise that decision under section 9 of the Social Security Act 1998, whether on an application made for that purpose, or on the Secretary of State's own initiative; or

    (ii) the claimant has appealed against that decision to the First-tier Tribunal and that appeal or any subsequent appeal to the Upper Tribunal or to a court has not been finally determined.

(6) Paragraphs [⁵ (6) to (9)] of article 4 of the No.9 Order apply in relation to the case of a claim for universal credit referred to in paragraph (2) (and any award that is made in respect of the claim) as they apply in relation to the case of a claim for universal credit referred to in sub-paragraphs (a) and (b) of article 4(2) of the No.9 Order (and any award that is made in respect of the claim).

[⁴ (7) Paragraphs (1) to (1B) of article 5 of the No.9 Order apply for the purposes of paragraph (2)(a) as they apply for the purposes of article 4(2) (a) of the No.9 Order.]

(8) Paragraphs (5) to (7) of article 5 of the No.9 Order apply for the purposes of sub-paragraphs (a) and (c) of paragraph (2) as they apply for the purposes of sub-paragraphs (a) and (g) of article 4(2) of the No.9 Order.

(9) Article 5(8) of the No.9 Order applies for the purposes of paragraph (3) as it applies for the purposes of article 4(3)(a) of the No.9 Order.]

AMENDMENTS

1. Welfare Reform Act 2012 (Commencement No.9, 11, 13, 14 and 16 and Transitional and Transitory Provisions (Amendment)) Order 2014 (SI 2014/1452) art.18(4) (June 16, 2014).

2. Welfare Reform Act 2012 (Commencement No.9, 11, 13 14, 16 and 17 and Transitional and Transitory Provisions (Amendment)) Order 2014 (SI 2014/1661) art. 5(c) (June 30, 2014).

3. Welfare Reform Act 2012 (Commencement No.9, 11, 13, 14, 16 and 17 and Transitional and Transitory Provisions (Amendment) (No.2)) Order 2014 (SI 2014/1923) art. 6(4) (July 28, 2014).

4. Welfare Reform Act 2012 (Commencement No.9, 11, 13 14, 16, 17 and 19 and Transitional and Transitory Provisions (Amendment)) Order 2014 (SI 2014/3067) art.6(4) (November 24, 2014).

5. Welfare Reform Act 2012 (Commencement No.9, 11, 13, 14, 16, 17 and 19 and Transitional and Transitory Provisions (Amendment)) Order 2015 (SI 2015/32) art.9 (January 26, 2015).

DEFINITIONS

"the amending provisions"–art. 2(1).
"contributory employment and support allowance"–*ibid*.
"employment and support allowance"–*ibid*.
"jobseeker's allowance"–*ibid*.
"No.2 relevant districts"–*ibid*.
"No.3 relevant districts"–*ibid*.
"the No.9 Order"–*ibid*.
"relevant period"—see para.(4).
"UC claim period"—see para.(5).

GENERAL NOTE

Para. (1)

3.186   This brings into force provisions relating to the abolition of income-related ESA and of income-based JSA where one of the different categories of case set out in para.(2) applies.

Para. (2) (a)

3.187   This provides that the new provisions come into force in relation to a claim for (and any subsequent award of) universal credit, ESA or JSA, where a person makes such a claim on or after July 1, 2013 for a period that begins on or after that date and, at the time that the claim is made, the claimant both lives in a No.2 or No.3 relevant district (see Part 1 of Schedule) and meets the Pathfinder Group (now gateway) conditions.

Para. (2) (b)

3.188   This is modelled on art.3(2)(b). As with art.3(2)(b), awards made on the basis of incorrect information as to residence or meeting the gateway conditions remain within the universal credit regime despite the error.

Para. (2) (c)

3.189   This covers universal credit claimants who make an ESA or JSA claim and are not otherwise covered by art.4(2)(a). See further art.4(4) and (5).

Para. (3)

3.190   The day appointed for the coming into force of the amending provisions in the above cases is the first day of the period in respect of which the claim is made.

Para. (7)

Article 5(1) of the Commencement No.9 Order provides that the Claims and   **3.191**
Payments Regulations 1987 determine whether and when a claim for employment
and support allowance or jobseeker's allowance is made or is treated as made.

Application of the No.9 Order

5. [¹ Articles] 9 to 22 of the No.9 Order apply in connection with the   **3.192**
coming into force of the amending provisions in relation to the case of a
claim referred to in article 4(2), and any award made in respect of the claim,
as they apply in connection with the coming into force of the amending
provisions in relation to the case of a claim referred to in [² sub-paragraphs
(a), (b) and (g) of article 4(2)] of the No.9 Order and any award made in
respect of the claim.

AMENDMENTS

1. Welfare Reform Act 2012 (Commencement No.9, 11, 13, 14 and 16 and
Transitional and Transitory Provisions (Amendment)) Order 2014 (SI 2014/1452)
art.18(5) (June 16, 2014).
2. Welfare Reform Act 2012 (Commencement No.9, 11, 13, 14, 16 and 17 and
Transitional and Transitory Provisions (Amendment) (No.2)) Order 2014 (SI
2014/1923) art. 6(5) (July 28, 2014).

DEFINITIONS

"the amending provisions"–art. 2(1).
"the No.9 Order"–*ibid*.

Amendment of article 7 of the No.9 Order – transitional provisions in relation to claimant responsibilities with respect to employment and support allowance and jobseeker's allowance

6.-(1) Paragraph (3) applies in relation to a case where, under any sec-   **3.193**
ondary legislation, in relation to a new style JSA award, the 1995 Act applies
as though the amending provisions had not come into force (which award
therefore continues as an old style JSA award) and where the day with effect
from which the 1995 Act so applies occurs on or after 1st July 2013.

(2) Paragraph (4) applies in relation to a case where, under any secondary legislation, in relation to a new style ESA award, Part 1 of the 2007 Act
applies as though the amending provisions had not come into force (which
award therefore continues as an old style ESA award) and where the day
with effect from which Part 1 of the 2007 Act so applies occurs on or after
1st July 2013.

(3) In relation to a case to which this paragraph applies, for article 7(2)
of the No.9 Order substitute—

"(2) Where, under any secondary legislation, in relation to a new
style JSA award, the 1995 Act applies as though the amending provisions had not come into force, then, with effect from the day on
which the 1995 Act so applies, the 1995 Act, the Social Security
Administration Act 1992 and the Social Security Act 1998 are to
apply in relation to the award as though the provisions referred to in
paragraph (1)(a), (b) and (e) had not come into force.".

(4) In relation to a case to which this paragraph applies, for article 7(3)
of the No.9 Order substitute—

"(3) Where, under any secondary legislation, in relation to a new style ESA award, Part 1 of the 2007 Act applies as though the amending provisions had not come into force, then, with effect from the day on which Part 1 of the 2007 Act so applies, Part 1 of the 2007 Act and the Welfare Reform Act 2009 are to apply in relation to the award as though the provisions referred to in paragraph (1)(c), (d) and (f) had not come into force.".

(5) For the purposes of this article, "secondary legislation" means an instrument made under an Act.

DEFINITIONS

"the 1995 Act"–art.2(1).
"the 2007 Act"–*ibid.*
"the amending provisions"–*ibid.*
"employment and support allowance"–*ibid.*
"new style ESA award"–*ibid.*
"new style JSA award"–*ibid.*
"the No.9 Order"–*ibid.*
"old style ESA award"–*ibid.*
"old style JSA award"–*ibid.*
"secondary legislation"–para.(5)

GENERAL NOTE

3.194 Article 7 of the Commencement No.9 Order (claimant responsibilities with respect to ESA and JSA) provides for the appointed day and transitional provisions for the measures in the 2012 Act that relate to claimant responsibilities in relation to a new style ESA or new style JSA awards. By virtue of art.7 of the Commencement No.9 Order, those new provisions come into force in relation to any case with respect to which the provisions of art.4(1)(a)-(c) of that Order come into force.

This provision amends Article 7 of the Commencement No.9 Order with respect to certain cases that are to occur after the Order is made. In relation to the case where, under any secondary legislation, Part 1 of the WRA 2007 or the Jobseekers Act 1995 applies in relation to a new style ESA award or a new style JSA award respectively as though the amending provisions had not come into force, then the amendments clarify that such awards remain governed by the previous primary legislation.

Amendment of Schedule 4 to the No.9 Order

3.195 7. With effect from 1st July 2013, Schedule 4 to the No.9 Order (modifications of the 2010 Transitional Regulations) is amended as follows—
(a) for paragraph 21(2)(b)(i) substitute—
"(i) for the definition of "contributory allowance" substitute—
"employment and support allowance" means an employment and support allowance to which a person is entitled by virtue of the Employment and Support Allowance (Transitional Provisions, Housing Benefit and Council Tax Benefit)(Existing Awards)(No.2) Regulations 2010 which was based on an award of incapacity benefit or severe disablement allowance to which the person was entitled.",
and for "; and" following that definition substitute "."; "; and
(b) after paragraph 21(2) insert—
"(2A) In paragraph 2A—

(a) in paragraph (1), omit "contributory"; and
(b) in paragraph (2), in the substituted section 1A
    (i) in paragraphs (1) and (3) to (5), for " a contributory allowance" substitute "an employment and support allowance"; and
    (ii) in paragraph (3), omit "Part 1 of".".

DEFINITIONS

"employment and support allowance"–art. 2(1).
"the No.9 Order"–*ibid.*

GENERAL NOTE

This simply amends Sch.4 to the Commencement No.9 Order to ensure con-   **3.196**
sistency between the wording of ss.1 and 1A of the WRA 2007 as modified by the
Transitional Provisions Regulations 2010, and the wording of that Act as amended
by the provisions of Sch.3, and Part 1 of Sch.14, to the WRA 2012 (that remove
references to an income-related allowance).

Amendment of the No.9 Order – transition from old style ESA to new style ESA

8.-(1) Paragraph (2) applies in relation to a case where—   **3.197**
  (a) (i) a person makes, or is treated as making, a claim for an employment and support allowance;
    (ii) under article 4 of the No.9 Order, Part 1 of the 2007 Act, as amended by the provisions of Schedule 3, and Part 1 of Schedule 14, to the Act that remove references to an income-related allowance, applies in relation to the claim; and
    (iii) the claim is made or treated as made on or after 1st July 2013; or
  (b) (i) a person has an old style ESA award immediately before the appointed day in relation to a case of a claim for universal credit referred to in article 4(2)(a) to (d) of the No.9 Order (and any award made in respect of the claim), or an award of universal credit referred to in article 4(2)(e) or (f) of the No.9 Order;
    (ii) the old style ESA award consists of or includes a contributory employment and support allowance (which allowance therefore continues as a new style ESA award); and
    (iii) the first day on which the person is entitled to an employment and support allowance under the new style ESA award occurs on or after 1st July 2013.

(2) Where this paragraph applies, article 10 of the No.9 Order is amended
as follows—
  (a) for the title substitute "Transition from old style ESA";
  (b) for paragraph (1) substitute—
     "(1) This article applies where a person—
       (a) makes, or is treated as making, a claim for an employment and support allowance and, under article 4, Part 1 of the 2007 Act, as amended by the provisions of Schedule 3, and Part 1 of Schedule 14, to the Act that remove references to an income-related allowance, applies in relation to the claim; or
      (b)(i) has an old style ESA award immediately before the appointed day in relation to a case of a claim for

universal credit referred to in article 4(2)(a) to (d) (and any award made in respect of the claim), or an award of universal credit referred to in article 4(2)(e) or (f); and

(ii) the old style ESA award consists of or includes a contributory employment and support allowance (which allowance therefore continues as a new style ESA award),

and, in the case of sub-paragraph (a), the condition referred to in paragraph (1A) is satisfied.

(1A) The condition is that—

(a) the person previously made, or was treated as having made, a claim for an employment and support allowance and Part 1 of the 2007 Act, as it has effect apart from the provisions of Schedule 3, and Part 1 of Schedule 14, to the Act that remove references to an income-related allowance, applied in relation to the claim;

(b) a notice was issued to the person under regulation 4 of the 2010 Transitional Regulations and Part 1 of the 2007 Act, as that Part has effect apart from the provisions of Schedule 3, and Part 1 of Schedule 14, to the Act that remove references to an income-related allowance, applied in relation to the notice; or

(c) the person previously had a new style ESA award and article 6(2) applied in relation to the award (which award therefore continued as an old style ESA award).";

(c) after paragraph (2)(g) omit "and" and insert—

"(ga) in regulation 39(6) (exempt work), the reference to an employment and support allowance included a reference to an old style ESA award;

(gb) in regulation 85(2)(a) (waiting days), where a claimant was entitled to an old style ESA award with effect from the first day of a period of limited capability for work by virtue of regulation 144(2)(a) of the ESA Regulations 2008 and, with effect from the second or third day of that period, that award continued as a new style ESA award in the circumstances referred to in paragraph (1)(b) of this article, the reference to an employment and support allowance included a reference to the old style ESA award;";

(d) after paragraph (2)(h) insert—

"(i) in regulation 89 (short absence), where—

(i) a claimant had an old style ESA award in the circumstances referred to in paragraph (1)(b) of this article;

(ii) a temporary absence from Great Britain commenced when regulation 152 of the ESA Regulations 2008 applied to the claimant; and

(iii) the first 4 weeks of the temporary absence had not ended immediately before the first day of entitlement to the new style ESA award,

the initial words of regulation 89 included a reference to the claimant being entitled to the new style ESA award during the remainder of the first 4 weeks of the temporary absence that commenced when regulation 152 of the ESA Regulations 2008 applied to the claimant;

(j) in regulation 90 (absence to receive medical treatment), where—
  (i) a claimant had an old style ESA award in the circumstances referred to in paragraph (1)(b) of this article;
  (ii) a temporary absence from Great Britain commenced when regulation 153 of the ESA Regulations 2008 applied to the claimant; and
  (iii) the first 26 weeks of the temporary absence had not ended immediately before the first day of entitlement to the new style ESA award,
  the initial words of paragraph (1) of regulation 90 included a reference to the claimant being entitled to the new style ESA award during the remainder of the first 26 weeks of the temporary absence that commenced when regulation 153 of the ESA Regulations 2008 applied to the claimant;
(k) in regulation 93 (disqualification for misconduct etc)—
  (i) in paragraph (3), for "Paragraph (2) does" there were substituted "Paragraphs (2) and (5) do"; and
  (ii) after paragraph (4) there were inserted—
    "(5) Subject to paragraph (3), a claimant is to be disqualified for receiving an employment and support allowance for any period determined by the Secretary of State under regulation 157(2) of the Employment and Support Allowance Regulations 2008 less any days during that period on which those Regulations applied to the claimant.
    (6) Where paragraph (5) applies to a claimant, paragraph (2) is not to apply to that claimant with respect to any matter referred to in paragraph (1) that formed the basis for the claimant's disqualification under regulation 157(2) of the Employment and Support Allowance Regulations 2008.";
(l) in regulation 95 (treating a claimant as not having limited capability for work), the existing words became paragraph (1) and—
  (i) at the beginning of paragraph (1), there were inserted "Subject to paragraph (2),"; and
  (ii) after paragraph (1), there were inserted—
    "(2) A claimant is to be treated as not having limited capability for work if—
      (a) under Part 1 of the Act as it has effect apart from the amendments made by Schedule 3, and Part 1 of Schedule 14, to the Welfare Reform Act 2012 that remove references to an income-related allowance ("the former law"), the claimant was disqualified for receiving a contributory employment and support allowance during a period of imprisonment or detention in legal custody;
      (b) Part 1 of the Act as amended by the provisions of Schedule 3, and Part 1 of Schedule 14, to the Welfare Reform Act 2012 that remove references to an income-related allowance ("the current law") applied to the claimant with effect from a day that occurred during the period of imprisonment or detention in legal custody referred to in sub-paragraph (a) and during the period of six weeks with effect from the day

on which the claimant was first disqualified as referred to in sub-paragraph (a); and

(c) the total of—

(i) the period for which the claimant was disqualified for receiving a contributory employment and support allowance during the period of imprisonment or detention in legal custody when the former law applied to the claimant; and

(ii) the period for which the claimant was disqualified for receiving an employment and support allowance during the period of imprisonment or detention in legal custody when the current law applied to the claimant,

amounts to more than six weeks."."; and

(e) after paragraph (2) insert—

"(3) Subject to paragraph (4), where this article applies, the 2007 Act is to be read as though—

(a) the reference to an employment and support allowance in section 1A(1) and (4) to (6);

(b) the first reference to an employment and support allowance in section 1A(3); and

(c) the first reference to an employment and support allowance in section 1B,

included a reference to a contributory employment and support allowance.

(4) Where this article applies and the 2010 Transitional Regulations apply to a person, paragraph (3)(c) becomes paragraph (3)(b) and, for paragraph (3)(a) and (b), there is substituted—

"(a) in section 1A as substituted by the 2010 Transitional Regulations—

(i) the reference to an employment and support allowance in section 1A(1), (4) and (5); and

(ii) the first reference to an employment and support allowance in section 1A(3); and".

(5) Where this article applies and a claimant—

(a) had an old style ESA award in the circumstances referred to in paragraph (1)(b); and

(b) the old style ESA award had not been preceded by a new style ESA award in the circumstances referred to in paragraph (1A)(c),

the 2007 Act is to be read as if, in section 24(2), the beginning of the assessment phase (subject to section 24(3)) was the first day of the period for which the claimant was entitled to the old style ESA award.".

DEFINITIONS

"the Act"–art. 2(1).
"the 2007 Act"–*ibid.*
"appointed day"–*ibid.*
"contributory employment and support allowance"–*ibid.*
"employment and support allowance"–*ibid.*
"new style ESA award"–*ibid.*
"the No.9 Order"–*ibid.*
"old style ESA award"–*ibid.*

General Note

This Article, together with arts.9-11, amends arts.10 and 11 of the Commencement   **3.198**
No.9 Order, and substitutes new articles 12 and 13 of the Commencement No.9
Order (transition from old style ESA to new style ESA and vice versa, and old style
JSA to new style JSA and vice versa) with respect to claims that are made on or after
July 1, 2013 and awards of old style ESA or JSA that continue as awards of new style
ESA or JSA (or vice versa) on or after that date. The amendments are intended to
clarify the cases to which the modifications made by those articles apply and provide
for additional modifications of legislation governing ESA and JSA.

Transition from new style ESA to old style ESA

9.-(1) Paragraph (2) applies in relation to a case where—   **3.199**
   (a) (i) a person makes, or is treated as making, a claim for an employ-
        ment and support allowance;
    (ii) Part 1 of the 2007 Act as it has effect apart from the provisions
        of Schedule 3, and Part 1 of Schedule 14, to the Act that remove
        references to an income-related allowance, applies in relation to
        the claim; and
    (iii) the claim is made or treated as made on or after 1st July 2013;
        or
   (b) (i) a person has a new style ESA award and article 6(2) of the No.9
        Order applies in relation to the award (which award therefore
        continues as an old style ESA award); and
    (ii) the first day on which the person in question is entitled to an
        employment and support allowance under the old style ESA
        award occurs on or after 1st July 2013.
  (2) Where this paragraph applies, article 11 of the No.9 Order is amended
as follows—
   (a) for the title substitute "Transition from new style ESA";
   (b) for paragraph (1) substitute—
      "(1) This article applies where a person—
        (a) makes, or is treated as making, a claim for an employment
          and support allowance and Part 1 of the 2007 Act, as it has
          effect apart from the provisions of Schedule 3, and Part
          1 of Schedule 14, to the Act that remove references to an
          income-related allowance, applies in relation to the claim;
          or
        (b) has a new style ESA award and article 6(2) applies in rela-
          tion to the award (which award therefore continues as an
          old style ESA award),
and, in the case of sub-paragraph (a), the condition referred to in paragraph
(1A) is satisfied.
  (1A) The condition is that—
  (a) the person previously made, or was treated as having made, a
    claim for an employment and support allowance and, under
    article 4, Part 1 of the 2007 Act, as amended by the provisions of
    Schedule 3, and Part 1 of Schedule 14, to the Act that remove ref-
    erences to an income-related allowance, applied in relation to the
    claim;
  (b) a notice was issued to the person under regulation 4 of the 2010
    Transitional Regulations and, under article 4, Part 1 of the 2007 Act,

as amended by the provisions of Schedule 3, and Part 1 of Schedule 14, to the Act that remove references to an income-related allowance, applied in relation to the notice; or

(c) the person previously—

(i) had an old style ESA award immediately before the appointed day in relation to a case of a claim for universal credit referred to in article 4(2)(a) to (d) (and any award made in respect of the claim), or an award of universal credit referred to in article 4(2) (e) or (f); and

(ii) the old style ESA award consisted of or included a contributory employment and support allowance (which allowance therefore continued as a new style ESA award).";

(c) after paragraph (2)(g), omit "and" and insert—

"(ga) in regulation 45(10) (exempt work), the reference to an employment and support allowance included a reference to a new style ESA award;

(gb) in regulation 144(2)(a) (waiting days), where the claimant was entitled to a new style ESA award with effect from the first day of a period of limited capability for work by virtue of regulation 85(2)(a) of the ESA Regulations 2013 and, with effect from the second or third day of that period, that award continued as an old style ESA award in the circumstances referred to in paragraph (1)(c) of this article, the reference to an employment and support allowance included a reference to the new style ESA award;";

(d) after paragraph (2)(h), insert—

"(i) in regulation 152 (short absence), where—

(i) a claimant had a new style ESA award in the circumstances referred to in paragraph (1)(b) of this article;

(ii) a temporary absence from Great Britain commenced when regulation 89 of the ESA Regulations 2013 applied to the claimant; and

(iii) the first 4 weeks of the temporary absence had not ended immediately before the first day of entitlement to the old style ESA award,

the initial words of regulation 152 included a reference to the claimant being entitled to the old style ESA award during the remainder of the first 4 weeks of the temporary absence that commenced when regulation 89 of the ESA Regulations 2013 applied to the claimant;

(j) in regulation 153 (absence to receive medical treatment)—

(i) a claimant had a new style ESA award in the circumstances referred to in paragraph (1)(b) of this article;

(ii) a temporary absence from Great Britain commenced when regulation 90 of the ESA Regulations 2013 applied to the claimant; and

(iii) the first 26 weeks of the temporary absence had not ended immediately before the first day of entitlement to the old style ESA award,

the initial words of paragraph (1) of regulation 153 included a reference to the claimant being entitled to the old style ESA award during the remainder of the first 26 weeks of the temporary absence that commenced when regulation 90 of the ESA Regulations 2013 applied to the claimant;

(k) in regulation 157 (disqualification for misconduct etc)—

    (i) in paragraph (3), for "Paragraph (2) does" there were substituted "Paragraphs (2) and (4) do"; and

    (ii) after paragraph (3) there were inserted—

"(4) Subject to paragraph (3), a claimant is to be disqualified for receiving an employment and support allowance for any period determined by the Secretary of State under regulation 93(2) of the Employment and Support Allowance Regulations 2013 less any days during that period on which those Regulations applied to the claimant.

(5) Where paragraph (4) applies to a claimant, paragraph (2) is not to apply to that claimant with respect to any matter referred to in paragraph (1) that formed the basis for the claimant's disqualification under regulation 93(2) of the Employment and Support Allowance Regulations 2013."; and

(l) in regulation 159 (treating a claimant as not having limited capability for work), the existing words became paragraph (1) and—

    (i) at the beginning of paragraph (1), there were inserted "Subject to paragraph (2),"; and

    (ii) after paragraph (1), there were inserted—

"(2) A claimant is to be treated as not having limited capability for work if—

(a) under Part 1 of the Act as amended by the provisions of Schedule 3, and Part 1 of Schedule 14, to the Welfare Reform Act 2012 that remove references to an income-related allowance ("the former law"), the claimant was disqualified for receiving an employment and support allowance during a period of imprisonment or detention in legal custody;

(b) Part 1 of the Act as it has effect apart from the amendments made by Schedule 3, and Part 1 of Schedule 14, to the Welfare Reform Act 2012 that remove references to an income-related allowance ("the current law") applied to the claimant with effect from a day that occurred during the period of imprisonment or detention in legal custody referred to in sub-paragraph (a) and during the period of six weeks with effect from the day on which the claimant was first disqualified as referred to in sub-paragraph (a); and

(c) the total of—

(i) the period for which the claimant was disqualified for receiving an employment and support allowance during the period of imprisonment or detention in legal custody when the former law applied to the claimant; and

(ii) the period for which the claimant was disqualified for receiving a contributory employment and support allowance during the period of imprisonment or detention in legal custody when the current law applied to the claimant, amounts to more than six weeks.".”; and

(e) after paragraph (2) insert—

"(3) Subject to paragraph (4), where this article applies, the 2007 Act is to be read as though—

(a) the reference to a contributory allowance in section (1A)(1) and (4) to (6);

(b) the first reference to a contributory allowance in section (1A)(3); and

(c) the first reference to a contributory allowance in section 1B, included a reference to a new style ESA award.

(4) Where this article applies and the 2010 Transitional Regulations apply to a person, paragraph (3)(c) becomes paragraph (3)(b) and, for paragraph (3)(a) and (b), there is substituted—

"(a) in section 1A as substituted by the 2010 Transitional Regulations—

(i) the reference to a contributory allowance in section 1A(1), (4) and (5); and

(ii) the first reference to a contributory allowance in section 1A(3); and".

(5) Where this article applies and a claimant—

(a) had a new style ESA award in the circumstances referred to in paragraph (1)(b); and

(b) the new style ESA award had not been preceded by an old style ESA award in the circumstances referred to in paragraph (1A)(c),

section 24(2) of the 2007 Act is to be read as if the beginning of the assessment phase (subject to section 24(3)) was the first day of the period for which the claimant was entitled to the new style ESA award.".

DEFINITIONS

"the Act"–art. 2(1).
"the 2007 Act"–*ibid.*
"appointed day"–*ibid.*
"contributory employment and support allowance"–*ibid.*
"employment and support allowance"–*ibid.*
"new style ESA award"–*ibid.*
"the No.9 Order"–*ibid.*
"old style ESA award"–*ibid.*

Transition from old style JSA to new style JSA

3.200   **10.**-(1) Paragraph (2) applies in relation to the case where—

(a) (i) a person makes, or is treated as making, a claim for a jobseeker's allowance;

(ii) under article 4 of the No.9 Order, the 1995 Act as amended by the provisions of Part 1 of Schedule 14 to the Act that remove references to an income-based jobseeker's allowance, applies in relation to the claim; and

(iii) the claim is made or treated as made on or after 1st July 2013; or

(b) (i) a person has an old style JSA award (whether or not the award was made to the person as a member of a joint-claim couple) immediately before the appointed day in relation to a case of a

claim for universal credit referred to in article 4(2)(a) to (d) of
the No.9 Order (and any award made in respect of the claim) or
an award of universal credit referred to in article 4(2)(e) or (f)
of the No.9 Order;

(ii) the old style JSA award consists of or includes a contributory
employment and support allowance (which allowance therefore
continues as a new style JSA award); and

(iii) the first day on which the person in question is entitled to a
jobseeker's allowance under the new style JSA award occurs on
or after 1st July 2013.

(2) Where this paragraph applies, for article 12 of the No.9 Order substitute—

"Transition from old style JSA

12.-(1) This article applies where a person—

(a) makes, or is treated as making, a claim for a jobseeker's
allowance and, under article 4, the 1995 Act, as amended
by the provisions of Part 1 of Schedule 14 to the Act that
remove references to an income-based jobseeker's allowance, applies in relation to the claim; or

(b) (i) has an old style JSA award (whether or not the
award was made to the person as a member of a joint-
claim couple) immediately before the appointed day
in relation to a case of a claim for universal credit
referred to in article 4(2)(a) to (d) (and any award
made in respect of the claim), or an award of universal
credit referred to in article 4(2)(e) or (f); and

(ii) the old style JSA award consists of or includes
a contribution-based jobseeker's allowance (which
allowance therefore continues as a new style JSA
award),

and, in the case of sub-paragraph (a), the condition referred to
in paragraph (2) is satisfied.

(2) The condition is that the person previously—

(a) made, or was treated as having made, a claim for a jobseeker's allowance (whether or not as a member of a joint-claim
couple) and the 1995 Act, as it has effect apart from the provisions of Part 1 of Schedule 14 to the Act that remove references
to an income-based jobseeker's allowance, applied in relation to
the claim; or

(b) had a new style JSA award and article 6(2) applied in relation to the award (which award therefore continued as an old
style JSA award).

(3) Where this article applies, the JSA Regulations 2013 are to be
read as if—

(a) in regulation 15(3)(b) (victims of domestic violence), the
reference to regulation 15 applying to the claimant included
a reference to the claimant having been treated as being available for employment under regulation 14A(2) or (6) of the JSA
Regulations 1996;

(b) in regulation 36(1) (waiting days), where a person was

entitled to an old style JSA award with effect from the first day of a jobseeking period by virtue of regulation 46(1)(a) of the JSA Regulations 1996 and, with effect from the second or third day of that period, that award continued as a new style JSA award in the circumstances referred to in paragraph (1)(b) of this article, the reference to a jobseeker's allowance included a reference to the old style JSA award;

(c) in regulation 37 (jobseeking period)—

(i) the jobseeking period in relation to a claimant included any period that, under regulation 47 of the JSA Regulations 1996 (jobseeking period), forms part of the jobseeking period for the purposes of the 1995 Act; and

(ii) in paragraph (3), the reference to a day that is to be treated as a day in respect of which the claimant was entitled to a jobseeker's allowance included a reference to any day that, under regulation 47(4) of the JSA Regulations 1996, is to be treated as a day in respect of which the claimant was entitled to a contribution-based jobseeker's allowance;

(d) in regulation 41 (persons temporarily absent from Great Britain), where a person had an old style JSA award in the circumstances referred to in paragraph (1)(b) of this article, the reference in paragraph (2)(b), (3)(a) and (c), (5)(a) and (6)(b) to entitlement to a jobseeker's allowance included a reference to the old style JSA award; and

(e) in regulation 46 (short periods of sickness), after paragraph (5) there were inserted—

"(6) Where—

(a) a person has been treated under regulation 55(1) of the Jobseeker's Allowance Regulations 1996 as capable of work or as not having limited capability for work for a certain period; and

(b) these Regulations apply to that person with effect from a day ("the relevant day") within that period,

the person is to be treated for the part of that period that begins with the relevant day as capable of work or as not having limited capability for work.

(7) Where paragraph (6) applies to a person and the conditions in paragraph (1)(a) to (c) are fulfilled in relation to that person on any day within the part of a period referred to in paragraph (6), the requirement of paragraph (1) to treat the person as capable of work or as not having limited capability for work is to be regarded as satisfied with respect to the fulfilment of those conditions on that day.

(8) For the purposes of paragraph (3), where paragraph (6) applies to a person, paragraph (3) is to apply to the person as though the preceding provisions of this regulation had applied to the person with respect to the person having been treated for a period, under regulation 55(1) of the Jobseeker's Allowance Regulations 1996 and paragraph (6), as capable of work or as not having limited capability for work.".

(4) Where this article applies, the 1995 Act is to be read as though, in

section 5 of the 1995 Act, the reference to a jobseeker's allowance in subsection (1) and the first reference to a jobseeker's allowance in subsection (2) included a reference to a contribution-based jobseeker's allowance.

(5) For the purposes of this article, "joint-claim couple" has the meaning given in section 1(4) of the 1995 Act.".

<small>DEFINITIONS</small>

"the Act"–art. 2(1).
"the 1995 Act"–*ibid.*
"appointed day"–*ibid.*
"contribution-based jobseeker's allowance"–*ibid.*
"contributory employment and support allowance"–*ibid.*
"jobseeker's allowance"–*ibid.*
"joint-claim couple"–*ibid.*
"new style JSA award"–*ibid.*
"the No.9 Order"–*ibid.*
"old style JSA award"–*ibid.*

Transition from new style JSA to old style JSA

11.-(1) Paragraph (2) applies in relation to a case where—   **3.201**
  (a) (i) a person makes, or is treated as making, a claim for a jobseeker's allowance (whether or not as a member of a joint-claim couple);
    (ii) the 1995 Act, as it has effect apart from the provisions of Part 1 of Schedule 14 to the Act that remove references to an income-based jobseeker's allowance, applies in relation to the claim; and
    (iii) the claim is made or treated as made on or after 1st July 2013; or
  (b) (i) a person has a new style JSA award and article 6(2) of the No.9 Order applies in relation to the award (which award therefore continues as an old style JSA award); and
    (ii) the first day on which the person in question is entitled to a jobseeker's allowance under the old style JSA award occurs on or after 1st July 2013.

(2) Where this paragraph applies, for article 13 of the No.9 Order substitute—

"Transition from new style JSA

    13.-(1) This article applies where a person—
        (a) makes, or is treated as making, a claim for a jobseeker's allowance (whether or not as a member of a joint-claim couple) and the 1995 Act, as it has effect apart from the provisions of Part 1 of Schedule 14 to the Act that remove references to an income-based jobseeker's allowance, applies in relation to the claim; or
        (b) has a new style JSA award and article 6(2) applies in relation to the award such that it continues as an old style JSA award,
    and, in the case of sub-paragraph (a), the condition referred to in paragraph (2) is satisfied.
    (2) the condition is that the person previously—
        (a) made, or was treated as having made, a claim for a jobseeker's allowance and, under article 4, the 1995 Act, as amended

by the provisions of Part 1 of Schedule 14 to the Act that remove references to an income-based jobseeker's allowance, applied in relation to the claim; or

(b) (i) had an old style JSA award immediately before the appointed day in relation to a case of a claim for universal credit referred to in article 4(2)(a) to (d) (and any award made in respect of the claim), or an award of universal credit referred to in article 4(2)(e) or (f); and

(ii) the old style JSA award consisted of or included a contributory employment and support allowance (which allowance therefore continued as a new style JSA award).

(3) Where this article applies, the JSA Regulations 1996 are to be read as if—

(a) in regulation 14A (victims of domestic violence), for the purposes of paragraph (3)(b) of that regulation, a person had been treated as available for employment on a day (under paragraph (2) of that regulation) where regulation 15 of the JSA Regulations 2013 applied to that person on that day;

(b) in regulation 46 (waiting days)—

(i) where a person was entitled to a new style JSA award with effect from the first day of a jobseeking period by virtue of regulation 36(1) of the JSA Regulations 2013 and, with effect from the second or third day of that period, that award continued as an old style JSA award in the circumstances referred to in paragraph (1)(b) of this article, the reference to a jobseeker's allowance in paragraph (1)(a) included a reference to the new style JSA award; and

(ii) the second reference to a jobseeker's allowance in paragraph (1)(d) included a reference to a new style JSA award;

(c) in regulation 47 (jobseeking period)—

(i) the jobseeking period in relation to a claimant included any period that, under regulation 37 of the JSA Regulations 2013 (jobseeking period) forms part of the jobseeking period for the purposes of the 1995 Act; and

(ii) in paragraph (4), the reference to any day that is to be treated as a day in respect of which the claimant was entitled to a contribution-based jobseeker's allowance included a reference to a day that, under regulation 37(3) of the JSA Regulations 2013 (jobseeking period), is to be treated as a day in respect of which the claimant was entitled to a jobseeker's allowance;

(d) in regulation 50 (persons temporarily absent from Great Britain), where a person had a new style JSA award in the circumstances referred to in paragraph (1)(b) of this article, the reference in paragraph (2)(b), (3)(a) and (c), (5)(a) and (c), (6AA)(a) and (6D)(b) to entitlement to a jobseeker's allowance included a reference to the new style JSA award; and

(e) in regulation 55 (short periods of sickness), after paragraph (5) there were inserted—

"(6) Where—

(a) a person has been treated under regulation 46(1) of the Jobseeker's Allowance Regulations 2013 as capable of work or as not having limited capability for work for a certain period; and

(b) these Regulations apply to that person with effect from a day ("the relevant day") within that period,

the person is to be treated for the part of that period that begins with the relevant day as capable of work or as not having limited capability for work.

(7) Where paragraph (6) applies to a person and the conditions in paragraph (1)(a) to (c) are fulfilled in relation to that person on any day within the part of a period referred to in paragraph (6), the requirement of paragraph (1) to treat the person as capable of work or as not having limited capability for work is to be regarded as satisfied with respect to the fulfilment of those conditions on that day.

(8) For the purposes of paragraph (3), where paragraph (6) applies to a person, paragraph (3) is to apply to the person as though the preceding provisions of this regulation had applied to the person with respect to the person having been treated for a period, under regulation 46(1) of the Jobseeker's Allowance Regulations 2013 and paragraph (6), as capable of work or as not having limited capability for work.".

(4) Where this article applies, the 1995 Act is to be read as though, in section 5 of the 1995 Act, the reference to a contribution-based jobseeker's allowance in subsection (1) and the first reference to a contribution-based jobseeker's allowance in subsection (2) included a reference to a new style JSA award.

(5) For the purposes of this article, "joint-claim couple" has the meaning given in section 1(4) of the 1995 Act.".

DEFINITIONS

"the Act"–art. 2(1).
"the 1995 Act"–*ibid.*
"appointed day"–*ibid.*
"contribution-based jobseeker's allowance"–*ibid.*
"contributory employment and support allowance"–*ibid.*
"jobseeker's allowance"–*ibid.*
"joint-claim couple"–*ibid.*
"new style JSA award"–*ibid.*
"the No.9 Order"–*ibid.*
"old style JSA award"–*ibid.*

Article 2(1)

SCHEDULE

PART I

THE NO.2 RELEVANT DISTRICTS

1. WN1 1 and WN1 2.
2. WN2 1 to WN2 5.
3. WN3 0.

3.202

4. WN3 4 to WN3 6.
5. WN5 0.
6. WN5 6 to WN5 9.
7. WN6 0.
8. WN6 7 to WN6 9.

PART I

THE NO.3 RELEVANT DISTRICTS

3.203
1. M35 0 to M35 4.
2. M35 6 and M35 7.
3. M35 9.
4. OL1 0 to OL1 6.
5. OL1 8 and OL1 9.
6. OL2 1.
7. OL2 3 to OL2 9.
8. OL3 1.
9. OL3 5 to OL3 7.
10. OL3 9.
11. OL4 0 to OL4 5.
12. OL8 and OL9.
13. WA1 and WA2.
14. WA3 4 to WA3 7.
15. WA4 and WA5.
16. WA13 0.
17. WA13 9.

The Welfare Reform Act 2012 (Commencement No.13 and Transitional and Transitory Provisions) Order 2013

(SI 2013/2657) (C.103) (AS AMENDED)

The Secretary of State, in exercise of the powers conferred by section 150(3) and (4)(a), (b)(i) and (c) of the Welfare Reform Act 2012, makes the following Order:

ARRANGEMENT OF ARTICLES

GENERAL NOTE

This Commencement Order ("the Commencement No.13 Order") extended   **3.204**
the universal credit scheme to certain postcode districts in West London
(Hammersmith), Manchester and Wigan ("the No.4 relevant districts") as from
October 28, 2013. In addition, of course, the claimant had initially to fall within the
Pathfinder Group, i.e. be a person who met the requirements of regs.5 to 12 of the
Transitional Provisions Regulations 2013, and now meets the gateway conditions in
Sch.5 to the Commencement No.9 Order.

Citation

1. This Order may be cited as the Welfare Reform Act 2012   **3.205**
(Commencement No.13 and Transitional and Transitory Provisions) Order
2013.

Interpretation

2. (1) In this Order—   **3.206**
"the Act" means the Welfare Reform Act 2012;
"the amending provisions" means the provisions referred to in article
    4(1)(a) to (c) of the No.9 Order (day appointed for the abolition of
    income-related employment and support allowance and income-based
    jobseeker's allowance);
[¹ ... [² . ...] ... [² . . .] . . .]
[⁴ "claimant"—
(a) in relation to an employment and support allowance, has the same
    meaning as in Part 1 of the Welfare Reform Act 2007, save as men-
    tioned in article 5(1A) of the No.9 Order as applied by article 4(7);
(b) in relation to a jobseeker's allowance, has the same meaning as in
    the Jobseekers Act 1995 (as it applies apart from the amendments
    made by Part 1 of Schedule 14 to the Act that remove references to
    an income-based jobseeker's allowance), save as mentioned in article
    5(1A) of the No.9 Order as applied by article 4(7);
(c) in relation to universal credit, has the same meaning as in Part 1 of
    the Act;]
"employment and support allowance" means an employment and support
    allowance under Part 1 of the Welfare Reform Act 2007;
[¹ "First-tier Tribunal" has the same meaning as in the Social Security
    Act 1998;
[² [³ "gateway conditions" means the conditions specified in Schedule 5
    to the No.9 Order]]]
[² "jobseeker's allowance" means a jobseeker's allowance under the
    Jobseekers Act 1995;]
""joint claimants" in relation to universal credit, has the same meaning
    as in Part 1 of the Act;"
"No.4 relevant districts" means the postcode part-districts specified in
    the Schedule;
"the No.9 Order" means the Welfare Reform Act 2012 (Commencement
    No.9 and Transitional and Transitory Provisions and Commencement
    No.8 and Savings and Transitional Provisions (Amendment)) Order
    2013.
[² "single claimant", in relation to universal credit, has the same meaning
    as in Part 1 of the Act;]

[¹ "Upper Tribunal" has the same meaning as in the Social Security Act 1998.]

[¹ (2) For the purposes of this Order, the Universal Credit, Personal Independence Payment, Jobseeker's Allowance and Employment and Support Allowance (Claims and Payments) Regulations 2013 apply for the purpose of deciding—

(a) whether a claim for universal credit is made; and

(b) the date on which such a claim is made.]

[² (3) [³ . . .]

(4) [³ . . .]]

AMENDMENTS

1. Welfare Reform Act 2012 (Commencement No.9, 11, 13, 14 and 16 and Transitional and Transitory Provisions (Amendment)) Order 2014 (SI 2014/1452) art.19(2) (June 16, 2014).

2. Welfare Reform Act 2012 (Commencement No.9, 11, 13 14, 16 and 17 and Transitional and Transitory Provisions (Amendment)) Order 2014 (SI 2014/1661) art.6(1)(a) and 6(3) (June 30, 2014).

3. Welfare Reform Act 2012 (Commencement No.9, 11, 13, 14, 16 and 17 and Transitional and Transitory Provisions (Amendment) (No.2)) Order 2014 (SI 2014/1923) art.7(2) (July 28, 2014).

4. Welfare Reform Act 2012 (Commencement No.9, 11, 13 14, 16, 17 and 19 and Transitional and Transitory Provisions (Amendment)) Order 2014 (SI 2014/3067) art.6(3) (November 24, 2014).

Day appointed for commencement of the universal credit provisions in Part 1 of the Act

3.207

3. (1) The day appointed for the coming into force of the provisions of the Act listed in Schedule 2 to the No.9 Order, in so far as they are not already in force, in relation to the case of a claim referred to in paragraph (2), and any award that is made in respect of the claim, is the day appointed in accordance with paragraph (3).

[¹(2) The claims referred to are—

(a) a claim for universal credit where, on the date on which the claim is made, the claimant resides in one of the No.4 relevant districts and meets the gateway conditions; and

[²(b) a claim for universal credit where—

(i) in the case of a single claimant, the claimant gives incorrect information regarding the claimant residing in a No.4 relevant district or meeting the gateway conditions and the claimant does not reside in such a district or does not meet the gateway conditions on the date on which the claim is made;

(ii) in the case of joint claimants, either or both of the joint claimants gives or give incorrect information regarding his or her (or their) residing in such a district or meeting the gateway conditions and one or both of them does not or do not reside in such a district or does not or do not meet those conditions on the date on which the claim is made; and

(iii) after a decision is made that the single claimant is, or the joint claimants are, entitled to universal credit and one or more payments have been made in respect of the single claimant or the joint claimants, the Secretary of State discovers that incorrect information has been given regarding residence or meeting the gateway conditions.]]

(3) The day appointed in relation to the case of a claim referred to in paragraph (2), and any award that is made in respect of the claim, is the first day of the period in respect of which the claim is made [² . . .].

(4) [¹. . .]

(5) Article 3(6) of the No.9 Order applies for the purposes of paragraph (3) as it applies for the purposes of article 3(4)(a) of the No.9 Order.

[¹ [² [³ (6) Article 3A of the No.9 Order applies in connection with a claim for universal credit where a single claimant, or, as the case may be, either or both of joint claimants, gives incorrect information regarding his or her (or their) residing in a No.4 relevant district or meeting the gateway conditions, as it applies in connection with the giving of incorrect information regarding a claimant residing in a relevant district (as defined in the No.9 Order) or meeting the gateway conditions.]]]

AMENDMENTS

1. Welfare Reform Act 2012 (Commencement No.9, 11, 13, 14 and 16 and Transitional and Transitory Provisions (Amendment)) Order 2014 (SI 2014/1452) art.19(3) (June 16, 2014).

2. Welfare Reform Act 2012 (Commencement No.9, 11, 13 14, 16 and 17 and Transitional and Transitory Provisions (Amendment)) Order 2014 (SI 2014/1661) art.6(1)(b) and 6(4) (June 30, 2014).

3. Welfare Reform Act 2012 (Commencement No.9, 11, 13, 14, 16 and 17 and Transitional and Transitory Provisions (Amendment) (No.2)) Order 2014 (SI 2014/1923) art.7(3) (July 28, 2014).

DEFINITIONS

"the Act"–art. 2(1).
"the No.4 relevant districts"–*ibid.*
"the No.9 Order"–*ibid.*

GENERAL NOTE

Para. (1)

This brings into force provisions relating to universal credit in Part 1 of the WRA 2012, as set out in Sch.2 to the Commencement No.9 Order, in so far as they are not already in force, in relation to the further categories of case set out in para.(2). **3.208**

Para. (2) (a)

This covers the making of a claim for universal credit on or after October 28, 2013, in respect of a period that begins on or after that date, where a person lives in a "No.4 relevant district" at the time that the claim is made. The "No.4 relevant districts" are those Manchester, Wigan but principally West London postcodes (the latter mainly dealt with by Hammersmith Jobcentre) set out in the Schedule. The other conditions for making a claim for universal credit, originally known as the "Pathfinder Group conditions", were set out in regs.5-12 of the Transitional Provisions Regulations 2013, and are now called "gateway conditions" (see Sch. 5 to the Commencement No.9 Order). **3.209**

Para. (2) (b)

This relates to the making of a claim for universal credit on or after October 28, 2013 in respect of a period that begins on or after that date but provides incorrect information as to their residence in a No.4 relevant district or meeting the gateway conditions. Such a claim remains within the universal credit regime despite the error. **3.210**

Para. (3)

3.211   The day appointed for the commencement of the universal credit provisions in the above cases is the first day of the period in respect of which the claim is made.

Para. (5)

3.212   Article 3(6) of the Commencement No.9 Order deals with the situation where there is an extension of time for making a claim.

Para. (6)

3.213   Article 3A of the Commencement No.9 Order makes consequential provision for cases where incorrect information has been given.

Day appointed for the abolition of income-related employment and support allow ance and income-based jobseeker's allowance

3.214   [¹ 4. (1) The day appointed for the coming into force of the amending provisions, in relation to the case of a claim referred to in paragraph (2) and any award that is made in respect of the claim, is the day appointed in accordance with paragraph (3).

(2) The claims referred to are—

(a) a claim for universal credit, an employment and support allowance or a jobseeker's allowance where, on the date on which the claim is made [³ or treated as made], the claimant—

  (i) resides in one of the No.4 relevant districts; and

  (ii) meets the gateway conditions;

[²(b) a claim for universal credit where—

  (i) in the case of a single claimant, the claimant gives incorrect information regarding the claimant residing in a No.4 relevant district or meeting the gateway conditions and does not reside in such a district or does not meet the gateway conditions on the date on which the claim is made;

  (ii) in the case of joint claimants, either or both of the joint claimants gives or give incorrect information regarding his or her (or their) residing in such a district or meeting those conditions and one or both of them does not or do not reside in such a district or does not or do not meet those conditions on the date on which the claim is made; and

  (iii) after a decision is made that the single claimant is, or the joint claimants are, entitled to universal credit and one or more payments have been made in respect of the single claimant or the joint claimants, the Secretary of State discovers that incorrect information has been given regarding residence or meeting the gateway conditions;

[³(c) a claim for an employment and support allowance or a jobseeker's allowance other than one referred to in sub-paragraph (a) that is made or treated as made during the relevant period by a single claimant of universal credit or by either of two joint claimants of universal credit who has or have made a claim for universal credit within sub-paragraph (a) or (b).]]

(3) The day appointed in relation to the case of a claim referred to in paragraph (2), and any award that is made in respect of the claim, is the first day of the period in respect of which the claim is made.

(4) For the purposes of paragraph (2)(c), "relevant period" means, in relation to a claim for universal credit referred to in paragraph (2)(a) or (b),

any UC claim period, and any period subsequent to any UC claim period in respect of which the claimant is entitled to an award of universal credit in respect of the claim.

(5) For the purposes of paragraph (4), a "UC claim period" is a period when—

(a) a claim for universal credit as referred to in paragraph (2)(a) [², (b)(i) or (ii)] has been made but a decision has not yet been made on the claim; or

(b) a decision has been made that the claimant is not entitled to universal credit and—

    (i) the Secretary of State is considering whether to revise that decision under section 9 of the Social Security Act 1998, whether on an application made for that purpose, or on the Secretary of State's own initiative; or

    (ii) the claimant has appealed against that decision to the First-tier Tribunal and that appeal or any subsequent appeal to the Upper Tribunal or to a court has not been finally determined.

(6) Paragraphs [⁵ (6) to (9)] of article 4 of the No.9 Order apply in relation to the case of a claim for universal credit referred to in paragraph (2) (and any award that is made in respect of the claim) as they apply in relation to the case of a claim for universal credit referred to in sub-paragraphs (a) and (b) of article 4(2) of the No.9 Order (and any award that is made in respect of the claim).

[² [³ . . .]] [⁴ (7) Paragraphs (1) to (1B) of article 5 of the No.9 Order apply for the purposes of paragraph (2)(a) as they apply for the purposes of article 4(2)(a) of the No.9 Order.]

(8) Paragraphs (5) to (7) of article 5 of the No.9 Order apply for the purposes of sub-paragraphs (a) and (c) of paragraph (2) as they apply for the purposes of sub-paragraphs (a) and (g) of article 4(2) of the No.9 Order.

(9) Article 5(8) of the No.9 Order applies for the purposes of paragraph (3) as it applies for the purposes of article 4(3)(a) of the No.9 Order.]

AMENDMENTS

1. Welfare Reform Act 2012 (Commencement No.9, 11, 13, 14 and 16 and Transitional and Transitory Provisions (Amendment)) Order 2014 (SI 2014/1452) art.19(4) (June 16, 2014).

2. Welfare Reform Act 2012 (Commencement No.9, 11, 13 14, 16 and 17 and Transitional and Transitory Provisions (Amendment)) Order 2014 (SI 2014/1661) art.6(5) (June 30, 2014).

3. Welfare Reform Act 2012 (Commencement No.9, 11, 13, 14, 16 and 17 and Transitional and Transitory Provisions (Amendment) (No.2)) Order 2014 (SI 2014/1923) art.7(4) (July 28, 2014).

4. Welfare Reform Act 2012 (Commencement No.9, 11, 13 14, 16, 17 and 19 and Transitional and Transitory Provisions (Amendment)) Order 2014 (SI 2014/3067) art.6(4) (November 24, 2014).

5. Welfare Reform Act 2012 (Commencement No.9, 11, 13, 14, 16, 17 and 19 and Transitional and Transitory Provisions (Amendment)) Order 2015 (SI 2015/32) art.9 (January 26, 2015).

DEFINITIONS

"the amending provisions"–art. 2(1)
"employment and support allowance"–*ibid.*
"jobseeker's allowance"–*ibid.*

"the No.4 relevant districts"–*ibid.*
"the No.9 Order"–*ibid.*
"a person who . . . falls within the Pathfinder Group"–art. 2(2).

GENERAL NOTE

Para. (1)

3.215 This brings into force provisions relating to the abolition of income-related ESA and of income-based JSA where the case falls within one of the categories set out in para.(2) (see also the incorporation by reference of other provisions as made by paras.(6)-(9) below).

Para. (2) (a)

3.216 This provides that the new provisions come into force in relation to a claim for (and any subsequent award of) universal credit, ESA or JSA, where a person makes such a claim on or after October 28, 2013 for a period that begins on or after that date and, at the time that the claim is made, the claimant both lives in a No.4 relevant district (see Schedule) and meets the Pathfinder Group conditions (now the gateway conditions).

Para. (2) (b)

3.217 This provides that the new provisions come into force in relation to a claim for (and any subsequent award of) universal credit where a person claims universal credit, again on or after October 28, 2013 for a period that begins on or after that date, but provides incorrect information as to either their residence in a No.4 relevant district (see Schedule) or as to their meeting the Pathfinder Group or gateway conditions. As with reg.3(2)(b), such a claim remains within the universal credit regime despite the error.

Para. (2) (c)

3.218 This covers universal credit claimants who make an ESA or JSA claim and are not otherwise covered by art.4(2)(a). See further art.4(4) and (5).

Para. (3)

3.219 The day appointed for the coming into force of the amending provisions in the above cases is the first day of the period in respect of which the claim is made or treated as made.

Para. (7)

3.220 Article 5(1) of the Commencement No.9 Order provides that the Claims and Payments Regulations 1987 determine whether and when a claim for ESA or JSA is made or is treated as made.

Amendment of the No.9 Order

3.221 5. With effect from 29th October 2013—
(a) in article 11(2)(f)(ii) of the No.9 Order, for "paragraph (2)(b)(iii)" substitute "paragraph (4)(c)"; and
(b) in article 5 of the Welfare Reform Act 2012 (Commencement No.11 and Transitional and Transitory Provisions and Commencement No.9 and Transitional and Transitory Provisions (Amendment)) Order 2013(1), the reference to article 11 of the No.9 Order is a reference to article 11 as amended by paragraph (a).

GENERAL NOTE

This article makes a minor amendment to the Commencement No.9 Order **3.222** (which is noted in the statutory text above) and makes a consequential clarification of the effect of a provision in the Commencement No.11 Order.

Application of the No.9 Order

6. [¹ Articles] 9 to 22 of the No.9 Order apply in connection with the **3.223** coming into force of the amending provisions in relation to the case of a claim referred to in article 4(2), and any award made in respect of the claim, as they apply in connection with the coming into force of the amending provisions in relation to the case of a claim referred to in [² sub-paragraphs (a), (b) and (g) of article 4(2)] of the No.9 Order and any award made in respect of the claim.

AMENDMENTS

1. Welfare Reform Act 2012 (Commencement No.9, 11, 13, 14 and 16 and Transitional and Transitory Provisions (Amendment)) Order 2014 (SI 2014/1452) art.19(5) (June 16, 2014).
2. Welfare Reform Act 2012 (Commencement No.9, 11, 13 14, 16 and 17 and Transitional and Transitory Provisions (Amendment)) Order 2014 (SI 2014/1661) art.6(6) (June 30, 2014).

DEFINITION

"the amending provisions"–art. 2(1).

GENERAL NOTE

This is in the same terms as art.5 of the Commencement No.11 Order. **3.224**

Article 2(1)

SCHEDULE

THE NO. 4 RELEVANT DISTRICTS

1. M35 5.
2. W6 0.
3. W6 6 to W6 9.
4. W14 0.
5. W14 4.
6. W14 8 and W14 9.
7. WN1 3.

The Welfare Reform Act 2012 (Commencement No.14 and Transitional and Transitory Provisions) Order 2013

SI 2013/2846 (C.114) (AS AMENDED)

The Secretary of State, in exercise of the powers conferred by section 150(3) and (4)(a), (b)(i) and (c) of the Welfare Reform Act 2012, makes the following Order:

543

GENERAL NOTE

3.225   This Commencement Order ("the Commencement No.14 Order") extended the universal credit scheme to certain postcode districts in Rugby, Inverness and Perth ("the No.5 relevant districts") as from November 25, 2013. In addition, of course, the claimant must fall within the Pathfinder Group, i.e. be a person who meets the requirements of regs.5 to 12 of the Transitional Provisions Regulations 2013, now the "gateway conditions" (see Sch.5 to the Commencement No.9 Order).

Citation

3.226   1. This Order may be cited as the Welfare Reform Act 2012 (Commencement No.14 and Transitional and Transitory Provisions) Order 2013.

Interpretation

3.227   2. (1) In this Order—
"the Act" means the Welfare Reform Act 2012;
"the amending provisions" means the provisions referred to in article 4(1)(a) to (c) of the No.9 Order (day appointed for the abolition of income-related employment and support allowance and income-based jobseeker's allowance);
[¹ ... [² · ...] ... [² ...] ...]
[⁴ "claimant"—
(a) in relation to an employment and support allowance, has the same meaning as in Part 1 of the Welfare Reform Act 2007, save as mentioned in article 5(1A) of the No.9 Order as applied by article 4(7);
(b) in relation to a jobseeker's allowance, has the same meaning as in the Jobseekers Act 1995 (as it applies apart from the amendments made by Part 1 of Schedule 14 to the Act that remove references to an income-based jobseeker's allowance), save as mentioned in article 5(1A) of the No.9 Order as applied by article 4(7);
(c) in relation to universal credit, has the same meaning as in Part 1 of the Act;]
"employment and support allowance" means an employment and support allowance under Part 1 of the Welfare Reform Act 2007;
[¹ "First-tier Tribunal" has the same meaning as in the Social Security Act 1998;
[² [³ "gateway conditions" means the conditions specified in Schedule 5 to the No.9 Order";]]
"jobseeker's allowance" means a jobseeker's allowance under the Jobseekers Act 1995;

[² "joint claimants" in relation to universal credit, has the same meaning as in Part 1 of the Act;]

"No.5 relevant districts" means the postcode part-districts specified in the Schedule;

"the No.9 Order" means the Welfare Reform Act 2012 (Commencement No.9 and Transitional and Transitory Provisions and Commencement No.8 and Savings and Transitional Provisions (Amendment)) Order 2013.

[² "single claimant", in relation to universal credit, has the same meaning as in Part 1 of the Act;]

[¹ "Upper Tribunal" has the same meaning as in the Social Security Act 1998.]

[¹ (2) For the purposes of this Order, the Universal Credit, Personal Independence Payment, Jobseeker's Allowance and Employment and Support Allowance (Claims and Payments) Regulations 2013 apply for the purpose of deciding—

(a) whether a claim for universal credit is made; and

(b) the date on which such a claim is made.]

[² (3) [³ . . .]]

AMENDMENTS

1. Welfare Reform Act 2012 (Commencement No.9, 11, 13, 14 and 16 and Transitional and Transitory Provisions (Amendment)) Order 2014 (SI 2014/1452) art.20(2) (June 16, 2014).

2. Welfare Reform Act 2012 (Commencement No.9, 11, 13 14, 16 and 17 and Transitional and Transitory Provisions (Amendment)) Order 2014 (SI 2014/1661) art.7(1)(a) and 7(3) (June 30, 2014).

3. Welfare Reform Act 2012 (Commencement No.9, 11, 13, 14, 16 and 17 and Transitional and Transitory Provisions (Amendment) (No.2)) Order 2014 (SI 2014/1923) art.8(2) (July 28, 2014).

4. Welfare Reform Act 2012 (Commencement No.9, 11, 13 14, 16, 17 and 19 and Transitional and Transitory Provisions (Amendment)) Order 2014 (SI 2014/3067) art.6(3) (November 24, 2014).

Day appointed for commencement of the universal credit provisions in Part 1 of the Act

3. (1) The day appointed for the coming into force of the provisions of the Act listed in Schedule 2 to the No.9 Order, in so far as they are not already in force, in relation to the case of a claim referred to in paragraph (2), and any award that is made in respect of the claim, is the day appointed in accordance with paragraph (3).   **3.228**

[¹ (2) The claims referred to are—

(a) a claim for universal credit where, on the date on which the claim is made, the claimant resides in one of the No.5 relevant districts and meets the gateway conditions; and

[²(b) a claim for universal credit where—

(i) in the case of a single claimant, the claimant gives incorrect information regarding the claimant residing in a No.5 relevant district or meeting the gateway conditions and the claimant does not reside in such a district or does not meet the gateway conditions on the date on which the claim is made;

      (ii) in the case of joint claimants, either or both of the joint claim-ants gives or give incorrect information regarding his or her (or their) residing in such a district or meeting the gateway condi-tions and one or both of them does not or do not reside in such a district or does not or do not meet those conditions on the date on which the claim is made; and

      (iii) after a decision is made that the single claimant is, or the joint claimants are, entitled to universal credit and one or more pay-ments have been made in respect of the single claimant or the joint claimants, the Secretary of State discovers that incorrect information has been given regarding residence or meeting the gateway conditions.]]

(3) The day appointed in relation to the case of a claim referred to in paragraph (2), and any award that is made in respect of the claim, is the first day of the period in respect of which the claim is made [² . . .].

(4) [¹ . . .]

(5) Article 3(6) of the No.9 Order applies for the purposes of paragraph (3) as it applies for the purposes of article 3(4)(a) of the No.9 Order.

[¹ [² [³ (6) Article 3A of the No.9 Order applies in connection with a claim for universal credit where a single claimant, or, as the case may be, either or both of joint claimants, gives incorrect information regarding his or her (or their) residing in a No.5 relevant district or meeting the gateway conditions, as it applies in connection with the giving of incorrect informa-tion regarding a claimant residing in a relevant district (as defined in the No.9 Order) or meeting the gateway conditions.]]]

AMENDMENTS

1. Welfare Reform Act 2012 (Commencement No.9, 11, 13, 14 and 16 and Transitional and Transitory Provisions (Amendment)) Order 2014 (SI 2014/1452) art.20(3) (June 16, 2014).

2. Welfare Reform Act 2012 (Commencement No.9, 11, 13 14, 16 and 17 and Transitional and Transitory Provisions (Amendment)) Order 2014 (SI 2014/1661) art.7(1)(b) and 7(4) (June 30, 2014).

3. Welfare Reform Act 2012 (Commencement No.9, 11, 13, 14, 16 and 17 and Transitional and Transitory Provisions (Amendment) (No.2)) Order 2014 (SI 2014/1923) art.8(3) (July 28, 2014).

DEFINITIONS

    "the Act"–art. 2(1).
    "the No.5 relevant districts"–*ibid.*
    "the No.9 Order"–*ibid.*

GENERAL NOTE

Para. (1)

3.229   This brought into force provisions relating to universal credit in Part 1 of the WRA 2012, as set out in Sch.2 to the Commencement No.9 Order, in so far as they were not already in force, in relation to the further categories of case set out in para. (2).

Para. (2)(a)

3.230   This covers the making of a claim for universal credit on or after November 25, 2013, in respect of a period that begins on or after that date, where a person lives in a "No.5 relevant district" at the time that the claim is made. The "No.5

relevant districts" are those postcodes in Rugby, Inverness and Perth set out in the Schedule. The other conditions for making a claim for universal credit, previously known as the "Pathfinder Group conditions", as set out in the Transitional Provisions Regulations 2013 are now the "gateway conditions" (see Sch.5 to the Commencement No.9 Order).

Para. (2) (b)

This relates to the making of a claim for universal credit on or after November 25, 2013 in respect of a period that also begins on or after that date but where the claimant provides incorrect information as to their residence in a No.5 relevant district or meeting the gateway conditions. Such a claim remains within the universal credit regime despite the error.   **3.231**

Para. (3)

The day appointed for the commencement of the universal credit provisions in the above cases is the first day of the period in respect of which the claim is made.   **3.232**

Para. (5)

Article 3(6) of the Commencement No.9 Order deals with the situation where there is an extension of time for making a claim.

Para. (6)

Article 3A of the Commencement No.9 Order makes consequential provision for cases where a claimant gives incorrect information about either their area of residence or meeting the gateway conditions.   **3.233**

Day appointed for the abolition of income-related employment and support allowance and income-based jobseeker's allowance

[¹ **4.** (1) The day appointed for the coming into force of the amending provisions, in relation to the case of a claim referred to in paragraph (2) and any award that is made in respect of the claim, is the day appointed in accordance with paragraph (3).   **3.234**

(2) The claims referred to are—

  (a) a claim for universal credit, an employment and support allowance or a jobseeker's allowance where, on the date on which the claim is made [³ or treated as made], the claimant—

    (i) resides in one of the No.5 relevant districts; and

    (ii) meets the gateway conditions;

[²(b) a claim for universal credit where—

    (i) in the case of a single claimant, the claimant gives incorrect information regarding the claimant residing in a No.5 relevant district or meeting the gateway conditions and does not reside in such a district or does not meet the gateway conditions on the date on which the claim is made;

    (ii) in the case of joint claimants, either or both of the joint claimants gives or give incorrect information regarding his or her (or their) residing in such a district or meeting those conditions and one or both of them does not or do not reside in such a district or does not or do not meet those conditions on the date on which the claim is made; and

    (iii) after a decision is made that the single claimant is, or the joint claimants are, entitled to universal credit and one or more payments have been made in respect of the single claimant or the joint claimants, the Secretary of State discovers that incorrect information has been given regarding residence or meeting the gateway conditions;

[³(c) a claim for an employment and support allowance or a jobseeker's allowance other than one referred to in sub-paragraph (a) that is made or treated as made during the relevant period by a single claimant of universal credit or by either of two joint claimants of universal credit who has or have made a claim for universal credit within sub-paragraph (a) or (b).]]

(3) The day appointed in relation to the case of a claim referred to in paragraph (2), and any award that is made in respect of the claim, is the first day of the period in respect of which the claim is made.

(4) For the purposes of paragraph (2)(c), "relevant period" means, in relation to a claim for universal credit referred to in paragraph (2)(a) or (b), any UC claim period, and any period subsequent to any UC claim period in respect of which the claimant is entitled to an award of universal credit in respect of the claim.

(5) For the purposes of paragraph (4), a "UC claim period" is a period when—

(a) a claim for universal credit as referred to in paragraph (2)(a) or [² (b) (i) or (ii)] has been made but a decision has not yet been made on the claim; or

(b) a decision has been made that the claimant is not entitled to universal credit and—

(i) the Secretary of State is considering whether to revise that decision under section 9 of the Social Security Act 1998, whether on an application made for that purpose, or on the Secretary of State's own initiative; or

(ii) the claimant has appealed against that decision to the First-tier Tribunal and that appeal or any subsequent appeal to the Upper Tribunal or to a court has not been finally determined.

(6) Paragraphs [⁵ (6) to (9)] of article 4 of the No.9 Order apply in relation to the case of a claim for universal credit referred to in paragraph (2) (and any award that is made in respect of the claim) as they apply in relation to the case of a claim for universal credit referred to in sub-paragraphs (a) and (b) of article 4(2) of the No.9 Order (and any award that is made in respect of the claim).

[² [³ ...]] [⁴ (7) Paragraphs (1) to (1B) of article 5 of the No.9 Order apply for the purposes of paragraph (2)(a) as they apply for the purposes of article 4(2)(a) of the No.9 Order.]

(8) Paragraphs (5) to (7) of article 5 of the No.9 Order apply for the purposes of sub-paragraphs (a) and (c) of paragraph (2) as they apply for the purposes of sub-paragraphs (a) and (g) of article 4(2) of the No.9 Order.

(9) Article 5(8) of the No.9 Order applies for the purposes of paragraph (3) as it applies for the purposes of article 4(3)(a) of the No.9 Order.]

Amendments

1. Welfare Reform Act 2012 (Commencement No.9, 11, 13, 14 and 16 and Transitional and Transitory Provisions (Amendment)) Order 2014 (SI 2014/1452) art.20(4) (June 16, 2014).

2. Welfare Reform Act 2012 (Commencement No.9, 11, 13 14, 16 and 17 and

Transitional and Transitory Provisions (Amendment)) Order 2014 (SI 2014/1661) art.7(5) (June 30, 2014).

3. Welfare Reform Act 2012 (Commencement No.9, 11, 13, 14, 16 and 17 and Transitional and Transitory Provisions (Amendment) (No.2)) Order 2014 (SI 2014/1923) art.8(4) (July 28, 2014).

4. Welfare Reform Act 2012 (Commencement No.9, 11, 13 14, 16, 17 and 19 and Transitional and Transitory Provisions (Amendment)) Order 2014 (SI 2014/3067) art.6(4) (November 24, 2014).

5. Welfare Reform Act 2012 (Commencement No.9,11, 13, 14, 16, 17 and 19 and Transitional and Transitory Provisions (Amendment)) Order 2015 (SI 2015/32) art.9 (January 26, 2015).

DEFINITIONS

"the amending provisions"–art. 2(1).
"employment and support allowance"–*ibid.*
"jobseeker's allowance"–*ibid.*
"the No.4 relevant districts"–*ibid.*
"the No.9 Order"–*ibid.*
"a person who . . . falls within the Pathfinder Group" –art. 2(2).

GENERAL NOTE

Para. (1)

This brought into force provisions relating to the abolition of income-related ESA   **3.235** and of income-based JSA where the case fell within one of the categories set out in para.(2) (see also the incorporation by reference of other provisions as made by paras.(6)-(9) below).

Para. (2) (a)

This provides that the new provisions come into force in relation to a claim for   **3.236** (and any subsequent award of) universal credit, ESA or JSA, where a person makes such a claim on or after November 25, 2013 for a period that begins on or after that date and, at the time that the claim is made, the claimant both lives in a No.5 relevant district (see Schedule) and meets the Pathfinder Group (now gateway) conditions.

Para. (2) (b)

This provides that the new provisions come into force in relation to a claim for   **3.237** (and any subsequent award of) universal credit where a person claims universal credit, again on or after November 25, 2013 for a period that begins on or after that date, but provides incorrect information as to either their residence in a No.5 relevant district (see Schedule) or as to their meeting the Pathfinder Group or gateway conditions. As with reg.3(2)(b), such a claim remains within the universal credit regime despite the error.

Para. (3)

The day appointed for the coming into force of the amending provisions in the   **3.238** above cases is the first day of the period in respect of which the claim is made.

Para. (7)

Article 5(1) of the Commencement No.9 Order provides that the Claims and   **3.239** Payments Regulations 1987 determine whether and when a claim for employment and support allowance or jobseeker's allowance is made or is treated as made.

Application of the No.9 Order

3.240   5. [¹Articles] 9 to 22 of the No.9 Order apply in connection with the coming into force of the amending provisions in relation to the case of a claim referred to in article 4(2), and any award made in respect of the claim, as they apply in connection with the coming into force of the amending provisions in relation to the case of a claim referred to in [² sub-paragraphs (a), (b) and (g) of article 4(2)] of the No.9 Order and any award made in respect of the claim.

AMENDMENTS

1. Welfare Reform Act 2012 (Commencement No.9, 11, 13, 14 and 16 and Transitional and Transitory Provisions (Amendment)) Order 2014 (SI 2014/1452) art.20(5) (June 16, 2014).
2. Welfare Reform Act 2012 (Commencement No.9, 11, 13 14, 16 and 17 and Transitional and Transitory Provisions (Amendment)) Order 2014 (SI 2014/1661) art.7(6) (June 30, 2014).

DEFINITION

"the amending provisions"–art. 2(1).

GENERAL NOTE

3.241   This provision is in the same terms as art.5 of the Commencement No.11 Order.

Article 2(1)

SCHEDULE

THE NO. 5 RELEVANT DISTRICTS

3.242   1. CV21 1 to CV21 4.
2. CV21 9.
3. CV22 5 to CV22 7.
4. IV1 1.
5. IV1 3.
6. IV1 9.
7. IV2 3 to IV2 7.
8. IV3 5.
9. IV3 8.
10. IV4 7.
11. IV5 7.
12. IV8 8.
13. IV9 8.
14. IV10 8.
15. IV11 8.
16. IV12 4 and IV12 5.
17. IV12 9.
18. IV13 7.
19. IV21 2.
20. IV22 2.
21. IV26 2.
22. IV54 8.
23. IV63 6 and IV63 7.
24. PH19 1.
25. PH20 1.
26. PH21 1.

27. PH22 1.
28. PH23 3.
29. PH24 3.
30. PH25 3.
31. PH26 3.
32. PH26 9.
33. PH32 4.

The Welfare Reform Act 2012 (Commencement No.16 and Transitional and Transitory Provisions) Order 2014

SI 2014/209 (C. 7) (AS AMENDED)

The Secretary of State, in exercise of the powers conferred by section 150(3) and (4)(a), (b)(i) and (c) of the Welfare Reform Act 2012, makes the following Order:

ARRANGEMENT OF ARTICLES

GENERAL NOTE

This Commencement Order ("the Commencement No.16 Order") extended the universal credit scheme to certain postcode districts in Bath and Harrogate ("the No.6 relevant districts") as from February 24, 2014 and to others in Shotton ("the No.7 relevant districts") as from April 7, 2014. In addition, of course, the claimant had to fall within the Pathfinder Group, i.e. be a person who meets the requirements of regs.5 to 12 of the Transitional Provisions Regulations 2013, now the "gateway conditions" (see Sch.5 to the Commencement No.9 Order).   **3.243**

Citation

1. This Order may be cited as the Welfare Reform Act 2012 (Commencement No.16 and Transitional and Transitory Provisions) Order 2014.   **3.244**

Interpretation

2. (1) In this Order—   **3.245**
"the Act" means the Welfare Reform Act 2012;
"the amending provisions" means the provisions referred to in article 4(1)(a) to (c) of the No.9 Order (day appointed for the abolition of

income-related employment and support allowance and income-based jobseeker's allowance);

[¹ ... [² · ...] ... [² ...] ...]

[⁴ "claimant"—

(a) in relation to an employment and support allowance, has the same meaning as in Part 1 of the Welfare Reform Act 2007, save as mentioned in article 5(1A) of the No.9 Order as applied by article 4(7);

(b) in relation to a jobseeker's allowance, has the same meaning as in the Jobseekers Act 1995 (as it applies apart from the amendments made by Part 1 of Schedule 14 to the Act that remove references to an income-based jobseeker's allowance), save as mentioned in article 5(1A) of the No.9 Order as applied by article 4(7);

(c) in relation to universal credit, has the same meaning as in Part 1 of the Act;]

"employment and support allowance" means an employment and support allowance under Part 1 of the Welfare Reform Act 2007;

[¹ "First-tier Tribunal" has the same meaning as in the Social Security Act 1998;

[² [³ "gateway conditions" means the conditions specified in Schedule 5 to the No.9 Order;]]]

"jobseeker's allowance" means a jobseeker's allowance under the Jobseekers Act 1995;

[² "joint claimants" in relation to universal credit, has the same meaning as in Part 1 of the Act;]

"No.6 relevant districts" means the postcode part-districts specified in Part 1 of the Schedule;

"No.7 relevant districts" means the postcode part-districts specified in Part 2 of the Schedule;

"the No.9 Order" means the Welfare Reform Act 2012 (Commencement No.9 and Transitional and Transitory Provisions and Commencement No.8 and Savings and Transitional Provisions (Amendment)) Order 2013;

[² "single claimant", in relation to universal credit, has the same meaning as in Part 1 of the Act;]

[¹ "Upper Tribunal" has the same meaning as in the Social Security Act 1998.]

[¹ (2) For the purposes of this Order, the Universal Credit, Personal Independence Payment, Jobseeker's Allowance and Employment and Support Allowance (Claims and Payments) Regulations 2013 apply for the purpose of deciding—

(a) whether a claim for universal credit is made; and

(b) the date on which such a claim is made.]

[² (3) [³ ...]]

AMENDMENTS

1. Welfare Reform Act 2012 (Commencement No.9, 11, 13, 14 and 16 and Transitional and Transitory Provisions (Amendment)) Order 2014 (SI 2014/1452) art.21(2) (June 16, 2014).

2. Welfare Reform Act 2012 (Commencement No.9, 11, 13 14, 16 and 17 and Transitional and Transitory Provisions (Amendment)) Order 2014 (SI 2014/1661) art.8(1)(a) and 8(3) (June 30, 2014).

3. Welfare Reform Act 2012 (Commencement No.9, 11, 13, 14, 16 and 17 and Transitional and Transitory Provisions (Amendment) (No.2)) Order 2014 (SI 2014/1923) art.9(2) (July 28, 2014).

4. Welfare Reform Act 2012 (Commencement No.9, 11, 13 14, 16, 17 and 19 and Transitional and Transitory Provisions (Amendment)) Order 2014 (SI 2014/3067) art.6(3) (November 24, 2014).

Day appointed for the coming into force of the universal credit provisions in Part 1 of the Act

3. (1) The day appointed for the coming into force of the provisions of the Act listed in Schedule 2 to the No.9 Order, in so far as they are not already in force, in relation to the case of a claim referred to in paragraph (2), and any award that is made in respect of the claim, is the day appointed in accordance with paragraph (3).   3.246

[¹ (2) The claims referred to are—

(a) a claim for universal credit where, on the date on which the claim is made or treated as made, the claimant resides in one of the No.6 or No.7 relevant districts and meets the gateway conditions; and

[²(b) a claim for universal credit where—

    (i) in the case of a single claimant, the claimant gives incorrect information regarding the claimant residing in a No.6 or a No.7 relevant district or meeting the gateway conditions and the claimant does not reside in such a district or does not meet the gateway conditions on the date on which the claim is made;

    (ii) in the case of joint claimants, either or both of the joint claimants gives or give incorrect information regarding his or her (or their) residing in such a district or meeting the gateway conditions and one or both of them does not or do not reside in such a district or does not or do not meet those conditions on the date on which the claim is made; and

    (iii) after a decision is made that the single claimant is, or the joint claimants are, entitled to universal credit and one or more payments have been made in respect of the single claimant or the joint claimants, the Secretary of State discovers that incorrect information has been given regarding residence or meeting the gateway conditions.]]

(3) The day appointed in relation to the case of a claim referred to in paragraph (2), and any award that is made in respect of the claim, is the first day of the period in respect of which the claim is made [² . . .].

(4) [¹ . . .]

(5) Article 3(6) of the No.9 Order applies for the purposes of paragraph (3) as it applies for the purposes of article 3(4)(a) of the No.9 Order.

[¹ [² [³ (6) Article 3A of the No.9 Order applies in connection with a claim for universal credit where a single claimant, or, as the case may be, either or both of joint claimants, gives incorrect information regarding his or her (or their) residing in a No.6 or a No.7 relevant district or meeting the gateway conditions, as it applies in connection with the giving of incorrect information regarding a claimant residing in a relevant district (as defined in the No.9 Order) or meeting the gateway conditions.]]]

AMENDMENTS

1. Welfare Reform Act 2012 (Commencement No.9, 11, 13, 14 and 16 and Transitional and Transitory Provisions (Amendment)) Order 2014 (SI 2014/1452) art.21(3) (June 16, 2014).

2. Welfare Reform Act 2012 (Commencement No.9, 11, 13 14, 16 and 17 and Transitional and Transitory Provisions (Amendment)) Order 2014 (SI 2014/1661) art.8(1)(b) and 8(4) (June 30, 2014).

3. Welfare Reform Act 2012 (Commencement No.9, 11, 13, 14, 16 and 17 and Transitional and Transitory Provisions (Amendment) (No.2)) Order 2014 (SI 2014/1923) art.8(3) (July 28, 2014).

DEFINITIONS

"claimant"–see art.2(1).
"gateway conditions"–*ibid.*
"joint claimant"–*ibid.*
"single claimant"–*ibid.*
"No.6 relevant districts"–*ibid.*
"No.7 relevant districts"–*ibid.*
"No.9 Order"–*ibid.*

GENERAL NOTE

3.247   See by analogy the General Note to art.3 of the Commencement No.14 Order.

Day appointed for the abolition of income-related employment and support allowance and income-based jobseeker's allowance

3.248   [¹ 4. (1) The day appointed for the coming into force of the amending provisions, in relation to the case of a claim referred to in paragraph (2) and any award that is made in respect of the claim, is the day appointed in accordance with paragraph (3).

(2) The claims referred to are—

(a) a claim for universal credit, an employment and support allowance or a jobseeker's allowance where, on the date on which the claim is made [³ or treated as made], the claimant—

  (i) resides in one of the No.6 or No.7 relevant districts; and
  (ii) meets the gateway conditions;

[²(b) a claim for universal credit where—

  (i) in the case of a single claimant, the claimant gives incorrect information regarding the claimant residing in a No.6 or a No.7 relevant district or meeting the gateway conditions and does not reside in such a district or does not meet the gateway conditions on the date on which the claim is made;

  (ii) in the case of joint claimants, either or both of the joint claimants gives or give incorrect information regarding his or her (or their) residing in such a district or meeting those conditions and one or both of them does not or do not reside in such a district or does not or do not meet those conditions on the date on which the claim is made; and

  (iii) after a decision is made that the single claimant is, or the joint claimants are, entitled to universal credit and one or more payments have been made in respect of the single claimant or the joint claimants, the Secretary of State discovers that incorrect information has been given regarding residence or meeting the gateway conditions;

[³(c) a claim for an employment and support allowance or a jobseeker's allowance other than one referred to in sub-paragraph (a) that is made or treated as made during the relevant period by a single claimant of universal credit or by either of two joint claimants of universal credit who has or have made a claim for universal credit within sub-paragraph (a) or (b).]]

(3) The day appointed in relation to the case of a claim referred to in paragraph (2), and any award that is made in respect of the claim, is the first day of the period in respect of which the claim is made.

(4) For the purposes of paragraph (2)(c), "relevant period" means, in relation to a claim for universal credit referred to in paragraph (2)(a) or (b), any UC claim period, and any period subsequent to any UC claim period in respect of which the claimant is entitled to an award of universal credit in respect of the claim.

(5) For the purposes of paragraph (4), a "UC claim period" is a period when—

(a) a claim for universal credit as referred to in paragraph (2)(a) [², (b)(i) or (ii)] has been made but a decision has not yet been made on the claim; or

(b) a decision has been made that the claimant is not entitled to universal credit and—

    (i) the Secretary of State is considering whether to revise that decision under section 9 of the Social Security Act 1998, whether on an application made for that purpose, or on the Secretary of State's own initiative; or

    (ii) the claimant has appealed against that decision to the First-tier Tribunal and that appeal or any subsequent appeal to the Upper Tribunal or to a court has not been finally determined.

(6) Paragraphs [⁵ (6) to (9)] of article 4 of the No.9 Order apply in relation to the case of a claim for universal credit referred to in paragraph (2) (and any award that is made in respect of the claim) as they apply in relation to the case of a claim for universal credit referred to in sub-paragraphs (a) and (b) of article 4(2) of the No.9 Order (and any award that is made in respect of the claim).

[² [³ . . .]] [⁴ (7) Paragraphs (1) to (1B) of article 5 of the No.9 Order apply for the purposes of paragraph (2)(a) as they apply for the purposes of article 4(2)(a) of the No.9 Order.]

(8) Paragraphs (5) to (7) of article 5 of the No.9 Order apply for the purposes of sub-paragraphs (a) and (c) of paragraph (2) as they apply for the purposes of paragraphs (a) and (g) of article 4(2) of the No.9 Order.

(9) Article 5(8) of the No.9 Order applies for the purposes of paragraph (3) as it applies for the purposes of article 4(3)(a) of the No.9 Order.]

AMENDMENTS

1. Welfare Reform Act 2012 (Commencement No.9, 11, 13, 14 and 16 and Transitional and Transitory Provisions (Amendment)) Order 2014 (SI 2014/1452) art.21(4) (June 16, 2014).

2. Welfare Reform Act 2012 (Commencement No.9, 11, 13 14, 16 and 17 and Transitional and Transitory Provisions (Amendment)) Order 2014 (SI 2014/1661) art.8(5) (June 30, 2014).

3. Welfare Reform Act 2012 (Commencement No.9, 11, 13, 14, 16 and 17 and Transitional and Transitory Provisions (Amendment) (No.2)) Order 2014 (SI 2014/1923) art.9(4) (July 28, 2014).

4. Welfare Reform Act 2012 (Commencement No.9, 11, 13 14, 16, 17 and 19 and Transitional and Transitory Provisions (Amendment)) Order 2014 (SI 2014/3067) art.6(4) (November 24, 2014).

5. Welfare Reform Act 2012 (Commencement No.9, 11, 13, 14, 16, 17 and 19 and Transitional and Transitory Provisions (Amendment)) Order 2015 (SI 2015/32) art.9 (January 26, 2015).

DEFINITIONS

"the amending provisions"–see art.2(1).
"claimant"–*ibid*.
"employment and support allowance"–*ibid*.
"First-tier Tribunal"–*ibid*.
"gateway conditions"–*ibid*.
"jobseeker's allowance"–*ibid*.
"joint claimant"–*ibid*.
"single claimant"–*ibid*.
"No.6 relevant districts"–*ibid*.
"No.7 relevant districts"–*ibid*.
"No.9 Order"–*ibid*.
"relevant period"–para.(4).
"UC claim period"–para.(5).
"Upper Tribunal"–see art.2(1).

GENERAL NOTE

3.249   See by analogy the General Note to art.4 of the Commencement No.14 Order.

Application of the No.9 Order

3.250   **5.** [¹ Articles] 9 to 22 of the No.9 Order apply in connection with the coming into force of the amending provisions in relation to the case of a claim referred to in article 4(2), and any award made in respect of the claim, as they apply in connection with the coming into force of the amending provisions in relation to the case of a claim referred to in [² sub-paragraphs (a), (b) and (g) of article 4(2)] of the No.9 Order and any award made in respect of the claim.

AMENDMENTS

1. Welfare Reform Act 2012 (Commencement No.9, 11, 13, 14 and 16 and Transitional and Transitory Provisions (Amendment)) Order 2014 (SI 2014/1452) art.21(5) (June 16, 2014).

2. Welfare Reform Act 2012 (Commencement No.9, 11, 13 14, 16 and 17 and Transitional and Transitory Provisions (Amendment)) Order 2014 (SI 2014/1661) art.8(6) (June 30, 2014).

DEFINITIONS

"the amending provisions"–see art.2(1).
"No.9 Order"–*ibid*.

GENERAL NOTE

3.251   See by analogy the General Note to art.5 of the Commencement No.11 Order.

Day appointed for the coming into force of section 139 of the Act

6. [*omitted as not relevant to this Volume*].   **3.252**

Article 2(1)

SCHEDULE 1

PART 1

THE NO.6 RELEVANT DISTRICTS

1. BA1 0 to BA1 7.   **3.253**
2. BA2 0 to BA2 6.
3. BA2 9.
4. BA3 2 and BA3 3.
5. BA3 9.
6. BS31 1.
7. BS31 3.
8. BS31 9.
9. BS39 4 and BS39 5.
10. BS39 7.
11. HG1 1 to HG1 5.
12. HG1 9.
13. HG2 0.
14. HG2 7 to HG2 9.
15. HG3 1 to HG3 4.
16. HG4 1 to HG4 3.
17. HG4 9.
18. HG5 0.
19. HG5 5.
20. HG5 8 and HG5 9.
21. LS17 0.
22. YO51 9.

PART 2

THE NO.7 RELEVANT DISTRICTS

1. CH5 1 to CH5 4.   **3.254**
2. CH5 9.

The Welfare Reform Act 2012 (Commencement No.9, 11, 13, 14 and 16 and Transitional and Transitory Provisions (Amendment)) Order 2014

(SI 2014/1452) (C.56)

The Secretary of State, in exercise of the powers conferred by section 150(3) and (4)(a), (b)(i) and (c) of the Welfare Reform Act 2012(1), makes the following Order:

Arrangement of Articles

Part 1

Citation, Interpretation And Application

Part 2

Amendment Of The No.9 Order

Part 3

Amendment Of The No.11, 13, 14 And 16 Orders

GENERAL NOTE

This volume includes here only Part 1 of this Order; this is because the myriad of   3.255
amendments made to the Commencement No.9 Order in Part 2 of this Order and
to other previous Commencement Orders (Nos.11, 13, 14 and 16 respectively) in
Part 3 are incorporated above in the text of the relevant Order.

Part 1 comprises just three articles. Articles 1 and 2 deal with citation and interpretation respectively. Article 3 sets out the types of cases for which amendments are
made to the existing Orders. The principal category of case (see art.3(1)(a)) is where
a claim is made on or after June 16, 2014 for universal credit, ESA or JSA and, on
the date on which the claim is made, the claimant resides in one of the "specified
districts" (on which see art.3(8)).

At the same time the Transitional Provisions Regulations 2013 were revoked and
replaced by the Transitional Provisions Regulations 2014. The "Pathfinder Group"
conditions that were formerly contained in regs.5 to 12 of the Transitional Provisions
Regulations 2013 were omitted from the Transitional Provisions Regulations 2014.
However, similar conditions appear in Sch.5 to the Commencement No.9 Order as
inserted by art.16 this Order (known as the "gateway conditions").

PART 1

CITATION, INTERPRETATION AND APPLICATION

Citation

1. This Order may be cited as the Welfare Reform Act 2012   3.256
(Commencement No.9, 11, 13, 14 and 16 and Transitional and Transitory
Provisions (Amendment)) Order 2014.

Interpretation

2.—(1) In this Order—   3.257
"the Act" means the Welfare Reform Act 2012;
"the 1995 Act" means the Jobseekers Act 1995;
"the 2007 Act" means the Welfare Reform Act 2007   ;
"the amending provisions" means the provisions referred to in article
    4(1)(a) to (c) of the No.9 Order, as inserted by article 6 of this
    Order;
"claimant", in relation to an employment and support allowance or a job-
    seeker's allowance, has the same meaning as in Part 1 of the 2007 Act
    and the 1995 Act (as it applies apart from the amendments made by
    Part 1 of Schedule 14 to the Act that remove references to an income-
    based jobseeker's allowance) respectively and, in relation to universal
    credit, has the same meaning as in Part 1 of the Act;
"the Claims and Payments Regulations 1987" means the Social Security
    (Claims and Payments) Regulations 1987;
"the Claims and Payments Regulations 2013" means the Universal

Credit, Personal Independence Payment, Jobseeker's Allowance and Employment and Support Allowance (Claims and Payments) Regulations 2013;

"employment and support allowance" means an employment and support allowance under Part 1 of the 2007 Act;

"First-tier Tribunal" has the same meaning as in the Social Security Act 1998;

"income-based jobseeker's allowance" means an income-based jobseeker's allowance under the 1995 Act;

"income-related employment and support allowance" means an income-related allowance under Part 1 of the 2007 Act;

"jobseeker's allowance" means a jobseeker's allowance under the 1995 Act;

"joint claimant" in relation to universal credit, has the same meaning as in Part 1 of the Act;

"new style ESA award" means an award of an employment and support allowance under Part 1 of the 2007 Act as amended by the provisions of Schedule 3, and Part 1 of Schedule 14, to the Act that remove references to an income-related allowance;

"new style JSA award" means an award of a jobseeker's allowance under the 1995 Act as amended by the provisions of Part 1 of Schedule 14 to the Act that remove references to an income-based allowance;

"the No.9 Order" means the Welfare Reform Act 2012 (Commencement No.9 and Transitional and Transitory Provisions and Commencement No.8 and Savings and Transitional Provisions (Amendment)) Order 2013;

"the No.11 Order" means the Welfare Reform Act 2012 (Commencement No.11 and Transitional and Transitory Provisions and Commencement No.9 and Transitional and Transitory Provisions (Amendment)) Order 2013;

"the No.13 Order" means the Welfare Reform Act 2012 (Commencement No.13 and Transitional and Transitory Provisions) Order 2013;

"the No.14 Order" means the Welfare Reform Act 2012 (Commencement No.14 and Transitional and Transitory Provisions) Order 2013;

"the No.16 Order" means the Welfare Reform Act 2012 (Commencement No.16 and Transitional and Transitory Provisions) Order 2014;

"relevant districts", "No.2 relevant districts", "No.3 relevant districts", "No.4 relevant districts", "No.5 relevant districts", "No.6 relevant districts" and "No.7 relevant districts" have the respective meanings given in the No.9 Order, the No.11 Order (with respect to the No.2 and No.3 relevant districts), the No.13 Order (with respect to the No.4 relevant districts), the No.14 Order (with respect to the No.5 relevant districts) and the No.16 Order (with respect to the No.6 and No.7 relevant districts);

"single claimant", in relation to universal credit, has the same meaning as in Part 1 of the Act;

"Upper Tribunal" has the same meaning as in the Social Security Act 1998.

(2) For the purposes of this Order—

(a) the Claims and Payments Regulations 2013 apply for the purpose of deciding—

(i) whether a claim for universal credit is made; and

(ii) the date on which the claim is made or is to be treated as made; and

(b) where a couple is treated, in accordance with regulation 9(8) of the Claims and Payments Regulations 2013, as making a claim for universal credit, references to the date on which the claim is treated as made are to the date of formation of the couple.

Amendment of the No.9, 11, 13, 14 and 16 Orders: cases to which the amendments apply

3.—(1) This article applies in relation to a case where—

3.258

(a) a claim is made for universal credit, an employment and support allowance or a jobseeker's allowance and, on the date on which the claim is made, the claimant resides in one of the specified districts;

(b) a claim for universal credit is made where—

    (i) the claimant gives incorrect information regarding the claimant residing in a specified district and does not reside in such a district on the date on which the claim is made; and

    (ii) after a decision is made that the claimant is entitled to universal credit and one or more payments have been made in respect of the claimant, the Secretary of State discovers that incorrect information regarding residence has been given;

(c) a claim for universal credit is treated as made by a couple in the circumstances referred to in regulation 9(8) of the Claims and Payments Regulations 2013 (claims for universal credit by members of a couple);

(d) a claim for universal credit is made by a former member of a couple who is not exempt from the requirement to make a claim by virtue of regulation 9(6) of the Claims and Payments Regulations 2013 (claims for universal credit by members of a couple), whether or not the claim is made jointly with another person, where the claim is made during the period of one month starting with the date on which notification is given to the Secretary of State that the claimants have ceased to be a couple;

(e) an award of universal credit is made without a claim in the circumstances referred to in regulation 6(1) or (2) of the Claims and Payments Regulations 2013 (claims not required for entitlement to universal credit in some cases); or

(f) an award of universal credit is made without a claim in the circumstances referred to in regulation 9(6), (7) or (10) of the Claims and Payments Regulations 2013 (claims for universal credit by members of a couple),

and the claim is made or treated as made, or, as the case may be, the award is made without a claim, on or after 16th June 2014.

(2) This article also applies in relation to a case where a claim for an employment and support allowance or a jobseeker's allowance, that does not fall within paragraph (1)(a), is made—

(a) during the relevant period by a single claimant of universal credit or, in the case of joint claimants of universal credit, by either of the joint claimants, where the single claimant has made or the joint claimants have made, or been treated as having made, a claim for universal credit within paragraph (1)(a) to (d);

561

(b) during the relevant period by a single claimant of universal credit or, in the case of joint claimants of universal credit, by either of the joint claimants, where the single claimant has been awarded, or the joint claimants have been awarded, universal credit without a claim within paragraph (1)(e) or (f);

(c) by a person who is entitled to make a claim for universal credit in the circumstances referred to in paragraph (1)(d) but has not yet done so; or

(d) by a person who may be entitled to an award of universal credit in the circumstances referred to in paragraph (1)(e) or (f) but where no decision has yet been made as to the person's entitlement.

(3) For the purposes of paragraph (2), "relevant period" means—

(a) in relation to a claim for universal credit within paragraph (1)(a) to (d), any UC claim period, and any period subsequent to any UC claim period in respect of which the single claimant or the joint claimants is or are entitled to an award of universal credit in respect of the claim;

(b) in relation to an award of universal credit within paragraph (1)(e) or (f), any period when the single claimant or the joint claimants to whom the award was made is or are entitled to the award.

(4) For the purposes of paragraph (3)(a), a "UC claim period" is a period when—

(a) a claim for universal credit within paragraph (1)(a), (b)(i) or (d) has been made but a decision has not yet been made on the claim;

(b) a claim for universal credit within paragraph (1)(c) has been treated as made and no decision has yet been made as to the joint claimants' entitlement; or

(c) a decision has been made that a single claimant or joint claimants is or are not entitled to universal credit and—

   (i) the Secretary of State is considering whether to revise that decision under section 9 of the Social Security Act 1998, whether on an application made for that purpose, or on the Secretary of State's own initiative; or

   (ii) the single claimant or the joint claimants has or have appealed against that decision to the First-tier Tribunal and that appeal or any subsequent appeal to the Upper Tribunal or to a court has not been finally determined.

(5) Subject to paragraph (6), for the purposes of paragraphs (1)(a) and (2), the Claims and Payments Regulations 1987 apply for the purpose of deciding—

(a) whether a claim for an employment and support allowance or a jobseeker's allowance is made; and

(b) the date on which the claim is made or is to be treated as made.

(6) For the purposes of paragraph (2)—

(a) a person makes a claim for an employment and support allowance or a jobseeker's allowance if they take any action which results in a decision on a claim being required under the Claims and Payments Regulations 1987; and

(b) except as provided in paragraph (7), it is irrelevant that the effect of any provision of the Claims and Payments Regulations 1987 is that, for the purposes of those Regulations, the claim is not made or treated as made during the relevant period or at a time referred to in paragraph (2)(c) or (d).

(7) The following provisions of the Claims and Payments Regulations 1987 apply for the purpose of deciding whether or not a claim for an employment and support allowance or a jobseeker's allowance is made or is to be treated as made during the relevant period or at a time referred to in paragraph (2)(c) or (d)—

(a) regulation 6(1F)(b) or (c); and

(b) regulation 6(4ZA) to (4ZD) and (4A)(a)(i) and (b).

(8) For the purposes of this article, "specified districts" means the relevant districts, No.2 relevant districts, No.3 relevant districts, No.4 relevant districts, No.5 relevant districts, No.6 relevant districts and No.7 relevant districts.

DEFINITIONS

"claimant"–see art.2(1).
"the Claims and Payments Regulations 1987"–*ibid.*
"the Claims and Payments Regulations 2013" –*ibid.*
"employment and support allowance"–*ibid.*
"First-tier Tribunal"–*ibid.*
"jobseeker's allowance"–*ibid.*
"joint claimant"–*ibid.*
"relevant districts"–*ibid.*
"relevant period"–para.(3).
"single claimant"–see art.2(1).
"specified districts"–para.(8).
"UC claim period"–para.(4).
"Upper Tribunal"–see art.2(1).

PART 2

AMENDMENT OF THE NO.9 ORDER

4.–16. [*These amendments are incorporated in the text of the Commencement No.9 Order above*].   3.259

PART 3

AMENDMENT OF THE NO.11, 13, 14 AND 16 ORDERS

17.–21. [*These amendments are incorporated in the text of the Commencement No.11, 13, 14 and 16 Orders above*].   3.260

The Welfare Reform Act 2012 (Commencement No.17 and Transitional and Transitory Provisions) Order 2014

SI 2014/1583 (C. 61) (AS AMENDED)

The Secretary of State, in exercise of the powers conferred by sections 150(3) and (4)(a), (b)(i) and (c) of the Welfare Reform Act 2012, makes the following Order:

ARRANGEMENT OF ARTICLES

1. Citation
2. Interpretation
3. Day appointed for commencement of the universal credit provisions in Part 1 of the Act
4. Day appointed for the abolition of income-related employment and support allowance and income-based jobseeker's allowance
5. Application of the No.9 Order

Schedule: Postcode Districts and part-districts

GENERAL NOTE

3.261   This Commencement Order ("the Commencement No.17 Order") extended the universal credit scheme to certain postcode districts and as from various dates in areas known as the No.8, No.9, No.10, No.11, No.12 and No.13 relevant districts (see Schedule). All the scheduled postcode districts are in the North West. "The No.8 relevant districts" are in Hyde, Stalybridge, Stretford and Altrincham (as from June 23, 2014). "The No.9 relevant districts" are in Southport, Crosby, Bootle, Bolton (Great Moor Street; Blackhorse Street) and Farnworth (as from June 30, 2014). "The No.10 relevant districts" are in the Wirral (as from July 7, 2014). "The No.11 relevant districts" are in Bolton, Bury and Preston (as from July 14, 2014). "The No.12 relevant districts" are in Liverpool, Greater Manchester and Warrington (as from July 21, 2014). "The No.13 relevant districts" are in Chester, Crewe, Stockport and Warrington (as from July 28, 2014). In addition, of course, the claimant had to fall within the Pathfinder Group, i.e. be a person who meets the requirements of regs.5 to 12 of the Transitional Provisions Regulations 2013, now the "gateway conditions" (see Sch.5 to the Commencement No.9 Order).

For an example of an Upper Tribunal appeal involving a case subject to this Commencement Order, see *AM v SSWP (UC)* [2017] UKUT 131 (and especially paragraphs 12–14).

Citation

3.262   **1.** This Order may be cited as the Welfare Reform Act 2012 (Commencement No.17 and Transitional and Transitory Provisions) Order 2014.

Interpretation

3.263   **2.** (1) In this Order—

"the Act" means the Welfare Reform Act 2012;

"the amending provisions" means the provisions referred to in article 4(1)(a) to (c) of the No.9 Order (day appointed for the abolition of income-related employment and support allowance and income-based jobseeker's allowance);

[¹...] [³ "claimant"—

(a) in relation to an employment and support allowance, has the same meaning as in Part 1 of the Welfare Reform Act 2007, save as mentioned in article 5(1A) of the No.9 Order as applied by article 4(7);

(b) in relation to a jobseeker's allowance, has the same meaning as in the Jobseekers Act 1995 (as it applies apart from the amendments made by Part 1 of Schedule 14 to the Act that remove references to an income-based jobseeker's allowance), save as mentioned in article 5(1A) of the No.9 Order as applied by article 4(7);

(c) in relation to universal credit, has the same meaning as in Part 1 of the Act;]

"employment and support allowance" means an employment and support allowance under Part 1 of the Welfare Reform Act 2007;

"First-tier Tribunal" has the same meaning as in the Social Security Act 1998;

[³ [⁴ ...] [⁵ "gateway conditions" means the conditions specified in Schedule 5 to the No.9 Order;]

"jobseeker's allowance" means a jobseeker's allowance under the Jobseekers Act 1995;

[² "joint claimants" in relation to universal credit, has the same meaning as in Part 1 of the Act;]

"the No.9 Order" means the Welfare Reform Act 2012 (Commencement No.9 and Transitional and Transitory Provisions and Commencement No.8 and Savings and Transitional Provisions (Amendment)) Order 2013;

"No.8 relevant districts" means the postcode districts and part-districts specified in Part 1 of the Schedule;

"No.9 relevant districts" means the postcode districts and part-districts specified in Part 2 of the Schedule;

"No.10 relevant districts" means the postcode districts and part-districts specified in Part 3 of the Schedule;

"No.11 relevant districts" means the postcode districts and part-districts specified in Part 4 of the Schedule;

"No.12 relevant districts" means the postcode districts and part-districts specified in Part 5 of the Schedule;

"No.13 relevant districts" means the postcode districts and part-districts specified in Part 6 of the Schedule;

[² "single claimant", in relation to universal credit, has the same meaning as in Part 1 of the Act;]

[⁴ [⁵...]]

"Upper Tribunal" has the same meaning as in the Social Security Act 1998.

(2) For the purposes of this Order, the Universal Credit, Personal Independence Payment, Jobseeker's Allowance and Employment and Support Allowance (Claims and Payments) Regulations 2013 apply for the purpose of deciding—

(a) whether a claim for universal credit is made; and

(b) the date on which such a claim is made.

[⁴ [³ (3) ...]]

AMENDMENTS

1. Welfare Reform Act 2012 (Commencement No.9, 11, 13 14, 16 and 17 and Transitional and Transitory Provisions (Amendment)) Order 2014 (SI 2014/1661) art.9 (June 30, 2014).

2. Welfare Reform Act 2012 (Commencement No.9, 11, 13, 14, 16 and 17 and Transitional and Transitory Provisions (Amendment) (No.2)) Order 2014 (SI 2014/1923) art.10(2) (July 28, 2014).

3. Welfare Reform Act 2012 (Commencement No.9, 11, 13 14, 16, 17 and 19 and Transitional and Transitory Provisions (Amendment)) Order 2014 (SI 2014/3067) art.5(a), (b) and 6(3) (November 24, 2014).

4. Welfare Reform Act 2012 (Commencement No.9, 11, 13, 14, 16, 17 and 19 and Transitional and Transitory Provisions (Amendment)) Order 2015 (SI 2015/32) art.8(1) (January 26, 2015).

5. Welfare Reform Act 2012 (Commencement No.9, 11, 13, 14, 16, 17 and 19 and Transitional and Transitory Provisions (Amendment)) Order 2015 (SI 2015/32) art.8(2) (March 2, 2015).

Day appointed for the coming into force of the universal credit provisions

3.264   **3.**(1) The day appointed for the coming into force of the provisions of the Act listed in Schedule 2 to the No.9 Order, in so far as they are not already in force, in relation to the case of a claim referred to in paragraph (2), and any award that is made in respect of the claim, is the day appointed in accordance with paragraph (3).

(2) The claims referred to are—

(a) a claim for universal credit that is made on or after 23rd June 2014 in respect of a period that begins on or after 23rd June 2014 where, on the date on which the claim is made, the claimant resides in one of the No.8 relevant districts and meets the gateway conditions;

[¹(b) a claim for universal credit that is made in respect of a period that begins on or after 23rd June 2014 where—

   (i) in the case of a single claimant, the claimant gives incorrect information regarding the claimant residing in a No.8 relevant district or meeting the gateway conditions and the claimant does not reside in such a district or does not meet the gateway conditions on the date on which the claim is made;

  (ii) in the case of joint claimants, either or both of the joint claimants gives or give incorrect information regarding his or her (or their) residing in such a district or meeting the gateway conditions and one or both of them does not or do not reside in such a district or does not or do not meet those conditions on the date on which the claim is made; and

 (iii) after a decision is made that the single claimant is, or the joint claimants are, entitled to universal credit and one or more payments have been made in respect of the single claimant or the joint claimants, the Secretary of State discovers that incorrect information has been given regarding residence or meeting the gateway conditions;]

(c) a claim for universal credit that is made on or after 30th June 2014 in respect of a period that begins on or after 30th June 2014 where, on the date on which the claim is made, the claimant resides in one of the No.9 relevant districts and meets the gateway conditions;

[¹(d) a claim for universal credit that is made in respect of a period that begins on or after 30th June 2014 where—

(i) in the case of a single claimant, the claimant gives incorrect information regarding the claimant residing in a No.9 relevant district or meeting the gateway conditions and the claimant does not reside in such a district or does not meet the gateway conditions on the date on which the claim is made;

(ii) in the case of joint claimants, either or both of the joint claimants gives or give incorrect information regarding his or her (or their) residing in such a district or meeting the gateway conditions and one or both of them does not or do not reside in such a district or does not or do not meet those conditions on the date on which the claim is made; and

(iii) after a decision is made that the single claimant is, or the joint claimants are, entitled to universal credit and one or more payments have been made in respect of the single claimant or the joint claimants, the Secretary of State discovers that incorrect information has been given regarding residence or meeting the gateway conditions;]

(e) a claim for universal credit that is made on or after 7th July 2014 in respect of a period that begins on or after 7th July 2014 where, on the date on which the claim is made, the claimant resides in one of the No.10 relevant districts and meets the gateway conditions;

[¹(f) a claim for universal credit that is made in respect of a period that begins on or after 7th July 2014 where—

(i) in the case of a single claimant, the claimant gives incorrect information regarding the claimant residing in a No.10 relevant district or meeting the gateway conditions and the claimant does not reside in such a district or does not meet the gateway conditions on the date on which the claim is made;

(ii) in the case of joint claimants, either or both of the joint claimants gives or give incorrect information regarding his or her (or their) residing in such a district or meeting the gateway conditions and one or both of them does not or do not reside in such a district or does not or do not meet those conditions on the date on which the claim is made; and

(iii) after a decision is made that the single claimant is, or the joint claimants are, entitled to universal credit and one or more payments have been made in respect of the single claimant or the joint claimants, the Secretary of State discovers that incorrect information has been given regarding residence or meeting the gateway conditions;]

(g) a claim for universal credit that is made on or after 14th July 2014 in respect of a period that begins on or after 14th July 2014 where, on the date on which the claim is made, the claimant resides in one of the No.11 relevant districts and meets the gateway conditions;

[¹(h) a claim for universal credit that is made in respect of a period that begins on or after 14th July 2014 where—

(i) in the case of a single claimant, the claimant gives incorrect information regarding the claimant residing in a No.11 relevant district or meeting the gateway conditions and the claimant does not reside in such a district or does not meet the gateway conditions on the date on which the claim is made;

(ii) in the case of joint claimants, either or both of the joint claimants gives or give incorrect information regarding his or her (or their) residing in such a district or meeting the gateway conditions and one or both of them does not or do not reside in such a district or does not or do not meet those conditions on the date on which the claim is made; and

(iii) after a decision is made that the single claimant is, or the joint claimants are, entitled to universal credit and one or more payments have been made in respect of the single claimant or the joint claimants, the Secretary of State discovers that incorrect information has been given regarding residence or meeting the gateway conditions;]

(i) a claim for universal credit that is made on or after 21st July 2014 in respect of a period that begins on or after 21st July 2014 where, on the date on which the claim is made, the claimant resides in one of the No.12 relevant districts and meets the gateway conditions;

[¹(j) a claim for universal credit that is made in respect of a period that begins on or after 21st July 2014 where—

(i) in the case of a single claimant, the claimant gives incorrect information regarding the claimant residing in a No.12 relevant district or meeting the gateway conditions and the claimant does not reside in such a district or does not meet the gateway conditions on the date on which the claim is made;

(ii) in the case of joint claimants, either or both of the joint claimants gives or give incorrect information regarding his or her (or their) residing in such a district or meeting the gateway conditions and one or both of them does not or do not reside in such a district or does not or do not meet those conditions on the date on which the claim is made; and

(iii) after a decision is made that the single claimant is, or the joint claimants are, entitled to universal credit and one or more payments have been made in respect of the single claimant or the joint claimants, the Secretary of State discovers that incorrect information has been given regarding residence or meeting the gateway conditions;]

(k) claim for universal credit that is made on or after 28th July 2014 in respect of a period that begins on or after 28th July 2014 where, on the date on which the claim is made, the claimant resides in one of the No.13 relevant districts and meets the gateway conditions;

[¹(l) a claim for universal credit that is made in respect of a period that begins on or after 28th July 2014 where—

(i) in the case of a single claimant, the claimant gives incorrect information regarding the claimant residing in a No.13 relevant district or meeting the gateway conditions and the claimant does not reside in such a district or does not meet the gateway conditions on the date on which the claim is made;

(ii) in the case of joint claimants, either or both of the joint claimants gives or give incorrect information regarding his or her (or their) residing in such a district or meeting the gateway conditions and one or both of them does not or do not reside in such a district or does not or do not meet those conditions on the date on which the claim is made; and

(iii) after a decision is made that the single claimant is, or the joint claimants are, entitled to universal credit and one or more payments have been made in respect of the single claimant or the joint claimants, the Secretary of State discovers that incorrect information has been given regarding residence or meeting the gateway conditions.]

(3) The day appointed in relation to the case of a claim referred to in paragraph (2), and any award that is made in respect of the claim, is the first day of the period in respect of which the claim is made.

(4) Article 3(6) of the No.9 Order applies for the purposes of paragraph (3) as it applies for the purposes of article 3(4)(a) of the No.9 Order.

[¹ (5) Article 3A of the No.9 Order applies in connection with a claim for universal credit where a single claimant, or, as the case may be, either or both of joint claimants, gives incorrect information regarding his or her (or their) residing in a No.8, No.9, No.10, No.11, No.12 or No.13 relevant district or meeting the gateway conditions, as it applies in connection with the giving of incorrect information regarding a claimant residing in a relevant district (as defined in the No.9 Order) or meeting the gateway conditions]

AMENDMENT

1. Welfare Reform Act 2012 (Commencement No.9, 11, 13, 14, 16 and 17 and Transitional and Transitory Provisions (Amendment) (No.2)) Order 2014 (SI 2014/1923) art.10(3) (July 28, 2014).

DEFINITIONS

"claimant"–see art.2(1).
"gateway conditions"–*ibid.*
"joint claimant"–*ibid.*
"single claimant"–*ibid.*
"No.8 relevant districts"–*ibid.*
"No.9 relevant districts"–*ibid.*
"No.10 relevant districts"–*ibid.*
"No.11 relevant districts"–*ibid.*
"No.12 relevant districts"–*ibid.*
"No.13 relevant districts"–*ibid.*
"No.9 Order"–*ibid.*

Day appointed for the abolition of income-related employment and support allowance and income-based jobseeker's allowance

4.(1) The day appointed for the coming into force of the amending provisions, in relation to the case of a claim referred to in paragraph (2), and any award that is made in respect of the claim, is the day appointed in accordance with paragraph (3).

3.265

(2) The claims referred to are—

(a) a claim for universal credit, an employment and support allowance or a jobseeker's allowance that is made [¹ or treated as made] on or after 23rd June 2014 in respect of a period that begins on or after 23rd June 2014 where, on the date on which the claim is made [¹ or treated as made], the claimant resides in one of the No.8 relevant districts and meets the gateway conditions;

[¹(b) a claim for universal credit that is made in respect of a period that begins on or after 23rd June 2014 where—

   (i) in the case of a single claimant, the claimant gives incorrect information regarding the claimant residing in a No.8 relevant district or meeting the gateway conditions and the claimant does not reside in such a district or does not meet the gateway conditions on the date on which the claim is made;

   (ii) in the case of joint claimants, either or both of the joint claimants gives or give incorrect information regarding his or her (or their) residing in such a district or meeting the gateway conditions and one or both of them does not or do not reside in such a district or does not or do not meet those conditions on the date on which the claim is made; and

   (iii) after a decision is made that the single claimant is, or the joint claimants are, entitled to universal credit and one or more payments have been made in respect of the single claimant or the joint claimants, the Secretary of State discovers that incorrect information has been given regarding residence or meeting the gateway conditions;]

(c) a claim for universal credit, an employment and support allowance or a jobseeker's allowance that is made [¹ or treated as made] on or after 30th June 2014 in respect of a period that begins on or after 30th June 2014 where, on the date on which the claim is made [¹ or treated as made], the claimant resides in one of the No.9 relevant districts and meets the gateway conditions;

[¹(d) a claim for universal credit that is made in respect of a period that begins on or after 30th June 2014 where—

   (i) in the case of a single claimant, the claimant gives incorrect information regarding the claimant residing in a No.9 relevant district or meeting the gateway conditions and the claimant does not reside in such a district or does not meet the gateway conditions on the date on which the claim is made;

   (ii) in the case of joint claimants, either or both of the joint claimants gives or give incorrect information regarding his or her (or their) residing in such a district or meeting the gateway conditions and one or both of them does not or do not reside in such a district or does not or do not meet those conditions on the date on which the claim is made; and

   (iii) after a decision is made that the single claimant is, or the joint claimants are, entitled to universal credit and one or more payments have been made in respect of the single claimant or the joint claimants, the Secretary of State discovers that incorrect information has been given regarding residence or meeting the gateway conditions;]

(e) a claim for universal credit, an employment and support allowance or a jobseeker's allowance that is made [¹ or treated as made] on or after 7th July 2014 in respect of a period that begins on or after 7th July 2014 where, on the date on which the claim is made [¹ or treated as made], the claimant resides in one of the No.10 relevant districts and meets the gateway conditions;

[¹(f) a claim for universal credit that is made in respect of a period that begins on or after 7th July 2014 where—

    (i) in the case of a single claimant, the claimant gives incorrect information regarding the claimant residing in a No.10 relevant district or meeting the gateway conditions and the claimant does not reside in such a district or does not meet the gateway conditions on the date on which the claim is made;

    (ii) in the case of joint claimants, either or both of the joint claimants gives or give incorrect information regarding his or her (or their) residing in such a district or meeting the gateway conditions and one or both of them does not or do not reside in such a district or does not or do not meet those conditions on the date on which the claim is made; and

    (iii) after a decision is made that the single claimant is, or the joint claimants are, entitled to universal credit and one or more payments have been made in respect of the single claimant or the joint claimants, the Secretary of State discovers that incorrect information has been given regarding residence or meeting the gateway conditions;]

(g) a claim for universal credit, an employment and support allowance or a jobseeker's allowance that is made [¹ or treated as made] on or after 14th July 2014 in respect of a period that begins on or after 14th July 2014 where, on the date on which the claim is made [¹ or treated as made], the claimant resides in one of the No.11 relevant districts and meets the gateway conditions;

[¹(h) a claim for universal credit that is made in respect of a period that begins on or after 14th July 2014 where—

    (i) in the case of a single claimant, the claimant gives incorrect information regarding the claimant residing in a No.11 relevant district or meeting the gateway conditions and the claimant does not reside in such a district or does not meet the gateway conditions on the date on which the claim is made;

    (ii) in the case of joint claimants, either or both of the joint claimants gives or give incorrect information regarding his or her (or their) residing in such a district or meeting the gateway conditions and one or both of them does not or do not reside in such a district or does not or do not meet those conditions on the date on which the claim is made; and

    (iii) after a decision is made that the single claimant is, or the joint claimants are, entitled to universal credit and one or more payments have been made in respect of the single claimant or the joint claimants, the Secretary of State discovers that incorrect information has been given regarding residence or meeting the gateway conditions;]

(i) a claim for universal credit, an employment and support allowance or a jobseeker's allowance that is made [¹ or treated as made] on or after 21st July 2014 in respect of a period that begins on or after 21st July 2014 where, on the date on which the claim is made [¹ or treated as made], the claimant resides in one of the No.12 relevant districts and meets the gateway conditions;

[¹(j) a claim for universal credit that is made in respect of a period that begins on or after 21st July 2014 where—

    (i) in the case of a single claimant, the claimant gives incorrect information regarding the claimant residing in a No.12 relevant district or meeting the gateway conditions and the claimant does not reside in such a district or does not meet the gateway conditions on the date on which the claim is made;

(ii) in the case of joint claimants, either or both of the joint claimants gives or give incorrect information regarding his or her (or their) residing in such a district or meeting the gateway conditions and one or both of them does not or do not reside in such a district or does not or do not meet those conditions on the date on which the claim is made; and

(iii) after a decision is made that the single claimant is, or the joint claimants are, entitled to universal credit and one or more payments have been made in respect of the single claimant or the joint claimants, the Secretary of State discovers that incorrect information has been given regarding residence or meeting the gateway conditions;]

(k) a claim for universal credit, an employment and support allowance or a jobseeker's allowance that is made [¹ or treated as made] on or after 28th July 2014 in respect of a period that begins on or after 28th July 2014 where, on the date on which the claim is made [¹ or treated as made], the claimant resides in one of the No.13 relevant districts and meets the gateway conditions;

[¹(l) a claim for universal credit that is made in respect of a period that begins on or after 28th July 2014 where—

(i) in the case of a single claimant, the claimant gives incorrect information regarding the claimant residing in a No.13 relevant district or meeting the gateway conditions and the claimant does not reside in such a district or does not meet the gateway conditions on the date on which the claim is made;

(ii) in the case of joint claimants, either or both of the joint claimants gives or give incorrect information regarding his or her (or their) residing in such a district or meeting the gateway conditions and one or both of them does not or do not reside in such a district or does not or do not meet those conditions on the date on which the claim is made; and

(iii) after a decision is made that the single claimant is, or the joint claimants are, entitled to universal credit and one or more payments have been made in respect of the single claimant or the joint claimants, the Secretary of State discovers that incorrect information has been given regarding residence or meeting the gateway conditions;]

[¹(m) a claim for an employment and support allowance or a jobseeker's allowance other than one referred to in sub-paragraph (a), (c), (e), (g), (i) or (k) that is made or treated as made during the relevant period by a single claimant of universal credit or by either of two joint claimants of universal credit who has or have made a claim for universal credit within one of sub-paragraphs (a) to (l).]

(3) The day appointed in relation to the case of a claim referred to in paragraph (2), and any award that is made in respect of the claim, is the first day of the period in respect of which the claim is made.

(4) For the purposes of paragraph (2)(m), "relevant period" means, in relation to a claim for universal credit within paragraph (2)(a) to (l), any UC claim period, and any period subsequent to any UC claim period in

respect of which the claimant is entitled to an award of universal credit in respect of the claim.

(5) For the purposes of paragraph (4), a "UC claim period" is a period when—

    (a) a claim for universal credit within paragraph [^{1} (2)(a), (b)(i) or (ii), (c), (d)(i) or (ii), (e), (f)(i) or (ii), (g), (h)(i) or (ii), (i), (j)(i) or (ii), (k) or (l)(i) or (ii)] has been made but a decision has not yet been made on the claim; or

    (b) a decision has been made that the claimant is not entitled to universal credit and—

        (i) the Secretary of State is considering whether to revise that decision under section 9 of the Social Security Act 1998, whether on an application made for that purpose, or on the Secretary of State's own initiative; or

        (ii) the claimant has appealed against that decision to the First-tier Tribunal and that appeal or any subsequent appeal to the Upper Tribunal or to a court has not been finally determined.

(6) Paragraphs [^{3} (6) to (9)] of article 4 of the No.9 Order apply in relation to a claim for universal credit referred to in paragraph (2) (and any award that is made in respect of the claim) as they apply in relation to a claim for universal credit referred to in sub-paragraphs (a) and (b) of article 4(2) of the No.9 Order (and any award that is made in respect of the claim).

[^{2} (7) Paragraphs (1) to (1B) of article 5 of the No.9 Order apply for the purposes of paragraph (2)(a), (c), (e), (g), (i) and (k) as they apply for the purposes of article 4(2)(a) of the No.9 Order.]

(8) Paragraphs (5) to (7) of article 5 of the No.9 Order apply for the purposes of sub-paragraphs (a), (c), (e), (g), (i), (k) and (m) of paragraph (2) as they apply for the purposes of sub-paragraphs (a) and (g) of article 4(2) of the No.9 Order.

(9) Article 5(8) of the No.9 Order applies for the purposes of paragraph (3) as it applies for the purposes of article 4(3)(a) of the No.9 Order.

AMENDMENTS

1. Welfare Reform Act 2012 (Commencement No.9, 11, 13, 14, 16 and 17 and Transitional and Transitory Provisions (Amendment) (No.2)) Order 2014 (SI 2014/1923) art.10(4) (July 28, 2014).

2. Welfare Reform Act 2012 (Commencement No.9, 11, 13 14, 16, 17 and 19 and Transitional and Transitory Provisions (Amendment)) Order 2014 (SI 2014/3067) art.6(5) (November 24, 2014).

3. Welfare Reform Act 2012 (Commencement No.9, 11, 13, 14, 16, 17 and 19 and Transitional and Transitory Provisions (Amendment)) Order 2015 (SI 2015/32) art.9 (January 26, 2015).

DEFINITIONS

"the amending provisions"–see art.2(1).
"claimant"–*ibid.*
"employment and support allowance"–*ibid.*
"First-tier Tribunal"–*ibid.*
"gateway conditions"–*ibid.*
"jobseeker's allowance"–*ibid.*
"joint claimant"–*ibid.*
"single claimant"–*ibid.*

"No.8 relevant districts"–*ibid.*
"No.9 relevant districts"–*ibid.*
"No.10 relevant districts"–*ibid.*
"No.11 relevant districts"–*ibid.*
"No.12 relevant districts"–*ibid.*
"No.13 relevant districts"–*ibid.*
"No.9 Order"–*ibid.*
"relevant period"–para.(4).
"UC claim period"–para.(5).
"Upper Tribunal"–see art.2(1).

Application of the No.9 Order

3.266   **5.** Articles 9 to 22 of the No.9 Order apply in connection with the coming into force of the amending provisions in relation to the case of a claim referred to in article 4(2), and any award made in respect of the claim, as they apply in connection with the coming into force of the amending provisions in relation to the case of a claim referred to in sub-paragraphs (a), (b) and (g) of article 4(2) of the No.9 Order and any award made in respect of the claim.

DEFINITIONS

"the amending provisions"–see art.2(1).
"No.9 Order"–*ibid.*

Article 2(1)

SCHEDULE

POSTCODE DISTRICTS AND PART-DISTRICTS

PART 1

THE NO.8 RELEVANT DISTRICTS

3.267   M31.
M32.
M33 2.
M33 4 to M33 7.
M34.
M41.
OL5.
SK14 1 and SK14 2.
SK14 4.
SK14 6.
SK14 9.
SK15.
WA14 1 and WA14 2.
WA14 5.
WA15 5 and WA15 6.
WA15 9.

PART 2

THE NO.9 RELEVANT DISTRICTS

3.268   BL1.
BL2.
BL3.
BL4.

BL5 1.
BL5 3.
BL6 4.
BL6 9.
L20 0.
L20 3 to L20 6.
L21.
L22.
L23.
L29.
L30.
L31 0.
L31 2 and L31 3.
L31 5 to L31 9.
L37 1 to L37 4.
L37 6 to L37 8.
L38.
M26 3.
PR8 1 and PR8 2.
PR8 6.
PR8 9.
PR9 0.
PR9 7.
PR9 9.

PART 3

THE NO.10 RELEVANT DISTRICTS

CH41.   **3.269**
CH42.
CH43.
CH44.
CH45.
CH46.
CH47.
CH48.
CH49.
CH60.
CH61.
CH62 0 to CH62 8.
CH63.

PART 4

THE NO.11 RELEVANT DISTRICTS

BL0 9.   **3.270**
BL8 1 to BL8 3.
BL8 9.
BL9 0.
BL9 5.
BL9 8 and BL9 9.
M25 1.
M25 3.
M25 9.
M26 1 and M26 2.
M26 4.
M45.
PR0.
PR1.
PR2.

PR4 4 and PR4 5.
PR5 4 and PR5 5.
PR11.
PR25 1 to PR25 3.
PR25 9.
PR26 6.

PART 5

THE NO.12 RELEVANT DISTRICTS

3.271   L10 0.
L10 2 and L10 3.
L10 6.
L10 8.
L28 3 to L28 7.
L32.
L33 0 to L33 2.
L33 5 to L33 9.
L34.
L35 0 to L35 5.
L35 7 to L35 9.
L36 0 to L36 4.
L36 6 to L36 9.
M17 1.
M17 8.
M27 0.
M27 5.
M27 8 and M27 9.
M28.
M30.
M38.
WA9.
WA10.
WA11 0.
WA11 8 and WA11 9.
WA12.

PART 6

THE NO.13 RELEVANT DISTRICTS

3.272   CH1.
CH2.
CH3.
CH4 7 and CH4 8.
CH62 9.
CW1.
CW2 6 to CW2 8.
CW3 0.
CW4.
CW5.
CW10.
CW11.
CW12 1 and CW12 2.
CW12 4.
CW12 9.
SK9.
WA 6.
WA14 3 and WA14 4.
WA16.

576

The Welfare Reform Act 2012 (Commencement No.9, 11, 13, 14, 16 and 17 and Transitional and Transitory Provisions (Amendment)) Order 2014

(SI 2014/1661) (C.69)

The Secretary of State, in exercise of the powers conferred by sections 150(3) and (4)(a), (b)(i) and (c) of the Welfare Reform Act 2012, makes the following Order:

ARRANGEMENT OF ARTICLES

GENERAL NOTE

This Commencement Order applies where claims for universal credit or for ESA or JSA were made on or after June 30, 2014, in relation to areas where claims for universal credit could already be made. It accordingly operates for the most part by way of amendments to previous Commencement Orders, which are incorporated into the relevant text above. Thus art.3 provides that that article applies where a claim for universal credit, ESA or JSA is made on or after June 30, 2014 and the claimant resides (or purports to reside) in one of the affected districts. However, art.4 of this Order amends Sch.5 to the Commencement No.9 Order (gateway conditions) where art.3 of this Order applies, making five main changes.   **3.273**

The first is that the condition that a person must not be entitled to certain benefits in order for the universal credit provisions to come into force is altered so that the list of benefits *excludes* housing benefit and a tax credit. This means that a person may claim universal credit where they are entitled to either housing benefit or a tax credit, subject to meeting the other gateway conditions in Sch.5.

Secondly, the condition that an old style ESA award or old style JSA award must not have terminated during the period of 2 weeks ending with the date on which the claim for universal credit is made is removed.

Thirdly, the condition as to the maximum income and capital that a claimant may have in order for the universal credit provisions to come into force is altered so that the claimant must declare that his or her earned income is not expected to exceed £330 during the period of one month starting with the date on which the claim for universal credit is made (previously £270 for a person aged under 25).

Fourthly, there is a new condition that a claimant must not be carrying on a trade, profession or vocation in respect of which he or she receives self-employed earnings.

Lastly, there is a new condition that the claimant must not be a company director or a member of a limited liability partnership.

Article 4 also provides that, in relation to the cases covered by art.3, any reference in the other relevant Orders to Sch.5 to the Commencement No.9 Order is to be construed as a reference to that Schedule as amended by art.4.

In addition, arts.6, 7 and 8 amend the Commencement No.13, No.14 and No.16 Orders respectively so that, for claims made with respect to certain areas where art.3 applies, the gateway conditions are treated as though the condition that a claimant must be a single person is removed. The effect is that in those cases claims for universal credit may be made by a couple as joint claimants, where both members of the couple reside in one of the relevant areas and meet the other gateway conditions. It also means that any claim for ESA or JSA by a member of a couple, where that member resides in one of the relevant areas and meet the other gateway conditions, will be a claim for new style ESA or new style JSA.

Citation

3.274   **1.** This Order may be cited as the Welfare Reform Act 2012 (Commencement No.9, 11, 13, 14, 16 and 17 and Transitional and Transitory Provisions (Amendment)) Order 2014.

Interpretation

3.275   **2.** (1) In this Order—
"the Act" means the Welfare Reform Act 2012;
"claimant", in relation to an employment and support allowance or a jobseeker's allowance, has the same meaning as in Part 1 of the Welfare Reform Act 2007 and the Jobseekers Act 1995 (as it applies apart from the amendments made by Part 1 of Schedule 14 to the Act that remove references to an income-based jobseeker's allowance) respectively and, in relation to universal credit, has the same meaning as in Part 1 of the Act;
"employment and support allowance" means an employment and support allowance under Part 1 of the Welfare Reform Act 2007;
"jobseeker's allowance" means a jobseeker's allowance under the Jobseekers Act 1995;
"joint claimants", in relation to universal credit, has the same meaning as in Part 1 of the Act;
"the No.9 Order" means the Welfare Reform Act 2012 (Commencement No.9 and Transitional and Transitory Provisions and Commencement No.8 and Savings and Transitional Provisions (Amendment)) Order 2013;
"the No.11 Order" means the Welfare Reform Act 2012 (Commencement No.11 and Transitional and Transitory Provisions and Commencement No.9 and Transitional and Transitory Provisions (Amendment)) Order 2013;
"the No.13 Order" means the Welfare Reform Act 2012 (Commencement No.13 and Transitional and Transitory Provisions) Order 2013;
"the No.14 Order" means the Welfare Reform Act 2012 (Commencement No.14 and Transitional and Transitory Provisions) Order 2013;
"the No.16 Order" means the Welfare Reform Act 2012 (Commencement No.16 and Transitional and Transitory Provisions) Order 2014;
"the No.17 Order" means the Welfare Reform Act 2012 (Commencement No.17 and Transitional and Transitory Provisions) Order 2014;
"relevant districts" has the meaning given in the No.9 Order;
"No.2 relevant districts" and "No.3 relevant districts" have the meanings given in the No.11 Order;
"No.4 relevant districts" has the meaning given in the No.13 Order;
"No.5 relevant districts" has the meaning given in the No.14 Order;

"No.6 relevant districts" and "No.7 relevant districts" have the meanings given in the No.16 Order;

"No.8 relevant districts", No.9 relevant districts", "No.10 relevant districts", "No.11 relevant districts", "No.12 relevant districts" and "No.13 relevant districts" have the meanings given in the No.17 Order;

"single claimant", in relation to universal credit, has the same meaning as in Part 1 of the Act;

"specified districts" means the relevant districts, No.2 relevant districts, No.3 relevant districts, No.4 relevant districts, No.5 relevant districts, No.6 relevant districts, No.7 relevant districts, No.8 relevant districts, No.9 relevant districts, No.10 relevant districts, No.11 relevant districts, No.12 relevant districts and No.13 relevant districts.

(2) For the purposes of this Order—

(a) the Universal Credit, Personal Independence Payment, Jobseeker's Allowance and Employment and Support Allowance (Claims and Payments) Regulations 2013 apply for the purpose of deciding—

    (i) whether a claim for universal credit is made; and

    (ii) the date on which such a claim is made; and

(b) the Social Security (Claims and Payments) Regulations 1987 apply for the purpose of deciding—

    (i) whether a claim for an employment and support allowance or a jobseeker's allowance is made; and

    (ii) the date on which the claim is made or is to be treated as made.

Amendment of the No.9, 11, 13, 14, 16 and 17 Orders: cases to which the amendments apply.

3. This article applies in relation to a case where—   3.276

(a) a claim is made for universal credit, an employment and support allowance or a jobseeker's allowance and, on the date on which the claim is made or treated as made, the claimant resides in one of the specified districts; or

(b) a claim for universal credit is made where—

    (i) in the case of a single claimant, the claimant gives incorrect information regarding the claimant residing in a specified district and does not reside in such a district on the date on which the claim is made;

    (ii) in the case of joint claimants, either or both of the joint claimants gives or give incorrect information regarding his or her (or their) residing in such a district and one or both of them does not or do not reside in such a district on the date on which the claim is made; and

    (iii) after a decision is made that the single claimant is, or the joint claimants are, entitled to universal credit and one or more payments have been made in respect of the single claimant or the joint claimants, the Secretary of State discovers that incorrect information has been given regarding residence,

and where the claim is made or treated as made on or after 30th June 2014.

DEFINITIONS

"claimant"–see art.2(1).
"employment and support allowance"–*ibid.*

"jobseeker's allowance"–*ibid.*
"joint claimant"–*ibid.*
"single claimant"–*ibid.*
"specified districts"–*ibid.*

Amendment of the No.9 Order

3.277   **4.** *[Amendments incorporated into No. 9 Order]*

Amendment of the No.11 Order

3.278   **5.** *[Amendments incorporated into No.11 Order]*

Amendment of the No.13 Order

3.279   **6.** *[Amendments incorporated into No. 13 Order]*

Amendment of the No.14 Order

3.280   **7.** *[Amendments incorporated into No. 14 Order]*

Amendment of the No.16 Order

3.281   **8.** *[Amendments incorporated into No. 16 Order]*

Amendment of the No.17 Order

3.282   **9.** *[Amendments incorporated into No. 17 Order]*

The Welfare Reform Act 2012 (Commencement No.9, 11, 13, 14, 16 and 17 and Transitional and Transitory Provisions (Amendment) (No.2)) Order 2014

(SI 2014/1923) (C.88)

The Secretary of State, in exercise of the powers conferred by section 150(3) and (4)(a), (b)(i) and (c) of the Welfare Reform Act 2012, makes the following Order:

ARRANGEMENT OF ARTICLES

GENERAL NOTE

The main change made by this Order was the removal of the condition that a
claimant had to be single in order for the universal credit provisions to come into
force where a claim is made for universal credit (and for the amending provisions
to come into force where a claim is made for universal credit, ESA or JSA). This
meant that as from July 28, 2014, the universal credit provisions (and the amending
provisions) came into force where a claim is made by members of a couple where
they reside in an area covered by the relevant Commencement Orders and each
member meets the remaining gateway conditions. These provisions were already in
force for claims made by members of a couple who resided in certain areas by virtue
of the Welfare Reform Act 2012 (Commencement No.9, 11, 13 14, 16 and 17 and
Transitional and Transitory Provisions (Amendment)) Order 2014 (SI 2014/1661).
To reflect the fact that the universal credit provisions (and the amending provisions) came into force where a claim is made by a couple who reside in one of the
"relevant districts", art.4 makes consequential changes to articles 3, 4 and 5 of the
Commencement No.9 Order and inserts a new article 3A into that Order.

3.283

Citation

1. This Order may be cited as the Welfare Reform Act 2012
(Commencement No.9, 11, 13, 14, 16 and 17 and Transitional and
Transitory Provisions (Amendment) (No.2)) Order 2014.

3.284

Interpretation

2. (1) In this Order—
"the Act" means the Welfare Reform Act 2012;
"the 1995 Act" means the Jobseekers Act 1995;
"the 2007 Act" means the Welfare Reform Act 2007;
"claimant", in relation to an employment and support allowance or a jobseeker's allowance, has the same meaning as in Part 1 of the 2007 Act
and the 1995 Act (as it applies apart from the amendments made by
Part 1 of Schedule 14 to the Act that remove references to an income-
based jobseeker's allowance) respectively and, in relation to universal
credit, has the same meaning as in Part 1 of the Act;
"the Claims and Payments Regulations 2013" means the Universal Credit,
Personal Independence Payment, Jobseeker's Allowance and Employment
and Support Allowance (Claims and Payments) Regulations 2013;
"employment and support allowance" means an employment and support
allowance under Part 1 of the 2007 Act;
"jobseeker's allowance" means a jobseeker's allowance under the 1995
Act;
"joint claimants", in relation to universal credit, has the same meaning as
in Part 1 of the Act;
"the No.9 Order" means the Welfare Reform Act 2012 (Commencement
No.9 and Transitional and Transitory Provisions and Commencement
No.8 and Savings and Transitional Provisions (Amendment)) Order
2013;
"the No.11 Order" means the Welfare Reform Act 2012 (Commencement
No.11 and Transitional and Transitory Provisions and Commencement
No.9 and Transitional and Transitory Provisions (Amendment)) Order
2013;
"the No.13 Order" means the Welfare Reform Act 2012 (Commencement
No.13 and Transitional and Transitory Provisions) Order 2013;

3.285

"the No.14 Order" means the Welfare Reform Act 2012 (Commencement No.14 and Transitional and Transitory Provisions) Order 2013;

"the No.16 Order" means the Welfare Reform Act 2012 (Commencement No.16 and Transitional and Transitory Provisions) Order 2014;

"the No.17 Order" means the Welfare Reform Act 2012 (Commencement No.17 and Transitional and Transitory Provisions) Order 2014;

"relevant districts" has the meaning given in the No.9 Order;

"No.2 relevant districts" and "No.3 relevant districts" have the meanings given in the No.11 Order;

"No.4 relevant districts" has the meaning given in the No.13 Order;

"No.5 relevant districts" has the meaning given in the No.14 Order;

"No.6 relevant districts" and "No.7 relevant districts" have the meanings given in the No.16 Order;

"No.8 relevant districts", "No.9 relevant districts", "No.10 relevant districts", "No.11 relevant districts", "No.12 relevant districts" and "No.13 relevant districts" have the meanings given in the No.17 Order;

"single claimant", in relation to universal credit, has the same meaning as in Part 1 of the Act;

"specified districts" means the relevant districts, No.2 relevant districts, No.3 relevant districts, No.4 relevant districts, No.5 relevant districts, No.6 relevant districts, No.7 relevant districts, No.8 relevant districts, No.9 relevant districts, No.10 relevant districts, No.11 relevant districts, No.12 relevant districts and No.13 relevant districts.

(2) For the purposes of this Order—

(a) the Claims and Payments Regulations 2013 apply for the purpose of deciding—

    (i) whether a claim for universal credit is made or treated as made; and

    (ii) the date on which such a claim is made;

(b) where a couple is treated, in accordance with regulation 9(8) of the Claims and Payments Regulations 2013, as making a claim for universal credit, references to the date on which the claim is treated as made are to the date of formation of the couple; and

(c) the Social Security (Claims and Payments) Regulations 1987 apply for the purpose of deciding—

    (i) whether a claim for an employment and support allowance or a jobseeker's allowance is made; and

    (ii) the date on which such a claim is made or is to be treated as made.

Amendment of the No.9, 11, 13, 14, 16 and 17 Orders: cases to which the amendments apply

3.286   **3.** This article applies in relation to a case where—

(a) a claim is made for universal credit, an employment and support allowance or a jobseeker's allowance and, on the date on which the claim is made or treated as made, the claimant resides in one of the specified districts;

(b) a claim for universal credit is made and it is subsequently discovered by the Secretary of State that—

    (i) in the case of a single claimant, the claimant gave incorrect information regarding the claimant residing in a specified district and the claimant did not reside in such a district on the date on which the claim was made; or

(ii) in the case of joint claimants, either or both of the joint claimants gave incorrect information regarding his or her (or their) residing in such a district and one or both of them did not reside in such a district on the date on which the claim was made;

(c) a claim for universal credit is treated as made by a couple in the circumstances referred to in regulation 9(8) of the Claims and Payments Regulations 2013 (claims for universal credit by members of a couple);

(d) a claim for universal credit is made by a former member of a couple who were joint claimants of universal credit, whether or not the claim is made jointly with another person, where the former member is not exempt from the requirement to make a claim by virtue of regulation 9(6) of the Claims and Payments Regulations 2013 (claims for universal credit by members of a couple), where the claim is made during the period of one month starting with the date on which notification is given to the Secretary of State that the former joint claimants have ceased to be a couple;

(e) an award of universal credit is made without a claim in the circumstances referred to in regulation 6(1) or (2) of the Claims and Payments Regulations 2013 (claims not required for entitlement to universal credit in some cases); or

(f) an award of universal credit is made without a claim in the circumstances referred to in regulation 9(6), (7) or (10) of the Claims and Payments Regulations 2013 (claims for universal credit by members of a couple),

and the claim for universal credit, an employment and support allowance or a jobseeker's allowance is made or treated as made, or, as the case may be, the award of universal credit is made without a claim, on or after 28th July 2014.

DEFINITIONS

"claimant"–see art.2(1).
"Claims and Payments Regulations 2013"–*ibid.*
"employment and support allowance"–*ibid.*
"jobseeker's allowance"–*ibid.*
"joint claimant"–*ibid.*
"single claimant"–*ibid.*
"specified districts"–*ibid.*

Amendment of the No.9 Order

4. *[Amendments incorporated into No. 9 Order]*   3.287

Application of parts of the No.9 Order amended by article 4

5. Where article 3 applies, any reference—   3.288

(a) in the No.11 Order and the No.17 Order to article 5(1) of, or Schedule 5 to, the No.9 Order is a reference to those provisions as amended by article 4(6)(a) and (7) respectively;

(b) in the No.11 Order, the No.13 Order, the No.14 Order, the No.16

Order and the No.17 Order to article 5(7) of the No.9 Order is a reference to that provision as amended by article 4(6)(c).

DEFINITIONS

"No.9 Order"–see art.2(1).
"No.11 Order"–*ibid.*
"No.13 Order"–*ibid.*
"No.14 Order"–*ibid.*
"No.16 Order"–*ibid.*
"No.17 Order"–*ibid.*

Amendment of the No.11 Order

3.289   **6.** *[Amendments incorporated into No.11 Order]*

Amendment of the No.13 Order

3.290   **7.** *[Amendments incorporated into No. 13 Order]*

Amendment of the No.14 Order

3.291   **8.** *[Amendments incorporated into No. 14 Order]*

Amendment of the No.16 Order

3.292   **9.** *[Amendments incorporated into No. 16 Order]*

Amendment of the No.17 Order

3.293   **10.** *[Amendments incorporated into No. 17 Order]*

The Welfare Reform Act 2012 (Commencement No.19 and Transitional and Transitory Provisions and Commencement No.9 and Transitional and Transitory Provisions (Amendment)) Order 2014

(SI 2014/2321) (C.99) (AS AMENDED)

The Secretary of State makes the following Order in exercise of the powers conferred by sections 150(3) and (4)(a), (b)(i) and (c) of the Welfare Reform Act 2012:

ARRANGEMENT OF ARTICLES

1.   Citation
2.   Interpretation
3.   Day appointed for the coming into force of the universal credit provisions
4.   Day appointed for the abolition of income-related employment and support allowance and income-based jobseeker's allowance
5.   Application of the No.9 Order
6.   Day appointed for the coming into force of section 41 of the Act.

7.   Amendment of the No.9 Order
SCHEDULE: POSTCODE DISTRICTS AND PART-DISTRICTS

GENERAL NOTE

This Commencement Order ("the Commencement No.19 Order") extended the   **3.294**
UC scheme to certain postcode districts in a wide range of different areas in the
North West of England (known as the No.14, No.15, No.16, No.17, No.18, No.19,
No.20, No.21, No.22, No.23, No.24, No.25, No.26 or No.27 relevant districts – see
Schedule). In addition, of course, the claimant must meet the gateway conditions in
Sch.5 to the Commencement No.9 Order.

Citation

1. This Order may be cited as the Welfare Reform Act 2012 (Commencement   **3.295**
No.19 and Transitional and Transitory Provisions and Commencement
No.9 and Transitional and Transitory Provisions (Amendment)) Order
2014.

Interpretation

2. (1) In this Order—   **3.296**
"the Act" means the Welfare Reform Act 2012;
"the amending provisions" means the provisions referred to in article
    4(1)(a) to (c) of the No.9 Order (day appointed for the abolition of
    income-related employment and support allowance and income-based
    jobseeker's allowance);
[¹ "claimant"—
(a)   in relation to an employment and support allowance, has the same
    meaning as in Part 1 of the Welfare Reform Act 2007, save as men-
    tioned in article 5(1A) of the No.9 Order as applied by article 4(7);
(b)   in relation to a jobseeker's allowance, has the same meaning as in
    the Jobseekers Act 1995 (as it applies apart from the amendments
    made by Part 1 of Schedule 14 to the Act that remove references to
    an income-based jobseeker's allowance), save as mentioned in article
    5(1A) of the No.9 Order as applied by article 4(7);
(c)   in relation to universal credit, has the same meaning as in Part 1 of
    the Act;]
"employment and support allowance" means an employment and support
    allowance under Part 1 of the Welfare Reform Act 2007;
"First-tier Tribunal" has the same meaning as in the Social Security Act
    1998;
"gateway conditions" means the conditions specified in Schedule 5 to the
    No.9 Order;
"jobseeker's allowance" means a jobseeker's allowance under the
    Jobseekers Act 1995;
"joint claimants", in relation to universal credit, has the same meaning as
    in Part 1 of the Act;
"the No.9 Order" means the Welfare Reform Act 2012 (Commencement
    No.9 and Transitional and Transitory Provisions and Commencement
    No.8 and Savings and Transitional Provisions (Amendment)) Order
    2013;
"No.14 relevant districts" means the postcode districts and part-districts
    specified in Part 1 of the Schedule;

"No.15 relevant districts" means the postcode districts and part-districts specified in Part 2 of the Schedule;

"No.16 relevant districts" means the postcode districts and part-districts specified in Part 3 of the Schedule;

"No.17 relevant districts" means the postcode districts and part-districts specified in Part 4 of the Schedule;

"No.18 relevant districts" means the postcode districts and part-districts specified in Part 5 of the Schedule;

"No.19 relevant districts" means the postcode districts and part-districts specified in Part 6 of the Schedule;

"No.20 relevant districts" means the postcode districts and part-districts specified in Part 7 of the Schedule;

"No.21 relevant districts" means the postcode districts and part-districts specified in Part 8 of the Schedule;

"No.22 relevant districts" means the postcode districts and part-districts specified in Part 9 of the Schedule;

"No.23 relevant districts" means the postcode districts and part-districts specified in Part 10 of the Schedule;

"No.24 relevant districts" means the postcode districts and part-districts specified in Part 11 of the Schedule;

"No.25 relevant districts" means the postcode districts and part-districts specified in Part 12 of the Schedule;

"No.26 relevant districts" means the postcode districts and part-districts specified in Part 13 of the Schedule;

"No.27 relevant districts" means the postcode districts and part-districts specified in Part 14 of the Schedule;

"single claimant", in relation to universal credit, has the same meaning as in Part 1 of the Act;

"Upper Tribunal" has the same meaning as in the Social Security Act 1998.

(2) For the purposes of this Order, the Universal Credit, Personal Independence Payment, Jobseeker's Allowance and Employment and Support Allowance (Claims and Payments) Regulations 2013 apply for the purpose of deciding—

(a) whether a claim for universal credit is made; and

(b) the date on which such a claim is made.

AMENDMENT

1. Welfare Reform Act 2012 (Commencement No.9, 11, 13 14, 16, 17 and 19 and Transitional and Transitory Provisions (Amendment)) Order 2014 (SI 2014/3067) art.6(3) (November 24, 2014).

Day appointed for the coming into force of the universal credit provisions

3.297   **3.** (1) The day appointed for the coming into force of the provisions of the Act listed in Schedule 2 to the No.9 Order, in so far as they are not already in force, in relation to the case of a claim referred to in paragraph (2), and any award that is made in respect of the claim, is the day appointed in accordance with paragraph (3).

(2) The claims referred to are—

(a) a claim for universal credit that is made on or after 15th September

2014 in respect of a period that begins on or after 15th September 2014 where, on the date on which the claim is made, the claimant resides in one of the No.14 relevant districts and meets the gateway conditions;

(b) a claim for universal credit that is made on or after 22nd September 2014 in respect of a period that begins on or after 22nd September 2014 where, on the date on which the claim is made, the claimant resides in one of the No.15 relevant districts and meets the gateway conditions;

(c) a claim for universal credit that is made on or after 29th September 2014 in respect of a period that begins on or after 29th September 2014 where, on the date on which the claim is made, the claimant resides in one of the No.16 relevant districts and meets the gateway conditions;

(d) a claim for universal credit that is made on or after 6th October 2014 in respect of a period that begins on or after 6th October 2014 where, on the date on which the claim is made, the claimant resides in one of the No.17 relevant districts and meets the gateway conditions;

(e) a claim for universal credit that is made on or after 13th October 2014 in respect of a period that begins on or after 13th October 2014 where, on the date on which the claim is made, the claimant resides in one of the No.18 relevant districts and meets the gateway conditions;

(f) a claim for universal credit that is made on or after 20th October 2014 in respect of a period that begins on or after 20th October 2014 where, on the date on which the claim is made, the claimant resides in one of the No.19 relevant districts and meets the gateway conditions;

(g) a claim for universal credit that is made on or after 27th October 2014 in respect of a period that begins on or after 27th October 2014 where, on the date on which the claim is made, the claimant resides in one of the No.20 relevant districts and meets the gateway conditions;

(h) a claim for universal credit that is made on or after 3rd November 2014 in respect of a period that begins on or after 3rd November 2014 where, on the date on which the claim is made, the claimant resides in one of the No.21 relevant districts and meets the gateway conditions;

(i) a claim for universal credit that is made on or after 10th November 2014 in respect of a period that begins on or after 10th November 2014 where, on the date on which the claim is made, the claimant resides in one of the No.22 relevant districts and meets the gateway conditions;

(j) a claim for universal credit that is made on or after 17th November 2014 in respect of a period that begins on or after 17th November 2014 where, on the date on which the claim is made, the claimant resides in one of the No.23 relevant districts and meets the gateway conditions;

(k) a claim for universal credit that is made on or after 24th November 2014 in respect of a period that begins on or after 24th November 2014 where, on the date on which the claim is made, the claimant resides in one of the No.24 relevant districts and meets the gateway conditions;

(l) a claim for universal credit that is made on or after 1st December 2014 in respect of a period that begins on or after 1st December 2014 where, on the date on which the claim is made, the claimant resides in one of the No.25 relevant districts and meets the gateway conditions;

(m) a claim for universal credit that is made on or after 8th December 2014 in respect of a period that begins on or after 8th December 2014 where, on the date on which the claim is made, the claimant resides in one of the No.26 relevant districts and meets the gateway conditions;

(n) a claim for universal credit that is made on or after 15th December 2014 in respect of a period that begins on or after 15th December 2014 where, on the date on which the claim is made, the claimant resides in one of the No.27 relevant districts and meets the gateway conditions;

(o) a claim for universal credit that is made on or after the date referred to in any of sub-paragraphs (a) to (n), in respect of a period that begins on or after that date where—

(i) in the case of a single claimant, the claimant gives incorrect information regarding the claimant residing in a district as referred to in the sub-paragraph in question or meeting the gateway conditions and the claimant does not reside in such a district or does not meet the gateway conditions on the date on which the claim is made;

(ii) in the case of joint claimants, either or both of the joint claimants gives or give incorrect information regarding his or her (or their) residing in such a district or meeting the gateway conditions and one or both of them does not or do not reside in such a district or does not or do not meet those conditions on the date on which the claim is made,

and after a decision is made that the single claimant is, or the joint claimants are, entitled to universal credit and one or more payments have been made in respect of the single claimant or the joint claimants, the Secretary of State discovers that incorrect information has been given regarding residence or meeting the gateway conditions.

(3) The day appointed in relation to the case of a claim referred to in paragraph (2), and any award that is made in respect of the claim, is the first day of the period in respect of which the claim is made.

(4) Article 3(6) of the No.9 Order applies for the purposes of paragraph (3) as it applies for the purposes of article 3(4)(a) of the No.9 Order.

(5) Article 3A of the No.9 Order applies in connection with a claim for universal credit where a single claimant, or, as the case may be, either or both of joint claimants, gives incorrect information regarding his or her (or their) residing in a No.14, No.15, No.16, No.17, No.18, No.19, No.20, No.21, No.22, No.23, No.24, No.25, No.26 or No.27 relevant district or meeting the gateway conditions, as it applies in connection with the giving of incorrect information regarding a claimant residing in a relevant district (as defined in the No.9 Order) or meeting the gateway conditions.

DEFINITIONS

"claimant"–see art.2(1).
"gateway conditions"–*ibid.*
"joint claimant"–*ibid.*
"single claimant"–*ibid.*
"No.9 Order"–*ibid.*
"No.14 relevant districts"–*ibid.*
"No.15 relevant districts"–*ibid.*
"No.16 relevant districts"–*ibid.*
"No.17 relevant districts"–*ibid.*
"No.18 relevant districts"–*ibid.*
"No.19 relevant districts"–*ibid.*
"No.20 relevant districts"–*ibid.*
"No.21 relevant districts"–*ibid.*
"No.22 relevant districts"–*ibid.*
"No.23 relevant districts"–*ibid.*
"No.24 relevant districts"–*ibid.*
"No.25 relevant districts"–*ibid.*
"No.26 relevant districts"–*ibid.*
"No.27 relevant districts"–*ibid.*

Day appointed for the abolition of income-related employment and support allowance and income-based jobseeker's allowance

4. (1) The day appointed for the coming into force of the amending provisions, in relation to the case of a claim referred to in paragraph (2), and any award that is made in respect of the claim, is the day appointed in accordance with paragraph (3).   3.298

(2) The claims referred to are—

(a) a claim for universal credit, an employment and support allowance or a jobseeker's allowance that is made or treated as made on or after 15th September 2014 in respect of a period that begins on or after 15th September 2014 where, on the date on which the claim is made or treated as made, the claimant resides in one of the No.14 relevant districts and meets the gateway conditions;

(b) a claim for universal credit, an employment and support allowance or a jobseeker's allowance that is made or treated as made on or after 22nd September 2014 in respect of a period that begins on or after 22nd September 2014 where, on the date on which the claim is made or treated as made, the claimant resides in one of the No.15 relevant districts and meets the gateway conditions;

(c) a claim for universal credit, an employment and support allowance or a jobseeker's allowance that is made or treated as made on or after 29th September 2014 in respect of a period that begins on or after 29th September 2014 where, on the date on which the claim is made or treated as made, the claimant resides in one of the No.16 relevant districts and meets the gateway conditions;

(d) a claim for universal credit, an employment and support allowance or a jobseeker's allowance that is made or treated as made on or after 6th October 2014 in respect of a period that begins on or after 6th October 2014 where, on the date on which the claim is made or treated as made, the claimant resides in one of the No.17 relevant districts and meets the gateway conditions;

(e) a claim for universal credit, an employment and support allowance or a jobseeker's allowance that is made or treated as made on or after 13th October 2014 in respect of a period that begins on or after 13th October 2014 where, on the date on which the claim is made or treated as made, the claimant resides in one of the No.18 relevant districts and meets the gateway conditions;

(f) a claim for universal credit, an employment and support allowance or a jobseeker's allowance that is made or treated as made on or after 20th October 2014 in respect of a period that begins on or after 20th October 2014 where, on the date on which the claim is made or treated as made, the claimant resides in one of the No.19 relevant districts and meets the gateway conditions;

(g) a claim for universal credit, an employment and support allowance or a jobseeker's allowance that is made or treated as made on or after 27th October 2014 in respect of a period that begins on or after 27th October 2014 where, on the date on which the claim is made or treated as made, the claimant resides in one of the No.20 relevant districts and meets the gateway conditions;

(h) a claim for universal credit, an employment and support allowance or a jobseeker's allowance that is made or treated as made on or after 3rd November 2014 in respect of a period that begins on or after 3rd November 2014 where, on the date on which the claim is made or treated as made, the claimant resides in one of the No.21 relevant districts and meets the gateway conditions;

(i) a claim for universal credit, an employment and support allowance or a jobseeker's allowance that is made or treated as made on or after 10th November 2014 in respect of a period that begins on or after 10th November 2014 where, on the date on which the claim is made or treated as made, the claimant resides in one of the No.22 relevant districts and meets the gateway conditions;

(j) a claim for universal credit, an employment and support allowance or a jobseeker's allowance that is made or treated as made on or after 17th November 2014 in respect of a period that begins on or after 17th November 2014 where, on the date on which the claim is made or treated as made, the claimant resides in one of the No.23 relevant districts and meets the gateway conditions;

(k) a claim for universal credit, an employment and support allowance or a jobseeker's allowance that is made or treated as made on or after 24th November 2014 in respect of a period that begins on or after 24th November 2014 where, on the date on which the claim is made or treated as made, the claimant resides in one of the No.24 relevant districts and meets the gateway conditions;

(l) a claim for universal credit, an employment and support allowance or a jobseeker's allowance that is made or treated as made on or after 1st December 2014 in respect of a period that begins on or after 1st December 2014 where, on the date on which the claim is made or treated as made, the claimant resides in one of the No.25 relevant districts and meets the gateway conditions;

(m) a claim for universal credit, an employment and support allowance or a jobseeker's allowance that is made or treated as made on or after 8th December 2014 in respect of a period that begins on or after 8th December 2014 where, on the date on which the claim is made or

treated as made, the claimant resides in one of the No.26 relevant
districts and meets the gateway conditions;

(n) a claim for universal credit, an employment and support allowance
or a jobseeker's allowance that is made or treated as made on or after
15th December 2014 in respect of a period that begins on or after
15th December 2014 where, on the date on which the claim is made
or treated as made, the claimant resides in one of the No.27 relevant
districts and meets the gateway conditions;

(o) a claim for universal credit that is made on or after the date referred
to in any of sub-paragraphs (a) to (n), in respect of a period that
begins on or after that date where—

    (i) in the case of a single claimant, the claimant gives incorrect
information regarding the claimant residing in a district as
referred to in the sub-paragraph in question or meeting the
gateway conditions and the claimant does not reside in such a
district or does not meet the gateway conditions on the date on
which the claim is made;

    (ii) in the case of joint claimants, either or both of the joint claim-
ants gives or give incorrect information regarding his or her (or
their) residing in such a district or meeting the gateway conditions and one or both of them does not or do not reside in such
a district or does not or do not meet those conditions on the
date on which the claim is made,

and after a decision is made that the single claimant is, or the joint claimants
are, entitled to universal credit and one or more payments have been made
in respect of the single claimant or the joint claimants, the Secretary of State
discovers that incorrect information has been given regarding residence or
meeting the gateway conditions;

(p) a claim for an employment and support allowance or a jobseeker's
allowance other than one referred to in sub-paragraphs (a) to (n)
that is made or treated as made during the relevant period by a single
claimant of universal credit or by either of two joint claimants of universal credit who has or have made a claim for universal credit within
one of sub-paragraphs (a) to (o).

(3) The day appointed in relation to the case of a claim referred to in
paragraph (2), and any award that is made in respect of the claim, is the first
day of the period in respect of which the claim is made.

(4) For the purposes of paragraph (2)(p), "relevant period" means, in
relation to a claim for universal credit within paragraph (2)(a) to (o), any
UC claim period, and any period subsequent to any UC claim period in
respect of which the claimant is entitled to an award of universal credit in
respect of the claim.

(5) For the purposes of paragraph (4), a "UC claim period" is a period
when—

(a) a claim for universal credit within one of sub-paragraphs (a) to (n)
of paragraph (2), or within sub-paragraph (o)(i) or (ii) of that paragraph, has been made but a decision has not yet been made on the
claim; or

(b) a decision has been made that the claimant is not entitled to universal credit and—

    (i) the Secretary of State is considering whether to revise that deci-
sion under section 9 of the Social Security Act 1998, whether

           on an application made for that purpose, or on the Secretary of State's own initiative; or

  (ii) the claimant has appealed against that decision to the First-tier Tribunal and that appeal or any subsequent appeal to the Upper Tribunal or to a court has not been finally determined.

(6) Paragraphs [² (6) to (9)] of article 4 of the No.9 Order apply in relation to a claim for universal credit referred to in paragraph (2) (and any award that is made in respect of the claim) as they apply in relation to a claim for universal credit referred to in sub-paragraphs (a) and (b) of article 4(2) of the No.9 Order (and any award that is made in respect of the claim).

[¹ (7) Paragraphs (1) to (1B) of article 5 of the No.9 Order apply for the purposes of paragraph (2)(a) to (n) as they apply for the purposes of article 4(2)(a) of the No.9 Order.]

(8) Paragraphs (5) to (7) of article 5 of the No.9 Order apply for the purposes of sub-paragraphs (a) to (n) and (p) of paragraph (2) as they apply for the purposes of sub-paragraphs (a) and (g) of article 4(2) of the No.9 Order.

(9) Article 5(8) of the No.9 Order applies for the purposes of paragraph (3) as it applies for the purposes of article 4(3)(a) of the No.9 Order.

AMENDMENTS

1. Welfare Reform Act 2012 (Commencement No.9, 11, 13 14, 16, 17 and 19 and Transitional and Transitory Provisions (Amendment)) Order 2014 (SI 2014/3067) art.6(6) (November 24, 2014).

2. Welfare Reform Act 2012 (Commencement No.9, 11, 13, 14, 16, 17 and 19 and Transitional and Transitory Provisions (Amendment)) Order 2015 (SI 2015/32) art.9 (January 26, 2015).

DEFINITIONS

"the amending provisions"–see art.2(1).
"claimant"–*ibid.*
"employment and support allowance"–*ibid.*
"First-tier Tribunal"–*ibid.*
"gateway conditions"–*ibid.*
"jobseeker's allowance"–*ibid.*
"joint claimant"–*ibid.*
"No.9 Order"–*ibid.*
"No.14 relevant districts"–*ibid.*
"No.15 relevant districts"–*ibid.*
"No.16 relevant districts"–*ibid.*
"No.17 relevant districts"–*ibid.*
"No.18 relevant districts"–*ibid.*
"No.19 relevant districts"–*ibid.*
"No.20 relevant districts"–*ibid.*
"No.21 relevant districts"–*ibid.*
"No.22 relevant districts"–*ibid.*
"No.23 relevant districts"–*ibid.*
"No.24 relevant districts"–*ibid.*
"No.25 relevant districts"–*ibid.*
"No.26 relevant districts"–*ibid.*
"No.27 relevant districts"–*ibid.*
"relevant period"–para.(4).
"UC claim period"–para.(5).
"Upper Tribunal"–see art.2(1).

Application of the No.9 Order

5. Articles 9 to 22 of the No.9 Order apply in connection with the coming into force of the amending provisions in relation to the case of a claim referred to in article 4(2), and any award made in respect of the claim, as they apply in connection with the coming into force of the amending provisions in relation to the case of a claim referred to in sub-paragraphs (a), (b) and (g) of article 4(2) of the No.9 Order and any award made in respect of the claim.

3.299

DEFINITIONS

"the amending provisions"–see art.2(1).
"No.9 Order"–*ibid.*

Day appointed for the coming into force of section 41 of the Act.

6. 15th September 2014 is the day appointed for the coming into force of section 41 of the Act (pilot schemes) for all purposes.

3.300

Amendment of the No.9 Order

7. *(Amendments incorporated into text of No. 9 Order)*

3.301

Article 2(1)

SCHEDULE

POSTCODE DISTRICTS AND PART-DISTRICTS

PART 1

THE NO.14 RELEVANT DISTRICTS

BL9 7.
L31 1.
L31 4.
L33 3 and L33 4.
L37 0.
L37 5.
L37 9.
L39.
L40 0 and L40 1.
L40 4 to L40 9.
M24 0 to M24 2.
M24 5 and M24 6.
OL10.
OL11.
OL12 6.
OL12 9.
OL15 0.
OL15 8.
OL16.
PR8 3 to PR8 5.
PR9 8.
WA11 7.
WN8.

3.302

PART 2

THE NO.15 RELEVANT DISTRICTS

3.303   L10 1.
L10 4 and L10 5.
L10 7.
L14.
L15.
L18 0 to L18 2.
L18 5.
L20 1 and L20 2.
L20 7 to L20 9.
L28 0 and L28 1.
L28 8.
L36 5.
M4.
M7 4.
M8.
M9.
M22 0 to M22 2.
M22 5.
M22 8 and M22 9.
M23.
M24 4.
M25 0.
M25 2.
M33 3.
M40.
WA15 0.
WA15 7 and WA15 8.

PART 3

THE NO.16 RELEVANT DISTRICTS

3.304   L1.
L2.
L3.
L4 0 to L4 4.
L4 7.
L5.
L6.
L7.
L8.
L17 1 to L17 4.
L17 7 to L17 9.

PART 4

THE NO.17 RELEVANT DISTRICTS

3.305   BB4.
BB5.
BB8.
BB9 0.
BB9 4 and BB9 5.
BB9 7 to BB9 9.
BB10.
BB11.

594

BB12 0.
BB12 6.
BB12 8.
BB18 5.
BB18 9.
BL0 0.
BL9 6.
OL12 0.
OL12 7 and OL12 8.
OL13.

PART 5

THE NO.18 RELEVANT DISTRICTS

BL5 2.   **3.306**
M29.
M46.
WA3 1 to WA3 3.
WN4.
WN7.

PART 6

THE NO.19 RELEVANT DISTRICTS

L4 6.   **3.307**
L4 8 and L4 9.
L11.
M15.
M16.
SK10.
SK11 6 to SK11 9.

PART 7

THE NO.20 RELEVANT DISTRICTS

L4 5.   **3.308**
L9.
L12.
L13.
L16.
L17 0.
L17 5 and L17 6.
L18 3 and L18 4.
L18 6 to L18 9.
L19.
L24 0 to L24 3.
L24 6 to L24 9.
L25.
L26.
L27.

PART 8

THE NO.21 RELEVANT DISTRICTS

FY5.   **3.309**
FY6.
FY7.
PR4 0.

PART 9

THE NO.22 RELEVANT DISTRICTS

3.310   M12.
M13.
M14.
M19 0.
M21.

PART 10

THE NO.23 RELEVANT DISTRICTS

3.311   L24 4 and L24 5.
L35 6.
M11.
M18.
M19 1 to M19 3.
M20.
M22 4.
SK1.
SK2.
SK3.
SK4.
SK5.
SK6.
SK7.
SK8.
SK12.
SK14 3.
SK14 5.
WA7.
WA8.

PART 11

THE NO.24 RELEVANT DISTRICTS

3.312   BB1.
BB2.
BB3.
BB6 7 and BB6 8.
BB9 6.
BB12 7.
BB12 9.
BL6 5 to BL6 7.
BL7.
BL8 4.
L40 2 and L40 3.
PR4 6.
PR5 0.
PR5 6.
PR5 8.
PR6.
PR7.
PR25 4 and PR25 5.
PR26 7 to PR26 9.

PART 12

THE NO.25 RELEVANT DISTRICTS

3.313   CH64.
CH65.

CH66.
CW6.
CW7.
CW8.
CW9.
M1.
M2.
M3.
M5.
M6.
M7 1 to M7 3.
M27 4.
M27 6.
M50.

PART 13

THE NO.26 RELEVANT DISTRICTS

FY1.   **3.314**
FY2.
FY3.
FY4.
FY8.
LA1.
LA2 0.
LA2 6.
LA2 9.
LA3.
LA4.
LA5 0.
LA5 8 and LA5 9.
LA6 1 and LA6 2.
LA7.
LA8.
LA9.
LA11.
LA12.
LA13.
LA14.
LA15.
LA16.
LA17.
LA18.
LA19.
LA20.
LA21.
LA22.
LA23.
M44.
PR3.
PR4 1 to PR4 3.

PART 14

THE NO.27 RELEVANT DISTRICTS

BB7.   **3.315**
CA1.
CA2.
CA3.
CA4.
CA5.

CA6.
CA7.
CA8 0 and CA8 1.
CA8 9.
CA10 1 to CA10 3.
CA11.
CA12.
CA13.
CA14.
CA15.
CA16.
CA17.
CA18.
CA19.
CA20.
CA21.
CA22.
CA23.
CA24.
CA25.
CA26.
CA27.
CA28.

The Welfare Reform Act 2012 (Commencement No.9, 11, 13 14, 16, 17 and 19 and Transitional and Transitory Provisions (Amendment)) Order 2014

SI 2014/3067 (C.129)

The Secretary of State for Work and Pensions makes the following Order in exercise of the powers conferred by sections 150(3) and (4) (a), (b) (i) and (c) of the Welfare Reform Act 2012:

ARRANGEMENT OF ARTICLES

GENERAL NOTE

3.316   The main effect of this Order was to amend the Commencement No.11 and the Commencement No.17 Orders so as to modify the "gateway conditions" specified in Sch.5 to the Commencement No.9 Order by (in large part) removing the condition that a claimant must not have responsibility for children or young persons in a case where the claimant resides in certain postcode districts or part-districts in the North West of England (as covered by those Commencement No.11 and No.17

598

Orders). As a consequence the provisions listed in Sch.2 to the No.9 Order come into force where, on the date on which a claim for universal credit is made, the claimant resides in one of those postcode districts or part-districts and meets the modified gateway conditions.

Citation

1. This Order may be cited as the Welfare Reform Act 2012 (Commencement No.9, 11, 13, 14, 16, 17 and 19 and Transitional and Transitory Provisions (Amendment)) Order 2014.

3.317

Interpretation

2. (1) In this Order—

"the Act" means the Welfare Reform Act 2012;

"claimant"—

(a) in relation to an employment and support allowance, has the same meaning as in Part 1 of the Welfare Reform Act 2007;

(b) in relation to a jobseeker's allowance, has the same meaning as in the Jobseekers Act 1995 (as it applies apart from the amendments made by Part 1 of Schedule 14 to the Act that remove references to an income-based jobseeker's allowance);

(c) in relation to universal credit, has the same meaning as in Part 1 of the Act;

"employment and support allowance" means an employment and support allowance under Part 1 of the Welfare Reform Act 2007;

"jobseeker's allowance" means a jobseeker's allowance under the Jobseekers Act 1995;

"joint claimants", in relation to universal credit, has the same meaning as in Part 1 of the Act;

"the No.9 Order" means the Welfare Reform Act 2012 (Commencement No.9 and Transitional and Transitory Provisions and Commencement No.8 and Savings and Transitional Provisions (Amendment)) Order 2013;

"the No.11 Order" means the Welfare Reform Act 2012 (Commencement No.11 and Transitional and Transitory Provisions and Commencement No.9 and Transitional and Transitory Provisions (Amendment)) Order 2013;

"the No.13 Order" means the Welfare Reform Act 2012 (Commencement No.13 and Transitional and Transitory Provisions) Order 2013;

"the No.14 Order" means the Welfare Reform Act 2012 (Commencement No.14 and Transitional and Transitory Provisions) Order 2013;

"the No.16 Order" means the Welfare Reform Act 2012 (Commencement No.16 and Transitional and Transitory Provisions) Order 2014;

"the No.17 Order" means the Welfare Reform Act 2012 (Commencement No.17 and Transitional and Transitory Provisions) Order 2014;

"the No.19 Order" means the Welfare Reform Act 2012 (Commencement No.19 and Transitional and Transitory Provisions and Commencement No.9 and Transitional and Transitory Provisions (Amendment)) Order 2014;

"prescribed districts" means the relevant districts and the areas each of which is described by a number preceding the expression "relevant districts" as specified in article 2(1) of the No.11 Order, the No.13

3.318

Order, the No.14 Order, the No.16 Order, the No.17 Order and the No.19 Order;

"relevant districts" has the same meaning as in the No.9 Order;

"single claimant", in relation to universal credit, has the same meaning as in Part 1 of the Act.

(2) For the purposes of this Order—

(a) the Universal Credit, Personal Independence Payment, Jobseeker's Allowance and Employment and Support Allowance (Claims and Payments) Regulations 2013 apply for the purpose of deciding—

    (i) whether a claim for universal credit is made; and

    (ii) the date on which such a claim is made; and

(b) the Social Security (Claims and Payments) Regulations 1987 apply for the purpose of deciding—

    (i) whether a claim for an employment and support allowance or a jobseeker's allowance is made; and

    (ii) the date on which such a claim is made or is to be treated as made.

Amendment of the No.9, No.11, No.13, No.14, No.16, No.17 and No.19 Orders: cases to which the amendments apply

3.319   **3.** Articles 4 to 6 apply where—

(a) a claim is made for universal credit, an employment and support allowance or a jobseeker's allowance and, on the date on which the claim is made or treated as made, the claimant resides in one of the prescribed districts; or

(b) a claim for universal credit is made where—

    (i) in the case of a single claimant, the claimant gives incorrect information regarding the claimant residing in a prescribed district and does not reside in such a district on the date on which the claim is made; or

    (ii) in the case of joint claimants, either or both of the joint claimants gives or give incorrect information regarding his or her (or their) residing in such a district and one or both of them does not or do not reside in such a district on the date on which the claim is made,

and where the claim is made or treated as made on or after 24th November 2014.

DEFINITIONS

"claimant"–see art.2(1).
"joint claimant"–*ibid.*
"prescribed districts"–*ibid.*
"single claimant"–*ibid.*

Amendment of the No.11 Order: the gateway conditions

3.320   **4.** *(Amendments incorporated into text of No. 11 Order)*

Amendment of the No.17 Order: the gateway conditions

3.321   **5.** *(Amendments incorporated into text of No. 17 Order)*

Meaning of "claimant": amendment of the No.9, No.11, No.13, No.14, No.16, No.17 and No.19 Orders

6. *(Amendments incorporated into text of No. 9, No. 11, No. 13, No. 14, No. 16, No. 17 and No. 19 Orders)*

3.322

Amendment of the No.9 Order: transitional provisions on waiting periods

7. With effect from 24th November 2014—

3.323

(a) in articles 10(2)(gb), 11(2)(gb), 12(3)(b) and 13(3)(b)(i) of the No.9 Order (transition from old style ESA to new style ESA and vice versa; transition from old style JSA to new style JSA and vice versa) (1), for "the second or third day of that period" substitute "a day between the second and the seventh day of that period (including the second and the seventh day)"; and

(b) any reference in the No.11 Order, the No.13 Order, the No.14 Order, the No.16 Order, the No.17 Order or the No.19 Order to article 10, 11, 12 or 13 of the No.9 Order is a reference to that article as amended by paragraph (a).

DEFINITIONS

"No.9 Order"–see art.2(1).
"No.11 Order"–*ibid.*
"No.13 Order"–*ibid.*
"No.14 Order"–*ibid.*
"No.16 Order"–*ibid.*
"No.17 Order"–*ibid.*
"No.19 Order"–*ibid.*

The Welfare Reform Act 2012 (Commencement No.20 and Transitional and Transitory Provisions and Commencement No.9 and Transitional and Transitory Provisions (Amendment)) Order 2014

(SI 2014/3094) (C.133)

The Secretary of State for Work and Pensions makes the following Order in exercise of the powers conferred by sections 150(3) and (4)(a), (b)(i) and (c) of the Welfare Reform Act 2012:

ARRANGEMENT OF ARTICLES

GENERAL NOTE

3.324 This Commencement Order ("the Commencement No.20 Order") extended the universal credit scheme to the part postcode district in Sutton (SM5 2) known as "the No.28 relevant district". This applied for a limited test period only, namely November 26, 2014 until December 20, 2014. In this instance there was no further requirement that the claimant had to meet the gateway conditions (in Sch.5 to the Commencement No.9 Order). This was because this extension involved the testing of the enhanced digital (or full) service for universal credit for the full scope of universal credit households in a limited area (i.e. the part postcode SM5 2). See also the Universal Credit (Digital Service) Amendment Regulations 2014 (SI 2014/2887), introduced with effect from 26 November 2014, which were limited to any claimant who lived in the digital trial area and who was referred to as a 'Digital service claimant'. There is no Schedule to this Commencement Order as the relevant part postcode area is simply defined by reference to the definition of "the No.28 relevant district" in art.2(1). Provision for universal credit new claims in Sutton was subsequently resumed under the Commencement No.21 Order.

Citation

3.325 **1.** This Order may be cited as the Welfare Reform Act 2012 (Commencement No.20 and Transitional and Transitory Provisions and Commencement No.9 and Transitional and Transitory Provisions (Amendment)) Order 2014.

Interpretation

3.326 **2.** (1) In this Order—
"the Act" means the Welfare Reform Act 2012;
"the 1998 Act" means the Social Security Act 1998;
"the amending provisions" means the provisions referred to in article 4(1)(a) to (c) of the No.9 Order (day appointed for the abolition of income-related employment and support allowance and income-based jobseeker's allowance);
"claimant"—
(a) in relation to an employment and support allowance, has the same meaning as in Part 1 of the Welfare Reform Act 2007, save as mentioned in article 5(1A) of the No.9 Order as applied by article 4(7);
(b) in relation to a jobseeker's allowance, has the same meaning as in the Jobseekers Act 1995 (as it applies apart from the amendments made by Part 1 of Schedule 14 to the Act that remove references to an income-based jobseeker's allowance), save as mentioned in article 5(1A) of the No.9 Order as applied by article 4(7);
(c) in relation to universal credit, has the same meaning as in Part 1 of the Act;
"the Claims and Payments Regulations 2013" means the Universal Credit, Personal Independence Payment, Jobseeker's Allowance and Employment and Support Allowance (Claims and Payments) Regulations 2013;
"the Digital Service Regulations 2014" means the Universal Credit (Digital Service) Amendment Regulations 2014;
"employment and support allowance" means an employment and support allowance under Part 1 of the Welfare Reform Act 2007;
"First-tier Tribunal" has the same meaning as in the 1998 Act;

"housing benefit" means housing benefit under section 130 of the Social Security Contributions and Benefits Act 1992;

"income support" means income support under section 124 of the Social Security Contributions and Benefits Act 1992;

"jobseeker's allowance" means a jobseeker's allowance under the Jobseekers Act 1995;

"joint claimants", in relation to universal credit, has the same meaning as in Part 1 of the Act;

"the No.9 Order" means the Welfare Reform Act 2012 (Commencement No.9 and Transitional and Transitory Provisions and Commencement No.8 and Savings and Transitional Provisions (Amendment)) Order 2013;

"the No.28 relevant district" means the postcode part-district SM5 2;

"single claimant", in relation to universal credit, has the same meaning as in Part 1 of the Act;

"specified condition" means the condition that a claimant is a British citizen who—

(d) has resided in the United Kingdom throughout the period of two years ending with the date on which the claim for universal credit is made; and

(e) has not, during that period, left the United Kingdom for a continuous period of four weeks or more;

"state pension credit" means state pension credit under the State Pension Credit Act 2002;

"tax credit" (including "child tax credit" and "working tax credit") and "tax year" have the same meanings as in the Tax Credits Act 2002;

"Upper Tribunal" has the same meaning as in the 1998 Act.

(2) For the purposes of this Order—

(a) the Claims and Payments Regulations 2013 apply for the purpose of deciding—

(i) whether a claim for universal credit is made or treated as made; and

(ii) the date on which such a claim is made; and

(b) where a couple is treated, in accordance with regulation 9(8) of the Claims and Payments Regulations 2013, as making a claim for universal credit, references to the date on which the claim is treated as made are to the date of formation of the couple.

Day appointed for the coming into force of the universal credit provisions

3. (1) The day appointed for the coming into force of the provisions of the Act listed in Schedule 2 to the No.9 Order, in so far as they are not already in force, in relation to the case of a claim referred to in paragraph (2), and any award that is made in respect of the claim, is the day appointed in accordance with paragraph (3).

3.327

(2) The claims referred to are—

(a) a claim for universal credit that is made on or after 26th November 2014 and before 20th December 2014 in respect of a period that begins on or after 26th November 2014 where, on the date on which the claim is made, the claimant resides in the No.28 relevant district and meets the specified condition;

(b) a claim for universal credit that is made on or after 26th November 2014 and before 20th December 2014, in respect of a period that begins on or after 26th November 2014 where—

(i) in the case of a single claimant, the claimant gives incorrect information regarding the claimant residing in the No.28 relevant district or meeting the specified condition and the claimant does not reside in that district or does not meet the specified condition on the date on which the claim is made;

(ii) in the case of joint claimants, either or both of the joint claimants gives or give incorrect information regarding his or her (or their) residing in that district or meeting the specified condition and one or both of them does not or do not reside in such a district or does not or do not meet the specified condition on the date on which the claim is made,

and after a decision is made that the single claimant is, or the joint claimants are, entitled to universal credit and one or more payments have been made in respect of the single claimant or the joint claimants, the Secretary of State discovers that incorrect information has been given regarding such residence or meeting the specified condition as the case may be.

(3) The day appointed in relation to the case of a claim referred to in paragraph (2), and any award that is made in respect of the claim, is the first day of the period in respect of which the claim is made.

(4) Article 3(6) of the No.9 Order applies for the purposes of paragraph (3) as it applies for the purposes of article 3(4)(a) of the No.9 Order.

(5) Article 3A of the No.9 Order applies in connection with a claim for universal credit where a single claimant, or, as the case may be, either or both of joint claimants, gives or give incorrect information regarding his or her (or their) residing in a No.28 relevant district or meeting the specified condition, as it applies in connection with the giving of incorrect information regarding a claimant residing in a relevant district (as defined in the No.9 Order) or meeting the gateway conditions (as defined in the No.9 Order).

DEFINITIONS

"claimant"–see art.2(1).
"joint claimant"–*ibid.*
"single claimant"–*ibid.*
"No.9 Order"–*ibid.*
"No.28 relevant district"–*ibid.*
"specified condition"–*ibid.*

Day appointed for the abolition of income-related employment and support allowance and income-based jobseeker's allowance

3.328   **4.** (1) The day appointed for the coming into force of the amending provisions, in relation to the case of a claim referred to in paragraph (2), and any award that is made in respect of the claim, is the day appointed in accordance with paragraph (3).

(2) The claims referred to are—

(a) a claim for universal credit that is made on or after 26th November 2014 and before 20th December 2014 in respect of a period that begins on or after 26th November 2014 where, on the date on which the claim is made, the claimant resides in the No.28 relevant district and meets the specified condition;

(b) a claim for universal credit that is made on or after 26th November 2014 and before 20th December 2014, in respect of a period that begins on or after 26th November 2014 where—

    (i) in the case of a single claimant, the claimant gives incorrect information regarding the claimant residing in the No.28 relevant district or meeting the specified condition and the claimant does not reside in that district or does not meet the specified condition on the date on which the claim is made;

    (ii) in the case of joint claimants, either or both of the joint claimants gives or give incorrect information regarding his or her (or their) residing in that district or meeting the specified condition and one or both of them does not or do not reside in such a district or does not or do not meet the specified condition on the date on which the claim is made,

and after a decision is made that the single claimant is, or the joint claimants are, entitled to universal credit and one or more payments have been made in respect of the single claimant or the joint claimants, the Secretary of State discovers that incorrect information has been given regarding such residence or meeting the specified condition as the case may be;

(c) a claim for an employment and support allowance or a jobseeker's allowance that is made or treated as made on or after 26th November 2014 and before 20th December 2014 where, on the date on which the claim is made or treated as made, the claimant resides in the No.28 relevant district and meets the specified condition;

(d) a claim for an employment and support allowance or a jobseeker's allowance other than one referred to in sub-paragraph (c) that is made or treated as made during the relevant period by a single claimant of universal credit or by either of two joint claimants of universal credit who has or have made a claim for universal credit within sub-paragraph (a) or (b).

(3) The day appointed in relation to the case of a claim referred to in paragraph (2), and any award that is made in respect of the claim, is the first day of the period in respect of which the claim is made.

(4) For the purposes of paragraph (2)(d), "relevant period" means, in relation to a claim for universal credit within paragraph (2)(a) or (b), any UC claim period, and any period subsequent to any UC claim period in respect of which the claimant is entitled to an award of universal credit in respect of the claim.

(5) For the purposes of paragraph (4), a "UC claim period" is a period when—

(a) a claim for universal credit within sub-paragraph (a) of paragraph (2), or within sub-paragraph (b)(i) or (ii) of that paragraph, has been made but a decision has not yet been made on the claim; or

(b) a decision has been made that the claimant is not entitled to universal credit and—

    (i) the Secretary of State is considering whether to revise that decision under section 9 of the 1998 Act, whether on an application made for that purpose, or on the Secretary of State's own initiative; or

(ii) the claimant has appealed against that decision to the First-tier Tribunal and that appeal or any subsequent appeal to the Upper Tribunal or to a court has not been finally determined.

(6) Paragraphs (6) and (7) of article 4 of the No.9 Order apply in relation to a claim for universal credit referred to in paragraph (2) (and any award that is made in respect of the claim) as they apply in relation to a claim for universal credit referred to in sub-paragraphs (a) and (b) of article 4(2) of the No.9 Order (and any award that is made in respect of the claim).

(7) Paragraphs (1A) and (1B) of article 5 of the No.9 Order apply for the purposes of paragraph (2)(c) as they apply for the purposes of article 4(2) (a) of the No.9 Order (but as if the reference in paragraph (1A) to Schedule 5 of the No.9 Order were omitted).

(8) Paragraphs (5) to (7) of article 5 of the No.9 Order apply for the purposes of sub-paragraphs (c) and (d) of paragraph (2) as they apply for the purposes of sub-paragraphs (a) and (g) of article 4(2) of the No.9 Order.

(9) Article 5(8) of the No.9 Order applies for the purposes of paragraph (3) as it applies for the purposes of article 4(3)(a) of the No.9 Order.

DEFINITIONS

"the amending provisions"–see art.2(1).
"claimant"–*ibid.*
"employment and support allowance"–*ibid.*
"First-tier Tribunal"–*ibid.*
"jobseeker's allowance"–*ibid.*
"joint claimant"–*ibid.*
"No.9 Order"–*ibid.*
"No.28 relevant district"–*ibid.*
"relevant period"–para.(4).
"specified condition"–see art.2(1).
"UC claim period"–para.(5).
"Upper Tribunal"–see art.2(1).

Application of the No.9 Order

3.329   **5.** Articles 9 to 22 of the No.9 Order apply in connection with the coming into force of the amending provisions in relation to the case of a claim referred to in article 4(2), and any award made in respect of the claim, as they apply in connection with the coming into force of the amending provisions in relation to the case of a claim referred to in sub-paragraphs (a), (b) and (g) of article 4(2) of the No.9 Order and any award made in respect of the claim.

DEFINITIONS

"the amending provisions"–see art.2(1).
"No.9 Order"–*ibid.*

Transitional provision: claims for housing benefit, income support or a tax credit

3.330   **6.** (1) Except as provided by paragraphs (2) to (5) and (8), a person may not make a claim for housing benefit, income support or a tax credit (in the latter case, whether or not as part of a Tax Credits Act couple) on any date where, if that person made a claim for universal credit on that date (whether or not as part of a couple), the provisions of the Act listed in Schedule 2 to the No.9 Order would come into force under article 3(1) and (2)(a) of this Order in relation to that claim for universal credit.

(2) Paragraph (1) does not apply to a claim for housing benefit in respect of specified accommodation.

(3) Paragraph (1) does not apply to a claim for housing benefit or a tax credit where—

(a) in the case of a claim for housing benefit, the claim is made by a person who has reached the qualifying age for state pension credit, or by a person who is a member of a State Pension Credit Act couple the other member of which has reached that age;

(b) in the case of a claim for a tax credit, the claim is made by—

(i) a person who has reached the qualifying age for state pension credit;

(ii) a Tax Credits Act couple both members of which have reached, or either member of which has reached, that age; or

(iii) in a case not covered by paragraph (i), a person who is a member of a State Pension Credit Act couple where the other member of the couple has reached that age.

(4) Paragraph (1) does not apply to a claim for a tax credit where a person or persons makes or make a claim for child tax credit or working tax credit and on the date on which he or she (or they) makes or make the claim he or she (or they) is or are entitled to working tax credit or child tax credit respectively.

(5) Paragraph (1) does not apply to a claim for a tax credit where a person is or was, or persons are or were, entitled to child tax credit or working tax credit in respect of a tax year and that person or those persons makes or make (or is or are treated as making) a claim for that tax credit for the next tax year.

(6) In paragraph (4), the reference to a person being entitled to a tax credit includes where a person is treated as being entitled to a tax credit in the circumstances referred to in regulation 11 of the Universal Credit (Transitional Provisions) Regulations 2014 but as if regulation 11 were amended as follows—

(a) in paragraph (1), for "For the purposes of regulations 7(7) and 8(4)" substitute "For the purposes of article 6(4) of the Welfare Reform Act 2012 (Commencement No.20 and Transitional and Transitory Provisions and Commencement No.9 and Transitional and Transitory Provisions (Amendment)) Order 2014"; and

(b) for paragraph (2)(d)(iii), substitute—

"(iii) the person's claim for child tax credit or working tax credit is made during the period of 30 days starting with the date on the notice referred to in paragraph (ii).".

(7) For the purposes of this article—

(a) a person makes a claim for income support, housing benefit or a tax credit if the person takes any action which results in a decision on a claim being required under the relevant Regulations; and

(b) except as provided in paragraph (8), it is irrelevant that the effect of any provision of the relevant Regulations is that, for the purpose of those Regulations, the claim is made or treated as made on a date that is earlier than the date on which that action was taken.

(8) Paragraph (1) does not apply to a claim for housing benefit or income support where—

(a) in the case of a claim for housing benefit—

    (i) first notification of the person's intention to make the claim is given (within the meaning of regulation 83(5)(d) of the Housing Benefit Regulations 2006 ("the 2006 Regulations") or, as the case may be, regulation 64(6)(d) of the Housing Benefit (Persons who have attained the qualifying age for state pension credit) Regulations 2006 ("the 2006 (SPC) Regulations")) before 26th November 2014; or

    (ii) a defective claim for housing benefit (within the meaning of the 2006 Regulations or the 2006 (SPC) Regulations) is made before 26th November 2014 and it is corrected or completed on or after that date;

(b) in the case of a claim for income support, first notification of the person's intention to make the claim is made, or deemed to be made, for the purposes of regulation 6(1A)(c) of the Social Security (Claims and Payments) Regulations 1987, before 26th November 2014.

(9) Paragraph (10) applies where a person makes a claim for universal credit and the provisions of the Act listed in Schedule 2 to the No.9 Order come into force under article 3(1) and (2)(a) or (b) of this Order in relation to that claim (and any award made in respect of the claim).

(10) Where this paragraph applies, regulation 6 of the Universal Credit (Transitional Provisions) Regulations 2014 applies in relation to the person who makes the claim as referred to in paragraph (9), in relation to any time when they are a "universal credit claimant" as referred to in paragraph (2) of that regulation, as if, in paragraphs (5) to (7) of that regulation, the reference to the date on which the claim for universal credit was made were a reference to 26th November 2014.

(11) For the purposes of this article—

(a) "couple" (apart from in the expressions "State Pension Credit Act couple" and "Tax Credit Act couple"), has the meaning given in section 39 of the Act;

(b) "qualifying age for state pension credit" means the qualifying age referred to in section 1(6) of the State Pension Credit Act 2002;

(c) the "relevant Regulations" means—

    (i) in the case of a claim for income support, the Social Security (Claims and Payments) Regulations 1987;

    (ii) in the case of a claim for housing benefit, the 2006 Regulations or, as the case may be, the 2006 (SPC) Regulations;

    (iii) in the case of a claim for a tax credit, the Tax Credits (Claims and Notifications) Regulations 2002;

(d) "specified accommodation" means accommodation to which one or more of sub-paragraphs (2) to (5) of paragraph 3A of Schedule 1 to the Universal Credit Regulations 2013 applies;

(e) "State Pension Credit Act couple" means a couple as defined in section 17 of the State Pension Credit Act 2002;

(f) "Tax Credits Act couple" means a couple as defined in section 3(5A) of the Tax Credits Act 2002.

DEFINITIONS

"the 2006 Regulations"–see art.2(1).
"the 2006 (SPC) Regulations"–*ibid.*
"child tax credit"–see art.2(1).

"couple"–para.11(a).
"housing benefit"–see art.2(1).
"income support"–*ibid.*
"qualifying age for state pension credit"–para.11(b).
"relevant Regulations"–para.11(c).
"specified accommodation"–para.11(d).
"state pension credit"–see art.2(1).
"State Pension Credit Act couple"–para.11(e).
"tax credit"–see art.2(1).
"Tax Credits Act couple"–para.11(f).
"working tax credit"–see art.2(1).

Amendment of the No.9 Order: claim for universal credit treated as made and awards of universal credit without a claim

7. (1) Paragraph (2) applies in relation to a case where— 3.331
   (a) an award of universal credit is made without a claim as a consequence of a couple forming or separating at a time when both members of the couple in question were entitled to an award of universal credit;
   (b) a claim for universal credit is treated as made as a consequence of a couple forming at a time when one member of the couple was entitled to an award of universal credit;
   (c) a claim for universal credit is made by a former member of a couple who were joint claimants of universal credit, whether or not the claim is made jointly with another person, where the former member is not exempt from the requirement to make a claim by virtue of regulation 9(6) of the Claims and Payments Regulations 2013 (claims for universal credit by members of a couple), as that provision has effect apart from the amendments made by the Digital Service Regulations 2014, where the claim is made during the period of one month starting with the date on which notification is given to the Secretary of State that the former joint claimants have ceased to be a couple; or
   (d) an award of universal credit is made without a claim in the circumstances referred to in regulation 6(1) or (2) of the Claims and Payments Regulations 2013 (claims not required for entitlement to universal credit in some cases),
and the claim for universal credit is made or treated as made, or, as the case may be, the award of universal credit is made without a claim, on or after 26th November 2014.

(2) *[Amendments are incorporated in No.9 Commencement Order]*

(3) For the purposes of paragraph (1), "couple" has the meaning given in section 39 of the Act.

DEFINITIONS

"Claims and Payments Regulations 2013"–see art.2(1).
"couple"–para.(3).
"Digital Service Regulations 2014"–see art.2(1).
"joint claimant"–*ibid.*

The Welfare Reform Act 2012 (Commencement No.9, 11, 13, 14, 16, 17 and 19 and Transitional and Transitory Provisions (Amendment)) Order 2015

(SI 2015/32) (C.3)

The Secretary of State for Work and Pensions makes the following Order in exercise of the powers conferred by section 150(3) and (4)(a) and (b)(i) of the Welfare Reform Act 2012:

ARRANGEMENT OF ARTICLES

1. Citation
2. Interpretation
3. Amendment of the No.9, No.11, No.13, No.14, No.16, No.17 and No.19 Orders: cases to which the amendments apply
4. Amendment of the No.9 Order
5. Amendment of paragraphs 4 and 7 of Schedule 5 to the No.9 Order
6. References to provisions of the No.9 Order amended by articles 4 and 5
7. Amendment of the No.11 Order – gateway conditions
8. Amendment of the No.17 Order – gateway conditions
9. Amendment of the No.11 Order, No.13 Order, No.14 Order, No.16 Order, No.17 Order and No.19 Order – consequential amendment

GENERAL NOTE

3.332   This Commencement Order provided for the introduction of universal credit claims from claimants with children in all live service areas. This was implemented in two stages, with effect from January 26 and March 2, 2015. Thus Art.4 amended Sch.5 to the Commencement No.9 Order so that there is no longer a general condition that a claimant must not have responsibility for children or young persons. In its place is a condition that a claimant must not have responsibility for certain children and young persons (e.g. most children or young persons who are looked after by a local authority and children or young persons who are entitled to DLA or PIP). Article 3(1) in turn provides that those amendments to permit claims by those with responsibility for children came into effect on January 26, 2015 where a claimant resides in any of the areas covered by the Commencement No.9 Order. In addition, these changes also come into effect on the same date where a claimant resides in the areas covered by the Commencement No.11, No.13, No.14, No.16 and No.17 Orders (save for postcode districts and part-districts BL1 to BL4, BL5 1, BL5 3, BL6 4, BL6 9 and M26 3 in the No.9 relevant districts and the No.13 relevant districts (other than postcode part-district CH62 9). Article 3(2) meanwhile provides that the same changes came into effect on March 2, 2015 where a claimant resides in postcode districts and part-districts in the No.9 relevant districts listed above or in one of the No.13 relevant districts, covered by the Commencement No.17 Order, or in the areas covered by the Commencement No.19 Order.

Citation

3.333   **1.** This Order may be cited as the Welfare Reform Act 2012 (Commencement No.9, 11, 13, 14, 16, 17 and 19 and Transitional and Transitory Provisions (Amendment)) Order 2015.

Interpretation

3.334   **2.**—(1) In this Order–

"the Act" means the Welfare Reform Act 2012;

"the Claims and Payments Regulations 1987" means the Social Security (Claims and Payments) Regulations 1987;

"employment and support allowance" means an employment and support allowance under Part 1 of the Welfare Reform Act 2007;

"jobseeker's allowance" means a jobseeker's allowance under the Jobseekers Act 1995;

"the No.9 Order" means the Welfare Reform Act 2012 (Commencement No.9 and Transitional and Transitory Provisions and Commencement No.8 and Savings and Transitional Provisions (Amendment)) Order 2013;

"the No.11 Order" means the Welfare Reform Act 2012 (Commencement No.11 and Transitional and Transitory Provisions and Commencement No.9 and

Transitional and Transitory Provisions (Amendment)) Order 2013;

"the No.13 Order" means the Welfare Reform Act 2012 (Commencement No.13 and Transitional and Transitory Provisions) Order 2013;

"the No.14 Order" means the Welfare Reform Act 2012 (Commencement No.14 and Transitional and Transitory Provisions) Order 2013;

"the No.16 Order" means the Welfare Reform Act 2012 (Commencement No.16 and Transitional and Transitory Provisions) Order 2014;

"the No.17 Order" means the Welfare Reform Act 2012 (Commencement No.17 and Transitional and Transitory Provisions) Order 2014;

"the No.19 Order" means the Welfare Reform Act 2012 (Commencement No.19 and Transitional and Transitory Provisions and Commencement No.9 and Transitional and Transitory Provisions (Amendment)) Order 2014.

(2) For the purposes of this Order, the Universal Credit, Personal Independence Payment, Jobseeker's Allowance and Employment and Support Allowance (Claims and Payments) Regulations 2013 apply for the purpose of deciding–

(a) whether a claim for universal credit is made; and

(b) the date on which such a claim is made.

(3) For the purposes of this Order, the Claims and Payments Regulations 1987 apply, subject to paragraphs (4) and (5), for the purposes of deciding–

(a) whether a claim for an employment and support allowance or a jobseeker's allowance is made; and

(b) the date on which the claim is made or treated as made.

(4) Subject to paragraph (5), for the purposes of this Order–

(a) a person makes a claim for an employment and support allowance or a jobseeker's allowance if he or she takes any action which results in a decision on a claim being required under the Claims and Payments Regulations 1987; and

(b) it is irrelevant that the effect of any provision of the Claims and Payments Regulations 1987 is that, for the purposes of those Regulations, the claim is made or treated as made at a date that is earlier than the date on which that action is taken.

(5) Where, by virtue of–

(a) regulation 6(1F)(b) or (c) of the Claims and Payments Regulations 1987,

in the case of a claim for an employment and support allowance; or

(b) regulation 6(4ZA) to (4ZD) and (4A)(a)(i) and (b) of those Regulations, in the case of a claim for a jobseeker's allowance, a claim for an employment and support allowance or a jobseeker's allowance is treated as made at a date that is earlier than the date on which the action referred to in paragraph (4)(a) is taken, the claim is treated as made on that earlier date.

Amendment of the No.9, No.11, No.13, No.14, No.16, No.17 and No.19 Orders: cases to which the amendments apply

3.335

3.—(1) Articles 4, 6(1) and (2), 7, 8(1) and 9 apply in relation to a case where–

(a) a claim for universal credit is made or treated as made;

(b) an award of universal credit is made without a claim; or

(c) a claim for an employment and support allowance or a jobseeker's allowance is made,

and the claim for universal credit, an employment and support allowance or a jobseeker's allowance is made or treated as made, or, as the case may be, the award of universal credit is made without a claim, on or after 26th January 2015.

(2) Articles 6(3) and 8(2) apply in relation to a case where a claim for universal credit, an employment and support allowance or a jobseeker's allowance is made or treated as made on or after 2nd March 2015.

(3) Articles 5 and 6(4) apply in relation to a case where a claim for universal credit, an employment and support allowance or a jobseeker's allowance is made or treated as made on or after 6th April 2015.

DEFINITIONS

"employment and support allowance"–see art.2(1).
"jobseeker's allowance"–*ibid.*

Amendment of the No.9 Order

3.336

4.— *(Amendments incorporated into text of No. 9 Order)*

Amendment of paragraphs 4 and 7 of Schedule 5 to the No.9 Order

3.337

5.— *(Amendments incorporated into text of No. 9 Order)*

References to provisions of the No.9 Order amended by articles 4 and 5

3.338

6.—(1) Where this paragraph applies, any reference in the No.11 Order, the No.13 Order, the No.14 Order, the No.16 Order, the No.17 Order and the No.19 Order to paragraphs (5) to (7) of article 5 of the No.9 Order is a reference to paragraphs (5) to (7) of article 5 as substituted by article 4(4).

(2) Where this paragraph applies, except where paragraph (4) applies, any reference in the No.11 Order, the No.13 Order, the No.14 Order or the No.16 Order to Schedule 5 to the No.9 Order is a reference to that Schedule as amended by article 4(5).

(3) Where this paragraph applies, except where paragraph (4) applies, any reference in the No.17 Order or the No.19 Order to Schedule 5 to the No.9 Order is a reference to that Schedule as amended by article 4(5).

(4) Where this paragraph applies, any reference in the No.11 Order, the No.13

Order, the No.14 Order, the No.16 Order, the No.17 Order or the No.19 Order to Schedule 5 to the No.9 Order is a reference to that Schedule as amended by articles 4(5) and 5.

DEFINITIONS

"No.9 Order"–see art.2(1).
"No.11 Order"–*ibid*.
"No.13 Order"–*ibid*.
"No.14 Order"–*ibid*.
"No.16 Order"–*ibid*.
"No.17 Order"–*ibid*.
"No.19 Order"–*ibid*.

Amendment of the No.11 Order – gateway conditions

7.— *(Amendments incorporated into text of No. 11 Order)*   3.339

Amendment of the No.17 Order – gateway conditions

8.— *(Amendments incorporated into text of No. 17 Order)*   3.340

Amendment of the No.11 Order, No.13 Order, No.14 Order, No.16 Order, No.17 Order and No.19 Order – consequential amendment

9.— *(Amendments incorporated into text of No. 11 Order, No. 13 Order, No.*   3.341
14 Order, No. 16 Order, No. 17 Order and No. 19 Order)

The Welfare Reform Act 2012 (Commencement No.21 and Transitional and Transitory Provisions) Order 2015

(SI 2015/33) (C.4)

The Secretary of State for Work and Pensions makes the following Order in exercise of the powers conferred by section 150(3) and (4)(a), (b)(i) and (c) of the Welfare Reform Act 2012:

ARRANGEMENT OF REGULATIONS

1. Citation
2. Interpretation
3. Day appointed for the coming into force of the universal credit provisions
4. Day appointed for the abolition of income-related employment and support allowance and income-based jobseeker's allowance
5. Application of the No.9 Order
6. Transitional provision: claims for housing benefit, income support or a tax credit

GENERAL NOTE

3.342   This Order (the Commencement No.21 Order) provided for the resumption of universal credit new claims in Sutton as from January 28, 2015, following the pilot in place there from November 26 to December 19, 2014 (by virtue of the Commencement No.20 Order).

Citation

3.343   **1.** This Order may be cited as the Welfare Reform Act 2012 (Commencement No.21 and Transitional and Transitory Provisions) Order 2015.

Interpretation

3.344   **2.**—(1) In this Order–

"the Act" means the Welfare Reform Act 2012;

"the 1998 Act" means the Social Security Act 1998;

"the amending provisions" means the provisions referred to in article 4(1)(a) to (c) of the No.9 Order (day appointed for the abolition of income-related employment and support allowance and income-based jobseeker's allowance);

"claimant"–

(a) in relation to an employment and support allowance, has the same meaning as in Part 1 of the Welfare Reform Act 2007, save as mentioned in article 5(1A) of the No.9 Order as applied by article 4(7) of this Order;

(b) in relation to a jobseeker's allowance, has the same meaning as in the Jobseekers Act 1995 (as it applies apart from the amendments made by Part 1 of Schedule 14 to the Act that remove references to an income-based jobseeker's allowance), save as mentioned in article 5(1A) of the No.9 Order as applied by article 4(7) of this Order;

(c) in relation to universal credit, has the same meaning as in Part 1 of the Act;

"the Claims and Payments Regulations 2013" means the Universal Credit, Personal Independence Payment, Jobseeker's Allowance and Employment and Support Allowance (Claims and Payments) Regulations 2013;

"employment and support allowance" means an employment and support allowance under Part 1 of the Welfare Reform Act 2007;

"First-tier Tribunal" has the same meaning as in the 1998 Act;

"jobseeker's allowance" means a jobseeker's allowance under the Jobseekers Act 1995;

"joint claimants", in relation to universal credit, has the same meaning as in Part 1 of the Act;

"the No.9 Order" means the Welfare Reform Act 2012 (Commencement No.9 and Transitional and Transitory Provisions and Commencement No.8 and Savings and Transitional Provisions (Amendment)) Order 2013;

"the No.28 relevant district" means the postcode part-district SM5 2;

"single claimant", in relation to universal credit, has the same meaning as in Part 1 of the Act;

[¹ . . .]

"Upper Tribunal" has the same meaning as in the 1998 Act.

(2) For the purposes of this Order, the Claims and Payments Regulations 2013 apply for the purpose of deciding–
(a) whether a claim for universal credit is made; and
(b) the date on which such a claim is made.

AMENDMENT

1. Welfare Reform Act 2012 (Commencement No.23 and Transitional and Transitory Provisions) Order 2015 (SI 2015/634) art.9(2) (June 10. 2015).

Day appointed for the coming into force of the universal credit provisions

3.—(1) The day appointed for the coming into force of the provisions of the Act listed in Schedule 2 to the No.9 Order, in so far as they are not already in force, in
relation to the case of a claim referred to in paragraph (2), and any award that is made in respect of the claim, is the day appointed in accordance with paragraph (3).

3.345

(2) The claims referred to are–
(a) a claim for universal credit that is made on or after 28th January 2015 in
respect of a period that begins on or after 28th January 2015 where, on the date on which the claim is made, the claimant resides in the No.28 relevant district [¹...];
(b) a claim for universal credit that is made on or after 28th January 2015 in respect of a period that begins on or after 28th January 2015 where–
　(i) in the case of a single claimant, the claimant gives incorrect information regarding the claimant residing in the No.28 relevant district [¹...] and the claimant does not reside in that district [¹...] on the date on which the claim is made;
　(ii) in the case of joint claimants, either or both of the joint claimants gives or give incorrect information regarding his or her (or their) residing in that district [¹...] and one or both of them does not or do not reside in that district [¹...] on the date on which the claim is made,
and after a decision is made that the single claimant is, or the joint claimants are, entitled to universal credit and one or more payments have been made in respect of the single claimant or the joint claimants, the Secretary of State discovers that incorrect information has been given regarding such residence [¹...].

(3) The day appointed in relation to the case of a claim referred to in paragraph (2), and any award that is made in respect of the claim, is the first day of the period in respect of which the claim is made.

(4) Article 3(6) of the No.9 Order applies for the purposes of paragraph (3) as it applies for the purposes of article 3(4)(a) of the No.9 Order.

(5) Article 3A of the No.9 Order applies in connection with a claim for universal credit where a single claimant, or, as the case may be, either or both of joint claimants, gives or give incorrect information regarding his or her (or their) residing in the No.28 relevant district [¹...], as it applies in connection with the giving of incorrect information regarding a claimant residing in one of the relevant districts (as defined in the No.9 Order) [¹...].

AMENDMENT

1. Welfare Reform Act 2012 (Commencement No.23 and Transitional and Transitory Provisions) Order 2015 (SI 2015/634) art.9(3) (June 10, 2015).

DEFINITIONS

"claimant"–see art.2(1).
"joint claimant"–*ibid.*
"single claimant"–*ibid.*
"No.9 Order"–*ibid.*
"No.28 relevant district"–*ibid.*
"specified condition"–*ibid.*

Day appointed for the abolition of income-related employment and support allowance and income-based jobseeker's allowance

3.346   **4.**—(1) The day appointed for the coming into force of the amending provisions, in relation to the case of a claim referred to in paragraph (2), and any award that is made in respect of the claim, is the day appointed in accordance with paragraph (3).

(2) The claims referred to are–

(a) a claim for universal credit that is made on or after 28th January 2015 in respect of a period that begins on or after 28th January 2015 where, on the date on which the claim is made, the claimant resides in the No.28 relevant district [² . . .];

(b) a claim for universal credit that is made on or after 28th January 2015 in respect of a period that begins on or after 28th January 2015 where–

(i) in the case of a single claimant, the claimant gives incorrect information regarding the claimant residing in the No.28 relevant district [² . . .] and the claimant does not reside in that district [² . . .] on the date on which the claim is made;

(ii) in the case of joint claimants, either or both of the joint claimants gives or give incorrect information regarding his or her (or their) residing in that district [² . . .] and one or both of them does not or do not reside in that district [² . . .] on the date on which the claim is made,

and after a decision is made that the single claimant is, or the joint claimants are, entitled to universal credit and one or more payments have been made in respect of the single claimant or the joint claimants, the Secretary of State discovers that incorrect information has been given regarding such residence [² . . .];

(c) a claim for an employment and support allowance or a jobseeker's allowance that is made or treated as made on or after 28th January 2015 where, on the date on which the claim is made or treated as made, the claimant resides in the No.28 relevant district [² . . .];

(d) a claim for an employment and support allowance or a jobseeker's allowance other than one referred to in sub-paragraph (c) that is made or treated as made during the relevant period by a single claimant of universal credit or by either of two joint claimants of universal credit who has or have made a claim for universal credit within sub-paragraph (a) or (b).

(3) The day appointed in relation to the case of a claim referred to in

paragraph (2), and any award that is made in respect of the claim, is the first day of the period in respect of which the claim is made.

(4) For the purposes of paragraph (2)(d), "relevant period" means, in relation to a

claim for universal credit within paragraph (2)(a) or (b), any UC claim period, and any period subsequent to any UC claim period in respect of which the claimant is entitled to an award of universal credit in respect of the claim.

(5) For the purposes of paragraph (4), a "UC claim period" is a period when–

(a) a claim for universal credit within sub-paragraph (a) of paragraph (2), or within sub-paragraph (b)(i) or (ii) of that paragraph, has been made but a decision has not yet been made on the claim; or

(b) a decision has been made that the claimant is not entitled to universal credit and–

(i) the Secretary of State is considering whether to revise that decision under section 9 of the 1998 Act, whether on an application made for that purpose, or on the Secretary of State's own initiative; or

(ii) the claimant has appealed against that decision to the First-tier Tribunal and that appeal or any subsequent appeal to the Upper Tribunal or to a court has not been finally determined.

(6) [¹ Paragraphs (6), (7), (9) and (10)] of article 4 of the No.9 Order apply in relation to a claim for universal credit referred to in paragraph (2) (and any award that is made in respect of the claim) as they apply in relation to a claim for universal credit referred to in sub-paragraphs (a) and (b) of article 4(2) of the No.9 Order (and any award that is made in respect of the claim).

(7) Paragraphs (1A) and (1B) of article 5 of the No.9 Order apply for the purposes of paragraph (2)(c) as they apply for the purposes of article 4(2)(a) of the No.9 Order (but as if the references in paragraph (1A) to Schedule 5 to the No.9 Order were omitted).

(8) Paragraphs (5) to (7) of article 5 of the No.9 Order apply for the purposes of sub-paragraphs (c) and (d) of paragraph (2) as they apply for the purposes of subparagraphs (a) and (g) of article 4(2) of the No.9 Order.

(9) Article 5(8) of the No.9 Order applies for the purposes of paragraph (3) as it applies for the purposes of article 4(3)(a) of the No.9 Order.

AMENDMENTS

1. Welfare Reform Act 2012 (Commencement No.22 and Transitional and Transitory Provisions) Order 2015 (SI 2015/101), art.7(2)(b) (February 11, 2015).

2. Welfare Reform Act 2012 (Commencement No.23 and Transitional and Transitory Provisions) Order 2015 (SI 2015/634) art.9(4) (June 10, 2015).

DEFINITIONS

"the amending provisions"–see art.2(1).
"claimant"–*ibid.*
"employment and support allowance"–*ibid.*
"First-tier Tribunal"–*ibid.*
"jobseeker's allowance"–*ibid.*
"joint claimant"–*ibid.*

"No.9 Order"–*ibid.*
"No.28 relevant district"–*ibid.*
"relevant period"–para.(4).
"specified condition"–see art.2(1).
"UC claim period"–para.(5).
"Upper Tribunal"–see art.2(1).

Application of the No.9 Order

3.347 **5.** Articles 9 to 22 of the No.9 Order apply in connection with the coming into force of the amending provisions in relation to the case of a claim referred to in article 4(2), and any award made in respect of the claim, as they apply in connection with the coming into force of the amending provisions in relation to the case of a claim referred to in sub-paragraph (a), (b) or (g) of article 4(2) of the No.9 Order and any award made in respect of the claim.

DEFINITIONS

"the amending provisions"–see art.2(1).
"No.9 Order"–*ibid.*

Transitional provision: claims for housing benefit, income support or a tax credit

3.348 **6.**—(1) Except as provided by paragraphs [¹1(2) to (5) and (11)], a person may not make a claim for housing benefit, income support or a tax credit (in the latter case, whether or not as part of a Tax Credits Act couple) on any date where, if that person made a claim for universal credit on that date (in the capacity, whether as a single person or as part of a couple, in which he or she is permitted to claim universal credit under the Universal Credit Regulations 2013), the provisions of the Act listed in Schedule 2 to the No.9 Order would come into force under article 3(1) and (2)(a) of this Order in relation to that claim for universal credit.

(2) Paragraph (1) does not apply to a claim for housing benefit in respect of specified accommodation.

(3) Paragraph (1) does not apply to a claim for housing benefit or a tax credit where–

(a) in the case of a claim for housing benefit, the claim is made by a person who has reached the qualifying age for state pension credit, or by a person who is a member of a State Pension Credit Act couple the other member of which has reached that age;

(b) in the case of a claim for a tax credit, the claim is made by–

(i) a person who has reached the qualifying age for state pension credit;

(ii) a Tax Credits Act couple both members of which have reached, or either member of which has reached, that age; or

(iii) in a case not covered by paragraph (i), a person who is a member of a State Pension Credit Act couple where the other member of the couple has reached that age.

(4) Paragraph (1) does not apply to a claim for a tax credit where a person or persons makes or make a claim for child tax credit or working

tax credit and on the date on which he or she (or they) makes or make the claim he or she (or they) is or are entitled to working tax credit or child tax credit respectively.

(5) Paragraph (1) does not apply to a claim for a tax credit where a person is or was, or persons are or were, entitled to child tax credit or working tax credit in respect of a tax year and that person or those persons makes or make (or is or are treated as making) a claim for that tax credit for the next tax year.

(6) In paragraph (4), the reference to a person being entitled to a tax credit includes where a person is treated as being entitled to a tax credit in the circumstances referred to in regulation 11 of the Universal Credit (Transitional Provisions) Regulations 2014 but as if regulation 11 were amended as follows–

(a) in paragraph (1), for "For the purposes of regulations 7(7) and 8(4)" substitute

"For the purposes of article 6(4) of the Welfare Reform Act 2012 (Commencement No.21 and Transitional and Transitory Provisions) Order 2015"; and

(b) for paragraph (2)(d)(iii), substitute–

"(iii) the person's claim for child tax credit or working tax credit is made during the period of 30 days starting with the date on the notice referred to in paragraph (ii).".

(7) Subject to paragraph (8), for the purposes of this article–

(a) a claim for housing benefit, income support or a tax credit is made by a person on the date on which he or she takes any action which results in a decision on a claim being required under the relevant Regulations; and

(b) it is irrelevant that the effect of any provision of the relevant Regulations is that, for the purpose of those Regulations, the claim is made or treated as made on a date that is earlier than the date on which that action is taken.

(8) Where under the provisions referred to in paragraph (9), a claim for housing benefit or income support is treated as made at a date that is earlier than the date on which the action referred to in paragraph (7)(a) is taken, the claim is treated as made on that earlier date.

(9) The provisions referred to are–

(a) in the case of a claim for housing benefit, regulation 83(4E), (4F), (5)(d) or (8) of the Housing Benefit Regulations 2006 ("the 2006 Regulations") or, as the case may be, regulation 64(5F), (5G), (6)(d) or (9) of the Housing Benefit (Persons who have attained the qualifying age for state pension credit) Regulations 2006 ("the 2006 (SPC) Regulations")); or

(b) in the case of a claim for income support, [² regulation 6(1A)(b) or 6A] of the Social Security (Claims and Payments) Regulations 1987.

(10) For the purposes of this article–

(a) "couple" (apart from in the expressions "State Pension Credit Act couple" and "Tax Credit Act couple"), has the meaning given in section 39 of the Act;

(b) "housing benefit" means housing benefit under section 130 of the Social Security Contributions and Benefits Act 1992;

(c) "income support" means income support under section 124 of the Social Security Contributions and Benefits Act 1992;

(d) "qualifying age for state pension credit" means the qualifying age referred to in section 1(6) of the State Pension Credit Act 2002;

(e) the "relevant Regulations" means–

   (i) in the case of a claim for housing benefit, the 2006 Regulations or, as the case may be, the 2006 (SPC) Regulations;

   (ii) in the case of a claim for income support, the Social Security (Claims and Payments) Regulations 1987;

   (iii) in the case of a claim for a tax credit, the Tax Credits (Claims and Notifications) Regulations 2002;

(f) "specified accommodation" means accommodation to which one or more of sub-paragraphs (2) to (5) of paragraph 3A of Schedule 1 to the Universal Credit Regulations 2013 applies;

(g) "state pension credit" means state pension credit under the State Pension Credit Act 2002;

(h) "State Pension Credit Act couple" means a couple as defined in section 17 of the State Pension Credit Act 2002;

(i) "tax credit" (including "child tax credit" and "working tax credit") and "tax year" have the same meanings as in the Tax Credits Act 2002;

(j) "Tax Credits Act couple" means a couple as defined in section 3(5A) of theTax Credits Act 2002.

[¹ (11) Paragraph (1) does not apply to a claim for housing benefit, income support or a tax credit where, by virtue of a determination made under regulation 4 [³, or by virtue of regulation 39,] of the Universal Credit (Transitional Provisions) Regulations 2014, the person in question would be prevented from making a claim for universal credit as referred to in that paragraph.]

AMENDMENTS

1. Welfare Reform Act 2012 (Commencement No.23 and Transitional and Transitory Provisions) Order 2015 (SI 2015/634) art.9(5) (March 18, 2015).

2. Welfare Reform Act 2012 (Commencement No.23 and Transitional and Transitory Provisions) (Amendment) Order 2015 (SI 2015/740) art.2(b) (March 18, 2015).

3. Welfare Reform Act 2012 (Commencement No.9 and 21 and Transitional and Transitory Provisions (Amendment)) Order 2017 (SI 2017/483) art.3 (April 6, 2017).

DEFINITIONS

"the 2006 Regulations"–para.(9)(a).
"the 2006 (SPC) Regulations"–*ibid.*
"child tax credit"–para.10(i).
"couple"–para.(10)(a).
"housing benefit"–para.(10)(b).
"income support"–para.(10)(c).
"qualifying age for state pension credit"–para.10(d).
"relevant Regulations"–para.10(e).
"specified accommodation"–para.10(f).
"state pension credit"–para.10(g).
"State Pension Credit Act couple"–para.10(h).
"tax credit"–para.(10)(i).
"Tax Credits Act couple"–para.10(j).
"working tax credit"–para.10(i).

The Welfare Reform Act 2012 (Commencement No.22 and Transitional and Transitory Provisions) Order 2015

(SI 2015/101) (C.6)

The Secretary of State for Work and Pensions makes the following Order, in exercise of the powers conferred by section 150(3) and (4)(a), (b)(i) and (c) of the Welfare Reform Act 2012:

ARRANGEMENT OF REGULATIONS

GENERAL NOTE

This Order made provision for the first phase of the national expansion of universal credit claims for single claimants for various dates (depending on the district concerned) between February 16 and July 20, 2015. It is important also to note that this Order has been subsequently modified for certain purposes by the Commencement No.26 and No.27 Orders, as well as by the Modification Order 2016. See further the commentary to art.3 below.

3.349

Citation

1. This Order may be cited as the Welfare Reform Act 2012 (Commencement No.22 and Transitional and Transitory Provisions) Order 2015.

3.350

Interpretation

2.—(1) In this Order—

3.351

"the 2015 Amendment Order" means the Welfare Reform Act 2012 (Commencement No.9, 11, 13, 14, 16, 17 and 19 and Transitional and Transitory Provisions (Amendment)) Order 2015;

"the Act" means the Welfare Reform Act 2012;

"the amending provisions" means the provisions referred to in article 4(1)(a) to (c) of the No.9 Order (day appointed for the abolition of income-related employment and support allowance and income-based jobseeker's allowance);

"the Claims and Payments Regulations 1987" means the Social Security (Claims and Payments) Regulations 1987;

"claimant"—

(a) in relation to an employment and support allowance, has the same meaning as in Part 1 of the Welfare Reform Act 2007;

(b) in relation to a jobseeker's allowance, has the same meaning as in the Jobseekers Act 1995 (as it applies apart from the amendments made by Part 1 of Schedule 14 to the Act that remove references to an income-based jobseeker's allowance);

(c) in relation to universal credit, has the same meaning as in Part 1 of the Act;

"employment and support allowance" means an employment and support allowance under Part 1 of the Welfare Reform Act 2007;

"First-tier Tribunal" has the same meaning as in the Social Security Act 1998;

"Index of Relevant Districts" means the Index of Relevant Districts issued by the Department for Work and Pensions on 10th February 2015;

"jobseeker's allowance" means a jobseeker's allowance under the Jobseekers Act 1995;

"the No.9 Order" means the Welfare Reform Act 2012 (Commencement No.9 and Transitional and Transitory Provisions and Commencement No 8 and Savings and Transitional Provisions (Amendment)) Order 2013;

"Upper Tribunal" has the same meaning as in the Social Security Act 1998.

(2) In this Order, "gateway conditions" means the conditions specified in Schedule 5 to the No.9 Order—

(a) as that Schedule has effect apart from the amendments made by article 4(5)(b) of the 2015 Amendment Order;

(b) as if that Schedule, as it has effect under sub-paragraph (a), were amended in accordance with paragraph (4) of this article; and

(c) in relation to a case where a claim for universal credit, an employment and support allowance or a jobseeker's allowance is made or treated as made on or after 6th April 2015, as if, in paragraph 4(1) of that Schedule, as that Schedule has effect under sub-paragraph (b), for "£330" there were substituted "£338".

(3) In this Order, references to numbered "relevant districts" are to the postcode districts and part-districts specified in the first column of the table in the Index of Relevant Districts corresponding to the number relating to those relevant districts that is specified in the third column of that table.

(4) The amendments to Schedule 5 to the No.9 Order (gateway conditions) referred to in sub-paragraph (2)(b) are—

(a) after paragraph 1(a) (personal characteristics) insert—

"(b) a single person (where that expression has the meaning given by section 40 of the Act);";

(b) for paragraph 4 (income and capital) substitute—

"4.—(1) The claimant must declare that, during the period of one month starting with the date on which the claim for universal credit is made, the claimant's earned income is expected not to exceed £330.

(2) The claimant's capital must not exceed £6,000.

(3) For the purposes of this paragraph, "earned income" and "capital" have the same meanings as they have in Part 6 of the Universal Credit Regulations.";

(c) in paragraph 8 (declarations)—

(i) in sub-paragraph (1) omit ", 4(2)";

(ii) omit sub-paragraph (2).

(5) For the purposes of this Order, the Universal Credit, Personal

Independence Payment, Jobseeker's Allowance and Employment and Support Allowance (Claims and Payments) Regulations 2013 apply for the purposes of deciding—

(a) whether a claim for universal credit is made; and

(b) the date on which such a claim is made.

(6) For the purposes of this Order, the Claims and Payments Regulations 1987 apply, subject to paragraphs (7) and (8), for the purposes of deciding—

(a) whether a claim for an employment and support allowance or a jobseeker's allowance is made; and

(b) the date on which the claim is made or treated as made.

(7) Subject to paragraph (8), for the purposes of this Order—

(a) a person makes a claim for an employment and support allowance or a jobseeker's allowance if he or she takes any action which results in a decision on a claim being required under the Claims and Payments Regulations 1987; and

(b) it is irrelevant that the effect of any provision of those Regulations is that, for the purposes of those Regulations, the claim is made or treated as made at a date that is earlier than the date on which that action is taken.

(8) Where, by virtue of—

(a) regulation 6(1F)(b) or (c) of the Claims and Payments Regulations 1987, in the case of a claim for an employment and support allowance; or

(b) regulation 6(4ZA) to (4ZD) and (4A)(a)(i) and (b) of those Regulations, in the case of a claim for a jobseeker's allowance,

a claim for an employment and support allowance or a jobseeker's allowance is treated as made at a date that is earlier than the date on which the action referred to in paragraph (7)(a) is taken, the claim is treated as made on that earlier date.

Day appointed for the coming into force of the universal credit provisions

3.—(1) The day appointed for the coming into force of the provisions of the Act listed in Schedule 2 to the No.9 Order, in so far as they are not already in force, in relation to a claim referred to in paragraph (2), and any award that is made in respect of the claim, is the day appointed in accordance with paragraph (3).

3.352

(2) The claims referred to are—

(a) a claim for universal credit that is made on or after 16th February 2015 in respect of a period that begins on or after 16th February 2015 where, on the date on which the claim is made, the claimant resides in one of the No.29 relevant districts and meets the gateway conditions;

(b) a claim for universal credit that is made on or after 23rd February 2015 in respect of a period that begins on or after 23rd February 2015 where, on the date on which the claim is made, the claimant resides in one of the No.30 relevant districts and meets the gateway conditions;

(c) a claim for universal credit that is made on or after 2nd March 2015 in respect of a period that begins on or after 2nd March 2015 where, on the date on which the claim is made, the claimant resides in one of the No.31 relevant districts and meets the gateway conditions;

(d) a claim for universal credit that is made on or after 9th March 2015 in respect of a period that begins on or after 9th March 2015 where, on the date on which the claim is made, the claimant resides in one of the No.32 relevant districts and meets the gateway conditions;

(e) a claim for universal credit that is made on or after 16th March 2015 in respect of a period that begins on or after 16th March 2015 where, on the date on which the claim is made, the claimant resides in one of the No.33 relevant districts and meets the gateway conditions;

(f) a claim for universal credit that is made on or after 23rd March 2015 in respect of a period that begins on or after 23rd March 2015 where, on the date on which the claim is made, the claimant resides in one of the No.34 relevant districts and meets the gateway conditions;

(g) a claim for universal credit that is made on or after 13th April 2015 in respect of a period that begins on or after 13th April 2015 where, on the date on which the claim is made, the claimant resides in one of the No.35 relevant districts and meets the gateway conditions;

(h) a claim for universal credit that is made on or after 20th April 2015 in respect of a period that begins on or after 20th April 2015 where, on the date on which the claim is made, the claimant resides in one of the No.36 relevant districts and meets the gateway conditions;

(i) a claim for universal credit that is made on or after 27th April 2015 in respect of a period that begins on or after 27th April 2015 where, on the date on which the claim is made, the claimant resides in one of the No.37 relevant districts and meets the gateway conditions;

(j) a claim for universal credit that is made on or after 4th May 2015 in respect of a period that begins on or after 4th May 2015 where, on the date on which the claim is made, the claimant resides in one of the No.38 relevant districts and meets the gateway conditions;

(k) a claim for universal credit that is made on or after 11th May 2015 in respect of a period that begins on or after 11th May 2015 where, on the date on which the claim is made, the claimant resides in one of the No.39 relevant districts and meets the gateway conditions;

(l) a claim for universal credit that is made on or after 18th May 2015 in respect of a period that begins on or after 18th May 2015 where, on the date on which the claim is made, the claimant resides in one of the No.40 relevant districts and meets the gateway conditions;

(m) a claim for universal credit that is made on or after 25th May 2015 in respect of a period that begins on or after 25th May 2015 where, on the date on which the claim is made, the claimant resides in one of the No.41 relevant districts and meets the gateway conditions;

(n) a claim for universal credit that is made on or after 1st June 2015 in respect of a period that begins on or after 1st June 2015 where, on the date on which the claim is made, the claimant resides in one of the No.42 relevant districts and meets the gateway conditions;

(o) a claim for universal credit that is made on or after 8th June 2015 in respect of a period that begins on or after 8th June 2015 where, on the date on which the claim is made, the claimant resides in one of the No.43 relevant districts and meets the gateway conditions;

(p) a claim for universal credit that is made on or after 15th June 2015 in respect of a period that begins on or after 15th June 2015 where, on the date on which the claim is made, the claimant resides in one of the No.44 relevant districts and meets the gateway conditions;

(q) a claim for universal credit that is made on or after 22nd June 2015 in respect of a period that begins on or after 22nd June 2015 where, on the date on which the claim is made, the claimant resides in one of the No.45 relevant districts and meets the gateway conditions;

(r) a claim for universal credit that is made on or after 29th June 2015 in respect of a period that begins on or after 29th June 2015 where, on the date on which the claim is made, the claimant resides in one of the No.46 relevant districts and meets the gateway conditions;

(s) a claim for universal credit that is made on or after 6th July 2015 in respect of a period that begins on or after 6th July 2015 where, on the date on which the claim is made, the claimant resides in one of the No.47 relevant districts and meets the gateway conditions;

(t) a claim for universal credit that is made on or after 13th July 2015 in respect of a period that begins on or after 13th July 2015 where, on the date on which the claim is made, the claimant resides in one of the No.48 relevant districts and meets the gateway conditions;

(u) a claim for universal credit that is made on or after 20th July 2015 in respect of a period that begins on or after 20th July 2015 where, on the date on which the claim is made, the claimant resides in one of the No.49 relevant districts and meets the gateway conditions;

(v) a claim for universal credit that is made on or after the date referred to in any of sub-paragraphs (a) to (u), in respect of a period that begins on or after that date where—

    (i) the claimant gives incorrect information regarding the claimant residing in a district as referred to in the sub-paragraph in question or meeting the gateway conditions and the claimant does not reside in such a district or does not meet the gateway conditions on the date on which the claim is made; and

    (ii) after a decision is made that the claimant is entitled to universal credit and one or more payments have been made in respect of the claimant, the Secretary of State discovers that incorrect information has been given regarding residence or meeting the gateway conditions.

(3) The day appointed in relation to a claim referred in paragraph (2), and any award that is made in respect of the claim, is the first day of the period in respect of which the claim is made.

(4) Article 3(6) of the No.9 Order applies for the purposes of paragraph (3) as it applies for the purposes of article 3(4)(a) of the No.9 Order.

(5) Article 3A of the No.9 Order applies in connection with a claim for universal credit where a claimant gives incorrect information regarding his or her residing in one of the No.29, No.30, No.31, No.32, No.33, No.34, No.35, No.36, No.37, No.38, No.39, No.40, No.41, No.42, No.43, No.44, No.45, No.46, No.47, No.48, or No.49 relevant districts or meeting the gateway conditions, as it applies in connection with the giving of incorrect information regarding a claimant residing in a relevant district (as defined in the No.9 Order) or meeting the gateway conditions (as defined in the No.9 Order).

DEFINITIONS

"the Act"–see art.2(1).
"claimant"–*ibid.*
"gateway conditions"–see art.2(2).
"joint claimant"–*ibid.*
"single claimant"–*ibid.*
"No.9 Order"–*ibid.*
"relevant districts"–see art.2(3).

GENERAL NOTE

3.353   This article brought into force provisions relating to universal credit in Part 1 of the 2012 Act as set out in Sch.2 to the Commencement No.9 Order, in relation to a number of different cases. Under art.3(2)(a) to (u), the universal credit provisions came into force in relation to any such claim and award that is made in respect of the claim, where the claim is made on or after a specified date with respect to a period that begins on or after that date. As originally enacted, the criteria were that on the date on which the claim is made, the claimant had to (i) reside in a specified area and (ii) comply with the modified gateway conditions as set out in Sch.5 to the Commencement No.9 Order. Separately, under article 3(2)(v), the provisions also came into force in relation to a claim for, and any award of, universal credit on or after the date specified in any of sub-paragraphs (a) to (u) of article 3(2), in respect of a period that begins on or after that date, where incorrect information was provided regarding the claimant residing in the area specified in that sub-paragraph or meeting the modified gateway conditions, but this was only discovered once payments of universal credit have been made. Article 3(3) provides that the day appointed for the commencement of the universal credit provisions in the above cases is the first day of the period in respect of which the claim is made. Paragraphs (4) and (5) apply the provisions of article 3(6) (period for which a claim for universal credit is made) and article 3A (incorrect information regarding entitlement to claim UC) of the Commencement No.9 Order respectively to the cases in paragraph (2).

However, in relation to claims made on or after January 27, 2016, article 6(1) and (2) of the Commencement No.26 Order modify the Commencement No.22 Order so that the restrictions on claiming universal credit applied in that Order (i.e. the gateway conditions) do not apply to the provisions of art.3(2) and 4(2) of that Order for the coming into force of the universal credit provisions and the amending provisions where claims are made (as the case may be) for universal credit, ESA or JSA by reference to residence in the designated postcodes (in Twickenham) in Parts 3 and 4 of the Schedule to the Commencement No.26 Order. Article 6(3) of the Commencement No.26 Order makes consequential modifications to a number of provisions of articles 3 and 4 to allow for claims by couples, which will become possible by virtue of the gateway conditions no longer applying.

Article 6 of the Commencement No.27 Order makes similar provision for other designated postcodes with effect from March 23, 2016 as does Art.5 of the Modification Order 2016.

Day appointed for the abolition of income-related employment and support allowance and income-based jobseeker's allowance

3.354   **4.**—(1) The day appointed for the coming into force of the amending provisions, in relation to a claim referred to in paragraph (2), and any award that is made in respect of the claim, is the day appointed in accordance with paragraph (3).

(2) The claims referred to are—

(a) a claim for universal credit that is made on or after 16th February 2015 in respect of a period that begins on or after 16th February 2015 where, on the date on which the claim is made or treated as made, the claimant resides in one of the No.29 relevant districts and meets the gateway conditions;

(b) a claim for an employment and support allowance or a jobseeker's allowance that is made or treated as made on or after 16th February 2015 where, on the date on which the claim is made or treated as made, the claimant resides in one of the No.29 relevant districts and meets the gateway conditions;

(c) a claim for universal credit that is made on or after 23rd February 2015 in respect of a period that begins on or after 23rd February 2015 where, on the date on which the claim is made or treated as made, the claimant resides in one of the No.30 relevant districts and meets the gateway conditions;

(d) a claim for an employment and support allowance or a jobseeker's allowance that is made or treated as made on or after 23rd February 2015 where, on the date on which the claim is made or treated as made, the claimant resides in one of the No.30 relevant districts and meets the gateway conditions;

(e) a claim for universal credit that is made on or after 2nd March 2015 in respect of a period that begins on or after 2nd March 2015 where, on the date on which the claim is made or treated as made, the claimant resides in one of the No.31 relevant districts and meets the gateway conditions;

(f) a claim for an employment and support allowance or a jobseeker's allowance that is made or treated as made on or after 2nd March 2015 where, on the date on which the claim is made or treated as made, the claimant resides in one of the No.31 relevant districts and meets the gateway conditions;

(g) a claim for universal credit that is made on or after 9th March 2015 in respect of a period that begins on or after 9th March 2015 where, on the date on which the claim is made or treated as made, the claimant resides in one of the No.32 relevant districts and meets the gateway conditions;

(h) a claim for an employment and support allowance or a jobseeker's allowance that is made or treated as made on or after 9th March 2015 where, on the date on which the claim is made or treated as made, the claimant resides in one of the No.32 relevant districts and meets the gateway conditions;

(i) a claim for universal credit that is made on or after 16th March 2015 in respect of a period that begins on or after 16th March 2015 where, on the date on which the claim is made or treated as made, the claimant resides in one of the No.33 relevant districts and meets the gateway conditions;

(j) a claim for an employment and support allowance or a jobseeker's allowance that is made or treated as made on or after 16th March 2015 where, on the date on which the claim is made or treated as made, the claimant resides in one of the No.33 relevant districts and meets the gateway conditions;

(k) a claim for universal credit that is made on or after 23rd March

2015 in respect of a period that begins on or after 23rd March 2015 where, on the date on which the claim is made or treated as made, the claimant resides in one of the No.34 relevant districts and meets the gateway conditions;

(l) a claim for an employment and support allowance or a jobseeker's allowance that is made or treated as made on or after 23rd March 2015 where, on the date on which the claim is made or treated as made, the claimant resides in one of the No.34 relevant districts and meets the gateway conditions;

(m) a claim for universal credit that is made on or after 13th April 2015 in respect of a period that begins on or after 13th April 2015 where, on the date on which the claim is made or treated as made, the claimant resides in one of the No.35 relevant districts and meets the gateway conditions;

(n) a claim for an employment and support allowance or a jobseeker's allowance that is made or treated as made on or after 13th April 2015 where, on the date on which the claim is made or treated as made, the claimant resides in one of the No.35 relevant districts and meets the gateway conditions;

(o) a claim for universal credit that is made on or after 20th April 2015 in respect of a period that begins on or after 20th April 2015 where, on the date on which the claim is made or treated as made, the claimant resides in one of the No.36 relevant districts and meets the gateway conditions;

(p) a claim for an employment and support allowance or a jobseeker's allowance that is made or treated as made on or after 20th April 2015 where, on the date on which the claim is made or treated as made, the claimant resides in one of the No.36 relevant districts and meets the gateway conditions;

(q) a claim for universal credit that is made on or after 27th April 2015 in respect of a period that begins on or after 27th April 2015 where, on the date on which the claim is made or treated as made, the claimant resides in one of the No.37 relevant districts and meets the gateway conditions;

(r) a claim for an employment and support allowance or a jobseeker's allowance that is made or treated as made on or after 27th April 2015 where, on the date on which the claim is made or treated as made, the claimant resides in one of the No.37 relevant districts and meets the gateway conditions;

(s) a claim for universal credit that is made on or after 4th May 2015 in respect of a period that begins on or after 4th May 2015 where, on the date on which the claim is made or treated as made, the claimant resides in one of the No.38 relevant districts and meets the gateway conditions;

(t) a claim for an employment and support allowance or a jobseeker's allowance that is made or treated as made on or after 4th May 2015 where, on the date on which the claim is made or treated as made, the claimant resides in one of the No.38 relevant districts and meets the gateway conditions;

(u) a claim for universal credit that is made on or after 11th May 2015 in respect of a period that begins on or after 11th May 2015 where, on the date on which the claim is made or treated as made, the claimant resides in one of the No.39 relevant districts and meets the gateway conditions;

(v) a claim for an employment and support allowance or a jobseeker's allowance that is made or treated as made on or after 11th May 2015 where, on the date on which the claim is made or treated as made, the claimant resides in one of the No.39 relevant districts and meets the gateway conditions;

(w) a claim for universal credit that is made on or after 18th May 2015 in respect of a period that begins on or after 18th May 2015 where, on the date on which the claim is made or treated as made, the claimant resides in one of the No.40 relevant districts and meets the gateway conditions;

(x) a claim for an employment and support allowance or a jobseeker's allowance that is made or treated as made on or after 18th May 2015 where, on the date on which the claim is made or treated as made, the claimant resides in one of the No.40 relevant districts and meets the gateway conditions;

(y) a claim for universal credit that is made on or after 25th May 2015 in respect of a period that begins on or after 25th May 2015 where, on the date on which the claim is made or treated as made, the claimant resides in one of the No.41 relevant districts and meets the gateway conditions;

(z) a claim for an employment and support allowance or a jobseeker's allowance that is made or treated as made on or after 25th May 2015 where, on the date on which the claim is made or treated as made, the claimant resides in one of the No.41 relevant districts and meets the gateway conditions;

(aa) a claim for universal credit that is made on or after 1st June 2015 in respect of a period that begins on or after 1st June 2015 where, on the date on which the claim is made or treated as made, the claimant resides in one of the No.42 relevant districts and meets the gateway conditions;

(bb) a claim for an employment and support allowance or a jobseeker's allowance that is made or treated as made on or after 1st June 2015 where, on the date on which the claim is made or treated as made, the claimant resides in one of the No.42 relevant districts and meets the gateway conditions;

(cc) a claim for universal credit that is made on or after 8th June 2015 in respect of a period that begins on or after 8th June 2015 where, on the date on which the claim is made or treated as made, the claimant resides in one of the No.43 relevant districts and meets the gateway conditions;

(dd) a claim for an employment and support allowance or a jobseeker's allowance that is made or treated as made on or after 8th June 2015 where, on the date on which the claim is made or treated as made, the claimant resides in one of the No.43 relevant districts and meets the gateway conditions;

(ee) a claim for universal credit that is made on or after 15th June 2015 in respect of a period that begins on or after 15th June 2015 where, on the date on which the claim is made or treated as made, the claimant resides in one of the No.44 relevant districts and meets the gateway conditions;

(ff) a claim for an employment and support allowance or a jobseeker's allowance that is made or treated as made on or after 15th June 2015 where, on the date on which the claim is made or treated as made, the claimant resides in one of the No.44 relevant districts and meets the gateway conditions;

(gg) a claim for universal credit that is made on or after 22nd June 2015 in respect of a period that begins on or after 22nd June 2015 where, on the date on which the claim is made or treated as made, the claimant resides in one of the No.45 relevant districts and meets the gateway conditions;

(hh) a claim for an employment and support allowance or a jobseeker's allowance that is made or treated as made on or after 22nd June 2015 where, on the date on which the claim is made or treated as made, the claimant resides in one of the No.45 relevant districts and meets the gateway conditions;

(ii) a claim for universal credit that is made on or after 29th June 2015 in respect of a period that begins on or after 29th June 2015 where, on the date on which the claim is made or treated as made, the claimant resides in one of the No.46 relevant districts and meets the gateway conditions;

(jj) a claim for an employment and support allowance or a jobseeker's allowance that is made or treated as made on or after 29th June 2015 where, on the date on which the claim is made or treated as made, the claimant resides in one of the No.46 relevant districts and meets the gateway conditions;

(kk) a claim for universal credit that is made on or after 6th July 2015 in respect of a period that begins on or after 6th July 2015 where, on the date on which the claim is made or treated as made, the claimant resides in one of the No.47 relevant districts and meets the gateway conditions;

(ll) a claim for an employment and support allowance or a jobseeker's allowance that is made or treated as made on or after 6th July 2015 where, on the date on which the claim is made or treated as made, the claimant resides in one of the No.47 relevant districts and meets the gateway conditions;

(mm) a claim for universal credit that is made on or after 13th July 2015 in respect of a period that begins on or after 13th July 2015 where, on the date on which the claim is made or treated as made, the claimant resides in one of the No.48 relevant districts and meets the gateway conditions;

(nn) a claim for an employment and support allowance or a jobseeker's allowance that is made or treated as made on or after 13th July 2015 where, on the date on which the claim is made or treated as made, the claimant resides in one of the No.48 relevant districts and meets the gateway conditions;

(oo) a claim for universal credit that is made on or after 20th July 2015 in respect of a period that begins on or after 20th July 2015 where, on the date on which the claim is made or treated as made, the claimant resides in one of the No.49 relevant districts and meets the gateway conditions;

(pp) a claim for an employment and support allowance or a jobseeker's allowance that is made or treated as made on or after 20th July 2015 where, on the date on which the claim is made or treated as made, the claimant resides in one of the No.49 relevant districts and meets the gateway conditions;

(qq) a claim for universal credit that is made on or after the date referred to in any of sub-paragraphs (a), (c), (e), (g), (i), (k), (m), (o), (q), (s), (u), (w), (y), (aa), (cc), (ee), (gg), (ii), (kk), (mm) or (oo), in respect of a period that begins on or after that date, where—

    (i) the claimant gives incorrect information regarding the claimant residing in a district as referred to in the sub-paragraph in question or meeting the gateway conditions and the claimant does not reside in such a district or does not meet the gateway conditions on the date on which the claim is made; and

    (ii) after a decision is made that the claimant is entitled to universal credit and one or more payments have been made in respect of the claimant, the Secretary of State discovers that incorrect information has been given regarding residence or meeting the gateway conditions;

(rr) a claim for an employment and support allowance or a jobseeker's allowance other than one referred to in sub-paragraphs (b), (d), (f), (h), (j), (l), (n), (p), (r), (t), (v), (x), (z), (bb), (dd), (ff), (hh), (jj), (ll), (nn) or (pp) that is made or treated as made during the relevant period by a claimant of universal credit who has made a claim for universal credit within this paragraph.

(3) The day appointed in relation to a claim referred to in paragraph (2), and any award that is made in respect of the claim, is the first day of the period in respect of which the claim is made.

(4) For the purposes of paragraph (2)(rr), the "relevant period" means, in relation to a claim for universal credit within paragraph (2), any UC claim period and any period subsequent to any UC claim period in respect of which the claimant is entitled to an award of universal credit in respect of the claim.

(5) For the purposes of paragraph (4), a "UC claim period" is a period when—

(a) a claim for universal credit within one of the sub-paragraphs (a), (c), (e), (g), (i), (k), (m), (o), (q), (s), (u), (w), (y), (aa), (cc), (ee), (gg), (ii), (kk), (mm), (oo) or (qq)(i) of paragraph (2) has been made but a decision has not yet been made on the claim; or

(b) a decision has been made that the claimant is not entitled to universal credit and—

    (i) the Secretary of State is considering whether to revise that decision under section 9 of the Social Security Act 1998, whether on an application made for that purpose or on the Secretary of State's own initiative; or

    (ii) the claimant has appealed against that decision to the First-tier Tribunal and that appeal or any subsequent appeal to the Upper Tribunal or to a court has not been finally determined.

(6) Paragraphs (6), (7), (9) and (10) of article 4 of the No.9 Order apply in relation to a claim for universal credit referred to in paragraph (2) (and any award that is made in respect of the claim) as they apply to a claim for universal credit referred to in sub-paragraphs (a) and (b) of article 4(2) of the No.9 Order (and any award that is made in respect of the claim).

(7) Article 5(1)(a) of the No.9 Order applies for the purposes of the

sub-paragraphs (relating to a claim for an employment and support allowance or a jobseeker's allowance) referred to in sub-paragraph (rr) as it applies for the purposes of article 4(2)(a) of the No.9 Order.

(8) Article 5(8) of the No.9 Order applies for the purposes of paragraph (3) as it applies for the purposes of article 4(3)(a) of the No.9 Order.

DEFINITIONS

"the amending provisions"–see art.2(1).
"claimant"–*ibid.*
"employment and support allowance"–*ibid.*
"First-tier Tribunal"–*ibid.*
"gateway conditions"–see art.2(2).
"jobseeker's allowance"–see art.2(1).
"joint claimant"–*ibid.*
"No.9 Order"–*ibid.*
"relevant districts"–*ibid.*
"relevant period"–para.(4).
"UC claim period"–para.(5).
"Upper Tribunal"–see art.2(1).

Application of the No.9 Order

3.355   **5.** Articles 9 to 22 of the No.9 Order apply in connection with the coming into force of the amending provisions in relation to a claim referred to in article 4(2), and any award made in respect of the claim, as they apply in connection with the coming into force of the amending provisions in relation to the case of a claim referred to in sub-paragraphs (a), (b) and (g) of article 4(2) of the No.9 Order and any award made in respect of the claim.

DEFINITIONS

"the amending provisions"–see art.2(1).
"No.9 Order"–*ibid.*

Modification of the Universal Credit (Digital Service) Amendment Regulations 2014

3.356   **6.** [¹ . . .]

AMENDMENT

1. Welfare Reform Act 2012 (Commencement No.24 and Transitional and Transitory Provisions and Commencement No.9 and Transitional and Transitory Provisions (Amendment)) Order 2015 (SI 2015/1537), art.8 (September 21, 2015).

Technical amendment — numbering in the 2015 Amendment Order

3.357   **7.**—(1) Paragraph (2) applies in relation to a case where a claim for universal credit is made or treated as made, or an award of universal credit is made without a claim, on or after 11th February 2015.

(2)(a) *[Amendments incorporated into the Welfare Reform Act 2012 (Commencement No. 9, 11, 13, 14, 16, 17 and 19 and Transitional and Transitory Provisions (Amendment)) Order 2015]*

(b) *[Amendment incorporated into the Welfare Reform Act 2012 (Commencement No. 21 and Transitional and Transitory Provisions) Order 2015].*

The Welfare Reform Act 2012 (Commencement No.23 and Transitional and Transitory Provisions) Order 2015

(SI 2015/634) (C.32)

The Secretary of State for Work and Pensions makes the following Order in exercise of the powers conferred by section 150(3) and (4)(a), (b)(i) and (c) of the Welfare Reform Act 2012:

ARRANGEMENT OF ARTICLES

GENERAL NOTE

This Commencement Order ("the Commencement No.23 Order") provides for   **3.358**
the expansion of universal credit to further postcode areas in the London Boroughs of Sutton, Croydon and Southwark in three phases. These are the No.50, No.51 and No.52 relevant districts (see art.2(1) for the definition of those areas). Thus e.g. under art.3(1) and (2)(a), the universal credit provisions come into force in relation to a claim for universal credit, and any award that is made in respect of the claim, where the claim is made on or after March 18, 2015 with respect to a period that begins on or after that date and, on the date on which the claim is made, the claimant resides in one of the "No.50 relevant districts". The same provision is made for claims made on or after June 10, 2015 where the claimant resides in one of the "No.51 relevant districts" and for claims made on or after November 4, 2015 where the claimant resides in one of the "No.52 relevant districts".

Citation

1. This Order may be cited as the Welfare Reform Act 2012   **3.359**
(Commencement No.23 and Transitional and Transitory Provisions) Order 2015.

Interpretation

2.—(1) In this Order—   **3.360**
"the Act" means the Welfare Reform Act 2012;
"the amending provisions" means the provisions referred to in article

633

4(1)(a) to (c) of the No.9 Order (day appointed for the abolition of income-related employment and support allowance and income-based jobseeker's allowance);

"claimant"—

(a) in relation to an employment and support allowance, has the same meaning as in Part 1 of the Welfare Reform Act 2007, save as mentioned in article 5(1A) of the No.9 Order as applied by article 4(7) of this Order;

(b) in relation to a jobseeker's allowance, has the same meaning as in the Jobseekers Act 1995 (as it applies apart from the amendments made by Part 1 of Schedule 14 to the Act that remove references to an income-based jobseeker's allowance), save as mentioned in article 5(1A) of the No.9 Order as applied by article 4(7) of this Order;

(c) in relation to universal credit, has the same meaning as in Part 1 of the Act;

"the Claims and Payments Regulations 1987" means the Social Security (Claims and Payments) Regulations 1987;

"employment and support allowance" means an employment and support allowance under Part 1 of the Welfare Reform Act 2007;

"jobseeker's allowance" means a jobseeker's allowance under the Jobseekers Act 1995;

"joint claimants", in relation to universal credit, has the same meaning as in Part 1 of the Act;

"the No.9 Order" means the Welfare Reform Act 2012 (Commencement No.9 and Transitional and Transitory Provisions and Commencement No.8 and Savings and Transitional Provisions (Amendment)) Order 2013;

"the No.11 Order" means the Welfare Reform Act 2012 (Commencement No.11 and Transitional and Transitory Provisions and Commencement No.9 and Transitional and Transitory Provisions (Amendment)) Order 2013;

"the No.13 Order" means the Welfare Reform Act 2012 (Commencement No.13 and Transitional and Transitory Provisions) Order 2013;

"the No.14 Order" means the Welfare Reform Act 2012 (Commencement No.14 and Transitional and Transitory Provisions) Order 2013;

"the No.16 Order" means the Welfare Reform Act 2012 (Commencement No.16 and Transitional and Transitory Provisions) Order 2014;

"the No.17 Order" means the Welfare Reform Act 2012 (Commencement No.17 and Transitional and Transitory Provisions) Order 2014;

"the No.19 Order" means the Welfare Reform Act 2012 (Commencement No.19 and Transitional and Transitory Provisions and Commencement No.9 and Transitional and Transitory Provisions (Amendment)) Order 2014;

"the No.21 Order" means the Welfare Reform Act 2012 (Commencement No.21 and Transitional and Transitory Provisions) Order 2015;

"the No.22 Order" means the Welfare Reform Act 2012 (Commencement No.22 and Transitional and Transitory Provisions) Order 2015;

"the No.50 relevant districts" means the postcode part-districts SM6 7 and SM6 8;

"the No.51 relevant districts" means the postcode part-districts CR0 4 and SM6 9;

"the No.52 relevant districts" means the postcode part-districts CR0 2 and SE1 5;

"single claimant", in relation to universal credit, has the same meaning as in Part 1 of the Act.

(2) For the purposes of this Order, the Universal Credit, Personal Independence Payment, Jobseeker's Allowance and Employment and Support Allowance (Claims and Payments) Regulations 2013 apply for the purpose of deciding—

(a) whether a claim for universal credit is made; and

(b) the date on which such a claim is made.

(3) For the purposes of this Order, the Claims and Payments Regulations 1987 apply, subject to paragraphs (4) and (5), for the purposes of deciding—

(a) whether a claim for an employment and support allowance or a jobseeker's allowance is made; and

(b) the date on which the claim is made or treated as made.

(4) Subject to paragraph (5), for the purposes of this Order—

(a) a person makes a claim for an employment and support allowance or a jobseeker's allowance if he or she takes any action which results in a decision on a claim being required under the Claims and Payments Regulations 1987; and

(b) it is irrelevant that the effect of any provision of those Regulations is that, for the purposes of those Regulations, the claim is made or treated as made at a date that is earlier than the date on which that action is taken.

(5) Where, by virtue of—

(a) regulation 6(1F)(b) or (c) of the Claims and Payments Regulations 1987, in the case of a claim for an employment and support allowance; or

(b) regulation 6(4ZA) to (4ZD) and (4A)(a)(i) and (b) of those Regulations, in the case of a claim for a jobseeker's allowance,

a claim for an employment and support allowance or a jobseeker's allowance is treated as made at a date that is earlier than the date on which the action referred to in paragraph (4)(a) is taken, the claim is treated as made on that earlier date.

Day appointed for the coming into force of the universal credit provisions

3.—(1) The day appointed for the coming into force of the provisions of the Act listed in Schedule 2 to the No.9 Order, in so far as they are not already in force, in relation to the case of a claim referred to in paragraph (2), and any award that is made in respect of the claim, is the day appointed in accordance with paragraph (3).

3.361

(2) The claims referred to are—

(a) a claim for universal credit that is made on or after 18th March 2015 in respect of a period that begins on or after 18th March 2015 where, on the date on which the claim is made, the claimant resides in one of the No.50 relevant districts;

(b) a claim for universal credit that is made on or after 10th June 2015 in respect of a period that begins on or after 10th June 2015 where, on the date on which the claim is made, the claimant resides in one of the No.51 relevant districts;

    (c) a claim for universal credit that is made on or after 4th November 2015 in respect of a period that begins on or after 4th November 2015 where, on the date on which the claim is made, the claimant resides in one of the No.52 relevant districts;

    (d) a claim for universal credit that is made on or after the date referred to in any of subparagraphs (a) to (c), in respect of a period that begins on or after that date where—

        (i) in the case of a single claimant, the claimant gives incorrect information regarding the claimant residing in a district as referred to in the sub-paragraph in question and the claimant does not reside in such a district on the date on which the claim is made;

       (ii) in the case of joint claimants, either or both of the joint claimants gives or give incorrect information regarding his or her (or their) residing in such a district and one or both of them does not or do not reside in such a district on the date on which the claim is made, and after a decision is made that the single claimant is, or the joint claimants are, entitled to universal credit and one or more payments have been made in respect of the single claimant or the joint claimants, the Secretary of State discovers that incorrect information has been given regarding residence.

(3) The day appointed in relation to the case of a claim referred to in paragraph (2), and any award that is made in respect of the claim, is the first day of the period in respect of which the claim is made.

(4) Article 3(6) of the No.9 Order applies for the purposes of paragraph (3) as it applies for the purposes of article 3(4)(a) of the No.9 Order.

(5) Article 3A of the No.9 Order applies in connection with a claim for universal credit where a single claimant, or, as the case may be, either or both of joint claimants, gives or give incorrect information regarding his or her (or their) residing in one of the No.50, No.51 or No.52 relevant districts, as it applies in connection with the giving of incorrect information regarding a claimant residing in one of the relevant districts (as defined in the No.9 Order).

DEFINITIONS

    "the Act"–see art.2(1).
    "claimant"–*ibid.*
    "joint claimant"–*ibid.*
    "single claimant"–*ibid.*
    "No.9 Order"–*ibid.*
    "the No.50 relevant districts"–*ibid.*
    "the No.51 relevant districts"–*ibid.*
    "the No.52 relevant districts"–*ibid.*

GENERAL NOTE

3.362   See by analogy the commentary to art.3 of the Commencement No.22 Order.

Day appointed for the abolition of income-related employment and support allowance and income-based jobseeker's allowance

3.363   **4.**—(1) The day appointed for the coming into force of the amending provisions, in relation to the case of a claim referred to in paragraph (2), and any award that is made in respect of the claim, is the day appointed in accordance with paragraph (3).

(2) The claims referred to are—

(a) a claim for universal credit that is made on or after 18th March 2015 in respect of a period that begins on or after 18th March 2015 where, on the date on which the claim is made, the claimant resides in one of the No.50 relevant districts;

(b) a claim for universal credit that is made on or after 10th June 2015 in respect of a period that begins on or after 10th June 2015 where, on the date on which the claim is made, the claimant resides in one of the No.51 relevant districts;

(c) a claim for universal credit that is made on or after 4th November 2015 in respect of a period that begins on or after 4th November 2015 where, on the date on which the claim is made, the claimant resides in one of the No.52 relevant districts;

(d) a claim for universal credit that is made on or after the date referred to in any of subparagraphs (a) to (c), in respect of a period that begins on or after that date where—

   (i) in the case of a single claimant, the claimant gives incorrect information regarding the claimant residing in a district as referred to in the sub-paragraph in question and the claimant does not reside in such a district on the date on which the claim is made;

   (ii) in the case of joint claimants, either or both of the joint claimants gives or give incorrect information regarding his or her (or their) residing in such a district and one or both of them does not or do not reside in such a district on the date on which the claim is made, and after a decision is made that the single claimant is, or the joint claimants are, entitled to universal credit and one or more payments have been made in respect of the single claimant or the joint claimants, the Secretary of State discovers that incorrect information has been given regarding residence;

(e) a claim for an employment and support allowance or a jobseeker's allowance that is made or treated as made on or after 18th March 2015 where, on the date on which the claim is made or treated as made, the claimant resides in one of the No.50 relevant districts;

(f) a claim for an employment and support allowance or a jobseeker's allowance that is made or treated as made on or after 10th June 2015 where, on the date on which the claim is made or treated as made, the claimant resides in one of the No.51 relevant districts;

(g) a claim for an employment and support allowance or a jobseeker's allowance that is made or treated as made on or after 4th November 2015 where, on the date on which the claim is made or treated as made, the claimant resides in one of the No.52 relevant districts;

(h) a claim for an employment and support allowance or a jobseeker's allowance other than one referred to in sub-paragraphs (e) to (g) that is made or treated as made during the relevant period by a single claimant of universal credit or by either of two joint claimants of universal credit who has or have made a claim for universal credit within any of subparagraphs (a) to (d).

(3) The day appointed in relation to the case of a claim referred to in

paragraph (2), and any award that is made in respect of the claim, is the first day of the period in respect of which the claim is made.

(4) For the purposes of paragraph (2)(h), "relevant period" means, in relation to a claim for universal credit within any of sub-paragraphs (a) to (d) of paragraph (2), any UC claim period, and any period subsequent to any UC claim period in respect of which the claimant is entitled to an award of universal credit in respect of the claim.

(5) For the purposes of paragraph (4), a "UC claim period" is a period when—

    (a) a claim for universal credit within any of sub-paragraphs (a) to (c) of paragraph (2), or within sub-paragraph (d)(i) or (ii) of that paragraph, has been made but a decision has not yet been made on the claim; or

    (b) a decision has been made that the claimant is not entitled to universal credit and—

        (i) the Secretary of State is considering whether to revise that decision under section 9 of the Social Security Act 1998, whether on an application made for that purpose, or on the Secretary of State's own initiative; or

        (ii) the claimant has appealed against that decision to the First-tier Tribunal and that appeal or any subsequent appeal to the Upper Tribunal or to a court has not been finally determined.

(6) Paragraphs (6), (7), (9) and (10) of article 4 of the No.9 Order apply in relation to a claim for universal credit referred to in paragraph (2) (and any award that is made in respect of the claim) as they apply in relation to a claim for universal credit referred to in sub-paragraphs (a) and (b) of article 4(2) of the No.9 Order (and any award that is made in respect of the claim).

(7) Paragraphs (1A) and (1B) of article 5 of the No.9 Order apply for the purposes of subparagraphs (e) to (g) of paragraph (2) as they apply for the purposes of article 4(2)(a) of the No.9 Order (but as if the references in paragraph (1A) to Schedule 5 to the No.9 Order were omitted).

(8) Article 5(8) of the No.9 Order applies for the purposes of paragraph (3) as it applies for the purposes of article 4(3)(a) of the No.9 Order.

DEFINITIONS

    "the amending provisions"–see art.2(1).
    "claimant"–*ibid.*
    "employment and support allowance"–*ibid.*
    "jobseeker's allowance"–*ibid.*
    "joint claimant"–*ibid.*
    "No.9 Order"–*ibid.*
    "the No.50 relevant districts"–*ibid.*
    "the No.51 relevant districts"–*ibid.*
    "the No.52 relevant districts"–*ibid.*
    "relevant period"–para.(4).
    "UC claim period"–para.(5).

Transitory provision – application of the "specified condition" for a period

3.364   **5.**—(1) Paragraphs (2) to (4) apply in relation to a case where a claim for universal credit, an employment and support allowance or a jobseeker's allowance is made on or after 18th March 2015 and before 10th June 2015.

(2) Where this paragraph applies, article 2(1) of this Order applies as if, after the definition of "single claimant" there were inserted—

";

"specified condition" means the condition that a claimant is a British citizen who—

(a) has resided in the United Kingdom throughout the period of two years ending with the date on which the claim for universal credit is made; and

(b) has not, during that period, left the United Kingdom for a continuous period of four weeks or more.".

(3) Where this paragraph applies, article 3 of this Order applies as if it were amended as follows—

(a) in sub-paragraph (a) of paragraph (2), after "relevant districts" insert "and meets the specified condition";

(b) in sub-paragraph (d)(i) of paragraph (2)—

(i) after "in question" insert "or meeting the specified condition"; and

(ii) after "in such a district" insert "or does not meet that condition";

(c) in sub-paragraph (d)(ii) of paragraph (2)—

(i) after "residing in such a district" insert "or meeting the specified condition"; and

(ii) after "reside in such a district" insert "or does not or do not meet that condition";

(d) in the closing words of sub-paragraph (d) of paragraph (2), after "regarding residence" insert "or meeting the specified condition as the case may be";

(e) in paragraph (5)—

(i) after "No.52 relevant districts" insert "or meeting the specified condition"; and

(ii) after "the No.9 Order)" insert "or meeting the gateway conditions (as defined in the No.9 Order)".

(4) Where this paragraph applies, article 4 of this Order applies as if it were amended as follows—

(a) in sub-paragraphs (a) and (e) of paragraph (2), after "relevant districts" insert "and meets the specified condition";

(b) in sub-paragraph (d)(i) of paragraph (2)—

(i) after "in question" insert "or meeting the specified condition"; and

(ii) after "in such a district" insert "or does not meet that condition";

(c) in sub-paragraph (d)(ii) of paragraph (2)—

(i) after "residing in a such a district" insert "or meeting the specified condition"; and

(ii) after "reside in such a district" insert "or does not or do not meet that condition";

(d) in the closing words of sub-paragraph (d) of paragraph (2), after "regarding residence" insert "or meeting the specified condition".

DEFINITIONS

"employment and support allowance"–see art.2(1).
"jobseeker's allowance"–*ibid.*

Application of the No.9 Order

3.365

6. Articles 9 to 22 of the No.9 Order apply in connection with the coming into force of the amending provisions in relation to the case of a claim referred to in article 4(2), and any award made in respect of the claim, as they apply in connection with the coming into force of the amending provisions in relation to the case of a claim referred to in sub-paragraph (a), (b) or (g) of article 4(2) of the No.9 Order and any award made in respect of the claim.

DEFINITIONS

"the amending provisions"–see art.2(1).
"No.9 Order"–*ibid.*

Transitional provision: claims for housing benefit, income support or a tax credit

3.366

7.—(1) Except as provided by paragraphs (2) to (6), a person may not make a claim for housing benefit, income support or a tax credit (in the latter case, whether or not as part of a Tax Credits Act couple) on any date where, if that person made a claim for universal credit on that date (in the capacity, whether as a single person or as part of a couple, in which he or she is permitted to claim universal credit under the Universal Credit Regulations 2013), the provisions of the Act listed in Schedule 2 to the No.9 Order would come into force under article 3(1) and [¹ (2)(a) to (c) of this Order in relation to that claim] for universal credit.

(2) Paragraph (1) does not apply to a claim for housing benefit, income support or a tax credit where, by virtue of a determination made under regulation 4 [², or by virtue of regulation 39,] of the Universal Credit (Transitional Provisions) Regulations 2014, the person in question would be prevented from making a claim for universal credit as referred to in that paragraph.

(3) Paragraph (1) does not apply to a claim for housing benefit in respect of specified accommodation.

(4) Paragraph (1) does not apply to a claim for housing benefit or a tax credit where—

    (a) in the case of a claim for housing benefit, the claim is made by a person who has reached the qualifying age for state pension credit, or by a person who is a member of a State Pension Credit Act couple the other member of which has reached that age;

    (b) in the case of a claim for a tax credit, the claim is made by—

        (i) a person who has reached the qualifying age for state pension credit;

        (ii) a Tax Credits Act couple both members of which have reached, or either member of which has reached, that age; or

        (iii) in a case not covered by paragraph (i), a person who is a member of a State Pension Credit Act couple where the other member of the couple has reached that age.

(5) Paragraph (1) does not apply to a claim for a tax credit where a person or persons makes or make a claim for child tax credit or working tax credit and on the date on which he or she (or they) makes or make the claim he or she (or they) is or are entitled to working tax credit or child tax credit respectively.

(6) Paragraph (1) does not apply to a claim for a tax credit where a

person is or was, or persons are or were, entitled to child tax credit or working tax credit in respect of a tax year and that person or those persons makes or make (or is or are treated as making) a claim for that tax credit for the next tax year.

(7) In paragraph (5), the reference to a person being entitled to a tax credit includes where a person is treated as being entitled to a tax credit in the circumstances referred to in regulation 11 of the Universal Credit (Transitional Provisions) Regulations 2014 but as if regulation 11 were amended as follows—

(a) in paragraph (1), for "For the purposes of regulations 7(7) and 8(4)" substitute "For the purposes of article 6(5) of the Welfare Reform Act 2012 (Commencement No.23 and Transitional and Transitory Provisions) Order 2015"; and

(b) for paragraph (2)(d)(iii), substitute—
   "(iii) the person's claim for child tax credit or working tax credit is made during the period of 30 days starting with the date on the notice referred to in paragraph (ii).".

(8) Subject to paragraph (9), for the purposes of this article—

(a) a claim for housing benefit, income support or a tax credit is made by a person on the date on which he or she takes any action which results in a decision on a claim being required under the relevant Regulations; and

(b) it is irrelevant that the effect of any provision of the relevant Regulations is that, for the purpose of those Regulations, the claim is made or treated as made on a date that is earlier than the date on which that action is taken.

(9) Where under the provisions referred to in paragraph (10), a claim for housing benefit or income support is treated as made at a date that is earlier than the date on which the action referred to in paragraph (8)(a) is taken, the claim is treated as made on that earlier date.

(10) The provisions referred to are—

(a) in the case of a claim for housing benefit, regulation 83(4E), (4F), (5)(d) or (8) of the 2006 Regulations or, as the case may be, regulation 64(5F), (5G), (6)(d) or (9) of the the 2006 (SPC) Regulations; or

(b) in the case of a claim for income support, [¹ regulation 6(1A)(b) or 6A] of the Claims and Payments Regulations 1987.

(11) For the purposes of this article—

(a) "couple" (apart from in the expressions "State Pension Credit Act couple" and "Tax Credit Act couple"), has the meaning given in section 39 of the Act;

(b) "housing benefit" means housing benefit under section 130 of the Social Security Contributions and Benefits Act 1992;

(c) "income support" means income support under section 124 of the Social Security Contributions and Benefits Act 1992;

(d) "qualifying age for state pension credit" means the qualifying age referred to in section 1(6) of the State Pension Credit Act 2002;

(e) "the 2006 Regulations" means the Housing Benefit Regulations 2006;

(f) "the 2006 (SPC) Regulations" means the Housing Benefit (Persons who have attained the qualifying age for state pension credit) Regulations 2006;

(g) "the relevant Regulations" means—
    (i) in the case of a claim for housing benefit, the 2006 Regulations or, as the case may be, the 2006 (SPC) Regulations;
    (ii) in the case of a claim for income support, the Claims and Payments Regulations 1987;
    (iii) in the case of a claim for a tax credit, the Tax Credits (Claims and Notifications) Regulations 2002;

(h) "specified accommodation" means accommodation to which one or more of subparagraphs (2) to (5) of paragraph 3A of Schedule 1 to the Universal Credit Regulations 2013 applies;

(i) "State Pension Credit Act couple" means a couple as defined in section 17 of the State Pension Credit Act 2002;

(j) "tax credit" (including "child tax credit" and "working tax credit") and "tax year" have the same meanings as in the Tax Credits Act 2002;

(k) "Tax Credits Act couple" means a couple as defined in section 3(5A) of the Tax Credits Act 2002.

AMENDMENTS

1. Welfare Reform Act 2012 (Commencement No.23 and Transitional and Transitory Provisions) (Amendment) Order 2015 (SI 2015/740), art.2(a) (March 17, 2015).
2. Social Security (Restrictions on Amounts for Children and Qualifying Young Persons) Amendment Regulations 2017 (2017/376) reg.4 (April 6, 2017).

DEFINITIONS

"the 2006 Regulations"–para.(11)(e).
"the 2006 (SPC) Regulations"–para.(11)(f).
"child tax credit"–para.11(j).
"couple"–para.(11)(a).
"housing benefit"–para.(11)(b).
"income support"–para.(11)(c).
"qualifying age for state pension credit"–para.11(d).
"relevant Regulations"–para.11(g).
"specified accommodation"–para.11(h).
"State Pension Credit Act couple"–para.11(i).
"tax credit"–para.(11)(j).
"Tax Credits Act couple"–para.11(k).
"working tax credit"–para.11(j).

Amendment of the Welfare Reform Act 2012 (Commencement No.9 and Transitional and Transitory Provisions and Commencement No.8 and Savings and Transitional Provisions (Amendment)) Order 2013

3.367

8.—(1) Paragraphs (2) and (3) apply in relation to a case where a claim for universal credit is made on or after 18th March 2015.

(2) Where this paragraph applies, in article 3A(3) of the No.9 Order, at the end insert "(and a determination had not been made under regulation 4 of the Universal Credit (Transitional Provisions) Regulations 2014, preventing a claim for universal credit being made with respect to the area in question or the category of case in question)".

(3) Where this paragraph applies, any reference in the No.11 Order, the No.13 Order, the No.14 Order, the No.16 Order, the No.17 Order, the

No.19 Order, the No.21 Order or the No.22 Order to article 3A of the No.9 Order is a reference to that article as amended by paragraph (2).

(4) Paragraph (5) applies in relation to a case where a claim for an employment and support allowance or a jobseeker's allowance is made on or after 18th March 2015.

(5) Where this paragraph applies, for paragraph (3) of article 5A of the No.9 Order substitute—

"(3) For the purposes of this article, paragraphs (5) to (7) of article 5(**b**) apply for the purpose of determining—

(a) whether a claim for ESA or JSA is made; and

(b) the date on which the claim is made or treated as made.".

Amendment of the Welfare Reform Act 2012 (Commencement No.21 and Transitional and Transitory Provisions) Order 2015

9.—(1) Paragraphs (2) to (4) apply in relation to a case where a claim for universal credit, an employment and support allowance or a jobseeker's allowance is made on or after 10th June 2015.

3.368

(2) Where this paragraph applies, in article 2(1) of the No.21 Order, omit the definition of "specified condition".

(3) Where this paragraph applies, article 3 of the No.21 Order is amended as follows—

(a) in paragraph (2)(a), omit "and meets the specified condition";

(b) in sub-paragraph (b) of paragraph (2)—

    (i) in paragraph (i), omit "or meeting the specified condition" and "or does not meet the specified condition";

    (ii) in paragraph (ii), omit "or meeting the specified condition" and "or does not or do not meet the specified condition"; and

    (iii) in the closing words, omit "or meeting the specified condition as the case may be"; and

(c) in paragraph (5), omit "or meeting the specified condition" and "or meeting the gateway conditions (as defined in the No.9 Order)".

(4) Where this paragraph applies, article 4 of the No.21 Order is amended as follows—

(a) in sub-paragraphs (a) and (c) of paragraph (2), omit "and meets the specified condition"; and

(b) in sub-paragraph (b) of paragraph (2)—

    (i) in paragraph (i), omit "or meeting the specified condition" and "or does not meet the specified condition";

    (ii) in paragraph (ii), omit "or meeting the specified condition" and "or does not or do not meet the specified condition"; and

    (iii) in the closing words, omit "or meeting the specified condition as the case may be".

(5) With effect from 18th March 2015, article 6 of the No.21 Order is amended as follows—

(a) in paragraph (1), for "(2) to (5)" substitute "(2) to (5) and (11)";

(b) in paragraph (9)(b), for "regulation 6(1A)(b)" substitute "regulations 6(1A)(b) and 6A"; and

(c) after paragraph (10) insert—

"(11) Paragraph (1) does not apply to a claim for housing benefit, income support or a taxcredit where, by virtue of a determination made under regulation 4 of the Universal Credit

(Transitional Provisions) Regulations 2014, the person in question would be prevented from making a claim for universal credit as referred to in that paragraph.".

Modification of the Universal Credit (Digital Service) Amendment Regulations 2014

3.369   **10.** With effect from 18th March 2015, the Universal Credit (Digital Service) Amendment Regulations 2014 have effect as if, in regulation 5(3)(a) of those Regulations (savings), for "the postcode part-district SM5 2" there were substituted "one of the postcode part-districts CR0 2 and CR0 4, SM5 2, SM6 7 to SM6 9 and SE1 5".

Modification of the Universal Credit (Surpluses and Self-employed Losses) (Digital Service) Amendment Regulations 2015

3.370   **11.** With effect from 18th March 2015, the Universal Credit (Surpluses and Self-employed Losses) (Digital Service) Amendment Regulations 2015 have effect as if, in regulation 4(3)(a) of those Regulations (savings), for "the postcode part-district SM5 2" there were substituted "one of the postcode part-districts CR0 2 and CR0 4, SM5 2, SM6 7 to SM6 9 and SE1 5."

The Welfare Reform Act 2012 (Commencement No.23 and Transitional and Transitory Provisions) (Amendment) Order 2015

(2015/740) (C.39)

The Secretary of State for Work and Pensions makes the following Order in exercise of the powers conferred by section 150(3) and (4)(a), (b)(i) and (c) of the Welfare Reform Act 2012:

ARRANGEMENT OF ARTICLES

Citation

3.371   **1.** This Order may be cited as the Welfare Reform Act 2012 (Commencement No.23 and Transitional and Transitory Provisions) (Amendment) Order 2015.

Amendment of the Welfare Reform Act 2012 (Commencement No.23 and Transitional and Transitory Provisions) Order 2015

3.372   **2.** The Welfare Reform Act 2012 (Commencement No.23 and Transitional and Transitory Provisions) Order 2015(1) is amended as follows—
   (a) in article 7 (transitional provision: claims for housing benefit, income support or a tax credit)—

    (i) in paragraph (1), for "(2)(a) of this Order in relation to a claim" substitute "(2)(a) to (c) of this Order in relation to that claim"; and

    (ii) in paragraph (10)(b), for "regulations 6(1A)(b) and 6A" substitute "regulation 6(1A)(b) or 6A"; and

(b) in article 9(5)(b) (amendment of the Welfare Reform Act 2012 (Commencement No.21 and Transitional and Transitory Provisions) Order 2015(2)), for ""regulations 6(1A)(b) and 6A"" substitute ""regulation 6(1A)(b) or 6A"".

The Welfare Reform Act 2012 (Commencement No.24 and Transitional and Transitory Provisions and Commencement No.9 and Transitional and Transitory Provisions (Amendment)) Order 2015

(SI 2015/1537) (C.87)

The Secretary of State makes the following Order, in exercise of the powers conferred by section 150(3) and (4)(a), (b)(i) and (c) of the Welfare Reform Act 2012:

ARRANGEMENT OF ARTICLES

GENERAL NOTE

The broad effect of this Commencement Order ("the Commencement No.24 Order") was to complete the national expansion of universal credit claims for single claimants in a series of stages from September 21, 2015 through to April 25, 2016.   **3.373**

Article 2 of the Order defines the gateway conditions, which are the requirements to be met to make a claim for universal credit. These are set out in Sch.5 to the Commencement No.9 Order (as amended). Article 5 of this Order amends para.7(e) of Sch.5 to allow the gateway condition requiring a universal credit claimant to have a particular type of account to be met in the case of a claim by a couple if either member of the couple has such an account.

It should be noted that para.(a) of the definition of the gateway conditions in Art.2 of this Order causes them to have effect apart from the amendments to Sch.5 made by art.4(5)(b) of the Welfare Reform Act 2012 (Commencement No.9, 11, 13, 14, 16, 17 and 19 and Transitional and Transitory Provisions (Amendment)) Order 2015 (S.I. 2015/32). That Order removed the condition that a claimant must not (at least for the great majority of cases) have responsibility for children or young persons. That particular gateway condition is reapplied for claims made with respect to the areas to which this Order applies. The gateway conditions are further modified by para.(b) of the definition and para.(3) to require that a claimant must be single, with consequent changes to alter or omit provisions relevant only to couples including the amendment by art.5 noted above ("the modified gateway conditions").

Article 3 then brought into force provisions relating to universal credit in Part 1 of the Act as set out in Sch.2 to the Commencement No.9 Order, in relation to a number of different types of cases and at different dates.

Citation

3.374   **1.** This Order may be cited as the Welfare Reform Act 2012 (Commencement No.24 and Transitional and Transitory Provisions and Commencement No.9 and Transitional and Transitory Provisions (Amendment)) Order 2015.

Interpretation

3.375   **2.**—(1) In this Order—

"the Act" means the Welfare Reform Act 2012;

"the amending provisions" means the provisions referred to in article 4(1)(a) to (c) of the No.9 Order (day appointed for the abolition of income-related employment and support allowance and income-based jobseeker's allowance);

"the Claims and Payments Regulations 1987" means the Social Security (Claims and Payments) Regulations 1987;

"claimant"—

(a) in relation to an employment and support allowance, has the same meaning as in Part 1 of the Welfare Reform Act 2007;

(b) in relation to a jobseeker's allowance, has the same meaning as in the Jobseekers Act 1995 (as it applies apart from the amendments made by Part 1 of Schedule 14 to the Act that remove references to an income-based jobseeker's allowance);

(c) in relation to universal credit, has the same meaning as in Part 1 of the Act;

"employment and support allowance" means an employment and support allowance under Part 1 of the Welfare Reform Act 2007;

"First-tier Tribunal" has the same meaning as in the Social Security Act 1998;

"gateway conditions" means the conditions specified in Schedule 5 to the No.9 Order—

(a) as that Schedule has effect apart from the amendments made by article 4(5)(b) of the Welfare Reform Act 2012 (Commencement No.9, 11, 13, 14, 16, 17 and 19 and Transitional and Transitory Provisions (Amendment)) Order 2015; and

(b) as if that Schedule, as it has effect under sub-paragraph (a), were amended in accordance with paragraph (3) of this article.

"Index of Relevant Districts" means the Index of Relevant Districts issued by the Department for Work and Pensions on 20th July 2015;

"jobseeker's allowance" means a jobseeker's allowance under the Jobseekers Act 1995;

"the No.9 Order" means the Welfare Reform Act 2012 (Commencement No.9 and Transitional and Transitory Provisions and Commencement

No. 8 and Savings and Transitional Provisions (Amendment)) Order 2013;

"the No. 11 Order" means the Welfare Reform Act 2012 (Commencement No. 11 and Transitional and Transitory Provisions and Commencement No. 9 and Transitional and Transitory Provisions (Amendment)) Order 2013;

"the No. 13 Order" means the Welfare Reform Act 2012 (Commencement No. 13 and Transitional and Transitory Provisions) Order 2013;

"the No. 14 Order" means the Welfare Reform Act 2012 (Commencement No. 14 and Transitional and Transitory Provisions) Order 2013;

"the No. 16 Order" means the Welfare Reform Act 2012 (Commencement No. 16 and Transitional and Transitory Provisions) Order 2014;

"the No. 17 Order" means the Welfare Reform Act 2012 (Commencement No. 17 and Transitional and Transitory Provisions) Order 2014;

"the No. 19 Order" means the Welfare Reform Act 2012 (Commencement No. 19 and Transitional and Transitory Provisions and Commencement No. 9 and Transitional and Transitory Provisions (Amendment)) Order 2014;

"the No. 20 Order" means the Welfare Reform Act 2012 (Commencement No. 20 and Transitional and Transitory Provisions and Commencement No. 9 and Transitional and Transitory Provisions (Amendment)) Order 2014;

"the No. 21 Order" means the Welfare Reform Act 2012 (Commencement No. 21 and Transitional and Transitory Provisions) Order 2015;

"the No. 22 Order" means the Welfare Reform Act 2012 (Commencement No. 22 and Transitional and Transitory Provisions) Order 2015;

"the No. 23 Order" means the Welfare Reform Act 2012 (Commencement No. 23 and Transitional and Transitory Provisions) Order 2015;

"the UC commencement orders" means the No. 9 Order, the No. 11 Order, the No. 13 Order, the No. 14 Order, the No. 16 Order, the No. 17 Order, the No. 19 Order, the No. 20 Order, the No. 21 Order, the No. 22 Order and the No. 23 Order;

"Upper Tribunal" has the same meaning as in the Social Security Act 1998.

(2) In this Order, references to numbered "relevant districts" are to the postcode districts and part-districts specified in the first column of the table in the Index of Relevant Districts corresponding to the number relating to those relevant districts that is specified in the third column of that table.

(3) The amendments to Schedule 5 to the No. 9 Order referred to in sub-paragraph (b) of the definition of gateway conditions in paragraph (1) are—

    (a) after paragraph 1(a) (personal characteristics)(20) insert—

        "(b) a single person (where that expression has the meaning given by section 40 of the Act);";

    (b) for paragraph 4 (income and capital) substitute—

        "4.—(1) The claimant must declare that, during the period of one month starting with the date on which the claim for universal credit is made, the claimant's earned income is expected not to exceed £338.

        (2) The claimant's capital must not exceed £6,000.

        (3) For the purposes of this paragraph, "earned income" and "capital" have the same meanings as they have in Part 6 of the Universal Credit Regulations.";

(c) in paragraph 7(e) (other requirements) omit "or, in the case of joint claimants, either member of the couple must have such an account"; and

(d) in paragraph 8 (declarations)—
   (i) in sub-paragraph (1) omit ", 4(2)";
   (ii) omit sub-paragraph (2).

(4) For the purposes of this Order, the Universal Credit, Personal Independence Payment, Jobseeker's Allowance and Employment and Support Allowance (Claims and Payments) Regulations 2013 apply for the purposes of deciding—

(a) whether a claim for universal credit is made; and

(b) the date on which such a claim is made.

(5) For the purposes of this Order, the Claims and Payments Regulations 1987 apply, subject to paragraphs (6) and (7), for the purposes of deciding—

(a) whether a claim for an employment and support allowance or a jobseeker's allowance is made; and

(b) the date on which the claim is made or treated as made.

(6) Subject to paragraph (7), for the purposes of this Order—

(a) a person makes a claim for an employment and support allowance or a jobseeker's allowance if he or she takes any action which results in a decision on a claim being required under the Claims and Payments Regulations 1987; and

(b) it is irrelevant that the effect of any provision of those Regulations is that, for the purposes of those Regulations, the claim is made or treated as made at a date that is earlier than the date on which that action is taken.

(7) Where, by virtue of—

(a) regulation 6(1F)(b) or (c) of the Claims and Payments Regulations 1987, in the case of a claim for an employment and support allowance; or

(b) regulation 6(4ZA) to (4ZD) and (4A)(a)(i) and (b) of those Regulations, in the case of a claim for a jobseeker's allowance,

a claim for an employment and support allowance or a jobseeker's allowance is treated as made at a date that is earlier than the date on which the action referred to in paragraph (7)(a) is taken, the claim is treated as made on that earlier date.

Day appointed for the coming into force of the universal credit provisions

3.376

3.—(1) The day appointed for the coming into force of the provisions of the Act listed in Schedule 2 to the No.9 Order, in so far as they are not already in force, in relation to a claim referred to in paragraph (2), and any award that is made in respect of the claim, is the day appointed in accordance with paragraph (3).

(2) The claims referred to are—

(a) a claim for universal credit that is made on or after 21st September 2015 in respect of a period that begins on or after 21st September 2015 where, on the date on which the claim is made, the claimant resides in one of the No.53 relevant districts and meets the gateway conditions;

(b) a claim for universal credit that is made on or after 28th September 2015 in respect of a period that begins on or after 28th September 2015 where, on the date on which the claim is made, the claimant resides in one of the No.54 relevant districts and meets the gateway conditions;

(c) a claim for universal credit that is made on or after 5th October 2015 in respect of a period that begins on or after 5th October 2015 where, on the date on which the claim is made, the claimant resides in one of the No.55 relevant districts and meets the gateway conditions;

(d) a claim for universal credit that is made on or after 12th October 2015 in respect of a period that begins on or after 12th October 2015 where, on the date on which the claim is made, the claimant resides in one of the No.56 relevant districts and meets the gateway conditions;

(e) a claim for universal credit that is made on or after 19th October 2015 in respect of a period that begins on or after 19th October 2015 where, on the date on which the claim is made, the claimant resides in one of the No.57 relevant districts and meets the gateway conditions;

(f) a claim for universal credit that is made on or after 26th October 2015 in respect of a period that begins on or after 26th October 2015 where, on the date on which the claim is made, the claimant resides in one of the No.58 relevant districts and meets the gateway conditions;

(g) a claim for universal credit that is made on or after 2nd November 2015 in respect of a period that begins on or after 2nd November 2015 where, on the date on which the claim is made, the claimant resides in one of the No.59 relevant districts and meets the gateway conditions;

(h) a claim for universal credit that is made on or after 9th November 2015 in respect of a period that begins on or after 9th November 2015 where, on the date on which the claim is made, the claimant resides in one of the No.60 relevant districts and meets the gateway conditions;

(i) a claim for universal credit that is made on or after 16th November 2015 in respect of a period that begins on or after 16th November 2015 where, on the date on which the claim is made, the claimant resides in one of the No.61 relevant districts and meets the gateway conditions;

(j) a claim for universal credit that is made on or after 23rd November 2015 in respect of a period that begins on or after 23rd November 2015 where, on the date on which the claim is made, the claimant resides in one of the No.62 relevant districts and meets the gateway conditions;

(k) a claim for universal credit that is made on or after 30th November 2015 in respect of a period that begins on or after 30th November 2015 where, on the date on which the claim is made, the claimant resides in one of the No.63 relevant districts and meets the gateway conditions;

(l) a claim for universal credit that is made on or after 7th December 2015 in respect of a period that begins on or after 7th December

2015 where, on the date on which the claim is made, the claimant resides in one of the No.64 relevant districts and meets the gateway conditions;

(m) a claim for universal credit that is made on or after 14th December 2015 in respect of a period that begins on or after 14th December 2015 where, on the date on which the claim is made, the claimant resides in one of the No.65 relevant districts and meets the gateway conditions;

(n) a claim for universal credit that is made on or after 11th January 2016 in respect of a period that begins on or after 11th January 2016 where, on the date on which the claim is made, the claimant resides in one of the No.66 relevant districts and meets the gateway conditions;

(o) a claim for universal credit that is made on or after 18th January 2016 in respect of a period that begins on or after 18th January 2016 where, on the date on which the claim is made, the claimant resides in one of the No.67 relevant districts and meets the gateway conditions;

(p) a claim for universal credit that is made on or after 25th January 2016 in respect of a period that begins on or after 25th January 2016 where, on the date on which the claim is made, the claimant resides in one of the No.68 relevant districts and meets the gateway conditions;

(q) a claim for universal credit that is made on or after 1st February 2016 in respect of a period that begins on or after 1st February 2016 where, on the date on which the claim is made, the claimant resides in one of the No.69 relevant districts and meets the gateway conditions;

(r) a claim for universal credit that is made on or after 8th February 2016 in respect of a period that begins on or after 8th February 2016 where, on the date on which the claim is made, the claimant resides in one of the No.70 relevant districts and meets the gateway conditions;

(s) a claim for universal credit that is made on or after 15th February 2016 in respect of a period that begins on or after 15th February 2016 where, on the date on which the claim is made, the claimant resides in one of the No.71 relevant districts and meets the gateway conditions;

(t) a claim for universal credit that is made on or after 22nd February 2016 in respect of a period that begins on or after 22nd February 2016 where, on the date on which the claim is made, the claimant resides in one of the No.72 relevant districts and meets the gateway conditions;

(u) a claim for universal credit that is made on or after 29th February 2016 in respect of a period that begins on or after 29th February 2016 where, on the date on which the claim is made, the claimant resides in one of the No.73 relevant districts and meets the gateway conditions;

(v) a claim for universal credit that is made on or after 7th March 2016 in respect of a period that begins on or after 7th March 2016 where, on the date on which the claim is made, the claimant resides in one of the No.74 relevant districts and meets the gateway conditions;

(w) a claim for universal credit that is made on or after 14th March 2016 in respect of a period that begins on or after 14th March 2016 where, on the date on which the claim is made, the claimant resides in one of the No.75 relevant districts and meets the gateway conditions;

(x) a claim for universal credit that is made on or after 21st March 2016 in respect of a period that begins on or after 21st March 2016 where, on the date on which the claim is made, the claimant resides in one of the No.76 relevant districts and meets the gateway conditions;

(y) a claim for universal credit that is made on or after 28th March 2016 in respect of a period that begins on or after 28th March 2016 where, on the date on which the claim is made, the claimant resides in one of the No.77 relevant districts and meets the gateway conditions;

(z) a claim for universal credit that is made on or after 11th April 2016 in respect of a period that begins on or after 11th April 2016 where, on the date on which the claim is made, the claimant resides in one of the No.78 relevant districts and meets the gateway conditions;

(aa) a claim for universal credit that is made on or after 18th April 2016 in respect of a period that begins on or after 18th April 2016 where, on the date on which the claim is made, the claimant resides in one of the No.79 relevant districts and meets the gateway conditions;

(bb) a claim for universal credit that is made on or after 25th April 2016 in respect of a period that begins on or after 25th April 2016 where, on the date on which the claim is made, the claimant resides in one of the No.80 relevant districts and meets the gateway conditions;

(cc) a claim for universal credit that is made on or after 25th April 2016 in respect of a period that begins on or after 25th April 2016 where, on the date on which the claim is made, the claimant resides in a postcode district or part-district in England and Wales or Scotland that is not referred to by one of the UC commencement orders or in sub-paragraphs (a) to (bb) and meets the gateway conditions;

(dd) a claim for universal credit that is made on or after the date referred to in any of sub-paragraphs (a) to (cc), in respect of a period that begins on or after that date where—

  (i) the claimant gives incorrect information regarding the claimant residing in a postcode district or part-district as referred to in the sub-paragraph in question or meeting the gateway conditions and the claimant does not reside in such a district or part-district or does not meet the gateway conditions on the date on which the claim is made; and

  (ii) after a decision is made that the claimant is entitled to universal credit and one or more payments have been made in respect of the claimant, the Secretary of State discovers that incorrect information has been given regarding residence or meeting the gateway conditions.

(3) The day appointed in relation to a claim referred to in paragraph (2), and any award that is made in respect of the claim, is the first day of the period in respect of which the claim is made.

(4) Article 3(6) of the No.9 Order applies for the purposes of paragraph (3) as it applies for the purposes of article 3(4)(a) of the No.9 Order.

(5) Article 3A of the No.9 Order applies in connection with a claim for universal credit where a claimant gives incorrect information regarding his or her residing in one of the numbered relevant districts referred to in

paragraph (2)(a) to (bb) or in a postcode district or part-district to which paragraph (2)(cc) applies or meeting the gateway conditions, as it applies in connection with the giving of incorrect information regarding a claimant residing in a relevant district (as defined in the No.9 Order) or meeting the gateway conditions (as defined in the No.9 Order).

DEFINITIONS

"the Act"–see art.2(1).
"claimant"–*ibid.*
"gateway conditions"–*ibid.*
"No.9 Order"–*ibid.*
"relevant districts"–see art.2(2).
"the UC commencement orders"–see art.2(1).

GENERAL NOTE

3.377   See by analogy the commentary to Art.3 of the Commencement No.22 Order.

Day appointed for the abolition of income-related employment and support allowance and income-based jobseeker's allowance

3.378   **4.**—(1) The day appointed for the coming into force of the amending provisions, in relation to a claim referred to in paragraph (2), and any award that is made in respect of the claim, is the day appointed in accordance with paragraph (3).

(2) The claims referred to are—

(a) a claim for universal credit that is made on or after 21st September 2015 in respect of a period that begins on or after 21st September 2015 where, on the date on which the claim is made, the claimant resides in one of the No.53 relevant districts and meets the gateway conditions;

(b) a claim for an employment and support allowance or a jobseeker's allowance that is made or treated as made on or after 21st September 2015 where, on the date on which the claim is made or treated as made, the claimant resides in one of the No.53 relevant districts and meets the gateway conditions;

(c) a claim for universal credit that is made on or after 28th September 2015 in respect of a period that begins on or after 28th September 2015 where, on the date on which the claim is made, the claimant resides in one of the No.54 relevant districts and meets the gateway conditions;

(d) a claim for an employment and support allowance or a jobseeker's allowance that is made or treated as made on or after 28th September 2015 where, on the date on which the claim is made or treated as made, the claimant resides in one of the No.54 relevant districts and meets the gateway conditions;

(e) a claim for universal credit that is made on or after 5th October 2015 in respect of a period that begins on or after 5th October 2015 where, on the date on which the claim is made, the claimant resides in one of the No.55 relevant districts and meets the gateway conditions;

(f) a claim for an employment and support allowance or a jobseeker's allowance that is made or treated as made on or after 5th October 2015 where, on the date on which the claim is made or treated as made, the claimant resides in one of the No.55 relevant districts and meets the gateway conditions;

(g) a claim for universal credit that is made on or after 12th October 2015 in respect of a period that begins on or after 12th October 2015 where, on the date on which the claim is made, the claimant resides in one of the No.56 relevant districts and meets the gateway conditions;

(h) a claim for an employment and support allowance or a jobseeker's allowance that is made or treated as made on or after 12th October 2015 where, on the date on which the claim is made or treated as made, the claimant resides in one of the No.56 relevant districts and meets the gateway conditions;

(i) a claim for universal credit that is made on or after 19th October 2015 in respect of a period that begins on or after 19th October 2015 where, on the date on which the claim is made, the claimant resides in one of the No.57 relevant districts and meets the gateway conditions;

(j) a claim for an employment and support allowance or a jobseeker's allowance that is made or treated as made on or after 19th October 2015 where, on the date on which the claim is made or treated as made, the claimant resides in one of the No.57 relevant districts and meets the gateway conditions;

(k) a claim for universal credit that is made on or after 26th October 2015 in respect of a period that begins on or after 26th October 2015 where, on the date on which the claim is made, the claimant resides in one of the No.58 relevant districts and meets the gateway conditions;

(l) a claim for an employment and support allowance or a jobseeker's allowance that is made or treated as made on or after 26th October 2015 where, on the date on which the claim is made or treated as made, the claimant resides in one of the No.58 relevant districts and meets the gateway conditions;

(m) a claim for universal credit that is made on or after 2nd November 2015 in respect of a period that begins on or after 2nd November 2015 where, on the date on which the claim is made, the claimant resides in one of the No.59 relevant districts and meets the gateway conditions;

(n) a claim for an employment and support allowance or a jobseeker's allowance that is made or treated as made on or after 2nd November 2015 where, on the date on which the claim is made or treated as made, the claimant resides in one of the No.59 relevant districts and meets the gateway conditions;

(o) a claim for universal credit that is made on or after 9th November 2015 in respect of a period that begins on or after 9th November 2015 where, on the date on which the claim is made, the claimant resides in one of the No.60 relevant districts and meets the gateway conditions;

(p) a claim for an employment and support allowance or a jobseeker's allowance that is made or treated as made on or after 9th November 2015 where, on the date on which the claim is made or treated as made, the claimant resides in one of the No.60 relevant districts and meets the gateway conditions;

(q) a claim for universal credit that is made on or after 16th November 2015 in respect of a period that begins on or after 16th November 2015 where, on the date on which the claim is made, the claimant resides in one of the No.61 relevant districts and meets the gateway conditions;

(r) a claim for an employment and support allowance or a jobseeker's allowance that is made or treated as made on or after 16th November 2015 where, on the date on which the claim is made or treated as made, the claimant resides in one of the No.61 relevant districts and meets the gateway conditions;

(s) a claim for universal credit that is made on or after 23rd November 2015 in respect of a period that begins on or after 23rd November 2015 where, on the date on which the claim is made, the claimant resides in one of the No.62 relevant districts and meets the gateway conditions;

(t) a claim for an employment and support allowance or a jobseeker's allowance that is made or treated as made on or after 23rd November 2015 where, on the date on which the claim is made or treated as made, the claimant resides in one of the No.62 relevant districts and meets the gateway conditions;

(u) a claim for universal credit that is made on or after 30th November 2015 in respect of a period that begins on or after 30th November 2015 where, on the date on which the claim is made, the claimant resides in one of the No.63 relevant districts and meets the gateway conditions;

(v) a claim for an employment and support allowance or a jobseeker's allowance that is made or treated as made on or after 30th November 2015 where, on the date on which the claim is made or treated as made, the claimant resides in one of the No.63 relevant districts and meets the gateway conditions;

(w) a claim for universal credit that is made on or after 7th December 2015 in respect of a period that begins on or after 7th December 2015 where, on the date on which the claim is made, the claimant resides in one of the No.64 relevant districts and meets the gateway conditions;

(x) a claim for an employment and support allowance or a jobseeker's allowance that is made or treated as made on or after 7th December 2015 where, on the date on which the claim is made or treated as made, the claimant resides in one of the No.64 relevant districts and meets the gateway conditions;

(y) a claim for universal credit that is made on or after 14th December 2015 in respect of a period that begins on or after 14th December 2015 where, on the date on which the claim is made, the claimant resides in one of the No.65 relevant districts and meets the gateway conditions;

(z) a claim for an employment and support allowance or a jobseeker's allowance that is made or treated as made on or after 14th December 2015 where, on the date on which the claim is made or treated as made, the claimant resides in one of the No.65 relevant districts and meets the gateway conditions;

(aa) a claim for universal credit that is made on or after 11th January 2016 in respect of a period that begins on or after 11th January 2016 where, on the date on which the claim is made, the claimant resides in one of the No.66 relevant districts and meets the gateway conditions;

(bb) a claim for an employment and support allowance or a jobseeker's allowance that is made or treated as made on or after 11th January 2016 where, on the date on which the claim is made or treated as made, the claimant resides in one of the No.66 relevant districts and meets the gateway conditions;

(cc) a claim for universal credit that is made on or after 18th January 2016 in respect of a period that begins on or after 18th January 2016 where, on the date on which the claim is made, the claimant resides in one of the No.67 relevant districts and meets the gateway conditions;

(dd) a claim for an employment and support allowance or a jobseeker's allowance that is made or treated as made on or after 18th January 2016 where, on the date on which the claim is made or treated as made, the claimant resides in one of the No.67 relevant districts and meets the gateway conditions;

(ee) a claim for universal credit that is made on or after 25th January 2016 in respect of a period that begins on or after 25th January 2016 where, on the date on which the claim is made, the claimant resides in one of the No.68 relevant districts and meets the gateway conditions;

(ff) a claim for an employment and support allowance or a jobseeker's allowance that is made or treated as made on or after 25th January 2016 where, on the date on which the claim is made or treated as made, the claimant resides in one of the No.68 relevant districts and meets the gateway conditions;

(gg) a claim for universal credit that is made on or after 1st February 2016 in respect of a period that begins on or after 1st February 2016 where, on the date on which the claim is made, the claimant resides in one of the No.69 relevant districts and meets the gateway conditions;

(hh) a claim for an employment and support allowance or a jobseeker's allowance that is made or treated as made on or after 1st February 2016 where, on the date on which the claim is made or treated as made, the claimant resides in one of the No.69 relevant districts and meets the gateway conditions;

(ii) a claim for universal credit that is made on or after 8th February 2016 in respect of a period that begins on or after 8th February 2016 where, on the date on which the claim is made, the claimant resides in one of the No.70 relevant districts and meets the gateway conditions;

(jj) a claim for an employment and support allowance or a jobseeker's allowance that is made or treated as made on or after 8th February 2016 where, on the date on which the claim is made or treated as made, the claimant resides in one of the No.70 relevant districts and meets the gateway conditions;

(kk) a claim for universal credit that is made on or after 15th February 2016 in respect of a period that begins on or after 15th February 2016 where, on the date on which the claim is made, the claimant resides in one of the No.71 relevant districts and meets the gateway conditions;

(ll) a claim for an employment and support allowance or a jobseeker's allowance that is made or treated as made on or after 15th February 2016 where, on the date on which the claim is made or treated as made, the claimant resides in one of the No.71 relevant districts and meets the gateway conditions;

(mm) a claim for universal credit that is made on or after 22nd February 2016 in respect of a period that begins on or after 22nd February 2016 where, on the date on which the claim is made, the claimant resides in one of the No.72 relevant districts and meets the gateway conditions;

(nn) a claim for an employment and support allowance or a jobseeker's allowance that is made or treated as made on or after 22nd February 2016 where, on the date on which the claim is made or treated as made, the claimant resides in one of the No.72 relevant districts and meets the gateway conditions;

(oo) a claim for universal credit that is made on or after 29th February 2016 in respect of a period that begins on or after 29th February 2016 where, on the date on which the claim is made, the claimant resides in one of the No.73 relevant districts and meets the gateway conditions;

(pp) a claim for an employment and support allowance or a jobseeker's allowance that is made or treated as made on or after 29th February 2016 where, on the date on which the claim is made or treated as made, the claimant resides in one of the No.73 relevant districts and meets the gateway conditions;

(qq) a claim for universal credit that is made on or after 7th March 2016 in respect of a period that begins on or after 7th March 2016 where, on the date on which the claim is made, the claimant resides in one of the No.74 relevant districts and meets the gateway conditions;

(rr) a claim for an employment and support allowance or a jobseeker's allowance that is made or treated as made on or after 7th March 2016 where, on the date on which the claim is made or treated as made, the claimant resides in one of the No.74 relevant districts and meets the gateway conditions;

(ss) a claim for universal credit that is made on or after 14th March 2016 in respect of a period that begins on or after 14th March 2016 where, on the date on which the claim is made, the claimant resides in one of the No.75 relevant districts and meets the gateway conditions;

(tt) a claim for an employment and support allowance or a jobseeker's allowance that is made or treated as made on or after 14th March 2016 where, on the date on which the claim is made or treated as made, the claimant resides in one of the No.75 relevant districts and meets the gateway conditions;

(uu) a claim for universal credit that is made on or after 21st March 2016 in respect of a period that begins on or after 21st March 2016 where, on the date on which the claim is made, the claimant resides in one of the No.76 relevant districts and meets the gateway conditions;

(vv) a claim for an employment and support allowance or a jobseeker's allowance that is made or treated as made on or after 21st March 2016 where, on the date on which the claim is made or treated as made, the claimant resides in one of the No.76 relevant districts and meets the gateway conditions;

(ww) a claim for universal credit that is made on or after 28th March 2016 in respect of a period that begins on or after 28th March 2016 where, on the date on which the claim is made, the claimant resides in one of the No.77 relevant districts and meets the gateway conditions;

(xx) a claim for an employment and support allowance or a jobseeker's allowance that is made or treated as made on or after 28th March 2016 where, on the date on which the claim is made or treated as made, the claimant resides in one of the No.77 relevant districts and meets the gateway conditions;

(yy) a claim for universal credit that is made on or after 11th April 2016 in respect of a period that begins on or after 11th April 2016 where, on the date on which the claim is made, the claimant resides in one of the No.78 relevant districts and meets the gateway conditions;

(zz) a claim for an employment and support allowance or a jobseeker's allowance that is made or treated as made on or after 11th April 2016 where, on the date on which the claim is made or treated as made, the claimant resides in one of the No.78 relevant districts and meets the gateway conditions;

(aaa) a claim for universal credit that is made on or after 18th April 2016 in respect of a period that begins on or after 18th April 2016 where, on the date on which the claim is made, the claimant resides in one of the No.79 relevant districts and meets the gateway conditions;

(bbb) a claim for an employment and support allowance or a jobseeker's allowance that is made or treated as made on or after 18th April 2016 where, on the date on which the claim is made or treated as made, the claimant resides in one of the No.79 relevant districts and meets the gateway conditions;

(ccc) a claim for universal credit that is made on or after 25th April 2016 in respect of a period that begins on or after 25th April 2016 where, on the date on which the claim is made, the claimant resides in one of the No.80 relevant districts and meets the gateway conditions;

(ddd) a claim for an employment and support allowance or a jobseeker's allowance that is made or treated as made on or after 25th April 2016 where, on the date on which the claim is made or treated as made, the claimant resides in one of the No.80 relevant districts and meets the gateway conditions;

(eee) a claim for universal credit that is made on or after 25th April 2016 in respect of a period that begins on or after 25th April 2016 where, on the date on which the claim is made, the claimant resides in a postcode district or part-district in England and Wales or Scotland that is not referred to by one of the UC commencement orders or in sub-paragraphs (a), (c), (e), (g), (i), (k), (m), (o), (q), (s), (u), (w), (y), (aa), (cc), (ee), (gg), (ii), (kk), (mm), (oo), (qq), (ss), (uu), (ww), (yy), (aaa) or (ccc) and meets the gateway conditions;

(fff) a claim for an employment and support allowance or a jobseeker's allowance that is made or treated as made on or after 25th April 2016 where, on the date on which the claim is made or treated as made, the claimant resides in a postcode district or part-district in England and Wales or Scotland that is not referred to by one of the UC commencement orders or in sub-paragraphs (b), (d), (f), (h), (j), (l), (n), (p), (r), (t), (v), (x), (z), (bb), (dd), (ff), (hh), (jj), (ll), (nn), (pp), (rr), (tt), (vv), (xx), (zz), (bbb) or (ddd) and meets the gateway conditions;

(ggg) a claim for universal credit that is made on or after the date referred to in any of sub-paragraphs (a), (c), (e), (g), (i), (k), (m), (o), (q), (s), (u), (w), (y), (aa), (cc), (ee), (gg), (ii), (kk), (mm), (oo), (qq), (ss), (uu), (ww), (yy), (aaa), (ccc) or (eee) or, in respect of a period that begins on or after that date, where—

    (i) the claimant gives incorrect information regarding the claimant residing in a postcode district or part-district as referred to in the sub-paragraph in question or meeting the gateway conditions and the claimant does not reside in such a district or part-district or does not meet the gateway conditions on the date on which the claim is made; and

    (ii) after a decision is made that the claimant is entitled to universal credit and one or more payments have been made in respect of the claimant, the Secretary of State discovers that incorrect information has been given regarding residence or meeting the gateway conditions;

(hhh) a claim for an employment and support allowance or a jobseeker's allowance other than one referred to in sub-paragraphs (b), (d), (f), (h), (j), (l), (n), (p), (r), (t), (v), (x), (z), (bb), (dd), (ff), (hh), (jj), (ll), (nn), (pp), (rr), (tt), (vv), (xx), (zz), (bbb), (ddd) or (fff) that is made or treated as made during the relevant period by a claimant of universal credit who has made a claim for universal credit within this paragraph.

(3) The day appointed in relation to a claim referred to in paragraph (2), and any award that is made in respect of the claim, is the first day of the period in respect of which the claim is made.

(4) For the purposes of paragraph (2)(hhh), the "relevant period" means, in relation to a claim for universal credit within paragraph (2), any UC claim period and any period subsequent to any UC claim period in respect of which the claimant is entitled to an award of universal credit in respect of the claim.

(5) For the purposes of paragraph (4), a "UC claim period" is a period when—

(a) a claim for universal credit within one of the sub-paragraphs (a), (c), (e), (g), (i), (k), (m), (o), (q), (s), (u), (w), (y), (aa), (cc), (ee), (gg), (ii), (kk), (mm), (oo), (qq), (ss), (uu), (ww), (yy), (aaa), (ccc), (eee) or (ggg)(i) of paragraph (2) has been made but a decision has not yet been made on the claim; or

(b) a decision has been made that the claimant is not entitled to universal credit and—

    (i) the Secretary of State is considering whether to revise that decision under section 9 of the Social Security Act 1998, whether on an application made for that purpose or on the Secretary of State's own initiative; or

    (ii) the claimant has appealed against that decision to the First-tier Tribunal and that appeal or any subsequent appeal to the Upper Tribunal or to a court has not been finally determined.

(6) Paragraphs (6), (7), (9) and (10) of article 4 of the No.9 Order(1) apply in relation to a claim for universal credit referred to in paragraph (2) (and any award that is made in respect of the claim) as they apply to

a claim for universal credit referred to in sub-paragraphs (a) and (b) of article 4(2) of the No.9 Order (and any award that is made in respect of the claim).

(7) Article 5(1)(a) of the No.9 Order applies for the purposes of the sub-paragraphs (relating to a claim for an employment and support allowance or a jobseeker's allowance) referred to in sub-paragraph (hhh) as it applies for the purposes of article 4(2)(a) of the No.9 Order.

(8) Article 5(8) of the No.9 Order applies for the purposes of paragraph (3) as it applies for the purposes of article 4(3)(a) of the No.9 Order.

DEFINITIONS

"the amending provisions"–see art.2(1).
"claimant"–*ibid.*
"employment and support allowance"–*ibid.*
"First-tier Tribunal"–*ibid.*
"gateway conditions"–*ibid.*
"jobseeker's allowance"–*ibid.*
"joint claimant"–*ibid.*
"No.9 Order"–*ibid.*
"relevant districts"–see art.2(2).
"relevant period"–para.(4).
"UC claim period"–para.(5).
"Upper Tribunal"–see art.2(1).
"the UC commencement orders"–*ibid.*

Amendment of the No.9 Order and cases to which the amendment applies

5.—(1) This article applies in relation to a case where a claim for universal credit, an employment and support allowance or a jobseeker's allowance is made or treated as made on or after 21st July 2015.

3.379

(2) Where this article applies—

(a) in paragraph 7(e) (other requirements) of Schedule 5 to the No.9 Order, at the end insert "or, in the case of joint claimants, either member of the couple must have such an account"; and

(b) any reference to Schedule 5 to the No.9 Order in the No.11 Order, the No.13 Order, the No.14 Order, the No.16 Order, the No.17 Order or the No.19 Order is a reference to that Schedule as amended by sub-paragraph (a).

DEFINITIONS

"employment and support allowance"–see art.2(1).
"jobseeker's allowance"–*ibid.*
"No.9 Order"–*ibid.*
"No.11 Order"–*ibid.*
"No.13 Order"–*ibid.*
"No.14 Order"–*ibid.*
"No.16 Order"–*ibid.*
"No.17 Order"–*ibid.*
"No.19 Order"–*ibid.*

Application of the No.9 Order

6. Articles 9 to 22 of the No.9 Order apply in connection with the coming into force of the amending provisions in relation to a claim referred to in

3.380

article 4(2), and any award made in respect of the claim, as they apply in connection with the coming into force of the amending provisions in relation to the case of a claim referred to in sub-paragraphs (a), (b) and (g) of article 4(2) of the No.9 Order and any award made in respect of the claim.

DEFINITIONS

"the amending provisions"–see art.2(1).
"No.9 Order"–*ibid.*

Modification of the Universal Credit (Digital Service) Amendment Regulations 2014

3.381   **7.** [¹ . . .]

AMENDMENT

1. Welfare Reform Act 2012 (Commencement No.25 and Transitional and Transitory Provisions) Order 2015 (SI 2015/1930) art.9 (December 2, 2015).

Revocation of modification of the Universal Credit (Digital Service) Amendment Regulations 2014

3.382   **8.** With effect from 21st September 2015, article 6 of the No.22 Order is revoked.

DEFINITION

"No.22 Order"–see art.2(1).

Modification of the Universal Credit (Surpluses and Self-Employed Losses) (Digital Service) Amendment Regulations 2015

3.383   **9.** [¹ . . .]

AMENDMENT

1. Welfare Reform Act 2012 (Commencement No.25 and Transitional and Transitory Provisions) Order 2015 (SI 2015/1930) art.9 (December 2, 2015).

The Welfare Reform Act 2012 (Commencement No.25 and Transitional and Transitory Provisions) Order 2015

(2015/1930) (C.118)

The Secretary of State for Work and Pensions makes the following Order in exercise of the powers conferred by section 150(3) and (4)(a), (b)(i) and (c) of the Welfare Reform Act 2012:

ARRANGEMENT OF ARTICLES

1.   Citation
2.   Interpretation

GENERAL NOTE

This Commencement Order provided for the expansion of universal credit to further designated postcodes in the London Borough of Sutton as from December 2, 2015 (see the definition of "the designated postcodes" in art.2(1)).

Citation

1. This Order may be cited as the Welfare Reform Act 2012 (Commencement No.25 and Transitional and Transitory Provisions) Order 2015.

3.384

Interpretation

2.—(1) In this Order—

3.385

"the Act" means the Welfare Reform Act 2012;

"the amending provisions" means the provisions referred to in article 4(1)(a) to (c) of the No.9 Order (day appointed for the abolition of income-related employment and support allowance and income-based jobseeker's allowance);

"claimant"—

(a) in relation to an employment and support allowance, has the same meaning as in 1 of the Welfare Reform Act 2007, save as mentioned in article 5(1A) of the No.9 Order as applied by article 4(7) of this Order;

(b) in relation to a jobseeker's allowance, has the same meaning as in the Jobseekers Act 1995 (as it applies apart from the amendments made by Part 1 of Schedule 14 to the Act that remove references to an income-based jobseeker's allowance), save as mentioned in article 5(1A) of the No.9 Order as applied by article 4(7) of this Order;

(c) in relation to universal credit, has the same meaning as in Part 1 of the Act;

"the Claims and Payments Regulations 1987" means the Social Security (Claims and Payments) Regulations 1987;

"employment and support allowance" means an employment and support allowance under Part 1 of the Welfare Reform Act 2007;

"jobseeker's allowance" means a jobseeker's allowance under the Jobseekers Act 1995;

"joint claimants", in relation to universal credit, has the same meaning as in Part 1 of the Act;

"the No.9 Order" means the Welfare Reform Act 2012 (Commencement No.9 and Transitional and Transitory Provisions and Commencement No.8 and Savings and Transitional Provisions (Amendment)) Order 2013;

"the No.23 Order" means the Welfare Reform Act 2012 (Commencement No.23 and Transitional and Transitory Provisions) Order 2015;

"the No.24 Order" means the Welfare Reform Act 2012 (Commencement No.24 and Transitional and Transitory Provisions and Commencement No.9 and Transitional and Transitory Provisions (Amendment)) Order 2015;

"the designated postcodes" means the postcode part-districts SM5 1, SM5 3, SM5 9, SM6 0 and SM6 6;

"single claimant", in relation to universal credit, has the same meaning as in Part 1 of the Act.

(2) For the purposes of this Order, the Universal Credit, Personal Independence Payment, Jobseeker's Allowance and Employment and Support Allowance (Claims and Payments) Regulations 2013 apply for the purpose of deciding—

(a) whether a claim for universal credit is made; and

(b) the date on which such a claim is made.

(3) For the purposes of this Order, the Claims and Payments Regulations 1987 apply, subject to paragraphs (4) and (5), for the purposes of deciding—

(a) whether a claim for an employment and support allowance or a jobseeker's allowance is made; and

(b) the date on which the claim is made or treated as made.

(4) Subject to paragraph (5), for the purposes of this Order—

(a) a person makes a claim for an employment and support allowance or a jobseeker's allowance if he or she takes any action which results in a decision on a claim being required under the Claims and Payments Regulations 1987; and

(b) it is irrelevant that the effect of any provision of those Regulations is that, for the purposes of those Regulations, the claim is made or treated as made at a date that is earlier than the date on which that action is taken.

(5) Where, by virtue of—

(a) regulation 6(1F)(b) or (c) of the Claims and Payments Regulations 1987, in the case of a claim for an employment and support allowance; or

(b) regulation 6(4ZA) to (4ZD) and (4A)(a)(i) and (b) of those Regulations, in the case of a claim for a jobseeker's allowance,

a claim for an employment and support allowance or a jobseeker's allowance is treated as made at a date that is earlier than the date on which the action referred to in paragraph (4)(a) is taken, the claim is treated as made on that earlier date.

Day appointed for the coming into force of the universal credit provisions

3.386   **3.**—(1) The day appointed for the coming into force of the provisions of the Act listed in Schedule 2 to the No.9 Order, in so far as they are not already in force, in relation to the case of a claim referred to in paragraph (2), and any award that is made in respect of the claim, is the day appointed in accordance with paragraph (3).

(2) The claims referred to are—

(a) a claim for universal credit that is made on or after 2nd December

2015 in respect of a period that begins on or after 2nd December 2015 where, on the date on which the claim is made, the claimant resides in one of the designated postcodes;

(b) a claim for universal credit that is made on or after 2nd December 2015, in respect of a period that begins on or after that date where—

    (i) in the case of a single claimant, the claimant gives incorrect information regarding the claimant residing in one of the designated postcodes and the claimant does not reside in such a postcode on the date on which the claim is made;

    (ii) in the case of joint claimants, either or both of the joint claimants gives or give incorrect information regarding his or her (or their) residing in such a postcode and one or both of them does not or do not reside in such a postcode on the date on which the claim is made,

and after a decision is made that the single claimant is, or the joint claimants are, entitled to universal credit and one or more payments have been made in respect of the single claimant or the joint claimants, the Secretary of State discovers that incorrect information has been given regarding residence.

(3) The day appointed in relation to the case of a claim referred to in paragraph (2), and any award that is made in respect of the claim, is the first day of the period in respect of which the claim is made.

(4) Article 3(6) of the No.9 Order applies for the purposes of paragraph (3) as it applies for the purposes of article 3(4)(a) of the No.9 Order.

(5) Article 3A of the No.9 Order applies in connection with a claim for universal credit where a single claimant, or, as the case may be, either or both of joint claimants, gives or give incorrect information regarding his or her (or their) residing in one of the designated postcodes, as it applies in connection with the giving of incorrect information regarding a claimant residing in one of the relevant districts (as defined in the No.9 Order).

DEFINITIONS

    "the Act"–see art.2(1).
    "claimant"–*ibid.*
    "the designated postcodes"–see art.2(2).
    "joint claimant"–*ibid.*
    "single claimant"–*ibid.*
    "No.9 Order"–*ibid.*

Day appointed for the abolition of income-related employment and support allowance and income-based jobseeker's allowance

4.—(1) The day appointed for the coming into force of the amending provisions, in relation to the case of a claim referred to in paragraph (2), and any award that is made in respect of the claim, is the day appointed in accordance with paragraph (3).

    3.387

(2) The claims referred to are—

(a) a claim for universal credit that is made on or after 2nd December 2015 in respect of a period that begins on or after 2nd December 2015 where, on the date on which the claim is made, the claimant resides in one of the designated postcodes;

 (b) a claim for universal credit that is made on or after 2nd December 2015, in respect of a period that begins on or after that date where—

  (i) in the case of a single claimant, the claimant gives incorrect information regarding the claimant residing in one of the designated postcodes and the claimant does not reside in such a postcode on the date on which the claim is made;

  (ii) in the case of joint claimants, either or both of the joint claimants gives or give incorrect information regarding his or her (or their) residing in such a postcode and one or both of them does not or do not reside in such a postcode on the date on which the claim is made,

and after a decision is made that the single claimant is, or the joint claimants are, entitled to universal credit and one or more payments have been made in respect of the single claimant or the joint claimants, the Secretary of State discovers that incorrect information has been given regarding residence;

 (c) a claim for an employment and support allowance or a jobseeker's allowance that is made or treated as made on or after 2nd December 2015 where, on the date on which the claim is made or treated as made, the claimant resides in one of the designated postcodes;

 (d) a claim for an employment and support allowance or a jobseeker's allowance other than one referred to in sub-paragraph (c) that is made or treated as made during the relevant period by a single claimant of universal credit or by either of two joint claimants of universal credit who has or have made a claim for universal credit within sub-paragraph (a) or (b).

(3) The day appointed in relation to the case of a claim referred to in paragraph (2), and any award that is made in respect of the claim, is the first day of the period in respect of which the claim is made.

(4) For the purposes of paragraph (2)(d), "relevant period" means, in relation to a claim for universal credit within sub-paragraph (a) or (b) of paragraph (2), any UC claim period, and any period subsequent to any UC claim period in respect of which the claimant is entitled to an award of universal credit in respect of the claim.

(5) For the purposes of paragraph (4), a "UC claim period" is a period when—

 (a) a claim for universal credit within sub-paragraph (a) of paragraph (2), or within sub-paragraph (b)(i) or (ii) of that paragraph, has been made but a decision has not yet been made on the claim; or

 (b) a decision has been made that the claimant is not entitled to universal credit and—

  (i) the Secretary of State is considering whether to revise that decision under section 9 of the Social Security Act 1998, whether on an application made for that purpose or on the Secretary of State's own initiative; or

  (ii) the claimant has appealed against that decision to the First-tier Tribunal and that appeal, or any subsequent appeal to the Upper Tribunal or to a court, has not been finally determined.

(6) Paragraphs (6), (7), (9) and (10) of article 4 of the No. 9 Order apply in relation to a claim for universal credit referred to in paragraph (2) (and any award that is made in respect of the claim) as they apply in relation to a claim for universal credit referred to in sub-paragraphs (a) and (b) of article 4(2) of the No. 9 Order (and any award that is made in respect of the claim).

(7) Paragraphs (1A) and (1B) of article 5 of the No.9 Order apply for the purposes of sub-paragraph (c) of paragraph (2) as they apply for the purposes of article 4(2)(a) of the No.9 Order (but as if the references in paragraph (1A) to Schedule 5 to the No.9 Order were omitted).

(8) Article 5(8) of the No.9 Order applies for the purposes of paragraph (3) as it applies for the purposes of article 4(3)(a) of the No.9 Order.

DEFINITIONS

"the amending provisions"–see art.2(1).
"claimant"–*ibid.*
"designated postcodes"–*ibid.*
"employment and support allowance"–*ibid.*
"jobseeker's allowance"–*ibid.*
"joint claimant"–*ibid.*
"No.9 Order"–*ibid.*
"relevant period"–para.(4).
"UC claim period"–para.(5).

Application of the No.9 Order

5. Articles 9 to 22 of the No.9 Order apply in connection with the coming into force of the amending provisions in relation to the case of a claim referred to in article 4(2), and any award made in respect of the claim, as they apply in connection with the coming into force of the amending provisions in relation to the case of a claim referred to in sub-paragraph (a), (b) or (g) of article 4(2) of the No.9 Order and any award made in respect of the claim.

3.388

DEFINITIONS

"the amending provisions"–see art.2(1).
"No.9 Order"–*ibid.*

Modification of the No.24 Order

6.—(1) Articles 3(2)(bb) and 4(2)(ccc) of the No.24 Order do not apply to a claim for universal credit to which articles 3(2)(a) and 4(2)(a) of this Order apply.

3.389

(2) Article 4(2)(ddd) of the No.24 Order does not apply to a claim for an employment and support allowance or a jobseeker's allowance to which article 4(2)(c) of this Order applies.

DEFINITIONS

"employment and support allowance"–see art.2(1).
"jobseeker's allowance"–*ibid.*
"No.24 Order"–*ibid.*

Transitional provision: claims for housing benefit, income support or a tax credit

7. Article 7 of the No.23 Order (prevention of claims for housing benefit, income support or a tax credit) applies as though the reference in paragraph (1) of that article to article 3(1) and (2)(a) to (c) of that Order included a reference to article 3(1) and (2)(a) of this Order.

3.390

DEFINITION

"No.23 Order"–see art.2(1).

Revocation of modifications made by the No.23 Order

3.391   **8.** With effect from 2nd December 2015, articles 10 (modification of the Universal Credit (Digital Service) Amendment Regulations 2014) and 11 (modification of the Universal Credit (Surpluses and Self-employed Losses) (Digital Service) Amendment Regulations 2015) of the No.23 Order are revoked.

DEFINITION

"No.23 Order"–see art.2(1).

Revocation of modifications made by the No.24 Order

3.392   **9.** With effect from 2nd December 2015, articles 7 (modification of the Universal Credit (Digital Service) Amendment Regulations 2014) and 9 (modification of the Universal Credit (Surpluses and Self-employed Losses) (Digital Service) Amendment Regulations 2015) of the No.24 Order are revoked.

DEFINITION

"No.24 Order"–see art.2(1).

The Welfare Reform Act 2012 (Commencement No.26 and Transitional and Transitory Provisions and Commencement No.22, 23 and 24 and Transitional and Transitory Provisions (Modification)) Order 2016

(2016/33) (C.3)

The Secretary of State for Work and Pensions makes the following Order in exercise of the powers conferred by section 150(3) and (4)(a), (b)(i) and (c) of the Welfare Reform Act 2012:

ARRANGEMENT OF ARTICLES

666

SCHEDULE   POSTCODE DISTRICTS AND PART-DISTRICTS

GENERAL NOTE

The effect of this Commencement Order was to provide for the introduction of the universal credit digital or full service in postcodes administered by Sutton, London Bridge, Hounslow and Croydon jobcentres with effect from January 27, 2016 and February 24, 2016.

3.393

Citation

1. This Order may be cited as the Welfare Reform Act 2012 (Commencement No.26 and Transitional and Transitory Provisions and Commencement No.22, 23 and 24 and Transitional and Transitory Provisions (Modification)) Order 2016.

3.394

Interpretation

2.—(1) In this Order—

3.395

"the Act" means the Welfare Reform Act 2012;

"the amending provisions" means the provisions referred to in article 4(1)(a) to (c) of the No.9 Order (day appointed for the abolition of income-related employment and support allowance and income-based jobseeker's allowance);

"claimant"—

(a) in relation to an employment and support allowance, has the same meaning as in Part 1 of the Welfare Reform Act 2007, save as mentioned in article 5(1A) of the No.9 Order as applied by article 4(7) of this Order;

(b) in relation to a jobseeker's allowance, has the same meaning as in the Jobseekers Act 1995 (as it applies apart from the amendments made by Part 1 of Schedule 14 to the Act that remove references to an income-based jobseeker's allowance), save as mentioned in article 5(1A) of the No.9 Order as applied by article 4(7) of this Order;

(c) in relation to universal credit, has the same meaning as in Part 1 of the Act;

"the Claims and Payments Regulations 1987" means the Social Security (Claims and Payments) Regulations 1987;

"employment and support allowance" means an employment and support allowance under Part 1 of the Welfare Reform Act 2007;

"jobseeker's allowance" means a jobseeker's allowance under the Jobseekers Act 1995;

"joint claimants", in relation to universal credit, has the same meaning as in Part 1 of the Act;

"the No.9 Order" means the Welfare Reform Act 2012 (Commencement No.9 and Transitional and Transitory Provisions and Commencement No.8 and Savings and Transitional Provisions (Amendment)) Order 2013;

"the No.22 Order" means the Welfare Reform Act 2012 (Commencement No.22 and Transitional and Transitory Provisions) Order 2015;

"the No.23 Order" means the Welfare Reform Act 2012 (Commencement No.23 and Transitional and Transitory Provisions) Order 2015;

"the No.24 Order" means the Welfare Reform Act 2012 (Commencement No.24 and Transitional and Transitory Provisions and Commencement

No. 9 and Transition and Transitory Provisions (Amendment)) Order 2015;

"the Part 1 designated postcodes" means the postcode districts and part-districts specified in Part 1 of the Schedule;

"the Part 2 designated postcodes" means the postcode part-districts specified in Part 2 of the Schedule;

"the Part 3 designated postcodes" means the postcode part-districts specified in Part 3 of the Schedule;

"the Part 4 designated postcode" means the postcode part-district specified in Part 4 of the Schedule;

"the Part 5 designated postcodes" means the postcode districts and part-districts specified in Part 5 of the Schedule;

"the Part 6 designated postcodes" means the postcode district and part-districts specified in Part 6 of the Schedule;

"the Part 7 designated postcodes" means the postcode districts and part-district specified in Part 7 of the Schedule;

"single claimant", in relation to universal credit, has the same meaning as in Part 1 of the Act.

(2) For the purposes of this Order, the Universal Credit, Personal Independence Payment, Jobseeker's Allowance and Employment and Support Allowance (Claims and Payments) Regulations 2013 apply for the purpose of deciding—

    (a) whether a claim for universal credit is made; and

    (b) the date on which such a claim is made.

(3) For the purposes of this Order, the Claims and Payments Regulations 1987 apply, subject to paragraphs (4) and (5), for the purposes of deciding—

    (a) whether a claim for an employment and support allowance or a jobseeker's allowance is made; and

    (b) the date on which the claim is made or treated as made.

(4) Subject to paragraph (5), for the purposes of this Order—

    (a) a person makes a claim for an employment and support allowance or a jobseeker's allowance if he or she takes any action which results in a decision on a claim being required under the Claims and Payments Regulations 1987; and

    (b) it is irrelevant that the effect of any provision of those Regulations is that, for the purposes of those Regulations, the claim is made or treated as made at a date that is earlier than the date on which that action is taken.

(5) Where, by virtue of—

    (a) regulation 6(1F)(b) or (c) of the Claims and Payments Regulations 1987, in the case of a claim for an employment and support allowance; or

    (b) regulation 6(4ZA) to (4ZD) and (4A)(a)(i) and (b) of those Regulations, in the case of a claim for a jobseeker's allowance,

a claim for an employment and support allowance or a jobseeker's allowance is treated as made at a date that is earlier than the date on which the action referred to in paragraph (4)(a) is taken, the claim is treated as made on that earlier date.

Day appointed for the coming into force of the universal credit provisions

3.—(1) The day appointed for the coming into force of the provisions of the Act listed in Schedule 2 to the No.9 Order, in so far as they are not already in force, in relation to the case of a claim referred to in paragraph (2), and any award that is made in respect of the claim, is the day appointed in accordance with paragraph (3).

3.396

(2) The claims referred to are—

(a) a claim for universal credit that is made on or after 27th January 2016 in respect of a period that begins on or after 27th January 2016 where, on the date on which the claim is made, the claimant resides in one of the Part 1 designated postcodes;

(b) a claim for universal credit that is made on or after 24th February 2016 in respect of a period that begins on or after 24th February 2016 where, on the date on which the claim is made, the claimant resides in one of the Part 2 designated postcodes;

(c) a claim for universal credit that is made on or after the date referred to in either sub-paragraph (a) or (b), in respect of a period that begins on or after that date where—

   (i) in the case of a single claimant, the claimant gives incorrect information regarding the claimant residing in a postcode as referred to in the sub-paragraph in question and the claimant does not reside in such a postcode on the date on which the claim is made;

   (ii) in the case of joint claimants, either or both of the joint claimants gives or give incorrect information regarding his or her (or their) residing in such a postcode and one or both of them does not or do not reside in such a postcode on the date on which the claim is made,

and after a decision is made that the single claimant is, or the joint claimants are, entitled to universal credit and one or more payments have been made in respect of the single claimant or the joint claimants, the Secretary of State discovers that incorrect information has been given regarding residence.

(3) The day appointed in relation to the case of a claim referred to in paragraph (2), and any award that is made in respect of the claim, is the first day of the period in respect of which the claim is made.

(4) Article 3(6) of the No.9 Order applies for the purposes of paragraph (3) as it applies for the purposes of article 3(4)(a) of the No.9 Order.

(5) Article 3A of the No.9 Order applies in connection with a claim for universal credit where a single claimant, or, as the case may be, either or both of joint claimants, gives or give incorrect information regarding his or her (or their) residing in one of the Part 1 or Part 2 designated postcodes, as it applies in connection with the giving of incorrect information regarding a claimant residing in one of the relevant districts (as defined in the No.9 Order).

DEFINITIONS

"the Act"–see art.2(1).
"claimant"–*ibid.*
"joint claimant"–*ibid.*
"the Part 1 designated postcodes"–*ibid.*

"the Part 2 designated postcodes"–*ibid.*
"No. 9 Order"–*ibid.*
"single claimant"–*ibid.*

Day appointed for the abolition of income-related employment and support allowance and income-based jobseeker's allowance

3.397   **4.**—(1) The day appointed for the coming into force of the amending provisions, in relation to the case of a claim referred to in paragraph (2), and any award that is made in respect of the claim, is the day appointed in accordance with paragraph (3).

(2) The claims referred to are—

(a) a claim for universal credit that is made on or after 27th January 2016 in respect of a period that begins on or after 27th January 2016 where, on the date on which the claim is made, the claimant resides in one of the Part 1 designated postcodes;

(b) a claim for universal credit that is made on or after 24th February 2016 in respect of a period that begins on or after 24th February 2016 where, on the date on which the claim is made, the claimant resides in one of the Part 2 designated postcodes;

(c) a claim for universal credit that is made on or after the date referred to in either sub-paragraph (a) or (b), in respect of a period that begins on or after that date where—

(i) in the case of a single claimant, the claimant gives incorrect information regarding the claimant residing in a postcode as referred to in the sub-paragraph in question and the claimant does not reside in such a postcode on the date on which the claim is made;

(ii) in the case of joint claimants, either or both of the joint claimants gives or give incorrect information regarding his or her (or their) residing in such a postcode and one or both of them does not or do not reside in such a postcode on the date on which the claim is made,

and after a decision is made that the single claimant is, or the joint claimants are, entitled to universal credit and one or more payments have been made in respect of the single claimant or the joint claimants, the Secretary of State discovers that incorrect information has been given regarding residence;

(d) a claim for an employment and support allowance or a jobseeker's allowance that is made or treated as made on or after 27th January 2016 where, on the date on which the claim is made or treated as made, the claimant resides in one of the Part 1 designated postcodes;

(e) a claim for an employment and support allowance or a jobseeker's allowance that is made or treated as made on or after 24th February 2016 where, on the date on which the claim is made or treated as made, the claimant resides in one of the Part 2 designated postcodes;

(f) a claim for an employment and support allowance or a jobseeker's allowance other than one referred to in sub-paragraphs (d) and (e) that is made or treated as made during the relevant period by a single claimant of universal credit or by either of two joint claimants of universal credit who has or have made a claim for universal credit within any of sub-paragraphs (a) to (c).

(3) The day appointed in relation to the case of a claim referred to in paragraph (2), and any award that is made in respect of the claim, is the first day of the period in respect of which the claim is made.

(4) For the purposes of paragraph (2)(f), "relevant period" means, in relation to a claim for universal credit within any of sub-paragraphs (a) to (c) of paragraph (2), any UC claim period, and any period subsequent to any UC claim period in respect of which the claimant is entitled to an award of universal credit in respect of the claim.

(5) For the purposes of paragraph (4), a "UC claim period" is a period when—

(a) a claim for universal credit within either sub-paragraph (a) or (b) of paragraph (2), or within sub-paragraph (c)(i) or (ii) of that paragraph, has been made but a decision has not yet been made on the claim; or

(b) a decision has been made that the claimant is not entitled to universal credit and—

   (i) the Secretary of State is considering whether to revise that decision under section 9 of the Social Security Act 1998, whether on an application made for that purpose or on the Secretary of State's own initiative; or

   (ii) the claimant has appealed against that decision to the First-tier Tribunal and that appeal, or any subsequent appeal to the Upper Tribunal or to a court, has not been finally determined.

(6) Paragraphs (6), (7), (9) and (10) of article 4 of the No.9 Order apply in relation to a claim for universal credit referred to in paragraph (2) (and any award that is made in respect of the claim) as they apply in relation to a claim for universal credit referred to in sub-paragraphs (a) and (b) of article 4(2) of the No.9 Order (and any award that is made in respect of the claim).

(7) Paragraphs (1A) and (1B) of article 5 of the No.9 Order apply for the purposes of sub-paragraphs (d) and (e) of paragraph (2) as they apply for the purposes of article 4(2)(a) of the No.9 Order (but as if the references in paragraph (1A) to Schedule 5 to the No.9 Order were omitted).

(8) Article 5(8) of the No.9 Order applies for the purposes of paragraph (3) as it applies for the purposes of article 4(3)(a) of the No.9 Order.

DEFINITIONS

"the amending provisions"–see art.2(1).
"claimant"–*ibid.*
"employment and support allowance"–*ibid.*
"jobseeker's allowance"–*ibid.*
"joint claimant"–*ibid.*
"No.9 Order"–*ibid.*
"the Part 1 designated postcodes"–*ibid.*
"the Part 2 designated postcodes"–*ibid.*
"relevant period"–para.(4).
"UC claim period"–para.(5).

Application of the No.9 Order

5. Articles 9 to 22 of the No.9 Order apply in connection with the coming into force of the amending provisions in relation to the case of a claim referred to in article 4(2), and any award made in respect of the claim, as they apply in connection with the coming into force of the amending provisions in relation to the case of a claim referred to in sub-paragraph (a), (b)

3.398

or (g) of article 4(2) of the No.9 Order and any award made in respect of the claim.

DEFINITIONS

"the amending provisions"–see art.2(1).
"No.9 Order"–*ibid.*

Modification of the No.22 Order: removal of the gateway conditions

3.399   **6.**—(1) This article applies in the case of a claim for universal credit, an employment and support allowance or a jobseeker's allowance that is made or treated as made on or after 27th January 2016.

(2) Where this article applies, the provisions of the No.22 Order referred to in sub-paragraphs (a) and (b) have effect, with respect to a claimant residing in the designated postcodes referred to in the sub-paragraph in question, as though the reference in those provisions to meeting the gateway conditions were omitted—

    (a) articles 3(2)(i) and 4(2)(q) and (r), in respect of the Part 3 designated postcodes; and

    (b) articles 3(2)(t) and 4(2)(mm) and (nn), in respect of the Part 4 designated postcode.

(3) With respect to any claim in relation to which provisions of the No.22 Order are modified under paragraph (2), the No.22 Order has effect as though—

    (a) in article 2(1), for the definition of "claimant" there were substituted—

    ""claimant"—

        (a) in relation to an employment and support allowance, has the same meaning as in Part 1 of the Welfare Reform Act 2007, save as mentioned in article 5(1A) of the No.9 Order as applied by article 4(7) of this Order;

        (b) in relation to a jobseeker's allowance, has the same meaning as in the Jobseekers Act 1995 (as it applies apart from the amendments made by Part 1 of Schedule 14 to the Act that remove references to an income-based jobseeker's allowance), save as mentioned in article 5(1A) of the No.9 Order as applied by article 4(7) of this Order;

        (c) in relation to universal credit, has the same meaning as in Part 1 of the Act;";

    (b) for article 3(2)(v) there were substituted—

    "(v) a claim for universal credit that is made on or after the date referred to in sub-paragraph (i) or (t), in respect of a period that begins on or after that date where—

        (i) in the case of a single claimant, the claimant gives incorrect information regarding the claimant residing in a district as referred to in the sub-paragraph in question and the claimant does not reside in such a district on the date on which the claim is made;

        (ii) in the case of joint claimants, either or both of the joint claimants gives or give incorrect information regarding his or her (or their) residing in such a district and one or both of them does not or do not reside in such a district on the date on which the claim is made, and after a decision is made that the single claimant is, or the joint claimants are, entitled to universal credit and one or more payments have been made in respect of the single claimant or the joint claimants, the Secretary of State discovers that incorrect information has been given regarding residence.";

(c) for article 3(5) there were substituted—

"(5) Article 3A of the No.9 Order applies in connection with a claim for universal credit where a single claimant, or, as the case may be, either or both of joint claimants, gives or give incorrect information regarding his or her (or their) residing in one of the No.37 or No.48 relevant districts, as it applies in connection with the giving of incorrect information regarding a claimant residing in one of the relevant districts (as defined in the No.9 Order).";

(d) for article 4(2)(qq) there were substituted—

"(qq) a claim for universal credit that is made on or after the date referred to in sub-paragraph (q) or (mm), in respect of a period that begins on or after that date where—

(i) in the case of a single claimant, the claimant gives incorrect information regarding the claimant residing in a district as referred to in the sub-paragraph in question and the claimant does not reside in such a district on the date on which the claim is made;

(ii) in the case of joint claimants, either or both of the joint claimants gives or give incorrect information regarding his or her (or their) residing in such a district and one or both of them does not or do not reside in such a district on the date on which the claim is made,

and after a decision is made that the single claimant is, or the joint claimants are, entitled to universal credit and one or more payments have been made in respect of the single claimant or the joint claimants, the Secretary of State discovers that incorrect information has been given regarding residence;";

(e) for article 4(7) there were substituted—

"(7) Paragraphs (1A) and (1B) of article 5 of the No.9 Order apply for the purposes of sub-paragraphs (r) and (nn) of paragraph (2) as they apply for the purposes of article 4(2)(a) of the No.9 Order (but as if the references in paragraph (1A) to Schedule 5 to the No.9 Order were omitted).".

DEFINITIONS

"employment and support allowance"–see art.2(1).
"jobseeker's allowance"–*ibid.*
"No.22 Order"–*ibid.*
"the Part 3 designated postcodes"–*ibid.*
"the Part 4 designated postcodes"–*ibid.*

Transitional provision: claims for housing benefit, income support or a tax credit

7. Article 7 of the No.23 Order (prevention of claims for housing benefit, income support or a tax credit) applies as though the reference in paragraph (1) of that article to article 3(1) and (2)(a) to (c) of that Order included—

(a) a reference to article 3(1) and (2)(a) and (b) of this Order; and

3.400

(b) a reference to paragraph (1) and sub-paragraphs (i) and (t) of paragraph (2) of article 3 of the No.22 Order, in respect only of claims in
relation to which sub-paragraphs (i) and (t) are modified by article
6(2) of this Order.

DEFINITIONS

"No.22 Order"–see art.2(1).
"No.23 Order" –*ibid.*

Modification of the No.24 Order

3.401   **8.**—(1) Articles 3(2)(bb) and 4(2)(ccc) of the No.24 Order do not apply
to a claim for universal credit to which articles 3(2)(a) and 4(2)(a) or articles 3(2)(b) and 4(2)(b) of this Order apply.

(2) Article 4(2)(ddd) of the No.24 Order does not apply to a claim for
an employment and support allowance or a jobseeker's allowance to which
sub-paragraph (d) or (e) of paragraph (2) of article 4 of this Order applies.

(3) With effect from 17th January 2016, the provisions of the No.24
Order set out in sub-paragraphs (a) to (c) have effect as though any reference in those provisions to numbered relevant districts (as defined in article
2(2) of that Order) does not include a reference to the designated postcodes
referred to in the sub-paragraph in question—

(a) articles 3(2)(o) and 4(2)(cc) and (dd), in respect of the Part 5 designated postcodes;

(b) articles 3(2)(s) and 4(2)(kk) and (ll), in respect of the Part 6 designated postcodes;

(c) articles 3(2)(v) and 4(2)(qq) and (rr), in respect of the Part 7 designated postcodes.

(4) Paragraph (3) does not apply for the purposes of articles 3(2)(cc) and
4(2)(eee) and (fff) of the No.24 Order.

DEFINITIONS

"employment and support allowance"–see art.2(1).
"jobseeker's allowance"–*ibid.*
"No.24 Order"–*ibid.*

Article 2(1)

SCHEDULE

POSTCODE DISTRICTS AND PART-DISTRICTS

PART 1

3.402   SE1 0 to SE1 4.
SE1 6.
SM1.
SM2 6.
SM3 9.
SM4.
TW3 2.
TW3 3.
TW4 5.
TW5 9.
TW7 7.
TW13 6.

PART 2

CR0 1.   **3.403**
CR0 3.
SM2 5.
SM2 7.
SM3 8.
SM5 4.
SM7 3.

PART 3

TW3 1.   **3.404**
TW3 4.
TW4 6 and TW4 7.
TW5 0.
TW7 4 to TW7 6.
TW7 9.
TW8 0.
TW8 1.
TW8 8.
TW13 4 and TW13 5.
TW13 7.
TW13 9.
TW14 0.
TW14 9.

PART 4

TW8 9.   **3.405**

PART 5

CR2.   **3.406**
CR3 0.
CR5 2.
CR7.
CR8 1 to CR8 4.
CR8 9.
SE25 6.

PART 6

CR3 5.   **3.407**
CR5 1.
CR5 3.
CR6.
CR8 5.

PART 7

NR13 3.   **3.408**
NR29.
NR30.
NR31.

The Welfare Reform Act 2012 (Commencement No.27 and Transitional and Transitory Provisions and Commencement No.22, 23 and 24 and Transitional and Transitory Provisions (Modification)) Order 2016

(SI 2016/407) (C.20)

The Secretary of State for Work and Pensions makes the following Order in exercise of the powers conferred by section 150(3) and (4)(a), (b)(i) and (c) of the Welfare Reform Act 2012:

ARRANGEMENT OF ARTICLES

GENERAL NOTE

3.409   This Commencement Order provided for the further expansion of the universal credit digital or full service in various designated postcode areas with effect from March 23, 2016 (Croydon, London Bridge and Musselburgh) and April 27, 2016 (Purley, Thornton Heath and Great Yarmouth).

Citation

3.410   **1.** This Order may be cited as the Welfare Reform Act 2012 (Commencement No.27 and Transitional and Transitory Provisions and Commencement No.22, 23 and 24 and Transitional and Transitory Provisions (Modification)) Order 2016.

Interpretation

3.411   **2.**—(1) In this Order—
"the Act" means the Welfare Reform Act 2012;
"the amending provisions" means the provisions referred to in article 4(1)(a) to (c) of the No.9 Order (day appointed for the abolition of income-related employment and support allowance and income-based jobseeker's allowance);
"claimant"—
(a) in relation to an employment and support allowance, has the same

meaning as in Part 1 of the Welfare Reform Act 2007, save as mentioned in article 5(1A) of the No.9 Order as applied by article 4(7) of this Order;

(b) in relation to a jobseeker's allowance, has the same meaning as in the Jobseekers Act 1995 (as it applies apart from the amendments made by Part 1 of Schedule 14 to the Act that remove references to an income-based jobseeker's allowance), save as mentioned in article 5(1A) of the No.9 Order as applied by article 4(7) of this Order;

(c) in relation to universal credit, has the same meaning as in Part 1 of the Act;

"the Claims and Payments Regulations 1987" means the Social Security (Claims and Payments) Regulations 1987;

"employment and support allowance" means an employment and support allowance under Part 1 of the Welfare Reform Act 2007;

"jobseeker's allowance" means a jobseeker's allowance under the Jobseekers Act 1995;

"joint claimants", in relation to universal credit, has the same meaning as in Part 1 of the Act;

"the No.9 Order" means the Welfare Reform Act 2012 (Commencement No.9 and Transitional and Transitory Provisions and Commencement No.8 and Savings and Transitional Provisions (Amendment)) Order 2013;

"the No.22 Order" means the Welfare Reform Act 2012 (Commencement No.22 and Transitional and Transitory Provisions) Order 2015;

"the No.23 Order" means the Welfare Reform Act 2012 (Commencement No.23 and Transitional and Transitory Provisions) Order 2015;

"the No.24 Order" means the Welfare Reform Act 2012 (Commencement No.24 and Transitional and Transitory Provisions and Commencement No.9 and Transitional and Transitory Provisions (Amendment)) Order 2015;

"the Part 1 designated postcodes" means the postcode district and part-districts specified in Part 1 of the Schedule;

"the Part 2 designated postcodes" means the postcode districts and part-districts specified in Part 2 of the Schedule;

"the Part 3 designated postcodes" means the postcode districts specified in Part 3 of the Schedule;

"single claimant", in relation to universal credit, has the same meaning as in Part 1 of the Act.

(2) For the purposes of this Order, the Universal Credit, Personal Independence Payment, Jobseeker's Allowance and Employment and Support Allowance (Claims and Payments) Regulations 2013 apply for the purpose of deciding—

(a) whether a claim for universal credit is made; and

(b) the date on which such a claim is made.

(3) For the purposes of this Order, the Claims and Payments Regulations 1987 apply, subject to paragraphs (4) and (5), for the purposes of deciding—

(a) whether a claim for an employment and support allowance or a jobseeker's allowance is made; and

(b) the date on which the claim is made or treated as made.

(4) Subject to paragraph (5), for the purposes of this Order—

(a) a person makes a claim for an employment and support allowance or

a jobseeker's allowance if he or she takes any action which results in a decision on a claim being required under the Claims and Payments Regulations 1987; and

(b) it is irrelevant that the effect of any provision of those Regulations is that, for the purposes of those Regulations, the claim is made or treated as made at a date that is earlier than the date on which that action is taken.

(5) Where, by virtue of—

(a) regulation 6(1F)(b) or (c) of the Claims and Payments Regulations 1987, in the case of a claim for an employment and support allowance; or

(b) regulation 6(4ZA) to (4ZD) and (4A)(a)(i) and (b) of those Regulations, in the case of a claim for a jobseeker's allowance,

a claim for an employment and support allowance or a jobseeker's allowance is treated as made at a date that is earlier than the date on which the action referred to in paragraph (4)(a) is taken, the claim is treated as made on that earlier date.

Day appointed for the coming into force of the universal credit provisions

3.412   **3.**—(1) The day appointed for the coming into force of the provisions of the Act listed in Schedule 2 to the No.9 Order, in so far as they are not already in force, in relation to the case of a claim referred to in paragraph (2), and any award that is made in respect of the claim, is the day appointed in accordance with paragraph (3).

(2) The claims referred to are—

(a) a claim for universal credit that is made on or after 23rd March 2016 in respect of a period that begins on or after 23rd March 2016 where, on the date on which the claim is made, the claimant resides in one of the Part 1 designated postcodes;

(b) a claim for universal credit that is made on or after 27th April 2016 in respect of a period that begins on or after 27th April 2016 where, on the date on which the claim is made, the claimant resides in one of the Part 2 designated postcodes;

(c) a claim for universal credit that is made on or after the date referred to in either sub-paragraph (a) or (b), in respect of a period that begins on or after that date where—

(i) in the case of a single claimant, the claimant gives incorrect information regarding the claimant residing in a postcode as referred to in the sub-paragraph in question and the claimant does not reside in such a postcode on the date on which the claim is made;

(ii) in the case of joint claimants, either or both of the joint claimants gives or give incorrect information regarding his or her (or their) residing in such a postcode and one or both of them does not or do not reside in such a postcode on the date on which the claim is made,

and after a decision is made that the single claimant is, or the joint claimants are, entitled to universal credit and one or more payments have been made in respect of the single claimant or the joint claimants, the Secretary of State discovers that incorrect information has been given regarding residence.

(3) The day appointed in relation to the case of a claim referred to in paragraph (2), and any award that is made in respect of the claim, is the first day of the period in respect of which the claim is made.

(4) Article 3(6) of the No.9 Order applies for the purposes of paragraph (3) as it applies for the purposes of article 3(4)(a) of the No.9 Order.

(5) Article 3A of the No.9 Order applies in connection with a claim for universal credit where a single claimant, or, as the case may be, either or both of joint claimants, gives or give incorrect information regarding his or her (or their) residing in one of the Part 1 or Part 2 designated postcodes, as it applies in connection with the giving of incorrect information regarding a claimant residing in one of the relevant districts (as defined in the No.9 Order).

DEFINITIONS

"the Act"–see art.2(1).
"claimant"–*ibid*.
"joint claimant"–*ibid*.
"the Part 1 designated postcodes"–*ibid*.
"the Part 2 designated postcodes"–*ibid*.
"No.9 Order"–*ibid*.
"single claimant"–*ibid*.

Day appointed for the abolition of income-related employment and support allowance and income-based jobseeker's allowance

4.—(1) The day appointed for the coming into force of the amending provisions, in relation to the case of a claim referred to in paragraph (2), and any award that is made in respect of the claim, is the day appointed in accordance with paragraph (3).

3.413

(2) The claims referred to are—

(a) a claim for universal credit that is made on or after 23rd March 2016 in respect of a period that begins on or after 23rd March 2016 where, on the date on which the claim is made, the claimant resides in one of the Part 1 designated postcodes;

(b) a claim for universal credit that is made on or after 27th April 2016 in respect of a period that begins on or after 27th April 2016 where, on the date on which the claim is made, the claimant resides in one of the Part 2 designated postcodes;

(c) a claim for universal credit that is made on or after the date referred to in either sub-paragraph (a) or (b), in respect of a period that begins on or after that date where—

(i) in the case of a single claimant, the claimant gives incorrect information regarding the claimant residing in a postcode as referred to in the sub-paragraph in question and the claimant does not reside in such a postcode on the date on which the claim is made;

(ii) in the case of joint claimants, either or both of the joint claimants gives or give incorrect information regarding his or her (or their) residing in such a postcode and one or both of them does not or do not reside in such a postcode on the date on which the claim is made,

and after a decision is made that the single claimant is, or the joint claimants are, entitled to universal credit and one or more payments have been made in respect of the single claimant or the joint claimants, the Secretary of State discovers that incorrect information has been given regarding residence;

    (d) a claim for an employment and support allowance or a jobseeker's allowance that is made or treated as made on or after 23rd March 2016 where, on the date on which the claim is made or treated as made, the claimant resides in one of the Part 1 designated postcodes;

    (e) a claim for an employment and support allowance or a jobseeker's allowance that is made or treated as made on or after 27th April 2016 where, on the date on which the claim is made or treated as made, the claimant resides in one of the Part 2 designated postcodes;

    (f) a claim for an employment and support allowance or a jobseeker's allowance other than one referred to in sub-paragraphs (d) and (e) that is made or treated as made during the relevant period by a single claimant of universal credit or by either of two joint claimants of universal credit who has or have made a claim for universal credit within any of sub-paragraphs (a) to (c).

(3) The day appointed in relation to the case of a claim referred to in paragraph (2), and any award that is made in respect of the claim, is the first day of the period in respect of which the claim is made.

(4) For the purposes of paragraph (2)(f), "relevant period" means, in relation to a claim for universal credit within any of sub-paragraphs (a) to (c) of paragraph (2), any UC claim period, and any period subsequent to any UC claim period in respect of which the claimant is entitled to an award of universal credit in respect of the claim.

(5) For the purposes of paragraph (4), a "UC claim period" is a period when—

    (a) a claim for universal credit within either sub-paragraph (a) or (b) of paragraph (2), or within sub-paragraph (c)(i) or (ii) of that paragraph, has been made but a decision has not yet been made on the claim; or

    (b) a decision has been made that the claimant is not entitled to universal credit and—

        (i) the Secretary of State is considering whether to revise that decision under section 9 of the Social Security Act 1998, whether on an application made for that purpose or on the Secretary of State's own initiative; or

        (ii) the claimant has appealed against that decision to the First-tier Tribunal and that appeal, or any subsequent appeal to the Upper Tribunal or to a court, has not been finally determined.

(6) Paragraphs (6), (7), (9) and (10) of article 4 of the No.9 Order apply in relation to a claim for universal credit referred to in paragraph (2) (and any award that is made in respect of the claim) as they apply in relation to a claim for universal credit referred to in sub-paragraphs (a) and (b) of article 4(2) of the No.9 Order (and any award that is made in respect of the claim).

(7) Paragraphs (1A) and (1B) of article 5 of the No.9 Order apply for the purposes of sub-paragraphs (d) and (e) of paragraph (2) as they apply for the purposes of article 4(2)(a) of the No.9 Order (but as if the references in paragraph (1A) to Schedule 5 to the No.9 Order were omitted).

(8) Article 5(8) of the No.9 Order applies for the purposes of paragraph (3) as it applies for the purposes of article 4(3)(a) of the No.9 Order.

Application of the No.9 Order

5. Articles 9 to 22 of the No.9 Order apply in connection with the coming
into force of the amending provisions in relation to the case of a claim
referred to in article 4(2), and any award made in respect of the claim, as
they apply in connection with the coming into force of the amending provisions in relation to the case of a claim referred to in sub-paragraph (a), (b)
or (g) of article 4(2) of the No.9 Order and any award made in respect of
the claim.

3.414

Modification of the No.22 Order: removal of the gateway conditions

6.—(1) This article applies in the case of a claim for universal credit, an
employment and support allowance or a jobseeker's allowance that is made
or treated as made on or after 23rd March 2016.

3.415

(2) Where this article applies, articles 3(2)(i) and 4(2)(q) and (r) of the
No.22 Order have effect, with respect to a claimant residing in the Part
3 designated postcodes, as though the reference in those provisions to
meeting the gateway conditions were omitted.

(3) With respect to any claim in relation to which provisions of the No.22
Order are modified under paragraph (2), the No.22 Order has effect as
though—

    (a) in article 2(1), for the definition of "claimant" there were substi-
tuted—

""claimant"—

      (a) in relation to an employment and support allowance, has the
same meaning as in Part 1 of the Welfare Reform Act 2007, save
as mentioned in article 5(1A) of the No.9 Order as applied by
article 4(7) of this Order;

      (b) in relation to a jobseeker's allowance, has the same meaning as
in the Jobseekers Act 1995 (as it applies apart from the amendments made by Part 1 of Schedule 14 to the Act that remove
references to an income-based jobseeker's allowance), save as
mentioned in article 5(1A) of the No.9 Order as applied by
article 4(7) of this Order;

      (c) in relation to universal credit, has the same meaning as in Part
1 of the Act;";

(b) for article 3(2)(v) there were substituted—

"(v) a claim for universal credit that is made on or after the date referred to in sub-paragraph (i), in respect of a period that begins on or after that date where—

    (i) in the case of a single claimant, the claimant gives incorrect information regarding the claimant residing in a district as referred to in that sub-paragraph and the claimant does not reside in such a district on the date on which the claim is made;

    (ii) in the case of joint claimants, either or both of the joint claimants gives or give incorrect information regarding his or her (or their) residing in such a district and one or both of them does not or do not reside in such a district on the date on which the claim is made,

and after a decision is made that the single claimant is, or the joint claimants are, entitled to universal credit and one or more payments have been made in respect of the single claimant or the joint claimants, the Secretary of State discovers that incorrect information has been given regarding residence.";

(c) for article 3(5) there were substituted—

"(5) Article 3A of the No.9 Order applies in connection with a claim for universal credit where a single claimant, or, as the case may be, either or both of joint claimants, gives or give incorrect information regarding his or her (or their) residing in one of the No.37 relevant districts, as it applies in connection with the giving of incorrect information regarding a claimant residing in one of the relevant districts (as defined in the No.9 Order).";

(d) for article 4(2)(qq) there were substituted—

"(qq) a claim for universal credit that is made on or after the date referred to in sub-paragraph (q), in respect of a period that begins on or after that date where—

    (i) in the case of a single claimant, the claimant gives incorrect information regarding the claimant residing in a district as referred to in that sub-paragraph and the claimant does not reside in such a district on the date on which the claim is made;

    (ii) in the case of joint claimants, either or both of the joint claimants gives or give incorrect information regarding his or her (or their) residing in such a district and one or both of them does not or do not reside in such a district on the date on which the claim is made,

and after a decision is made that the single claimant is, or the joint claimants are, entitled to universal credit and one or more payments have been made in respect of the single claimant or the joint claimants, the Secretary of State discovers that incorrect information has been given regarding residence;"; and

(e) for article 4(7) there were substituted—

"(7) Paragraphs (1A) and (1B) of article 5 of the No.9 Order apply for the purposes of sub-paragraph (r) of paragraph (2) as they apply for the purposes of article 4(2)(a) of the No.9 Order (but as if the references in paragraph (1A) to Schedule 5 to the No.9 Order were omitted).".

"employment and support allowance"–see art.2(1).
"jobseeker's allowance"–*ibid.*
"No.22 Order"–*ibid.*
"the Part 3 designated postcodes"–*ibid.*

Modification of the No.23 Order: claims for housing benefit, income support or a tax credit

7. Article 7 of the No.23 Order (prevention of claims for housing benefit,   3.416
income support or a tax credit)(1) applies as though the reference in
paragraph (1) of that article to article 3(1) and (2)(a) to (c) of that Order
included—

   (a) a reference to article 3(1) and (2)(a) and (b) of this Order; and
   (b) a reference to paragraph (1) and sub-paragraph (i) of paragraph (2)
       of article 3 of the No.22 Order, in respect of claims in relation to
       which sub-paragraph (i) is modified by article 6(2) of this Order.

"No.22 Order"–see art.2(1).
"No.23 Order" –*ibid.*

Modification of the No.24 Order

8.—(1) Articles 3(2)(bb) and 4(2)(ccc) of the No.24 Order do not apply   3.417
to a claim for universal credit to which articles 3(2)(a) and 4(2)(a) of this
Order apply.

(2) Article 4(2)(ddd) of the No.24 Order does not apply to a claim for
an employment and support allowance or a jobseeker's allowance to which
article 4(2)(d) of this Order applies.

"employment and support allowance"–see art.2(1).
"jobseeker's allowance"–*ibid.*
"No.24 Order"–*ibid.*

Article 2(1)

SCHEDULE

POSTCODE DISTRICTS AND PART-DISTRICTS

PART 1

CR0 0.   3.418
CR0 5 to CR0 9.
CR9.
SE1 7 to SE1 9.
SE16 2.
SE16 4 to SE16 7.
SE25 4.
SE25 5.
TW14 8.

PART 2

3.419   CR2.
             CR3 0.
             CR3 5.
             CR5.
             CR6.
             CR7.
             CR8.
             NR13 3.
             NR29.
             NR30.
             NR31.
             SE25 6.

PART 3

3.420   EH21.
             EH31.
             EH32.
             EH33.
             EH34.
             EH35.
             EH36.
             EH39.
             EH40.
             EH41.
             EH42.

The Welfare Reform Act 2012 (Commencement No.13, 14, 16, 19, 22, 23 and 24 and Transitional and Transitory Provisions (Modification)) Order 2016

(SI 2016/596) (C.41)

The Secretary of State for Work and Pensions makes the following Order in exercise of the powers conferred by section 150(3) and (4)(a), (b)(i) and (c) of the Welfare Reform Act 2012:

ARRANGEMENT OF ARTICLES

1.   Citation
2.   Interpretation
3.   Modification of the No.14, 16, 22 and 24 Orders: removal of the gateway conditions from 25th May 2016
4.   Modification of the No.13, 14, 16, 22 and 24 Orders: removal of the gateway conditions from 29th June 2016
5.   Modification of the No.13, 19 and 22 Orders: removal of the gateway conditions from 27th July 2016
6.   Modifications in consequence of removal of the gateway conditions: the No.13 Order
7.   Modifications in consequence of removal of the gateway conditions: the No.14 Order

SCHEDULE   POSTCODE DISTRICTS AND PART-DISTRICTS

GENERAL NOTE

This Order, amending and modifying a range of earlier Commencement Orders, provides for the expansion of the full or digital universal credit service in a number of designated postcode areas with effect from May 25, June 29 and July 27, 2016.   3.421

Citation

1. This Order may be cited as the Welfare Reform Act 2012 (Commencement No.13, 14, 16, 19, 22, 23 and 24 and Transitional and Transitory Provisions (Modification)) Order 2016.   3.422

Interpretation

2.—(1) In this Order—   3.423
"the Act" means the Welfare Reform Act 2012;
"claimant"—
(a) in relation to an employment and support allowance, has the same meaning as in Part 1 of the Welfare Reform Act 2007;
(b) in relation to a jobseeker's allowance, has the same meaning as in the Jobseekers Act 1995 (as it applies apart from the amendments made by Part 1 of Schedule 14 to the Act that remove references to an income-based jobseeker's allowance);
(c) in relation to universal credit, has the same meaning as in Part 1 of the Act;
"the Claims and Payments Regulations 1987" means the Social Security (Claims and Payments) Regulations 1987;
"employment and support allowance" means an employment and support allowance under Part 1 of the Welfare Reform Act 2007;
"jobseeker's allowance" means a jobseeker's allowance under the Jobseekers Act 1995;
"the No.9 Order" means the Welfare Reform Act 2012 (Commencement No.9 and Transitional and Transitory Provisions and Commencement No.8 and Savings and Transitional Provisions (Amendment)) Order 2013;
"the No.13 Order" means the Welfare Reform Act 2012 (Commencement No.13 and Transitional and Transitory Provisions) Order 2013;
"the No.14 Order" means the Welfare Reform Act 2012 (Commencement No.14 and Transitional and Transitory Provisions) Order 2013;
"the No.16 Order" means the Welfare Reform Act 2012 (Commencement No.16 and Transitional and Transitory Provisions) Order 2014;
"the No.19 Order" means the Welfare Reform Act 2012 (Commencement

No.19 and Transitional and Transitory Provisions and Commencement No.9 and Transitional and Transitory Provisions (Amendment)) Order 2014;

"the No.22 Order" means the Welfare Reform Act 2012 (Commencement No.22 and Transitional and Transitory Provisions) Order 2015;

"the No.23 Order" means the Welfare Reform Act 2012 (Commencement No.23 and Transitional and Transitory Provisions) Order 2015;

"the No.24 Order" means the Welfare Reform Act 2012 (Commencement No.24 and Transitional and Transitory Provisions and Commencement No.9 and Transitional and Transitory Provisions (Amendment)) Order 2015.

(2) In this Order, references to "designated postcodes", by numbered "Part", are to the postcode districts and part-districts in the corresponding numbered Part of the Schedule to this Order.

(3) For the purposes of this Order, the Universal Credit, Personal Independence Payment, Jobseeker's Allowance and Employment and Support Allowance (Claims and Payments) Regulations 2013 apply for the purpose of deciding—

(a) whether a claim for universal credit is made; and

(b) the date on which such a claim is made.

(4) For the purposes of this Order, the Claims and Payments Regulations 1987 apply, subject to paragraphs (5) and (6), for the purposes of deciding—

(a) whether a claim for an employment and support allowance or a jobseeker's allowance is made; and

(b) the date on which the claim is made or treated as made.

(5) Subject to paragraph (6), for the purposes of this Order—

(a) a person makes a claim for an employment and support allowance or a jobseeker's allowance if he or she takes any action which results in a decision on a claim being required under the Claims and Payments Regulations 1987; and

(b) it is irrelevant that the effect of any provision of those Regulations is that, for the purposes of those Regulations, the claim is made or treated as made at a date that is earlier than the date on which that action is taken.

(6) Where, by virtue of—

(a) regulation 6(1F)(b) or (c) of the Claims and Payments Regulations 1987, in the case of a claim for an employment and support allowance; or

(b) regulation 6(4ZA) to (4ZD) and (4A)(a)(i) and (b) of those Regulations, in the case of a claim for a jobseeker's allowance,

a claim for an employment and support allowance or a jobseeker's allowance is treated as made at a date that is earlier than the date on which the action referred to in paragraph (5)(a) is taken, the claim is treated as made on that earlier date.

Modification of the No.14, 16, 22 and 24 Orders: removal of the gateway conditions from 25th May 2016

3.424   **3.**—(1) This article applies in the case of a claim for universal credit, an employment and support allowance or a jobseeker's allowance that is made or treated as made on or after 25th May 2016.

(2) Where this article applies, the provisions referred to in sub-paragraphs (a) to (i) have effect, with respect to a claimant residing in the designated postcodes referred to in the sub-paragraph in question, as though the reference in those provisions to meeting the gateway conditions were omitted—

(a) articles 3(2)(a) and 4(2)(a) of the No.14 Order, in respect of the Part 1 designated postcodes;

(b) articles 3(2)(a) and 4(2)(a) of the No.16 Order, in respect of the Part 2 designated postcodes;

(c) articles 3(2)(e) and 4(2)(i) and (j) of the No.22 Order, in respect of the Part 3 designated postcodes;

(d) articles 3(2)(f) and 4(2)(k) and (l) of the No.22 Order, in respect of the Part 4 designated postcodes;

(e) articles 3(2)(h) and 4(2)(o) and (p) of the No.22 Order, in respect of the Part 5 designated postcodes;

(f) articles 3(2)(i) and 4(2)(q) and (r) of the No.22 Order, in respect of the Part 6 designated postcodes;

(g) articles 3(2)(c) and 4(2)(e) and (f) of the No.24 Order, in respect of the Part 7 designated postcode;

(h) articles 3(2)(n) and 4(2)(aa) and (bb) of the No.24 Order, in respect of the Part 8 designated postcodes;

(i) articles 3(2)(bb) and 4(2)(ccc) and (ddd) of the No.24 Order, in respect of the Part 9 designated postcodes.

DEFINITIONS

"claimant"–see art.2(1).
"designated postcodes"–see art.2(2).
"employment and support allowance"–see art.2(1).
"jobseeker's allowance"–*ibid.*
"No.14 Order"–*ibid.*
"No.16 Order"–*ibid.*
"No.22 Order"–*ibid.*
"No.24 Order"–*ibid.*

Modification of the No.13, 14, 16, 22 and 24 Orders: removal of the gateway conditions from 29th June 2016

4.—(1) This article applies in the case of a claim for universal credit, an employment and support allowance or a jobseeker's allowance that is made or treated as made on or after 29th June 2016.

3.425

(2) Where this article applies, the provisions referred to in sub-paragraphs (a) to (f) have effect, with respect to a claimant residing in the designated postcodes referred to in the sub-paragraph in question, as though the reference in those provisions to meeting the gateway conditions were omitted—

(a) articles 3(2)(a) and 4(2)(a) of the No.13 Order, in respect of the Part 10 designated postcodes;

(b) articles 3(2)(a) and 4(2)(a) of the No.14 Order, in respect of the Part 11 designated postcodes;

(c) articles 3(2)(a) and 4(2)(a) of the No.16 Order, in respect of the Part 12 designated postcodes;

(d) articles 3(2)(a) and 4(2)(a) and (b) of the No.22 Order, in respect of the Part 13 designated postcodes;

(e) articles 3(2)(k) and 4(2)(u) and (v) of the No.22 Order, in respect of the Part 14 designated postcodes;

(f) articles 3(2)(a) and 4(2)(a) and (b) of the No.24 Order, in respect of the Part 15 designated postcode.

DEFINITIONS

"claimant"–see art.2(1).
"designated postcodes"–see art.2(2).
"employment and support allowance"–see art.2(1).
"jobseeker's allowance"–*ibid.*
"No.13 Order"–*ibid.*
"No.14 Order"–*ibid.*
"No.16 Order"–*ibid.*
"No.22 Order"–*ibid.*
"No.24 Order"–*ibid.*

Modification of the No.13, 19 and 22 Orders: removal of the gateway conditions from 27th July 2016

3.426   **5.**—(1) This article applies in the case of a claim for universal credit, an employment and support allowance or a jobseeker's allowance that is made or treated as made on or after 27th July 2016.

(2) Where this article applies, the provisions referred to in sub-paragraphs (a) to (d) have effect, with respect to a claimant residing in the designated postcodes referred to in the sub-paragraph in question, as though the reference in those provisions to meeting the gateway conditions were omitted—

(a) articles 3(2)(a) and 4(2)(a) of the No.13 Order, in respect of the Part 16 designated postcodes;

(b) articles 3(2)(j) and 4(2)(j) of the No.19 Order, in respect of the Part 17 designated postcodes;

(c) articles 3(2)(m) and 4(2)(m) of the No.19 Order, in respect of the Part 18 designated postcodes;

(d) articles 3(2)(e) and 4(2)(i) and (j) of the No.22 Order, in respect of the Part 19 designated postcodes.

DEFINITIONS

"claimant"–see art.2(1).
"designated postcodes"–see art.2(2).
"employment and support allowance"–see art.2(1).
"jobseeker's allowance"–*ibid.*
"No.16 Order"–*ibid.*
"No.17 Order"–*ibid.*
"No.18 Order"–*ibid.*
"No.19 Order"–*ibid.*

Modifications in consequence of removal of the gateway conditions: the No.13 Order

3.427   **6.**—(1) This article applies in the case of a claim in relation to which provisions of the No.13 Order are modified under articles 4(2)(a) or 5(2)(a).

(2) Where this article applies, the No.13 Order has effect as though—

(a) in article 2(1) (interpretation), the definition of "gateway conditions" were omitted;

(b) in article 3(2)(b) (coming into force of the universal credit provisions and incorrect information)—

> (i) in paragraph (i), "or meeting the gateway conditions" and "or does not meet the gateway conditions" were omitted;
> (ii) in paragraph (ii), "or meeting the gateway conditions" and "or does not or do not meet those conditions" were omitted;
> (iii) in paragraph (iii), "or meeting the gateway conditions" were omitted;

(c) in article 3(6) (article 3A of the No.9 Order and incorrect information), "or meeting the gateway conditions" were omitted in both places it occurs;

(d) in article 4(2)(b) (abolition of income-related employment and support allowance and income-based jobseeker's allowance and incorrect information)—

> (i) in paragraph (i), "or meeting the gateway conditions" and "or does not meet the gateway conditions" were omitted;
> (ii) in paragraph (ii), "or meeting those conditions" and "or does not or do not meet those conditions" were omitted;
> (iii) in paragraph (iii), "or meeting the gateway conditions" were omitted; and

(e) for article 4(7) (claims by couples) there were substituted—

> "(7) Paragraphs (1A) and (1B) of article 5 of the No.9 Order apply for the purposes of paragraph (2)(a) as they apply for the purposes of article 4(2)(a) of the No.9 Order (but as if the references in paragraph (1A) to Schedule 5 to the No.9 Order were omitted).".

DEFINITION

"No.13 Order"–see art.2(1).

Modifications in consequence of removal of the gateway conditions: the No.14 Order

7.—(1) This article applies in the case of a claim in relation to which provisions of the No.14 Order are modified under articles 3(2)(a) or 4(2)(b).

3.428

(2) Where this article applies, the No.14 Order has effect as though—

(a) in article 2(1) (interpretation), the definition of "gateway conditions" were omitted;

(b) in article 3(2)(b) (coming into force of the universal credit provisions and incorrect information)—

> (i) in paragraph (i), "or meeting the gateway conditions" and "or does not meet the gateway conditions" were omitted;
> (ii) in paragraph (ii), "or meeting the gateway conditions" and "or does not or do not meet those conditions" were omitted;
> (iii) in paragraph (iii), "or meeting the gateway conditions" were omitted;

(c) in article 3(6) (article 3A of the No.9 Order and incorrect information), "or meeting the gateway conditions" were omitted in both places it occurs;

(d) in article 4(2)(b) (abolition of income-related employment and support allowance and income-based jobseeker's allowance and incorrect information)—

> (i) in paragraph (i), "or meeting the gateway conditions" and "or does not meet the gateway conditions" were omitted;

689

  (ii) in paragraph (ii), "or meeting those conditions" and "or does not or do not meet those conditions" were omitted;

  (iii) in paragraph (iii), "or meeting the gateway conditions" were omitted; and

 (e) for article 4(7) (claims by couples) there were substituted—

   "(7) Paragraphs (1A) and (1B) of article 5 of the No.9 Order apply for the purposes of paragraph (2)(a) as they apply for the purposes of article 4(2)(a) of the No.9 Order (but as if the references in paragraph (1A) to Schedule 5 to the No.9 Order were omitted).".

DEFINITION

"No.14 Order"–see art.2(1).

Modifications in consequence of removal of the gateway conditions: the No.16 Order

3.429   **8.**—(1) This article applies in the case of a claim in relation to which provisions of the No.16 Order are modified under articles 3(2)(b) or 4(2)(c).

 (2) Where this article applies, the No.16 Order has effect as though—

 (a) in article 2(1) (interpretation), the definition of "gateway conditions" were omitted;

 (b) in article 3(2)(b) (coming into force of the universal credit provisions and incorrect information)—

  (i) in paragraph (i), "or meeting the gateway conditions" and "or does not meet the gateway conditions" were omitted;

  (ii) in paragraph (ii), "or meeting the gateway conditions" and "or does not or do not meet those conditions" were omitted;

  (iii) in paragraph (iii), "or meeting the gateway conditions" were omitted;

 (c) in article 3(6) (article 3A of the No.9 Order and incorrect information)—

  (i) "or a No.7" were omitted;

  (ii) "or meeting the gateway conditions" were omitted in both places it occurs;

 (d) in article 4(2)(b) (abolition of income-related employment and support allowance and income-based jobseeker's allowance and incorrect information)—

  (i) in paragraph (i), "or meeting the gateway conditions" and "or does not meet the gateway conditions" were omitted;

  (ii) in paragraph (ii), "or meeting those conditions" and "or does not or do not meet those conditions" were omitted;

  (iii) in paragraph (iii), "or meeting the gateway conditions" were omitted; and

 (e) for article 4(7) (claims by couples) there were substituted—

   "(7) Paragraphs (1A) and (1B) of article 5 of the No.9 Order apply for the purposes of paragraph (2)(a) as they apply for the purposes of article 4(2)(a) of the No.9 Order (but as if the references in paragraph (1A) to Schedule 5 to the No.9 Order were omitted).".

"No.16 Order"–see art.2(1).

Modifications in consequence of removal of the gateway conditions: the No.19 Order

9.—(1) This article applies in the case of a claim in relation to which provisions of the No.19 Order are modified under article 5(2)(b) or (c).

(2) Where this article applies, the No.19 Order has effect as though—

(a) in article 2(1) (interpretation), the definition of "gateway conditions" were omitted;

(b) in article 3(2)(o) (coming into force of the universal credit provisions and incorrect information)—

   (i) for "any of sub-paragraphs (a) to (n)" there were substituted "sub-paragraph (j) or (m)";

   (ii) in paragraph (i), "or meeting the gateway conditions" and "or does not meet the gateway conditions" were omitted;

   (iii) in paragraph (ii), "or meeting the gateway conditions" and "or does not or do not meet those conditions" were omitted;

   (iv) in the words after paragraph (ii), "or meeting the gateway conditions" were omitted;

(c) in article 3(5) (article 3A of the No.9 Order and incorrect information)—

   (i) for "No.14, No.15, No.16, No.17, No.18, No.19, No.20, No.21, No.22, No.23, No.24, No.25, No.26 or No.27" there were substituted "No.23 or No.26";

   (ii) "or meeting the gateway conditions" were omitted in both places it occurs;

(d) in article 4(2)(o) (abolition of income-related employment and support allowance and income-based jobseeker's allowance and incorrect information)—

   (i) for "any of sub-paragraphs (a) to (n)" there were substituted "sub-paragraph (j) or (m)";

   (ii) in paragraph (i), "or meeting the gateway conditions" and "or does not meet the gateway conditions" were omitted;

   (iii) in paragraph (ii), "or meeting the gateway conditions" and "or does not or do not meet those conditions" were omitted;

   (iv) in the words after paragraph (ii), "or meeting the gateway conditions" were omitted; and

(e) for article 4(7) (claims by couples) there were substituted—

"(7) Paragraphs (1A) and (1B) of article 5 of the No.9 Order apply for the purposes of paragraph (2)(a) as they apply for the purposes of article 4(2)(a) of the No.9 Order (but as if the references in paragraph (1A) to Schedule 5 to the No.9 Order were omitted).".

3.430

"No.19 Order"–see art.2(1).

Modifications in consequence of removal of the gateway conditions: the No.22 Order

3.431
10.—(1) This article applies in the case of a claim in relation to which provisions of the No.22 Order are modified under articles 3(2)(c), (d), (e) or (f), 4(2)(d) or (e) or 5(2)(d).

(2) Where this article applies, the No.22 Order has effect as though—

(a) in article 2(1) (interpretation), for the definition of "claimant" there were substituted—

""claimant"—

(a) in relation to an employment and support allowance, has the same meaning as in Part 1 of the Welfare Reform Act 2007, save as mentioned in article 5(1A) of the No.9 Order as applied by article 4(7) of this Order;

(b) in relation to a jobseeker's allowance, has the same meaning as in the Jobseekers Act 1995 (as it applies apart from the amendments made by Part 1 of Schedule 14 to the Act that remove references to an income-based jobseeker's allowance), save as mentioned in article 5(1A) of the No.9 Order as applied by article 4(7) of this Order;

(c) in relation to universal credit, has the same meaning as in Part 1 of the Act;";

(b) paragraphs (2) and (4) of article 2 (definition of, and amendments to, the "gateway conditions") were omitted;

(c) for article 3(2)(v) there were substituted—

"(v) a claim for universal credit that is made on or after the date referred to in sub-paragraph (a), (e), (f), (h), (i) or (k), in respect of a period that begins on or after that date where—

(i) in the case of a single claimant, the claimant gives incorrect information regarding the claimant residing in a district as referred to in the sub-paragraph in question and the claimant does not reside in such a district on the date on which the claim is made;

(ii) in the case of joint claimants, either or both of the joint claimants gives or give incorrect information regarding his or her (or their) residing in such a district and one or both of them does not or do not reside in such a district on the date on which the claim is made,

and after a decision is made that the single claimant is, or the joint claimants are, entitled to universal credit and one or more payments have been made in respect of the single claimant or the joint claimants, the Secretary of State discovers that incorrect information has been given regarding residence.";

(d) for article 3(5) there were substituted—

"(5) Article 3A of the No.9 Order applies in connection with a claim for universal credit where a single claimant, or, as the case may be, either or both of joint claimants, gives or give incorrect information regarding his or her (or their) residing in one of the No.29, No.33, No.34, No.36, No.37 or No.39 relevant districts, as it applies in connection with the giving of incorrect information regarding a claimant residing in one of the relevant districts (as defined in the No.9 Order).";

(e) for article 4(2)(qq) there were substituted—

"(qq) a claim for universal credit that is made on or after the date referred to in sub-paragraph (a), (i), (k), (o), (q) or (u), in respect of a period that begins on or after that date where—

(i) in the case of a single claimant, the claimant gives incorrect information regarding the claimant residing in a district as referred to in the sub-paragraph in question and the claimant does not reside in such a district on the date on which the claim is made;

(ii) in the case of joint claimants, either or both of the joint claimants gives or give incorrect information regarding his or her (or their) residing in such a district and one or both of them does not or do not reside in such a district on the date on which the claim is made,

and after a decision is made that the single claimant is, or the joint claimants are, entitled to universal credit and one or more payments have been made in respect of the single claimant or the joint claimants, the Secretary of State discovers that incorrect information has been given regarding residence;"; and

(f) for article 4(7) (claims by couples) there were substituted—

"(7) Paragraphs (1A) and (1B) of article 5 of the No.9 Order apply for the purposes of sub-paragraphs (b), (j), (l), (p), (r) and (v) of paragraph (2) as they apply for the purposes of article 4(2)(a) of the No.9 Order (but as if the references in paragraph (1A) to Schedule 5 to the No.9 Order were omitted).".

DEFINITION

"No.22 Order"–see art.2(1).

Modifications in consequence of removal of the gateway conditions: the No.24 Order

11.—(1) This article applies in the case of a claim in relation to which provisions of the No.24 Order are modified under articles 3(2)(g), (h) or (i) or 4(2)(f).

3.432

(2) Where this article applies, the No.24 Order has effect as though—

(a) in article 2(1) (interpretation)—

(i) for the definition of "claimant" there were substituted—

""claimant"—

(a) in relation to an employment and support allowance, has the same meaning as in Part 1 of the Welfare Reform Act 2007, save as mentioned in article 5(1A) of the No.9 Order as applied by article 4(7) of this Order;

(b) in relation to a jobseeker's allowance, has the same meaning as in the Jobseekers Act 1995 (as it applies apart from the amendments made by Part 1 of Schedule 14 to the Act that remove references to an income-based jobseeker's allowance), save as mentioned in article 5(1A) of the No.9 Order as applied by article 4(7) of this Order;

(c) in relation to universal credit, has the same meaning as in Part 1 of the Act;";

(ii) the definition of "gateway conditions" were omitted;

(b) article 2(3) (amendments to the gateway conditions) were omitted;

(c) for article 3(2)(dd) there were substituted—

"(dd) a claim for universal credit that is made on or after the date referred to in sub-paragraph (a), (c), (n) or (bb), in respect of a period that begins on or after that date where—

(i) in the case of a single claimant, the claimant gives incorrect information regarding the claimant residing in a district as referred to in the sub-paragraph in question and the claimant does not reside in such a district on the date on which the claim is made;

(ii) in the case of joint claimants, either or both of the joint claimants gives or give incorrect information regarding his or her (or their) residing in such a district and one or both of them does not or do not reside in such a district on the date on which the claim is made,

and after a decision is made that the single claimant is, or the joint claimants are, entitled to universal credit and one or more payments have been made in respect of the single claimant or the joint claimants, the Secretary of State discovers that incorrect information has been given regarding residence.";

(d) for article 3(5) there were substituted—

"(5) Article 3A of the No.9 Order applies in connection with a claim for universal credit where a single claimant, or, as the case may be, either or both of joint claimants, gives or give incorrect information regarding his or her (or their) residing in one of the No.53, No.55, No.66 or No.80 relevant districts, as it applies in connection with the giving of incorrect information regarding a claimant residing in one of the relevant districts (as defined in the No.9 Order).";

(e) for article 4(2)(ggg) there were substituted—

"(ggg) a claim for universal credit that is made on or after the date referred to in sub-paragraph (a), (e), (aa) or (ccc), in respect of a period that begins on or after that date where—

(i) in the case of a single claimant, the claimant gives incorrect information regarding the claimant residing in a district as referred to in the sub-paragraph in question and the claimant does not reside in such a district on the date on which the claim is made;

(ii) in the case of joint claimants, either or both of the joint claimants gives or give incorrect information regarding his or her (or their) residing in such a district and one or both of them does not or do not reside in such a district on the date on which the claim is made,

and after a decision is made that the single claimant is, or the joint claimants are, entitled to universal credit and one or more payments have been made in respect of the single claimant or the joint claimants, the Secretary of State discovers that incorrect information has been given regarding residence;"; and

(f) for article 4(7) (claims by couples) there were substituted—

"(7) Paragraphs (1A) and (1B) of article 5 of the No.9 Order apply for the purposes of sub-paragraphs (b), (f), (bb) and (ddd) of paragraph (2) as they apply for the purposes of article 4(2)(a) of the No.9

Order (but as if the references in paragraph (1A) to Schedule 5 to the No.9 Order were omitted).".

DEFINITION

"No.24 Order"–see art.2(1).

Modification of the No.23 Order: claims for housing benefit, income support or a tax credit

12. Article 7 of the No.23 Order (prevention of claims for housing benefit, income support or a tax credit) applies as though the reference in paragraph (1) of that article to article 3(1) and (2)(a) to (c) of that Order included— 3.433
  - (a) a reference to paragraph (1) and sub-paragraph (a) of paragraph (2) of article 3 of the No.13 Order, in respect of claims in relation to which sub-paragraph (a) is modified by articles 4(2)(a) and 5(2)(a) of this Order;
  - (b) a reference to paragraph (1) and sub-paragraph (a) of paragraph (2) of article 3 of the No.14 Order, in respect of claims in relation to which sub-paragraph (a) is modified by articles 3(2)(a) and 4(2)(b) of this Order;
  - (c) a reference to paragraph (1) and sub-paragraph (a) of paragraph (2) of article 3 of the No.16 Order, in respect of claims in relation to which sub-paragraph (a) is modified by articles 3(2)(b) and 4(2)(c) of this Order;
  - (d) a reference to paragraph (1) and sub-paragraphs (j) and (m) of paragraph (2) of article 3 of the No.19 Order, in respect of claims in relation to which sub-paragraphs (j) and (m) are modified respectively by article 5(2)(b) and (c) of this Order;
  - (e) a reference to paragraph (1) and sub-paragraphs (a), (f), (h), (i) and (k) of paragraph (2) of article 3 of the No.22 Order, in respect of claims in relation to which those sub-paragraphs are modified respectively by articles 4(2)(d), 3(2)(d), (e) and (f) and 4(2)(e) of this Order;
  - (f) a reference to paragraph (1) and sub-paragraph (e) of paragraph (2) of article 3 of the No.22 Order, in respect of claims in relation to which sub-paragraph (e) is modified by articles 3(2)(c) and 5(2)(d) of this Order; and
  - (g) a reference to paragraph (1) and sub-paragraphs (a), (c), (n) and (bb) of paragraph (2) of article 3 of the No.24 Order, in respect of claims in relation to which those sub-paragraphs are modified respectively by articles 4(2)(f) and 3(2)(g), (h) and (i) of this Order.

DEFINITION

"No.23 Order"–see art.2(1).

The Welfare Reform Act 2012 (Commencement No.19, 22, 23 and 24 and Transitional and Transitory Provisions (Modification)) Order 2016

SI 2016/963

The Secretary of State for Work and Pensions makes the following Order in exercise of the powers conferred by section 150(3) and (4)(a), (b)(i) and (c) of the Welfare Reform Act 2012:

ARRANGEMENT OF ARTICLES

Citation

3.434   **1.** This Order may be cited as the Welfare Reform Act 2012 (Commencement No.19, 22, 23 and 24 and Transitional and Transitory Provisions (Modification)) Order 2016.

Interpretation

2.—(1) In this Order— 3.435
"the Act" means the Welfare Reform Act 2012;
"claimant"—
(a) in relation to an employment and support allowance, has the same meaning as in Part 1 of the Welfare Reform Act 2007;
(b) in relation to a jobseeker's allowance, has the same meaning as in the Jobseekers Act 199 (as it applies apart from the amendments made by Part 1 of Schedule 14 to the Act that remove references to an income-based jobseeker's allowance);
(c) in relation to universal credit, has the same meaning as in Part 1 of the Act;
"the Claims and Payments Regulations 1987" means the Social Security (Claims and Payments) Regulations 1987;
"employment and support allowance" means an employment and support allowance under Part 1 of the Welfare Reform Act 2007;
"jobseeker's allowance" means a jobseeker's allowance under the Jobseekers Act 1995;
"the No.9 Order" means the Welfare Reform Act 2012 (Commencement No.9 and Transitional and Transitory Provisions and Commencement No.8 and Savings and Transitional Provisions (Amendment)) Order 2013;
"the No.19 Order" means the Welfare Reform Act 2012 (Commencement No.19 and Transitional and Transitory Provisions and Commencement No.9 and Transitional and Transitory Provisions (Amendment)) Order 2014;
"the No.22 Order" means the Welfare Reform Act 2012 (Commencement No.22 and Transitional and Transitory Provisions) Order 2015;
"the No.23 Order" means the Welfare Reform Act 2012 (Commencement No.23 and Transitional and Transitory Provisions) Order 2015;
"the No.24 Order" means the Welfare Reform Act 2012 (Commencement No.24 and Transitional and Transitory Provisions and Commencement No.9 and Transitional and Transitory Provisions (Amendment)) Order 2015.

(2) In this Order, references to "designated postcodes", by numbered "Part", are to any postcode district or part-district in the corresponding numbered Part of the Schedule to this Order.

(3) For the purposes of this Order, the Universal Credit, Personal Independence Payment, Jobseeker's Allowance and Employment and Support Allowance (Claims and Payments) Regulations 2013 apply for the purpose of deciding—
(a) whether a claim for universal credit is made; and
(b) the date on which the claim is made.

(4) For the purposes of this Order, the Claims and Payments Regulations 1987 apply, subject to paragraphs (5) and (6), for the purposes of deciding—
(a) whether a claim for an employment and support allowance or a jobseeker's allowance is made; and
(b) the date on which the claim is made or treated as made.

(5) Subject to paragraph (6), for the purposes of this Order—
(a) a person makes a claim for an employment and support allowance or

a jobseeker's allowance if he or she takes any action which results in a decision on a claim being required under the Claims and Payments Regulations 1987; and

(b) it is irrelevant that the effect of any provision of those Regulations is that, for the purposes of those Regulations, the claim is made or treated as made at a date that is earlier than the date on which that action is taken.

(6) Where, by virtue of—

(a) regulation 6(1F)(b) or (c) of the Claims and Payments Regulations 1987, in the case of a claim for an employment and support allowance; or

(b) regulation 6(4ZA) to (4ZD) and (4A)(a)(i) and (b) of those Regulations, in the case of a claim for a jobseeker's allowance,

a claim for an employment and support allowance or a jobseeker's allowance is treated as made at a date that is earlier than the date on which the action referred to in paragraph (5)(a) is taken, the claim is treated as made on that earlier date.

Modification of the No.19 and 24 Orders: removal of the gateway conditions from 5th October 2016

3.436

3.—(1) This article applies in the case of a claim for universal credit that is made, or a claim for an employment and support allowance or a jobseeker's allowance that is made or treated as made, on or after 5th October 2016.

(2) Where this article applies, the provisions referred to in sub-paragraphs (a) and (b) have effect, with respect to a claimant residing in the designated postcodes referred to in the sub-paragraph in question, as though the reference in those provisions to meeting the gateway conditions were omitted—

(a) articles 3(2)(j) and 4(2)(j) of the No.19 Order, in respect of the Part 1 designated postcodes;

(b) articles 3(2)(r) and 4(2)(ii) and (jj) of the No.24 Order, in respect of the Part 2 designated postcodes.

DEFINITIONS

"claimant"–art.2(1).
"designated postcodes"–art.2(2).
"employment and support allowance"–art.2(1).
"jobseeker's allowance"–*ibid.*
"the No.19 Order"–art.2(1).
"the No.24 Order"–*ibid.*

Modification of the No.22 and 24 Orders: removal of the gateway conditions from 12th October 2016

3.437

4.—(1) This article applies in the case of a claim for universal credit that is made, or a claim for an employment and support allowance or a jobseeker's allowance that is made or treated as made, on or after 12th October 2016.

(2) Where this article applies, the provisions referred to in sub-paragraphs (a) to (g) have effect, with respect to a claimant residing in the designated postcodes referred to in the sub-paragraph in question, as though the reference in those provisions to meeting the gateway conditions were omitted—

(a) articles 3(2)(a) and 4(2)(a) and (b) of the No.22 Order, in respect of the Part 3 designated postcodes;

(b) articles 3(2)(h) and 4(2)(o) and (p) of the No.22 Order, in respect of the Part 4 designated postcodes;

(c) articles 3(2)(k) and 4(2)(u) and (v) of the No.22 Order, in respect of the Part 5 designated postcodes;

(d) articles 3(2)(h) and 4(2)(o) and (p) of the No.24 Order, in respect of the Part 6 designated postcodes;

(e) articles 3(2)(j) and 4(2)(s) and (t) of the No.24 Order, in respect of the Part 7 designated postcodes;

(f) articles 3(2)(k) and 4(2)(u) and (v) of the No.24 Order, in respect of the Part 8 designated postcodes;

(g) articles 3(2)(r) and 4(2)(ii) and (jj) of the No.24 Order, in respect of the Part 9 designated postcodes.

DEFINITIONS

"claimant"–art.2(1).
"designated postcodes"–art.2(2).
"employment and support allowance"–art.2(1).
"jobseeker's allowance"–*ibid.*
"the No.22 Order"–art.2(1).
"the No.24 Order"–*ibid.*

Modification of the No.24 Order: removal of the gateway conditions from 19th October 2016

5.—(1) This article applies in the case of a claim for universal credit that is made, or a claim for an employment and support allowance or a jobseeker's allowance that is made or treated as made, on or after 19th October 2016.

(2) Where this article applies, articles 3(2)(r) and 4(2)(ii) and (jj) of the No.24 Order have effect, with respect to a claimant residing in the Part 10 designated postcodes, as though the reference in those provisions to meeting the gateway conditions were omitted.

3.438

DEFINITIONS

"claimant"–art.2(1).
"designated postcodes"–art.2(2).
"employment and support allowance"–art.2(1).
"jobseeker's allowance"–*ibid.*
"the No.24 Order"–art.2(1).

Modification of the No.22 and 24 Orders: removal of the gateway conditions from 26th October 2016

6.—(1) This article applies in the case of a claim for universal credit that is made, or a claim for an employment and support allowance or a jobseeker's allowance that is made or treated as made, on or after 26th October 2016.

(2) Where this article applies, the provisions referred to in sub-paragraphs (a) to (c) have effect, with respect to a claimant residing in the designated postcodes referred to in the sub-paragraph in question, as though the reference in those provisions to meeting the gateway conditions were omitted—

3.439

(a) articles 3(2)(h) and 4(2)(o) and (p) of the No.22 Order, in respect of the Part 11 designated postcodes;
(b) articles 3(2)(e) and 4(2)(i) and (j) of the No.24 Order, in respect of the Part 12 designated postcodes;
(c) articles 3(2)(h) and 4(2)(o) and (p) of the No.24 Order, in respect of the Part 13 designated postcodes.

DEFINITIONS

"claimant"–art.2(1).
"designated postcodes"–art.2(2).
"employment and support allowance"–art.2(1).
"jobseeker's allowance"–*ibid.*
"the No.22 Order"–art.2(1).
"the No.24 Order"–*ibid.*

Modification of the No.19, 22 and 24 Orders: removal of the gateway conditions from 2nd November 2016

3.440   **7.**—(1) This article applies in the case of a claim for universal credit that is made, or a claim for an employment and support allowance or a jobseeker's allowance that is made or treated as made, on or after 2nd November 2016.

(2) Where this article applies, the provisions referred to in sub-paragraphs (a) to (d) have effect, with respect to a claimant residing in the designated postcodes referred to in the sub-paragraph in question, as though the reference in those provisions to meeting the gateway conditions were omitted—
(a) articles 3(2)(n) and 4(2)(n) of the No.19 Order, in respect of the Part 14 designated postcodes;
(b) articles 3(2)(b) and 4(2)(c) and (d) of the No.22 Order, in respect of the Part 15 designated postcodes;
(c) articles 3(2)(j) and 4(2)(s) and (t) of the No.24 Order, in respect of the Part 16 designated postcodes;
(d) articles 3(2)(m) and 4(2)(y) and (z) of the No.24 Order, in respect of the Part 17 designated postcodes.

DEFINITIONS

"claimant"–art.2(1).
"designated postcodes"–art.2(2).
"employment and support allowance"–art.2(1).
"jobseeker's allowance"–*ibid.*
"the No.19 Order"–art.2(1).
"the No.22 Order"–*ibid.*
"the No.24 Order"–*ibid.*

Modification of the No.19, 22 and 24 Orders: removal of the gateway conditions from 9th November 2016

3.441   **8.**—(1) This article applies in the case of a claim for universal credit that is made, or a claim for an employment and support allowance or a jobseeker's allowance that is made or treated as made, on or after 9th November 2016.

(2) Where this article applies, the provisions referred to in sub-paragraphs (a) to (e) have effect, with respect to a claimant residing in the designated postcodes referred to in the sub-paragraph in question, as though the reference in those provisions to meeting the gateway conditions were omitted—

(a) articles 3(2)(n) and 4(2)(n) of the No.19 Order, in respect of the Part 18 designated postcodes;

(b) articles 3(2)(b) and 4(2)(c) and (d) of the No.22 Order, in respect of the Part 19 designated postcodes;

(c) articles 3(2)(f) and 4(2)(k) and (l) of the No.22 Order, in respect of the Part 20 designated postcodes;

(d) articles 3(2)(r) and 4(2)(ii) and (jj) of the No.24 Order, in respect of the Part 21 designated postcodes;

(e) articles 3(2)(s) and 4(2)(kk) and (ll) of the No.24 Order, in respect of the Part 22 designated postcodes.

DEFINITIONS

"claimant"–art.2(1).
"designated postcodes"–art.2(2).
"employment and support allowance"–art.2(1).
"jobseeker's allowance"–*ibid.*
"the No.19 Order"–art.2(1).
"the No.22 Order"–*ibid.*
"the No.24 Order"–*ibid.*

Modification of the No.22 and 24 Orders: removal of the gateway conditions from 23rd November 2016

9.—(1) This article applies in the case of a claim for universal credit that is made, or a claim for an employment and support allowance or a jobseeker's allowance that is made or treated as made, on or after 23rd November 2016.　　3.442

(2) Where this article applies, the provisions referred to in sub-paragraphs (a) to (c) have effect, with respect to a claimant residing in the designated postcodes referred to in the sub-paragraph in question, as though the reference in those provisions to meeting the gateway conditions were omitted—

(a) articles 3(2)(a) and 4(2)(a) and (b) of the No.22 Order, in respect of the Part 23 designated postcodes;

(b) articles 3(2)(t) and 4(2)(mm) and (nn) of the No.22 Order, in respect of the Part 24 designated postcodes;

(c) articles 3(2)(d) and 4(2)(g) and (h) of the No.24 Order, in respect of the Part 25 designated postcodes.

DEFINITIONS

"claimant"–art.2(1).
"designated postcodes"–art.2(2).
"employment and support allowance"–art.2(1).
"jobseeker's allowance"–*ibid.*
"the No.22 Order"–art.2(1).
"the No.24 Order"–*ibid.*

Modification of the No.22 and 24 Orders: removal of the gateway conditions from 30th November 2016

10.—(1) This article applies in the case of a claim for universal credit that is made, or a claim for an employment and support allowance or a jobseeker's allowance that is made or treated as made, on or after 30th November 2016.　　3.443

(2) Where this article applies, the provisions referred to in sub-paragraphs

(a) to (d) have effect, with respect to a claimant residing in the designated postcodes referred to in the sub-paragraph in question, as though the reference in those provisions to meeting the gateway conditions were omitted—

   (a) articles 3(2)(a) and 4(2)(a) and (b) of the No.22 Order, in respect of the Part 26 designated postcodes;

   (b) articles 3(2)(b) and 4(2)(c) and (d) of the No.22 Order, in respect of the Part 27 designated postcodes;

   (c) articles 3(2)(e) and 4(2)(i) and (j) of the No.22 Order, in respect of the Part 28 designated postcodes;

   (d) articles 3(2)(p) and 4(2)(ee) and (ff) of the No.24 Order, in respect of the Part 29 designated postcodes.

DEFINITIONS

"claimant"–art.2(1).
"designated postcodes"–art.2(2).
"employment and support allowance"–art.2(1).
"jobseeker's allowance"–*ibid.*
"the No.22 Order"–art.2(1).
"the No.24 Order"–*ibid.*

Modification of the No.22 and 24 Orders: removal of the gateway conditions from 7th December 2016

3.444   **11.**—(1) This article applies in the case of a claim for universal credit that is made, or a claim for an employment and support allowance or a jobseeker's allowance that is made or treated as made, on or after 7th December 2016.

(2) Where this article applies, the provisions referred to in sub-paragraphs (a) to (g) have effect, with respect to a claimant residing in the designated postcodes referred to in the sub-paragraph in question, as though the reference in those provisions to meeting the gateway conditions were omitted—

   (a) articles 3(2)(a) and 4(2)(a) and (b) of the No.22 Order, in respect of the Part 30 designated postcodes;

   (b) articles 3(2)(b) and 4(2)(c) and (d) of the No.22 Order, in respect of the Part 31 designated postcodes;

   (c) articles 3(2)(a) and 4(2)(a) and (b) of the No.24 Order, in respect of the Part 32 designated postcodes;

   (d) articles 3(2)(c) and 4(2)(e) and (f) of the No.24 Order, in respect of the Part 33 designated postcodes;

   (e) articles 3(2)(d) and 4(2)(g) and (h) of the No.24 Order, in respect of the Part 34 designated postcodes;

   (f) articles 3(2)(h) and 4(2)(o) and (p) of the No.24 Order, in respect of the Part 35 designated postcodes;

   (g) articles 3(2)(r) and 4(2)(ii) and (jj) of the No.24 Order, in respect of the Part 36 designated postcodes.

DEFINITIONS

"claimant"–art.2(1).
"designated postcodes"–art.2(2).
"employment and support allowance"–art.2(1).
"jobseeker's allowance"–*ibid.*
"the No.22 Order"–art.2(1).
"the No.24 Order"–*ibid.*

Modification of the No.22 and 24 Orders: removal of the gateway conditions from 14th December 2016

12.—(1) This article applies in the case of a claim for universal credit   3.445
that is made, or a claim for an employment and support allowance or a
jobseeker's allowance that is made or treated as made, on or after 14th
December 2016.

(2) Where this article applies, the provisions referred to in sub-paragraphs
(a) to (g) have effect, with respect to a claimant residing in the designated
postcodes referred to in the sub-paragraph in question, as though the reference in those provisions to meeting the gateway conditions were omitted—

   (a) articles 3(2)(a) and 4(2)(a) and (b) of the No.22 Order, in respect of
      the Part 37 designated postcodes;

   (b) articles 3(2)(e) and 4(2)(i) and (j) of the No.22 Order, in respect of
      the Part 38 designated postcodes;

   (c) articles 3(2)(h) and 4(2)(o) and (p) of the No.22 Order, in respect of
      the Part 39 designated postcodes;

   (d) articles 3(2)(j) and 4(2)(s) and (t) of the No.22 Order, in respect of
      the Part 40 designated postcodes;

   (e) articles 3(2)(n) and 4(2)(aa) and (bb) of the No.22 Order, in respect
      of the Part 41 designated postcodes;

   (f) articles 3(2)(d) and 4(2)(g) and (h) of the No.24 Order, in respect of
      the Part 42 designated postcodes;

   (g) articles 3(2)(p) and 4(2)(ee) and (ff) of the No.24 Order, in respect
      of the Part 43 designated postcodes.

DEFINITIONS

   "claimant"–art.2(1).
   "designated postcodes"–art.2(2).
   "employment and support allowance"–art.2(1).
   "jobseeker's allowance"–*ibid.*
   "the No.22 Order"–art.2(1).
   "the No.24 Order"–*ibid.*

Modifications in consequence of removal of the gateway conditions: the No.19 Order

13.—(1) This article applies in the case of a claim in relation to which   3.446
provisions of the No.19 Order are modified under articles 3(2)(a), 7(2)(a)
or 8(2)(a).

(2) Where this article applies, the No.19 Order has effect as though—

   (a) in article 2(1) (interpretation), the definition of "gateway condi-
      tions" were omitted;

   (b) in article 3(2)(o) (coming into force of the universal credit provisions
      and incorrect information)—

      (i) in the opening words, for "any of sub-paragraphs (a) to (n)"
         there were substituted "the relevant preceding sub-paragraph";

      (ii) in paragraph (i), "or meeting the gateway conditions" and "or
         does not meet the gateway conditions" were omitted;

      (iii) in paragraph (ii), "or meeting the gateway conditions" and "or
         does not or do not meet those conditions" were omitted;

      (iv) in the closing words, "or meeting the gateway conditions" were
         omitted;

(c) in article 3(5) (article 3A of the No.9 Order and incorrect information)—

    (i) for the text from "No.14" to "No.27 relevant district" there were substituted "numbered relevant district referred to in paragraph (2)";

    (ii) "or meeting the gateway conditions" were omitted in both places it occurs;

(d) in article 4(2)(o) (abolition of income-related employment and support allowance and income-based jobseeker's allowance and incorrect information)—

    (i) in the opening words, for "any of sub-paragraphs (a) to (n)" there were substituted "the relevant preceding sub-paragraph";

    (ii) in paragraph (i), "or meeting the gateway conditions" and "or does not meet the gateway conditions" were omitted;

    (iii) in paragraph (ii), "or meeting the gateway conditions" and "or does not or do not meet those conditions" were omitted;

    (iv) in the closing words, "or meeting the gateway conditions" were omitted; and

(e) for article 4(7) (claims by couples)(1) there were substituted—

"(7) Paragraphs (1A) and (1B) of article 5 of the No.9 Order apply for the purposes of sub-paragraphs (a) to (n) of paragraph (2) as they apply for the purposes of article 4(2)(a) of the No.9 Order (but as if the references in paragraph (1A) to Schedule 5 to the No.9 Order were omitted).".

DEFINITIONS

"the No.9 Order"–art.2(1).
"the No.19 Order"–*ibid.*

Modifications in consequence of removal of the gateway conditions: the No.22 Order

3.447

14.—(1) This article applies in the case of a claim in relation to which provisions of the No.22 Order are modified under—

(a) article 4(2)(a), (b) or (c);

(b) article 6(2)(a);

(c) article 7(2)(b);

(d) article 8(2)(b) or (c);

(e) article 9(2)(a) or (b);

(f) article 10(2)(a), (b) or (c);

(g) article 11(2)(a) or (b); or

(h) article 12(2)(a), (b), (c), (d) or (e).

(2) Where this article applies, the No.22 Order has effect as though—

(a) in article 2(1) (interpretation), for the definition of "claimant" there were substituted—

""claimant"— (a) in relation to an employment and support allowance, has the same meaning as in Part 1 of the Welfare Reform Act 2007, save as mentioned in article 5(1A) of the No.9 Order as applied by article 4(7) of this Order;

(b) in relation to a jobseeker's allowance, has the same meaning as in the Jobseekers Act 1995 (as it applies apart from the amendments made by Part 1 of Schedule 14 to the Act that remove references to an income-based jobseeker's allowance), save as mentioned in article 5(1A) of the No.9 Order as applied by article 4(7) of this Order;

(c) in relation to universal credit, has the same meaning as in Part 1 of the Act;";

(b) paragraphs (2) and (4) of article 2 (definition of, and amendments to, the "gateway conditions") were omitted;

(c) for article 3(2)(v) (coming into force of the universal credit provisions and incorrect information) there were substituted—

"(v) a claim for universal credit that is made on or after the date referred to in the relevant preceding sub-paragraph, in respect of a period that begins on or after that date where—

(i) in the case of a single claimant, the claimant gives incorrect information regarding the claimant residing in a district as referred to in the sub-paragraph in question and the claimant does not reside in such a district on the date on which the claim is made;

(ii) in the case of joint claimants, either or both of the joint claimants gives or give incorrect information regarding his or her (or their) residing in such a district and one or both of them does not or do not reside in such a district on the date on which the claim is made,

and after a decision is made that the single claimant is, or the joint claimants are, entitled to universal credit and one or more payments have been made in respect of the single claimant or the joint claimants, the Secretary of State discovers that incorrect information has been given regarding residence.";

(d) for article 3(5) (article 3A of the No.9 Order and incorrect information) there were substituted—

"(5) Article 3A of the No.9 Order applies in connection with a claim for universal credit where a single claimant, or, as the case may be, either or both of joint claimants, gives or give incorrect information regarding his or her (or their) residing in a numbered relevant district referred to in paragraph (2), as it applies in connection with the giving of incorrect information regarding a claimant residing in one of the relevant districts (as defined in the No.9 Order).";

(e) for article 4(2)(qq) (abolition of income-related employment and support allowance and income-based jobseeker's allowance and incorrect information) there were substituted—

"(qq) a claim for universal credit that is made on or after the date referred to in the relevant preceding sub-paragraph, in respect of a period that begins on or after that date where—

(i) in the case of a single claimant, the claimant gives incorrect information regarding the claimant residing in a district as referred to in the sub-paragraph in question and the claimant does not reside in such a district on the date on which the claim is made;

(ii) in the case of joint claimants, either or both of the joint claimants gives or give incorrect information regarding his or her (or their) residing in such a district and one or both of them does not or do not reside in such a district on the date on which the claim is made,

and after a decision is made that the single claimant is, or the joint claimants are, entitled to universal credit and one or more payments have been made in respect of the single claimant or the joint claimants, the Secretary of State discovers that incorrect information has been given regarding residence;"; and

(f) for article 4(7) (claims by couples) there were substituted—

"(7) Paragraphs (1A) and (1B) of article 5 of the No.9 Order apply for the purposes of the sub-paragraphs referred to in sub-paragraph (rr) as they apply for the purposes of article 4(2)(a) of the No.9 Order (but as if the references in paragraph (1A) to Schedule 5 to the No.9 Order were omitted).".

"the No.9 Order"–art.2(1).
"the No.22 Order"–*ibid.*

Modifications in consequence of removal of the gateway conditions: the No.24 Order

3.448

15.—(1) This article applies in the case of a claim in relation to which provisions of the No.24 Order are modified under—

(a) article 3(2)(b);
(b) article 4(2)(d), (e), (f) or (g);
(c) article 5(2);
(d) article 6(2)(b) or (c);
(e) article 7(2)(c) or (d);
(f) article 8(2)(d) or (e);
(g) article 9(2)(c);
(h) article 10(2)(d);
(i) article 11(2)(c), (d), (e), (f) or (g); or
(j) article 12(2)(f) or (g).

(2) Where this article applies, the No.24 Order has effect as though—

(a) in article 2(1) (interpretation)—

(i) for the definition of "claimant" there were substituted—

""claimant"—

(a) in relation to an employment and support allowance, has the same meaning as in Part 1 of the Welfare Reform Act 2007, save as mentioned in article 5(1A) of the No.9 Order as applied by article 4(7) of this Order;

(b) in relation to a jobseeker's allowance, has the same meaning as in the Jobseekers Act 1995 (as it applies apart from the amendments made by Part 1 of Schedule 14 to the Act that remove references to an income-based jobseeker's allowance), save as mentioned in article 5(1A) of the No.9 Order as applied by article 4(7) of this Order;

(c) in relation to universal credit, has the same meaning as in Part 1 of the Act;";

(ii) the definition of "gateway conditions" were omitted;

(b) article 2(3) (amendments to the gateway conditions) were omitted;

(c) for article 3(2)(dd) (coming into force of the universal credit provisions and incorrect information) there were substituted—

"(dd) a claim for universal credit that is made on or after the date referred to in the relevant preceding sub-paragraph, in respect of a period that begins on or after that date where—

(i) in the case of a single claimant, the claimant gives incorrect information regarding the claimant residing in a district as referred to in the sub-paragraph in question and the claimant does not reside in such a district on the date on which the claim is made;

(ii) in the case of joint claimants, either or both of the joint claimants gives or give incorrect information regarding his or her (or their) residing in such a district and one or both of them does not or do not reside in such a district on the date on which the claim is made,

and after a decision is made that the single claimant is, or the joint claimants are, entitled to universal credit and one or more payments have been made in respect of the single claimant or the joint claimants, the Secretary of State discovers that incorrect information has been given regarding residence.";

(d) for article 3(5) (article 3A of the No.9 Order and incorrect information) there were substituted—

"(5) Article 3A of the No.9 Order applies in connection with a claim for universal
credit where a single claimant, or, as the case may be, either or both of joint claimants, gives or give incorrect information regarding his or her (or their) residing in
a numbered relevant district referred to in paragraph (2), as it applies in connection with the giving of incorrect information regarding a claimant residing in one
of the relevant districts (as defined in the No.9 Order).";

(e) for article 4(2)(ggg) (abolition of income-related employment and
support allowance and income-based jobseeker's allowance and
incorrect information) there were substituted—

"(ggg) a claim for universal credit that is made on or after the date referred to
in the relevant preceding sub-paragraph, in respect of a period that begins on or
after that date where—

(i) in the case of a single claimant, the claimant gives incorrect information
regarding the claimant residing in a district as referred to in the sub-paragraph in question and the claimant does not reside in such a district on the
date on which the claim is made;
(ii) in the case of joint claimants, either or both of the joint claimants gives or
give incorrect information regarding his or her (or their) residing in such a
district and one or both of them does not or do not reside in such a district
on the date on which the claim is made,

and after a decision is made that the single claimant is, or the joint claimants are,
entitled to universal credit and one or more payments have been made in respect
of the single claimant or the joint claimants, the Secretary of State discovers that
incorrect information has been given regarding residence;"; and

(f) for article 4(7) (claims by couples) there were substituted—

"(7) Paragraphs (1A) and (1B) of article 5 of the No.9 Order apply for the purposes of the sub-paragraphs referred to in sub-paragraph (hhh) as they apply
for the purposes of article 4(2)(a) of the No.9 Order (but as if the references in
paragraph (1A) to Schedule 5 to the No.9 Order were omitted).".

DEFINITIONS
"the No.9 Order"–art.2(1).
"the No.24 Order"–*ibid.*

Modification of the No.23 Order: claims for housing benefit, income support or a tax credit

16. Article 7 of the No.23 Order (prevention of claims for housing
benefit, income support or a tax credit)(1) applies as though the reference
in paragraph (1) of that article to article 3(1) and (2)(a) to (c) of that Order
included—

    3.449

(a) a reference to paragraph (1) and sub-paragraph (j) of paragraph (2)
of article 3 of the No.19 Order, in respect of claims in relation to
which sub-paragraph (j) is modified by article 3(2)(a) of this Order;
(b) a reference to paragraph (1) and sub-paragraph (n) of paragraph (2)
of article 3 of the No.19 Order, in respect of claims in relation to
which sub-paragraph (n) is modified by articles 7(2)(a) and 8(2)(a)
of this Order;
(c) a reference to paragraph (1) and sub-paragraphs (f), (j), (k), (n)

and (t) of paragraph (2) of article 3 of the No.22 Order, in respect of claims in relation to which those sub-paragraphs are modified respectively by articles 8(2)(c), 12(2)(d), 4(2)(c), 12(2)(e) and 9(2)(b) of this Order;

(d) a reference to paragraph (1) and sub-paragraphs (a), (b), (e) and (h) of paragraph (2) of article 3 of the No.22 Order, in respect of claims in relation to which those sub-paragraphs are modified respectively by articles 4(2)(a), 9(2)(a), 10(2)(a), 11(2)(a) and 12(2)(a), articles 7(2)(b), 8(2)(b), 10(2)(b) and 11(2)(b), articles 10(2)(c) and 12(2)(b) and articles 4(2)(b), 6(2)(a) and 12(2)(c) of this Order;

(e) a reference to paragraph (1) and sub-paragraphs (a), (c), (e), (k), (m) and (s) of paragraph (2) of article 3 of the No.24 Order, in respect of claims in relation to which those sub-paragraphs are modified respectively by articles 11(2)(c), 11(2)(d), 6(2)(b), 4(2)(f), 7(2)(d) and 8(2)(e) of this Order; and

(f) a reference to paragraph (1) and sub-paragraphs (d), (h), (j), (p) and (r) of paragraph (2) of article 3 of the No.24 Order, in respect of claims in relation to which those sub-paragraphs are modified respectively by articles 9(2)(c), 11(2)(e) and 12(2)(f), articles 4(2)(d), 6(2)(c) and 11(2)(f), articles 4(2)(e) and 7(2)(c), articles 10(2)(d) and 12(2)(g) and articles 3(2)(b), 4(2)(g), 5(2), 8(2)(d), and 11(2)(g) of this Order.

DEFINITIONS

"the No.19 Order"–art.2(1).
"the No.22 Order"–*ibid.*
"the No.23 Order"–*ibid.*
"the No.24 Order"–*ibid.*

Amendment of the Welfare Reform Act 2012 (Commencement No.13, 14, 16, 19, 22, 23 and 24 and Transitional and Transitory Provisions (Modification)) Order 2016

3.450   17.—(1) With effect from the day after the date of making of this Order, article 9 of the Welfare Reform Act 2012 (Commencement No.13, 14, 16, 19, 22, 23 and 24 and Transitional and Transitory Provisions (Modification)) Order 2016 (consequential modifications of the No.19 Order) is amended as follows.

(2) In the text substituted by paragraph (2)(e), for "paragraph (2)(a)" substitute "sub-paragraphs (j) and (m) of paragraph (2)".

Article 2(2)

SCHEDULE

POSTCODE DISTRICTS AND PART-DISTRICTS

PART 1

3.451   WA8 4 and WA8 5.

PART 2

3.452   SE16 3.
SE16 9.

SE21.
SE22.

PART 3

BD23.   **3.453**
BD24.
DL6 1.
DL6 3.
DL7 7 to DL7 9.
DL8 2.
LA2 7 and LA2 8.
LA6 3.
TS9 5
YO7.

PART 4

TA4 4.   **3.454**
TA23.
TA24.

PART 5

DL6 2.   **3.455**
DL7 0.
DL8 1.
DL8 3 to DL8 5.

PART 6

TA22.   **3.456**

PART 7

DL8 9.   **3.457**
PART 8
BD20 7 and BD20 8.

PART 9

TS9 7.   **3.458**

PART 10

SE5 0.   **3.459**
SE5 5.
SE11 9.
SE17.

PART 11

TA1.   **3.460**
TA2.
TA3 5 and TA3 6.
TA4 1.
TA4 3.
TA10 0 and TA10 1.
TA19.
TA20 1 and TA20 2.
TA20 9.
TA21 1.
TA21 8.

PART 12

3.461   TA20 4.

PART 13

3.462   TA3 7.
TA4 2.
TA20 3.
TA21 0.
TA21 9.

PART 14

3.463   CA18.
CA19.
CA20.
CA21.
CA22.
CA23.
CA24.
CA25.
CA26.
CA27.
CA28.

PART 15

3.464   NN6 6 to NN6 8.
NN11 0 to NN11 2.
NN11 4.
NN11 7 to NN11 9.

PART 16

3.465   NN7 4.
NN11 3.
NN11 6.

PART 17

3.466   G64 4.
G64 9.
G66.

PART 18

3.467   CA7 1 to CA7 4.
CA12.
CA13.
CA14.
CA15.

PART 19

3.468   LE13.
LE14 2.
LE14 4.

PART 20

3.469   NG32 1.

PART 21

SE5 7 and SE5 8.   **3.470**
SE15.

PART 22

LE14 3.   **3.471**
NG13 0.

PART 23

W12 2.   **3.472**
W12 6 to W12 9.

PART 24

NW10 6.   **3.473**
W12 0.

PART 25

PA11.   **3.474**
PA13.
PA14.
PA15 1 to PA15 4.
PA15 9.
PA16.
PA18.
PA19.

PART 26

SN1.   **3.475**
SN2.
SN3.
SN5 1.
SN5 6 and SN5 7.
SN25 1.
SN25 6.
SN26.
SN38.
SN99.

PART 27

LE8 8 and LE8 9.   **3.476**
LE17 6.

PART 28

SN25 3 to SN25 5.   **3.477**

PART 29

LE8 0.   **3.478**

PART 30

SW6.   **3.479**
SW7 1 to SW7 3.
TS24.
TS25 1 to TS25 4.
TS26.

PART 31

3.480   B95 6.
B95 8.
CV35 0.
CV36.
CV37 0 and CV37 1.
CV37 6 and CV37 7.
CV37 9.

PART 32

3.481   TS27 3.

PART 33

3.482   B95 5.
CV35 9.

PART 34

3.483   B50.
CV37 8.

PART 35

3.484   SW5.
SW7 4.
SW10.

PART 36

3.485   SW3.

PART 37

3.486   SN5 0.
SN5 8.

PART 38

3.487   SN4.
SN5 3 to SN5 5.
SN25 2.

PART 39

3.488   SN6 7.
TN31 6.
TN31 9.
TN32.
TN33 0.
TN34.
TN35.
TN36.
TN37.
TN38.

PART 40

3.489   SN6 6.

PART 41

PART 42

PART 43

The Welfare Reform Act 2012 (Commencement No.11, 13, 16, 22, 23 and 24 and Transitional and Transitory Provisions (Modification)) Order 2017

(SI 2017/57) (C.5)

The Secretary of State for Work and Pensions makes the following Order in exercise of the powers conferred by section 150(3) and (4)(a), (b)(i) and (c) of the Welfare Reform Act 2012:

ARRANGEMENT OF ARTICLES

SCHEDULE   POSTCODE DISTRICTS AND PART-DISTRICTS

Citation

3.493   **1.** This Order may be cited as the Welfare Reform Act 2012 (Commencement No.11, 13, 16, 22, 23 and 24 and Transitional and Transitory Provisions (Modification)) Order 2017.

Interpretation

3.494   **2.** (1) In this Order—

"claimant"—

(a) in relation to an employment and support allowance, has the same meaning as in Part 1 of the Welfare Reform Act 2007;

(b) in relation to a jobseeker's allowance, has the same meaning as in the Jobseekers Act 1995 (as it applies apart from the amendments made by Part 1 of Schedule 14 to the Welfare Reform Act 2012 that remove references to an income-based jobseeker's allowance);

(c) in relation to universal credit, has the same meaning as in Part 1 of the Welfare Reform Act 2012;

"the Claims and Payments Regulations 1987" means the Social Security (Claims and Payments) Regulations 1987;

"employment and support allowance" means an employment and support allowance under Part 1 of the Welfare Reform Act 2007;

"jobseeker's allowance" means a jobseeker's allowance under the Jobseekers Act 1995;

"the May 2016 Order" means the Welfare Reform Act 2012 (Commencement No.13, 14, 16, 19, 22, 23 and 24 and Transitional and Transitory Provisions (Modification)) Order 2016;

"the September 2016 Order" means the Welfare Reform Act 2012 (Commencement No.19, 22, 23 and 24 and Transitional and Transitory Provisions (Modification)) Order 2016;

"the No.9 Order" means the Welfare Reform Act 2012 (Commencement No.9 and Transitional and Transitory Provisions and Commencement No.8 and Savings and Transitional Provisions (Amendment)) Order 2013;

"the No.11 Order" means the Welfare Reform Act 2012 (Commencement No.11 and Transitional and Transitory Provisions and Commencement No.9 and Transitional and Transitory Provisions (Amendment)) Order 2013;

"the No.13 Order" means the Welfare Reform Act 2012 (Commencement No.13 and Transitional and Transitory Provisions) Order 2013;

"the No.16 Order" means the Welfare Reform Act 2012 (Commencement No.16 and Transitional and Transitory Provisions) Order 2014;

"the No.22 Order" means the Welfare Reform Act 2012 (Commencement No.22 and Transitional and Transitory Provisions) Order 2015;

"the No.23 Order" means the Welfare Reform Act 2012 (Commencement No.23 and Transitional and Transitory Provisions) Order 2015;

"the No.24 Order" means the Welfare Reform Act 2012 (Commencement No.24 and Transitional and Transitory Provisions and Commencement No.9 and Transitional and Transitory Provisions (Amendment)) Order 2015.

(2) In this Order, references to "designated postcodes", by numbered "Part", are to any postcode district or part-district in the corresponding numbered Part of the Schedule to this Order.

(3) For the purposes of this Order, the Universal Credit, Personal Independence Payment, Jobseeker's Allowance and Employment and Support Allowance (Claims and Payments) Regulations 2013 apply for the purpose of deciding—

(a) whether a claim for universal credit is made; and

(b) the date on which the claim is made.

(4) For the purposes of this Order, the Claims and Payments Regulations 1987 apply, subject to paragraphs (5) and (6), for the purposes of deciding—

(a) whether a claim for an employment and support allowance or a jobseeker's allowance is made; and

(b) the date on which the claim is made or treated as made.

(5) Subject to paragraph (6), for the purposes of this Order—

(a) a person makes a claim for an employment and support allowance or a jobseeker's allowance if that person takes any action which results in a decision on a claim being required under the Claims and Payments Regulations 1987; and

(b) it is irrelevant that the effect of any provision of those Regulations is that, for the purposes of those Regulations, the claim is made or treated as made at a date that is earlier than the date on which that action is taken.

(6) Where, by virtue of—

(a) regulation 6(1F)(b) or (c) of the Claims and Payments Regulations 1987, in the case of a claim for an employment and support allowance; or

(b) regulation 6(4ZA) to (4ZD) and (4A)(a)(i) and (b) of those Regulations, in the case of a claim for a jobseeker's allowance,

a claim for an employment and support allowance or a jobseeker's allowance is treated as made at a date that is earlier than the date on which the action referred to in paragraph (5)(a) is taken, the claim is treated as made on that earlier date.

Modification of the No.22 and 24 Orders: removal of the gateway conditions from 1st February 2017

3.—(1) This article applies in the case of a claim for universal credit that is made, or a claim for an employment and support allowance or a jobseeker's allowance that is made or treated as made, on or after 1st February 2017.

3.495

715

(2) Where this article applies, the provisions referred to in sub-paragraphs (a) to (h) have effect, with respect to a claimant residing in the designated postcodes referred to in the sub-paragraph in question, as though the reference in those provisions to meeting the gateway conditions were omitted—

  (a) articles 3(2)(f) and 4(2)(k) and (l) of the No.22 Order, in respect of the Part 1 designated postcodes;

  (b) articles 3(2)(h) and 4(2)(o) and (p) of the No.22 Order, in respect of the Part 2 designated postcodes;

  (c) articles 3(2)(n) and 4(2)(aa) and (bb) of the No.22 Order, in respect of the Part 3 designated postcodes;

  (d) articles 3(2)(b) and 4(2)(c) and (d) of the No.24 Order, in respect of the Part 4 designated postcodes;

  (e) articles 3(2)(c) and 4(2)(e) and (f) of the No.24 Order, in respect of the Part 5 designated postcodes;

  (f) articles 3(2)(h) and 4(2)(o) and (p) of the No.24 Order, in respect of the Part 6 designated postcodes;

  (g) articles 3(2)(l) and 4(2)(w) and (x) of the No.24 Order, in respect of the Part 7 designated postcodes;

  (h) articles 3(2)(m) and 4(2)(y) and (z) of the No.24 Order, in respect of the Part 8 designated postcodes.

DEFINITIONS

  "claimant"–art.2(1).
  "designated postcodes"–art.2(2).
  "employment and support allowance"–art.2(1).
  "jobseeker's allowance"–*ibid.*
  "the No.22 Order"–art.2(1).
  "the No.24 Order"–*ibid.*

Modification of the No.22 and 24 Orders: removal of the gateway conditions from 8th February 2017

3.496   **4.**—(1) This article applies in the case of a claim for universal credit that is made, or a claim for an employment and support allowance or a jobseeker's allowance that is made or treated as made, on or after 8th February 2017.

(2) Where this article applies, the provisions referred to in sub-paragraphs (a) and (b) have effect, with respect to a claimant residing in the designated postcodes referred to in the sub-paragraph in question, as though the reference in those provisions to meeting the gateway conditions were omitted—

  (a) articles 3(2)(i) and 4(2)(q) and (r) of the No.22 Order, in respect of the Part 9 designated postcodes;

  (b) articles 3(2)(j) and 4(2)(s) and (t) of the No.24 Order, in respect of the Part 10 designated postcodes.

DEFINITIONS

  "claimant"–art.2(1).
  "designated postcodes"–art.2(2).
  "employment and support allowance"–art.2(1).
  "jobseeker's allowance"–*ibid.*
  "the No.22 Order"–art.2(1).
  "the No.24 Order"–*ibid.*

Modification of the No. 11, 22 and 24 Orders: removal of the gateway conditions from 22nd February 2017

5.—(1) This article applies in the case of a claim for universal credit   3.497
that is made, or a claim for an employment and support allowance or a
jobseeker's allowance that is made or treated as made, on or after 22nd
February 2017.

(2) Where this article applies, the provisions referred to in sub-paragraphs
(a) to (h) have effect, with respect to a claimant residing in the designated
postcodes referred to in the sub-paragraph in question, as though the reference in those provisions to meeting the gateway conditions were omitted—

(a) articles 3(2)(a) and 4(2)(a) of the No.11 Order, in respect of the Part
11 designated postcodes;

(b) articles 3(2)(c) and 4(2)(e) and (f) of the No.22 Order, in respect of
the Part 12 designated postcodes;

(c) articles 3(2)(e) and 4(2)(i) and (j) of the No.22 Order, in respect of
the Part 13 designated postcodes;

(d) articles 3(2)(j) and 4(2)(s) and (t) of the No.22 Order, in respect of
the Part 14 designated postcodes;

(e) articles 3(2)(a) and 4(2)(a) and (b) of the No.24 Order, in respect of
the Part 15 designated postcodes;

(f) articles 3(2)(l) and 4(2)(w) and (x) of the No.24 Order, in respect of
the Part 16 designated postcodes;

(g) articles 3(2)(s) and 4(2)(kk) and (ll) of the No.24 Order, in respect
of the Part 17 designated postcodes;

(h) articles 3(2)(y) and 4(2)(ww) and (xx) of the No.24 Order, in
respect of the Part 18 designated postcodes.

DEFINITIONS

"claimant"–art.2(1).
"designated postcodes"–art.2(2).
"employment and support allowance"–art.2(1).
"jobseeker's allowance"–*ibid.*
"the No.11 Order"–art.2(1).
"the No.22 Order"–*ibid.*
"the No.24 Order"–*ibid.*

Modification of the No. 22 and 24 Orders: removal of the gateway conditions from 8th March 2017

6.—(1) This article applies in the case of a claim for universal credit that   3.498
is made, or a claim for an employment and support allowance or a jobseeker's allowance that is made or treated as made, on or after 8th March 2017.

(2) Where this article applies, the provisions referred to in sub-paragraphs
(a) and (b) have effect, with respect to a claimant residing in the designated
postcodes referred to in the sub-paragraph in question, as though the reference in those provisions to meeting the gateway conditions were omitted—

(a) articles 3(2)(f) and 4(2)(k) and (l) of the No.22 Order, in respect of
the Part 19 designated postcodes;

(b) articles 3(2)(p) and 4(2)(ee) and (ff) of the No.24 Order, in respect
of the Part 20 designated postcodes.

DEFINITIONS

"claimant"–art.2(1).
"designated postcodes"–art.2(2).
"employment and support allowance"–art.2(1).
"jobseeker's allowance"–*ibid.*
"the No.22 Order"–art.2(1).
"the No.24 Order"–*ibid.*

Modification of the No.22 and 24 Orders: removal of the gateway conditions from 15th March 2017

3.499   **7.**—(1) This article applies in the case of a claim for universal credit that is made, or a claim for an employment and support allowance or a jobseeker's allowance that is made or treated as made, on or after 15th March 2017.

(2) Where this article applies, the provisions referred to in sub-paragraphs (a) to (c) have effect, with respect to a claimant residing in the designated postcodes referred to in the sub-paragraph in question, as though the reference in those provisions to meeting the gateway conditions were omitted—

(a) articles 3(2)(i) and 4(2)(q) and (r) of the No.22 Order, in respect of the Part 21 designated postcodes;

(b) articles 3(2)(p) and 4(2)(ee) and (ff) of the No.22 Order, in respect of the Part 22 designated postcodes;

(c) articles 3(2)(t) and 4(2)(mm) and (nn) of the No.24 Order, in respect of the Part 23 designated postcodes.

DEFINITIONS

"claimant"–art.2(1).
"designated postcodes"–art.2(2).
"employment and support allowance"–art.2(1).
"jobseeker's allowance"–*ibid.*
"the No.22 Order"–art.2(1).
"the No.24 Order"–*ibid.*

Modification of the No.22 Order: removal of the gateway conditions from 22nd March 2017

3.500   **8.**—(1) This article applies in the case of a claim for universal credit that is made, or a claim for an employment and support allowance or a jobseeker's allowance that is made or treated as made, on or after 22nd March 2017.

(2) Where this article applies, articles 3(2)(i) and 4(2)(q) and (r) of the No.22 Order have effect, with respect to a claimant residing in the Part 24 designated postcodes, as though the reference in those provisions to meeting the gateway conditions were omitted.

DEFINITIONS

"claimant"–art.2(1).
"designated postcodes"–art.2(2).
"employment and support allowance"–art.2(1).
"jobseeker's allowance"–*ibid.*
"the No.22 Order"–art.2(1).

Modification of the No.22 and 24 Orders: removal of the gateway conditions from 29th March 2017

9.—(1) This article applies in the case of a claim for universal credit that is made, or a claim for an employment and support allowance or a jobseeker's allowance that is made or treated as made, on or after 29th March 2017.

3.501

(2) Where this article applies, the provisions referred to in sub-paragraphs (a) to (d) have effect, with respect to a claimant residing in the designated postcodes referred to in the sub-paragraph in question, as though the reference in those provisions to meeting the gateway conditions were omitted—

(a) articles 3(2)(c) and 4(2)(e) and (f) of the No.22 Order, in respect of the Part 25 designated postcodes;

(b) articles 3(2)(a) and 4(2)(a) and (b) of the No.24 Order, in respect of the Part 26 designated postcodes;

(c) articles 3(2)(h) and 4(2)(o) and (p) of the No.24 Order, in respect of the Part 27 designated postcodes;

(d) articles 3(2)(y) and 4(2)(ww) and (xx) of the No.24 Order, in respect of the Part 28 designated postcodes.

DEFINITIONS

"claimant"–art.2(1).
"designated postcodes"–art.2(2).
"employment and support allowance"–art.2(1).
"jobseeker's allowance"–*ibid.*
"the No.22 Order"–art.2(1).
"the No.24 Order"–*ibid.*

Modification of the No.16 Order: removal of the gateway conditions from 5th April 2017

10.—(1) This article applies in the case of a claim for universal credit that is made, or a claim for an employment and support allowance or a jobseeker's allowance that is made or treated as made, on or after 5th April 2017.

3.502

(2) Where this article applies, articles 3(2)(a) and 4(2)(a) of the No.16 Order have effect, with respect to a claimant residing in the Part 29 designated postcodes, as though the reference in those provisions to meeting the gateway conditions were omitted.

DEFINITIONS

"claimant"–art.2(1).
"designated postcodes"–art.2(2).
"employment and support allowance"–art.2(1).
"jobseeker's allowance"–*ibid.*
"the No.16 Order"–art.2(1).

Modification of the No.22 Order: removal of the gateway conditions from 12th April 2017

11.—(1) This article applies in the case of a claim for universal credit that is made, or a claim for an employment and support allowance or a jobseeker's allowance that is made or treated as made, on or after 12th April 2017.

3.503

(2) Where this article applies, the provisions referred to in sub-paragraphs (a) and (b) have effect, with respect to a claimant residing in the designated

postcodes referred to in the sub-paragraph in question, as though the reference in those provisions to meeting the gateway conditions were omitted—
- (a) articles 3(2)(b) and 4(2)(c) and (d) of the No.22 Order, in respect of the Part 30 designated postcodes;
- (b) articles 3(2)(t) and 4(2)(mm) and (nn) of the No.22 Order, in respect of the Part 31 designated postcodes.

DEFINITIONS

"claimant"–art.2(1).
"designated postcodes"–art.2(2).
"employment and support allowance"–art.2(1).
"jobseeker's allowance"–*ibid*.
"the No.22 Order"–art.2(1).

Modification of the No.22 and 24 Orders: removal of the gateway conditions from 19th April 2017

3.504

12.—(1) This article applies in the case of a claim for universal credit that is made, or a claim for an employment and support allowance or a jobseeker's allowance that is made or treated as made, on or after 19th April 2017.

(2) Where this article applies, the provisions referred to in sub-paragraphs (a) to (c) have effect, with respect to a claimant residing in the designated postcodes referred to in the sub-paragraph in question, as though the reference in those provisions to meeting the gateway conditions were omitted—
- (a) articles 3(2)(h) and 4(2)(o) and (p) of the No.22 Order, in respect of the Part 32 designated postcodes;
- (b) articles 3(2)(r) and 4(2)(ii) and (jj) of the No.22 Order, in respect of the Part 33 designated postcodes;
- (c) articles 3(2)(e) and 4(2)(i) and (j) of the No.24 Order, in respect of the Part 34 designated postcodes.

DEFINITIONS

"claimant"–art.2(1).
"designated postcodes"–art.2(2).
"employment and support allowance"–art.2(1).
"jobseeker's allowance"–*ibid*.
"the No.22 Order"–art.2(1).
"the No.24 Order"–*ibid*.

Modification of the No.11 and 13 Orders: removal of the gateway conditions from 26th April 2017

3.505

13.—(1) This article applies in the case of a claim for universal credit that is made, or a claim for an employment and support allowance or a jobseeker's allowance that is made or treated as made, on or after 26th April 2017.

(2) Where this article applies, the provisions referred to in sub-paragraphs (a) and (b) have effect, with respect to a claimant residing in the designated postcodes referred to in the sub-paragraph in question, as though the reference in those provisions to meeting the gateway conditions were omitted—
- (a) articles 3(2)(a) and 4(2)(a) of the No.11 Order, in respect of the Part 35 designated postcodes;
- (b) articles 3(2)(a) and 4(2)(a) of the No.13 Order, in respect of the Part 36 designated postcodes.

DEFINITIONS

"claimant"–art.2(1).
"designated postcodes"–art.2(2).
"employment and support allowance"–art.2(1).
"jobseeker's allowance"–*ibid.*
"the No.11 Order"–art.2(1).
"the No.13 Order"–*ibid.*

Modifications in consequence of removal of the gateway conditions: the No.11 Order

14.—(1) This article applies in the case of a claim in relation to which   **3.506** provisions of the No.11 Order are modified under articles 5(2)(a) or 13(2) (a).

(2) Where this article applies, the No.11 Order has effect as though—

(a) in article 2(1) (interpretation), the definition of "gateway conditions" were omitted;

(b) in article 3(2)(b) (coming into force of the universal credit provisions and incorrect information)—

   (i) in paragraph (i), "or meeting the gateway conditions" and "or does not meet the gateway conditions" were omitted;

   (ii) in paragraph (ii), "or meeting the gateway conditions" and "or does not or do not meet those conditions" were omitted;

   (iii) in paragraph (iii), "or meeting the gateway conditions" were omitted;

(c) in article 3(6) (article 3A of the No.9 Order and incorrect information), "or meeting the gateway conditions" were omitted in both places it occurs;

(d) in article 4(2)(b) (abolition of income-related employment and support allowance and income-based jobseeker's allowance and incorrect information)—

   (i) in paragraph (i), "or meeting the gateway conditions" and "or does not meet the gateway conditions" were omitted;

   (ii) in paragraph (ii), "or meeting those conditions" and "or does not or do not meet those conditions" were omitted;

   (iii) in paragraph (iii), "or meeting the gateway conditions" were omitted; and

(e) for article 4(7) (claims by couples) there were substituted—

"(7) Paragraphs (1A) and (1B) of article 5 of the No.9 Order apply for the purposes of paragraph (2)(a) as they apply for the purposes of article 4(2)(a) of the No.9 Order (but as if the references in paragraph (1A) to Schedule 5 to the No.9 Order were omitted).".

DEFINITIONS

"the No.9 Order"–art.2(1).
"the No.11 Order"–*ibid.*

Modifications in consequence of removal of the gateway conditions: the No.13 Order

15.—(1) This article applies in the case of a claim in relation to which   **3.507** provisions of the No.13 Order are modified under article 13(2)(b).

(2) Where this article applies, the modifications to the No.13 Order made by article 6(2) of the May 2016 Order have effect.

DEFINITIONS

"the May 2016 Order"–art.2(1).
"the No.13 Order"–*ibid.*

Modifications in consequence of removal of the gateway conditions: the No.16 Order

3.508   **16.**—(1) This article applies in the case of a claim in relation to which provisions of the No.16 Order are modified under article 10(2).

(2) Where this article applies, the modifications to the No.16 Order made by paragraph (2) of article 8 of the May 2016 Order have effect, apart from the modification made by sub-paragraph (c)(i) of that paragraph.

DEFINITIONS

"the May 2016 Order"–art.2(1).
"the No.16 Order"–*ibid.*

Modifications in consequence of removal of the gateway conditions: the No.22 Order

3.509   **17.**—(1) This article applies in the case of a claim in relation to which provisions of the No.22 Order are modified under—

(a) article 3(2)(a), (b) or (c);
(b) article 4(2)(a);
(c) article 5(2)(b), (c) or (d);
(d) article 6(2)(a);
(e) article 7(2)(a) or (b);
(f) article 8(2);
(g) article 9(2)(a);
(h) article 11(2)(a) or (b); or
(i) article 12(2)(a) or (b).

(2) Where this article applies, the modifications to the No.22 Order made by article 14(2) of the September 2016 Order have effect.

DEFINITIONS

"the No.22 Order"–art.2(1).
"the September 2016 Order"–*ibid.*

Modifications in consequence of removal of the gateway conditions: the No.24 Order

3.510   **18.**—(1) This article applies in the case of a claim in relation to which provisions of the No.24 Order are modified under—

(a) article 3(2)(d), (e), (f), (g) or (h);
(b) article 4(2)(b);
(c) article 5(2)(e), (f), (g) or (h);
(d) article 6(2)(b);
(e) article 7(2)(c);
(f) article 9(2)(b), (c) or (d); or
(g) article 12(2)(c).

(2) Where this article applies, the modifications to the No.24 Order made by article 15(2) of the September 2016 Order have effect.

DEFINITIONS

"the No.24 Order"–art.2(1).
"the September 2016 Order"–*ibid.*

Modification of the No.23 Order: claims for housing benefit, income support or a tax credit

19. Article 7 of the No.23 Order (prevention of claims for housing   3.511
benefit, income support or a tax credit) applies as though the reference in
paragraph (1) of that article to article 3(1) and (2)(a) to (c) of that Order
included—
(a) a reference to paragraph (1) and sub-paragraph (a) of paragraph (2) of
    article 3 of the No.11 Order, in respect of claims in relation to which
    sub-paragraph (a) is modified by articles 5(2)(a) and 13(2)(a) of this
    Order;
(b) a reference to paragraph (1) and sub-paragraph (a) of paragraph (2) of
    article 3 of the No.13 Order, in respect of claims in relation to which
    sub-paragraph (a) is modified by article 13(2)(b) of this Order;
(c) a reference to paragraph (1) and sub-paragraph (a) of paragraph (2) of
    article 3 of the No.16 Order, in respect of claims in relation to which
    sub-paragraph (a) is modified by article 10(2) of this Order;
(d) a reference to paragraph (1) and sub-paragraphs (b), (e), (j), (n), (p), (r)
    and (t) of paragraph (2) of article 3 of the No.22 Order, in respect
    of claims in relation to which those sub-paragraphs are modified
    respectively by articles 11(2)(a), 5(2)(c), 5(2)(d), 3(2)(c), 7(2)(b),
    12(2)(b) and 11(2)(b) of this Order;
(e) a reference to paragraph (1) and sub-paragraphs (c), (f), (h) and (i) of
    paragraph (2) of article 3 of the No.22 Order, in respect of claims in
    relation to which those sub-paragraphs are modified respectively by
    articles 5(2)(b) and 9(2)(a), articles 3(2)(a) and 6(2)(a), articles 3(2)
    (b) and 12(2)(a) and articles 4(2)(a), 7(2)(a) and 8(2) of this Order;
(f) a reference to paragraph (1) and sub-paragraphs (b), (c), (e), (j), (m),
    (p), (s) and (t) of paragraph (2) of article 3 of the No.24 Order, in
    respect of claims in relation to which those sub-paragraphs are modi-
    fied respectively by articles 3(2)(d), 3(2)(e), 12(2)(c), 4(2)(b), 3(2)
    (h), 6(2)(b), 5(2)(g) and 7(2)(c) of this Order; and
(g) a reference to paragraph (1) and sub-paragraphs (a), (h), (l) and (y) of
    paragraph (2) of article 3 of the No.24 Order, in respect of claims in
    relation to which those sub-paragraphs are modified respectively by
    articles 5(2)(e) and 9(2)(b), articles 3(2)(f) and 9(2)(c), articles 3(2)
    (g) and 5(2)(f) and articles 5(2)(h) and 9(2)(d) of this Order.

DEFINITIONS

"the No.11 Order"–art.2(1).
"the No.13 Order"–*ibid.*
"the No.16 Order"–*ibid.*
"the No.22 Order"–*ibid.*
"the No.23 Order"–*ibid.*
"the No.24 Order"–*ibid.*

SCHEDULE

POSTCODE DISTRICTS AND PART-DISTRICTS

PART 1

3.512   LE16 7.
LE16 9.
NN17 1 and NN17 2.
NN17 4.
NN18 0.
NN18 9.

PART 2

3.513   SN6 8.

PART 3

3.514   NN18 8.

PART 4

3.515   NN6 9.

PART 5

3.516   LE16 8.
NN17 3.
NN17 5.

PART 6

3.517   SW7 5.

PART 7

3.518   TS25 5.

PART 8

3.519   PE8 4 and PE8 5.

PART 9

3.520   NE6 1 and NE6 2.
NE6 5.

PART 10

3.521   NE6 3.
NE7.

PART 11

3.522   WA1.
WA2.
WA3 4 to WA3 7.
WA4.
WA5.

WA13 0.
WA13 9.

PART 12

E3 4 and E3 5.   **3.523**
E3 9.
E14.

PART 13

SO14.   **3.524**
SO15.
SO16 2.
SO16 4 to SO16 6.
SO17.
SO18 1.
SO18 4.
SO18 6.
SO18 9.
SO19 1 and SO19 2.
SO19 4 and SO19 5.
SO19 7 to SO19 9.

PART 14

SO18 2 and SO18 3.   **3.525**
SO18 5.
SO19 0.
SO19 6.
SO30 0.
SO30 3 and SO30 4.
SO30 9.

PART 15

SO16 0.   **3.526**
SO16 3.
SO16 7 to SO16 9.
SO30 2.

PART 16

SO40 0.
SO40 2 and SO40 3.
SO40 8.
SO43.

PART 17

E3 2 and E3 3.   **3.527**

PART 18

SO31 4 and SO31 5.   **3.528**
SO31 8.

PART 19

CV13 0.   **3.529**
LE9 8.
LE10.

PART 20

3.530   LE9 4.
LE9 7.

PART 21

3.531   NE4.
NE5 1 and NE5 2
NE5 5.
NE5 9.
NE15 6 and NE15 7.

PART 22

3.532   NE15 8 and NE15 9.

PART 23

NE15 0.

PART 24

3.533   EH18.
EH19.
EH20.
EH22.
EH23.
EH24.
EH25.
EH26.
EH37.

PART 25

3.534   E1 0 to E1 5.
E1 7 and E1 8.
EC2N 2.
EC2V 8.
EC2Y 5.
EC3A 1.
EC3A 4 and EC3A 5.
EC3M 2 and EC3M 3.
EC3M 8.
EC3N 4.
EC3R 6.
EC3V 0 and EC3V 1.
EC3V 4.
EC4M 5 and EC4M 6.
EC4M 9.
EC4R 2.
EC4V 2.

PART 26

3.535   E1W.

PART 27

3.536   EC2A 1.
EC2M 3 to EC2M 7.
EC2N 1.
EC2N 3 and EC2N 4.

726

EC2R.
EC2V 5 to EC2V 7.
EC2Y 8 and EC2Y 9.
EC3A 2 and EC3A 3.
EC3A 6 to EC3A 8.
EC3M 1.
EC3M 4 to EC3M 7.
EC3N 1 to EC3N 3.
EC3R 5.
EC3R 7 and EC3R 8.
EC3V 3.
EC3V 9.
EC4A.
EC4M 7 and EC4M 8.
EC4N.
EC4R 0 and EC4R 1.
EC4R 3.
EC4R 9.
EC4V 3 to EC4V 6.
EC4Y.

PART 28

E1 6.   **3.537**
EC2A 2 to EC2A 4.
EC2M 1 and EC2M 2.

PART 29

CH5 1 to CH5 4.   **3.538**
CH5 9.

PART 30

CH6.   **3.539**
CH7 1 to CH7 3.
CH7 6.
CH7 9.

PART 31

CH7 4.   **3.540**
CH8 8.

PART 32

BA9.   **3.541**
BA10.
BA20.
BA21 3 and BA21 4.
BA22 7 and BA22 8.
TA10 9.
TA11 .
TA12.
TA13.
TA14.
TA15.
TA16.
TA17.
TA18 7.
TA18 9.

PART 33

3.542   BA7.
        BA8.
        SP7 0.
        SP7 7 to SP7 9.
        SP8 4 and SP8 5.
        SP8 9.

PART 34

3.543   BA21 5.
        BA22 9.
        DT9.
        TA18 8.

PART 35

3.544   M35 0.
        M35 9.
        OL1 1 to OL1 4.
        OL1 9.
        OL2 5 to OL2 8.
        OL3 5 to OL3 7.
        OL4 1 to OL4 5.
        OL8.
        OL9.

PART 36

M35 5.

The Welfare Reform Act 2012 (Commencement No.9 and 21 and Transitional and Transitory Provisions (Amendment)) Order 2017

(SI 2017/483)

The Secretary of State for Work and Pensions makes the following Order in exercise of the powers conferred by section 150(3) and (4)(a), (b)(i) and (c) of the Welfare Reform Act 2012:

ARRANGEMENT OF ARTICLES

1. Citation
2. Amendment of the Welfare Reform Act 2012 (Commencement No.9 and Transitional and Transitory Provisions and Commencement No.8 and Savings and Transitional Provisions (Amendment)) Order 2013
3. Amendment of the Welfare Reform Act 2012 (Commencement No.21 and Transitional and Transitory Provisions) Order 2015

Citation

3.545   1. This Order may be cited as the Welfare Reform Act 2012 (Commencement No.9 and 21 and Transitional and Transitory Provisions (Amendment)) Order 2017.

Amendment of the Welfare Reform Act 2012 (Commencement No.9 and Transitional and Transitory Provisions and Commencement No.8 and Savings and Transitional Provisions (Amendment)) Order 2013

[2. Omitted–see the amendments to arts. 5A(1) and 6(1)) of the Welfare Reform Act 2012 (Commencement No.9 and Transitional and Transitory Provisions and Commencement No.8 and Savings and Transitional Provisions (Amendment)) Order 2013   **3.546**

Amendment of the Welfare Reform Act 2012 (Commencement No.21 and Transitional and Transitory Provisions) Order 2015

[3. Omitted–see the amendments to art. 6(11) of the Welfare Reform Act 2012 (Commencement No.21 and Transitional and Transitory Provisions) Order 2015   **3.547**

PART IVC

SAVINGS PROVISIONS

The Universal Credit (Digital Service) Amendment Regulations 2014

(2014/2887)

The Secretary of State for Work and Pensions, in exercise of the powers conferred by section 1(1) of the Social Security Administration Act 1992(1) and sections 4(3), 7(3), 8(3), 9(2), 10(3), 11(4), 12(1) and (3), 19(2)(d), 32(1) and (4), 42(2) and (3) of, and paragraph 3(2) of Schedule 1 to, the Welfare Reform Act 2012(2), makes the following Regulations:

In accordance with section 173(1)(b) of the Social Security Administration Act 1992, the Social Security Advisory Committee has agreed that the proposals for these Regulations need not be referred to it.

[In force November, 26 2014]

Citation and commencement

1. These Regulations may be cited as the Universal Credit (Digital Service) Amendment Regulations 2014 and, subject to regulation 5 (saving), come into force on 26th November 2014.

3.548

Universal credit - childcare costs

2. *[Omitted: see the amendments to regs. 33, 34 and 34A of the Universal Credit Regulations 2013, above.]*

3.549

Universal Credit - assessment periods

3. *[Omitted: see the amendments to regs 15, 21 and 22A of the Universal Credit Regulations 2013; regs 6, 9 and 26 of the Universal Credit, Personal Independence Payment, Jobseeker's Allowance and Employment and Support Allowance (Claims and Payments) Regulations 2013 above and reg.7of the Universal Credit (Transitional Provisions) Regulations 2013 below.]*

3.550

Universal Credit – calculation of unearned income

4. *[Omitted: see the amendment to reg.73 of the Universal Credit Regulations 2013, above.]*

3.551

Saving

[⁴ **5.**—(1) The amendments made by these Regulations do not apply to an award of universal credit unless it is—

3.552

(a) an award to which a person has become entitled by reference to residence in a digital service area (whether or not the person is still living in that area);

(b) an award to which a person who is living in a digital service area is entitled (whether or not the person was living in that area at the time that person became entitled);

(c) an award, not falling within sub-paragraph (a) or (b), to which a person who has lived in a digital service area at any time after it became a digital service area is entitled but only if that award has been administered on the digital service computer system;

(d) an award not falling within sub-paragraphs (a) to (c)—
    (i) which is made to members of a couple jointly as a consequence of a previous award having ended when the couple formed, or
    (ii) which is made to a single claimant as a consequence of a previous award having ended when the claimant ceased to be a member of a couple,
where that previous award was administered on the digital service computer system.

(2) Where the date on which these Regulations first apply to an existing award of universal credit by virtue of paragraph (1)(b) is not the first day of an assessment period, they are not to have effect in relation to that award until the first day of the next assessment period.

(3) In this regulation—
"a digital service area" means—
(a) postcode districts SM5 2, SM6 7 and SM6 8; and
(b) an area in respect of which no restrictions have been imposed in order for the universal credit provisions to come into force on a claim for universal credit (apart from with respect to residence and the date on which, or period in respect of which, universal credit is claimed) by an order under section 150 of the Welfare Reform Act 2012 or an area (apart from that referred to in (a)) in respect of which such restrictions have been, but are no longer, imposed;
"the digital service computer system" is the computer system operated by the Secretary of State in digital service areas;
"universal credit provisions" means the provisions listed in Schedule 2 to the Welfare Reform Act 2012 (Commencement No.9 and Transitional and Transitory Provisions and Commencement No.8 and Savings and Transitional Provisions (Amendment)) Order 2013.]

AMENDMENT

1. Welfare Reform Act 2012 (Commencement No.22 and Transitional and Transitory Provisions) Order 2015 (SI 2015/101) art 6 (February 16, 2015).
2. Welfare Reform Act 2012 (Commencement No.23 and Transitional and Transitory Provisions) Order 2015 (SI 2015/634) art.10 (March 18, 2015).
3. Welfare Reform Act 2012 (Commencement No.24 and Transitional and Transitory Provisions and Commencement No.9 and Transitional and Transitory Provisions (Amendment)) Order 2015 (SI 2015/1537) arts 7 and 8 (September 21, 2015).
4. Universal Credit and Miscellaneous Amendments Regulations 2015 (SI 2015/1754) reg.20 (October 28, 2015).

The Shared Parental Leave and Statutory Shared Parental Pay (Consequential Amendments to Subordinate Legislation) Order 2014

(2014/3255)

In force in accordance with art. 1(2) and (3)
The Secretary of State makes the following Order in exercise of the powers

conferred by section 135(3) and 136(1) and (2) of the Children and Families Act 2014.

Citation and commencement

1.-(1) This Order may be cited as the Shared Parental Leave and Statutory Shared Parental Pay (Consequential Amendments to Subordinate Legislation) Order 2014.

(2) The provisions of this Order specified in article 37 come into force on 31st December 2014.

(3) The remaining provisions of this Order come into force on 5th April 2015

3.553

Amendment of Miscellaneous Regulations

2.-34. *[Omitted—Where relevant the amendments have been noted in the text of the Universal Credit Regulations (above) and in Vols I-IV]*

3.554

Transitional provisions

35.-(1) The amendments made by this Order in those articles which come into force on 5th April 2015 in accordance with 1(3) (amendments relating to references to ordinary and additional paternity leave and to ordinary and additional statutory paternity pay) do not have effect in relation to—

3.555

(a) ordinary statutory paternity pay which is paid;

(b) additional statutory paternity pay which is paid;

(c) a period in respect of which additional statutory paternity pay is payable which begins, or continues;

(d) ordinary paternity leave which is taken; or

(e) additional paternity leave which is taken;

on or after 5th April 2015.

(2) In this article—

"additional paternity leave" means leave under section 80AA or 80BB of the Employment Rights Act 1996;

"additional statutory paternity pay" means pay under section 171ZEA or 171ZEB of the Social Security Contributions and Benefits Act 1992;

"ordinary paternity leave" means leave under section 80A or 80B of the Employment Rights Act 1996;

"ordinary statutory paternity pay" means pay under section 171ZA or 171ZB of the Social Security Contributions and Benefits Act 1992.

36. *[Omitted as relating solely to Northern Ireland]*
Provisions coming into force on 31st December 2014

3.556

37. The provisions specified in article 1(2) are—

3.557

(a) this article;

(b) article 1;

(c)-(y) *[Omitted]*

(z) article 28(1), (2)(c), (3)(c) and (4)(c) and (d);

(aa)-(hh) *[Omitted]*

(gg) article 35;

(hh) *[Omitted]*.

The Social Security (Housing Costs Amendments) Regulations 2015

(SI 2015/1647)

Made by the Secretary of State for Work and Pensions under ss. 123(1)(a), 135(1), 137(1) and 175(1), (3) and (4) of the Social Security Contributions and Benefits Act 1992, ss. 4(5), 35(1) and 36(2) and (4) of the Jobseekers Act 1995, ss. 4(2)(a), 24(1) and 25(2), (3) and (5) of the Welfare Reform Act 2007 and ss. 11(4) and (5)(b), 40, 42(1), (2) and (3) of, and para. 1 of Sch. 6 to, the Welfare Reform Act 2012.

[In force April 1, 2016]

Citation and commencement

3.558   **1.** These Regulations may be cited as the Social Security (Housing Costs Amendments) Regulations 2015 and come into force on 1st April 2016.

Amendment of the Income Support (General) Regulations 1987, the Jobseeker's Allowance Regulations 1996 and the Employment and Support Allowance Regulations 2008

3.559   **2-4.** *[Omitted]*

Amendment of the Universal Credit Regulations 2013

3.560   **5.** *[Omitted – see the amendments to para. 5(2)(a) and (b) of Sch. 5 to the Universal Credit Regulations 2013 in Pt. III]*

Amendment of the Universal Credit (Transitional Provisions) Regulations 2014

3.561   **6.** *[Omitted – see the amendment to reg. 29 of the Universal Credit (Transitional Provisions) Regulations 2014 in Pt. IV]*

Revocation

3.562   **7.** *[Omitted as not relevant to universal credit]*

Saving provision

3.563   **8.**—(1) This regulation applies to a person ("P") where, for the purpose of determining whether P's entitlement to a relevant benefit includes an amount for housing costs, the Secretary of State determines that P is entitled or required to be treated as entitled to one or more relevant benefits for a continuous period which includes 31st March 2016.

(2) Where this regulation applies to P, the provisions of—

(a) Schedule 6 to the Employment and Support Allowance Regulations 2008;

(b) Schedule 3 to the Income Support (General) Regulations 1987; and

(c) Schedule 2 to the Jobseeker's Allowance Regulations 1996,

as modified by the Social Security (Housing Costs Special Arrangements)

(Amendment and Modification) Regulations 2008 are to have effect in relation to P as if the amendments made by regulations 2 to 4 of these Regulations and the revocation made by regulation 7(1) had not been made.

(3) Where this regulation applies to P, the provisions of Schedule 5 to the Universal Credit Regulations 2013 are to have effect in relation to P as if the amendments made by regulations 5 and 6 of these Regulations had not been made.

(4) In this regulation, "relevant benefit" means—

(a) an employment and support allowance under Part 1 of the Welfare Reform Act 2007;

(b) income support under the Income Support (General) Regulations 1987;

(c) a jobseeker's allowance under the Jobseeker's Allowance Regulations 1996; and

(d) universal credit under Part 1 of the Welfare Reform Act 2012.

The Employment and Support Allowance and Universal Credit (Miscellaneous Amendments and Transitional and Savings Provisions) Regulations 2017

(SI 2017/204)

In Force April 3, 2017

REGULATIONS REPRODUCED

The Secretary of State for Work and Pensions makes the following Regulations in exercise of the powers conferred by sections 12(1), 17(4), 18(3), 19(2)(d), 25(a) and 42(3)(a) of the Welfare Reform Act 2012 and sections 15(4) and (5) and 34(1) of the Welfare Reform and Work Act 2016.

In accordance with section 173(5)(b) of the Social Security Administration Act 1992, this instrument contains only regulations made by virtue of, or consequential upon, sections 15, 16, 17 and 34 of the Welfare Reform and Work Act 2016 and is made before the end of the period of 6 months beginning with the coming into force of those sections.

In accordance with section 176(1) of the Social Security Administration Act 1992 the Secretary of State has consulted with organisations appearing to him to be representative of the authorities concerned.

GENERAL NOTE

Parts 1-3 of, and Sch.1 to, these Regulations, taken together and ss.15-17 of the Welfare Reform and Work Act 2016, abolish the LCW element of universal credit **3.564** (and the work-related activity component of ESA) with effect from April 3, 2017 and make a number of consequential amendments. However, for universal credit, the abolition is subject to the transitional and savings provisions in Sch.2, Pt.2, to which effect is given by reg.2. Part 1 of the Schedule contains equivalent provisions for ESA and is reproduced in Vol.II.

Under Pt.2 of Sch.2, claimants who are found to have—or are treated as having—limited capability for work, but not limited capability for work-related activity, continue to be entitled to the LCW component in the following circumstances:

- There was an award of universal credit immediately before April 3, 2017 and that award included the LCW element, or would have done so if that element were not excluded by the three-month waiting period in reg.28(1) of the Universal Credit Regulations (para.9).

- There was an award of universal credit immediately before April 3, 2017 and that award included the LCWRA element, and it is subsequently decided that the claimant only has limited capability for work (para.10). This only applies where the claimant has had both limited capability for work and limited capability for work-related activity throughout the period from April 3, 2017 to the date on which it is determined that s/he only has limited capability for work.

- There was a claim for universal credit before April 3, 2017 and—also before that date—the claimant provided medical evidence of having limited capability for work. In those circumstances, the claimant will be entitled to the LCW element even if the determination that s/he has limited capability for work is not made until after April 3, 2017 and even if that determination is made on revision by the Secretary of State or on appeal by the First-tier Tribunal or Upper Tribunal (para.11).

- Article 24 of the Welfare Reform Act 2012 (Commencement No 9 and Transitional and Transitory Provisions and Commencement No 8 and Savings and Transitional Provisions (Amendment)) Order 2013 (see Part IVB below) provides that, where an award of universal credit is made and subsequently a decision is made to revise or supersede and earlier decision about old style ESA (or old style JSA) (or there is a final decision on an appeal against such a decision) the Secretary of State must consider whether to revise (or, in some circumstances, supersede) the universal credit decision. Where the claim for old style ESA was made, or treated as made, before April 3, 2013 and a decision is made to revise the universal credit decision after that date, then, if the revising decision includes a determination that the claimant has limited capability for work, the LCW element is to be included in the universal credit award (para.12).

- The claimant was entitled to employment and support allowance immediately before April 3, 2017 and remains so entitled until the date on which a subsequent claim for universal credit is made or treated as made (para.13).

- The claimant does not fall within the previous paragraph but was entitled to incapacity credits immediately before April 3, 2017 and remains so entitled until the date on which a subsequent claim for universal credit is made or treated as made (para.14).

- The claimant is entitled to income support on the grounds of incapacity for work or disability, or incapacity benefit or severe disablement allowance immediately before April 3, 2017 and regs 22-24, 26 or 27 of the Universal Credit (Transitional Provisions) Regulations 2014 applies to him or her from then until the date on which a subsequent claim for universal credit is made or treated as made (para.15).

The LCW element continues to be payable under Sch,2, Pt.2 for as long as continues to be entitled to universal credit and to have limited capability for work (para.8(1)(b)). Continuity of entitlement is not broken (i) where the award of universal credit but a further award begins immediately because the claimant ceased to be a member of a couple or became a member of a couple (para.8(2)(a)); or (ii) the award ends because the claimant's income (or the joint claimants' combined income) was too high but a further award is made within six months (para.8(2)(b)).

Citation and commencement

1. These Regulations may be cited as the Employment and Support Allowance and Universal Credit (Miscellaneous Amendments and Transitional and Savings Provisions) Regulations 2017 and come into force on 3rd April 2017.

3.565

PART 4

CONSEQUENTIAL, TRANSITIONAL AND SAVINGS PROVISIONS

Consequential, transitional and savings provisions

7.—(1) [Omitted]

3.566

(2) Schedule 2 contains transitional and savings provisions.

Regulation 7(2)

SCHEDULE 2

TRANSITIONAL AND SAVINGS PROVISIONS

PART 2

UNIVERSAL CREDIT: TRANSITIONAL AND SAVINGS PROVISIONS

Transitional and savings provisions: General

8.—(1) The amendments made by regulations 4 and 5 and paragraphs 13, 16 and 17 of Schedule 1 do not apply—

3.567

    (a) where a claimant has an award of universal credit in any of the circumstances in the following paragraphs; and

    (b) for so long as the claimant continues to be entitled to universal credit and to have limited capability for work.

(2) For the purposes of sub-paragraph (1)(b), the reference to continuous entitlement to universal credit includes where an award has terminated and a further award is made and—

    (a) immediately before the further award commences, the previous award has terminated because the claimant ceased to be a member of a couple or became a member of a couple; or

    (b) within the six months beginning with the date that the further award commences, the previous award has terminated because the financial condition in section 5(1)(b) or, if it was a joint claim, section 5(2)(b), of the Welfare Reform Act 2012 was not met.

(3) In this Part—

"employment and support allowance" means an employment and support allowance under Part 1 of the Welfare Reform Act 2007;

"LCW element" and "LCWRA element" have the meanings in regulation 27 of the Universal Credit Regulations 2013 as it has effect apart from the amendments made by regulation 4(4) (which remove references to the LCW element);

"limited capability for work" has the meaning given in section 37(1) of the Welfare Reform Act 2012.

(4) The Universal Credit, Personal Independence Payment, Jobseeker's Allowance and Employment and Support Allowance (Claims and Payments) Regulations 2013 apply for the purpose of deciding the date on which a claim for universal credit is made or is to be treated as made.

Claimants entitled to the LCW element before 3rd April 2017

3.568   9. The first circumstance is where immediately before 3rd April 2017 the award included the LCW element, or would have but for regulation 28(1) of the Universal Credit Regulations 2013, as it has effect apart from the amendments made by regulation 4(5)(a) (which removes the reference to the LCW element).

Claimants entitled to the LCWRA element before 3rd April 2017

3.569   10. The second circumstance is where—
   (a)   immediately before 3rd April 2017 the award included the LCWRA element;
   (b)   on or after 3rd April 2017 a determination that the claimant has limited capability for work is made; and
   (c)   the claimant had limited capability for work and work-related activity throughout the period beginning immediately before 3rd April 2017 and ending with the date on which the determination that the claimant has limited capability for work is made.

Claimants who are providing evidence of having limited capability for work before 3rd April 2017

3.570   11. The third circumstance is where—
   (a)   before 3rd April 2017—
        (i)   it falls to be determined whether the claimant has limited capability for work; and
        (ii)   the claimant has provided evidence of having limited capability for work in accordance with the Social Security (Medical Evidence) Regulations 1976; and
   (b)   on or after 3rd April 2017 a determination that the claimant has limited capability for work is made on the basis of an assessment under Part 5 of the Universal Credit Regulations 2013, on revision under section 9 of the Social Security Act 1998 or on appeal.

Claimants who appeal or seek revision of a decision relating to employment and support allowance

3.571   12. The fourth circumstance is where—
   (a)   the claimant appeals or seeks revision under section 9 of the Social Security Act 1998 of a decision relating to the entitlement of the claimant to an employment and support allowance, where the claim for employment and support allowance was made or treated as made before 3rd April 2017; and
   (b)   on or after 3rd April 2017, in accordance with article 24 of the Welfare Reform Act 2012 (Commencement No 9 and Transitional and Transitory Provisions and Commencement No 8 and Savings and Transitional Provisions (Amendment)) Order 2013, the Secretary of State considers it appropriate to revise under section 9 of the Social Security Act 1998 an award of universal credit so as to include the LCW element.

Claimants entitled to employment and support allowance before 3rd April 2017

3.572   13. The fifth circumstance is where immediately before 3rd April 2017 the claimant was entitled to employment and support allowance and remains so entitled throughout the period beginning with 3rd April 2017 and ending with the date on which the claim for universal credit is made or treated as made.

Claimants entitled to be credited with earnings under the Social Security (Credits) Regulations 1975 before 3rd April 2017

3.573   14. The sixth circumstance is where—
   (a)   immediately before 3rd April 2017—
        (i)   the claimant entitled to the award was entitled to be credited with earnings equal to the lower earnings limit then in force in respect of a week to which regulation 8B(2)(a)(iv), (iva) or (v) of the Social Security (Credits) Regulations 1975 applies; and
        (ii)   paragraph 13 does not apply to that claimant; and
   (b)   the claimant is so entitled in respect of each week that falls in the period beginning

with 3rd April 2017 and ending with the date on which the claim for universal credit is made or treated as made.

Claimants entitled to income support or other incapacity benefits before 3rd April 2017

15. The seventh circumstance is where regulation 22, 23, 24, 26 or 27 of the Universal Credit (Transitional Provisions) Regulations 2014 applies to the claimant throughout the period beginning immediately before 3rd April 2017 and ending with the date on which the claim for universal credit is made or treated as made.

3.574

The Universal Credit (Housing Costs Element for claimants aged 18 to 21) (Amendment) Regulations 2017 The Universal Credit (Amendment) Regulations 2017

(SI 2017/252)

In Force April 1, 2017

Regulations Reproduced

General Note

See the commentary to paras 4A-4C of Sch.4 to the Universal Credit Regulations.   3.574.1
The Secretary of State, in exercise of the powers conferred by sections 11(5)(a) and 42(2) and (3) of the Welfare Reform Act 2012, makes the following Regulations.
In accordance with section 173(1)(b) of the Social Security Administration Act 1992, the Social Security Advisory Committee has agreed that the proposals for these Regulations need not be referred to it.

Citation and commencement

1. These Regulations may be cited as the Universal Credit (Housing   3.575
Costs Element for claimants aged 18 to 21) (Amendment) Regulations 2017 and come into force on 1st April 2017.

Entitlement to housing costs element

2. *[See the amendments to reg.6(1A) of, and Sch.4, para.1(3) and Pt.2 to, the*   3.576
Universal Credit Regulations (above)]

Saving for claimants not living in a digital service area

3.—(1) The amendments made by these Regulations do not apply to an   3.577
award of universal credit unless it is—
  (a) an award to which a person has become entitled by reference to residence in a digital service area (whether or not the person is still living in that area);

741

   (b) an award to which a person who is living in a digital service area is entitled (whether or not the person was living in that area at the time that person became entitled);

   (c) an award, not falling within sub-paragraph (a) or (b), to which a person who has lived in a digital service area at any time after it became a digital service area is entitled but only if that award has been administered on the digital service computer system;

   (d) an award not falling within sub-paragraphs (a) to (c)—

      (i) which is made to members of a couple jointly as a consequence of a previous award having ended when the couple formed; or

      (ii) which is made to a single claimant as a consequence of a previous award having ended when the claimant ceased to be a member of a couple,

where that previous award was administered on the digital service computer system.

(2) Where the date on which these Regulations first apply to an existing award of universal credit by virtue of paragraph (1)(b) is not the first day of an assessment period, they are not to have effect in relation to that award until the first day of the next assessment period.

(3) In this regulation—

"a digital service area" means—

   (a) postcode districts SM5 2, SM6 7 and SM6 8; and

   (b) an area in respect of which no restrictions have been imposed in order for the universal credit provisions to come into force on a claim for universal credit (apart from with respect to residence and the date on which, or period in respect of which, universal credit is claimed) by an order under section 150 of the Welfare Reform Act 2012 or an area (apart from that referred to in (a)) in respect of which such restrictions have been, but are no longer, imposed;

"the digital service computer system" is the computer system operated by the Secretary of State in digital service areas;

"universal credit provisions" means the provisions listed in Schedule 2 to the Welfare Reform Act 2012 (Commencement No.9 and Transitional and Transitory Provisions and Commencement No.8 and Savings and Transitional Provisions (Amendment)) Order 2013.

Saving for claimants entitled to housing benefit or with an award that includes the housing costs element

3.578   **4.**—(1) These Regulations do not apply to an award of universal credit if, immediately before the first day on which they would otherwise apply, the claimant was entitled to—

   (a) an award of universal credit that included the housing costs element; or

   (b) an award of housing benefit under section 130 of the Social Security Contributions and Benefits Act 1992.

(2) Paragraph (1) does not apply to an award with effect from the day after the day on which it ceases to include the housing costs element.

(3) In this regulation, "housing costs element" has the meaning in regulation 25 of the Universal Credit Regulations 2013 (the housing costs element).

PART V

UNIVERSAL CREDIT: CLAIMS & PAYMENTS AND DECISIONS & APPEALS

The Universal Credit, Personal Independence Payment, Jobseeker's Allowance and Employment and Support Allowance (Claims and Payments) Regulations 2013

(SI 2013/380)

The Secretary of State, in exercise of the powers conferred upon him by the provisions set out in Schedule 1 to these Regulations, makes the following Regulations.

In accordance with section 172(1) of the Social Security Administration Act 1992, the Secretary of State has referred the proposals for these Regulations to the Social Security Advisory Committee.

The Secretary of State has consulted with organisations representing qualifying lenders likely to be affected by the fee specified in paragraph 9(2) of Schedule 5 to the Regulations (direct payment to lender of deductions in respect of interest on secured loans).

In accordance with section 176(2)(b) of the Social Security Administration Act 1992 and in so far as these Regulations relate to housing benefit, the Secretary of State has obtained the agreement of organisations appearing to him to be representative of the authorities concerned that proposals in respect of these Regulations should not be referred to them.

ARRANGEMENT OF REGULATIONS

PART I

GENERAL

PART III

EVIDENCE, INFORMATION AND NOTIFICATION OF CHANGES OF CIRCUMSTANCES

PART IV

PAYMENTS

PART V

THIRD PARTIES

PART VI

MOBILITY COMPONENT OF PERSONAL INDEPENDENCE PAYMENT

4.2   These Regulations are included in Vol.III. However, they are also reproduced in full below (except for Sch.3 which made consequential amendments to other legislation). The provisions which relate to universal credit are annotated in this volume. Readers are referred to Vol.III for commentary on the provisions which relate to personal independence payment or are of general application. These Regulations are in force from April 8, 2013 in relation to personal independence payment and April 29, 2013 in relation to universal credit, new-style ESA and new-style JSA.

PART I

GENERAL

Citation and commencement

4.3   **1.**—(1) These Regulations may be cited as the Universal Credit, Personal Independence Payment, Jobseeker's Allowance and Employment and Support Allowance (Claims and Payments) Regulations 2013.

(2) For the purpose of personal independence payment these Regulations come into force on 8th April 2013.

(3) For the purposes of universal credit, jobseeker's allowance and employment and support allowance these Regulations come into force on 29th April 2013.

Interpretation

4.4   **2.** In these Regulations—
"the 1991 Act" means the Child Support Act 1991;
"the 2012 Act" means the Welfare Reform Act 2012;
"the Administration Act" means the Social Security Administration Act 1992;
"the Contributions and Benefits Act" means the Social Security Contributions and Benefits Act 1992;
"the Jobseeker's Allowance Regulations" means the Jobseeker's Allowance Regulations 2013;
"the Personal Independence Payment Regulations" means the Social Security (Personal Independence Payment) Regulations 2013;
"the Universal Credit Regulations" means the Universal Credit Regulations 2013;
"appropriate office" means—
(a) an office of the Department for Work and Pensions or any other place designated by the Secretary of State in relation to any case or class of case as a place to, or at which, any claim, notice, document, evidence or other information may be sent, delivered or received for the purposes of these Regulations and includes a postal address specified by the Secretary of State for that purpose; or
(b) in the case of a person who is authorised or required by these Regulations to use an electronic communication for any purpose, an

address to which such communications may be sent in accordance with Schedule 2;

"assessment period" has the meaning given by regulation 21 of the Universal Credit Regulations;

"attendance allowance" means an allowance payable by virtue of section 64 of the Contributions and Benefits Act;

"benefit", except in regulation 60 and Schedules 5 and 6, means universal credit, personal independence payment, a jobseeker's allowance or an employment and support allowance;

"child" has the meaning given by section 40 of the 2012 Act;

"claimant" in relation to—

(a) universal credit, has the meaning given by section 40 of the 2012 Act;

(b) personal independence payment, means any person who is a claimant for the purposes of regulations made under Part 4 (personal independence payment) of that Act;

(c) a jobseeker's allowance, has the meaning given by section 35(1) of the Jobseekers Act 1995; and

(d) an employment and support allowance, has the meaning given by section 24(1) of the Welfare Reform 2007 Act;

"couple" has the meaning given by section 39 of the 2012 Act;

"disability living allowance" means an allowance payable by virtue of section 71 of the Contributions and Benefits Act;

"earned income" has the meaning given by regulation 52 of the Universal Credit Regulations;

"electronic communication" has the meaning given by section 15(1) of the Electronic Communications Act 2000;

"employment and support allowance" means an allowance under Part 1 of the Welfare Reform Act 2007 as amended by the provisions of Schedule 3, and Part 1 of Schedule 14, to the 2012 Act that remove references to an income-related allowance;

"jobseeker's allowance" means an allowance under the Jobseekers Act 1995 as amended by the provisions of Part 1 of Schedule 14 to the 2012 Act that remove references to an income-based allowance;

"limited capability for work" has the meaning given by section 1(4) of the Welfare Reform Act 2007;

"local authority" has the meaning given by section 191 of the Administration Act;

"maternity allowance" means an allowance payable by virtue of section 35 of the Contributions and Benefits Act;

"official computer system" means a computer system maintained by or on behalf of the Secretary of State to—

(a) send or receive any claim or information; or

(b) process or store any claim or information;

"partner" means one of a couple;

"personal independence payment" means the allowance under Part 4 of the 2012 Act;

"qualifying young person" has the meaning given by regulation 5 of the Universal Credit Regulations;

"regular and substantial caring responsibilities for a severely disabled person" has the meaning given by regulation 30 of the Universal Credit Regulations;

"universal credit" means the benefit under Part 1 of the 2012 Act;
"writing" includes writing produced by means of electronic communications used in accordance with Schedule 2.

Use of electronic communications

4.5   **3.** Schedule 2 makes provision as to the use of electronic communications.

DEFINITION

"electronic communication"—see reg.2.

Consequential amendments

4.6   **4.** Schedule 3 makes amendments to other regulations which are consequential upon these Regulations.

Disapplication of section 1(1A) of the Administration Act

4.7   **5.** Section 1(1A) of the Administration Act (requirements in respect of a national insurance number) is not to apply to a child or a qualifying young person in respect of whom universal credit is claimed.

DEFINITIONS

"the Administration Act"—see reg.2.
"universal credit"—*ibid.*

PART II

CLAIMS

Claims not required for entitlement to universal credit in certain cases

4.8   **6.** [¹ . . .]

AMENDMENT

1. Universal Credit (Digital Service) Amendment Regulations 2014 (SI 2014/2887) reg.3(2)(a) (November 26, 2014). The amendment is subject to the saving provision in reg.5 of SI 2014/2887 (see Pt IV).

GENERAL NOTE

4.9   SSAA 1992 s.1(1) provides that except in such cases as may be prescribed, no person shall be entitled to any benefit unless, in addition to satisfying any other conditions of entitlement, he or she "makes a claim for it in the manner, and within the time, prescribed in relation to that benefit by regulations" under SSAA Pt 1.

From April 29, 2014, reg.6 set out the exceptions to that general rule, in which a former entitlement to universal credit could revive without a claim being made, if not more than six months had elapsed since the previous entitlement ended. As a result of the saving provision in reg.5 of SI 2014/2887, those exceptions continue in "Live Service" cases and readers are referred to pp.432-3 of the 2013/14 edition for the text of the revoked regulation.

However, in "Full Service" or "Digital Service" cases (see *Universal Credit—An Introduction* (above)) reg.6 has been revoked from November 26, 2014. and the only such exceptions relate to people who cease to be—or become—members of a couple and are to be found in reg.9(6) and (7). Claimants who are subject to the Full Service rules, who were formerly entitled to universal credit and become so entitled again must now make a new claim. However, more favourable rules apply if the claim is made within six months of the old entitlement ending and (if applicable) within seven days of any claimant ceasing paid work: see UC Regulations regs 21(3C) and 22A.

Claims not required for entitlement to an employment and support allowance in certain cases

[1 **7.**—(1) It is not to be a condition of entitlement to an employment and support allowance that a claim be made for it where—   **4.10**

(a) the claimant has made and is pursuing an appeal against a relevant decision of the Secretary of State, and

(b) the appeal relates to a decision to terminate or not to award an employment and support allowance for which a claim was made.

(2) In this regulation—

"appellate authority" means the First-tier Tribunal, the Upper Tribunal, the Court of Appeal, the Court of Session, or the Supreme Court; and

"relevant decision" means—

(a) a decision that embodies the first determination by the Secretary of State that the claimant does not have limited capability for work; or

(b) a decision that embodies the first determination by the Secretary of State that the claimant does not have limited capability for work since a previous determination by the Secretary of State or appellate authority that the claimant does have limited capability for work.]

AMENDMENT

1. Employment and Support Allowance (Repeat Assessments and Pending Appeal Awards) (Amendment) Regulations 2015 (SI 2015/437) reg.6 (March 30, 2015).

DEFINITIONS

"claimant"—see reg.2.
"employment and support allowance"—*ibid.*

Making a claim for universal credit

8.—(1) Except as provided in paragraph (2), a claim for universal credit must be made by means of an electronic communication in accordance with the provisions set out in Schedule 2 and completed in accordance with any instructions given by the Secretary of State for that purpose.   **4.11**

(2) A claim for universal credit may be made by telephone call to the telephone number specified by the Secretary of State if the claim falls within a class of case for which the Secretary of State accepts telephone claims or where, in any other case, the Secretary of State is willing to do so.

(3) A claim for universal credit made by means of an electronic communication in accordance with the provisions set out in Schedule 2 is defective if it is not completed in accordance with any instructions of the Secretary of State.

(4) A claim made by telephone in accordance with paragraph (2) is properly completed if the Secretary of State is provided during that call with all the information required to determine the claim and the claim is defective if not so completed.

(5) If a claim for universal credit is defective the Secretary of State must inform the claimant of the defect and of the relevant provisions of regulation 10 relating to the date of claim.

(6) The Secretary of State must treat the claim as properly made in the first instance if—

(a) in the case of a claim made by telephone, the person corrects the defect; or

(b) in the case of a claim made by means of an electronic communication, a claim completed in accordance with any instructions of the Secretary of State is received at an appropriate office,

within one month, or such longer period as the Secretary of State considers reasonable, from the date on which the claimant is first informed of the defect.

DEFINITIONS

"appropriate office"—see reg.2.
"claimant"—*ibid.*
"electronic communication"—*ibid.*
"universal credit"—*ibid.*

GENERAL NOTE

4.12   Regulation 8 and Sch.2 prescribe the manner in which a claim for universal credit must be made. The general rule (in accordance with the aspiration that universal credit is to be "digital by default") is that the claim must be made by "an electronic communication" in accordance with Sch.2. In brief, the claim must be made by completing and submitting an online claim form (para.(1)). However, a claim may instead be made by telephone if the Secretary of State is prepared to accept it in that form (para.(2)). An online claim that is not completed in accordance with the Secretary of State's instructions, or a telephone claim where the Secretary of State is not provided with all the information required to determine the claim during the phone call, is defective (paras (3) and (4)). On receipt of a defective claim, the Secretary of State must inform the claimant of the defect and of the relevant provisions of reg.10 (i.e., para.(2) of that regulation) (para.(5)). If the claimant then corrects the defect within a month (or longer if the Secretary of State considers it reasonable), then the claim is treated as having been properly made in the first place (para.(6)).

Claims for universal credit by members of a couple

4.13   **9.**—(1) Where a person is a member of a couple and may make a claim as a single person by virtue of regulation 3(3) (couples) of the Universal Credit Regulations, but instead makes a claim for universal credit jointly, that claim is to be treated as a claim made by that person as a single person.

(2) Where a claim for universal credit is made jointly by a member ("M1") of a polygamous marriage with another member of the polygamous marriage ("M2"), that claim is to be treated as a claim made by M1 as a single person where—

(a) M1 is not a party to an earlier marriage in the polygamous marriage, and

(b) any party to an earlier marriage is living in the same household as M1 and M2.

(3) In paragraph (2) "polygamous marriage" means a marriage during which a party to it is married to more than one person and which took place under the laws of a country which permits polygamy.

(4) The Secretary of State may treat a claim made by members of a couple as single persons as a claim made jointly by the couple where it is determined by the Secretary of State that they are a couple.

(5) Where the Secretary of State considers that one member of a couple is unable to make a joint claim with the other member of that couple, the other member of the couple may make a claim jointly for both of them.

[² (6) Where an award of universal credit to joint claimants is terminated because they cease to be a couple an award may be made, without a claim, to either or each one of them—

(a) as a single person; or

(b) if either of them has formed a new couple with a person who is already entitled to universal credit, jointly with that person.]

(7) Where awards of universal credit to two single claimants are terminated because they form a couple who are joint claimants, it is not to be a condition of entitlement to universal credit that the couple make a claim for it and universal credit may be awarded to them jointly.

(8) A couple who are joint claimants are to be treated as making a claim for universal credit where—

[² (a) one of them ceased to be entitled to an award of universal credit (whether as a single person or as a member of a different couple) on the formation of that couple;]

(b) the other member of the couple did not have an award of universal credit as a single person before formation of the couple

[¹ and the claim is to be treated as made on the day after the member of the couple mentioned in sub-paragraph (a) ceased to be entitled to universal credit.]

(9) In relation to an award which may be made by virtue of paragraph (6) or (7) without a claim being required, a claimant and every person by whom or on whose behalf, sums by way of universal credit are receivable must supply in such manner and at such times as the Secretary of State may determine such information or evidence as the Secretary of State may require in connection with the formation or dissolution of a couple.

(10) Where an award of universal credit to joint claimants is terminated because one of them has died it is not to be a condition of entitlement to universal credit that the surviving partner makes a claim for it.

<small>DEFINITIONS</small>

"couple"—see reg.2 and WRA 2012 s.39.
"universal credit"—see reg.2.

<small>AMENDMENT</small>

1. Social Security (Miscellaneous Amendments) (No.2) Regulations 2013 (SI 2013/1508) reg.6(1) and (2) (July 29, 2013).

2. Universal Credit (Digital Service) Amendment Regulations 2014 (SI 2014/2887) reg.3(2)(b) (November 26, 2014). The amendment is subject to the saving provision in reg.5 of SI 2014/2887 (see Pt IV).

GENERAL NOTE

4.14   See the commentary to reg.3 of the Universal Credit Regulations. The effect of the saving provision in reg.5 of SI 2014/2887 is that the amendments with effect from November 26, 2014 only apply in "Full Service" (aka "Digital Service") cases), see *Universal Credit—An Introduction* above. For the text of the regulation before those amendments, which continues to apply in "Live Service" cases, see pp.435-6 of the 2013/14 edition.

Date of claim for universal credit

4.15   **10.**—(1) Where a claim for universal credit is made, the date on which the claim is made is—

   (a) subject to sub-paragraph (b), in the case of a claim made by means of an electronic communication in accordance with regulation 8(1), the date on which the claim is received at an appropriate office;

   (b) in the case of a claim made by means of an electronic communication in accordance with regulation 8(1), where the claimant receives assistance at home or at an appropriate office from the Secretary of State, or a person providing services to the Secretary of State, which is provided for the purpose of enabling that person to make a claim, the date of first notification of a need for such assistance;

   (c) subject to sub-paragraph (d), in the case of a claim made by telephone in accordance with regulation 8(2), the date on which that claim is properly completed in accordance with regulation 8(4); or

   (d) where the Secretary of State is unable to accept a claim made by telephone in accordance with regulation 8(2) on the date of first notification of intention to make the claim, the date of first notification, provided a claim properly completed in accordance with regulation 8(4) is made within one month of that date,

or the first day in respect of which the claim is made if later than the above.

   (2) In the case of a claim which is defective by virtue of regulation 8, the date of claim is to be the first date on which the defective claim is received or made but is treated as properly made in the first instance in accordance with regulation 8(6).

DEFINITIONS

   "appropriate office"—see reg.2.
   "claimant"—*ibid.*
   "electronic communication"—*ibid.*
   "universal credit"—*ibid.*

GENERAL NOTE

4.16   Regulation 10 identifies the date on which a claim for universal credit is made. Online claims are made when received by the DWP (para.(1)(a)), unless the person received assistance to complete the form from an officer of the Department (or a contractor providing services to the Secretary of State) in which case the date of claim is the date on which the Secretary of State was told that assistance was needed (para.(1)(b)). A telephone claim is made on the day reg.8(4) is satisfied (i.e., when the Secretary of State is provided with all the information required to determine the claim) (para.(1)(c)). But if the Department cannot accept a telephone claim on the same day as the claimant first notifies it that it would like to make one, then the claim is made on that day as long as a properly completed telephone claim is made within a month of that day (para.(1)(d)).

Paragraph (2) applies where a defective claim is treated as properly made in the first instance under reg.8(6). Such a claim is made on the first date the defective claim was received.

Making a claim for personal independence payment

11.—(1) A claim for personal independence payment must be made—   **4.17**

(a) in writing on a form authorised by the Secretary of State for that purpose and completed in accordance with the instructions on the form;

(b) by telephone call to the telephone number specified by the Secretary of State; or

(c) by receipt by the claimant of a telephone call from the Secretary of State made for the purpose of enabling a claim for personal independence payment to be made,

unless in any case or class of case the Secretary of State decides only to accept a claim made in one of the ways specified in paragraph (a), (b) or (c).

(2) In the case of a claim made in writing the claim must be sent to or received at the appropriate office.

(3) A claim for personal independence payment made in writing is defective if it is not completed in accordance with any instructions of the Secretary of State.

(4) A claim made by telephone in accordance with paragraph (1) is properly completed if the Secretary of State is provided during that call with all the information required to determine the claim and the claim is defective if not so completed.

(5) If a claim for personal independence payment is defective the Secretary of State must inform the claimant of the defect and of the relevant provisions of regulation 12 relating to the date of claim.

(6) The Secretary of State must treat the claim as properly made in the first instance if a claim completed in accordance with any instructions of the Secretary of State is received within one month, or such longer period as the Secretary of State may consider reasonable, from the date on which the claimant is first informed of the defect.

(7) Paragraph (8) applies where—

(a) a person ("P1") makes a claim for personal independence payment on behalf of another person ("P2") whom P1 asserts to be a person unable for the time being to act; and

(b) the Secretary of State makes a decision not to appoint P1 under regulation 57.

(8) The Secretary of State must treat the claim made by P1 as properly made by P2 in the first instance if a further claim made by P2 is received within one month, or such longer period as the Secretary of State may consider reasonable, from the date the Secretary of State notified the decision not to appoint P1 under regulation 57.

DEFINITIONS

"claimant"—see reg.2.
"personal independence payment"—*ibid.*
"writing"—*ibid.*

Date of claim for personal independence payment

4.18   **12.**—(1) Subject to paragraph (4), where a claim for personal independence payment is made in accordance with regulation 11 the date on which the claim is made is—

(a) in the case of a claim in writing made by means of an electronic communication in accordance with the provisions set out in Schedule 2, the date on which the claim is received at the appropriate office;

(b) in the case of a claim made by telephone, the date on which a claim made by telephone is properly completed; or

(c) where a person first notifies an intention to make a claim and provided that a claim made in writing produced other than by means of an electronic communication is properly completed and received at the appropriate office designated by the Secretary of State in that claimant's case within one month or such longer period as the Secretary of State considers reasonable of the date of first notification, the date of first notification,

or the first day in respect of which the claim is made if later than the above.

(2) In the case of a claim which is defective by virtue of regulation 11(3) or (4)—

(a) subject to sub-paragraph (b) and paragraph (4), the date of claim is to be the first date on which the defective claim is received or made but is treated as properly made in the first instance in accordance with regulation 11(6);

(b) the date of claim is to be the date of first notification of an intention to make a claim where a claim made by a person to whom paragraph (1)(c) applies is defective but is treated as properly made in the first instance in accordance with regulation 11(6).

(3) In the case of a claim which is treated as properly made by the claimant in accordance with regulation 11(8), the date on which the claim is made is the date on which it was received in the first instance.

(4) Where a further claim made by a person ("P2") in the circumstances set out in regulation 11(8) is defective and that further claim is treated as properly made in the first instance in accordance with regulation 11(6), the date of claim is to be the date on which the claim made by the person ("P1") whom the Secretary of State decided not to appoint under regulation 57 was received in the first instance.

(5) In a case where the Secretary of State decides not to award personal independence payment following a claim for it being made on behalf of another expressly on the ground of terminal illness (which has the meaning given by section 82(4) of the 2012 Act), the date of claim is to be—

(a) the date that claim was made if a further claim, made in accordance with regulation 11, is received within one month, or such longer period as the Secretary of State may consider reasonable, from the date the Secretary of State notified the decision not to award personal independence payment on the ground of terminal illness; or

(b) the date that claim was made where the further claim is defective but is treated as properly made in the first instance in accordance with regulation 11(6).

DEFINITIONS

  "appropriate office"—see reg.2.
  "claimant"—*ibid.*
  "electronic communication"—*ibid.*
  "personal independence payment"—*ibid.*
  "writing"—*ibid.*

Making a claim for an employment and support allowance by telephone

13.—(1) Except where the Secretary of State directs in any case or class   4.19
of case that a claim must be made in writing, a claim for an employment
and support allowance may be made by telephone call to the telephone
number specified by the Secretary of State.

(2) Where the Secretary of State, in any particular case, directs that the
person making the claim approves a written statement of the person's circumstances provided for the purpose by the Secretary of State, a telephone
claim is not a valid claim unless the person complies with the direction.

(3) A claim made by telephone in accordance with paragraph (1) is properly completed if the Secretary of State is provided during that call with all
the information required to determine the claim and the claim is defective
if not so completed.

(4) Where a telephone claim is defective, the Secretary of State must
advise the person making it of the defect and of the effect on the date of
claim of the provisions of regulation 14.

(5) If the person corrects the defect so that the claim then satisfies the
requirements of paragraph (3) and does so within one month, or such
longer period as the Secretary of State considers reasonable, of the date the
Secretary of State first drew attention to the defect, the Secretary of State
must treat the claim as if it had been properly made in the first instance.

DEFINITION

  "employment and support allowance"—see reg.2.

Date of claim for an employment and support allowance where claim made by telephone

14. In the case of a telephone claim, the date on which the claim is made   4.20
is to be the first date on which—

  (a) a claim made by telephone is properly completed;
  (b) a person first notifies the Secretary of State of an intention to make
      a claim, provided that a claim made by telephone is properly com-
      pleted within one month or such longer period as the Secretary of
      State considers reasonable of first notification; or
  (c) a defective claim is received but is treated as properly made in the
      first instance in accordance with regulation 13(5),

or the first day in respect of which the claim is made if later than the
above.

Making a claim for an employment and support allowance in writing

4.21   **15.**—(1) A claim for an employment and support allowance may be made to the Secretary of State in writing on a form authorised by the Secretary of State for that purpose and must be completed in accordance with the instructions on the form.

(2) A written claim for an employment and support allowance, which is made on the form approved for the time being, is properly completed if completed in accordance with the instructions on the form and defective if not so completed.

(3) If a written claim is defective when first received, the Secretary of State must advise the person making it of the defect and of the effect on the date of claim of the provisions of regulation 16.

(4) If the person corrects the defect so that the claim then satisfies the requirements of paragraph (2) and does so within one month, or such longer period as the Secretary of State considers reasonable, of the date the Secretary of State first drew attention to the defect, the Secretary of State must treat the claim as if it had been properly made in the first instance.

DEFINITIONS

    "employment and support allowance"—see reg.2.
    "writing"—*ibid.*

Date of claim for an employment and support allowance where claim made in writing

4.22   **16.** In the case of a written claim for an employment and support allowance, the date on which the claim is made is to be the first date on which—

    (a) a properly completed claim is received in an appropriate office;

    (b) a person first notifies an intention to make a claim, provided that a properly completed claim form is received in an appropriate office within one month, or such longer period as the Secretary of State considers reasonable, of first notification; or

    (c) a defective claim is received but is treated as properly made in the first instance in accordance with regulation 15(4),

or the first day in respect of which the claim is made if later than the above.

DEFINITIONS

    "appropriate office"—see reg.2.
    "employment and support allowance"—*ibid.*

Claims for an employment and support allowance where no entitlement to statutory sick pay

4.23   **17.**—(1) Paragraph (2) applies to a claim for an employment and support allowance for a period of limited capability for work in relation to which the claimant gave the claimant's employer a notice of incapacity under regulation 7 of the Statutory Sick Pay (General) Regulations 1982 and for which the claimant has been informed in writing by the employer that there is no entitlement to statutory sick pay.

(2) A claim to which this paragraph applies is to be treated as made on the date accepted by the claimant's employer as the first day of incapacity,

provided that the claimant makes the claim within the period of 3 months beginning with the day on which the claimant is informed in writing by the employer that the claimant was not entitled to statutory sick pay.

DEFINITIONS

"claimant"—see reg.2.
"employment and support allowance"—*ibid.*
"limited capability for work"—*ibid.*
"writing"—*ibid.*

Special provisions where it is certified that a woman is expected to be confined or where she has been confined

18. Where, in a certificate issued or having effect as issued under the Social Security (Medical Evidence) Regulations 1976, it has been certified that it is to be expected that a woman will be confined and she makes a claim for maternity allowance in expectation of that confinement, any such claim may, unless the Secretary of State otherwise directs, be treated as a claim for an employment and support allowance, made in respect of any days in the period beginning with either—

  (a) the beginning of the sixth week before the expected week of confinement; or

  (b) the actual date of confinement,

whichever is the earlier, and ending in either case on the 14th day after the actual date of confinement.

(2) Where, in a certificate issued under the Social Security (Medical Evidence) Regulations 1976 it has been certified that a woman has been confined and she claims maternity allowance within three months of the date of her confinement, her claim may be treated in the alternative or in addition as a claim for an employment and support allowance for the period beginning with the date of her confinement and ending 14 days after that date.

DEFINITIONS

"employment and support allowance"—see reg.2.
"maternity allowance"—*ibid.*

Making a claim for a jobseeker's allowance: attendance at an appropriate office

19. A person wishing to make a claim for a jobseeker's allowance, unless the Secretary of State otherwise directs, is required to attend for the purpose of making a claim for that allowance, in person at an appropriate office or such other place, and at such time, as the Secretary of State may specify in that person's case.

DEFINITIONS

"appropriate office"—see reg.2.
"jobseeker's allowance"—*ibid.*

Date of claim where a person claiming a jobseeker's allowance is required to attend at an appropriate office

20.—(1) Subject to regulation 29(6), where a person is required to attend in accordance with regulation 19, if the person subsequently attends for the

4.24

4.25

4.26

purpose of making a claim for a jobseeker's allowance at the place and time specified by the Secretary of State and, if so requested, provides a properly completed claim form at or before the time when the person is required to attend, the claim is to be treated as made on whichever is the later of the date of first notification of intention to make that claim or the first day in respect of which the claim is made.

(2) Where a person who is required to attend in accordance with regulation 19 without good cause fails to attend at either the place or time specified in that person's case, or does not, if so requested, provide a properly completed claim form at or before the time when the person is required to attend, the claim is to be treated as made on the first day on which the person does attend at the specified place or time or does provide a properly completed claim form, or if later the first day in respect of which the claim is made.

(3) The Secretary of State may direct that the time for providing a properly completed claim form may be extended to a date no later than the date one month after the date of first notification of intention to make that claim.

DEFINITION

"jobseeker's allowance"—see reg.2.

Making a claim for a jobseeker's allowance in writing

4.27   **21.**—(1) Except where a person is required to attend in accordance with regulation 19, a claim for a jobseeker's allowance may be made in writing on a form authorised by the Secretary of State for that purpose and may be delivered or sent to the Secretary of State at an appropriate office.

(2) A claim made in accordance with paragraph (1) must be completed in accordance with the instructions on the form.

(3) A written claim for a jobseeker's allowance made under this regulation or regulation 20, which is made on the form approved for the time being, is properly completed if completed in accordance with the instructions on the form and defective if not so completed.

(4) If a written claim made under this regulation is defective when first received, the Secretary of State must advise the person making it of the defect and of the effect on the date of claim of the provisions of regulation 22.

(5) If that person corrects the defect so that the claim then satisfies the requirements of paragraph (3) and does so within one month, or such longer period as the Secretary of State considers reasonable, from the date the Secretary of State first drew attention to the defect, the claim must be treated as having been properly made in the first instance.

DEFINITIONS

"appropriate office"—see reg.2.
"jobseeker's allowance"—*ibid.*
"writing"—*ibid.*

Date of claim for a jobseeker's allowance where claim made in writing

4.28   **22.** Subject to regulation 29(6), in the case of a written claim for a jobseeker's allowance made under regulation 21, the date on which the claim is made or treated as made is to be the first date on which—

(a) a properly completed claim is received in an appropriate office;

(b) a person first notifies an intention to make a claim, provided that a properly completed claim form is received in an appropriate office within one month or such longer period as the Secretary of State considers reasonable of first notification; or

(c) a defective claim is received but is treated as properly made in the first instance in accordance with regulation 21(5),

or the first day in respect of which the claim is made if later than the above.

DEFINITIONS

"appropriate office"—see reg.2.
"jobseeker's allowance"—*ibid.*

Making a claim for a jobseeker's allowance by telephone

23.—(1) Except where a person is required to attend in accordance with regulation 19, or where the Secretary of State in any case directs that the claim must be made in writing in accordance with regulation 21, a claim for a jobseeker's allowance may be made by telephone call to the telephone number specified by the Secretary of State where such a claim falls within a class of case for which the Secretary of State accepts telephone claims or in any other case where the Secretary of State is willing to do so.

4.29

(2) A claim made by telephone in accordance with paragraph (1) is properly completed if the Secretary of State is provided during that call with all the information required to determine the claim and the claim is defective if not so completed.

(3) Where a telephone claim is defective, the Secretary of State must advise the person making it of the defect and of the effect on the date of claim of the provisions of regulation 24.

(4) If the person corrects the defect so that the claim then satisfies the requirements of paragraph (2) and does so within one month, or such longer period as the Secretary of State considers reasonable, of the date the Secretary of State first drew attention to the defect, the Secretary of State must treat the claim as if it had been properly made in the first instance.

DEFINITIONS

"jobseeker's allowance"—see reg.2.
"writing"—*ibid.*

Date of claim for a jobseeker's allowance where claim made by telephone

24. Subject to regulation 29(6), in the case of a telephone claim made under regulation 23, the date on which the claim is made or treated as made is to be the first date on which—

4.30

(a) a claim made by telephone is properly completed;

(b) a person first notifies an intention to make a claim, provided that a claim made by telephone is properly completed within one month or such longer period as the Secretary of State considers reasonable of first notification; or

(c) a defective claim is received but is treated as properly made in the first instance in accordance with regulation 23(4),

or the first day in respect of which the claim is made if later than the above.

Interchange with claims for other benefits

4.31   **25.**—(1) The Secretary of State may treat a claim for an employment and support allowance by a woman in addition or in the alternative as a claim for maternity allowance.

(2) The Secretary of State may treat a claim for a maternity allowance in addition or in the alternative as a claim for an employment and support allowance.

(3) Where it appears that a person who has made a claim for personal independence payment is not entitled to it but may be entitled to disability living allowance or attendance allowance, the Secretary of State may treat any such claim alternatively, or in addition, as a claim for either disability living allowance or attendance allowance as the case may be.

(4) Where it appears that a person who has made a claim for disability living allowance or attendance allowance is not entitled to it but may be entitled to personal independence payment, the Secretary of State may treat any such claim alternatively, or in addition, as a claim for personal independence payment.

(5) In determining whether the Secretary of State should treat a claim as made alternatively or in addition to another claim ("the original claim") under this regulation the Secretary of State must treat the alternative or additional claim, whenever made, as having been made at the same time as the original claim.

DEFINITIONS

"attendance allowance"—see reg.2.
"disability living allowance"—*ibid.*
"employment and support allowance"—*ibid.*
"maternity allowance"—*ibid.*
"personal independence payment"—*ibid.*

Time within which a claim for universal credit is to be made

4.32   **26.**—(1) Subject to the following provisions of this regulation, a claim for universal credit must be made on the first day of the period in respect of which the claim is made.

(2) Where the claim for universal credit is not made within the time specified in paragraph (1), the Secretary of State is to extend the time for claiming it, subject to a maximum extension of one month, to the date on which the claim is made, if—

(a) any one or more of the circumstances specified in paragraph (3) applies or has applied to the claimant; and

(b) as a result of that circumstance or those circumstances the claimant could not reasonably have been expected to make the claim earlier.

(3) The circumstances referred to in paragraph (2) are—

(a) the claimant was previously in receipt of a jobseeker's allowance or an employment and support allowance and notification of expiry of entitlement to that benefit was not sent to the claimant before the date that the claimant's entitlement expired;

(b) the claimant has a disability;

(c) the claimant has supplied the Secretary of State with medical evidence that satisfies the Secretary of State that the claimant had an illness that prevented the claimant from making a claim;

(d) the claimant was unable to make a claim in writing by means of an electronic communication used in accordance with Schedule 2 because the official computer system was inoperative;

[¹ . . .]

(f) where—

(i) the Secretary of State decides not to award universal credit to members of a couple jointly because one of the couple does not meet the basic condition in section 4(1)(e) of the 2012 Act;

(ii) they cease to be a couple; and

(iii) the person who did meet the basic condition in section 4(1)(e) makes a further claim as a single person;

(g) where—

(i) an award of universal credit to joint claimants has been terminated because one of the couple does not meet the basic condition in section 4(1)(e) of the 2012 Act;

(ii) they cease to be a couple; and

(iii) the person who did meet the basic condition in section 4(1)(e) makes a further claim as a single person.

(4) In the case of a claim for universal credit made by each of joint claimants, the prescribed time for claiming is not to be extended under paragraph (2) unless both claimants satisfy that paragraph.

[¹ (5) In the case of a claim for universal credit referred to in regulation 21(3C) of the Universal Credit Regulations (assessment period applied from a previous award within the last 6 months) the claim for universal credit must be made before the end of the assessment period in respect of which it is made]

AMENDMENT

1. Universal Credit (Digital Service) Amendment Regulations 2014 (SI 2014/2887) reg.3(2)(c) (November 26, 2014). The amendment is subject to the saving provision in reg.5 of SI 2014/2887 (see Pt IV). The absence of a full-stop at the end of para.(5) is a consequence of the amending instrument and is not an editorial error.

MODIFICATION

With effect from June 16, 2014, para.(3) is modified by reg.15 of the Universal Credit (Transitional Provisions) Regulations 2014 (SI 2014/1230). The modification applies where a claim for universal credit is made by a person who was previously entitled to an "existing benefit" (namely JSA(IB), ESA(IR), IS, HB and CTC, WTC and, in some circumstances, incapacity benefit and severe disablement allowance: see regs 2(1) and 25(2) of SI 2014/1230). The modified text includes the following sub-para.(aa) after sub-para.(a):

""(aa) the claimant was previously in receipt of an existing benefit (as defined in the Universal Credit (Transitional Provisions) Regulations 2014) and notification of expiry of entitlement to that benefit was not sent to the claimant before the date that the claimant's entitlement expired;"

DEFINITIONS

> "the 2012 Act"—see reg.2.
> "benefit"—*ibid.*
> "claimant"—*ibid.*
> "couple"—see reg.2 and WRA 2012, s.39.
> "jobseeker's allowance"—see reg.2.
> "universal credit"—*ibid.*

GENERAL NOTE

4.33   The effect of the saving provision in reg.5 of SI 2014/2887 is that the amended text of reg.26 only applies in "Full Service" (aka "Digital Service" cases), see *Universal Credit—An Introduction* above. For the text of the unamended regulation, which continues to apply in "Live Service" cases, see pp.445-6 of the 2013/14 edition.

A claim for universal credit must normally be made on the first day for which the claimant wishes to receive it (para.(1)). However, under para.(2), the Secretary of State must extend that time limit by up to one month (but no more) if at least one circumstances in para.(3) applies, or has applied, to the claimant; and, as a result of that circumstance or those circumstances, the claimant could not reasonably have been expected to make the claim earlier. In the case of joint claimants, both must satisfy para.(2) before the time limit can be extended (para.(4)).

For a discussion of the circumstances in which a computer can be said to have been "inoperative" (para.(3)(d)), see *AM v SSWP (UC)* [2017] UKUT 131 (AAC).

Time within which a claim for personal independence payment is to be made

4.34   **27.** A claim for personal independence payment must be made on the first day of the period in respect of which the claim is made.

DEFINITION

> "personal independence payment"—see reg.2.

Time within which a claim for an employment and support allowance is to be made

4.35   **28.** A claim for an employment and support allowance must be made on the first day of the period in respect of which the claim is made or within the period of three months immediately following that day.

DEFINITION

> "employment and support allowance"—see reg.2.

Time within which a claim for a jobseeker's allowance is to be made

4.36   **29.**—(1) Subject to paragraphs (2) and (4), a claim for a jobseeker's allowance must be made on the first day of the period in respect of which the claim is made.

(2) In a case where the claim is not made within the time specified in paragraph (1), the Secretary of State is to extend the time for claiming a jobseeker's allowance, subject to a maximum extension of three months, to the date on which the claim is made, where—

(a) any one or more of the circumstances specified in paragraph (3) applies or has applied to the claimant; and

(b) as a result of that circumstance or those circumstances the claimant could not reasonably have been expected to make the claim earlier.

(3) The circumstances referred to in paragraph (2) are—

(a) the claimant has difficulty communicating because—

    (i) the claimant has learning, language or literacy difficulties; or

    (ii) the claimant is deaf or blind,

and it was not reasonably practicable for the claimant to obtain assistance from another person to make the claim;

(b) the claimant was caring for a person who is ill or disabled and it was not reasonably practicable for the claimant to obtain assistance from another person to make the claim;

(c) the claimant was given information by an officer of the Department for Work and Pensions which led the claimant to believe that a claim for a jobseeker's allowance would not succeed;

(d) the claimant was given written advice by a solicitor or other professional adviser, a medical practitioner, a local authority or a person working in a Citizens Advice Bureau or a similar advice agency, which led the claimant to believe that a claim for a jobseeker's allowance would not succeed;

(e) the claimant was required to deal with a domestic emergency affecting the claimant and it was not reasonably practicable for the claimant to obtain assistance from another person to make the claim; or

(f) the claimant was prevented by adverse weather conditions from attending an appropriate office.

(4) In a case where the claim is not made within the time specified in paragraph (1), the prescribed time for claiming a jobseeker's allowance is to be extended, subject to a maximum extension of one month, to the date on which the claim is made, where—

(a) any one or more of the circumstances specified in paragraph (5) applies or has applied to the claimant; and

(b) as a result of that circumstance or those circumstances the claimant could not reasonably have been expected to make the claim earlier.

(5) The circumstances referred to in paragraph (4) are—

(a) the appropriate office where the claimant would be expected to make a claim was closed and alternative arrangements were not available;

(b) the claimant was unable to attend the appropriate office due to difficulties with the claimant's normal mode of transport and there was no reasonable alternative available;

(c) there were adverse postal conditions;

(d) the claimant was previously in receipt of an employment and support allowance and notification of expiry of entitlement to that benefit was not sent to the claimant before the date that the entitlement expired;

(e) the claimant had ceased to be a member of a couple within the period of one month before the claim was made;

(f) during the period of one month before the claim was made a close relative of the claimant had died and for this purpose "close relative" means partner, parent, son, daughter, brother or sister;

(g) the claimant was unable to make telephone contact with the appropriate office where the claimant would be expected to notify an intention of making a claim because the telephone lines to that office were busy or inoperative;

(h) the claimant was unable to make contact by means of an electronic communication used in accordance with Schedule 2 where the claimant would be expected to notify an intention of making a claim because the official computer system was inoperative.

(6) In a case where the time for claiming a jobseeker's allowance is extended under paragraph (2) or (4), the claim is to be treated as made on the first day of the period in respect of which the claim is, by reason of the operation of those paragraphs, timeously made.

DEFINITIONS

"appropriate office"—see reg.2.
"claimant"—*ibid.*
"electronic communication"—*ibid.*
"jobseeker's allowance"—*ibid.*
"official computer system"—*ibid.*
"partner"—*ibid.*

Amendment of claim

4.37   **30.**—(1) A person who has made a claim for benefit may amend it at any time before a determination has been made on the claim by notice in writing received at an appropriate office, by telephone call to a telephone number specified by the Secretary of State or in such other manner as the Secretary of State may decide or accept.

(2) Any claim amended in accordance with paragraph (1) may be treated as if it had been so amended in the first instance.

DEFINITIONS

"benefit"—see reg.2.
"writing"—*ibid.*

Withdrawal of claim

4.38   **31.**—(1) A person who has made a claim for benefit may withdraw it at any time before a determination has been made on it by notice in writing received at an appropriate office, by telephone call to a telephone number specified by the Secretary of State or in such other manner as the Secretary of State may decide or accept.

(2) Any notice of withdrawal given in accordance with paragraph (1) has effect when it is received.

DEFINITION

"appropriate office"—see reg.2.

Advance claim for and award of universal credit

4.39   **32.**—(1) This regulation applies where—
(a) although a person does not satisfy the conditions of entitlement to universal credit on the date on which a claim is made, the Secretary of State is of the opinion that unless there is a change of circumstances that person will satisfy those conditions for a period beginning on a day not more than one month after the date on which the claim is made; and
(b) the case falls within a class for which Secretary of State accepts

advance claims or is a case where Secretary of State is otherwise willing to do so.

(2) The Secretary of State is to treat the claim as if made on the first day of that period.

(3) The Secretary of State may award universal credit accordingly, subject to the requirement that the person satisfies the conditions for entitlement on the first day of that period.

DEFINITION

"universal credit"—see reg.2.

GENERAL NOTE

Regulation 32 permits claims for universal credit to be made up to one month in advance.   4.40

Advance claim for and award of personal independence payment

33.—(1) Where, although a person does not satisfy the requirements for entitlement to personal independence payment on the date on which the claim is made, the Secretary of State is of the opinion that unless there is a change of circumstances the person will satisfy those requirements for a period beginning on a day ("the relevant day") not more than 3 months after the date on which the decision on the claim is made, the Secretary of State may award personal independence payment from the relevant day subject to the condition that the person satisfies the requirements for entitlement on the relevant day.   4.41

(2) A person who has an award of personal independence payment may make a further claim for personal independence payment during the period of 6 months immediately before the existing award expires.

(3) Where a person makes a claim in accordance with paragraph (2) the Secretary of State may—

 (a) treat the claim as if made on the first day after the expiry of the existing award; and

 (b) award personal independence payment accordingly, subject to the condition that the person satisfies the requirements for entitlement on that first day after the expiry of the existing award.

DEFINITION

"personal independence payment"—see reg.2.

Advance claim for and award of an employment and support allowance or a jobseeker's allowance

34. Where, although a person does not satisfy the requirements of entitlement to an employment and support allowance or a jobseeker's allowance on the date on which a claim is made, the Secretary of State is of the opinion that unless there is a change of circumstances that claimant will satisfy those requirements for a period beginning on a day ("the relevant day") not more than three months after the date on which the claim is made, then the Secretary of State may—   4.42

 (a) treat the claim as if made for a period beginning with the relevant day; and

(b) award an employment and support allowance or a jobseeker's allowance accordingly, subject to the condition that the person satisfies the requirements for entitlement when those benefits become payable under an award.

DEFINITIONS

"employment and support allowance"—see reg.2.
"jobseeker's allowance"—*ibid.*

Attendance in person

4.43   **35.** Except in a case where regulation 9 of the Personal Independence Payment Regulations applies, every person who makes a claim for benefit, other than a jobseeker's allowance, or any person entitled to benefit, other than a jobseeker's allowance, and any other person by whom, or on whose behalf, payments by way of such a benefit are receivable, must attend at such place and on such days and at such times as the Secretary of State may direct, for the purpose of supplying any information or evidence under regulations 37, 38, 39 and 41, if reasonably so required by the Secretary of State.

DEFINITIONS

"benefit"—see reg.2.
"jobseeker's allowance"—*ibid.*

Duration of awards

4.44   **36.**—(1) A claim for universal credit is to be treated as made for an indefinite period and any award of universal credit on that claim is to be made for an indefinite period.

(2) The provisions of Schedule 4 are to have effect in relation to claims for a jobseeker's allowance made during periods connected with public holidays.

GENERAL NOTE

4.45   Under para.(1), claims for universal credit are treated as made for an indefinite period and any award made is also for an indefinite period. However, this does not prevent the Secretary of State from revising the decision making the award, or from superseding that decision so as to change the award or bring it to an end if there is a subsequent change of circumstances. For revision and supersession of decisions about universal credit see ss.9 and 10 SSA 1998 and regs. 5–37 of the Decisions and Appeals Regulations 2013.

PART III

EVIDENCE, INFORMATION AND NOTIFICATION OF CHANGES OF
CIRCUMSTANCES

DEFINITION

"universal credit"—see reg.2.

Evidence and information in connection with a claim

37.—(1) Subject to regulation 8 of the Personal Independence Payment   **4.46**
Regulations, paragraphs (2) and (3) apply to a person who makes a claim
for benefit, other than a jobseeker's allowance, or on whose behalf a claim
is made.

(2) The Secretary of State may require the person to supply information
or evidence in connection with the claim, or any question arising out of it,
as the Secretary of State considers appropriate.

(3) The person must supply the Secretary of State with the information
or evidence in such manner as the Secretary of State determines within one
month of first being required to do so or such longer period as the Secretary
of State considers reasonable.

(4) Where joint claimants have made a claim for universal credit, information relating to that claim may be supplied by the Secretary of State to
either or both members of the couple for any purpose connected with the
claim.

(5) Where a person is a member of a couple and may make a claim as a
single person by virtue of regulation 3(3) (couples) of the Universal Credit
Regulations and entitlement to or the amount of any universal credit is or
may be affected by the circumstances of their partner, the Secretary of State
may require the partner to do any of the following, within one month of
being required to do so or such longer period as the Secretary of State may
consider reasonable—

(a) to confirm the information given about the partner's circumstances;
(b) to supply information or evidence in connection with the claim, or
     any question arising out of it, as the Secretary of State may require.

(6) The Secretary of State may require a landlord or a rent officer to
supply information or evidence in connection with a claim for universal
credit that may include in the calculation of an award an amount in respect
of housing costs, and any information or evidence so requested must be
supplied within one month of the request or such longer period as the
Secretary of State considers reasonable.

(7) Every person providing relevant childcare as defined in regulation
35 of the Universal Credit Regulations, in a case where the calculation of
a claimant's award of universal credit may include an amount in respect of
childcare costs under regulation 31 of those Regulations, must supply such
information or evidence in connection with the claim made by the claimant, or any question arising out of it, as may be required by the Secretary
of State, and must do so within one month of being required to do so or
such longer period as the Secretary of State may consider reasonable.

(8) In this regulation any reference to a person or joint claimants making
a claim for a benefit, other than a jobseeker's allowance, is to be interpreted
as including a person or joint claimants in a case where it is not a condition
of entitlement to benefit that a claim be made for it.

(9) In this regulation any reference to a claim for a benefit, other than a
jobseeker's allowance, is to be interpreted as including a potential award of
benefit in a case where it is not a condition of entitlement to benefit that a
claim be made for it.

DEFINITIONS

"the Personal Independence Payment Regulations"—see reg.2.
"the Universal Credit Regulations"—*ibid.*

"benefit"—*ibid.*
"claimant"—*ibid.*
"couple"—see reg.2 and WRA 2012 s.39.
"jobseeker's allowance"—see reg.2.
"partner"—*ibid.*
"personal independence payment"—*ibid.*
"universal credit"—see reg.2.

Evidence and information in connection with an award

4.47   **38.**—(1) This regulation, apart from paragraph (7), applies to any person entitled to benefit, other than a jobseeker's allowance, and any other person by whom, or on whose behalf, payments by way of such a benefit are receivable.

(2) Subject to regulation 8 of the Personal Independence Payment Regulations, a person to whom this regulation applies must supply in such manner as the Secretary of State may determine and within the period applicable under regulation 45(4)(a) of the Universal Credit, Personal Independence Payment, Jobseeker's Allowance and Employment and Support Allowance (Decisions and Appeals) Regulations 2013 such information or evidence as the Secretary of State may require for determining whether a decision on the award of benefit should be revised under section 9 of the Social Security Act 1998 or superseded under section 10 of that Act.

(3) A person to whom this regulation applies must supply in such manner and at such times as the Secretary of State may determine such information or evidence as the Secretary of State may require in connection with payment of the benefit awarded.

(4) A person to whom this regulation applies must notify the Secretary of State of any change of circumstances which the person might reasonably be expected to know might affect—

(a) the continuance of entitlement to benefit;
(b) the amount of benefit awarded; or
(c) the payment of benefit,

as soon as reasonably practicable after the change occurs.

(5) A notification of any change of circumstances under paragraph (4) must be given—

(a) in writing or by telephone (unless the Secretary of State determines in any case that notice must be given in a particular way or to accept notice given otherwise than in writing or by telephone); or
(b) in writing if in any class of case the Secretary of State requires written notice (unless the Secretary of State determines in any case to accept notice given otherwise than in writing),

and must be sent or delivered to, or received at, the appropriate office.

(6) Where universal credit has been awarded to joint claimants, information relating to that award may be supplied by the Secretary of State to either or both members of the couple for any purpose connected with that award.

(7) Every person providing relevant childcare as defined in regulation 35 of the Universal Credit Regulations, in a case where the claimant's award of universal credit includes an amount in respect of childcare costs under regulation 31 of those Regulations, must supply such information or evidence in connection with the award, or any question arising out of it, as

the Secretary of State may require, and must do so within one month of being required to do so or such longer period as the Secretary of State may consider reasonable.

(8) Where the calculation of an award of universal credit includes, by virtue of regulation 29 of the Universal Credit Regulations, an amount in respect of the fact that a claimant has regular and substantial caring responsibilities for a severely disabled person, the Secretary of State may require a person to whom this regulation applies to furnish a declaration signed by such severely disabled person confirming the particulars respecting the severely disabled person which have been given by that person.

DEFINITIONS

"the Universal Credit Regulations"—see reg.2.
"benefit"—*ibid.*
"claimant"—*ibid.*
"jobseeker's allowance"—*ibid.*
"personal independence payment"—*ibid.*
"regular and substantial caring responsibilities for a severely disabled person"—*ibid.*
"universal credit"—*ibid.*
"writing"—*ibid.*

Alternative means of notifying changes of circumstances

39. In such cases and subject to such conditions as the Secretary of State   4.48
may specify, the duty in regulation 38(4) to notify a change of circumstances may be discharged by notifying the Secretary of State as soon as reasonably practicable—

(a) where the change of circumstances is a birth or death, through a local authority, or a county council in England, by personal attendance at an office specified by that authority or county council, provided the Secretary of State has agreed with that authority or county council for it to facilitate such notification; or

(b) where the change of circumstances is a death, by telephone to a telephone number specified for that purpose by the Secretary of State.

DEFINITION

"local authority"—see reg.2.

Information to be provided to rent officers

40.—(1) The Secretary of State must provide to the rent officer such   4.49
information as the rent officer may reasonably require to carry out functions under section 122 of the Housing Act 1996.

(2) The information referred to in paragraph (1) may include information required to make a determination under the Rent Officers Order and may include—

(a) the name and address of a universal credit claimant in respect of whom the Secretary of State has applied for a determination;

(b) the amount of any rent (within the meaning of paragraph 2 of Schedule 1 to the Universal Credit Regulations) (meaning of payments in respect of accommodation);

(c) the amount of any service charge payments (within the meaning of paragraph 2 of Schedule 1 to the Universal Credit Regulations);

(d) the number of bedrooms in the accommodation in respect of which a determination is made;

(e) the name and address of a claimant's landlord.

(3) A landlord must provide to the rent officer such information or evidence as the rent officer may reasonably require to make a determination in accordance with the Rent Officers Order and which the rent officer is not able to obtain from the Secretary of State.

(4) The evidence referred to in paragraph (3) may include evidence as to whether a property is let at an Affordable Rent within the meaning in Schedule 2 to the Rent Officers Order.

(5) In this regulation and regulation 37 "landlord" means any person to whom a claimant or partner is liable to make payments in respect of the occupation of the claimant's accommodation.

(6) In this regulation "the Rent Officers Order" means the Rent Officer (Universal Credit Functions) Order 2013.

DEFINITIONS

"the Universal Credit Regulations"—see reg.2.
"claimant"—*ibid.*
"universal credit"—*ibid.*

Evidence and information required from pension fund holders

4.50

41.—(1) Where a claimant or the claimant's partner is aged not less than 60 and is a member of, or a person deriving entitlement to a pension under a personal pension scheme or an occupational pension scheme, such a person must, where the Secretary of State so requires, furnish the following information—

(a) the name and address of the pension fund holder;

(b) such other information including any reference or policy number as is needed to enable the personal pension scheme or occupational pension scheme to be identified.

(2) Where the pension fund holder receives from the Secretary of State a request for details concerning the personal pension scheme or occupational pension scheme relating to a person to whom paragraph (1) refers, the pension fund holder must provide the Secretary of State with any information to which the following paragraph refers.

(3) The information to which this paragraph refers is—

(a) where the purchase of an annuity under a personal pension scheme or occupational pension scheme has been deferred, the amount of any income which is being withdrawn from the personal pension scheme or occupational pension scheme;

(b) in the case of—

    (i) a personal pension scheme or occupational pension scheme where income withdrawal is available, the maximum amount of income which may be withdrawn from the scheme; or

    (ii) a personal pension scheme or occupational pension scheme where income withdrawal is not available, the maximum amount of income which might be withdrawn from the fund if the fund were held under a personal pension scheme or occupational pension scheme where income withdrawal was available, calculated by or on behalf of the pension fund holder by means of tables prepared from time to time by the Government Actuary which are appropriate for this purpose.

(4) In this regulation any reference to a claimant is to be interpreted as including a person in a case where it is not a condition of entitlement to benefit that a claim be made for it.

(5) This regulation does not apply to a person claiming personal independence payment.

(6) In this regulation—

(a) "pension fund holder" means with respect to a personal pension scheme or an occupational pension scheme, the trustees, managers or scheme administrators of the scheme concerned;

(b) "personal pension scheme" means—

(i) a personal pension scheme as defined by section 1 of the Pension Schemes Act 1993;

(ii) an annuity contract or trust scheme approved under section 620 or 621 of the Income and Corporation Taxes Act 1988 or a substituted contract within the meaning of section 622(3) of that Act which is treated as having become a registered pension scheme by virtue of paragraph 1(1)(f) of Schedule 36 to the Finance Act 2004;

(iii) a personal pension scheme approved under Chapter 4 of Part 14 of the Income and Corporation Taxes Act 1988 which is treated as having become a registered pension scheme by virtue of paragraph 1(1)(g) of Schedule 36 to the Finance Act 2004;

(c) "occupational pension" means any pension or other periodical payment under an occupational pension scheme but does not include any discretionary payment out of a fund established for relieving hardship in particular cases.

DEFINITIONS

"claimant"—see reg. 2.
"partner"—*ibid.*

Notification for purposes of sections 111A and 112 of the Administration Act

42. Regulations 43 to 44 below prescribe the person to whom, and manner in which, a change of circumstances must be notified for the purposes of sections 111A(1A) to (1G) and 112(1A) to (1F) of the Administration Act (offences relating to failure to notify a change of circumstances).   4.51

DEFINITION

"the Administration Act"—see reg. 2.

Notification of changes of circumstances affecting a jobseeker's allowance or an employment and support allowance for purposes of sections 111A and 112 of the Administration Act

43.—(1) Subject to paragraphs (2) and (3), where the benefit affected by the change of circumstances is a jobseeker's allowance or an employment and support allowance, notice must be given to the Secretary of State at the appropriate office—   4.52

(a) in writing or by telephone (unless the Secretary of State determines in any case that notice must be in writing or may be given otherwise than in writing or by telephone); or

(b) in writing if in any class of case the Secretary of State requires written notice (unless the Secretary of State determines in any case to accept notice given otherwise than in writing).

(2) Where the notice in writing referred to in paragraph (1) is given or sent by an electronic communication that notice must be given or sent in accordance with the provisions set out in Schedule 2 to these Regulations (electronic communications).

(3) In such cases and subject to such conditions as the Secretary of State may specify, the duty in regulation 38(4) of these Regulations or regulation 31(4) of the Jobseeker's Allowance Regulations to notify a change of circumstances may be discharged by notifying the Secretary of State as soon as reasonably practicable—

(a) where the change of circumstances is a birth or death, through a local authority, or a county council in England, by personal attendance at an office specified by that authority or county council, provided the Secretary of State has agreed with that authority or county council for it to facilitate such notification; or

(b) where the change of circumstances is a death, by telephone to a telephone number specified for that purpose by the Secretary of State.

DEFINITIONS

"the Jobseeker's Allowance Regulations"—see reg.2.
"appropriate office"—*ibid.*
"benefit"—*ibid.*
"electronic communication"—*ibid.*
"employment and support allowance"—*ibid.*
"jobseeker's allowance"—*ibid.*
"writing"—*ibid.*

Notification of changes of circumstances affecting personal independence payment or universal credit for purposes of sections 111A and 112 of the Administration Act

4.53   **44.**—(1) Subject to paragraphs (2) and (3), where the benefit affected by the change of circumstances is personal independence payment or universal credit, notice must be given to the Secretary of State ("S") at the appropriate office—

(a) in writing or by telephone (unless S determines in any case that notice must be in writing or may be given otherwise than in writing or by telephone); or

(b) in writing if in any class of case S requires written notice (unless S determines in any case to accept notice given otherwise than in writing).

(2) Where the notice in writing referred to in paragraph (1) is given or sent by an electronic communication that notice must be given or sent in accordance with the provisions set out in Schedule 2 to these Regulations (electronic communications).

(3) In such cases and subject to such conditions as the Secretary of State may specify, the duty in regulation 38(4) to notify a change of circum-

stances may be discharged by notifying the Secretary of State as soon as reasonably practicable—

(a) where the change of circumstances is a birth or death, through a local authority, or a county council in England, by personal attendance at an office specified by that authority or county council, provided the Secretary of State has agreed with that authority or county council for it to facilitate such notification; or

(b) where the change of circumstances is a death, by telephone to a telephone number specified for that purpose by the Secretary of State.

DEFINITIONS

"the Administration Act"—see reg.2.
"electronic communication"—*ibid.*
"local authority"—*ibid.*
"personal independence payment"—*ibid.*
"universal credit"—*ibid.*
"writing"—*ibid.*

GENERAL NOTE

SSAA ss.111A(1A) to (1F) and 112(1A) to (1D) create various offences where a person "fails to give a prompt notification of [a change of circumstances] in the prescribed manner to the prescribed person". The main difference between the two sections is that offences under s.111A require proof of dishonesty whereas those under s.112 do not. Regulation 44 provides that the "prescribed person" to whom notice must be given is the Secretary of State and that the "prescribed manner" of giving notice is as set out in paras (1)–(3). The general rule (para.(1)) is that notice may be given by telephone or in writing unless the Secretary of State requires notice to be given in writing. That is subject to the special rules about reporting births and deaths in para.(3). Written notices that are "given or sent by an electronic communication" (i.e., by email and, when the technology permits, online) must satisfy the rules in Sch.2 (para.(2)).

4.54

PART IV

PAYMENTS

Time of payment: general provision

45. Subject to the other provisions of this Part, benefit is to be paid in accordance with an award as soon as is reasonably practicable after the award has been made.

4.55

DEFINITION

"benefit"—see reg.2.

Direct credit transfer

46.—(1) The Secretary of State may arrange for benefit to be paid by way of direct credit transfer into a bank or other account—

4.56

(a) in the name of the person entitled to benefit, the person's partner, a person appointed under regulation 57(1) or a person referred to in regulation 57(2);

    (b) in the joint names of the person entitled to benefit and the person's partner;

    (c) in the joint names of the person entitled to benefit and a person appointed under regulation 57(1) or a person referred to in regulation 57(2); or

    (d) in the name of such persons as are mentioned in regulation 57(2).

(2) A Jobseeker's Allowance or an Employment and Support Allowance are to be paid in accordance with paragraph (1) within seven days of the last day of each successive period of entitlement.

DEFINITIONS

"benefit"—see reg.2.
"partner"—*ibid.*

Payment of universal credit

4.57

47.—(1) Universal credit is payable monthly in arrears in respect of each assessment period unless in any case or class of case the Secretary of State arranges otherwise.

(2) Where universal credit is to be paid in accordance with regulation 46, it is to be paid within seven days of the last day of the assessment period but if it is not possible to pay universal credit within that period of seven days, it is to be paid as soon as reasonably practicable thereafter.

(3) In respect of an award of universal credit which is the subject of an arrangement for payment under regulation 46, the Secretary of State may make a particular payment by credit transfer otherwise than is provided by paragraph (2), if it appears to the Secretary of State appropriate to do so for the purpose of—

    (a) paying any arrears of benefit; or

    (b) making a payment in respect of a terminal period of an award or for any similar purpose.

(4) Where the Secretary of State has arranged for universal credit to be paid in accordance with regulation 46, joint claimants may nominate a bank or other account into which that benefit is to be paid.

(5) Where joint claimants of universal credit have not nominated a bank or other account into which that benefit is to be paid, the Secretary of State may nominate a bank or other account.

(6) The Secretary of State may, in any case where the Secretary of State considers it is in the interests of—

    (a) the claimants;

    (b) a child or a qualifying young person for whom one or both of the claimants are responsible; or

    (c) a severely disabled person, where the calculation of an award of universal credit includes, by virtue of regulation 29 of the Universal Credit Regulations, an amount in respect of the fact that a claimant has regular and substantial caring responsibilities for that severely disabled person,

arrange that universal credit payable in respect of joint claimants be paid wholly to only one member of the couple or be split between the couple in such proportion as the Secretary of State considers appropriate.

(7) Where a superseding decision takes effect in accordance with paragraph 26 of Schedule 1 to the Universal Credit, Personal Independence Payment, Jobseeker's Allowance and Employment and Support Allowance

(Decisions and Appeals) Regulations 2013, the amount payable in respect of that last assessment period is to be calculated as follows—

$$N \times \left(\frac{A \times 12}{365} \right)$$

where N is the number of days in the period and A is the amount calculated in relation to that period as if it were an assessment period of one month.

DEFINITIONS

"assessment period"—see reg.2 and Universal Credit Regs reg.21.
"benefit"—see reg.2.
"child"—see reg.2 and WRA 2012 s.40.
"couple"—see reg.2 and WRA 2012 s.39.
"employment and support allowance"—see reg.2.
"jobseeker's allowance"—*ibid.*
"qualifying young person"—*ibid.*
"regular and substantial caring responsibilities for a severely disabled person"—*ibid.*
"universal credit"—*ibid.*

GENERAL NOTE

Regulation 47 contains important rules about the payment of universal credit.

4.58

Para. (1)
Universal credit is normally paid monthly in arrears after the end of the relevant assessment period. This is in contrast to the rules for income support, income-based JSA and income-related ESA. The change in policy is linked to the provisions under which earned income for each assessment period is taken to be the amount reported to HMRC by the claimant's (or claimants') employers. Monthly payment in arrears after the end of the assessment period is intended to ensure that no payment is made until after changes in circumstances relating to earned income have been reported and that overpayments will be reduced.

Paras (2) to (5)
These apply where universal credit is paid by direct transfer under reg.46 which will be the usual method of payment. They are largely administrative. However, the rule in para.(2) that payment by direct transfer must be paid within seven days of the last day of the assessment period or as soon as reasonably practicable thereafter will be important to claimants.

Para. (6)
Allows the Secretary of State pay universal credit to one of two joint claimants or to split that payment between them in the circumstances specified. See also reg.58(1).

Para. (7)
Changes of circumstance relating to universal credit normally take effect from the first day of the assessment period in which they occur. However, Sch.1, para.26 of the Decisions and Appeals Regulations 2013 provides that where a claimant reaches the qualifying age for state pension credit during an assessment period and has made an advance claim for SPC, the change in circumstances takes effect when it occurs. In those circumstances, it is necessary to make a payment which covers less than a full assessment period and para.(7) specifies how that payment is to be calculated. The rule is the same as that which applies under reg.21(6) of the Universal Credit Regulations where a payment has to be made covering less than

a full assessment period because the time limit for claiming has been extended and entitlement therefore begins before the date of claim.

Payment of personal independence payment

4.59   **48.**—(1) Subject to the following provisions of this regulation and regulation 50, personal independence payment is to be paid at intervals of four weeks in arrears.

(2) In the case of any person to whom section 82 of the 2012 Act(terminal illness) applies, the Secretary of State may arrange that personal independence payment is to be paid at intervals of one week in advance.

(3) Where the amount of personal independence payment payable is less than £5.00 a week the Secretary of State may arrange that it is to be paid in arrears at such intervals as may be specified not exceeding 12 months.

DEFINITION

"personal independence payment"—see reg.2.

Days for payment of personal independence payment

4.60   **49.**—(1) Subject to the following provisions of this regulation, a personal independence payment is payable on the day of the week on which the Secretary of State makes a decision to award that benefit, except that where that decision is made on a Saturday or a Sunday the benefit is to be paid on such day of the week as the Secretary of State may direct in any case.

(2) The Secretary of State may, in any case or class of case, arrange that personal independence payment or any part of it be paid on any day of the week.

(3) Where personal independence payment is in payment to any person and the day on which it is payable is changed, it is to be paid at a daily rate of 1/7th of the weekly rate in respect of any of the days for which payment would have been made but for that change.

(4) Where there is a change in the amount of any personal independence payment payable, or where entitlement to personal independence payment ends, and these events do not occur on the day of the week referred to in paragraph (1) or (2), personal independence payment is to be paid at a daily rate of 1/7th of the weekly rate.

DEFINITIONS

"benefit"—see reg.2.
"personal independence payment"—*ibid.*

Payment of personal independence payment at a daily rate between periods in hospital or other accommodation

4.61   **50.**—(1) Personal independence payment is to be paid in respect of any person, for any day falling within a period to which paragraph (2) applies, at the daily rate (which is to be equal to 1/7th of the weekly rate) and personal independence payment payable in pursuance of this regulation is to be paid weekly or as the Secretary of State may direct in any case.

(2) This paragraph applies to any period which is not a period of residence—

(a) but which commences immediately following such a period; and

(b) on the first day of which it is expected that, before the expiry of the term of 28 days beginning with that day, the person will commence another period of residence.

(3) Where paragraph (2) applies, the period referred to in that paragraph is to end—

(a) at the expiry of the term of 28 days beginning with the first day of the period referred to in that paragraph; or

(b) if earlier, on the day before the day which is the first day of a period of residence.

(4) In this regulation a "period of residence" means a period of residence where—

(a) the person is a resident of a care home, as defined in section 85(3) of the 2012 Act, and no amount of personal independence payment which is attributable to the daily living component is payable in respect of the person by virtue of regulation 28(1) of the Personal Independence Payment Regulations; or

(b) the person is undergoing medical or other treatment as an in-patient at a hospital or similar institution and no amount of personal independence payment which is attributable to the daily living component or the mobility component is payable in respect of the person by virtue of regulation 29 of the Personal Independence Payment Regulations,

and such period is to be deemed to begin on the day after the day on which the person enters the care home, hospital or similar institution and to end on the day before the day on which the person leaves the care home, hospital or similar institution.

DEFINITIONS

"the 2012 Act"—see reg.2.
"the Personal Independence Payment Regulations"—*ibid.*
"personal independence payment"—*ibid.*

Payment of an employment and support allowance

51.—(1) Subject to paragraphs (3) to (8), an employment and support allowance paid in accordance with regulation 46 is to be paid fortnightly in arrears on the day of the week determined in accordance with paragraph (2).

4.62

(2) The day specified for the purposes of paragraph (1) is the day in column (2) which corresponds to the series of numbers in column (1) which includes the last two digits of the claimant's national insurance number—

(1)	(2)
00 to 19	Monday
20 to 39	Tuesday
40 to 59	Wednesday
60 to 79	Thursday
80 to 99	Friday

(3) The Secretary of State may, in any case or class of case, arrange that the claimant be paid otherwise than fortnightly.

(4) In respect of an award of an employment and support allowance which is the subject of an arrangement for payment under regulation 46, the Secretary of State may make a particular payment by credit transfer otherwise than as provided by paragraph (1), if it appears to the Secretary of State appropriate to do so for the purpose of—
  (a) paying any arrears of benefit; or
  (b) making a payment in respect of a terminal period of an award or for any similar purpose.

(5) The Secretary of State may, in any case or class of case, arrange that an employment and support allowance be paid on any day of the week and where it is in payment to any person and the day on which it is payable is changed, it is to be paid at a daily rate of 1/7th of the weekly rate in respect of any of the days for which payment would have been made but for that change.

(6) Where the weekly amount of an employment and support allowance is less than £1.00 it may be paid in arrears at intervals of not more than 13 weeks.

(7) Where the weekly amount of an employment and support allowance is less than 10 pence that allowance is not payable.

(8) Where an employment and support allowance is normally payable in arrears and the day on which that benefit is payable by reason of paragraph (2) is affected by office closure, it may for that benefit week be paid wholly in advance or partly in advance and partly in arrears and on such day as the Secretary of State may direct.

(9) Where under paragraph (8) an employment and support allowance is paid either in advance or partly in advance and partly in arrears it is for any other purposes to be treated as if it were paid in arrears.

(10) For the purposes of paragraph (8), "benefit week" means a period of seven days beginning or ending with such day as the Secretary of State may direct.

(11) For the purposes of paragraph (8), "office closure" means a period during which an appropriate office is closed in connection with a public holiday.

(12) For the purposes of paragraph (11), "public holiday" means—
  (a) in England and Wales, Christmas Day, Good Friday or a bank holiday under the Banking and Financial Dealings Act 1971;
  (b) in Scotland, a bank holiday under the Banking and Financial Dealings Act 1971 or a local holiday.

DEFINITIONS

  "appropriate office"—see reg.2.
  "benefit"—*ibid.*
  "claimant"—*ibid.*
  "employment and support allowance"—*ibid.*

Payment of a jobseeker's allowance

4.63   **52.**—(1) Subject to paragraphs (2) to (4), a jobseeker's allowance paid in accordance with regulation 46 is to be paid fortnightly in arrears unless in any case or class of case the Secretary of State arranges otherwise.

(2) In respect of an award of a jobseeker's allowance which is the subject of an arrangement for payment under regulation 46, the Secretary of State

may make a particular payment by credit transfer otherwise than as provided by paragraph (1), if it appears to the Secretary of State appropriate to do so for the purpose of—

(a) paying any arrears of benefit; or

(b) making a payment in respect of a terminal period of an award or for any similar purpose.

(3) Where the amount of a jobseeker's allowance is less than £1.00 a week the Secretary of State may direct that it is to be paid at such intervals, not exceeding 13 weeks, as may be specified in the direction.

(4) Where a jobseeker's allowance is normally payable in arrears and the day on which that benefit is normally payable is affected by office closure, it may for that benefit week be paid wholly in advance or partly in advance and partly in arrears and on such day as the Secretary of State may direct.

(5) Where under paragraph (4) a jobseeker's allowance is paid either in advance or partly in advance and partly in arrears it is for any other purposes to be treated as if it were paid in arrears.

(6) For the purposes of paragraph (4), "benefit week" means a period of seven days ending with a day determined in accordance with the definition of that term in regulation 2(2) (general interpretation) of the Jobseeker's Allowance Regulations.

(7) For the purposes of paragraph (4), "office closure" means a period during which an appropriate office is closed in connection with a public holiday.

(8) For the purposes of paragraph (7), "public holiday" means—

(a) in England and Wales, Christmas Day, Good Friday or a bank holiday under the Banking and Financial Dealings Act 1971;

(b) in Scotland, a bank holiday under the Banking and Financial Dealings Act 1971 or a local holiday.

DEFINITIONS

"benefit"—see reg.2.
"jobseeker's allowance"—*ibid.*

Fractional amounts of benefit

53. Where the amount of any benefit payable would, but for this regulation, include a fraction of a penny, that fraction is to be disregarded if it is less than half a penny and is otherwise to be treated as a penny.   **4.64**

DEFINITION

"benefit"—see reg.2.

Payment to persons under age 18

54. Where a benefit is paid to a person under the age of 18, a direct credit transfer under regulation 46 into any such person's account, or the receipt by the person of a payment made by some other means, is sufficient discharge for the Secretary of State.   **4.65**

Extinguishment of right to payment if payment is not obtained within the prescribed period

4.66   **55.**—(1) The right to payment of any sum by way of benefit is to be extinguished where payment of that sum is not obtained within the period of 12 months from the date on which the right is treated as having arisen.

(2) For the purposes of this regulation, the right to payment of any sum by way of benefit is to be treated as having arisen—

(a) where notice is given or sent that the sum contained in the notice is ready for collection, on the date of the notice or, if more than one such notice is given or sent, the date of the first such notice;

(b) in relation to any such sum which the Secretary of State has arranged to be paid by means of direct credit transfer in accordance with regulation 46 into a bank or other account, on the due date for payment of the sum or in the case of universal credit on the date of payment of the sum; or

(c) in relation to any such sum to which neither sub-paragraph (a) or (b) applies, on such date as the Secretary of State determines.

(3) The giving or sending of a notice under paragraph (2)(a) is effective for the purposes of that paragraph, even where the sum contained in that notice is more or less than the sum which the person concerned has the right to receive.

(4) Where a question arises whether the right to payment of any sum by way of benefit has been extinguished by the operation of this regulation and the Secretary of State is satisfied that—

(a) the Secretary of State first received written notice requesting payment of that sum after the expiration of 12 months from the date on which the right is treated as having arisen;

(b) from a day within that period of 12 months and continuing until the day the written notice was given, there was good cause for not giving the notice; and

(c) no payment has been made under the provisions of regulation 46 (direct credit transfer),

the period of 12 months is extended to the date on which the Secretary of State decides that question, and this regulation is to apply accordingly as though the right to payment had arisen on that date.

(5) This regulation applies to a person appointed under regulation 57(1) to act on behalf of a claimant or a person referred to in regulation 57(2) as it applies to a claimant.

DEFINITIONS

"benefit"—see reg.2.
"claimant"—*ibid.*

Payments on death

4.67   **56.**—(1) On the death of a person who has made a claim for benefit, the Secretary of State may appoint such person as the Secretary of State thinks fit to proceed with the claim and any related issue of revision, supersession or appeal under the Social Security Act 1998.

(2) Subject to paragraphs (6) and (7), any sum payable by way of benefit which is payable under an award on a claim proceeded with under para-

graph (1) may be paid or distributed by the Secretary of State to or amongst persons over the age of 16 claiming as personal representatives, legatees, next of kin or creditors of the deceased and the provisions of regulation 55 (extinguishment of right to payment if payment is not obtained within the prescribed period) are to apply to any such payment or distribution.

(3) Subject to paragraphs (2), (6) and (7), any sum payable by way of benefit to the deceased, payment of which the deceased had not obtained at the date of the deceased's death, may, unless the right to payment was already extinguished at that date, be paid or distributed to or amongst any persons mentioned in paragraph (2), and regulation 55 is to apply to any such payment or distribution, except that, for the purpose of that regulation, the period of 12 months is to be calculated from the date on which the right to payment of any sum is treated as having arisen in relation to any such person and not from the date on which that right is treated as having arisen in relation to the deceased.

(4) A direct credit transfer under regulation 46 into an account in the name of any person mentioned in paragraph (2), or the receipt by such a person of a payment made by some other means, is sufficient discharge for the Secretary of State for any sum so paid.

(5) Where the Secretary of State is satisfied that any sum payable by way of benefit under paragraph (2) or (3), or part of it, is needed for the well-being of any person under the age of 16, the Secretary of State may obtain sufficient discharge for it by paying the sum or part of it to a person over that age who satisfies the Secretary of State that that person will apply the sum so paid for the well-being of the person under the age of 16.

(6) Paragraphs (2) and (3) are not to apply in any case unless written application for the payment of any sum is made to the Secretary of State within 12 months from the date of the deceased's death or within such longer period as the Secretary of State may allow in any case.

(7) The Secretary of State may dispense with strict proof of the title of any person claiming in accordance with the provisions of this regulation.

(8) In paragraph (2) "next of kin" means—

(a) in England and Wales, the persons who would take beneficially on an intestacy;

(b) in Scotland, the persons entitled to the moveable estate of the deceased on intestacy.

DEFINITION

"benefit"—see reg. 2.

PART V

THIRD PARTIES

Persons unable to act

57.—(1) Where a person ("P1") is, or may be, entitled to benefit (whether or not a claim for benefit has been made by P1 or on P1's behalf) but P1 is unable for the time being to act, the Secretary of State may, if all

4.68

the conditions in paragraph (2) and the additional conditions in paragraph (3) are met, appoint a person ("P2") to carry out the functions set out in paragraph (4).

(2) The conditions are that—

(a) no deputy has been appointed by the Court of Protection under Part 1 of the Mental Capacity Act 2005;

(b) no receiver has been appointed under Part 7 of the Mental Health Act 1983 who is treated as a deputy by virtue of the Mental Capacity Act 2005 with power to claim or receive benefit on P1's behalf;

(c) no attorney with a general power, or a power to claim or receive benefit, has been appointed by P1 under the Powers of Attorney Act 1971, the Enduring Powers of Attorney Act 1985, the Mental Capacity Act 2005 or otherwise; and

(d) in Scotland, P1's estate is not being administered by a judicial factor or any guardian acting or appointed under the Adults with Incapacity (Scotland) Act 2000 who has power to claim or receive benefit on P1's behalf.

(3) The additional conditions are that—

(a) P2 has made a written application to the Secretary of State to be appointed; and

(b) if P2 is a natural person, P2 is over the age of 18.

(4) The functions are exercising on behalf of P1 any right to which P1 may be entitled and receiving and dealing on behalf of P1 with any sums payable to P1.

(5) Anything required by these Regulations to be done by or in relation to P1 may be done by or in relation to P2 or any person mentioned in paragraph (2).

(6) Where a person has been appointed under regulation 82(3) of the Housing Benefit Regulations 2006 by a relevant authority within the meaning of those Regulations to act on behalf of another in relation to a benefit claim or award, the Secretary of State may, if the person so appointed agrees, treat that person as if the Secretary of State had appointed that person under paragraph (1).

(7) A direct credit transfer under regulation 46 into the account of P2 or any person mentioned in paragraph (2), or the receipt by such a person of a payment made by some other means, is sufficient discharge for the Secretary of State for any sum paid.

(8) An appointment under paragraph (1) or (6) comes to an end if—

(a) the Secretary of State at any time revokes it;

(b) P2 resigns P2's office having given one month's notice in writing to the Secretary of State of an intention to do so; or

(c) the Secretary of State is notified that any condition in paragraph (2) is no longer met.

DEFINITION

"benefit"—see reg.2.

Payment to another person on the claimant's behalf

4.69   **58.**—(1) The Secretary of State may direct that universal credit be paid wholly or in part to another person on the claimant's behalf if this appears to the Secretary of State necessary to protect the interests of—

(a) the claimant;

(b) their partner;
(c) a child or qualifying young person for whom the claimant or their partner or both are responsible; or
(d) a severely disabled person, where the calculation of the award of universal credit includes, by virtue of regulation 29 of the Universal Credit Regulations, an amount in respect of the fact that the claimant has regular and substantial caring responsibilities for that severely disabled person.

(2) The Secretary of State may direct that personal independence payment be paid wholly to another person on the claimant's behalf if this appears to the Secretary of State necessary to protect the interests of the claimant.

DEFINITIONS

"the Universal Credit Regulations"—see reg.2.
"claimant"—*ibid.*
"partner"—*ibid.*
"regular and substantial caring responsibilities for a severely disabled person"—*ibid.*
"universal credit"—*ibid.*

GENERAL NOTE

Para. (1)
Universal credit may be paid to third parties in the specified circumstances.   **4.70**

Direct payment to lender of deductions in respect of interest on secured loans

59. Schedule 5 has effect where section 15A(1) of the Administration Act   **4.71** (payment out of benefit of sums in respect of mortgage interest etc.) applies in relation to a case where a claimant is entitled to universal credit.

GENERAL NOTE

Where an award of universal credit includes the housing costs element based on   **4.72** loan interest payments, that part of the award will normally be paid directly to the lender under the provisions of Sch.5.

Deductions which may be made from benefit and paid to third parties

60. Except as provided for in regulation 59 and Schedule 5, deduc-   **4.73** tions may be made from benefit and direct payments may be made to third parties on behalf of a claimant in accordance with the provisions of Schedule 6 and Schedule 7.

DEFINITIONS

"benefit"—see reg.2.
"claimant"—*ibid.*
"personal independence payment"—*ibid.*

GENERAL NOTE

4.74   Regulation 60 gives effect to Schs 6 and 7. Under Sch.6, the Secretary of State may make deductions from certain benefits (including universal credit) and pay them to third parties where the claimant is in arrears of mortgage payments, rent or service charge, charges for fuel, water charges, or the payments due under certain loans. It also allows deductions to be made in respect of payments in lieu of child support due under s.43 Child Support Act 1991 and reg.28 Child Support (Maintenance Assessments and Special Cases) Regulations 1992, and to recover integration loans made to refugees.

Under Sch.7, deductions from universal credit may be made to enforce payment of child support maintenance due under the Child Support Act 1991. Deductions under that schedule are then paid to the person with care of the qualifying child.

PART VI

MOBILITY COMPONENT OF PERSONAL INDEPENDENCE PAYMENT

Cases where mobility component of personal independence payment not payable

4.75   **61.**—(1) Subject to the following provisions of this regulation, personal independence payment by virtue of entitlement to the mobility component is not payable to any person who would otherwise be entitled to it during any period in respect of which that person has received, or is receiving, any payment—

   (a) by way of grant under section 5 of, and paragraph 10 of Schedule 1 to, the National Health Service Act 2006, section 5 of, and paragraph 10 of Schedule 1 to, the National Health Service (Wales) Act 2006 or section 46 of the National Health Service (Scotland) Act 1978 towards the costs of running a private car;

   (b) of mobility supplement under—

      (i) the Naval, Military and Air Forces etc., (Disablement and Death) Service Pensions Order 2006;

      (ii) the Personal Injuries (Civilians) Scheme 1983; or

      (iii) the Order referred to in paragraph (i) by virtue of the War Pensions (Naval Auxiliary Personnel) Scheme 1964, the Pensions (Polish Forces) Scheme 1964, the War Pensions (Mercantile Marine) Scheme 1964 or an Order of Her Majesty in relation to the Home Guard dated 21st or 22nd December 1964 or in relation to the Ulster Defence Regiment dated 4th January 1971; or

   (c) out of public funds which the Secretary of State is satisfied is analogous to a payment under sub-paragraph (a) or (b).

(2) Paragraph (3) applies where a person in respect of whom personal independence payment is claimed for any period has received any such payment as is referred to in paragraph (1) for a period which, in whole or in part, covers the period for which personal independence payment is claimed.

(3) Such payment referred to in paragraph (1) is to be treated as an aggregate of equal weekly amounts in respect of each week in the period for which it is made and, where in respect of any such week a person is

treated as having a weekly amount so calculated which is less than the weekly rate of mobility component of personal independence payment to which, apart from paragraph (1), they would be entitled, any personal independence payment to which that person may be entitled for that week is to be payable at a weekly rate reduced by the weekly amount so calculated.

Payment of personal independence payment on behalf of a claimant (Motability)

62.—(1) This regulation applies where—
    (a) personal independence payment is payable in respect of a claimant by virtue of entitlement to the mobility component at the enhanced rate; and
    (b) under arrangements made or negotiated by Motability, an agreement has been entered into by or on behalf of the claimant for the hire or hire-purchase of a vehicle.

    (2) Where this regulation applies, the Secretary of State may arrange that any personal independence payment by virtue of entitlement to the mobility component at the enhanced rate be paid in whole or in part on behalf of the claimant in settlement of liability for payments due under the agreement mentioned in paragraph (1).

    (3) Subject to regulations 63 and 64, in the case of the hire of a vehicle, an arrangement made by the Secretary of State under paragraph (2) terminates—
    (a) where the vehicle is returned to the owner at or before the expiration of the term of hire or any agreed extension of the term of hire, on expiry of the period of the term or extended term;
    (b) where the vehicle is retained by or on behalf of the claimant with the owner's consent after the expiration of the term of hire or any agreed extension of the term of hire, on expiry of the period of the term or extended term; or
    (c) where the vehicle is retained by or on behalf of the claimant otherwise than with the owner's consent after the expiration of the term of hire or any agreed extension of the term of hire, or its earlier termination, on expiry of whichever is the longer of the following periods—
        (i) the period ending with the return of the vehicle to the owner; or
        (ii) the period of the term of hire or any agreed extension of the term of hire.

    (4) Subject to regulations 63 and 64 in the case of a hire-purchase agreement, an arrangement made by the Secretary of State under paragraph (2) terminates—
    (a) on the purchase of the vehicle; or
    (b) where the vehicle is returned to, or is repossessed by, the owner under the terms of the agreement before the completion of the purchase, at the end of the original period of the agreement.

    (5) In this regulation "Motability" means the company, set up under that name as a charity and originally incorporated under the Companies Act 1985 and subsequently incorporated by Royal Charter.

Power for the Secretary of State to terminate an arrangement (Motability)

4.76

63. The Secretary of State may terminate an arrangement under regulation 62(2) on such date as the Secretary of State decides—

(a) if requested to do so by the owner of the vehicle to which the arrangement relates; or

(b) if it appears to the Secretary of State that the arrangement is causing undue hardship to the claimant and that it should be terminated earlier than provided for by regulation 62(3) or (4).

Restriction on duration of arrangements by the Secretary of State (Motability) 64. The Secretary of State must terminate an arrangement under regulation 62(2) where the Secretary of State is satisfied that—

(a) the vehicle to which the arrangement relates has been returned to the owner; and

(b) the expenses of the owner arising out of the hire or hire-purchase agreement have been recovered following the return of the vehicle.

DEFINITIONS

"claimant"—see reg.2.
"personal independence payment"—*ibid.*

[¹ **Recovery of expenses**

4.77

62A.—(1) Paragraph 2 applies where—

(a) an agreement referred to in regulation 62(1)(b) has been entered into; and

(b) a relevant provider is receiving payments of personal independence payment in settlement of liability for payments due under that agreement.

(2) The Secretary of State may require the relevant provider to make payments to meet the reasonable expenses of the Secretary of State in administering the making of the payments of personal independence payment to the relevant provider.

(3) The method by which the expenses under paragraph (2) are to be met is for the Secretary of State to issue an invoice to the relevant provider setting out the expenses that have been incurred and for the relevant provider to pay the sum stated to the Secretary of State.

(4) The first invoice issued by the Secretary of State may recover expenses incurred between 21st July 2016 and the date of the invoice.

(5) Subsequently the Secretary of State may issue invoices no more frequently than annually and only in respect of expenses incurred since the period covered by the previous invoice.

(6) The expenses that the Secretary of State may take into account for the purposes of paragraph (2) include—

(a) the salaries and other costs relating to the employment of staff wholly engaged in the administering of the payments of personal independence payment and where staff have other responsibilities, an apportioned amount of those costs; and

(b) overheads, including rent and other shared costs, relating to those staff.

(7) In determining what expenses were reasonably incurred in administering the making of payments of personal independence payment to a relevant provider, the Secretary of State must have regard to any agreement between the Secretary of State and the relevant provider concerning the

level of service to be provided by the Secretary of State in the making of such payments to that relevant provider.]

AMENDMENT

1. Social Security (Expenses of Paying Sums in Relation to Vehicle Hire) Regulations 2016 (SI 2016/674) regs 4 and 5 9 (July 21, 2016).

Preamble

SCHEDULE 1

POWERS EXERCISED IN MAKING THESE REGULATIONS

1. The following provisions of the Administration Act—   **4.78**
  (a) section 1(1), (1C);
  (b) section 5(1)(a), (b), (c), (d), (g), (i), (j), (k), (l), (m), (p), (q), (1A), (2A), (2B), (2C), (3B);
  (c) section 7A(2)(b);
  (d) section 15A(2);
  (e) section 111A(1A)(d), (1B)(d), (1D)(c), (1E)(c);
  (f) section 112(1A)(d), (1B)(d), (1C)(c), (1D)(c);
  (g) section 189(1) and (5) to (6);
  (h) section 191.
2. Paragraph 7A of Schedule 2 to the Abolition of Domestic Rates etc. (Scotland) Act 1987.
3. Paragraph 6 of Schedule 4 to the Local Government Finance Act 1988.
4. Section 24(2)(b), (c) and (d) and section 30 of the Criminal Justice Act 1991.
5. Section 43(2) of the 1991 Act.
6. Paragraphs 1 and 6(2)(b) of Schedule 4 and paragraph 6 of Schedule 8 to, the Local Government Finance Act 1992.
7. Sections 32 and 92 of, and paragraph 3(1)(a), (b), (2)(a), (b) and (c) of Schedule 1 to the 2012 Act.

DEFINITIONS

"the Administration Act"—see reg. 2.
"electronic communication"—*ibid.*

Regulation 3

SCHEDULE 2

ELECTRONIC COMMUNICATIONS

PART I

USE OF ELECTRONIC COMMUNICATIONS

Use of electronic communications by the Secretary of State
1. The Secretary of State may use an electronic communication in connection with claims   **4.79**
for, and awards of, any benefit.

Conditions for the use of electronic communications by other persons
2.—(1) A person other than the Secretary of State may use an electronic communication in connection with the matters referred to in paragraph 1 if the conditions specified in sub-paragraphs (2) to (5) are satisfied.

(2) The first condition is that the person is for the time being permitted to use an electronic communication for the purpose in question by an authorisation given by means of a direction of the Secretary of State.

(3) The second condition is that the person uses an approved method of—
  (a) authenticating the identity of the sender of the communication where required to do so;

    (b) electronic communication;

    (c) authenticating any claim or information delivered by means of an electronic communication; and

    (d) subject to sub-paragraph (6), submitting any claim or information to the Secretary of State.

(4) The third condition is that any claim or information sent by means of an electronic communication is in an approved form.

(5) The fourth condition is that the person maintains such records as may be specified in a direction given by the Secretary of State.

(6) Where the person uses any method other than the method approved by the Secretary of State of submitting any claim or information, it is to be treated as not having been submitted.

(7) In this paragraph "approved" means approved by means of a direction given by the Secretary of State for the purposes of this Schedule.

Use of intermediaries

3. The Secretary of State may use intermediaries in connection with—

    (a) the delivery of any claim or information by means of an electronic communication; and

    (b) the authentication or security of anything transmitted by such means,

and may require other persons to use intermediaries in connection with those matters.

PART II

EVIDENTIAL PROVISIONS

Effect of delivering information by electronic communications

4.80   4.—(1) Any claim or information which is delivered by means of an electronic communication is to be treated as having been delivered in the manner or form required by any provision of these Regulations on the day on which the conditions imposed—

    (a) by this Schedule; and

    (b) by or under an applicable enactment (except to the extent that the condition thereby imposed is incompatible with this Schedule), are satisfied.

(2) The Secretary of State may, by a direction, determine that any claim or information is to be treated as delivered on a different day (whether earlier or later) from the day specified in sub-paragraph (1).

(3) Any claim or information is not to be taken to have been delivered to an official computer system by means of an electronic communication unless it is accepted by the system to which it is delivered.

Proof of delivery

4.81   5.—(1) The use of an approved method of electronic communication is to be presumed, unless the contrary is proved, to have resulted in delivery—

    (a) in the case of any claim or information falling to be delivered to the Secretary of State, if the delivery of that claim or information is recorded on an official computer system; or

    (b) in the case of any information that falls to be delivered by the Secretary of State, if the despatch of that information is recorded on an official computer system.

(2) The use of an approved method of electronic communication is to be presumed, unless the contrary is proved, not to have resulted in delivery—

    (a) in the case of any claim or information falling to be delivered to the Secretary of State, if the delivery of that claim or information is not recorded on an official computer system; or

    (b) in the case of information that falls to be delivered by the Secretary of State, if the despatch of that information is not recorded on an official computer system.

(3) The time and date of receipt of any claim or information sent by an approved method of electronic communication is to be presumed, unless the contrary is proved, to be that recorded on an official computer system.

Proof of identity

4.82   6.—(1) The identity of—

    (a) the sender of any claim or information delivered by means of an electronic communication to an official computer system; or

    (b) the recipient of any claim or information delivered by means of an electronic communication from an official computer system, is to be presumed, unless the contrary is proved, to be the person whose name is recorded as such on that official computer system.

(2) Any claim or information delivered by an approved method of electronic communication on behalf of another person ("P") is to be deemed to have been delivered by P unless P proves that it was delivered without P's knowledge or connivance.

Proof of content

7. The content of any claim or information sent by means of an electronic communication is to be presumed, unless the contrary is proved, to be that recorded on an official computer system.

DEFINITIONS

"electronic communication"—see reg.2.
"official computer system"—*ibid.*

Regulation 36(2)

SCHEDULE 4

SPECIAL PROVISIONS RELATING TO CLAIMS FOR A JOBSEEKER'S ALLOWANCE
DURING PERIODS CONNECTED WITH PUBLIC HOLIDAYS

1. In this Schedule and regulation 36(2)— **4.83**
    (a) "public holiday" means—
        (i) in England and Wales, Christmas Day, Good Friday or a bank holiday under the Banking and Financial Dealings Act 1971,
        (ii) in Scotland, a bank holiday under the Banking and Financial Dealings Act 1971 or a local holiday;
    (b) "Christmas and New Year holidays" means—
        (i) in England and Wales, the period beginning at the start of Christmas Day and terminating at the end of New Year's Day, or if New Year's Day is a Sunday at the end of 2nd January,
        (ii) in Scotland, the period beginning at the start of Christmas Day and terminating at the end of 2nd January, or where New Year's Day is a Saturday or a Sunday terminating at the end of 3rd January;
    (c) "Easter Holidays" means the period beginning at the start of Good Friday and terminating at the end of Easter Monday;
    (d) "office closure" means a period during which an appropriate office is closed in connection with a public holiday.
2. Where a claim for a jobseeker's allowance is made during any period set out in paragraph 3, the Secretary of State may treat that claim as a claim for a period, to be specified in a decision of the Secretary of State, not exceeding—
    (a) 35 days after the date of the claim where the claim is made during the period specified in sub-paragraph (a) of paragraph 3; or
    (b) 21 days after the date of claim where the claim is made during the period specified in either sub-paragraph (b) or (c) of paragraph 3.
3. For the purposes of paragraph 2 the periods are—
    (a) in the case of Christmas and New Year holidays, a period beginning with the start of the 35th day before the first day of office closure and terminating at the end of the last day of office closure;
    (b) in the case of Easter Holidays, a period beginning with the start of the 16th day before the first day of office closure and terminating at the end of the last day of office closure;
    (c) in the case of any other public holiday, a period beginning with the start of the 14th day before the first day of office closure and terminating at the end of the last day of office closure.

DEFINITIONS

"appropriate office"—see reg.2.
"jobseeker's allowance"—*ibid.*

SCHEDULE 5

DIRECT PAYMENT TO LENDER OF DEDUCTIONS IN RESPECT OF INTEREST ON
SECURED LOANS

Interpretation

4.84   1.—(1) In this Schedule—

"housing costs element" means an amount in respect of housing costs which is included in a claimant's award of universal credit under section 11(1) of the 2012 Act;

"qualifying lender" means (subject to paragraph 10)—

   (a) the bodies or persons listed in paragraphs (a) to (g) of section 15A(3) of the Administration Act;

   (b) the Regulator of Social Housing;

   (c) the Greater London Authority; and

   (d) any body incorporated under the Companies Act 1985, the main objects of which include the making of loans secured by—

      (i) a mortgage of or charge over land, or

      (ii) in Scotland a heritable security;

"loan interest payments" has the meaning given by paragraph 5 of Schedule 1 to the Universal Credit Regulations;

"relevant claimant" has the meaning given in paragraph 2(1);

"specified benefits", in relation to a relevant claimant, means the benefits specified in paragraph 2(2)—

   (a) to which the relevant claimant is entitled; or

   (b) where the relevant claimant is a member of a couple, to which the other member of the couple is entitled;

"standard rate" means the standard rate of interest determined under paragraph 12 of Schedule 5 to the Universal Credit Regulations.

(2) References in this Schedule to a relevant claimant who meets the payment condition or the liability condition are to a claimant who meets those conditions in accordance with regulation 25 of the Universal Credit Regulations (the housing costs element).

Relevant claimants and benefits from which payments are to be made

    2.—(1) For the purposes of this Schedule, "relevant claimant" means a claimant—

   (a) who is entitled to universal credit;

   (b) whose maximum amount for the purposes of universal credit includes the housing costs element; and

   (c) whose amount of housing costs element is calculated by reference to loan interest payments (whether or not that amount is calculated by reference to any other description of payment).

(2) Direct payments of loan interest may be made under paragraph 3 from any of the following benefits—

   (a) universal credit; and

   (b) if the maximum amount to which the relevant claimant is entitled for the purposes of universal credit is insufficient for the purposes of this Schedule—

      (i) a jobseeker's allowance, or

      (ii) an employment and support allowance.

Circumstances in which direct payments of loan interest to be made

4.85   3.—(1) If the circumstances set out in sub-paragraph (2) apply to a relevant claimant in respect of a loan, the Secretary of State is to pay part of the specified benefits directly to the qualifying lender to whom the loan interest payments in respect of the loan are payable.

(2) The circumstances are that—

   (a) a loan was made in respect of which loan interest payments are payable to a qualifying lender;

   (b) the relevant claimant (or either joint claimant) meets the payment condition and liability condition in respect of loan interest payments on the loan;

   (c) those payments are taken into account in calculating the amount of housing costs element to be included in the relevant claimant's award of universal credit; and

   (d) the amount included in respect of those payments is calculated by reference to the standard rate.

(3) The part of the specified benefits which is to be paid under sub-paragraph (1) is the amount calculated under paragraphs 4 and 5 in respect of the relevant claimant.

Determining the amount to be paid to a qualifying lender

4.—(1) Where the circumstances set out in paragraph 3(2) apply to a relevant claimant in respect of one loan only, the amount that is to be paid under paragraph 3 directly to the qualifying lender is to be calculated as follows. **4.86**

Step 1

Find the amount in respect of the loan interest payments which is calculated under paragraph 10 of Schedule 5 to the Universal Credit Regulations (amount in respect of interest on loans).

Step 2

Deduct from the amount resulting from step 1 a sum equivalent to so much of any amount payable in the circumstances described in sub-paragraph (2) as represents payments in respect of loan interest.

(2) This sub-paragraph applies where a payment is being made under a policy of insurance taken out by a relevant claimant to insure against the risk of not being able to maintain repayments of loan interest to a qualifying lender.

(3) The amount to be paid directly to the qualifying lender in respect of the relevant claimant is—

    (a) the amount resulting from sub-paragraph (1); or

    (b) where the aggregate amount of all of the specified benefits is less than the amount resulting from sub-paragraph (1), the aggregate amount of all those benefits less one penny.

Determining the amount to be paid to a qualifying lender: more than one loan

5.—(1) Where the circumstances set out in paragraph 3(2) apply to a relevant claimant in respect of more than one loan, the amount that is to be paid under paragraph 3 directly to each of the qualifying lenders to whom loan interest payments are payable is to be calculated as follows. **4.87**

(2) Where loan interest payments on two or more loans are payable to the same qualifying lender, the amount to be paid directly to that lender is found by—

    (a) in respect of each of those loans, calculating an amount in accordance with Steps 1 and 2 of paragraph 4(1); and

    (b) adding those amounts together.

(3) Where loan interest payments are payable to more than one qualifying lender, the amount to be paid directly to each lender is found by—

    (a) where loan interest payments are payable to a qualifying lender in respect of one loan only, calculating an amount in accordance with Steps 1 and 2 of paragraph 4(1) in respect of the loan;

    (b) where loan interest payments are payable to a qualifying lender in respect of more than one loan, calculating an amount in accordance with sub-paragraph (2).

(4) The amount to be paid directly to the qualifying lender in respect of the relevant claimant is—

    (a) the amount resulting from sub-paragraph (2) or (3) in respect of that lender; or

    (b) where the aggregate amount of all of the specified benefits is less than the sum of the amounts resulting from sub-paragraph (2) or (3), the amount determined under sub-paragraph (5).

(5) For the purposes of sub-paragraph (4)(b)—

    (a) the overall total of the amounts to be paid directly to the qualifying lenders is the aggregate amount of all of the specified benefits less one penny; and

    (b) that amount is to be paid directly to qualifying lenders as follows—

        (i) the qualifying lender in whose case the amount resulting from sub-paragraph (2) or (3) is the largest is to be paid first,

        (ii) if anything remains, the qualifying lender in whose case the amount resulting from sub-paragraph (2) or (3) is next largest is to be paid next, and so on until nothing remains.

(6) In the application of sub-paragraph (5)(b) in any case where the amount resulting from sub-paragraph (2) or (3) is the same in respect of two or more qualifying lenders, the available amount is to be divided equally between them.

Qualifying lenders to apply direct payments in discharge of borrower's liability

4.88   **6.** Where a direct payment is made under paragraph 3 to a qualifying lender in respect of a relevant claimant, the lender must apply the amount of the payment towards discharging the liability to make loan interest payments in respect of which the direct payment was made.

Application by qualifying lenders of any amount which exceeds liability

4.89   **7.**—(1) This paragraph applies where, in respect of a relevant claimant—

    (a) any direct payment is made under paragraph 3 to a qualifying lender; and

    (b) the amount paid exceeds the amount of the loan interest payments payable.

(2) Unless sub-paragraph (3) applies, the qualifying lender must apply the amount of the excess as follows—

    (a) first, towards discharging the amount of any liability of the relevant claimant for arrears of loan interest payments in respect of the loan in question; and

    (b) if any amount of the excess is then remaining, towards discharging any liability of the relevant claimant to repay—

        (i) the principal sum in respect of the loan, or

        (ii) any other sum payable by the relevant claimant to that lender in respect of the loan.

(3) Where loan interest payments on two or more loans are payable to the same qualifying lender, the lender must apply the amount of the excess as follows—

    (a) first, towards discharging the amount of any liability of the relevant claimant for arrears of loan interest payments in respect of the loan in respect of which the excess amount was paid; and

    (b) if any amount of the excess is then remaining, towards discharging any liability of the relevant claimant to repay—

        (i) in respect of the loan referred to in paragraph (a), the principal sum or any other sum payable by the relevant claimant to that lender, or

        (ii) in respect of any other loan, any sum payable by the relevant claimant to that lender where the liability to pay that sum has not already discharged under this Schedule.

Time and manner of payments

4.90   **8.** Direct payments under paragraph 3 are to be made in monthly instalments in arrears.

Fees payable by qualifying lenders

4.91   **9.**—(1) A fee is payable by a qualifying lender to the Secretary of State for the purpose of meeting the expenses of the Secretary of State in administering the making of direct payments to qualifying lenders under paragraph 3.

(2) The fee is [¹[² [³ [⁴ £0.39]]]] in respect of each occasion on which a direct payment is made to the qualifying lender.

Election not to be regarded as a qualifying lender

4.92   **10.**—(1) A body or person who would otherwise be within the definition of "qualifying lender" in paragraph 1(1)—

    (a) may elect not to be regarded as such by giving notice to the Secretary of State in writing; and

    (b) may revoke any such notice by giving a further notice in writing.

(2) In respect of any financial year, a notice under sub-paragraph (1) which is given not later than the 1st February before the start of the financial year takes effect on 1st April following the giving of the notice.

(3) Where a body or person becomes a qualifying lender in the course of a financial year—

    (a) any notice of an election by the body or person under sub-paragraph (1)(a) must be given within 6 weeks ("the initial period") of the date of their becoming a qualifying lender; and

    (b) no direct payments may be made under paragraph 3 to the body or person before the expiry of the initial period.

(4) But sub-paragraph (3)(b) does not apply in any case where—

    (a) the body or person gives the Secretary of State notice in writing that that provision should not apply; and

    (b) that notice is given before the start of the initial period or before that period expires.

(5) In relation to a notice under sub-paragraph (1)—

    (a) where the notice is given by an electronic communication, it must be given in accordance with the provisions set out in Schedule 2 (electronic communications);

    (b) where the notice is sent by post, it is to be treated as having been given on the day the notice was received.

Provision of information

11.—(1) A qualifying lender must, in respect of a relevant claimant, provide the Secretary of State with information as to—

   (a) the loan interest payments in respect of which the relevant claimant meets the payment condition and the liability condition;

   (b) the amount of the loan;

   (c) the purpose for which the loan was made;

   (d) the amount outstanding on the loan;

   (e) the amount of arrears of loan interest payments due in respect of the loan;

   (f) any change in the amount of the loan interest payable; and

   (g) the redemption of the loan.

(2) The information referred to in sub-paragraph (1)(a) to (e) must be provided at the request of the Secretary of State where—

   (a) a claim is made for universal credit; or

   (b) the housing costs element is to be included in an award of universal credit otherwise than on the making of a claim,

and loan interest payments payable to the qualifying lender are taken into account in determining the amount of the relevant claimant's housing costs element.

(3) The information referred to in sub-paragraph (1)(f) must be provided at such times, or in the case of the information referred to in sub-paragraph (1)(d) at such other times, as the Secretary of State may determine.

(4) The information referred to in sub-paragraph (1)(g) must be provided to the Secretary of State immediately once the qualifying lender has received notice that the loan is to be redeemed.

Recovery of sums wrongly paid

12.—(1) In the following circumstances, a qualifying lender must at the request of the Secretary of State repay any amount paid to the lender under paragraph 3 which ought not to have been paid.

(2) Those circumstances are that, in respect of a relevant claimant—

   (a) an amount calculated by reference to loan interest payments payable to the qualifying lender ceases to be included in the relevant claimant's housing costs element;

   (b) a specified benefit ceases to be paid to a relevant claimant;

   (c) the loan in respect of which loan interest payments are payable has been redeemed; or

   (d) both of the conditions set out in sub-paragraphs (3) and (4) are met.

(3) The first condition is that the amount of the relevant claimant's housing costs element is reduced as a result of—

   (a) the standard rate having been reduced; or

   (b) the amount outstanding on the loan having been reduced.

(4) The second condition is that no corresponding reduction was made to the amount calculated in respect of the qualifying lender under paragraph 4 or 5.

(5) A qualifying lender is not required to make a repayment in the circumstances described in sub-paragraph (2)(a) or (b) unless the Secretary of State's request is made before the end of the period of two months starting with the date on which the thing described in that provision ceased.

Amendment

   1. Social Security (Fees Payable by Qualifying Lenders) (Amendment) Regulations 2014 (SI 2014/485) reg.3 (April 1, 2014).

   2. Social Security (Fees Payable by Qualifying Lenders) (Amendment) Regulations 2015 (SI 2015/343) reg.3 (April 1, 2015).

   3. Social Security (Fees Payable by Qualifying Lenders) (Amendment) Regulations 2016 (SI 2016/228) reg.3 (April 1, 2016).

   4. Social Security (Fees Payable by Qualifying Lenders) (Amendment) Regulations 2017 (SI 2017/270) reg.3 (April 1, 2017).

Definitions

   "the 2012 Act"—see reg.2.
   "benefit"—*ibid.*
   "claimant"—*ibid.*
   "couple"—see reg.2 and WRA 2012, s.39.

"electronic communication"—see reg.2.
"universal credit"— *ibid.*
"the Universal Credit Regulations"—*ibid.*
"writing"—*ibid.*

GENERAL NOTE

4.95   From April 1, 2014 to March 31, 2015, the fee prescribed by para.9(2) was £0.40: see reg.3 of SI 2014/485. From April 1, 2015 to March 31, 2016, it was £0.46. Since April 1, 2017 it has been £0.39.

Regulation 60

SCHEDULE 6

DEDUCTIONS FROM BENEFIT AND DIRECT PAYMENT TO THIRD PARTIES

Interpretation

4.96   **1.**[²(1)] In this Schedule—
"assessment period" has the meaning given by regulation 21 (assessment periods) of the Universal Credit Regulations;
"the work allowance" means, in relation to any claimant, the amount applicable to that claimant under regulation 22(2) (deduction of income and work allowance) of the Universal Credit Regulations;
"child element" means, in relation to any claimant, any amount included in the claimant's award of universal credit under regulation 24 (the child element) of the Universal Credit Regulations;
"the Community Charges Regulations" means the Community Charges (Deductions from Income Support) (No. 2) Regulations 1990;
"the Community Charges (Scotland) Regulations" means the Community Charges (Deductions from Income Support) (Scotland) Regulations 1989;
"the Council Tax Regulations" means the Council Tax (Deductions from Income Support) Regulations 1993;
"the Fines Regulations" means the Fines (Deductions from Income Support) Regulations 1992;
"standard allowance" means, in relation to any claimant, any amount included in the claimant's award of universal credit under section 9(1) of the 2012 Act;
"water charges" means—
  (a) as respects England and Wales, any water and sewerage charges under Chapter 1 of Part 5 of the Water Industry Act 1991;
  (b) as respects Scotland, any such charges established by Scottish Water under a charges scheme made under section 29A of the Water Industry (Scotland) Act 2002;
  [² ...]
  [² (2) For the purposes of this Schedule, where the relevant percentage of the standard allowance results in a fraction of a penny, that fraction is to be disregarded if it is less than half a penny and otherwise it is to be treated as a penny.]

General

4.97   **2.**—(1) The Secretary of State may deduct an amount from a claimant's award of universal credit and pay that amount to a third party in accordance with the following provisions of this Schedule to discharge (in whole or part) a liability of the claimant to that third party.
(2) A payment made to a third party in accordance with this Schedule may be made at such intervals as the Secretary of State may direct.

Limitations applicable to deductions made under this Schedule

4.98   **3.**—(1) The Secretary of State may not deduct an amount from a claimant's award of universal credit under this Schedule and pay that amount to a third party if, in relation to any assessment period, that would—
  (a) reduce the amount payable to the claimant to less than one penny; or
  (b) result in more than three deductions being made, in relation to that assessment period, under one or more of the provisions mentioned in sub-paragraph (2).
(2) The provisions are—
  (a) paragraph 6 (housing costs) of this Schedule;

(b) paragraph 7 (rent and service charges included in rent) of this Schedule;
(c) paragraph 8 (fuel costs) of this Schedule;
(d) paragraph 9 (water charges) of this Schedule;
(e) paragraph 10 (payments in place of payments of child support maintenance) of this Schedule;
(f) paragraph 11 (eligible loans) of this Schedule;
(g) paragraph 12 (integration loans) of this Schedule;
(h) regulation 3 (deductions from income support etc.) of the Community Charges Regulations;
(i) regulation 3 (deductions from income support etc.) of the Community Charges (Scotland) Regulations;
(j) regulation 5 (deduction from debtor's income support etc.) of the Council Tax Regulations; and
(k) regulation 4 (deductions from offender's income support etc.) of the Fines Regulations.

(3) The aggregate amount deducted from a claimant's award of universal credit in relation to any assessment period and paid to a third party under paragraphs 8 (fuel costs) and 9 (water charges) of this Schedule must not, without the claimant's consent, exceed a sum equal to [² 25%] of the aggregate of the standard allowance and any child element.

Maximum amount

4.—(1) Except as provided for in sub-paragraph (4), the Secretary of State may not deduct an amount from a claimant's award of universal credit under a provision mentioned in paragraph 5(2) of this Schedule if, in relation to any assessment period, that would result in the Secretary of State deducting an amount in excess of [² 40%] of the standard allowance ("the maximum amount") from the claimant's award under one or more relevant provisions. **4.99**

(2) The relevant provisions are—
(a) those mentioned in paragraph 5(2) of this Schedule;
(b) section 26 (higher-level sanctions) of the 2012 Act;
(c) section 27 (other sanctions) of the 2012 Act;
(d) section 71ZG (recovery of payments on account) of the Administration Act;
(e) section 6B of the Social Security Fraud Act 2001 ("the 2001 Act");
(f) section 7 of the 2001 Act; and
(g) section 9 of the 2001 Act.

(3) For the purposes of determining whether the maximum amount would be exceeded, no account is to be taken of any liability for continuing need mentioned in—
(a) paragraph 8(4)(b) (fuel costs) of this Schedule; or
(b) paragraph 9(6)(b) or (7)(b)(water charges) of this Schedule.

(4) Subject to paragraph 3 of this Schedule, the Secretary of State may deduct an amount from the claimant's award under paragraph 6 (housing costs), [⁵ . . .] paragraph 8 (fuel costs) [⁵ , or the minimum amount which may be deducted under paragraph 7 (rent and service charges included in rent)] of this Schedule and pay that amount to a third party where the deduction appears to the Secretary of State to be in the claimant's best interests, even though the deduction would result in the maximum amount being exceeded.

Priority as between certain debts

5.—(1) This paragraph applies to a claimant ("C") where, in relation to any assessment period— **4.100**
(a) a deduction could otherwise be made from C's award under more than one of the provisions mentioned in sub-paragraph (2); and
(b) the amount of universal credit payable to C in relation to that assessment period is insufficient to enable the Secretary of State to meet all of the liabilities for which in C's case deductions may be made under those provisions or the deduction, were it to be made, would mean that the maximum amount referred to in paragraph 4(1) would be exceeded.

(2) The provisions are—
(a) paragraph 6 (housing costs) of this Schedule;
(b) paragraph 7 (rent and service charges included in rent) of this Schedule [⁵ where the amount of the deduction equals 10% of the standard allowance];
(c) paragraph 8 (fuel costs) of this Schedule;
(d) regulation 3 (deductions from income support etc.) of the Community Charges Regulations, regulation 3 (deductions from income support etc.) of the Community Charges (Scotland) Regulations or (because no such payments are being made in C's case) regulation 5 (deduction from debtor's income support etc.) of the Council Tax Regulations;

   (e) regulation 4 (deductions from offender's income support etc.) of the Fines Regulations where the amount of the deduction equals 5% of the standard allowance;

   (f) paragraph 9 (water charges) of this Schedule;

   (g) paragraph 10 (payments in place of child support maintenance) of this Schedule;

   (h) Schedule 7 (deductions from benefit in respect of child support maintenance and payment to persons with care) to these Regulations;

   (i) section 78(2) (recovery of social fund awards) of the Administration Act;

   (j) section 71ZH(1)(a) or (b) (recovery of hardship payments etc.) of the [⁶Administration Act];

   (k) section 115A (penalty as alternative to prosecution) of the Administration Act where an overpayment is recoverable from a person by, or due from a person to, the Secretary of State or an authority under or by virtue of section 71 (overpayments – general), section 75 (overpayments of housing benefit) or section 71ZB (recovery of overpayments of certain benefits) of that Act;

   (l) section 71 (overpayments – general), section 71ZC (deduction from benefit) or section 75(4) (overpayments of housing benefit) of the Administration Act or an over-payment of working tax credit or child tax credit, where in each case, the overpayment (or part of it) is the result of fraud;

   (m) section 115C(4) (incorrect statements etc.) and section 115D(4) (failure to disclose information) of the Administration Act;

   (n) section 71 (overpayments – general), section 71ZC (deduction from benefit) or section 75(4) (overpayments of housing benefit) of the Administration Act or an over-payment of working tax credit or child tax credit, where in each case, the overpayment (or part of it) is not the result of fraud;

   (o) paragraph 12 (integration loans) of this Schedule;

   (p) paragraph 11 (eligible loans) of this Schedule;

[⁵ (pa) paragraph 7 (rent and service charges included in rent) where the amount of deduc-tion exceeds the minimum amount that may be deducted under that paragraph;]

   (q) regulation 4 (deductions from offender's income support etc.) of the Fines Regulations where the amount of the deduction exceeds the minimum amount that may be deducted in accordance with those Regulations.

(3) Where this paragraph applies to a claimant, the Secretary of State must make a deduc-tion under any of the provisions mentioned sub-paragraph (2) in accordance with sub-para-graphs (4) and (5).

(4) The Secretary of State must give priority to any such deductions in the order in which they are listed in sub-paragraph (2), with housing costs having the priority.

(5) Where two or more provisions mentioned in any single paragraph of sub-paragraph (2) apply to the claimant, unless the Secretary of State directs otherwise, those deductions have equal priority with each other and the amount of such deductions are to be apportioned accordingly.

(6) For the purposes of sub-paragraph (2)(l) and (n), an overpayment is the result of fraud if, in relation to that overpayment or that part of it, the claimant—

   (a) has been found guilty of an offence whether under statute or otherwise;

   (b) made an admission after caution of deception or fraud for the purpose of obtaining benefit under the Administration Act, or in the case of a tax credit, under the Tax Credits Act 2002; or

   (c) agreed to pay a penalty under section 115A of the Administration Act (penalty as an alternative to prosecution) and the agreement has not been withdrawn.

Housing costs

4.101   **6.**—(1) This paragraph applies where the following condition is met.

(2) The condition is that in any assessment period the claimant is in debt for any item of housing costs which is included in the claimant's award of universal credit under Schedule 5 (housing costs element for owner-occupiers) to the Universal Credit Regulations.

(3) Where this paragraph applies, but subject to sub-paragraph (4), the Secretary of State may, in such cases and circumstances as the Secretary of State may determine, in relation to that assessment period deduct an amount from the claimant's award equal to 5% of the stand-ard allowance in respect of any debt mentioned in sub-paragraph (2) and pay that amount or those amounts to the person to whom any such debt is owed.

(4) Before the Secretary of State may commence (or re-commence) making deductions in respect of any such debt, the claimant's earned income (or in the case of joint claimants their combined earned income) in relation to the previous assessment period must not exceed the work allowance.

(5) No amount may be deducted under this paragraph in respect of owner-occupier payments within the meaning of paragraph 4 of Schedule 1 (meaning of payments in respect of accommodation) to the Universal Credit Regulations in any case where those payments—

(a) are required to be paid directly to a qualifying lender under regulation 59 of these Regulations; or

(b) would have been required to be paid to a body which, or a person who, would otherwise have been a qualifying lender but for an election given under paragraph 10 of Schedule 5 to these Regulations.

(6) As between liability for items of housing costs to which this paragraph applies, liabilities in respect of owner-occupier payments (within the meaning of paragraph 4(1) of Schedule 1 (meaning of payments in respect of accommodation) to the Universal Credit Regulations) are to have priority over all other items.

Rent and service charges included in rent

7.—(1) This paragraph applies where all of the following conditions are met.   **4.102**

(2) The first condition is that in any assessment period the claimant—

(a) has an award of universal credit which includes an amount under Schedule 4 (housing costs element for renters) to the Universal Credit Regulations; or

(b) occupies exempt accommodation and has an award of housing benefit under section 130 (housing benefit) of the Contributions and Benefits Act.

(3) The second condition is that the claimant is in debt for any—

(a) rent payments;

(b) service charges which are paid with or as part of the claimant's rent.

(4) The third condition is that the claimant occupies the accommodation to which the debt relates.

(5) Where this paragraph applies, but subject to sub-paragraphs (6) and (7), the Secretary of State may, in such cases and circumstances as the Secretary of State may determine, deduct in relation to that assessment period an amount from the claimant's award [⁵ which is no less than 10% and no more than 20%] of the standard allowance and pay that amount to the person to whom the debt is owed.

(6) Before the Secretary of State may commence (or re-commence) making deductions in respect of such a debt, the claimant's earned income (or in the case of joint claimants their combined earned income) in relation to the previous assessment period must not exceed the work allowance.

(7) The Secretary of State must stop making such deductions if, in relation to the three assessment periods immediately preceding the date on which the next deduction could otherwise be made, the claimant's earned income (or in the case of joint claimants their combined earned income) equals or exceeds the work allowance.

(8) In this paragraph—

"exempt accommodation" has the meaning given by paragraph 1 of Schedule 1 (interpretation) to the Universal Credit Regulations;

"rent payments" includes any elements included in the claimant's rent which would not fall to be treated as rent under the Housing Benefit Regulations 2006 or as rent payments under the Universal Credit Regulations;

"service charges" includes any items in a charge for services in respect of the accommodation occupied by the claimant which would not fall to be treated as service charges under the Universal Credit Regulations.

Fuel costs

8.—(1) This paragraph applies where the following condition is met.   **4.103**

(2) The condition is that in any assessment period the claimant is in debt for any [¹ fuel item].

(3) Where this paragraph applies, but subject to sub-paragraphs (5) and (6), the Secretary of State may, in such cases and circumstances as the Secretary of State may determine, deduct in relation to that assessment period the following amounts from the claimant's award and pay them to the person to whom the payment is due.

(4) The amount which may be deducted in respect of any fuel item is—

(a) an amount equal to 5% of the standard allowance; and

(b) an additional amount which the Secretary of State estimates is equal to the average monthly cost necessary to meet the claimant's continuing need for [¹ the fuel in respect of which the debt arose, plus such monthly amount as is required to meet any payments required to be made under a green deal plan within the meaning of section 1 of the Energy Act 2011 ("the 2011 Act")], except where current consumption is paid for by other means such as a pre-payment meter.

(5) Before the Secretary of State may commence (or re-commence) making deductions in respect of such a debt, the claimant's earned income (or in the case of joint claimants their combined earned income) in relation to the previous assessment period must not exceed the work allowance.

(6) The Secretary of State must stop making such deductions if, in relation to the three assessment periods immediately preceding the date on which the next deduction could otherwise be made, the claimant's earned income (or in the case of joint claimants their combined earned income) equals or exceeds the work allowance.

(7) As between liabilities for items of gas or electricity, the Secretary of State must give priority to whichever liability the Secretary of State considers it would, having regard to the circumstances and to any requests of the claimant, be appropriate to discharge.

[¹(8) In this paragraph, "fuel item" means—
    (a) any charge for mains gas, including for the reconnection of mains gas;
    (b) any charge for mains electricity and including any charge for the disconnection and reconnection of mains electricity and including any payments required to be made under a green deal plan within the meaning of section 1 of the 2011 Act.]

Water charges

4.104

9.—(1) This paragraph applies where the following condition is met.

(2) The condition is that in any assessment period the claimant is in debt for water charges, including any charges for reconnection ("the original debt").

(3) Where this paragraph applies, but subject to sub-paragraphs (4) and (5), the Secretary of State may, in such cases and circumstances as the Secretary of State may determine, deduct an amount from the claimant's award in accordance with sub-paragraphs (6) to (8) and pay it to a water undertaker to whom the payment is due or to the person or body authorised to collect water charges for that undertaker.

(4) Before the Secretary of State may commence (or re-commence) making deductions in respect of such a debt, the claimant's earned income (or in the case of joint claimants their combined earned income) in relation to the previous assessment period must not exceed the work allowance.

(5) The Secretary of State must stop making such deductions if, in relation to the three assessment periods immediately preceding the date on which the next deduction could otherwise be made, the claimant's earned income (or in the case of joint claimants their combined earned income) equals or exceeds the work allowance.

(6) Where water charges are determined by means of a water meter, the amount to be deducted under this paragraph in relation to any assessment period is to be—
    (a) an amount equal to 5% of the standard allowance towards discharging the original debt; and
    (b) an additional amount which the Secretary of State estimates to be the average monthly cost necessary to meet the claimant's continuing need for water consumption.

(7) Where water charges are determined otherwise than by means of a water meter, the amount to be deducted in relation to any assessment period under this paragraph is to be—
    (a) the amount referred to in sub-paragraph (6)(a); and
    (b) an additional amount equal to the cost necessary to meet the continuing need for water consumption in that assessment period.

(8) Where the claimant is in debt to two water undertakers—
    (a) only one amount under sub-paragraph (6)(a) or (7)(a) may be deducted;
    (b) a deduction in respect of an original debt for sewerage may only be made after the whole debt in respect of an original debt for water has been paid; and
    (c) deductions in respect of continuing charges for both water and for sewerage may be made at the same time.

(9) In this paragraph "water undertaker" means—
    (a) in relation to any area in England and Wales, a company holding an appointment as a water undertaker or a sewerage undertaker under the Water Industry Act 1991; or
    (b) in relation to any area in Scotland, Scottish Water.

Payments in place of payments of child support maintenance

4.105

10.—(1) This paragraph applies where the Secretary of State has determined that section 43 (contribution to maintenance by deduction from benefit) of the 1991 Act and regulation 28 (contribution to maintenance by deduction from benefit) of the Child Support (Maintenance Assessments and Special Cases) Regulations 1992 apply in relation to the claimant.

(2) Where this paragraph applies, the Secretary of State must, if satisfied that there is suf-

ficient universal credit in payment (but subject to paragraphs 1, 4 and 5 of this Schedule), determine that an amount is to be deducted from the claimant's award for transmission to the person or persons entitled to receive that amount under or by virtue of the 1991 Act.

(3) Not more than one deduction may be made under this paragraph in relation to any assessment period.

(4) The amount of universal credit which may be deducted in relation to any assessment period and paid to a third party under this paragraph is to be an amount equal to 5% of the standard allowance.

Eligible loans

11.—(1) This paragraph applieswhere [⁴ in any assessment period the claimant is in arrears in respect of a loan entered into (whether solely or jointly) with an eligible lender in respect of an eligible loan].

(2) [⁴ . . .]

(3) [⁴ . . .]

(4) Where the claimant has an award of universal credit, the Secretary of State may, in such cases and circumstances as the Secretary of State may determine, deduct in relation to the assessment period referred to in sub-paragraph (2) an amount from the claimant's award equal to 5% of the standard allowance and pay that amount to the eligible lender towards discharging the amount owing under the loan agreement.

(5) In a case where the claimant has an award of universal credit but the amount payable to the claimant in relation to that assessment period is insufficient to enable such a deduction to be made, the Secretary of State may instead deduct a weekly amount equal to 5% of the personal allowance for a single claimant aged not less than 25 from any employment and support allowance or jobseeker's allowance awarded to the claimant and pay that amount to the eligible lender.

(6) In a case where the claimant does not have an award of universal credit, but has an award of an employment and support allowance or a jobseeker's allowance, the Secretary of State may deduct a weekly amount equal to 5% of the personal allowance for a single claimant aged not less than 25 from any such award and pay that amount to the eligible lender.

(7) The Secretary of State must not make deductions from a claimant's employment and support allowance or a jobseeker's allowance under this paragraph if that would reduce the amount payable to the claimant to less than 10 pence.

(8) In this paragraph—

"eligible benefit" means—

(a) an employment and support allowance;

(b) a jobseeker's allowance;

(c) universal credit;

"eligible lender" means—

(a) a body registered under section 1 (societies which may be registered) of the Industrial and Provident Societies Act 1965;

(b) a credit union within the meaning of section 1 (registration under the Industrial and Provident Societies Act 1965) of the Credit Unions Act 1979;

(c) a charitable institution within the meaning of section 58(1) (interpretation of Part 2) of the Charities Act 1992;

(d) a body entered on the Scottish Charity Register under section 3 (Scottish Charities Register) of the Charities and Trustee Investment (Scotland) Act 2005;

(e) a community interest company within the meaning of Part 2 of the Companies (Audit, Investigations and Community Enterprise) Act 2004,

which, except for a credit union, [³ has permission under the Financial Services and Markets Act 2000 to enter into a contract of the kind mentioned in paragraph 23 or paragraph 23B of Schedule 2 to that Act (credit agreements and contracts for hire of goods)] and which the Secretary of State considers is an appropriate body to which payments on behalf of the claimant may be made in respect of loans made by that body;

"eligible loan" means a loan made by a lender who is, at the time the loan agreement is made, an eligible lender, to a claimant except a loan which—

(a) is secured by a charge or pledge;

(b) is for the purpose of business or self-employment; or

(c) was made by means of a credit card;

"loan agreement" means an agreement between the eligible lender and the claimant in respect of an eligible loan;

"5% of the personal allowance" means 5% of the personal allowance applicable in the claimant's case, rounded up (in any case where that calculation produces a result which is not a multiple of five pence) to the next higher multiple of five pence.

4.106

[³ (9) The definition of "eligible lender" must be read with—
  (a) section 22 of the Financial Services and Markets Act 2000,
  (b) any relevant order under that section, and
  (c) Schedule 2 to that Act.]

Integration loans

12.—(1) This paragraph applies where [⁴ the claimant has an integration loan which is recoverable by deductions].

(2) The first condition is that the claimant has an integration loan which is recoverable by deductions.

(3) The second condition is that, as at the date on which the Secretary of State receives an application for deductions to be made under this paragraph, no deductions are being made from the claimant's universal credit in respect in respect of an amount recoverable under—
  (a) section 71 (overpayments – general) or 71ZB (recovery of overpayments of certain benefits) of the Administration Act; or
  (b) section 78 (recovery of social fund awards) of that Act.

(4) Where this paragraph applies, the amount payable by deductions in any assessment period is to be equal to 5% of the standard allowance.

(5) In this paragraph, "integration loan which is recoverable by deductions" means an integration loan which is made under the Integration Loans for Refugees and Others Regulations 2007 and which is recoverable from the claimant by deductions from the claimant's award of universal credit under regulation 9 of those Regulations.

AMENDMENTS

1. Social Security (Miscellaneous Amendments) Regulations 2013 (SI 2013/443) reg.10 (April 29, 2013).

2. Social Security (Miscellaneous Amendments) (No. 2) Regulations 2013 (SI 2013/1508) reg.6(1) and (3) (July 29, 2013).

3. Financial Services and Markets Act 2000 (Regulated Activities) (Amendment) (No.2) Order 2013 (SI 2013/1881) art.28 and Sch. para.45 (April 1, 2014).

4. Universal Credit and Miscellaneous Amendments Regulations 2014 (SI 2014/597) reg.5 (April 28, 2014).

5. Universal Credit and Miscellaneous Amendments (No.2) Regulations 2014 (SI 2014/2888) reg.6 (Assessment periods beginning on or after November 26, 2014).

6. Universal Credit and Miscellaneous Amendments Regulations 2015 (SI 2015/1754) reg.9 (Assessment periods beginning on or after November 4, 2015).

DEFINITIONS

"the 1991 Act"—see reg.2.
"the 2012 Act"—*ibid.*
"the Administration Act"—*ibid.*
"assessment period"—see reg.2 and Universal Credit Regs., reg.21.
"benefit"—see reg.2.
"child" —see reg.2 and WRA 2012 s.40.
"claimant"—see reg.2.
"earned income"—see reg.2 and Universal Credit Regs., reg.52.
"employment and support allowance"—see reg.2.
"jobseeker's allowance"—*ibid.*
"universal credit"—*ibid.*
"the Universal Credit Regulations"— *ibid.*

4.107

SCHEDULE 7

DEDUCTIONS FROM BENEFIT IN RESPECT OF CHILD SUPPORT MAINTENANCE AND
PAYMENT TO PERSONS WITH CARE

Interpretation
1. In this Schedule—   **4.108**
"beneficiary" means a person who has been awarded a specified benefit;
"maintenance", except in paragraph 3, means child support maintenance which a non-resident parent is liable to pay under the 1991 Act at a flat rate (or would be so liable but for a variation having been agreed to) where that rate applies (or would have applied) because the non-resident parent falls within paragraph 4(1)(b), (c) or (2) of Schedule 1 to the 1991 Act, and includes such maintenance payable at a transitional rate in accordance with regulations made under section 29(3)(a) of the Child Support, Pensions and Social Security Act 2000;
"person with care" has the same meaning as in section 3 (meaning of certain terms used in this Act) of the 1991 Act;
"specified benefit" means—
(a) an employment and support allowance;
(b) a jobseeker's allowance;
(c) universal credit.

Deductions
2.—(1) Subject to the following provisions of this paragraph and to paragraph 5 (flat rate   **4.109**
maintenance), the Secretary of State may deduct from any specified benefit awarded to a beneficiary, an amount equal to the amount of maintenance which is payable by the beneficiary and pay the amount deducted to or among the person or persons with care in discharge (in whole or in part) of the liability to pay maintenance.
(2) A deduction may only be made from one specified benefit in respect of the same period.
(3) No amount may be deducted under this Schedule from any employment and support allowance or any jobseeker's allowance awarded to the claimant if that would reduce the amount of the benefit payable to the claimant to less than 10 pence.
(4) No amount may be deducted from any universal credit awarded to the claimant under this Schedule if that would reduce the amount payable to the claimant to less than one penny.

Arrears
3.—(1) Except where universal credit is awarded to the beneficiary, the Secretary of State   **4.110**
may deduct the sum of £1 per week from any employment and support allowance or job-seeker's allowance which the beneficiary has been awarded and, subject to sub-paragraph (2), pay the amount deducted to or among the person or persons with care in discharge (in whole or in part) of the beneficiary's liability to pay arrears of maintenance.
(2) Deductions made under sub-paragraph (1) may be retained by the Secretary of State in the circumstances set out in regulation 8 of the Child Support (Arrears, Interest and Adjustment of Maintenance Assessments) Regulations 1992.
(3) In sub-paragraph (1) "maintenance" means child support maintenance as defined by section 3(6) of the 1991 Act whether before or after the amendment of the definition of such maintenance by section 1(2)(a) of the Child Support, Pensions and Social Security Act 2000, and includes maintenance payable at a transitional rate in accordance with regulations made under section 29(3)(a) of that Act.

Apportionment
4. Where maintenance is payable to more than one person with care, the amount deducted   **4.111**
must be apportioned between the persons with care in accordance with paragraphs 6, 7 and 8 of Schedule 1 (maintenance assessments) to the 1991 Act.

Flat rate maintenance
5.—(1) This paragraph applies where the beneficiary and that person's partner are each   **4.112**
liable to pay maintenance at a flat rate in accordance with paragraph 4(2) of Schedule 1 to the 1991 Act and either of them has been awarded universal credit (whether as a single claimant or as joint claimants).
(2) Where this paragraph applies, an amount not exceeding an amount equal to the flat rate of maintenance may be deducted from such an award in respect of the total liability of both partners to pay maintenance, in the proportions described in regulation 4(3)

of the Child Support (Maintenance Calculations and Special Cases) Regulations 2001 or regulation 44(3) of the Child Support Maintenance Calculation Regulations 2012 and must be paid in discharge (in whole or in part) of the respective liabilities to pay maintenance.

Notice

4.113   **6.** Where the Secretary of State commences making deductions under this Schedule, the Secretary of State must notify the beneficiary in writing of the amount and frequency of the deduction and the benefit from which the deduction is made and must give further such notice when there is a change to any of the particulars specified in the notice.

DEFINITIONS

"the 1991 Act"—see reg.2.
"beneficiary"—see para.(1).
"benefit"—see reg.2.
"child"—see reg.2 and WRA 2012 s.40.
"claimant"—see reg.2.
"employment and support allowance"—*ibid.*
"jobseeker's allowance"—*ibid.*
"maintenance"—see para.(1).
"person with care"—*ibid.*
"specified benefit"—*ibid.*
"universal credit"—see reg.2.

The Universal Credit, Personal Independence Payment, Jobseeker's Allowance and Employment and Support Allowance (Decisions and Appeals) Regulations 2013

(SI 2013/381)

4.114   *The Secretary of State makes the following Regulations in exercise of the powers conferred by sections: 5(1A), 159D(1) and (6), 189(1), (4) to (6) and section 191 of the Social Security Administration Act 1992; 9(1), (4) and (6), 10(3) and (6), 10A, 11(1), 12(2), (3), (3A), (3B), (6) and (7)(b), 16(1), 17, 18(1), 21(1) to (3), 22 and 23, 25(3)(b) and (5)(c), 26(6)(c), 28(1), 31(2), 79(1) and (4) to (7) and 84 of, and paragraph 9 of Schedule 2, paragraphs 1, 4 and 9 of Schedule 3 and Schedule 5 to, the Social Security Act 1998.*

A draft of this instrument was laid before and approved by a resolution of each House of Parliament in accordance with section 80(1) of the Social Security Act 1998.

The Social Security Advisory Committee has agreed that the proposals in respect of these Regulations should not be referred to it.

ARRANGEMENT OF REGULATIONS

PART I

GENERAL

PART VI

TERMINATION

PART VII

APPEALS

GENERAL NOTE

An annotated version of these Regulations is included in Vol.III. They are repeated   **4.115**
in this volume so as to provide a complete text of the law governing universal credit.
Readers are referred to Vol.III for commentary on the individual provisions. These
Regulations are in force from April 8, 2013 in relation to personal independence
payment and April 29, 2013 in relation to universal credit, new-style employment
and support allowance and new-style jobseeker's allowance.

PART I

GENERAL

Citation, commencement and application

   1.—(1) These Regulations may be cited as the Universal Credit, Personal   **4.116**
Independence Payment, Jobseeker's Allowance and Employment and
Support Allowance (Decisions and Appeals) Regulations 2013.

(2) They come into force—

(a) in so far as they relate to personal independence payment and for the purposes of this regulation, on 8th April 2013;

(b) for all remaining purposes, on 29th April 2013.

(3) These Regulations apply in relation to—

(a) an employment and support allowance payable under Part 1 of the 2007 Act as amended by Schedule 3 and Part 1 of Schedule 14 to the 2012 Act (to remove references to an income-related allowance);

(b) a jobseeker's allowance payable under the Jobseekers Act as amended by Part 1 of Schedule 14 to the 2012 Act (to remove references to an income-based allowance);

(c) personal independence payment; and

(d) universal credit.

Interpretation

4.117   **2.** In these Regulations—

"the 1998 Act" means the Social Security Act 1998;

"the 2007 Act" means the Welfare Reform Act 2007;

"the 2012 Act" means the Welfare Reform Act 2012;

"the Administration Act" means the Social Security Administration Act 1992;

"appeal", except where the context otherwise requires, means an appeal to the First-tier Tribunal established under the Tribunals, Courts and Enforcement Act 2007;

"appropriate office" means—

(a) in the case of a contributions decision which falls within Part 2 (contributions decisions) of Schedule 3 (decisions against which an appeal lies) to the 1998 Act, any National Insurance Contributions office of HMRC or any office of the Department for Work and Pensions; or

(b) in any other case, the office of the Department for Work and Pensions, or other place, the address of which is specified on the notification of the original decision referred to in regulation 5(1) (revision on any grounds);

"assessment period" is to be construed in accordance with regulation 21 (assessment periods) of the Universal Credit Regulations;

"benefit" means a benefit or an allowance in relation to which these Regulations apply;

"benefit week" has the same meaning as in—

(a) regulation 2 (interpretation) of the Employment and Support Allowance Regulations 2013 in the case of an employment and support allowance;

(b) regulation 2 (general interpretation) of the Jobseeker's Allowance Regulations 2013, in the case of a jobseeker's allowance;

"child" means a person under the age of 16;

"claimant" means—

(a) any person who has claimed—

    (i) an employment and support allowance;

    (ii) a jobseeker's allowance;

    (iii) personal independence payment;

(b) in the case of universal credit, any person who is a claimant for the purposes of section 40 (interpretation) of the 2012 Act; and

(c) any other person from whom an amount of benefit is alleged to be recoverable;

"the Claims and Payments Regulations 2013" means the Universal Credit, Personal Independence Payment, Jobseeker's Allowance and Employment and Support Allowance (Claims and Payments) Regulations 2013;

"the Contributions and Benefits Act" means the Social Security Contributions and Benefits Act 1992;

"the date of notification", in relation to a decision of the Secretary of State, means the date on which the notification of the decision is treated as having been given or sent in accordance with—

(a) regulation 3 (service of documents); or

(b) where the notification is given or sent using an electronic communication, Schedule 2 (electronic communications) to the Claims and Payments Regulations 2013;

"designated authority" means—

(a) the Secretary of State; or

(b) a person providing services to the Secretary of State;

"electronic communication" has the same meaning as in section 15(1) of the Electronic Communications Act 2000;

"employment and support allowance" means an employment and support allowance in relation to which these Regulations apply;

"the Fraud Act" means the Social Security Fraud Act 2001;

"fraud penalty", in relation to any claimant of an employment and support allowance, a jobseeker's allowance or universal credit, means any period during which the provisions of section 6B, 7 or 9 of the Fraud Act apply to the award;

"family" means the claimant's partner and any—

(a) child; or

(b) qualifying young person, within the meaning of regulation 5 (meaning of "qualifying young person") of the Universal Credit Regulations, who is a member of the same household as the claimant and for whom the either the claimant or their partner is, or both of them are, responsible;

"HMRC" means Her Majesty's Revenue and Customs;

"the Jobseekers Act" means the Jobseekers Act 1995;

"jobseeker's allowance" means a jobseeker's allowance in relation to which these Regulations apply;

"limited capability for work" has the same meaning as in—

(a) section 1(4) of the 2007 Act in relation to an employment and support allowance;

(b) section 37(1) of the 2012 Act in relation to universal credit;

"limited capability for work determination" means—

(a) where the determination relates to an employment and support allowance, a determination whether a person has limited capability for work following a limited capability for work assessment in accordance with regulation 15(1) (determination of limited capability for work) of the Employment and Support Allowance Regulations 2013, or a determination that a person is to be treated as having limited capability for work in accordance with regulation 16 (certain claimants to be treated as having limited capability for work) or 25 (exceptional circumstances) of those Regulations;

(b) where the determination relates to universal credit, a determination whether a person has limited capability for work following a limited capability for work assessment referred to in regulation 39(2) (limited capability for work) of the Universal Credit Regulations, or a determination that a person is to be treated as having limited capability for work in accordance with regulation 39(6) of those Regulations;

"official error" means an error made by—

(a) an officer of the Department for Work and Pensions or HMRC acting as such which was not caused or materially contributed to by any person outside the Department or HMRC;

(b) a person employed by, and acting on behalf of, a designated authority which was not caused or materially contributed to by any person outside that authority,

but excludes any error of law which is shown to have been such by a subsequent decision of the Upper Tribunal, or of the court as defined in section 27(7) of the 1998 Act;

"partner" means one of a couple within the meaning of section 39 (couples) of the 2012 Act;

"personal independence payment" means an allowance payable under Part 4 (personal independence payment) of the 2012 Act;

"relevant benefit" has the same meaning as in Chapter 2 (social security decisions and appeals) of Part 1 (decisions and appeals) of the 1998 Act;

"the Rent Officers Order 2013" means the Rent Officers (Universal Credit Functions) Order 2013;

"terminally ill", in relation to a claimant, means that the claimant is suffering from a progressive disease and that death in consequence of that disease can reasonably be expected within 6 months;

"the Tribunal Procedure Rules" means the Tribunal Procedure (First-tier Tribunal) (Social Entitlement Chamber) Rules 2008;

"the Universal Credit Regulations" means the Universal Credit Regulations 2013;

"universal credit" means the benefit payable under Part 1 (universal credit) of the 2012 Act;

"writing" includes writing produced by means of electronic communications used in accordance with regulation 4 (electronic communications).

Service of documents

4.118   **3.**—(1) Where, under any provision of these Regulations, any notice or other document is given or sent by post to the Secretary of State, it is to be treated as having been given or sent on the day on which it is received by the Secretary of State.

(2) Where, under any provision of these Regulations, the Secretary of State sends a notice or other document by post to a person's last known address, it is to be treated as having been given or sent on the day on which it was posted.

Electronic communications

4.119   **4.** Schedule 2 (electronic communications) to the Claims and Payments Regulations 2013 applies to the delivery of electronic communications to or by the Secretary of State for the purposes of these Regulations in the same manner as it applies to the delivery of electronic communications for the purposes of the Claims and Payments Regulations 2013.

PART II

REVISION

CHAPTER 1

REVISION ON ANY GROUNDS

Revision on any grounds

5.—(1) Any decision of the Secretary of State under section 8 or 10 of   4.120
the 1998 Act ("the original decision") may be revised by the Secretary of
State if—
   (a) the Secretary of State commences action leading to the revision
       within one month of the date of notification of the original decision;
       or
   (b) an application for a revision is received by the Secretary of State at an
       appropriate office within—
       (i) one month of the date of notification of the original deci-
           sion (but subject to regulation 38(4)(correction of accidental
           errors));
       (ii) 14 days of the expiry of that period if a written statement of the
           reasons for the decision is requested under regulation 7 (con-
           sideration of revision before appeal) or regulation 51 (notice of
           a decision against which an appeal lies) and that statement is
           provided within the period specified in paragraph (i);
       (iii) 14 days of the date on which that statement was provided if the
           statement was requested within the period specified in para-
           graph (i) but was provided after the expiry of that period; or
       (iv) such longer period as may be allowed under regulation 6 (late
           application for a revision).
   (2) Paragraph (1) does not apply—
   (a) in respect of a relevant change of circumstances which occurred since
       the decision had effect or, in the case of an advance award under reg-
       ulation 32, 33 or 34 of the Claims and Payments Regulations 2013,
       since the decision was made;
   (b) where the Secretary of State has evidence or information which indi-
       cates that a relevant change of circumstances will occur;
   (c) in respect of a decision which relates to an employment and support
       allowance or personal independence payment where the claimant is

terminally ill, unless the application for a revision contains an express statement that the claimant is terminally ill.

Late application for a revision

4.121   **6.**—(1) The Secretary of State may extend the time limit specified in regulation 5(1) (revision on any grounds) for making an application for a revision if all of the following conditions are met.

(2) The first condition is that the person wishing to apply for the revision has applied to the Secretary of State at an appropriate office for an extension of time.

(3) The second condition is that the application—

(a) explains why the extension is sought;

(b) contains sufficient details of the decision to which the application relates to enable it to be identified; and

(c) is made within 13 months of the latest date by which the application for revision should have been received by the Secretary of State in accordance with regulation 5(1)(b)(i) to (iii).

(4) The third condition is that the Secretary of State is satisfied that it is reasonable to grant the extension.

(5) The fourth condition is that the Secretary of State is satisfied that due to special circumstances it was not practicable for the application for revision to be made within the time limit specified in regulation 5(1)(b)(i) to (iii) (revision on any grounds).

(6) In determining whether it is reasonable to grant an extension of time, the Secretary of State must have regard to the principle that the greater the amount of time that has elapsed between the end of the time limit specified in regulation 5(1)(b)(i) to (iii) (revision on any grounds) and the date of the application, the more compelling should be the special circumstances on which the application is based.

(7) An application under this regulation which has been refused may not be renewed.

Consideration of revision before appeal

4.122   **7.**—(1) This regulation applies in a case where—

(a) the Secretary of State gives a person written notice of a decision under section 8 or 10 of the 1998 Act (whether as originally made or as revised under section 9 of that Act); and

(b) that notice includes a statement to the effect that there is a right of appeal in relation to the decision only if the Secretary of State has considered an application for a revision of the decision.

(2) In a case to which this regulation applies, a person has a right of

appeal under section 12(2) of the 1998 Act in relation to the decision only if the Secretary of State has considered on an application whether to revise the decision under section 9 of that Act.

(3) The notice referred to in paragraph (1) must inform the person—

(a) of the time limit under regulation 5(1) (revision on any grounds) for making an application for a revision; and

(b) that, where the notice does not include a statement of the reasons for the decision ("written reasons"), the person may, within one month of the date of notification of the decision, request that the Secretary of State provide written reasons.

(4) Where written reasons are requested under paragraph (3)(b), the Secretary of State must provide that statement within 14 days of receipt of the request or as soon as practicable afterwards.

(5) Where, as the result of paragraph (2), there is no right of appeal against a decision, the Secretary of State may treat any purported appeal as an application for a revision under section 9 of the 1998 Act.

DEFINITIONS

"the 1998 Act"—see reg.2.
"appeal"—*ibid.*

CHAPTER 2

REVISION ON SPECIFIC GROUNDS

Introduction

8. A decision of the Secretary of State under section 8 or 10 of the 1998 Act may be revised at any time by the Secretary of State in any of the cases and circumstances set out in this Chapter.

4.123

Official error, mistake etc.

9. A decision may be revised where the decision—

4.124

(a) arose from official error; or

(b) was made in ignorance of, or was based on a mistake as to, some material fact and as a result is more advantageous to a claimant than it would otherwise have been.

DEFINITION

"official error"—see reg.2.

Decisions against which no appeal lies

10. A decision·may be revised where the decision is one which is—

4.125

(a) specified in Schedule 2 (decisions against which no appeal lies) to the 1998 Act; or

(b) prescribed by regulation 50(2) (decisions which may or may not be appealed).

DEFINITIONS

"the 1998 Act"—see reg.2.
"appeal"—*ibid.*

Decisions where there is an appeal

4.126   **11.**—(1) A decision may be revised where there is an appeal against the decision within the time prescribed by the Tribunal Procedure Rules but the appeal has not been decided.

(2) Where—

(a) the Secretary of State makes a decision under section 8 or 10 of the 1998 Act or such a decision is revised under section 9(1) of the 1998 Act ("decision A");

(b) the claimant appeals against decision A;

(c) after the appeal has been made, but before it results in a decision by the First-tier Tribunal, the Secretary of State makes another decision ("decision B") which—

   (i) supersedes decision A; or

   (ii) decides a further claim by the claimant;

(d) after the making of decision B, the First-tier Tribunal makes a decision on the appeal ("decision C"); and

(e) the Secretary of State would have made decision B differently if, at the time, the Secretary of State had been aware of decision C,

the Secretary of State may revise decision B.

DEFINITIONS

"the 1998 Act"—see reg.2.
"appeal"—*ibid.*
"claimant"—*ibid.*

Award of another benefit

4.127   **12.** Where—

(a) the Secretary of State makes a decision to award a benefit to a claimant ("the original award"); and

(b) an award of another relevant benefit or of an increase in the rate of another relevant benefit is made to the claimant or, in the case of universal credit, to a member of their family, for a period which includes the date on which the original award took effect,

the Secretary of State may revise the original award.

DEFINITIONS

"benefit"—see reg.2.
"claimant"—*ibid.*
"relevant benefit"—*ibid.*
"universal credit"—*ibid.*

Advance awards etc.

4.128   **13.** A decision pursuant to regulation 32, 33 or 34 of the Claims and Payments Regulations 2013 to make an advance award of benefit may be revised if the conditions for entitlement are found not to have been satisfied at the start of the period for which the claim is treated as having been made.

"the Claims and Payments Regulations 2013"—see reg.2.

Sanctions cases etc.

14.—(1) The following decisions may be revised—

4.129

(a) a decision that the amount of an employment and support allowance is to be reduced by virtue of section 11J(1) (sanctions) of the 2007 Act;

(b) a decision that the amount of a jobseeker's allowance is to be reduced by virtue of section 6J (higher-level sanctions) or 6K(1) (other sanctions) of the Jobseekers Act;

(c) a decision that the amount of universal credit is to be reduced by virtue of section 26(1) (higher-level sanctions) or 27(1) (other sanctions) of the 2012 Act.

(d) A decision under section 6B, 7 or 9 ("the loss of benefit provisions") of the Fraud Act that benefit ceases to be payable or falls to be reduced as a result of the person—

(e) being convicted of an offence; or

(f) agreeing to pay a penalty as an alternative to prosecution,

may be revised where that conviction is quashed or set aside by a court or where the person withdraws the agreement to pay the penalty.

DEFINITIONS

"the 2007 Act"—see reg.2.
"benefit"—*ibid.*
"employment and support allowance"—*ibid.*
"the Fraud Act"—*ibid.*
"the Jobseekers Act"—*ibid.*
"jobseeker's allowance"—*ibid.*

Other decisions relating to an employment and support allowance

15.—(1) A decision awarding an employment and support allowance may be revised in any of the following circumstances.

4.130

(2) The first circumstance is where—

(a) the decision was made on the basis that the claimant had made and was pursuing an appeal against a decision of the Secretary of State that the claimant did not have limited capability for work ("the original decision"); and

(b) the appeal in relation to the original decision is successful.

(3) The second circumstance is where—

(a) the decision incorporates a determination that the conditions in regulation 26(2) (conditions for treating claimant as having limited capability for work until a determination about limited capability for work has been made) of the Employment and Support Allowance Regulations 2013 are satisfied;

(b) those conditions were not satisfied when the claim was made; and

(c) a decision falls to be made concerning entitlement to that award in respect of a period before the date on which the award took effect.

(4) The third circumstance is where the claimant's current period of

limited capability for work is treated as a continuation of another such period under regulation 86 (linking period) of the Employment and Support Allowance Regulations 2013.

[¹ (4A) The fourth circumstance is where the decision—

(a) immediately follows the last day of a period for which the claimant was treated as capable of work or as not having limited capability for work under regulation 55ZA of the Jobseeker's Allowance Regulations or regulation 46A of the Jobseeker's Allowance Regulations 2013 (extended period of sickness) and that period lasted 13 weeks; and

(b) is not a decision which embodies a determination that the person is treated as having limited capability for work under regulation 26 of the Employment and Support Allowance Regulations 2013 (conditions for treating a claimant as having limited capability for work until a determination about limited capability for work has been made).]

(5) A decision terminating a person's entitlement to an employment and support allowance may be revised where—

(a) that entitlement was terminated because of section 1A (duration of contributory allowance) of the 2007 Act; and

(b) it is subsequently determined, in relation to the period of entitlement before that decision, that the person had or is treated as having had limited capability for work-related activity.

AMENDMENT

1. Jobseeker's Allowance (Extended Period of Sickness) Amendment Regulations 2015 (SI 2015/339) reg.8(1) and (2) (March 30, 2015).

DEFINITIONS

"appeal"—see reg.2.
"claimant"—*ibid.*
"employment and support allowance"—*ibid.*
"limited capability for work"—*ibid.*

Other decisions relating to a jobseeker's allowance

4.131

16.—(1) A decision awarding a jobseeker's allowance may be revised in any of the following circumstances.

(2) The first circumstance is where—

(a) the Secretary of State makes a conversion decision (within the meaning of regulation 5(2)(b) of the Employment and Support Allowance (Transitional Provisions, Housing Benefit and Council Tax Benefit) (Existing Awards) (No.2) Regulations 2010 (deciding whether an existing award qualifies for conversion)) in respect of a person;

(b) the person appeals against that decision;

(c) before or after the appeal is made, there is a decision to award a job-seeker's allowance as the result of a claim being made by that person; and

(d) the appeal in relation to the conversion decision referred to in sub-paragraph (a) is successful.

(3) The second circumstance is where—

(a) a person's entitlement to an employment and support allowance is terminated because of a decision which embodies a determination that the person does not have limited capability for work;

(b) the person appeals against that decision;

(c) before or after the appeal is made, there is a decision to award a job-seeker's allowance as the result of a claim being made by that person; and

(d) the appeal in relation to the termination decision referred to in sub-paragraph (a) is successful.

<small>DEFINITIONS</small>

"appeal"—see reg.2.
"benefit"—*ibid.*
"employment and support allowance"—*ibid.*
"jobseeker's allowance"—*ibid.*

Contributions cases

17.—(1) A decision ("the original decision") may be revised where—   **4.132**
(a) on or after the date of the original decision—
  (i) a late paid contribution is treated under regulation 5 (treatment of late paid contributions where no consent, connivance or negligence by the primary contributor) of the Social Security (Crediting and Treatment of Contributions and National Insurance Numbers) Regulations 2001 ("the Crediting Regulations") as paid on a date which falls on or before the date on which the original decision was made;
  (ii) a direction is given under regulation 6 (treatment of contributions paid late through ignorance or error) of those Regulations that a late paid contribution is to be treated as paid on a date which falls on or before the date on which the original decision was made; or
  (iii) an unpaid contribution is treated under regulation 60 (treatment of unpaid contributions where no consent, connivance or negligence by the primary contributor) of the Social Security (Contributions) Regulations 2001 as paid on a date which falls on or before the date on which the original decision was made; and
(b) either an award of benefit would have been made or the amount of benefit awarded would have been different.

(2) A decision may be revised where, by virtue of regulation 6C (treatment of Class 3 contributions paid under section 13A of the Act) of the Crediting Regulations, a contribution is treated as paid on a date which falls on or before the date on which the decision was made.

[¹ (3) A decision in relation to a claim for a jobseeker's allowance or an employment and support allowance may be revised at any time where—
(a) on or after the date of the decision a contribution is treated as paid as set out in regulation 7A of the Social Security (Crediting and Treatment of Contributions, and National Insurance Numbers) Regulations 2001 (treatment of Class 2 contributions paid on or before the due date); and
(b) by virtue of the contribution being so treated, the person satisfies the contribution conditions of entitlement specified in paragraph (6) in relation to that benefit.

(4) A decision to award a jobseeker's allowance or an employment and support allowance may be revised at any time where on or after the date of the decision—

(a) any of the circumstances in paragraph (5) occur; and

(b) by virtue of the circumstance occurring, the person ceases to satisfy the contribution conditions of entitlement specified in paragraph (6) in relation to that benefit.

(5) The circumstances are—

(a) a Class 2 contribution is repaid to a person in consequence of an amendment or correction of the person's relevant profits under section 9ZA or 9ZB of the Taxes Management Act 1970 (amendment or correction of return by taxpayer or officer of the Board);

(b) a Class 2 contribution is returned to a person under regulation 52 of the Social Security (Contributions) Regulations 2001 (contributions paid in error); or

(c) a Class 1 or a Class 2 contribution paid by a person to Her Majesty's Revenue and Customs under section 223 of the Finance Act 2014 (accelerated payment in respect of notice given while tax enquiry is in progress) is repaid to the person.

(6) The contribution conditions of entitlement are—

(a) in relation to a jobseeker's allowance, the conditions set out in section 2(1)(a) and (b) of the Jobseekers Act (the contribution-based conditions); or

(b) in relation to an employment and support allowance, the first and second conditions set out in paragraphs 1(1) and 2(1) of Schedule 1 to the 2007 Act (conditions relating to national insurance).

(7) In this regulation "relevant profits" has the meaning given in section 11(3) of the Contributions and Benefits Act]

AMENDMENT

1. Social Security (Credits, and Crediting and Treatment of Contributions) (Consequential and Miscellaneous Amendments (SI 2016/1145) reg.6 (January 1, 2017).

DEFINITION

"benefit"—see reg.2.

Other decisions relating to personal independence payment

4.133
18.—(1) Where the Secretary of State makes a decision awarding personal independence payment which takes effect immediately after the expiry of an existing award under regulation 33(3) (advance claim for and award of personal independence payment) of the Claims and Payments Regulations 2013, that decision may be revised if the requirements for entitlement are found not to have been met on the date on which the decision takes effect.

(2) A decision that personal independence payment is not payable to a person for any period may be revised where—

(a) the Secretary of State determines that the person meets the condition in section 85(2) of the 2012 Act (care home residents where the costs of qualifying services are borne out of local or public funds) on incomplete evidence in accordance with regulation 39(5); and

(b) after that determination is made, any of the costs of the qualifying services are recovered from the person for whom they are provided.

(3) A decision of the Secretary of State made in consequence of a negative determination may be revised at any time if it contains an error to which the claimant did not materially contribute.

DEFINITIONS

"the 2012 Act"—see reg.2.
"personal independence payment"—*ibid.*

Other decisions relating to universal credit

19.—(1) Where the Secretary of State has reduced the amount of an award of universal credit as a consequence of regulation 81 (reduction of universal credit) of the Universal Credit Regulations, that decision may be revised. 4.134

(2) A decision in relation to universal credit which adopts a determination made under the Rent Officers Order 2013 may be revised at any time in consequence of a rent officer's redetermination made under that Order which resulted in an increase in the amount which represents rent for the purposes of calculating the housing costs element in universal credit.

DEFINITIONS

"the Universal Credit Regulations"—see reg.2.
"universal credit"—*ibid.*

CHAPTER 3

PROCEDURE AND EFFECTIVE DATE

Procedure for making an application for a revision

20.—(1) The Secretary of State may treat an application for a supersession under section 10 of the 1998 Act as an application for a revision under section 9 of that Act. 4.135

(2) The following paragraph applies where the Secretary of State, in order to consider all the issues raised by the application, requires further evidence or information from a person who has applied for a revision ("the applicant").

(3) The Secretary of State must notify the applicant that—
(a) the further evidence or information specified in the notification is required;
(b) if the applicant provides the relevant evidence or information within one month of the date of notification or such longer period as the Secretary of State may allow, the decision may be revised taking such evidence or information into account; and

(c) if the applicant does not provide such evidence or information within that period, the decision may be revised using such evidence or information as was submitted with the application for revision.

DEFINITION

"the date of notification"—see reg.2.

Effective date of a revision

4.136   **21.** Where, on a revision under section 9 of the 1998 Act, the Secretary of State decides that the date from which the decision under section 8 or 10 of that Act ("the original decision") took effect was wrong, the revision takes effect from the date from which the original decision would have taken effect had the error not been made.

DEFINITION

"the 1998 Act"—see reg.2.

PART III

SUPERSESSIONS

CHAPTER 1

GROUNDS FOR SUPERSESSION

Introduction

4.137   **22.** Subject to regulation 32 (decisions which may not be superseded), the Secretary of State may make a decision under section 10 ("a superseding decision") of the 1998 Act in any of the cases and circumstances set out in this Chapter.

Changes of circumstances

4.138   **23.**—(1) The Secretary of State may supersede a decision in respect of which—
    (a) there has been a relevant change of circumstances since the decision to be superseded had effect or, in the case of an advance award under regulation 32, 33 or 34 of the Claims and Payments Regulations 2013, since it was made; or
    (b) it is expected that a relevant change of circumstances will occur.
    (2) The fact that a person has become terminally ill is not a relevant change of circumstances for the purposes of paragraph (1) unless an application for supersession is made which contains an express statement that the person is terminally ill.

DEFINITIONS

"the Claims and Payments Regulations 2013"—see reg.2.
"terminally ill"—*ibid.*

Error of law, ignorance, mistake etc.

24. A decision of the Secretary of State, other than one to which regula-   4.139
tion 25 (decisions against which no appeal lies) refers, may be superseded
where—

(a) the decision was wrong in law, or was made in ignorance of, or was
based on a mistake as to, some material fact; and

(b) an application for a supersession was received, or a decision was taken
by the Secretary of State to act on the Secretary of State's own initiative, more than one month after the date of notification of the decision to be superseded or after the expiry of such longer period as may
have been allowed under regulation 6 (late application for a revision).

Decisions against which no appeal lies

25. A decision specified in Schedule 2 (decisions against which no appeal   4.140
lies) to the 1998 Act or prescribed in regulation 50(2) (decisions which may
or may not be appealed) may be superseded.

DEFINITIONS

"the 1998 Act"—see reg.2.
"appeal"—*ibid.*

Medical evidence and limited capability for work etc.

26.—(1) An employment and support allowance decision, a personal   4.141
independence payment decision or universal credit decision may be
superseded where, since the decision was made, the Secretary of State
has—

(a) received medical evidence from a healthcare professional or other
person approved by the Secretary of State; or

[¹ (b) made a determination that the claimant is to be treated as having—

(i) limited capability for work in accordance with regulation
16, 21, 22 or 29 of the Employment and Support Allowance
Regulations 2013; or

(ii) limited capability for work or for work and work-related activity
in accordance with Part 5 (capability for work or work-related
activity) of the Universal Credit Regulations.]

(2) The decision awarding personal independence payment may be
superseded where there has been a negative determination.

(3) In this regulation—

"an employment and support allowance decision", "personal independence payment decision" and "universal credit decision" each has the
meaning given in Schedule 1 (effective dates for superseding decisions
made on the ground of a change of circumstances);

"healthcare professional" means—

(a) a registered medical practitioner;

(b) a registered nurse; or

(c) an occupational therapist or physiotherapist registered with a regulatory body established by an Order in Council under section 60 (regulation of health professions, social workers, other care workers etc.) of the Health Act 1999.

AMENDMENT

1. Universal Credit and Miscellaneous Amendments Regulations 2014 (SI 2014/597) reg.6 (April 28, 2014).

DEFINITIONS

"claimant"—see reg.2.
"employment and support allowance"—*ibid.*
"limited capability for work"—*ibid.*
"personal independence payment"—*ibid.*
"universal credit"—*ibid.*

Sanctions cases

4.142   **27.**—(1) A decision as to the amount of an award of benefit may be superseded where the amount of that award is to be reduced by virtue of—

(a) section 11J(1) (sanctions) of the 2007 Act;
(b) section 6J(1) (higher-level sanctions) or 6K(1) (other sanctions) of the Jobseekers Act; or
(c) section 26(1) (higher-level sanctions) or 27(1) (other sanctions) of the 2012 Act.

(2) A decision reducing an award of benefit by virtue of any of those provisions may be superseded where the reduction falls to be suspended or terminated.

DEFINITIONS

"the 2007 Act"—see reg.2.
"benefit"—*ibid.*

Loss of benefit cases

4.143   **28.** A decision that a benefit is payable to a claimant may be superseded where that benefit ceases to be payable or falls to be reduced by virtue of section 6B, 7 or 9 of the Fraud Act (loss of benefit provisions).

DEFINITION

"benefit"—see reg.2.

Contributions cases

4.144   **29.** The Secretary of State may supersede a decision ("the original decision") where, on or after the date on which the decision is made, a late or an unpaid contribution is treated as paid under—

(a) regulation 5 of the Social Security (Crediting and Treatment of Contributions and National Insurance Numbers) Regulations 2001 (treatment of late paid contributions where no consent, connivance or negligence by the primary contributor) on a date which falls on or before the date on which the original decision was made;

(b) regulation 6 of those Regulations (treatment of contributions paid late through ignorance or error) on a date which falls on or before the date on which the original decision was made; or

(c) regulation 60 of the Social Security (Contributions) Regulations 2001 (treatment of unpaid contributions where no consent, connivance or negligence by the primary contributor) on a date which falls on or before the date on which the original decision was made.

Housing costs: universal credit

30.—(1) A decision in relation to universal credit which adopts a deter-   4.145
mination made under the Rent Officers Order 2013 may be superseded where, in consequence of a rent officer's redetermination made in under that Order, the amount which represents rent for the purposes of calculating the housing costs element in universal credit is reduced.

DEFINITIONS

"the Rent Officers Order 2013"—see reg.2.
"universal credit"—*ibid.*

Tribunal decisions

31. The Secretary of State may supersede a decision of the First-tier   4.146
Tribunal or Upper Tribunal which—
   (a) was made in ignorance of, or was based upon a mistake as to, some material fact; or
   (b) in a case where section 26(5) (appeals involving issues that arise in other cases) of the 1998 Act applies, was made in accordance with section 26(4)(b)of that Act.

CHAPTER 2

SUPERSEDING DECISIONS: LIMITATIONS AND PROCEDURE

Decisions which may not be superseded

32. A decision which may be revised under section 9 of the 1998 Act may   4.147
not be superseded under Chapter 1 of this Part unless—
   (a) circumstances arise in which the Secretary of State may revise the decision under Part 2; and
   (b) further circumstances arise in relation to that decision which—
       (i) are not set out in that Part; but
       (ii) are set out in Chapter 1 of this Part or are ones where a superseding decision may be made in accordance with regulation 33(3).

DEFINITION

"the 1998 Act"—see reg.2.

Procedure for making an application for a supersession

4.148   **33.**—(1) The Secretary of State may treat an application for a revision under section 9 of the 1998 Act, or a notification of a change of circumstances, as an application for a supersession under section 10 of that Act.

(2) The following paragraph applies where the Secretary of State, in order to consider all the issues raised by the application, requires further evidence or information from a person who has applied for a supersession ("the applicant").

(3) The Secretary of State must notify the applicant that—

(a) the further evidence or information specified in the notification is required;

(b) if the applicant provides the relevant evidence or information within one month of the date of notification or such longer period as the Secretary of State may allow, the decision may be superseded taking such information or evidence into account; and

(c) if the applicant does not provide such evidence or information within that period, the decision to be superseded may be superseded taking into account only such evidence or information as was submitted with the application for a supersession.

DEFINITION

"the date of notification"—see reg.2.

CHAPTER 3

EFFECTIVE DATES FOR SUPERSESSIONS

Introduction

4.149   **34.** This Chapter and Schedule 1 (effective dates for superseding decisions made on the ground of a change of circumstances) contains exceptions to the provisions of section 10(5) of the 1998 Act as to the date from which a decision under section 10 of that Act which supersedes an earlier decision takes effect.

DEFINITION

"the 1998 Act"—see reg.2.

Effective dates: Secretary of State decisions

4.150   **35.**—(1) Schedule 1 (effective dates for superseding decisions made on the ground of a change of circumstances) makes provision for the date from which a superseding decision takes effect where there has been, or it is anticipated that there will be, a relevant change of circumstances since the earlier decision took effect.

(2) This paragraph applies where the Secretary of State supersedes a decision—

(a) on the ground that the decision was wrong in law, or was made in ignorance of, or was based on a mistake as to, some material fact, in accordance with regulation 24 (error of law, ignorance, mistake etc.); or

(b) under regulation 25 (decisions against which no appeal lies).

(3) In a case where paragraph (2) applies and the superseding decision relates to a jobseeker's allowance or an employment and support allowance, the superseding decision takes effect from the first day of the benefit week in which the superseding decision, or where applicable, the application for supersession, was made.

(4) In a case where paragraph (2) applies and the superseding decision relates to universal credit, the superseding decision takes effect from the first day of the assessment period in which the superseding decision, or where applicable, the application for supersession, was made.

(5) A superseding decision made in consequence of a decision which is a relevant determination for the purposes of section 27 of the 1998 Act (restrictions on entitlement to benefit in certain cases of error) takes effect from the date of the relevant determination.

(6) In the case of an employment and support allowance, a superseding decision made in accordance with regulation 26(1) (medical evidence and limited capability for work etc.), following an application by the claimant, that embodies a determination that the claimant has limited capability for work-related activity, takes effect from the date of the application.

(7) In the case of an employment and support allowance, a superseding decision made on the Secretary of State's own initiative in accordance with regulation 26(1) that embodies a determination that the claimant has—
  (a) limited capability for work; or
  (b) limited capability for work-related activity; or
  (c) limited capability for work and limited capability for work-related activity,
takes effect [¹ the day after the last day of the relevant period as defined in regulation 5(4) of the Employment and Support Allowance Regulations 2013] where the determination is the first such determination.

(8) In the case of an employment and support allowance where regulation 6 of the Employment and Support Allowance Regulations 2013 (assessment phase – previous claimants) applies, a superseding decision made in accordance with regulation 26(1) of these Regulations that embodies a determination that the claimant has—
  (a) limited capability for work; or
  (b) limited capability for work-related activity; or
  (c) limited capability for work and limited capability for work-related activity,
takes effect from the beginning of the 14th week of the claimant's continuous period of limited capability for work.

(9) In the case of universal credit, a superseding decision made in accordance with regulation 26(1) that embodies a determination that the claimant has limited capability for work or limited capability for work and work-related activity takes effect—
  (a) in a case to which regulation 28(1) (period for which the LCW or LCWRA element is not to be included) of the Universal Credit Regulations applies, from the beginning of the assessment period specified in that paragraph; or
  (b) in any other case, from the beginning of the assessment period in which the decision (if made on the Secretary of State's own initiative) or the application for a supersession was made.

(10) A superseding decision to which regulation 27(1) (sanctions cases: reduction in an award) applies takes effect from the beginning of the period specified in—

(a) regulation 54 of the Employment and Support Allowance Regulations 2013, where the decision relates to the start of a reduction in the amount of an employment and support allowance;

(b) regulation 56 of the Employment and Support Allowance Regulations 2013, where the decision relates to ending the suspension of a such a reduction where a fraud penalty ceases to apply;

(c) regulation 22 of the Jobseeker's Allowance Regulations 2013, where the decision relates to the start of a reduction in the amount of a jobseeker's allowance;

(d) regulation 24 of the Jobseeker's Allowance Regulations 2013, where the decision relates to ending the suspension of such a reduction where a fraud penalty ceases to apply;

(e) regulation 106 of the Universal Credit Regulations, where the decision relates to the start of a reduction in the amount of universal credit;

(f) regulation 108 of the Universal Credit Regulations, where the decision relates to ending the suspension of such a reduction where a fraud penalty ceases to apply.

(11) A superseding decision to which regulation 27(2) (sanctions cases: suspension and termination of a reduction) applies takes effect from the beginning of the period specified in—

(a) regulation 56 of the Employment and Support Allowance Regulations 2013, where the decision relates to the start of a suspension where a fraud penalty applies;

(b) regulation 57 of the Employment and Support Allowance Regulations 2013, where the decision relates to the termination of a reduction in the amount of an employment and support allowance;

(c) regulation 24 of the Jobseeker's Allowance Regulations 2013, where the decision relates to the start of a suspension where a fraud penalty applies;

(d) regulation 25 of the Jobseeker's Allowance Regulations 2013, where the decision relates to the termination of a reduction in the amount of a jobseeker's allowance;

(e) regulation 108 of the Universal Credit Regulations, where the decision relates to the start of a suspension where a fraud penalty applies;

(f) regulation 109 of the Universal Credit Regulations, where the decision relates to the termination of a reduction in the amount of an award of universal credit.

(12) A superseding decision to which regulation 28 (loss of benefit provisions) applies takes effect from the date prescribed for the purposes of section 6B or 7 of the Fraud Act.

(13) Where a decision is superseded in accordance with regulation 29 (contributions cases), the superseding decision takes effect from the date referred to in regulation 29(a), (b) or (c) on which the late or unpaid contribution is treated as paid.

(14) A superseding decision made in consequence of a redetermination in accordance with regulation 30 (housing costs: universal credit) takes effect on the first day of the first assessment period following the day on which that redetermination is received by Secretary of State.

1. Jobseeker's Allowance (Extended Period of Sickness) Amendment Regulations 2015 (SI 2015/339) reg.8(1) and (3) (March 30, 2015).

DEFINITIONS

"assessment period"—see reg.2 and Universal Credit Regs reg.21.
"benefit"—see reg.2.
"claimant"—*ibid.*
"employment and support allowance"—*ibid.*
"the Fraud Act"—*ibid.*
"fraud penalty"—*ibid.*
"jobseeker's allowance"—*ibid.*
"limited capability for work"—*ibid.*
"the Universal Credit Regulations"—*ibid.*
"universal credit"—*ibid.*

Effective dates for superseding decisions where changes notified late

36.—(1) For the purposes of regulation 35(1) (effective dates: Secretary of State decisions) and paragraphs 6, 14 and 21 of Schedule 1 (effective dates for superseding decisions made on the ground of a change of circumstances), the Secretary of State may extend the time allowed for a person ("the applicant") to give notice of a change of circumstances in so far as it affects the effective date of the change if all of the following conditions are met.

4.151

(2) The first condition is that an application is made to the Secretary of State at an appropriate office for an extension of time.

(3) The second condition is that the application—

(a) contains particulars of the change of circumstances and the reasons for the failure to give notice of the change of circumstances on an earlier date; and

(b) is made—

(i) within 13 months of the date on which the change occurred; or

(ii) in the case of personal independence payment where a notification is given under paragraph 15 of Part 2 of Schedule 1 (effective dates for superseding decisions made on the ground of a change of circumstances), within 13 months of the date on which the claimant first satisfied the conditions of entitlement to the particular rate of personal independence payment.

(4) The third condition is that the Secretary of State is satisfied that it is reasonable to grant the extension.

(5) The fourth condition is that the change of circumstances notified by the applicant is relevant to the decision which is to be superseded.

(6) The fifth condition is that the Secretary of State is satisfied that, due to special circumstances, it was not practicable for the applicant to give notice of the change of circumstances within the relevant notification period.

(7) In determining whether it is reasonable to grant an extension of time—

(a) the Secretary of State must have regard to the principle that the greater the amount of time that has elapsed between the end of the relevant notification period and the date of the application, the more compelling should be the special circumstances on which the application is based;

(b) no account must be taken of the fact that the applicant or any person acting for them was unaware of, or misunderstood, the law applicable to the case (including ignorance or misunderstanding of the time limits imposed by these Regulations); and

(c) no account must be taken of the fact that the Upper Tribunal or a court has taken a different view of the law from that previously understood and applied.

(8) An application under this regulation which has been refused may not be renewed.

(9) In this regulation, "the relevant notification period" means—

(a) in the case of universal credit, the assessment period in which the change of circumstances occurs; or

(b) in any other case, a period of one month, beginning with the date on which the change of circumstances occurred.

DEFINITION

"personal independence payment"—see reg.2.

Effective dates: tribunal cases

4.152

37.—(1) This paragraph applies where—

(a) the Secretary of State supersedes a decision of the First-tier Tribunal or the Upper Tribunal on the ground that it is made in ignorance of, or based on a mistake as to, a material fact in accordance with regulation 31(a) (tribunal decisions), and

(b) as a result of that ignorance or mistake, the decision to be superseded was more advantageous to the claimant than it would otherwise have been.

(2) In a case where paragraph (1) applies where the decision relates to—

(a) a jobseeker's allowance;

(b) personal independence payment,

the superseding decision takes effect from the date on which the decision of the First-tier Tribunal or the Upper Tribunal took, or was to take, effect.

(3) In a case where paragraph (1) applies and the decision relates to an employment and support allowance or universal credit where—

(a) the material fact does not relate to a limited capability for work determination embodied in or necessary to the decision; or

(b) the material fact does relate to such a determination and the Secretary of State is satisfied that at the time the decision was made the claimant knew or could reasonably be expected to know of it and that it was relevant,

the superseding decision takes effect from the first day of the benefit week or (as the case may be) the assessment period in which in the Tribunal's decision took or was to take effect.

(4) Where the Secretary of State supersedes a decision of the First-tier Tribunal or the Upper Tribunal in accordance with regulation 31(b) (tribunal decisions), the decision takes effect—

(a) if the decision relates to personal independence payment, from the date on which the decision of the First-tier Tribunal or the Upper Tribunal would have taken effect had it been decided in accordance with the determination of the Upper Tribunal or the court in the appeal referred to in section 26(1)(b) of the 1998 Act;

(b) if the decision relates to a jobseeker's allowance or an employment and support allowance, from the first day of the benefit week in which the Tribunal's decision would have taken effect had it been so decided;

(c) if the decision relates to universal credit, from the first day of the assessment period in which the Tribunal's decision would have taken effect had it been so decided.

(5) Paragraph (6) applies where—

(a) the Upper Tribunal, or the court as defined in section 27(7) (restrictions on entitlement to benefit in certain cases of error) of the 1998 Act, determines an appeal as mentioned in subsection (1)(a) of that section ("the relevant determination");

(b) the Secretary of State makes a decision of the kind specified in subsection (1)(b) of that section;

(c) there is an appeal against the relevant determination;

(d) after the Secretary of State's decision, payment is suspended in accordance with regulation 44 (suspension in prescribed cases); and

(e) on appeal a court, within the meaning of section 27, reverses the relevant determination in whole or part.

(6) A consequential decision by the Secretary of State under section 10 of the 1998 Act which supersedes an earlier decision of the Secretary of State under paragraph (5)(b) takes effect from the date on which the earlier decision took effect.

DEFINITIONS

"the 1998 Act"—see reg.2.
"appeal"—*ibid.*
"assessment period"—see reg.2 and Universal Credit Regs reg.21.
"benefit"—see reg.2.
"benefit week"—*ibid.*
"claimant"—*ibid.*
"employment and support allowance"—*ibid.*
"jobseeker's allowance"—*ibid.*
"personal independence payment"—*ibid.*
"universal credit"—*ibid.*

PART IV

OTHER MATTERS RELATING TO DECISION- MAKING

Correction of accidental errors

38.—(1) An accidental error in a decision of the Secretary of State, or in any record of such a decision, may be corrected by the Secretary of State at any time.

(2) Such a correction is to be treated as part of that decision or of that record.

(3) The Secretary of State must give written notice of the correction as soon as practicable to the person to whom the decision was given.

(4) In calculating the time within which an application may be made

4.153

under regulation 5 (revision on any grounds) for a decision to be revised, no account is to be taken of any day falling before the day on which notice of the correction was given.

Determinations on incomplete evidence

4.154   **39.**—(1) The following provisions of this regulation apply for the purposes of a decision under section 8 or 10 of the 1998 Act.

(2) Where—

(a) a determination falls to be made by the Secretary of State concerning the matter mentioned in paragraph (3); and

(b) it appears to the Secretary of State that the Secretary of State is not in possession of all of the evidence or information which is relevant for the purposes of the determination,

the Secretary of State must make the determination on the assumption that the relevant evidence or information which is not in the Secretary of State's possession is adverse to the claimant.

(3) The matter is whether, for the purposes of regulation 45 (relevant education) of the Jobseeker's Allowance Regulations 2013 a person is by virtue of that regulation to be treated as receiving relevant education.

(4) Where—

(a) a determination falls to be made by the Secretary of State as to what costs are to be included in claimant's award of universal credit under section 11 (housing costs) of the 2012 Act; and

(b) it appears to the Secretary of State that the Secretary of State is not in possession of all of the evidence or information which is relevant for the purposes of the determination,

the Secretary of State may make the determination on the assumption that the costs to be included in the claimant's award under that section are those that the Secretary of State is able to determine using such evidence or information as is in the Secretary of State's possession.

(5) Where, in the case of personal independence payment—

(a) a determination falls to be made by the Secretary of State as to whether a person meets the condition in section 85(2) (care home residents where the costs of qualifying services are borne out of local or public funds) of the 2012 Act; and

(b) it appears to the Secretary of State that, having made reasonable enquiries, the Secretary of State is not in possession of all of the evidence or information which is or could be relevant for the purposes of the determination,

the Secretary of State may make the determination using such information or evidence as is in the Secretary of State's possession.

DEFINITIONS

"the 2012 Act"—see reg.2.
"claimant"—*ibid.*

Determinations as to limited capability for work

4.155   **40.**—(1) Where, in relation to an award of an employment and support allowance, the Secretary of State makes a determination (including a determination made following a change of circumstances) whether a person—

(a) has or does not have limited capability for work; or

(b) is to be treated as having or not having limited capability for work,

which is embodied in or necessary to a decision under Chapter 2 of Part 1 of the 1998 Act (decisions and appeals) or on which such a decision is based, that determination is to be conclusive for the purposes of any further decision relating to such an allowance.

(2) Paragraph (1) applies to determinations made in relation to universal credit as it applies in the case of an employment and support allowance.

(3) Where, in relation to any purpose for which Part 1 (employment and support allowance) of the 2007 Act or Part 1 (universal credit) of the 2012 Act applies, a determination falls to be made as to whether a person—

(a) is, or is to be treated as, having or not having limited capability for work; or

(b) is terminally ill,

that issue is to be determined by the Secretary of State, notwithstanding the fact that any other matter falls to be determined by another authority.

DEFINITIONS

> "the 1998 Act"—see reg.2.
> "employment and support allowance"—*ibid.*
> "limited capability for work"—*ibid.*
> "universal credit"—*ibid.*

Effect of alterations affecting universal credit

41.—(1) Subject to paragraph (3), an alteration in the amount of a person's employed earnings (within the meaning of regulation 55(1) of the Universal Credit Regulations) made in accordance with Chapter 2 of Part 6 (earned income) of the Universal Credit Regulations in consequence of information provided to the Secretary of State by HMRC is prescribed for the purposes of section 159D(1)(b)(vi) (effect of alterations affecting universal credit) of the Administration Act.   **4.156**

(2) For the purposes of this regulation, "alteration" means an increase or decrease in such earnings.

(3) Where the person disputes the figure used in accordance with regulation 55 (employed earnings) of the Universal Credit Regulations to calculate employed earnings in relation to any assessment period, the Secretary of State must—

(a) inform the person that they may request that the Secretary of State gives a decision in relation to the amount of universal credit payable in relation to that assessment period; and

(b) where such a decision is requested, give it within 14 days of receiving the request or as soon as practicable afterwards.

(4) Paragraph (3) does not affect the validity of anything done under section 159D(2) or (3) of the Administration Act in relation to the person's award.

(5) A decision made in accordance with paragraph (3) takes effect on the date on which the alteration under section 159(D)(2) or (3) came into force in relation to the person.

DEFINITIONS

> "the Administration Act"—see reg.2.
> "assessment period"—see reg.2 and Universal Credit Regs reg.21.

"the Universal Credit Regulations"—see reg.2.
"universal credit"—*ibid.*

Issues for HMRC

4.157　　**42.**—(1) Where, on consideration of any claim or other matter, it appears to the Secretary of State that an issue arises which, by virtue of section 8 of the Transfer Act, falls to be decided by an officer of HMRC, the Secretary of State must refer that issue to HMRC.

(2) Where—

(a) the Secretary of State has decided any claim or other matter on an assumption of facts—

    (i) which appeared to the Secretary of State not to be in dispute, but

    (ii) concerning which, had an issue arisen, that issue would have fallen, by virtue of section 8 of the Transfer Act, to be decided by HMRC;

(b) an application for a revision or supersession is made, or an appeal is brought, in relation to that claim or other matter; and

(c) it appears to the Secretary of State on receipt of that application or appeal that such an issue arises,

the Secretary of State must refer that issue to HMRC.

(3) Pending the final decision of any issue which has been referred to HMRC in accordance with paragraph (1) or (2), the Secretary of State may—

(a) determine any other issue arising on consideration of the claim, application or other matter,

(b) seek a preliminary opinion from HMRC on the issue referred and decide the claim, application or other matter in accordance with that opinion; or

(c) defer making any decision on the claim, application or other matter.

(4) On receipt by the Secretary of State of the final decision of an issue which has been referred to HMRC under paragraph (1) or (2), the Secretary of State must—

(a) in a case where the Secretary of State made a decision under paragraph (3)(b), decide whether to revise the decision under section 9 of the 1998 Act or to supersede it under section 10 of that Act;

(b) in a case to which paragraph (3)(a) or (c) applies, decide the claim, application or other matter in accordance with the final decision of the issue so referred.

(5) In this regulation—

(a) "final decision" means the decision of HMRC under section 8 (decisions by officers of Board) of the Transfer Act or the determination of any appeal in relation to that decision; and

(b) "the Transfer Act" means the Social Security Contributions (Transfer of Functions, etc.) Act 1999.

DEFINITIONS

"appeal"—see reg.2.
"HMRC"—*ibid.*

Appeals raising issues for HMRC

4.158　　**43.**—(1) This regulation applies where—

(a) a person has appealed to the First-tier Tribunal and it appears to the

First-tier Tribunal that an issue arises which, by virtue of section 8 of the Transfer Act, falls to be decided by HMRC; and

(b) the tribunal has required the Secretary of State to refer that issue to HMRC.

(2) Pending the final decision of any issue which has been referred to HMRC in accordance with paragraph (1), the Secretary of State may revise the decision under appeal under section 9 of the 1998 Act, or make a further decision under section 10 of that Act superseding that decision, in accordance with the Secretary of State's determination of any issue other than one which has been so referred.

(3) On receipt by the Secretary of State of the final decision of an issue which has been referred to HMRC in accordance with paragraph (1), the Secretary of State must consider whether the decision under appeal ought to be revised or superseded under the 1998 Act, and—

(a) if so, revise it or make a further decision which supersedes it; or

(b) if not, invite the First-tier Tribunal to determine to appeal.

(4) In this regulation, "final decision" and "Transfer Act" have the same meaning as in regulation 42 (issues for HMRC).

DEFINITIONS

"the 1998 Act"—see reg.2.
"appeal"—*ibid.*
"HMRC"—*ibid.*

PART V

SUSPENSION

Suspension in prescribed cases

44.—(1) The Secretary of State may suspend, in whole or part, payment of any benefit to a person ("P") in the circumstances described in paragraph (2).

(2) The circumstances are where—

(a) it appears to the Secretary of State that—

    (i) an issue arises whether the conditions for entitlement to the benefit are or were fulfilled;

    (ii) an issue arises whether a decision relating to an award of the benefit should be revised under section 9 or superseded under section 10 of the 1998 Act,

    (iii) an issue arises whether any amount of benefit paid to P is recoverable under or by virtue of section 71ZB, 71ZG or 71ZH of the Administration Act,

    (iv) the last address notified to the Secretary of State of P is not the address at which P resides,

(b) an appeal is pending in P's case against a decision of the First-tier Tribunal, the Upper Tribunal or a court; or

(c) an appeal is pending against a decision given by the Upper Tribunal or a court in a different case and it appears to the Secretary of State that, if the appeal were to be decided in a particular way, an issue

4.159

would arise as to whether the award of any benefit to P (whether the same benefit or not) ought to be revised or superseded.

(3) For the purposes of section 21(2)(c) (suspension in prescribed circumstances) of the 1998 Act, where an appeal against the decision has not been brought or an application for permission to appeal against the decision has not been made but the time for doing so has not yet expired, an appeal is pending in the circumstances described in paragraph (4).

(4) The circumstances are where a decision of the First-tier Tribunal, the Upper Tribunal or a court has been made and the Secretary of State—

    (a) is awaiting receipt of that decision; or

    (b) in the case of a decision of the First-tier Tribunal, is considering whether to apply for a statement of reasons for the decision or has applied for such a statement and is awaiting receipt; or

    (c) has received that decision or, if it is a decision of the First-tier Tribunal has received the statement of reasons for it, and is considering whether to apply for permission to appeal, or where permission to appeal has been granted, is considering whether to appeal.

(5) Where payment of any benefit is suspended as the result of paragraph (2)(b) or (c), the Secretary of State must, as soon as reasonably practicable, give written notice to P of any proposal to—

    (a) request a statement of the reasons for a tribunal decision;

    (b) apply for permission to appeal; or

    (c) make an appeal.

DEFINITIONS

    "the 1998 Act"—see reg.2.
    "appeal"—*ibid.*
    "benefit"—*ibid.*

Provision of information or evidence

4.160   **45.**—(1) This regulation applies where the Secretary of State requires information or evidence from a person mentioned in paragraph (2) ("P") in order to determine whether a decision awarding a benefit should be revised under section 9 of the 1998 Act or superseded under section 10 of that Act.

(2) The persons are—

    (a) a person in respect of whom payment of any benefit has been suspended in the circumstances set out in regulation 44(2)(a) (suspension in prescribed cases);

    (b) a person who has made an application for a decision of the Secretary of State to be revised or superseded;

    (c) a person from whom the Secretary of State requires information or evidence under regulation 38(2) (evidence and information in connection with an award) of the Claims and Payments Regulations 2013;

    (d) a person from whom the Secretary of State requires documents, certificates or other evidence under regulation 31(3) (evidence and information) of the Jobseeker's Allowance Regulations 2013;

    (e) a person whose entitlement to an employment and support allowance or universal credit is conditional on their having, or being treated as having, limited capability for work.

(3) The Secretary of State must notify P of the requirements of this regulation.

(4) P must either—

(a) supply the information or evidence within—

  (i) a period of 14 days beginning with the date on which the notification under paragraph (3) was given or sent to P or such longer period as the Secretary of State allows in that notification, or

  (ii) such longer period as P satisfies the Secretary of State is necessary in order to comply with the requirements, or

(b) satisfy the Secretary of State within the period applicable under sub-paragraph (a)(i) that either—

  (i) the information or evidence does not exist, or

  (ii) it is not possible for P to obtain it.

(5) In relation to a person to whom paragraph (2)(d) refers, paragraph (4)(a)(i) has effect as if for "14 days" there were substituted "7 days".

(6) The Secretary of State may suspend the payment of a benefit, in whole or part, to any person to whom paragraph (2)(b), (c), (d) or (e) applies who fails to satisfy the requirements of paragraph (4).

(7) In this regulation, "evidence" includes evidence which a person is required to provide in accordance with regulation 2 (evidence of incapacity for work, limited capability for work and confinement) of the Social Security (Medical Evidence) Regulations 1976.

<small>DEFINITIONS</small>

"benefit"—see reg.2.
"jobseeker's allowance"—*ibid.*
"limited capability for work"—*ibid.*

Making of payments which have been suspended

46. The Secretary of State must pay a benefit which has been suspended where— 4.161

(a) in a case where regulation 44(2)(a) (suspension in prescribed cases) applies, the Secretary of State is satisfied that the benefit is properly payable and that there are no outstanding issues to be resolved;

(b) in a case to which regulation 45(6) (provision of information or evidence) applies, the Secretary of State is satisfied that the benefit is properly payable and that the requirements of regulation 45(4) have been satisfied;

(c) in a case to which regulation 44(2)(b) (suspension in prescribed cases) applies, the Secretary of State—

  (i) does not, in the case of a decision of the First-tier Tribunal, apply for a statement of the reasons for that decision within the period specified under the Tribunal Procedure Rules;

  (ii) does not, in the case of a decision of the First-tier Tribunal, the Upper Tribunal or a court, make an application for permission to appeal or (where permission to appeal is granted) make the appeal within the time prescribed for the making of such application or appeal;

  (iii) withdraws an application for permission to appeal or withdraws the appeal; or

  (iv) is refused permission to appeal, in circumstances where it is not open to the Secretary of State to renew the application for permission or to make a further application for permission to appeal;

(d) in a case to which regulation 44(2)(c) (suspension in prescribed cases) applies, the Secretary of State, in relation to the decision of the Upper Tribunal or a court in a different case—

(i) does not make an application for permission to appeal or (where permission to appeal is granted) make the appeal within the time prescribed for the making of such application or appeal;

(ii) withdraws an application for permission to appeal or withdraws the appeal;

(iii) is refused permission to appeal, in circumstances where it is not open to the Secretary of State to renew the application for permission or to make a further application for permission to appeal.

DEFINITIONS

"appeal"—see reg.2.
"benefit"—*ibid.*
"the Tribunal Procedure Rules"—*ibid.*

PART VI

TERMINATION

Termination for failure to furnish information or evidence

4.162   47.—(1) This regulation applies where payment of a benefit to a person ("P") has been suspended in full under—

(a) regulation 44 (suspension in prescribed cases) and P subsequently fails to comply with a requirement for information or evidence under regulation 45 (provision of information or evidence) and more than one month has elapsed since the requirement was made; or

(b) regulation 45(6) and more than one month has elapsed since the first payment was suspended.

(2) In a case to which this regulation applies, except where entitlement ceases on an earlier date other than under this regulation, the Secretary of State must decide that P ceases to be entitled to that benefit with effect from the date on which the payment of the benefit was suspended.

DEFINITION

"benefit"—see reg.2.

Termination in the case of entitlement to alternative benefits

4.163   48.—(1) This paragraph applies where an award of a jobseeker's allowance ("the existing benefit") exists in favour of a person and, if that award did not exist and a claim was made by that person for an employment and support allowance ("the alternative benefit"), an award of the alternative benefit would be made on that claim.

(2) This paragraph applies where an award of an employment and support allowance ("the existing benefit") exists in favour of a person and, if that award did not exist and a claim was made by that person for a jobseeker's allowance ("the alternative benefit"), an award of the alternative benefit would be made on that claim.

(3) In a case where paragraph (1) or (2) applies, if a claim for the alternative benefit is made, the Secretary of State may bring to an end the award of the existing benefit if satisfied that an award of the alternative benefit will be made.

(4) Where the Secretary of State brings an award of the existing benefit to an end under paragraph (3), the Secretary of State must end the award on the day immediately preceding the first day on which an award of the alternative benefit takes effect.

(5) Where an award of a jobseeker's allowance is made in accordance with this regulation, paragraph 4 of Schedule 1 to the Jobseekers Act (waiting days) does not apply.

(6) Where an award of an employment and support allowance is made in accordance with this regulation, paragraph 2 (waiting days) of Schedule 2 (supplementary provisions) to the 2007 Act does not apply.

DEFINITIONS

"the 2007 Act"—see reg.2.
"benefit"—*ibid.*
"employment and support allowance"—*ibid.*
"the Jobseekers Act"—*ibid.*
"jobseeker's allowance"—*ibid.*

PART VII

APPEALS

Other persons with a right of appeal

49. In addition to the claimant, but subject to regulation 7 (consideration of revision before appeal), the following persons have the right of appeal under section 12(2) of the 1998 Act— 4.164

  (a) any person appointed by the Secretary of State under regulation 56 (payments on death) of the Claims and Payments Regulations 2013 to proceed with the claim of a person who claimed benefit and subsequently died;

  (b) any person appointed by the Secretary of State under regulation 57 (persons unable to act) of those Regulations to act on behalf of another;

  (c) any person claiming personal independence payment on behalf of another under section 82(5) of the 2012 Act (terminal illness); and

  (d) in the case of a decision under section 71ZB, 71ZG or 71ZH of the Administration Act to recover any amount paid by way of benefit, any person from whom such an amount is recoverable, but only if their rights, duties or obligations are affected by that decision.

DEFINITIONS

"the 1998 Act"—see reg.2.
"the 2012 Act"—*ibid.*
"the Administration Act"—*ibid.*

"appeal"—*ibid.*
"benefit"—*ibid.*
"the Claims and Payments Regulations 2013"—*ibid.*
"personal independence payment"—*ibid.*

Decisions which may or may not be appealed

4.165   **50.**—(1) An appeal lies against a decision set out in Schedule 2 (decisions against which an appeal lies).

(2) No appeal lies against a decision set out in Schedule 3 (decisions against which no appeal lies).

(3) In paragraph (2) and Schedule 3, "decision" includes a determination embodied in or necessary to a decision.

DEFINITION

"appeal"—see reg.2.

Notice of a decision against which an appeal lies

4.166   **51.**—(1) This regulation applies in the case of a person ("P") who has a right of appeal under the 1998 Act or these Regulations.

(2) The Secretary of State must—

(a) give P written notice of the decision and of the right to appeal against that decision; and

(b) inform P that, where that notice does not include a statement of the reasons for the decision, P may, within one month of the date of notification of that decision, request that the Secretary of State provide a written statement of the reasons for that decision.

(3) If the Secretary of State is requested under paragraph (2)(b) to provide a written statement of reasons, the Secretary of State must provide such a statement within 14 days of the request or as soon as practicable afterwards.

DEFINITION

"appeal"—see reg.2.

Appeals against decisions which have been revised

4.167   **52.**—(1) An appeal against a decision of the Secretary of State does not lapse where—

(a) the decision is revised under section 9 of the 1998 Act before the appeal is decided; and

(b) the decision of the Secretary of State as revised is not more advantageous to the appellant than the decision before it was revised.

(2) In a case to which paragraph (1) applies, the appeal must be treated as though it had been brought against the decision as revised.

(3) The Secretary of State must inform the appellant that they may, within one month of the date of notification of the decision as revised, make further representations as to the appeal.

(4) After the end of that period, or within that period if the appellant consents in writing, the appeal to the First-tier Tribunal must proceed, except where—

(a) the Secretary of State further revises the decision in light of further representations from the appellant; and

(b) that decision is more advantageous to the appellant than the decision before it was revised.

(5) Decisions which are more advantageous for the purpose of this regulation include those where—

(a) the amount of any benefit payable to the appellant is greater, or any benefit is awarded for a longer period, as a result of the decision;

(b) the decision would have resulted in the amount of benefit in payment being greater but for the operation of any provision of the Administration Act or the Contributions and Benefits Act restricting or suspending the payment of, or disqualifying a claimant from receiving, some or all of the benefit;

(c) as a result of the decision, a denial or disqualification for the receipt of any benefit is lifted, wholly or in part;

(d) the decision reverses a decision to pay benefit to a third party instead of to the appellant;

(e) in consequence of the decision, benefit paid is not recoverable under section 71ZB, 71ZG or 71ZH of the Administration Act or regulations made under any of those sections, or the amount so recoverable is reduced; or

(f) a financial gain accrued or will accrue to the appellant in consequence of the decision.

DEFINITIONS

"the 1998 Act"—see reg.2.
"the Administration Act"—*ibid.*
"appeal"—*ibid.*
"benefit"—*ibid.*
"claimant"—*ibid.*
"the date of notification"—*ibid.*
"writing"—*ibid.*

Decisions involving issues that arise on appeal in other cases

53.—(1) For the purposes of section 25(3)(b) of the 1998 Act (prescribed cases and circumstances in which a decision may be made on a prescribed basis)—   4.168

(a) a prescribed case is a case in which the claimant would be entitled to the benefit to which the decision relates, even if the other appeal referred to in section 25(1)(b) of the 1998 Act were decided in a way which is the most unfavourable to the claimant; and

(b) the prescribed basis on which the Secretary of State may make the decision is as if—

  (i) the other appeal referred to in section 25(1)(b) of the 1998 Act had already been decided; and

  (ii) that appeal had been decided in a way which is the most unfavourable to the claimant.

(2) For the purposes of section 25(5)(c) of the 1998 Act (appeal treated as pending against a decision in a different case, even though an appeal against the decision has not been brought or an application for permission to appeal against the decision has not been made but the time for doing so has not yet expired), the prescribed circumstances are that the Secretary of State—

(a) certifies in writing that the Secretary of State is considering appealing against that decision; and

(b) considers that, if such an appeal were to be decided in a particular way—

    (i) there would be no entitlement to benefit in that case; or

    (ii) the appeal would affect the decision in that case in some other way.

DEFINITIONS

"the 1998 Act"—see reg.2.
"appeal"—*ibid.*
"benefit"—*ibid.*
"claimant"—*ibid.*

Appeals involving issues that arise in other cases

4.169   **54.** For the purposes of section 26(6)(c) of the 1998 Act (appeal is treated as pending against a decision in a different case, even though an appeal against the decision has not been brought or an application for permission to appeal has not been made but the time for doing so has not yet expired) the prescribed circumstances are that the Secretary of State—

(a) certifies in writing that the Secretary of State is considering appealing against that decision; and

(b) considers that, if such an appeal were already decided, it would affect the determination of the appeal referred to in section 26(1)(a) of the 1998 Act.

DEFINITIONS

"the 1998 Act"—see reg.2.
"appeal"—*ibid.*
"writing"—*ibid.*

Consequential amendments

4.170   **55.** [Omitted]

Regulation 35

SCHEDULE 1

EFFECTIVE DATES FOR SUPERSEDING DECISIONS MADE ON THE
GROUND OF A CHANGE OF CIRCUMSTANCES

PART I

EMPLOYMENT AND SUPPORT ALLOWANCE AND JOBSEEKER'S ALLOWANCE

4.171   1. Subject to the following provisions of this Part and to Part 4, in the case of an employment and support allowance or a jobseeker's allowance, a superseding decision made on the ground of a change of circumstances takes effect from the first day of the benefit week in which the relevant change of circumstances occurs or is expected to occur.

2. Paragraph 1 does not apply where—

    (a) the superseding decision is not advantageous to the claimant; and

    (b) there has been an employment and support allowance decision where the Secretary of State is satisfied that, in relation to a limited capability for work determination, the claimant—

(i) failed to notify an appropriate office of a change of circumstances which the claimant was required by regulations under the Administration Act to notify; and

(ii) could not reasonably have been expected to know that the change of circumstances should have been notified.

3. Where a relevant change of circumstances results, or is expected to result, in a reduced award and the Secretary of State is of the opinion that it is impracticable for a superseding decision to take effect from the day set out in paragraph 1, that superseding decision takes effect—

(a) where the relevant change has occurred, from the first day of the benefit week following that in which that superseding decision is made; or

(b) where the relevant change is expected to occur, from the first day of the benefit week following that in which that change of circumstances is expected to occur.

4. Where entitlement ends, or is expected to end, as the result of a change of circumstances, the superseding decision takes effect from the day on which the relevant change of circumstances occurs or is expected to occur.

5. In the case of an employment and support allowance where a person who is subject to—

(a) section 45A or 47 of the Mental Health Act 1983 (power of higher courts to direct hospital admission; removal to hospital of persons serving sentences of imprisonment etc.);

(b) section 59A (hospital direction) of the Criminal Procedure (Scotland) Act 1995; or

(c) section 136 (transfer of prisoners for treatment for mental disorder) of the Mental Health (Care and Treatment) (Scotland) Act 2003,

ceases, or is expected to cease, to be detained in a hospital (as defined in the Act, or the Act of the Scottish Parliament, to which the person is subject) for a period of less than a week, a superseding decision related to that person's departure from, or return to, hospital takes effect from the day on which that change of circumstances occurs or is expected to occur.

6. Where the superseding decision is advantageous to the claimant and the change of circumstances was notified to an appropriate office more than one month after the change occurred or after the expiry of such longer period as may be allowed under regulation 36 (effective dates for superseding decisions where changes notified late), the superseding decision takes effect from the beginning of the benefit week in which the notification was given.

7. In the case of an employment and support allowance decision where the Secretary of State is satisfied that, in relation a limited capability for work determination, the claimant—

(a) failed to notify an appropriate office of a change of circumstances which the claimant was required by regulations under the Administration Act to notify; and

(b) could reasonably have been expected to know that the change of circumstances should have been notified,

the superseding decision takes effect in accordance with paragraph 8.

8. The superseding decision takes effect—

(a) from the date on which the claimant ought to have notified the change of circumstances; or

(b) if more than one change has taken place between the date from which the decision to be superseded took effect and the date of the superseding decision, from the date on which the first change ought to have been notified.

9. In the case of a claimant who makes an application for a supersession which contains an express statement that they are terminally ill, the superseding decision takes effect from the date on which the claimant became terminally ill.

10. Where the superseding decision is advantageous to the claimant and is made on the Secretary of State's own initiative, the decision takes effect from the beginning of the benefit week in which the Secretary of State commenced action with a view to supersession.

11. In this Part—

"employment and support allowance decision" means a decision to award an employment and support allowance embodied in or necessary to which is a determination that the claimant has, or is to be treated as having, limited capability for work;

"week" means a period of 7 days, beginning with midnight between Saturday and Sunday.

PART II

PERSONAL INDEPENDENCE PAYMENT

12. Subject to the following provisions of this Part and to Part 4, in the case of personal independence payment, a superseding decision made on the ground of a change of circumstances

4.172

takes effect on the date on which the relevant change of circumstances occurs or is expected to occur.

13. Paragraph 12 does not apply where—

    (a) the superseding decision is not advantageous to the claimant; and

    (b) there has been a personal independence payment decision where the Secretary of State is satisfied that, in relation to such a decision, the claimant—

        (i) failed to notify an appropriate office of a change of circumstances which the claimant was required by regulations under the Administration Act to notify; and

        (ii) could not reasonably have been expected to know that the change of circumstances should have been notified.

14. Except in a case where paragraph 15 or 31 applies, where the superseding decision is advantageous to the claimant and the change of circumstances was notified to an appropriate office more than one month after the change occurred or after the expiry of such longer period as may be allowed under regulation 36 (effective dates for superseding decisions where changes notified late), the superseding decision takes effect from the date of notification of the change.

15. Where—

    (a) the change is relevant to entitlement to a particular rate of personal independence payment; and

    (b) the claimant notifies an appropriate office of the change no later than one month after the date on which they first satisfied the conditions of entitlement to that rate or within such longer period as may be allowed by regulation 36 (effective dates for superseding decisions where changes notified late),

the superseding decision takes effect from the date on which the claimant first satisfied those conditions.

16. Where the Secretary of State is satisfied that, in relation to a personal independence payment decision, the claimant—

    (a) failed to notify an appropriate office of a change of circumstances which the claimant was required by regulations under the Administration Act to notify; and

    (b) could reasonably have been expected to know that the change of circumstances should have been notified,

the superseding decision takes effect in accordance with paragraph 17.

17. The superseding decision takes effect—

    (a) from the date on which the claimant ought to have notified the change of circumstances; or

    (b) if more than one change has taken place between the date from which the decision to be superseded took effect and the date of the superseding decision, from the date on which the first change ought to have been notified.

18. Where the superseding decision is advantageous to the claimant and is made on the Secretary of State's own initiative, the decision takes effect from the date on which the Secretary of State commenced action with a view to supersession.

19. In paragraphs 13 and 16, "personal independence payment decision" means a decision to award personal independence payment, embodied in or necessary to which is a determination whether the claimant satisfies any of the requirements in section 78(1) and (2) (daily living component) or section 79(1) and (2) (mobility component) of the 2012 Act.

PART III

UNIVERSAL CREDIT

4.173

20. Subject to the following paragraphs and to Part 4, in the case of universal credit, a superseding decision made on the ground of a change of circumstances takes effect from the first day of the assessment period in which that change occurred or is expected to occur.

21. Except in a case to which paragraph 22 or 31 applies, where the superseding decision is advantageous to the claimant and the change of circumstances was notified to an appropriate office after the end of the assessment period in which the change occurred or after the expiry of such longer period as may be allowed under regulation 36 (effective dates for superseding decisions where changes notified late), the superseding decision takes effect from the first day of the assessment period in which the notification was given.

22. In the case of a person to whom regulation 61 (information for calculating earned income) of the Universal Credit Regulations applies, where—

    (a) the relevant change of circumstances is that the person's employed earnings are reduced; and

(b) the person provides such information for the purposes of calculating those earnings at such times as the Secretary of State may require,

the superseding decision takes effect from the first day of the assessment period in which that change occurred.

23. In the case of a universal credit decision where the Secretary of State is satisfied that, in relation to a limited capability for work determination, the claimant—

(a) failed to notify an appropriate office of a change of circumstances which the claimant was required by regulations under the Administration Act to notify; and

(b) could reasonably have been expected to know that the change of circumstances should have been notified,

the superseding decision takes effect in accordance with paragraph 24.

24. The superseding decision takes effect—

(a) from the first day of the assessment period in which the claimant ought to have notified the change of circumstances; or

(b) if more than one change has taken place between the date from which the decision to be superseded took effect and the date of the superseding decision, from the first day of the assessment period in which the first change ought to have been notified.

25. Where—

(a) the superseding decision is not advantageous to the claimant; and

(b) there has been a universal credit decision where the Secretary of State is satisfied that, in relation to a limited capability for work determination, the claimant—

(i) failed to notify an appropriate office of a change of circumstances which the claimant was required by regulations under the Administration Act to notify; and

(ii) could not reasonably have been expected to know that the change of circumstances should have been notified,

the superseding decision takes effect on the first day of the assessment period in which the Secretary of State makes that decision.

26. Where, in any assessment period, a claimant—

(a) reaches the qualifying age for state pension credit under the State Pension Credit Act 2002; and

(b) has made an advance claim for an award of state pension credit,

a superseding decision made in consequence of the person reaching that age takes effect on the date on which that change of circumstances occurs or is expected to occur.

27. A superseding decision of the Secretary of State to make or to cease making a hardship payment takes effect in accordance with regulation 117 (period of hardship payments) of the Universal Credit Regulations.

28. In the case of a claimant who makes an application for a supersession which contains an express statement that they are terminally ill, the superseding decision takes effect from the first day of the assessment period in which the claimant became terminally ill.

29. Where the superseding decision is advantageous to a claimant and is made on the Secretary of State's own initiative, it takes effect from the first day of the assessment period in which the Secretary of State commenced action with a view to supersession.

30. In this Part, "a universal credit decision" means a decision to award universal credit embodied in or necessary to which is a determination that the claimant has or is to be treated as having limited capability for work.

PART IV

COMMON PROVISIONS

31.—(1) This paragraph applies in relation to an award of personal independence payment   **4.174**
or universal credit where the change of circumstances is that the claimant or, in the case of universal credit, a member of their family, becomes entitled to another relevant benefit, ceases so to be entitled or the rate of another such benefit alters.

(2) Where this paragraph applies, the superseding decision takes effect from—

(a) where the superseding decision concerns universal credit, the first day of the assessment period in which—

(i) the entitlement to the other benefit arises;

(ii) the entitlement to the other benefit ends; or

(iii) entitlement to a different rate of the other benefit arises;

(b) where the superseding decision concerns personal independence payment, the date on which—

    (i) the entitlement to the other benefit arises;
    (ii) the entitlement to the other benefit ends; or
    (iii) entitlement to a different rate of the other benefit arises.

(3) For the purpose of sub-paragraph (1), where the superseding decision relates to personal independence payment, "relevant benefit" includes any payment made under any of the provisions mentioned in regulation 61(1) (cases where mobility component of personal independence payment not payable) of the Claims and Payments Regulations 2013.

32. Where the change of circumstances is that there has been a change in the legislation in relation to any benefit, the superseding decision takes effect from the date on which that change in the legislation had effect.

33. Where the change of circumstances is the expected coming into force of a change in the legislation in relation to any benefit, the superseding decision takes effect from the date on which that change in the legislation takes effect.

DEFINITIONS

    "the Administration Act"—see reg.2.
    "appropriate office"—*ibid.*
    "assessment period"—see reg.2 and Universal Credit Regulations, reg.21.
    "benefit week"—see reg.2.
    "benefit"—*ibid.*
    "claimant"—*ibid.*
    "employment and support allowance"—*ibid.*
    "family"—*ibid.*
    "jobseeker's allowance"—*ibid.*
    "limited capability for work determination"—*ibid.*
    "limited capability for work"—*ibid.*
    "personal independence payment"—*ibid.*
    "relevant benefit"—*ibid.*
    "terminally ill"—*ibid.*
    "universal credit"—*ibid.*

Regulation 50(1)

SCHEDULE 2

DECISIONS AGAINST WHICH AN APPEAL LIES

4.175   **1.** A decision as to whether a person is entitled to a benefit for which no claim is required by virtue of regulation 6, 7 or 9(6) and (7) of the Claims and Payments Regulations 2013.

DEFINITIONS

    "appeal"—see reg.2.
    "the Claims and Payments Regulations 2013"—*ibid.*

Regulation 50(2)

SCHEDULE 3

DECISIONS AGAINST WHICH NO APPEAL LIES

Claims and Payments

4.176   **1.** A decision under any of the following provisions of the Claims and Payments Regulations 2013—

    (a) regulation 18 (special provisions where it is certified that a woman is expected to be confined or where she has been confined);
    (b) regulation 25 (interchange with claims for other benefits);
    (c) regulation 37 (evidence and information in connection with a claim);
    (d) regulation 46 (direct credit transfer);
    (e) regulation 47 (payment of universal credit);

(f) regulation 48 (payment of personal independence payment);

(g) regulation 49 (days for payment of personal independence payment);

(h) regulation 50(1) (payment of personal independence payment at a daily rate between periods in hospital or other accommodation);

(i) regulation 51 (payment of an employment and support allowance);

(j) regulation 52 (payment of a jobseeker's allowance);

(k) regulation 55, except a decision under paragraph (4) (extinguishment of right to payment if payment is not obtained within the prescribed period);

(l) regulation 56 (payments on death);

(m) regulation 57 (persons unable to act);

(n) regulation 58 (payment to another person on the claimant's behalf);

(o) regulation 59 (direct payment to lender of deductions in respect of interest on secured loans);

(p) Part 6 (mobility component of personal independence payment).

Other Jobseeker's Allowance Decisions

2. A decision made in accordance with regulation 39(2) (jobseeker's allowance determinations on incomplete evidence) of these Regulations.

4.177

Other Decisions relating to Universal Credit

3. A decision in default of a nomination under regulation 21(4) (assessment periods) of the Universal Credit Regulations.

4.178

4. A decision in default of an election under regulation 29 (award to include the carer element) of the Universal Credit Regulations.

5. A decision as to the amount of universal credit to which a person is entitled, where it appears to the Secretary of State that the amount is determined by reference to the claimant's entitlement to an increased amount of universal credit in the circumstances referred to in section 160C(2) (implementation of increases in universal credit due to attainment of a particular age) of the Administration Act.

6. So much of a decision as adopts a decision of a rent officer under an order made by virtue of section 122 of the Housing Act 1996 (decisions of rent officers for the purposes of universal credit).

Suspension

7. A decision of the Secretary of State relating to suspending payment of benefit, or to the payment of a benefit which has been suspended, under Part 5 (suspension) of these Regulations.

4.179

Decisions Depending on Other Cases

8. A decision of the Secretary of State in accordance with section 25 or 26 of the 1998 Act (decisions and appeals depending on other cases).

4.180

Expenses

9. A decision of the Secretary of State whether to pay travelling expenses under section 180 of the Administration Act.

4.181

Deductions

10. A decision of the Secretary of State under the Fines (Deductions from Income Support) Regulations 1992, other than a decision whether benefit is sufficient for a deduction to be made.

4.182

11. Any decision of the Secretary of State under the Community Charges (Deductions from Income Support) (No. 2) Regulations 1990, the Community Charges (Deductions from Income Support) (Scotland) Regulations 1989 or the Council Tax (Deductions from Income Support) Regulations 1993, except a decision—

(a) whether there is an outstanding sum due of the amount sought to be deducted;

(b) whether benefit is sufficient for the deduction to be made; or

(c) on the priority of the deductions.

Loss of Benefit

12.—(1) In the circumstances referred to in sub-paragraph (2), a decision of the Secretary of State that a sanctionable benefit as defined in section 6A(1) of the Fraud Act is not payable (or is to be reduced) pursuant to section 6B, 7 or 9 of that Act as a result of—

4.183

(a) a conviction for one or more benefit offences in one set of proceedings;

(b) an agreement to pay a penalty as an alternative to prosecution;

(c) a caution in respect of one or more benefit offences; or

(d) a conviction for one or more benefit offences in each of two sets of proceedings, the later offence or offences being committed within the period of 5 years after the date of any of the convictions for a benefit offence in the earlier proceedings.

(2) The circumstances are that the only ground of appeal is that any of the convictions was erroneous, or that the offender (as defined in section 6B(1) of the Fraud Act) did not commit the benefit offence in respect of which there has been an agreement to pay a penalty or a caution has been accepted.

Payments on Account, Overpayments and Recovery

4.184　**13.** In the case of personal independence payment, a decision of the Secretary of State under the Social Security (Payments on account, Overpayments and Recovery) Regulations 1988, except a decision of the Secretary of State under the following provisions of those Regulations—

   (a)　regulation 5, as to the offsetting of a prior payment against a subsequent award;

   (b)　regulation 11(1), as to whether a payment in excess of entitlement has been credited to a bank or other account;

   (c)　regulation 13, as to the sums to be deducted in calculating recoverable amounts.

14. A decision of the Secretary of State under the Social Security (Payments on Account of Benefit) Regulations 2013, except a decision under regulation 10 (bringing payments on account of benefit into account) of those Regulations.

15. A decision of the Secretary of State under the Social Security (Overpayments and Recovery) Regulations 2013, except a decision of the Secretary of State under the following provisions of those Regulations—

   (a)　regulation 4(3), as to the person from whom an overpayment of a housing payment is recoverable;

   (b)　regulation 7, as to the treatment of capital to be reduced;

   (c)　regulation 8, as to the sums to be deducted in calculating recoverable amounts;

   (d)　regulation 9 (sums to be deducted: change of dwelling).

Reciprocal Agreements

4.185　**16.** A decision of the Secretary of State made in accordance with an Order made under section 179 (reciprocal agreements with countries outside the United Kingdom) of the Administration Act.

European Community Regulations

4.186　**17.** An authorisation given by the Secretary of State in accordance with Article 22(1) or 55(1) of Council Regulation (EEC) No 1408/71 on the application of social security schemes to employed persons, to self-employed persons and to members of their families moving within the European Union.

Up-rating

4.187　**18.** A decision of the Secretary of State relating to the up-rating of benefits under Part 10 (review and alteration of benefits) of the Administration Act.

DEFINITIONS

   "the Administration Act"—see reg.2.

   "assessment period"—see reg.2 and Universal Credit Regs., reg.21.

   "benefit"—see reg.2.

   "claimant"—*ibid.*

   "the Fraud Act"—*ibid.*

   "jobseeker's allowance"—*ibid.*

   "personal independence payment"—*ibid.*

   "universal credit"—*ibid.*

   "the Universal Credit Regulations"—*ibid.*

INDEX

(All references are to paragraph number)